Marriage & Family

MARRIAGE & FAMILY
THE QUEST FOR INTIMACY

Seventh Edition

Robert H. Lauer

Jeanette C. Lauer

Alliant International University, San Diego

Mc Graw Hill **Higher Education**

Boston   Burr Ridge, IL   Dubuque, IA   New York   San Francisco   St. Louis
Bangkok   Bogotá   Caracas   Kuala Lumpur   Lisbon   London   Madrid   Mexico City
Milan   Montreal   New Delhi   Santiago   Seoul   Singapore   Sydney   Taipei   Toronto

Higher Education

Published by McGraw-Hill, an imprint of The McGraw-Hill Companies, Inc., 1221 Avenue of the Americas, New York, NY 10020. Copyright © 2009, 2007, 2004, 2000, 1997, 1994, 1991. All rights reserved. No part of this publication may be reproduced or distributed in any form or by any means, or stored in a database or retrieval system, without the prior written consent of The McGraw-Hill Companies, Inc., including, but not limited to, in any network or other electronic storage or transmission, or broadcast for distance learning.

This book is printed on acid-free paper

1 2 3 4 5 6 7 8 9 0 DOW/DOW 0 9 8

ISBN: 978-0-07-340428-8
MHID: 0-07-340428-4

Editor in Chief: *Michael Ryan*
Publisher: *Frank Mortimer*
Sponsoring Editor: *Gina Boedeker*
Executive Marketing Manager: *Leslie Oberhuber*
Developmental Editor: *Larry Goldberg*
Senior Production Editor: *Karol Jurado*
Production Service: *Pine Tree Composition, Inc.*
Manuscript Editor: *Kathy Whittier*
Text Designer: *Kay Lieberherr*
Cover Designer: *Ashley Bedell*
Cover Image: *Digital Vision/Getty Images*
Media Project Manager: *Jennifer Barrick*
Production Supervisor: *Louis Swaim*
Composition: *10/12 Minion by Laserwords*
Printing: *PMS 180, 45# Pub Matte Plus, R.R. Donnelley & Sons*

Credits: The credits section for this book begins on page 435 and is considered an extension of the copyright page.

Library of Congress Cataloging-in-Publication Data

Lauer, Robert H.
   Marriage and family : the quest for intimacy / Robert H. Lauer, Jeanette C. Lauer.—7th ed.
      p. cm.
   ISBN-13: 978-0-07-340428-8 (alk. paper)
   ISBN-10: 0-07-340428-4 (alk. paper)
  1. Marriage—United States. 2. Family—United States. I. Lauer, Jeanette C. II. Title.
   HQ536.L39 2009
   306.80973—dc22

                            2008023145

The Internet addresses listed in the text were accurate at the time of publication. The inclusion of a Web site does not indicate an endorsement by the authors or McGraw-Hill, and McGraw-Hill does not guarantee the accuracy of the information presented at these sites.

www.mhhe.com

To Jeffrey Mathew, Krista Julianne, Benjamin Brindle,
David Christopher, and John Robert
Who are embarking on the quest

Brief Contents

CONTENTS

vii

FIGURES

TABLES

PREFACE

What do you want out of life? If you are like most Americans, you would probably include happiness in your answer. But where can you find happiness? We wrote this text because we believe your personal happiness is crucially tied up with the quality of your intimate relationships. The text not only will provide you with a basic understanding of marriage and family life, but it also will show you how you can apply the knowledge you gain to enrich your life. In other words, this is not only a text; it's a practical guide as well. It is conceptual and theoretical social science, but it is also *applied* social science. The former comes from the wealth of information and the empirical work of the hundreds of researchers we discuss. The latter is found in the "Principles for Enhancing Intimacy" sections presented in each chapter as well as in the "Personal," "Comparison," and "What Do You Think?" inserts. Hopefully, by the time you complete this book, you will have a thorough understanding of marriage and family life today and an understanding of the steps you can take to enhance the quality of your own intimate relationships.

ORGANIZATION

We have organized the book to answer a series of questions: What is the context in which intimate relationships occur? What is the meaning of intimate relationships and how do we establish them? What is the nature of intimacy for married couples? What is the nature of intimacy in the family? What kinds of things threaten intimate relationships, and how do people cope with those threats?

Part One addresses *context,* discussing beliefs and dreams about marriage and the family, the diversity of family life, and the gender roles and sexuality that are integral to intimacy.

Part Two explores the *meaning of intimate relationships* and how they are established. We discuss the process of getting involved with someone and falling in love. We also note the special case of those who remain single, and how they deal with intimate relationships.

Part Three looks at the *nature of, and problems with, intimacy* for married couples. We discuss such issues as making the transition from singlehood to marriage, communication, conflict, and work.

In Part Four, we examine *intimacy in the family*— the differences that children make in our intimate lives, and the challenges and changes in intimacy over the family life cycle.

Finally, Part Five is an examination of various *threats to intimate relationships.* Family crises, including alcoholism and violence as well as numerous other stressors, put strains on the family. Separation and divorce are one way of dealing with the strains. Those who do get divorced are likely to remarry at some point, so the final chapter explores the reconstituted family.

CHANGES IN THE SEVENTH EDITION

We have updated this edition throughout with the latest available information. First, we have incorporated the latest available research—more than 500 new references from the professional literature. Second, we have utilized the most recent government data. The new references and government data, in addition to updating our knowledge about intimate relationships, provide increasingly more information on racial and ethnic differences in those relationships. This information, integrated throughout the chapters as appropriate, shows how Americans of various racial and ethnic backgrounds have similar as well as dissimilar experiences in their family relationships.

In addition to updating every chapter's research base and statistical data, we have made a number of other enhancements to the text's coverage. Here is a sampling:

- We eliminated one chapter in order to make the book easier to use in one semester; important materials have been incorporated into other chapters.

- We revised all the On the Web sections at the end of each chapter to suggest better sites and more challenging projects.
- We expanded the glossary.
- Chapter 1 has a new introductory section.
- Chapter 2 has a new section on the social context of family life and expanded materials on the Hispanic family.
- Chapter 3 has new information on gender similarities and differences in the kind of interaction that builds intimacy.
- Chapter 4 has a new Comparison box on unwanted sex in China.
- Chapter 5 has a new Comparison box on dating violence in Russia.
- Chapter 6 has new materials on people's beliefs about love and a new Comparison box on love styles among British, Indian, and Portuguese college students.
- A new section on the wedding is in chapter 8.
- Chapter 11 has expanded information on day care and new materials on social policy for working mothers.
- A new Comparison box on corporal punishment and aggression in Singapore is in chapter 12.
- Chapter 13 has expanded materials on the sandwich generation and new material on "boomerang" children.
- Chapter 14 has new information on the battered woman syndrome.
- Expanded materials on covenant marriage and separation have been added to chapter 15.
- Chapter 16 has new materials on styles of positive stepmothering.

LEARNING AIDS

The World Wide Web has become a tool that can enrich our understanding of marriages and families around the world. The seventh edition takes full advantage of online resources with updated and completely revised *On the Web* exercises at the end of every chapter and a unique book-specific Web site (see below for more).

We have retained many other important pedagogical aids from previous editions—learning objectives, chapter overviews, and end-of-chapter summaries. Finally, we have included four unique tools to promote active learning and critical thinking:

- "Personal" inserts feature an actual experience that has been shared with the authors. We have changed the names, but the people and the circumstances are real. The "Personal" inserts illustrate some principle or principles in the chapters. They should help you to

grasp the principles more fully by seeing them at work in a real situation. The "Personal" inserts could also form the basis for interesting class discussions and analysis.
- "Comparison" inserts examine some topic in each chapter in terms of what happens in other societies. Our understanding is incomplete as long as we know only about our own society. The materials range from how certain Inuit children learn to be male and female to how the Japanese divorce. These cross-cultural data reveal both similarities and differences with current U.S. practices. Seeing the similarities makes us feel less alone, more a part of all humankind. Seeing the differences helps us become more tolerant and more appreciative of the rich diversity of humans.
- "Principles for Enhancing Intimacy" inserts draw on the materials in each chapter to create practical courses of action students can take to make their own intimate relationships more meaningful and more fulfilling. The principles turn academic knowledge into practical tools for intimate relationships. As a result, students will gain not only understanding but also the skills necessary for constructing a rich life of intimacy.
- Finally, the "What Do You Think?" inserts present you with the arguments made on each side of a series of controversial issues. We make no effort to resolve the issues or to give you our own position. The issues reflect value differences as well as disagreement about interpretation of data. As you reflect on the various controversies, think about the arguments on both sides. Which ones seem to you to be most persuasive? Can you think of additional arguments? Can you understand the thinking of the side with which you disagree? Did seeing both sides of the issues help clarify your own position? These inserts should help you understand the complexity of many issues as well. Hopefully, they will also help you respect the position of those with whom you disagree as you recognize that both sides have thoughtful points to make.

SUPPLEMENTS

As a full-service publisher of quality educational products, McGraw-Hill does much more than just sell textbooks. The company creates and publishes an extensive array of print, video, and digital supplements for students and instructors. This edition of *Marriage & Family* is accompanied by a robust supplements package.

For the Student

Student's Online Learning Center Web site. This innovative, book-specific Web site features unique interactive activities that give students an opportunity to explore some of the most compelling issues faced by today's families. Multiple-choice tests, chapter summaries, Internet exercises, and more are also included. All of this material is organized by chapter for ease of use and can be found at www. mhhe.com/lauer7e.

For the Instructor

Instructor's Online Learning Center Web site. The password-protected instructor side of the Online Learning Center Web site includes an instructor's manual, test bank, computerized test bank, Powerpoint presentations, and other support materials. Online content for *Marriage & Family* is supported by WebCT, eCollege.com, Blackboard, and other course management systems. Go to www.mhhe.com/lauer7e.

ACKNOWLEDGMENTS

We are grateful to the personnel at McGraw-Hill, who have been most helpful and supportive during the writing of this book, and particularly our editors, Sherith Pankratz and Gina Boedeker. We are grateful to each of the academic reviewers. Their suggestions have, we believe, enhanced the quality of the book:

Jeffrey Basham, College of the Sequoias

Sampson Lee Blair, The State University of New York

Adriana Leela Bohm, Delaware County Community College

Kevin R. Bush, Miami University

Jarilyn Gess, Minnesota State University Moorhead

George W. Glann, Jr., Fayetteville Technical Community College

Jim Guinee, University of Central Arkansas

Rudolph Harris, Des Moines Area Community College

Susan Hoerbelt, Hillsborough Community College

Joseph W. Ruane, University of the Sciences in Philadelphia

Robert H. Lauer
Jeanette C. Lauer

A GUIDED TOUR

Divided into *five parts,* the **seventh edition of** *Marriage & Family: The Quest for Intimacy* combines a positive and practical approach to the study of marriage and family life with a manageable amount of sociological theory and research citations. The text not only provides students with a basic understanding of marriage and family life but helps them apply the knowledge to enrich their lives and nurture their own intimate relationships.

Thorough, Diversified Coverage

The seventh edition offers **thorough, diversified coverage** of racial and ethnic differences in intimacy, including a new section on the social context of family life and expanded coverage of the Hispanic family; updated treatment on gender similarities and differences; new information on people's beliefs about love; and greater emphasis on other issues important to today's student.

part two

~ SEEKING INTIMATE RELATIONSHIPS ~

The Chinese have a word, *jen,* that refers to a quality of humans that leads them to live in society. In other words, humans by nature seek to live with others. Only unnatural and abnormal people, according to Confucian teachings, live outside of human communities, for it is in society that humans are able to fully develop and realize their potential.

We agree with this ancient Chinese view of our need for relationships. Of course, most of us begin life in the context of family relationships. But sooner or later we begin to establish relationships beyond the family. In part two, we shall look at some of the issues, the alternatives, and the problems that arise as we step outside the family and establish additional intimate relationships. Issues, or points of dispute, include such matters as whether cohabitation is a good preparation for marriage, romantic love can last, and singleness is a healthy option. The issues arise, in part, because we do so many alternatives—singlehood, sex or celibacy, cohabitation, marriage, and the choice of different possible marriage partners. The alternatives and issues mean that some people face problems, times of doubt, and uncertainty about which choices to make.

105

4

~ SEXUALITY ~

LEARNING OBJECTIVES

After reading and studying chapter 4, you should be able to

1 Relate the meaning of sex as both a physical and a social phenomenon.
2 Describe the impact of sex on intimate relationships.
3 Discuss the extent of teenage sex and the consequences of early childbearing.
4 Explain the various methods of contraception and the degree to which they are used and by whom.

5 Outline the role and the practices of sex in marriage.
6 Identify the changing patterns of marital sex.
7 Review the functions and consequences of extra-marital sex.
8 Describe the nature and consequences of the major sexually transmitted diseases.
9 Outline the primary types of sexual dysfunction.
10 Summarize the important guidelines for engaging in safe sex.

As we look at sexual beliefs and practices throughout the world, we find both similarities with and differences from our own society. Investigate some kinds of sexual beliefs and/or practices in another society that differ from those in your society (e.g., frequency and/or positions of intercourse, the meaning of sex, attitudes about premarital and/or extra-marital sex, what techniques and practices are considered erotic). Compare them with your society and with your personal values. How do you feel about the beliefs and/or practices of the other society? Do you think that they are more or less preferable to those of your own? Why?

One way to carry on your investigation is through the library. You can check journals, such as the *Journal of Sex Research.* Or

you can use the *Social Science Index* or *Psychological Abstracts* to locate appropriate articles. Studies by anthropologists are also excellent sources.

Another way to carry on the investigation is to interview someone from another country. If that person is willing to discuss the topic with you, ask him or her to describe sexual attitudes and/or behavior in some area such as premarital sex or sexual techniques.

If the entire class engages in this project, each student could be responsible for a different society. Discuss the findings in terms of the questions given in the first column.

77

5

~ GETTING INVOLVED ~

LEARNING OBJECTIVES

After reading and studying chapter 5, you should be able to

1 Discuss the ways in which people get together as they search for intimate possibilities.
2 Relate the factors that make someone attractive as a potential partner.
3 Explain the functions of dating.
4 Describe the patterns of dating.

5 Identify the factors associated with dating violence.
6 Discuss the factors that build intimacy in a growing relationship.
7 Explain why relationships break up.
8 Describe how people respond when a split occurs.
9 Identify the reasons that some people stay single.
10 Discuss how single people meet their intimacy needs.

Patterns of dating have changed over time. To get a better sense of the changes that have occurred recently, interview three men or three women about their dating experiences. Select one who is under 20 years of age, another between 35 and 40, and a third over 60. In each case, explore the dating experiences of the individual during adolescence. Ask such questions as, "Who initiated dates, males or females? What did you typically do on a date? What influence did your parents

have over your dates? What did you feel were the purposes of dating? What was one of your most memorable dates?"

Compare the results from the three different generations. What did you find that was similar and what was different? If the entire class participates in this project, see if there are gender differences as well as age differences. Did those who interviewed men find different answers from those who interviewed women?

107

The authors have incorporated the latest available research—**more than 500 new references** from the professional literature and have utilized **the most recent government data.** The government data—integrated throughout the chapters and often displayed in color charts and graphs—shows how Americans of various racial and ethnic backgrounds have similar as well as dissimilar experiences in their family relationships.

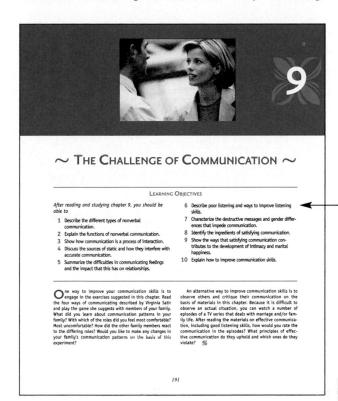

Chapter Previews

Chapter-opening vignettes capture student interest, and chapter overviews and objectives help keep students on track as they work through the chapters.

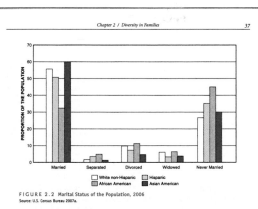

FIGURE 2.2 Marital Status of the Population, 2006
Source: U.S. Census Bureau 2007a.

Theory Icons

Marginal icons correlate the theories presented in chapter 1 with the examples discussed in later chapters.

Boxed Features and Photos

The ***Personal, Comparison, What Do you Think?,*** and ***Principles for Enhancing Intimacy*** **boxes** throughout the text facilitate active learning and critical thinking through real-life scenarios and presenting cross-cultural data. **Photos** bring the topics and concepts alive for the student.

Chapter 3 / Gender Roles 73

Personal

"We Worked It Out"

Gender roles and gender-role orientations can change over time both in a society and in an individual's life. Marcie, for example, is a middle-aged woman who began her married life as a traditional wife and mother. She stayed at home and raised her family. When the last of her four children began school, Marcie felt the need to do something more. Because her husband, David, was also traditional in his views, they went through periods of struggle before, as Marcie put it, they finally "worked it out":

> I was only 35 when my last child started school. The first thought that hit me was that I could now go to college. Maybe I could have a career. I knew I had to do something. At first, David couldn't understand why I was so restless. He argued that the kids still needed me at home. He particularly wanted me to be there when they got home from school. I agreed with this, but I told him that I could take night classes. He was appalled.
>
> Eventually, though, he agreed that one class at night was not unreasonable. But after the first semester, I wanted to take two classes. This made him angry again. I pointed out that I would be an old woman before I ever finished my degree. He said that he and the kids would never see me if I took on more. I suggested that we ask the children how they felt about it. We did, and he was really surprised when they all supported my wishes.
>
> Eventually, I found that I could take a combination of day and night classes and still be home when the children came in from school. Our next struggle was over housework. I told David that I needed his help. He had never done housework. I guess he saw how happy I was working on my degree, so he agreed. But he wouldn't take any initiative. I had to tell him everything to do. And he didn't do things right. Finally, we worked that out. I gave him a list of specific tasks he needed to do each week. He agreed to do them, and I agreed not to complain about the way he did them.
>
> I'm about to graduate now. I have a couple of prospects for jobs. We've already talked about how we can each manage to work and still take care of the children's needs. I'm excited about going to work. I loved being a traditional wife and mom. But now I love the idea of being a working mom. Fortunately, David has changed his views as much as I have. So our marriage and our family are both stronger than ever.

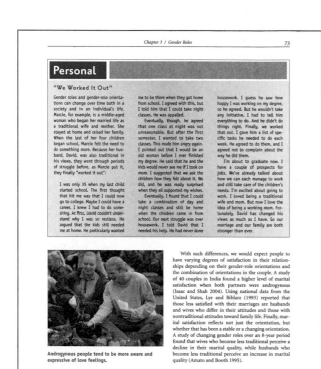

Androgynous people tend to be more aware and expressive of love feelings.

With such differences, we would expect people to have varying degrees of satisfaction in their relationships depending on their gender-role orientations and the combination of orientations in the couple. A study of 40 couples in India found a higher level of marital satisfaction when both partners were androgynous (Isaac and Shah 2004). Using national data from the United States, Lye and Biblarz (1993) reported that those less satisfied with their marriages are husbands and wives who differ in their attitudes and those with nontraditional attitudes toward family life. Finally, marital satisfaction reflects not just the orientation, but whether that has been a stable or a changing orientation. A study of changing gender roles over an 8-year period found that wives who become less traditional perceive a decline in their marital quality, while husbands who become less traditional perceive an increase in marital quality (Amato and Booth 1995).

Chapter 3 / Gender Roles 63

What Do You Think?

There is disagreement about ***whether women should reject current standards of beauty and accept their bodies as they are.*** *What follows are pro and con arguments. What do you think?*

Pro

Women should accept their bodies as they are because

- self-acceptance is crucial to emotional well-being.
- the standards reflect a sexist culture, not inherent beauty.
- women have injured their health and even died in an effort to meet the standards.
- the standards lower the self-esteem of women who believe they don't or can't meet the standards.
- the standards overemphasize the importance of bodily appearance to the detriment of other qualities.

Con

Women should not accept their bodies as they are because

- the standards (thinness, e.g.) reflect good health as well as beauty.
- achieving the standards will make them attractive to men.
- resisting the culture will hinder career advancement.
- the closer they come to the standards, the higher their self-esteem and self-confidence.
- modern medicine has developed techniques to allow women to remake their bodies.

One final example involves housework. Traditionally, the woman was the homemaker and the man was the breadwinner. While the majority of women now work outside the home, most of them retain major responsibility for doing the housework (Spain and Bianchi 1996). Whatever people's ideals may be, traditional gender roles continue to influence their behavior.

Gender-Role Orientation

As we pointed out, few if any people have conformed precisely to the traditional roles. Most people have some combination of the qualities or traits of each role. Social scientists call those traits associated with the traditional male role **instrumental traits** and those associated with the traditional female role **expressive traits.** Instrumental traits, such as aggressiveness, competitiveness, self-confidence, and logic, enable people to achieve goals. Expressive traits, such as warmth, caring, sensitivity, and nurturance, enable people to establish good interpersonal relationships.

The way to find people's gender-role orientation is to ask them to describe themselves in terms of the various traits. Those who select predominantly instrumental traits are masculine, while those who select predominantly expressive traits are feminine in their orientation. For example, the Personal Attributes Questionnaire, developed by Spence and Helmreich (1978), asks respondents to rate themselves on a number of traits, such as the following:

Not at all aggressive	A...B...C...D...E	Very aggressive
Not at all emotional	A...B...C...D...E	Very emotional
Very rough	A...B...C...D...E	Very gentle

A strong masculine response would be E on the aggressive scale and A on the emotional and rough/gentle scales. A strong feminine response would be the opposite.

At first, it seems reasonable to assume that masculine and feminine are the two extremes of one dimension. That is, the more masculine you are, the less feminine and vice versa. But social scientists agree that masculinity and femininity are not opposites that exclude each other. Instead of a continuum, with masculine at one end and feminine at the other, gender-role orientation must be understood as two-dimensional (figure 3.3). Thus, an individual can be high on both, low on both, or high on one and low on the other dimension. The smallest category, in terms of numbers of people, is the **undifferentiated,** in which an individual sees himself or herself as low on both masculine and feminine traits. You would be undifferentiated if you saw yourself as moderately aggressive (in between "very" and "not at all"), moderately independent, moderately emotional, and so on.

As figure 3.3 indicates, an individual can be aggressive and competitive and independent and also gentle and sensitive. Such people are called *androgynous.* **Androgyny** is a term coined by Sandra Bem (1974) to describe those people who possess both masculine, or instrumental, and feminine, or expressive, traits. Bem has argued that androgynous individuals are healthier and more adaptable than others. This makes sense, because

178 *Part Three / The Intimate Couple*

with most of the dimensions of their relationship but have at least one source of dissatisfaction. Traditional couples tend to be very strong in their relationships with family and friends and satisfied on most other dimensions but dissatisfied with communication patterns and their sexual relationship.

Balanced Couples. Balanced couples (8 percent of the total) are quite satisfied on such dimensions as leisure activities, children, and sex. They are particularly strong in their communication patterns and conflict resolution skills. However, they have ongoing problems with financial management. Money issues vex them even though they are able to talk about them and do well in solving other kinds of problems.

Harmonious Couples. Eight percent of the couples were classified as harmonious. On the whole, this type expresses great satisfaction with each other and with their relationship. The one area that is troublesome for them is parenting. They find the children to be as much of a burden as a blessing. They enjoy each other, but parenthood is not a source of gratification for them.

Vitalized Couples. The final type, the vitalized, comprised 9 percent of the sample. These couples are highly satisfied on all nine dimensions of their life together. They are not problem free, but they are able to work together to deal with any problems in a way that is satisfying to each partner. In essence, they have

Comparison

Types of Marriage in Togo

The people of the Moba-Gurma society, who are located in the northern, rural part of the African nation of Togo, live in domestic groups. The groups consist of about nine people on the average and are headed by an older male. Fertility is a central value for the Moba-Gurma people. Thus, a woman's status depends on her ability to bear children, and a man's status depends on the number of wives and children he has.

Marriages in this society can be classified by the manner in which a husband obtains a wife. Seven types of marriage are found:

1. *Marriage by exchange* occurs when two heads of domestic groups agree to exchange young women. Such an agreement may arise out of friendship or out of a desire to form an alliance. Nearly a third of marriages occur by this method, which enables all men (including those with physical disabilities) to have a wife as long as they have a woman to exchange.
2. *Brideservice marriage* comprises almost 5 percent of the total. In this type, a man who does not have a woman to exchange offers something else. He may, for example, work in the fields of the family from whom he expects to get a wife.
3. *Child betrothal* occurs in a little over one in five marriages. Under this arrangement, the head of the family gives a woman to a man in gratitude for his services (farm work) or as an expression of friendship. Typically, a young daughter is given or an unborn daughter is promised.
4. Nearly a fourth of unions involve *marriage by abduction.* This is a somewhat misleading term, since the woman allows herself to be abducted. She may have been promised to someone else, or she may be already married. But she agrees to meet the man in an arranged place and he "abducts" her. The situation is called *abduction* in the male-dominated Moba-Gurma society because they cannot imagine, or acknowledge, a woman doing such a thing of her own volition.
5. About 9 percent of marriages are *leviratic.* The levirate is a common practice in Africa. It requires a man to marry the wife or wives of a deceased brother. If the deceased man had no brother, another male relative is required to marry the widow or widows.
6. *Marriage by reimbursement* also comprises about 9 percent of all unions. This type occurs after a man has obtained a wife through brideservice or child betrothal. Even though the man has paid for his wife under these two methods, he still must give a woman back at some later date to replace the one taken.
7. Finally, a very small number of marriages are *bridewealth* unions, a marriage formed when a well-to-do man arranges the purchase of a wife. The few men who practice this arrangement tend to use it to get a woman from another ethnic group (Pilon 1994).

Chapter 11 / Work and Home 255

SUMMARY

Since industrialization, "his" work has mainly been to function as a provider and "her" work has been to care for the home. But in the industrial economy, only paid labor has been defined as work.

Since the 1960s, women have gone into the labor force in increasing numbers. Most married as well as single women now work outside the home; the most dramatic increase in labor force participation has occurred among married women with children under the age of 6. Women may take jobs or enter careers. Those who are employed become part of either a dual-earner or dual-career family. Dual-career families include three types of marital roles: traditional, participant, and role-sharing. The commuter marriage is a special form of the dual-career family and poses a serious challenge to the maintenance of intimacy.

Women who choose employment outside the home do so for a variety of reasons. They work for economic reasons (including consumerism and the desire for financial security), for the fulfillment that work brings, or for the power gained.

Home and work affect each other. Problems can arise from home-to-work spillover or work-to-home spillover. Both men and women experience conflicting demands from home and work.

Dual-income families face a number of challenges. One is the issue of equity, especially in relationship to household responsibilities. Progress has been made, but husbands and wives still do not assume equal shares of the responsibilities even when the wife as well as the husband is involved in a career. Other important challenges include the issue of children and child care, the costs of both parents working (including the effects on children), time management, and role negotiation.

Dual-income families can have as much satisfaction as single-income families. If the various challenges are addressed successfully, the couple can have high marital satisfaction as well as a number of other benefits from the arrangement.

Work is an integral part of our well-being. Wives and mothers who want to work and gain employment tend to find themselves assuming a heavier load of responsibilities. They still prefer to work and are more satisfied if they have employment. Men still tend to think of themselves as responsible to be providers and may have ambivalent feelings about cutting back on their hours or becoming house-husbands. But the life satisfaction of both men and women in dual-income families can be as high as it is for those in other arrangements.

Both social policy and individual coping strategies are important in helping the dual-income family to cope with their challenges. Family-friendly social policies, including those mandated by government and those instituted by companies, facilitate the ability of dual-income couples to construct a meaningful family life. Individual coping strategies, such as time-management skills and self care, are also important.

Principles for Enhancing Intimacy

1. Women today have numerous role options available to them. Women can choose among career, marriage, and motherhood—or any combination of these. They can decide to stay at home or continue to work outside the home after they have children. Increased confusion, however, often accompanies enlarged options as individuals struggle to decide what is the best pattern for their lives. When faced with such choices, it is vital for you to gain an understanding of your needs as well as those of your spouse and to consider carefully your personal and your shared goals.
2. It is very important to negotiate role expectations before marriage. Each person needs to define clearly what role he or she expects to play in the marriage and what the role of the other will be. Then, compromises need to be negotiated. Be aware that the roles you decide on are not etched in stone. The process of negotiation and compromise will be repeated throughout your marriage as circumstances change.
3. Women who decide to combine the responsibilities of job, children, and home must recognize and come to terms with the enormity of their tasks and their own limitations. They can't do everything equally well all of the time. If you choose to assume these roles, you need to make a list of priorities, reduce your expectations, eliminate the less valuable tasks, and seek help when necessary.

Chapter Reviews

End-of-chapter **summaries, key terms lists, and Internet activities** provide students with ample review and study materials.

KEY TERMS

birth rate 11
cohabitation 10
conflict theory 21
definition of the situation 21
emotional loneliness 4
exchange theory 20
extended family 6

familism 16
family of origin 4
integration 5
intimacy 4
loneliness 4
myth 6
nuclear family 7

social class 21
social loneliness 4
symbolic interaction theory 21
systems theory 20
theory 20
values 16

ON THE WEB   Marriage and Family in America: Needs, Myths, and Dreams

As noted in the text, we get our information about marriage and family from both experience and the mass media. An important source of information among the mass media is the Internet. There is also a certain amount of misinformation, so you must be careful about which sources you use. It's a good idea to begin with sites that are provided by experts such as researchers. Two very good sites are:

National Council on Family Relations
http://www.ncfr.org

This site, sponsored by a prestigious organization that publishes two of the better journals, not only posts various news items and information about professional activities but also gives you access to press reports based on articles published in their professional journals.

The National Marriage Project
http://marriage.rutgers.edu

Based at Rutgers University in New Jersey, the National Marriage Project engages in ongoing research into various aspects of marriage and family life. The site offers access to their varied publications.

Using these two sites, enlarge your understanding with the following projects:

1. Go to the NCFR site and click on "press release." You will have access to releases that describe articles published in the *Journal of Marriage and Family* and in *Family Relations*. Select one that interests you, then try to put the findings into the theoretical perspectives described in this chapter. Which theoretical perspective seems most useful? Which one or ones appear not to be useful? Why?

2. A number of important trends are noted in this chapter ("changing patterns of intimate relationships"). Check the press releases for both journals at the NCFR site, and examine the recent publications at the National Marriage Project site. To what extent are either of these sites addressing the trends? What new or updated information can you find related to the trends? Which trends seem to be ignored, and how could you explain the omissions?

3. Imagine you have to speak to a group of high school teenagers about what they can expect in terms of their own future marriages and family life. Use information from the two sites to outline a 45-minute talk that you think would be useful for them.

Online Learning Center Web Site

Go to **www.mhhe.com/lauer7e** to reach this book-specific Web site that includes multiple-choice quizzes, Internet exercises, and other coursewide content, all organized by chapter for students to use easily when studying for exams and writing papers.

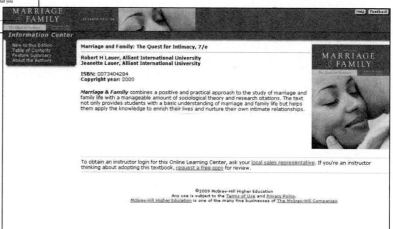

part one

~ THE CONTEXT OF INTIMACY ~

*I*magine that you have been on a date and your date asks if you had a good time. You not only have had a good time, but you also want to pursue the relationship, so you nod, smile, and suggest a good-night kiss. In most cases, the kiss would be an encouragement. But if your date happened to arrive here recently from any of a number of preindustrial societies, the offer of a kiss might be viewed as strange, unhealthy, or even disgusting.

Our quest for intimacy occurs in particular social contexts. We must understand the context in order to establish meaningful relationships. In part one, we examine the context of intimacy in our society. What is happening in the realm of intimate relationships? What effects does our multicultural society have on such relationships? How do sex roles and sexuality bear upon the quest for intimacy? The answers to these questions are crucial for both understanding and pursuing meaningful intimate relationships.

~ MARRIAGE AND FAMILY IN AMERICA ~

NEEDS, MYTHS, AND DREAMS

LEARNING OBJECTIVES

After reading and studying chapter 1, you should be able to

1 Explain what is meant by the statement, "we are social creatures."

2 Discuss the need for, and meaning of, intimacy.

3 Recognize and evaluate myths about family life.

4 Describe the changing patterns of intimate relationships in contemporary society.

5 Identify what Americans want in family life in light of the conflicting evidence.

6 Discuss the factors that explain long-term, satisfying marriages.

7 Briefly outline some of the theories used to research and understand family life.

Although most Americans agree that the family is a highly important part of their personal lives and well-being, many know little about their extended families. One of the ways we get a better sense of who we are is to know more about the kind of family of which we are a part. In this exercise, therefore, get to know your extended family better. Inquire about members of the family that you both know and don't know—whether grandparents, cousins, or whatever—and try to get pictures of those people. Ask questions of family members to whom you have access: "Who is or was the most colorful member of this family in your estimation? What

is one of the most interesting stories that you know about our family? What did your parents tell you about their parents or other members of the family?"

Summarize your experience by answering the following questions: What have you learned about your family that you didn't know before? How does that make you feel? What difference does it make in the way you think about yourself?

If the entire class engages in this project, share some of the more colorful stories with each other and discuss as a group both the benefits and the pitfalls of discovering more about our families. 🌼

Think about a time when you were in love. How would you describe the feeling of being in love? Or think about a time when you had a particularly joyous experience with your family. How would you describe the feelings associated with this positive family experience? As you reflect on these occasions, you may re-experience something of the vibrant emotional high you felt at the time. And you may realize something that social scientists repeatedly find in their research; namely, that close, personal relationships are crucial to your well-being (Myers 2004; Corrigan and Phelan 2004; Kaplan and Kronick 2006). In other words, you have a basic need for **intimacy,** which involves love, affection, caring, and deep attachment to a friend, lover, spouse, or relative. Because such close, vital connections are crucial to a fulfilling life, the major theme of this book is understanding and enhancing the quality of intimate relationships.

Achieving well-being through intimate relationships is, however, neither a simple nor an inevitable process. Your first experience of intimacy occurs in the family into which you were born—your **family of origin.** If that family breaks up because of divorce or death, your intimacy occurs in a single-parent family, and eventually you may live in a stepfamily. You may go through various other changes, including your own marriage, divorce, and remarriage. Thus, you could experience numerous different family situations as you pursue your quest for intimacy. One couple told us that while they were growing up, they had nine different fathers between them. Clearly, different people have differing experiences of family life.

In subsequent chapters, you will encounter the theme of intimacy in marriage and family life again and again as we discuss various issues, showing how such matters as gender roles, dating, communication, and parenting affect your experience of intimacy. We make it all very concrete and practical by ending each chapter with "Principles for Enhancing Intimacy," which illustrate how you can use the chapter's materials to maximize the quality of your own intimate relationships. We also personalize the materials with examples from our research and work with couples as well as the "Personal" boxes that offer a longer account of some topic. Three other features in each chapter reflect our belief in the importance of challenging you to think and of giving you opportunities to participate in the learning process: The "What Do You Think" box presents two different ways of thinking about an issue and asks you to weigh in on the debate; the "Comparison" box gives you an opportunity to reflect on the beliefs and behavior about intimate relationships in other societies and cultures; and the vignettes at the beginning of the chapters suggest activities and projects that enable you and the class to engage in your own research.

In this chapter, we lay the foundation of our quest for fulfilling intimate relationships by exploring the need for intimacy and the myths and dreams about intimate relationships in our society. We examine the trends occurring in marriage and family life as well as the debate about the future of marriage. We point out the strengths and benefits of marriage and family, and, finally, discuss the prospects for those who want a lasting and satisfying marriage and family life.

THE NEED FOR INTIMACY: WE ARE SOCIAL CREATURES

Earlier, we asked you to think about a time when you were in love or when you had a joyous experience with your family. Now try something else. Think of a time when you were in the midst of a group of strangers, or a time when you felt acutely lonely. Can you imagine what it would be like if your entire life were like that, if you never had any experiences of intimacy? Clearly, intimacy is a need, not an option. And it is a need because you, like all other people, are a social creature. There are many ways to illustrate the fact that humans are social creatures. For our purposes, two contrary aspects of human life make the point: the experiences of loneliness and of gaining well-being through intimate relationships.

Loneliness

The experience of **loneliness,** the feeling of being isolated from desired relationships, dramatizes the fact that we are social creatures. Everyone feels lonely at some time. For some people, however, loneliness is a serious problem.

The Meaning of Loneliness.   Social scientists distinguish between **social loneliness** and **emotional loneliness** (Van Baarsen et al. 2001). Social loneliness means you have less interpersonal interaction than you desire. Emotional loneliness means you have fewer intimate relationships than you desire. Emotional loneliness can result from a lack of romantic intimacy or family intimacy or both.

It is important to keep in mind that loneliness is not the same as aloneness. Most people prefer and benefit from a certain amount of solitude (Rokach 2001). At the same time, we also want and require relationships that fulfill our intimacy needs. But it isn't enough to interact with people, even a lot of people. That may cure social loneliness, but it doesn't necessarily address emotional loneliness. For example, a young woman who complained of loneliness pointed out that she was part of a large family but "everyone is busy." And at her work she had some friends that she saw socially on occasions, but "I can't say that I feel really close to any of them." Being around the same people on a regular basis is not equivalent to having intimate relationships with those people.

The Sources of Loneliness.   Some people are lonely for temporary periods because of such things as the breakup of a relationship, a move to a new location, or an accident or illness that confines them to home. More persistent loneliness may be rooted in certain social and individual factors.

As far as social factors are concerned, loneliness may reflect a failure of **integration** (Rokach and Sharma 1996). That is, the individual may not feel that he or she is a meaningful and significant part of any group. Such a situation, Emile Durkheim (1933) argued in a classic study, is inherent in modern society. In more primitive societies, he asserted, people are alike in their ideas, values, and aspirations. The entire society is like a close-knit family. But as the population grows and the society becomes more complex, the familial nature inevitably breaks down. Differences between people grow. The society becomes heterogeneous. Society is no longer an integrated whole, but a conglomeration of diverse individuals. People still need to be an integral part of some group or groups, but it is more difficult to do so.

Recent studies support Durkheim's observations. For example, Putnam (2001) presented evidence that Americans are involved in fewer social activities of all kinds, from Sunday picnics with friends to participation in organizations like the PTA and the League of Women Voters. Putnam claims that community ties have eroded, leading to less trust, less collective caring for each other, and more isolation. Another study showed, as did Durkheim's data, that suicidal behavior is more prevalent among the depressed when they have no religious affiliation (Dervic et al. 2004).

With regard to individual factors, childhood characteristics and experiences may be involved in loneliness. Low self-esteem of adolescents is associated with loneliness and the loneliness may continue into adulthood (Olmstead et al. 1991). Those who had a parent die when they were children, or who lacked warm and supporting parents while growing up, are more likely to suffer from

chronic loneliness as adults (Johnson, LaVoie, and Mahoney 2001). Whatever the source or sources, however, loneliness is a serious problem because the consequences are serious for people's quality of life.

The Consequences of Loneliness.   Persistent loneliness results in various negative consequences. Lonely people report higher rates of physical and emotional health problems (Hawkley et al. 2003; Pressman et al. 2005). Depression, for example, is a common outcome of loneliness (Adams, Sanders, and Auth 2004). A study of university freshmen reported that those with high levels of loneliness also had higher levels of psychological stress and negative emotions, poorer quality of sleep, and lower levels of antibody response to influenza immunization (Pressman et al. 2005).

If the loneliness is severe, the depression may also be severe and may be associated with thoughts of suicide. Moreover, the lonely individual can get caught in a vicious, downward cycle as depression leads the person to isolate himself or herself from others, which deepens the depression and intensifies the isolation.

Loneliness is emotionally debilitating.

Well-Being and Intimacy

Another aspect of life that demonstrates the fact that humans are social creatures is the way in which well-being is tied up with intimate relationships. A psychotherapist who works with severely mentally disturbed patients in a private hospital told us that she can "mark the beginning of health and recovery in a patient from the time he or she commits to interacting with others." She noted that when patients first arrive, they avoid contact with others and refuse to interact in group therapy settings. Disturbed people are unable to relate intimately or even casually to others. Lonely people relate casually but have few or no intimate relationships. Healthy, fulfilled people operate from a base of intimacy.

Because well-being is tied up with intimate relationships, as Carolyn Cutrona (2004:992) put it, the "drive to establish connection and intimacy with another person is powerful" and universal—all people in all societies are driven to make intimate connections with others. To be sure, not every intimate connection is an unfailing or continuous source of well-being, as anyone who has experienced an abusive relationship or a troubled relationship or one that breaks up will attest to. Indeed, those who remain in such relationships suffer various kinds of emotional and physical health problems (Hawkins and Booth 2005; Whisman and Uebelacker 2006; Umberson et al. 2006). Nevertheless, there is an abundance of evidence that links intimate marital and family relationships with well-being.

The link between the individual's well-being and his or her intimate relationships exists from birth. The quality of the relationship with the parents exerts crucial influence on the infant's healthy development. During childhood, feeling close to mother and to teachers and having friendships are associated with higher levels of self-esteem and with greater emotional strength in adulthood (Flaste 1991; Burnett and Demnar 1996).

The need for intimacy continues into adulthood. And the more committed the relationships, the higher is people's sense of well-being. Thus, a study of people in differing phases of life reported that the highest level of subjective well-being occurred in those who were married (Dush and Amato 2005). Successively lower levels were found among those who were cohabiting; who were in a steady dating relationship; who had casual dating relationships; and, at the lower end of perceived well-being, those who dated infrequently or not at all. Nor is it merely a matter of feeling better. People actually do better when they have satisfying intimate relationships. For example, adults in various crisis situations deal with them much better if they have the social support of intimate relationships (Bosworth et al. 2000; Viscoli et al. 2001). We shall give additional evidence later in this chapter when we note the health benefits of marriage.

MYTHS ABOUT FAMILY LIFE

It is important not only to be aware of the importance of the intimate relationships experienced in marriage and family, but also to understand the realities of family life. So how much do you know about American families? And, more importantly, *how* do you know what you know? We raise such questions because Americans "know" a certain number of things about family life that are myths rather than facts.

Where do our notions about the family come from? One way we get information is through experience. We know of our own experience and that of our friends and relatives. Another important source of information is the mass media. Consider, for instance, the family life portrayed on television. If you were a foreigner and the only thing you knew about American families came from television programs, how would you describe a typical family?

For example, if you watch any soap operas (if not, ask someone who does), think about the family life portrayed. How would you characterize it? How stable are the relationships? How much conflict occurs? How many celebrations or gratifying experiences are there? How much of what is portrayed is an accurate reflection of your experiences in your family or of other families with whom you are familiar?

Such programs are likely to generate a certain amount of misunderstanding about the nature of family life. The combination of misleading information in the mass media, misinterpretations of correct information, and inferences made from our own limited experiences creates and leads to the acceptance of various myths. We use **myth** here in the sense of one of its dictionary meanings— a belief about something that is accepted uncritically. Myths usually contain at least a germ of truth but are accepted without question by many people as the whole truth. Because myths help shape our perceptions, expectations, and hopes, they are important and must be considered carefully. Let us look at a few of those concerning marriage and the family.

We've Lost the Extended Family

The **extended family** refers to a group of three or more generations formed as an outgrowth of the parent–child relationship. Grandparents, parents, and children together comprise an extended family. Was that a typical family arrangement earlier in U.S history? Many people think so. But mounting evidence indicates that three generations gathered around a common hearth is a romanticization of the past. It seems that both in America and elsewhere, the **nuclear family** (husband, wife, and any children) has been the most common arrangement since at least the sixteenth century (Laslett 1977).

There are a number of reasons why the extended family has not been common. First, life expectancy in the past was much lower. Infectious diseases claimed the lives of many individuals before they were old enough to be grandparents. Second, children tended to leave home when they married. Like young people today, they preferred to establish their own homes, rather than to live with their parents.

Opposites Attract

We'll explore this myth in detail in chapter 7. The bottom line, however, is that you are very unlikely to be attracted to someone who is your "opposite." The more alike you are with someone in terms of your social background, your lifestyle, your values, and so forth, the more likely you are to be attracted to that person. More importantly, the more alike you are, the better your chances of having a lasting and satisfying relationship.

Of course, sometimes people who are unlike each other do get romantically involved and marry. Such marriages have a lower probability of being both lasting and satisfying (National Marriage Project 2004). The differences that seemed attractive at the beginning of a relationship may become irritations, frustrations, and sources of conflict in day-to-day living in marriage.

People Marry Because They Love Each Other

Why did you, or will you, get married? Your answer probably includes, or will include, the fact of being in love. But love, as we will see in chapter 6, is a complex emotion. It is difficult to define. And the feeling we call *love* might really be something different or at least involve some other emotions. As Lederer and Jackson (1968:42) point out, we all like to think that we marry for love, "but by and large the emotion [we] interpret as love is in reality some other emotion—often a strong sex drive, fear, or a hunger for approval."

Lederer (a writer) and Jackson (a therapist) go on to point out that we generally lose all judgment during courtship. We are driven by an "ecstatic paralysis" to mate with someone and reproduce ourselves. We may

Love is one, but not the only, reason people marry.

also wed because parents and other important people expect us to marry, because we are lonely, because we want economic security, or for various other reasons.

It is not that love is absent when people are considering marriage, but it is a mistake to believe that love is the only or even the dominant reason that people marry (Razdan 2003). Love may be the outgrowth as well as the foundation of a good marriage, but many other factors and feelings are involved when we are wrestling with the decision of whether to marry.

Having Children Increases Marital Satisfaction

"Just Molly and me and baby makes three," goes an old song. The outcome is a kind of personal "heaven." Most married people plan on having children, and most expect that those children will enrich their lives. But whatever the effect of children on people's lives as a whole, they clearly do not always increase satisfaction with the marital relationship.

Most studies show that marital satisfaction decreases for one or both spouses during the child-rearing years (Twenge, Campbell, and Foster 2003). The demands of raising children are such that parents often do not have the time or energy for cultivating their own relationship. Children frequently add financial strains. They require a great deal of energy. They may leave one or both parents exhausted and short-tempered. When children eventually grow up and leave home, the parents may find their marital satisfaction increasing again as they enter into a kind of second honeymoon.

This is not to say that children inevitably detract from the quality of one's life or marriage. It is important to keep in mind that *decreased* satisfaction is not the same as *dis*satisfaction. Furthermore, many couples report stable and some even report increased marital satisfaction after they have children (Belsky and Kelly 1994; Shapiro, Gottman, and Carrere 2000). The impact of children seems to depend on the quality of the marriage: A good marriage enhances the benefits and reduces the liabilities of children. If the marriage deteriorates with the addition of children, the couple probably already had a troubled relationship.

A Good Sex Life Is the Best Predictor of Marital Satisfaction

Tom, a counselor in a university, married when he was 29. When we talked with him before the wedding, he seemed somewhat ambivalent. He was already having some problems with his fiancée about money and in-laws. He shared very few interests with her. "Why," we asked, "are you marrying her?" "We have a great sex life," he replied. "We're terrific in bed together." One year later, Tom divorced his wife. "Great sex" was not enough to save the marriage.

What about marriages that start off better than Tom's, those in which the couples have shared values, interests, and goals? Is sex the best predictor of satisfaction? Again, the answer is no. The way you communicate with your spouse, the way you solve problems, and the way in which you spend your leisure time are all more important than sex. Sexual compatibility and sexual fulfillment are important and desirable, but they are not even essential to a meaningful and satisfying marriage. In a survey of 300 couples who had long-term (15 years or more), satisfying marriages, we found that agreement about sex was not among the top 10 reasons people gave for the quality of their marriages (Lauer and Lauer 1986:179–80). One woman who said she was "extremely

happy" with her marriage reported very little sexual activity over the past 10 years. This was her second marriage. Her first had been "totally sex and little else." Her second husband's health problems contributed to the decline in sexual activity. "So I suppose a kind of trade-off exists here," she said. "I like absolutely everything else about my current marriage."

In other words, you can have a great sex life and an unhappy marriage. You can even have an unfulfilling sex life and a happy marriage. And, as we shall see in chapter 4, some people have both a fulfilling sex life and a happy marriage. But it isn't the sex that is the most important reason for their marital satisfaction.

Having said this, however, it is important to note one thing more: married sex is more satisfying both emotionally and physically than is sex between the unmarried (National Marriage Project 2004). Contrary to the notion of the "swinging single" life that is filled with exciting sexual adventures, you are more likely to find sexual fulfillment in marriage than in either being single or cohabiting.

Happily Married People Don't Have Conflict

A young wife told us that in the early months of her marriage she was devastated each time she and her husband would argue. "I had assumed," she admitted, "that if you had a good marriage there would be no reason to fight. So every time we had an argument, I was afraid that our marriage was doomed." Eventually, she came to realize something that we will discuss in detail in chapter 10: Not only is conflict normal, but when it is handled properly, it strengthens rather than threatens the marriage (Driver and Gottman 2004).

"Happily ever after," then, does *not* mean "with never a difference or disagreement." In fact, a little reflection shows how unrealistic it is to expect a conflict-free union. Any sustained, close relationship has times of strain, disagreement, and argument. Parents fight with their children. Close friends disagree and are hurt by each other. People who work closely together on a daily basis find themselves getting frustrated and angry. Why should you expect anything different in marriage?

Of course, the amount of disagreement will vary. But it is highly unlikely that any long-term, close relationship can totally avoid conflict. In fact, conflict theorists go farther, and assert that conflict can facilitate creative solutions and increase solidarity over the long run. Studies of long-term marriages confirm the positive contribution that effective conflict resolution makes to a union (Lauer and Lauer 1986; Alford-Cooper 1998).

Half of All Marriages End in Divorce

In the past, more marriages ended because of the death of a spouse than because of divorce. Now the opposite is true. But just how many marriages actually end in divorce? Millions of Americans, including many professionals, assert that half of all marriages will fail. The statistic causes many people anxiety as they contemplate marriage. Ironically, the statistic isn't true.

It is true that the divorce rate is quite high and that there has been about one divorce for every two marriages in the United States in recent decades. But such rates do not mean a 50 percent failure rate. Actually, the failure rate is very difficult to calculate. To illustrate the problems, let's say that 2 million couples are married in a particular year and 1 million divorce. There are 55 million other couples who remain married from previous years. And there are millions of people who are single because they divorced in previous years. How does one calculate the failure rate?

The point is, predicting failure rates is very complex. Among other things, divorce rates vary considerably among generations and among people in the same generation from differing social backgrounds. With regard to generational differences, rates were quite low until the dramatic rise in the 1960s. But since 1982, divorce rates have tended to decline again. The rate is now lower than it has been since the early 1970s. Had the rates of the early 1980s continued, half or more of all marriages would indeed fail (National Marriage Project 2003:25).

With regard to differing social backgrounds, the lower your education and income, the higher your chances are of divorce. Rates also vary among religious groups. Catholics are far less likely than Protestants to divorce. And a national survey showed that the proportion ever divorced varied from 44 percent of Pentecostals to 28 percent of Presbyterians (Barna Group 2004). As a group, Pentecostals are lower in education and income than Presbyterians, so we can't be sure to what extent such differences reflect the religion itself or the socioeconomic status of the two groups. At any rate, in the national survey, which was a representative sample of the U.S. population, 35 percent of those ever married also had been divorced. It is not true that half of all marriages fail, and if the declining rates continue, the proportion of those divorced will be far less than 50 percent.

Taking all such factors into account, what are your chances? If marriage and divorce rates remained at the same level indefinitely, it would be easy to answer the question. All we can say at this point is that, if you marry now or in the near future, your chances of a lasting marriage (i.e., until one of you dies) are better than even.

And if you are among the educated going into a first marriage, are at least in your mid-20s to marry, are strongly religious and marrying someone of the same faith, and haven't lived with many different partners before getting married, your chances of divorce go down dramatically (National Marriage Project 2004).

The Dangers of Myths

There are more myths than those we have discussed. The important point is to recognize that many of the common beliefs about marriage and family living are wrong. Do not take for granted the truth of something simply because a lot of people agree that it is true. Myths are more than simple mistakes. Accepting myths can detract from the quality of your life.

Consider, for example, the myth that people marry only because they are in love. Americans like to think that arranged marriages and marriages of convenience belong to an earlier era or to a less modernized culture and that love is the sole reason people wed today. Yet even in contemporary U.S. society, as we shall see in chapter 7, individuals choose a mate for a variety of factors and not just because they are deeply in love. And even when they marry because of feelings of love, they often find that the feelings are fleeting and question whether they were ever "in love" in the first place.

The experience of Bart, a 30-year-old businessman who married when he was 23, illustrates this point well. At the time of his wedding, he believed he was "madly in love." But four years later, the "feeling of love" no longer existed. Bart had an affair. His wife found out about it and divorced him. Bart was so upset over the divorce that he went into therapy. There he discovered that his feeling of being "madly in love" was a mix of many different emotions and really wasn't love at all. And he learned that he had gone into the union with very unrealistic expectations about the nature of love and marriage. Like many people, he was certain that being "madly in love" would last a lifetime and didn't realize that these initial feelings needed to be nourished and eventually replaced by something more substantial. Bart has not remarried. He deeply regrets the mistakes he made and fears another relationship. He is somewhat bitter about the myth that led him to this point: "I think I have a better sense of what love means now. I wish someone had drilled that into me 10 years ago."

Myths can ruin a good relationship. They blind us to the realities of intimacy. They give us false expectations about the nature of marriage and family life. As such, they are impediments in our quest for well-being.

CHANGING PATTERNS OF INTIMATE RELATIONSHIPS

How do you achieve intimacy before you are married? What does it mean to be a husband or wife? What does it mean to be a parent? When are you likely to get married? How many, if any, children will you probably have? The answers to such questions vary, depending on when they are asked. Social life, including patterns of intimacy, is dynamic. Young people in their 20s today, for example, may not have yet contemplated marriage at an age when their parents already had two or three children. In this section, we will look at some of the important changes that have been occurring in intimate relationships in recent years. As you come to understand the dynamic nature of intimate living, you will develop the realistic grounding necessary to enhance the quality of your own life.

Premarital Sex

There has always been premarital sex. Records indicate that even some of our Puritan forebears were pregnant when they were joined in marriage (Demos 1968). But the approval of, and proportion of those engaging in premarital sex, increased considerably during the 1960s and 1970s. By the late 1980s, the proportion began to decline. Still, a recent national survey reported that 46.8 percent (compared to 54.1 percent in 1991) of high-school teenagers have had sexual intercourse at least once (Federal Interagency Forum on Child and Family Statistics 2007). The proportion varied by gender and by racial/ethnic background. More male students (47.9 percent) than female (45.7 percent) reported having sex. And more black students (67.6 percent) than Hispanic (51.0 percent) or white (43.0 percent) had sexual intercourse.

The rates also varied by age, with older teenagers more likely to have sexual experience than are the younger ones. By grade level, the rates were the following: ninth grade, 34.3 percent; tenth grade, 42.8 percent; eleventh grade, 51.4 percent; and twelfth grade, 63.1 percent.

Births to Unmarried Women

The number and proportion of births to unmarried women has increased enormously since 1960 (table 1.1). In 2006, 38.5 percent of all births were to unmarried women. In 2005, more than two-thirds of women under 25 having a first child were not married (Federal Interagency Forum on Child and Family Statistics 2007). Even a significant number of older mothers were unmarried:

TABLE 1.1 Births to Unmarried Women, By Race and Hispanic Origin, 1960–2006

Race	1960	1970	1980	1990	2000	2006
Number (1,000)						
White*	82	175	320	556	524	614
Black**	142	224	346	456	425	436
Asian				n.a.	n.a.	39
Hispanic				218	347	518
Births as a Percent of All Births in Racial Group						
White*	2.3	5.7	11.0	16.9	22.1	26.6
Black**	21.6	34.9	48.4	66.7	68.5	70.7
Asian				n.a.	n.a.	16.3
Hispanic				36.7	42.5	49.9

*Prior to 2000, "white" includes white Hispanic.
**Figures for 1960, 1970, and 1980 are for blacks and other races.
Source: U.S. Census Bureau 1988:62 and National Center for Health Statistics Web site.

15.8 percent of those aged 35 to 39, and 19.0 percent of those 40 years or older. As table 1.1 shows, birth rates for unmarried mothers also differ by racial and ethnic origin, with Asian mothers having the lowest rates and black mothers having the highest.

Living Alone

Increasing numbers of people are living alone. In 2006, 30.5 million Americans lived alone (figure 1.1). More women than men live alone, and African Americans are more likely than those of other racial/ethnic groups to live alone. People live alone because they are widowed, divorced, separated, or never married. Some of them will eventually marry. Others will opt—willingly or unwillingly—to remain single.

Living alone poses serious questions about fulfilling one's intimate needs. Of course, living with someone doesn't necessarily mean that those needs *are* fulfilled. The point is, rather, that just because a person lives alone does not mean that he or she can exist without intimate relationships. Rather, it means that the individual must find alternative means of fulfilling his or her needs.

Cohabitation

One way that some people fulfill their intimacy needs without getting married is through **cohabitation,** living with someone in an intimate, sexual relationship without

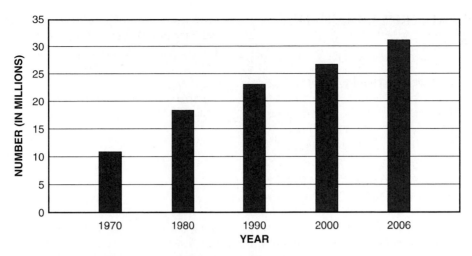

FIGURE 1.1 Number of Americans Living Alone
Sources: U.S. Census Bureau 1987:45 and 2008:55.

being legally married. By 2005, nearly 6 million unmarried couples, including 777,000 same-sex couples, were living together (U.S. Census Bureau 2008:62). This represents a dramatic increase over the 430,000 reported in 1960. The majority of unmarried couples living together are younger than 40 years of age, and a substantial proportion of them have children under the age of 18 living with them.

Some of those who cohabit will eventually marry. Many of those who opt for cohabitation think it is a way to test their compatibility for marriage, thus beating the odds on the high divorce rate. This is another of the myths that prevail today. We shall see why in chapter 7.

Delayed Marriage

Between 1950 and 1970, half of the females who married did so by the time they were 20.5 years old, and half of the males who married did so by the time they were 22.5 years old. In the 1970s, the median age at which people married (that is, the age by which half were married) began to increase. By 2005, the figures were about 26 for females and 27 for males (National Marriage Project 2007). The figure for women is the highest ever officially recorded in the United States (statistics for this have been kept since 1890).

Most people will eventually marry. But they are delaying marriage. Among whites, marriage is likely to be delayed for those spending part or all of their childhood without a father in the home (Li and Wojtkiewicz 1994). In addition, the availability of sexual relations among singles, the emphasis on personal growth and

freedom, the unwillingness to "settle down" before one has many experiences, and fears about commitment and the high divorce rate are factors that may have contributed to the higher age at first marriage.

Birth Rates

An increasing number of women are delaying having their first child until their mid- or even late 30s. This means that they will likely have fewer children. Moreover, because the capacity for getting pregnant tends to decrease with age, some women are involuntarily childless. Others choose to remain childless (see chapter 12). They do not view children as necessary to a fulfilling life.

As a result of later marriages, delayed first births, and an increasing number of childless marriages, the **birth rate** declined considerably from the 1950s, though it leveled off after 1995 (figure 1.2). In 2005, the rate was 14.0 births per 1,000 women aged 15 to 44 years, a little more than half of what it was in 1954 and less than half of what it was in 1910. In fact, the rate is now lower than what is necessary for the natural replacement of the population (Bachu and O'Connell 2001). Without immigration, the U.S. population will eventually decline if birth rates remain at the present low level.

Household Size

As would be expected from the increasing number of people living alone and the lower birth rates, the average household size in the country has declined. In 1790, the average household contained 5.8 people. The number

Comparison

Asian Women Are Marrying at a Later Age

Delaying marriage until a later age is not unique to women in the United States. In many Asian countries, where women have typically married during or even before adolescence, average age at marriage has been increasing. Since the mid-1990s, the proportion of Japanese women who have never married has risen from 40 to 54 percent in those aged 25 to 29 years, and from 14 to 27 percent in those aged 30 to 34 years. In fact, the average age at first marriage for Japanese women has surpassed that of U.S. women. While the average age at first marriage in many other Asian countries is still lower than that in the United States, it has tended to be on the rise throughout Asia. For example, among those aged 30 to 34 years, the proportion who have never married increased from 1960 to 2000 from 11.6 percent to 14.8 percent in the Philippines, from 6.7 to 16.1 percent in Thailand, from 2.1 percent to over 11 percent in Taiwan, and from 0.5 percent to 10.7 percent in the Republic of Korea.

In some countries, there is an interval between the wedding ceremony and the time when a couple begins living together and consummates their marriage through sexual intercourse. In Nepal, for instance, the union is generally not consummated during the first year of marriage. During this time, the young bride is trained to be an accomplished, subservient housewife before she moves in with her in-laws. In other words, she spends a year learning how to make the transition from being a daughter to being a wife and a daughter-in-law.

What differentiates those women who marry earlier from those who marry later? Generally, women with higher levels of education tend to marry at a later age. And closely related to education is profession: Women who work in nonagricultural jobs tend to marry later than those engaged in agriculture or those who do not work outside the home. Professional women are particularly likely to marry at a later age. Average age at first marriage will no doubt continue to rise, therefore, in Asian countries as the educational and occupational levels of women continue to rise.

Sources: Chowdhury and Trovato 1994; Niraula 1994; Women in Development 1999; Retherford, Ogawa, and Matsukura 2001; Kagemaya 2004; Jones 2005.

reflects not only the tendency to have more children but also may have included boarders, lodgers, and apprentices who lived with the family. By 1960, the average was 3.3 people, and by 2006 the figure was 2.57 (U.S. Census Bureau 2008:60).

The changes in average household size are due to changes in the types of households formed (married couple, single parent, nonfamily) as well as in the size of the specific types. The size of specific types of households varies depending on fertility rates. Changes in

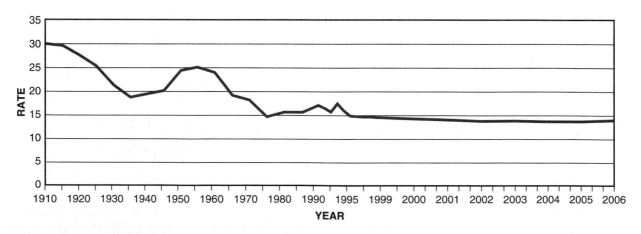

FIGURE 1.2 Birth Rate per 1,000 Population, 1910–2006
Sources: U.S. Census Bureau 1989:59 and 2008:79.

Increasing numbers of women leave their children in day care while they work.

types and in size of types account for the decline (Santi 1987). In the early 1970s, average household size went down mainly because of declining fertility rates. In the second half of the 1970s, fertility rates leveled out, but changes in living arrangements (increasing numbers of nonfamily and single-parent households) kept average household size in a continual decline. Since then, living arrangements continue to be an important factor in declining household size.

Employed Mothers

Women have been participating in the economy in growing numbers since the 1950s. Census Bureau figures show that the proportion of married women (with a husband in the home) who are employed increased from 23.8 percent in 1950 to 60.2 percent in 2005 (U.S. Census Bureau 2008:581). The most dramatic increase occurred among women who had children under 6 years of age. In 1987, for the first time, more than half of the new mothers (those with children under the age of 1) stayed in the labor force.

Some mothers are employed out of necessity; their husbands do not earn enough to support the family. Others work outside the home because they want a better lifestyle than they could afford with only one income. And still others define their jobs or careers as important to their own fulfillment. Whatever the reasons, homes with an employed father, a stay-at-home mother, and children are now only a small fraction of all U.S. households.

Divorce

Even though the number of people who divorce is exaggerated in popular belief, it is true that the divorce rate has risen dramatically since 1965. By the mid-1970s, the United States had the highest divorce rate in the Western world. After 1981, divorce rates tended to level off and even decline. Since the late 1980s, the rate has been on a slightly downward trend and is now around the level it was in the early 1970s.

A Concluding Note on Changing Patterns

Clearly, there are both long-term trends and short-term fluctuations in patterns of intimate behavior. Making firm conclusions about the future is therefore hazardous. Some experts, for instance, believe that marriage and family patterns will continue to evolve and to diverge from the traditional nuclear family type. They are convinced that we are entering into a new age in which new forms of family are emerging. Others believe that we are on the verge of a conservative trend that will renew the emphasis on traditional patterns. We will make our own position clear when we discuss what people want.

Personal

"I Had to Go to Work"

Maria and Luis are a Hispanic couple in their 30s. They married young and now have four children. Maria has become one of the millions of mothers who are now in the workforce. She tells of the struggles that led her to decide to find employment. Contrary to what she had hoped, getting a job outside the home did not immediately resolve the intimacy issues that Maria had been experiencing with her husband and her children.

When Luis and I were married, right after I graduated from high school, we both agreed that I would take care of our home and our children and he would earn our living. That's the way it was in both of our families when we were growing up. Even the priest who married us urged us to accept those roles because it was God's way of ensuring the best for our children.

Well, it worked okay for a number of years. But when the children were all in school and our expenses kept going up, we just couldn't make it on Luis's paycheck. We were getting deeper and deeper in debt.

We had to tell our children that we couldn't afford for them to have the same things and do the same things as their friends. How do you tell a teenaged girl that she can't go to her school prom unless she wears one of her old dresses? How do you tell your son that he can't join the competitive soccer league because we can't afford the fee?

And it wasn't just a problem with the kids. We found ourselves getting more and more irritated with each other. I made a big mistake one evening when I told Luis that, if he only had a better job, money wouldn't always be so tight. He got real angry and stalked out of the house. I knew I had hurt him. It wasn't his fault. He was doing the best he could. But I also knew something more. I had to go to work. We were going to have to change our ideas of what an ideal family is like. After all, other mothers I knew were working. Why shouldn't I? In fact, the more I thought about it, the more I was convinced that it would solve all our problems.

So when Luis finally came home, I told him I was sorry for blaming him and that we could fix things if I went to work. Well, he just took that as another slam at him for not bringing home more money than he did. We argued about it for a couple of weeks before he finally came around and agreed that I was only trying to help and that my working was probably the only way for us to solve our money problems.

I thought we were going to fix everything at last. But the only job I could find was in the evenings. That helped our finances, but Luis and the children complained that I wasn't around. I began to feel like a bad wife and mother who had abandoned her family. Then I got a day job. Things are much better now. But we still struggle. I'm tired when I come home and don't feel like cooking and doing housework. Luis and my kids are starting to help more. Even though they complain, it's making a big difference. I really love my family. It's tough. But we're going to get through this.

WHAT DO WE WANT? WHAT DO WE NEED?

Social scientists are engaged in an intense debate about what Americans need in the way of marriage and family life. We will look at that debate and then examine the evidence that can help answer the questions.

The Great Debate

The debate is often framed in terms of the liberal versus the conservative view of marriage and the family. The former is exemplified by the Alternatives to Marriage Project, an organization founded in 1998 to advocate "equality and fairness for unmarried people, including people who choose not to marry, cannot marry, or live together before marriage" (Alternatives to Marriage Project 2002). The organization does not oppose marriage. Rather, it strives to gain equal rights for the unmarried. Those rights would include such things as

- equal support for all families in which children live.
- legal recognition of all types of families, so that all may receive the benefits offered to any.
- legalization of same-sex marriages.
- support of research on unmarried relationships and families in order to identify and address their needs.
- legislation that makes discrimination on the basis of marital status illegal.

Those who advocate such rights argue that all "alternative" forms of the family, including single-parent and same-sex families and cohabiting couples, are as valid and as fulfilling as the heterosexual, married-couple family. And they argue that they are valid and fulfilling for any children involved as well as for the adults.

The conservative position is represented by organizations like the Institute for American Values and The National Marriage Project. Their aims include such things as

- promoting marriage as the best basis for family life.
- strengthening existing marriages.
- reducing the divorce rate.
- discouraging such alternative forms of family life as cohabitation and single-parent families.
- researching the state of marriage and family life in the United States today, including the attitudes of young people.

For example, the Institute for American Values (2002) issued a report on "why marriage matters," based on the work of 13 family scholars. The report summarizes evidence that the benefits of marriage extend to husbands, wives, children, and society as a whole.

In essence, then, one side argues that changes in marriage and the family over the past half-century are to be affirmed and celebrated. The other side argues that the changes pose a serious threat to individual and social well-being. Let's review some of those changes.

Changes in Traditional Arrangements

If we define a traditional family as one that stays intact except for death and is composed of an employed father (the breadwinner), a stay-at-home mother (the homemaker), and children, then it is clear it is now the choice of a minority of Americans. Most people no longer regard that arrangement as practical. Moreover, the woman's movement and women's experience in the labor force have sensitized women to the value of employment outside the home. The experience of non-family living, which an increasing number of young Americans who leave the parental home before marrying have, also contributes to a change in the traditional pattern. Using a national sample of young adults, Waite, Goldscheider, and Witsberger (1986) discovered an erosion of traditional family orientation among those who had spent time in nonfamily living. This period of independent living affects personal plans and goals about marriage and family life. In particular, young women who lived independently were more likely to make plans for employment, expect fewer children, be more accepting of employed mothers, and hold nontraditional views of what it means to be a wife and mother in a family. Young men who lived independently also acquired nontraditional views, but the effects were not as dramatic for them as for the women.

Adding to the evidence of change, Glenn (1987, 1992) analyzed national polls taken between 1969 and 1986 and found a number of ways in which Americans were moving away from the traditional ideal, including having less emphasis on marital permanence as an ideal. Certainly, the data we have given in this chapter support the notion that traditional arrangements are being replaced by new forms of family life. Figure 1.3 shows the

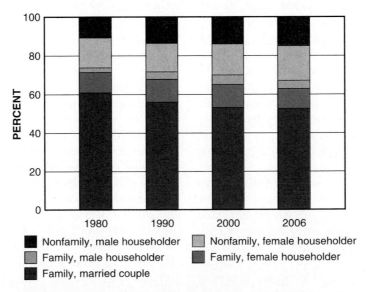

FIGURE 1.3 Household Composition, 1980–2006
Source: U.S. Census Bureau 2008:58, 60.

dramatic change in household composition from 1980 to 2006. Note the decline of married-couple families, and the increasing proportion of nonfamily households. In the last decade of the twentieth century, the rate of increase of nonfamily households was twice that of family households, and families headed by women with no husband present grew three times as fast as married-couple families (Gibson 2001).

Such trends raise a question about the future of traditional forms of marriage and the family. Will they be a minority of all arrangements in the near future, or will they even die out? Some scholars argue for *marital decline,* while others affirm *marital resilience* (Amato 2004). Those who see continuing decline point out that U.S. culture is increasingly individualistic with an increasingly strong emphasis on personal happiness. Many Americans define a commitment to marriage as the imposition of restraints and obligations that can interfere with the individual's pursuit of happiness. In such a context, marriage is unlikely to last beyond the point where the individual no longer feels happy and fulfilled by the relationship.

In contrast, those who affirm resilience deny the trend toward increasing individualism and the personal obsession with happiness. They argue that we can't really be sure that the proportion of troubled marriages has increased. What has changed is that it is easier to get out of marriage and there is no longer a stigma attached to divorce. Marriages that once would have continued in a state of mutual misery now break up. But the majority of those who divorce will remarry at some point. Even many of those who are single parents would like to marry or remarry. In other words, the growing number of singles (never married, divorced, widowed) and single-parent families does not reflect a preferred state in order to pursue happiness, but the problems of finding a suitable mate. Most Americans still regard marriage and family life as an integral part of happiness, not a state that inhibits the individual's quest for happiness.

Given such differing perspectives by the experts, what can we say about the future of marriage and family life? Cherlin (2004) suggests three possibilities (based on his contention that marriage is not as strongly governed by social expectations as it once was but has become more tied up with individual choice and personal development). One possibility is that marriage will revert to what it was in the past—a social institution governed by strong expectations. As such, present trends would reverse and increasing numbers of people would be in stable marriages and two-parent families. Cherlin doubts this will happen.

A second possibility is that marriage will remain important to people but will not be as dominant as it was in the past. Marriage, Cherlin asserts, still has a high symbolic status in U.S. society because it is a marker of prestige and personal achievement. The third possibility is that marriage will become merely one of many alternative ways of experiencing an intimate relationship. It will be no less nor no more valued than any of the other alternatives. As Cherlin notes, some observers believe the third possibility is already emerging, while others expect the second possibility to hold for the foreseeable future.

Our own position lies somewhere between the first two possibilities articulated by Cherlin. We believe that a renewed emphasis on the value of marriage and family life will occur in the future. **Values** are things that are preferred because people define them as worthy and desirable. We expect, in other words, an increasing proportion of Americans to prefer marriage and family because they will define them as desired states that are worthy of their commitment. For this to happen, Americans must come to terms with the contrary values—what we call "me or we?"—that now exist. They also must recognize the strengths and benefits of marriage and family life, which we will explore. Let's look first at the issue of contrary values.

Me or We?

Americans are caught up in contradictory feelings that derive from contrary values. On the one hand, there is **familism,** a value on family living. Familism leads us to cherish our families, to subordinate our personal desires if necessary for the good of the family group, and to view marriage as that which demands our commitment and fidelity.

On the other hand, we are a nation that values individualism, the well-being of the individual. American individualism has two strains, one of which—utilitarian individualism—emphasizes personal achievement and the other of which—expressive individualism—emphasizes personal happiness and fulfillment (Bellah et al. 1985). Utilitarian individualism stresses getting ahead for yourself, while expressive individualism focuses on fulfillment by doing those things that satisfy you.

Expressive individualism has been particularly strong for the past few decades, buttressed by a humanistic psychology that has urged people to search for self-fulfillment above all. There is some evidence that we may be retreating from this strong emphasis on expressive individualism. As we heard one therapist put it, "We've been through the *me* generation and now we're trying to go back to a *we* generation." Americans struggle between "me" and "we." As Bellah et al. (1985:111) point out, our individualistic ideology makes it hard for us to understand why we should even be concerned about giving to each other:

> Now we are all supposed to be conscious primarily of our assertive selves. To reappropriate a language in which we could all, men and women, see that dependence and independence are deeply related, and that we can be independent persons without denying that we need one another, is a task that has only begun.

In sum, we believe that Americans value marriage and family but are struggling between familial and individualistic values. We value and need intimacy, but many are not convinced that marriage and family living are the only ways to fulfill those intimacy needs. Indeed, they are not the only arrangements that will satisfy all people. Thus, we are in process of making a variety of arrangements legitimate. The majority of people, and we believe an increasing majority, will continue to opt for marriage and family living; a minority will find alternative arrangements.

Strengths and Benefits of Marriage and Family

Increasing numbers of studies show the strengths and benefits of marriage and family. As the results of these studies pervade the population, we believe that increasing numbers of people will place a higher value on stable marriages and family life. Clearly, some marriages and some families are more stressful and destructive than beneficial, but those in satisfying relationships reap many benefits. A large and growing body of research underscores the advantages that the married have over the unmarried. Overall, both married men and married women are happier; have lower rates of alcoholism, suicide, and depression; are physically and emotionally healthier; are less likely to engage in binge drinking or use marijuana; are less sexually frustrated; are better off financially; and live longer than the unmarried (Pienta, Hayward, and Jenkins 2000; Waite and Gallagher 2000; Kim and McKenry 2002; Simon 2002; Lee and Bulanda 2005; Duncan, Wilkerson, and England 2006; Jaffe et al. 2007; The National Marriage Project 2007; Proulx, Helms, and Buehler 2007). The reasons for the advantages of marriage are a matter of some debate, but most observers would agree on one point: A satisfying marriage provides you with a built-in support system to help you deal with the varied challenges and struggles of your life (Dehle, Larsen, and Landers 2001).

The benefits of a stable marriage for physical and emotional well-being also have been found in other nations such as Japan and Great Britain (Kawakami et al. 1995; Murphy, Glaser, and Grundy 1997). And a 17-nation study reported that in 16 of the countries (Northern Ireland was the only exception), marriage was significantly related to happiness and that marriage increases happiness equally among men and women (Stack and Eshleman 1998). Clearly, a satisfying marital relationship enhances happiness and is a strong buffer against the negative effects of stress.

The strengths of marriage and family are evident in the high value that people continue to place upon them. Most teenagers regard a good marriage and family life as extremely important (Martin et al. 2003). In a national survey of the values of 14- to 29-year-olds, "having a lifelong partner" and "getting married" received more ratings of "top importance" than did "having sex" (Youthography 2007). Eighty-one percent of females and 76.2 percent of males rated "having a lifelong partner" as of top importance to them, and 67.0 percent of females and 60.9 percent of males gave top ratings to getting married. In contrast, having sex got top ratings from 40.8 percent of the females and 52.3 percent of the males.

People also affirm the importance of marriage and family in other ways. A Pew Research Center (2006b) survey reported that family continues to be the greatest source of satisfaction in people's lives. About 73 percent of the respondents said that they speak on an average day with a family member who doesn't live in their house. And family members (including spouses) are the most likely source to which people turn for help when facing problems.

In short, most Americans, including those who have been victimized by dysfunctional marriages and family lives, continue to value marriage and family. They want good marriages and satisfying family lives for themselves. And a large majority of those living in a family situation affirm that it is the source of their greatest satisfaction in life.

'TIL DEATH?

For the majority who opt for marriage and family, what are the prospects? To the extent that our expressive individualistic values prevail, people will enter and remain in a marriage only so long as it is perceived to be personally beneficial to them. They will then divorce and may seek to fulfill their intimacy needs through another marriage. Indeed, some have raised the question of whether any other pattern is realistic if people are to have their needs fulfilled. That is, can two people maintain a long-term relationship that is not only stable but also satisfying to them both?

What Do You Think?

*There is disagreement about **whether the decline of the traditional family (father, stay-at-home mother, and children) will lead to the breakdown of U.S. society.** What follows are pro and con arguments. What do you think?*

Pro

The decline of the traditional family will

- foster continuing high divorce rates.
- lead to more sexual promiscuity and unwanted pregnancies.
- result in a greater number of people living in poverty.
- increase the number of neglected, latchkey kids.
- increase juvenile delinquency.
- increase the number of overworked and overstressed single parents who don't function well at home or on the job.

Con

The decline of the traditional family will

- mean change but not breakdown—other societies function well with diverse styles of family life.
- result in more equitable arrangements for women.
- afford families a more prosperous lifestyle when both spouses work outside the home.
- give people a choice in the type of family they want.
- allow people to be parents without forcing them to marry.
- affirm and support the diversity Americans cherish.

Over four decades ago, Levinger (1965) argued that relationships can be described in terms of their stability and satisfaction. Some marriages are high on both (a "full-shell" marriage), some are low on both ("no-shell"), and some have one without the other ("half-shell" marriages are those that are happy but for some reason cannot survive; "empty-shell" marriages are those that last but do not bring satisfaction). All four of these types can still be found. For some, the marriage proves to be unsatisfactory almost from the start. Like the young man who married a woman because of the "great sex" they had, the no-shell marriages break up in a short time (half of all marriages that break up do so within the first seven years).

But are there empty-shell marriages, those that are unsatisfactory yet stable? The answer is yes. In our study of 351 long-term marriages (Lauer and Lauer 1986), the only criterion for being included in the sample was a minimum of 15 years of marriage. We anticipated that virtually all would have a satisfying union, since people tend not to remain in an unhappy marriage. But in nearly 15 percent (51) of the couples, one or both of the partners were unhappy to some extent. Why did they stay together? The two major reasons were a sense of duty (religious beliefs or family tradition) and children. A study employing a national sample and looking directly for reasons for stability in unhappy marriages found that those in the more stable unions (as measured by perceived chances for separation or divorce) tended to be older, be committed to marriage as an institution, and believe that divorce would only further detract from

Play strengthens family life.

their happiness. Compared to those in less stable marriages, they also had less social activity and less sense of control over their lives (Heaton and Albrecht 1991).

It is the first pattern noted previously, of course, the highly stable *and* satisfying marriage, that Levinger called "full-shell," that has been the ideal in modern American life. But can it happen? Can people live together in a vital, meaningful relationship "'til death do us part"? Again, the answer is yes. For some people, marriage is still an experience that enhances their physical and mental health and their general sense of well-being:

> Marriage places more demands on people than friendship, but the rewards are enormous for those who are able to work through the differences and annoyances and maintain a growing relationship. For some, the rewards are so immense that marriage is a watershed in their lives (Lauer and Lauer 1988:86).

What are the ingredients of such a marriage? We asked our happy couples to select from 39 factors those that they regarded as most important in their own experience. In order of the frequency with which they were named, the following are the reasons given by husbands and wives:

Husbands

1. My spouse is my best friend.
2. I like my spouse as a person.
3. Marriage is a long-term commitment.
4. Marriage is sacred.
5. We agree on aims and goals.
6. My spouse has grown more interesting.
7. I want the relationship to succeed.
8. An enduring marriage is important to social stability.
9. We laugh together.
10. I am proud of my spouse's achievement.
11. We agree on a philosophy of life.
12. We agree about our sex life.

Wives

1. My spouse is my best friend.
2. I like my spouse as a person.
3. Marriage is a long-term commitment.
4. Marriage is sacred.
5. We agree on aims and goals.
6. My spouse has grown more interesting.
7. I want the relationship to succeed.
8. We laugh together.
9. We agree on a philosophy of life.
10. We agree on how and how often to show affection.
11. An enduring marriage is important to social stability.
12. We have a stimulating exchange of ideas.

Even though husbands and wives were interviewed or filled out their questionnaires separately, the first seven items are exactly the same! The order varies somewhat after that, but there are no striking differences between husbands and wives. There seems to be considerable consensus on what it takes to forge a union that is both long-lasting and fulfilling to both partners.

A follow-up study of 100 couples married 45 years or more found virtually the same results and the same general consensus between men and women (Lauer, Lauer, and Kerr 1990). And other researchers have come to the same conclusion that the factors involved in marital stability and marital satisfaction are similar for husbands and wives (Sharlin 1996; Kurdek 2005).

Note that the most important factor is liking your spouse, liking the kind of person to whom you are married, appreciating the kind of person that he or she is. Three of the first six factors relate to the individual's perception of the kind of person the spouse is. It is not only a myth but a dangerous myth that people marry each other purely out of love. As one wife, who rated her marriage as "extremely happy," told us,

> I feel that liking a person in marriage is as important as loving that person. I have to like him so I will love him when things aren't so rosy. Friends enjoy each other's company—enjoy doing things together . . . That's why friendship really ranks high in my reasons for our happy marriage.

A husband summed up the importance of friendship and liking when he said, "Jen is just the best friend I have. I would rather spend time with her, talk with her, be with her than anyone else." And a wife noted that she liked the kind of person her husband was so much that she would want to be friends with him even if she wasn't married to him.

Next to liking and being friends with one's spouse, people talked about the importance of commitment. Couples in unhappy marriages also ranked commitment high, but there was a difference in their commitment. They were committed primarily to the institution of marriage. Once in a particular union, therefore, they were determined to make it last, regardless of how unhappy they were. In other words, they were committed to maintaining a marriage but were not really committed to each other. Couples in happy marriages, on the other hand, are committed to marriage and to their spouses. This involves a determination to work through whatever problems might cause dissatisfaction. As expressed by one wife,

> We've remained married because 40 years ago our peer group just did. We worked our way through problems that today we might walk away from. Our marriage is firm and

filled with respect and love, but it took time and work. In a marriage today, we might have separated. I'm glad we didn't. I can't emphasize this too strongly. I have two children who are divorced. They are still searching for a magical something that isn't obtainable in the real world. Marriage grows through working out problems and going on. Our marriage took 40 years and we are still learning.

There are many other factors that are important, such as humor and the ability to handle conflict constructively. The point is that a long-term and satisfying marriage is not merely a matter of finding just the right person who can make you happy. It is a matter of two people who have some positive factors going for them (such as liking each other and sharing similar values) working together in a committed relationship to achieve a mutually satisfying life. Even in an age of rapid change and high divorce rates, the full-shell marriage can be a reality for those who wish it.

A NOTE ON THEORY

In simplest terms, a **theory** is an explanation. For example, the myth that people marry simply because they love each other may be based on the theory that love is a dominant emotion in human life. It is an emotion that we can recognize and one that structures the nature of our relationships. More formally, a theory is a set of logically related propositions that explain some phenomenon (see, for example, Sternberg's triangular theory of love in chapter 6).

Social scientists use theories not only to explain but also to guide research. Consequently, theory is an important part of the study of intimate relationships. There is, however, no single theory that encompasses the field of marriage and the family. In fact, most theoretical perspectives used to study intimate relationships are borrowed from other disciplines. In this section, we will briefly describe the more commonly used theories and note a few places in the text where they apply. Because we stress practical application, we will not elaborate on theory in the remaining chapters. For an interesting exercise, try to read through one of the subsequent chapters and see which of the following theories seem to apply to the various findings in that chapter.

Systems Theory

A variety of theories fall under the general heading of **systems theory,** but all share certain assumptions. As applied to intimate relationships, systems theory asserts that the intimate group must be analyzed as a whole; the

group has boundaries that distinguish it from other groups. Thus, particular people form the system and have particular rules and roles that apply to their system. Furthermore, the group is composed of interrelated parts (individuals). That is, the parts are not independent but influence each other and work together in such a way that the system tends to be maintained; outside influences generally cause minimal change. If the system is composed of three or more individuals (as in a family with children), various subsystems may arise (e.g., parent and child may form a coalition against the other parent). Although such subsystems may appear to be threatening, they actually tend to maintain the system. For instance, a woman may remain in a marriage only because she and her child support and protect each other when the alcoholic husband and father becomes abusive.

Family therapists use systems theory. Among the well-known theories of family therapists is that of Murray Bowen (1978), who built his theory on the premise that humans respond primarily at the emotional rather than the cognitive level (Crosby 1991). In this theory, two tasks are important for healthy development. The first is to develop our cognitive functioning so that our behavior is not driven mainly by our emotions. The second is to develop our individuality so that we have separate identities from our family of origin even while remaining members of that family (Charles 2001).

These tasks may be complicated by certain family processes, such as the formation of coalitions (subsystems) and the tendency to transmit unhealthy patterns from one generation to another (the system maintaining itself). Thus, what appears to be an individual's problem may be a problem arising out of the family system. In order to help the individual, a therapist should treat the family, for it is the system itself and not merely one of its parts that is not functioning in a healthy way. Bowen's theory is, of course, far more complex than we can discuss here, but see our discussion of the use and misuse of power in chapter 10 for an example of its application.

Exchange Theory

"You owe me one" is a popular expression of **exchange theory,** which asserts that we all attempt to keep our costs lower than our rewards in interaction (Nye 1988). *Costs* refer to such things as time, money, emotional or intellectual energy, or anything else that an individual defines as part of his or her investment in a relationship. Similarly, *rewards* include emotional or intellectual gratification, money, a sense of security, or anything else an individual defines as a satisfying outcome of a relationship. If a relationship consistently costs us more than it rewards us, we are likely to avoid the person or break the relationship.

Exchange theory posits a rational assessment of a situation. The individual weighs the pros and cons, the costs and rewards, of a situation. He or she tries to determine if the situation is fair or appealing or worthwhile. To some extent, this happens in selecting a life partner (see the discussion in chapter 7). It happens in the negotiation of responsibilities of dual-career couples (chapter 11). It occurs in many other areas of family life, such as decision making, child rearing, and division of labor in the home. Exchange theory does not explain all of family life, but it is clearly of value in our efforts to understand.

Symbolic Interaction Theory

Symbolic interaction theory views humans primarily as cognitive creatures who are influenced and shaped by their interaction experiences (Lauer and Handel 1983). That is, what happens in interaction is a result not merely of what individuals bring to it but also of the interaction itself. Like systems theorists, symbolic interactionists believe that the whole is greater than the sum of its parts. Thus, a young woman who has determined to devote herself to a career rather than marry may find herself changing her mind as she interacts with a particular man. Or a man who is negative about parenthood may find himself becoming enthusiastic and committed as he interacts with his child.

An important concept in symbolic interactionism is **definition of the situation.** According to this concept, when we define a situation as real, it has real consequences. That is, our interpretation of a situation is as important as anything that is objectively true about that situation. For example, a man may be very jealous of his girlfriend because he believes she is flirting with other men. In point of fact, she may be completely faithful to her boyfriend. But if he perceives her to be flirting, there will be real—and perhaps damaging—consequences to the relationship.

Depending on how they define their situation, then, people may be satisfied in a relationship that outsiders view as undesirable or dissatisfied in one that outsiders view as very good. Our discussion of spouse abuse in chapter 14 points out how abused women perceive their situation in a variety of ways that justify staying in the relationship.

Symbolic interactionism can be combined with exchange theory. For example, what is important is not that rewards exceed costs in some objective sense or as assessed by an outside observer but that the people involved in a relationship perceive the rewards to exceed the costs (see the discussion of equity in chapter 8).

Conflict Theory

Conflict theory asserts that all societies are characterized by inequality, conflict, and change as groups within the society struggle over scarce resources. These groups have differing and even contradictory interests, needs, and goals. Because of the contradictions and because the things for which people strive may not be available in sufficient number for all, everyone cannot be satisfied. Individuals from the differing groups therefore struggle with each other, using whatever resources they have, each striving to meet his or her own interests, needs, and goals.

In family studies, conflict theory is seen in explanations that focus on two types of groups: social class and gender. A **social class** is a group of people with similar levels of income, education, and occupational prestige and a similar lifestyle. The higher your social class, the more resources you have available to you. At various points in this book, you will encounter some class differences in family life. Class differences are prominent in chapter 2, where we discuss the disadvantages faced by those (single parents and most racial/ethnic groups) who have a disproportionate number of their families in the lower classes.

Conflict theory also is used to explain gender differences. Feminists argue that the traditional family is a patriarchal arrangement that men use to maintain their power over women. Some believe that men have an inherent advantage in the power struggle because they possess more of a crucial resource—money. Typically, men have brought more money than women have into the household, thereby establishing their power over women and having the final say in any decisions that matter to them.

In various parts of this book, we will employ conflict theory to look at gender differences in terms of "his" experience and "her" experience (e.g., of marriage in chapter 8 and of parenting in chapter 12). Conflict theory also can be used to explain such phenomena as power struggles (chapter 10).

Theory and Intimacy

A common reaction from students when we talk about theory is, "I'm interested in the practical stuff, but not in theory. What use is theory to me?"

Actually, theory can be used to understand all the topics in this book. Some theories, of course, work better than others for explaining particular topics. But all are useful in enhancing your understanding of intimate relationships.

One of our students provided us with an interesting example of the utility of theory. Here is her story:

I went through a series of relationships, finally got married, and within a few years was divorced. I thought I would never find "Mr. Right." So I decided to get my college degree. When I took a social psychology class and studied symbolic interactionism, I had a revelation: I divorced my husband because he was a man!

I know that sounds silly. What I mean is, I learned that our behavior reflects the gender roles that we learn in our society. I thought my ex-husband was just a bad catch. Now I realize that he was only acting like most men who learn the traditional male role in our society. I know now that I could have accepted this and that we could have worked together to iron out the things that were vexing me.

It's just too bad I didn't take the course before I got married.

The student learned a better way to understand behavior than simply concluding, "I married a jerk." The point is, the theories alert you to look for certain things in intimate relationships and to understand them in particular ways. For example, understanding of a theory may prompt you to ask, "What was the family system in which my partner grew up and how can my knowledge of that help me in our relationship?" (systems theory); "Is our relationship less satisfying because one of us feels that it costs more than it's worth?" (exchange theory); "Is money an issue with us because we define its use and importance differently rather than because one of us is right and the other is wrong?" (symbolic interactionism); and "Are we arguing so long and hard because we are engaged in a power struggle rather than in a conflict over a single issue?" (conflict theory).

These examples are only illustrations, but they underscore the fact that an understanding of theory is an important tool for you to use in building and maintaining meaningful intimate relationships. Because theory is important, therefore, we identify specifically at one or more places in each chapter the way a particular theory applies and note in the margin the theory being used. These notations provide you with many more examples of how you can use theory to better understand and thereby enhance your own intimate relationships.

SUMMARY

Humans are social creatures and have, therefore, a basic need for close, personal relationships. The experiences of loneliness, both social and emotional loneliness, and of gaining well-being through intimate relationships illustrate our social nature and our need for intimacy.

We learn about family life through our own experiences and through the mass media. But some of what we know is mythical. Some of the common myths today include (1) we've lost the extended family, (2) opposites attract, (3) people marry because they love each other, (4) having children increases marital satisfaction, (5) a good sex life is the best predictor of marital satisfaction, (6) happily married people don't have conflict, and (7) half of all marriages end in divorce. Such myths are dangerous because they can ruin good relationships.

Patterns of intimate relationships change over time. In recent years, there has been an increase in premarital sex, out-of-wedlock births, the number of people living alone, the number of people cohabiting, age at first marriage, and the proportion of mothers who work. The divorce rate has declined, but is still much higher than it was through most of the twentieth century. Birth rates and average household size have both declined.

Social scientists debate what Americans need in the way of marriage and family life. Some argue that alternative forms of the family are as valid and as fulfilling as the heterosexual, married-couple family, while others insist that the heterosexual, married-couple family is crucial to both individual and social well-being.

For various reasons, only a minority of Americans now live in a family that has an employed father, a stay-at-home mother, and children. Some experts believe this is a trend that will continue, lessening the importance of marriage, while others assert the trend will reverse. Americans are seeking to work out what they want in the context of the contrary values of familism and individualism. But the strengths and benefits of marriage and family are so clear that most Americans continue to value them and to indicate satisfaction with their own marriage and family life. Those who desire a stable and satisfying marriage and family are still able to achieve them.

KEY TERMS

birth rate *11*
cohabitation *10*
conflict theory *21*
definition of the situation *21*
emotional loneliness *4*
exchange theory *20*
extended family *6*

familism *16*
family of origin *4*
integration *5*
intimacy *4*
loneliness *4*
myth *6*
nuclear family *7*

social class *21*
social loneliness *4*
symbolic interaction theory *21*
systems theory *20*
theory *20*
values *16*

ON THE WEB   Marriage and Family in America: Needs, Myths, and Dreams

As noted in the text, we get our information about marriage and family from both experience and the mass media. An important source of information among the mass media is the Internet. There is also a certain amount of misinformation, so you must be careful about which sources you use. It's a good idea to begin with sites that are provided by experts such as researchers. Two very good sites are:

National Council on Family Relations
http://www.ncfr.org

This site, sponsored by a prestigious organization that publishes two of the better journals, not only posts various news items and information about professional activities but also gives you access to press reports based on articles published in their professional journals.

The National Marriage Project
http://marriage.rutgers.edu

Based at Rutgers University in New Jersey, the National Marriage Project engages in ongoing research into various aspects of marriage and family life. The site offers access to their varied publications.

www.mhhe.com/lauer7e

Using these two sites, enlarge your understanding with the following projects:

1. Go to the NCFR site and click on "press release." You will have access to releases that describe articles published in the *Journal of Marriage and Family* and in *Family Relations*. Select one that interests you, then try to put the findings into the theoretical perspectives described in this chapter. Which theoretical perspective seems most useful? Which one or ones appear not to be useful? Why?

2. A number of important trends are noted in this chapter ("changing patterns of intimate relationships"). Check the press releases for both journals at the NCFR site, and examine the recent publications at the National Marriage Project site. To what extent are either of these sites addressing the trends? What new or updated information can you find related to the trends? Which trends seem to be ignored, and how could you explain the omissions?

3. Imagine you have to speak to a group of high school teenagers about what they can expect in terms of their own future marriages and family life. Use information from the two sites to outline a 45-minute talk that you think would be useful for them.

~ DIVERSITY IN FAMILIES ~

LEARNING OBJECTIVES

After reading and studying chapter 2, you should be able to

1 Briefly discuss how families vary across time and among and within societies.

2 Define what a *family* is.

3 Explain the problems of the single-parent family.

4 Discuss the various ways the single-parent family copes with its problems.

5 Outline the similarities and differences among African American, Hispanic, Asian American, Native American, and white families in U.S. society.

6 Describe life in the contemporary black family.

7 Discuss the strengths as well as the problems of the Hispanic family.

8 Explain how the Asian culture shapes the structure and experience of Asian American families.

9 Identify two factors that affect Native American family life.

10 Understand the difficulties of interracial families and the ways in which they cope with these problems.

11 Describe the similarities and differences between heterosexual and homosexual families in developing lasting intimate relationships.

Have you ever played the game of word association? For example, when you hear the word *fun*, what is the first word that comes to your mind? How about *happiness? Dating? Marriage?* Jot down your first response to each word.

Now respond to the word *family*. Instead of just one response, however, write down five words that come to mind. Then think about your responses. Why do you think you made these particular associations? Are there any common elements in your choices? Did your responses to *fun, happiness, dating, and marriage* have anything to do with family life? Based on your responses, what is your family like?

How do you think other people would respond to the words? Would they respond differently depending on their family situations or backgrounds? Ask 10 others to play the game of word association with you. If possible, select two different groups of five people each, such as five married people and five single parents, or five white and five black married people, or five heterosexuals and five homosexuals. If that isn't possible, get people who come from as many of the groups discussed in this chapter as possible.

Write down their responses. Then compare the two groups or those from differing groups. What kinds of meaning of family life seem to emerge from the words they chose? Do you see any differences among them? If so, how would you explain the differences? If not, why do you think there are no differences?

If the entire class participates in this project, you can specify the groups you want to investigate (perhaps three or four different groups) and pool the results. What conclusions would you now draw about the meaning of *family?* ❧

Imagine that you are an artist and that you have been asked to draw or paint a picture of a family. You may use any setting you like. What would you draw? Whatever the setting, you would probably draw an adult man, an adult woman, and one or more children. And for many of you, these people would probably be white.

But some families are composed of only two people—an adult and a child. Some are composed of nonwhites. Others are racially mixed. And others are composed of two adults of the same sex, with or without children. Because there are so many variations, the question arises as to what is meant by *family*. One way to define it is to identify the functions that all families fulfill. Anthropologists identify four functions: sexual relations, reproduction, socialization of children, and economic cooperation. However, each of these functions, except the socialization of children, is lacking in families in one or more societies in the world (Reiss and Lee 1988). And even socialization is lacking in those families that are childless.

Our definition of **family,** therefore, is a group united by marriage or cohabitation, blood, and/or adoption in order to satisfy intimacy needs and/or bear and socialize children. Satisfying intimacy needs and rearing children always take place in a social context, however. Such factors as social class, race, sexual orientation, religious affiliation, and type of community (urban or rural) all have some bearing upon marriage and family life.

THE SOCIAL CONTEXT OF FAMILY LIFE

Let's go back to the picture of a family. Does social context make any difference? That is, does it make any difference in the family life if the people are white or Hispanic or part of a nonwhite racial group, **heterosexual** or **homosexual,** a couple, or a single parent? In many ways, the answer is "no," because whatever the social context, Americans want most of the same things: a marriage that is satisfying and that lasts, children who grow up with both parents and who do well in their lives, a family with strong and meaningful bonds, and so on. Thus, a study of white and Hispanic mothers in a northern California community found differences between the two groups in income and educational attainment, but found no differences between the values placed on, and the amount of time given to, work, marriage, and parenting (Franco, Sabattini, and Crosby 2004). And a study of high school seniors reported similar, high long-term educational and occupational goals among all

racial/ethnic groups—white, African American, Asian American, and Hispanic (Chang et al. 2006).

At the same time, the extent to which people are able to live out their values for marriage and family life is affected by the social context. In particular, lower social class position, prejudice, and discrimination adversely affect those striving to realize their ideals. For example, while Americans generally value high educational achievement for themselves and their children, the factor most strongly associated with that achievement is social class position (Fang and Sen 2006). The lower your social class position, the lower your educational achievement is likely to be. Another example is spousal violence, which is also more likely—independently of race or ethnicity—among the poor (Frias and Angel 2005).

Culture is another part of social context that can affect family life. For example, Asian culture stresses the subordination of the individual to the group. As we shall point out later in this chapter, that translates into such things as the socialization of children into the values of obedience, loyalty, and self-control to a greater extent than is true of other groups. Similarly, Native American culture has a strong emphasis on custom and tradition and the extended family.

Some of the families we examine in this chapter are diverse because of such cultural emphases. But the most important factor in the diversity found in them is the fact that they are disproportionately in the lower social classes and/or the victims of prejudice and discrimination. Their diverse experiences of marriage and family life occur in a corrosive social context. We will point out differences between families from varying racial/ethnic groups in subsequent chapters (that is, wherever research has identified differences). Here, we want to look at how families fare in the struggle to build intimate relationships in the face of low social class position, prejudice and discrimination, and variant cultural traditions.

We will first look briefly at how families vary among and within human societies generally. Then we will examine various U.S. families that are affected by low social class position and/or prejudice and discrimination. As table 2.1 shows, a disproportionate number of single-parent, African American, Hispanic, and Native American families are in the lowest social class (below the poverty level in income). They are also, like those in interracial and in gay and lesbian families, subject to a certain amount of prejudice and discrimination. They have, therefore, additional pressures and constraints as they strive to maintain a meaningful family life.

TABLE 2.1   Percent of People Below the Poverty Level, 2006

	Percent
All people	12.3
People in families	10.6
In white families	8.5
In black families	23.1
In Hispanic families	19.5
In Asian American families	8.0
In families with female householder, no husband present	30.5

Source: DeNavas-Walt, Proctor, and Smith 2007:44–45.

THE VARIABILITY OF FAMILY LIFE

Families vary across time, among societies, and within societies. It would require a number of volumes to fully discuss such variations. In this section, we only want to illustrate the variability with a few examples.

Variations among Societies

In some ways, people everywhere are alike. People everywhere, for example, need intimate relations and form family units to fulfill some of their intimacy needs. When we talk about variations, then, we are not overlooking the similarities among peoples. Rather, we are stressing the important points that intimacy needs can be fulfilled in diverse ways and diverse kinds of family units can be formed.

The variations among societies underscore the fact that some differ from what we may regard as normal, natural, right, or typical. For example, our ideal is for marriage to be "'til death do us part." Marco Polo reported a tribe in Asia in which a wife could take another husband if her first husband was away from home for 20 days; the husband could also take another wife if he was staying in a different place (Durant 1954:38).

Another of our ideals is choice—individuals should personally choose whom they marry. But many cultures have or have had the practice of **arranged marriage,** in which the parents choose marital partners for their children. The bride and groom may not even see each other before the wedding. We discuss more about arranged marriages in chapter 7.

Finally, the ideal of most Americans is **monogamy,** union with one person at a time. We say "most" Americans because the early Mormons, as a part of their belief system, practiced a form of polygamy. **Polygamy** is the

marriage of one person to two or more people of the opposite sex. **Polygyny** is the marriage of a man to two or more wives, while **polyandry** is the marriage of a woman to two or more husbands. Although illegal in the United States, a small splinter group of Mormons still practices polygyny in accord with their religious beliefs (Altman and Ginat 1996).

Polygyny has been practiced by more human societies than any other form of marriage. Most preindustrial societies as well as modern Muslim societies allow polygyny. While Americans are prone to see polygyny as a form of female oppression, women who are part of such unions sometimes define them quite differently. Many Mormon wives in the nineteenth century vigorously tried to get the federal government to allow polygyny. A study of polygynous wives in the African nation of Cameroon found that the wives most satisfied with the arrangement were junior (newer and younger) wives rather than senior wives, those with more children (a status symbol in the society), and those whose husbands had a higher economic status (Gwanfogbe et al. 1997). For many polygynous wives, it is *their* situation that is the ideal, not the monogamous union that is idealized in U.S. society.

On the other hand, some women find the polygynous arrangement very unsatisfying. Interviews with ten polygynous families in an Arab town in the south of Israel reported that half of the families seemed to be well-functioning and half were functioning poorly. But the experience was painful to some extent for the wives in both kinds of families (Slonim-Nevo and Al-Krenawi 2006).

Other variations are based not so much in ideals as in common practices. In our society, at least until recent times, a woman typically assumed the surname of the man she married. Couples establish their own residence, and the family tree is traced through both the husband's and the wife's line. However, anthropologists have discovered a wide range of patterns in other societies. In some societies, for example, the man takes the woman's name. In others, the husband continues to live with his family, rather than with his wife, or couples may alternate residence between the man's and the woman's families. People in some societies trace their line only through the man, while others trace it only through the woman.

There are, in sum, a wide range of practices that people have developed to satisfy their intimacy needs in families. No evidence exists that any particular practice works best for people generally. In fact, one could argue

A polygamous Mormon family illustrates the diversity of U.S. family life.

that the diversity of family life is both necessary and desirable if the maximum number of people are to find satisfying family relationships.

Variations within Societies

Within any particular society, family life varies over time. And in a complex, modern society, it varies among groups at any particular point in time as well. The core of this chapter will explore these variations among groups. Here,we want to illustrate how the family has varied over time by looking at a few aspects of white families in colonial America (Queen, Habenstein, and Quadagno 1985). You can compare the following materials with what you know about white family life today.

The American colonists generally believed that it was important for every individual to be a part of a household. Single people were not merely encouraged to be married but were stigmatized if they remained single too long. In some cases, they were even penalized; Maryland, for instance, imposed a tax on bachelors.

In spite of the stigma on singlehood, it was not easy to get married. In the early years of the southern colonies, there were about four men for every woman. And in all the colonies, a young man was expected to be financially independent before he married. This meant that he had to have a home on his own land. Once financially secure, he had to secure the permission of the prospective bride's father before he could even begin the courtship.

When a couple was ready to marry, they would make their intention known publicly. This could be done by a posted notice in a public place or the reading of the banns (a public notice, normally given three times) in a public meeting or a church. New Englanders initially regarded marriage as a civil affair. Magistrates, not clergy, performed wedding ceremonies. Not until 1692 were clergymen allowed to perform weddings in Massachusetts. In the southern colonies, except for Maryland, the clergy were required to perform the marriage services.

Because of lack of birth control, marriage was likely to lead quickly to children, and families tended to be large. Seven or more children were not uncommon. Colonial families were not likely to face an "empty nest" at middle age under such circumstances. Unmarried children could be living at home until the parents were fairly old.

Sexual standards were strict. In New England, unmarried people caught in the act of having intercourse could be fined, whipped, forced to marry, or any combination of the three. Some of the colonies were even stricter in the matter of adultery. Some offenders were required to wear publicly a scarlet letter. Some were whipped or sentenced to time in the pillory. And a few were put to death. The standards were the same in the South, but the penalties were far less severe. Even in the South, however, an offender could be publicly censured and punished.

As in modern America, marriage did not always work out well in the colonies. Divorce was much rarer, however. In the southern colonies, divorce was not legal; unhappy couples might eventually separate, or one or the other spouse might desert. In contrast, since marriage was a civil contract among the early Puritans of New England, the contract could be dissolved by a local court. Adultery, cruelty, and a long period of absence were among the reasons for which a court might grant a divorce. The court also gave the divorcing parties the right to remarry. Desertion was more common than divorce in early New England, leaving some women to raise their children alone.

Clearly, then, the colonial family differed from most families today in a number of important ways. If we had time to trace the family throughout American history, we would discover variations at each time period. Let's examine some of the diversity in family life in America today.

THE SINGLE-PARENT FAMILY

Single-parent families may occur in various ways, including divorce, death of a spouse, and the decision to have or adopt a child on one's own without getting married. An increasing number of people, particularly women, have opted for parenthood without marriage in recent years, in many cases with support from family, friends, employers, clergy, and physicians (Downs 2003).

In the case of divorce, *single-parent* does not mean that the child has no contact with the other parent but that the child lives primarily with one parent. In other cases, contact with the other parent or with the biological parents (in the case of adoption) may not be possible. *Single-parent* also does not mean a permanent arrangement. In fact, using national data, Aquilino (1996) found that, among children born to unmarried mothers, only one in five spent their entire childhood in a single-parent home and nearly half had grandparents or other relatives living with them during their childhood.

Extent of Single-Parent Families

Single-parent families have increased considerably over the past decades, from roughly 3.5 million in 1970 to 12.9 million in 2006, representing nine percent of all households (U.S. Census Bureau 2008). Most of the single parents (10.4 million) are mothers. African Americans and Hispanics have higher rates of single-parent families than do whites or Asian Americans.

People may be single parents by default: those abandoned or divorced by spouses, those left alone because the other parents were incarcerated, those left alone because the other parents didn't want to marry them,

Single-parent families are an increasing proportion of all families.

and those widowed. Becoming a single parent by default can pose severe problems for both parent and child. Hamer and Marchioro (2002) interviewed 24 black men in an impoverished area who were single parents because the mothers weren't interested in parenting or had had their children taken away because they abused or neglected them. Although the men used their kin networks to help with the parenting, a combination of low wages and minimal assistance from social service agencies diminished their effectiveness as fathers.

Single parenting also may be a choice. A woman may want to be a mother, but may not want to get married or not yet have found a suitable candidate for marriage. Such a choice is easier than it was in the past because single parenthood is less stigmatized.

Thus, in the 1960s and 1970s the increase in single-parent families came about largely as a result of divorce, but the subsequent increase is due more to nonmarital

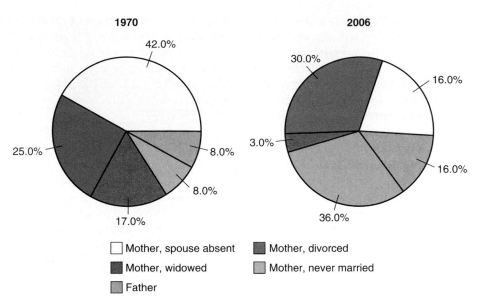

FIGURE 2.1 Children Living with One Parent
Sources: U.S. Census Bureau 1994:66; 2007a.

births (Sawhill 2006). Figure 2.1 shows the dramatic increase in the proportion of single-mother families that involve women who have never been married. Many single fathers have also never been married (Eggebeen, Snyder, and Manning 1996).

Women who opt to be single parents have various motives. A minority are financially well off, want to have children, but do not want or cannot find a husband (Hertz 2006). Many more are poor and are likely to be even poorer or to remain in poverty because of the children. What drives them? In interviews with 162 low-income, single mothers in the Philadelphia area, Edin and Kefalas (2005) assert that most of the mothers say their children "saved" them because motherhood brought them out of a chaotic, self-destructive lifestyle and gave meaning and focus to their lives.

Finally, it is important to keep in mind that when we talk about the number of children living in a one-parent home in any year, we are only talking about a fraction of the children who will live with one parent at some point in their lives. Depending on what happens to marriage and divorce rates, as many as half of all children may ultimately spend some time in a one-parent household.

Challenges of the Single-Parent Family

What kinds of challenges are you more likely to encounter if you are a single parent or a child in a single-parent family? As we discuss the challenges, keep in mind that these are challenges you are *more likely* to experience. As we

shall see in the next section, *more likely* does not mean *most likely;* it only means your chances of dealing with certain difficulties are somewhat higher if you live in a one-parent family.

Challenges of Single Parents. Parenthood is challenging and difficult even when there are two parents in the home. With just one parent, the challenges increase greatly. Raising a child as a single parent has rewards, but it also has more costs and problems associated with it than does two-parent child rearing (Nomaguchi and Milkie 2003). A basic problem is the inadequacy of resources available to the single parent and the consequent overload (Brennan et al. 2007). This basic problem faces single parents of all racial/ethnic groups and those living in rural as well as urban areas (Nelson 2005). In particular, the single parent is likely to face three kinds of overload: responsibility, task, and emotional.

Responsibility overload may result from having too few financial resources. The problem is especially acute for mothers who are single parents. In fact, much of the disadvantage of single-mother households, including the academic performance of the children, is accounted for by economic disadvantages. The economic disadvantage is particularly severe for single mothers who have never been married, and for grandmothers who function as a single parent (Franklin, Smith, and McMiller 1995; Park 2006). Overall, single-mother households have higher rates of poverty than any other group (table 2.1).

Task overload arises from the fact that one parent must do the work of two parents. If the parent works full-time outside the home as well as takes care of the children and manages the household, he or she is likely to feel overwhelmed by the sheer number of tasks that need to be done. Olson and Banyard (1993) found that general parenting tasks such as discipline and getting children to do household tasks were the most frequent sources of stress for low-income single mothers.

Emotional overload can occur when the single parent neglects his or her own needs. Single, employed mothers, who are likely to have less time for such matters as personal care, and leisure activities than either the nonemployed single mother or the mother in a two-parent home, report particularly high levels of distress (Hildebrandt and Kelber 2005). The working single parent may also have an intimacy deficit, a deficit that cannot be alleviated by friends if the parent has little time for anything but his or her job and family work. And the deficit cannot be made up by the children, for they are a responsibility as well as a source of companionship. In addition, the parent needs the intimacy of a peer, the closeness of an adult relationship.

Alone or in combination, the three kinds of overload can result in loneliness, a feeling of hopelessness, or various emotional problems. Anxiety and depression are common problems of single mothers who are two to three times more likely than married mothers to seek professional help for mental health problems (Cairney et al. 2004). Even when the single mother has some social support, she may still succumb to depression because of the numerous stressors with which she must cope every day (Turner 2006).

Comparison

Single Parents in Iceland

If you are a single parent in the United States, you are likely to deal with more challenges and problems than married parents. How does this compare with single parents in a small nation like Iceland? Juliusdottir (1997) conducted a study of a national random sample of 846 Icelandic parents. A number of interesting findings emerged about Icelandic single parents:

- Ninety-five percent of the single parents are women.
- Nearly a third of the single parents have obtained or are obtaining further education.
- Single mothers on the average work about eight hours a week more than widowed mothers but about the same number of hours a week (approximately 43) as married mothers.
- Single parents have a lower average income than married parents, widowed parents, or noncustodial divorced parents—about 74 percent as much as the average of the other three groups.

- Among all parents, visits with grandparents are frequent; about 44 percent of all parents visit grandparents three times a week or more, with single parents visiting somewhat more often than the other three groups.
- When the parents were asked about their health, the single parents complained more about emotional and psychosomatic health problems than did the married parents; the healthiest group was the married parents, followed by never-married single parents, divorced single parents, widowed single parents, and non-custodial divorced parents.

Icelandic single parents show both similarities with and differences from U.S. single parents. Like their U.S. counterparts, the Icelandic single parents are overwhelmingly female, have fewer financial resources, and are likely to have more health problems. Among the health problems cited more often by the Icelandic single parents than by the married parents were

insecurity, anxiety attacks, headaches, and fatigue. Interestingly, however, the noncustodial divorced parents had the most severe health problems, complaining about sleeplessness, depression, and pessimism more than the other groups.

The high level of health problems among the noncustodial divorced parents may reflect a grieving process. Family relations in Iceland—as indicated by the high visitation rate—are very strong. The noncustodial divorced parents are not only separated from their ex-spouses and children but also have substantially fewer visits with or calls to grandparents than do the single parents. In a society with a high value on family relations, there are adverse health consequences for those deprived of those relations.

Finally, Icelandic single parents tend to be more involved with family than their U.S. counterparts. This gives them a stronger social support network and helps insulate them from some of the problems faced by their American counterparts.

Challenges of Children of Single Parents. Children of single parents generally do not have, from infancy on, the same level of social, emotional, relational, and financial care as children in two-parent homes (Aronson and Huston 2004). It is not surprising, then, that these children are more likely to exhibit a variety of problematic behaviors (Amato 2001; Ellis et al. 2003; Berger 2005; Barton 2006; Hollist and McBroom 2006; Bramlett and Blumberg 2007; Turner, Finkelhor, and Ormrod 2007); compared to those in two-parent families, they

- have higher rates of antisocial behavior, aggression, anxiety, depression and school problems.
- are less likely to complete high school.
- are more likely to get involved in early sexual activity and adolescent pregnancy.
- are more likely to be the victims of abuse.
- are more likely to use illicit drugs.
- are likely to have poorer mental and physical health.

And, again, these result are true for all racial/ethnic groups and in both urban and rural communities (Hoffmann 2006).

But it is important to reiterate that these tendencies *do not mean that most children in single-parent families will suffer such consequences.* Higher rates do not mean a majority; they only mean that children in single-parent homes are more likely than those in two-parent homes to have such problems. Still, if your chances of being seriously depressed are, say, three in ten rather than one in ten, the difference is sufficiently large to warrant concern.

The children in single-parent homes have more difficulties within the family as well as within themselves and in their outside relationships. Because the bulk of single-parent families are headed by females, it is not surprising that both primary school children and adolescents in single-parent homes report less support, control, and punishment from their fathers than do other children (Amato 1987). They also report more conflict with siblings, more family stress, and less family cohesion. Cohesion, the sense of emotional bonding that family members have toward each other, is important. Fewer behavioral problems occur when family members define themselves as part of a cohesive unit (Dreman and Ronen-Eliav 1997).

Single parents do attempt to build cohesion through various kinds of family rituals (Moriarty and Wagner 2004). And one might expect the bond to be stronger with the remaining parent when a divorce or separation has occurred. So why do children in single-parent families feel less cohesion? One possibility is that single-parent children begin to establish their independence earlier than those from intact homes. And when children are in the phase of establishing their own separate identities, they typically perceive less family cohesion.

Interestingly, the children may feel greater cohesion if the mother is working (Alessandri 1992). Mothers who are unemployed are more likely to get depressed, leading to more frequent punishment of and increased distress and depression in the children (McLoyd et al. 1994). In such a situation, it is understandable that the children will not sense their home to be very cohesive.

Finally, children in single-parent homes are less likely to achieve higher levels of education, occupation, and income and to maintain stable marriages (Mueller and Cooper 1986; Caspi et al. 1998). McLanahan and Sandefur (1994) found that, compared to those who grew up with both biological parents, teenagers who spend part of their childhood apart from their biological father are twice as likely to drop out of high school, twice as likely to become parents while still in their teens, and one and a half times as likely to be both out of school and without work into their early 20s.

To some extent, these effects reflect the fact that those in single-parent homes are more likely to be in a lower socioeconomic level. But even when we look at those who come from the same socioeconomic levels, the children from the single-parent homes are at a disadvantage. Growing up with two parents appears to increase our level of motivation to achieve. Perhaps the harried single parent simply cannot give the attention to the child's achievements that is necessary to motivate the child to higher and higher levels.

Problems Between Parents and Children. "Anyone who thinks that children are helpless creatures," a weary parent remarked, "should remember that it takes at least two adults to handle one child." Parenting is not an easy responsibility even when there are two in the home. When there is one, relationships with children present even more severe challenges.

Consider some of the problems that can arise when the single parent interacts with the child or children. In a mother-daughter home, there may be more open competition, with the daughter wanting to stay up as late as the mother and measuring her success with boys against her mother's success with men (Bohannan 1985:169–70). The daughter also may lack an appropriate understanding of male-female relationships. As noted family therapist Virginia Satir put it,

Her attitudes about being female can range all the way from being the servant girl—giving everything, receiving nothing—to feeling she has to do everything herself and be completely independent (1972:172).

Boys seem to present even greater problems than girls (Hetherington 2003). Recently divorced mothers of sons report less control of their children than do mothers of girls or married mothers (Mednick 1987:196). Sons have a harder time adjusting to divorce than do daughters and express some of their anger in disobedience and aggressiveness against the mother. The aggression tends to reach a peak at about a year after the divorce but is still higher after two years than that of boys in intact families.

Some of the problems between mothers and sons arise not from the son's feelings about the situation but from the mother's decisions about how to relate to the son now that the father is absent (Satir 1972). A single mother may try to get an older son to assume some of the role responsibilities of the missing father. That distorts both the parent–child relationship and the son's relations with any siblings. If the son feels an obligation to nurture and care for his mother and defend her against her own helplessness, he may not be able to establish his own independence and pursue his own needs for intimate heterosexual relationships. Or he may rebel against the situation and leave home but wrestle for years or even a lifetime with a feeling of women as enemies. On the other hand, a single mother might tend to "over-mother" the son, who then may form an image of females as dominant and males as insignificant.

Most single-parent families are headed by a mother. The single mother, therefore, has been studied far more than the single father. Do single fathers have similar problems with their sons or daughters? We cannot say with certainty. In a small sample, Richards and Schmiege (1993) found that both mothers and fathers identified at least one *significant* problem of being a single parent, but the fathers identified fewer total problems than did the mothers. A larger study, of 912 single-father households, reported that fathers of preadolescent girls reported significantly fewer problems than fathers with boys, with girls and boys, or with adolescent girls (DeMaris and Greif 1992). Finally, a study comparing father-headed with mother-headed single families in Israel found no differences in well-being between the two groups (Fitchen and Cohen 1995). The single fathers were handling the situation as well as the single mothers.

An advantage of single fathers is the likelihood of higher income. In the Richards and Schmiege (1993)

research, nearly 80 percent of single mothers but less than 20 percent of single fathers identified money as a problem. Single mothers also may be rewarded less than are fathers by their children (Ambert 1982). The children of single fathers are more likely to express their appreciation than are the children of single mothers. This tendency may reflect the belief that it is the mother's responsibility to care for the children. When the father assumes that responsibility, he is going beyond what is expected of him, and he earns special praise and appreciation. There is, of course, no reason why the mother should be any more responsible than the father for rearing the children. Nevertheless, as long as people believe this, the single father is likely to continue receiving more rewards in the form of appreciation and admiration than is the single mother.

Finally, dating can be a vexing problem. If a single parent has problems and issues with regard to interpersonal relationships, those problems and issues may be intensified and added to by the presence of children (Anderson et al. 2004). The parent may feel guilty about leaving the child alone to go out on a date. This may cause some resentment toward the child, who consumes so much of the parent's time and energy. The child, in turn, may decide that the parent is considering remarriage and that he or she may have to adapt to a stepparent. In spite of the difficulties of the single-parent home, some children resist the idea of a stepparent. The potential stepparent is defined as an intruder and one who reminds the child again of the pain of the breakup of the family.

Single parents who perceive their children to be less positive about their dating agree that the children react with both anger and resentment toward the dates. Some parents, recognizing the potential problems, delay introducing their dates to their children, though a majority do so immediately or soon after dating someone. Single mothers are more quick to introduce dates to children than are single fathers. This may reflect women's greater concern with relationships and the sense that it is easier for a woman than a man to accept a nurturing relationship with someone else.

The problem of dating is compounded by the fact that the children not only do not like the parent's dates, but the dates also may be less than enthusiastic about the children. If the parent is strongly attracted to a date who dislikes the children and/or who is disliked by the children, the parent may have to struggle with frustration, disappointment, and resentment toward both the date and the children.

The Successful Single-Parent Family

The challenges and problems we have discussed reflect the special circumstances of parenting without a partner. Again, these challenges and problems are *more* likely to face single-parent than two-parent families but are not experienced by all or even the majority of single-parent families. And even those families that face these challenges may provide a healthier context for children than intact families with a high level of conflict or other severe problems.

To balance the picture, we need to look at some of the positive results found by researchers. For one thing, some two-parent families (e.g., those in which a father has a high level of antisocial behavior) are more damaging to children than are single-parent families (Jaffee et al. 2003).

Personal

"I Chose to Do It Alone"

Most people are not single parents by choice. They become single parents because of separation, divorce, or death or because of a sexual relationship that for some reason did not result in marriage. Emma is a 50-year-old teacher who became a single parent by choice, eventually provided her children with a father, but then returned to singlehood again. She regrets none of her decisions:

My experience with raising children has been deeply colored by the fact that I chose to do it alone. My children were not the result of a love relationship gone sour, but of deliberate planning. Having been raised in a highly dysfunctional family, I left home at an early age with a really negative concept of marriage.

After a few years of living on my own, I realized I badly wanted to have children. But I still had a very negative attitude about marriage. To make a long story short, I managed to have two children in the space of 16 months amidst violent protest from both friends and family. I expected the protest, and I was prepared to deal with it. I knew there would be rough times ahead and that whatever happened, I was going to have to do it entirely alone.

I also knew my children would have to be strong and independent if they were to survive. So as infants, I gave them all the cuddling, stimulation, and nurturing I could, and I found babysitters who did the same. I had to work full-time to support us. So it was important to make what time we had together really count. I did as much as possible with them.

Life was tough, mostly because money was short. But my children seemed secure and well adjusted. Then, when the oldest was eight, I reassessed my situation and soon found myself married to a man who seemed to be what we all needed to make life really complete. Eventually, my "prince" turned out to be a real toad. But he was a good father to my children, and we had a third child. He told me I could stop working and stay home with the children. That was my first mistake. After four years, I got increasingly bored, restless, and irritable. My husband, meanwhile, turned out to be an alcoholic like my father. That awful kind of family life that I was so determined to avoid had developed right under my nose!

When my husband was transferred to another city I stayed behind with the children. I told them we would be on welfare for a while, that I wanted to go back to school and get a degree to teach. They agreed. I went to school days while they were in school and worked nights while they slept. It wasn't ideal, but we made the most of it. They were understanding, and I began to feel better than I had in years. Eventually, I divorced my husband, got my degree, and improved our financial situation by going back to work.

My children agree that there were times when they felt angry and wished that I was more like the mothers of their friends. But they also feel they grew up stronger, more self-confident and independent than most of the people they see around them. It's been a rough life, but I believe it's been a highly successful one. I am pleased with the way my children are conducting their lives and with the relationships I have with them. My two daughters are married and have their own children. My son is having some problems developing a relationship with a woman, but maybe he will work that out.

If I had it to do all over again, I think the only thing I would change would be to go to school first and then get artificially inseminated. Otherwise, I have no regrets in spite of the painful times. I have discovered quite happily that motherhood does not end when a child leaves home. Being a mother to an adult is quite different from mothering an infant. But it's still mothering.

But even when compared to children in well-functioning two-parent families, those in single-parent families report similar levels of well-being on many measures. For example, while those in single-parent homes are likely to experience less closeness than those in intact homes, this does not mean a serious intimacy deficit. Children living with a mother only report about the same levels of both support and punishment as those living with both parents (Amato 1987).

Moreover, in spite of the greater likelihood of mental health problems, the majority of single parents and their children have fairly high levels of both physical and mental health. In her study of 42 single parents and their children, however, Hanson (1986) found some sex differences in health status. Single mothers had poorer health than single fathers. But children living with a mother reported higher overall health than those living with a father. Interestingly, boys living with their mothers had the best overall health, while girls living with their fathers had the least. We should note that the sample was small and the health status was based on self-reports of eating and sleeping habits, use of drugs, smoking, self-care, use of preventive health measures, history of illness and accidents, and other indicators of well-being. In part, the results probably reflect the fact that women generally report lower health levels than men. They also reflect some of the interaction problems discussed. Thus, mothers with sole custody of sons reported the lowest levels of mental health.

Looking at social skills, Kesner and McKenry (2001) found no differences among 68 preschool children between those from single-parent and those from two-parent families. The children were equally competent in such things as cooperation, assertion, responsibility, empathy, and self-control.

As these findings suggest, single parents can take measures to provide their children with the necessary resources to do well. Single parents who pursue education beyond high school, particularly those who get a college degree, can eliminate the economic deprivation in which many of the children now live (Zhan and Pandey 2004). Positive attitudes and good parenting skills can enable children from single-parent families to perform as well academically as their peers from two-parent families (Ricciuti 2004).

With regard to their experience of being single parents, Richards and Schmiege (1993) found that about two-thirds report that parenting becomes easier over time. And while all the single parents in their sample had at least one significant problem, all but two of the 71 mothers and

fathers also identified at least one parenting strength. They most frequently mentioned a parenting skill as a strength, such as being supportive and fostering independence.

Studies of single fathers report that most of them feel comfortable and competent with their roles (Risman 1986; Nieto 1990). Other studies indicate that both single fathers and single mothers like being parents, feel competent, and are basically satisfied with the parenting experience (Mednick 1987).

In spite of the extra demands on their time and energy, single parents also function well at work. Single parents indicate high levels of satisfaction with their work, and they are not absent from work significantly more than others (Burden 1986). In fact, having a job that provides both meaningful work and a predictable source of income enhances the mental health of single mothers (Mednick 1987).

Finally, based on in-depth interviews of 26 single parents whom professionals had identified as successful, Olson and Haynes (1993) identified a number of factors that contribute to successful single parenthood. The parent must accept the responsibilities and challenges of single parenthood. The parenting role must be given priority. Open communication is essential, as is consistent but nonpunitive discipline. Successful parents are supportive and they foster individuality. At the same time, they maintain a sense of family by creating and maintaining rituals and traditions. Finally, they continue to nurture their own needs, knowing that if they neglect those needs they will be less capable of adequately parenting their children.

RACIAL/ETHNIC FAMILIES

Diversity in racial/ethnic families reflects a history of prejudice and discrimination, a greater proportion of families in the lower social classes, and, to some extent, differing cultural traditions. With regard to the latter, for example, Hispanics may feel a greater responsibility to members of the extended family than do their non-Hispanic peers. Asian American children may be subject to greater pressure from parents than are their non-Asian peers to excel academically.

But the most significant factor in racial/ethnic diversity is the history of prejudice and discrimination and the higher proportion of families in the lower social classes. Thus, a black counselor listed nine habits that "every black dad should have," one of which was the habit of building self-esteem by talking with children about the ways African Americans have had to deal with racism and poverty (Hutchinson 2000). Looking at the lives of black leaders, he argued, provides models that can be used to build confidence and pride.

In this section, then, we will look at the ways in which racial/ethnic families maintain ties with their cultural heritage and cope with prejudice and discrimination. We will see both negative and positive outcomes.

The African American Family

People who differ from the majority have never had an easy time in this country. Prejudice and discrimination have been their lot—from the Irish Catholic immigrants in the nineteenth century to the Vietnamese refugees in the last quarter of the twentieth century. Yet of all those who have struggled for acceptance in the larger society, none has had a more tortured journey than African Americans. Consider how their experience has affected their family life.

The Demographics of African American Families.
Census Bureau estimates put the black population at 40.2 million in mid-2006, representing 13.4 percent of the total population. African Americans are the second largest U.S. minority. Table 2.2 shows some striking

TABLE 2.2   Households by Race, Hispanic Origin, and Type, 2006

Race, Hispanic Origin	Number (1,000)	Percent Distribution
All households		
Total	114,384	100
White	93,588	82
Black	14,002	12
Asian and Pacific Islander	4,273	4
Hispanic (of any race)	12,519	11
Family households		
White, total	63,401	100
Married couple	50,363	79
Male householder	3,903	6
Female householder	9,136	14
Black, total	9,047	100
Married couple	4,126	46
Male householder	805	9
Female householder	4,117	46
Asian and Pacific Islander, total	3,208	100
Married couple	2,590	81
Male householder	235	7
Female householder	383	12
Hispanic (of any race), total	9,862	100
Married couple	6,642	67
Male householder	969	10
Female householder	2,252	23

Source: U.S. Census Bureau 2007.

TABLE 2.3   Living Arrangements of Children under 18 years, by Race and Hispanic Origin, 2006 (Numbers in thousands)

Living Arrangement	Number	Percent Distribution
White		
Children under 18 years	56,332	100.0
Living with		
Two parents	41,599	73.8
Mother only	10,090	17.9
Father only	2,604	4.6
Neither parent	2,040	3.6
Black		
Children under 18 years	11,225	100.0
Living with		
Two parents	3,886	34.6
Mother only	5,742	51.2
Father only	541	4.8
Neither parent	1,056	9.4
Hispanic		
Children under 18 years	14,697	100.0
Living with		
Two parents	9,686	65.9
Mother only	3,674	25.0
Father only	603	4.1
Neither parent	734	5.0
Asian		
Children under 18 years	2,869	100.0
Living with		
Two parents	2,403	83.8
Mother only	278	9.7
Father only	104	3.6
Neither parent	86	3.0

Source: U.S. Census Bureau 2007a.

differences between black families and the others. A smaller proportion of black families consists of married couples. Over half of all black families with children are single-parent families. Figure 2.2 shows that African Americans are the only group in which a minority of adults are married, and African Americans have the highest proportion of people who are divorced or who have never married.

These data mean that black children are more likely than those of any other group to be living in a single-parent family (table 2.3). Black children are also far more likely to be living with a mother who has never been married. To understand such differences, we must explore briefly the black experience in America, particularly the way in which black families have been affected by American institutions.

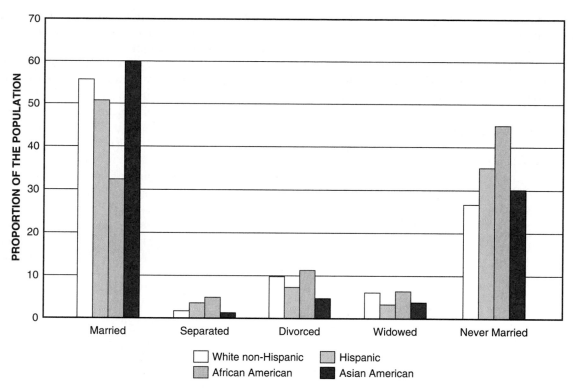

FIGURE 2.2 Marital Status of the Population, 2006
Source: U.S. Census Bureau 2007a.

Social Institutions and African American Family Life.
From slavery through segregation to present-day discrimination, African Americans have waged a long battle in the United States for justice and equality. Even after slavery was ended and African Americans had won certain fundamental rights, such as the right to vote, they faced various kinds of pressures to keep them from exercising their rights. Indeed, efforts to keep blacks from voting appeared even in the 1990s (Lauer and Lauer 2008). Politically, then, African Americans have had difficulties exercising the power needed to press their causes and redress their griev-

Conflict Theory Applied

ances. *Conflict theory* helps us understand their long struggle and its consequences for family life, for much of the segregation and discrimination experienced by African Americans is rooted in the competition between racial groups for economic and political advantage.

Various means have been used to keep African Americans economically disadvantaged (Lauer and Lauer 2008). Economic deprivation, in turn, places great strains on family life. The higher rates of divorce and single-parent families among African Americans become more understandable when we realize that for decades black unemployment rates have been at least double those of whites, and the median income of black families has been less than two-thirds that of whites. In 2006, the median black household income was 61 percent that of white households, down from 66.3 percent in 2000 (DeNavas-Walt, Proctor, and Smith 2007).

Such figures belie the not uncommon belief that African Americans have made great strides economically since the civil rights movement of the 1960s. It is true that an increasing proportion of African Americans are in the middle and upper income brackets. The increasing number of black families who are prospering financially, however, should not obscure the fact that African Americans as a group continue to have the lowest median income of all groups.

A number of factors, all of which have some basis in this economic situation, have affected what one researcher calls the "black marriage crisis," the continuing decline in the rate and quality of black marriages (Malone-Colon 2007).

The decline does not reflect a devaluation of marriage and family. In fact, more blacks than whites say that marriage is very important. And more blacks than whites say that children are very important for a successful marriage (Pew Research Center 2007a). Nevertheless, the proportion of blacks who are married is strikingly lower than that of any other group, and the proportions of separated, divorced, and never married are higher than those of any other group (figure 2.2).

One important factor in understanding these figures is economic—the black male is more likely than the white to be unemployed, or, if employed, to be in a lower income bracket. He is therefore less likely than his white counterpart to be able to offer secure and adequate financial support. Black women, aware of the situation, put more importance than white women on a potential husband being able to offer good financial support (Bulcroft and Bulcroft 1993).

The situation is compounded by the disproportionate number of black men in jails or prisons, the higher mortality rate for young black males compared to that of other racial groups, and the fact that some black men marry women of other races (Crowder and Tolnay 2000; Harris and Miller 2003). African American women who look for a mate within their race, then, have a smaller pool from which to choose. It is this combination of factors that accounts for the lower rate of marriage and the high proportion of female-headed households among African Americans (Rolison 1992; Fossett and Kiecolt 1993).

Those who do marry face some problems that other groups do not, at least not to the same extent. Because of the high rate of unemployment among black men, many black women provide a greater proportion of income to their families than do white women. This can cause strain, because one of the factors in marital satisfaction on the part of wives is the perception that their husbands are good providers. It also may help explain the higher rate of depression among black wives than among white wives (Gazmararian, James, and Lepkowski 1995).

As the economic problems of the black family diminish, the black husband and father assumes a more active role in family life (McAdoo 1985/1986; Hossain and Roopnarine 1993). He becomes more involved with teaching his children and with making child-rearing decisions. Moreover, the black father seems, more than those of other races, to try to socialize daughters to be competent and independent at an early age.

In other words, the fate of the black family, like that of all families, is tied up with its position in the U.S. economy. And its position in the economy, in turn, depends in part on what happens in the government. Various governmental actions in the past, such as school desegregation, voter registration laws, and affirmative action programs, have helped many black families. Affirmative action programs increased the participation of African Americans and other minorities in business, industry, and education. But the programs were dismantled in the 1990s. Organizations can no longer require timetables or quotas for minority hiring. Advocates for the dismantling of affirmative action claim that we have reached a point at which such programs are not needed. Critics, on the other hand, argue that minorities will suffer new setbacks. If the critics are correct, new government programs will be required to reverse the discrimination that has adversely affected black families.

Life in the African American Family. If you are African American, then you are more likely than others to grow up in a family that is impoverished, that is disrupted by divorce, or that is headed by a mother who has never married. Black adolescents mature earlier and have their first sexual experience at earlier ages than others, putting them at greater risk for sexually transmitted disease and unwanted pregnancy (Ohalete 2007). If there is pregnancy and nonmarital birth, black fathers are less likely to provide the amount of support needed by the mother and child (Wiemann et al. 2006). Rates of violent disagreements, spouse abuse, and the maltreatment (including neglect) of children are higher among black families than others (Schuck 2005; Moore et al. 2007). And blacks are more likely to live in a violent neighborhood context. A study of 18- to 25-year-olds living in various Chicago neighborhoods reported that the odds of perpetrating violence were 85 percent higher for blacks than for whites (Sampson, Morenoff, and Raudenbush 2005). Both at home and in their neighborhoods, black parents and children experience more violence than those of other races.

Finally, more black marriages than those of other races are characterized by what one researcher calls an "incomplete merger" (Whyte 1990). In his study of a sample of Detroit families, Whyte found that whites and blacks were similar in terms of division of power and labor in the home. In other ways, however, there were significant differences. In comparison to the white wives, the black wives put more value on a good income and less value on sexual fidelity. The black wives reported less togetherness (in terms of such things as spending free time together, confiding in each other, and having a joint banking account) and, in general, lower marital satisfaction. As Whyte (1990:162) sums it up, the differences "point to a more incomplete 'merger' of the two spouses into the conjugal relationship . . . producing a greater maintenance of separate activities and resources." Other studies also report lower satisfaction among black wives than those of other racial groups or Hispanics (Dillaway and Broman 2001; Bulanda and Brown 2007). And blacks are less likely than others to perceive their marriages as harmonious.

It is important to keep in mind that these problematic aspects of family life are particularly characteristic of that disproportionate number of black families in the lower income brackets. The problems are rooted in economic deprivation and/or experiences of prejudice and discrimination (Cutrona et al. 2003; Jackson and Scheines 2005). Thus, in black families in which there are children living with both parents, rates of poverty and delinquency are lower, the children are more likely to delay sexual activity, and children have higher self-esteem and higher levels of educational achievement (Malone-Colon 2007).

Even among lower-income black families, many parents are able to raise children who are well-adjusted and who achieve upward mobility (Black, Dubowitz, and Starr 1999; Hill 2001). There are, therefore, many strengths and positive aspects of life in the black family. In fact, in some areas black families have advantages over white families. A study of 290 women from two-parent families found that while both whites and African Americans reported good childhood family environments, the black women, compared to the white, rated their families of origin as more cohesive, organized, and expressive, and as lower in conflict (Clay et al. 2007).

Moreover, compared to white families, black families have a greater amount of equality. Black couples are more egalitarian than white couples in the sharing of household tasks (Kamo and Cohen 1998). There is a high degree of cooperation and shared decision making among African American couples (McAdoo 1993). And a higher proportion of black wives (70.3 percent) than of white wives (56.6 percent) report that their husbands or partners act as child care providers (John 1996).

In part, the egalitarianism results from the fact that black wives are more likely than white wives to work, and black husbands are more likely than white husbands to approve of their wives working. Black women have a more consistent history of being employed outside the home than do white women, so that there is more of an expectation than a mere acceptance of their working. Perhaps because of such an expectation, black husbands are willing to adjust their own schedules in order to help their working wives (e.g., by staying home with a sick child).

Extended family relationships are very important to black families. African Americans are likely to live near relatives, possess a strong sense of familial obligations, interact frequently with relatives, have frequent get-togethers with relatives on special occasions and holidays, and expect mutual aid among extended family members (Parke 2004). The kind of aid given and received tends to vary somewhat from white families. African Americans are more likely to give and receive practical help such as transportation or child care, while whites are more likely to give and receive financial and emotional support (Sarkisian and Gerstel 2004).

African Americans differ in some ways from whites in parenting styles. Compared to white fathers, black fathers show less warmth, but more closely monitor their children (Hofferth 2003). Because of continuing prejudice and discrimination, black parents also face the problem of their children's self-esteem. One way they raise that self-esteem is by stressing pride and knowledge about African American culture (Constantine and Blackmon 2002).

Finally, a survey of a group of white and black single parents reported that the blacks were more positive about parenting and were more certain that their children added satisfaction to their lives (Jacobsen and Bigner 1991). And results from the National Survey of Families and Households show no racial differences among single mothers in parenting behavior or involvement with their children (McKenry and Fine 1993). The survey did find, however, that African American single mothers had higher expectations than did whites for their children to be independent, to control their temper, and to be obedient.

Three factors help account for some of these strengths of black single parents: greater extended family support among African Americans, the way children are viewed, and a greater acceptance of single parenthood (McCabe, Clark, and Barnett 1999; Jambunathan, Burts, and Pierce 2000). Thus, there are likely to be additional resources available to the black single parent.

Life in the black family, in sum, is likely to have certain problematic aspects primarily because of the effects of discrimination and deprivation in U.S. society. But many black families are strong and viable and in some areas even have an advantage over other families.

The Hispanic Family

Like African Americans, Hispanics have also had to grapple with prejudice and discrimination, and with lower social class positions. Cultural factors also play a strong role in Hispanic family life.

The Demographics of Hispanic Families. By mid-2006, the U.S. Census Bureau estimated the Hispanic population to be 44.3 million, or 14.8 percent of the total population. Hispanics are the largest minority in the United States. Hispanic families are not as poor as black families, but in 2006 the median household income of Hispanics was only 72.1 percent of that of white non-Hispanics (DeNavas-Walt, Proctor, and Smith 2007). And the poverty rate for Hispanics was more than double that of white families (table 2.1). Moreover, as with African Americans, even at the same educational levels Hispanics fall short of the income levels of non-Hispanic whites (Cavalcanti and Schleef 2001).

There is a strong emphasis on family in Hispanic culture. Thus, 78.8 percent of all Hispanic households are family households (compared to 64.6 percent of black, 67.7 percent of white, and 75.1 percent of Asian households; see table 2.2). Although fewer Hispanics than whites or Asians are married, they are less likely than whites or African Americans to be divorced (figure 2.2). A study of Mexican American women found that they are more likely than whites to live with or close to the extended family and to give each other household and child care help (Sarkisian, Gerena, and Gerstel 2007). The differences between the two groups, however, seem to be related more to differing social class positions than to culture.

A higher proportion of Hispanics (69 percent) than any other group believe that children are very important for a successful marriage (Pew Research Center 2007a). It is not surprising, then, that Hispanics have the highest birth rate of any group—99.1 births per 1,000 women aged 15–44, compared to 67.2 for African Americans, 66.6 for Asians, and 58.4 for whites (Hamilton, Martin, and Ventura 2006). Hispanic teens have higher birth rates than other teenagers (Gilliam 2007). Hispanics also have the third highest rate of births to unmarried women: 47.9 percent of all births, compared to 69.5 percent for African Americans, 63.3 percent for Native Americans, 25.4 percent for whites, and 16.2 percent for Asians (Hamilton, Martin, and Ventura 2006).

In part, the high rates of unmarried mothers among African Americans, Native Americans, and Hispanics reflect the high unemployment rates among their men,

Studies of Hispanic families show more egalitarianism than male dominance.

leaving the women with fewer potential marriage partners than white women have (Catanzarite and Ortiz 2002). However, Hispanic women are about 2.5 times more likely than black women and nearly as likely as white women to marry within 30 months after a nonmarital birth (Harknett and McLanahan 2004).

Life in the Hispanic Family. Evidence regarding the quality of Hispanic marriages is mixed. A study comparing Hispanic with non-Hispanic white and mixed-ethnicity couples found higher levels of distress in the Hispanic couples (Negy and Snyder 2000). A set of representative surveys of the U.S. population indicated that Mexican American wives were not as happy as non-Hispanic white wives (Weaver 2003). Both sets of wives were between 18 and 30 years of age and economically well-off, so the lower happiness of the Hispanic women was not due to age or socioeconomic differences.

In contrast, using data from a national survey of families, and five measures of marital quality, Bulanda and Brown (2007) found that Mexican Americans and whites reported similar levels of marital quality. Additional research is needed to resolve these contradictory results. It may be that the results differ depending on the mix of national origins in the Hispanic sample. That is, we know that somewhat differing results are obtained from, say, those of Cuban or Puerto Rican origin versus those of

Mexican origin. For example, Puerto Rican parents score higher on nurturance and consistency than do Mexican Americans and El Salvadoran Americans (Figueroa-Moseley et al. 2006). And a study of intimate-partner abuse among poor Hispanic women reported significantly lower rates of abuse among Dominican, Puerto Rican, and other Hispanics than among Mexican-origin women (Frias and Angel 2005).

If many Hispanic women do have less satisfaction from marriage, it may be rooted in the higher levels of conflict and abuse in their homes. A national survey of children's health reported that a slightly higher proportion of Hispanic children (11.3 percent) lived in homes where violent disagreements occurred than did U.S. children as a whole (10.3 percent) (Moore et al. 2007). And a study of Hispanic women in the southeast found that 54.9 percent reported violent victimization by an intimate partner (Murdaugh et al. 2004).

Such abuse is linked in the popular imagination with the notion of *machismo,* male power and dominance. However, while machismo may be a characteristic of Latin American culture, studies of Hispanic families in the United States fail to show a pattern of male dominance (Zinn and Wells 2000). There is more egalitarianism than male dominance. Hispanics value egalitarianism in family life as much as do non-Hispanic whites (Franco, Sabattini, and Crosby 2004). And there is a growing movement among Hispanic men to meet in small groups and discuss how they can work cooperatively with their wives, being helpmates rather than bosses in the home (Wood 2001). These men want to redefine *machismo* to mean not a man who rules over his family, but a man who takes proper care of his wife and children in an egalitarian setting.

Parenting in Hispanic families reflects four cultural values: *familismo, respeto, personalismo,* and *simpatía* (Guilamo-Ramos et al. 2007). *Familismo* means familism, an emphasis on family values and family well-being more than on individual desires. In line with this, Hofferth (2003) found that Hispanic fathers take more responsibility for raising their children than do white fathers. *Respeto* is respect for, and responsibility toward, elders. *Personalismo* is a value on individual character and inner qualities. And *simpatía* refers to the value of harmony in relationships, gained by such things as politeness, agreeableness, and respect for others.

Thus, in his study of Dominican and Puerto Rican mothers and their children, Guilamo-Ramos and his associates found a number of practices related to these cultural values. First, the mothers asserted the need to closely monitor and control their adolescents. Loyalty, support, and obedience by their adolescent children was very important to them. Second, although the mothers stressed the importance of strictness rather than leniency, they also insisted on striving to build warm and supportive relationships with their children. At times, that means participating in activities (games, watching television, etc.) that are important to the child.

Third, the mothers said that it is important to explain parental decisions to the children. They do not expect children to obey simply "because I say so." Children deserve an explanation. Fourth, the mothers desire close and trusting relationships with their children. They encourage their children to be open with them. The openness is not total, however. Hispanic parents discuss sexual issues with their children less than parents of other groups do (Guilamo-Ramos et al. 2006); the mothers were raised in a culture that does not support open discussions of sexual matters in the home. Finally, the mothers admitted to making distinctions between their daughters and their sons. Perhaps reflecting some remnant of the *machismo* tradition, they agreed that boys should have more freedom than girls to do things outside the home on their own.

One parenting problem in the Hispanic family involves education. Hispanics have the highest school dropout rate of any group. In part, the problem may reflect the tendency for Hispanic children to have negative experiences in school such as feeling they are treated unfairly by either school policies or treatment by teachers (Villalba et al. 2007). The problem may also be due to less adequate preparation for school by parents. Although reading to preschool children is highly beneficial for their literacy development, for reasons unknown Hispanic parents read less than others to their preschoolers. A national study reported that overall 60 percent of 3- to 5-year-old children not yet in kindergarten benefitted from a daily reading, but only 45 percent of Hispanic children (compared to 68 percent of white and 66 percent of Asian Americans) had someone read to them each day (Whelan 2007).

The problem of dropouts is a serious one, but parenting can address the issue, as underscored by the research of Ceballo (2004). She studied Hispanic students from impoverished, immigrant families who had achieved academic success, raising the question of what parenting practices contributed to that success. She found three. First, the parents were strongly committed to the importance of education. Second, the parents encouraged their children to be autonomous, not diverted by others who were neglecting or abandoning their education. Third, the parents both verbally and nonverbally supported educational goals and tasks of their children.

Finally, as with African Americans, Hispanics are more family (including the extended family) and community oriented than are whites. The community orientation is illustrated in the experience of immigrants, who form social networks of mutual help (Garcia 2005). They establish the networks through family, friends, coworkers, and church.

The family orientation has four components (Zinn and Wells 2000; Parke 2004). First, the value on family life is one factor in the larger family size of Hispanics. A second component involves living arrangements. Among Hispanics, there is a tendency to cluster together in the same community and for homes to be composed of people from two or three generations. Hispanics are also less geographically mobile than are non-Hispanic whites.

The third component is a high value on family closeness in the context of a respect for authority. That is, children are expected to obey their parents and show respect for them. This respectful attitude is to be maintained even when the children are grown and have their own families. Finally, the family orientation is seen in the value on living near relatives. And the extended family is extended even more by the practice of *el compadrazco*, asking special friends to become godparents of children when the latter are baptized. The friends who participate in this practice become, in effect, a part of the extended family, with obligations similar to those of brothers and sisters.

In general, then, Hispanics are more integrated into community and family life than are non-Hispanic whites. This integration assures them of an extensive network of others who are available for help and support of various kinds.

The Asian American Family

Comparatively little research has been done on Asian American families. However, Asian Americans are a rapidly growing minority in the United States, numbering about 13.1 million, or 4.4 percent of the total population in 2006. The countries from which most Asian Americans come are China, the Philippines, India, Vietnam, and Korea. More than half of Asian Americans live in the West. As a minority group, they fare extremely well. Among other things, they attain more in education and income than any other group, including white Americans (Osborne 2004). In education, for example,

87 percent of adults are high school graduates, compared to 84 percent of all U.S. adults. And 47 percent of Asians and Pacific Islanders have a college degree, compared to 27 percent of all U.S. adults. Asian American parents are the only group that *expects* their children to obtain graduate degrees (Kuhn 2006). With regard to income, the median household income for Asian Americans is about 23 percent higher than the median for all U.S. households.

Asian American families tend to be large, with 23 percent of married-couple families having five or more members (McKinnon and Grieco 2001). The great majority of family households are married-couple households (table 2.2). And Asian Americans have a smaller proportion of divorced people than any other group (figure 2.2).

Asian culture tends to influence Asian American family life (Hamilton 1996; Parke 2004). In traditional Asian culture, the individual's needs are subordinated to the group's needs. Thus, Asian Americans are likely to socialize their children into the values of obedience, loyalty, and self-control. Obedience and loyalty to the family are strongly emphasized (Xiong et al. 2005). A study of Taiwanese American girls reported that the mothers tried to exercise strong influence over their daughters' decisions, and daughters who went against their mothers' advice suffered mental strain (Kao, Guthrie, and Loveland-Cherry 2007). The value of self-control is seen, among other things, in the greater emotional restraint found among Asian American youth (Rothbaum et al. 2000). The emphasis on obedience and self-control also helps explain the fact that Asian adolescents find it more difficult than do their white peers to discuss problems with their parents (Rhee, Chang, and Rhee 2003).

Asian American parents also instill a high value on education in their children (Asakawa 2001). A study of 140 Chinese adolescents found that the youth tended to balance family obligations with academic demands rather than with their social life with friends (Fuligni, Yip, and Tseng 2002). A study of Asian Americans from a number of different countries of origin reported three factors that help account for the high level of educational attainment: "(*a*) Children are expected to defer to parental authority without question; (*b*) there is a strong interdependence among family members, both within and beyond the nuclear unit; and (*c*) children are reared to believe that their success in school will affect the honor of their family directly" (Blair and Qian 1998:371).

The emphasis on respect for authority is undoubtedly a factor in another characteristic of Asian Americans. Namely, their adolescents have lower rates of deviance in the form of delinquency and misbehavior at school than the adolescents of any other group (Jang 2002; Le and Stockdale 2005).

Traditional Asian culture elevates males over females. The husband is expected to be the breadwinner, while the wife is expected to manage the children and the home. Wives are expected to defer to their husbands' wishes, while children are supposed to defer to both parents' wishes. There is also emphasis on extended family obligations; elderly Chinese and Japanese are more likely than whites to live in an extended family household, particularly in a married child's household (Phua, Kaufman, and Park 2001).

The qualities of obedience and self-restraint among Asian children have consequences for sexual development and behavior. A sample of Asian college students reported receiving very little information from parents about sexual matters other than the message (particularly for daughters) to refrain from any premarital sexual activity (Kim and Ward 2007). Surveys of the initiation of sexual behavior show that Asian Americans who adhere to traditional Asian values, tend to have their first sexual experience at a later age than those of other groups, particularly those who have strong ties with parents (Hahm, Lahiff, and Barreto 2006).

Because of their high levels of educational and occupational attainment, Asian Americans have been called the "model minority." But Asians escape neither prejudice and discrimination nor the problems that all groups must confront. With regard to prejudice and discrimination, Asians may not be as widely mistreated as are African Americans and Hispanics, but those who are victimized are more likely than others to report suffering from depression or anxiety (Gee et al. 2007). With regard to common problems, although the Asian family is more stable than others in terms of marriage and divorce rates, levels of domestic violence are high. For example, a study of South Asian women found that 40 percent reported intimate partner violence (Raj and Silverman 2003). The abuse reflects such things as the tradition of male dominance and disagreements about proper male and female roles in the U.S. setting (Morash et al. 2007).

There are, of course, variations both among and within various Asian American groups in all matters, from educational attainment and financial status to adherence to family traditions. For example, Chinese students perform best academically, and Korean and Southeast Asian students do better than do Japanese and Filipino students (Blair and Qian 1998). As another example, the large number of Vietnamese who came to the United States after the Vietnam war, like other Asians, lived in male-dominated, extended families. However, the Vietnamese appear to be rapidly adopting such Western patterns as women working outside the home, small family size, and use of day care (Gold 1993).

In some ways, the traditional Vietnamese pattern is strengthened in the United States—Vietnamese maintain even stronger kin ties out of economic necessity (Kibria 1993, 1994). But family relations have become more egalitarian. The Vietnamese man encounters problems of earnings and status in the United States. His wife is likely to gain power in the marital relationship. At the same time, parental control over the children tends to diminish, increasing the amount of conflict in the family (Kibria 1993). More quickly than other groups, the Vietnamese find themselves struggling with adapting family style and structure to U.S. ways.

With regard to variations within groups, the Hmong, an ethnic subgroup from Vietnam, have clung more persistently to their traditional pattern, which includes male dominance, early marriage for females, and early and frequent childbearing (Hutchison and McNall 1994). Interestingly, at the same time, the Hmong maintain high educational expectations for their women, which will increase pressures to change the traditional pattern.

The longer Asian American families are in this country, the more likely they are to be acculturated. Acculturation can be slow because of the tendency for people to cluster together and to provide for themselves a continuing Asian cultural context. For instance, New York's Chinatown has an extensive Chinese-language media, including newspapers, magazines, radio, and television, that can satisfy the family's information and entertainment needs. Nevertheless, the younger generation will inevitably become Americanized to some extent.

The process already shows up in the second generation. A study of Chinese immigrant families reported that filial piety remains alive but undergoes a change (Lin and Liu 1993). The children of the immigrants continue to provide help and resources to their parents, but they resist parental control over matters having to do with their personal freedom and self-development. Among other things, the children want to make their own choice in marriage. Thus, as *systems theory* emphasizes, the children are

Systems Theory Applied

struggling with how to establish their own identity while remaining a part of their family, a struggle that is more painful because of the contradiction between U.S. and traditional Chinese values.

Similarly, Chinese American women who are successful occupationally have, like their white counterparts, fewer children than Chinese American women who remain more traditional (Espenshade and Ye 1994).

Finally, a study of southeast Asian adolescents reported tensions between the young people, who are increasingly accepting U.S. ways, and their parents, who strive to continue living with traditional Asian values (Xiong and Detzner 2004–2005). For example, the young people complained about parents being too protective and controlling and the lack of overt affection from their parents. The longer Asian American families are in the United States, the more they are American rather than Asian.

The Native American Family

The 2.15 million American Indians, Eskimos, and Aleuts make up about 0.75 percent of the U.S. population (U.S. Census Bureau 2007b). Compared to the rest of the nation, they are a relatively young population, with a median age of 31.9 years compared to 36.2 years for the nation as a whole. Like Asian Americans, Native Americans tend to cluster in the West. The largest numbers of Native American households are found in Arizona, Oklahoma, and California. The majority of Native American households, 68 percent, consist of families, although only 40.5 percent of those are married couple families. Overall, 42.3 percent of Native Americans are married.

Native Americans are lower than other groups on such measures of well-being as education and income (U.S. Census Bureau 2007b). Only about 77 percent have a high school education, and 14 percent have a college degree. Median income is lower than that of other groups. About a fourth of all Native Americans live in poverty.

As in the case of the educational and economic status of African Americans, that of Native Americans must be understood in terms of a history of prejudice and discrimination by the larger society. Historically, the government has made and arbitrarily broken treaties with the various tribes, seized tribal lands, attempted to obliterate native culture, and confined tribes to reservations where they have restricted educational and economic opportunities (see, e.g., Layng 2000 and Red Horse et al. 2000). When Native Americans have tried to participate in the larger society, they have faced prejudice and discrimination in the schools and the workplace. In sum,

Native Americans today are one of the most impoverished of all minorities.

The high poverty rate is one important factor that circumscribes family life among Native Americans. Their families generally exhibit the same characteristics of people who live in poverty, including higher rates of fertility, alcoholism, drug use, health problems, crime rates (including the highest murder rates of any group), child neglect, and so on (Red Horse et al. 2000; Kaufman et al. 2004; Lanier and Huff-Corzine 2006; U.S. Census Bureau 2007b). Native American children have lower rates of well-being than any other group (Willeto 2007). They have higher rates of neglect than others (Donald et al. 2003). They have a high rate of alcohol use and abuse (which is associated with the large number of single-parent families) (Lonczak et al. 2007). And the alcohol use and abuse is one of the factors associated with early initiation of sexual behavior (Mitchell et al. 2007). Alcohol

Tribal tradition is important in Native American family life.

abuse in the family increases the chances of child abuse; Native American families have one of the highest rates of abuse of women and children (Earle 2000; Wahab and Olson 2004). Native American adolescents, growing up in a context of high rates of drug abuse, child abuse, and troubled family life, have high rates of depression and of thoughts about and attempts at suicide (King et al. 1992; Sack et al. 1994).

The severity of these problems is underscored by a survey of 14,000 Native Americans in grades 7 through 12, living on reservations in 15 states.[1] The Native Americans were twice as likely as other teenagers to have attempted suicide (22 percent of the girls and 12 percent of the boys admitted they had tried). Eleven percent said that at least one of their parents was dead; fewer than half lived with both parents. Twenty-two percent of the twelfth-grade girls reported being victims of sexual abuse.

The other important factor in Native American family life is tribal tradition. About 300 different tribes exist. As Staples (1988:350) points out, we cannot talk about a Native American family: "There are only tribes and family systems, which vary from tribe to tribe." For example, some tribes are **patrilineal** (descent is traced through the male line), while others are **matrilineal** (descent is traced through the female line).

The Hopi, who live mainly in northern Arizona, are an example of a matrilineal group (Queen, Habenstein, and Quadagno 1985). In the traditional Hopi family, one's lineage was traced through one's mother, grandmother, and so on, and the females owned most of the property and directed tribal ceremonies. The husband was considered a guest in his wife's home.

Nevertheless, while acknowledging the tribal variations, we can make some general points about Native American families. Their culture emphasizes custom and tradition, the extended family, and communalism rather than individualism (Red Horse et al. 2000). They select life partners on the basis of romantic love (John 1997); their rate of intermarriage is high, particularly involving white men and Native American women; and divorce is likely to be a less guilt-ridden and recriminating process than it is among whites (John 1997).

Given the high fertility rates and the low proportion who are married, it is not surprising that more Native American children than those of other groups are being raised by grandparents (U.S. Census Bureau 2007b). One study found that almost half of those who were raising a grandchild had been doing so for five years or more (Fuller-Thomson and Minkler 2005). Unfortunately, the grandparents were disproportionately female, poor, and disadvantaged by some kind of functional disability that made the child-rearing tasks even more challenging for them.

These varied problems facing the Native American family are particularly severe for those living on reservations rather than in urban areas (Stiffman et al. 2007). But whether living in an urban or a rural setting, the hopeful news is that those young Native Americans who can draw on strengths in their social environments have better academic records and higher levels of mental health (Stiffman et al. 2007). Until the issues of poverty and discrimination are resolved, however, the Native American family is likely to continue to exhibit severe problems rather than to be a dependable nurturing environment for the young.

The Interracial Family

The vast majority of Americans marry within their own racial group. In fact, through most of our history, Americans have disapproved, and in some cases even made illegal, interracial marriages. A 1958 national survey found that only 4 percent of whites approved of intermarriage with African Americans (Qian 2005). But attitudes have changed, laws forbidding interracial marriage no longer exist, and the number of interracial marriages is increasing. As late as 1970, only 0.5 percent of all marriages were classified by the Census Bureau as interracial. By 2006, however, 7.1 percent of marriages involved people who were either from differing racial groups or one spouse was Hispanic and the other was non-Hispanic (U.S. Census Bureau 2007a).

Some interesting variations exist in interracial marriages. Asians and Hispanics are more likely to intermarry than are whites or African Americans (Fu 2007). About 97 percent of white and black women, and 98 percent of white and 92 percent of black men, are married to those of their own race. Hispanics and Native Americans who intermarry are most likely to do so with whites, while African Americans are least likely among the racial minorities to intermarry with whites (Qian and Lichter 2007). Nevertheless, the number of white-black marriages has increased considerably, with the dominant pattern being a black man with a white woman (Batson, Qian, and Lichter 2006).

A survey of U.S.-raised Asian Americans reported the following percentages of the Asian American wives who married whites: Chinese, 31.7 percent; Japanese, 29.2 percent; Koreans, 49.4 percent; and Vietnamese,

---

[1]*Facts on File*, 2 April 1992, p. 235BZ.

23.6 percent (Le 2005). Finally, research on Arab American intermarriages also found a very high rate: Over 80 percent of U.S.-born Arabs marry non-Arabs (Kulczycki and Lobo 2002). Arabs with high levels of education and those of Lebanese ancestry have the highest rates of intermarriage.

In addition to more favorable public attitudes, several factors are related to the growing number of interracial marriages. One is education. Those who have a college education are more likely to intermarry than those with less education (Qian 2005). Another factor is the later age at marriage, which generally means a lower likelihood of living with parents and less parental influence over the choice of a mate (Rosenfeld and Kim 2005). Thus, interracial couples are more geographically mobile and more urban than couples of the same race.

Interracial marriages are more challenging and more fragile than marriages that are racially homogamous (Fu 2000). A comparison of black, white non-Hispanic, and interracial couples showed that the latter focused more on their emotional attachments to each other and also on the amount of work needed to maintain the marriage (Dainton 1999). In some cases, the stability of the marriage depends on which spouse is of which race. For example, marriages with a black husband and white wife are more stable than those with a white husband and black wife. The probability of an interracial marriage lasting depends on a number of factors. As with other marriages, interracial unions are more likely to last when there are children and when the couple marry at a relatively later age. And they are more likely to be satisfying when each spouse has pride in, and identifies with, his or her own race while at the same being accepting of other races (Leslie and Letiecq 2004).

Because we are likely to be attracted to those who are like us (the principle of **homogamy,** or marriage between people who are similar in social and demographic characteristics) and because interracial marriages are more likely to fail, why do people marry across racial lines? In essence, their reasons are the same as those of others. That is, when asked about the motives for their marriages, interracial couples primarily mention love and compatibility (Kouri and Lasswell 1993). Compatibility, of course, suggests a homogamous relationship, and an interracial marriage might seem to have **heterogamy** (be between people who are dissimilar in social and demographic characteristics). However, people of different races in our country may have similar values and attitudes, and people may prefer someone of another race who is similar in values and attitudes to someone of their own race who is different in values and

attitudes. An in-depth study of 21 black-white marriages found that none of the individuals had intended to have an interracial relationship (Rosenblatt, Karis, and Powell 1995). Rather, the two people met and "clicked" with each other and pursued the relationship as individuals rather than as members of particular races.

A few of those in interracial marriages indicate that they are motivated by rebellion against the conventions of society or by an attraction to the opposite sex of another race. While a deeper study of the couples might identify some more subtle forces at work, we have no other answers at present. Some people are so much in love and so compatible with a person of another race that they are willing to assume the risk of lower stability and perhaps go counter to pressures from friends and family in order to enter an interracial union.

The risk of breakup and the pressure to refrain from interracial marriages vary from place to place. In a multicultural setting, interracial marriages may be more common and more acceptable. There may be more support for the couple, enabling them to maintain the union. In some places, children of an interracial union are stigmatized; they may not be fully accepted by either of their parents' races. But they may escape the stigma and its negative psychological consequences in a multicultural setting.

On the other hand, even in a more accepting, multicultural setting, the marital relationship itself is problematic. Researchers who compared interracial couples with racially homogamous couples in a multiracial, multicultural community in Hawaii found that those in the interracial unions reported lower levels of happiness (Fu, Tora, and Kendall 2001). The lower levels were more commonly reported by wives than by husbands.

An older, but still valid and useful, study of interracial Hawaiian families with children with emotional problems illustrates the kinds of struggles couples have (McDermott and Fukunaga 1977). One of the problems the interracial couples had was that of trying to establish consensual parental roles. A number of Asian men married to white women tried to assume the traditional Asian role of male leadership. But some of their white wives "repeatedly competed for this role, undercut their husbands, or attempted to act as co-leader with the husband" (McDermott and Fukunaga 1977:84). In such cases, the husband often either ignored his wife or treated her as one of the children. The reaction of the children tended to be withdrawal and mild depression.

Another problem arising in the interracial families was the differing value systems of the parents. Some cultures value accuracy over creativity, while others have the opposite value. Husbands and wives with differing values put their children into the difficult situation of having to obey contradictory parental expectations.

The troubled families had tried to cope with their differences in various ways. Three coping efforts were dysfunctional. First, some of the families had settled into a kind of cold war in which, for the most part, the parents no longer attempted to accommodate their differences but rather each maintained a different and contrary approach to dealing with the children. Second, in other families, there was a "competitive adjustment," in which each parent tried to get the other to acknowledge his or her leadership in the family. Finally, some of the families engaged in a "reluctant adjustment," in which the parents withdrew from trying to establish leadership and allowed the children to govern themselves most of the time.

Eventually, the families in this research learned better ways of coping with their differences. *Complementary adjustment* in an interracial family involves letting one parent be the primary leader in the family while the other engages in supplementary functions. For example, one parent makes a decision and the other supports it, encourages the children to support it, and models supportive behavior to the children. In *additive adjustment,* the parents try to take elements from each of their cultures that they both define as desirable and use these in making decisions about family life.

In sum, interracial families face the same problems as others plus some additional problems that are unique. But they can work through their problems and maintain a strong and meaningful family life. When the family lives in a hostile environment (among people who resist or resent interracial unions), the prospects for long-term stability are not encouraging. In a more accepting atmosphere, the family will still have its unique problems to solve, but it will be better able to do so.

FAMILIES WITH SAME-SEX PARENTS

Although many people do not think of homosexual relationships as resulting in a family, same-sex couples are the heads of 777,000 households in the United States (U.S. Census Bureau 2008:62). **Gays** and **lesbians** have been striving for decades to gain the legal recognition now enjoyed by heterosexual couples. Those who live in areas where they cannot legally marry often put together (sometimes with the aid of clergy) a non-legal ceremony that publicly affirms their commitment to each other (Hull 2006).

The majority of Americans do not believe that same-sex marriages should be legal. Some states have passed laws expressly forbidding same-sex marriages, and some Americans are asking for a constitutional ban on such unions. Nevertheless, a significant change occurred in 2003 when seven same-sex couples sued in the Massachusetts courts for the right to be married. In February 2004, the Massachusetts Supreme Court declared that gays have the right to nothing less than marriage. It took the stand that civil unions, like those available in Vermont (see below), did not fulfill the rights of gay couples. The law took effect in May 2004.

What Do You Think?

*There is disagreement about **whether same-sex marriages should be legalized.** What follows are pro and con arguments. What do you think?*

Pro

Same-sex marriages should be legal because they

- give homosexuals equal rights with heterosexuals.
- strengthen the bonds of homosexual unions, cutting down on promiscuity.
- provide homosexual partners with the same kinds of employee benefits, tax benefits, and inheritance rights as opposite-sex couples.
- permit homosexual partners to legally adopt children.
- give the homosexual couple a sense of acceptance and legitimacy in the larger society.

Con

Same-sex marriages should not be legal because they

- contradict the nation's Judeo-Christian heritage.
- are contrary to nature, which makes heterosexual relations the basis for continuing the race.
- make young people think that, since such unions are sanctioned by law, they are an acceptable alternative.
- allow homosexual partners to adopt children and raise them as homosexuals.
- and deprive children of the opportunity to learn proper gender roles.

Same-sex couples and families have gained some other legal rights in recent years. One right involves the benefits of domestic partnerships (Partners Task Force for Gay & Lesbian Couples 2002). Employment benefits can amount to as much as a fourth or more of an individual's total compensation, including such things as health benefits extended to the worker's spouse. The first business to give such benefits to same-sex partners was the *Village Voice Newspaper* in 1982. Beginning in 1997, San Francisco required all companies doing business with the city and/or county to offer the same benefits to same-sex partners that they gave to opposite-sex partners. Many large corporations now offer such benefits to same-sex partners of their employees.

The other legal right gained by homosexuals occurred in the state of Vermont, where, since July 2000, gay couples may enter into a "civil union." A civil union is a legal relationship that gives same-sex couples all the benefits accorded to married heterosexual couples in the state. However, those in a civil union still do not receive the benefits given by the federal government to married couples, and it is likely that most or all the other states will deny legal recognition to such unions for the near future.

Although these unions are not legally recognized in any other state as of this writing, a considerable number of homosexuals commit themselves to marriage. They may or may not have a formal ceremony. If they have a ceremony, they may have a member of the clergy conduct the service. They also may exchange and wear wedding rings to symbolize and affirm their relationship.

Moreover, millions of gays and lesbians have children. The children may have been born when one member of the couple was part of a heterosexual marriage. Subsequently, the individual "came out"; that is, he or she openly acknowledged his or her homosexual orientation. Some of the children of such parents are being raised in homosexual families. In other cases, the homosexual parent has joint custody.

Homosexual couples have to work through the same problems as heterosexual couples. They face issues about household division of labor, power, sexual relationships, and money (Patterson 2000). In addition, like interracial couples, they face the problem of being in a stigmatized relationship. Nationally, 57 percent of Americans believe that homosexuals should not be allowed to be legally married (Polling Report 2008). Homosexual families, then, must not only deal with the same issues as other families but also with a hostile environment and with problems that are unique to the homosexual relationship.

Problems in Gay and Lesbian Families

Gay male couples have some unique sources of stress. One is the stereotypical male role. Men in our society are expected to be relatively unemotional, strong, competitive, independent, and in control. If the partners in a gay relationship each attempts to live by the stereotype, they will encounter serious problems. How can they maintain a loving relationship if they are constantly competing with each other? Or if both want to win all the time? Or if both want to be in control?

Many gay couples want a family life with children.

Another source of stress is the stereotypical sexual role of the male. In our society, men are expected to be sexually active, experienced, and prepared to engage in a sexual relationship at almost any time. This can create performance anxiety, an anxiety that may be intensified by the spread of AIDS and the knowledge that homosexual relationships are particularly vulnerable to AIDS.

Homophobia, the irrational fear of homosexuality, is a third possible source of stress (Cortez 1996). U.S. attitudes about homosexuality have grown somewhat more tolerant in recent years, but a substantial number assert that homosexuality is not an acceptable lifestyle. Most homosexuals have grown up hearing such derogatory labels as "fag" and "queer." It is very difficult not to incorporate some of the negative societal messages into one's own self-concept. One of the partners in a homosexual relationship may, therefore, be struggling with self-esteem and his or her identity as homosexual. And that can diminish the quality of the relationship (Otis et al. 2006). Or the partners may feel it necessary to refrain from behavior that is meaningful and acceptable for heterosexual couples, such as public displays of their affection for each other (Brewer 1997). And if one or both partners are from a racial/ethnic minority, the prejudice and discrimination hitting them on two fronts at once, they are even more vulnerable to high levels of stress and mental health problems (Guarnero 2007; Zamboni and Crawford 2007).

Finally, there is the stress of **sexual dysfunctions.** Contrary to the popular image and to the general pattern of the homosexual male, some gays suffer from inhibited sexual desire. The problem intersects with the stereotypical male sex role and with homophobia. That is, a man might have inhibited sexual desire because he is still battling his feelings of guilt or his ambiguity about his sexual orientation. But the inhibited desire intensifies his stress because he also may accept the stereotype of himself as one who is supposed to be a sexually active individual.

What about children who are being raised by two adults of the same sex? In essence, the children appear to do as well as those in heterosexual settings (Patterson 2000). Homosexual, like heterosexual, parents tend to report few serious problems in child rearing and generally satisfactory relationships with the children (Turner, Scadden, and Harris 1990). Homosexual fathers do not differ from heterosexual fathers in their reported involvement or intimacy level with their children (Bigner and Jacobsen 1989). The children of gay fathers may need help to understand their own feelings about homosexuality, and

some experience anger and a sense of isolation (Barret and Robinson 1990:91). But they also report their relationships with their fathers to be honest and open (Barret and Robinson 1990:91).

Gay fathers have more difficulty disclosing their homosexual orientation to their children than do lesbian mothers (Bozett 1989). Once disclosed, however, both gay and lesbian parents say that their children generally have a positive attitude about the homosexuality. O'Connell (1993) studied 11 young adults whose mothers came out as lesbians either before or after divorcing the fathers. She found "profound loyalty and protectiveness" toward the mothers even though the subjects remained sad about the parental breakup.

Homosexual parents do not indicate a preference for their children also to be homosexual. In fact, Javaid (1993) found, in a small sample, that the lesbian mothers preferred their children, and particularly their sons, to marry and procreate. In another study, two researchers compared 25 adults raised in lesbian families with 21 adults raised by single heterosexual mothers (Golombok and Tasker 1996). They found that while those raised by lesbian mothers were more likely to explore same-sex relationships, the large majority identified themselves as heterosexual when they were young adults (only two women identified themselves as lesbian as young adults). Finally, a survey of 55 gay or bisexual men found that more than 90 percent of their sons were heterosexual (Bailey et al. 1995).

As far as the children's general well-being is concerned, those raised by same-sex parents are as psychologically healthy and well-adjusted as their peers who are reared in a heterosexual family (Golombok et al. 2003; Lambert 2005). In one study, lesbian mothers reported more severe disputes with children than did the heterosexual mothers, but no differences in socioemotional development or parent–child warmth existed (MacCallum and Golombok 2004). And a national study of gay and lesbian parents found more similarities than differences between them and heterosexual parents (Johnson and O'Connor 2002). Where they did find differences, moreover, the gay and lesbian parents had, in a number of areas, more positive child-rearing practices: They were, compared to the heterosexual parents, more responsive to their children, more child oriented, and more egalitarian in sharing household tasks between the partners.

Finally, an interesting longitudinal study compared those raised by lesbian couples and single heterosexual mothers (Tasker and Golombok 1997). The two groups were first studied as adolescents and then again some 15 years later as young adults. The researchers found no differences between the two groups in their acceptance of their family identity during adolescence. The children raised by lesbian parents, in other words, were not traumatized by their family situation when they were adolescents, particularly those who had close relationships with their mothers and their mothers' partners. Problems did arise for those who were stigmatized by their peers and those who felt that their mothers were too open about their lesbian identity in front of their friends. By the time they were young adults, however, those raised in lesbian families were more positive about their background than were those raised by single heterosexual mothers.

Such evidence of well-being in homosexual families led the American Academy of Pediatrics to support the right of gays and lesbians to adopt their partners' children (Perrin 2002). The recommendation came after a review of two decades of studies showed that children in homosexual families were as well-adjusted socially and psychologically as those in heterosexual families. As of this writing, only a few states allow such adoptions.

Intimacy in the Gay or Lesbian Family

What do homosexuals want in an intimate relationship? In fact, long-term homosexual relationships are indistinguishable from their heterosexual counterparts in most respects (Gottman et al. 2003). Like heterosexuals, homosexuals value such things in an intimate relationship as being able to talk about feelings, being able to laugh together, having a supportive group of friends, and sharing as many activities as possible with one's partner. Whatever their sexual orientation, people expect family life to provide them with a measure of emotional support, love, security, and companionship.

It is more difficult for a homosexual couple to fulfill its intimacy needs, however, because of the hostile environment. As a result, homosexual couples may receive more emotional support from friends, including other homosexuals, than they do from their extended families. Homosexual couples, then, are more dependent on friends for support than are other couples. Those with a high degree of emotional support from friends are less psychologically distressed than those who report less emotional support from friends.

Other than a support system, the factors that add to the quality of a homosexual relationship are the same as those for a heterosexual union (Gottman et al. 2003; Mackey, Diemer, and O'Brien 2004). The quality of the relationship, regardless of the type of couple, depends on such things as perceived investment in the relationship, few alternatives to the relationship, commitment to the relationship, and shared decision making. In most respects, in short, the homosexual couple is no different from the heterosexual. In both kinds of relationships, the partners are seeking to fulfill their intimacy needs. And many of the same kinds of factors determine the extent to which those needs are fulfilled.

There are, however, some differences. While both homosexual and heterosexual couples argue about the same issues, Kurdek (1994) found differences in frequency of conflict over particular issues. Heterosexual couples argue more frequently over politics and social issues, while homosexual couples argue more frequently over distrust or lying (about, e.g., previous lovers, which may be especially troublesome when the ex-lovers are still part of their social support network).

Two additional differences that affect intimacy are the greater probability of equality among homosexuals and the way in which fidelity is defined by gays and lesbians. Equality facilitates intimacy. Women, regardless of their sexual orientation, are more likely than men to value equality. But equality in such matters as decision making and sharing of household tasks is more likely between homosexual than heterosexual partners (Kurdek 2001; Sullivan 2005; Goldberg and Perry-Jenkins 2007). Patterson (1995) studied 26 lesbian couples who had at least one child in their home. She found that the partners agreed that they shared household tasks and decision making equally. But biological mothers reported more child care, and nonbiological mothers reported more hours in paid work outside the home. In other words, equality doesn't have to involve an equal sharing of every task.

With regard to fidelity, gay men are less monogamous than married, heterosexual men (Solomon, Rothblum, and Balsam 2005). In part, this may reflect the partners' choice of an open rather than a closed relationship. In an open relationship, the partners retain their commitment to each other while allowing occasional outside relationships. In a closed relationship, the partners are expected to be sexually faithful to each other. Those in an open relation-

Symbolic Interactionist Theory Applied

ship say that monogamy cannot meet all of an individual's needs, interests, and fantasies. They say that an occasional outside contact enhances their enjoyment of their partner and strengthens their bond. *Fidelity,* then, may be defined as emotional commitment rather than sexual exclusivity. Such a definition of fidelity is contrary to that of most heterosexuals. But recall that *symbolic interactionist* theory argues that we must understand people's own definitions of the situation. Thus, gay and lesbian partners who allow for occasional outside sexual activity still feel that they are being faithful to each other.

Long-Term Gay and Lesbian Relationships

In spite of the social stigma, many gays and lesbians not only form families but remain in long-term, satisfying relationships (Dang and Frazer 2005). Riedmann (1995) estimated that 75 percent of lesbians and 50 percent of gay men are in stable, monogamous relationships at any given time. A comparison of heterosexual and homosexual relationships that lasted for an average of 30 years reported that the same factors affected the quality of intimacy of the couples regardless of sexual orientation (Mackey, Diemer, and O'Brien 2000). In fact, the highest degree of psychological intimacy (defined as being open with the partner about matters not usually shared with others) was attained by the lesbian couples.

SUMMARY

A good deal of diversity in family life stems from such factors in the social context as cultural background, religion, social class position, and the experience of prejudice and discrimination. A disproportionate number of single-parent families are in the lower social classes. The number of single-parent families has increased considerably in recent decades. Single parents face the problems of responsibility, task, and emotional overload. The children of single parents are more likely to have both personal and interpersonal difficulties than are children who live with both parents. They perceive their homes as less cohesive, and they are likely to achieve less in education, occupation, and income than those from intact homes.

Boys seem to present more problems than girls for single parents. Single mothers may try to get their older sons to assume the responsibilities of the missing father, or they may go to the opposite extreme and "overmother" their sons. There is not a great deal of research on single fathers, but children tend to reward single fathers more than single mothers.

Problems may arise when a single parent begins to date. Children may be angry and resentful about the parent's dating. The problem may be compounded by the fact that the dates may be less than enthusiastic about the children.

In spite of the problems, most single-parent homes function reasonably well. The majority of single parents and their children have good physical and mental health. Single parents also function well at work.

Racial/ethnic families are similar to white families in many ways, but they face special problems because of their situation in society. African Americans make up the second largest racial minority in the United States. They have a higher rate of single-parent families than either whites or Hispanics. They are also more likely to be single, widowed, or divorced. Black children are far more likely than others to be living with a mother who has never been married.

The problems of the black family must be viewed in the context of centuries of political and economic disadvantages. African Americans have lower incomes and higher rates of unemployment than whites, making the role of provider a more difficult one for the black male. Those African Americans who have fewer economic problems also have fewer family problems. Although disproportionately disadvantaged, black families have a number of strengths and, in some cases, even advantages over other groups.

Hispanics, the largest minority, are also disadvantaged economically. They have a strong emphasis on family life, including loyalty to the extended family. They have the highest fertility rates of any group. Evidence on the quality of married life among Hispanics is mixed, although Hispanics do have high rates of domestic abuse. Parenting in Hispanic families reflects four cultural values: *familismo, respeto, personalismo,* and *simpatía.* Education of the young is a serious problem because Hispanic adolescents have a high dropout rate. The tendency to cluster in the same community, along with the high value on family life, gives Hispanics an extensive network of others who can offer support of various kinds.

Asian American families are better off in some ways than those of other races. They have higher educational attainment and higher median income than any other group. The families tend to be large and stable—they have the lowest divorce rate of any group. Influenced by Asian culture, Asian American families tend to subordinate individual needs to group needs and stress such values as obedience, loyalty, and self-control. They also tend to be male dominated.

Native Americans are one of the most impoverished groups in the nation. Native American family life is circumscribed by the high poverty rate (leading to such things as high rates of fertility, alcoholism, and drug use) but also by tribal traditions (seen in such things as matrilineal versus patrilineal descent and the importance of the extended family). The rate of intermarriage is high. Like other Americans, Native Americans tend to select life partners on the basis of romantic love.

Interracial families have increased dramatically in recent decades. There is a higher rate of divorce in interracial marriages. People are attracted to mates of other races because of such things as love and compatibility. Even in an accepting environment, however, interracial unions face some unique problems. One problem is which parental roles and values to adopt when the husband and wife come from different cultural traditions.

Same-sex couples have to work through the same problems as heterosexual couples. In addition, they face problems arising from a hostile environment and from the nature of their relationship. For example, gay male couples may be stressed as their relationship is affected by the stereotypical male role (including the male sexual role), by homophobia, or by sexual dysfunctions.

Lesbian couples may not have the same kind of problems as either gay male or heterosexual couples. They report less conflict over money management and income and more egalitarianism than other couples.

Same-sex couples trying to raise children report few serious problems and generally satisfying relationships. Children of homosexuals are likely to be heterosexual when they grow up.

In general, homosexuals want the same thing as heterosexuals in an intimate relationship. And the same factors enhance the quality of both homosexual and heterosexual relationships: commitment, shared decision making, and perceived investment in the relationship.

Principles for Enhancing Intimacy

Beginning with this chapter, we will briefly note some of the principles that can be derived from materials in the chapter and used to enhance the quality of your own intimate relationships. A major premise of the chapter, of course, is the point that intimate relationships are a necessary part of our well-being. Some of the important principles are as follows:

1. People fulfill many of their intimacy needs within the context of the family. If you are in a nontraditional or nonwhite family, affirm your family so that it can be a vital source of satisfaction and well-being.
2. Although nontraditional and racial/ethnic families encounter a host of obstacles, strong bonds of affection and shared values, interests, and goals help minimize the difficulties and produce fulfilling relationships.
3. The same factors—love, respect, support, and sharing—are vital in all types of families. These are the bonds in any strong, enduring intimate relationship and thus should be cultivated. If you are in a nontraditional family, it may require extra effort to develop these bonds, but the end result will be worth the struggle.
4. Racial/ethnic families have special problems, but they also have some special strengths, such as the resource of strong extended-family relationships. As a member of one of these families, you can tap into these strengths and use them to maximize intimacy.

KEY TERMS

arranged marriage *27*
family *26*
gays *47*
heterogamy *46*
heterosexual *26*
homogamy *46*

homophobia *49*
homosexual *26*
lesbians *47*
matrilineal *45*
monogamy *27*
patrilineal *45*

polyandry *27*
polygamy *27*
polygyny *27*
sexual dysfunction *49*

ON THE WEB   Diversity in Families

Diversity in family life occurs both within and between societies. One of the differences between societies involves polygamy. Americans view monogamous marriage as the ideal form, but many societies have practiced, and some continue to practice, polygamy. A Web site that is a good resource for nonmonogamous people of all sexual orientations is

www.mhhe.com/lauer7e

Polygamy.com
http://www.polygamy.com

You can also find information on the Internet on all the types of families discussed in this chapter. An interesting site for exploring Hispanic life is

Journal of Hispanic Sciences
http://hjb.sagepub.com

Here you can access issues of a journal that specializes in Hispanic research, including abstracts of all articles.

Explore some of the topics in this chapter with the following projects:

1. Use the polygamy Web site to research Mormon polygamy in the United States or polygamy in another society. Describe the polygamous arrangement and discuss its advantages and disadvantages. Based on your findings, how would you respond to those who argue that polygamy should be an acceptable, legal arrangement in the United States?

2. Go to the Journal of Hispanic Sciences Web site to see the kinds of topics covered over the past two years' issues. Categorize the articles by topic (such as family life, education, health, sexual issues, political orientation, etc.) and summarize the findings in each topic. How do your results add to, contradict, or fail to be relevant to the materials in the text?

3. Using a search engine (such as Google or Yahoo), explore the topic of family life in another society, ancient or modern. Note the differences and similarities with family life in the United States today. From the point of view of your own values, what (if any) aspects of family in the society you researched would you like to see incorporated into U.S. family life today?

~ GENDER ROLES ~

FOUNDATION FOR INTIMACY

LEARNING OBJECTIVES

After reading and studying chapter 3, you should be able to

1 Describe psychological and social similarities and differences that exist between men and women.

2 Define *gender, gender role,* and *gender-role orientation.*

3 Discuss traditional gender roles and their social consequences.

4 Explain the four types of gender-role orientation—masculine, feminine, undifferentiated, and androgynous.

5 Discuss the extent to which gender roles are a product of biology or environment.

6 Describe the functions of the family, school, and media in gender-role development.

7 Evaluate the extent to which people are becoming less traditional in their gender-role orientation.

8 Understand how gender-role orientation affects communication patterns.

9 Explain how attitudes about love, sex, and self are shaped by gender-role orientation.

10 Discuss the relationship between gender-role orientation and mental health.

Write a personal account of your own gender-role development. You can organize your paper along the lines of answers to the following questions:

1. What does it mean to you to be someone of your gender? That is, what kinds of traits and qualities do you have as a male or female?
2. To what extent are you similar and different from your same-sex parent? Describe that parent. If you didn't grow up with a same-sex parent, describe the person whom you believe was most influential in shaping your ideas.
3. What messages did you get from your parents about appropriate traits? What kinds of things did they encourage? Discourage?

4. What school experiences do you recall that shaped your development?
5. Who are some of the same-sex people you admire and some that you dislike on television? How do you think they influenced you?
6. What is your ideal for someone of your sex? To what extent are you like your ideal?
7. How do you think you will continue to develop? What can you do to further your development along the lines you desire?

If the entire class does this project, it would be useful to have a few males and a few females share their answers. Compare and contrast the male with the female accounts. ❊

According to a Harvard physician, Dr. Dudley Sargent, the physique of women has changed. He observed, "Twenty years ago women were the very antithesis of men in physical proportions." But now women have begun looking more like men. "It is to be hoped," said Dr. Sargent, "that women do not grow to be more like men than they are today. . . . The danger of women becoming too mannish is imminent."[1] The doctor also pointed out that men have changed and are in danger of becoming too "effeminate."

Dr. Sargent's remarks were made in 1910. They illustrate the ongoing concern that people have about men being men and women being women. But what does it mean to be a man? What does it mean to be a woman? In this chapter, we will explore this complex issue. We will look at similarities and differences between the sexes. We will explore the meaning of gender roles and the way in which we develop those roles. Finally, we will examine the consequences of gender roles, including the implications of those roles for intimate relationships.

MEN AND WOMEN: HOW DO THEY DIFFER?

As an interesting exercise, write down five ways you believe that men and women are alike and five ways in which they differ. When you have finished this chapter, look at your list again and see if you want to make any changes to it. Keep in mind that even social scientists do not completely agree on how the two sexes differ and in what ways they are similar.

Men and Women: Some Commonalities

While we will focus more on differences than similarities, we want to underscore the fact that there are some similarities. Both men and women have some of the same fundamental needs: survival, self-esteem, intimacy, and growth. Both need the sense of having some control over their lives. Both need to achieve. Both need recreation. When we talk about the basic needs of humans, neither sex is exempt, even though each may fulfill those needs in somewhat different ways.

In addition, some research shows that men and women are similar in areas in which we once thought they were different. For example, women have typically

been viewed as more emotional than men. Studies using a variety of different methods all show that women express their feelings verbally more than men do (Goldschmidt and Weller 2000; Zakowski et al. 2003).

But a greater degree of *expressing* feelings does not mean that women have a greater degree of *experiencing* feelings. A national study of self-reports of both the experience and the expression of feelings reported that, in general, there is little difference between men and women in the frequency of everyday feelings (Simon and Nath 2004). There are differences in the kinds of emotions they tend to experience. Women, for example, tend to have a greater number of negative emotional experiences. And their experience of negative feelings, particularly when associated with relational problems, may be more intense and of longer duration than those of men (Birditt and Fingerman 2003). Nevertheless, overall men and women seem to experience a similar amount of emotion in daily life.

Many people also believe that men and women differ in their responses to erotic stimuli. Presumably, men are more aroused than women by such stimuli. But the matter is not that straightforward. A small-scale study that had men and women watch erotic films reported that men's sexual arousal depended upon the attractiveness of the female actor, being interested, and imagining themselves as a participant (Janssen, Carpenter, and Graham 2003). For women, only imagining themselves as a participant heightened their sexual arousal.

A third example of presumed differences involves the giving and receiving of support during times of personal troubles. In a series of experiments, researchers concluded that the notion that men and women are totally different creatures in dealing with "troubles talk" is false (MacGeorge et al. 2004). In fact, they found very little difference in the way that men and women provided support (mainly by expressing sympathy and offering advice), or in the way that men and women react emotionally to a message of advice (mainly positively, though men were slightly more likely to react negatively), or in the reaction of men and women to person-centered comforting messages (both sexes valued highly person-centered messages more positively than low person-centered messages). In short, in interaction involving "troubles talk," the researchers found no significant difference between the ways that men and women behave.

Finally, women are thought to conform more than men. Even many social scientists have asserted that women are easier to persuade and more prone to comply with group pressures than are men. Indeed, some experimental

---

[1]Reported in the *St. Louis Post-Dispatch,* 28 November 1910.

evidence supported such a position. Yet, as long ago as the 1970s, Alice Eagly (1978) carefully reviewed the literature and concluded that women are not more easily influenced than men. Only a third of the studies she reviewed showed women to be more conforming in group settings than men. Most found no male–female differences. Where women do conform, it may reflect the fact that they face greater pressures than do men to comply with the group. One researcher of small-group interaction reported that women, but not men, who deviated from the group opinion were negatively evaluated (Doherty 1998).

The point is that there are similarities, including some that go against the conventional wisdom. Men and women do differ, but they also are similar in many ways. In fact, an analysis of a vast number of psychological studies concluded that there are more similarities than differences (Hyde 2005). You are not a totally different kind of creature from those of the opposite sex. Having said this, let's look at the ways in which males and females differ.

Gender Differences

Researchers use a number of different terms as they explore male–female similarities and differences. **Sex** refers to your biological identification as a male or female. But since so much of our behavior is based on social rather than biological factors, we use the term **gender** to refer to males and females as social creatures. **Gender role** refers to the behavior associated with being either male or female. And **gender-role orientation** refers to the conception of yourself has having some combination of masculine and feminine traits.

As we discuss gender differences, it is important to keep in mind that these differences are not absolute. That is, every man is not different from every woman in the same way. For instance, men tend to be more aggressive than women. But if we were to plot the aggression level of all males and all females, we might get a result something like figure 3.1. As the figure illustrates, rather than the absolute statement that men are more aggressive than women, it is more accurate to say that a greater number of men than of women are highly aggressive. Some women are more aggressive than some men, but, on the average, men are the more aggressive gender.

With this caveat in mind, we note that men and women differ in numerous ways, ranging from the physiological to the social. Among other things, men and women differ in their attention span, their aspirations, the strategies they use in competitive games, the amount they smile, their vulnerability to particular diseases and addictions, their life expectancy, the structure and functioning of their brains, their attitudes on social issues, and their sexual interests (Kreeger 2002; Marano and Strand 2003; Goldman et al. 2004). Let's examine a few of the social and psychological differences in detail.

Ability.   If you read a poem, a story, or an article, do you think your evaluation of it would be influenced by the gender of the author? You probably think not. But even among people who affirm a belief in gender equality, there is a persistent belief that males are better at some pursuits than are females and vice versa (Rashotte and Webster 2005). Males are believed to be better in such matters as exercising leadership, running a business, pursuing scientific work, and

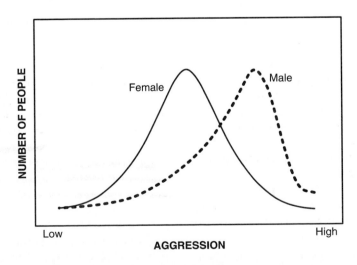

FIGURE 3.1 Male-Female Differences

creating art, while females are believed to do better at nurturing and at managing domestic matters.

Beliefs that attach certain abilities and qualities differentially to gender begin early in life. Researchers asked a group of 170 children aged 8 to 12 years to draw a picture of an intelligent and of an ordinary person (Raty and Snellman 1997). The most common portrait of the intelligent person was an adult male. And reflecting the belief that males are more skilled at leadership, a study involving 150 adults with egalitarian beliefs reported that males were more likely than females to be selected as task leaders (Sapp, Harrod, and Zhao 1996).

Despite these beliefs, it is not true that male abilities are generally superior to those of females. On tests of cognitive ability, women outscore men on some and men outscore women on others (Maylor et al. 2007). On tests of language and verbal ability, girls score better than boys (Nelson and Van Meter 2007). They score higher than boys on tests that demand an understanding of complex language, creative writing, analogies, fluency, and spelling. Among the very young, girls are as likely as boys to use, and be competent with, computers (Calvert et al. 2005). And young women are now doing as well as, or even better than, young men in academic performance (National Center for Education Statistics 2004). Among other things, females are less likely to repeat a grade or to drop out of high school; are closing the gap in math and science course-taking; have higher educational aspirations as high school seniors than do males; have a higher proportion who go to college; and are more likely to complete a college degree.

Boys, on the other hand, have better spatial and quantitative ability. They score higher on math tests and do better on tasks that require visual and spatial perception. However, these conclusions need to be qualified. By the twelfth grade, boys' superiority in math is only slight and is most pronounced in geometry (Leahey and Guo 2001). In fact, a good deal of research debunks the presumed superiority of men in math and science and concludes that men and women have equal capacity for them (Spelke 2005; Hyde and Linn 2006; Ding, Song, and Richardson 2007).

Boys' higher scores on tests of spatial perception may reflect the extent of interest in spatial tasks rather than innate ability. In a sample of college students, the males outperformed the females on spatial tests only because a number of the males had a strong preference for spatial sports (Voyer, Nolan, and Voyer 2000). Such a preference, in turn, may reflect the influence of **socialization,** the process by which people learn to function effectively in a group. In this case, it means that boys are socialized to think of spatial sports as a masculine endeavor. This may be changing somewhat. But think of a soccer player. If the first image you get is that of a male rather than a female, you may still regard spatial sports as more of a masculine than a feminine activity.

The notion that men can perform better than women in all occupations is also untrue. One reason some people give for the presumed difference is that women are less involved with the workplace than are men. Some businessmen have been reluctant to promote women into the upper ranks of management because they assume that women are not as committed to their careers as are men. We will discuss women and work more fully in chapter 11. Here, we will simply point out that women may be less committed to work than they are to family (Friedman and Weissbrod 2005). This means, among other things, that women are more stressed than men when work demands and family demands conflict. But given the same opportunities as men, both their competence and their motivation are equal to men's. Both sexes can perform well in nearly all kinds of work.

The fact that this has not been fully accepted, however, is illustrated in the extent to which **occupational sex segregation,** the clustering of men and women in different occupations, exists. As a result of the 1964 Civil Rights Act, occupational sex segregation has declined considerably (Tomaskovic-Devey et al. 2006). Nevertheless, as table 3.1 shows, many occupations are still dominated by one sex or the other.

Aggression.   It appears universally true that men are more aggressive than women. Anthropologists have reported that violence typically occurs at the hands of men in all societies. The difference appears even in people's dreams. Men in tribal societies are more likely to dream of sexual intercourse, wives, weapons, and animals, while women are more likely to dream of husbands and children, mothers and fathers, and crying (Konner 1982).

The gender differences in aggressive tendencies are apparent from infancy. A study of physical aggression by children between the ages of 17 and 29 months of age found that 5 percent of boys, compared to 1 percent of girls, frequently engaged in aggressive behaviors (Baillarageon et al. 2007). Studies of children in various societies show that boys exhibit a much higher preference for sports as a leisure activity than do girls (Lightbody et al. 1996; Gibbons, Lynn, and Stiles 1997). Boys, in other words, prefer a more aggressive kind of activity.

TABLE 3.1 Percent of Females Employed in Selected Occupations, 2006

Occupation	Percent Female
All Occupations	46.3
Managerial and Professional	50.6
Chief executives	23.4
Human resources managers	65.8
Architects	22.2
Civil engineers	11.9
Physicians	32.2
Elementary/Middle school teachers	82.2
Lawyers	32.6
Librarians	84.2
Service Occupations	57.3
Dental assistants	95.4
Waiters and waitresses	71.5
Maids and housekeeping cleaners	90.3
Recreation and fitness workers	68.7
Child care workers	94.2
Firefighting and fire prevention	3.5
Police and sheriff patrol officers	12.8
Sales and Office Occupations	63.3
Cashiers	74.8
Retail salespersons	51.4
File clerks	79.2
Secretaries	96.9
Natural Resources, Construction and Maintenance Occupations	4.7
Highway maintenance workers	3.8
Electricians	1.9
Construction and building inspectors	8.8
Production, Transportation, and Material Occupations	22.8
Bakers	57.9
Sewing machine operators	77.9
Machinists	6.7
Aircraft pilots and flight engineers	3.2

Source: U.S. Census Bureau (2008:598).

Males are more aggressive by almost any measure. Men commit more violent crimes than women. They are more likely to assault someone. In social psychological experiments, men are typically more aggressive than women in their responses. Men even dream about physical aggression more often than do women (Schredl et al. 2004). And men prefer movies with sex and violence significantly more than do women, while women prefer love stories significantly more than do men (Emmers-Sommer et al. 2006).

This does not mean that men are more aggressive than women in every kind of situation. In a study of anger while driving, researchers reported that while high anger and low anger drivers drove equally often and as many miles, the high anger drivers were more often and more intensely angry and more likely to engage in aggressive and risky kinds of driving (Deffenbacher et al. 2003). Interestingly, however, there were few gender differences. Thus, while men are generally more aggressive than women, the differences can disappear in some circumstances.

Interaction: Quantity and Quality. Females are more relationship oriented than males. It isn't that males have less need of intimacy, nor that they are incapable of forming close relationships. In fact, a small study of undergraduates reported that males and females had similar levels of emotional closeness for both same- and cross-sex friendships (Johnson et al. 2007). But males tend to value independence more than females, while females value connectedness and intimacy more than males (Christensen et al. 2006). A study of e-mail communication with friends regarding a recent holiday found that the e-mails from females, compared to those from males, contained more material that would maintain rapport and intimacy (Coley and Todd 2002). In troubling situations, females are more likely than males to reach out to others for support, while males are more likely to try to solve the problem on their own (McCall and Struthers 1994). And while most adult sibling relationships involve frequent contact and positive feelings, women are more likely than men to say they feel close to their siblings (Spitze and Trent 2006). In fact, sisters make contact and exchange advice more than other kinds of pairs of siblings.

Generally, females appear to be more skilled than males in maintaining quality interaction, in part because of certain aspects of their conversational style. Women do much of the work in starting and maintaining conversations. Women have a questioning style that includes a number of characteristics (Kohn 1988):

- Women ask more questions than men. One analysis of conversations between professional couples reported that the women asked three times as many questions as the men.
- Women have a questioning tone to their statements. The tone asks for confirmation from the listener that the speaker is correct.
- Women use more tag questions. Tag questions occur at the end of sentences and encourage the listener to respond. Some examples are "This is a beautiful day, isn't it?" and "School gets to be a drag sometimes, don't you think?"

Adolescent girls report higher levels of intimacy than do boys, and girls tend to have their highest level with their girlfriends.

- Women are more likely to begin with a question. "Guess what?" and other leading questions are meant to capture the listener's attention.
- Women use more qualifiers ("sort of," "maybe") and intensifiers ("really") than men. The qualifiers and intensifiers give hints to the listener about how to react.

The interpersonal skills of females emerge early in their lives (Leman, Ahmed, and Ozarow 2005). A study of 38 preschool children found that the girls were more likely than the boys to share play stickers and to negotiate and cooperate with each other (Burford et al. 1996).

On the other hand, there are more gender similarities than differences in the kind of interaction that builds intimacy. In their studies of a group of seventh- and eighth-graders and a sample of first-year college students, Radmacher and Azmitia (2006) categorized the behaviors and feelings that create intimacy into two types: the *expressive* (such as giving emotional support, feeling trust and loyalty, and disclosing personal matters) and the *instrumental* (such as engaging in shared activities and giving nonemotional help). As figure 3.2 illustrates, there were some differences, but the differences were not large. The researchers had expected expressive experiences to

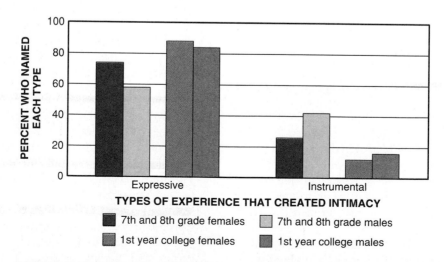

FIGURE 3.2 Gendered Pathways to Intimacy
Source: Adapted from Radmacher and Azmitia 2006.

be much more important to young girls than to young boys and instrumental experiences to be much more important to the boys than to the girls. But the gender differences were not statistically significant in either age group. With the exception of the seventh- and eighth-grade boys, expressive experiences were more important than instrumental ones for building intimacy (although the young boys did name more expressive than instrumental experiences, the difference was not statistically significant).

The researchers found another difference among the college students. For the women, the degree of emotional closeness they felt to a friend depended upon the extent to which they disclosed personal matters. For the men, the degree of emotional closeness depended upon both the extent to which they disclosed personal matters and on the number of shared activities they had. In fact, the men, but not women, were more likely to talk about personal matters while engaged in some shared activity. As one college student put it, "I don't usually open up," but he and a friend shared a room on a high school senior trip to Mexico, and one evening as they sat in their room they began talking about such things as their plans and hopes for the future. It was in the context of the shared activity that they each disclosed personal matters that they typically kept to themselves.

Finally, one additional finding of interest was that the college men indicated higher levels of emotional closeness with female than with male friends. This is consistent with other research that shows that men are more comfortable discussing personal matters with females than with other males.

Conflict Theory Applied

Nonverbal Behavior. It has been estimated that anywhere between 50 and 80 percent of the meaning in a conversation is communicated nonverbally. The same words can take on quite different meanings depending on one's facial expression, gestures, voice tone, and inflection. For example, depending on the nonverbal cues, the three words "I love you" could mean sarcasm, indifference (suggesting that the speaker said them only to try to placate the other), disbelief (I love *you*?), true devotion, or a variety of things in between. Nonverbal behavior, then, is a crucial part of intimate relationships.

Gender differences exist in nonverbal behavior. Women are more sensitive to nonverbal cues than are men. Women are better able to recall the nonverbal behavior of someone (Hall, Murphy, and Mast 2006). And women are more skilled at interpreting nonverbal behavior. *Conflict theorists* explain this as a protective measure. They note that those who are less powerful (women and minorities) have a greater need to know what the more powerful people with whom they interact are really thinking and planning. But women also use somewhat different kinds of nonverbal behavior, and they use differences both in communicating and interpreting nonverbal behavior to enhance their ability to form and maintain intimate relationships. For example, eye contact is an important nonverbal component of intimacy. Researchers who have watched videotapes of people conversing note that pairs of women have more eye contact than do pairs of men (Kahn 1984). And women are more likely to maintain eye contact when they are sitting close to each other, while men are more likely to maintain eye contact when farther apart from each other.

From an early age, females seem to use eye contact to communicate intimacy more than do males (Leeb and Rejskind 2004). And from an early age, females are superior in communicating nonverbal emotional messages. In fact, boys seem to get poorer at sending nonverbal emotional messages as they get older. Overall, then, women's nonverbal behavior suggests that they are warm, friendly, and attentive to others. Men's nonverbal behavior suggests that they have high status and are important and somewhat distant.

Keeping Differences in Perspective. Clearly, not every woman is warm, friendly, and attentive to others. Nor does every man act superior and distant. Similarly, every man is not more aggressive than any woman. There are differences, but the differences refer to averages in whole groups (recall figure 3.1). Thus, it is more accurate to say that more women than men are warm, friendly, and attentive to others, than to say that women are warmer, more friendly, and more attentive than men.

The difference in language may seem subtle, but it is an important difference. It helps us keep in mind that there are numerous similarities between the sexes and that at least some of the differences are relatively small.

SEX, GENDER, GENDER ROLE, AND GENDER-ROLE ORIENTATION

Are you male or female? How much does the answer tell us about your behavior? As the previous discussion indicates, it tells us some things but not a great deal. We need to ask some additional questions of you. What kinds of behavior do you see as appropriate for someone of your sex? And to what extent do you see yourself having both masculine and feminine traits?

Many people think that being male or female is a major factor in determining behavior. Indeed, we all do tend to treat people differently by gender. But for many kinds of behavior, gender roles and gender-role orientations are even more important than gender.

Gender Roles

To test your understanding of your own gender role, answer each of the following as true or false:

1. I plan on a long and successful career.
2. I will be responsible for most or all of the income for my family.
3. Becoming a parent is *not* one of my highest priorities.
4. I don't see myself doing much housework.
5. I expect my spouse to support me in whatever career decisions I make.
6. I will be in charge of the checkbook in my home.
7. When crucial decisions need to be made in my family, I will have the final word.
8. If I have children, I will follow the rule that it is more important for boys than for girls to participate in sports.
9. In a well-functioning home, the wife takes care of the inside and the husband takes care of the yard and cars.

A traditional female would answer false and a traditional male would answer true to most of the above statements. How did you score? Let's look a little more closely at traditional gender roles.

Traditional Gender Roles. For many decades, researchers have found a tendency for agreement by men and women on the "typical" attributes of each sex. In essence, men are held to be strong, independent, successful, courageous, aggressive, and logical (Harris 1995). In a classic statement, Brannon (1976) described the traditional male role in terms of four norms: "no sissy stuff," "the big wheel," "the sturdy oak," and "give 'em hell." "No sissy stuff" means that men must not do anything that might appear to be feminine. The "big wheel" means that men should act in a way to command respect and admiration. The "sturdy oak" means that men should be strong, calm in the midst of turmoil and difficulty. And "give 'em hell" means that men love adventure, risk, danger, and violence.

Women, by contrast, are viewed as more gentle, nurturing, emotional, submissive, and dependent on men for support and protection (Viki, Abrams, and Hutchison 2003). As such, they can expect to be treated with courtesy and consideration by men, but they must behave within the bounds of what the dominant males consider appropriate for females. Traditional roles—men as breadwinners and women as homemakers—reflect these perspectives.

In short, then, the traditional male is someone who is in control of his life, who acts with reason and determination to achieve goals and complete tasks. The traditional female is someone who is dependent on that male, who tries to protect the male from any threats to his ego, and who must resort to emotions rather than reason when she tries to influence him. And these roles have been affirmed and encouraged in self-help, etiquette, and advice books from the 1950s through the end of the twentieth century (McDaniel 2001).

Consequences of the Traditional Roles. To some extent the traditional roles are stereotypes. That is, few if any people have followed them precisely. But to the extent that people have approximated those roles, certain consequences for a wide range of behavior follow, one of which is illustrated in table 3.1—the tendency to consider certain occupations as more appropriate for one sex than the other.

Numerous additional consequences arise. Men who agree with the traditional roles expect to be the providers in their families and expect their wives to be the nurturers (Haynes 2000). They are more inclined toward Type A behavior, such as rapid speaking, preoccupation with one's work, impatience, and a generally aggressive, competitive approach to life (Thompson, Grisanti, and Pleck 1985). They are less inclined to disclose intimate matters to women and more concerned about being in control in an intimate relationship. They tend to be negative about the idea of women's equality, and their attitudes are conducive to the **sexual harassment** of women (Wade and Brittan-Powell 2001).

Even though our ideas about gender roles have been changing, many people still react to others on the basis of those traditional roles. For instance, a man who acts passive and dependent or a woman who insists on pursuing a career in a male-dominated occupation may be defined as maladjusted. And even though most wives work, and some are the household's major source of income, both men and women continue to value the ability of a man to be a good provider (Loscocco and Spitze 2007).

What Do You Think?

*There is disagreement about **whether women should reject current standards of beauty and accept their bodies as they are.** What follows are pro and con arguments. What do you think?*

Pro

Women should accept their bodies as they are because

- self-acceptance is crucial to emotional well-being.
- the standards reflect a sexist culture, not inherent beauty.
- women have injured their health and even died in an effort to meet the standards.
- the standards lower the self-esteem of women who believe they don't or can't meet the standards.
- the standards overemphasize the importance of bodily appearance to the detriment of other qualities.

Con

Women should not accept their bodies as they are because

- the standards (thinness, e.g.) reflect good health as well as beauty.
- achieving the standards will make them attractive to men.
- resisting the culture will hinder career advancement.
- the closer they come to the standards, the higher their self-esteem and self-confidence.
- modern medicine has developed techniques to allow women to remake their bodies.

One final example involves housework. Traditionally, the woman was the homemaker and the man was the breadwinner. While the majority of women now work outside the home, most of them retain major responsibility for doing the housework (Spain and Bianchi 1996). Whatever people's ideals may be, traditional gender roles continue to influence their behavior.

Gender-Role Orientation

As we pointed out, few if any people have conformed precisely to the traditional roles. Most people have some combination of the qualities or traits of each role. Social scientists call those traits associated with the traditional male role **instrumental traits** and those associated with the traditional female role **expressive traits.** Instrumental traits, such as aggressiveness, competitiveness, self-confidence, and logic, enable people to achieve goals. Expressive traits, such as warmth, caring, sensitivity, and nurturance, enable people to establish good interpersonal relationships.

The way to find people's gender-role orientation is to ask them to describe themselves in terms of the various traits. Those who select predominantly instrumental traits are masculine, while those who select predominantly expressive traits are feminine in their orientation. For example, the Personal Attributes Questionnaire, developed by Spence and Helmreich (1978), asks respondents to rate themselves on a number of traits, such as the following:

| Not at all aggressive | A...B...C...D...E | Very aggressive |

| Not at all emotional | A...B...C...D...E | Very emotional |
| Very rough | A...B...C...D...E | Very gentle |

A strong masculine response would be E on the aggressive scale and A on the emotional and rough/gentle scales. A strong feminine response would be the opposite.

At first, it seems reasonable to assume that masculine and feminine are the two extremes of one dimension. That is, the more masculine you are, the less feminine and vice versa. But social scientists agree that masculinity and femininity are not opposites that exclude each other. Instead of a continuum, with masculine at one end and feminine at the other, gender-role orientation must be understood as two-dimensional (figure 3.3). Thus, an individual can be high on both, low on both, or high on one and low on the other dimension. The smallest category, in terms of numbers of people, is the **undifferentiated,** in which an individual sees himself or herself as low on both masculine and feminine traits. You would be undifferentiated if you saw yourself as moderately aggressive (in between "very" and "not at all"), moderately independent, moderately emotional, and so on.

As figure 3.3 indicates, an individual can be aggressive and competitive and independent and also gentle and sensitive. Such people are called *androgynous.* Androgyny is a term coined by Sandra Bem (1974) to describe those people who possess both masculine, or instrumental, and feminine, or expressive, traits. Bem has argued that androgynous individuals are healthier and more adaptable than others. This makes sense, because

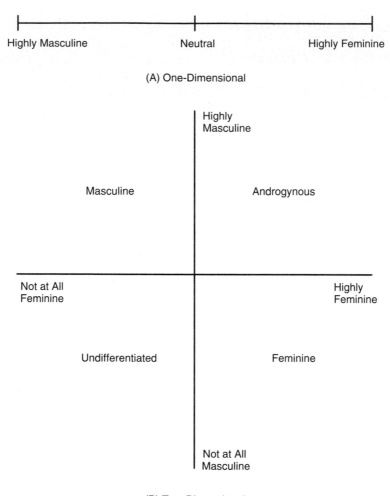

FIGURE 3.3 One- or Two-Dimensional Gender-Role Orientation

they should have a greater range of behaviors available to them to meet diverse demands of differing situations. We shall see to what extent androgyny does facilitate people's functioning.

GENDER ROLES: NATURE OR NURTURE?

One of the controversies surrounding gender roles is whether they reflect human nature. Are women more expressive than men because there is something in their biological makeup that leads them to behave in that way? Or do gender roles reflect socialization, the way in which children are nurtured? Those who stress nature may prefer to use the term *sex role,* which suggests that the differences are innate. We use the term *gender role* because we believe the evidence shows that male–female differences

reflect nurture as much as, or perhaps even somewhat more than, they do nature.

Differences between males and females develop quite early in life. There are certain differences even in infants (girl babies, for example, tend to smile more than boy babies). By the time they are 3 years old, children think of themselves as male or female (Brown 1995). There are gender differences in the communicative gestures of infants between 13 and 18 months of age, and the vocabularies of those 18 months and older (Stennes et al. 2005). Girls use the kind of gestures and the words that adults would typically describe as feminine, and boys use gestures and words that adults define as masculine. And from an early age, boys and girls differ in their preferences for toys, games, and various kinds of activities (Jervolino et al. 2005). Boys, for example, usually prefer cars and trains to dolls and jewelry, while girls prefer the dolls and jewelry. Girls tend to prefer play involving nurturing and caring for others, while boys tend to prefer play revolving about adventure and fighting. How can we account for these differences?

How Much Is Biological?

Sigmund Freud (1949) set forth an influential case for the biological basis of gender roles. Freud's arguments were summed up in his famous idea that *anatomy is destiny*. He argued that girls reach the point in their development when they realize that they are anatomically different from boys. They lack a penis, and therefore they feel severely deprived. This leads to "penis envy." According to Freud, only in the act of conceiving and giving birth to a child can a woman find fulfillment. But she never fully overcomes her penis envy, so that jealousy and envy are more prominent in women than in men. Without going into the details of his theory, we should note that Freud also concluded that women are naturally more passive, submissive, and neurotic than men. All of this, according to Freud, results from women's psychological reaction to their physiology.

A more recent biological approach looks at the hormonal differences between males and females and the differences in the structure and functioning of the brain (Kreeger 2002; Pfaff 2002). Some researchers have even gone so far as to argue that most behavior can be understood in terms of innate biological differences. Increasingly, this is an untenable position. An increasing amount of research shows that social and biological factors both contribute to behavior (Sapolsky 2004; Sinha 2004). In fact, the human environment affects the way that genes express themselves (Ridley 2003). For example, humans are genetically built for language, but they do not acquire language unless there are other humans around to teach it to them. Another example is the fact that girls raised in fatherless homes go through puberty earlier than those with fathers. The timing seems to be the reaction of genes to the environment, though we still can't explain exactly why it happens.

Behavior, then, is both a biological and a social phenomenon. As a final example, Grossman and Wood (1993) conducted two experiments; in one, females reported more emotional intensity than did males. The researchers manipulated the situation in the second experiment so that males and females reported about the same emotional intensity, but physiological measures showed that the females had a stronger bodily reaction. Both biological and social factors were at work in the emotional experiences.

The Importance of Nurture

Most social scientists argue that nurture is an important part of gender-role behavior. *Symbolic interactionists* and *systems theorists* both stress the importance of roles in shaping human behavior. That is, the way we behave is due more to social expectations involved in the roles we assume than to any genetic or biological imperatives. Some of the evidence for such a position comes from history and from the observation of other cultures. Historically, American men and women have not always behaved in strict accord with what we have called the traditional sex roles. In the American colonies, married and single women functioned

Symbolic Interactionist and Systems Theories Applied

as innkeepers, printers, and the head of dame schools. Further, they were actively involved in the economics of their family and social affairs of their community. In the mid-nineteenth century, as the nation industrialized and the middle classes grew, new ideas about proper gender roles developed. Indeed, women's roles narrowed significantly. Women were to be freed from hard work so that they could engage in the more feminine pursuits of music, art, and embroidery. Greater emphasis was placed on the proper dress, appearance, and decorative function of women. Increasingly, as men's work took them away from the home, the women's place became the home. They were to create and maintain the home as a refuge for their husbands and children in the face of an increasingly impersonal and hostile environment.

Looking at other cultures, we also find deviations from traditional roles in America. In her study of three primitive cultures in New Guinea, Margaret Mead (1969) concluded that the meaning of being male or female is largely a matter of cultural conditioning. Many of the traits we think of as masculine or feminine are "as lightly linked to sex as are the clothing, the manners, and the form of headdress that a society at a given period assigns to either sex" (Mead 1969:260). Among the Tchambuli, for example, the women were in command and were concerned with the practical matters of tribal life, such as fishing and trading. They also took the initiative in mating. The men, in contrast, concerned themselves with their personal appearance, their jewelry, and their rivalries and jealousies in their efforts to get the attention of women.

Finally, there is some evidence from research in developmental psychology that underscores the importance of socialization. According to the stereotype, females are more emotional and more nurturing than males. With regard to emotions, there is evidence that male infants are more emotional than female infants—laughing, crying, and showing joy and anger more—but parents tend to teach their sons to suppress their emotions from about one year on (Levant and Kopecky 1994). Similarly, girls do not appear to be *naturally* more nurturing than boys (Melson and Fogel 1988). Until about the age of 4 or 5, boys tend to be equally as interested as girls in babies and their care. As they get older and become more aware of their gender identity, boys become less involved and less interested in babies. They *learn* to engage in the traditional less-nurturing male role.

In sum, the evidence we have supports the earlier conclusions of Chafetz (1974:27–28) about the relative influence of biological and social factors:

1. Most of the traits and behaviors identified as masculine or feminine in a society are not innate. Those defined as masculine in one society may be feminine in another, and vice versa.
2. A few *tendencies* are innately linked to gender, such as the male tendency to greater aggression. But social factors can virtually eliminate the effects of the tendencies.
3. Whatever innate differences exist, they are quantitative rather than qualitative. That is, we cannot say that men are aggressive and women are passive. But, as we stated earlier, more men than women are highly aggressive.

Socialization and Gender-Role Orientation

Since socialization is important in gender-role development, we need to identify the major sources of that socialization. Reflect back on your own experience. How did you learn what it means to be masculine and feminine? Probably the three most important sources were family, school, and the mass media. And these three sources may have agreed with and reinforced each other. We will illustrate the impact of socialization by the phenomenon of body image among men and women. Then we will discuss the various ways in which family, school, and the media shape gender roles.

Body Image.   When you look in a full-length mirror, how does your body appear to you? Do you like the way it looks? If you're like most people, you're dissatisfied with something about your body image. This dissatisfaction can affect you negatively. For example, both male

and female adolescents who perceive themselves to be overweight have a higher risk of depression and bodily aches and pains and lower self-esteem (Ge et al. 2001). Some people become so distressed over their appearance that they resort to such things as extreme diets, exhausting exercise, eating disorders, body piercings, tattoos, or cosmetic surgery in order to change their appearance.

What is the ideal? In essence, men want to be lean and muscular and women want to be curvaceous but thin (Jones 2004; Frederick et al. 2007). People learn these cultural ideals in the family, in school, among friends, and from the media. And the learning occurs early in life; children as young as 9 years of age can express dissatisfaction with their body image (Gardner, Sorter, and Friedman 1997).

Learning in the family occurs in various ways. A child may hear the parents complain about their weight or their shape. They see their parents react to people who are closer to the ideal with envy or desire. The father who lifts weights in order to become more muscular is teaching his son something about the preferred body type, particularly if he is doing it for reasons of appearance rather than of health. A mother who engages in rigorous dieting or cosmetic surgery in order to alter her appearance is teaching her daughter something about the preferred body type.

Friends, schoolmates, and the media reinforce the cultural ideals. Conversations among friends and schoolmates about appearances reflect a commitment to the cultural ideals (Jones 2004). When young girls are teased about their appearance, they are strongly affected in adolescence and adulthood about the way they perceive their bodies (Kostanski and Guilone 2006).

Not surprisingly, the ideal of muscular males and thin females pervades the media. Magazines and television both portray the cultural ideals in ways that clearly show them to be the most desirable and attractive of body types (Hatoum and Belle 2004; Jones, Vigfusdottir, and Lee 2004; Schooler et al. 2004). These portrayals adversely affect both men and women, for hardly anyone has a body that perfectly matches the ideal. A study of 126 women found that seeing magazine advertisements containing the thin-idealized female body led to increased negative mood and higher dissatisfaction with the readers' own bodies (Tiggemann and McGill 2004). And a survey of nearly 600 white women reported that the more the women watched television, the more negative was their image of their own bodies (Schooler et al. 2004). Finally, an experiment that exposed 158 men to television ads concluded that those who saw ideal-image ads became significantly more depressed and dissatisfied with their own muscularity than did those men who saw ads without such images (Agliata and Tantleff-Dunn 2004).

Both sexes, then, are affected by cultural ideals of body image. Among men, gay men have greater body dissatisfaction than heterosexual men (Tiggemann, Martins, and Kirkbride 2007). But whether gay or straight, those who see themselves as overweight may engage in unhealthy dieting behaviors (Markey and Markey 2005). And those who are obsessed with becoming more muscular may use a combination of exercise, dieting, and bodybuilding techniques. If the desired result is still not achieved, they may try drugs, particularly anabolic steroids (Pope, Phillips, and Olivardia 2000).

Women report more body dissatisfaction than do men (Markey, Markey, and Birch 2004; Frederick, Forbes, Grigorian, and Jarcho 2007). And rates of women's dissatisfaction tend to remain stable across the adult lifespan (Bessenoff and Del Priore 2007). Although both men and women compare themselves with professional models, college women do so more frequently than college men (Franzoi and Klaiber 2007). The pressure to be thin but shapely and to have attractive facial features leads women to engage in various measures designed to achieve the ideal, measures that are often harmful or even hazardous to their health. Some resort to smoking as a way to lose weight or to maintain a low weight (Zucker et al. 2001). Some develop eating disorders, such as anorexia or bulimia, as they struggle to be thin (Hesse-Biber 1996). The eating disorders occur in all racial and ethnic groups, though African Americans may be at higher risk than others (Walcott, Pratt, and Patel 2003).

According to a study of 79 adolescent girls, aged 15 to 18, dissatisfaction with their bodies led many of them to get body piercings and tattoos (Carroll and Anderson 2002). Nearly half of the girls had at least one form of body modification and were willing to accept the associated risks (infection, viral transmission, allergic reactions, etc.) in order to alter their appearance. The researchers found that the more tattoos and piercings a girl had, the higher her score on a measure of anger and the greater her dissatisfaction with her body.

Women and men also use cosmetic surgery to create the desired body image (Sullivan 2001; Kiser and Whitehorne 2005). But, again, women are far more likely than men to opt for such surgery. Around 11.5 million cosmetic procedures were performed in 2005, 85 to 90 percent of which involved women as patients (Carr 2007). The most common procedures are liposuction

(the removal of unwanted fat from such areas as the abdomen, hips, buttocks, and thighs), breast augmentation, eyelid surgery, reshaping of the nose, and tummy tucks. Cosmetic surgery has become a growth industry, fueled by cultural ideals but also by the constant advertising of cosmetic surgeons. It is virtually impossible for a woman today to avoid being reminded not only of the ideal, but also of ways to achieve the ideal and of the benefits that will ensue.

There are two ways in which the quest for the ideal body type is ironic. First, while the quest reflects a desire to be attractive and to form enriching intimate relationships, the individual's effort may yield little in the way either of increased self-esteem or of enhanced intimate relationships. In fact, as in the case of women who develop eating disorders, the quest may become so extreme that it becomes an impediment to meaningful intimacy.

Second, a good deal of misperception exists among both men and women about the views of the opposite sex. In one study, researchers found that women overestimate the extent to which men prefer thinness in women, and men overestimate the extent to which women prefer muscularity in men (Forbes et al. 2001). In another study of 172 wives, the women were much more dissatisfied with their bodies than were their

Girls learn from magazines and other forms of the mass media the "ideal" way to look.

husbands, and they believed their husbands to be more dissatisfied than they actually were (Markey, Markey, and Birch 2004). As with much else in social life, however, it is the perceptions that motivate the behavior, even though the perceptions are *mis*perceptions.

Particular body images are one aspect of what it means to be masculine and feminine. Let's explore the ways in which family, school, and the media teach you other facets of your gender role.

Family.   Our earliest exposure to what it means to be masculine and feminine comes from our parents. We learn from them and tend to model ourselves after them. We learn not only from listening to them but also by observing their attitudes and behavior. For example, your attitudes about the appropriate division of labor in the household grow out of both the attitudes your mother held and the way your parents divided up household chores between them (Cunningham 2001).

Parents teach gender roles by the different ways they treat their male and female children. Both fathers and mothers use a greater range and number of emotional terms with their daughters than with their sons (Adams et al. 1995; Garner, Robertson, and Smith 1997; Fivush 2000). They engage in more physical play with sons than with daughters and more pretend play with daughters than with sons (Lindsey and Mize 2001). They use different discipline strategies for boys and girls (Leve and Fagot 1997). Parents tend to encourage their children to engage in gender-typed activities. For example, they assume that science is less interesting and more difficult for daughters than for sons and act accordingly when talking with their children about science. As a result, their daughters are lower both in their interest and their sense of competence in science (Tenenbaum and Leaper 2003).

Such differential treatment occurs from birth. Observations of mothers' speech and play behavior in the first year of their children's lives show that mothers interact more, speak more, and make more interpretations with their daughters than they do with their sons and give more instructions to their sons than they do to their daughters (Clearfield and Nelson 2006). In our culture, there are also definite ideas of the differing kinds of toys appropriate for boys and girls (Blakemore and Centers 2005). Thus, in the early years of life, parents tend to give boys such things as sports equipment, tools, and large and small vehicles of various kinds, while they give girls dolls, children's furniture, and similar toys. Parents need to be aware of the implications of their gifts to their children. Even such a seemingly neutral gift as a picture book has an impact, because the books, while becoming less stereotyped, still tend to portray girls as dependent and submissive and boys as independent, active, and creative (Diekman and Murnen 2004).

Another factor that affects gender-role socialization is the type of family. Support for nontraditional gender roles is more likely to come from women employed full-time outside the home than from women employed part-time outside the home. And it is least likely to come from homemakers (Cassidy and Warren 1996). In single-parent families, father-headed families have the most traditional gender attitudes and mother-headed families have the most egalitarian attitudes (Wright and Young 1998). However, a study of mother-headed black families found that girls scored higher on perceived masculinity than did boys (Mandara, Murray, and Joyner 2005). The researchers speculated that the mothers' tendency to rely on and pressure their daughters made the latter more masculine, while the lack of a father for socialization made the boys less masculine.

School.   Schools teach equality between the sexes if they group boys and girls together and apply the same standards to both. In practice, however, such equal treatment is absent. Using participant observation, Martin (1998) studied five preschools and found five kinds of practices that differentiate boys from girls. First, parents sent their children to preschool in gendered clothing (61 percent of the girls wore something pink; boys never wore pink). The children observed each other and learned that boys and girls dress in different colors as well as different kinds of clothing. Second, the teachers encouraged girls to behave more formally than boys (girls, e.g., were more likely to be told to "sit on your bottom" during circle while boys might be allowed to squat or be on their knees). Third, teachers were more likely to tell girls than boys to be quiet or to repeat something in a quieter and "nicer" voice. Fourth, teachers gave more directives to girls than to boys about changing their behavior ("talk to her, don't yell, sit here, pick that up, be careful," etc.). Finally, the children taught each other the meaning of being masculine and feminine by engaging in roughhouse (boys) or by trying to be nice (girls). Thus, children in preschool learn the meaning of being male or female from both teachers and their peers.

They also learn from the books they read in school. An examination of elementary school reading books found that males are still portrayed as aggressive, argumentative, and competitive (Evans and Davies 2000).

Comparison

Inuit Youth Learn to Be Males and Females

The community of Holman lies some 300 miles north of the Arctic Circle on Victoria Island. A few hundred Eskimos, mostly of the Copper Inuit, live there. Until they settled in Holman during the 1960s, these Inuit Eskimos lived in scattered, isolated hunting and trapping camps. In the camps, males and females had fairly well-defined gender roles that were distinct yet complementary, and both roles were necessary to their joint survival.

What does it now mean to be a male or female Inuit in the more settled and secure community of Holman? As two researchers discovered when they interviewed 41 Inuit youth between the ages of 11 and 19, gender roles have changed, although, as in the past, clear distinctions between the sexes remain. When asked to identify the characteristics of males and females, the youths largely agreed that females are sexy, shy, clean, quiet,

friendly, and nice, while males are bullies, scary, aggressive, dirty, show-offs, and mean. They also agreed that young males, compared to young females, have higher social status, greater freedom to do as they like, and fewer household responsibilities and are indulged more by their parents. The females, nevertheless, preferred their own roles, seeing themselves as more mature and adultlike than the males.

These images of maleness and femaleness are acquired through various socialization techniques. Females are given an increasing number of household chores as they mature. They are treated as adults at a relatively early age. For example, a mother at a community dance told her 11-year-old daughter that she was running around "like a little kid." The daughter sat down and remained sedate like her parents. In contrast,

young sons are given few, if any, chores. They are sometimes taken by their fathers to learn how to hunt and fish, but only if the youths feel like doing so. Finally, when they are teenagers, Inuit youths do have some opportunities to work and earn money. The females tend to spend all or a portion of what they earn on things that will benefit the family, while the males usually spend everything they earn on themselves.

The gender roles the Inuit youth learn make the transition to adulthood somewhat easier for females. Teenage females have already begun to function as adults, while teenage males engage in largely nonproductive and irresponsible peer group activities. As a result, the males have more behavioral and psychological adjustments to make as they assume the responsibilities of adulthood (Condon and Stern 1993).

Boys who read them, then, are learning that this is part of what it means to be a traditional male.

The differential treatment of males and females tends to continue even into college. A study of photographs in college-level human sexuality and marriage and family textbooks concluded that there was more egalitarianism in the 1990s than in the 1970s, but traditional roles for women still dominated the photos used in the 1990s (Low and Sherrard 1999). Some college advisors still try to steer women into traditional female occupations or traditional female specialties (e.g., become a pediatrician, not a surgeon). In various ways, then, a woman can still encounter pressures throughout her educational career to accept a more traditional role.

The Media.   The media also are influential in shaping our notions of appropriate gender roles. Consider, for example, children's picture books. Over time, the

books have become more egalitarian in their portrayal of males and females. However, an examination of 200 top-selling and award-winning children's picture books reported a number of ways in which **sexism** remains a problem (Hamilton et al. 2006). The researchers found nearly twice as many males as females in title and main character roles. There were more male characters in the illustrations. The female main characters were more nurturing than the male main characters, and they were shown more often in indoor rather than outdoor situations. Occupations were also gender stereotyped, with more women than men seeming to have no paid work.

Another study, this time of 200 children's picture books, examined how the books depicted parenting (Anderson and Hamilton 2005). The researchers found that fathers were underrepresented in the books. When fathers did appear, they tended to be withdrawn and ineffective in their parenting.

Moving on to elementary-level novels, two researchers analyzed the differences between books that were recommended to teachers and parents as "nonsexist" books and those categorized as sexist (Diekman and Murnen 2004). The researchers had raters read the books and note any examples of sexism such as stereotypical personality types, gender-specific work and family roles, and various kinds of inequality. The nonsexist books were more likely than the sexist to portray women in nontraditional roles and activities. However, both types of books still tended to portray women in traditional terms in their personality, in doing household chores, and in their leisure activities.

Other investigations of the print media have examined popular magazines and comic strips. An analysis of the meaning of work in a popular young woman's magazine concluded that men are the norm for workers and hold the power in the work world, and the highest form of women's work is fashion modeling (Massoni 2004). A study of how women are portrayed in ads in a general interest and a women's fashion magazine reported that women still tend to appear in stereotypically traditional roles (Lindner 2004). And an analysis of 50 comic strips found that, compared to men, women were underrepresented, more likely to be married and have children, less likely to have a job, and more likely to be engaged in child care and household chores (Glascock and Preston-Schreck 2004).

Finally, four researchers looked at how gender in parenting was treated in six best-selling, self-help books on parenting (Krafchick et al. 2005). They found that 82 percent of implicit gender messages in the books reflected traditional gender roles, and two of the books were highly prescriptive about gender in their advice. For example, one of the highly prescriptive books advocated a breadwinner father and stay-at-home mother, asserted that working mothers are selfish and inadequate as mothers, and stated that the use of child care harms children.

Television is probably the most influential of all the media. An analysis of 18 prime-time situation comedies reported that thin females were overrepresented and that the heavier a female character, the more the remarks made about her were negative (Fouts and Burggraf 2000). In television commercials, men tend to appear as strong and women appear as sex objects (Coltrane 2000). Also, fewer men than women appear in commercials for domestic products, while fewer women than men appear in commercials for nondomestic products (Bartsch et al. 2000).

The mass media in other nations also may support traditional ideas about gender roles. An analysis of 106 Australian radio ads concluded that the way men and women were portrayed tended to reflect traditional gender role stereotypes (Hurtz and Durkin 1997).

Women may have come a long way. But there is a long way to go if equality is the goal. The mass media, along with school and family practices, continue to support traditional roles.

CHANGING GENDER ROLES AND ORIENTATIONS

As noted, what we have called the traditional roles emerged in the mid-nineteenth century. Gender roles vary over time and among societies. Gender-role orientations also change over time and may even vary over an individual's life span.

Changing Patterns

Evidence exists that people are becoming less traditional in their attitudes about gender roles. As noted, although the media continue to reinforce traditional roles, they do so less than in the past. And although many occupations continue to be dominated by one sex or the other, they are less so than they were in the past.

In essence, those who reject the traditional model tend to affirm more egalitarian roles. They believe that women should have the same opportunities as men and that men can and should engage in some of the traditional female pursuits (such as the nurturing of children). Thus, Hispanic women who hold to more nontraditional gender roles, for example, are more likely than others to delay marriage, go to college, and pursue a career (Cardoza 1991). And children who affirm gender egalitarianism in all racial/ethnic groups are more likely to aspire to a college education and to graduate or professional degrees (Davis and Pearce 2007).

With such changes in attitudes, we would expect changes in gender-role orientations. There is some evidence that orientations have been changing, and the change may be in the direction of increasing androgyny (Strough et al. 2007).

Lingering Traditionalism

Traditional roles are not dead. Recall the occupational sex ratios (table 3.1), the reactions of people at horror movies, and the fact that women who work still bear the brunt of the responsibility for housework and child rearing. Women, including women in other nations, tend to be more egalitarian than men in their views (Bryant 2003; Frieze et al. 2003). But both men and women show

Thus, wives ... chores than ... bs (Bittman ... re free time ... 03).

... in attitudes. ... ool students ... ce between ... male gender ... of students ... an a female ... person in a ... nalism even ... t difference ... ns change or ... t of orienta-

... ate handling of your emotions, understanding the emotional states of others, and responding to those emotional states in a way that builds good relationships. In general, women have higher emotional intelligence than men. But men who are androgynous have higher emotional intelligence than those who are masculine in their gender-role orientation (Guastello and Guastello 2003). Similar effects of gender-role orientation can be seen in such areas as communication, self-concepts, and mental health.

Communication

We have noted that women tend to have a different conversational style than men. Differences also exist, however, depending on the individual's gender-role orientation. Androgynous individuals exhibit greater communication skills than those with other gender-role orientations (Hirokawa, Yagi, and Miyata 2004). Individuals with a masculine orientation tend to talk more in small groups and to overlap or interrupt the speech of others (Drass 1986; Jose and McCarthy 1988).

More importantly, gender-role orientation affects such things as our ability to handle conflict and the way in which we will try to influence someone. With regard to conflict, Yelsma and Brown (1985) found gender-role orientation to be more important than sex. They studied 91 married couples and found that androgynous and masculine spouses tended to handle conflict more constructively than did feminine spouses.

With regard to influence, a variety of tactics can be used. *Manipulation* involves such things as dropping hints, flattering someone, and behaving seductively. *Supplication* includes pleading, crying, and acting helpless. *Bullying* is the use of threats, insults, and ridicule. *Autocracy* refers to such things as insisting and asserting one's authority. *Bargaining* involves reasoning and the willingness to compromise. Finally, *disengagement* is withdrawing in some way (sulking, leaving the scene).

In a study of 235 intimate couples, researchers found that more feminine spouses are more likely to use supplication, while more masculine spouses tend to avoid both supplication and bargaining (Howard, Blumstein, and Schwartz 1986). Supplication is a relatively weak tactic. Thus, those with a feminine orientation are less likely to be influential and more likely to be influenced by a partner.

Self-Concept

Symbolic interactionists define **self-concept** as the totality

Symbolic Interactionist Theory Applied

of the beliefs and attitudes you have about yourself. Your self-concept is important because the way you think about yourself is an integral part of your psychological health. You can't be a healthy individual if you don't think well of yourself and if you don't have a high degree of self-esteem.

Who is likely to have the higher self-esteem? The research consistently indicates that both males and females who are high in masculine traits have higher self-esteem than others. Adolescents who score high on masculinity see themselves as more socially and physically competent and have higher self-esteem scores than those low on masculinity (Cate and Sugawara 1986). Among adult women, masculinity is a better predictor of self-esteem than a woman's educational or occupational achievements (Long 1986). Finally, a study of 215 undergraduates reported that those with an androgynous or masculine orientation saw themselves as more academically capable than did those with a feminine or undifferentiated orientation (Choi 2004).

Four things are important to keep in mind here. First, androgynous as well as masculine people score high on masculinity. The point is that it is the masculinity, rather than the androgyny per se, that makes the difference. Second, masculinity refers to the perception of traits that are associated with the traditional male role; that is, to instrumental traits. Masculinity and femininity are unfortunate choices for terms, because we are not saying that a masculine gender-orientation in a woman means that she is any less of a woman or that she is "mannish." Rather, a masculine orientation for either males or females simply means the possession of such traits as independence, being active rather than passive, competitiveness, and the ability to make decisions. Third, such traits understandably lead to high self-esteem because they are highly valued in American culture. They are the traits that are believed necessary for success in any venture. And fourth, having such traits does not mean that the individual lacks kindness or sensitivity or a willingness to be helpful.

Mental Health

In the past, some researchers expected psychological health to be highest when there was congruence between gender and gender-role orientation (males would be masculine and females would be feminine in their orientation). Research shows that is not true. Others expected androgynous people to have the best mental health. That also appears to be untrue. Rather, masculinity tends to be associated with such things as high self-esteem, high levels of adjustment, subjective well-being, and less depression and anxiety (Markstrom-Adams 1989; Harris and Schwab 1990; Kleinplatz, McCarrey, and Kateb 1992; Williams and D'Alessandro 1994; Obeidallah, McHale, and Silbereisen 1996). In fact, a study of adolescents found that having a relatively high and increasing masculinity during adolescence was associated with fewer depressive symptoms in early adulthood for both males and females (Barrett and Raskin 2002).

Are, then, the feminine traits a handicap? The answer is no, because androgynous individuals have both the masculine and feminine traits and the same advantages as masculine types in terms of self-concept and mental health. Is there, then, any advantage at all

to androgyny? We would say there is. The expressive traits can help with social adjustment by increasing interpersonal skills (Payne 1987; Aylor and Dainton 2004). Those with strong expressive traits also score higher on the well-being that comes from positive interpersonal relationships (September et al. 2001). In a sample of 100 elderly subjects, those who were androgynous were significantly more satisfied with life (Dean-Church and Gilroy 1993). Research on the adjustment of women to the death of a spouse reported that androgynous widows had a more positive adjustment than those who were feminine, masculine, or undifferentiated (Solie and Fielder 1987/1988). Finally, a study of 412 French-speaking Canadian women who gave birth found a positive relationship between androgyny on the one hand and self-esteem and satisfaction with social support on the other (Berthiaume et al. 1996). Social support, in turn, lessened the chances of postpartum depression.

GENDER-ROLE ORIENTATION AND INTIMACY

Gender-role orientation may be more important than whether one is male or female in explaining differences in relating to someone intimately. Three researchers surveyed 286 undergraduates and found differences between males and females in their love styles (Bailey, Hendrick, and Hendrick 1987). But they found more and stronger effects for gender-role orientation. Androgynous subjects were more likely and undifferentiated subjects less likely than others to endorse physical and sexual aspects of love. Masculine subjects gave the strongest support and feminine subjects gave the weakest to a view of love as enjoyable and noncommittal. Feminine and androgynous subjects gave strong support to an unselfish love that is concerned with the other's well-being. Masculine and undifferentiated subjects were the most and feminine subjects the least permissive in their sexual attitudes.

Other research underscores the importance of gender-role orientation for intimate love relationships. Androgyny facilitates the development of close friendships (Jones, Bloys, and Wood 1990). It also is associated with the awareness and expression of love feelings and with greater comfort in dating and sexual situations (Ganong and Coleman 1987; Quackenbush 1990).

Personal

"We Worked It Out"

Gender roles and gender-role orientations can change over time both in a society and in an individual's life. Marcie, for example, is a middle-aged woman who began her married life as a traditional wife and mother. She stayed at home and raised her family. When the last of her four children began school, Marcie felt the need to do something more. Because her husband, David, was also traditional in his views, they went through periods of struggle before, as Marcie put it, they finally "worked it out":

I was only 35 when my last child started school. The first thought that hit me was that I could now go to college. Maybe I could have a career. I knew I had to do something. At first, David couldn't understand why I was so restless. He argued that the kids still needed me at home. He particularly wanted me to be there when they got home from school. I agreed with this, but I told him that I could take night classes. He was appalled.

Eventually, though, he agreed that one class at night was not unreasonable. But after the first semester, I wanted to take two classes. This made him angry again. I pointed out that I would be an old woman before I ever finished my degree. He said that he and the kids would never see me if I took on more. I suggested that we ask the children how they felt about it. We did, and he was really surprised when they all supported my wishes.

Eventually, I found that I could take a combination of day and night classes and still be home when the children came in from school. Our next struggle was over housework. I told David that I needed his help. He had never done housework. I guess he saw how happy I was working on my degree, so he agreed. But he wouldn't take any initiative. I had to tell him everything to do. And he didn't do things right. Finally, we worked that out. I gave him a list of specific tasks he needed to do each week. He agreed to do them, and I agreed not to complain about the way he did them.

I'm about to graduate now. I have a couple of prospects for jobs. We've already talked about how we can each manage to work and still take care of the children's needs. I'm excited about going to work. I loved being a traditional wife and mom. But now I love the idea of being a working mom. Fortunately, David has changed his views as much as I have. So our marriage and our family are both stronger than ever.

Androgynous people tend to be more aware and expressive of love feelings.

With such differences, we would expect people to have varying degrees of satisfaction in their relationships depending on their gender-role orientations and the combination of orientations in the couple. A study of 40 couples in India found a higher level of marital satisfaction when both partners were androgynous (Isaac and Shah 2004). Using national data from the United States, Lye and Biblarz (1993) reported that those less satisfied with their marriages are husbands and wives who differ in their attitudes and those with nontraditional attitudes toward family life. Finally, marital satisfaction reflects not just the orientation, but whether that has been a stable or a changing orientation. A study of changing gender roles over an 8-year period found that wives who become less traditional perceive a decline in their marital quality, while husbands who become less traditional perceive an increase in marital quality (Amato and Booth 1995).

SUMMARY

Both similarities and differences exist between men and women. Both have some of the same fundamental needs, and both respond to some situations in similar ways. The differences include superior verbal ability of females and superior spatial and quantitative ability of males; a greater proportion of men who are highly aggressive; more interpersonal skills among females; and better ability by females to interpret nonverbal cues.

We need to distinguish between sex (biological males and females), gender (social males and females), gender role (behavior associated with being male or female), and gender-role orientation (conception of the self as having some combination of male and female traits). The traditional gender roles suggest that men are strong, independent, aggressive, and logical, while women are gentle, dependent, nurturing, and emotional. Your gender-role orientation may be masculine (primarily instrumental traits), feminine (primarily expressive traits), androgynous (high on both masculine and feminine traits), or undifferentiated (low on both kinds of traits).

Whether gender roles reflect nature or nurture is a matter of controversy. Evidence from biologists and psychologists as well as cross-cultural studies indicate that most of the traits and behaviors identified as masculine or feminine are not innate but reflect social factors such as socialization. We have gender-related tendencies, but these can be modified by social factors. Our gender-role orientation is also social, the result of socialization by the family, school, and media.

Gender roles and gender-role orientations change over time. People are becoming less traditional in their attitudes about gender roles. There is some lingering traditionalism, however, that affects both attitudes and behavior.

Gender-role orientations make a difference in various areas of our lives, including the way we communicate, our self-concepts, and our mental health. Androgynous people have a number of advantages over others, although for some things such as mental health, it is the masculine component that leads to the advantage. Gender-role orientations also affect intimacy and the extent of satisfaction with intimate relationships.

Principles for Enhancing Intimacy

1. Although traditionally many vocations and professions have been closed to them, women should no longer be deterred from pursuing what they most want to do. When women are given the same opportunities as men, they perform as well as men at most tasks.

2. The skills of effective communication and interaction with others can be learned. And because they are more proficient in these skills, women provide appropriate models of behavior for men.

3. If you should choose a behavior or way of life that goes beyond the traditional norms of how a male or female should act, realize that you may encounter criticism.

Even though our ideas about sex roles have expanded, many people still react to others on the basis of traditional expectations.

4. An important way to gain self-esteem is to cultivate the traits—such as independence, decisiveness, and competitiveness—that are typically labeled masculine.

5. Those traits—warmth, caring, sensitivity, and nurturance—that are traditionally labeled as female are as appropriate for men as they are for women. These traits help people meet their needs for intimacy. Remember that most of the traits that we generally label as masculine or feminine are not innate but learned.

KEY TERMS

androgyny *63*
expressive traits *63*
gender *57*
gender role *57*
gender-role orientation *57*

instrumental traits *63*
occupational sex segregation *58*
self-concept *71*
sex *57*
sexism *69*

sexual harassment *62*
socialization *58*
undifferentiated *63*

ON THE WEB   Gender Roles: Foundation for Intimacy

If you would like to take a test to measure your own gender-role orientation, go to http://androgyne.0catch.com/gentest1.htm, where you will find an easily taken and self-scored set of questions. It will be interesting to see if your orientation is what you believed it to be before taking the test.

www.mhhe.com/lauer7e

Of course, gender roles and gender-role orientations are more than merely interesting. They have serious, practical consequences. Two good sites for further study are:

Sex Roles

http://www.springerlink.com/content/0360-0025

This is the site of the journal, *Sex Roles,* a major source of research results for the topics in this chapter. You can access the abstracts of all volumes up to the present.

Gender and Society: A Matter of Nature or Nurture?

http://www.trinity.edu/~mkearl/gender.html

This site has much basic information plus a host of links to other resources for exploring a variety of issues related to gender roles.

Using these two sites and others, enlarge your understanding with the following projects:

1. Look at the latest issue of *Sex Roles.* Select one of the articles that interests you and read the abstract. See how many other articles you can find related to the same topic over the past two to three years. Summarize the findings and what you have learned about the topic. Imagine that you are asked to teach a class about the topic. What additional information would you like to have? Identify some additional Web sites that would help you gather the information.
2. Using the Gender and Society site and others, learn about gender roles in some other society (past or present). Compare your findings with materials in the text on gender roles in American society. Identify similarities and differences between the two societies. From the point of view of your values, are there elements of the roles in the other society that you would like to see incorporated into American society? Why or why not?
3. Use a search engine to explore the topic of sexual harassment. Get any information you can on the nature of the harassment, how prevalent it is, and people's attitudes toward it. Using the text materials on gender roles, write an essay that explains your findings about sexual harassment.

∼ SEXUALITY ∼

LEARNING OBJECTIVES

After reading and studying chapter 4, you should be able to

1 Relate the meaning of *sex* as both a physical and a social phenomenon.

2 Describe the impact of sex on intimate relationships.

3 Discuss the extent of teenage sex and the consequences of early childbearing.

4 Explain the various methods of contraception and the degree to which they are used and by whom.

5 Outline the role and the practices of sex in marriage.

6 Identify the changing patterns of marital sex.

7 Review the functions and consequences of extramarital sex.

8 Describe the nature and consequences of the major sexually transmitted diseases.

9 Outline the primary types of sexual dysfunction.

10 Summarize the important guidelines for engaging in safe sex.

As we look at sexual beliefs and practices throughout the world, we find both similarities with and differences from our own society. Investigate some kinds of sexual beliefs and/or practices in another society that differ from those in your society (e.g., frequency and/or positions of intercourse, the meaning of sex, attitudes about premarital and/or extramarital sex, what techniques and practices are considered erotic). Compare them with your society and with your personal values. How do you feel about the beliefs and/or practices of the other society? Do you think that they are more or less preferable to those of your own? Why?

One way to carry on your investigation is through the library. You can check journals, such as the *Journal of Sex Research*. Or you can use the *Social Science Index* or *Psychological Abstracts* to locate appropriate articles. Studies by anthropologists are also excellent sources.

Another way to carry on the investigation is to interview someone from another country. If that person is willing to discuss the topic with you, ask him or her to describe sexual attitudes and/or behavior in some area such as premarital sex or sexual techniques.

If the entire class engages in this project, each student could be responsible for a different society. Discuss the findings in terms of the questions given in the first column. 🞇

What is the most intense form of human intimacy? Some people would answer "sex." But sex can be alienating as well as bonding, meaningless as well as exhilarating. Even when it is highly gratifying, sex may not hold a relationship together. Hank got married when he was in his early 30s. When we discussed his impending marriage with him, he told us that he knew it would require a lot of work because he and his future wife had a lot of differences. "What do you have in common?" we asked. The only thing Hank could think of was, "We have great sex together." Hank's marriage was built on little else. Within a year of the marriage, Hank and his wife were divorced. "Great sex" didn't make a lasting marriage.

In this chapter we will look at the meaning of sex and how it affects our relationships. We will examine some of the problems involved with teenage sex, including unwanted pregnancies. We will discuss such issues as contraception, abortion, sexual diseases and dysfunctions, and extramarital sex. And we will see the role of sex in marriage, including long-term marriage.

THE MEANING OF SEX

Like gender roles, sex is social as well as biological. And, as there is in gender roles, there is variation in sexual orientation. We begin with sexual orientation.

Heterosexuality and Homosexuality

Most people are heterosexual, preferring male–female sexual relations only. Others are exclusively homosexual, preferring only those of their own sex. And a small percentage are bisexual, finding gratification with both sexes and having no strong preference for either.

How many people are homosexual? According to a national survey of Americans 18–44 years of age, which asked people whether they thought of themselves as heterosexual, homosexual, **bisexual,** or something else, 2.3 percent of men identified themselves as homosexual and 1.8 percent said they were bisexual (Mosher, Chandra, and Jones 2005). For women, the figures were 1.3 percent homosexual and 2.8 percent bisexual. However, when asked whether they had any same-sex sexual contact in the past 12 months, 2.9 percent of men and 4.4 percent of women said they had. And when asked about their attraction to those of the same sex, 3.2 percent of the men and 3.4 percent of the women said they were attracted mostly or only to those of the same sex or equally to both sexes. Millions of Americans, then, are exclusively homosexual and many more have had some homosexual experience.

Why are some people homosexual? Controversy surrounds the issue, but studies of brain structure and of twins suggest a genetic basis for homosexuality, while findings on peer group relationships and on patterns of sexual behavior over the life span suggest that sociocultural factors also underlie homosexual behavior (Swaab et al. 2001; Lauer and Lauer 2008). It seems clear that given the strong pressures to be heterosexual and the stigma often attached to being homosexual, the genetic component is strong. That is, some people by virtue of their genetic makeup are only attracted to same-sex relationships.

Apart from their differing preferences for relationships, however, heterosexuals and homosexuals share many of the same meanings of sex. They are alike in their physical responses and in a number of social aspects such as motives and variations in activity.

Sex as Physical: The Response Cycle

In the 1960s, William Masters and Virginia Johnson pioneered the investigation of the responses of the body to sex. The researchers identified four stages of human sexual response: excitement, plateau, orgasm, and resolution (Masters, Johnson, and Kolodny 1988:80–95). During the response, there are two basic physiological reactions. One involves an increased concentration of blood in bodily tissues in the genitals and the female breasts. The other is increased energy in the nerves and muscles throughout the body.

Excitement, the first stage of arousal, is the result of some kind of physical or psychological stimulation. You can become excited by someone stroking your body, by kissing, by reading erotic literature, by having someone look at you seductively, by remembering a previous sexual experience, by fantasizing about sex, and so on. In the woman, excitement leads to lubrication of the **vagina,** usually within 10 to 30 seconds, along with various other physiological changes. In the man, similar physiological reactions result in erection of the **penis,** usually within three to eight seconds in young males.

The excitement stage may or may not lead to the next phase. Something may interfere with continued response, such as a telephone ringing, something that the partner says or does, or a thought that suddenly comes into your mind. But if the process continues, you move into the second stage, the *plateau.* As figure 4.1 shows, in the plateau stage there is a continuing high level of arousal, preparing the way for orgasm. The actual length of the plateau varies from individual to individual. For men who have trouble controlling **ejaculation,** the plateau may be extremely

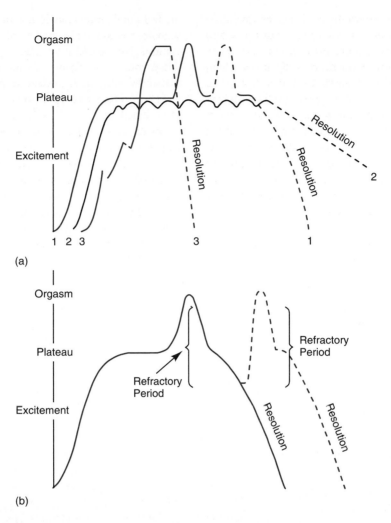

(a) Three types of female response. Pattern 1 is multiple orgasm. Pattern 2 is arousal without orgasm. Pattern 3 involves a number of small declines in excitement and a very rapid resolution.

(b) The typical male pattern of response. The dotted line indicates the possibility of a second orgasm and ejaculation after the refractory period.

FIGURE 4.1 The Sexual Response Cycle

Source: William H. Masters and Virginia E. Johnson, *Human Sexual Response,* Boston: Little, Brown, 1966, p. 5. Reprinted by permission.

short. For women, a brief plateau sometimes precedes an intense orgasm. Others find a longer plateau to be a kind of sexual high that is very satisfying.

Both men and women continue to experience physiological changes during the plateau. The woman's vagina becomes increasingly moist and the tissues swell with blood. The portion of the vagina nearest the opening becomes so congested that during intercourse the penis tends to be gripped because of the reduced size of

the vaginal opening. The back part of the vagina opens up and out to accommodate the erect penis. In the male, the penis is fully erect, and the **testes** are fluid-swollen, enlarged, and pulled up closer to the body. During the plateau stage, both males and females have increased heart rates, faster breathing, and increased blood pressure.

Orgasm, the third stage, is a discharge of the sexual tension that has been built up and maintained during the plateau. The orgasm takes the least time of any of the stages. Usually it involves muscular contractions and intense physical feelings that occur in the matter of a few seconds and are followed by rapid relaxation. Again, there are physiological changes that occur in both men and women. In both, there is a good deal of involuntary muscular contraction throughout the body. Sometimes the contractions happen in the facial muscles, making the face appear to be frowning or in pain. But normally such an expression reflects a high level of arousal, rather than any pain or displeasure.

Women may have anywhere from 3 to 15 muscular contractions during orgasm. These contractions occur in various muscles throughout their bodies. They also have changes in their brain wave patterns. Women may have multiple orgasms if they have continuing stimulation and interest (pattern 1 in figure 4.1). For men, orgasm occurs in two distinct phases. In the first phase, muscular contractions force **semen** through the penis. The man experiences a sense of having gotten to the point where he can no longer control himself; ejaculation is inevitable. In the second phase, additional muscular contractions lead to ejaculation.

Following orgasm, there is a **refractory period** for the male, a time following orgasm in which the individual needs to recover and is incapable of having an additional orgasm or ejaculation. The refractory period may last anywhere from minutes to hours. As the male ages, the refractory period gets longer. For the male, the refractory period is part of the fourth stage, *resolution*. Resolution is a return to a state of being sexually unaroused. In both males and females, the various physiological changes reverse and the individual becomes like he or she was prior to arousal. If the individual has been highly aroused without orgasm having occurred, the resolution will take longer.

Sex as Social Behavior

Although sex is one of the basic drives in humans, the expression of sex is still a social phenomenon. That is, we learn how to behave as sexual beings. Despite the notion that sex involves "doing what comes naturally," there is more learned than unlearned sexual activity. Even the meaning of *sex* is learned, and what you learn depends on when and where you live. In the United States, for instance, the dominant notions about sex from colonial days through the nineteenth to the twentieth centuries changed from "a decorous enjoyment to a morbid suppression to an uneasy liberation" (Lauer and Lauer 1983:20). Nineteenth-century Americans would be shocked by the views of both their forebears and their progeny. And consider the wife who said, "I get irritable when I don't have sex. Sex makes

me feel good about myself and my marriage." This frank statement would not have been made openly in earlier generations. Nor would it be made openly in some societies today. Your views about sex and your sexual activity are shaped by your social context. In American society today, most adults find sexual relations to be a significant aspect of a fulfilled life.

Both gender roles and gender-role orientation affect sexual activity. For example, men tend to have a stronger sex drive than do women (Baumeister, Catanese, and Vohs 2001). Compared to women, they think more often about sex, they have more and more varied sexual fantasies, they desire sexual intercourse more frequently, and they are more likely to initiate sexual activity. Men are also more sexually permissive than are women in terms of such matters as number of partners and having casual sex (Fischtein, Herold, and Desmarais 2007).

Males also tend to begin sexual relations at an earlier age than women do. For those under the age of 13, 8.8 percent of boys compared to 3.7 percent of girls have had sexual intercourse (Eaton et al. 2006). The proportions vary considerably by race/ethnicity: for whites, 5.0 percent of boys and 2.9 percent of girls; for African Americans, 26.8 percent of boys and 7.1 percent of girls; and for Hispanics, 11.1 percent of boys and 3.6 percent of girls.

One other gender difference is that through most of U.S. history, it has been more of a stigma for a woman than for a man to be sexually promiscuous. That may no longer be true. A survey of over 8,000 people reported disapproval of both men and women who had multiple sexual partners (Marks and Fraley 2005).

Gender-role orientations also may influence sexual behavior. Although there has not been much research, one study reported that the masculine gender-role orientation

Sex is an important part of intimacy.

for both men and women was associated with more frequent sexual intercourse (Leary and Snell 1988). Those scoring high on instrumental traits also tended to have more oral sex and more relaxed feelings about sex.

Finally, a number of different motives enter into sexual behavior (Browning et al. 2000; Meston and Buss 2007). Sexual relations are more than a response to the sexual drive. People also engage in sex because they love each other, they desire the pleasure sex brings, they conform to each other's expectations, and they desire recognition and acceptance.

Thus, a variety of factors affect our sexual behavior. There are variations in behavior both within and among societies. Differences in arousal, techniques, and the experience of unwanted sex further underscore the social nature of our sexual behavior.

Variations in Sexual Activity. There is enormous variation in the extent to which people in differing societies and within a particular society are aroused. Levels of sexual activity among societies vary from the extremely low level of the Grand Valley Dani to the unusually high level of the people of Mangaia (both groups are in the South Pacific; Lauer and Lauer 1983). The Dani do not begin to have sexual relations until about two years after marriage. Weddings are held only about once every four to six years. The frequency of sexual relations is so low that the population is barely maintained. A couple will abstain from sex for four to six years after the birth of a child. Moreover, there is little extramarital sex and no evidence of homosexuality or masturbation. The Dani simply seem to have little interest.

By contrast, sex is a principal interest among the Mangaians. Nearly all, both male and female, have considerable premarital experience with a variety of partners. The Mangaians claim that a typical 18-year-old male will have, on the average, three orgasms per night each night of the week. A 28-year-old male will have about two orgasms per night, five to six times each week. In their late 40s, males have an orgasm two to three times a week.

From a *symbolic interactionist* point of view, there are no sexual techniques that are inherently more appealing than others. What matters is how people define those techniques. Thus, you proba-

Symbolic Interactionist Theory Applied

bly regard mouth-to-mouth kissing as erotic. The Mangaians did not regard it as such until Westerners influenced them. Most Americans regard foreplay as essential to satisfying sex. In other societies, however, foreplay varies from being virtually absent to consuming even more time than it does among Americans (Ford and Beach 1951:41).

The preferred position for intercourse also varies from one society to another. Among the Trobriand Islanders, the man squats and draws the woman toward him until her legs rest on his hips or his elbows. Islanders maintain that this position gives the man considerable freedom of movement and that it does not inhibit the woman in her movements of response (Malinowski 1932:285).

There are also different preferences within a society. Some people, for example, like or even prefer oral sex, while others do not enjoy or find oral sex satisfying (Brady and Halpern-Feisher 2007). Nationally, among 18- to 26-year-olds, about 80 percent of those in a sexual relationship have had oral sex as well as vaginal intercourse (Kaestle and Halpern 2007). Oral sex was much more likely among those couples who said they had a mutually loving relationship.

Such diversity underscores the fact that sexual behavior is learned. What is defined as erotic by some people may be defined as disgusting by others. What is defined as good and pleasurable by some will be defined as evil by others. Social factors are powerful, and they may modify, facilitate, or suppress the expression of the sex drive.

Unwanted and Coerced Sex. In an ideal world, there would be reciprocal desire between two people. People in love would desire sexual relations with each other at the same time so that all sexual activity would reflect the

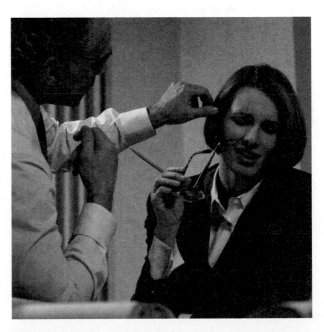

Nearly everyone experiences some unwanted sexual activity.

desire growing out of mutual love. In the real world, there is a great deal of unwanted and coerced sex, ranging from **sexual harassment** to **rape**. "Unwanted" means that the sexual activity is contrary to the individual's desires. Sexual harassment falls into this category. Another example is the individual who is exhausted and not at all in the mood but who agrees to sex in order to please a partner. "Coerced" means forced sexual activity of some kind, where the coercion can range from the verbal and emotional to the physical (Adams-Curtis and Forbes 2004). Coerced intercourse or attempted intercourse is rape. When an individual forcibly touches, fondles, or kisses another, it is not technically rape, but it is both unwanted and coerced sexual behavior.

Sexual harassment occurs in all kinds of settings and among all ages. Among students and workers in every capacity from professionals (e.g, lawyers, professors) to blue-collar workers (e.g., autoworkers), experiences of sexual harassment abound (Swim et al. 2001;

Bronner, Peretz, and Ehrenfield 2003; Hinze 2004). Harassment includes such things as unwelcome sexual advances, unwanted touching by someone, requests for sexual favors, or other sexual behavior that creates discomfort or worse in the victim. Unless a dramatic shift occurs, at least half of all women will be harassed at some point during their academic or working lives, and that harassment will be experienced as degrading, frightening, and sometimes violent (Fitzgerald 1993; Wyatt and Riederle 1995).

Coerced sex is also common, and may begin early in life. Forty percent of girls who have sex before the age of 15 say they were forced into it (Mackay 2001). A national survey reported that about 28 percent of young women described their first sexual experience as not wanted (Houts 2005). In another national survey, three researchers found that a fourth of women who had intercourse at age 13 or younger and 20 percent of those between 19 and 24 years of age at first intercourse said they were coerced

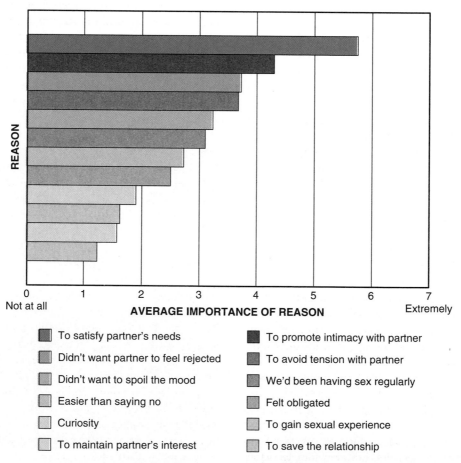

FIGURE 4.2 Reasons for Agreeing to Unwanted Sex
Source: Adapted from Impett and Peplau 2002.

(Abma, Driscoll, and Moore 1998). And a national survey of 7,545 adolescent women found that 7 percent reported that they had been forced into intercourse at some time in their lives (Raghavan et al. 2004).

Coerced sex can have long-term adverse consequences for women. A comparison of adolescents who had experienced early forced intercourse with those who had not found the former to be more depressed and anxious, lower in self-esteem, and more likely to use drugs and engage in delinquent activities (Lanz 1995).

Coerced sex is not merely a problem of women. They are far more likely than men to be coerced, but women also engage in sexual coercion (Russell and Oswald 2001). And sexual coercion is not merely an American problem. A study of Filipino adolescents found that the great majority had been coerced, and 64.6 percent of the victims were females and 42.3 percent were males (Serquina-Ramiro 2005) (see also the Comparison box in this chapter).

Why do people submit to unwanted sex? Why would someone who has no sexual desire agree to kissing, petting, and even intercourse? One factor is the abuse of alcohol and drugs. Under the influence of too much alcohol or the use of various other drugs, people may passively submit to sexual advances that they would otherwise reject (Davis, George, and Norris 2004). Other factors emerged in a study of college women who consent to unwanted sex with a dating partner (Impett and Peplau 2002). As shown in figure 4.2, those factors ranged from the desire or willingness to satisfy a partner's needs to the fear of the relationship breaking up if the individual rejected the advances.

SEX AND INTIMATE RELATIONSHIPS

Human love, according to Erich Fromm (1956), does not reflect a Freudian sexual instinct. Rather, Fromm argued, sexual desire reflects the human need for love and union. In other words, the need for intimacy has primacy over sex. We agree that intimacy is a more fundamental need than the need for sex. The sex drive is strong, and we need to find some outlet for sexual tension. But that tension can be dealt with in ways other than sexual intercourse, if necessary. There are, after all, healthy celibates. You can be celibate and be fulfilled. But you cannot be fulfilled without intimacy.

Sexual relations, then, while involving such things as pleasure and stress relief, are an important way to fulfill intimacy needs (Metz and McCarthy 2007). In fact, those who engage in sex may find themselves feeling less stress and more positive in mood the next day (Burleson, Trevathan, and Todd 2007). And this positive mood enhances the quality of the relationship, leading to more physical affection and more sexual activity. It is true, of course, that some people have sex simply for the sake of sex. But a number of experts have argued that sex without intimacy, like the casual sex of the one-night stand, is of little or no value (Fromm 1956). In fact, drug and alcohol use are prominent reasons given by people for casual sex (Harvey and Weber 2002). At best, casual sex fails to fulfill our intimacy needs. At worst, it leaves us feeling more empty and lonely than we were before the experience. Instead of enhancing the quality of our intimate lives, sex without intimacy can become an impediment to the development of relationships that add to our well-being.

Actually, most people seem to sense the fact that sex needs to be an expression of an intimate relationship, and that the emotional satisfaction of sex is strongly associated with being in a committed, exclusive relationship (Waite and Joyner 2001). Most Americans, for example, neither approve of nor engage in **promiscuity**, frequent and indiscriminate sexual relations with many partners. In a national survey of adults 15–44 years of age, 62.2 percent said that they had only one opposite-sex sexual partner in the past 12 months, and 0.7 percent said that they had only one same-sex sexual partner (Mosher, Chandra, and Jones 2005). In the 30–44 age group, males reported an average of 6 to 8 female sexual partners in their lifetimes; females reported an average of 4 male partners. It may be that promiscuous sexual behavior diminishes an individual's capacity to eventually form a fully satisfying marital relationship. Garcia and Markey (2007) found that a large discrepancy between a husband and wife in the numbers of sexual partners each had before they met was associated with lower levels of love, satisfaction, and commitment.

Feelings of intimacy often express themselves in sexual activity. In most societies, people continue to have sexual relations throughout life (May and Riley 2002; Nicolosi et al. 2005). Sexual desire and frequency of sexual relations do decline with age, but they do not stop for those with good health and a partner (Araujo, Mohr, and McKinlay 2004). In a study of older adults (57 to 85 years of age) in the United States, the proportions reporting sexual relations in the past year were 73 percent of those aged 57–64, 53 percent of those aged 65–74, and 26 percent of those aged 75–85 (Lindau et al. 2007). Those with excellent or good health were twice as likely to have sex as those with fair or poor health. Women were less likely than men to be sexually active, but far more of them were widowed. In short, aged people tend to continue sexual intimacy as long as they are healthy and have a partner.

Personal

Sex and the Search for Intimacy

Charles, a young single man, has tried for years to find a fulfilling intimacy solely through sex. He shares with us the conclusions he has reached in his 28th year:

> While I was in college, I lived on campus for two years. I was really promiscuous. I had sex relations with many women. I thoroughly enjoyed it. I thought of myself as a real stud, and I enjoyed the envy of some of my male friends. In time, my sexual experiences had an unexpected and interesting effect on me. I discovered that my so-called manhood, though sexually fulfilled, lacked a quality of intimacy that became more profound as my need for emotional closeness increased. I had thought that what I—and any real man—needed was a lot of good sex. But the more sex I had, the more I came to realize that something was missing. I would never have believed it a few years earlier, but one day I admitted to myself that sex wasn't enough. I wanted to have something more with a woman than her body.
>
> Unfortunately, I had gotten the label of being a "player." So it became more and more difficult to develop closeness in a relationship. The women I wanted to go out with had the idea that I was a shallow person only looking for a good time. My reputation was established, and it was keeping me from developing the intimacy that I now yearned for. The only women who were interested were the ones just like me. Or just like I used to be. They didn't even appeal to me any more.
>
> I couldn't do anything until I moved away. After graduation, I went to work in another city. I knew I had to change my lifestyle. I decided to play it cool with women. I was still hot to trot. I really missed having sex. But I finally realized that it wasn't going to help me to keep on the way I had been in college. I wanted to make love and please myself and my lover. But more than that, I wanted to emotionally caress a woman and understand her and relate to her. And I wanted her to do that to me as well.
>
> I'm in a kind of limbo right now. I have dated some women, and I am starting to develop a relationship with one that I think may lead to what I need. In any case, I know that I can't let sex be a deterrent to intimacy anymore. I know what I need. And I know that I can't get it in a one-night stand.

TEENAGE SEX

Pregnancy and sexually transmitted diseases (including AIDS) are serious problems among teenagers, with black girls having high rates of disease and Hispanic girls having the highest rate of births before the age of 20 (Abma et al. 2004; DiClemente et al. 2004). How many teenagers have sex, and at what age do they start? What are some of the consequences of being sexually active as a teenager?

Extent of Sex among Teenagers

The majority of teenagers, both in the United States and scores of other countries, become sexually active between the ages of 15 and 19 (Wellings et al. 2006). Substantial numbers, however, begin sexual activity earlier. Nationally, 6.2 percent of U.S. youth have sexual intercourse before the age of 13 (Eaton et al. 2006). By the time they are in the 15- to- 17-year age group, 30.3 percent of females and 42.6 percent of males have had sexual intercourse (Abma et al. 2004). And the proportions go up to 68.8 percent of females and 64.3 percent of males in the 18 to 19 age group. Compare these figures with those from previous years. In 1995, for example, the proportions for 15- to 17-year-olds was 38.0 percent for females and 43.1 percent for males, and the proportions for 18- to 19-year-olds was 68.0 percent for females and 75.4 percent for males.

The probability of being sexually active varies by a number of factors, including racial/ethnic groups. In 2002, the proportion of 15- to 19-year-old never-married teens who had sexual intercourse was, for Hispanics, 37.4 percent of females and 54.8 percent of males; for non-Hispanic whites, 45.1 percent of females and 40.8 percent of males; and for non-Hispanic blacks, 56.9 percent of females and 63.3 percent of males (Abma et al. 2004). The age at which sex begins also varies among the racial/ethnic groups. African Americans tend to begin earlier than others, followed by whites, Hispanics, and Asian Americans (Regan et al. 2004).

Sexually active teenagers face the prospect of an unwanted pregnancy.

Among all racial/ethnic groups, adolescents who are sexually active are more likely than those who are not to differ in a number of ways. Specifically, those who are sexually active are more likely to rarely attend church, live with only one parent, have a troubled relationship with parents or lack close relationships with parents, use drugs (including tobacco and alcohol), have close friends who are sexually active, and be in the lower social classes (McBride, Paikoff, and Holmbeck 2003; Meier 2003; Fingerson 2005; Adamczyk and Felson 2006; Regnerus and Luchies 2006; Sieving et al. 2006; Sandfort, Morr, Hirsch, and Santelli 2008). There are also some long-term negative consequences of early sexual activity, including a higher probability of risky sexual behavior.

Unwanted Pregnancy and Early Childbearing

One consequence of teenage sex is a high rate of unwanted pregnancies and giving birth at an early age.

Eighty-eight percent of births to teens, age 17 or younger, were unwanted or mistimed (Abma et al. 2004). Birth rates among teenagers have declined, however, from a peak rate of 116.8 per 1,000 in 1990 to 76.4 per 1,000 in 2002 (Ventura et al. 2006). The rates declined for all racial/ethnic groups and dramatically so for white, non-Hispanic and black teenagers. Still, hundreds of thousands of teenagers get pregnant each year, the majority of them unmarried.

Many teenagers give birth to children who are unwanted at the time of conception, in part because of the mother being unmarried. But married people also bear children who are unwanted at the time of conception. The fact that a child is not wanted at the time of conception does not mean that the child is still unwanted at birth, of course. But we can justly wonder about the well-being of the children who remain unwanted at birth.

Why Pregnancy? Birth control measures are readily available in most communities. In fact, the decline in teenage pregnancy is attributed to an improved use of contraceptives (Santelli et al. 2006). Why, then, do so many teenagers continue to get pregnant?

First, no contraceptive is foolproof. Failure rates during the first year of use vary from a low of 8 percent for users of the pill to 15 percent for condom users and 25 percent for users of spermicides (Jones and Forrest 1992).

Second, although the use of contraceptives at the time of first and times of subsequent intercourse has increased, the failure to use any method of birth control is still a significant factor in teenage pregnancies (Abma et al. 2004; Lance 2004). Birth control measures are readily available, but the sex may be an unplanned response to the strong drive of teenagers. Or the teenagers may be too embarrassed or too poor to purchase birth control measures. Or they may believe that using such things as condoms reduces pleasure (Parsons et al. 2000).

Third, not all teenagers find the prospect of pregnancy to be unsettling (Unger, Molina, and Teran 2000). While the majority of teenage women who become mothers say they did not intend it, about 7.5 percent of the female adolescents in a national survey indicated that they *expected* to bear a child in adolescence out of wedlock (Trent and Crowder 1997). Those more likely to have such an expectation came from families that were black or Hispanic rather than non-Hispanic white, in the lower social classes, and single-parent rather than two-parent (Blake and Bentov 2001). Why would they want to get pregnant out of wedlock? Many of such teenagers had troubled childhoods. In a small sample of whites and Mexican Americans, half had lost a parent during their childhood years (de Anda, Becerra, and Fielder 1990). A study of 535 young women reported that two-thirds of those who became pregnant had been sexually abused (Boyer and Fine 1992). With such experiences, teenagers may feel isolated and alone and that a baby is the one way to find someone to love. Others may use pregnancy to get attention, to assert their independence from their parents, or, particularly for those in the lower social classes, to do something creative in a world of very limited opportunities. Perhaps that is why there is more tolerance for unmarried parenthood in economically distressed communities (South and Baumer 2000).

Fourth, certain parental attitudes and behaviors can significantly reduce the likelihood of out-of-wedlock pregnancy (Fingerson 2005; Regnerus and Luchies 2006). Teenage girls who have close relationships with their parents, who can talk to their parents about sexual matters, and whose parents teach them to be responsible are less likely to get pregnant.

Finally, among both whites and African Americans, the chances of pregnancy are much higher if a girl is going steady and if she has had discipline problems in school. In essence, then, girls who feel good about themselves, have high expectations and aspirations for their lives, and have good relationships with concerned parents are much less likely to get pregnant than others. This is only partly due to a lower amount of sexual activity. It is also due to a greater probability of using birth control.

Some Consequences of Teenage Births. Whether wanted or not, the children of teenagers differ in important ways from other children. And the parents of those children differ from parents who wait at least until their 20s to have children.

Teenagers who father or give birth to children are more likely than those who become parents at later ages to experience a variety of negative consequences (Hanna 2001; Mirowsky 2005; Henretta 2007; Mollborn 2007). If they are in high school, they are less likely to complete their education, due largely to a lack of such resources as housing, child care, and financial support. They are more likely to be and remain poor, to suffer from chronic unemployment, and, when they do find work, to get low-paying jobs. They have higher levels of health problems (including heart disease, lung disease, and cancer), and a higher risk of dying early.

Detrimental consequences affect not just the teenage parents but their children as well (Jaffee et al. 2000; Gueorguieva et al. 2001; Levine, Pollack, and Comfort 2001; Abel, Kruger, and Burd 2002; Pogarsky, Thornberry, and Lizotte 2006). The children are more likely to be preterm and low weight, which are factors in infant mortality. They are more likely to exhibit learning disabilities when they begin school. During their school years, they are more likely to be involved in truancy, fighting, early sexual activity, and other kinds of problem behavior. And when the children grow up, they are more likely than others to repeat the same kind of pattern—leave school early, be unemployed, and become parents in their teens.

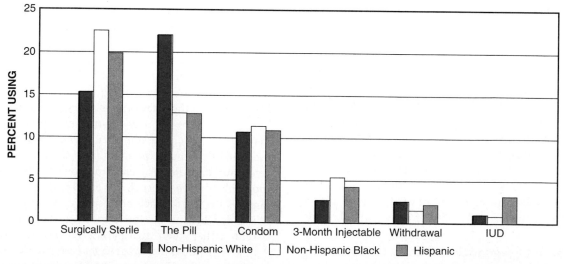

FIGURE 4.3 Percent Distribution of Women 15–44 Years of Age Using Contraceptive Methods
Source: U.S. Census Bureau 2008:95.

Clearly, little positive can be said for teenage pregnancy and childbearing. Both parents and children are likely to suffer a wide variety of negative consequences. Your chances for maximizing your well-being and the quality of your intimate relationships are much less if you bear children in your teens.

CONTRACEPTION

Contraception, a method of birth control, is the use of devices or techniques to prevent fertilization. When a couple wants to avoid pregnancy, knowledge and use of effective contraception can enhance sexual pleasure and intensify sexual intimacy by removing the fear of conception.

Amount and Kinds of Contraceptive Use

Although few women desire to get pregnant when they first become sexually active, about a fourth use no contraceptive method (Abma et al. 2004). This represents a dramatic decrease since 1980, when half used no method. As sexual activity continues, contraceptive use is even more likely. **Sterilization** is the most commonly used method, followed by the oral contraceptive pill (figure 4.3). The pill is the leading method among women under 30, while ster-

TABLE 4.1 Methods of Birth Control

Popular Name	Description	Effectiveness (pregnancies per 100 women using method for 1 year)	Advantages	Disadvantages
The pill (oral contraceptive; consultation with physician required)	Contains synthetic hormones (estrogens and progestin) to inhibit ovulation. The body reacts as if pregnancy has occurred and so does not release an egg. No egg—no conception. The pills are usually taken for 20 or 21 consecutive days; menstruation begins shortly thereafter.	2* (for combination pills)	Simple to take, removed from sexual act, highly reliable, reversible. Useful side effects: relief of premenstrual tension, reduction in menstrual flow, regularization of menstruation, relief of acne.	Weight gain (5–50 percent of users), breast enlargement and sensitivity; some users have increased headaches, nausea, and spotting. Increased possibility of vein thrombosis (blood clotting) and slight increase in blood pressure. Must be taken regularly. A causal relationship to cancer can neither be established nor refuted.
IUD (intrauterine device; consultation with physician required)	Metal or plastic object that comes in various shapes and is placed within the uterus and left there. Exactly how it works is not known. Hypotheses are that endocrine changes occur, that the fertilized egg cannot implant in the uterine wall because of irritation, and that spontaneous abortion is caused.	3–6	Once inserted, user need do nothing more about birth control. High reliability, reversible, relatively inexpensive. Must be checked periodically to see if still in place.	Insertion procedure requires specialist and may be uncomfortable and painful. Uterine cramping, increased menstrual bleeding. Between 4 and 30 percent are expelled in first year after insertion. Occasional perforation of the uterine wall. Occasional pregnancy that is complicated by the presence of the IUD. Associated with pelvic inflammatory disease.
Diaphragm and jelly (consultation with physician required)	Flexible hemispherical rubber dome inserted into the vagina to block entrance to the cervix, thus providing a barrier to sperm. Usually used with spermicidal cream or jelly.	10–16	Can be left in place up to 24 hours. Reliable, harmless, reversible. Can be inserted up to 2 hours before intercourse.	Disliked by many women because it requires self-manipulation of genitals to insert and is messy because of cream. If improperly fitted, it will fail. Must be refitted periodically, especially after pregnancy. Psychological aversion may make its use inconsistent.

(continued)

TABLE 4.1 Continued

Popular Name	Description	Effectiveness (pregnancies per 100 women using method for 1 year)	Advantages	Disadvantages
Condom	Thin, strong sheath or cover, usually of latex, worn over the penis to prevent sperm from entering the vagina.	7–14	Simple to obtain and use; free of objectionable side effects. Quality control has improved with government regulation. Protection against various sexually transmitted diseases.	Must be applied just before . intercourse. Can slip off, especially after ejaculation when penis returns to flaccid state. Occasional rupture. Interferes with sensation and spontaneity.
Chemical methods	Numerous products to be inserted into the vagina to block sperm from the uterus and/or to act as a spermicide. Vaginal foams are creams packed under pressure (like foam shaving cream) and inserted with an applicator. Vaginal suppositories are small cone-shaped objects that melt in the vagina; vaginal tablets also melt in the vagina.	13–17 (more effective when used in conjunction with another method, such as the diaphragm)	Foams appear to be most effective, followed by creams, jellies, suppositories, tablets. Harmless, simple, reversible, easily available.	Minor irritations and temporary burning sensations. Messy. Must be used just before intercourse and reapplied for each act of intercourse.
Sponge	Small sponge that fits over the cervix, blocking and killing sperm.	9–11	Simple to purchase and use. Can be inserted hours before intercourse and left in place up to 24 hours.	Possible health problems, including toxic shock syndrome and vaginitis. Difficult to remove. May make intercourse dry.
Sterilization	Surgical procedure to make an individual sterile.	Less than 1	Safest method. Does not affect sexual drive. No planning or additional steps before intercourse necessary.	May be irreversible. Possibility of postoperative infections for women.
Natural family planning (rhythm method)	Abstinence from intercourse during fertile period each month.	10–29	Approved by the Roman Catholic church. Costless, requires no other devices.	Woman's menstrual period must be regular. Demands accurate date keeping and strong self-control. Difficult to determine fertile period exactly.

Note: Individuals vary in their reaction to contraceptive devices. Advantages and disadvantages listed are general ones.
*If taken regularly pregnancy will not occur. If one or more pills are missed, there is a chance of pregnancy. Combination pills contain both estrogen and progesterone.
Sources: U.S. Department of Health and Human Services, *Contraceptive Efficacy among Married Woman Aged 15–44 Years.* Publication no. (PHS) 80–1981 (Hyattsville, MD: U.S. National Center for Health Statistics, 1980). Pamphlets published by Planned Parenthood Federation.

ilization is the leading method for women aged 30 to 44 years. Table 4.1 shows the more common methods, how they work, and some of their benefits and limitations.

There are a number of other methods that are newer and less commonly used (Neergaard 2000; Schwetz 2002; Clark 2005). Injections of the drug Depo-Provera provide 99 percent protection for three months. Norplant (capsules implanted under the skin of a woman's upper arm) protects for about five years. A female condom is available, though it does not seem to be as effective as the male condom. In 2000, the Food and Drug Administration approved use in this country of the abortion pill RU-486, which is taken under a physician's supervision. In 2004, however, the Food and Drug Administration said the warning label should be strengthened because a number of women died after taking the pills (Harrison 2004). There is also a contraceptive patch that releases hormone compounds that prevent ovulation (Clark 2005). As with all of the above methods, the patch carries the risk of serious side effects, including an elevated risk of blood clots, and its long-term effects are unknown. Finally, there is Plan B, the "morning after" pill, which may prevent pregnancy after another contraceptive has failed or a woman has had unprotected sex (Payne 2007). The pill is to be taken within 72 hours after sex. It can prevent the release of an egg from the ovary, or the union of sperm and egg, or a fertilized egg attaching itself to the womb. It will not work if a fertilized egg is already attached. As of this writing, there are no known serious side effects, but the user may experience some mild effects such as nausea, headache, and stomach pain.

People also try a number of other techniques that have little or no use. For example, some people believe that a woman cannot get pregnant the first time she has intercourse and, therefore, no device need be used. That belief has resulted in many pregnancies. Still others try withdrawal (removing the penis from the vagina before ejaculation) or a vaginal douche immediately after intercourse. These were the two most popular methods in the nineteenth century. Neither is reliable. Even if withdrawal occurs before ejaculation, many men have a leakage of seminal fluid prior to ejaculation that can result in pregnancy. And the vaginal douche, ironically, may actually facilitate pregnancy. Rather than flushing out, the douche may force sperm up into the cervix. Moreover, some of the sperm may have already traveled into the cervix, making the douche useless.

Thus, there are both effective and ineffective methods of contraception. Some of the modern methods may not be quite as ineffective or hazardous as the ancient Egyptian mixture that contained crocodile dung, but people continue to use methods that are not effective. In part, this is due to a lack of education. A substantial proportion of adolescents get no formal sexual education in the years when most are becoming sexually active. Of course, not all who receive the information make use of it. An unwanted pregnancy is a painful experience. Today, there is ample information available; no one need get pregnant out of ignorance.

Who Uses Contraceptives?

We can distinguish the groups most likely to use some form of contraception on the basis of age and other characteristics.

Age Differences. As the discussion so far indicates, contraceptive use is less likely among younger people who are sexually active. A national survey found that the proportion of women using some contraceptive method was 31.5 percent of those aged 15 to 19, 60.7 percent of those aged 20 to 24, 68.0 percent of those aged 25 to 29, 69.2 percent of those aged 30 to 34, 70.8 percent of those aged 35 to 39 years, and 69.1 percent of those aged 40 to 44 years (Mosher et al. 2004). The proportion of women who use a contraceptive method varies by racial/ethnic background. In a national study of high school students, more African Americans (68.9 percent) than whites (62.6 percent) or Hispanics (57.7 percent) said they had used a condom during their last sexual intercourse (Eaton et al. 2006). In the same survey, the use of birth control pills was higher among whites (22.3 percent) than African Americans (10.0 percent) or Hispanics (9.8 percent).

One reason for the lower rate of contraceptive use by the young may be what someone has called the "illusion of unique invulnerability." The illusion means that a young woman thinks of herself as, for some reason, less likely than others to get pregnant. This sense of invulnerability is the same thing that leads people into various kinds of self-destructive behavior. For example, many people who smoke or have an unhealthy diet feel that they will escape the negative consequences of their behavior even though others do not.

Similarly, the young woman who adopts the stance of "I just don't think that I will get pregnant" is less likely to use birth control methods . . . and quite likely to get pregnant.

Some younger people, of course, do use contraceptives, and the proportion is increasing. Younger people more likely to use contraceptives are those who have good communication with their parents about sexual matters generally and contraceptives in particular (Wilson et al. 1994; Miller 2002). Peer influence is also important. Those who perceive their peers as using contraceptives are more likely to use them for themselves.

One other important related factor is the age at which the individual first has sexual intercourse. Those who have intercourse early (age 16 or younger) are less likely than those who begin sexual relations later to know about and use effective methods of contraception. The early experimenters are also less likely to use effective contraception at the time of first intercourse (Abma and Sonenstein 2001). Ironically, they may not use contraceptives out of fear that their parents will discover them and know that they are sexually active (Iuliano, Speizer, Santelli, and Kendall 2006).

Other Factors. The proportion of religious women who practice birth control is about the same as for the nonreligious (Goldscheider and Mosher 1991). And the proportion is about the same for Protestants, Catholics, and Jews. However, there are differences in the preferred method; the most frequently used methods are sterilization for Protestants, the pill for Catholics, and diaphragms for Jews.

Religion has another interesting effect. Some religions hold that contraception is wrong. Married people in those religions may refrain from using contraceptives (although many do use them), with resulting large families. Some of the younger, unmarried people, however, may refrain from contraception but not from sexual relations (Zaleski and Schiaffino 2000). It is as though they are willing to violate one but not two of their religions' precepts.

A number of other factors also affect people's likelihood of using contraceptives (Whitley 1990; Luster and Small 1994; Langer, Warheit, and McDonald 2001; Frisco 2005; Shafii, Stovel, and Holmes 2007). In particular, usage is more likely among those who

- used a contraceptive at the time of their first sexual experience.
- have a partner who supports the use.
- hold positive attitudes about contraception.

- have high self-esteem.
- do well in school.
- have parents who monitor and support them.
- come from two-parent families.
- use alcohol, if at all, only in moderation.

ABORTION

Abortion, the expulsion of the fetus from the uterus, is a highly controversial subject. Abortion may be either spontaneous (so-called *natural abortion* or *miscarriage*) or induced by some medical or surgical procedure. We include the topic here because induced abortion is used as a method of birth control. That is, women have abortions for the same kinds of reasons that they use birth control (Finer et al. 2005). They claim that a child would interfere with their education or work or other responsibilities, or that they can't afford a baby, or that they are single and do not want to be a single parent, or that they already have as many children as they want.

Abortion has been used throughout history to deal with unwanted pregnancies. In the United States, abortion was illegal in most states until the Supreme Court's famous 1973 decision in the *Roe v. Wade* case. That case allowed abortion on demand in the first trimester of a pregnancy. The case was the result of increasing pressures from various groups to give legitimacy to the procedure and protect women from the pain and risks of back-alley abortions. Some women died and many others nearly died from illegal abortions, which could be performed by people who ranged from midwives to bookies.

How many pregnancies end in abortion? Table 4.2 shows that for every 10 pregnancies, between 2 and 3 are aborted. The number of abortions has tended to decline since about 1980, due possibly to the aging of the population (younger women are most likely to have abortions), fewer abortion services (a result of violence and harassment by pro-life activists), and perhaps some change in attitudes.

Abortion will probably continue to divide the nation into *conflicting camps* for some time. A *New York Times* poll found that 34 percent agree that abortion should

 Conflict Theory Applied

be generally available to those who want it, 39 percent agree that it should be available but would impose stricter limits than now exist, and 25 percent said it should not

TABLE 4.2 **Legal Abortions, by Selected Characteristics**

Characteristic	Number (1,000)	Percent distribution	Abortion ratio*
Total legal abortions	1,287	100	238
Age of woman:			
Less than 15 years	8	1	537
15–19 years old	212	17	337
20–24 years old	430	33	293
25–29 years old	294	23	211
30–34 years old	196	15	167
35–39 years old	108	8	186
40 years old and over	40	3	268
Race of woman:			
White	715	56	181
Black and other	572	44	395
Marital status of woman:			
Married	229	18	79
Unmarried	1,058	82	422

*Number of abortions per 1,000 abortions and live births.
Source: U.S. Census Bureau 2008:97.

be permitted (2 percent weren't sure of their position) (The Polling Report 2008).

Abortion poses psychological risks for some women. At the least, there is likely to be a short-term grief response, a sense of loss and anxiety about death (Williams 2001). There is also the possibility of the "postabortion syndrome," which includes four components: (1) perceiving the abortion as a painful, intentional destruction of one's unborn child; (2) negative reexperiencing of the abortion; (3) failure to avoid or deny traumatic recollections of the abortion; and (4) varying negative emotions such as guilt (Speckhard and Rue 1992). Many clinics have both pre- and postprocedure counseling in order to help with such problems. One young woman who had two abortions told us that she is now ready to bear a child: "But I'm having trouble getting pregnant. I'm beginning to feel like I had my children and they died." She was clearly grieving over losses that had occurred some years earlier. Only in a few cases, however, are the problems severe enough to warrant psychiatric care.

PREMARITAL SEX

Most religious traditions link sex with marriage. But premarital sex occurs in all societies. How much occurs in the United States, and how do Americans feel about it?

The Double Standard

As *conflict theory* suggests, men and women have differing interests, and their interaction often takes the form of a power struggle. One outcome of the struggle

What Do You Think?

There is disagreement about **whether abortion should be legal and readily available**. What follows are pro and con arguments. What do you think?

Pro

Abortion should be legal and readily available because

- women should have control over their own bodies.
- no one should be forced to accept a child conceived through rape.
- abortion is a better alternative than an unwanted child.
- no one should bring a child into the world who cannot afford to meet that child's needs for food, clothing, etc.
- "back-alley" abortions would otherwise replace legal abortions and some women will die from the procedure.

Con

Abortion should be neither legal nor available because

- it violates the rights of the unborn child.
- it contradicts moral and religious beliefs that prohibit killing.
- when mothers kill their own children, the entire society degenerates morally.
- women who abort suffer emotional and physical distress.
- the child who is unwanted can be adopted by people who are desperate to have their own family.

is the double standard, a long-standing fixture of U.S. society that favors male interests. Thus, in terms of

Conflict Theory Applied

premarital sex, this means that boys traditionally were expected to have some experience, while girls were expected to remain virgins until marriage. In his classic study of a small Missouri town, James West (1945:194) captured the essence of the double standard:

> It is expected . . . that most boys will acquire a limited amount of sexual experience before marriage, as they are expected to experiment with drinking and "running around." All these "outlaw traits" are associated with a young man's "sowing his wild oats." It is better if he sows his wild oats outside the community, if possible . . . A girl who sows any wild oats, at home or abroad, is disgraced, and her parents are disgraced.

Has the double standard changed? To some extent it has. Premarital sexual activity is nearly as acceptable for females as for males. Nevertheless, experimental studies continue to show that the standard still exists for many people, so that men are rewarded and women are stigmatized to some extent for premarital sexual activity (Crawford and Popp 2003; Marks and Fraley 2006).

Changing Attitudes

Although the double standard accepted the fact that most boys would have premarital sexual experience, it did not mean that such behavior was considered ideal. Surveys from the first half or so of the twentieth century found that less than a third of Americans agreed that premarital sex was all right (Hyde and DeLamater 2007). And fewer agreed that it was all right for a woman than those who agreed it was all right for a man. Such attitudes have changed rapidly in the last few decades, however (Harding and Jencks 2003). In national surveys, the proportion of women who agreed that premarital sex is always or almost always wrong declined from 56.4 percent in the early 1970s to 40 percent in the late 1990s, while the proportion of men agreeing declined from 46 percent to 29.8 percent (Thornton and Young-DeMarco 2001:1022).

Whether people believe that premarital sex is wrong depends on a number of factors, including sex, age, education, race, and religion. And there are variations even within those groups. For example, the proportion agreeing that premarital sex is always wrong varies among religious groups from 68.8 percent of conservative Christians

to 25.6 percent of religious moderates to 5.7 percent of religious liberals (McConkey 2001:165).

It is interesting that a majority of Catholics agree that premarital sex is "not wrong." Officially, the Catholic church continues to teach that premarital relationships are a sin. A 1976 declaration from the Congregation for the Doctrine of the Faith noted that many people justify premarital sex in cases in which people intend to marry and in which they have an affection for each other that is like that in the marital state. But even in those cases, the declaration pointed out, the belief was contrary to Catholic doctrine, which continued to affirm that all sexual intercourse must take place in the context of marriage (Hyde and DeLamater 2007).

Traditionally, all Christian groups have taught that premarital sex is morally wrong. Whatever the official teachings, however, belief in the immorality of premarital sex has declined among members of all groups except conservative Protestants who attend church often (Petersen and Donnenwerth 1997). Mainline Protestants, Catholics, and conservative Protestants who attend church infrequently have all followed the national trend of increasing acceptance of premarital sex.

Some male–female differences in attitudes exist. Males tend to be more permissive and even expect sex in casual relationships (Wilson and Madora 1990; Cohen and Shotland 1996). Males and females are similar in their attitudes about sex, however, when the couple is in love or engaged. Both tend to approve of sexual relations under such circumstances.

Changing Behavior

Attitudes do not necessarily reflect behavior. That is, because people approve of premarital sex does not mean that they are actually engaging in it. How much premarital sexual behavior actually occurs, and how does the amount now compare with the past?

Extent of Premarital Sex.   We pointed out in chapter 1 that the amount of premarital sex has increased considerably in recent decades. In the famous Kinsey studies of the 1940s, the data showed that about a third of all females and 71 percent of all males had premarital sexual relations by the age of 25 (Hyde and DeLamater 2007). After the 1960s, the proportions rose dramatically. By the first decade of the present century, a survey reported that 95 percent of Americans who were 44 years of age (94 percent of women and 96 percent of men) had had premarital sex (Finer 2007). That is, they were still unmarried but had had sex, or they reported having had sex before they were married at some point earlier in their lives. Figure 4.4 breaks this research down by various age cohorts and at which age they first had sex. Note that the probability of having premarital sex—at any age—tends to increase with each succeeding generation. Also note that the proportions of those having premarital sex increases in each cohort as the people age.

Of course, some people remain celibate for many years before engaging in sexual relationships. Women who refuse to have premarital sex do so for a variety of reasons and handle the pressure in various ways. For instance, a student who had decided to wait for sex until marriage told us,

> I'm up front with the guys I date. I tell them that I don't have hangups. I really look forward to sex. But I just believe that it should wait until marriage. That turns some guys off. At first, I was troubled by some guys that I liked who didn't want to date me any more because of my attitude. But I decided that if a guy didn't respect me for my stand on sex, we probably shouldn't be together anyway.

Premarital Sex and Social Background. As in the case of dating patterns, premarital sexual patterns vary depending on background factors. *Religion* is one such factor. In general, the more religious the individual (in

terms of such things as regular attendance at church, praying, etc.), the less likely is that individual to have premarital sex (O'Connor 1998; Rostosky et al. 2004). The effects are stronger for females than for males, however.

Another factor in premarital sexual activity is *family background,* including the family atmosphere, parenting styles, and the marital status of the parents. With regard to atmosphere, the more conflict in the home, the more a young person is likely to have early sexual experience (McBride, Paikoff, and Holmbeck 2003). With regard to parenting styles, when parents are more heavily involved in their children's lives, the children are less likely to have early sexual experience (Roche et al. 2005). Parental attitudes are also important. Although young people have more permissive sexual attitudes and behavioral patterns than their parents, children tend to reflect the attitudes of their parents. Thus, mothers with more permissive attitudes are likely to have children who have permissive attitudes and who therefore are more sexually active (Small and Luster 1994; Hovell et al. 1994; Whitbeck et al. 1999).

Also important is the extent to which parents monitor the child's behavior (Longmore, Manning, and Giordano 2001). Sexual activity is less likely when the child is not allowed to be home alone, when the child is required to let parents know where he or she is when not at home, and when some restrictions are placed on the amount and

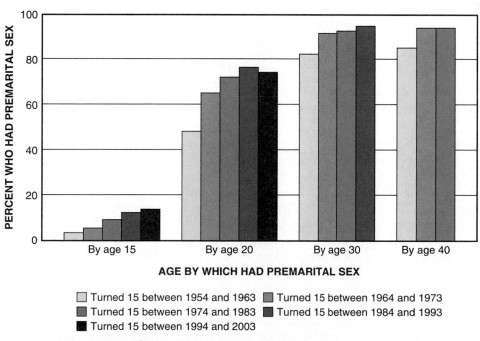

FIGURE 4.4 Proportion Having Premarital Sex
Source: Adapted from Finer 2007.

kind of television the child can watch. Parents need to monitor the child's peer relationships as well. Children whose involvement with friends leads to delinquent behavior and alcohol consumption are more likely to be sexually active (Whitbeck et al. 1999; Woodward, Fergusson, and Horwood 2001).

Such close monitoring becomes more difficult in a single-parent home. So it is not surprising that a higher rate of sexual activity and premarital pregnancy occurs among children who live with one parent (Upchurch et al. 1999; Moore and Chase-Lansdale 2001).

Other important factors related to family background include the behavior of siblings. Older brothers' behavior significantly affects the time of younger siblings' initiation of sexual relations (Widmer 1997). And a study of 455 girls, the majority of them Hispanics and African Americans, reported that those with sexually active sisters and/or an adolescent childbearing sister were more likely to be sexually active (East, Felice, and Morgan 1993).

SEX IN MARRIAGE

Among the things necessary for a successful marriage, how would you rate a good sex life? Most Americans would say it is very important. As we noted in chapter 1, however, sex is not among the top 10 reasons people give for a satisfying, long-term marriage. The point is, sex itself is unlikely to either break up a marriage or keep it together. At the same time, given such things as a sense of friendship, satisfying communication, mutual respect, and admiration, a good sex life can greatly enhance the quality of a couple's intimacy. But what does it mean to have a "good" sex life? Is that measured by frequency of sex? By the number of orgasms? By variety? The relationship between sex and marriage is not a simple one.

Sexual Practices in Marriage

The sex life of married couples has changed considerably over the last few decades. As the famed Kinsey studies reported (Kinsey, Pomeroy, and Martin 1948; Kinsey et al. 1953) in the 1940s, only a minority of married people engaged in oral sex, either **fellatio** or **cunnilingus.** By the time of Morton Hunt's 1974 survey, however, a majority of married people engaged in oral sex at least some of the time (Hunt 1974). Hunt also reported that married couples, compared with those in earlier decades, engaged in much more foreplay and experimented with a greater number of positions in intercourse. These changes may reflect an increased concern with the woman's enjoyment and orgasm, both of which tend to be enhanced if more time is given to sexual activity.

On the average, Americans have sexual relations from two to four times a month (Blanchflower and Oswald 2004). And although comics have talked about marriage as the end of romance and sex, and a popular image of the single person includes frequent sex with many different partners, married people have more and better sex than do singles. And this is true not only in the United States but in scores of other nations that have been studied (Wellings et al. 2006). The frequency varies by such things as age and work (Robinson and Godbey 1998). In general, reported sexual activity is higher among the younger than the older, among those who work 40 hours or more a week than those who work fewer hours, and among those identifying themselves as liberals than those identifying themselves as conservatives.

While many people are interested (perhaps for comparison purposes—how well am I doing compared to others?) in the average number of times Americans have sex, the average is misleading, because the range of activity is considerable. Some couples never have sex relations while others may have them every day or a number of times each day. It is also important to realize that *average* does not mean *normal*. People sometimes read such statistics and believe that something is wrong with them if they do not follow the average practice. But sexual needs and desires vary widely. There is no "normal" frequency.

Sexual Satisfaction and Marital Satisfaction

How important is sexual satisfaction to marital satisfaction? A number of things can be said. First, a high degree of sexual satisfaction early in marriage tends to increase the quality and the stability of the marriage (Yeh et al. 2006). Indeed, 70 percent of Americans agree that a happy sexual relationship is very important for a successful marriage (Pew Research Center 2007a). Keep in mind, however, that the meaning of a "happy" or "satisfying" sexual relationship can vary considerably. For one couple it may mean frequent sexual relations and frequent experimentation with varied sexual techniques, while for another couple the sex may be occasional and routine.

Second, sexual satisfaction involves more than intercourse. A man married 25 years told us that he "remembers little about sexual intercourse" in the early years of his marriage. But he does remember "laying at night in my wife's arms. In that way, she was telling me that I was all right. That was very important." Sex, he noted, was not as important as caring and affection. In fact, it is precisely such caring and affection that enables couples to have a satisfying sex life. Once again, we can have intimacy without sex, but we cannot have satisfying sex without intimacy. In other words, sexual satisfaction is likely to be the result of, rather than the cause of, marital satisfaction (Henderson-King and Veroff 1994).

Third, although sexual satisfaction is important, it is less important than other things in the quality of an intimate relationship. More important than sex in intimacy are such things as the ease with which differences are handled, the extent to which the partners express affection, the degree of commitment to the marriage, and the amount of self-disclosure.

Fourth, the relationship between sexual satisfaction and marital satisfaction is one of mutual influence. That is, marital satisfaction affects sexual satisfaction and vice versa (Young 2000). In other words, it is true both that sexual dissatisfaction can detract from marital intimacy and that a troubled marriage can detract from sexual satisfaction.

Finally, in our study of long-term married couples, we came to three conclusions about the role of sex that are in accord with the findings of other researchers (Lauer and Lauer 1986:73; Mackey and O'Brien 1995; Alford-Cooper 1998; Hinchliff and Gott 2004):

1. A couple can have a meaningful sexual relationship for the duration of their marriage; neither age nor amount of years together necessarily diminishes the quality of sex.
2. Some couples have long-term, satisfying marriages even though one or both have a less-than-ideal sex life.
3. The most important thing in a couple's sexual relationship is agreement about the arrangement.

The last point stresses something we mentioned earlier—there is no such thing as a normal or ideal sex life for all couples. It isn't the kind or frequency of sexual activities that is most important but the extent to which the couple agrees on whatever arrangement they make.

Changes in Marital Sex over the Life Span

Perhaps the most obvious change in sexual activity over the course of a marriage is the decline in frequency. That decline is a function of a number of factors. First, as people age, their sexual needs and desires change (Birnbaum, Cohen, and Wertheimer 2007). For most, sex becomes somewhat less urgent. In addition, people come to recognize that other things are as important or more important in their relationships.

Still, sexual activity remains strong and important to many people as they age. And its importance is not merely for physical release. As an 84-year-old woman said, "Sex means more to me than just physical satisfaction. I need to have my husband near to me. I need to hold him and have him hold and hug me." As such needs become increasingly

Sexual activity tends to remain important to people as they age.

important, the preferred form of sexual activity may change. A study of 99 men and women aged 60 to 85 investigated changes in preferred sexual activity over the course of the adult years (Turner and Adams 1988). The researchers found that for 47 of their subjects, there was no change. They still preferred the same activity they did in their earlier years (for 40 of the 47, intercourse; for the others, such things as petting and masturbation). Some who had preferred petting in earlier years now preferred intercourse. And some who had preferred intercourse now preferred petting, masturbation, or fantasies.

Health is the second factor that can alter a couple's sexual pattern. People who must take painkilling drugs or medication for high blood pressure may find their sexual functioning impaired. Chronic health problems, such as arthritis and diabetes, can diminish sexual desire and activity. A hysterectomy may make intercourse more painful for a woman.

A third factor, the arrival of children, can drastically alter a couple's sex life. Typically, there is a decline in sexual relations after couples become parents (Ahlborg, Persson, and Hallberg 2005). New parents may experience a decline in sexual desire because the demands of parenthood leave them feeling exhausted at day's end. The decline in frequency of sexual relations, incidentally, may be frustrating to one or both partners, but it does not necessarily mean a decline in commitment or affection. In fact, new parents may assert that their love for each other is stronger than ever even though the frequency of their sexual relations has declined.

Finally, our study of long-term marrieds identified three patterns in sexual functioning (Lauer and Lauer 1986). In one pattern, the level and satisfaction with the couple's sex life remained fairly stable over time. A second pattern involved a decline in sexual frequency. Sometimes that was associated with less sexual satisfaction, but in other cases it was not. Third, the sex life of some couples improved over time. In some cases, even the frequency increased. Independently of frequency, however, some couples perceived the quality of their sex life as improving over time. As a woman married 40 years told us, "It's better than ever."

EXTRAMARITAL SEX

What do you think about someone who is married having sex with a partner other than his or her spouse? How does that affect marital intimacy? In a 1997 Gallup poll of attitudes about extramarital sex, 79 percent said it is "always" wrong, 11 percent said it is "almost always" wrong, 6 percent said it is wrong "only sometimes," and 3 percent said it is not wrong at all. Most people feel that extramarital sex damages the marital relationship. Nevertheless, a substantial number of people have extramarital sex. One national survey reported that about a fourth of married men and 15 percent of married women admit to ever having an affair (Laumann et al. 1994), while another found that 8.5 percent of men and 4.3 percent of women reported an affair within the past five years (Leigh, Temple, and Trocki 1993).

Clearly, most Americans practice fidelity. Just as clearly, many people engage in extramarital sex who say they do not approve of it. And because only one of the partners in some marriages has the extramarital relationship, a great many couples are affected. Tens of millions of Americans face the problem of a spouse who has been unfaithful. The extent of the unfaithfulness varies, of course. Extramarital sex may involve either an affair or a one-night stand. Affairs may continue for weeks or even years, with regular or periodic sexual relations. The one-night stand involves a single encounter. Clearly, an affair is much more difficult to maintain than the single encounter.

Why Extramarital Sex?

Many married people fantasize about what it would be like to have sex with someone other than their spouse. But fantasies are not usually enough to motivate someone to have extramarital sex. Most Americans express disapproval of extramarital sex. The disapproval is often rooted in religious beliefs, and, in fact, those who are very religious are less likely than others to have extramarital sex (Burdette, Ellison, Sherkat, and Gore 2007).

Nevertheless, a substantial number of Americans will have an affair at some point in their married life. A large-scale, national study of married individuals reported a rate of infidelity of 2.3 percent in any one year (Whisman, Gordon, and Chatav 2007). Of course, that does not tell us the proportion who will have extramarital sex over a lifetime, but it's probable that at least 10 percent of all married people will be unfaithful one or more times. Women are likely to justify the infidelity on the basis of emotional need. Men tend to assert a need for more variety and more frequency of sex (which helps explain the fact that pregnancy raises the risk of infidelity).

People give other reasons. They may be sexually frustrated (a substantial proportion of women indicate sexual dissatisfaction with their husbands). They may believe that they were seduced. They may use an affair or one-night stand to get revenge against a mate who has cheated or who has angered them. In general, the lower an individual evaluates his or her marriage and the quality of his or her sex life, the more likely that individual is to have extramarital activity (Wiederman and Allgeier 1996; Treas and Giesen 2000; Previti and Amato 2004). In other words, the rate of extramarital sex in the nation is an indicator of marital problems. Extramarital sex causes problems, but it also reflects a troubled relationship.

Some Consequences of Extramarital Sex

On the positive side, some people report that the extramarital experience provided them with a brief but meaningful thrill. But for the most part, extramarital sex doesn't solve people's problems; it only intensifies them (Previti and Amato 2004).

As a therapist who has dealt with many cases of infidelity notes, most affairs involve "a little bad sex and hours on the telephone" (Pittman 1993:36). The thrill of engaging in the forbidden turns out to be disappointing.

Those who get involved in extramarital sex because they have "fallen in love" are also likely to be disappointed. "Romantic affairs lead to a great many divorces, suicides, homicides, heart attacks, and strokes, but not to very many successful remarriages" (Pittman 1993:35).

In addition, there is the crisis in the marriage if the extramarital activity is discovered. The betrayed spouse is likely to undergo a time of great trauma. He or she may have trouble concentrating, sleeping, and eating. There may be a preoccupation with the betrayal and an agonizing effort to try to understand it. There may be a feeling of having been victimized to the extent that marital trust is no longer possible. A wife who discovered her husband's extramarital activity told an interviewer that, in the week following her discovery, she found herself standing in a department store with no idea why she had come there. She said that she felt "as if the very floor I stood on were moving, waving and buckling underneath me. It was as if I myself, and the world around me, were completely unreal" (Scarf 1987:138).

Various outcomes of infidelity are possible (Charny and Parnass 1995). The harm may be irreparable; the couple may divorce. The marriage may survive but provide a low level of satisfaction and little or no intimacy. And in a few cases, the marriage may survive and improve. If the latter is to occur, the main problems that the couple must work through are the factors in their relationship that might have contributed to the infidelity and the problem of a spouse who was emotionally involved with someone else (having your spouse emotionally involved seems harder to cope with than the purely sexual involvement).

At times, both spouses may be having extramarital activity, sometimes with both knowing this and sometimes not. Even in those cases, the marriage might survive. A professional woman shared the following account with us:

> We have a two-career marriage. We seemed to have less and less time for each other. I got involved in an affair with a man at work. Then one day I discovered that my husband was also having an affair. That made me furious! Suddenly we had to confront the fact that our marriage was on the rocks. We both agreed that we didn't want it to end. We were both hurt, but we got counseling and worked through the pain. That was three years ago. So far, it's working well. And I intend for that to continue.

SEXUAL DISEASES AND DYSFUNCTIONS

Our examination of sexual diseases and dysfunctions is necessarily brief. But it is important that you at least be familiar with them. Getting, or the fear of getting, a disease can lower or even eliminate the intimacy of sexual relations. You also should be aware of some of the rules of safe sex, our final topic in this chapter.

Sexual Diseases

Sexually transmitted diseases (a term now preferred to *venereal diseases*) have plagued humankind throughout history. Some believe that with the advent of AIDS, the risk is greater than ever, but many people died of sexual diseases before the advent of modern medicines that can cure or control most of those diseases.

Major Types of Sexually Transmitted Diseases. *AIDS*, or acquired immunodeficiency syndrome, is caused by a virus that attacks certain white blood cells, eventually

causing an individual's immune system to stop functioning. The individual then falls prey to one infection after another. Even normally mild diseases can prove fatal. Many AIDS patients develop rare cancers or suffer serious brain damage. HIV, the virus that causes AIDS, spreads in a number of ways, including through anal or vaginal intercourse with an infected person, blood transfusions, accidental exchange of blood from a contaminated hypodermic needle, and contact of infected mothers with their infants before or during birth. Initially, those most likely to get infected with HIV and develop AIDS were homosexual and bisexual men and intravenous drug users. Increasingly, however, HIV is being passed on through heterosexual contacts and women and children comprise a growing number of the victims (Hosain and Chatterjee 2005; Merchant and Lala 2005). Worldwide, young people aged 15 to 24 years account for half of all new AIDS cases (Dolan and Niven 2005). In the United States, a disproportionate number of Hispanics and black women are HIV-infected (Essien et al. 2005; Peragallo et al. 2005).

No cure exists for AIDS, but certain preventive measures can enable people to avoid HIV infection and those who are infected can take measures to delay and perhaps stop the virus from developing into AIDS. Safe sexual practices and the use of clean needles for injections are important preventive measures. For those infected, a variety of drugs and a healthy lifestyle (including diet and exercise) are effective in slowing the disease for at least some people. Efforts are also underway to develop an AIDS vaccine, though no one knows when or if such a vaccine might be available.

Gonorrhea is one of the oldest forms of sexual disease. It can be transmitted by any kind of sexual contact, including kissing. In men, gonorrhea causes a thick discharge from the penis and burning while urinating. In women, it has no visible symptoms, but it can damage their fallopian tubes—causing them to become infertile—and also cause lower abdominal pain, nausea, and pain during intercourse. Gonorrhea is treated with penicillin.

Syphilis appeared in Europe in the fifteenth century (Masters, Johnson, and Kolodny 1988:563), killing hundreds of thousands of people. It is transmitted by sexual contact but also can be transmitted in a blood transfusion or, if a pregnant woman acquires it, to the fetus. The first symptom of syphilis is a sore on some part of the body. The sore usually heals and goes away, but untreated syphilis will go into a second stage involving rash, fever, and pains. If still untreated, it can result in brain damage, heart problems, and ultimately death.

Pregnant women with untreated syphilis may experience stillbirth or neonatal death or give birth to babies that are deaf or have neurologic or bone disorders (Centers for Disease Control 2001). Syphilis also is treated with penicillin.

Genital herpes is caused by a virus. It is transmitted by sexual intercourse and shows up in the form of painful blisters on or in the area of the genitals. The blisters eventually disappear, but they may reappear periodically because the virus continues to live in the human body. Some people suffer repeated 7- to 14-day periods of the sores. At the present, there is no cure for genital herpes.

Finally, *chlamydial infections* are caused by a bacterium. Chlamydia usually has no symptoms. It can cause infection of the urethra in males and infections in the reproductive system of females. It can lead to a fatal tubal pregnancy or infertility in women (Miller et al. 2004). If caught early, chlamydia is readily treatable with antibiotics. If untreated, it can contribute to a number of diseases, including pneumonia and blindness (Ojcius, Darville, and Bavoil 2005).

Incidence. A substantial number of Americans suffer from one or more sexually transmitted diseases. Nationally, in 2005, 0.8 percent of all Americans aged 12 years and older and 2.1 percent of young adults (those aged 18 to 25 years) had a sexually transmitted disease (Substance Abuse and Mental Health Services Administration 2007). The rates of infection among young adults varied considerably by racial/ethnic background. African Americans had the highest rates (3.7 percent), followed by Native Americans (3.5 percent), whites and Hispanics (2.0 percent), and Asian Americans (0.2 percent).

Table 4.3 shows the number of new cases of four sexually transmitted diseases reported each year to the Centers for Disease Control. Declines in some of the rates

reflect people's growing awareness of risks and increasing use of protective measures.

More than a million Americans either have AIDS or the HIV that causes AIDS (Centers for Disease Control 2007). Among those who have AIDS, a little less than 1 percent of the victims are children under the age of 13. The rates of infection (number per 100,000 population) vary among racial/ethnic groups: 68.7 for African Americans, 24.0 for Hispanics, 9.3 for Native Americans, 6.9 for white, non-Hispanics, and 4.3 for Asian Americans. The majority of male AIDS victims involves homosexual relationships. The majority of female AIDS victims involves heterosexual relationships with men who have HIV or AIDS.

Clearly, while some racial/ethnic groups have higher rates of certain diseases, a considerable number of Americans of all races suffer from a sexually transmitted disease at one time or another in their lives. "Suffer" is the appropriate word, because, depending on the particular disease acquired, people may experience fear, anger, guilt, and a damaged self-esteem in addition to the physical consequences (Swanson and Chentiz 1993).

Sexually Transmitted Diseases and Sexual Behavior. The possibility of acquiring a sexually transmitted disease has done little in the past to change sexual behavior. An individual's sexual behavior may change once he or she has contracted the disease, of course. But few people have abstained from sexual relations or from having a variety of sexual partners out of the fear of disease. When concern about, and fear of, AIDS first arose, there may have been some modification of risky sexual behavior. But most researchers find that despite knowledge about AIDS, many people continue to engage in high-risk sexual behavior (Morrison-Beedy 1997; Kalichman et al. 2007). Some do so because there is an increased belief that newer HIV treatments reduce the chances of transmitting the virus. Some do so because they apply the "illusion of unique invulnerability" (discussed in the section on contraceptive use) to their risk of contracting HIV/AIDS (Dolcini et al. 1996). Whatever the reasons, risky behavior continues at a high level. For example, a study of older men who either have, or are at risk for, HIV infection reported that only 58 percent of the HIV-positive men always used condoms with their sexual partners (Cooperman, Arnsten, and Klein 2007).

Worse, some of those already infected do not inform sexual partners of their condition. A study of HIV-positive

T A B L E 4.3 Reported Cases of Sexually Transmitted Diseases, 1960–2005

Disease	Year				
	1960	1970	1980	1990	2005
Gonorrhea (1,000)	259	600	1004	690	340
Syphilis (1,000)	122	91	69	134	33
AIDS (1,000)				42	41
Chlamydia					976

Source: U.S. Census Bureau 1989:111 and 2008:173.

Unprotected sex has left millions of Americans struggling with deadly AIDS.

adults found that 42 percent of gay or bisexual men, 19 percent of heterosexual men, and 17 percent of all women admitted having sex without telling the partner of their condition (Ciccarone et al. 2003).

Sexual Dysfunctions

Famed English author and reformer John Ruskin courted a young woman to whom he wrote such flowery phrases as, "You are like the bright—soft—swelling—lovely fields of a high glacier covered with fresh morning snow" (Rose 1983:54). Ruskin won her heart, and they were married. A few years later, they were divorced because Ruskin could never consummate the union. He was one of many people for whom sex is more of a problem than an experience of intimacy.

Types of Sexual Dysfunctions. A **sexual dysfunction** is any impairment of the physical responses in sexual activity. For males, the major sexual dysfunctions have to do with penile *erection* and *ejaculation* (Mackay 2001). A man may be unable to have or maintain an erection that is firm enough for intercourse. Or he may ejaculate before the woman is sufficiently aroused for orgasm or even before inserting his penis into her vagina. In a few cases, the man's problem may be the opposite: difficulty ejaculating or even an inability to ejaculate within the vagina. Gay men also have problems with erection and ejaculation. In a large-scale study, gay

men reported erectile problems more frequently than did heterosexual men, while heterosexual men reported the problem of rapid ejaculation more than did gay men (Bancroft et al. 2005).

For women, the main kinds of sexual dysfunction include *vaginismus* (involuntary spasms of the muscles around the vagina, preventing penetration by the penis or making it painful), *anorgasmia* (difficulty reaching or an inability to reach orgasm), and *painful intercourse.*

From 10 to 20 percent of sexual dysfunctions have organic causes, such as diabetes, drug abuse, and infections. A variety of psychological and social factors are involved in most cases. The individual may have developed negative sexual attitudes, suffer from anxiety or guilt, feel hostile or alienated from the sexual partner, and so forth. Stress, such as that resulting from unemployment, can affect sexual functioning (Morokoff and Gilliland 1993). Therapy often can help people recapture a satisfying sex life.

Prevalence of Sexual Dysfunctions. Many people have to deal with sexual dysfunction at some point in their lives. The prevalence of sexual dysfunction in community studies varies widely, from 10 to 52 percent of men and 25 to 63 percent of women; a national sample reported rates of 31 percent for men and 43 percent for women (Heiman 2002). **Impotence,** the inability to get or sustain an erection, is the most common problem among men, while low sex drive is the most common problem for women. The prevalence among both men and women tends to increase with age (Lewis et al. 2004).

In 1998, the drug Viagra appeared on the market to help men with erectile problems (Mitka 1998). The drug caused quite a stir, including testimonials from well-known people about its efficacy, conflict over whether HMOs should pay for the drug, and reports of some deaths among men also taking medication for coronary artery disease.

Inhibited Sexual Desire

Inhibited sexual desire is a problem but not, strictly speaking, a dysfunction because it does not necessarily involve a physical impairment. It occurs in both men and women, though it is more often reported by women (Gregoire 2000). Like sexual dysfunctions, it may be rooted in such things as hostility, fear, and anxiety. It also may result from drug abuse or be a side effect of certain drugs such as those used to reduce high blood pressure or depression. A temporary lowering of sexual desire also occurs in the majority of women during pregnancy (Regan et al. 2003).

Inhibited sexual desire can lead to a distressed relationship and even to major conflict between husband and wife (Gregoire 2000). A study of 90 married women with sexual problems found a number of differences between those with inhibited desire and those with various dysfunctions but normal desire (Stuart, Hammond, and Pett 1987). Those with inhibited desire, compared to the others, perceived their partners to have less affectionate interaction and more negative attitudes toward sex. They were more likely than those with normal desire to have had premarital intercourse. And, most importantly, those with inhibited desire reported far greater dissatisfaction with the quality of the marital relationship, including such factors as trust, commitment, emotional closeness, love, and attractiveness of the spouse. For these women, inhibited desire grew out of poor marital interaction, a conclusion underscored by the fact that most of the women developed the problem gradually after they were married.

We do not know how many people have inhibited sexual desire. Probably anywhere from 20 to 50 percent of people experience it at some point in their lives, some more severely than others. The problem may go away if the couple can outlast it and build or maintain a generally good marital relationship. For some, however, the problem will require therapy.

Safe Sex

The only truly safe sex is no sex. Few people are so concerned about safety that they will opt for celibacy; for all others, it is helpful to consider some guidelines for maximizing safety:

1. Be careful about whom you allow to be a sexual partner. How well do you know the person and his or her sexual history? Does the person have any signs of infection?
2. Minimize the number of sexual partners you have. Having multiple partners greatly enhances the risk of acquiring a sexually transmitted disease, including AIDS. The safest sex is between two people who have an exclusive relationship.
3. Discuss health and sexual concerns with the partner before you have sexual relations. It isn't an invasion of privacy to question someone about his or her sexual history when the issue is one of your health and even your life.
4. Use available protection during sexual relations. In particular, experts recommend that males always use a condom, even if the woman is using another birth control device. Condoms do not give absolute protection, but they maximize the safety of sexual intercourse. Experts also recommend that you wash your genitals carefully and thoroughly both before and after sexual relations.
5. Have regular medical checkups. You should be specifically checked for sexually transmitted diseases if you or your partner have sexual relations with more than one person.
6. Know the symptoms of the various diseases. We have briefly noted many of them. But you should be familiar with all the symptoms. Some of the diseases are insidious in that they may appear to go away, only to return in a more advanced and damaging phase.
7. Consult a physician immediately if you have contracted or been exposed to a sexually transmitted disease. You may be embarrassed, but keep in mind that you are dealing with your health, your reproductive capacity, and perhaps even your life.

Comparison

Unwanted Sex in China

Unwanted sex occurs among married people as well as those not married. The sex may involve verbal or physical coercion. Or it may be a matter of the wife passively acceding to the husband's desires even though she doesn't want to have sex at the time. In a national study of Americans, Basile (2002) found that 34 percent said they had had unwanted sex with a husband or partner at some time in their lives, and 20 percent had unwanted sex with their current husband one or more times. Among the reasons given for the unwanted sex were a sense of duty, being persuaded by begging and pleading, and submitting after being bullied.

How much unwanted marital sex is there in other nations? Although there is little available research, one team of researchers surveyed a national sample of 1,127 married women in China (Parish et al. 2007). The women's age ranged from 20 to 64 years. Thirty-two percent of the women reported unwanted sexual intercourse during their current marriage, with a fifth of those saying that force was involved. In addition to intercourse, the researchers asked about unwanted sex acts (such as oral sex and touching the genital area). Twenty-two percent indicated unwanted sex acts in the past year. Finally, the researchers asked the women if they ever agreed to sex just to please their husbands, and 72 percent said they did at least sometimes.

There is, then, a good deal of unwanted marital sex among Chinese wives. "Unwanted," however, does not mean that the wives were sexually repressed or lacking in sexual desire. Rather, a number of factors determined whether the sex was wanted. One important factor was the quality of the relationship. Women who indicated that their husbands gave them daily experiences of intimacy, engaged in sexual foreplay, and attended to their sexual needs were less likely to report unwanted sex. Interestingly, Chinese women may not be as receptive to sexual experimentation as women in some other nations, because wives who said their husbands engaged them in varied positions (such as the wife on top of the husband), who caressed their breasts, or who gave them oral sex were more likely to also say the sex was unwanted.

Another factor in sex being unwanted were attitudes and expectations. Some of the wives did admit they regarded sex as dirty, and they were also more likely to say that the sex was unwanted. A curious finding, however, is that wives with more education and more permissive sexual attitudes (such as approving of premarital sex) also had higher reported rates of unwanted sex. The researchers speculated that such women may have higher standards of what is acceptable and appropriate, or may be victimized by husbands who equate their permissiveness with desire and willingness.

A third factor involves bargaining position. Women with higher levels of income reported more unwanted sexual activity. While this would appear to give them greater bargaining power (in other words, the power to resist unwanted sex), it is consistent with findings in the United States about women whose income is relatively high compared to their husbands as having an elevated risk of being abused. Such behavior is an effort by the husband to maintain control and authority in the marriage.

One other question emerged about unwanted marital sex. If it occurs in the context of marriage, does unwanted sex become only an annoyance or does it have more serious consequences? When the sex is the result of physical force, it is emotionally damaging to the woman. But even if no physical force is involved, having unwanted sex tends to diminish the emotional well-being of women.

In short, although the Chinese and American cultures differ on many dimensions, the amount and consequences of unwanted sex are comparable. The techniques used by husbands to persuade or coerce their wives are also comparable. In both societies, there are husbands who seem oblivious or indifferent to the fact that unwanted sexual activity may provide them with short-term relief, but it is detrimental both to the well-being of their wives and of their marriages.

SUMMARY

Sex is both a physical and a social phenomenon. The social nature of sex is illustrated by variations in sexual arousal and techniques and by the amount of unwanted sex in which people engage.

Sex is an important part of intimate relationships. The need for intimacy has primacy over the need for sex. Sexual activity is a natural expression of the feeling of intimacy with someone.

The majority of teenagers become sexually active between the ages of 15 and 19. One consequence of teenage sex is a high rate of unwanted pregnancies at an early age. Teenagers get pregnant for a variety of reasons, including a lack of responsible use of birth control measures. Some teenagers may want to get pregnant because of loneliness, alienation from parents, or the need to assert their independence or to do something creative.

The consequences of teenage childbearing are mostly negative. The parents are less likely to complete their education and more likely to remain poor. Only a minority of women marry the father, so the woman assumes the child-rearing responsibilities. Some of the mothers will escape poverty, but the risks of a poorer quality of life for them and their children are much higher than they are for those who bear children after their teen years.

Contraception refers to methods of preventing fertilization. Some, such as the rhythm method and withdrawal, are of little use. The pill, condoms, and the diaphragm are common devices. Among married women, there has been a dramatic increase in sterilization since 1965.

Abortion is a form of birth control for some people. The proportion of legal abortions has risen dramatically since 1973. A slight majority of Americans favor the woman's right to choose whether to have an abortion. There are some psychological risks; many clinics have both pre- and postabortion counseling.

The double standard still exists to some extent with regard to premarital sex, but sexual activity is now nearly as acceptable for females as for males. Over half of Americans believe premarital sex is not wrong. The majority of American women have sexual intercourse before marriage.

The sex life of married people has changed over the past few decades, with an increasing amount of foreplay and variations in technique. The frequency of sex varies considerably among the married. Sexual satisfaction is not essential to marital satisfaction, though most happy couples do have meaningful sex lives. Frequency tends to decline for various reasons, but quality can remain high or even increase as the couple ages.

Although the great majority of Americans disapprove of extramarital sex, a substantial number have at least one extramarital experience. Emotional need tends to motivate women, while men are more likely to have a purely sexual motivation.

A substantial number of Americans suffer from one or more sexually transmitted diseases. Gonorrhea, syphilis, genital herpes, chlamydial infections, and AIDS are the most common diseases. Sexual dysfunctions are also common.

Widespread concern about disease, particularly AIDS, raises the question of safe sex. While there are no guarantees, a number of steps can be taken to minimize the chances of acquiring a sexually transmitted disease.

Principles for Enhancing Intimacy

1. Sex is a vital and human function, but it is a very complex one as well. If you want to experience the fullness of your sexual potential, it is important to develop an understanding about the physical and emotional factors that are involved in sex.

2. Sex is not a substitute for intimacy. To be most satisfying, sex needs to be the expression of an intimate relationship, rather than an effort to create intimacy.

3. An unwanted pregnancy is a difficult and painful experience. Knowledge about sexuality and the use of effective contraceptives are the best ways to avoid unwanted pregnancies.

4. Extramarital affairs generally create more problems than they solve for people. In fact, they often cause great personal trauma for the people involved. It is more satisfying to work through the problems in your marriage than to seek escape in an affair.

5. Sexually transmitted diseases pose a significant danger for the sexually active. It is important that you know about the symptoms and consequences of these various diseases as well as the ways you can avoid them.

6. Although sexual dysfunctions are fairly common, they are treatable and need not detract from the quality of an intimate relationship.

7. Sex can be one of the more gratifying of human experiences. But satisfying sex is ultimately responsible sex. Learn the seven guidelines to safe sex and make them a part of your intimate interactions with others.

KEY TERMS

abortion   *90*
bisexual   *78*
contraception   *87*
cunnilingus   *94*
ejaculation   *78*
fellatio   *94*

impotence   *99*
orgasm   *79*
penis   *78*
promiscuity   *83*
rape   *82*
refractory period   *80*

semen   *80*
sexual dysfunction   *99*
sexual harassment   *82*
sterilization   *87*
testes   *79*
vagina   *78*

ON THE WEB   Sexuality

Compared to many societies, sex is a very open topic in the United States. Yet there is still a great deal of ignorance and misinformation about sex. A social worker told the authors about a young pregnant girl who kept denying that she had ever had sex. It turned out that she was actually ignorant of the relationship between sex and pregnancy. This was not an isolated case. The social worker said that she had encountered numerous misunderstandings and misinformation in the areas of birth control and sexually transmitted diseases.

Two useful sites for further exploring various facets of sexuality are:

Planned Parenthood
http://www.plannedparenthood.org

The site of Planned Parenthood has information on many aspects of sexuality, including a test called "Your Sex IQ."

www.mhhe.com/lauer7e

Centers for Disease Control
http://www.cdc.gov

The Centers for Disease Control gathers data on sexuality, including the latest data on, and comprehensive information about, sexually transmitted diseases.

Use these two sites to enlarge your understanding with the following projects:

1. Take the "Your Sex IQ" test on the Planned Parenthood site. As it says on the site, even one wrong answer means you need additional information about sexuality. If you got any wrong answers, explore the topic further on the site.
2. The Planned Parenthood site has information, illustrated with cartoons, about teen sex. Supplement the information with materials from the text and prepare a presentation that would be helpful for eighth graders.
3. Use the search engine on the Centers for Disease Control site to research one of the sexually transmitted diseases. Prepare and deliver a 15-minute lecture to your class on the disease, covering whatever information and data you believe will be both interesting and helpful.

part two

~ Seeking Intimate Relationships ~

The Chinese have a word, *jen,* that refers to a quality of humans that leads them to live in society. In other words, humans by nature seek to live with others. Only unnatural and abnormal people, according to Confucian teachings, live outside of human communities, for it is in society that humans are able to fully develop and realize their potential.

We agree with this ancient Chinese view of our need for relationships. Of course, most of us begin life in the context of family relationships. But sooner or later we begin to establish relationships beyond the family. In part two, we shall look at some of the issues, the alternatives, and the problems that arise as we step outside the family and establish additional intimate relationships. Issues, or points of dispute, include such matters as whether cohabitation is a good preparation for marriage, romantic love can last, and singleness is a healthy option. The issues arise, in part, because we do have so many alternatives—singlehood, sex or celibacy, cohabitation, marriage, and the choice of different possible marriage partners. The alternatives and issues mean that some people face problems, times of doubt, and uncertainty about which choices to make.

~ Getting Involved ~

LEARNING OBJECTIVES

After reading and studying chapter 5, you should be able to

1 Discuss the ways in which people get together as they search for intimate possibilities.
2 Relate the factors that make someone attractive as a potential partner.
3 Explain the functions of dating.
4 Describe the patterns of dating.
5 Identify the factors associated with dating violence.
6 Discuss the factors that build intimacy in a growing relationship.
7 Explain why relationships break up.
8 Describe how people respond when a split occurs.
9 Identify the reasons that some people stay single.
10 Discuss how single people meet their intimacy needs.

Patterns of dating have changed over time. To get a better sense of the changes that have occurred recently, interview three men or three women about their dating experiences. Select one who is under 20 years of age, another between 35 and 40, and a third over 60. In each case, explore the dating experiences of the individual during adolescence. Ask such questions as, "Who initiated dates, males or females? What did you typically do on a date? What influence did your parents have over your dates? What did you feel were the purposes of dating? What was one of your most memorable dates?"

Compare the results from the three different generations. What did you find that was similar and what was different? If the entire class participates in this project, see if there are gender differences as well as age differences. Did those who interviewed men find different answers from those who interviewed women? 🕸

An acquaintance of ours was eager, almost desperate, to find someone with whom to share his life. He had established himself professionally and was eager to settle into marriage and family life. But he felt that he hadn't the time for dating a variety of women in the search for a mate. So he decided to short circuit the process by getting a mail-order bride from Asia. It worked well for a short time, then turned into a disaster. He learned, to his distress, that there is no short cut to the process of getting acquainted, getting to know each other, and building intimacy.

Indeed, getting involved with someone is not merely an interpersonal but also a social process. There are **norms,** shared patterns of behavior, in every society that govern the process. The social nature of getting involved is underscored by the fact that we do not date merely in accord with biological needs but also according to social imperatives. That is, it is not sexual maturation alone that determines when we shall start dating. Rather, there are also social pressures and norms that tell us when it is appropriate to enter the world of dating. And the norms differ for various groups. For example, a study of 683 young adults reported that the average age at first date varied from 14.5 for whites to 18.8 for Asian Americans (Regan et al. 2004).

In this chapter, we look first at how people go about trying to link up with others. We examine the factors involved in being attracted to someone. We then discuss the varied aspects of dating, including dating problems. Finally, we look at the single life, including the issues of intimacy and life satisfaction for singles.

GETTING TOGETHER: THE SEARCH FOR INTIMATE POSSIBILITIES

The first task in beginning an intimate relationship is to identify someone whom you find attractive and available. Where do you look? In contrast to our acquaintance who looked overseas, you may find the love of your life very near to where you live.

Beginning Where You Are

Propinquity, nearness in place, is a major factor in finding intimate possibilities. We tend to like people who live near us or who are close to us in some setting (the neighborhood, classroom, workplace, etc.), and at least some of them are likely to be candidates for an intimate relationship.

Why do people like those who live and work near them? As we shall see later when we discuss the factors involved in attraction, similarity is very important. And people who are alike in important ways tend to live in the same area, engage in similar kinds of work, have similar leisure interests, and belong to similar kinds of organizations. The probability is, in other words, that those who are around are also similar to you in many ways. In particular, people are likely to grow up in neighborhoods and go to school with those from the same social class. People in the same class also tend to have similar values and attitudes.

Thus, there are social factors that lead to clusterings of relatively similar people. Of course, the more mobile you are, the more likely you are to sense dissimilarities with others. Moving from a rural area to the city or from one part of the country to another part can make you more aware of differences among people. A Midwestern student who attended a school in California said, "I lived in California for three years before I felt like I was no longer in a foreign country." Gradually, the student got involved in some organizations and found people who shared his interests. As he got to know like-minded people, he no longer felt he was in a foreign country.

This may all sound obvious, but it addresses one of the myths surrounding romantic relationships—that there is a "one-and-only" for you, an ideal mate for whom you have to search far and wide so that you can have the perfect match. On the contrary, there are probably a good number of "one-and-only" people with whom you could have a satisfying relationship, and many of them are nearby.

Hanging Out and Hooking Up

In the past, when a young person met someone with whom he or she would like to pursue a relationship, the two would go out on a date. In recent years, many young people have gotten involved in **hanging out** and **hooking up** before, or instead of, dating (Marquardt and Glenn 2001). "Hanging out" refers to casual and sometimes spontaneous getting together of groups at parties, parking lots, bars, or other locales. "Hooking up" may result from the get-together and can include anything from kissing to sexual intercourse between two people who are not committed to each other. Both high school and college students hang out and hook up.

A study of 555 college students compared three groups: 120 students who had never hooked up, 266 who had had at least one hookup but without any sexual intercourse, and 169 who had at least one hookup that involved sexual intercourse (Paul, McManus, and Hayes 2000). Significantly more males than females in the study had sexual intercourse when they hooked up, and nearly half of those who had sex never saw the hookup partner again. On the average, those who had hooked up did so 11 times a year.

The researchers also found that heavy drinking played a role in hookups. Significantly more intoxication occurred among those who had sex during hookups than those who did not have sex. And there was a higher degree of alcohol abuse among all who hooked up than among those who did not. Students who did not hook up also had significantly higher self-esteem than those who hooked up.

Another study, using a sample of 178 students at a small liberal arts university, reported that 23 percent of the women and 7 percent of the men had one or more experiences of unwanted sexual intercourse (Flack 2007). Seventy-eight percent of those who had unwanted intercourse did so while hooking up, and the most frequent reason given for the intercourse was impaired judgment because of heavy drinking.

Why do some students opt for hanging out and hooking up while others do not? Research has not provided any definitive answers. But at least some of those who do not engage in these activities recognize that hanging out and hooking up are not effective ways to meet a potential mate—one of the functions of dating (Marquardt and Glenn 2001). In contrast, at least some of those who do hang out and hook up do not want to expend the time and energy necessary for a romantic relationship because of a higher commitment to education and career. One other factor may be the extent to which students misperceive the comfort level of those involved in hanging out and hooking up. A study of college students reported that men were more comfortable than women with the practices (Lambert, Kahn, and Apple 2003). However, both men and women thought their peers were more comfortable than they themselves were, and both men and women overestimated the extent to which the opposite sex was comfortable with hooking up. In other words, the researchers note, hooking up occurs in the context of "pluralistic ignorance," a situation in which everyone is making false assumptions about the attitudes and beliefs of others. If students had a more realistic understanding of the comfort level of others, they might be more hesitant to engage in the practice.

THE SELECTION PROCESS

Despite the hanging out and hooking up that occurs, getting involved with someone frequently begins with, or eventually entails, dating (Kuttler and La Greca 2004).

In fact, dating is a primary way to select the person with whom you want to pursue a serious relationship.

What Attracts?

A first question is, what makes someone attractive to you as a dating partner? What qualities do you look for in the person? A researcher studied TV dating games and also interviewed 204 people to ascertain the kinds of things that makes a person attractive as a dating partner (Hetsroni 2000). The criteria used by those in the TV dating games are shown in figure 5.1. Note that men and women differed somewhat in the extent to which they used the various criteria. Still, the three most commonly used by both men and women were intelligence/education, personal traits, and physical appearance.

Physical appearance is one of the important factors in interpersonal attraction that social scientists have studied. Similarity is another important factor. What is crucial about such criteria as intelligence/education and others shown in figure 5.1 is whether you and the other person are similar or different. The importance of physical appearance and similarity emerged in a study of college students who were dating (Peretti and Abplanalp 2004). The researchers asked what kinds of things comprised the "chemistry" in the students' relationships. Two of the most frequent things named were physical attractiveness and similarity. The students talked about similarity in terms of "alikeness" and having various things in common (such as ethnicity, religion, education, socioeconomic status, morals, norms, values, and attitudes). Let's look at these two important factors in more detail.

Physical Attractiveness. Beauty may be only skin deep, but it is an important factor in attraction. It is particularly important in first impressions, when there is little other available information about a person. Both men and women use physical attractiveness to evaluate someone's appeal, although it is more important to men than to women (Berry and Miller 2001; Urbaniak and Kilmann 2003; Lippa 2007). Physical attractiveness diminishes in importance, although it doesn't completely lose its importance, in longer-term relationships or when other information is available. The importance of physical attractiveness is illustrated by an account that Nancy, a female student, shared with us:

> Until I was 16, I was very unattractive. Actually, I was pretty ugly. I was overweight, wore nerdy glasses, had very bad skin, and my hair was always messy looking. I didn't date anybody until I was 16, and even then it was only a few times. When I was 14, I had begun pursuing a guy I thought

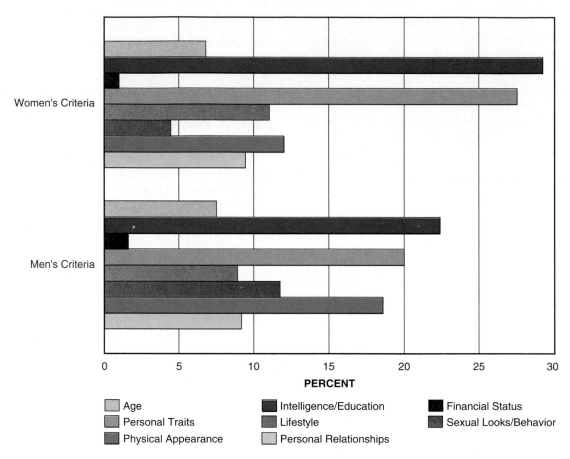

FIGURE 5.1 Criteria for Screening Dating Candidates
Source: Adapted from Hetsroni 2000.

I was madly in love with. But it went nowhere. He was the hunk of our class and out of my league. Everybody liked him, and he could have had any girl in my class. So I didn't expect him to go out with me, although I wanted it very much. His rejection reinforced my belief that I was unattractive, and that hurt my self-esteem. It was a vicious cycle. The more my self-esteem went down, the more unattractive I became.

Everything suddenly changed when I was 16 and a half. I lost weight. I got contact lenses. And I got a haircut that looked good on me. I became a different person. Every time I looked in the mirror, my self-esteem went up. In a matter of months, a number of guys asked me to go out with them, and people seemed generally friendlier. Just by changing my looks, I ended the whole vicious cycle that had been so painful.

Nancy's experience illustrates some of the findings of research. Attractive persons are more self-accepting, and self-acceptance enhances attractiveness. The more we see ourselves as attractive, the more self-esteem we have at all ages. When we see someone who is physically attractive to us, we are likely to define that person as more likable, friendly, confident, sensitive, and flexible than someone who is less attractive. Obviously, then, we perceive physically attractive people as more desirable dating partners.

Similarity. Do opposites attract? This may work for magnets, but for people, it is similarity rather than differences that attracts us to each other. At later stages, some differences may enhance an intimate relationship, as we shall discuss in subsequent chapters. Initially, however, we are attracted to people who are like us in their attitudes, their values, and even their personalities, and we are put off by those who are different from us (Hester 1996; Jones et al. 2004; Peretti and Abplanalp 2004).

In fact, when we perceive someone to be different, we may communicate with that person in a way that says, "I am not available." Unavailability may be communicated directly in words, or by various **nonverbal cues.** The nonverbal cues include such things as aloofness and body posture. Women are generally better than men at picking up on and correctly interpreting nonverbal cues (Rosip and Hall 2004). So a woman who wants to communicate unavailability may have to do so verbally as well as nonverbally; a man who wants to communicate unavailability is more likely able to do it with nonverbal cues alone.

Why does similarity lead to attraction? In the Peretti and Abplanalp (2004) study, students gave a number of reasons. They said it increased their liking of the partner, made communication and conversation more meaningful, and made the relationship more stable and satisfying. In short, similarity increases your attraction to someone because it makes for a more comfortable relationship, it builds self-esteem (someone agrees with your attitudes and values and thereby validates you), and it facilitates the development of intimacy because of the ease of sharing thoughts, feelings, and ideas.

Finding People to Date

Where do you meet people to date? For those in school, another student is a likely prospect. Once out of school, many single adults discover that it is harder to find dates. Indeed, even celebrities may find it difficult, as illustrated by the fact that professional matchmakers are available to help celebrities with dating (Waxman 2007). For non-celebrities, the workplace is a possible source, as are various clubs and organizations, singles bars, and mutual friends.

Another possibility is the great number of dating services now available throughout the nation and the increasing use of personal ads. Dating services may use computer analysis to match people or videotapes to help people choose someone who appeals to them.

Many newspapers now feature large numbers of personal ads in their classified section. The advertisers normally give information on their sex, race, marital status (single or divorced), and interests. People of all ages use the ads, and some become creative in their efforts, as the following two examples from a Southwestern newspaper illustrate:

> Catholic widow, 57, 5'5", 128 lbs., healthy, employed, lonely, honest, sincere, would like to meet 58–65-year-old gentleman, healthy, honest, sincere for friend/companion.
>
> Couch potatoes pass this ad! Attractive, single white female, 5'5", 122 lbs., brown/brown, seeking a go-getter, 22 to 31. Must be tender, fun-loving, like dancing, dining out, football and much more. No drugs or diseases, please.

Analyses of personal ads show that men tend to seek attractive women and offer financial security, while women tend to seek financial security and offer attractiveness (Cicerello and Sheehan 1995; Sheldon 2007).

Still another possibility is to find someone online. Use of the Internet to find possible romantic relationships is

Co-workers are one source of dating partners.

widespread. A national survey reported that 31 percent of American adults know someone who has used a dating Web site, while 26 percent know someone who has dated a person he or she met on a dating site (Gottlieb 2006). The survey also found that of those singles looking for a partner, 37 percent had tried an online dating site.

Thus, millions of Americans visit sites where they can place ads or search for possible relationships in chat rooms. As with newspaper ads, the online ads give information about both the individual and what the individual is seeking. An analysis of personal ads placed by men found that black, Hispanic, and Asian men were more likely than white men to have a race preference for a partner (Phua and Kaufman 2003). This was more true for heterosexual than for gay men, however. An experiment in which "female seeking male" ads were placed on two large Internet bulletin boards reported 500 e-mail responses in six weeks (Strassberg and Holty 2003). Interestingly, the largest response was to a woman described as successful, financially independent, and ambitious. The next largest came to a woman described as "lovely . . . very attractive and slim."

A romance can develop online through continued meetings in the chat room or by e-mail. Eventually, the couple may decide to telephone each other and/or meet face-to-face. One young woman who met a man on the Internet and married him five months later told us, "As soon as we started e-mailing, we knew we had so much in common that we wanted to meet. And at our first face-to-face meeting he proposed marriage and I accepted."

There are both advantages and disadvantages to meeting someone on the Internet and then pursuing the relationship further. A major disadvantage is that you miss the nonverbal signals that can provide so much information about a person. If you decide to meet face to face, you may find that you have started a relationship with someone who is disturbed or even dangerous; it is important to know how to protect yourself before getting involved online (Gwinnell 1998). Another disadvantage is that you may want to pursue a relationship with someone who lives at a great distance from you. We heard an online account of a Canadian woman who met and fell in love with a Swedish man via the Internet. They now were engaged and struggling with the logistics of where to live.

On the other hand, it is an advantage that you get to know something about each other before being distracted by physical appearance. As we noted in the last chapter, your feelings about someone, including your evaluation of that person's attractiveness, can change considerably as you get to know the person. Perhaps many potentially fulfilling relationships never develop because there is no initial physical attraction.

One other advantage to Internet meetings is that they provide an opportunity to meet and pursue a relationship with someone when other avenues seem to be closed or less accessible. In a word, many people have found love through Internet meetings. There are even books available to guide people on the proper use of the Internet to locate a potential life partner (see, e.g., Booth and Jung 1998).

Functions of Dating

We have already indicated that people date for differing reasons. We will examine the various functions of dating separately, but keep in mind that a particular date may serve more than one of the following functions and that we date for different reasons at different ages.

Recreation. We all have a need for recreation, for a time when we can relax and have fun. One way to do this is to date. Dating takes us out of the world of work or study and into a world of relating and enjoying. Early and middle adolescents (sixth through eleventh graders) are likely to see dating primarily in terms of recreation. For them, the major purpose of dating may be to secure some degree of personal gratification. For older individuals, however, dating is likely to serve additional purposes.

Intimacy and Companionship. While recreation continues to be a function of dating, those who are in college or beyond emphasize the importance of companionship and intimacy (Dickson, Hughes, and Walker 2005; Lawson and Leck 2006). Males may look for sexual intimacy more than females do, and females may hope for interpersonal intimacy more than males do, but intimacy and the companionship are important to both males and females.

Dating, we should note, is not confined to the young. People date after a divorce or after the death of a spouse. Two researchers who studied dating patterns among those over 60 reported that companionship and intimacy were primary purposes of dating. Older people date in order to have an emotional and sexual outlet not otherwise available to them (Kilborn 2004). And they do some of the same things on dates as younger people. They go to the movies, go out for pizza, attend dances,

What Do You Think?

There is disagreement about **whether the Internet is a good place to meet potential dates.** What follows are pro and con arguments. What do you think?

Pro

The Internet is a good place to meet potential dates because

- it greatly expands your choices.
- a person with a computer and Internet access is more likely to be educated and respectable.
- you can learn a great deal about someone before you ever agree to go out on a date.
- you can more openly talk online with the other person about sensitive and embarrassing matters.
- many people are developing successful relationships via the Internet.

Con

The Internet is not a good place to meet potential dates because

- people aren't truthful about themselves on the Internet.
- you are more likely to meet someone who is mentally ill or dangerous on the Internet.
- you can't see online the nonverbal signals that are so important in understanding and evaluating someone.
- you might get serious about someone who lives at a great distance, making the relationship impractical.
- only losers resort to the Internet.

and even camp and travel together. Clearly, dating enhances the quality of life for older people.

Mate Selection.   Mate selection is the most obvious function of dating. We date others in the hope of eventually finding someone to marry (Marquardt and Glenn 2001). In fact, one of the predictors of stability in a dating relationship is whether the two people believe that there is a chance of marriage.

Status Attainment.   *Conflict theorists* stress the competition involved in all human relationships. From this perspective, we would expect dating relationships to involve some efforts to enhance one's position in society. And, indeed, one of the findings of the study of older dating couples was that dating enhances the **status,** or prestige, of the female. Dating serves the same purpose for younger

Conflict Theory Applied

people. Those who date during early and middle adolescence are likely to gain prestige. They enhance their status with their peers

because they show themselves to be not only more grown up but also desirable individuals. That this is important is illustrated by the young woman who told us of her severe embarrassment in high school because no boy asked her out on a date when most of the other girls her age were already dating.

It is not just dating per se but dating particular people that can enhance status. Among adolescents, for example, the young man who dates a cheerleader or a very popular classmate or the young woman who dates an athlete or prominent classmate gains even more status.

Socialization.   The process of learning to function effectively in a group is known as **socialization.** We are not born with the knowledge of how to be a student, an employee, a member of a church, or a member of a family. We learn how to function in the various groups in which we participate. One of the things we have to learn is how to get along with people of the opposite sex, and dating is a way of doing this. The lack of socialization into heterosexual relationships early in life (we interact mostly with same-sex others before puberty) is one of the reasons for the awkwardness of first-dating situations. In dating, we begin to learn how to relate more meaningfully to someone of the opposite sex. That means we are learning the skills necessary for future long-term relationships.

Patterns of Dating

As a social phenomenon, dating differs not only across generations but across societies and among different groups within a particular society as well. In any society, of course, there are norms about dating that are supposed to apply to all groups. Individuals and groups may break these norms, but those who do will probably pay a price. For example, take the issue of who initiates a date in our society. For the most part, men are expected to take the initiative and ask the female for a date. Even though the women's movement has rectified some of the inequalities in relationships, it has not eliminated this expectation. A majority of both men and women agree that it is the man who initiates the date, makes the plans, picks the woman up, pays for the occasion, and begins any romantic moves (Laner and Ventrone 2000).

Of course, there are many who reject the idea that a woman must wait for a man to ask her out. And many women also insist on sharing the expenses of a date. The acceptability of shared expenses may vary by race, however. Using small samples from a predominantly black and a predominantly white university, two researchers found that the African Americans were more traditional than whites about dating protocol (Ross and Davis 1996).

Sharing expenses is based in part on the belief that the woman who allows a man to assume all of the costs of a date may be under some obligation to provide him with sexual favors in return. In a shared-cost date, the two people are equal and may each decide whether the relationship should include sexual activity. The egalitarian nature of the shared-expense date gives a woman more discretion about her behavior. She does not have to feel that she "owes" her date anything sexually. She can ask a man out, share the costs of the evening, and feel free to engage or not engage in sexual activity.

Although, according to the prevailing social norms, a woman does not generally initiate a date, it is acceptable for her to indicate interest in a man. In fact, one researcher who observed men and women in restaurants, in singles bars, and at parties concluded that women give nonverbal cues that initiate flirtation far more often than do men (Lott 1999). A good many verbal and nonverbal cues are used to let a man know of a woman's interest in him. The nonverbal include glancing, maintaining eye contact, preening, smiling, licking her lips, leaning toward the man, touching him, laughing, and nodding. Verbal cues include compliments, continuation rather than termination of a conversation, giving one's telephone number, listening to a man without interrupting him, giving extended rather than terse answers to a man's questions, and commenting on things he says. All of these cues suggest an interest in dating the man. A woman can use all of them with impunity, but if she decides to initiate the date, she faces the possibility of a misinterpretation of her character.

Fun and intimacy are two of the reasons that people date.

Dating Problems

Someone you find attractive asks you for a date. You accept gladly and with anticipation. You expect to return home feeling exhilarated by the experience. What are the chances that your date will wind up abusing you on this or a subsequent date? The chances may be greater than you think.

Dating always has its problematic aspects. At the least, there is usually some anxiety about how well things will go and whether you will both have a good time. But our concern here is for those serious problems that may arise. Dating can, and too frequently does, involve violence between the partners.

Violence in Dating.   Violence is the use of force to injure or abuse someone. Physical violence that occurs in dating situations includes pushing, grabbing, shoving, slapping, kicking, biting, hitting with the fist, and date rape (which we will discuss shortly). Psychological

Comparison

Dating Violence in Russia

People who date do not expect to be the victims of aggression or violence. Yet, if you date long enough in the United States, your chances of being victimized are fairly high. As the text points out, dating violence is not an exclusively U.S. problem. A survey of 475 college students in three Russian universities underscores the point (Lysova 2007). The researcher included only those who were spending active time together and had already formed an emotional attachment (rather than those who only had casual dating experience). The violence included everything from the relatively mild (slapping a partner) to the severe (use of a weapon or rape).

More than a fourth of the students experienced violence from a partner in the year preceding the survey. And nearly 9 percent said they had been subjected to severe violence. As in the United States, the rates of violent victimization were about the same for men and women.

About 3 percent of the students indicated that the violence was sufficiently severe to inflict injury. While most of the injuries were relatively mild (bruises, small cuts), about 1 percent suffered a severe injury such as loss of consciousness, a fracture, or other injuries that required medical attention. Again as in the United States, although the rates of victimization were roughly equal for men and women, the women were far more likely than the men to suffer some kind of injury.

Sexual assault also occurred. Sexual assault includes various kinds of behavior designed to force the partner to have sexual relations against his or her will. About a fourth of the students said they had been sexually assaulted in the preceding year. The rates differed considerably by gender, however: 36.6 percent of the women, compared to 14.5 percent of the men, reported some kind of sexual assault. The assaults included coercion, threats, and force.

Finally, the students reported a great deal of psychological aggression, which is behavior that inflicts emotional suffering. It ranges from insults and yelling to physically damaging the person's belongings to threatening to hit or throw something at the person. Psychological aggression was reported by more than half the students. Again, women were more likely to be victimized: 67.1 percent of the women compared to 55.3 percent of the men said they had suffered some kind of psychological aggression.

Thus, there are high rates of dating violence in Russia. Generally, the rates and patterns are comparable to those in the United States. Lower rates have been found in some countries, such as Portugal, Israel, and Australia (Lysova 2007). But the problem exists in all nations that have been studied.

violence also occurs in the form of verbal abuse, threats, and such hostile nonverbal behavior as scowls and the "silent treatment."

How much violence occurs in dating? A national survey of adolescents in heterosexual, romantic relationships found that a third experienced some kind of victimization: 20 percent reported psychological violence and another 12 percent reported physical violence or a combination of physical and psychological violence (Halpern et al. 2001). Combined with other experiences in which violence occurs, the great majority of women will be victims of violence during their lifetimes. Among college women, 88 percent experienced at least one incident of physical or sexual victimization by the end of their four years in college (National Institute of Justice 2004).

Dating violence occurs worldwide. A survey of students in 31 universities in 16 different countries found that 29 percent admitted physically assaulting a dating partner in the 12 months prior to the survey (Straus 2004). Seven percent had physically injured a partner. And males and females had roughly the same rates of assaulting a partner.

Men and women in the United States also experience similar rates of victimization. They differ, however, depending on various sociodemographic characteristics. Figure 5.2 shows the percentage of females reporting physical violence while dating in the past 12 months. The data come from a national survey of female students in the ninth through twelfth grades. Females who are older and black or Hispanic have the highest rates. Not shown in the figure are additional data on regional differences: the highest rates occur in the South (10.9 percent) and the lowest in the Northeast (7.3 percent) (Silverman, Raj, and Clements 2004).

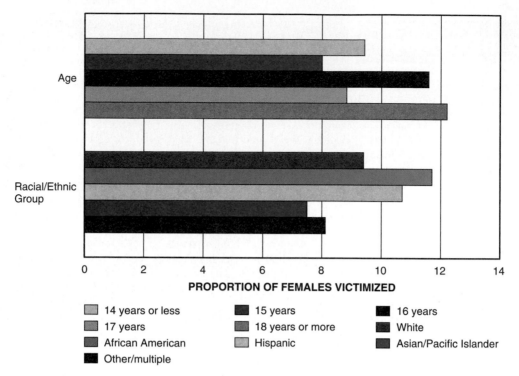

FIGURE 5.2   Dating Violence against Adolescent Females
Source: Adapted from Silverman, Raj, and Clements 2004.

Other researchers used national data and found that 9.2 percent of female adolescents experienced dating violence (Howard and Wang 2003). Higher rates occurred among those females who were in the twelfth grade; were black or Hispanic; had used drugs over the previous month; reported regular binge drinking; and engaged in risky sexual behavior, such as having multiple sex partners and not using condoms. Other research supports the fact that violence in dating tends to be associated with the use of alcohol and other drugs (O'Keefe 1997; Eaton et al. 2007).

What kind of people are the perpetrators of violence? Initially, they may seem no different than anyone else. But they have a number of background experiences and motivations that distinguish them from others. Men who use violence, for instance, may do so out of the belief that violence enables them to win arguments and control the relationship (Riggs and Caulfield 1997). For both men and women, dissatisfaction with the amount of control they have—the power they are able to exert over the partner—can lead to psychological and/or physical violence (Ronfeldt, Kimerling, and Arias 1998; Kaura and Allen 2004).

In addition, those who use violence are more likely to have experienced violence as children from parents or observed their parents being violent with each other (Simons, Lin, and Gordon 1998; Shook et al. 2000; Kinsfogel and Grych 2004; Lichter and McCloskey 2004). Knowing that one's friends engaged in dating violence is also associated with an individual's own likelihood of being violent (Arriaga and Foshee 2004). Not only those who witness troubled relationships among family and friends, but those who have problems of their own with interpersonal relationships generally or who are prone to jealousy are more likely to be aggressive in a dating situation (Riggs 1993).

Finally, certain attitudes are associated with violence. A study of 147 college men reported that those who had participated in aggressive high school sports engaged in more verbal and physical aggression with dating partners than did other men (Forbes, Adams-Curtis, Pakalka, and White 2006). The researchers also found that the more aggressive men had a distinctive set of attitudes: They were more accepting of violence, more sexist in their thinking, more hostile toward women, and more accepting of various rape myths (such as, "she really wanted it," or "she led me on").

How can you avoid getting involved with someone who has the potential to be violent? Based on research such as that noted above and experience in dealing with victims, a university counseling service suggests that you attend to the following cues when you are getting to know someone. They are the warning signs of the potential for dating violence. Specifically, be careful of a dating partner who

- abuses you emotionally by such things as insults, putting you down, or acting perturbed when you take the initiative.
- tries to control such things as whom you befriend, how you dress, or how you conduct other matters in your life.
- speaks in a derogatory way or tells "put-down" jokes about those of the opposite sex.
- expresses groundless jealousy.
- abuses alcohol or uses other drugs or tries to get you to be a user against your wishes.
- pressures you to have sex regardless of whether you want to.
- acts in a physically aggressive way toward you or others in order to get his or her way.
- gets excessively angry when frustrated by something.
- considers you as inferior or subservient in some way.
- has extreme mood shifts.
- is sufficiently volatile that you tend to change what you do or say in order to avoid your partner's angry reaction.

The more of these characteristics a dating partner has, the more you are at risk of being the victim of his or her violence.

One final point: The rates of violent behavior are about the same for males and females. In one study, 32 percent of dating college females acknowledged that they had used physical aggression against a dating partner (Hettrich and O'Leary 2007). The main reasons given were poor communication and anger at the partner (for such things as trying to force the woman to engage in oral sex). And both male and female victims may suffer various physical and emotional harm as a result of the aggression (Anderson and Savage 2005; Kaura and Lohman 2007).

Nevertheless, there is one significant difference between male and female aggression; namely, female victims are likely to be more severely abused than are male victims. And they are also more at risk for long-term negative outcomes such as drug use, unhealthy weight control behavior, risky sexual behavior, pregnancy, and

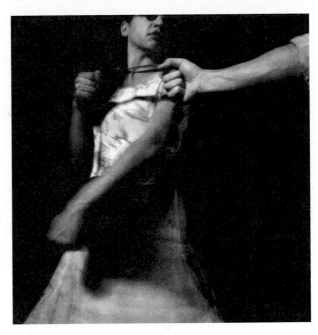

There is a significant amount of dating violence.

attempted suicide (Silverman et al. 2001). Why would women remain in abusive relationships? As *symbolic interactionism* stresses, the crucial factor is not the existence of violence, which seldom leads quickly to the end of a relationship (Kasian and Painter 1992). The crucial factor is how the victims define their violent situation. Those in dating situations, like those in abusive marriages, may believe they have no better alternative, may blame themselves for provoking their partners, or may believe the abusers' promises that the violent behavior will stop. Some even think that once they marry, the violence will cease. But marital abuse often begins during dating and courtship; marriage will not change a violent man into a gentle husband.

 Symbolic Interactionist Theory Applied

Date Rape. **Sexual aggression** occurs frequently in dating. Sexual aggression refers to any kind of unwanted sexual activity, from kissing to sexual intercourse. A majority of intimate partners (including those married, cohabiting, and dating) in the United States experience sexual aggression to some extent. Over a 10-year period, the average annual proportion of victims of threats or attempted attacks was 67.8 percent of females and 63.9 percent of males (Bureau of Justice Statistics 2007). In the same period, 32.2 percent of females and 36.1 percent of males said they had actually been physically attacked. College women have higher rates of victimization than those not in college, probably a reflection of the tendency for college women to engage more in two risk factors: heavy episodic drinking and multiple sex partners (Buddie and Testa 2005).

The most severe form of sexual aggression is **rape,** which is defined by the Federal Bureau of Investigation as the "carnal knowledge of a female forcibly and against her will" (Federal Bureau of Investigation 2002:454). The force need not be overt if the act is against the woman's will. Thus, some rapes occur when the victim is secretly given a date rape drug. A number of such drugs exist. They have no color or odor or taste, and can be easily mixed into a flavored drink. The victim becomes physically helpless, unable to resist sex, and afterwards can't remember what happened. The number of rapes involving date rape drugs is unknown, but a Canadian survey of 1,400 women who reported a sexual assault found that a fourth of the women said that drugs were a factor in the rape (Weir 2001).

According to self-reports of American women, as many as 15 to 20 percent have been raped on a date (Patterson and Kim 1991; Schubot 2001; Rickert et al. 2004). The victims suffer emotional and physical trauma (Shapiro and Schwarz 1997). Virtually every area of a woman's life is negatively affected by the experience of rape. The majority will suffer from posttraumatic stress disorder at some time in their lives, and some of them will develop various kinds of chronic medical conditions (Solomon and Davidson 1997; Ullman and Brecklin 2003). They are also at risk for an unwanted pregnancy and a sexually transmitted disease (Silverman, Raj, and Clements 2004). Relationships, work, health habits, and sense of personal well-being may be adversely affected, including the ability to relate intimately and/or to have sexual relationships (Thompson et al. 2002).

A number of factors increase the chances of date rape. Alcohol abuse, especially binge drinking, is often involved in date rape (Dunn, Bartee, and Perko 2003). Men who are more traditional in their gender-role orientation and who oppose feminism are more likely than others to hold attitudes and beliefs supportive of date rape (Truman, Tokar, and Fischer 1996). And men who accept various rape myths are more likely than others to believe that date rape is acceptable (McDonald and Kline 2004). Rape myths include the idea that the woman "really wants it even though she says no," and that a healthy woman can fight off the man if she truly objects to intercourse.

BUILDING INTIMACY

When you start to date the same person frequently or exclusively, you become increasingly intimate with that person through a number of mechanisms. We will look at three that are an integral part of the process: self-disclosure, intimacy as an exchange relationship, and interdependence and commitment.

Self-Disclosure

Self-disclosure, one of the most important mechanisms for developing intimacy, is an honest revealing of oneself to another person (Clark et al. 2004). At first, people reveal things about themselves that are relatively safe. This is important because self-disclosure always carries risks. Disclosing distressing information, for example, to someone you don't know well can increase your blood pressure, heighten your anxiety, and lead to a depressed mood (Kurylo and Gallant 2000). Disclosing things you don't want to be widely known makes you vulnerable to another person, who might betray your confidence. Disclosing your flaws and faults may lessen the respect another has for you. Most people, therefore, engage in self-disclosure cautiously. They usually expect the other person to reciprocate in the self-disclosure. And in the early part of a relationship, there tends to be an equal amount of self-disclosure from each partner. As intimacy develops, an increasing amount of private information may be shared.

Self-disclosure is more than a sharing of information. As stressed by a *symbolic interactionist* point of view, an intimate relationship is created and maintained by ongoing communication in which personal meanings such as values and attitudes are constructed and shared (Duck 1994). That is, the two people are not merely opening up a part of themselves to each other, but are helping shape each other and are growing in their understanding both of themselves and each other. Self-disclosure links you with another person in a mutually growing process.

Symbolic Interactionist Theory Applied

Pioneering work by Waring and Chelune (1983) identified four kinds of self-disclosure. First, there is a sharing of emotions. Intimates tell each other how they feel about matters. Second, there is a sharing of needs. Intimates reveal what they see as their personal needs in the relationship as well as more general needs. Third, there is a sharing of thoughts, beliefs, attitudes, and even fantasies. And finally, there is a sharing of self-awareness, the way each feels and thinks about himself or herself as a person.

Sharing our feelings, needs, thoughts, and self-awareness with someone else is both a result of intimacy and a creator of greater intimacy (Vittengi and Holt 2000). The more that partners engage in self-disclosure, the more feelings of closeness and love they have for each other. The more that partners engage in self-disclosure early in the relationship, the more they are likely to stay together.

Because self-disclosure is tied so closely with the development of intimacy, we tend to disclose ourselves only to a few (we cannot have intimate relations with a great many people) and only to those with whom we expect to have intimacy. Self-disclosure is, as noted earlier, a risky process. The more you disclose, the more vulnerable you are to being manipulated, controlled, scorned, and embarrassed.

In terms of *systems theory,* we may think of self-disclo-

Systems Theory Applied

sure as a "form of boundary regulation" in which there are two boundaries involved (Derlega et al. 1993:67). One boundary is the couple, the boundary within which it is safe to share something without fear that the information will disrupt the relationship or pass on to others. The other boundary is the personal boundary, which maintains certain information within the individual. Intimacy development means a progressive shrinking (though not an obliteration) of the personal boundary. In other words, more and more is shared. And because of the risks, the sharing requires trust. We trust the other *not* to react negatively, to support us, and to hold what we say in confidence.

As we disclose ourselves in a relationship, trust tends to grow, enhancing the sense of intimacy. As a result, self-disclosure also increases the level of satisfaction with the relationship and enhances the sense of compatibility as partners become increasingly aware of their similarities and at ease with each other's views.

We should note that there are some sex and racial differences in self-disclosure. Girls tend to seek intimate disclosures in their friendships at an earlier age than boys do. A study of 122 white and black adolescents found differences by both sex and race (Pagano and Hirsch 2007). The researchers looked at patterns of self-disclosure among the youth in both their romantic relationships and their same-sex friendships. White girls had significantly higher levels of self-disclosure in their friendships

than in their romantic relationships, whereas white boys had nearly equal levels in each kind of relationship. Among the African Americans, both the boys and girls had equal levels of self-disclosure in the two kinds of relationships.

Gender-role orientations also make a difference. A survey of 302 undergraduates found the highest levels of self-disclosure among feminine and androgynous females, followed by (in decreasing levels of self-disclosure) masculine females, masculine males, androgynous males, undifferentiated females, undifferentiated males, and feminine males (Foubert and Sholley 1996). As we saw in chapter 3, gender, gender roles, and gender-role orientation all make a difference in how people behave.

Intimacy as an Exchange Relationship

Exchange Theory Applied

Exchange theory argues that a one-sided intimate relationship will probably not last. One form of exchange theory, equity theory, asserts that a satisfying relationship requires each partner to have a sense of **equity.** That is, neither partner should be overbenefitted (which can lead to guilt) nor underbenefitted (which can lead to anger) by the relationship.

The theory makes intuitive sense. However, research with 101 couples over a roughly five-year period by Susan Sprecher (2001) found only the sense of being underbenefitted to be associated with lower satisfaction, lesser commitment, and a higher likelihood of breaking up. Being overbenefitted in the relationship did not have the expected adverse consequences.

Sprecher found other aspects of exchange theory to be supported in her research. In particular, rewards were a stronger predictor of commitment to the relationship than was a sense of equity. Each individual was asked to assess the extent to which he or she found the partner's contribution to seven resources as rewarding. The seven resources were love, status, money, material goods, services (such as giving favors or comfort), information, and sex. The more an individual felt rewarded in resources by the relationship, the greater was the individual's satisfaction with and commitment to the relationship.

Finally, research on the partners' emotional involvement in the relationship concluded that it was common for people to perceive unequal emotional involvement between themselves and their partners (Sprecher, Schmeeckle, and Felmlee 2006). Those who thought they had less emotional involvement than their partners also believed they had more control over the continuation of the relationship. But when partners perceived their emotional involvement as equal, they also had greater relationship satisfaction and stability.

Interdependence and Commitment

We noted in chapter 1 that commitment is important to a lasting, satisfying marriage. It is also important to a dating couple if the relationship is to be maintained. Those who perceive that their partners have a fluctuating kind of commitment to them (one that is alternately strong and weak) are more likely to eventually break up than those who perceive the commitment as relatively stable (Arriaga, Reed, Goodfriend, and Agnew 2006).

As intimacy grows, there is an increasing sense of interdependence. Each partner is dependent on the other to fulfill some of his or her needs. Each has some power in the relationship, therefore, because of the dependence of the other. Yet the power may not be equal because of differing amounts of commitment to the relationship. That is, the relationship may be more important to one partner than the other. The one with the most interest in maintaining the relationship is likely to be the most committed to it. And the person who is the most committed can be exploited because that person has the most to lose if the relationship breaks up.

In an ideal situation, issues of power and inequity would not arise. But human life is not ideal. People bring varying amounts of commitment to a relationship. Interdependence seldom, if ever, means an equal amount of dependence of each partner, particularly in the early stages of the relationship. Thus, power issues, as we shall see in chapter 10, come into most of our intimate relationships.

In essence, then, interdependence and commitment are both essential elements of a developing intimacy. But they are also problem areas that can lead to the dissolution of a relationship.

MAINTAINING OR BREAKING UP THE RELATIONSHIP

A point comes in every intimate relationship when the couple must decide whether to continue on with each other or break up. In long-term relationships, there may be a number of such points. If the partners decide to maintain the relationship, they will continue using the mechanisms we have discussed to deepen their intimacy. But most, if not all, people will have at least one

experience of breaking up. Among adolescents, whites are likely to have more such experiences than are African Americans, because the latter tend to have relationships of somewhat longer duration (Giordano, Manning, and Longmore 2005).

When people do break up, it is a painful experience (usually, even for the person wanting out of it). Indeed, the loss of any intimate relationship is likely to involve a grieving process (Viorst 1998). Once you have broken up with someone, you are likely to find yourself coping with volatile emotions, including sadness and anger (Sbarra and Emery 2005). Women tend to cope by confiding in a close friend, while men try to cope by quickly starting to date others (Sorenson et al. 1993). Let's look at who is likely to break up and how people deal with the problem of a deteriorating relationship before the breakup occurs.

Who Breaks Up?

On the basis of factors we have discussed that keep a relationship going, we could make some reasonable inferences about when a relationship is likely to break up. If, for instance, there is perceived inequity, the lack of self-disclosure, or the absence of other factors that enhance intimacy, we would expect a relationship not to last.

There are other factors as well. Cheating on one's partner, which occurs equally by men and women, is a reason many people break up (Brand, Markey, Mills, and Hodges 2007). But the reason for breaking up is not always as dramatic as infidelity. Some people break up simply because they are unhappy in the relationship or because they find a more desirable partner. In contrast, couples are less likely to break up when they spend more time together, are of the same race, and perceive social support for their relationship from family and friends (Felmlee, Sprecher, and Bassin 1990).

Responding to Deterioration

Typically, a breakup is preceded by a deteriorating relationship. One or both partners sense that the quality of the relationship has lessened to a point where the question of continuing or breaking up must be faced. As the quality diminishes, partners can react in a variety of ways. In a classic study of the matter, Rusbult (1987) identified four kinds of responses: exit, voice, loyalty, and neglect.

Exit refers to a response of withdrawal or threatened withdrawal from the relationship. Those who decide to stop going or living together, to try being "just friends" instead of lovers, or to stop seeing each other altogether have chosen the response of exit.

Voice is the response of facing up to, and trying to talk through, the problems. Discussion, compromise, counseling, and efforts to change oneself or one's partner are ways of dealing with the problems by voice.

Loyalty is the response of staying with the partner in spite of the problems. Those who opt for loyalty do not try to resolve the problems; they simply try to endure them. They may believe that the situation will improve in time. They may insist that they must have faith in the relationship and the partner.

Finally, *neglect* is a refusal to face the problems and a willingness to let the relationship die. Some examples of behavior that fit the category of neglect are

> ignoring the partner or spending less time together, refusing to discuss problems, treating the partner badly emotionally or physically, criticizing the partner for things unrelated to the real problem, "just letting things fall apart," chronically complaining without offering solutions to problems . . . (Rusbult 1987:213).

As Rusbult notes, the terms used may be a little misleading. For example, *voice* does not refer only to talking. Rather, *voice* represents active and constructive reactions. *Exit* refers to active and destructive behavior. *Loyalty* is passive, constructive behavior. And *neglect* is passive, destructive behavior.

Differing personalities will prefer different responses, but there are also other reasons for selecting a response (Rusbult 1987:227–28). Research has shown that people exit when they believe that they have nothing to lose by doing so and that the relationship is not worth saving. A combination of dissatisfaction with the relationship, a sense of minimal investment in the relationship, and a belief that there are good alternatives will make exit a likely response. Exit tends to be used more by younger people in relationships that have been going on for only a short time.

Voice is a response that is appropriate when the relationship is valued but in danger. People who have been satisfied with the relationship and invested themselves in it are more likely to try the response of voice. Females are more likely than males to use voice.

Loyalty is an effort to maintain the status quo. People who have been satisfied with the relationship, feel invested in it, perceive few or no better alternatives, and believe the problems are relatively minor may opt for loyalty. Loyalty tends to be used more by older people who have been in a relationship for a longer period of time. Females are also more likely than males to use loyalty.

Most people have the painful experience of breaking an intimate relationship.

Neglect is a destructive response that is used by those who don't know how to mend the relationship and are probably not motivated to do so in any case. Neglect is more common when both satisfaction and investment in the relationship have been low. Males are more likely than females to use neglect.

There may be additional gender differences in reactions to, and methods of coping with, a breakup. Using a small sample of 73 male and 173 female students who had been passionately in love, dated, and then broke up, three researchers found a number of gender differences (Choo, Levine, and Hatfield 1996). The women were more likely than the men to experience joy or relief immediately after the breakup. As a coping style, the women were more likely than the men to blame their partners, while the men were more likely to bury themselves in work or sports. Other researchers found that women reported more personal growth as a result of a breakup than did men (Tashiro and Frazier 2003).

Although breaking up is difficult, we should beware of a tendency to think that it is always bad for relationships to break up. It is generally always painful, but it is not always bad. There are relationships that are destructive to the individuals involved. They *should* break up. Each case must be judged on its own merits in order to determine whether staying together or breaking up is best for the individuals involved.

STAYING SINGLE

Most people have the experience of dating and breaking up. A large and increasing number experience cohabitation. The great majority eventually marry. But a minority remain single. In 2006, the Census Bureau reported

Personal

The Birth, Life, and Death of a Relationship

Frank is a graduate student whose account of a relationship illustrates many of the points we made in this chapter. When Frank came face to face with a problem that he believed too great for the relationship to continue, he used the response of exit:

I enjoy working out at a local health spa. One day while running around the track I saw a very physically attractive female. She had an excellent build, a tan, and blond hair. I decided to talk to her as we ran. After chatting a bit, I took a risk and asked her if she would be interested in getting some yogurt. She responded with an enthusiastic "yes."

I was dating a few other women at the time. But I wasn't really interested in developing an intimate relationship with any of them. But I wanted to get more involved. I was ready for an intimate relationship. I thought this beautiful blond woman might be the one.

We hit it off really well from the beginning. I found it easy to talk to her. I felt very comfortable being with her. We both shared things about our families, values, school, work, and other interests. We sat at the table in the yogurt shop for an hour. As we were leaving, I asked her if she would like to go out some night for dinner. Again, she said "yes" enthusiastically. And she gave me a hug. That hug, along with her facial expressions and the way she looked at me told me that she was interested in getting to know me better.

For the next month, we dated three or four times a week. We went to the beach, the mountains, parks, movies, dinner, and sometimes we just went to her place or mine and talked about our lives and our aspirations. I fell head-over-heels in love with her. I bought her clothes, flowers, cards—all kinds of things to let her know how I felt. Being in love with her made me feel more satisfied, more secure, and more peaceful.

It turned out that we had similar political, religious, and social perspectives. And we were in the same graduate program, though at different universities. We had a lot to talk about, and the more we talked the more we realized how much alike we were. The relationship soon became sexual, and that deepened our love for each other. I had truly found the intimate relationship that I had wanted.

After a month, we agreed to date each other exclusively. I felt a growing commitment to her. We only lived about a mile apart, so we began to spend most of our evenings together. It was a natural thing to make the decision to live together. I felt that we had the "chemistry" necessary to make the thing go. And I believed that living together would deepen our commitment and our intimacy.

I moved into her apartment. We then had to figure out the finances. We agreed on a plan for paying for specific items like rent and food. Everything seemed to be going well. Then, about a month after I had moved in with her, I found out that she had problems with cocaine. She had somehow kept that part of her life separate from me. I asked her to stop snorting the stuff and to get treatment. She refused. I felt betrayed. I asked her what or who was first in her life. I was stunned when she said it was the cocaine.

I was in agony. I had a lot of beautiful memories already, and we had only known each other for a few months. But as she became more irresponsible with her money and failed to pay specific bills, our relationship deteriorated. Finally, I decided to simply walk away from the relationship. That was tough, because I had really committed myself to her and I expected this to be a long-term relationship. But she had made it clear that I was not her first commitment in life. Maybe I should have tried to stay and help her. But I thought I knew her, and I guess I never really did.

---

92 million unmarried and single Americans, comprising 42 percent of the adult population (18 years and older)(U.S. Census Bureau 2007c). Of those, 60 percent had never been married, while the others were either divorced or widowed.

Why People Are Single

There is both a voluntary and an involuntary singlehood. That is, some people are single by choice, and some are single because of various barriers to marriage (Frazier et al. 1996). Those who are involuntarily single may struggle to find some kind of positive spin on their singlehood (Reynolds, Wetherell, and Taylor 2007).

Singles offer a variety of reasons for not marrying (Straus 2006). For some, it is preferable to being in an unhappy or unfulfilling relationship. For some, it is an impediment to a valued career. They may delay marriage in order to establish themselves firmly in a career, or they may forego marriage completely in order to devote themselves totally to a career.

Another reason is the (mistaken) belief that single people have better sex lives than married people. Maintaining personal freedom is still another reason; 62 percent of the unmarried men in one study believed that they risked losing their personal freedom if they married (Whitehead and Popenoe 2004). Personal freedom means such things as the freedom to be spontaneous, to travel, to pursue interests, and to change careers without having to worry about the consequences of those actions for a family. Desire for personal growth is yet another reason. For instance, one reason given by never-married Chinese and Japanese American women was that marriage would interfere with their educational aspirations (Ferguson 2000).

In addition to the reasons people give, a number of social factors affect the likelihood of staying single. Those who are gay cannot marry in most states; they remain single but not by choice. For heterosexuals, wars, depressions, and changing sex ratios affect marriage rates. The **sex ratio,** the number of males per 100 females, varies from decade to decade. In 2006, there were 86 unmarried men age 18 and older for every 100 unmarried women in the United States (U.S. Census Bureau 2007c). The sex ratio among African Americans is particularly severe. Compared to whites, young black men have higher rates of mortality, imprisonment, and homosexuality. Black women, in consequence, have reduced choices and are more likely than whites to find themselves in a state of involuntary singlehood (Crowder and Tolnay 2000).

Intimacy and Life Satisfaction

While our needs for intimacy differ, all of us require intimate relationships. How do singles handle their intimacy needs? Although it is reasonable to think that all singles are looking for a romantic partner, a national survey by the Pew Research Center reported that among all singles only 16 percent say they are currently looking for such a partner (Rainie and Madden 2006). Does this indicate that most singles are content with their situation? How do singles compare with those who are married in terms of intimacy and life satisfaction?

Intimacy. Singles may fulfill some of their intimacy needs by living with parents, friends, or acquaintances or by cohabiting. Those who live alone have a greater challenge. Whatever their living arrangements, however, singles employ a variety of means to establish relationships with others. They use the more traditional means of meeting people through family, friends, school, and religious groups. They also employ the relatively newer methods of singles' bars, groups, ads, and dating services. The popularity of such methods shows that singles are aware of their needs for intimacy and are anxious to establish and maintain intimate relationships. By establishing a number of relationships, singles in effect may create their own families. A **network family** is a support group of nonkin. One does not live with the network family, but the members are always available to help and support each other in the same way as a family related by blood or marriage.

Friends are particularly important for singles. In essence, a friend is someone whom you like as a person; enjoy being with; feel comfortable and relaxed around; can share thoughts, feelings, cares, and hopes with; and feel free to call on in time of need (Lauer and Lauer 1999b). Close friends provide singles with a number of benefits. Because friendships are intimate relationships, they enhance singles' health. Friends can encourage and support personal growth, help with difficult decisions, and provide various kinds of support and help in difficult times. In a study of 99 adults living alone in a retirement community, Potts (1997) found that those with high-quality friendships had lower levels of depression. Another study of 796 residents in retirement communities reported that interacting with friends was related to life satisfaction (Hong and Duff 1997).

Of course, friends are important to singles whatever their age. In her study of the lives of never married women, Simon (1987) pointed out the crucial importance of friendships. The women had pictures of their friends on display in their homes or apartments. They would talk about their friends when discussing such things as work, travel, recreation, and retirement. A common pattern involved having a close, daily, long-term friendship with another person (usually another woman) while also joining a circle of two to five additional friends. The circle might meet once or twice a week, either as a group or in pairs.

The women tended to develop their bonds during their 30s, when it began to appear that they would not marry. They found other women who had made the same choice (or who had the choice forced on them by circumstances) and cemented what would be long-term relationships. As the friendships developed, the women made long-term plans, including plans about what they would do after retirement. Thus, the women have a number of close companions, at least some of whom have shared a series of experiences with them. They have established effective network families that provide them with many of the intimate needs of marriage.

A more recent study, of single, middle-class women, reported that each of the 46 women in the sample struggled early on with her singleness (Trimberger 2005). Seven to nine years later, the researcher interviewed the women again. Of the 27 who were still single, each had made peace with her situation and indicated a contentedness with singleness. Among the important factors in their adjustment were intimate friend networks, satisfying work, and a supportive community. In other words, having meaningful relationships and satisfying work were crucial to their adjustment.

Two areas of concern remain. What about the fulfillment to be found in sexual relationships and in children? Of course, many single women do have sexual relationships. But we have already pointed out that singles have sex less often than marrieds and report less sexual satisfaction than marrieds. It seems that, at least in terms of the sexual aspect of intimacy, singles are less likely than marrieds to find fulfillment. Even those who choose to be single may find themselves struggling with their sexual needs.

There is also the question of children. We explore more fully the role of children in meeting our intimacy needs in chapter 12. However, it is important to note here that some people, regardless of whether they are married, regard children as an important part of their fulfillment.

Victor Callan (1986) studied 42 single women who said they wanted to remain childless and 60 who wanted one or more children. He found that those who preferred to be childless tended to be more pessimistic and less loving than the others. Those who preferred either no children or only one child were more concerned about their financial and social independence than those who desired two children. Thus, various factors enter into our desire to have or not have children. As in the case of getting married, one factor is the concern about one's independence and freedom. Interestingly, even some of those women who were more concerned about independence still wanted to have one child.

Increasing numbers of single women are having children. The proportion of births to unmarried mothers varies considerably by race and ethnicity, but, as pointed out in chapter 1, it has increased among all groups. In 2006, as shown in table 1.1, the percentage of births to unmarried mothers was 26.6 percent for non-Hispanic whites, 49.9 percent for Hispanics, 70.7 percent for African Americans, and 16.9 percent for Asian Americans.

Single women who have children are more likely to be in the lower socioeconomic levels. As such, they are doubly handicapped in their efforts at parenting. Not only do they lack the help of husbands and fathers, but they also must deal with the problem of limited financial resources. Single mothers are the most impoverished group in the nation. They may fulfill some of their intimacy needs through their children, but the costs in terms of financial and emotional stress are high.

Those who do not have children appear to adapt well in the long run. Using national data, Zhang and Hayward (2001) found that being childless did not increase either the loneliness or the depression among elderly divorced, widowed, and never-married individuals.

Life Satisfaction.   How do singles fare in terms of life satisfaction? When singles are asked about the factors that go into their life satisfaction, their answers are similar to those of other Americans. Good health is one of the most important factors, although singles are less likely than marrieds to enjoy good health. Other factors mentioned by singles or discovered by researchers include career, personal growth, financial security, love, sex, and a social support network (Barrett 1999; Taylor et al. 2001).

A study of male and female never-marrieds focused on the role of social support and loneliness in life satisfaction (Cockrum and White 1985). The researchers found that friends were important to both males and females. Visiting friends enabled them to deal with loneliness. There were gender differences, however. For men, life satisfaction depended on having a network of individuals with whom they could share their interests and their values. For women, life satisfaction was higher when they had people with whom they could establish close, emotional bonds.

So how satisfied are singles? In their interviews with a small sample of never-married and divorced women, Lewis and Moon (1997) found mixed results in terms of life satisfaction. The women identified advantages to being single, including not having to be a caretaker for a man and freedom to do as they pleased. At the same time, they expressed concerns about the lack of intimacy, the lack of children, and growing old alone. On the whole, they were content with being single but also acknowledged a sense of loss in not having a mate or children.

Mixed results also appeared in a study of never-married older women in a Canadian city (Baumbusch 2004). The women valued their independence, their ability to be alone, and were generally satisfied with their single status. They did, however, acknowledge some problems with loneliness and the lack of a social support network.

Finally, surveys consistently show that more married people than single people are happy with their lives. In a National Opinion Research Center (1999) survey, for example, the proportions who said they were very happy were 40 percent of married men and 41 percent of married women; 19 percent of divorced men and 20 percent of divorced women; and 20 percent of both men and women who had never been married. Similarly, in a survey by the Pew Research Center (2006a) far more married (43 percent) than unmarried (24 percent) said they were very happy. To sum up, although some singles—whether never-married, divorced, or widowed—prefer their lifestyle and find it satisfying, overall, singles are less likely than the married to perceive themselves as being very happy.

SUMMARY

A first problem for those who want to develop an intimate relationship is to find people with whom to connect. Such people are likely to be near the places you normally frequent. Some young people try to facilitate the process by hanging out and hooking up.

Dating is the typical way to develop intimate relationships. Two of the most important qualities that make someone an appealing dating partner are physical attractiveness and similarity. People find dates at school, at work, at recreational facilities, through friends, through newspaper ads or Web sites, and by using dating services.

Dating has numerous functions, including recreation, companionship, gaining status, socialization, and mate selection. Every society has norms about dating that regulate such things as who initiates the date. Patterns of dating differ, however, among various groups in the society.

Violence occurs in many dating situations. A substantial number of people are victimized by some kind of violence while on a date. Men and women both are perpetrators of violence. In many cases, the violence takes the form of sexual aggression, ranging from the use of verbal threats and coercion to engage in sexual behavior to date rape.

As a couple dates more frequently or exclusively, they use various mechanisms to build intimacy. Three very important mechanisms are self-disclosure, treating intimacy as an exchange relationship, and nurturing interdependence and commitment.

The breakup of a relationship is a common experience. Four ways that people respond to a deteriorating relationship are exit (leaving), voice (confronting and attempting to work through problems), loyalty (sticking it out), and neglect (refusal to admit problems, allowing the relationship to die).

Some Americans voluntarily or involuntarily remain single. A number of factors are involved in people remaining single: career aspirations, the belief that sex is better and readily available to singles, the belief that marriage is a threat to personal freedom, and the desire for personal growth. Social conditions like the sex ratio also affect marriage rates. Singles have various ways to establish and maintain intimate relationships. Many singles prefer their lifestyle and find it satisfying, but overall, singles are less likely than the married to agree that they have happy and exciting lives.

Principles for Enhancing Intimacy

1. If you are dating for purposes of potential mate selection, do not make the mistake of looking for perfection. As Sills (1984) points out, we sometimes sabotage ourselves by limiting our choices. From a field of 10, we only will date the top 2. Even if 2 of the 10 are totally unacceptable to us, this still leaves 6 remaining possibilities whom we also reject. Sills suggests that a mate could probably be found among the 6, while a status symbol will be found in those top 2.

2. If you are female, support equality in relationships, and are attracted to a certain male, ask him for a date. This is one way to overcome his shyness or to find out

quickly whether he is interested in you. However, do recognize that some people may label your actions as aggressive, unfeminine, or even as a sexual come-on.

3. Because violence is an all-too-frequent occurrence in dating, avoid relationships with troubled individuals. Learn the warning signs of potential relationship violence. And if violence should occur, don't persist in the relationship and do seek the aid and advice of a parent, friend, or counselor.

4. Longer courtships generally result in more satisfying marriages. Get to know the person you plan to marry;

that is, find out about his or her values, interests, goals, patterns of behavior, and familial relationships. Every indicator suggests that this will improve your chances for a successful and lasting marriage.

5. Although the breaking up of a relationship is often a painful process, it is also often a necessary and, in the long run, beneficial one.

6. If you decide to remain single, attend to your intimacy needs by cultivating and maintaining close friendships.

KEY TERMS

equity   *119*
hanging out   *108*
hooking up   *108*
network family   *123*
nonverbal cues   *111*

norms   *108*
propinquity   *108*
rape   *118*
self-disclosure   *118*
sex ratio   *123*

sexual aggression   *117*
socialization   *113*
status   *113*

ON THE WEB   Getting Involved

The prospect of dating presents a number of challenges for the individual wishing to find a suitable partner, particularly when hoping for a long-term relationship. Increasingly, the Internet is seen as a viable source for making contact with potential partners as well as for finding information about how to meet and date successfully.

Two interesting Web sites are:

Directory of Dating
http://www.directoryofdating.com

This site lists and provides links to online dating services by category, rates them, posts reviews, and names any sites that are not recommended because of complaints received.

Youth Resource
http://www.youthresource.com

This site is for lesbian, gay, and transgendered teeenagers. It includes many resources, including a gallery, chat room,

www.mhhe.com/lauer⁷e

and links to HIV-awareness and political activist sites.

Use these two sites to enlarge your understanding with the following projects:

1. Study the Directory of Dating site and explore some of the links. Make a report to the class on the following topic: how the Directory of Dating site illustrates, adds to, or disagrees with materials in the text on what attracts someone as a dating partner, the functions of dating, and ways to build intimacy.

2. Based on your examination of the Youth Resources site, list the potential difficulties and dangers that lesbian, gay, and transgendered youth face when confronting the dating issue. What advice would you give to a group of such youth about the dating process?

~ FALLING IN LOVE ~

LEARNING OBJECTIVES

After reading and studying chapter 6, you should be able to

1. Define *love* in terms of the ancient Greek words for it—*storge, philia, eros,* and *agape.*
2. Describe the process of falling in love.
3. Discuss how people can tell whether they're falling in love.
4. Distinguish between passionate and companionate love.
5. Outline the historical development of the concept of passionate love.

6. Explain the measures of passionate love.
7. Describe the process of moving from passionate to companionate love.
8. Distinguish between what it means to love and to like someone.
9. Define the different styles of loving and their implications for relationships.
10. Discuss the causes and consequences of jealousy.

Millions of American men and women of all ages watch soap operas on television. What is shown is important, because such programs help shape people's expectations and values about love relationships. Watch one of the programs, such as *Days of Our Lives* or *As the World Turns.* Look at each of the love relationships shown and write up an analysis by addressing the following questions.

1. What kinds of love do family members show each other? How does that square with your ideals?
2. What kinds of heterosexual love relationships exist? To what extent do they agree or disagree with materials in

this chapter? How would you evaluate the relationships in terms of your own values?
3. What, if any, kinds of love relationships are missing? Why do you think they are not a part of the program?
4. If the love relationships shown were typical of real life, how would you summarize the nature of love today?

If the entire class participates in this project, have different members watch different programs. Compare the results. Are soap operas giving a consistent portrait of love? If so, why? If not, what are the implications?

How many times have you been in love? This was one of the love-related questions a researcher (Montgomery 2005) asked of a group of young men and women aged 12 to 24 years Think for a moment about the answers you would give. Then look at figure 6.1. It shows the responses to the number of times the young people said they had been in love, broken down by age group and gender. Note that males in all the age groups tended to fall in love more often than did the females. Also note that the older the group, the less often they believed they had been in love. For all ages, incidentally, a majority said they had been in love no more than once or twice.

So if your answer was once or twice, you are typical. If you said "never," however, you have missed out, so far, on one of the more important experiences of life. For scientists have studied not only the experience of love and beliefs about love, but also the way in which love affects emotional and physical health. And the conclusion is that love is crucial to your well-being. All of us, heterosexual or homosexual, male or female, have a need for the love that is found in romantic relationships (Isay 2006). Thus, a survey of psychologists working in academia, university counseling centers, and community mental health centers identified the experience and expression of love as one of the important factors in the "good life" (Kernes and Kinnier 2005). And research on the brain indicates that humans are "hard-wired" for love, so that your well-being depends as much on love as it does on food, water, and air to breathe (Lewis, Lannon, and Amini 2001; Fisher 2004). It is not surprising, then, that the more deeply you are in love, the happier you are likely to be (Willi 1997). But if you look for love, what

exactly is it you're seeking? What does it mean to love? We use the term in many different ways, obviously. We say that we love pizza, love our new car, love to ski, love our parents, love our spouses, and so forth.

In this chapter, we will try to bring some clarity to this "love" that people agree is so important in their lives. We will discuss the multifaceted nature of loving another person. We will look at the different ways of loving. And we will examine one of the barriers to a loving relationship—jealousy.

THE MEANING OF LOVE

When we use the same word to express our feelings for food, activities, possessions, and people, it is little wonder that it is difficult to define what we mean by love. When applied to a lover or spouse, the term means, among other things, a deep and passionate affection. But there is more to love than passion. In fact, there is more to love than feelings.

The richness of the term *love* is illustrated by four ancient Greek words that are all translated as love (Lewis 1960). **Storge** (pronounced store-gay) is the kind of love found in the affection between parents and their children. It is, Lewis (1960:54) pointed out, the least discriminating kind of love, because "almost anyone can become an object of affection: the ugly, the stupid, even the exasperating." As such, it is to be cherished, because it is love in spite of the lack of those qualities we discussed earlier as the main factors in attraction.

The second word is **philia** (fill-ee-ah). It is the kind of love that exists between friends. To the Greeks, this

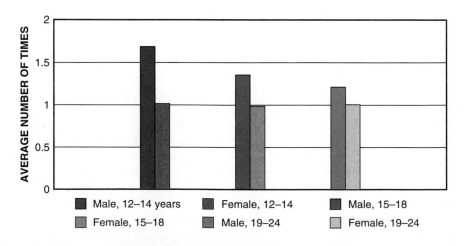

FIGURE 6.1 **How Many Times Have You Been In Love?**
Source: Adapted from Montgomery 2005.

was the highest form of love, for *philia* referred to a warm and close relationship that has the characteristics of intimacy we have discussed—sharing, affection, and commitment. It is an intense sharing between two people who have similar perspectives on life.

Eros (air-os) is the third love. *Eros,* from which we get "erotic," is love between men and women. It includes sexual love. Aristotle said that *eros* makes people long to be in each other's presence. In other words, *eros* is more than lust. It is more than a desire for sex. It is desire for sex with a particular person. In *eros,* one is preoccupied with thoughts about the person and longing to be with the person. As Lewis (1960:150) put it, "it is the very mark of Eros that . . . we had rather share unhappiness with the Beloved than be happy on any other terms."

Finally, there is **agape** (a-gah-pay), a love that is independent of one's feelings for another. To practice *agape* is to act on behalf of the well-being of someone else, whether you like that person or not. Like *storge, agape* does not depend on the attractiveness of the other. Rather, it is a love in which we *will* to act beneficially toward another.

We will meet these types again as we discuss recent studies of love. Modern research underscores the wisdom in the ancient distinctions. Love, as an old song puts it, is a "many-splendored" rather than a simple thing. Or as *symbolic interactionists* argue, love can mean different

Symbolic Interaction Theory Applied

things to different people. Hendrick and Hendrick (1992:113) point out that love "is complex, varied, and means different things to different people at different times." To understand the place of love in any individual's life, we must know what love means to that person. Thus, for one person "love" may be primarily a cognitive obsession with someone, while for another person "love" may mean an intense emotional yearning to be with someone, and for still another "love" may mean trying to care for and please someone.

WHEN YOU FALL IN LOVE

When you fall in love, exactly what is it into which you are falling? In terms of our discussion so far, most people no doubt have *eros* in mind. But how do we fall in love? How do we get to the point with someone at which we feel intensely and are preoccupied with him or her? And how can we tell if it is really love or something else that we feel?

The Process of Falling

In *How to Make Anyone Fall in Love with You* (Lowndes 1997), the author asserts that falling in love results from

Love is expressed in many different ways.

a chemical secreted by the nervous system. To make someone fall in love with you, you have to somehow get the other person's nervous system to produce the chemical. The author suggests 85 techniques that will trigger the production, thereby convincing the other person that he or she is in love with you.

Many of the techniques are simple, such as the use of compliments. Do they work? Clearly, when you do such things as compliment someone, you are likely to enhance positive feelings between the two of you. Whether you can actually "make" someone fall in love with you by using these various techniques is questionable. But the popularity of such books (this is only one of many) illustrates the desire of people for love relationships. The books make the assumption that falling in love is something more than a chance event that occurs when two people suddenly realize there is "chemistry" between them. Indeed, falling in love is, for most of us, a complex process.

The Love Prone.   As noted earlier, most young people have at least one experience of falling in love. Typically it occurs around the age of 17 (Regan et al. 2004). And this is true for all racial/ethnic groups and for both males and females. There are differences in how quickly people fall in love. Men are more likely to believe in, and to experience, "love at first sight" (Bowman 2001; Montgomery 2005).

Some people, however, go beyond just falling in love at first sight. They are love prone. One could even call them love addicted. Sometimes they are in love with several individuals at the same time. They also tend to fall in love for the first time at a younger age than do others. They believe that sex and chemistry, rather than qualities like trust, are important to an enduring romance. Although they tend to have sex more frequently than others, they report less satisfaction with their love lives.

The Rest of Us.   Although some people do experience "love at first sight," including some who are not love prone, falling in love is a process for most of us. Ira Reiss (Reiss and Lee 1988) characterized the development of love in terms of four separate but interrelated processes: rapport, self-revelation, mutual dependency, and intimacy need fulfillment.

When two people first meet, they assess the extent to which they feel comfortable and attracted to each other. Is the other person easy to talk with? Do you like being around that person? Do you seem to have certain attitudes, values, and interests in common? If so, you may quickly develop a **rapport,** a harmonious and comfortable relationship.

Once rapport is established, you feel relaxed with the other person and the two of you are likely to engage in self-revelation (or, in terms we have used, self-disclosure). We have pointed out that increasing self-disclosure is a characteristic of a developing intimacy. Except for in those rare cases of love at first sight, it is difficult for us to feel love for another until there is some mutual knowledge about each other. You may feel strongly attracted to someone. You may have sexual desire for someone. But falling in love is more than attraction and sexual desire. It is attraction to and desire for a person with certain qualities, attitudes, and mannerisms.

Self-disclosure not only provides two people with the knowledge about each other that is an essential ingredient to falling in love. It also leads to the next process—mutual dependency. You become mutually dependent because you do things that require the other person to be present:

One needs the other person as an audience for one's jokes, as a confidant(e) for the expression of one's fears and wishes, as

a partner for one's sexual experiences, and so on. Thus, habits of behaving develop that cannot be fulfilled alone, and in this way one becomes dependent on the other person (Reiss and Lee 1988:101).

Finally, then, mutual dependency leads to the fulfillment of our intimacy needs. We all need someone to love, someone in whom we can confide, someone with whom we can share experiences, someone who loves and appreciates us. As such intimacy needs are fulfilled, we are falling in love.

Reiss points out that the four processes are interdependent. If something happens to any one of them, it will adversely affect the development or maintenance of a love relationship. For example, if problems of some sort lead to conflict and a reduction in self-disclosure, mutual dependency and the fulfillment of intimacy needs tend to be reduced also. That leads to a breakdown of rapport, which may in turn depress the amount of self-disclosure. The relationship could go into a downward spiral toward breaking up if something doesn't happen to reverse the process.

His Falling and Her Falling.   Although the process described by Reiss applies to both males and females, some gender differences exist in experiences of falling in love. Women report being in love fewer times than do men and are less likely than men to believe in love at first sight (Montgomery 2005). Men tend to say "I love you" earlier in a relationship than do women, and to say it with a sexual agenda in mind (Brantley, Knox, and Zusman 2002). An analysis of 300 Valentine Day announcements found that women stressed love and fidelity more than men did, while men stressed praise and commitment (but not fidelity) somewhat more than women did (Quintero and Koestner 2006). Typically, women are more concerned with relationships than are men. Thus, they come to a relationship with greater concerns about emotional closeness and communication, while men have greater concerns about practical help and sex.

These differences appear in different cultural settings. A study of an ethnically diverse sample of university students (Anglo-Celtic, Chinese, other Asian, and European) reported that the women generally viewed love as more friendship oriented and less permissive than did men (Dion and Dion 1993). And a study of Mexican American students found that the women gave more importance than did the men to mutual respect (treating each other with special regard or consideration) in love relationships (Castaneda 1993).

Personal

Falling in Love—Twice

Laura is a vibrant woman in her late thirties. She talks about falling in and out of love and then back in love again. She also tells about the ways in which her parents influenced her love relationships and her need for intimacy:

My first experience with falling in love came in college. I married my first real love. Prior to that I don't recall having had serious feelings about anyone. Except, of course, for a few infatuations.

My initial attraction to Brian was his understanding and ability to listen and respond to me. I missed this kind of intimacy with my parents. I was never close to either of them. I don't think they know, or ever did know, much about me. Mother was not a good listener, and I didn't talk much with my father. They were close with each other, but I wasn't included. I grew up without learning how to be intimate with another person.

So I was immediately hooked by Brian because he paid attention to me. He looked like a hippie, with his beard and worn jeans. My parents didn't like him, and mother told me I would get bored with him. We were just good friends for several years. Then he went away for a year. He kept in touch through his letters. I lost 20 pounds while he was gone. I really missed him. But I guess the weight loss was good. When he returned, he obviously found me even more attractive than before and started pursuing a love relationship.

Our romance was an adventure. My parents had never been interested in cultural activities. Brian took me to poetry readings, classical concerts, and dinners with fascinating people. We stayed up some nights talking and discussing ideas until dawn. He wrote stories and poetry and shared them with me. We dreamed of him as an English professor in a university some day.

Brian eventually proposed and I accepted. But there was a price to pay. Brian put his dream of being a professor on hold and went into business. We were married soon after. It was wonderful at first. I felt like we were little kids playing house. It was fun to cook, to have friends over, to be together. It was the first time in my life that I could share my thoughts and feelings with someone.

After some years, however, I got restless. There were times that I felt too close to Brian. I shared so much of myself with him that I began to feel the need for space and distance. The intimacy I had longed for was now suffocating me. I didn't share my feelings with Brian, though. I didn't understand what was happening to me, only that I felt closed in. I felt trapped and knew that I had to get out. The intimacy of our relationship seemed more painful to me than the estrangement with which I had grown up. Brian was shocked when I told him. But he finally agreed to a separation and, before the year was over, to a divorce.

I adjusted to being single, I guess. But within a year, a new man entered my life. Kent was divorced. He was sophisticated, traveled to France once a year to buy wine, and owned horses. I truly believed I had found my white knight. This time I fell in love with a beautifully decorated, intriguing package. The only thing missing was the closeness that I had experienced with Brian. My intimacy level with Kent was more like that with my parents. I had all the space I needed. Kent had a family much like mine, so he was also comfortable with less intimacy.

Kent and I lived together for two years, and the experience caused me to reevaluate myself as well as my marriage and relationship with Brian. Frankly, I was confused. I missed him and the intimacy we had shared. Yet I still remembered my feelings of suffocation and of being too close. My confusion led me to several months of counseling, a good deal of soul-searching, and finally to a better understanding of myself. I also began to realize that I still loved Brian and wanted to share my life with him. Fortunately, Brian and I had maintained our friendship, despite the divorce, and gradually our relationship once again became an intimate one. We were remarried two years later—that was over 10 years ago. At times it hasn't been easy. I have had to work at keeping the barriers down, and Brian has had to work at allowing me enough space. But this time, it's for keeps!

How Can You Tell If It's Love?

When a student told us that she was "madly in love" with a young man, we asked her how she knew what she felt was really love. She looked startled for a moment and then replied, "You just *know*. You *know* when you're in love." However, others have offered more specific ways of knowing. For example, a group of German undergraduates included the following among the ways they "knew" they were in love with someone: positive feelings when they were with the person; trust in the other person; and sexual arousal (Lamm and Wiesmann 1997). Actually, it isn't as easy as it might seem to know when we are feeling love or something else.

Misattribution of Arousal.   Two social psychologists, Ellen Berscheid and Elaine Walster (1974), have set forth a "two-component" theory of love. The theory is based on the fact that differing emotions can produce similar kinds of physical arousal (such as a pounding heart or sweating). In a classic experiment, Schachter and Singer (1962) injected volunteer subjects with adrenaline. Among other things, the drug increases heart and breathing rates. The subjects were told that they were testing a new vitamin. Some were told that they would have physical symptoms. Others were told nothing or were led to expect symptoms (such as numbness) that they would not experience. Each group was sent to a waiting room for a 20-minute period. While there, a confederate of the experimenter acted extremely happy in some cases and angry in others. The confederate's behavior did not affect those who had been correctly informed of what symptoms to expect. But those who had been misinformed or not informed tended to feel the same kind of emotion displayed by the confederate. In other words, exactly the same kind of physical symptoms were defined as happiness by some and anger by others.

Building on the work of Schachter and Singer, Berscheid and Walster (1974) suggested that at least in some cases the feeling of love may be a case of **misattribution of arousal,** attributing the wrong emotion to physical arousal. In other words, there may be times when we believe we feel passionate love because we are aroused and the conditions are such that the conclusion is reasonable. Additional research supports this theory.

A series of subsequent experiments continued to confirm the notion that people can wrongly attribute an arousal to romantic feelings. For example, in one experiment the researchers questioned people at amusement parks (Meston and Frohlich 2003). They questioned some as they were waiting to ride a roller coaster and others as they were emerging from the ride. They showed the men who participated a photograph of a woman and the women a photograph of a man. They then asked the respondents to rate those shown in the photos on their attractiveness and desirability as a date. Among those respondents with a nonromantic partner for the ride, both males and females rated the person in the photo as more attractive and more desirable as a date when exiting the ride than when waiting to go on it. In other words, the arousal caused by the ride enhanced romantic-type feelings toward the people in the photos.

In another experiment, researchers paired up males and females who were strangers to each other in a number of game-like physical activities (Lewandowski and Aron 2004). The activities varied in the degree to which they were arousing. Afterward, the subjects filled out a questionnaire that measured romantic attraction. Those who had participated in the highly arousing activities were significantly more attracted romantically to their partners than were those in the less arousing activities.

Clearly, then, in some situations we may mistakenly attribute arousal to a feeling of love. It may not be wise to define your feelings as love when you meet someone after just being aroused in some way. Arousal can occur through exercise, drinking, caffeine, stimulating movies, and so forth. Perhaps some of the cases of love at first sight are the result of just such circumstances.

Some Tests of Love.   So how can you tell if it's love? Peele and Brodsky (1976) offer some interesting questions to consider. These questions will help you decide if what you are feeling is a loving and healthy relationship or what they call a form of addiction. They point out that some people get into a relationship in order to deal with problems. Such relationships are not really love. Rather, people experiencing a healthy love should be able to respond positively to most of the following six questions (Peele and Brodsky 1976:83–84):

1. Do you and your lover each believe in your own personal value? That is, do you think well of yourself as a person? Do you have high self-esteem?

2. Has your relationship improved each of you? Are you in some way a better, stronger, more attractive individual? Do you value the relationship because of that improvement?

3. Do you each maintain some separate interests? Do you have meaningful relationships apart from your lover?

4. Is your relationship an integral part of your total life rather than a kind of side interest?

5. Are you each capable of respecting the other's growth and interests without being possessive or jealous?

6. Are you friends? Would you still want to relate to each other even if you weren't lovers?

Such questions take us beyond *eros*, the passionate kind of love we have been discussing so far. It may not be possible to answer all of the questions early in a relationship. But neither can you answer the question of whether it's love you feel for someone very early in a relationship. The ultimate test of a loving relationship is time. If it is possible to respond positively to the questions over a period of time, you will be able to look back and say, "I fell in love."

PASSIONATE VERSUS COMPANIONATE LOVE

If someone had all the qualities you desired in another person, would you marry that person even if you were not in love with him or her? The answer is, probably not. In fact, some of our students think the question itself is an odd one. They argue that love is the foundation for marriage, and that anyone would be foolish to even consider marriage for any other reason.

But what kind of love? The love that most people have in mind when they think of the precondition for an exclusive relationship, living together, or marriage is *eros*. Such love is sometimes called romantic love or passionate love. We will use the term **passionate love** and define it as

TABLE 6.1   Passionate versus Companionate Love

Passionate love	Companionate love
Intensely emotional	Strong emotional bonds
Persistent, strong sexual desire	Varying sexual desire
Emphasis on being great lovers	Emphasis on being best friends
Volatile	Stable
Need to idealize the other	Effort to be realistic about the other
Consuming—dominates one's life	Supporting—frees one to grow
Subject to strong jealousy	Minimal jealousy, if any
Limited in duration	Can last a lifetime

a preoccupation and intense longing for union with a particular other. Passionate love can throw you into a state of obsession with someone, awaken emotions (e.g., intense joy and jealousy) that you don't usually experience, and affect your sleep patterns and your appetite (Fischer et al. 2006; Brand et al. 2007).

In contrast, **companionate love** is affection for and commitment to someone with whom one is deeply involved. Thus, companionate love is similar to *philia*. Table 6.1 lists the important qualities of the two kinds of love.

But does everyone agree that passionate love is necessary for marriage or some other kind of exclusive commitment? And how long can passionate love last? In this section, we will address these questions. Then we will look a little more closely at the experience of passionate love.

Is it love or misattribution of arousal?

The Emergence of Passionate Love

People have always experienced passionate love, but the notion that passionate love is a precondition for a relationship like marriage is a relatively new idea in human history. In fact, in Greek and Roman mythology love and marriage were not connected with each other. The goddess of marriage was different from the goddess of love. In the past, writers extolled sexual love, and some extolled nonsexual kinds of love, but in neither case was marriage the context. Marriages, throughout most of human history, were contracted for various purposes, such as security, help, and procreation, but not for love.

Then something happened during the twelfth century in Europe. A new ideal about the relationship between men and women emerged, the ideal of "courtly love." At first, the ideal was confined mainly to the aristocracy and spread by troubadours, knights who composed and sang poems. The love they wrote and sang about was something new: It involved a preoccupation with the beloved, a longing for union with the beloved, a proclamation of the lover's undying commitment and loyalty.

No single explanation exists for the sudden appearance and spread of the ideal of passionate love. It may have been due, in part, to the rediscovery of ancient Greek and Roman writings, to a reaction against the brutality of the era, to the shortage of noble women compared to the number of knights, and to antichurch feelings (Reiss and Lee 1988:98). At any rate, sex was placed in a new context, a new kind of relationship between men and women. And while originally the relationship was one that was cultivated outside of marriage, the ideal gradually spread to the premarital state. Romantic liaisons eventually became romantic courtships. The ideals expressed by the twelfth-century troubadours ultimately became the experience expected by young people as the route to marriage.

Romantic, or passionate, love as a precondition of marriage is still not universal. However, romantic love is increasingly the preferred and actual basis for selecting someone as a dating or marriage partner (Hatfield and Rapson 1993; Jones 2007).

There are those who bemoan rather than applaud this emphasis on passionate love. Some even consider it an enemy of a lasting marriage because it cannot be maintained over an indefinite period of time. It is an exhilarating experience while it lasts, and for many people it is a time of personal growth as the individual exposes himself or herself to new risks, new possibilities, and new experiences (Person 2006). But the point is that it does not and cannot last indefinitely. The unrealistic expectations of bliss created by our emphasis on passionate love can lead to a considerable amount of "misery, disappointment, and disillusionment" in marriage or long-term relationships (Crosby 1991:20).

The Experience of Passionate Love

How often have you had the experience of passionate love? Not everyone has had such an experience. And among those who have, some experience it only once, while others experience it many times in their lifetime. Often it is a bittersweet experience—the individual may have trouble concentrating on other matters or may be frustrated because of separation from the loved one. Adolescents, those from about 12 or 13 to 21 or 22 years of age, are particularly prone to falling into a state of passionate love.

Measuring Passionate Love. Passionate love has been compared with the "high" of certain drugs (amphetamines). But more than feelings are involved. We also think and behave in certain ways when we have passionate love for someone. Hatfield and Sprecher (1986) have developed a scale for measuring these various facets. The scale helps us better understand the nature of passionate love.

In brief, if you are passionately in love with someone, according to the scale you would tend to do the following:

Think in certain ways, such as
- persistently reflecting about the other person.
- idealizing his or her qualities (such as kindness and beauty).
- desiring to know and be known by the other person.

Feel in certain ways, such as
- having sexual desires for the other person.
- feeling bad when things are not going well between the two of you.
- desiring a close and permanent relationship.
- feeling physically aroused by the other person.

Behave in certain ways, such as
- trying to find out how the person feels about you.
- studying the other person.
- serving and helping the other person.

You can measure the extent to which you are now, or have been, passionately in love with someone by taking the short form of the test (figure 6.2). Score your feelings for both someone you believe you love or loved passionately and someone you like. The former score should be much higher. Do the items on the test capture your experience of passionate love? Keep in mind that no two people's experiences are ever precisely the same. Let's look at some research that underscores the point.

Please think of the person whom you love most passionately right now. If you are not in love right now, please think of the last person you loved passionately. If you have never been in love, think of the person whom you came closest to caring for in that way. Keep this person in mind as you complete this section of the questionnaire. (The person you choose should be of the opposite sex if you are heterosexual or of the same sex if you are homosexual.) Try to tell us how you felt at the time when your feelings were most intense.

Mark a number beside each question in accord with the following:

| 1 | 2 | 3 | 4 | 5 | 6 | 7 | 8 | 9 |

Not at all true   Moderately true   Definitely true

_____ 1. I would feel despair if _____ left me.
_____ 2. Sometimes I feel I can't control my thoughts; they are obsessively on _____.
_____ 3. I feel happy when I am doing something to make _____ happy.
_____ 4. I would rather be with _____ than anyone else.
_____ 5. I'd get jealous if I thought _____ were falling in love with someone else.
_____ 6. I yearn to know all about _____.
_____ 7. I want _____—physically, emotionally, mentally.
_____ 8. I have an endless appetite for affection from _____.
_____ 9. For me, _____ is the perfect romantic partner.
_____ 10. I sense my body responding when _____ touches me.
_____ 11. _____ always seems to be on my mind.
_____ 12. I want _____ to know me—my thoughts, my fears, and my hopes.
_____ 13. I eagerly look for signs indicating _____'s desire for me.
_____ 14. I possess a powerful attraction for _____.
_____ 15. I get extremely depressed when things don't go right in my relationship with _____.

FIGURE 6.2 Passionate Love Scale
Source: From Elaine Hatfield and Susan Sprecher, "Measuring Passionate Love in Intimate Relationships" in *Journal of Adolescence* 9:391, December 1986. Copyright © 1986 Academic Press, London, England. Reprinted by permission.

Different Kinds of Lovers. When you were an infant, you became emotionally attached to your mother or other primary caregiver, and you were distressed if you were separated. Depending on your experiences, you may have developed one of three kinds of attachment styles with your mother: secure, avoidant, or anxious/ambivalent (Johnson 1994). These three styles carry over into adult relationships. They predict the nature and quality of intimate relationships, including sexual experiences (Collins et al. 2002; Banse 2004; Schachner and Shaver 2004). Let's look at each style and how each bears on the nature of passionate love.

Secure infants are able to explore and play apart from the mother. They may show distress when left with a stranger but will soon resume exploring and playing. Their security comes from a sense that the mother is sensitive and responsive to their needs. For the adult, a **secure attachment style** means the willingness to get close to others and feel secure in the relationship.

Insecure infants can be either avoidant (somewhat detached from the mother and showing little preference for her over a stranger) or anxious/ambivalent (tending to cling to the mother and showing anxiety around new situations or people). The avoidant infant experiences the mother as somewhat cold, rejecting, and nonresponsive, while the anxious/ambivalent infant has a mother who is inconsistent in her care. As adults, an **avoidant attachment style** is the effort to retain control of one's life by maintaining a certain amount of distance from one's partner. The avoidant adult is more comfortable with self-reliance than with intimacy. The **anxious/ambivalent attachment style** is the opposite: an effort to maintain high levels of closeness and love in the context of anxiety over rejection or abandonment.

The three attachment styles have been found in the love relationships of a nationally representative sample of U.S. adults (Mickelson, Kessler, and Shaver 1997). Most people fell into one of these three styles: 59 percent were secure, 25 percent were avoidant, and 11 percent were anxious/ambivalent (figure 6.3). Those with a secure attachment style have more positive and more secure experiences of love as adults (McCarthy 1999).

With regard to romantic lovers, secure lovers are those who find it fairly easy to get close to others. They feel more trust toward their partners than do those with other styles (Mikulincer 1998). Secure lovers are comfortable depending on others and having others depend on them. They don't worry frequently about a relationship either getting

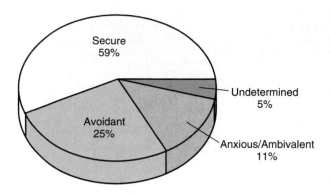

FIGURE 6.3 Types of Lovers
Source: Based on data from Mickelson, Kessler, and Shaver 1997.

too close or being terminated. They have higher levels of commitment and satisfaction in their relationships than do either of the other two types (Simpson 1990).

Avoidant lovers are somewhat uncomfortable about a close relationship with others; they may even structure their social activities in order to minimize closeness (Tidwell, Reis, and Shaver 1996). They don't trust people and are therefore unwilling to depend on others. Compared with the other two types, they report lower levels of intimacy, enjoyment, and positive emotions and higher levels of negative emotions in their relationships. They feel that others often want more intimacy than they are willing to provide.

Finally, anxious/ambivalent lovers perceive a reluctance on the part of others to get close to them. They worry about a partner not staying with them or not loving them. In choosing a mate, they are less willing to compromise with their ideals than are those who are secure or avoidant (Tolmacz 2004). And they desire to "merge completely" with someone else, a desire that may frighten rather than attract the other person.

From Passionate Love to Companionate Love

As we noted, passionate love does not last indefinitely. This is fortunate, because the passionate lover might accomplish very little else in his or her life. Generally, within the first few years of the relationship, passionate love gradually yields to companionate love as the dominant form of a relationship (Hyde and DeLamater 2007). Note, however, that we say the "dominant" form. The two types are not an "either-or" matter. Companionate love exists during the passionate love stage, just as passionate love can remain during the time when companionate love is dominant (Sprecher and Regan 1998). Tucker and Aron (1993) measured the two kinds of love in a small sample

of couples and found a decline in the level of passionate love from engagement to marriage, from childlessness to parenthood, and from parenting to the empty nest. But the decline was relatively small; at least a moderate level of passionate love existed at each stage.

What kind of changes occur, then, as companionate love becomes dominant? Among other things, the lovers stop idealizing each other. They notice imperfections. They find things that are annoying. They may experience periods of boredom and irritation. They may begin to question whether they want to remain in the relationship. They may wonder whether the relationship will ultimately be the satisfying experience they had expected and hoped for. In other words, the realities of life set in. The lovers come down from the mountaintop of romantic fantasy and start coping with the vexations of two imperfect humans trying to establish a long-term, meaningful relationship.

We have known students who lament the inevitability of the process. "I would like to live forever in a state of passionate love," one declared with fervor. But such a statement overlooks a number of things. For one, the state of passionate love has its own vexations, as we have noted. Second, passionate love consumes time and energy. It may divert us from other things that are important to our growth. And third, the passing of passionate love is not the same as the death of passion. As we shall note, people in long-term marriages frequently report a passion for each other (including strong sexual desire) that lasts for 40 years or more. But the passion in a long-term relationship is episodic rather than continuing. As such, it allows people to engage in other matters with their full attention and faculties.

Companionate love, then, does not mean that a relationship has lost its fire. Rather, it means that two people have found a firm basis for a lasting relationship. And that relationship is likely to have times of passion as well as times of friendship. In a real sense, the transition to companionate love is not a loss but a gain. Companionate love is more important for life satisfaction than is passionate love (Kim and Hatfield 2004). And a study of 144 undergraduates reported that those couples experiencing high levels of companionate love had higher-quality relationships (Hecht, Marston, and Larkey 1994). The value of companionate love is illustrated in the following excerpt from an account shared with us by a 50-year-old woman who has been married for over 20 years:

> We couldn't get enough of each other during courtship and for the first year of our marriage. But increasingly after that other responsibilities—our professional commitments and then the kids—seemed to intrude on our lovemaking. We often joked about having to make a date for sex. We warned

What Do You Think?

*There is disagreement about **whether you can fall in love at first sight.** What follows are pro and con arguments. What do you think?*

Pro

You can fall in love at first sight because

- love is based on feelings, which tell you from the first whether you love someone.
- there is someone out there just "made for you" and you'll recognize him or her when you meet.
- initial attraction is the best predictor of a long-term relationship.
- there are people married for decades who agree that they fell in love at first sight.

Con

You can't fall in love at first sight because

- it takes time and reflection to know how you feel about the other person, yourself, and your relationship.
- love is based on shared experiences, not just attraction.
- strong initial feelings for someone are lust not love.
- your feelings of the moment are never a safe guide to a long-term relationship.

---

each other about using it or losing it. At times our hit-or-miss love life was a source of real anxiety. But I am happy to report that we have come to terms with the problem. We are more deeply committed to each other than ever before. True, we find ourselves having sex less frequently than we want, but now we don't worry about it. We know each other well, and we are about as intimate as any couple could be.

LOVING AND LIKING

Can you like someone without loving that person? You probably would answer yes. And can you love someone without liking that person? A lot of people answer no to that question. But recall that *agape* love is independent of feelings for the other, which means that it is possible to love without liking.

Such thoughts raise the question of the relationship between loving and liking. Both the passionate and companionate love styles we have discussed imply that you like as well as love the other. But exactly what does it mean to like someone? Is liking merely a milder form of loving? Are loving and liking similar in some ways? Or are they completely different?

Rubin's Love Scale

One useful way to understanding the relationship between liking and loving is Zick Rubin's (1970) Love Scale. Rubin developed a series of questions that measure both love and liking. The love questions tap into three dimensions of loving: attachment, caring, and intimacy. *Attachment* refers to the desire to be with and

approved by the loved one. *Caring* is the desire to give to the loved one, and *intimacy* is close and confidential communication. Two examples of the kind of questions that measure love are, "I would do almost anything for _____" and "If I could never be with _____, I would feel miserable." Clearly, such statements reflect intense emotion.

The measures of liking are less emotional in tone. They reflect the attitudes and feelings we are likely to have for friends. Two examples are, "In my opinion, _____ is an exceptionally mature person" and "I have great confidence in _____'s good judgment." To like someone, then, means to respect, admire, and enjoy being with that person.

In research using the Rubin scales, there is some overlap between loving and liking (Sternberg 1987). That is, subjects are likely to score the person they are rating relatively high on both scales or low on both scales. But there is a difference between the scores for friends and those for lovers. Both the love and liking scores tend to be higher for dating partners than for same-sex friends. But whereas the liking score for partners is only slightly higher than that for friends, the love score is considerably higher. In other words, when we love someone, we tend to like that person as well and even more than we like our friends.

Love and Friendship

Keith Davis (1985) also has addressed the question of loving and liking. He put it in terms of the characteristics of love versus those of friendship. There are, he says, eight qualities in friendship. According to Davis, friends

1. enjoy being with each other most of the time.
2. accept each other as they are.
3. trust each other to act out of concern for the other's best interest.
4. respect the judgments of each other.
5. help and support each other.
6. share experiences and feelings.
7. understand each other's feelings and thoughts.
8. feel at ease with each other, so that the relationship is based on openness and honesty rather than pretense.

The preceding list adds a few dimensions to the respect, admiration, and enjoyment in the Rubin scale. Liking also means a desire to help and a willingness to share. Love includes all of the eight qualities plus two more. Lovers are characterized by a passion cluster and a caring cluster. The passion cluster includes those

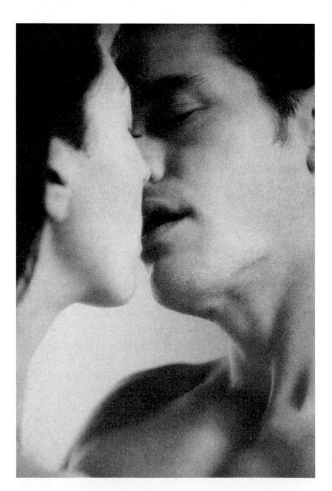

Passionate love is like a "high."

qualities of passionate love that we have already discussed. The caring cluster includes a willingness to give "to the point of extreme self-sacrifice" and a "championing of each other's interests" to ensure the success of each (Davis 1985:24–25).

In Davis's research, spouses and lovers tended to score higher than friends on all the characteristics. However, friends got slightly higher scores on trust and feeling at ease and substantially higher scores on acceptance. Apparently, lovers and spouses make more efforts to change each other than do friends. And they are more likely to be critical of each other than are friends.

Both friends and lovers enhance our well-being. And they do so in some similar and different ways. To be liked by a friend provides us with some experiences that are desirable. We may or may not like our friends quite as strongly as we like our lovers, but liking and being liked by a friend add to the quality of our lives.

A TRIANGULAR THEORY OF LOVE

Liking and loving, passionate love and companionate love—how are they all related? Or are they? Robert J. Sternberg (1987, 1999) believes they are. He developed what he calls a triangular theory of love that shows how various kinds of love are related. His theory asserts that we can understand love best by viewing it in terms of three components. These components can be thought of as the vertices of a triangle. At the top is intimacy. On the left is passion. And on the right is decision/commitment.

Intimacy is a feeling of being connected or bonded to another. Passion is the type of love we have discussed. The decision/commitment component has two factors. In the short run, there is the factor of deciding that you love someone. In the long run, there is the factor of committing yourself to maintain the love over time. As Sternberg noted, these two factors are separable. That is, you can decide you love someone without committing yourself to maintain that love over an extended period of time. And there are people who are committed and have never consciously decided or admitted their love.

Each of these three components is an important factor for relational satisfaction (Lemieux and Hale 2000). A study of 446 couples who were dating, or engaged, or married found that passion does tend to diminish over time, but that commitment tends to increase as the relationship continues (Lemieux and Hale 2002). The commitment scores were highest for the married couples. And a study of 435 Dutch adolescents (12 to 18 years of age) found that the three components were all important factors in both the satisfaction with, and the endurance of, their romantic relationships (Overbeek et al. 2007).

Sternberg used the three components to identify a number of different types of love, ranging from the lack of all three (nonlove) to the "consummate love" that involves the presence of all three (table 6.2). Sternberg defined *liking* as intimacy without either passion or decision/commitment. There is a closeness, a bonding in the experience of liking someone, but there is no passion or long-term commitment.

When you feel highly aroused by someone whom you don't know and for whom you have no commitment, you experience **infatuation.** Infatuation tends to last anywhere from six weeks to six months (Applewhite 2005). It can be confused with falling in love, which means that the inevitable diminishing intensity in the infatuation may be interpreted as decreasing love.

If for some reason you commit yourself to a person without knowing or feeling passion for him or her, your love is an *empty* one. This may occur in some long-term relationships that have become stagnant. The two partners no longer feel much for each other and no longer share a great deal, but for reasons of religion or convenience or because of economic and family pressure they stay in the relationship.

In *romantic* love, you feel intimate and passionate but have not yet committed yourself to the other. *Companionate* love has intimacy and commitment but not passion. It is the kind of love that characterizes long-term friendships and some marriages in which the passion has died.

An interesting type that emerges from Sternberg's scheme is *fatuous* love, in which there is passion and commitment but no intimacy. Sternberg (1987:340) said that this is the kind of love that is "sometimes associated with

Hollywood and with whirlwind courtships." He called it *fatuous* because the people make a commitment in the midst of the dizzying experience of passion, rather than in the context of a stabilizing experience of intimacy.

Finally, there is *consummate* love, in which all three components exist. This is the complete love, the love that most of us desire and strive for. The fact that you attain consummate love with someone, unfortunately, does not mean that you will maintain it. But it is attainable, and it is the most rewarding of all love experiences.

Sternberg's typology is very useful for understanding differing kinds of experiences of love. He showed us the complexity of love. For example, we have noted that the idea that there is a transition from passionate to companionate love in long-term relationships is misleading if it is taken to mean that all passion dies. Sternberg's findings agree as reflected in the idea of consummate love in which passion and long-term commitment can coexist. Indeed, we found such love in our study of long-term marriages. Companionate love was the dominant form for some of the couples who had been married 15 or more years. But others spoke of continuing passion in the relationship. As one woman put it, "We knew that if the passion died we would still have a friendly relationship. Thank God, the passion hasn't died. In fact, it has gotten more intense" (Lauer and Lauer 1986:71).

Applying Sternberg's typology to your own experience can help you better understand the nature of your relationships and why a particular relationship either is rewarding or is in some way falling short of your expectations. Which of the various types of love have you experienced? Which are you experiencing at the present time?

STYLES OF LOVING

Another useful way to understand love is found in the typology of John Alan Lee (1973). Lee used three of the Greek terms we discussed at the beginning of the chapter—*eros, storge,* and *agape.* He added three more—*ludus, mania,* and *pragma*—to get six different styles of loving. **Ludus** is playful love. **Mania** is a possessive, dependent love. And **pragma** is a logical kind of love.

Six Types of Lovers

The *erotic lover* tends to focus on the physical, and particularly the sexual, aspects of the relationship. Erotic lovers may have ideal partners in mind and may fall immediately in love when meeting someone who fits the ideal image.

TABLE 6.2 Types of Love

Type of love	Intimacy	Presence of passion	Decision/ commitment
Nonlove	—	—	—
Liking	Yes	—	—
Infatuation	—	Yes	—
Empty	—	—	Yes
Romantic	Yes	Yes	—
Companionate	Yes	—	Yes
Fatuous	—	Yes	Yes
Consummate	Yes	Yes	Yes

Source: Robert J. Sternberg, "Liking versus Loving: A Comparative Evaluation of Theories" in *Psychological Bulletin* 102:340. Copyright 1987 by the American Psychological Association. Reprinted by permission.

The *ludic lover* views love as a pleasant pastime but not something in which to get deeply involved. Ludic lovers have little or no commitment to the other; they tend instead to value highly their autonomy, freedom, privacy, and self-sufficiency (Dion and Dion 1991). They value variety and are likely to have a larger number of sexual partners than are the other types (Hensley 1996). And women who use verbal or physical coercion to engage in sexual behavior are more likely than other women to have a ludic style in intimate relationships (Russell and Oswald 2001). *Storgic lovers* have a kind of quiet affection for the other. A storgic relationship tends to develop slowly but to be stable. There is no overwhelming passion, no points of exhilaration. Rather, a storgic love is a slow, perhaps unwitting, process of development.

The *manic lover* combines something of *eros* and *ludus.* The manic lover is intensely preoccupied with the beloved, feels intense jealousy, and alternates between ecstasy and despair in the relationship. The manic lover feels the passion of *eros* but plays the games of *ludus* as he or she tries to cope with swinging feelings and fear of loss.

A *pragmatic lover* is a combination to some extent of *ludus* and *storge.* The pragmatic lover may take careful stock of the other, consciously assessing the characteristics of the other. The pragmatic lover tries to find a partner who has a particular set of characteristics that he or she desires in another. To that extent, the pragmatic lover is playing a game. But *pragma* also can be a stable and growing kind of love.

Finally, the *agapic lover* acts on behalf of the well-being of the other without demanding or perhaps even expecting any benefits in return. *Agape* is other-focused, patient, and kind. It makes no demands for itself. It seeks only to serve the other. It is the kind of love that psychoanalyst Erich Fromm (1956:22) wrote about: "Love is the active concern for the life and the growth of that which we love."

These six styles are found among people throughout the world (Neto et al. 2000). *Pragma, storge,* and *ludus* vary somewhat depending on the culture, but *eros, mania,* and *agape* are the same in all cultures studied.

Gender differences exist in love styles, though the differences are not the same in all cultures. A comparative study of American and Chinese subjects reported that, among the Americans, the men were more *ludic* and *agapic* but less *erotic* and *pragmatic* than the women (Sprecher and Toro-Morn 2002). Among the Chinese, the men were more romantic, *agapic,* and *storgic* than the women. Other research also has found American men to be more ludic and agapic than women, and women to be more erotic and pragmatic than men (Lacey et al. 2004).

Styles also vary by religious commitment (Hendrick and Hendrick 1987; Montgomery and Sorell 1997). Those who define themselves as very religious score higher than others on *storge, pragma,* and *agape* and lower on *ludus.* Those neutral about religion have the highest scores on *eros* and *ludus.* There are no differences between the groups on *mania* scores.

While it is important to understand the six different styles and six different types of lovers, it is also important to keep in mind that in practice we use at least some of each of the styles. But there can be a dominant style. And that can change over time or from one relationship to another.

The extent to which you use each of the styles is important. You form your own unique style out of a mixture of the six. But the result is not merely a matter of personal preference. It has serious implications for your well-being and for your relationships.

Implications of Differing Styles of Loving

If you are now in love, to what extent do each of the styles characterize your relationship? And if you are not in love at the present, to what extent have you used each of the styles in past relationships? It turns out that people who are in love use different styles from those who have a romantic relationship but do not think of themselves as in love (Erwin 1999; Kanemasa et al. 2004). In essence, those in love are higher in *eros* and *agape* and lower on *ludus* than those not in love.

Love styles are related to people's attitudes about sexual behavior. A study of university students found that those who were tolerant of most kinds of sexual behavior and said religious beliefs did not guide their sexual behavior preferred a *ludic* love style (Lacey et al. 2004). Those who were more traditional and conservative in their attitudes toward sexual behavior were more *storgic* and *pragmatic* in their love styles than the liberals.

Love styles also are related to people's experiences of intimacy. Hendrick, Hendrick, and Adler (1988) found *eros* associated with higher levels of satisfaction for both men and women and *ludus* associated with lower levels. Clearly, people like passion but dislike games. A survey of 147 undergraduates reported that those with a ludic style were most likely and those with an erotic style were least likely to be lonely (Rotenberg and Korol 1995). And a study of 86 couples who were parents of college-age children reported a positive relationship between marital satisfaction and *eros* and *agape* and a negative relationship between satisfaction and *ludus* (Inman-Amos, Hendrick, and Hendrick 1994). In both studies, the partners tended

Comparison

Love Styles of British, Indian, and Portuguese College Students

Do the six love styles identified by Lee apply only to Americans, or do they help us understand love in other societies as well? To answer the question, Neto (2007) surveyed 231 British, 154 Indian, and 177 Portuguese college students. He found both similarities and differences among the three cultures, as well as between males and females within each country.

First, there were no differences in the amount of *eros* in the three countries. Nor were there differences in the extent to which males and females in each country indicated an erotic love style. This is consistent with most American studies that also show no gender differences. Thus, it seems that the experience of, and emphasis on, passionate love is about the same for all people and all societies (at least those that have been studied). Another finding consistent with those of American studies is that the men

were more agapic than were the women. Perhaps this reflects the widespread value that men are to be the protectors of and providers for women, and should, therefore, be more willing to sacrifice their own needs for those of their families.

There were some cultural differences on the other types of love. Students in India indicated higher levels of *pragma, mania,* and *agape* than did the students in Britain and Portugal. And the students in India reported lower scores on *ludus* than the British students and higher scores on *storge* than the Portuguese students. These results probably reflect differences between two diverse kinds of cultures. That is, the British and Portuguese cultures have more individualistic values, while Indian culture has a greater communal emphasis.

In most studies, males report themselves as more ludic than do

females. In this research, that was true of the Indian and Portuguese students, but not the British. The result for the British students is puzzling and cannot be explained without more research.

Some of the results appear to reflect rather clearly the differences in cultures. For example, the Indian students scored significantly higher on *pragma* than either the British or the Portuguese. That is understandable in view of the fact that pragmatic love was measured by such things as considering, when choosing a potential mate, how the person will reflect on one's family. In India, the choice of a life partner is more of a family than a private matter. Indian men also had the highest scores on *storge* of any other group, reflecting an emphasis in Indian culture on friendship in love relationships.

to be alike in their scores on the various love scales. It seems that we gravitate toward those who are similar to us not only in background, values, and attitudes but also in styles of loving.

Finally, some gender differences exist in the way that love styles relate to intimate experiences. Using a sample of 826 male and female students, three researchers examined how love style and gender related to self-silencing in romantic relationships (Collins, Cramer, and Singleton-Jackson 2005). Self-silencing refers to such things as putting the needs of the other first and repressing the expression of emotions that might strain the relationship. Self-silencing can be detrimental to your health, lowering your self-esteem and increasing the risk of depression.

The researchers found that certain love styles tended to be associated with self-silencing, but there were gender differences. In particular, only *mania* was associated with self-silencing in males, while *eros, ludus, mania,* and *agape* were all associated with self-silencing among females. In short, whatever their love

styles, women are more likely than men to engage in self-silencing. For men, only those who are involved in the possessive, dependent kind of love will likely engage in self-silencing.

LOVE THREATENED—JEALOUSY

A male graduate student told us that one of the more unsettling experiences of his life occurred when he took his girlfriend to a party: "She spent most of the evening talking to and laughing with some guy she met there. I was so mad I could feel myself shaking. It literally made me sick to my stomach." What the student experienced was an intense case of **jealousy,** which is a negative emotional reaction to a real or imagined threat to a love relationship. In the case of the student, the threat was imagined. His girlfriend had met someone who shared her interest in French literature. But she was not romantically attracted to the man. The fact that the threat was imagined, however, did not lessen the intensity of the reaction.

There are those who consider a certain amount of jealousy to be normal and even good. A survey of undergraduates reported that 35 percent said they were jealous individuals and over half believed that jealousy is normal (Knox, Breed, and Zusman 2007). David Buss (2000) argued that the lack of jealousy may be a more dangerous sign than its presence, because the jealousy—as long as it is not excessive or inappropriate—can strengthen the relationship and intensify the commitment. We agree that there are situations where jealousy would be an understandable, if not an appropriate, response; for example, when a partner flirts with others or seems emotionally closer to someone else other than you. Such jealousy could lead you to act in a way that would eventually strengthen your relationship. However, it could also spur you to act in a way that would end the relationship, because jealous feelings are not conducive to a reasonable, helpful discussion of an issue. On balance, therefore, we believe that jealousy is most likely to be a destructive rather than a helpful factor in a relationship.

The jealousy may be emotional, sexual, or both. That is, you can be jealous because you fear that your partner is becoming emotionally involved with someone else or because your partner is sexually attracted to or sexually involved with someone else or because your partner is both sexually and emotionally involved with someone else. Interestingly, although both kinds of jealousy are stressful, a study of those who had experienced infidelity by a partner reported that the emotional infidelity was even more distressful than the sexual (Harris 2002).

Who Is Most Jealous?

If the frequency and intensity of jealousy varies, what kind of people get most jealous? Some people, both men and women, have a "jealous personality" (Pines and Aronson 1983). They are likely to experience jealousy throughout their lives. And their jealousy can take the destructive form of expecting and demanding the total being of the partner (Maggini, Lundgren, and Leuci 2006). For such a person, jealousy is like a chronic illness that is severely vexing and corrosive of his or her quality of life. This, of course, represents an extreme. There are many others who experience less severe (but still painful) kinds of jealousy. What are the typical sources of such jealousy?

As you might expect, people who are insecure or who believe they are powerless in their love relationships are more likely to feel jealous (Rotenberg, Shewchuk, and Kimberley 2001). Those who believe that they have few alternatives also tend to be more jealous. Hansen

(1985b) studied 220 married people and reported that, regardless of the quality of the marriage, those who saw themselves as having few alternatives to the marriage were more likely to experience jealousy.

Finally, gender differences exist in jealousy. Most of the research that has investigated gender differences have found that a greater proportion of women than men report feelings of jealousy, including extreme jealousy in the area of romantic relationships (Sagarin and Guadagno 2004). A study of both an older (mean age of 67 years) and a younger (mean age of 20 years) sample reported that men tended to be more distressed by a partner's sexual infidelity, while women, particularly the young women, were more distressed by a partner's emotional infidelity (Shackelford et al. 2004). Note that the subjects were not concerned about just one kind of infidelity, but that they ranked one as more distressing than the other.

Finally, research with 291 college students showed a number of gender differences (Knox, Breed, and Zusman 2007). The men were more likely than the women to drink alcohol or use other drugs when they felt jealous, while the women were more likely than the men to seek comfort in eating. The men were more likely than the women to believe that their jealousy was a sign of love. And the women were more likely than the men to confide in friends about the jealousy they were feeling.

Situations That Provoke Jealousy

From the point of view of *conflict theory*, we would expect a fair amount of jealousy. Jealousy can be conceptualized as a reaction to a potential loss in the competition for an

 Conflict Theory Applied intimate relationship. Given the amount of flirting and sexual attraction that occurs in all kinds of situations, jealousy should be fairly common. Indeed, for the person who is intensely jealous, virtually anything can arouse feelings of jealousy. Certain situations, however, appear to provoke jealousy in most people. The party situation noted at the beginning of this section is an example. Basically, any situation in which one partner feels that something is happening that threatens the relationship will provoke jealousy.

One way to think about jealousy-provoking situations is that they violate our expectations for our relationships. Marriage is for most people an exclusive relationship. So is cohabitation. Even dating partners may develop such expectations early in the relationship. Hansen (1985a) studied dating jealousy among more than 300 students. He found that a significant proportion expected their partners to give up close personal friendships with people of the opposite sex. And most expected sexual exclusiveness from the earliest stages of their relationships. When our expectations are violated, we feel threatened. Jealousy is a sign that we want to protect the relationship.

Consequences of Jealousy

How an individual reacts when feeling jealous depends in part upon attachment style (Sharpsteen and Kirkpatrick 1997). When jealous, anxious lovers are more likely than others to resist expressing anger. Avoidant lovers tend to express anger against and blame the person they feel has intruded into the relationship. Secure lovers are more likely to be angry with the partner but also to try to maintain the relationship.

As we noted earlier, jealousy can actually strengthen a relationship. A study of 134 dating couples showed that jealousy levels were higher among those more satisfied than those less satisfied with their relationship (Dugosh 2000).

Nevertheless, when it is too intense and too frequent, jealousy can be destructive. There are, therefore, consequences for personal well-being:

> For most subjects, extreme jealousy was associated with feeling hot, nervous, and shaky; and experiencing fast heartbeat, and emptiness in the stomach. The emotional reactions felt most strongly were anxiety, fear of loss, pain, anger, vulnerability, and hopelessness (Pines and Aronson 1983:131).

In addition, jealousy may lead to a loss of self-esteem (Buunk and Bringle 1987; Peretti and Pudowski 1997). When the threat is real, when there is a particular third person involved, the jealous individual is likely to compare himself or herself with the rival. Is the rival inferior or superior? If superior, the rival is an assault on the jealous person's self-esteem. And the assault on self-esteem is particularly strong if the rival is seen as superior in sexual abilities (Buunk and Bringle 1987).

Finally, jealousy may lead to the loss of the partner. Ironically, it is the fear of loss that creates jealousy in the first place. When jealousy is too intense and too frequent (and perhaps for reasons too frequently imagined rather than real), it becomes a self-fulfilling prophecy. The individual creates the very loss that he or she had feared by distrusting and accusing the partner. In the Pines and Aronson (1983) study, the more jealousy the subjects reported at the time, the more relationships they had experienced that had ended because of their jealousy.

SUMMARY

The multifaceted meaning of *love* is illustrated by four ancient Greek words that are all translated as "love." *Storge* is love between parents and children. *Philia* is love between friends. *Eros* involves sexual and romantic love between men and women. *Agape* is a love that is independent of feelings, working on behalf of the well-being of the other.

Falling in love is a complex process. A few people are love prone, falling in love over and over again and often at first sight. Most people go through a series of phases when falling in love: rapport, self-revelation, mutual dependency, and the fulfillment of intimacy needs. There are some gender differences in falling in love. Women report being in love fewer times than do men and are less likely than men to believe in love at first sight. And women come to a relationship with greater concerns about emotional closeness and communication, while men have greater concerns about practical help and sex.

It is not easy to know when we are in love. In some cases, we may mistakenly attribute physiological arousal to feelings of love. Tests are available that are more useful than one's own feelings for determining if one is in love.

We may distinguish between passionate love, a preoccupation and intense longing for someone, and companionate love, affection and commitment to someone with whom one is deeply involved. Passionate love as a precondition for marriage is a relatively new idea in human history. It affects our feelings, thoughts, and behavior. Companionate love is a gain rather than a loss in the relationship. It can anchor two people in a lasting and meaningful union.

When we love someone, we tend to like that person as well. In the most meaningful love relationships, the liking is stronger than the liking we have for friends.

Intimacy, passion, and decision/commitment are the three components of Sternberg's triangular theory of love. The most rewarding love has all three. Various other kinds of love have one or two of the three.

John Alan Lee identified six styles of love. Erotic lovers focus on the physical and sexual. Ludic lovers view love as a game. Storgic lovers have a quiet affection for another. Manic lovers have the passion of *eros* but play the games of *ludus*. Pragmatic lovers take a rational approach, assessing the other for desirable traits. Agapic lovers act on behalf of the well-being of the other, expecting nothing in return.

Jealousy seems to afflict both men and women. It may be the result of personality problems and/or may be provoked by certain situations that are defined as threatening to the relationship. Jealousy is destructive when it is too intense and too frequent.

Principles for Enhancing Intimacy

1. Although "love at first sight" seems romantic, enduring love needs time to develop. Shared interests, shared confidences, and shared experiences take time to evolve. But the intimacy and love they produce are worth the wait.

2. Don't confuse arousal with love. Remember that such things as vigorous exercise, heavy drinking, or sexy movies can arouse and trick our emotions into thinking that we are in love.

3. To verify your own feelings, use the six indicators of a healthy love found in this chapter to examine your relationships. Remember, however, that a love relationship takes time to develop and that initially it may not measure up to all the indicators.

4. Don't expect passionate love to be unending. It may be the story-book ideal, but it tends to give way to something even better—companionate love. Companionate love maintains the passion but moves beyond the

obsessions and irritations of passionate love. Companionate love not only provides you with the intimacy and security that each of us needs; it also frees you to deal with other areas of your life.

5. Because love relationships that are built on friendship seem to be the most satisfying and enduring, it is important to like as well as love a person before you make a commitment. If you feel a strong passion for someone but like nothing about that person, recognize that the relationship is going to have problems and will likely not last.

6. Work at overcoming jealousy; if jealousy is a serious problem, books on it and on self-change are available that can help you overcome it. Jealousy can wreck a relationship. The "green-eyed monster," even if it is a response to a real threat, can cause you to react irrationally and excessively. And, in the process, you may lose the love relationship you are trying to protect.

KEY TERMS

ON THE WEB Falling in Love

Love has been portrayed in countless songs, paintings, and works of literature. It has been portrayed as both one of the loftiest as well as one of the more devastating of human experiences. Indeed, few if any of us escape at least a bit of both kinds of love experiences. The following two sites reflect these contrary experiences:

www.mhhe.com/lauer7e

Romantic Love Letters
http://www.theromantic.com/LoveLetters/main.htm

This site features portions of love letters written by men and women. The letters cover a period of almost 2000 years and illustrate the kinds of thoughts and feelings that people have when they are in love.

The Jealousy Test
http://www.britishcouncil.it/students/rome/Jealousy_Quiz.htm

This site has a jealousy test that you may take. It isn't a scientifically validated test, but it poses various realistic and interesting situations and asks for your responses. You are then given a jealousy score.

Use these two sites to enlarge your understanding with the following projects:

1. Go to the Romantic Love Letters site and select 20 letters from various times. Read them carefully, then address the following questions. What, if any, differences do you detect in the way love letters were written over time? What similarities do you find? Use quotes from the letters to illustrate points made in the text about such matters as the meaning of love, passionate versus companionate love, loving and liking, Sternberg's three components of love, and Lee's six styles of loving.

2. Take the jealousy test and calculate your score. Think about the questions, your answers, and your score. Do you agree that the score you received accurately reflects your tendency to be jealous? Why or why not? Ask some other students to take the same test, then compare and discuss your responses with them.

~ SELECTING A LIFE PARTNER ~

LEARNING OBJECTIVES

After reading and studying chapter 7, you should be able to

1 Define the role and patterns of cohabitation.
2 Evaluate the extent to which cohabitation is a preparation for marriage.
3 Discuss the ways in which people select a life partner.
4 Describe the qualities that people look for in a life partner.
5 Summarize the process of exchange and role equity in developing a lasting relationship.

6 Define the concepts of *assortative mating, homogamy, heterogamy, and hypergamy.*
7 Understand the impact of various social factors on the selection of a life partner.
8 Describe how family traditions and pressures contribute to the selection process.
9 Know the best predictors of marital satisfaction.
10 Understand why long-term satisfaction with the choice of a life partner is ultimately difficult to predict.

Have you ever thought about the kind of person you want to marry? What kinds of qualities do you want him or her to possess? How does this compare with the kind of person you prefer to date? Are there differences? Do you think that these findings are typical of your peers as well?

Interview six students. Ask three of them to make a list of the qualities they prefer in someone they date. Ask three others to list the qualities they want in someone they marry. Compare the two sets of lists. What similarities and

differences are there? What do you see as the implications of your findings for the quality of relationships? Do people look for qualities in dates that are likely to lead to satisfying marriages? How do your lists compare with those given in table 7.1?

If the entire class participates in this project, have half the class interview males only and the other half females only. Then compare the results along the lines suggested, but note gender differences in preferences for both dating and mating. ✳

I s there a "one and only" for you? Is there a perfect match out there, just waiting to be discovered by you? If you believe such things, you have very romantic and unrealistic notions about love and marriage. You could have a satisfying long-term relationship with a number of people. This is not to say that you could have a happy relationship with just anyone, however. In this chapter, we will look briefly at some notions of how selecting a life partner should proceed. We'll begin with an examination of cohabitation, which is increasingly a way for people to "test the waters" with someone before marriage. We'll then discuss people's expectations for a life partner and the various factors that can narrow the field (many of which you might be unaware). Finally, we will look at how you can hedge your bets by being sensitive to the factors that predict marital satisfaction.

COHABITATION: THE BEST WAY TO SELECT?

While there are a variety of reasons people cohabit, increasing numbers of Americans are engaging in cohabitation as a part of the selection process for a **life partner** and as a test of how they might fare as a married couple. Table 7.1 shows the dramatic increase since 1970.

This number will no doubt continue to grow. A survey of adolescents found that they expect to cohabit at some point in their future, but rarely consider cohabitation as a substitute for marriage (Manning, Longmore, and Giordano 2007).

When cohabitation is a testing for a subsequent marriage, it may occur before or after the engagement. That is, some couples decide to get married only after they have cohabited for a time, while others do not cohabit until they have decided to get married.

Who Cohabits?

Not everyone is equally likely to cohabit (Whitehead and Popenoe 2001; King and Scott 2005). Compared with married couples, cohabitors tend to be younger, less educated, and more likely to be unemployed (in part, because many are still in college). Compared to those who do not cohabit, they also tend to be less religious and are more likely to have grown up in a single-parent home. There are older cohabitors, of course, mostly people who were previously married (Brown, Lee, and Bulanda 2006). They are more likely to view their living together as an alternative to marriage, while younger cohabitors are more likely to expect marriage at some point in the future.

Patterns of Cohabitation

Many couples cohabit on the grounds that it permits them to be sure they are compatible before they marry. In some cases, the relationship leads to marriage when the woman gets pregnant.

People cohabit for reasons other than to check on their compatibility. Using data from a national sample, Casper and Sayer (as reported in Brown [2005]) identified four types of cohabitation. The most common type, involving almost half of the sample, was the *precursor to marriage* group. These cohabitors had definite plans to marry and expressed a high degree of satisfaction with, and commitment to, the relationship. A little less than 30 percent of the sample fit the category of *coresidential daters.* They basically disliked living the single life and opted to move in with someone even though they were uncertain about how long term the relationship might be. We should note that it is very likely that some, if not most, of these eventually raised the question of marriage. A survey of college students found that those cohabiting typically decided to live together for practical reasons, and most did not discuss marriage before moving in with each other (Kramer 2004). Nevertheless, for most the subject of marriage came up within the first two years of living together.

Casper and Sayer called the third group *trial cohabitors.* About 15 percent of the sample fell into this category. Trial cohabitors intend at some point to marry, but they are not sufficiently committed to their current partner to expect the cohabitation to end up in marriage. Finally, about a tenth of the cohabitors fell into the *alternative to marriage* group. For various reasons, the students in this group had more of a commitment to their partners than they did to marriage. Even though they were interested in a long-term relationship with their current partner, they were not interested in getting married.

These four types are a useful way to categorize cohabiting relationships. But they do not capture the full variety of patterns. They focus on motives, purposes, and styles of

T A B L E   7 . I   Number of Unmarried Couples Living Together, 1970–2006 (in Thousands)

	1970	1980	1990	2000	2006
Number of couples	523	1,589	2,856	3,822	5,012
Number with children under 15 years old	196	431	891	1,563	2,108

Source: U.S. Census Bureau Web site 2008.

relating. We also could categorize relationships according to whether they include children. As table 7.1 shows, there were 2,108,000 couples cohabiting in 2006 who had children under the age of 15 in their home. In some cases, the partners began cohabiting when the woman became pregnant. Such cohabitors may view their cohabitation as a practical way to parent the child and share expenses without making the commitment to marriage (Reed 2006). In other cases, children were brought into the relationship by one or both partners. And in still other cases, the children were conceived in cohabitation. Conceiving a child while cohabiting tends to make the relationship more stable (Manning 2004). About a fifth of all nonmarital births in the United States are to women who were formerly married but are now cohabiting (Brown 2000a).

Hispanic and black women are more likely than white women to conceive a child while cohabiting, and the conception is more likely to be intended (Manning 2001). Hispanic and black women are also far more likely than white women to remain with their cohabiting partner after the child is born. What differences does it make for children to grow up in a home where the parents are cohabiting? Research on the topic is sparse. One researcher found that children between the ages of 6 and 17 who were living with cohabiting parents (either two biological parents or a stepparent and a biological parent) had lower levels of emotional and behavioral well-being than children living with both biological, married parents (Brown 2004, 2006). However, another researcher studied only kindergarten-aged children (Artis 2007), and she took into account factors such as income and parenting practices. She found no differences in child well-being between those in cohabiting families and those in two-biological-parent, married families who were relatively equal in such resources as income and parenting skills with one exception: The children in the cohabiting families lagged behind those in the married families in their reading skills.

Finally, we could discuss differing patterns of relationships among heterosexual and homosexual partners. What, if any, are the differences between cohabiting heterosexual, gay, and lesbian couples? A national survey reported that gay male couples have a higher level of violence than heterosexual couples (Tjaden, Thoennes, and Allison 1999). In most respects, however, there are few differences. Comparing gay and lesbian cohabiting couples with heterosexual cohabiting couples, Kurdek (2004) found that the two types of couples had similar levels of psychological adjustment and that their relationships were similar in many ways. The gay and lesbian couples did appear to do better at resolving conflict, while the heterosexual couples had more support from their families.

In sum, cohabitation is not the same experience for everyone. The nature of any individual's experience depends on such things as the motives and purposes of the two partners, the length of time the two have been together, and whether the relationship is heterosexual or homosexual.

Cohabitation Compared to Marriage

For many couples, cohabitation is a testing ground for marriage. How accurate is the test? How much is marriage like cohabitation? Married and cohabiting couples face the same kinds of problems—money, sex, division of labor in the home, and so forth. Nevertheless, just as there are differences among varying kinds of cohabitors, there are differences between the experiences of marriage and cohabitation.

In the great bulk of the research comparing marriage and cohabitation, it is the married couples who have the advantage. Consider some of the findings:

- Married couples report more sex and more satisfying sex (Popenoe and Whitehead 1999).
- Married couples have a better-quality relationship than do cohabiting couples, particularly than do those cohabiting couples who do not plan on marrying (Brown and Booth 1996; Dush, Cohan, and Amato 2003).
- A woman is nine times more likely to be killed by her partner in a cohabiting than in a married relationship (Shackelford and Mouzos 2005).
- Married couples report greater happiness, less depression, higher levels of commitment to the relationship, and better relationships with parents (Kurdek 1991; Nock 1995; Skinner et al. 2002).
- Marital unions are more stable and durable than cohabiting unions (Binstock and Thornton 2003; Bouchard 2006).
- Children born to cohabiting parents are five times more likely than those born to married parents to experience parental separation; the instability is higher for white than for black or Hispanic children (Osborne, Manning, and Smock 2007).
- Cohabiting-parent families spend more than married-parent families on alcohol and tobacco but less on education (DeLeire and Kalil 2005).

The greater amount of depression among those who cohabit reflects the greater degree of instability in their relationship (Brown 2000b). Cohabitors' reports of instability are about 25 percent higher than are those of married couples. And if there are children (either stepchildren or the couple's own children) in the cohabitors' home, depression levels tend to be even higher. In contrast, children do not affect the depression scores of married couples.

There are a number of ways in which long-term cohabiting and married couples are similar. Based on a national survey, Willetts (2006) concluded that significant differences do not exist on such things as frequency of conflict, perceptions of equity, and relationship satisfaction. If the relationship—whether cohabitation or marriage—does break up, men experience a moderate decline in their economic status, while women experience a much more dramatic decline (Avellar and Smock 2005). The decline for women is particularly high among African Americans and Hispanics.

Finally, there are a few areas in which cohabiting couples have an advantage over the married. In the area of household work, cohabiting men report performing more household labor than do married men, and cohabiting women report doing less household labor than do married women (Davis, Greenstein, and Marks 2007). This suggests that it is not merely the presence of a man but of a husband that makes the difference in a woman's household responsibilities. On the other hand, if the couple has widely differing beliefs about the appropriate division of labor in the home, the cohabiting couple is much more likely to end the relationship (Hohmann-Marriott 2006).

Another area in which cohabiting couples have at least a small advantage is the amount of time spent together as a couple. Initially, cohabiting couples spend more time alone together. Eventually, however, their time together resembles that of married people (Willetts 2006).

In spite of the differences noted, it seems reasonable that cohabitation might provide a good preparation for marriage for those who want to use it as a testing ground. Granted, those who cohabit may be disadvantaged relative to the married. However, once the cohabitors get married, don't they have a better chance of making it because they have tested the waters and decided they want to jump in? Let's examine how well cohabitation prepares couples who eventually marry.

Cohabitation as a Preparation for Marriage

One way to test the extent to which cohabitation helps people have a more satisfying marriage is to compare the experiences of those who cohabited with those who did not. Here, again, the findings are not encouraging to those who cohabit or plan on cohabiting. Those who cohabit before marriage exhibit poorer marital problem-solving skills and are less supportive of each other than

are those who did not cohabit (Cohan and Kleinbaum 2002). The rate of infidelity is higher among couples who cohabited before marriage than those who did not (Forste and Tanfer 1996). National surveys conclude that those who cohabit before marriage have a marriage of lesser quality and are far more likely to perceive the possibility of divorce than are those who do not cohabit (Thomson and Colella 1992; Stets 1993; Dush, Cohan, and Amato 2003). And with the exception of African American and Mexican American women, actual divorce rates, among both Americans and Canadians, are higher among those who cohabit before they marry (DeMaris and Rao 1992; Smock 2000; Phillips and Sweeney 2005).

At best, then, cohabitation brings no advantage to those who desire marriage. At worst, cohabitors are at a higher risk for problems and breakups. In spite of the logic of the arrangement, there is nothing to suggest that cohabitation yields the benefits that people expect from it.

Why not? This is a question we can't yet answer. A number of possibilities have been suggested (Popenoe and Whitehead 1999). Those who cohabit may be more unconventional and less inclined to view marriage as a sacred institution. They may be less willing to commit themselves to one person. Being less bothered by the tradition of marrying before living together, they also may be more accepting of divorce. One study found that men who cohabited with their wives before engagement were less committed to their partners than men who cohabited only after engagement or not at all before the marriage (Rhoades, Stanley, and Markman 2006). Whatever the reasons, however, the consequences are clear: Cohabiting before marriage makes a poorer-quality and less stable marriage more likely.

IS THERE A BEST WAY TO SELECT A LIFE PARTNER?

If cohabitation doesn't improve the selection process, is there something else that will? What about an arranged marriage? As noted in chapter 2, many cultures have, or still do, practice arranged marriages (Ezra 2003; Hoelter, Axinn, and Ghimire 2004; Kanaan and Avraham 2005). For example, it is estimated that 95 percent of marriages in India are still arranged (Lall 2006). In some countries, such as Turkey, many people agree that arranged marriages have no place in a modern society, but they still are not uncommon (Hart 2007).

Arranged marriages also take place in modern Western societies among some immigrants who come from countries where the arranged marriage is the norm. For instance, even though many young people in Canada whose parents are from India prefer to choose their own partners, their marriages are frequently arranged (Netting 2006). And in the United States, arranged marriages occur among some Muslim immigrant families. A study of such marriages in the Houston area found that none of the couples who entered an arranged marriage had ever met before their parents or other relatives brought them to each other's attention (Al-Johar 2005).

Arranged marriages occur in one of two ways, and both ways may be used in the same society. One way is for the parents to take the initiative and directly negotiate the union. The other way is for the parents to use some form of help such as a matchmaker or the placement of marriage advertisements (Majumdar 2004) (see the Comparison box).

How well do arranged marriages work? If we judge by such things as divorce rates or rates of abuse, they work at least as well as marriages of choice. In fact, in India the divorce rate is very low. Moreover, a comparison of 45 people in India in arranged marriages with Americans in marriages of choice found no difference in levels of satisfaction (Myers, Madathil, and Tingle 2005). One potential hazard, however, of arranged marriages is the possibility of excessive inbreeding. In the Palestinian territories, for example, 40 to 50 percent of marriages are arranged within the extended family or between first cousins (Kanaan and Avraham 2005). This inbreeding has resulted in a number of adverse effects on physical health, including high rates of hearing loss and blood disorders.

With increasing education and economic development, arranged marriages tend to give way to those based on romantic attraction and love (Hoelter, Axinn, and Ghimire 2004). The ideal in most modern societies is for young people to select their own life partners. In societies where people choose their life partners, the result is a love match that brings greater satisfaction to both partners. At least that's the assumption. But to return to the original question, which method is best? If we use stability of the marriage as a criterion, arranged marriages are best. If we use satisfaction with the relationship as a criterion, we do not have much evidence, but what there is suggests that people in arranged marriages are as satisfied as those in marriages of choice.

In short, whether you choose your own life partner or have one chosen for you by your parents and/or relatives, there will be both advantages and disadvantages. There probably is no best way. But since in our society choosing a life partner is a matter of individual determination, we should at least be aware of the problems and processes involved in the choices we make.

What We Expect in a Life Partner

What do you regard as the qualities in an ideal life partner? More importantly, what qualities do you want in your own life partner? A male undergraduate student offered his list of qualities for an ideal wife[1]:

1. *Intelligence* is easily the most important virtue . . . I could never be happy and married to a dumbbell.
2. *Character.* I use this term in a general way and subdivide it to make my meaning clear.

We are attracted to people who share our interests.

[1]From Alba Bales, "A Course in Home Economics for College Men" in *Journal of Home Economics* 21:427–28. Copyright © 1929 American Home Economics Association, Alexandria, VA. Reprinted by permission.

a. *Unselfishness,* in my opinion, is the first requisite to married happiness. I don't mean that I expect a wife to forget herself in bovine devotion to me but I am certain that I have no sympathy for the woman whose first thought is of herself.

b. *Loyalty* can be the most beautiful of traits. The trials of a man's life can be met with greater courage and left with fewer scars because of the staunch comradeship of a loyal wife.

c. *Honesty* is of self-evident importance. I refer to absence of deceit and to frankness.

d. *Sympathy* . . . I know that I can be more successful if my wife has some understanding of me and the difficulties of my work.

e. *Energy.* Personal laziness is unforgivable.

f. *Sex purity.*

3. *Disposition.* I refer to buoyancy of nature.

4. *Health.*

5. *Appearance.* My humble wish is that my wife be sufficiently handsome so that no one will pity me. Neatness and taste are far more important than natural beauty.

6. *Education,* in itself, is not especially admirable but it does lead to similarity of taste.

7. *Business ability.* I have seen too many men driven to grayness and imminent insanity by their wives' faulty financial cooperation.

8. *Domesticity.* I still believe in the tradition that a woman's chief function is that of a homemaker if she chooses to marry.

The preceding was written in 1929. Clearly, at least some of our ideals have changed. A list given us by a

Comparison

Looking for a Mate in India

In India, the world's second most populous country, marriages are still arranged by parents rather than according to the choice of young people. Many young women are taught and practice a ritual that includes fasting, bathing, and chanting, in order to secure a good husband, loving in-laws, and a happy marriage. Yet it is their parents, not they, who will make the choice of a mate.

How do parents go about finding mates for their children? They may enlist the services of a matchmaker or a relative to find a mate. However, before the two young people ever meet, the parents investigate the family background of the prospective mate and meet with the other parents.

Parents also may take charge of the process on their own. One way to do so is to place an ad in the matrimonial columns of a national newspaper. Every week, for example, hundreds of ads appear in *The Times of India*. They are organized by the community,

caste, language, or religion of the family seeking a mate for a child. An ad might run like this:

Matrimonial correspondence invited from parents of Brahmin girls from good family background, good looking and accomplished, as match for only son, a businessman, non smoker, vegetarian, 28. References. No dowry. Give horoscope.

The ads contain some different and also some of the same kinds of information found in personal ads in American newspapers. Race (or skin color in India), age, physical attributes, and other qualities are typical in ads of both countries. In India, however, the ads are likely to include caste preference (or indicate that caste is no bar to a match). They also frequently include educational and occupational preferences. And some request horoscopes because some parents believe that mismatched stars will result in a troubled marriage.

Interestingly, the ads suggest that parents look for some of the same qualities that their children would want in a mate. They indicate that those searching for brides for their sons prefer a woman at least five years younger than the son, with at least some education, who is physically attractive. Those searching for grooms for their daughters want a man who is a good provider and who comes from a good family.

Many Indians who now live in other countries seek mates from their native land. They may look not only at newspapers but also at Internet sites that carry ads. In addition to other qualities, therefore, the ads may specify whether an individual is willing to live in another country. In particular, a prospective bride may need to be not only young and good looking, but also educated, employable, and willing to live in a foreign land.

Source: Divakaruni 2000.

female student had the following qualities for her ideal husband:

1. Have a strong religious commitment.
2. Be career-oriented with hopes and plans for the future.
3. Be physically attractive, have a healthy body.
4. Come from an emotionally healthy family.
5. Be sexually satisfying.
6. Enjoy being physically active.
7. Be independent.
8. Be committed to the relationship and want security and trust within the marriage.
9. Be romantic. Bring me flowers and cards. Take me out to dinner. Dance alone with me at home.
10. Be exciting and enjoy change.

These two lists do not, of course, represent what people generally expect in a life partner. We use them only as illustrations of the preferences of two individuals. They do raise the question, however, of what most Americans do want in a life partner. Let's look at the evidence.

Qualities Desired in a Life Partner

Both popular and professional sources have addressed the question of what we look for in a life partner. In a survey of men conducted by *Ladies' Home Journal,* one of the questions asked was what they valued most in a wife (Kiger 2003). The two most frequently named qualities were that the wife understood her husband and listened to him, and that she was a great mother to their children. The men also said that two of the rewarding things about being married was the assurance that their wives would always be there for them emotionally and that they would have "someone to grow old with."

David Buss and his associates compared data from surveys of samples of students taken at six times from 1939 to 1996 (Buss et al. 2001). The students were asked to rate the importance of 18 different qualities in a potential life partner. The top 10 qualities as rated by men and women in 1996 are shown in table 7.2.

The researchers noted a number of changes between 1939 and 1996. In 1996 both men and women placed a higher value on mutual attraction and love, education and intelligence, sociability, and good looks. And both placed a lower value on refinement, neatness, and chastity. Also, men and women were more similar in their choices in 1996 than they were in 1939.

Note that "good looks" is in the top 10 qualities selected by men, while qualities that would enable a man to be a good provider (ambition, dependability,

TABLE 7.2   Most-Valued Qualities in a Mate

By men	By women
1. Mutual attraction, love	1. Mutual attraction, love
2. Dependable character	2. Dependable character
3. Emotional stability, maturity	3. Emotional stability, maturity
4. Pleasing disposition	4. Pleasing disposition
5. Education, intelligence	5. Education, intelligence
6. Good health	6. Desire for home, children
7. Sociability	7. Ambition, industriousness
8. Good looks	8. Sociability
9. Desire for home, children	9. Good health
10. Ambition, industriousness	10. Similar education background

Source: Adapted from Buss et al. 2001.

education) are in the top 10 selected by women. This accords with other research that shows that men look for physically attractive females, while women look for men who will be good providers (Stewart, Stinnett, and Rosenfeld 2000; Fletcher et al. 2004).

Such qualities are not just valued in the United States. A British Internet survey of over 200,000 people from 53 different nations found a great deal of similarity in what people value in a mate in terms of character traits (Lippa 2007). The most frequently chosen traits from a list of 23 were intelligence, sense of humor, honesty, kindness, general good looks, face attractiveness, values, communication skills, and dependability. Men tended to value good looks and facial attractiveness in a partner more than did the women. And the women ranked honesty, sense of humor, kindness, and dependability as of more importance than did the men. Thus, people everywhere value many of the same qualities in a mate.

Exchange and Equity

If you asked people what they expect in a life partner, they will name the kind of qualities just discussed. They are

Exchange Theory Applied

not likely to say that they also expect someone who will strike a good bargain with them in the relationship. But as *exchange theorists* argue, there is a sense in which we can talk about mate selection as a process of exchange in which people seek equity.

In an exchange relationship, people seek to maximize their rewards and minimize their costs. This does not mean that people seek to take advantage of others, for most of us also believe in equity and are most comfortable in relationships in which there is relative equity. But two different relationships could offer equity while also offering differing rewards. For example, a man may propose a traditional marriage to a woman. He offers to be the breadwinner. In return for giving her economic security, he expects her to take care of the home and the children. They also, of course, will provide each other with emotional support and a sexual relationship. The two people might both see this as an equitable arrangement and be willing to engage in the exchange. Another man might offer the same woman an egalitarian marriage. They both will be employed outside the home and share in the responsibilities around the house. This, too, is an equitable arrangement. But depending on the woman's values and aspirations, the rewards are very different. If she values a career for herself, she will define the second proposal as one that is much more rewarding.

Even though we don't consciously think in terms of bargaining and exchange, there are always assumptions about what each mate will give and what each will receive. There are likely to be assumptions about who will handle which tasks in the home. In an era of changing roles, the assumptions of the two partners may be different. The result will be bargaining and negotiation after marriage. As one student told us,

> When I was married, I thought he would do all the repairs around the house and he thought I would do all the cleaning and washing. I had no intention of doing all the housework and he didn't have the faintest idea about how to repair things. But I not only know how, I also love to do this kind of work. We had some arguments about it all. But now we share the housework and cooking. And I do a lot of the repair work.

It is interesting to ponder how many marriages begin with differing expectations on the part of the partners. When those expectations confront reality, the bargaining process begins. The partners must try to clarify the nature of the exchange and bring about consensual equity in the marriage.

NARROWING THE FIELD: ASSORTATIVE MATING

Theoretically, there are millions of people you might marry. Realistically, there are relatively few. The choices for women are even fewer than those for men because of the sex composition of the population. As figure 7.1 shows, after age 24 and increasingly after age 30, there is less than one male for each female in the United States. The sex ratio also varies by race. For all people of marriageable age, only Hispanics have more males than

females. African Americans have the lowest number of males per 100 females because of high death rates among young black men.

The proportion of men to women changes over time because of such things as war (thus, there was a lower proportion of men to women in 1950 than in 2000 because of World War II). The lower proportion of males to females in the older groups reflects the life expectancy gap between men and women (women, on the average, live longer), a gap that has narrowed over time but is still wide at the higher age levels.

Life Partner Selection as a Filtering Process

It would, then, be impossible for everyone of marriageable age in the nation to be married at the same time. But even if there were equal numbers of men and women, not everyone would be equally desirable. We are selective about choosing a life partner. In particular, we tend to select someone who is like us in various ways. This is the principle of **homogamy,** which refers to marriage between two people who are similar in social and demographic characteristics, such as age, race, ethnicity, and religion. Some social scientists use the term **assortative mating,** which is a broader concept that refers to marriage between two people who are similar on one or more characteristics. In addition to social and demographic characteristics, assortative mating may be based on personality traits, values, attitudes, and various other factors that we shall discuss. Sometimes the term homogamy is used to include these other characteristics, but we prefer to restrict it to social and demographic factors.

Assortative mating stresses the fact that mate selection is nonrandom. That is, if we used no such criterion as age or race or any of the others to select a mate, then married partners should have a lot of differences between them. But the similarities are far greater than the differences, and this is true for all societies that have been studied (Bereczkei 1996). Mate selection is clearly not a random affair.

Some people, of course, do marry in the whirl of romantic infatuation (Lykken and Tellegen 1993). And some marry others who are unlike themselves. **Heterogamy** is marriage between two people who are dissimilar in some social and demographic characteristics. The difference may be along one dimension, such as is the case for a 50-year-old woman who marries a 25-year-old man who is like her in most respects except age. Or the dissimilarities may be more pronounced, such as is the case for a black Baptist man who marries a white

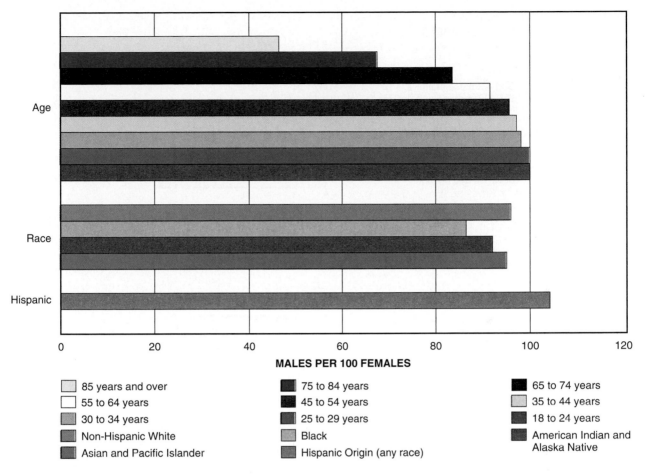

FIGURE 7.1 Sex Ratios by Age, Race, and Hispanic Origin
Source: Spraggins 2003.

Jewish woman who is 10 years younger than he is. Sometimes a person will "marry up." **Hypergamy** is marriage with someone who is from a higher socioeconomic background. In other words, hypergamy is a particular kind of heterogamy.

To get a sense of your own perspectives on these ideas, make a list of the qualities of the person you would prefer as a life partner. Write down the person's race, ethnic background, age, nationality, religion, and educational level. Also list any preferences you have in terms of height, weight, other physical characteristics, personality characteristics, and particular attitudes and values. Then make a second list of what you feel you would *accept* (as opposed to prefer) on each of the characteristics. To what extent are you similar to the person you have in mind? To what extent would you accept heterogamy?

Basically, what you have done is put people through a filtering system. In fact, we can think of life partner

selection as a kind of filtering process in which we sort out people according to various characteristics (figure 7.2). In the following sections, we will look at some of the more common characteristics that are used.

Age

Age is the most prominent factor along which we sort people out in life partner selection. Men's age, on the average, is about two years older than that of women at the time of marriage. The similarity in age is especially common among younger couples. Those who marry at older ages or those going into second marriages are more likely to have a larger age gap between the two partners (Gelissen 2004).

Age homogamy increased during the twentieth century (Qian and Preston 1993). Women increasingly tended to marry men who were within four years of their own

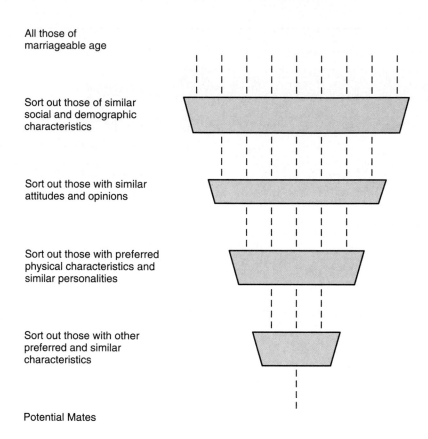

All those of
marriageable age

Sort out those of similar
social and demographic
characteristics

Sort out those with similar
attitudes and opinions

Sort out those with preferred
physical characteristics and
similar personalities

Sort out those with other
preferred and similar
characteristics

Potential Mates

FIGURE 7.2   Life Partner Selection as a Filtering Process

age, and the number of older women who married younger men declined. By 2006, nearly two-thirds of all married couples were no more than three years apart in age (U.S. Census Bureau 2007a). In only 1.2 percent of marital unions was one spouse 20 or more years older than the other.

There is no evidence, nevertheless, that age homogamy results in greater marital satisfaction than does age heterogamy. And in at least one study of another society—a study of 1,831 middle-aged Hungarians—age homogamy *was* associated with higher marital quality (Bereczkei 1996).

Ethnic Background

Does it matter if your ancestry is Irish or German or Chinese when it comes to getting married? In a small Illinois agricultural community over a 50-year period, 21 of 23 Germans married other Germans and 16 of 25 Irish married other Irish (Davis-Brown, Salamon, and Surra 1987). Ethnic background is becoming less of a criterion of selection, however. Since World War II, the rate of intermarriage among many ethnic groups has

risen considerably, although there are still strong tendencies to stay within one's own ethnic group. Unfortunately, the Census Bureau does not collect data on ethnic backgrounds of married couples other than those involving Hispanics. In 2006, only 3.7 percent of couples involved a Hispanic and a non-Hispanic (U.S. Census Bureau 2007a). An older study by Alba and Golden (1986) examined 27,597 marriages among couples with differing ethnic backgrounds. The couples were not people who had immigrated from other countries but those who had been Americans for at least one or more generations. While the rates were not as high as they were before World War II, there is still a considerable amount of marriage within ethnic groups.

More Europeans intermarried with other groups than married within their own group. Still, a third of those of British background married other Britishers, and the rates of marriage within the ethnic group were around 25 percent for Irish, Germans, French, and Scandinavians. Among non-Europeans, the rates within ethnic groups were generally higher. Over 72 percent of Mexicans and 74.4 percent of Asians married within their own groups.

Those who are dissimilar in age have marriages as good as those who are homogamous.

Race

Race imposes more constraints than ethnic background on our marital choices. As table 7.3 shows, the proportion of all married couples who are interracial has increased considerably (from 1.3 percent in 1980 to 3.9 percent in 2006), although the proportion is still quite small. People are far more likely to marry within rather

TABLE 7.3 **Number of Married Couples of Mixed Races and Origins, 1980–2006 (in Thousands)**

Race and origin of spouses	1980	1990	2006
Married couples, total	49,714	53,256	59,528
Interracial Couples	651	964	2,288
Black/White	167	211	403
White/other race	450	720	1,722
Black/other race	34	33	108
Other or mixed racial origin	n.a.	n.a.	55
Hispanic origin/other origin	891	1,193	2,227

Source: U.S. Census Bureau 2004/2005 and 2007a.

Conflict Theory Applied

than across racial and ethnic lines. As *conflict theorists* point out, a good deal of the competition for valued resources takes place along racial lines in the United States. Consequently, we would not expect racial boundaries to be often crossed in marriage, because people of differing races tend to approach each other as competitors rather than as potential mates.

Still, some intermarriage occurs, and Asian Americans tend to intermarry at a higher rate than either African Americans or Hispanics (Lee and Yamanaka 1990). In 2006, 20 percent of marriages involving Asians were interracial marriages (U.S. Census Bureau 2007a). Those who are born in the United States and attain higher educational and occupational levels are more likely than others to intermarry (Sung 1990; Lee and Yamanaka 1990). The majority of Asian Americans, however, like the great bulk of all Americans, marry within their own racial group.

Religion

Since the 1920s, the number of Protestant-Catholic marriages has increased dramatically (Kalmijn 1991). Nevertheless, religion has been and remains a strong homogamous factor (Watson et al. 2004). As figure 7.3, which is based on the research of Sherkat (2004) illustrates, however, religious homogamy is less likely among those born in 1933 or later than it was for those born before 1933.

Figure 7.3 also shows that the extent of religious homogamy varies significantly among the different religious groups. Episcopalians are least likely to be in a homogamous union. Jewish people are most likely to marry those of their same faith, followed closely by Mormons. It is also interesting to note that the proportion of religiously homogamous unions increased for Mormons, those of "other religions," and those with no religion.

Sherkat (2004) pointed out that overall religious homogamy characterized 48 percent of marriages in the pre-1933 cohort and 42.9 percent of those in the 1933 and later cohort. He also noted that religious homogamy tends to decrease with increasing educational attainment. In other words, the more educated the population, the more religious intermarriage occurs.

As with other kinds of homogamy, religious homogamy tends to increase both satisfaction and stability in marriage (Brandt 2004; Myers 2006). An exception, however, may be Roman Catholics, for whom

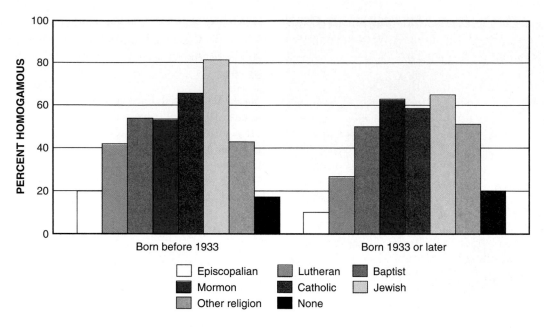

FIGURE 7.3   Religious Homogamy
Source: Sherkat 2004.

heterogamy is not related to marital happiness (Shehan, Bock, and Lee 1990). That is, Catholics report as much happiness whether they are married to other Catholics or to non-Catholics.

Education

Men tend to marry women who are either at or somewhat below their own educational level. Educational homogamy is fairly strong. It decreased from 1940 to 1960, but has increased again since that time (Qian and Preston 1993; Schwartz and Mare 2005). As table 7.4 shows, husbands and wives have the same amount of education in a little over half of all marriages. In the others, the proportion of wives with more education than their husbands is nearly equal to that of the proportion of husbands with more education than their wives.

TABLE 7.4   Educational Homogamy, 2006

Education difference	Number (in thousands)	Percent
Husband and wife same education	32,836	55.2
Husband more education than wife	13,432	22.6
Wife more education than husband	13,260	22.3

Source: U.S. Census Bureau 2007a.

Although most people marry those who have a similar amount of education, national surveys have found that both men and women are willing to marry someone with more education (Raley and Bratter 2004). Interestingly, the same surveys revealed that men who are willing to marry women with less education, however, are more likely to actually get married.

And So Forth

The list goes on and on. We are likely to choose a life partner who shares our sense of humor (Murstein and Brust 1985). That is, we tend to like and love those who find the same things funny as we do. We prefer those with similar leisure interests (Houts, Robins, and Huston 1996), the same love style (Hahn and Blass 1997), and the same attachment style (Quinsey et al. 1996).

We even may be drawn to people who share some kind of negative characteristic with us. People with anxiety disorders or alcohol or other drug dependence tend to mate with those with the same problem (Olmsted, Crowell, and Waters 2003; Grant et al. 2007). People who struggle with emotional problems such as manic-depressive illness or clinical depression tend to marry those dealing with the same problems (Mathews and Reus 2001). Those whose parents divorced tend to marry other children of divorce (Wolfinger 2003). Obese people tend to choose others who are obese for their life partners

(Speakman, Djafarian, Stewart, and Jackson 2007). And, finally, people tend to choose others with the same eye color (Laeng, Mathisen, and Johnsen 2007).

In going from age to similar eye color we have traveled from the significant to the trivial. Clearly, not all factors are equally important nor equally strong. The strongest include age, education, race, religion, and ethnic background. The bottom line, however, is that we are attracted to, and tend to choose for a life partner from, those who are similar to us in a variety of ways.

Why Assortative Mating?

What factors are at work in assortative mating? Why do we tend to select someone who is like us along so many dimensions? Is it indeed a case of narcissism, or is something else operating in the decision-making process?

Propinquity. As someone has said, even if there is a "one and only" for you, he or she is likely to live within driving distance. Most of us marry someone who is located nearby. The "nearby" may be a neighborhood, a city, a college campus, or a workplace. Thus, we are likely to marry someone of the same age and educational level because many people meet a future spouse in school. We are likely to marry someone of the same religion because many meet at a church or synagogue. Racial and ethnic housing patterns make it more likely that we will interact with, be attracted to, and eventually marry someone within our own racial and ethnic group.

To a large extent, propinquity reflects social class differences. Your class position is reflected in your lifestyle, including where you live and the kind of work you do. To be in a social class means to be enmeshed in a network of others who are mostly similar to you. And you are most likely to find your mate in the network of people with whom you regularly interact (McPherson, Smith-Lovin, and Cook 2001). Whether in school, at work, or in the community, you are less likely to interact much with those of other classes. In other words, you have fewer opportunities to meet and find a mate among people who are dissimilar than you do among those who are similar to you (Kalmijn and Flap 2001).

Attraction. As noted in chapter 5, we tend to be attracted to those who are like us. This is not necessarily the same as narcissism, however. Rather, it may be a case of feeling more comfortable with the familiar. We know how to relate to people who are like us. We have more experience with them, both in the family and among those nearby in neighborhoods, schools, and churches.

Many stories and movies have illustrated the discomfort and difficulties people face who try to function in a foreign land or even among people of a different social class in their own country. Such terms as *snobbish, common, uppity, cliquish,* and *rude* sometimes may be rooted in the uncomfortable outsider's feelings as much as in the behavior of the group. A young woman whose brother acquired great wealth in business told about her own problem with his new set of friends:

> He wanted to fix me up with one of his single friends. I said I'd rather meet this fellow in a group setting. So I went to one of their parties. I thought they were all really snooty. My brother said they liked me a lot. I couldn't believe that at first. But I guess he was right. I just didn't feel comfortable with them. They didn't talk about things that I knew anything about. I still haven't let my brother fix me up. I don't know if I ever will.

Some people cross such social boundaries as class, race, nationality, and ethnicity with relative ease. Others find that they can relate to people who are different, but they are not sufficiently comfortable with them to form intimate relationships. In other words, the principle of attraction means that we reject those who are dissimilar as much as it means that we choose those who are similar to us. This is not necessarily a judgment about the worth of other people. It may be simply a matter of sorting out people according to how much we feel at ease with them.

Family Traditions and Pressures. We like to think that selecting a life partner is purely a matter of personal choice. But there is still the factor of your family's reaction to the selection. As *systems theorists* point out, one

Systems Theory Applied

of your tasks is to develop your individuality while remaining a part of your family of origin. If your family opposes your individual choice of a life partner, you will be caught in a painful dilemma, as Shakespeare's *Romeo and Juliet* and numerous other works of literature illustrate. And in point of fact, your family probably does not give you complete freedom to make your own choice. Both male and female students have reported pressure to marry someone of the same race or religion or social status (Prather 1990). It is unlikely that you will completely ignore such pressures. Rather, you may reject some possible life partners before a relationship gets started because you know that your parents would strongly disapprove.

Family traditions and pressures are one reason why matters such as race, religion, and ethnicity are still important. It is in the family that we first learn about the importance of religion, for example. And we also learn about the problems that will attend an interreligious, interracial, or interethnic marriage.

Family traditions and pressures can work in the opposite direction as well. That is, you may be pressured to marry someone about whom you have doubts because all of your family members like and approve of that person. The authors once counseled with a couple who had virtually no interests in common. They came from the same town, had the same socioeconomic background, and were members of the same church. But he had a college degree and she was only a high school graduate. And they were dramatically different in the kinds of things they enjoyed doing, in their beliefs about family finances, in their child-rearing philosophies, and in a variety of attitudes about life. We asked them why they had married in the first place. The man reflected a moment and then said, "I guess because everybody expected us to get married. Both our families thought it was a good match, so we just went along with them." They are now divorced.

When you marry, you do not just marry an individual. You marry into a family. That family, therefore, will have some voice in deciding whether you are an appropriate choice.

PREDICTORS OF MARITAL SATISFACTION

Even if you select someone who is similar to you, it doesn't guarantee that the marriage will be a happy or lasting one. The nineteenth-century philosopher John Stuart Mill was so impressed with the problems of finding a suitable mate that he called marriage a lottery. He said that those who calculate the odds of winding up in a happy union would probably not even take the risk of trying (Rose 1983). We do not believe that the odds are that great. But we do agree that there is always a risk and that people should make the effort to minimize the risk of a bad match. One way to do that is to attend to the principle of similarity. That is, the more alike you are on social, demographic, and various other factors, including attitudes and values, the more likely the marriage will succeed (Amato et al. 2003; Wilson and Cousins 2003; Luo and Klohnen 2005; Gaunt 2006). The attitudes and values that are important include lifetime commitment to the relationship, a strong moral stance, the desire to be a good parent, a religious commitment,

and the willingness to practice forgiveness in the marriage (Rosen-Grandon, Myers, and Hattie 2004; Brimhall and Butler 2007). Marital satisfaction also is higher among those couples who have an egalitarian relationship, with the husband sharing in the housework and the two partners being equals in making decisions (Amato et al. 2003).

One factor that might be overlooked is the quality of the relationship prior to marriage. Three researchers who studied 100 couples over a 13-year period found that those who remained happily married, compared to the others, had reported high premarital satisfaction and fewer premarital problems. As the researchers summed it up: "This study supports the hypothesis that the seeds of marital distress and divorce are sown for many couples before they say 'I do'" (Clements, Stanley, and Markman 2004:621). Marriage, then, will not solve your problems. If your relationship is troubled prior to marriage, you are more likely to end up in a divorce rather than in a happy union.

There are, then, numerous predictors of marital satisfaction. No single predictor is crucial, in the sense that if it is lacking the marriage is doomed. Still, we know a good deal about the kinds of things that are liabilities and those that are assets for marital satisfaction (Larson and Holman 1994; Larson 2000; Patrick, Sells, Giordano, and Tollerud 2007). These liabilities and assets can be divided into those of context (social and demographic), individual factors, and couple characteristics. Among the liabilities are the following:

- *Context:* marrying at a younger age, coming from a dysfunctional family or a broken home, marrying in the face of parental disapproval, and having lower levels of education and inadequate preparation for a career.
- *Individual:* having some kind of mental disorder such as a neurosis or chronic depression, having a hostile personality, and dealing inadequately with stress.
- *Couple:* being dissimilar, knowing each other a short time before marrying, cohabiting, and possessing poor communication and conflict-resolution skills.

In contrast, assets in the quest for marital satisfaction include the following:

- *Context:* coming from an intact, nurturing family; marrying at a later age; being supported by family and friends in your marital choice; and having a good educational background and career preparation.
- *Individual:* possessing physical and emotional health, having good interpersonal skills, and being flexible.
- *Couple:* being similar, knowing each other for a long time before marrying, communicating well with each other, and solving problems together satisfactorily.

Family traditions help shape our sense of who we are and the kind of person we would be comfortable with as a life partner.

Here we will look briefly at three predictors to illustrate how and why they are important.

Timing

By *timing* we refer to three things: how long a couple has known and dated each other; age at marriage; and general readiness—the sense that one is prepared to commit to marriage. With regard to the first, there are whirlwind romances that lead to marriage after a matter of days or weeks. Although many last and are satisfying unions, the odds are against such marriages. The longer you date someone before marriage, the more likely you are to have a rewarding marriage (Grover et al. 1985).

The second strong predictor of stability and satisfaction is age at marriage. Again, there are some who marry as teenagers and wind up in long-term, happy unions. But it is a great risk. There is also, however, a popular notion that later marriages may be problematic because people get "set in their ways." Robert Bitter (1986) used a national sample of married people to investigate the question of whether late marriages are less stable. His conclusions are fascinating. He found that there is a marriage "squeeze" as people delay getting married until their 30s or 40s. That is, there are fewer homogamous choices available. People who marry later, therefore, are more likely to have a heterogamous union. And it is the heterogamy rather than the later age that results in a higher level of instability. If you marry later and have a homogamous union, your chances of breaking up are less than if you married at an earlier age.

Finally, the third aspect of timing—general readiness—means that getting married is not merely a matter of finding the right partner but of being at a point in your life at which you feel equipped for the challenges and adventure of marriage. Thus, Holman and Li (1997:141) conclude the following from their study of 2,508 young adults:

> When a person is older, is financially and educationally in a position to get married, and feels that she or he has support from friends and family for the chosen partner, and when the quality of that couple's relationship is good, then he or she feels ready to marry.

Or, as a young man told us, the woman he was dating wanted to get married, and he believed she was the "right" partner for him. But "it's not the right time. I'm just getting started in my career." From the point of view of their compatibility, it was a great match. From the point of view of general readiness, she was ready but he was not. They ended their relationship.

Equity

We have frequently mentioned the importance of perceived equity in a relationship. It is important for marriage as well as other intimate relationships (Stafford and Canary 2006; Wilcox and Nock 2006). The point we want to make here is that if you don't feel equity in

Personal

Should I Marry My Baby's Father?

Patti is a 26-year-old single mother. The father of the child wanted to marry Patti, but she refused. Her story shows how some of the things that might initially attract us to another person are not sufficient for a long-term relationship. Patti's marriage would have been a heterogamous one. She decided that it wouldn't work:

I guess I am an idealistic person, but I always pictured myself in a wonderful life with a loving spouse with whom I would share things. I was attracted to Paul, my daughter's father, because he was so good looking. I thought that anyone that good looking would have a lot of other good qualities. So I didn't pay attention to some of the warning signs, like the fact that he dressed carelessly and didn't take care of himself very well.

Anyway, we had a whirlwind relationship that quickly involved sex. And I got pregnant. He suggested that we should get married. We weren't even living together

yet. I guess the idea of getting married and living with Paul made me think about the kind of relationship we had. I had felt, but hadn't even admitted to myself, that there were some serious problems. We were so different in so many ways. Paul has no interest in reading or learning anything. He can sit for hours and just watch television. He is also not very good at just sitting and talking about things. When I thought about the things we had in common, they didn't seem as important as the things we didn't have in common.

During my pregnancy, I felt physically and emotionally unable to break up with him. I tried a couple of times. But each time, he would talk pleadingly with me, send me flowers and cards, and promise to become more like the person I wanted him to be. I was so afraid of being alone that I agreed to continue the relationship. But I kept putting him off

about the marriage. Besides, I needed his help and wanted to share parenthood with him.

For a while, because he didn't want our relationship to end, I thought that being a father might change him. But he wasn't as involved or as enthusiastic as I was about the baby. Finally, I guess I realized that he wouldn't change. It hit me one day that the worst part of each day was the time I spent with Paul. I got tense as soon as I saw him. He had little to say to me; I had to carry on the conversation. One day I just told him that it was over. He tried to persuade me again and sent the usual flowers and cards. But I wouldn't see him again.

I certainly don't regret breaking up with him. He's never tried to see his daughter. She's three now, and I love her dearly. I guess my major problem with her now is trying to decide what I'm going to tell her about her father some day when she asks.

your relationship now, it is unlikely that you will do so after marriage. In fact, problems of equity may come up after marriage even when they didn't exist before the marriage.

Home responsibilities are one area in which the question of equity may arise. Some couples never discuss matters before marriage that are likely to be sources of conflict afterward: Who will take care of the laundry, the cooking, the housecleaning, the finances, and all of the multitude of other things that must be done? It is important that both husband and wife be satisfied with the way these tasks are allocated (Himsel and Goldberg 2003). In fact, a survey by the Pew Research Center (2007c) found that 62 percent agreed that sharing household chores is very important, and another 30 percent agreed that it is rather important, to a happy marriage. The importance of equity continues

into later life. Wives over 50 years of age who perceive the division of household tasks to be fair are more likely to report higher levels of marital happiness (Ward 1993). The importance of equity may vary by social class, however. Analysis of a national survey showed that middle-class wives who perceived inequity in the division of household tasks also reported higher levels of marital conflict, but working-class wives reported less conflict when they did most of the traditionally female tasks (Perry-Jenkins and Folk 1994). Working-class wives may not have the same notions as middle-class wives as to what constitutes fairness in a marriage.

Problems of equity also may arise in such areas as emotional support. In fact, in their study of women, Wilcox and Nock (2006) found that among the predictors of a wife's happiness, the most important is the extent to

What Do You Think?

There is disagreement about **whether opposites attract and make the best matches.** What follows are pro and con arguments. What do you think?

Pro	Con
Opposites attract and make the best matches because	Opposites neither attract nor make the best matches because
• such matches are more diverse and, therefore, more exciting. • they make up for each other's weaknesses. • they have a broader range of experiences to draw on to deal with the challenges of marriage. • they are exposed to new and different facets of life. • they don't get bored with each other.	• contrary interests and values generate arguments, not excitement. • you are more comfortable with people who share your own background and goals in life. • the more alike you are, the easier it is to understand and appreciate each other. • the more interests you share, the stronger your relationship. • they tend to do their own thing and spend too little time together.

which her husband is emotionally engaged with her—affectionate, empathetic, and tuned into her feelings. For both men and women, if one is always giving and the spouse is always receiving the major part of the support, the giver is likely to grow weary of the inequity. In most cases, the germs of such problems are already evident in the intimate relationship that exists before the marriage. It is wise, therefore, for those contemplating marriage to ask to what extent they feel equity in the relationship.

Communication

One of the most important factors in marriage is the pattern of communication. The ability to talk over problems and resolve differences effectively is particularly important (Schwartz 2002). We discuss communication in depth in chapter 9 and ways of handling conflict in chapter 10. Here we want to underscore the importance of communication as a predictor of marital success. Those who insult their partners or talk in ways that are unsupportive and those who are unable to communicate in ways that lead to effective resolution of problems are unlikely to have happy marriages (Clements, Stanley, and Markman 2004).

Good communication involves not only the ability to discuss problems but also self-disclosure, a sharing of daily events, interesting "small talk," and positive conversation about the spouse (words that convey respect, affection,

love, etc.). A study of working couples found that the husband's ability to share his thoughts and feelings and to give his wife emotional support enhanced the wife's marital satisfaction even more than his participation in household and child care tasks (Erickson 1993). Again, the point is to examine the relationship prior to marriage to see to what extent it is characterized by good communication patterns. As Patti said in the Personal boxed feature, one of the reasons she decided not to marry Paul was his inability to sustain meaningful conversation with her. Paul seemed to become articulate only when he saw that the relationship was in jeopardy. It is unlikely that he would have easily altered his style after marriage.

PREPARE: A Multifactor Approach

As in the case of assortative mating, a good many other factors go into a satisfying marriage. Problems can arise from a great many things, ranging from dissimilar attitudes to incompatible body clocks (one spouse may be a morning and the other an evening person). Predicting marital satisfaction requires a variety of factors.

However, not all factors are equally important. For those contemplating marriage, there are a variety of premarital counseling programs that can help a couple understand various facets of their relationship and how the attitudes, values, and behavior patterns they now

Strong ties with family and friends help a marriage last.

have are likely to affect their future marriage (Williams 2007). One effective and widely used program (particularly in churches) is PREPARE, which uses an instrument devised by Dr. David Olson and his colleagues to predict marital success among those contemplating marriage. PREPARE was developed in 1977 and validated by David Fournier in 1978 on the basis of 1,000 premarital couples and 200 clergy who had used the instrument. Following this validation, some revisions were made and a second version appeared in 1979. Results from subsequent research are impressive. For example, Fowers and Olson (1986) tested 164 engaged couples and then studied them again three years later. They found that satisfied couples had scored considerably higher on the instrument than those who had canceled their engagement or who married and were dissatisfied or who had divorced. They point out that PREPARE scores predicted with 80 to 90 percent accuracy which couples were separated and divorced and which were happily married! Subsequent longitudinal research with nearly 400 couples supports the predictive power of PREPARE scores (Fowers 1996).

PREPARE measures 11 different areas: the extent to which the couple has realistic expectations, personality issues, communication, conflict resolution, management of finances, leisure activities, the sexual relationship, children and marriage, family and friends, equalitarian roles, and religious orientation. For example, the sexual relationship is evaluated by such measures as the extent to which you would be willing to try almost any sexual activity your partner wanted and the extent to which you

believe the two of you talk freely about sexual expectations and interests. The religious orientation is evaluated by such measures as the extent to which you feel it is important to pray with your partner and believe that you and your partner find the same meaning in religion.

The researchers not only measured each partner's score but also looked at the extent to which the partners agreed in each area. The 11 areas are all important in predicting marital satisfaction. In many cases, the important thing is not that you believe a particular way about something but that you and your partner believe the same thing (religious orientation, for example). In other cases, you may believe the same thing, but it can be dysfunctional for a stable, satisfying marriage (for example, both may believe that good marriages are free of conflict).

It is important to keep in mind that no instrument is perfect. You may have serious differences with someone on one or more of the 11 areas prior to marriage. You may continue to have those differences afterward yet have a meaningful and stable relationship. But the odds are not with you. The more agreement you have in these 11 areas, the more likely you are to have a satisfying marriage.

A FINAL CAUTION

Even with an instrument like PREPARE, it is difficult to predict long-term satisfaction. After all, the researchers only did a three-year follow-up. We don't know if the instrument also will predict much longer relationships. A number of factors make long-term satisfaction difficult to predict prior to marriage.

One is that our knowledge of another person is always limited. Even though a good deal of self-disclosure goes on in a relationship, there is usually also a good deal of "putting your best foot forward" during courtship. People may not reveal some of the more problematic aspects of their lives until after the marriage.

Second, everyone changes over time. You may seem to be perfectly compatible with a partner now. But both of you will be different people in 10 years. What if you change in ways that make you less compatible? One couple shared with us problems they were having in the tenth year of their marriage that they couldn't have anticipated. The wife had decided to go to college to pursue a degree and a career. Their two children were both in school, and she was not satisfied staying at home. Her husband had not attended college and felt threatened by her plans. Moreover, he could not understand her excitement about her classes and her interest in a variety of subjects that meant nothing to him. Eventually, he began to ridicule the things she would tell him. She, in turn, stopped talking to him about her interests. Soon, they fell into a pattern of living separate lives while sharing a house and two children. They were different people than when they were first married. And the differences led to less rather than more compatibility.

Our needs as well as our interests change over time. In some cases, something that attracted two people initially becomes a problem as time passes. For example, Janice is a data processor who married Frank because he was strong and assertive. He seemed like the kind of person who would not be defeated by life, and who would always be able to support his family. But after a few years, Frank's strength began to look more like domination to her. He wanted complete control of their finances. Even though she worked, he insisted on giving her an allowance and managing the rest of the budget himself. At the time of their marriage, Janice felt she needed a strong and assertive husband. Some years later, she felt able to care for herself if necessary. Frank's aggressive nature had become a liability because of her changing needs.

Such changes cannot be predicted. We can never be certain, therefore, that a relationship will be lasting and satisfying. But we can increase our odds by attending to the things that we know are part of long-term, satisfying marriages.

SUMMARY

Cohabitation is increasingly a part of the selection process for a life partner. Those who cohabit rather than going directly from dating into marriage tend to be younger, less educated, less religious, more likely to be unemployed, and more likely to have been raised in a single-parent home. There are various ways to categorize people who cohabit. One useful way is to place them in four groups: the precursor to marriage group, coresidential daters, trial cohabitors, and the alternative to marriage group. The kind of experience one has in cohabiting depends upon the motives and purposes involved, the length of time the partners have been together, and whether the relationship is heterosexual or homosexual. In comparing cohabiting couples with those who are married, the married couples have far more advantages for their relationship and their personal well-being. Contrary to popular thought, the evidence suggests that those who cohabit, compared to those who do not, are likely to have a poorer quality of marriage and a greater risk of divorce.

There is no single best way to select a life partner. In some societies, and among some groups in societies such as ours, marriages are arranged by parents rather than the individuals getting married. For such people, traditions and/or political and economic considerations may be more important than love. In most modern societies, however, the ideal is for people to select their own life partners.

Most of us know the kinds of things we prefer and those we dislike in a life partner. The unmarried prefer such qualities as kindness, understanding, an exciting personality, intelligence, attractiveness, and good health. Married people have some of the same and some different preferences. Some gender differences also occur in preferences. In addition, people are more satisfied when they are in a relationship of equity.

While the number of eligible life partners is theoretically enormous, practically there are only a few for each of us. Because of the sex ratio, women have fewer choices than men. Mate selection is a filtering process. We engage in assortative mating, which means that most people have homogamous rather than heterogamous marriages. Assortative mating takes place along the lines of age, ethnic background, race, religion, education, and a variety of other factors. Assortative mating occurs because of a number of factors, including propinquity, attraction, and family traditions and pressures.

A homogamous marriage doesn't guarantee stability or satisfaction. Homogamous marriages are more likely than heterogamous to last and to be happy, but a number of additional factors enhance your chances for success. A longer courtship and later age at marriage both increase the probability of a lasting and satisfying union. Other factors include perceived equity, good communication patterns, and the various areas covered in the PREPARE instrument.

Long-term satisfaction is difficult to predict for two reasons. First, our knowledge of someone is always limited. People may not reveal problematic aspects of their lives until after the marriage. Second, our needs and interests change over time. They may change in a way that makes a couple more compatible, but they also can change in a way that makes the couple diverge from each other.

Principles for Enhancing Intimacy

1. Although most Americans reject the notion of arranged marriages, it is a good idea to talk over your choice of a prospective life partner with a trusted older or more experienced person. This person should be someone who knows you well and who has your best interests at heart. If he or she has major reservations about your choice, listen and consider the comments carefully.

2. If you haven't selected a life partner as yet or even if you already have someone in mind, take the time to seriously consider what kind of person you want him or her to be. Make a list of those characteristics that you really feel are essential in someone with whom you plan to spend your life, and refer to it often.

3. If you are contemplating marriage in the near future, it is vital to know what your prospective spouse expects from you and from your relationship. Talk about your shared and individual goals, about your respective roles in the marriage, about if and when you are going to have children, and so forth.

4. The old adage says that opposites attract, but it doesn't acknowledge that opposites often produce an unsatisfactory union. The evidence shows that the greater the similarity between you and your spouse, the greater your chances for a happy and enduring marriage.

5. Take time before you marry to get to know your future spouse. A longer courtship gives you a greater opportunity to know more fully your spouse-to-be and to establish the patterns of communication that are so essential to a successful marriage.

KEY TERMS

assortative mating *154*

heterogamy *154*

homogamy *154*

hypergamy *155*

life partner *148*

ON THE WEB   Selecting a Life Partner

Many students are intrigued by the PREPARE instrument. You can find more information about PREPARE at http://www.prepare-enrich.com/indexm.cfm. Many students are also skeptical of the findings about cohabitation discussed in the text. At least, they believe that the negative effects will not apply to them. Actually, there is a good deal of debate about the value of cohabitation and about the reasons for the negative effects reported by researchers. Two sites that offer contrary perspectives are:

www.mhhe.com/lauer7e

Alternatives to Marriage

www.unmarried.org/cohabitation.php

The Alternatives to Marriage site acknowledges some of the negative findings, but argues in favor of cohabitation, and includes such things as a list of ways to improve your chances of a good marriage after cohabiting.

All About Cohabiting Before Marriage

http://members.aol.com/cohabiting

This site argues strongly against cohabitation, offering reasons ranging from the legal to the sociological and psychological to the religious. It also has links to other resources.

Using these two sites and others, enlarge your understanding with the following projects:

1. Compare the arguments and the evidence used on the two cohabitation sites. Imagine you are a counselor and a young couple asks you about the advisability of living together to see if they should get married. How would you respond?
2. Write a letter to your school or your local newspaper. Tell why you believe or do not believe in cohabitation and include things that parents and schools can do that support your position.
3. Enter "personal ads" into a search engine. There are free sites where you may enter your preference for a romantic partner and get lists of possibilities. Look at 20 of the people suggested for you. Make a frequency list of the qualities they profess to have. Compare your list with the qualities noted in the text as desirable for a dating partner. How effectively are the people presenting themselves?

part three

~ THE INTIMATE COUPLE ~

Whatever the attractions of singlehood and cohabitation may be, the fact is that most of us will eventually marry. And marriage means a different experience of intimacy than is likely to occur in other kinds of relationships. Even couples who cohabit tend to report a noticeable change in their relationship after they marry.

In this section, we will look at what is involved in the transition from singlehood to marriage. Then we will examine the challenges that people face as they seek to deepen their intimacy in marriage. What is the role of communication? What is the meaning of conflict, and how and why do couples fight? How will the couple deal with the division of labor both in and outside of the home? These are some of the questions that young adults face when they begin their quest for mature intimacy.

~ GETTING MARRIED ~

LEARNING OBJECTIVES

After reading and studying chapter 8, you should be able to

1 Characterize the marital status of the population.
2 Distinguish between those who do and don't marry and summarize why people marry.
3 Describe the various kinds of marriages.
4 Discuss what people expect from marriage.
5 Explain the role of negotiation and marriage contracts in working through conflicting expectations.

6 Contrast and compare the types of adjustments men and women have to make when they marry.
7 Discuss how teenage, student, and heterogamous marriages begin with certain disadvantages.
8 Describe the process of establishing equity and consensus and adjusting to in-laws.
9 Explain the kinds of changes that are likely to occur during the first year of marriage.
10 Show the importance of commitment in building an enduring and satisfying marriage.

Do you think you are typical or different from other people in your attitudes about marriage? Make copies of the test in figure 8.2 (p. 176) and conduct your own research to see how other people feel. One way to do such research is to ask a number of questions about who is most likely to prefer the traditional and who is most likely to prefer the nontraditional union.

For example, do you think that males or females will be more traditional? Will there be differences between older and younger people? Will the more or less educated people prefer a traditional union? Will there be any differences by race?

Decide on which of the questions you would like to try to answer. Of course, you will not have a large enough sample to make a firm conclusion, but if the entire class participates in the project, you could have a sufficient number of responses to be comfortable with your results.

It is important to research only one of the questions. For example, if you are interested primarily in gender differences, try to have an equal number of males and females. Select people who are all of the same race. And select those who are as close as possible in age and education. Otherwise, you can't be sure if any differences you find are due to gender or one of the other factors.

After you score the questionnaires, answer the following questions. Were there any differences between the two groups you studied? If so, which group was the most traditional? How can you account for your results? Did your results turn out differently from how you anticipated? What conclusions would you draw or what are the implications of your findings (assuming that a larger survey of the population would produce similar results)? ✖

In his classic work, *Utopia,* Sir Thomas More wrote that the Utopians severely punished anyone engaging in premarital sex. The Utopians believed, he pointed out, that if people could have sex outside of marriage no one would ever get married. If not for the opportunity to have sexual relations, why, More asked, would one put up with all the inconveniences of being married?

There are some people, like the young man we discussed at the beginning of chapter 4, who marry primarily for sexual reasons. But, as we shall see, there are many other reasons for getting married. In spite of Sir Thomas's dire warning, the bulk of Americans marry despite readily available sexual relations outside marriage.

In this chapter, in addition to looking at reasons that people marry, we shall look at some different types of marriages and explore our various expectations when we marry. We will discuss the wedding, which is the way that people in all cultures validate and celebrate a marriage. We will see some of the common adjustments that people have to make when they marry, along with changes in the first year of marriage. Finally, we will discuss the meaning of *commitment* and the way in which it affects the quality of married life.

WHAT ARE YOUR CHANCES OF GETTING MARRIED?

Most Americans want to marry, and the great majority will. However, your chances vary depending on a number of factors.

Marital Status of the Population

The **marriage rate,** which is defined by the Census Bureau as the proportion of unmarried women aged 15 and over who get married in a year, fluctuates considerably over time (figure 8.1). Marriage rates have been dropping since 1970, not only in the United States but in most other nations as well (United Nations Statistics Division 2005). The rate for the United States is the highest in the Western hemisphere and is higher than most other nations. Still, the proportion of Americans who ever marry is likely to be somewhat lower than it was in the past. Projections based on the trends indicate that about 90 percent of women will marry at some time in their life, down from the 95 percent level that existed during most of the nation's history (Goldstein and Kenney 2001).

The lower marriage rate combined with the rates of divorce and widowhood means that the currently married proportion of the population has declined over the last few decades. In 1970, 65.4 percent of men and 59.7 percent of women were currently married. By 2006, the figures were 56.8 percent of men and 54.1 percent of women. Table 8.1 gives the breakdown by sex and age. The dramatic decline in the proportion of women married, compared to that of men, after age 65 reflects the higher death rates of men. Marital status also varies by race and ethnic origin. In 2006, the proportion of those married was 55.6 percent for whites, 50.7 percent for Hispanics, 32.4 percent of African Americans, and 60.1 percent for Asian Americans (U.S. Census Bureau 2007a).

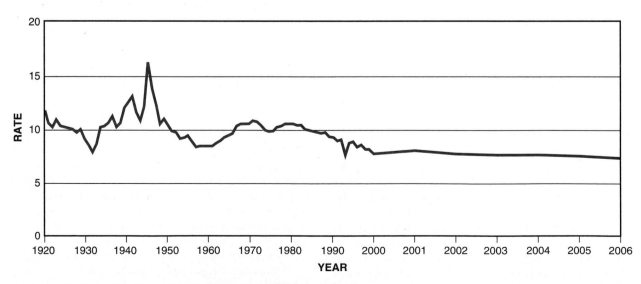

FIGURE 8.1 Marriage Rates (Rate per 1,000 Population)
Source: National Center for Health Statistics Web site.

TABLE 8.1 Proportion of the Population Married, by Sex and Age, 2006

Age	Percent	
	Males	Females
Total	56.8	54.1
15 to 17 years old	0.3	0.5
15 to 64 years old	53.7	56.0
65+ years old	74.9	45.6
85+ years	62.8	18.4

Source: U.S. Census Bureau 2007a.

Who Does and Who Doesn't Marry?

Who will and who will not marry is not merely one of preference. Some people are involuntarily single because of the **marriage squeeze,** a shortage of acceptable mates for one sex or the other. Thus, women have lower rates of marriage when they live in an area where there is a shortage in the number and quality (i.e., men whom they define as acceptable as mates) of available men (Lichter et al. 1992). The marriage squeeze affects women more than men at this point. However, the sex ratio has been changing and, according to Census Bureau projections, the number of men relative to the number of women will continue to increase. It may be men rather than women who face the greater chance of involuntary singlehood in the future.

A number of social factors and conditions in addition to the marriage squeeze affect marriage rates. First, the norm that a man should be somewhat older than a woman he marries limits the choices of both men and women. Second, the lingering belief among some people that wives should be homemakers leads to lower rates of marriage among those women who hold this belief but who also aspire to a college degree (Barber and Axinn 1998). Third, those men who expect to be the breadwinner or at least the primary provider of income for the family are likely to marry only when they believe their income is at a sufficiently high level to fulfill their responsibility (Koball 2004). Finally, for both men and women marriage rates are higher among the well educated than those who are poorly educated (Schoen and Cheng 2006).

Interestingly, some have argued that women's increasing economic independence depresses the marriage rate because women no longer are pressured into a union in order to survive economically. However, a comparative study of three nations found that women's higher levels of income are associated with lower first marriage rates in Japan but with higher rates in the United States and Sweden (Ono 2003).

WHY DO PEOPLE MARRY?

In a national survey, both men and women said they believed that men need to be married more than do women (Kaufman and Goldscheider 2007). However, a study of young, single men and women found that the women had a higher drive to marry than did the men (Blakemore, Lawton, and Vartanian 2005). Given the high proportion of people who do eventually marry, it is safe to say that marriage is desired by most people. Why?

To be sure, if someone says to you, "I'm going to get married," you are not likely to ask why. You no doubt assume that the two people are in love and want to live together and perhaps have children together. But as we noted in chapter 1, people marry for reasons other than love. In fact, some social scientists believe that the full meaning of love only emerges during the course of a marriage, not prior to marriage. This isn't to say that the two people do not feel that they are in love. However, there are other reasons for getting married.

The Need for Intimacy

The question of why get married would be answered very differently in various societies and in different generations (Coontz 2005). In ancient Greece and Rome, and in Europe through the eighteenth century, marriage was tied up more with politics and money than with love. The elite in medieval Europe, for example, used marriage as a way to increase wealth, to form political alliances, and to prevent illegitimate children from trying to claim a share of a family's wealth. Among the middle classes, marriage was largely a business matter, a way for a man to raise capital (from the dowry) and for the woman to gain economic security.

Gradually, marriage came to be considered a matter of love rather than money or politics. Men increasingly sought intimacy in their wives rather than in mistresses or courtesans. Women increasingly looked to their husbands for intimacy and not merely for economic security. This is not to say that there were no love matches prior to modern times. But the dominant motivation for marriage was not to fulfill the need for intimacy.

We have noted in previous chapters the importance of intimacy for your well-being. Of course, you need not get married in order to fulfill your intimacy needs. But the drive to establish an intimate relationship is powerful (Cutrona 2004). And most people believe that the best way to have and to maintain intimacy is through marriage. Thus, in contrast to the past, intimacy is a primary goal of marriage today (Shumway 2003).

Social Expectations

The expectation is that you will get married, as illustrated by the fact that there are still some negative attitudes toward people who opt to remain single. All societies have the **institution** of marriage, which is a societal way of regulating heterosexual relationships. Even people in preindustrial societies have well-defined rules about people getting married and generally expect that most will marry.

In other words, to say that marriage is a social institution is to point out that there are norms and expectations that govern it. These vary from one society to another, but they serve the same basic functions. Among other things, the institution of marriage prevents heterosexual relationships from deteriorating into chaos (a married person is, at least theoretically, off-limits to others who might be sexually attracted to that person). It provides a

normative way of perpetuating the group, by specifying a context in which sexual relations and the bearing and care of children will occur.

Thus, marriage as an institution is important to the well-being of the total group. Individuals who scorn such an institution are a threat to the group and to its survival. It is understandable, then, that we are raised with the expectation that we will marry. That expectation is communicated to us through family and friends.

If quiet expectations do not motivate an individual, a family may resort to more overt expectations in the form of pressures of various kinds. Parents may pressure their children into marriage because they are embarrassed by their children's single status or because they feel that the children will be happier if married. Unfortunately, sometimes the pressures lead to a marriage that is premature and doomed to failure.

Social Ideals and Personal Fulfillment

We have seen that most Americans still value a monogamous union that results in children and lasts a lifetime. To grow up in a society with that kind of ideal means

What Do You Think?

There is disagreement about **whether marriage is more beneficial for men than for women.** *What follows are some pro and con arguments. What do you think?*

Pro	Con
Marriage is more beneficial for men than for women because	Marriage is not more beneficial for men than for women because
• women have to make more adjustments after marriage than men do.	• men today are just as involved in time-consuming household chores as women are.
• married women have less time for personal growth than do married men or single women.	• it fulfills women's unique relationship and nesting needs.
• married men are healthier than either single men or married women.	• it provides women with greater economic security.
• it frees men from household chores and enables them to focus on a career.	• it broadens a woman's career choices—she can be a stay-at-home wife and/or mother or a working wife and/or mother.
• it gives men someone to bear and care for their children.	• it gives a woman a personal domain that she can shape and govern to suit her whims.

that you are likely to accept it for your own. It becomes not merely the ideal of most people, as portrayed in stories, television, and family conversations, but your own ideal as well. In other words, through socialization you develop the sense that marriage is the way to fulfill some of your basic needs and to attain the highest reaches of happiness.

Some people carry this to an extreme and expect marriage to fulfill *all* their basic needs (Crosby 1991; Silliman and Schumm 2004). They look to a mate for emotional support, romantic and sexual fulfillment, meeting their companionship needs, and so on. This is what we call the "you're my everything" expectation. It is, of course, unrealistic, and can lead to serious marital problems.

At the same time, it is reasonable to expect marriage to contribute to your personal fulfillment. And the fact that there is a greater amount of life satisfaction among the married than among single people is evidence that marriage does indeed contribute to fulfillment.

Desire for Children

As those who are involved with premarital counseling know, most people who get married say that one of the reasons is to have children. They have reached a stage of their lives in which they desire to form their own families. As we have seen, some people have children outside of marriage. However, there are many difficulties for those who take that option. If you want to have and raise children, it is a far easier task if you are married.

The desire for children is one reason people marry.

Marriage as a Practical Solution

Some people view marriage as a practical solution to various problems and challenges. Some want to get away from an undesirable home situation. Some believe a spouse will help them realize their ambitions. Some want a dependable and steady sex life. And some realize that being single is too lonely and/or difficult for them. Marriage is a practical and acceptable way to deal with these problems.

TYPES OF MARRIAGE

Because people get married for a variety of reasons and because their experiences of marriage are quite diverse, we would expect to find different types of marriage. However, there is no single way to classify marriage by differing types. We could divide them up on the basis of communication styles, amount of conflict, degree of homogamy, or any other basis we choose. Some of the more useful classification schemes, we believe, use lifestyles or the nature of the relationship as the basis for categorization.

Classified by Lifestyles

Which is most appealing to you, a traditional marriage or some other lifestyle? Before answering, take the test in figure 8.2, and see how you score. The traditional marriage is one in which the husband is the breadwinner and major decision maker, the wife is the homemaker, there are children, the spouses have sexual relations only with each other, and the union lasts a lifetime. You may, of course, prefer some of the elements of the traditional marriage, but not others.

In a study of college women, Billingham, Perera, and Ehlere (2005) put the issue of preference in reverse, giving the students a list of various forms of marriage and family life and asking them in which of the forms they would *never* be willing to participate. A number of the forms were rejected by 85 percent or more of the women, including a polygamous union and a marriage in which the husband has the right to have sex with others. Only 43.7 percent said they would never participate in a five-year evaluation and renewal, and a third would not participate in a child-free marriage. Just under 11 percent, however, rejected completely the traditional marriage, and 6.7 percent rejected long-term cohabitation with the intent of eventual marriage. But not a single woman rejected the

Would you prefer a more traditional or nontraditional kind of marriage? Circle your answer to the statements below, then read the directions beneath the statements on how to score yourself.

1. A wife should respond to her husband's sexual overtures even when she is not interested.

   1. Agree strongly   2. Agree mildly   3. Disagree mildly   4. Disagree strongly

2. In general, the father should have greater authority than the mother in the bringing up of children.

   1. Agree strongly   2. Agree mildly   3. Disagree mildly   4. Disagree strongly

3. Only when the wife works should the husband help with housework.

   1. Agree strongly   2. Agree mildly   3. Disagree mildly   4. Disagree strongly

4. Husbands and wives should be equal partners in planning the family budget.

   4. Agree strongly   3. Agree mildly   2. Disagree mildly   1. Disagree strongly

5. In marriage, the husband should make the major decisions.

   1. Agree strongly   2. Agree mildly   3. Disagree mildly   4. Disagree strongly

6. If both husband and wife agree that sexual fidelity isn't important, there's no reason why both shouldn't have extramarital affairs if they want to.

   4. Agree strongly   3. Agree mildly   2. Disagree mildly   1. Disagree strongly

7. If a child gets sick and the wife works, the husband should be just as willing as she to stay home from work and take care of that child.

   4. Agree strongly   3. Agree mildly   2. Disagree mildly   1. Disagree strongly

8. In general, men should leave the housework to women.

   1. Agree strongly   2. Agree mildly   3. Disagree mildly   4. Disagree strongly

9. Married women should keep their money and spend it as they please.

   4. Agree strongly   3. Agree mildly   2. Disagree mildly   1. Disagree strongly

10. In the family, both of the spouses ought to have as much say on important matters.

   4. Agree strongly   3. Agree mildly   2. Disagree mildly   1. Disagree strongly

Add your total. Note that "agree strongly" is sometimes worth one and sometimes worth four. It is your total score that is important, not whether you agreed or disagreed more often. Your score may vary from 10 to 40. If you score 30 to 40, you are nontraditional. A score of 20 to 30 means you take a middle-of-the-road position. A score of 10 to 20 puts you into the traditional category.

FIGURE 8.2 Rate Your Marital Preference

Source: Karen Oppenheim Mason, *Sex-Role Attitude Items and Scales from U.S. Sample Surveys* (Rockville, MD: National Institute of Mental Health) 1975:16–19.

egalitarian marriage, which is one in which husband and wife can both be employed and have an equal voice in making decisions.

Another study of college students' attitudes toward marital roles reported similar preferences (Kaufman 2005). The majority of the students expected to marry and to have children. The majority also indicated that they would not like to stay at home rather than work, nor would they like their spouse to stay at home. In fact, they tended to be egalitarian in their attitudes (figure 8.3). Only a minority of both men and women agreed that the woman should be the primary caretaker of the children and the man should be the primary financial provider, while a majority of both men and women agreed that it's important for the man to help care for the children and for the woman to be financially self-supporting.

Classified by Nature of the Relationship

In chapter 7, we discussed PREPARE, an instrument for assessing couples before they marry. A similar instrument, ENRICH, was developed to assess the relationships of people who are already married. Lavee and Olson (1993) used nine dimensions of a couple's relationship measured by ENRICH to develop a typology

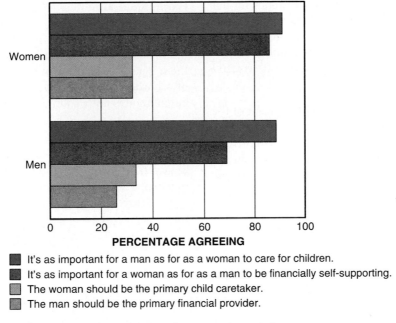

FIGURE 8.3 Attitudes about Marriage Roles
Source: Adapted from Kaufman (2005).

of marriages. The nine dimensions are the extent of satisfaction with the partner's personality traits and habits, the amount and kind of communication the couple has, the way conflict is handled, how the finances are managed, the amount and kind of leisure activities, sex, children and parenting issues, relationships with family and friends, and the role of religion in the couple's life.

The researchers used data from 8,383 couples across the nation who took ENRICH in either marital therapy or marriage enrichment programs. On the average, the couples were in their early 30s, had been married for 10 years, and had two to three children. Eighty percent were in a first marriage. Seven types of couples emerged from the analysis.

Devitalized Couples. Forty percent of the couples fell into this category (keep in mind that the sample was not random and included many couples who were in therapy). Devitalized couples are dissatisfied to some extent with all nine dimensions of their relationship. Nothing is working well for them. They are probably thinking about separation or divorce.

Financially Focused Couples. Eleven percent of the couples were financially focused. This group scores high on financial management. They agree with each other on how to manage their money. They are dissatisfied on a number of the other dimensions, so the major reason they stay together is because of the financial rewards involved and/or the financial penalties incurred by splitting up.

Conflicted Couples. Conflicted couples comprised 14 percent of the sample. Conflicted couples, like the financially focused, are dissatisfied on a number of dimensions. But, unlike the financially focused, they are satisfied with more than a single dimension. They may, for example, be unhappy about their communication patterns and the way they deal with conflict, but may be satisfied with such things as leisure activities and the parenting of their children.

Traditional Couples. Ten percent of the couples were traditional. Along with the next two types (the balanced and the harmonious), traditional couples are satisfied with most of the dimensions of their relationship but have at least one source of dissatisfaction. Traditional couples tend to be very strong in their relationships with family and friends and satisfied on most other dimensions but dissatisfied with communication patterns and their sexual relationship.

Balanced Couples. Balanced couples (8 percent of the total) are quite satisfied on such dimensions as leisure activities, children, and sex. They are particularly strong in their communication patterns and conflict resolution skills. However, they have ongoing problems with financial management. Money issues vex them even though they are able to talk about them and do well in solving other kinds of problems.

Harmonious Couples. Eight percent of the couples were classified as harmonious. On the whole, this type expresses great satisfaction with each other and with their relationship. The one area that is troublesome for them is parenting. They find the children to be as much of a burden as a blessing. They enjoy each other, but parenthood is not a source of gratification for them.

Vitalized Couples. The final type, the vitalized, comprised 9 percent of the sample. These couples are highly satisfied on all nine dimensions of their life together. They are not problem free, but they are able to work together to deal with any problems in a way that is satisfying to each partner. In essence, they have

Comparison

Types of Marriage in Togo

The people of the Moba-Gurma society, who are located in the northern, rural part of the African nation of Togo, live in domestic groups. The groups consist of about nine people on the average and are headed by an older male. Fertility is a central value for the Moba-Gurma people. Thus, a woman's status depends on her ability to bear children, and a man's status depends on the number of wives and children he has.

Marriages in this society can be classified by the manner in which a husband obtains a wife. Seven types of marriage are found:

1. *Marriage by exchange* occurs when two heads of domestic groups agree to exchange young women. Such an agreement may arise out of friendship or out of a desire to form an alliance. Nearly a third of marriages occur by this method, which enables all men (including those with physical disabilities) to have a wife as long as they have a woman to exchange.

2. *Brideservice marriage* comprises almost 5 percent of the total. In this type, a man who does not have a woman to exchange offers something else. He may, for example, work in the fields of the family from whom he expects to get a wife.

3. *Child betrothal* occurs in a little over one in five marriages. Under this arrangement, the head of the family gives a woman to a man in gratitude for his services (farm work) or as an expression of friendship. Typically, a young daughter is given or an unborn daughter is promised.

4. Nearly a fourth of unions involve *marriage by abduction*. This is a somewhat misleading term, since the woman allows herself to be abducted. She may have been promised to someone else, or she may be already married. But she agrees to meet the man in an arranged place and he "abducts" her. The situation is called *abduction* in the male-dominated Moba-Gurma society because they cannot imagine, or acknowledge, a

woman doing such a thing of her own volition.

5. About 9 percent of marriages are *leviratic*. The levirate is a common practice in Africa. It requires a man to marry the wife or wives of a deceased brother. If the deceased man had no brother, another male relative is required to marry the widow or widows.

6. *Marriage by reimbursement* also comprises about 9 percent of all unions. This type occurs after a man has obtained a wife through brideservice or child betrothal. Even though the man has paid for his wife under these two methods, he still must give a woman back at some later date to replace the one taken.

7. Finally, a very small number of marriages are *bridewealth* unions, a marriage formed when a well-to-do man arranges the purchase of a wife. The few men who practice this arrangement tend to use it to get a woman from another ethnic group (Pilon 1994).

the kind of marriage that fulfills their needs and their expectations.

Diversity in Relationships. As you read about the seven types, you probably have varied reactions to each. Which types appeal to you? Which ones do you think would be "good enough" in order for you to stay in a marriage? The point is that there are diverse ways of relating to each other in the intimacy of marriage. Most of these ways probably fall short of your ideal, but many of them are sufficiently satisfying for the people involved to remain together.

Interestingly, the researchers found some background differences among the various types. The devitalized tended to be younger, married fewer years, in a lower income bracket than the other types, and have parents who were divorced. Those in the traditional and vitalized groups tended to be older and married a greater number of years. The vitalized couples also were more likely to be in a first marriage, to come from an intact home, and to be in higher income brackets than the other types.

EXPECTATIONS

When people marry, they have certain expectations about what their marriage will involve. Among other things, they tend to expect that marriage will make them happy and fulfilled, that it will last, and that their spouse will be faithful. Some of these expectations may be unrealistic. If, for instance, you expect that your spouse is always going to make you happy or that your relationship will be invulnerable to infidelity, your expectations are unrealistic. A survey of high school students reported that 60 percent agreed that when they married, the spouse would fulfill nearly all their needs for security, support, and companionship (Silliman and Schumm 2004). If they retain such expectations, they are expecting more than they are likely to get.

Yet even if your expectations are all realistic, it doesn't mean that your marriage will be free of problems. You may or may not have the same expectations as the person you marry. You each may have realistic expectations, but they may be incompatible with each other. Unfortunately, sometimes we don't communicate what we expect until after we are married.

Our Private Contracts

Marriage is a contract between two people. It is a legal contract in the sense that the partners can bring each other to court to require performance or to dissolve the relationship. It is a social contract in the sense that family and friends feel that they have a stake in the relationship and the right to intervene or at least to bring pressure to bear on the couple. It is an interpersonal contract in the sense that the partners agree to commit themselves to each other for the duration of their lives. All of these contracts may result in anguish because the spouses also bring to the marriage their private contracts, which basically involve assumptions that each makes about the nature of the relationship and their mutual obligations. Each partner has a private contract, then, in the sense that each *assumes* that there is agreement about various matters that were never discussed (Lauer and Lauer 1993).

For example, Kevin and Beth, a young dual-career couple, shared with us the reason they went for marriage counseling in their fifth year together. They had a marriage that was working well for the first four years. Each was doing well in a career. They had an egalitarian relationship: They shared chores around their apartment and decisions about budgeting their income. Both loved to travel, and they planned a venture into someplace new each year.

In the fifth year, however, their marriage ran into trouble. Kevin was ready to buy a home. He also expected that a new home would mean it was time to begin their family, though at first he didn't mention that. Beth was not happy about buying a home. She preferred to travel a few more years rather than to be saddled with a mortgage.

For the first time in their marriage, they began to argue strenuously about money. He wanted to save for a down payment for a home. He accused Beth of "going crazy" with credit cards. During one of the arguments, he accused her of reneging on the understanding they had before they got married: to begin their family within the first five years of marriage. Beth was astonished. He hadn't said anything about children when he suggested they buy a home. "I'm not sure I can afford to take time off from my work to have a baby," she said. "It could really hurt my career at this point."

"But," Kevin insisted, "that was our agreement."

"No, it wasn't," Beth retorted. "We agreed only that we would have children, not that we would have them in five years. You know how important it is for me to get another promotion before I take time off for a baby." Kevin reminded her that he was already 35 years old. "If I wait for another five years," he said, "I'll be retired before my children are grown."

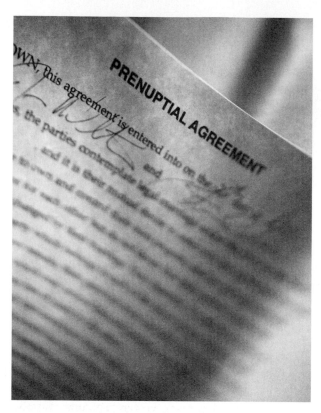

Some couples formalize their expectations with a prenuptial agreement.

Beth was unmoved by his argument. "I just want another couple of years. Then we can settle down, get our home, and start our family." Kevin threw his hands up in dismay and stalked out of the house.

They were at an impasse because they were the victims of their private contracts. Each accused the other of not living up to an agreement. But the "agreement" was a myth, a set of two private contracts that contradicted each other. He assumed that they agreed that they would have children by the time he was 35. She assumed they agreed that they would have children only after they had traveled extensively and that she was at a point in her career where she could take time off. Neither of them had told the other about their "agreements."

Role Expectations

When private contracts clash, it is frequently over role expectations. Kevin assumed that Beth, even though she had a career, would revert to being a more traditional wife who would willingly sacrifice her career to bear and

care for their children. Beth assumed that Kevin was thoroughly committed to an egalitarian marriage in which her role as a professional was as important as his.

Kevin and Beth are not unique in their problem. The **Symbolic Interactionist Theory Applied** question of the husband role and the wife role is a vexing one in many marriages. It is vexing when, in *symbolic interactionist* terms, we define our own expectations as legitimate and those of our partner as not legitimate when they clash with our own. That defines the situation as one of right and wrong rather than as a difference that needs to be worked out to the mutual satisfaction of the partners.

What, then, are people's expectations about those roles? One thing is clear: Expectations have become more egalitarian than they were in the middle of the twentieth century and earlier. Two researchers who analyzed data collected from female college students at six different points in time between 1961 and 1996 found that women have become more egalitarian in their expectations about marital matters (Botkin and Weeks 2000). The researchers compared the women's marriage role expectations overall as well as their expectations about authority, homemaking, child care, personal characteristics, social participation, education, and employment and support.

They found a significant increase in overall egalitarianism as well as in the various specific areas of marriage over the time period. Interestingly, the greatest change occurred between 1961 and 1972, with a 58.9 percent increase in egalitarian responses. Subsequent generations continued to show increases, but not to the same extent. And the proportion who expected husband and wife to share equally in child care actually declined slightly from the 1984 high of 95.9 percent of the women to the 1996 figure of 91.6 percent.

Compared to women in the 1961 survey, then, those in subsequent years were far more egalitarian in their expectations. A majority agreed that husband and wife should have equal responsibility for such matters as decision making, caring for children, household chores, supporting of each other's employment/career in the workforce, and educational aspirations.

Of course, whether those expectations are realized when they actually marry is another matter. Some will have an egalitarian union. Others will find that there is more egalitarianism in attitude than in practice, as we will see in chapter 11. The discrepancies between what husbands expect and what wives expect, along with the discrepancies between expectations and practice, account for a good deal of discontent and conflict in marriages. Couples who want to avoid problems will find themselves engaging in a process of negotiation about marital roles.

Negotiation: Changing Personal Contracts

Kevin and Beth had problems because neither was aware of the other's private contract, neither discussed the fact that the original contracts had been broken, and neither tried to initiate a process of negotiation to try to clarify and rework expectations. They desperately needed to understand and work with each other's private contract.

Negotiation is a process of working through clashing expectations. In negotiation, the expectations of each partner are brought out into the open. That is, the private contracts must become joint knowledge. Sometimes the individuals are not even aware of their own private contracts. They only recognize that something the partner has done has frustrated, angered, or disappointed them. Once the differing expectations are acknowledged, then the process of give-and-take can begin as the couple examines their various options and comes to a satisfactory compromise.

Consider the following example of clashing expectations and successful negotiation. A married student told us that she was appalled when she found that her new husband threw his clothes on the floor at night. "I thought that any civilized man would either hang his clothes up or put them in the wash." At first, she picked them up herself. Then she grew angry with him. When she became somewhat cold and distant, he asked her what was bothering her. He was surprised at her response. He expected her, as his wife, to pick up his clothes. His mother had done that. She curtly informed him that she would not be a mother to him.

They soon were able to negotiate a settlement. He agreed that he could change a lifelong habit, and she agreed to remind him and to be patient until he had established a new habit. She became aware of the fact that her private contract included a provision about her husband's neatness and help in keeping the house clean. She was unaware of that until she saw the clothes on the floor. His private contract included the expectation that his wife would behave like his mother in some ways. He, too, was unaware of that until his wife confronted him with her anger.

Not all clashing expectations are negotiated that easily. It is important for couples to recognize the existence of private contracts, the probability of differences in expectations, and the importance of negotiation for working through the differences.

The Marriage Contract: Clarifying Expectations

Instead of waiting until problems arise to clarify and negotiate private contracts, a couple can avoid at least some of the problems of marriage by formulating a marriage contract prior to the wedding. This can be a formal, legal document, such as a **prenuptial agreement** that is drawn up by a lawyer. A prenuptial agreement normally specifies such matters as how assets will be distributed in the event of divorce or death, how premarital debts will be paid, and what kind of insurance coverage to have. However, the agreement also can specify various nonfinancial matters such as child care, household division of labor, limits on work hours, and education (Shellenbarger 2003). As long as the agreements are fair and reasonable (which means, among other things, that both partners have made full disclosure), they are valid in all 50 states and the District of Columbia.

Legally, prenuptial agreements are particularly important for people who have considerable assets, who own all or part of a business, who have children from a previous marriage, who are pursuing a professional degree, or who expect a sizable inheritance. The prenuptial agreement takes precedence over any state laws such as community property.

Increasingly, married people are also turning to a **postnuptial agreement,** a legal document that specifies how the couple's assets will be divided if they divorce, but it is entered into after the couple is married (Frank 2007). The postnuptial is usually drawn up by couples who were not wealthy when they married, but who accumulated a good deal of wealth thereafter. If one of the spouses was the primary reason for the newfound wealth, that spouse may want protection in case of divorce.

For many people, either a prenuptial or a postnuptial agreement suggests a lack of trust in the relationship and the partner. They are not comfortable turning love into a contractual matter. Even if you find a legal agreement offensive, however, you still need to clarify the expectations you each have for the marriage. An alternative to the legal agreement is to write an informal marriage contract that clarifies your expectations (Garrett 1982). These contracts are not legally binding, but they do help the couple begin their married life with a better understanding of what each expects and, consequently, with less likelihood of friction and conflict over some common issues in marriage. Garrett (1982) suggests that, among other things, you discuss and include the following in your marriage contract:

1. Will the wife use the husband's last name, her own name, or a hyphenated name?
2. What will be the division of labor in the home? Who will do the cooking, cleaning, washing, repairs, and so on?
3. Will you have children? If so, how many and when?
4. Will you use contraception? What kind?
5. If you have children, how will you divide up the child care responsibilities? What kind of discipline will you use?
6. What will you do about housing? Will housing decisions be made in light of the husband's career, the wife's career, or both?
7. Who will be the breadwinner? How will financial decisions be made and who will be responsible for paying bills?
8. What will be your relationships with in-laws? Will you spend part or all of your vacation time with parents or relatives?
9. How much of your leisure will you spend together and how much separately?
10. What are your sexual expectations?
11. How will you change the terms of this contract over the course of your marriage?

The last point is important because no contract should be unalterable. A marriage contract reflects the way you feel at a certain point in time. One or both partners may want to change the terms. The points should always be open to negotiation. Informal contracts are meant to facilitate the ongoing development of intimacy, not bind partners to an inflexible pattern.

THE WEDDING

The **wedding** is a public ceremony that validates and celebrates a couple's marriage. Various traditions are associated with the wedding, and those traditions differ considerably between societies and eras. In a preindustrial society, the wedding may consist of little more than the sharing of a common meal and a ritualistic transfer of the bride from her parents' home to that of her husband. In Puritan New England, a couple had to make an announcement at three successive public meetings about their intent to marry or

attach a written announcement on the meetinghouse door for 14 days (Morgan 1966). And until 1686, the wedding was conducted by a civil magistrate rather than a minister. The celebration included a feast, but dancing and excessive "merrymaking" were forbidden.

In the United States today, the wedding has become a lucrative business as well as an elaborate affair. The law requires certain procedures prior to the wedding, and various family and religious traditions as well as contemporary norms are likely to define the nature of the wedding itself.

Legal Considerations

Laws regulate a number of steps prior to the wedding (Cornell Law School 2007). These laws are mainly state laws, and they vary from one state to another. We say "mainly" because the Supreme Court has ruled that the states can prescribe who is allowed to marry but cannot prohibit marriage where there is no valid reason to do so. For example, a state cannot prohibit an interracial marriage because that violates the Equal Protection Clause of the Constitution.

The main legal considerations at the state level are the age at which people can marry, what, if any, medical examinations are required, and how the couple obtains a marriage license. In most states, you can marry without parental consent if you are 18 years or over. In Mississippi, the age without parental consent is 15 for females and 17 for males, and in Nebraska you have to be 19 years or older. The age with parental consent drops to 16 in a majority of the states, although some allow it at an earlier age and some only drop down a year to 17. In Massachusetts, a girl can marry at age 12 if she has both parental consent and the permission of a judge.

States may also require a medical exam, although most do not. Most do require a license, however. Generally, you must apply in person for the license at the local clerk's office. There is a fee for the license, and some states have a waiting period between the time of the application and the time the license takes effect. Licenses also have an expiration time if the wedding does not take place. Expiration times vary from 30 days to a year.

Planning and Carrying Out the Wedding

As we noted earlier, weddings in the United States today tend to be elaborate affairs. While both the bride and the groom may have responsibilities in planning the wedding, the bride is likely to bear the brunt of the work

(Sniezek 2005). The planning has become so extensive, however, that there are professional wedding planners who can be hired to take care of both the broad plan and the details (Mead 2007).

Consider some of the questions involved in the planning. Where will the ceremony take place? Who should be invited? Who will determine the attire of the bridesmaids and groomsmen? If the bride's parents are divorced and the mother has remarried, who will give the bride away? Where should the reception be held? Who will secure the music and the food? What are the seating arrangements at the reception? What kind of photography and video recording of the event should be utilized? And so on. It is little wonder that some couples opt for a wedding planner.

Even without a wedding planner, a wedding is likely to be an expensive affair. In 2007, the average cost of weddings in the United States was $30,000 (Blalik 2007). It is estimated that the wedding "industry" is a $161 billion business (Mead 2007). Because the average age at marriage has risen, many couples are already established in their careers. Rather than the parents of the bride paying most of the cost, therefore, about three-fourths of couples expect to pay at least part of the bill themselves (Kwiatoski 2007).

The cost can increase considerably for those who plan a "destination wedding" (McMullen-Coyne 2005). The destination wedding is a product from luxury hotel chains that offer couples help, including lists of professional planners, in designing and carrying out weddings at one of their sites throughout the world. Thus, a couple living in, say, Missouri could decide to have their wedding and their honeymoon take place at a luxury resort in Hawaii. This would mean that the entire wedding party, including all guests, would travel to Hawaii instead of attending a wedding in their home state of Missouri. The destination wedding has the appeal of something unique and exotic but also can add considerably to the total cost.

Unfortunately, an elaborate wedding can generate tension between the bride and the groom as well as between the couple and their parents. If, for example, the bride and the groom have contrary ideas about what kind of wedding they prefer, or if one or both sets of parents try to impose things on the couple that the couple do not want, some lasting conflict and hurt may result. Although they do not necessarily produce conflict and hurt feelings, such differences may be common. A survey of 196 undergraduates reported some significant gender differences about weddings (Knox,

Zusman, McGinty, and Abowitz 2003). In particular, compared to the men, women indicated that they would spend more time thinking about and preparing for the wedding, were more likely to hire a professional photographer to take photos and videotape the wedding, and were more likely to want a formal wedding rather than something simple like a civil wedding conducted by a justice of the peace.

This is not to say that the modern wedding is inherently detrimental to the quality of the couples' relationship. We have known many couples for whom the wedding day was a highlight of their life. Yet we have also known some for whom the seeds of ongoing discontent and conflict were sown in the nettlesome tasks of an elaborate wedding.

ADJUSTING TO MARRIAGE

To get married is to enter a new social world. Even those who have cohabited for a number of years frequently say that their relationship changes when they get married. There are adjustments to be made, whether or not you have lived together prior to marriage. In part, adjustments reflect the differing expectations we discussed. In part, they reflect the nature of the new social world into which people enter—a world of new responsibilities, new options such as child-bearing, and new relationships such as with in-laws.

His Marriage and Her Marriage

Jessie Bernard (1972) argued that every marriage is really two marriages: his and hers. That is, men and women have

Conflict Theory Applied

substantially different experiences in marriage. Or, in terms of *conflict theory*, men and women have different interests and must to some extent vie with each other to successfully pursue those interests. For example, we all need to have some sense of control over our lives. But when women get married, they tend to have a greater sense of control in terms of increased income but a diminished sense of control in terms of being autonomous (Ross 1991). Given the same income, non-married women have a greater sense of control than either married women or men.

Bernard also argued that men derive more from marriage than do women. Research on more than 7,000 married couples reported that men are somewhat more satisfied with their marriages than are

Even when both spouses affirm egalitarianism, the wife tends to assume the major responsibility for child care.

women and seem to get greater mental health benefits from marriage than do women (Fowers 1991). It is also true that women have to make more adjustments in marriage than do men.

Why must women make more adjustments? Consider some of the typical things that happen in marriage. A man is less likely than a woman to change his vocation or to drop out of the labor force. He is unlikely to move his residence to accommodate his wife's career, while she may move frequently to accommodate him. In spite of egalitarian attitudes, women still bear the brunt of housekeeping chores in most homes. When children come, women tend to assume the major responsibility for their care.

Furthermore, women are more likely than men to have their private contracts violated. For women, talking things over is an important part of an intimate relationship, and men tend to talk to them in an intimacy-building fashion during courtship (Goleman 1986). But after marriage, the husband may spend less and less time talking with his wife about their relationship. She may find herself deprived of an important source of meeting her intimacy needs. Worse, she may have been led to believe by her husband's behavior that the intimate communication would be a part of their marriage.

Starting with Two Strikes

Adjustment in some marriages is more difficult because they begin at a disadvantage. We have discussed the problems with teenage marriages, for instance. Teenage couples truly begin their married life with two strikes already against them. They frequently face the problem of low income and perhaps of thwarted educational and career hopes at a time in life when they lack the maturity to cope effectively with such things.

Student marriages also begin with some disadvantages, whether the student is married to an employed spouse or another student. There are likely to be problems over the use of time and other strains associated with student marriages (Dyk 1987). The time problems become acute if the student is also employed part- or full-time. School schedules are relatively inflexible. An employed spouse may get weary of always having to accommodate to the demands that professors make on his or her partner. When the employed spouse is the husband and he has more traditional gender-role attitudes, the probability of conflict increases even more (Dyk 1987). The strains associated with student marriages arise from the student being so stressed or preoccupied with schoolwork that the marital relationship suffers. Students can get emotionally, intellectually, and physically weary. If the spouse does not understand and fully support the student, marital problems are more likely.

Various other marriages begin at a disadvantage. If the woman is pregnant at the time of marriage, there is the additional adjustment of becoming parents. If the couple is not homogamous, there will be many adjustments to make. The quality of the family life in which the partners grew up also affects their adjustment to marriage (Sabatelli and Bartle-Haring 2003). The point is that, even under the best of circumstances, learning to live intimately with another person requires adjustments. It is unfortunate if the couple begins with disadvantages as well as challenges.

Establishing Equity and Consensus

As argued by *exchange theorists,* if you have not worked out a marriage contract, you will have to work on the problems of equity and consensus in such areas as the division of labor around the home, your sex life, your social life, and other matters. A sense of equity is vital to making a satisfying adjustment (Huppe and Cyr 1997;

Voydanoff and Donnelly 1999). A certain amount of consensus is also important. That is, the spouses must

Exchange Theory Applied

agree, or at least perceive that they agree, on various attitudes and behaviors. Couples in long-term, satisfying marriages do not agree on everything, but in our research, 84.4 percent felt that they always or almost always agreed on aims, goals, and things they believed important (Lauer and Lauer 1986:97). A husband put it this way:

> I think the success of our marriage is due in large part to having many common values and that we agree on basically most things that are important in our lives together. This is particularly true for issues related to careers, money, and family life-style.

A relationship based on equity and consensus seems to come rather easily to some couples. Others have a more difficult time. One way those who are struggling can establish equity and consensus is for each spouse to make a list of preferences. For example, in considering the division of labor in the home, the couple can first make a list of the various chores. Then each spouse ranks the chores from most to least desirable. The rankings are compared and the final division of labor negotiated.

Adjustment and In-Law Relationships

A marriage and family therapist told us that he believes as many as 60 percent of all marriages have some tension because of the relationship between the mother-in-law and daughter-in-law. Popular magazines regularly carry articles that tell people how to deal with in-law problems. A study of 451 couples in rural areas found that the quality of relationships with in-laws predicted the extent to which the partners perceived their marriages to be stable and satisfying (Bryant, Conger, and Meehan 2001). Thus, in-laws are important factors in many marriages. You don't marry an individual. You marry into a family.

In spite of their importance, in-law relationships have been the focus of little research. In some unpublished research, we asked 233 people, with a mean age of 38.3 years and married a mean of 11.4 years, to discuss their in-law relationships. Specifically, we asked which in-law relationship had been the most significant for them, in either a positive or negative sense, and how the in-law relationships had affected their marriage. Only seven said that they didn't regard any of their in-laws as significant (because they lived at too great a distance

from them). All of the others acknowledged that an in-law had been significant in some way in their lives.

We found the mother-in-law most likely to be named as the significant in-law relationship (table 8.2). Significant in what sense? We found that about half of those who said their mother-in-law was most significant indicated the relationship was a negative one and half said it was positive. Three researchers who used in-depth interviews to study the relationship of wives with their mothers-in-law found that a major challenge is feeling "a part of the family" of the in-laws (Turner, Young, and Black 2006). Some of the daughters-in-law were painfully disillusioned by the difficulty they experienced trying to be an integral part of their in-laws' family. Some, however, felt fully accepted and relished the relationship. The majority fell somewhere between the two extremes, expressing ambivalence or uncertainty or thinking of themselves as making progress but not yet experiencing what they had hoped for in the relationship.

Considering all the varied in-law relationships, it is important to note that they are more likely to be positive than negative.

In-laws, then, can help couples in their adjustment. Some in-laws are problems and make adjustment more difficult. However, in-laws are more likely to be resources than problems. The help that in-laws give may be monetary and/or emotional (Goetting 1990). As a young husband told us,

> When I got married, I got, in my father-in-law, the father to whom I could finally talk. He has been invaluable to me over the years. I could never go to my own father with some of the problems I've faced. I can always go to my father-in-law. He's been a security net.

TABLE 8.2 Most Significant In-Law Relationship

	Sex of respondent		
Relationship	Male (N = 88)	Female (N = 138)	Total (N = 226)
	Percent		
Mother-in-law	39.8	52.2	47.3
Father-in-law	26.1	14.5	19.0
Both mother- and father-in-law	13.6	12.3	12.8
Brother- or sister-in-law	20.5	15.9	17.8
Other	0.0	5.1	3.1
Total	100.0	100.0	100.0

Source: Copyright © 1986 Jeanette C. Lauer and Robert H. Lauer. Reprinted by permission.

FIRST-YEAR CHANGES

When a young couple returned from their honeymoon, a friend said to them, "Well, it's all downhill from here on." The friend was disillusioned with her marriage, and her disillusionment was rooted in her unrealistic expectations. She had thought of marriage as a kind of endless honeymoon. It isn't. Changes in a couple's relationship begin in the first year of marriage (Huston, McHale, and Crouter 1986). These changes reflect the realities of intimate living in a complex society.

For one thing, the feelings of the spouses change. By the end of the first year, you are likely to feel somewhat less satisfied with the amount of interaction you have with your spouse. You will probably feel less satisfied with the extent to which your spouse initiates activity that pleases you and the frequency with which you have physical intimacy. Wives tend to report less satisfaction in these areas than husbands, both at the beginning of the marriage and at the end of the first year (Huston, McHale, and Crouter 1986:121). It is important to keep in mind that we are *not* saying that people are dissatisfied with their marriages after a year. Most couples still feel positive about their interaction, but they are not as euphoric as they were at the time of their wedding. The positive feelings are still there, but they have moderated.

Behavior and activities also tend to change. Spouses report a diminished amount of joint household and leisure activities. There tends to be an increase in household and other kinds of work activity and a decrease of about 20 percent in joint leisure activity. The decline in leisure and increase in work activity is particularly strong if the couple has a baby during the first year.

The amount of time spouses spend talking with each other declines slightly. More importantly, there is a significant decline in behavior that reflects affection. Married people report that by the end of the first year, their spouses less frequently engaged in such things as

- approving and complimenting the partner.
- doing or saying something to make the partner laugh.
- telling the partner, "I love you."
- taking the initiative in sex.
- doing something nice for the partner.
- showing physical affection and having sexual relations.
- discussing their feelings and problems.
- talking over things that happened during the day.

Personal

In-Laws: The Good and the Bad

Henry is 61 years old. He has been married for 35 years. He has experienced both the good and the bad in in-law relationships. Both his father- and mother-in-law have had an impact on his life and his marriage. He had great admiration for his father-in-law. His mother-in-law is another matter:

My father-in-law is dead now, but he was the most significant in-law I had. He was 73 when I met him. His wife was 58 and she supported the family until she retired at 65. He adapted well to the role of taking care of the house. He did the cooking and cleaning, never complained about anything to anyone, and was always there to talk with me about my problems.

He lived for the first 10 years of my marriage. He encouraged me to pursue my goals, and taught me to be compassionate. Every night, he massaged his wife's feet. He had lived through a great deal of poverty and stress, but I never heard him gripe about it and I never heard him curse. He was a kind and gentle man who made me feel welcome into the family and supported me when I was getting my own career going.

My mother-in-law, on the other hand, is still alive and still a problem. She is selfish and thoughtless. Never in the 35 years of our marriage has she offered to help us or anyone that I know of. I can count the number of dinners I have had in her house on one hand. Because of her self-centered behavior and her constant demands on my wife, I have gotten—I still get—very depressed and angry. In the early years of our marriage, we argued a lot about her mother. If it hadn't been for my father-in-law, we would have had a much more difficult time. For about the last five years, we have learned to ignore her self-centered ways. We try to remember that she is very old and we reach out to her even though she will not reciprocate.

The number of such activities declined by about 40 percent from the beginning of the marriage (Huston, McHale, and Crouter 1986:123). Again, it is important to underscore the fact that this does not mean that such things were absent, but only that they were less frequent after a year. The overall amount of companionship does not change much, but it becomes more instrumental, more task-oriented, and less focused on romance and affection.

In other words, by the end of the first year, couples are well on their way to a realistic mode of living together. Their time and energy are devoted not only to each other but also to building careers and perhaps to beginning a family. Our intimacy needs are fundamental, but we also have needs for achievement and for security. Human life is not a honeymoon. Marriage is not a honeymoon. On the other hand, it is important to keep in mind that the exhilaration of the honeymoon can be periodically recaptured in a long-term relationship.

COMMITMENT

Why discuss commitment at the end of the chapter on getting married? Doesn't commitment come when a couple is seriously considering marriage? Yes and no. Commitment is certainly a part of the process leading up to marriage. However, even in this process commitment can vary. Surra and Hughes (1997) looked at the commitment to wed among 113 young adults and found two different types. "Relationship-driven commitment" evolved smoothly in a mainly harmonious relationship. "Event-driven commitment" featured sharp increases and decreases in the commitment to wed as a result of such things as episodes of conflict and having different networks of friends.

Commitment, in other words, can vary over time, both in the process leading up to the decision to wed and in the marriage itself. As far as marriage is concerned, those with higher levels of commitment are more likely to be satisfied with the union and less likely to have thoughts about divorce or other possible partners (Stanley, Markman, and Whitton 2002). In fact, there is a reciprocal relationship between commitment and the satisfaction and stability of the union. That is, commitment facilitates satisfaction and stability, and in turn, satisfaction and stability foster commitment. Commitment is a living part of the marriage, not an insurance policy that is irrevocable.

The Meaning of Commitment

For Americans, commitment in marriage seems to mean three things: promise, dedication, and attachment (Quinn 1982; Weigel, Bennett, and Ballard-Reisch 2003). There is

a promise or pledge to engage in something that will include some difficult times (for better or worse, says the traditional marriage vow). There is a dedication to the joint goal of staying together and forming a meaningful family unit. This means there is an attachment between the two people, an emotional attachment that results from joint dedication to their goal. There also can be an element of constraint in the commitment—the fear of the social, financial, and emotional costs of the union breaking up (Adams and Jones 1997). Such constraints, however, are unlikely to maintain a union if the other elements of commitment are lacking.

In essence, then, **commitment** means "a promise of dedication to a relationship in which there is an emotional attachment to another person who has made the same promise" (Lauer and Lauer 1986:50). It is important to note that the commitment is to the person and not simply to the institution of marriage. One difference between long-term satisfying marriages and those that are long-term but unsatisfying is that people in the former are committed more to the spouse while people in the latter are committed more to the institution (Lauer and Lauer 1986). Commitment to the institution means that there are family pressures or religious beliefs that make the person unwilling to break the union even though he or she is unhappy with it.

The Role of Commitment

Commitment is a valuable resource in marriage. Those who are committed to their spouses as persons have fewer marriage problems, express their love for their mates more often, and have higher levels of marital satisfaction (Swensen and Trahaug 1985; Clements and Swensen 2000). Commitment to the person means that you are determined to work through troubled times. In contrast, commitment to the institution means a willingness to simply endure troubles rather than to work through them. Those who work through problems, rather than endure or wait them out, find the quality of their relationship greatly enhanced.

Commitment also gives the partners a sense of security. A wife told us that she occasionally experienced a "flash of emotion" that could turn into jealousy. Nevertheless, she views that as her own problem and not the fault of her husband, because she knows that they are committed to each other. Neither of them, she said with confidence, would put the marriage into jeopardy. Each has a sense of security with the other.

Commitment has benefits that go beyond enriching the marital relationship. A happy marriage in which there is a firm sense of commitment becomes a strong resource for dealing with the stresses of life. For instance, two researchers studied thousands of Israeli men over a five-year period to try to determine how a particular heart problem, angina pectoris, develops.[1] They found that one of the better predictors of those men who were at high risk was the answer to the question, "Does your wife show you her love?" Those who answered "no" were more likely to develop the heart disorder. Or as a husband told us, "To know that you have someone that loves you, and on whom you can depend no matter what problems may arise, is really important. It's like having a crutch under a broken leg that you can rely on to support you."

Building Commitment

People enter marriage with varying degrees of commitment. Men who cohabited with their wives before engagement have lower levels of commitment than men who cohabited only after engagement or not at all (Rhoades, Stanley, and Markman 2006). The level of commitment, as we have noted earlier, can also change. Married people can act in a way that intensifies the commitment of each to the union or in ways that erode that commitment. One way to build commitment is to make sure that each partner feels a sense of equity in the relationship (Sabatelli and Cecil-Pigo 1985). It is very difficult to maintain commitment to a person if you feel that

you are seriously underrewarded, that you are giving far more to the relationship than the other. There are times in any relationship, of course, when one person has to give more, perhaps far more, than the other. But that should balance out over time. Few, if any, people can maintain commitment in the face of long-term inequity.

Commitment also grows as people's satisfaction with their relationship increases. While some decline in the affectional behavior noted is both normal and necessary after the honeymoon period, it is important for the couple to guard romance. The expression of affection is important throughout the marriage. It isn't enough to merely *feel* affectionate. That affection must be *expressed*. There is an old story about a reticent New Englander who said that he loved his wife so much it was all he could do to keep from telling her about it. Men generally have a more difficult time than women in openly expressing affection. But it is the expression, not merely the presence, of affectionate feelings that is necessary for building commitment.

Finally, commitment can be built by planning shared activities that are gratifying to both partners (Lauer and Lauer 1986). Sharing times of fun, achievement, or adventure intensifies people's commitment as well as provides them with intimate experiences. The more you have a history of shared, gratifying experiences, the deeper your commitment is likely to become.

SUMMARY

Although most Americans marry, your own chances vary depending on a number of factors. The marriage rate fluctuates over time, and reflects more than the preference of people to marry or not. Sex ratios and age are factors in the rates. The longer you wait, the less your chances are of being married.

People marry for various reasons in addition to being in love. One is the need for intimacy. Another is conformity to social expectations. Others include the idea that marriage and family are the ideal and most fulfilling state for humans, the desire to have children, and the definition of marriage as a practical solution to various problems and challenges.

We may classify marriages by lifestyles or by the nature of the relationship. Among the lifestyles are traditional and egalitarian marriages. Egalitarian marriages may be fur-

ther classified as home-centered, balanced, or career/job-centered. Marriages classified by the nature of the relationship include devitalized, financially focused, conflicted, traditional, balanced, harmonious, and vitalized.

We all have expectations when we marry. Even if we marry with all realistic expectations, we will not have a problem-free relationship. Each partner tends to bring a private contract to the marriage, a set of assumptions about various matters that have not been discussed. When private contracts clash, it is frequently over role expectations.

Negotiation is necessary to work through clashing expectations. In negotiation, private contracts must become joint knowledge. Negotiations also can occur before marriage, as the couple formulates a marriage contract to avoid some problems after they are married.

When you marry, you enter a new social world. There are many adjustments to make, even if you have lived together. The adjustments are not the same for both sexes.

---

[1]*New York Times*, 5 June 1988.

There is "his" marriage and "her" marriage. Women generally have to make more adjustments than men. Adjustment is more difficult when the marriage begins with disadvantages. Student, teenage, and heterogamous marriages all begin with some disadvantages. One important facet of adjustment is establishing equity and consensus in the relationship. In-laws also require adjustment, although overall they are more likely to be resources than problems.

During the first year of marriage, feelings and patterns of behavior change. Satisfaction tends to decline somewhat. Interaction tends to become more instrumental, more task oriented, and less focused on romance and affection.

Commitment is not only the basis for marriage but the outcome of a satisfying relationship. Commitment means promise, dedication, and attachment. In stable and satisfying marriages, there is commitment to the spouse as an individual instead of commitment to marriage as an institution. Commitment can be built up by attending to the kinds of things that enhance the quality of the relationship.

Principles for Enhancing Intimacy

1. When, why, and who you marry should be your personal decision. But you need to be aware of the risks involved in marrying too early. Teenage and student marriages face unique difficulties that can place an intolerable burden on the relationship. There are also risks, however, in waiting too long. If you are a female, the chances of marriage after age 40 are slim. It is important to be aware of these risks, but not to let them dictate your decision in this important matter.

2. It is important, before your wedding, to talk about the kind of marriage you and your future life partner want. Do you both agree that you want a relationship based on traditional roles or on egalitarian roles? Do you have "private contracts," assumptions, and expectations that you have not shared with each other? A thorough discussion of these can minimize difficulties after you are married.

3. The first year of marriage generally seems to challenge the popular expectation of "happily ever after." All too frequently, the demands of building a life together change the patterns of interaction and intimacy that characterized your courtship. It is vital, first of all, to understand and prepare to deal with these changes.

Then it is important to begin a lifelong process of working to maintain the romance and to deepen the intimacy in your relationship.

4. Remember that when you marry, you not only gain a spouse but also another family. Learn as much as you can about your future life partner's relationship with his or her family before your wedding. This will not only tell you much about your spouse but also about the kinds of problems you are likely to encounter when you become a member of the family. Recognize potential problem areas, and plan to deal with them in a constructive manner. But keep yourself open to the benefits of an additional family; the benefits will likely outweigh the difficulties.

5. Commitment frightens many people today. Yet it is an essential ingredient in a successful marriage. Commitment to the institution of marriage provides you with the time to work out and grow through the problems that inevitably assault any relationship. Even more important is commitment to your spouse. The goal of this kind of commitment is both the happiness and well-being of your life partner and also a growing and dynamic relationship.

KEY TERMS

commitment   *187*
egalitarian marriage   *176*
institution   *174*

marriage rate   *172*
marriage squeeze   *173*
postnuptial agreement   *181*

prenuptial agreement   *181*
wedding   *182*

ON THE WEB   Getting Married

Two sections in the text underscore the complex nature of getting married. One is the discussion of the various types of marriage. There are actually many more ways to classify marriage than those in the text, and a number of different types that are not discussed. The other discussion that illustrates the complex nature of getting married is the section on the wedding.

Two sites that are useful for exploring these two topics in greater detail are:

About.com:Marriage

http://marriage.about.com/od/lifestylechoices/Different_Types_of_Marriages.htm

This site has information and links about various types of marriage, including common-law marriages, military marriages, arranged marriages, and prison marriages.

www.mhhe.com/lauer7e

Get Married

http://www.getmarried.com

The Get Married site has a wealth of information about the wedding, including links to various resources needed for planning and carrying out a wedding.

Using these two sites, enlarge your understanding with the following projects:

1. Go to the About.com: Marriage site and investigate one of the types of marriage that interests you. Use a search engine to get additional information on that type and write a paper on how it differs from, or is similar to, other types.

2. Using the Get Married site, compile a detailed list of the tasks involved in planning and carrying out an elaborate wedding. Set up a class debate. Assign two students to a pro position and two to a con position on the proposition: Elaborate weddings are an appropriate celebration of marriage in an affluent society. Give all those in the debate the materials you have compiled on the tasks.

~ The Challenge of Communication ~

LEARNING OBJECTIVES

After reading and studying chapter 9, you should be able to

1 Describe the different types of nonverbal communication.

2 Explain the functions of nonverbal communication.

3 Show how communication is a process of interaction.

4 Discuss the sources of static and how they interfere with accurate communication.

5 Summarize the difficulties in communicating feelings and the impact that this has on relationships.

6 Describe poor listening and ways to improve listening skills.

7 Characterize the destructive messages and gender differences that impede communication.

8 Identify the ingredients of satisfying communication.

9 Show the ways that satisfying communication contributes to the development of intimacy and marital happiness.

10 Explain how to improve communication skills.

One way to improve your communication skills is to engage in the exercises suggested in this chapter. Read the four ways of communicating described by Virginia Satir and play the game she suggests with members of your family. What did you learn about communication patterns in your family? With which of the roles did you feel most comfortable? Most uncomfortable? How did the other family members react to the differing roles? Would you like to make any changes in your family's communication patterns on the basis of this experiment?

An alternative way to improve communication skills is to observe others and critique their communication on the basis of materials in this chapter. Because it is difficult to observe an actual situation, you can watch a number of episodes of a TV series that deals with marriage and/or family life. After reading the materials on effective communication, including good listening skills, how would you rate the communication in the episodes? What principles of effective communication do they uphold and which ones do they violate?

"When I use a word," said Humpty Dumpty in Lewis Carroll's *Through the Looking-Glass,* "it means just what I choose it to mean—neither more nor less." But Humpty Dumpty was mistaken. We would all like for our words to mean exactly what we choose for them to mean, in the sense that those who hear us understand us perfectly. However, communication is a complicated process. We will define **communication** as the use of language and nonverbal signs to create shared meaning between two or more people. But the meaning we convey to others depends on more than our intention.

It is important, therefore, to understand the complexities of communication. Much of the satisfaction and dissatisfaction of marriage and family life is rooted in the way that people communicate. In fact, a four-nation (Brazil, Italy, Taiwan, and the United States) study reported that constructive communication is positively associated with satisfaction in romantic relationships in these countries (Christensen et al. 2006). In this chapter we will look at communication as an intricate process that has manifold possibilities for miscommunication. We will discuss the importance of listening as a part of effective communication. We will look at impediments to good communication and the kinds of communication that are satisfying to people. Communication is integrally tied up with marital intimacy and satisfaction, another topic that we will explore. Finally, we will suggest some ways to improve communication between partners.

THE NATURE OF COMMUNICATION

At the outset, we must underscore the point that it is impossible *not* to communicate. Some people use what they call the "silent treatment" as a method of dealing with conflict. The victim of the silent treatment may complain that his or her spouse "won't communicate with me." Still the silent treatment itself is a powerful form of communication, telling the partner that the silent one is angry and unwilling to discuss the problem. We are always communicating to each other, in the sense that our words, our lack of words, and our expressions are interpreted by others to say something about our mood, our feelings, and perhaps our relationships.

Verbal Communication

When most people use the term *communication,* they probably are thinking of verbal communication, the use of words to convey our ideas to others. All animals

Symbolic Interactionist Theory Applied

engage in communication of some kind. But, as *symbolic interactionists* have shown, humans are symbolic creatures; we create, manipulate, and employ symbols to direct our own behavior and to influence the behavior of others (Lauer and Handel 1983:80). Symbols are shared meanings. Language is a system of these symbols. When we use a particular symbol, such as "love," we engage in a certain amount of shared meaning with others.

One way to examine and evaluate an intimate relationship is to view it as an "ongoing conversation," a process in which the partners strive to influence and understand each other and establish consensual meanings in their life together (Alford-Cooper 1998:20). One of the difficulties in this process is that words—even common words—do not have a standardized and single meaning that is the same for everyone. For instance, if you say, "I love you" to someone, you may mean that you feel a deep attachment, that you are sexually attracted to the person, or that you find being with the other person a delightful experience or some combination of these or other meanings. Also the meaning that the other person imputes to your statement may be different from what you intended. As we shall see in the discussion that follows, we have multiple opportunities to miscommunicate with each other, no matter how precise we try to be with our words.

Nonverbal Communication

"I love you" may not only mean something positive but something negative as well. Depending on the inflection you put on the words, you could give quite contrary meanings to them. They could be put in the form of a question, a surprised reaction to someone's inquiry. They could be stated with sarcasm, indicating not only a lack of love but a degree of contempt for the other. They could be said with an air of indifference, suggesting a failed effort to appease an anxious and unloved inquirer. They could be stated with passion, conveying an intensity of feeling for the other.

Thus, words are only a part of the meaning in communication. Equally important as the words we use is the way in which we express them—the numerous **nonverbal cues** we use while communicating, cues that are crucial to understanding and building fulfilling intimate relationships (Quilliam 2005). Estimates are that anywhere from 50 to 80 percent of the meaning we convey is through the nonverbal part of our communication. One psychologist even puts the figure at 90 percent (Nelson 2004). Whatever the exact amount, it is clear that nonverbal communication is responsible for a significant amount of the shared meaning that is created.

Kinds of Nonverbal Communication. You offer many different kinds of nonverbal cues to others when communicating. One cue is the clothing you wear. If you go out on a date, what you wear may tell the other person something about how you feel or about the kind of person you are. The message is not necessarily what you intend to give. For example, a student told us that she broke up with her boyfriend because he was always so sloppily dressed when they dated. She said that he tried to reconcile with her, insisting that he thought he was being "cool" and casual rather than sloppy. She interpreted his dress as a lack of interest in himself and a lack of respect for her. In spite of his protests, she refused to date him any more.

Facial expressions and eye behavior are important aspects of nonverbal communication (Smith et al. 2005). They are difficult to control, although some people learn to control their facial expressions. They exercise such control in order to mask some kind of emotion they are feeling (Malandro and Barker 1983). Eye behavior is even more difficult to control. Our eyes tell others about how we are feeling, how interested we are, how much self-confidence we have, and how trustworthy we are (e.g., no one wants to be known as "shifty eyed").

Touching is still another important kind of nonverbal behavior. Between lovers, a decline in touching is an important message about feelings. Touching someone while talking to them may indicate affection or remorse. Gripping someone may indicate anger or frustration. It is important to keep in mind that these meanings may be independent of any words that are being said. For example, a man may proclaim, "I love you" to a woman while holding her arm in a viselike grip. The woman is likely to define the sentence as threatening rather than as an expression of affection.

Finally, all of the cues we give in oral speech apart from the content of the words themselves are some of the most important kinds of nonverbal communication. As illustrated previously by the diverse and contrary meanings that can be given to the phrase "I love you," the tone of voice and the emphasis given to words radically affect the meaning that is communicated (LaPlante and Ambady 2003). For instance, a woman says to her husband, "How about a movie tonight?" Think of the different meanings

he can give to her by responding with the following: "Oh, okay" (interpreted by her as willingness but no enthusiasm); "Oh *kay*" (interpreted by her as an idea he loves); "*Oh* kay" (interpreted by her to mean "we're doing what *you* want to do again"); and "*Ohhh* kay" (hesitation in his voice, interpreted by her to mean, "I'll do it, but I had something else in mind that I prefer doing").

Functions of Nonverbal Behavior. Nonverbal cues have a number of functions in communication (Malandro and Barker 1983; Knapp and Hall 2001). First, they *complement* our words. If you say, "I love you" and touch or embrace the other, you are reinforcing the meaning of your words. Sometimes people may not really believe what we say or at least may have doubts, unless we reinforce the words with some kind of nonverbal behavior.

Second, nonverbal cues may *contradict* our words. A student told us how happy he was to be married, but the pained look on his face contradicted what he was saying. Eventually, he admitted to some serious problems that he and his new wife were having. At times, the nonverbal rather than the verbal message is more reliable.

Third, nonverbal cues *repeat* the message. Repeating differs from complementing because the latter cannot stand alone. To touch or hug someone may have diverse meanings from the words "I love you." But if two lovers have developed their own special language, such as touching the fingers to the lips as a way of saying, "I love you," then they are using a nonverbal cue to repeat the message of love. The message is given without the words. They may be at a party, catch each other's eye, and give the nonverbal signal of love. No words need be spoken.

Fourth, nonverbal cues *regulate* communication. People develop signals to let each other know when they approve of what the other says (such as nodding the head), when they disapprove (frowning), and when they want to interrupt and speak themselves (such as lifting a finger). Such nonverbal cues help to regulate the verbal interaction between them.

Fifth, nonverbal cues may *substitute* for words. A man may ask his wife if she still loves him, and she may respond by smiling and kissing him; her response, while affirmative, is wordless.

Sixth, nonverbal cues may *accent* the verbal message. A pause, an emphasis on a particular word, a touch—all can be used to stress a particular point that is being made verbally. "I love you," spoken slowly and with a slight pause between each word, may be a way of reassuring a lover who has had doubts about the relationship.

Seventh, nonverbal cues may *trigger attributions*. That is, your partner will pick up on nonverbal cues and attribute various motivations and feelings to you. In a study of the interaction of 60 couples, three researchers found that positive cues contributed to satisfaction with the relationship (Manusov, Floyd, and Kerssen-Griep 1997). However, they also noted that the couples tended to notice negative cues more than they did positive cues.

Interpreting Nonverbal Behavior.   Given the importance of nonverbal behavior, it would be great if you could simply remind yourself to watch for cues and then use them to build meaningful relationships. But as we shall see with communication generally, much can go wrong in the process of one person saying something and the other hearing and interpreting it. In particular, gender and your closeness to the other person affect your interpretation of nonverbal cues.

Gender affects your interpretation because males and females learn to function somewhat differently in the use of nonverbal cues (Nelson 2004). For example, females generally smile more than males. For women, smiling is a way to acknowledge the presence of someone else in a nonthreatening way. A man, however, may interpret a woman's smile to mean that she finds him sexually attractive. If the nonverbal cue is ambiguous, you are

Nonverbal cues are important. What are the nonverbal messages sent by this couple to each other?

likely to interpret it in accord with the gender of the person and of your stereotype of males and females. Thus, three researchers had students rate the emotions of people in photographs who were trying to show both anger and sadness (Plant, Kling, and Smith 2004). The photos were morphed so that the facial expressions were identical for the men and the women. Nevertheless, the students rated the women as sadder than the men, in accord with the stereotype that women express sadness more than men. The men, in turn, were rated higher on anger and lower on sympathy than the women.

There is another way in which gender affects the interpretation of nonverbal behavior: *Women, compared to men, are more sensitive to, and more likely to accurately recall, nonverbal cues* (Hall, Murphy, and Mast 2006). Women, in other words, are likely to be more accurate in understanding men than are men in understanding women. We do not know the reason or reasons for this gender difference, although some social scientists believe it reflects the tendency for the man to have more power in the relationship. And in any relationship marked by power differences, the person with less power has a greater need to accurately understand the person with more power than vice versa.

Your closeness to the other person also affects your interpretation, but probably not in the way you would expect. That is, would you expect to be more accurate in interpreting the nonverbal cues of a stranger, a friend, or a very close friend? And would you expect that being in love would make you more accurate in perceiving the nonverbal cues of love in others? With regard to the first question, researchers found that friends were more accurate than strangers at identifying concealed sadness and anger of someone, but that less close friends were more accurate in their interpretations than were closer friends (Sternglanz and Depaulo 2004). With regard to the second question, researchers had subjects look at video clips of couples, some of whom were in love, and identify those they believed to be in love (Aloni and Bernleri 2004). The subjects who were in love themselves at the time and who reported having had a long, romantic relationship believed that they would be more accurate in perceiving the cues of love. But they were actually less accurate.

It seems, in short, that you are not better able to interpret the nonverbal cues of those who are closest to you, and being in an intimate, romantic relationship does not make you more accurate at picking up the cues of love. Clearly, it is a good idea to check out verbally the way you interpret nonverbal cues.

COMMUNICATION AS AN INTERACTION PROCESS

What you communicate to someone depends not only on what you say and how you say it but also on how the other person interprets what you say and how you say it. Figure 9.1 shows a model of communication as a process of interaction. Begin at the left side, labeled the "sender." This is the person who initiates the conversation, who wants to share some idea or feeling. The first step is to **encode** the idea and/or feeling into language, that is, into words that will hopefully convey the meaning to the other person. If you're angry with someone, for example, you could phrase your anger in various ways. You could be subtle: "I'm not in a good mood." Or you could be direct: "I'm angry with you just now." Or you could phrase it in any number of other ways. The point is, you must encode your ideas and feelings in a way that will best convey what you want the other person to know.

The encoded message is transmitted through the **media,** which, in communication, are the verbal and nonverbal means of conveying meaning to someone. Thus, you can express your anger both in words and in your demeanor and gestures (e.g., a scowl, a clenched fist, and a loud voice). The dotted line from "encode message" back to ideas and feelings in figure 9.1 indicates that as you transmit the message you hear your own words and evaluate them. That gives you an opportunity to revise what you say in order to clarify the message. For example, if you blurt out "I'm not in a good mood," you may realize as you hear the words that they are not adequate, and say, "No, that's not what I mean. I'm really angry with you."

The other person, the receiver, must **decode** your message—interpret your words so that he or she understands your ideas and feelings. The receiver filters the message through his or her own ideas and feelings before encoding a response. In responding to your anger, the other person may realize that he or she is perplexed and encode that message ("Why are you angry with me? What did I do?"), or similarly angry and encode that message ("You have no right to be angry; I'm the one who should be angry"), and so on. The receiver, in other words, is now a sender and the process continues. Let us take a concrete example to underscore the fact that at each phase of the process there can be **static,** interference of some kind that hinders accurate communication.

A Discussion about Sex

Chuck and Linda are a fictitious married couple who are having a discussion about their sexual relationship. Our commentary on their dialogue is enclosed in brackets:

Chuck: I think that women don't have as strong a sexual drive as men. [Chuck desires to have sex more often than Linda. He is upset but isn't sure if he feels anger, frustration, or both. He also wants to avoid offending Linda. He knows she is frequently stressed from dealing with both her career and their family. He encodes his desire into a statement that is a "feeler." He wants to know how she will respond to the idea. Yet when he hears his words, he thinks he might have chosen a better way to start the conversation. He prepares himself to back off if she reacts badly.]

Linda: I don't know why you would say that. [She notices a slight edge to Chuck's voice. She decodes what he has said as a personal complaint. She knows he has wanted sex more often than she has. She isn't sure if that's why he made the statement. If that's why, it will open the way to a larger discussion. She feels that he doesn't understand the strain of being both a mother and a career woman. Perhaps if he helped around the

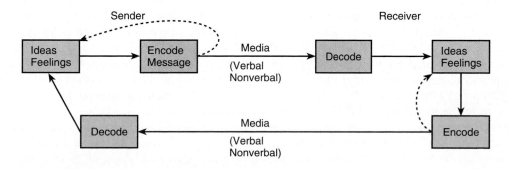

FIGURE 9.1 The Communication Process

house more, she would have more energy. But she, too, doesn't want to offend. Basically, they have a satisfying marriage. She makes her response as terse and neutral as possible.]

Chuck: I just think it's true. [He saw her mouth tighten when she replied. He interprets that as a warning signal that pursuing the topic could lead to an argument. Even though her words suggest that she would not agree that she has a weaker sex drive, her nonverbal cues warn him that this is an emotional topic. He decides to be neutral in his response.]

Linda: Well, I've got too much to do to talk about something silly like that. [Hearing a softening in his voice, she defines him as unwilling to confront the issue directly. This angers her. She decides to force him to cut off the discussion or get to the point. In case he wants to pursue it, she has opened the door to what she regards as the real problem—an inequity in household responsibilities.]

Such conversations can go on endlessly without the couple ever directly discussing the real issue. They communicated, but Linda was never certain what Chuck really wanted to say. And he felt that she was unaware of his feelings about their sex life. Merely because people are talking together does not mean that they are communicating accurately with each other.

Communication Static

Chuck and Linda illustrate some of the manifold ways in which static gets into the communication process. The sender, the media of transmission, and the receiver are all sources of static (Pneuman and Bruehl 1982). Senders may transmit with static because they aren't certain of their own feelings or ideas. Because Chuck was unsure of his own feelings, it was difficult for him to open the conversation in a helpful way. As a result, he sent ambiguous information to Linda. Ambiguous or insufficient information also can result from poor communication habits, such as assuming that one's thoughts or feelings can be inferred accurately without careful communication.

Sender static also can result from certain mannerisms. For instance, a sender who uses "you know" or "uh" repeatedly or who uses exaggerated nonverbal gestures while speaking may so distract the listener that accurate communication is very difficult.

Static occurs in the media when there is a discrepancy between the nonverbal and verbal communication. Chuck and Linda each noticed nonverbal signs that feelings were more intense than the words would indicate. Discrepancies between the verbal and nonverbal leave the hearer somewhat bewildered as to which medium of

communication to accept. The man who insists he is not angry when his face is distorted with emotion is sending an ambiguous message. His wife knows that his words do not tell all, but she is not sure if the emotion expressed on his face is anger or something else. Media static also may occur if there are too many distractions in the environment (noisy children, for example, who keep grabbing the attention of one or both parents who are trying to discuss an interpersonal issue).

Receiver static occurs when the listener filters the message through his or her own ideas and feelings—selecting, expanding, and interpreting the words and nonverbal cues to make sense of the message. Chuck interpreted Linda's frequent lack of sexual desire as insufficient passion for him. Linda interpreted Chuck's ambiguity as an unwillingness to confront the issue directly. He never knew that she resented having a disproportionate share of responsibility for the home. She never knew he was sufficiently sensitive to her needs to recognize that she felt stressed over her workload. Each assumed things about the other, because it was important for each to make sense of the situation. Lacking sufficient and accurate information from the other, each interpreted the other in a way that made sense, even though neither reached a satisfying conclusion.

Communicating Feelings

As Chuck and Linda illustrate, when we talk with others we inevitably communicate feelings as well as ideas. Feelings are very important in the marital relationship. The way you think your spouse feels about things may be more crucial to your relationship than what your spouse says. Research has shown that the accurate communication of feelings is as complicated and as subject to distortion as the communication of ideas (Gaelick, Bodenhausen, and Wyer 1985). As figure 9.2 shows, a circular process is involved in the communication of feelings. The feelings you intend to communicate are interpreted by the other and may or may not be perceived correctly. The other person has an affective reaction to his or her perception of your feelings and communicates that to you. You interpret the other's feelings, compare them with what you expected, and have your own affective reaction. You then communicate additional feelings, and the cycle continues.

Because of the interpretation that always occurs, the cycle has both intended and unintended communication. Thus, in their study of 29 couples, psychologists Gaelick, Bodenhausen, and Wyer (1985) found that people believe they reciprocate both positive and negative

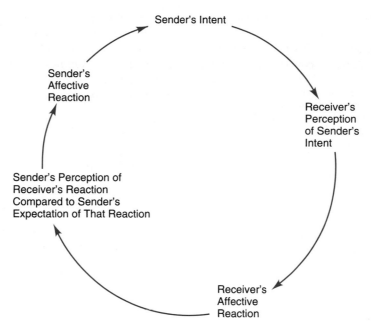

FIGURE 9.2 Intended and Unintended Communication of Feelings

Source: Data from L. Gaelick, G. V. Bodenhausen, and R. S. Wyer Jr., *Journal of Personality and Social Psychology* 49:1248, 1985.

feelings that they perceive from their partners. They had the couples engage in three conversations. One dealt with the events of the day, the second with a conflict they were having, and the third with what they liked best about living together. Although the subjects believed that they generally reciprocated the feeling they perceived their partners to convey and that their partners reciprocated their own expression of emotion, the researchers concluded that, in actuality, they only reciprocated hostility. Among these 29 couples, at least, there was not much accuracy in perceiving the expression of positive emotions.

The researchers also found two interesting gender differences in the communication of feelings. The men tended to distort the messages of their female partners in a negative direction, interpreting the lack of positive feelings as an indication of hostility. The women tended to distort the messages of their male partners in a positive direction, interpreting the lack of hostility as an indication of positive feelings. Clearly, neither feelings nor ideas are easily and accurately communicated to those we love. Effective communication is a complex and difficult task. One thing that is essential is effective listening.

LISTENING

Psychiatrist Karl Menninger (1942:275) once wrote that listening may be even more important than talking:"I believe listening to be one of the most powerful and influential techniques of human intercourse." Indeed, good listening has been found to be important in all kinds of relationships, from preserving the dignity of the elderly to satisfaction in married couples (Skaldeman 2006; Anderberg, Lepp, Berglund, and Segesten 2007). Note that we said "good" listening, because there are various ways we can listen to others, not all of which are helpful to effective communication.

Styles of Poor Listening

A number of styles of listening impede effective communication (Burley-Allen 1995). Some people habitually listen in one or more of these ways, while others may fall into them on occasion.

The Faker. Fakers only pretend to be listening. They may smile while you talk to them. They may nod their heads. They may appear to be intent, but they are either thinking about something else or are so intent on appearing to be listening that they do not hear what you are saying.

Ellen, an undergraduate, broke her engagement because she found that her fiancé consistently faked his listening:

> I realized how little he paid attention to me when I told him one day my doctor wanted me to have another test. He had found some suspicious cells in my cervix. Mike just looked at me and smiled. I really exploded. I was scared to death. He apologized. Said he was worried about an exam. I began probing into some other things I thought we had talked about. He couldn't remember half the things I had told him!

The Dependent Listener. Some people primarily want to please the speaker. They are so concerned about whether the speaker has a good impression of them that they are unable to listen and respond appropriately. Dependent listeners may agree excessively with what the speaker says, not because they really agree but because they want to maintain the goodwill of the speaker.

A woman, for example, who is overly dependent on her husband may not listen to what he is saying because she is concerned primarily with pleasing him rather than understanding and helping him. Unfortunately, she does not realize that the relationship she is so desperate to maintain may be jeopardized rather than strengthened by her behavior. By striving to please, dependent listeners are frustrating at best. They may be valued by the individual who only wants someone to support whatever he or she says and does, but they are unable to build fulfilling relationships.

The Interrupter. Interrupters never allow the other to finish. They may be afraid that they will forget something important they want to say. Or they may feel that it is necessary to respond to a point as soon as it is made. Or they may simply be more concerned with their own thoughts and feelings than with those of others. In any case, they barrage the other with words rather than offering the other an understanding ear.

Here is how an interrupter might function:

Wife: I really had a rough day today. I thought my boss was going to . . .

Husband: I bet your day wasn't any worse than mine. I couldn't believe the way my clerks were fouling up today. I think I'm going to have to bring them in one by one for some additional training.

Wife: Yeah, those people can drive you up a wall at times. Well, my boss just about went through the ceiling. . . .

Husband: You've got to stop letting him get to you. Just tell him you'll quit if he keeps on.

Wife: I can understand why he got upset. I didn't have the report ready. But he doesn't realize that . . .

Husband: He gets upset at anything. I don't know how you stand working for him.

Note that the interrupting husband never lets his wife completely finish. The wife has no opportunity to talk out her feelings and frustrations. The husband simply breaks in with his own problems or tries to give her a quick-fix solution. He isn't listening, because he is making no effort to fully understand her and the experience of her day.

The Self-Conscious Listener. Some people are concerned primarily with their own status in the eyes of the other rather than with the ideas and feelings of the other. Trying to impress the other person, they don't listen with understanding.

A woman who wants her husband to think of her as intelligent, for example, might be so concerned with that image that she doesn't really listen to him. Instead of trying to understand what he is saying, she will be thinking about how to respond in order to impress him with the quality of her mind. Or she may want to impress him with the fact that she is indispensable to him, that she can help him with any of his problems. Again, instead of listening carefully and trying to understand him, she may be constantly framing her replies in order to appear helpful.

The Intellectual Listener. Intellectual listeners attend only to the words of the other. They make a rational appraisal of what the other has said verbally, but they ignore the nonverbal cues (including the feelings that are communicated nonverbally).

The intellectual listener may develop this style because of the type of work in which he or she engages. Consider the case of Frank, a computer programmer, who had learned to be thoroughly logical and systematic in order to succeed in his work. He tried to apply the same procedure to his marriage, however, and found himself in trouble:

> He was so busy analyzing what was communicated to him, he didn't have time to just be there with the other person. His wife often told him he was a nitpicker. She felt he was overly critical of her and the children because he seldom accepted what she said. He would challenge her thought processes. He spent most of their communication time analyzing what she said as if he had to turn it into a program (Burley-Allen 1995).

Frank was a highly intelligent person, but he had to learn how to listen.

Improving Listening Skills

How do you learn to listen? How can you learn to listen so that you understand the other person and the other knows you understand? One thing is to avoid the problematic styles we have described. Beyond that, Madelyn Burley-Allen (1995) suggests a number of things you can do to improve your listening skills generally. Some of those particularly appropriate for intimate relationships follow:

1. Take the initiative in communication. Unfortunately, we tend to think of listening as a passive activity. But effective listening has to be active. You have to look at your partner and concentrate on what he or she is saying. You need to watch the nonverbal cues and listen to the words carefully and strive to understand exactly what he or she is trying to communicate. It is also helpful to respond to various things with noncommittal remarks such as "I see," or "That's interesting."

2. Resist distractions. The distractions may be in the environment, such as noise in the home, or they may be in your mind, such as preoccupation with some problem or concern. In either case, you must consciously decide to put aside the distractions for a while and focus on what your partner is saying.

3. Control your emotions and your tendency to respond before your partner is finished. We all have certain "hot buttons," words or ideas that create an emotional reaction in us. When those buttons are pushed, we are likely to stop listening and start formulating a reply. Your emotions, in other words, can turn you into an interrupter. It is important to resist that tendency. Hear your partner out completely.

4. Ask questions and rephrase to clarify your partner's meaning. In effective listening, questions are used not to cast suspicion on motives ("Are you saying that just to annoy me?") but to get clarification ("Are you saying then that you are really hurt because I was late?"). Effective listeners are particularly aware of the value of rephrasing what the other has said. Rephrasing is done to clarify, to check for accuracy, to check for feelings, or simply to show interest and understanding.

   For example, a husband says to his wife, "We have blown our budget to bits this month. You've got to stop spending so much money." She could respond angrily, "What about the money you spend? It's not all my fault." That is likely to start an argument. An effective listening response would rephrase the husband's statement. She might say, "You feel that our budget problems are due mainly to my spending habits?" (clarification); or "You're angry because of the way I spend money" (check for feelings). This provides her

Good listening skills can be practiced everywhere, including the home.

husband with the opportunity to respond in a constructive way to their budget difficulties.

5. Make use of the speed of your thoughts by summarizing. We think faster than we can speak. You can make use of this by periodically summarizing what your partner has said. It is important that you use your thinking not only to formulate responses but also to summarize in an effort to understand exactly what your partner is getting at.

6. Practice. You can enhance your listening skills by practicing with everyone, not merely your intimate partner. The more you try to be an effective listener with people, the more skill you will gain and, we might add, the more you will enhance the quality of your relationships.

IMPEDIMENTS TO COMMUNICATION

"If people would only learn to communicate" is a complaint that has been uttered numberless times. The implication is that many of our problems could be solved through effective communication. Why, then, don't people communicate? As we have seen, it isn't just a matter of not talking. Not many relationships fall into a silent pattern. But the misunderstandings and speculations that characterized people who don't speak with one another plague even many of those who *are* talking to each other. What happens?

The failure to listen is one obvious impediment to effective communication. In addition, we need to be aware of certain kinds of destructive messages and of important gender differences in communication patterns.

Destructive Messages

When people communicate effectively, they are able to build intimacy, to share meaningful times together, and to understand each other more fully. Ineffective communication, on the other hand, impedes intimacy and facilitates misunderstanding, feelings of rejection, and conflict. A number of common destructive messages characterize ineffective communication (Gottman 1994). Some destructive messages are particularly hazardous to a relationship. Gottman (1994:414) calls four of the most corrosive ways of sending destructive messages the "Four Horsemen of the Apocalypse." They are complain/criticize, contempt, defensiveness, and stonewalling. These four, he notes, are likely to be a sequence, with each one giving way to the next as the communication deteriorates.

For example, a husband begins by complaining that his wife has forgotten to pay a bill again. The complaint becomes a criticism as he adds the point that her neglect makes more work for him. As she tries to defend herself by pointing out that she had an unusually demanding week, he adds insult: "You're just irresponsible. Admit it!" She reacts to his contempt by pointing out ways in which he, too, has failed. He becomes defensive, ignoring her point and listing other ways in which she exhibits irresponsibility. She gets very upset and demands that he stop attacking her. At that point, he stonewalls her by storming out of the house. Stonewalling, or withdrawing from the argument, incidentally, is more likely to be done by men than by women (Christensen et al. 2006).

This example makes it clear why the Four Horsemen of the Apocalypse are so destructive to a relationship. But there are a number of other ways of communicating that are also hazardous to a good relationship.

Ordering may be occasionally necessary with children, but it is likely to generate such things as fear, anger, resistance, or resentment in an intimate partner. "Stop doing that," "You have to . . . ," and "You must . . ." are the kinds of phrases used in ordering. Ironically, the partner may be quite willing to do what you want but will resist and perhaps refuse simply because you ordered rather than requested. Ordering turns the interaction into a power struggle rather than an opportunity for effective communication between equals.

Threatening tends to generate the same emotions as ordering. It also can lead to passivity or despair. Again, to threaten the other is to engage in a power struggle rather than effective communication.

Moralizing sends a message that the partner should feel guilty or morally inferior or that the partner needs guidance and direction from others. "You ought not . . ." and "You should . . ." are moralizing phrases. Moralizing also can be accomplished nonverbally by a look of disgust or disapproval.

Providing solutions is a parental approach to a relationship. The words may sound like a suggestion, but the nonverbal cues can indicate a kind of parental guidance and even the superiority of the questioner: "Why don't you clean off the table during the commercial?" or "Why don't you balance your checkbook each time you write a check?"

Lecturing is a more forceful way of providing guidance and solutions to problems. "You will have to learn how to keep the house clean if you want to be a good wife." "You will have to be more forceful at work and demand a raise if you are going to be a good father and husband." Lecturing also tends to diminish the self-esteem of the partner and underscore the superiority of the one giving the lecture.

Ridiculing is sometimes used with good intentions (in the mistaken belief that the other person will see how ridiculous his or her behavior or ideas are and change). Sometimes the intentions are not so good (the person who uses ridicule may be demonstrating his or her own superiority over the other). In either case, ridicule will generate more resistance and resentment than change and intimacy. "You're talking like an idiot" and "You're a slob" are examples of ridicule. You can't engage in effective communication with someone who hurls such biting phrases.

Analyzing is the attribution of motives to someone. The world is full of amateur psychoanalysts who tell others why they behave the way they do and why they think and feel as they do. "You're only doing that to hurt me" and "You're only smiling to cover up your hostility" are examples of analyzing. This angers us, because the analyst invades our privacy and suggests motivations that we believe to be wrong. If the analyst is a very powerful and admired person in our lives, we may believe the analysis and lose self-esteem. In either case, effective communication breaks down.

Finally, *interrogating* is another power tactic that conveys a sense of distrust of the other. "Can you give me one good reason why you won't go to the party?" and "You're not telling the truth, are you?" are examples of interrogation. Interrogation is used to coerce information rather than to foster dialogue.

Conflict Theory Applied

Why do people engage in such destructive messages? In some cases they reflect a *conflict of interests* and the consequent efforts to coerce the partner in order to pursue one's own interests. Criticism of another, for example, can be a way to build up one's own flagging self-esteem. Ordering can be a way of maintaining control in the relationship. On the other hand, it is important to note that there may be times when some of the messages are appropriate and even necessary. But if they become part of a style of communication or if they are used too frequently or at inappropriate times, they impede effective communication and corrode the relationship.

Gender Differences as an Impediment

In the play *My Fair Lady,* Henry Higgins sings a song of bewilderment in which he asks why a woman can't be more like a man. Higgins doesn't understand women and particularly doesn't understand why they react differently from his male friends. His perplexity symbolizes that of many who run into problems of communication because they do not understand basic gender differences.

According to the conventional wisdom, one gender difference is simply that women talk more than men. However, an analysis of 396 college students, who wore voice recorders that took samples of their speech for a number of days, found virtually no difference between

What Do You Think?

There is disagreement about **whether, when it comes to communication, "men are from Mars and women are from Venus."** What follows are pro and con arguments. What do you think?

Pro

In matters of communication, men are from Mars and women are from Venus because

- men want "bottom-line" communication, while women want extended conversations.
- men are reason oriented and women are feelings oriented.
- men and women have different goals and different needs in communication.
- men give advice and women give understanding.

Con

In matters of communication, men and women are not from "different planets" because

- both seek deeper intimacy through communication.
- both have the same need to self-disclose.
- communication is a primary way to maintain contact with another person, regardless of gender.
- effective and meaningful communication is a gender-free skill that anyone can learn.

males and females in the number of words spoken per day (Mehl et al. 2007). Both males and females averaged around 16,000 words each day (the female average was a little higher than the male, but the difference was not significant).

Psychiatrist Aaron Beck (1988) has noted some of the important differences in male–male versus female–female communication, such as that men rarely talk about personal matters. Beck wrote that he only learned one of his close male friends was going to be a grandfather when the man's wife told Beck's wife about it. Beck also pointed out that a woman is likely to think her marriage is working as long as she and her husband can keep talking about it; but her husband may think that it is not working if they have to keep talking about it. Beck's observation holds true within the marital relationship as well as between friends. In their study of 120 people who had been married at least 20 years, Mackey and O'Brien (1995) found that a frequent source of tension even of those married many years was husbands' discomfort with talking about their inner thoughts and feelings. And because of their discomfort, husbands often try to control the content and emotional depth of discussions, an effort that is not pleasing to their wives (Ball, Cowan, and Cowan 1995).

Deborah Tannen (1990) has analyzed gender differences in conversational styles in detail. She points out that men approach life as a contest in which each party is striving to "preserve independence and avoid failure" (Tannen 1990:25). Women, by contrast, approach life as a community affair in which the goal is to maintain intimacy and avoid being isolated. In conversations, therefore, men attempt to sustain or gain status, while women strive for relational closeness. As a result, the same behavior can have very different meanings for men and women. For instance, checking with her partner before making plans may make a woman feel good because her life is intertwined with someone else's. Checking with his partner may make a man feel that he has lost his independence. Men, therefore, are more likely than women to make decisions without consulting their partners.

Tannen discusses various other ways in which men and women differ, differences that lead to misunderstandings and problems. For example, women tend to respond to someone else's trouble with understanding and sympathy; men tend to give advice or try to solve the problem. Women tend to listen and give support; men tend to lecture and give authoritative information and opinions. Women find details about minor daily activities to be a sign of intimacy and caring; men may find such details boring or even irritating.

Tannen makes all of these differences a matter of gender: Men communicate one way and women communicate another. More recent research suggests that cross-sex communication is more complex than that (Edwards and Hamilton 2004). Using university students as the subjects, the researchers found that gender-role orientation is a significant factor in communication. In particular, when an individual interprets whether a message from someone is cooperative or not, the interpretation depends not as much on whether the individual is male or female as on whether the individual is androgynous, feminine, or masculine in gender-role orientation. Men who are high on nurturance (femininity) are likely to interpret the message as cooperative—in the way Tannen argues that women generally interpret messages. By the same token, women who are low in nurturance (a more masculine gender-role orientation) are unlikely to interpret the message as cooperative. Those who are androgynous, on the other hand, have a greater likelihood of making a correct interpretation and, therefore, are more effective in cross-sex communications.

Finally, research over seven decades shows that men and women tend to have somewhat different preferences for topics of conversation. An analysis of the preferences of 253 men and women reported that the most popular topic for both genders was work and money. For men, that choice was followed closely by the topic of leisure activity (including sports). For women, the second most popular topic was equally divided between leisure activity and persons of the opposite sex (Bischoping 1993). In fact, women were almost four times as likely to talk about men as men were to talk about women.

Clearly, not every woman or every man can be characterized in these ways. But it is also clear that gender differences are widespread and fundamental. It is important to understand the differences as a couple tries to build a meaningful intimate relationship.

Why Husbands and Wives Don't Talk to Each Other

"He doesn't talk to me" is one of the most common complaints. Why does communication sometimes lapse into a kind of silent tolerance? Why do some couples lapse into silence? Any of the previously discussed factors may come into play in a marriage. One or both partners may develop a style of sending out destructive messages. There may be a lack of understanding of gender differences. The result of such things is that conversations become a form of punishment rather than reward. And few of us are willing to engage consistently in behavior that we define as punishing.

For instance, Faye is a homemaker with two preschool children. Her husband, Tom, is an architect. They have a stable marriage of ten years, though they do not converse as readily as they once did. In particular, Faye complains about Tom's reluctance to talk:

I'm hungry for adult conversation and companionship by the time Tom comes home from work. But sometimes it's like I have to yank every word out of him. I feel like he could spend the rest of his life with me without ever initiating a conversation.

Tom is educated, knowledgeable, and interested in a variety of topics from sports to politics. Why doesn't he talk with Faye? Tom told the marriage enrichment group that he and Faye were attending one night, "Sometimes people don't talk to each other because of the way one of them responds." When pressed about what he meant, he said,

Suppose I come home and tell Faye that I'm thinking of starting my own firm, or even of getting out of architecture all together and trying a different career that will be more satisfying to me. Then she tells me that's a dumb idea because I have a wife and two kids to support and a good job and I ought to be thinking about more productive things.

Faye admitted that it sounded like something she would say. She got frightened when he talked about such things. So she would cut him off and ridicule the idea. As a result, Tom had unwittingly fallen into the habit of initiating very little conversation. Tom and Faye are working on improving their communication. They have a

Personal

All the Talk Was Useless

One of the important points in this chapter is that talking together doesn't necessarily mean that effective communication is occurring. Jenny is a nurse who was married for 15 years to Phil, a psychologist. She was 22 and he was 30 when they married. They talked a lot, but it didn't save their marriage. Jenny recalls the relationship with a tinge of sadness in her words:

We were both introspective kinds of people. When I was a child I was lonely and I rarely, if ever, confided totally in another person. Phil also had a difficult childhood. So we were both insecure. The result was that, though we talked a lot, we didn't talk about anything that would threaten our security.

Before we were married, we talked about where we would live and how our careers would go and how our marriage would be a good one. But we didn't discuss things like potential problems or things we liked and didn't like about each other. And we certainly didn't talk about how we would make decisions and who would control the finances. That was unfortunate, because a lot of the troubles we had later on really were the result of a power struggle between us. While we were married, we argued, we discussed, and we hit impasses on many things. We disagreed about our in-laws. I thought he should be more accepting of my parents, and he thought I should feel more warmly toward his parents. We argued about money constantly. We fought about each other's spending habits. We also talked a lot about things we agreed on. We both loved movies, and we discussed them. We told each other about our work and the

things that happened on the job. Phil was supportive when I was stressed at work, and I think I helped him when he was worn down by some of his patients. But the arguments consumed an increasing amount of our conversation as the years went by.

So in the end, all the talk was useless. Because we didn't talk about the really crucial things. We never discussed our own fears and vulnerabilities with each other. We never talked about our differences for what they were—a struggle for control in the relationship. We just fought more and more. The final breakup came within two months of our 15th anniversary. We never even discussed the breakup. We didn't talk about the reasons for it. We never talked about how we each felt. We just slipped quietly apart. And the marriage ended.

basically sound relationship, but effective communication has deteriorated because neither has understood the other, and Tom has chosen the typical male response of lapsing into relative silence.

We should note that while it is true that lack of communication is a common complaint, it is also true that for many couples the quality of communication improves over the course of the marriage. Mackey and O'Brien (1995) reported in their study of lasting marriages that 68 percent of their respondents identified their communication as positive in the third phase of marriage (after the youngest child was at least 18 years of age), while 44 percent recalled their communication as positive before their children were born. Their respondents also identified the child-rearing years as the most difficult for good marital communication.

SATISFYING COMMUNICATION

If you have a satisfying pattern of communication, will that guarantee a satisfying marriage? The answer is no. Satisfying communication is not sufficient. On the other hand, it *is* necessary. You can't have a satisfying marriage without satisfying communication, even though the latter won't guarantee a happy union. We should note that what is "satisfying" will differ somewhat for various couples. Nevertheless, people who come to therapists with marital problems report a variety of communication problems, including too little conversation, too few things to talk about, too much criticism, and general dissatisfaction with conversations. Overall, then, it is the *quality* of communication and not the mere *quantity* that is important for marital satisfaction (Emmers-Sommer 2004).

What kind of things go into satisfying communication? What makes people happy with the communication pattern of their relationship? Communication is more satisfying to us when we feel understood and when we have agreement with the other (Allen and Thompson 1984). It is likely to be more satisfying with those we regard as good communicators; that is, people who avoid such negative things as insults, complaints, and setting verbal traps, and are interested, interesting, comfortable people with whom to talk (Schrader 1990; Eckstein 2004). It is more satisfying when it is what psychologists call "nonviolent communication" (Rosenberg and Leu 2003; Eckstein and Grassa 2005). Nonviolent communication stresses such things as being nonthreatening, showing respect for each other, being honest with each other, and striving for fairness and trust. It emphasizes the need to make requests without blaming the partner or causing the partner to feel guilty.

Perhaps we can best sum up satisfying communication by looking at the kinds of items in the most frequently used measure of marital communication, the Marital Communication Inventory developed by Bienvenu (1978). This inventory is used by researchers and therapists to study and improve communication. A sampling of items shows that marital communication is more satisfying and effective the more often the spouses do the following:

- Discuss the way they will spend their income.
- Discuss their work and interests with each other.
- Express their feelings to each other.
- Avoid saying things that irritate each other.
- Have pleasant mealtime conversations.
- Listen to each other.
- Perceive that they are understood by the other.
- Support each other.
- Communicate affection and regard.
- Avoid the silent treatment.
- Confide in each other.

COMMUNICATION, MARITAL SATISFACTION, AND INTIMACY

Satisfying communication is essential for a healthy marriage. When a national sample of married people 40 to 50 years of age was asked about areas of desired change, one of the more frequent things desired was improved communication (Christensen and Miller 2006). Satisfying communication is so crucial because it facilitates the growth of both marital satisfaction and intimacy. Couples that are satisfied with their relationship, who define their marriage as a happy one, and who indicate high levels of intimacy also report satisfying patterns of communication (Pollock, Die, and Marriott 1990).

In fact, satisfying marital communication can act as preventive medicine for some marital ills. For example, adult children of alcoholics are at greater risk than others for marital problems. However, a study of female, adult children of alcoholics found that those with satisfying marital communication had higher levels of intimacy, a stronger sense of equity in the relationship, and less marital conflict (Jennison and Johnson 2001). Let's examine some of the aspects of communication that contribute to the well-being of marriage.

Everyday Conversations

We saw that the marriage of Jenny and Phil (in the Personal feature) ended because they never talked about the serious issues in their relationship. We should not

Pleasant mealtime conversations make both communication and the marriage more satisfying.

conclude that *only* the serious issues are an important part of the communication pattern of a couple, however. Everyday conversations and discussing the events of the day are significant for marital satisfaction (Vangelisti and Banski 1993). Couples who are highly satisfied with their relationship engage in both a greater amount of conversation and a broader range of topics than do those who are less satisfied (Richmond 1995).

Everyday conversation includes not only topics about what's going on in the world, the community, the workplace, and so forth, but also relational matters. Satisfied couples talk about their marriages and their families. They discuss their dreams and goals for the future. And they continue to affirm each other through expressions of appreciation and compliments. More compliments mean greater satisfaction with the relationship, because a compliment is a way of saying "I notice what you're doing and saying and I respect and admire you" (Doohan and Manusov 2004).

Self-Disclosure

We have seen that self-disclosure comes up repeatedly as an essential factor in an intimate relationship. In marriage, **self-disclosure** enhances both satisfaction and intimacy. The more a spouse engages in self-disclosure, the more both partners are likely to be highly satisfied with the relationship (King 1993; Yelsma and Marrow 2003; Gable et al. 2004). Self-disclosure accounts for more than half the variation in intimacy among couples (Waring and Chelune 1983).

Of course, self-disclosure must be practiced by both partners. And when it is, the result is a higher level of

intimacy and satisfaction, as a study of 96 married couples showed (Laurenceau, Barrett, and Rovine 2005). Each spouse was asked to complete a daily diary that assessed his or her own self-disclosure, that of the partner, and perceived level of intimacy. They kept the diaries for 42 consecutive days. The researchers found that self-disclosure by both the individual and the individual's partner enhanced the sense of intimacy, which, in turn, increased marital satisfaction.

In other words, when you practice self-disclosure you not only make your partner feel better about the relationship, you also find yourself feeling better because you have disclosed something about yourself. A husband of 14 years expressed it this way to us:

> I grew up in a family that didn't practice much self-disclosure. We were a pretty tight-mouthed, stiff-upper-lip group. When I met my wife, I found out that she was raised in a very different kind of family. She expected both of us to talk about our feelings and our ideas. That was hard for me. But one thing made it a lot easier. To my surprise, I discovered that when I shared my feelings with her, it not only made her feel closer to me. It also made me feel closer to her. We both gained by my self-disclosure! And of course, we both gain by hers. I have to tell you, I came to believe that self-disclosure is as important to marriage as food and water is to a person's body.

But what, exactly, do you disclose? We are not suggesting that you make your life an open book. You do not tell your spouse everything that pops into your mind, or every passing emotion you feel. Self-disclosure does not mean that there is an indiscriminate and continuous flow of words and feeling between the partners. Rather, two things are important.

 Exchange Theory Applied First, *exchange theory* suggests that self-disclosure, as we have already indicated, should be by both partners and should be equitable (Derlega et al. 1993). A study of troubled versus satisfied marriages reported that there was a relatively equal amount of self-disclosure among the satisfied couples (Chelune, Rosenfeld, and Waring 1985). In the troubled marriages, the wives tended to disclose more than the husbands.

Secondly, self-disclosure should always be done with discretion. A general guideline is that in a satisfying marriage you can disclose anything to your spouse, but you never disclose everything. Exactly what should and should not be disclosed may vary from one couple to another. It is always appropriate to disclose such things as feelings of pleasure and love. (Perhaps we should say it is imperative to express those feelings. It isn't enough to feel them internally.) Marital satisfaction is enhanced by the *disclosure,* not just the experience, of pleasure and love. It is appropriate to disclose your needs in the relationship, including your sexual needs and desires. In spite of the presumably open sexual nature of our society, many couples still find it difficult to talk freely about sexual matters with each other. It is also appropriate to disclose things that are troubling you or matters of serious concern. Sharing your feelings about a serious illness, for example, can enable you to cope better with that illness (Kelley, Lumley, and Leisen 1997). It also can help your partner to understand you better and to give you the support you need.

Self-disclosure, in sum, enhances both your personal and your marital well-being when you and your mate share a substantial part of your lives with each other. But there are always some things that should not be shared. Thus, as long as the disclosures can be handled by you in other ways, it is usually better not to disclose those things that you know will hurt or anger your spouse.

Other Aspects of Communication

Certain other aspects of communication are also related to marital satisfaction and intimacy. In our study of long-term marriages, we found three differences between those in happy, unhappy, and mixed (one partner happy and one unhappy) marriages (tables 9.1, 9.2, and 9.3). Couples in happy marriages tend more frequently to have a stimulating exchange of ideas, to laugh together, and to calmly discuss something. In other words, in happy marriages there are more—and also more stimulating and fun-filled—conversations.

Comparison

Couple Talk in Brisbane and Munich

Troubled couples in many different countries complain about communication problems in their marriage. Skilled communicators are likely to have more satisfying marriages than are those who are less skilled. But specifically what kinds of communication skills are important? And are the same skills important in different countries?

Three researchers attempted to answer these questions by comparing how 81 couples in Brisbane, Australia, and Munich, Germany, communicated during a problem-solving discussion. Forty-nine of the couples were in unhappy marriages, while 32 said they were happily married.

In some ways, the Australians and Germans communicated alike. Compared to the unhappy couples, the happy couples in both countries

agreed significantly more often with each other (e.g., "Yes, you're right," "I agree that I started the argument," etc.) and accepted each other (indicated by paraphrasing what the partner said and affirming the partner). The happy couples also made significantly more neutral statements and asked more neutral questions (e.g., "I think we have a problem with the kids," "Would you say that again, please?" etc.). In contrast, unhappy couples in both countries criticized their spouses and disagreed significantly more often than did happy couples. And finally, the happy couples had far more positive, nonverbal interaction (such as smiling at the partner).

But there was an important cross-national difference. German couples, whether happy or unhappy, used sig-

nificantly more negative responses than did the Australians. In part, this resulted from the fact that the Germans were more likely than the Australians to respond to a partner's negative statement with a negative statement of their own. In terms of the escalation of a negative interchange, the happy German couples were very similar to the unhappy Australian couples!

In other words, there was far more negativity generally in the German than in the Australian couples. In both countries a major problem of couples who defined themselves as unhappy was their inability to terminate negative interaction quickly. Happy couples, in contrast, knew how to either avoid such a process in the first place or reverse it once it started (Halford, Hahlweg, and Dunne 1990).

TABLE 9.1   Marital Happiness and Stimulating Exchange of Ideas

Frequency of discussions	Degree of Happiness		
	Both happy	One unhappy	Both unhappy
	Percent		
At least daily	28.3	21.9	18.4
Once or twice a week	47.3	29.7	26.3
Once or twice a month	17.8	28.1	18.4
Less than once a month	6.5	20.3	36.8
	99.9	100.0	99.9
	(N = 505)	(N = 64)	(N = 38)

Source: Copyright © 1986 Jeanette C. Lauer and Robert H. Lauer. Reprinted by permission.

TABLE 9.2   Marital Happiness and Laughing Together

Frequency of discussions	Degree of Happiness		
	Both happy	One unhappy	Both unhappy
	Percent		
At least daily	72.8	32.8	34.2
Once or twice a week	23.7	37.5	23.7
Once or twice a month	1.8	25.0	26.3
Less than once a month	1.8	4.7	15.8
	100.1	100.0	100.0
	(N = 506)	(N = 64)	(N = 38)

Source: Copyright © 1986 Jeanette C. Lauer and Robert H. Lauer. Reprinted by permission.

TABLE 9.3   Marital Happiness and Calm Discussions

Frequency of discussions	Degree of Happiness		
	Both happy	One unhappy	Both unhappy
	Percent		
At least daily	61.7	35.9	21.1
Once or twice a week	29.6	28.1	28.9
Once or twice a month	7.3	28.1	18.4
Less than once a month	1.4	7.8	31.6
	100.0	99.9	100.0
	(N = 506)	(N = 64)	(N = 38)

Source: Copyright © 1986 Jeanette C. Lauer and Robert H. Lauer. Reprinted by permission.

IMPROVING COMMUNICATION SKILLS

There are numerous books, workshops, and courses designed to help people improve their communication skills. Couples who attend premarital programs say that improved communication skills are one of the most helpful outcomes (Valiente, Belanger, and Estrada 2002). Marriage and family therapists spend a good deal of their time helping troubled clients with their communication patterns. In addition, you also can improve your own skills by attending to some basic rules and practicing them at every opportunity.

Rules

All rules for improving communication skills revolve about the goals of making us more effective senders and more effective receivers. Effective senders are those who

Some couples must go through counseling in order to learn to communicate in a nonthreatening way.

transmit clear messages and who do so in a nonthreatening way. To transmit a clear message, you need to listen to your own words carefully (figure 9.1) and continue to modify what you say until the message accurately reflects your feelings and ideas. At the same time, the message should be an invitation to dialogue and not an attack. Those who send their messages using some of the destructive styles discussed will threaten their partners in one way or another.

Unfortunately, a clear message sent in a nonthreatening manner does not guarantee accurate communication. When you communicate with someone, you are engaging in a process of interaction in which each of you is interpreting the verbal and nonverbal cues of the other. That interpretation may or may not be accurate. It can only be accurate when each of you has learned to be an effective receiver as well as an effective sender. To be an effective receiver means, above all, to be a good listener. Family therapist Virginia Satir (1972:70) pointed out that one of the common communication types she observed was the *distractor*. A distractor is someone who never responds directly to what is said by the other. The distractor tries to avoid the issue by ignoring it and bringing up something more pleasant. For example, a wife may say to her husband, "I was really hurt when you didn't tell me you would be so late." He might respond, "How about taking in a movie tonight?" In doing so, he is not actively listening to her. He has played the role of

distractor. You only actively listen when your response indicates that you understand and follow through in the direction suggested by the sender.

Practice

You can improve your own communication skills by attending to the ideas in this chapter when you talk with others. Even when you listen to a lecture, you can hone your skills by using some of the ideas discussed in the section on listening (e.g., summarizing the speaker's points in your mind).

In addition, certain exercises are specifically designed to improve communication skills. Lederer and Jackson (1968:277–84) suggest a number of exercises, one of which requires intimate partners to acknowledge everything the other says for a two-week period. In fact, they suggest that each acknowledge and in turn have the acknowledgment acknowledged. This should be done no matter how trivial the original statement seems to be. For instance, one of the partners may say, "It is cold today." The other should acknowledge the observation in some way, such as, "Yes, I noticed that it is cold also" or "You're right. It's colder than yesterday." The one who made the original statement could then acknowledge the acknowledgment: "So you noticed it too."

The exercise may seem silly at times. But two points are important. First, it will be done for more serious as well as trivial matters. And second, it is good practice in developing "confirmation" in communication (Montgomery 1981). Confirmation is a way of letting the other know that you are listening and that you understand and accept his or her feelings.

One further example of a helpful exercise is the communication game suggested by Satir (1972:80–95). In addition to the distractor, Satir identified three communication types that she found common in her work as a therapist: the *placator* is always agreeable, always trying to please; the *blamer* is always finding fault and acts superior to others; and the *computer* is the ultrarational individual who logically analyzes everything. Most people play one or more of those roles at some time.

Satir suggests playing the game with three people (to represent a family of mother, father, and child), but it also can be played with two as well. Play the game with someone with whom you are intimate. Let us say that it is a spouse or an intimate partner. Decide on a topic of conversation, perhaps a problem you are currently having or plans for a date or vacation. Then each selects a way of communicating. For example, you might begin as the blamer and your partner could be the distractor. Discuss the topic for about five minutes or so. Then talk about how each of you felt when you were playing that role.

After the discussion, each partner assumes a second way of communicating, and so on until each has played all four roles. An interesting aspect of this game, Satir noted, is the ease with which people construct an appropriate dialogue. That is because most of us have had practice already in each of the ways of communicating. In the course of playing the game, however, people learn a great deal about themselves and their relationships. You will probably find some of the ways of communicating very repugnant or very difficult for you. Some men react strongly to being a placator, and some women find it very difficult to be a blamer.

The major point is that communication skills are like any other. They can be improved by practice. For those who wish to enhance the quality of their intimate relationships, good communication skills are imperative.

SUMMARY

It is impossible not to communicate. We communicate nonverbally as well as verbally. Clothing, facial expressions, eye behavior, touching, and various oral cues such as inflection are a part of nonverbal communication. Nonverbal cues may complement, contradict, repeat, regulate, substitute for, or accent our verbal messages. Gender and interpersonal closeness both affect the way we interpret nonverbal cues.

Communication is an interaction process in which the sender encodes feelings and ideas and transmits them to the receiver who must decode them in the context of his or her own feelings and ideas. Communication static can occur in any part of this process. Feelings as well as ideas are subject to the process of interpretation by each party in the communication.

Listening is a crucial part of communication. Some listening styles impede effective communication, including the faker, the dependent listener, the interrupter, the self-conscious listener, and the intellectual listener. There are various techniques that anyone can use to improve listening skills.

A number of destructive messages are impediments to effective communication. Ordering, threatening, moralizing, providing solutions, lecturing, criticizing, ridiculing, analyzing, interrogating, and withdrawing are forms of destructive messages. These messages may be appropriate and useful at times, but they are destructive when used regularly or at inappropriate times.

It is important to recognize gender differences in communication in order to minimize problems. Women tend to believe the marriage is working as long as they can keep discussing it with their husbands. Men tend to believe the marriage is not working if they have to keep discussing it.

Satisfying communication is crucial to a satisfying marriage, although the former will not guarantee the latter. Communication is satisfying when we feel that we are understood and that the other agrees with us. Marital communication is more satisfying to the extent that the partners discuss both trivial and important matters, avoid irritating each other, and listen to each other.

Satisfying communication facilitates the development of both marital satisfaction and intimacy. Everyday conversations and self-disclosure are particularly important to satisfaction and a deepening intimacy. People in happy marriages have, more frequently than others, a stimulating exchange of ideas, calm discussions, and times of laughing together.

Communication skills can improve by attending to some basic rules and practicing. A good communicator must be both an effective sender and an effective receiver. Various exercises can help make you a more effective communicator.

Principles for Enhancing Intimacy

1. Effective communication is essential to a successful relationship, but it doesn't seem to come naturally or easily. It takes determination and effort. Effective communication requires commitment and hard work for the duration of the relationship.

2. Many people complain that it is the lack of communication that is hurting or even destroying their relationship. It is important to remember, however, that you are always communicating something. Even when you refuse to talk to your partner and give him or her the "silent treatment," you are communicating a powerful message. Unfortunately, what you seem to be saying is that this relationship is not worth talking about. And, not surprisingly, the relationship will be worthless if the silence persists.

3. There is some truth to the old adage "Actions speak louder than words." For example, your facial expressions, body language, tone of voice, and physical appearance convey a message. At times, it is not the message you intend. Yet to the recipient of the message, nonverbal communication is often a more forceful indicator of your feelings than the words you use. Be open to your partner's readings of your nonverbal cues; you can both learn something about your true feelings.

4. Cultivate the capacity of effective listening. Generally, we master easily the technique of ineffective listening—partial attention, premature conclusions, misunderstood intentions, and so forth. Effective listening, however, involves the need to understand what the other person is really saying and to respond in a way that demonstrates this understanding.

5. Effective communication is not a cure-all for every troubled relationship. At times, effective communication convincingly reveals that the relationship cannot or should not be salvaged. As a necessary ingredient of a vital intimate relationship, however, effective communication is worth the risk.

KEY TERMS

communication *192*
decode *195*
encode *195*

media *195*
nonverbal cues *192*

self-disclosure *205*
static *195*

ON THE WEB   The Challenge of Communication

The text points out that satisfying marital communication is essential for a fulfilling marriage. What is "satisfying" will vary somewhat for different people, of course, but there are some aspects of communication that all people view as important to marital communication. And nonverbal communication is as important as the verbal. Two sites that are useful for further exploring some of these ideas are:

www.mhhe.com/lauer7e

Exploring Nonverbal Communication
http://nonverbal.ucsc.edu

This site, maintained by a professor at the University of California, Santa Cruz, offers an opportunity to test your nonverbal skills in such areas as body language, gestures, the face, and the voice.

Relationship Communication Test
http://www.drphil.com/articles/article/339

Dr. Phil, the psychologist who writes books and hosts a television program, offers a relationship communication test on this site. There is no score, but every "true" answer indicates some area of communication that needs improvement.

Using these two sites and others, enlarge your understanding with the following projects:

1. Go to the "Exploring Nonverbal Communication" site and test yourself. Use a search engine to explore other sites dealing with nonverbal communication. Using materials from the text and from the other sites, how would you design a site that would give a comprehensive test of nonverbal skills?
2. Use the Relationship Communication Test on Dr. Phil's site to test 10 students—five males and five females. Analyze your results. Do the males or females have higher communication skills? What are the areas that most need improvement? Are there differences between the areas most needing improvement named by females and those most named by males? Use materials from the text to draw some conclusions about the 10 students you tested.

~ POWER AND CONFLICT IN MARRIAGE ~

LEARNING OBJECTIVES

After reading and studying chapter 10, you should be able to

1 Discuss the meaning, measurement, and importance of marital power.
2 Explain the sources of power in light of the resource theory.
3 Analyze the six types of power that can be used in a marriage.

4 Show the ways in which marriage is a power struggle.
5 Define the six types of power interaction in marriage.
6 Discuss the functions of marital conflict.
7 Summarize the primary issues about which couples fight.
8 Describe the sources of marital tension.
9 Outline the common styles of conflict.
10 Relate the principles of "good fighting."

The amount of conflict and the things that people fight about vary over the course of a marriage. A man married 30 years told us, "We have arguments from time to time. But we fought more in the first six months of our marriage than we did over the next 30 years."

How much difference is there over time in the frequency of conflict and the kinds of things that people fight about? Interview six people who have been married 5 years or less, six who have been married 15 to 20 years, and six who have been married 30 or more years. (You may want to work with two others, and each of you can interview six people in one of the categories.)

Prepare a questionnaire for your subjects (your instructor can help with this). Tell them that you are researching the amount and kinds of conflict in marriages. Point out that their names will not be on the questionnaire and that you would appreciate a frank response. On the questionnaire, have them record their age, sex, and number of years married. Have them circle their response to the following:

How frequently do you and your spouse have arguments?

1. Never
2. Less than once a month
3. Once or twice a month
4. Once or twice a week
5. Daily

Then let them respond to an open-ended question: What are the issues or topics about which you and your spouse argue?

Tabulate the responses by number of years married. Are there any differences in frequency or in the kinds of things that people say they argue about? What are they? How would you explain the differences or lack of differences? Also note if there are any differences in the responses given by men and women.

If the entire class participates in this project, group all of the responses for each of the three categories (number of years married). The larger number of responses will give you more confidence in answering the questions. ❊

213

In our fantasies, marriage is a romantic adventure. In reality, marriage is a struggle as well as an adventure. It is a struggle in a number of ways. Consider the explanation of John Ruskin, famed nineteenth-century author and reformer, for the unhappy state of his own union:

> I married her thinking her so young and affectionate that I might influence her as I chose, and make of her just such a wife as I wanted. It appeared that *she* married *me* thinking she could make of me just the *husband she* wanted. I was grieved and disappointed at finding I could not change her, and she was humiliated and irritated at finding she could not change me (quoted in Rose 1983:61).

As Ruskin found to his chagrin, marriage can involve conflict and a struggle for power within the relationship. Power and conflict are a normal part of intimate relationships. They can, however, wreck a relationship. Nonetheless, they need not lead to dissatisfaction in marriage and can, in fact, enhance the quality of the relationship if the partners handle them well.

In this chapter, we will examine those aspects of marriage that *conflict theorists* regard as central to all human interaction—issues of power and conflict. We will look at power in terms of its meaning, importance, sources, and role in the struggles of marriage. We also will discuss the meaning and role of conflict. We will see the kinds of things that people fight about, the way in which they fight, and some methods of "good fighting."

POWER IN MARRIAGE

Conflict Theory Applied

Who is the head of the house? Who is in control in the marriage? Americans like to think of marriage as a relationship of equals. Yet how equal are marriages? We can only answer the question after we look at power in relationships and at the way in which marriage can become a struggle over power.

The Meaning of Power

What do you actually do when you exert power in a relationship? That is, what does it mean to have interpersonal power? And how can you tell who has the power in a relationship?

Defining Power.   A dictionary definition equates power with the possession of such things as authority, influence, and control. Social psychologists make a finer distinction. In general, they define *power* as the capacity to

influence others and to resist being influenced by others (Worchel, Cooper, and Goethals 1991:397). Note that power is the *capacity* to exercise influence. The power may or may not be used in specific situations.

We will define **power** in a similar but slightly different way as the ability to get someone to think or feel or act in a way that he or she would not have done spontaneously. It is important to note that this does not imply that the person didn't want to think, feel, or act in that way. Power doesn't necessarily involve coercion. It doesn't necessarily mean that you influence your partner in a way that is contrary to his or her inclination. In other words, we should not think of the use of power as something inherently negative or wrong. Of course, power can be abused and misused. However, it also can be used to enhance the well-being of others, as illustrated by the work of therapists and the influence of physical fitness experts.

Measuring Power.   Think about any marital relationship you know fairly well. Which spouse has the most power? How do you know? Researchers have struggled with these questions but have generally measured marital power on the basis of who makes the major decisions. For example, who has the final say on such matters as buying a house, the kind of car to purchase, the vacation, and the choice of work for either spouse? In a classic study, Blood and Wolfe (1960) used the responses to such questions to identify patterns of power in marriages. They found four different patterns (figure 10.1). The wife-dominant was the least frequent pattern, comprising about 3 percent of the couples. About a fourth were husband-dominant. The rest, the great majority, were relatively egalitarian in their decision making. There were two types of egalitarian marriages, however. In the "autonomic," the decision making was equal but separate. That is, each spouse had authority over certain areas. In the "syncratic," the spouses shared authority over all decisions.

The methodology of Blood and Wolfe has been criticized on a number of grounds. For one thing, they gave equal weight to all kinds of decisions. But we may question whether the decision about the weekly food budget is as significant as the question of whether and where each spouse works. Another criticism is that they didn't include many important decisions (they used only eight), for example, decisions about sexual matters and the number of children, if any, to have. A third criticism is that they interviewed only the wives in the marriages. What differences might they have found if they also had asked husbands about who made the decisions?

Finally, the work of Blood and Wolfe (and others) has been criticized on the grounds that power involves

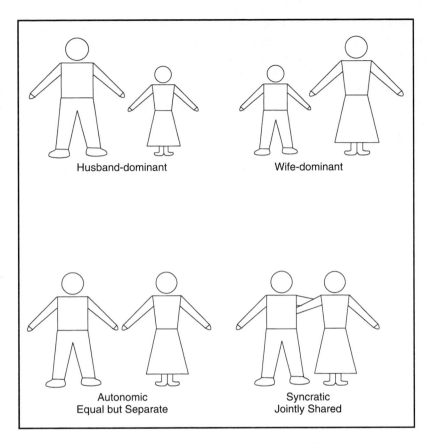

Husband-dominant

Wife-dominant

Autonomic
Equal but Separate

Syncratic
Jointly Shared

FIGURE 10.1 Types of Marital Power Relationships

more than simply who makes the final decisions on specific issues. What about the division of labor in the household? What about the way in which conflicts are handled and resolved? What about the ability to use techniques to influence the partner, such as in the case of the spouse who makes good sexual relations contingent on the other's behaving in a particular way? The point is that power issues do go beyond such things as who decides which car to buy. Power, whether in a marriage or any other social situation, is difficult to measure. For the sake of clarity, therefore, it is preferable to specify the kind of power we are measuring. In the Blood and Wolfe study, for instance, we could classify the marriages as husband-dominant in eight decision-making areas, wife-dominant in eight decision-making areas, and so forth. Their research may not have measured the full scope of power, but their findings are not trivial.

Why Is Power Important?

A student told us that he didn't believe in power in a marriage. "I wouldn't want to have any power over my

wife, and I wouldn't want her to have any power over me. Power contradicts the very meaning of marriage." His ideal was of a totally equal relationship in which power is banished by mutual consent. But that overlooks the point that power is an integral part of human relationships. It also overlooks the point that to be equal does not mean to be powerless.

 Symbolic Interactionist Theory Applied In fact, we need power. At a more general level, to have power, to have some sense of control over our lives, is important to our mental health. The important point is not whether an outside observer would detect power, but whether people *define their situation* as one in which they have some power. If they feel helpless, they are likely to become depressed and vulnerable to various kinds of physical and mental ills (Seligman 1998).

Those who feel that they have some degree of control over the circumstances of their lives, on the other hand, are better able not only to cope but also to master the various crises of life (Lauer and Lauer 1988). A sense of power is also important in maintaining self-esteem. A study of 90 couples found that those with satisfying marriages divided up decision making so that each spouse had some power in the relationship; that power, in turn, supported the needs of each partner for self-esteem (Beach and Tesser 1993).

There are many matters over which partners might want to exert power and influence each other. They include seemingly trivial things such as picking up clothes or using the remote control and deciding which television programs to watch (Walker 1996). We say "seemingly trivial" because if there is an effort to control many things, it suggests that the couple is locked in a general power struggle of which they may or may not be aware. Such struggles manifest themselves in everything from the seemingly trivial to weightier matters like major purchases or decisions about work. Apart from engaging in a fundamental power struggle, however, partners may wish to exert power and influence each other for different reasons: for personal benefit, for the benefit of the partner, or for the smooth functioning of the household and/or the relationship.

Thus, the use of power is inevitable in an intimate relationship. The way the power is used and the perceived balance of power are important to marital satisfaction. Those who perceive power inequality are likely to be less satisfied with the marriage (Whisman and Jacobson 1990). One way that the less powerful partner may deal with the inequality is to develop a physical or

emotional disorder that forces the more powerful partner to accede to his or her wishes out of consideration for the handicap (Bagarozzi 1990). Another way the less powerful partner may react is to engage in behavior that is counterproductive to a healthy relationship. Thus, when one partner feels relatively powerless in a marriage, that person may keep quiet about his or her complaints (Solomon, Knobloch, and Fitzpatrick 2004). Keeping quiet, of course, means that the issues will not be resolved and that the relationship will continue to be unsatisfying or will deteriorate and ultimately break up.

But how do we know who has the most power? We can, of course, ask the partners, but on what do they base their conclusion? One way to measure power is by who makes the final decisions on various matters. If one partner typically has the final word, that is the person with the most power. Another way to measure power is by who has control over the division of labor in the home. Again, if one partner typically makes the final decision over such things as who performs which chores, that is the more powerful of the two. Of course, if both partners agree to these kinds of arrangements, there is power inequality but not a power struggle.

We have known couples who, for religious or practical reasons, were accepting of an unequal power arrangement. Most couples, however, prefer a more egalitarian marriage. As we noted earlier, in fact, the more egalitarian the arrangement, the more likely the couple is to experience high levels of marital satisfaction.

Marriage is a struggle as well as an adventure.

Sources of Power

Where do we get power? What would give you more power than your partner or your partner more power than you?

Traditionally, and in virtually all societies, men have the greater power simply by virtue of being males. In the United States, male dominance has been reinforced by books that advise couples how to construct a meaningful marriage. Even recent books continue to give advice that maintains the traditional division of power. For example, an analysis of the best-selling books touting the notion that men are from Mars and women from Venus concludes that the descriptions and recommendations given in the books support and encourage power differences between men and women (Zimmerman, Haddock, and McGeorge 2001).

What is the basis for this strong tradition of male dominance? The answers vary. One is the anthropological argument that, from the beginning of human history, women have been dependent on men to provide food and other necessities for them and their children. In support of that argument, Lee and Petersen (1983) found, in

Comparison

The Power of Egyptian Husbands and Wives

In Egypt, the Muslim marriage contract requires a husband to support his wife and a wife to obey her husband. The husband also agrees to a "dower," a substantial sum that must be paid to the wife, usually in installments over a lifetime. If he divorces her, he must pay any balance—a strong deterrent to divorce.

The requirement to obey one's husband would make most Americans automatically regard an Egyptian marriage as unacceptably inequitable. However, as in the United States, Egyptian marriages exhibit varying degrees of power inequality. Egyptian women do have some power in family matters, including in the decision-making process. Those who live with their husband's relatives tend to have less power in family matters. Those who are educated have more power and more influence on decisions.

Husbands are expected to treat their wives well, but married women may be victimized by spousal abuse. A survey of wives in Minya found that 26.8 percent had been beaten and 4.1 percent said they had been severely beaten. Rates of abuse are lower among the wealthy and more educated and among those couples who live near the wife's relatives. Abused women who are dependent upon their husbands because they have sons are more likely to be abused and somewhat more likely to tolerate the abuse (in Egypt, a women depends upon her sons for support in her old age; if she divorces her husband, however, he gets custody of the sons). And women who have less education than their husbands, and therefore less likelihood of being able to become financially independent, also have higher rates of abuse.

If a woman is abused, what are her alternatives? Until relatively recent times, a wife who abandoned an abusive husband and fled to relatives could be returned to her husband by the police upon the husband's request. Her return was justified on the basis that she had pledged obedience to him. Now, however, a judge can declare the request for obedience to be unjustified if there are sufficient grounds for doing so.

Egyptian husbands continue to seek obedience orders in the courts against their wives. Wives who resist the order to return to their husbands generally do so on one of two grounds: clear evidence of abuse or inadequate provision of a home.

What is "inadequate provision of a home"? An adequate home, as one judge outlined it, includes the wife's right to have quarters that reflect the husband's social standing; refuses to allow members of her husband's family residence in the house; has good neighbors, such that the home is safe; and has a kitchen, bath, and private conveniences that aren't shared with others.

As far as abuse is concerned, a wife who can show either actual or threatened harm from her husband can legally withdraw from him. She can also divorce him, and in fact the most frequent reason for judicial divorce is proven abuse. At the time of the divorce, the husband must pay his wife the balance of the financial obligation he made at the time of their marriage (which could be a substantial amount of money).

Thus, although Muslim marriages are often perceived by Westerners to involve great inequality in power, in Egypt husbands and wives both have strong obligations and some degree of power. A husband must support and treat his wife well. As long as he does, she is obligated to remain with him and fulfill her responsibilities as a wife. By American standards, this is an inequitable arrangement, giving far more power to the husband. By Egyptian standards, however, the arrangement is considered an appropriate one (Fluehr-Lobban and Bardsley-Sirois 1990; Yount 2005a, 2005b).

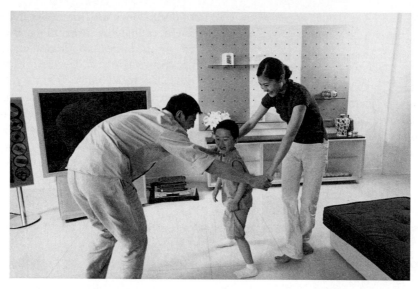

The ability to maintain an orderly home is one resource women can use to gain power.

113 nonindustrial societies, that the more wives contribute to food production, the more they tend to have power in marriage. Resource theory provides another answer to the question of male dominance. Let's examine it in detail.

Resource Theory.   **Resource theory** was formulated by Blood and Wolfe (1960), who argued that the balance of power in a marriage will reflect the relative resources that each partner has. The power over the decision-making process, they said,

> stems primarily from the resources which the individual can provide to meet the needs of his marriage partner and to upgrade his decision-making skills (Blood and Wolfe 1960:44).

Whoever has the most resources will have the most power. For example, one important resource is money. The spouse with the highest income (which normally means the one with the most education and highest-status occupation as well) will probably have the most power in the relationship.

Because money is one of the more important resources, it is understandable that the male generally has had the most power in American family life. To the extent that the husband has been the breadwinner or has been the main contributor to the family's financial resources, he has also assumed the authority to decide how the income will be spent. In this case, power refers to authority over the family's financial resources. That power, however, tended to spill over into other areas as well.

Logically, you might expect that if a woman brings more money into the home than the man does, the power will shift to her. Yet this doesn't necessarily happen. Even when the woman earns substantially more than the man, the man may act in ways to maintain his dominant position in the relationship (Tichenor 2005). Nor do wives necessarily resist or resent the husbands' power. Comparing 22 couples in which the wife earned at least 50 percent more than the husband with 8 couples in which the husband earned about the same as or more than his wife, Tichenor (1999) found that the high-earning wives gained some privileges. However, they were uncomfortable with the notion that money would bring them power in their marriage and refrained from making claims for more say in household decisions.

There are, of course, important resources other than material ones. For women, educational attainment is typically associated with a greater degree of power in the marital relationship. Thus, a study of wives in Mexico reported that those with higher levels of education were less likely to be victims of violence, more likely to have an equal say in decisions, and more likely to be satisfied with their influence in the decision-making process (Oropesa 1997). It also has been suggested that women can and do use sex to achieve a balance of power with the economically dominant men in their lives. Historically, sex was the main commodity that women could withhold or bestow in order to achieve their desires, which often went far beyond personal sexual gratification (Brown 1995). However, men can also use sex as a weapon in the struggle for power by claiming that they suffer from sexual dissatisfaction (Betchen 2006). Such a claim can neutralize or negate a wife's belief that she is underbenefitted and her husband is overbenefitted in their relationship.

In addition, emotional support, budgeting skills, the ability to organize and maintain an efficient home, and parenting skills may be important resources (Gatrell 2007). In other words, whatever you have that can help meet the needs of your partner is a resource in your marriage. For example, a female executive told us that she accorded her husband equal authority to make decisions in their marriage because, among other things, "he is such a good father." Although she contributed much more income than he did to the family, she valued his ability to be a good father to her children (he was the stepfather to her children from a previous marriage). His parenting skills were a resource that balanced out her greater financial contribution.

An important nonmaterial resource is a person's interest in maintaining the relationship. Waller (1951) formulated the "principle of least interest," which states that the partner who is least interested in maintaining the relationship has the most power. Consider the situation from the point of view of the one with the most interest. If you are more concerned than your spouse in keeping a marriage going, you are likely to defer to your spouse in various decisions and to strive to please your spouse in diverse matters. In other words, your spouse will have more power in the relationship than you. Even if your spouse does not intentionally exploit the situation, your behavior will be that of a less powerful person interacting with a more powerful person.

It is vital to keep in mind that resources are only resources if they meet the needs of the other. That is, to bring a large income to a marriage may or may not be an important resource. If the partner has a large income of his or her own, money may not be as important as other things. Or if the spouse who earns the income, or most of the income, is abusive or lacks good communication skills or has difficulty expressing affection, the money may be insufficient to hold the marriage together. In other words, we must look at all of the resources each individual has. It is your resource profile, not a particular resource, that will determine your potential power. And it is your resource profile in the context of the needs of your partner that will determine your actual power in the relationship.

Types of Power.   Raven, Centers, and Rodrigues (1975) identified six different kinds of power that people can exert in a marriage (table 10.1). Note that the six types represent differing kinds of resources that people have. Research on gender differences shows that men generally have more **expert** and **legitimate power** than do women, while women tend to have more **referent power** than do men (Carli 1999). Either spouse may also use **coercive power, reward power,** or **informational power.** In general, women tend to find it more difficult to exercise power. Of course, the type of power used depends on the situation. A decision about whether to visit a friend or relative is likely to be settled on the basis of legitimate or referent power. A decision about cleaning or repairing something in the home is likely to be settled by legitimate or expert power.

The type of power also varies by how satisfied the individual is with the marriage. Those in less satisfactory marriages are far more likely to ascribe coercive power to their mates than are those in satisfying unions.

TABLE 10.1 Types of Power in Marriage

Type	Reason for compliance	Example
Coercive	To avoid punishment by spouse	Tired wife agrees to sex to avoid husband's verbal abuse.
Reward	To obtain rewards from spouse	Husband becomes less messy as wife praises him for helping keep a clean house.
Legitimate	Spouse has the right to ask and you have the duty to comply	Husband agrees to share household tasks with working wife because he is committed to equality.
Expert	Spouse has special knowledge or expertise	Wife trusts husband's judgment about cars and lets him decide which one to buy.
Referent	Identification with, and admiration of, spouse and desire to please him or her	Husband goes to opera and tries to learn more about and enjoy operatic music that wife loves.
Informational	Persuasion by spouse that what spouse wants is in your own best interests	Wife votes Democratic even though she is a Republican because husband convinces her that women will benefit more under Democrats.

What Do You Think?

*There is disagreement about **whether marriage always involves a power struggle**. What follows are pro and con arguments. What do you think?*

Pro

Marriage always involves a power struggle because

- men and women come to marriage with fundamentally different goals.
- men have a basic drive to be dominant.
- decision making requires someone to be the final authority.
- all people are driven by self-interest, and the pursuit of self-interest requires power.
- we are products of a highly competitive culture in which we learn to strive for the top position.

Con

Marriage is not always a power struggle because

- most people are committed to an egalitarian union.
- in strongly homogamous marriages, differences are too few to warrant a power struggle.
- love rather than power is the key to fulfillment.
- people soon learn that cooperation and mutual understanding work much better than power in decision making.
- most people want to please rather than dominate their mates.

MARRIAGE AS A POWER STRUGGLE

A wife says to her husband, "We're going to the movies tonight." He likes to go to the movies and is not even averse to going that night. Still, he doesn't like the way she has put it. She didn't ask whether he wanted to go. She simply informed him that they were going. He responds, therefore, "Not me. You can go if you want, but I'm staying home."

What has happened in this situation illustrates **reactance theory,** which states that when someone tries to force us to engage in a behavior, even though the behavior is consistent with our attitudes, we are likely to resist and may even change our attitudes (Brehm 1966). As stated earlier, we all need to have some control over our lives. At any time, there are a limited number of areas in which we feel we have a choice. We will not take lightly to someone trying to take one of those areas of choice away from us.

Thus, this couple had the beginnings of a power struggle over the choice of how to spend a free evening. It was an unnecessary struggle in that particular case, being spurred on by an unfortunate way of stating a desire. In other cases, the struggle can be more intense. Every marriage has some power struggles. Some are ongoing struggles for power as long as the marriage lasts. Power struggles involve conflict and are particularly

likely to result in destructive conflict. When power is shared, in contrast, the marriage is likely to be more harmonious and less caught up in conflict, a relationship that holds in other societies such as Taiwan as well as in the United States (Eckstein 2004; Xu and Lai 2004).

Types of Power Interaction

There are various ways that spouses can attempt to either exert or avoid power when communicating with each other. First, a conversation can be either *symmetrical* or *complementary.*

In a symmetrical discussion, the two spouses send similar messages, messages designed to control how the relationship is defined. There are, in turn, three types of symmetrical discussions. In *competitive symmetry,* the couple is engaged in a situation of escalating conflict. For example, the husband may say, "I don't want to go out tonight. I've worked hard today." The wife responds, "You never want to go anywhere. I've worked hard, too, but you don't care how I feel about it." Each is trying to control the definition of the situation, and each is doing it in a way that escalates the conflict. In *neutralized symmetry,* the spouses have respect for each other, and each tries to avoid exerting control. The wife says, "It looks like snow tonight." The husband responds, "If we go out, we better leave early and drive slowly." Each has left the way open for the other to express feelings about going out on a snowy night before they both come to a final decision. In *submissive symmetry,* both spouses try to give control to the other. A husband may say, "How are we going to pay all of our bills this month?" The wife may respond, "Please don't get upset. What do you think we should do?" Neither wants to take control of the situation.

In *complementary interaction,* the two spouses indicate agreement that one is dominant and the other submissive. For example, a husband may say, "Why don't you return this spotted shirt? You're better at that than I am." The wife responds, "Yes, I am. I'll do it." Or a husband may say, "Let's go to the ball game tonight. I don't feel like staying home." The wife responds, "Okay," even though baseball is not her favorite sport.

As these examples illustrate, people do not always try to exert power. Sometimes they deliberately refrain from it, trying to relate to the spouse as an equal. Sometimes they try to give the power to the spouse or submit to a spouse who is exercising power. But sometimes both spouses try to take control. And in some marriages, the struggle goes on more or less continuously as every issue becomes a battleground on which to test the relative power of each.

CONFLICT IN MARRIAGE

If a couple is engaged in a power struggle, they are, by definition, having conflict. However, even if they are not in an ongoing power struggle, they will likely have conflict. Lack of conflict is not necessarily the sign of a good marriage. In fact, marriage counselors note that many of the couples who come to them have not been fighting. Some marriages die because the partners no longer care enough about each other even to fight. A healthy marriage, then, has some degree of conflict. The most important thing is how the conflict is handled. Kurdek (1995) studied 155 couples and found marital satisfaction related to styles of dealing with conflict. Other researchers, doing longitudinal research, have concluded that the most powerful predictor of whether a couple will break up or stay together is the way they handle their differences (Markman, Stanley, and Blumberg 1994; Gottman 1994).

The Positive Functions of Conflict

Conflict can have both positive and negative consequences for a marriage. Few people enjoy interpersonal conflict, so it is easier for most of us to think of the negative rather than the positive consequences.

However, people who have some conflict and who handle it well tend to have higher levels of marital adjustment than others (Gottman and Krokoff 1989; Noller et al. 1994). By handling conflict appropriately, they enhance the quality of their relationship and create a more intense sense of intimacy. Their marriage is strengthened rather than threatened by the conflict. Well-managed conflict also has a number of other positive functions:

1. Conflict brings issues out into the open. The couple that engages in good fighting will avoid an interpersonal cold war and the resentments that tend to build and corrode the relationship.
2. Conflict helps clarify issues. Jack, a 29-year-old chemical engineer, is married to Donna, a teacher. He told us about a conflict that helped clarify an issue for them:

    We were on our way back from a ski trip. We've found that our car trips are often ideal times for marital communication. On this trip, Donna brought up the issue of cleaning up the dog's mess in the backyard. Before we got the dog, she had promised she would clean up after it. It was a job I didn't want. But now she was apparently tired of it. I told her I would only consider a change if she would offer me something in return. "Let's negotiate," I said. "If I clean it up, what will you do for me in return?" At that she got really angry. And we argued for most of the way home.

    Well, it turned out that she was really upset because she thought I wasn't carrying my share of the work around the house. The dog's mess allowed us to get to the heart of the matter, and we spent the last part of our trip working out an arrangement that made both of us feel better.

3. We can grow through conflict. We grow by striving, not by easing along. Handled properly, conflict will increase your awareness of the kind of person you are and can become.
4. Small conflicts help to defuse more serious conflict. Molehills can become mountains. Ignoring small problems can lead to a buildup of resentment that will eventually explode in a more serious fight.
5. Conflict can create and maintain an equitable balance of power. Two spouses who carry on conflict as equals, each affirming his or her own position and striving to understand the position of the other, demonstrate that each has power in the relationship. In other words, while conflict can be a manifestation of a power struggle, it also can be a means of establishing a power balance. Balanced power means a more satisfying relationship.

The Negative Consequences of Severe Conflict

When the conflict is severe, that is, when it is persistent and intense and not handled in a way that is constructive and satisfactory to one or both partners, the consequences are likely to be destructive. Severe conflict can be destructive to the partners' emotional and physical health and leads to an unhappy marriage or divorce.

Severe conflict is equally destructive to children and, in fact, can have long-term negative consequences. This occurs because parents who have a highly conflicted relationship tend to function poorly in most areas of child rearing (Krishnakumar and Buehler 2000). They are particularly prone to use harsh punishment and to be deficient in making their children feel accepted. This poor functioning as parents, in turn, results in various kinds of personal and relational problems for the children (Buehler and Gerard 2002). These problems include the following:

- poor health behavior, including higher rates of substance use and abuse (Repetti, Taylor, and Seeman 2002; Caughlin and Malis 2004).
- lower competence in relating to others (Repetti, Taylor, and Seeman 2002; Riggio 2004).
- more negative self feelings and more self-destructive (suicidal) thoughts (Shagle and Barber 1993; Doyle and Markiewicz 2005).
- higher levels of anxiety and aggression (Cummings 1994; Riggio 2004).
- higher rates of depression (Constantine 2006; Turner and Kopiec 2006).
- higher levels of parental negativity and adolescent antisocial behavior (Feinburg, Kan, and Hetherington 2007).
- greater likelihood of feeling caught between the parents, which is associated with lower subjective well-being and poorer relationships with the parents (Amato and Afifi 2006).
- greater likelihood of having lower-quality or troubled romantic relationships and marriages of their own (Amato and Booth 2001; Doucet and Aseltine 2003; Crockett and Randall 2006).

The negative effects of parental conflict have been found in infants as young as 30 months (Pauli-Pott and Beckmann 2007). And the problems are exacerbated by the fact that mutual influence exists between parental conflict and children's behavior problems (Jenkins et al. 2005). That is, the conflict contributes to the behavior problems that, in turn, fuel the conflict, which prolongs and intensifies the behavior problems. And so on. The family is caught up in a destructive spiral.

The question arises: Would children be better off in a two-parent home that has a high level of conflict or a single-parent home with a lower level of conflict? James Peterson and Nicholas Zill (1986) addressed the question using a national sample of 1,400 children ages 12 to 16. The researchers looked at such things as rates of depression, antisocial behavior, and school problems among children in various kinds of home situations. They found generally that children who lived with both parents were the least depressed and withdrawn. But for those children in homes of high, persistent conflict, the levels of depression and withdrawal were even higher than for those who lived with just one of their biological parents. Antisocial behavior also tended to be higher among those in two-parent homes with high, persistent conflict. Thus, as painful as divorce is, remaining in an intact family with high and persistent conflict can be even more painful.

What People Fight About

Have you ever had an argument with someone knowing that what you supposedly were fighting about was not the real issue? For instance, we noted previously that although Jack and Donna started arguing over who was going to clean up after the dog, they were really fighting about a larger issue: the division of labor in the home. We need to be careful in conflict, therefore, to distinguish between overt and underlying issues. Sometimes what people initially argue about is the real issue, and sometimes it isn't. Conflict can only be constructive if you learn to focus on the real issue. Couples, of course, can fight over anything and everything. However, the most common sources of conflict include money (e.g., spending styles, the budget, the amount of money spent on various items), children (e.g., how many to have, when to have them, discipline), and sex (e.g., how often, techniques, birth control) (Oggins 2003; Christensen and Miller 2006; Dew 2007).

If the marriage is generally a satisfying one, the amount of conflict tends to diminish over time (Hatch and Bulcroft 2004). In her survey of 1,152 spouses who had been married 50 or more years, Alford-Cooper (1998:86–7) found that the most common sources of conflict reported were "finances (29 percent), relatives (24 percent), ill health (24 percent), raising the children (21 percent), and the spouse's annoying habits (everything from snoring to alcoholism, 17 percent)."

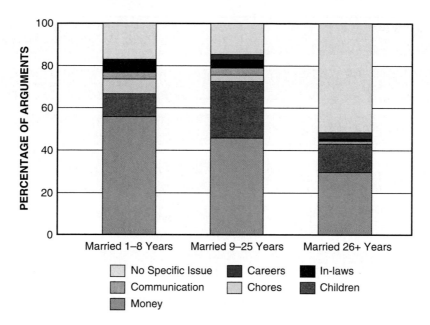

FIGURE 10.2 What Starts Arguments
Source: Adapted from Stanley, Markman, and Whitton 2002.

What people fight about as well as the amount they fight also tends to change over time. Figure 10.2 shows the kinds of things that people married for various amounts of time reported as most frequently starting their arguments. In the early years of marriage, money looms large as the most frequent source of conflict. Children are an increasingly important source of conflict during the middle years (9 to 25). Those married 26 years or more were more likely to indicate that no single issue emerged as the most frequent reason for arguing, though money was still a fairly common source.

Finally, what about couples who are in serious trouble, serious enough to be seeing a therapist? What kinds of conflict do therapists see in couples they counsel? Research on 160 couples who came to a family therapy clinic focused on a number of matters: the kinds of problems the couples named, how often the problems surfaced, whether males and females differed in their perceptions of the problems, and whether the problems most likely named varied by how long the couples had been married (Miller, Yorgason, Sandberg, and White 2003). With regard to the length of marriage, the problems identified were similar whatever the stage of marriage (the number of years of marriage ranged from 1 to 20).

With regard to the kinds of problems named, figure 10.3 shows the eight areas most frequently identified. There were a few additional areas that were not

named as often, including parents-in-law, spiritual matters, values, and differences over gender roles. Note two things about the eight areas in the figure. First, the ordering of the problems by males and females is remarkably similar. Thus, both named communication as the most troubling area, finances as the second, emotional intimacy as the third, and so on. The second thing to note is that the wives reported a greater frequency of the problems arising than did the husbands. It would appear that the wives believed that the problems were more troubling than did the husbands.

What, then, do people fight about? In general, everything and anything. But some problems are clearly more common than others, and some are more damaging to the relationship than others. The one problem that stands out as of overriding importance if the marriage is to survive and be healthy is communication. Both spouses must have, or learn, good communication skills or the conflict is likely to be destructive to the marriage.

Sources of Tension

To know what people fight about is not necessarily to know why they fight. As we have pointed out, few people fight because they enjoy conflict. Rather, a number of sources of tension in our lives make conflict inevitable. These sources are at various levels of social life. We are

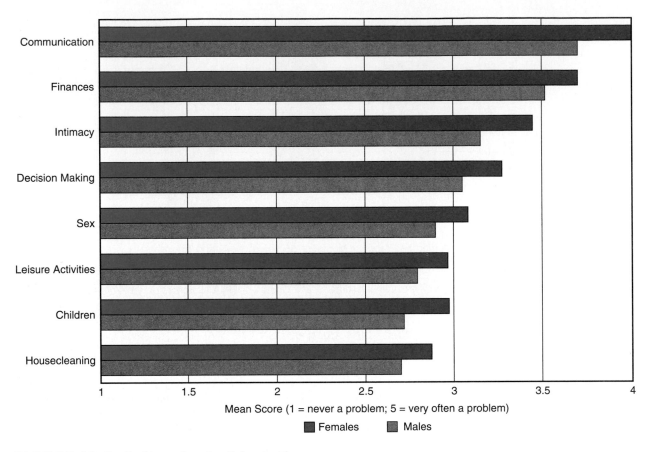

FIGURE 10.3 Problems Couples Bring to Therapy
Source: Adapted from Miller, Yorgason, Sandberg, and White (2003).

affected not only by our relationships but also by the organizations and the social institutions in which we necessarily function. Accordingly, we will look at social, interpersonal, and personal sources of tension.

Social Sources. Issues about money are a common battleground in marriages. Those issues become more widespread and more acute in times of economic depression. In the years following the Great Depression of 1929, economic problems led to a serious decline in marital quality among working-class and middle-class couples (Liker and Elder 1983). Men who were no longer able to find work to support their families became tense, irritable, and even explosive. In general, tension and conflict increased in families as couples tried to adjust to diminished income. The lack of income led to another source of conflict for those couples forced to move into parental homes—often in cramped quarters. They found themselves facing problems with relatives and having conflict over those problems (Alford-Cooper 1998). We

should note that the negative effects of the Depression were not nearly so pronounced among those who had strong marriages before the economic hard times. A strong marriage is a buffer against the stress of social adversity, although even in those marriages the difficult times increased the tension.

Thus, changes in the national economy can have a severe impact on marriage and family life. Financial stress increases the amount of both personal and interpersonal problems. Unemployment, for instance, can lead to mental illness, problems of physical health, depression, and violent behavior in the family, including child abuse (Lauer and Lauer 2008). Unemployment, unfortunately, is something over which many people have little control. National recessions, depressed local economies, and such things as plant closings confront many people with short- or long-term unemployment. This is likely to mean tension and increased conflict in the marriage. However, work problems include more than unemployment. Even if an individual is secure in the job, such things as overload and negative interactions at work can spill over into the marriage as husbands or wives come home angry, frustrated, and short-tempered (Story and Repetti 2006). It is not uncommon for someone so stressed by work to be angry or withdrawn in the home as a result.

The economy brings about adverse consequences in ways other than unemployment. A high rate of inflation can add to a couples' financial distress. Buying a first home, which is depicted in the media as a joyous event, can actually be extremely stressful (Meyer 1987). Moving to a new home is often disruptive and may create more financial stress than the couple anticipated. In some areas of the country, the price of new housing is so high that young couples despair of ever owning their own home, and some obtain a home only by going into an indebtedness that strains their relationship as well as their pocketbook.

Another social factor that creates tension in marriage is the illusions that prevail in our society. One such illusion is the notion that a marriage can be conflict-free. Whoever first coined that unfortunate phrase "happily ever after" has done a disservice to countless couples who are startled to find out that it can't be done. Starry-eyed young people who have such unrealistic expectations about marriage may find it difficult to cope with even minor disagreements with their spouses.

A second illusion is the belief that whatever problems there are, they will improve with time (Lasswell 1985). "Time heals all wounds" is another poor choice for a principle of life. In point of fact, a significant number of problems do not get better merely because of the passage of time. In a marriage, unless the spouses attend to them, minor problems can escalate into major problems rather than dissipating with time. Half of all serious marital problems arise in the first two years of marriage, but couples who come to marriage counselors have, on the average, been married for seven years.

Other illusions are the various unrealistic expectations we hold about marriage or the meaning of being a husband and a wife. The point here is that these illusions are rooted in our social context. The culture itself gives birth to these expectations through folklore, movies, books, and magazines. In that sense, our culture has not adequately prepared us for the realities of marriage.

Finally, various kinds of change in the society can combine to create tensions in the family. For example, many couples assume that their children will get a college education. Indeed, the job market seems to demand such an education. Yet the cost has soared in recent years. Yearly tuition and living expenses for a student at some

Financial strains can create both personal and marital distress.

private universities equals the total annual family income of a large number of Americans.

Or consider the following combination of changes. Young people are delaying marriage, and after they marry, they often wind up divorced. In addition, the cost of housing has increased dramatically and has made it difficult for young people to obtain a home of their own. The combination of these factors means that a good many adult children are living with their parents. For many parents, this is fundamentally an enjoyable experience. But it can also be frustrating (the children continue to require a great deal of time and energy) and can increase the amount of conflict the parents have with each other (Turcotte 2006).

Thus, a number of sources of tension in the society come to bear on marriages. The tensions increase the frequency of marital conflict. Sometimes we fight because we are strained by factors that are beyond our control.

Interpersonal and Personal Sources. Of course conflict also arises from tensions within the relationship and within the individual spouses. Psychiatrist Martin Goldberg (1987) points out six areas of marital interaction that underlie much of the conflict in a marriage. These include the areas of power and control, nurturance, intimacy and privacy, trust, fidelity, and differences in style. Goldberg says that while money, sex, child rearing, in-laws, decisions about whether to have children, and substance abuse are the most common topics of disagreement, frequently we can understand arguments over such matters better by looking at the possible underlying causes.

First, then, there is the area of *power and control,* which is a matter of "who tells whom what to do and when." This is the area of interaction in which power struggles occur, though they are often disguised. For instance, arguments about discipline of children may reflect the struggle of two competing philosophies of child rearing for control of the situation. It becomes more than a matter of disagreement over the appropriate way to discipline; it becomes a matter of who will have the final say in how the children are reared.

Second, there is the area of *nurturance,* which is a matter of "who takes care of whom and how." Ideally, of course, each spouse takes care of the other's needs. When that happens, there is not likely to be conflict arising from this area. But if one of the partners feels neglected, conflict is likely. Goldberg (1987) gives the example of a couple, Ron and Jill, who had a harmonious marriage for the first five years. Ron was an insurance salesman. His job was sufficiently stressful and uncertain so that he needed, and received, Jill's continuing reassurance and emotional support. Then they had a baby. Their relationship began steadily to deteriorate. Jill increasingly focused her nurturing on the baby, and Ron became increasingly hostile and discontented. He began staying out late and drinking to excess. When Jill and Ron fought about his drinking and absence from the home, what was the real issue? Clearly, it was his need for nurturance, which was no longer being fulfilled.

Third, there is the area of *intimacy and privacy,* which involves the amount of interaction versus the amount of aloneness that each partner desires. People who complain that their spouses won't give them "their space," that their spouses tend to "smother" them, or that their spouses are detached and distant all have problems in this area of intimate interaction. If both partners have roughly the same needs for intimacy and privacy, their relationship will be harmonious in this area. If their needs are widely different, they are likely to have serious

conflict. A divorced woman told us that she finally left her husband of seven years because she had to have her space:

> Phil is a loving, caring man. But I grew up in a home where we just didn't do a lot of touching and feeling. I was the only child, and I spent a lot of time by myself. I still prefer to spend hours alone. Phil couldn't handle that. And I couldn't handle his wanting to be around me all the time. Even when we were fighting about other things, like going somewhere or whether to have friends over, the real problem was the difference in how much we wanted to be together and with other people.

Trust is the fourth area of interaction that can give rise to problems. Trust is basic to a marriage. Couples can argue about many things and still have a satisfying marriage if there is a basic foundation of trust. When trust declines or is lacking, the relationship is likely to deteriorate and may sink into a series of severe arguments. If you don't trust your spouse, if you don't have a firm sense that your spouse is honest, supportive, and loyal, you will probably find yourself continually challenging your spouse on a variety of issues. When a spouse isn't trusted, all sorts of behavior become suspect—being late, going somewhere alone, being with a friend of the opposite sex, mild criticism of your behavior, and so on. The real issue is not the behavior of the spouse but the lack of trust. Thus, a husband says to his wife, "That color of red doesn't look very good on you." In a situation of little trust, she may translate his statement into something like, "He is criticizing me. He finds other women more attractive than he finds me. He doesn't really like me any more."

The fifth area of interaction involves *fidelity,* which means more than sexual faithfulness: "It can be more precisely defined as general adherence to one's marital vows" (Goldberg 1987:48–49). In other words, it is faithfulness to the expectations that the spouses had for each other when they were married. That means that you can commit infidelity without ever having a sexual relationship with someone else. Goldberg provides the example of Rita and Jeff, who have been married for three turbulent years. When they were married, they wrote their wedding vows and pledged to put each other first above all other people. Each claims that the other has broken the vows. Jeff insists that Rita is spending an inordinate amount of time with her parents, who live a short distance from them. He says that she has given them priority over him. Rita, on the other hand, says that Jeff gives priorities to three of his old friends, with whom he spends a good deal of time at local bars. Neither has been sexually unfaithful to the other, but their marriage is in serious trouble in the area of fidelity.

Finally, there are *differences in style* that underlie many conflicts. Differences in style include diverse preferences for recreation and for order versus clutter. Differences in style also involve diverse ways of thinking and dealing with problems. Some people are more emotional than others. Some are more rational. Some people confront anxiety-provoking situations head on; some shrink from them and try to deny their existence. There are numerous ways in which people differ from each other that can result in conflicts (recall our earlier discussion about the importance of homogamy for a satisfying marriage). The important point for couples is to recognize when these differences in style are the actual issue rather than something else about which they are fighting.

For example, Vern and Sally, two young professionals, fought continually about leisure time. He preferred to stay home and read the paper, plan his investments, and watch television. She preferred to have dinner out and then go dancing or attend a movie. Each thought the other was being obstinate and dull. Neither thought of the problem in terms of differences in style, neither of which was inherently bad or wrong. Neither thought in terms of some compromise that would accord the other a measure of leisure satisfaction until they worked through their problem with a marriage counselor.

These six areas of interaction can be sources of tension in a marriage. When the tension erupts into conflict, the fighting will be most productive if the couple recognizes the underlying issue.

STYLES OF CONFLICT

How do you handle conflict? That is, do you see yourself as basically a "no-holds-barred" type of person, a conflict avoider, a reasonable individual who will fight only if necessary, or something else? You probably have a dominant style, and you will use that style consistently in various situations of interpersonal conflict (Sternberg and Dobson 1987). Whether the conflict is with a lover, a spouse, a relative, a boss, a coworker, or a neighbor, we tend to be consistent in our style of fighting.

Social scientists who specialize in interpersonal conflict have identified five different styles (Wilmot and Hocker 2000). Each of us tends primarily to use one or two of them with which we feel most comfortable. The styles differ in terms of how concerned we are with our own interests versus how concerned we are about the interests of the people with whom we are fighting.

One style is **competition,** which involves a high concern for oneself and a low concern for the other. If this is your dominant style, you view conflict as a kind of war. The object is to win the fight, not to be concerned about the other person. A competitive spouse is a dominant spouse, one who has to always be ahead in the struggle for power in the marriage. If both spouses are competitive in their conflict style, the fighting may become vicious and protracted. It is easy for Americans to enter a marriage as competitors, of course, because our culture teaches us to be competitive. We are socialized through school and the media to approach life as competitors. Unfortunately, it isn't the best preparation for marriage. In fact, the lowest marital satisfaction occurs among couples in which one or both partners use the competitive style in conflict (Greeff and De Bruyne 2000).

Avoidance is the second style. If you are an avoider, you have little concern either for your own interests or for the interests of the other. You are mainly concerned about maintaining peace, even if the peace is a hollow or destructive one because differences are never resolved. Such peace will be hollow or destructive because the interests of the partners may be thwarted by the lack of conflict (Weger 2005). For example, a woman who resents her husband's lack of affection may say nothing because she doesn't want to engage in an argument. She values peace highly. But she is serving neither her own interests nor those of her husband well. Instead, she is putting her marriage into jeopardy. The hazards of avoidance are underscored in research by Crohan (1992), who studied 133 African American and 149 white couples. She found that those couples who believed that conflict should be avoided were less happy over the two-year period of the research than couples who used other styles. And there is a higher rate of verbal and physical abuse among couples in which one partner is an avoider and the other is a competitor (Sagrestano, Heavey, and Christensen 1999).

Third, **accommodation** is the opposite of competition. It is a neglect of one's own interests in order to pursue the interests of the other. If you are an accommodator, you may engage in the conflict, but you will always give in to your partner. Unlike the avoider, you do not shrink away from all conflict. But neither can you assert your own interests in the face of those of your partner. Ultimately, you give in because you do not want to offend or deny your partner.

Compromise involves some concern about both one's own interests and the interests of the other. "Some"

Some kinds of competition enhance a relationship.

concern means a moderate amount, enough to seek a solution that is satisfactory to both people but not enough to struggle for an optimal solution. If you are a compromiser, you will assert yourself in conflict, but you will moderate your position when necessary in order to reach an outcome that is acceptable to both yourself and your partner.

The importance and usefulness of compromise is illustrated in the research of Samuel Vuchinich (1985), who videotaped dinner conversations in 52 families and analyzed their patterns of arguing. He found four ways in which a verbal attack by one member on another ended: withdrawal, submission, standoff, or compromise.

In *withdrawal* (a form of avoidance), one of the participants simply withdraws from the conflict by either refusing to talk any more or by leaving the room. *Submission* (also a form of avoidance) is giving in. Submission may not be the end of the disagreement, however. It may just be the beginning of a cold war that will erupt at a later time if the winning party doesn't handle the situation well—such as when the "winner" gloats over his or her "victory" and the "loser" submits merely because he or she feels pressured by other family members.

A *standoff* (a combination of avoidance and competition) occurs when no progress is being made and the opponents simply drop the matter without resolving it. *Compromise* occurs when one family member offers a concession to the other. If there is a reciprocal concession, and both agree, the conflict ends.

Each method has implications for family intimacy. Withdrawal may alienate family members from each other. They may feel that they simply cannot get along or communicate effectively with each other. Submission can lead to resentment or to dominance relations if the same member always tends to be the one to submit. Standoffs may lead to family members getting increasingly frustrated and angry with each other. Compromise, on the other hand, tends to build intimacy. The family members see that they are able to work through their disagreements. Unfortunately, less than 10 percent of the conflicts that Vuchinich studied ended in compromise. Very few ended in withdrawal. About a fourth ended with submission, and the rest ended in standoff. Clearly, family members need to develop the ability to compromise.

Finally, **collaboration** is the opposite of avoidance. It is a high degree of concern both for one's own interests and for the interests of the partner. If you are a collaborator, you will pursue your own interests vigorously while still maintaining a high degree of concern for the interests of your partner. You will not allow your partner to accommodate himself or herself to you. You will not want him or her even to compromise. You want to continue the struggle until you have an optimal solution, one that is in the best interests of each of you. As may be evident, collaboration is time and energy consuming.

In some cases, it may not even be possible to collaborate (when one of the spouses strongly prefers to keep things as they are, so that any new arrangement will be a compromise for that spouse). Still, when it is possible, collaboration is the best way to work out conflict in marriage. Couples who use a collaborative style report the highest degree of both marital satisfaction and satisfaction with the way they settle their disagreements (Greeff and De Bruyne 2000).

We will illustrate the styles with an example. A husband and wife both work. They have two children. For years, the wife has done the cooking and assumed the major burden of responsibility for the home. The husband believes that this is appropriate. The wife resents it. What might she do about it? If she is an avoider, she will say nothing. She will continue to agonize inwardly and battle with her growing resentment. If she were a competitor, she would have confronted her husband early in their marriage and insisted that he do his share of work. She might even have tried to get him to do more than would have satisfied her. If she is an accommodator, she might have stood up to him initially but backed down when he insisted that the home was her responsibility. If she is a compromiser, she would have battled with him until they had worked out a division of labor that was acceptable to each. If she is a collaborator, she would have persisted until they not only had an acceptable division of labor but each also was convinced that the solution enhanced their individual and their interpersonal well-being.

Of course, the outcome would depend on the husband's style as well as the wife's. Some combinations, such as two competitors or two avoiders, can be disastrous for a marriage. Some combinations, such as a competitor and an accommodator, may be efficient but not necessarily conducive to maximizing the well-being of both partners. Other combinations, such as two collaborators or a collaborator and a compromiser or two compromisers, are more conducive to a stable and satisfying relationship.

We should note two things here. First, you can change your style. It is important to know what your dominant style is, how you tend to approach interpersonal conflict. But if that style does not help your relationships, you can change it. Second, each of the styles is appropriate at some time or other. There are times when a spouse who is typically, say, a compromiser should be an accommodator (if the issue is more important to the partner). There are times when it is best to avoid certain conflicts (when one or both spouses are too tired or agitated to be reasonable). No single style is appropriate for every situation, but some are better than others as a dominant style.

GOOD FIGHTING

Whatever your dominant style for handling conflict, you can still learn the principles of good fighting. In our study of long-term marriages, we discovered eight principles that couples in happy marriages use to engage in constructive conflict. Each principle is not necessarily appropriate for every conflict, but the principles comprise a set of tools that can be used to ensure that marital conflict is "good fighting" rather than destructive.

Maintain Your Perspective

There are some things not worth fighting about. "We don't treat everything as a disaster," as one husband put it. People who fight over trivial matters are probably engaging in a power struggle. Couples who have a strong relationship save their energies for the issues that are really important. This means that sometimes one spouse simply accommodates the other or that both spouses recognize that an issue is trivial and decide to avoid it.

Develop Tension Outlets

We have noted that there are tensions in life that can lead to marital conflict. Whether you are a student, a businessperson, or a homemaker, you probably have a sufficient amount of tension in your life so that you need some kind of outlet for it. Humor, exercise, meditation, and sports are some of the tension outlets that people use. You need to find something that works for you and use it to get rid of some of the tension that otherwise can erupt into conflict in your intimate relationships.

Avoid Festering Resentment

If accommodating your partner means you have maintained your perspective on an issue that is trivial to you, the accommodation is useful. If it means that you are denying your own interests and building resentment, the accommodation is destructive. It is vital to openly confront those things that are important to you and to resolve them. People in long-term, happy marriages do not allow their conflict to continue indefinitely on a hot- or cold-war basis.

Avoiding the buildup of resentment means that the partners must practice forgiveness. To be hurt by an intimate is very stressful. There is a tendency to be resentful and to punish the offender in some way. But because the hurtful behavior cannot be undone, the only healthy resolution (assuming the offender regrets the behavior) is forgiveness. Such forgiveness is actually a healthier response for the person who has been hurt (Worthington and Scherer 2004). It reduces anger, anxiety, and depression, and it increases the individual's satisfaction with the relationship and with life (Thompson et al. 2005).

Avoiding the buildup of resentment also requires each partner to be open and honest about his or her feelings. Spouses should not have to speculate or guess about the feelings of each other. That can lead to misinterpretation and more serious conflict. For example, a man may have a grim look on his face. He has had some serious problems at work and is concerned about job security. But he says nothing. His wife tries to interpret his grimness and decides that he is angry at her for some reason. That makes her angry. He senses this and becomes even moodier, wondering why he can't have some warmth and security at home when his work is so problematic. They speak curtly and coldly with each other. Each resents what the other is doing, but neither has any understanding of what has happened.

Be Sensitive to Timing

Many conflicts that could otherwise have been handled constructively work out badly for a couple simply because they occurred at the wrong time:

> Openly confronting conflict does not necessarily mean immediate attention to an issue. Some people are receptive to problem-solving in the morning and some in the evening. Few if any people can handle conflict well when they are exhausted. In addition, there are times when it is simply inappropriate to raise an issue. The wife who criticizes her husband's appearance just as they are walking into a party, or the husband who angrily tells his wife in front of friends that she neglects his needs both illustrate insensitivity to timing (Lauer and Lauer 1986:125).

Personal

Learning How to Fight

Joshua was married three years ago while he was still in graduate school. He and his wife, Kay, each began their marriage with a dominant style of conflict. Both found that they had to change their styles if their marriage was to survive and be mutually satisfying. Joshua talks about the way in which they discussed their styles and agreed to change:

> Kay and I had a rough way to go for a while. She came from a large family where she learned to handle conflict primarily by avoiding it. I, on the other hand, preferred the "bull-in-the-china-shop" approach. I tended to try to control other people by rational argument, by persuasive charm, or by open hostility. I did whatever it took to win.
>
> It didn't take long for us to realize that our approaches to our differences were very destructive. But it wasn't easy to give them up.

We had used them for too many years. We talked about our ways of fighting. I told her that she made me furious by not confronting our differences. I resented it when she would clam up or shut down if she felt threatened. She said that I intimidated and frustrated her by my aggressiveness. She said that sometimes she even felt rage because I was willing to "hit below the belt" if necessary to control things.

We got some books and read what the experts had to say.

Then we talked about whether we could change and learn how to solve our differences by listening, caring, and negotiation. That's what the books told us to do, but neither of us had tried those methods before. We started working on our differing approaches about a year ago. For me, it has mainly been a matter of learning to shut up and listen, *really* listen

with compassion and acceptance. I have to learn not to come at our differences like a prizefighter. For her, it has been a matter of becoming more assertive, open, and confident about verbalizing her feelings and her thoughts.

It hasn't been easy. We still break the rules at times. But we're getting better at it. We are learning to fight effectively. Actually, we don't even fight as much any more. Some of our fights were about the ways we were fighting and not about other things. Now that we're better at handling conflict, we feel a much more intense intimacy. That's something new for me. I always felt good about winning fights before. It's been a kind of a thrill to feel more intimate when we've handled an argument well together. I still feel like a winner, even if I don't get what I wanted.

Another time at which it is usually best to avoid conflict is when one of the spouses is extremely angry. Conflict can only be constructive to the relationship when both people can function rationally as well as emotionally.

Communicate without Ceasing

While communication is not a cure-all, it is important not to handle conflict with the silent treatment or by simply hoping that everything will turn out well with the passage of time. Couples who avoid confronting a problem, who rely on the passage of time to dissipate the issue, tend to have a lower quality of intimacy and marriages that are less satisfying (Alford-Cooper 1998:94). In resolving issues, of course, it is the quality of communication and not simply the fact of communication that is important. Recall from the last chapter that listening is a crucial part of effective communication. In conflict, we are particularly prone to want to make our own point rather than to listen carefully to what the other is saying.

In addition, the communication must possess a certain calmness. A study of 130 newlyweds found that those couples in the happiest unions dealt with their problems by discussing them with "gentleness, soothing, and de-escalation of negativity" (Gottman et al. 1998:17). De-escalation of negativity means that if one partner exhibits negative emotions, such as anger, the other tries to de-escalate by not becoming angry in turn. Rather than fueling the process of anger, the partner responds with relative calmness.

De-escalating a process of increasing negative emotion is crucial. The most satisfied couples—however long they have been married—use more affection (see the next point) and less negative emotion to resolve their differences (Carstensen, Gottman, and Levenson 1995). It's easy to see why. Anger, for example, can result in verbal aggression, in saying things that one will later regret and that reflect the anger of the moment rather than fundamental feelings. Nearly every one of the 300 happily married couples in our long-term marriage project advised against arguing when one or both of the spouses is very angry. As one wife of 33 years said, "Find something to do until you are both calm and then talk things out."

Be Flexible, Willing to Compromise

People who are happily married for many years believe in the importance of both accommodation and compromise in conflict. Give in when the issue does not matter that much to you and prepare to compromise when the issue is important to you. Collaboration is desirable but not always practical. Compromise is not a surrender and not an acceptance of an inferior solution. Rather, compromise may frequently be the only realistic way to handle differences between two people, each of whom understands both his or her own needs and interests and those of the spouse.

Use Conflict to Attack Problems, Not Your Spouse

This is one of the most important principles. It stresses the fact that a couple needs to approach conflict as a problem-solving rather than a spouse-bashing exercise (Gottman 1994). Distressed couples show more anger and blaming and less ability to focus on the problem than do satisfied couples (Sillars et al. 2000). But if the conflict is severe, even satisfied couples can fall into the trap of attacking each other rather than the problem, blaming each other for the distress they are experiencing. Your energies will better serve your relationship if they are directed toward the problem. Define the conflict as a disagreement, as a problem that must be solved together, rather than as a battle of personalities (Markman, Stanley, and Blumberg 1994). As a husband put it, "We always have good outcomes from our arguments if we remember one simple rule—namely, that we each must approach our disagreement by saying to the other, 'We have a problem,' rather than 'You are a problem.'"

Keep Loving while You Are Fighting

Marital therapists point out that at times spouses are going to fight unfairly. Exaggerated positions, extreme statements, and some "low blows" are likely to occur at times in any relationship. Nevertheless, the couples in our study insisted that the goal is to keep loving while you are fighting. Loving and fighting may sound like incompatible activities. But two things should be kept in mind. First, in line with the last principle, good fighting involves an attack on a problem rather than on the spouse. And second, the love we are talking about here is agapic love, acting out of concern for the well-being of the other independently of our feelings at the moment. Thus, when you refuse to hurt your partner during conflict (by, e.g., not throwing out cutting remarks that you know will injure him or her), you are continuing to love. To keep the conflict within the bounds of reason, to avoid attacking the spouse, and to, as one wife put it, keep in mind the things you like about your spouse even while you are fighting are some of the ways that you can continue to love during conflict.

Tension outlets, such as shared humor, are an important part of "good fighting."

SUMMARY

Power is the ability to get someone to think or feel or act in a way that he or she would not have done spontaneously. The use of power is not inherently negative or wrong. It can be used to help as well as to control others. Marital power has typically been measured on the basis of which spouse makes the final decisions. Power is important to both our personal and our marital well-being.

Resource theory asserts that we get power from the resources we bring to a relationship, including income, emotional support, sexual availability, and parenting skills. The principle of least interest says that the partner with the least interest in maintaining the relationship has the most power. Six types of power can be used in marriage: coercive, reward, legitimate, expert, referent, and informational.

Marriage may be analyzed as a power struggle. Spouses attempt to exert or avoid power when communicating with each other. In a symmetrical discussion, the two spouses send similar messages that are designed to control how the relationship is defined. In complementary discussion, the two spouses indicate agreement that one is dominant and the other is submissive.

Like power, conflict can have both positive and negative consequences for a marriage. Among the positive results are that issues are brought into the open and clarified, people may grow through conflict, small conflicts

diffuse more serious conflict, and conflict can create and maintain an equitable balance of power. Severe marital conflict has negative consequences both for the couple and for children.

People tend to have conflict over money, children, and other issues, such as sex. Couples who go to therapists report communication problems as the most frequently occurring problem, followed by finances, emotional intimacy, decision making, sex, leisure activities, child-rearing matters, and housecleaning.

A number of sources of tension make marital conflict inevitable. Social sources include the vagaries of the economy, cultural illusions about marriage, and various kinds of social change. Interpersonal and personal sources include such things as issues of power and control, nurturance, intimacy and privacy, trust, fidelity, and differences in style.

Common styles of conflict include competition, avoidance, accommodation, compromise, and collaboration. "Good fighting" occurs when a couple follows certain principles, such as maintaining perspective, developing tension outlets, avoiding festering resentment, being sensitive to timing, continuing to communicate, being willing to compromise, using conflict to attack problems rather than one another, and continuing to love each other even while fighting.

Principles for Enhancing Intimacy

1. Individuals need power; that is, each of us needs some degree of control over our lives. This need for power extends into our marriages. There are situations—some critical, others less so—when we need to influence or wield power over our spouse. Power, of course, can be abused. We unfortunately may attempt to dominate or totally control our partner. In a satisfying marriage, however, each spouse has power and shares it on a generally equal basis.

2. Power struggles and conflict in a marriage are not necessarily destructive. In fact, they can be an indication of a healthy and vital relationship and should be treated as such. When a conflict arises, it should be viewed as a shared problem that needs a solution and not as a sign that the relationship is doomed.

3. In order to deal positively with a conflict in marriage, it is essential to identify the true source of the difficulty. If, for example, the problem concerns financial arrangements, then you need to focus on money matters, not on extraneous factors, such as your in-laws' overindulgence of your spouse or the tax policies of the federal government.

Instead, examine your spending patterns: Are you overextending yourselves financially? Are you trying to buy too large a house or too expensive a car too quickly? Are you buying too much on credit? Concentrating on the real nature of your conflict takes insight, determination, and courage. But it is essential to a meaningful resolution of your problems.

4. Effective handling of conflict takes patience and persistence. However, you can build your skills by consulting the experts—books and articles written by professionals in marriage and the family, marriage enrichment seminars, as well as mature and successful couples. Learn the secrets of "good fighting" from them and then consistently apply them in your marriage.

5. People deal with conflict in different ways. In order to deal constructively with problems and power struggles, it is important for you to understand your own as well as your partner's style of handling conflict. You may find that it is essential for you to accommodate, to some extent, your style to that of your partner if solutions are to be found.

KEY TERMS

ON THE WEB   Power and Conflict in Marriage

Power is an inevitable aspect of every marriage. Each of the six types of power—coercive, reward, legitimate, expert, referent, and informational—is likely to appear at some point in a couple's marital life. Similarly, conflict is also inevitable. Both power and conflict can be either destructive or productive, depending upon the kind and the situation. A Web site with a good deal of information on both power and conflict is:

www.mhhe.com/lauer7e

About.com:Marriage
http://marriage.about.com

This site draws on various resources to provide ideas and excerpts on aspects of married life, including issues relating to power and conflict.

Using the above site, enlarge your understanding with the following projects:

1. Go to the About.com:Marriage site and search the materials on power. The materials won't use the six terms identified in the text, but you can usually infer the kind of power being discussed. Tabulate the frequency of use of each of the six types of power. Which is most frequently dealt with? Are any neglected? Are there examples of power as a positive as well as a negative factor? Using materials in the text, draw some conclusions about the adequacy of the site for teaching people what they need to know about power in marriage.

2. Go to the About.com:Marriage site and search the materials on conflict. Use the materials to draw up a list of both the positive and the negative consequences of conflict. Present your findings to the class, and lead a discussion in which the students talk about the consequences of conflict from the realm of their own experience.

~ WORK AND HOME ~

After reading and studying chapter 11, you should be able to

1 Outline the historical trends in female employment and the impact of these trends on male and female roles.

2 Identify the differences between the dual-earner and the dual-career family.

3 Discuss the reasons that some women prefer to work outside the home and others prefer to stay at home.

4 Show the extent to which female employment outside the home has resulted in more egalitarian marriages.

5 Characterize the various types of dual-income families.

6 Understand the problems as well as the satisfactions of dual-income families.

7 Describe the challenges that dual-income couples face and the extent to which they can achieve marital satisfaction.

8 Explain how dual-income couples negotiate conflicting role demands.

9 Discuss the effect that working outside the home has on women's physical and emotional health.

10 Relate the various coping strategies that are available to employed women.

If you have grown up in a dual-income family, reflect on the materials in this section and write up an account of your experiences. How do your experiences compare with the materials presented? Based on your experience, what are the major problems and the greatest rewards and satisfactions in a dual-income family, particularly for the children? What changes in our society would you suggest in order to help dual-income families cope with their challenges?

If you have not grown up in a dual-income family, look through six or so issues of a women's magazine, such as *Working Woman*. Find a number of articles that address the issue of the dual-income family. What are the problems identified in the articles? What are the rewards and satisfactions? How do they compare with the materials in this chapter? Interview a woman who is in a dual-income family. Ask her what she believes to be the most serious problems and the greatest benefits from such an arrangement. Then tell her about the kinds of problems and satisfactions discussed in this chapter. Ask her to comment on them in terms of her own experiences. What kinds of things did she identify as problems and satisfactions? How does her experience compare with the materials in the chapter? If a number of students do this project, each one should choose a different magazine and a different person to interview. Then compare all the results. What are your overall conclusions?

If you are female and get married in the near future, will it be acceptable for you to work outside the home? If this question sounds foolish, consider the following. For about a century, from the middle of the nineteenth to the middle of the twentieth centuries, white middle-class women who married were expected to stay at home and care for their houses, their husbands, and their children. Some Americans still disapprove of married women working, especially if the women have children in the home (Brescoll and Uhlmann 2005). Religious conservatism is particularly associated with such disapproval, and white women who are members of conservative denominations are more likely than others to drop out of the labor market after getting married or after giving birth (Glass and Nath 2006). Black women who are members of conservative denominations, in contrast, are likely to remain in or enter the workforce.

Working-class women and women from racial/ethnic minorities have typically sought outside employment. In fact, Landry (2002) argues that black middle-class wives pioneered the now-common dual-income family by rejecting the notion that married women should not work and committing themselves to career, family, and community. Since the middle of the twentieth century, middle-class white women have followed the pattern of black women in growing numbers. In this chapter, we will discuss why women have entered the **labor force** in large numbers and the impact that employed wives and mothers have on individual and family well-being.

HIS WORK AND HER WORK

Throughout most of human history, the great majority of people lived on farms or in peasant villages. As historian Carl Degler (1980:5) has pointed out, for nearly everyone

> the family was a cooperative economic unit, with children and mother working along with husband, even though usually there was a division of labor by gender. . . . Even those relatively few families which lived and worked in towns acted as cooperative enterprises in their shops, inns, and other businesses. Home and work were close together, and wife and husband participated in both.

This situation changed rapidly and dramatically with the rise of industrialization. Industrialization meant that some of the things women did in the home, such as making clothes, would increasingly be done in the factory or shop. Women did continue, of course, to cook and clean and nurture their families. But in the emerging industrial economy, paid labor became a primary source of income and the essence of the meaning of *work*. What women did in the home was no longer defined as *work*.

The role of "housewife," or homemaker, developed in this context. It is a role that can be described in terms of four characteristics (Oakley 1974). First, it is allocated almost exclusively to women. Second, it is associated with economic dependence, because the homemaker must lean on her husband for support. Third, it is defined generally as *nonwork,* or at least as not *real* work. This is illustrated by the response to "Do you work?" often given by some homemakers: "No, I'm just a homemaker." Of course, even those who respond in this way recognize that homemaking is every bit as demanding and exhausting as any work outside the home. Indeed, men who spend time taking care of a house and children understand that homemaking is *real* work. Nevertheless, one characteristic of the role of homemaker is the definition of it as non-work. The fourth characteristic of the role is that it is given priority by women over other roles. Housework and child care are considered the primary responsibilities of the homemaker, responsibilities that take priority over anything else that a woman might wish to do (such as outside employment or a career). Around 1900, if a married woman was employed, people thought that something was wrong. "Her husband was absent, crippled, or incompetent" (Degler 1980:386).

Industrialization, then, created the tendency among white, middle-class families for "his" work to be paid labor outside the home and "her" work to be that of the homemaker. While there are some who still prefer this pattern, the majority of women now opt for employment or career roles as well as the roles of wife and mother.

CHANGING PATTERNS OF WORKING

Earlier in our history, some people argued that "his" work and "her" work reflected human nature. That is, they believed that men are programmed for work outside the home and women are programmed for being homemakers. Yet the forces that kept most women in the home in the past were social and cultural, not biological. In recent decades, the situation has changed dramatically.

Women in the Labor Force

At the turn of the century, only about one of five adult women was in the labor force. The labor force is defined by the government as those who are employed (whether part-time or full-time) and those who are unemployed but looking for work. By 1940, the rate was still less than

TABLE 11.1 The Female Labor Force, 1940–2006 (persons 14 years old and over through 1965; 16 years old and older thereafter)

Year	Number (1,000)	Percent of Female Population
1940	12,887	25.4
1950	18,412	33.9
1960	23,272	37.8
1970	31,560	43.4
1980	45,487	51.5
1990	56,829	57.5
2000	66,303	59.9
2006	70,173	59.4

Source: U.S. Census Bureau 1975:128 and Bureau of Labor Statistics Web site.

a third of the female population. The rate increased during World War II and then fell again after the war. In the 1960s and 1970s, however, the proportion of women going into the labor force increased rapidly (table 11.1). Nearly 6 out of 10 women aged 16 and above are now in the labor force. As noted earlier, working- and lower-class women have been more likely than middle-class women to be in the labor force. For example, the famous "Middletown" study found that almost half of working-class wives in Muncie, Indiana, were employed full-time during the early 1920s (Caplow et al. 1982).

Interestingly, while the participation of women went up from 1940 through the early 2000s, that of men went down after 1950 (figure 11.1). The trend was toward a labor force equally divided between men and women and toward families in which very few men function as the sole breadwinner. The trend is dramatized by the fact that in 1970 nearly 90 percent of couples had a more conventional arrangement (Raley, Mattingly, and Bianchi 2006). That is, the husband was the sole provider in 56 percent of married-couple homes and contributed 60 percent or more of the income in another 31 percent of married-couple homes. By 2001, the husband was the sole provider in only 25 percent and brought in the larger proportion of the income in 39 percent of the homes. In 2001, wives accounted for an equal amount of income in a fourth of homes and were the primary or sole providers in 12 percent of homes.

Some people interpret this trend as evidence of the "decline" of the family and a deviation from the historic pattern. But as Stephanie Coontz (1997) has pointed out, it was not until the 1920s that the majority of U.S. children lived in a home where the husband was the sole breadwinner, the wife was a homemaker, and the children could attend school rather than work for wages. In other words, the male as sole breadwinner is a deviation, not the norm, in the history of U.S. family life.

Married Women and Employment

The figures in table 11.1 are for all women, whether single, married, separated, divorced, or widowed. Moreover, some of the women are in jobs and some are pursuing

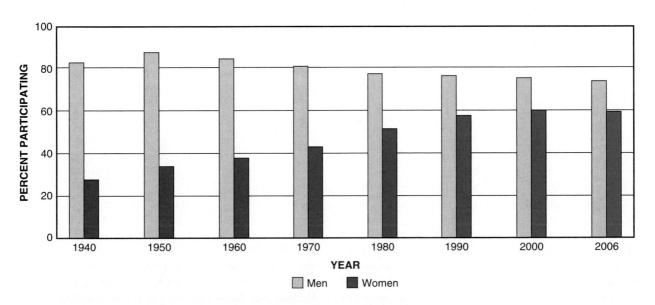

FIGURE 11.1 Civilian Labor Force Participation Rates, by Sex
Sources: U.S. Census Bureau 1975:131–32 and Bureau of Labor Statistics Web site.

TABLE 11.2 Marital Status and Labor Force Participation Rates of Women with Children, 1960–2005 (for women 14 years and older in 1960; thereafter, 16 years and older)

Year	Total			Children 6 to 17			Children under 6		
	Single	Married	Other	Single	Married	Other	Single	Married	Other
1960	(NA)	27.6	56.0	(NA)	39.0	65.9	(NA)	18.6	40.5
1970	(NA)	39.7	60.7	(NA)	49.2	66.9	(NA)	30.3	52.2
1980	52.0	54.1	69.4	67.6	61.7	74.6	44.1	45.1	60.3
1990	55.2	66.3	74.2	69.7	73.6	79.7	48.7	58.9	63.6
2005	72.9	68.1	79.8	79.8	75.0	82.2	68.4	59.8	73.6

NA Not available
Source: U.S. Bureau of the Census 2001:373 and 2008:580.

careers. These are important distinctions that need to be addressed.

Marital and Family Status of Employed Women. Table 11.2 shows the increasing participation in the labor force of women with children, including those with preschool children. The most dramatic increase in participation rates occurred among married women with children under the age of 6—the proportion more than tripled from 1960 to 2005. However, the rates have leveled off or declined in recent years (Cohany and Sok 2007). The rate for mothers with children under a year old reached a peak of 59.2 percent in 1997, then fell to 53.3 percent in 2000 and has shown no clear trend since then. The decline reflects the fact that there has been an associated decline in the proportion of mothers who want to stay in full-time work (Pew Research Center 2007b). Among working mothers, the proportion who prefer full-time work declined from 32 percent in 1997 to 21 percent in 2007, and the proportion of non-working mothers who preferred to work full-time dropped from 24 percent to 16 percent. Sixty percent of working mothers said that part-time work would be their ideal.

Figure 11.2 shows the most recent rates of employment by racial/ethnic groups. Note that there are variations in the extent to which mothers participate in the labor force, but in all groups the highest rates of participation are those with children between the ages of 6 and 17. Some of those who are employed only work part-time, but most are full-time workers.

While the proportion of working mothers who want full-time work has declined, most would still like to remain in the labor force. They have opted for worker as well as homemaker roles. Again, we need to keep in mind that substantial numbers of married women are not in the labor force. While a slight majority of women with infants prefer to work, a considerable number prefer to

stay home and care for their children themselves. The important point is that women have options, and many of them are opting for different roles than those of their mothers and grandmothers.

Jobs and Careers.   Some women who work have jobs; others are in careers. We can distinguish between jobs and careers in a number of ways. Careers normally require extensive training—a college education or even graduate school. Careers tend to be more structured in that there is a pattern of mobility people tend to follow. In the university, for instance, you may begin as an instructor and gradually move up to the position of full professor. Moving up through the ranks is a common pattern in education, business, government, and social service agencies. Careers also may be pursued by individuals such as therapists. In such cases, mobility may involve moving from being an assistant to a therapist, to starting one's own practice, to becoming the head of one's own clinic. Finally, a career involves commitment. You can frequently take or leave a particular job, but if you are in a career, you probably have a commitment to go as far as you can. You want to get to the top of your field or as close to the top as possible.

The distinction between job and career requires us to distinguish among different kinds of families. A **dual-income family** is one in which both spouses have paid work outside the home. There are two types of dual-income families. In a **dual-earner family,** one or both spouses view their outside work as a job rather than a career. In a **dual-career family,** both spouses are engaged in careers, which means that both are committed to employment that has a long-term pattern of mobility. There are a number of different kinds of dual-career families, which we will discuss below. We don't know how many of the dual-income families are dual-earner versus dual-career, but over three-fourths of all married

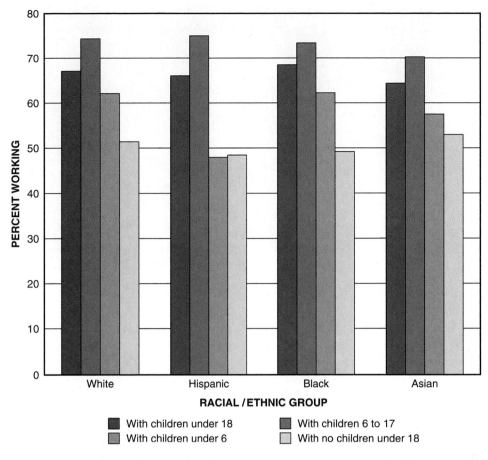

FIGURE 11.2 Employment Status among Mothers 16 Years and Older
Source: U.S. Department of Labor 2007.

people who have paid work outside the home live in a dual-income family (Bond 2002).

Dual-earner and dual-career families share many of the same challenges, such as who will do the "family work"—the housekeeping and child care that formerly were the responsibility of the homemaker. Most of our discussion in this chapter, therefore, will apply to dual-income families generally. For some matters, however, the distinction between dual-earner and dual-career is important. In the dual-career family, for example, there is no assumption that either spouse will subordinate his or her career to the interests of the other. Both partners are committed to combining professional and family roles. In contrast, when one of the partners is pursuing a career while the other holds a job (a dual-earner family), the job-holder will be expected to make concessions to the career of the partner. One such concession is moving

to a new location that is important for career mobility. The couple would not remain where they are simply because the job-holder "loves" the work that he or she is doing.

Types of Dual-Career Families

While all dual-career families by definition involve a twofold commitment, there are variations in the way that the spouses handle their work and family roles. Moreover, there are differing structural arrangements, perhaps the most radical of which is the commuter marriage.

Three Types of Marital Roles. In her study of dual-career families, Gilbert (1993) identified three different types of arrangements: the traditional, the participant, and the role-sharing. In the *traditional* dual-career family, the wife simply adds a new role—that of a career

The majority of women are in the labor force.

woman. She continues to be responsible for the family work. The problems of coordination and time that emerge are problems that she must resolve. This arrangement, of course, violates the principle of equity that underlies the idea of two careers. Nevertheless, it is one pattern that some couples have adopted.

In the *participant* dual-career family, the husband assumes some of the responsibilities of child care. Husband and wife may even share equally the parenting of the children. But the wife still retains the responsibility for housework. As suggested by the studies on time use, this type is fairly common.

Finally, in the *role-sharing* dual-career family, both spouses are actively involved in family work, both child care and household tasks. The role-sharing family implements the principle of equity. The spouses share family power and responsibilities equally as each pursues a meaningful career.

Which of the three patterns is adopted by any particular couple depends on a variety of personal, interpersonal, and social factors. For example, a personal factor may be the attitudes and values of the spouses. If their values are still somewhat traditional, the couple may feel most comfortable with a participant family. An interpersonal factor could be the balance of power in the relationship. If the male has been dominant, he may insist on something less than role-sharing in order to accept his wife's career. She may accede because she has become habituated to his dominance in important decisions. Furthermore, such things as occupational demands and

structures as well as social support systems are examples of social factors. One of the partners may have less flexibility than the other. For instance, the wife may be a busy lawyer and unable to pursue her career fully without role-sharing. Or the parents of the couple may exert pressure one way or another.

In other words, the type of family arrangement that the couple works out reflects more than their preference. A host of factors come to bear on them as they seek to cope with the difficult task of maintaining two careers and a family. The roles they finally work out may or may not be in accord with their preference, but they may perceive the arrangement as the only one that is viable for them. For example, a university professor who is married to an attorney told us,

> My husband spends many more hours at his office than I do at mine. We didn't have our degrees when we were first married. I knew that he would have long hours as an attorney, but I didn't realize that I would wind up doing more than my share of housework. But I have come to terms with that. I know that if he was the professor and I was the attorney, he would do most of the housework. That's just the way it is.

Commuter Marriages.   The **commuter marriage** is a dual-career marriage in which the spouses live in different locations and still maintain their dual commitment to work and to family. They do not prefer to live apart, but they don't want to give up their careers or each other. It is estimated that there are 3.6 million or more couples who have such marriages (Cullen 2007).

While the arrangement is not ideal even from the point of view of those who have it, and while most people would not want a commuter marriage, the couples involved point to a number of advantages (Guldner 2003). In the first place, each spouse is likely to have more discretionary time during the separation. This means that a spouse is free to spend as much time as he or she wants at work during the day without worrying that the partner will resent the long hours. It also means that a spouse has more time for pursuing interests not shared by the partner.

Second, someone in a commuter marriage may experience enhanced self-esteem and self-confidence because of living independently on most days and, at the same time, have the security of knowing that loving support is available when life is difficult. And, third, the anticipation of getting together can intensify appreciation for one's partner and make the reunion something of a honeymoon experience.

But there are also disadvantages. How do you fulfill your intimacy needs when you are with your spouse less than half the time? Some couples discover that the reunions require a period of time for re-establishing intimacy rather than being like a honeymoon experience. And there are a number of negative emotions that are likely to arise when the reunion is over and it is time to separate again. Guldner (2003) has identified three kinds of reactions to the separation: protest, depression, and detachment. In the protest stage, the spouses may find themselves angry. The depression stage follows and may require some kind of deliberate action or pattern of thinking in order to break through into the final stage of detachment. During protest and depression, the partners may also experience anxiety and guilt. But in the detachment phase, the partners deliberately distance themselves emotionally from each other in order to cope with the separation.

Given the emotional swings and intimacy challenges, commuter marriages work better if there are no children involved. But hundreds of thousands of children are living in homes where the parents are separated for reasons other than marital problems (Cullen 2007). Little research has been done on life in the commuter-marriage family, but one study found that commuter couples, compared to dual-career couples living together, report more work satisfaction but lower family satisfaction and less satisfaction with life as a whole (Bunker et al. 1992).

We don't have evidence about the long-term consequences of such marriages. Can they survive decades of separation? If they do, what kind of relationship will the couple have when one or both retire? How will they adjust to living together all the time?

WHY WOMEN WORK OUTSIDE THE HOME

Married women who work outside the home face the prospect of less leisure time for themselves and less leisure time than their husbands have. They are likely to get additional help from their husbands but not enough to make their total work load equitable. According to the Bureau of Labor Statistics (2007a) time-use survey, employed men work an average of about an hour a day more than employed women. But employed women still assume the bulk of household duties. The wives spend, on the average, around 35 minutes more on housework each day. They spend twice as much time as do their husbands on food preparation and cleanup. And they devote more time to caring for children (about 48 minutes more per day for children under 6 and 19 minutes per day when the children are 6 to 17 years old). As a result, working wives have between 35 and 45 minutes per day less time for leisure activities than do working husbands. What, then, is the motivation for a married woman to work outside the home?

One motivation is the consumerism that is an integral part of U.S. culture (Stoneley 2003; Kyvig 2004). As illustrated by the notion of "shop till you drop," many Americans equate a high quality of life with the quantity of things they own. A young husband, for example, shared with us his wife's and his own entanglement with consumerism:

> We'd like to start raising a family. But my wife wants to stop working when we have a baby, and frankly we just can't afford that. Well, I guess we really could afford it if we changed our lifestyle and cut back on some of the things we do and buy. But neither one of us wants to do that. We're having too much fun. So I guess we'll wait a few more years before we have any kids.

Even if consumerism isn't a dominant factor, there's another economic motivation, namely, the desire for financial security. Whether the woman has a job or a career, she is likely to be more committed to the work to the extent that she perceives her income as necessary for her family's financial security. She also may see her work as necessary to her future security, giving her an independent pension should she become a widow (Uchitelle 1998). Of course, there are costs involved in working, particularly when there are children in the home. One of the largest costs is child care, which can decrease the advantage of the dual-income family over the single-income family considerably. Nevertheless, two incomes do give the dual-income family advantages both in income and home ownership.

Women, like men, work for a variety of reasons other than economic. A poll found that even if women felt they had enough money to live comfortably without working, a majority would either work or volunteer—15 percent would continue working full-time, 33 percent would work part-time, and 20 percent would do volunteer work (Boyle 1995). Obviously, women, like men, reap important benefits from employment, including "the opportunity to develop the instrumental part of themselves and to establish a sense of self apart from a man and children, economic independence, increased self-esteem, and better overall health" (Gilbert 1993:85). It is not surprising, then, that while African American women are more likely than whites to work out of economic necessity, both groups of women offer reasons other than economic necessity for employment (Herring and Wilson-Sadberry 1993).

Still another reason to work is the power gained (Bullers 1999). We have noted before that power is an important resource to all of us. We each need to feel that we have some control over the circumstances of our lives. Women may work in order to get their own income and thus increase their sense of power. That increased power may make their marriage a more equitable one. It may give a woman a sense of security in case her marriage fails or her husband dies.

Finally, what about the effects of employment on marital and family relations? We will explore these in more detail, but here we want to note that employed women generally do not believe that their marriages or families suffer because of their work outside the home. Whether they are correct is increasingly important, because both partners work in an ever-growing number of marriages.

HOME VERSUS THE WORKPLACE

A major part of your life takes place in the realms of work and home and in the interplay between these two realms. This interplay can be both positive and negative. On the positive side, satisfaction in either realm helps create the emotional strength and positive attitudes that enable you to deal more effectively with the challenges and demands in the other realm (Stevens, Minnotte, Mannon, and Kiger 2007). Satisfaction in both realms is

at the core of a happy, fulfilling life. On the negative side, problems in either realm tend to adversely affect life in the other realm. For example, feeling overworked or having negative kinds of interaction at work can spill over into negative emotions and interaction in the home (Story and Repetti 2006). Marital problems, on the other hand, can adversely affect the quality of your work.

A common reason for negative consequences is the conflict between the demands of the workplace and the demands of home. In **family-to-work spillover,** family demands or problems negatively affect work performance. Women are twice as likely as men to report adverse work consequences because of family demands (Keene and Reynolds 2005; Mennino, Rubin, and Brayfield 2005). In part, women experience more adverse consequences because they are more likely than men to adjust their workload (e.g., by turning down assignments or overtime) in order to accommodate family needs.

In **work-to-family spillover,** work demands or problems negatively affect family life. For example, work-related stress may adversely affect the quality of the marital relationship (Matthews, Conger, and Wickrama 1996), and excessive time demands at work may leave an individual with too little time or energy to care for the needs of a spouse and children. Men and women, according to one study, react somewhat differently to negative experiences at work. Women tend to exhibit angrier marital behavior, while men tend to become more withdrawn (Schulz et al. 2004).

Both men and women experience these conflicting demands. As table 11.3 shows, employed husbands and employed wives report about the same amount of conflict overall, though employed husbands with nonemployed wives have somewhat less conflict than those whose wives work outside the home.

A possible consequence of work-home conflict is that more and more women will spend increasing hours at work in order to escape the demands of home—both the physical demands of the various tasks and the emotional demands of maintaining a meaningful family life. At least that is the conclusion of Hochschild (1997) on the basis of her study of 130 female factory and clerical workers. Hochschild argues that growing numbers of women who work outside the home are fleeing "a world of unresolved quarrels and unwashed laundry for the reliable orderliness, harmony, and managed cheer of work." However, using national data, Kiecolt (2003) concluded that quite the opposite resolution of work-home conflict is happening: Increasing numbers of women are looking to home life as a haven rather than to work as more satisfying than home.

TABLE 11.3 Frequency of Work–Family Conflict

Group (in percent)	Not at all	Not too much	Somewhat	A lot
Total sample	24.3	41.3	24.0	10.4
Employed husbands	25.9	40.4	23.6	10.1
Wife employed	26.7	41.8	21.0	10.5
No children	35.1	37.1	20.3	7.4
Youngest 0–5 years	22.9	41.3	22.9	12.8
Youngest 6–17 years	20.0	46.8	20.7	12.3
Wife not employed	25.0	38.7	26.6	9.7
No children	35.0	38.7	20.0	6.3
Youngest 0–5 years	20.4	32.8	37.1	9.7
Youngest 6–17 years	20.3	45.6	20.9	13.3
Employed wives	22.5	40.5	26.5	10.5
Husband employed	22.9	39.1	27.7	10.4
No children	37.1	33.7	18.5	10.7
Youngest 0–5 years	11.8	40.3	36.1	11.8
Youngest 6–17 years	16.3	43.5	31.0	9.2
Husband not employed	18.6	55.8	14.0	11.6
Employed women in one-parent families	17.0	58.0	13.6	11.4
Youngest 0–5 years	18.6	55.8	9.3	16.3
Youngest 6–17 years	15.6	60.0	17.8	6.7

Source: U.S. Bureau of Labor Statistics 1991, "Conflicts between Work and Family Life" in *Monthly Labor Review*, p. 103.

CHALLENGES OF DUAL-INCOME FAMILIES

According to the Bureau of Labor Statistics (2007b), over half of all married-couple families are dual-income families. And among those with children, 62 percent are dual-income (including 67.2 percent of those with children between the ages of 6 and 17, and 55.6 percent of those with children younger than 6). The second income does not resolve all problems, however. Dual-income families must confront a number of what are sometimes vexing challenges.

More or Less Equal?

We have seen repeatedly that equity is a crucial part of a satisfying, intimate relationship. Researchers have found equity to be related to marital quality in preindustrial as well as modernized societies. In essence, whatever their working status outside the home, women want equity in marital and family arrangements (Stohs 1995; Hendrix 1997; Rosenbluth, Steil, and Whitcomb 1998). By definition, it would seem that the dual-income family is an equitable relationship. The assumption underlying such an arrangement is that each spouse will be committed both to the work of the other and to the family.

The implication is that, if the spouses spend equal amounts of time at their place of employment, they must take equal responsibility for family work. Otherwise, the

 Exchange Theory Applied

costs of the relationship may become greater than the rewards, and, in accord with *exchange theory,* the spouse who perceives the costs to be far greater than the rewards will not find the marriage sufficiently satisfying. This is true for other societies as well as the United States. A study of Lebanese couples found that wives whose husbands were minimally involved with housework, compared to those whose husbands were highly involved, were 1.6 times more likely to be distressed, 2.69 times more likely to be unhappy, and 2.96 times more likely to be uncomfortable with their husbands (Khawaja and Habib 2007). These results are consistent with a national U.S. survey that found an equitable division of household work to be associated with marital happiness (Frisco and Williams 2003).

To what extent is such equity becoming more common? Research on British, German, and U.S. dual-income couples found that the relative share of household work done by husbands and wives is becoming more equal in all three countries (Gershuny, Bittman, and Brice 2005). However, wives still do more of the work, and wives also make more adjustments (such as reducing work hours and refusing work-related travel) for their husbands' work schedules than do husbands for their wives' schedules (Maume 2006).

Who's Minding the House?

How many dual-income couples achieve an equitable arrangement in household responsibilities? A concern for equity, after all, is not the only driving force for a sharing of household responsibilities. The declining proportion of men in the labor force, the increasing number of women who work outside the home and contribute to the support of the family, and the decline in the proportion of Americans who believe that women rather than men should take care of the home (Spain and Bianchi 1996) all should result in a greater sharing by men and women of family work.

And in point of fact there is less inequality than there was in the past. The amount of time married mothers spend on household tasks has declined steadily since the 1960s, while the amount of time spent by married fathers has increased substantially (Bianchi et al. 2000).

Increasing numbers of husbands assume some share of the housework.

Fathers today tend to be more involved in child care tasks than were previous generations of fathers (Barnett and Rivers 1996). A fourth or more of men with preschoolers and wives who work outside the home provide some care for their children, and nearly a fifth are the major care providers (Casper 1997).

Systems Theory Applied

Whether a man shares household responsibility depends on a number of factors. One factor is the awareness of the disproportionate share of household responsibilities that fall on his wife. Husbands who are oblivious to this fact are unlikely to help. They and their wives may get into what *systems theorists* call *circularity*. For example, a man complained that his wife was not sufficiently supportive, which caused him to do poorly at his sales job. For him, the problem was simple—she needed to be more supportive so that he could perform better at work. She responded that his performance, which resulted in a lower paycheck, forced her to work more hours at her part-time job. For her, too, the problem was simple—he needed to do a better job so she could work less. The real problem was not simple but circular. When his commissions were lower, she worried more and spent more hours at her part-time job, which took time and energy away from their marital relationship. Thus, his poor performance caused her stress, which caused her lowered support, which caused his continued poor performance. The problem was circular, and their arguments were endless and fruitless until they recognized the circularity into which they had fallen.

A number of other factors bear on a husband's probability of sharing household responsibility. In particular, husbands are likely to assume increased responsibility when they have high levels of education; have wives with educational levels similar to theirs; have egalitarian attitudes about gender and family roles; are in, along with their wives, professional or managerial occupations; earn about the same as, rather than significantly more than, their wives; have somewhat different work schedules than their wives, so that they are the only parent at home during certain hours of the day or evening; and have wives who have been employed for a long rather than relatively short period of time (Presser 1994; Brayfield 1995; Harpster and Monk-Turner 1998; Cunningham 2007).

Progress but Not Equality. In spite of the gains, wives who work outside the home are still likely to spend substantially more hours than their husbands on housework.

Comparison

Household Tasks and Equity in China

Since the Communist takeover of China in 1949, the official ideology has advocated the equality of the sexes. Following the revolution, women were brought into the labor force in massive numbers, doing generally the same kinds of work and receiving the same pay as men. How does this equality translate into the division of labor within the home? How does it compare with the United States, where women who work outside the home still assume a disproportionate number of household tasks?

Zuo and Bian (2001) addressed such questions in their interviews with 39 couples living in Beijing. In 37 of the couples, the wife worked outside the home. The other two wives were full-time homemakers. The researchers interviewed husbands and wives separately to determine their views on the division of labor among both routine and nonroutine tasks. The routine tasks were management of the home, budgeting, shopping, cleaning house, cooking, child care, child education, dishwashing, and laundry. Nonroutine tasks included such things as repairing appliances and setting up the stove and smoke pipes for winter heating.

Most (33) of the couples agreed that the husband did more of the non-routine work. And a majority of the couples agreed that the wife did more of the routine tasks except for shopping for items other than groceries (19 couples said the wife did more and 20 said they shared the task equally). If a couple indicated that a husband did more of a particular task, it was most likely to be cooking (nine couples). As for child care, 17 couples said the wife did more, 10 said they shared the task equally, and 5 said the husband did more. Clearly, there is inequity among these Chinese families. In fact, 11 of the 13 wives who earned more than their husbands assumed most of the responsibility for household tasks.

What did the couples think of this situation? For one thing, both the men and the women agreed that it is appropriate for each partner to contribute to the family income. Both agreed that a career is a legitimate pursuit for women. But they also both agreed that the wife should continue to have the major responsibility for household tasks. One of the wives, for example, acknowledged that her career in a government agency meant she would have less time for her family and a greater potential for conflict with her husband. This did not mean, she said, that women shouldn't pursue a career, "but they should be able to combine the career with the family" (Zuo and Bian 2001:1128).

In sum, inequity exists, but the women did not perceive themselves as being treated unfairly. They agreed that the home is still the woman's primary responsibility even when she works as much as the man. The only sense of unfairness expressed by wives was for their husbands' failure to be good providers. Even in those cases, however, the women affirmed their own responsibility for the home.

The Bureau of Labor Statistics (2007a) time-use survey reported that, on the average, women spend 2.7 hours on household activities (chores, management, food preparation and cleanup), compared to 2.1 hours for men. And, as noted earlier, they spend considerably more time in child care activities. This inequity occurs in other nations as well. A study of 115 dual-income Canadian couples reported that the mothers in the labor force did twice as many family chores as did their husbands (Huppe and Cyr 1997). And an Australian national survey also reported that married women spent more time on, and did a greater proportion of, housework than did their husbands (Baxter 2005). And the workload gets worse for women after the birth of a child. In a study of 128 couples who had their first child, the researchers found that the mothers' responsibilities increased by 64 percent, while the fathers' increased by 37 percent (Gjerdingen and Center 2005). The couples reported less sharing and less satisfaction with work sharing after childbirth.

While there is still a tendency for men and women to engage in the traditional kinds of household tasks, men are increasingly taking on such tasks as cooking, cleaning, and daily child care (Sayer 2005; Bianchi, Robinson, and Milkie 2006). Those men who are more willing to assume some of the traditional female tasks tend to be urban, nonwhite, well-educated, and egalitarian in their attitudes (Harpster and Monk-Turner 1998).

In short, there appears to be ongoing progress toward equality, but equality does not yet exist. The trend towards equality exists in many nations. Whether the trend will continue is an open question, but the egalitarian attitudes expressed by both males and females suggests that it will.

The Dual-Career Wife. The problem of an equitable household division of labor is particularly severe for the dual-career wife, who is more likely than the husband to bear the brunt of the conflicts among work, spouse, and children. Dual-career wives try to do all of the tasks that homemakers do even though they may not spend as much time on them. And even though they have careers, they may believe they have no choice about the various homemaking tasks in which they engage (DeMeis and Perkins 1996).

Some women try to deal with the conflict by trying to be the "superwoman"—the perfect mother, the best homemaker, the ideal wife, and the high-achieving career woman (Tiedje 2004). Whatever the motivation for such unrealistic aspirations, the woman who holds them is likely to fall victim to various consequences of stress: depression, anxiety, irritability, and problems with eating and sleeping. One such woman, Margaret, has an administrative position in health services. She seems to have it all—career and family. But one day she told us, "I never thought I'd be saying this. But I'd like to chuck it all—my work, my kids, even my husband. I'm tired. My most prevalent fantasy is to have my own apartment with only myself to take care of." Margaret has reached a point of exhaustion.

In sum, while there has been some change, considerable inequity exists for both dual-career and dual-earner wives when measured by sheer number of hours. As noted earlier, a sense of equity is important to marital satisfaction. Indeed, women who perceive inequity in household tasks are more likely than others to feel distressed and depressed (Bird 1999). Why, then, does the inequality persist?

Why Inequality Persists. One reason for the inequality is differences in income. Money is power in our society. A study of 60 dual-career couples reported that those partners who had the higher income viewed their careers as more important than those of their spouses, were somewhat less involved in child care responsibilities, and had more say in financial decisions (Steil and Weltman 1991).

Inequality also may persist because of the tendency for some aspects of traditional role expectations to persist. Whatever the reasons for the inequality, we should note that inequality in such things as time spent on household tasks is not always defined as inequity by people. In studying marital quality of 41 people in dual-career marriages, three researchers found that the respondents gave more importance to such matters as mutual respect, support, commitment, and reciprocity over time than they did to current sharing of household tasks and responsibilities (Rosenbluth, Steil, and Whitcomb 1998). In other words, there does not have to be a 50-50 sharing of household tasks and decision making in order for people to have a sense of equity in the relationship.

Finally, inequality persists where wives do not define their unequal share of household tasks as unfair. Using data from married couples expecting their first child, three researchers found that women who did not equate greater household responsibility as inequity did so because they enjoyed the household tasks and/or they and their husbands believed they were particularly competent in doing such tasks (Grote, Naylor, and Clark 2002).

Children and the Challenge of Child Care

If a dual-income couple has children, they face the question of who will care for them. Will they use day care service, the help of relatives, or the services of a nanny? Or will they try to care for the children themselves?

The majority will opt for some kind of child care. Roughly 61 percent of pre-kindergarten children receive some kind of nonparental child care on a regular basis (Federal Interagency Forum on Child and Family Statistics 2007). About 48 percent of children under the age of 5 whose mothers are employed are cared for by a relative; the rest are cared for by nonrelatives or organizations, or they care for themselves. Two challenges face the couple who opt for child care. One is the challenge of finding satisfactory care and the other is the challenge of spending sufficient time parenting.

The Challenge of Finding Satisfactory Care. Parents who use a child care center look for such things as the quality of facilities and programs, ratio of children to staff, cost, convenience of the location, and hours of operation (Leslie 2000). They also monitor how their children appear to be adjusting and developing. Many parents find such care satisfactory (Van Horn et al. 2001; Teleki and Buck-Gomez 2002).

There are, nevertheless, reasons for concern. The children, after all, are spending a great deal of time with nonfamily members during crucial developmental years. Some evidence exists that a number of physical and developmental risks are involved in child care. Children 3 years of age and younger in child care have higher rates of communicable illnesses (respiratory and ear infections and gastrointestinal illness) than do children reared in their homes (National Institute of Child Health

Parents strive to find quality day care for their children.

and Human Development 2001; Gordon, Kaestner, and Korenman 2007). Generally, children are safe from physical injuries in child care facilities. However, child care centers are much safer than are private homes and, although few children ever die in child care, are far less likely than private homes to put a child at risk of death from some kind of violence (Wrigley and Dreby 2005).

There are also behavioral consequences for children in child care. Children who have early, extensive child care are at greater risk for more conflicted parent-child relationships and higher levels of aggression (Belsky 2002). Research by the National Institute of Child Health and Human Development shows that the more hours per day a child is in day care, the more likely the child is to exhibit behavior problems at age 5 (Lang 2005). And a preschool child who attends a day care center for a year or more is more likely than others to become disruptive in school, an effect that lasts through the sixth grade (Belsky et al. 2007).

On the other hand, the higher rate of communicable illnesses did not adversely affect the children as they grew older. And in another study of cognitive and language development, researchers found that children in high-quality child care fared as well in their development as those cared for at home (Burchinal et al. 2000).

The Challenge of Sufficient Parenting Time.   A national survey showed that mothers whose children were in child care for more than 30 hours per week spent about 12 fewer hours per week interacting with their infants than did mothers who cared for their infants themselves (Booth et al. 2002). However, the mothers who used child care gave as much quality time to their children, and the fathers of the children were more involved with them than were fathers married to stay-at-home mothers. Overall, therefore, the children did well. The mothers did suffer some separation anxiety, so the major question seems to be whether the parenting time is sufficient from the child's or the mother's point of view.

Other Options.   What if couples decide not to use child care? In some cases, because of their own values and preferences, the parents may decide to care for the children themselves. In a minority of cases, the father may become the primary caregiver (Riley and Glass 2002). In other cases, the couple may revert to more traditional roles with the mother as caregiver and the father as breadwinner.

Some women opt to be stay-at-home mothers for a limited period and then return to work. Maternity leaves and more flexible schedules facilitate such a choice. Of course, not working or working part-time also may be a woman's preference. A study of 391 female managers reported that those who were unemployed or working part-time said they were forgoing full-time employment for the time being because they wanted to spend more time with their preschool children (Rosin and Korabik 1990).

Clearly, the issue of children presents the dual-income couple with difficult decisions. A survey of nearly 1,000 professional women found that they tended to make sacrifices in family life or career or both (Olson, Frieze, and Detlefsen 1990). Many of the childless women said they would like to have children. Those who had children reported that they made various kinds of career sacrifices. Interestingly, women in the male-dominated business world reported more difficulty in combining children and career than those in the female-dominated area of library science.

Social practices and pressures thus work against an equal sharing of child rearing. This may be one reason there are fewer children on the average in dual-career than in more traditional marriages. There is also a tendency in dual-career families for the spouses to postpone childbearing until they have established themselves in their careers.

When the children reach school age, problems of child care are lessened somewhat but not eliminated. Who will stay at home on the days when there is no school? Who will respond if the school calls and says that the child is sick? Again, the burden is likely to fall on the mother. The woman, therefore, is likely to make more career adjustments and sacrifices than the man.

The Costs of Both Parents Working

Stress arises if people perceive that their families are suffering in some way because of their employment. Many believe that a woman who works outside the home cannot care for her children as well as can the woman who is a homemaker. The belief that children suffer may be greater when there are sons rather than daughters involved (Downey, Jackson, and Powell 1994). Parents tend to believe that sons need more supervision than do daughters.

If children suffer from too little maternal care, then, we have a problem of massive proportions. What does the evidence show? Actually, it is conflicting and sometimes confusing. A review of research conducted throughout the 1990s concluded that there was little relationship between maternal employment and child outcomes (Perry-Jenkins, Repetti, and Crouter 2000). A number of studies that focused on the impact on adolescents also found that maternal employment has no negative consequences on such things as cognitive and social competence, emotional well-being, and amount of communication and conflict between mother and child (Armistead, Wierson, and Forehand 1990; Orthner 1990). But a great many studies find either positive or negative consequences for children.

Positive Outcomes of Maternal Employment. A number of researchers have reported positive effects of maternal employment. Other things being equal, the children of working mothers have, at age 4, less hyperactivity, more prosocial behavior, and less anxiety than the children of nonworking mothers (Nomaguchi 2006). A study of 52 mothers and their adolescent children found higher self-esteem and less depression among adolescents whose mothers were highly educated and employed (Joebgen and Richards 1990). A survey of 97 low-income mothers reported that their children were in better health than those whose mothers were unemployed and on public assistance (Secret and Peck-Heath 2004). The researchers also found better school performance among those children whose mothers had either long-term employment or long-term unemployment, suggesting that stability in the mother's role was more important than whether the mother worked or stayed at home.

What Do You Think?

*There is disagreement about **whether young children suffer when both parents work outside the home.** What follows are pro and con arguments. What do you think?*

Pro

Young children suffer when both parents work outside the home because

- they feel that they take second place to their parents' careers.
- they have inadequate supervision.
- they have too little time with their parents.
- they miss out on having their mothers' continuing presence, which is so vital in the early years of life.
- nonparental caregivers don't give children the love and attention they need to thrive.

Con

Young children do not suffer when both parents work outside the home because

- they learn self-sufficiency at an early age.
- even young children need their "space."
- parents find caregivers who provide their children with the needed supervision and loving attention.
- it is quality of time, not quantity of time, with parents that is crucial to children's development.
- the parents have more financial resources with which to provide the children with a better quality of life.

Maternal employment may have positive effects on children by encouraging higher levels of educational attainment (Kalmijn 1994; Haveman and Wolfe 1994). This may be particularly true when mothers work in occupations that are complex (such as the professions); these mothers may "create home environments that are more cognitively enriched and more affectively and physically appropriate" than those created by mothers who work in less complex occupations (Parcel and Menaghan 1994:61).

There may also be some indirect benefits to the children. The full-time employment of wives is associated with greater marital stability, and husbands whose mothers worked during their childhood are more likely to spend time on housework as adults (Gupta 2006; Schoen, Rogers, and Amato 2006). Both the stability and the greater equality are likely to create stronger and more satisfying marriages, which, in turn, are likely to enhance parenting skills.

Negative Outcomes of Maternal Employment. Unfortunately, there is more evidence of negative than of positive effects. A study of third- and fourth-grade children whose mothers worked during the first year of the children's lives reported that they, compared to children whose mothers were not employed, had less tolerance for frustration, more behavioral problems, and were more likely to be named by their peers for hitting others and "being mean" (Youngblade 2003). We noted earlier research that reported more conflicted parent–child relationships and higher levels of problem behavior among children whose mothers work when they are very young. There is also a slower rate of cognitive development (such as lower vocabulary scores) when mothers work during the first three years (Han 2005). Muller (1995) examined national data and found that children perform better on achievement tests when mothers are either employed part-time or not employed. And researchers who studied 200 seventh graders found that daughters, though not sons, reported greater closeness with both parents when the mother was not employed (Paulson, Koman, and Hill 1990). A study of eighth graders reported that those who had to care for themselves for 11 hours a week or more because of parental work reported more anger, stress, and family conflict than others (Dwyer 1990). And Baum (2004) reported that adolescents whose mothers had recently gone to work experienced a decline in their grades.

It may be that it is not simply whether both parents work that is crucial but rather the extent to which working parents can still supervise, interact with, and adequately support their children. Such a conclusion is consistent with the fact that children have more behavior problems when their parents work overtime (Parcel and Menaghan 1994). In fact, any kind of nonstandard work schedule—working overtime, evenings, nights, or weekends—can be detrimental for children (Strazdins et al. 2006). The parents themselves report worse family functioning, more symptoms of depression, and lower parenting effectiveness. And the children are more likely than others to have such social and emotional difficulties as hyperactivity/inattention, aggression, anxiety, and unhappiness.

Obviously, working parents cannot give as much time in support and guidance as those who do not work (Nomaguchi and Milkie 2006). But some of the negative effects may be mitigated if one or both parents can limit the hours worked. Hill and his associates (2006) have proposed an ideal of a total of 60 hours per week for the combined work hours of both parents. They compared three groups of married couples with children. Both parents worked full-time in one group. One worked full-time and one worked part-time (60 hours or less combined) in the second group. And only one worked in the third group. The latter two groups, compared to the first, reported enhanced family satisfaction and less work-family conflict.

The negative behavioral and cognitive outcomes we have discussed do not occur among all groups. For reasons that are unclear, the negative outcomes appear to affect white but not black children (Han, Waldfogel, and Brooks-Gunn 2001). The slower cognitive development is also puzzling in light of the fact that parents in homes where mothers have outside employment engage in reading and homework activities more frequently than do parents in homes where the mother is not employed (Zick, Bryant, and Osterbacka 2001).

Finally, to add to the complexity as well as to the controversy, Sugar (1994) studied 253 mothers between the ages of 25 and 45. Those whose own mothers had worked were more likely to struggle with depression. They also felt less effective as parents and indicated less satisfaction with their work and with life generally. If Sugar's conclusions are generally valid, they indicate that negative consequences of mothers working may appear mainly when the children become adults and parents themselves.

Our own conclusion from the varied pieces of evidence is that maternal employment, whether because of the quality of child care available or other reasons, poses risks (but not inevitable negative consequences) to the child's well-being. This is particularly true if the employment occurs during the preschool years. On the other hand, some women may function better as mothers if they also have paid employment. For some couples, a stay-at-home father may serve the child as well as a stay-at-home mother. For some couples, high-quality care may enable the child to thrive while the mother and father both work outside the home. In short, parents must be aware of the risks as well as the benefits of both working and make a decision that will maximize the well-being of all the family members.

Time Management

One of the common complaints of those in dual-income marriages is that they have too little time for each other and for their children (Tiedje 2004; Roxburgh 2006). Only a minority are satisfied with the time they have available for family activities. The problem is intensified for those with children and if one or both parents have a high need for achievement in a career. The problem is also intensified by the fact that the average workweek for dual-income couples increased from about 78 hours in 1970 to 82 hours in 2000 (Gerson and Jacobs 2004).

The perception of too little time means that the individual experiences **time pressure,** feelings of frustration and anxiety because of insufficient time to fulfill one's responsibilities and desires. Working mothers with minor age children (41 percent) are more likely to experience time pressure than are working fathers with minor age children (26 percent) (Pew Research Center 2006c). Such time pressure can result in family strains and individual stress. It is associated with higher rates of depression and a lower sense of well-being among employed women (Roxburgh 2004; Nomaguchi, Milkie, and Bianchi 2005).

Careful planning and cooperation by all family members are important in order to deal with time pressures and to minimize conflicts over time (Haddock et al. 2001). Some couples resolve the problem by following detailed schedules. Others try to depend on the goodwill and good sense of each member of the family, hoping that all of the demands of work and home will be met without the rigid structuring of time. The latter may not succeed. Those who try to operate without a schedule are likely to find that household tasks get neglected or that family members become increasingly hostile toward or alienated from each other as home life becomes more chaotic. Scheduling enables the family members to see the challenges they face as they try to meet each member's needs, and it helps them to meet those needs in a satisfying way.

Role Negotiation

All of the challenges we have discussed above may require the couple to negotiate their roles, or to engage in what *symbolic interactionists* call **role-making,** the process of working out the nature of particular roles in the Course of interaction (Lauer and Handel 1983:124).

 Symbolic Interactionist Theory Applied "Role-making" suggests that we do not slip easily into ready-made roles but must work together to construct what our roles will be. That can happen through role negotiation, which has become increasingly common and necessary as the number of dual-income families has grown. The questions are "Who does what?" and "How can a couple achieve an equitable division of labor?" As we might expect, there is little, if any, agreement on the answers. Each couple must negotiate its own compromise about family roles.

Not only is there no social consensus, but specific couples also are likely to disagree with one another. The problems are illustrated by research of 83 dual-income couples who each had at least one preschool child (Chassin et al. 1985). The researchers investigated the perceptions of spousal, parental, and worker roles held by the partners.

They found general agreement on perceptions of worker and husband roles but a considerable amount of disagreement on wife and parental roles. Women saw the wife's role as more powerless, more dependent, more child oriented, and less glamorous than their husband's role. Men viewed the father role as more dependent, more tied down, and more child oriented than did the women. Women viewed the mother role as more sensitive, warmer, and less glamorous than did the men.

Generally, the partners saw a lot of overlap between the wife and mother roles. But women rated the employed-woman role as more unfeeling, more independent, more sophisticated and glamorous, and more interesting and tense than the roles of wife and mother. Men rated the employed-woman role as meaner, less good, more independent, more sophisticated, more serious, and colder than the roles of wife and mother.

The researchers also found that women perceived the wife role as less desirable than did the men, suggesting that "the men in this dual-worker sample may underestimate their wives' discontent with the wife role" (Chassin et al. 1985:308). That difference is a potential source of

Career-oriented women are more satisfied with their lives when they combine work with marriage and family.

conflict. Another possible source of conflict is the women's lower evaluation than the men's of the father role, suggesting that the wives may undervalue their husbands' contribution to child rearing. Finally, the overlap between wife and mother and the gap between those roles and the employed woman role indicate conflict between the home and work roles. In particular, women in dual-income families may see themselves as involved in a "'trade-off' between the independence, freedom, and glamour of the worker role and the sensitivity, warmth, and relaxation of the wife and mother roles" (Chassin et al. 1985:308). The wife and mother roles, of course, are more consistent with traditional notions of femininity.

"Whatever works for you" is probably a good rule to follow as partners negotiate such differences. What you settle on as acceptable roles for you and your spouse is not as important as the fact that you settle on something. Agreement about roles is crucial to your marital satisfaction.

SATISFACTIONS OF DUAL-INCOME FAMILIES

Despite potential problems, the dual-income family arrangement also offers a number of satisfactions. To be sure, serious problems arise if one or both spouses give work high priority and family low priority. Thus, Orbuch and Custer (1995) found that when women defined their work as one of the most important aspects of their lives, their husbands reacted negatively. African American husbands rated their marriages lower in quality, while white husbands reported higher levels of anxiety. Clearly, husbands are troubled by wives who give top priority to career or job. But if you successfully negotiate family roles, achieve an equitable division of labor in the home (particularly important for women), and have an equitable sharing of bread-winning (particularly important for men), you have resolved some of the major problems of the dual-income family and you are likely to have a satisfying marriage (Wilkie, Ferree, and Ratcliff 1998; Stevens, Kiger, and Riley 2001; Saginak and Saginak 2005).

Marital Satisfaction

Marital satisfaction among dual-income couples is common, particularly when the spouses are able to work the number of hours they prefer (whether full-time or part-time) (Carr, Gareis, and Barnett 2003). Smith (1985) examined 27 studies that involved 4,602 subjects and compared those in dual-income and single-income families. The studies looked at overall marital adjustment and four specific areas of adjustment: physical (love, affection, sexual relations), companionship (sharing interests, tasks, activities), communication (self-disclosure, small talk, listening), and tensions and regrets (conflict, willingness to marry same person again). The bulk of the studies show no differences in overall adjustment between dual-income families and those in which the woman is a homemaker. In fact, the majority of studies show no difference in any of the specific areas. In the areas of physical relations and companionship, where a substantial proportion of studies found differences, the results tended to favor families with homemakers over the dual-income families. But it is clear that the majority of couples seem to be working out the problems faced by the dual-income family (Blair 1993).

Other Benefits

In addition to marital satisfaction, a number of other benefits can accrue to the dual-income family. One relates to the need for a sense of control over our lives. A woman who has a sense of her own separate identity and a feeling of being independent will be healthier and more satisfied than one who cannot separate herself from her family and who is economically and emotionally dependent on her husband.

There are benefits to the family generally as well. The higher income level will give family members options that they might not otherwise have. Moreover, to the extent that they resolve the issue of an equitable division of labor in the home, they will have the opportunity to share in an experience of equality that many Americans value but miss. They also will have the opportunity to experience a lifestyle in which the constraints of traditional gender roles are no longer operative. Also the children may develop a sense of responsibility, independence, and competence earlier in life and more completely because they too must assume a certain share of family work.

In sum, the potential satisfactions and rewards of the dual-income family are as plentiful as those of the single-income family. Neither type is inherently superior to the other. Neither type is free of risks, challenges, and demands. Couples must determine for themselves what will work best for them.

WORK AND WELL-BEING

What would you do if you won a lottery? Would you retire and live happily ever after in glorious leisure? Probably not. Many people who have won lotteries have continued to work. Others have quit their jobs, but they have gone into other kinds of work or have found some way to spend their time. Humans do not generally function well without some kind of meaningful activity to occupy them.

Meaningful work, as Freud once observed, is one of the crucial bases of our well-being. Of course, not everyone who has a job has "meaningful" work. Yet one of the characteristics of Americans is the increasing expectation that work should facilitate self-fulfillment rather than merely provide a source of income (McCormack 2007). They want their work to be enjoyable and even exciting. Americans are also less interested in work that totally consumes them than in having limited hours at the workplace that allows the pursuit of other activities. The question is, to what extent can people find such personal fulfillment in a dual-income family?

Life Satisfaction

Even though women in dual-income families are likely to carry a heavier share of the responsibility for household tasks and to have fewer leisure hours than their husbands, women who are employed tend to be more satisfied with their lives. A large-scale survey of the wives of physicians, for example, reported that those who worked outside the home had higher levels of both marital and life satisfaction (Sotile and Sotile 2004). Similarly, men still tend to think of themselves as responsible for being providers for their families. Even if the wife brings in sufficient income, a husband may be ambivalent about becoming a house-husband. As a man told us:

> We decided that since Kelly can make so much more money than I can, I would stop working and stay at home with the kids, at least until they're all in school. For the most part, I love it. I really do. And I do an occasional job that brings in some income. But I have to admit that I also am embarrassed when we're at a social function and someone asks me what I do. It's like I'm not a *real* man because I don't have a regular job. Still, I wouldn't have it any other way with our family.

In sum, men and women in dual-income families can achieve as much life satisfaction as those with other arrangements. In particular, as noted earlier, when they each work the number, or close to the number, of hours they prefer, and limit the total hours they work if they have children, their work will enhance their lives.

Mental and Physical Health

In a sense, work presents us with one of the dilemmas of human life. On the one hand, work-induced stress is associated with such physical health problems as coronary heart disease, migraines, peptic ulcers, and hypertension (Lauer and Lauer 2008). On the other hand, the stress of being forcibly unemployed can be as serious as the stress of working in undesirable conditions or in an unfulfilling job. Unemployment leads to higher rates of suicide, mental illness, and various physical problems. The way to deal with the dilemma, of course, is to find work that is meaningful and fulfilling.

Having the option to work outside the home is important for wives. Women have higher rates of both physical and mental ailments than do men. For many women, it is the restrictive nature of the traditional role of wife and mother that creates stress and leads to high rates of illness (Lauer and Lauer 2008). Thus, women who are dissatisfied with the homemaker role and not employed have

Personal

Employed and Married and Loving Both

Phyllis is a high-school counselor in her 40s. She and Roger have four children. They have had their share of difficult times, but overall, she sees the marriage as a very good one and believes that working outside the home has enhanced the quality of their family life:

During our 21 years of marriage, being happily employed has probably contributed as much to our happiness as anything else. I taught for two years before we married. It was very fulfilling, and the idea of my quitting to be a "good wife" was neither discussed nor considered. Because of my job, I felt a sense of accomplishment, competence, pride, and independence, all of which contributed to my being a very happy person. Roger was just as fortunate in his career choice. He found excitement and challenge in being an architect.

In our 20s, life was amazingly wonderful. Everything was new and thrilling—our jobs, our marriage, our friends, and the babies. We both worked hard and were very conscientious about our jobs. Roger was willing from the beginning to help out a great deal with the children, everything from changing diapers to getting up for middle-of-the-night feedings. We shared chores around the house but with no particular division of labor. Having his help with the mundane, routine aspects of home life endeared him to me greatly and helped me to continue working.

Our jobs were important to both of us because they gave us a sense of our individuality. We have never been suffocated or stifled by each other. Most of the time, we have worked at having enough togetherness to know that we were married. Our careers help us to view each other as competent people and this creates a mutual respect for each other as spouses and as professional people.

During our 30s, however, our professions brought about some frustrations and tensions. Roger had become a licensed architect and opened his own office. I had gone back to college to get my master's degree so that I could change from teaching to counseling. We had two more children, but Roger's work week had gone from 50 to what seemed like 90 hours a week. Time together became scarce. Our relationship became strained. I felt neglected. I was so busy that it took a while, but I gradually realized that I was terribly frustrated and angry. It all came out when we took a vacation. We spent most of the time talking about our situation. We both felt like we needed a vacation after the vacation. But it did help us to make some adjustments. We hired a cleaning lady, planned to spend a number of weekends away from home with just the two of us, and tried to do more things together. We realized that intimacy didn't just happen for us as it did in the first years of our marriage. We now had to put energy and effort into maintaining our intimate relationship.

In our 40s, life has quieted down a bit. Roger is somewhat burned out with his work. He's looking for new challenges. I think I am too. So we're talking about what we can do to make our lives more exciting. We've got some ideas and are looking forward to the future.

There's no doubt about it. In spite of the frustrations we've had, the net effect of both of us being employed is that we have been able to maintain a high quality of intimacy during most of our years of marriage.

more problems with depression than do other women (Shehan, Burg, and Rexroat 1986; Bromberger and Matthews 1994). Women with meaningful employment, on the other hand, have less psychological distress (Barnett et al. 1993; Barnett and Rivers 1996; Elliott 1996). Moreover, a national survey of women and their physical health reported that the healthiest women are those who are employed and married, followed by those employed and not married, those married but not in the labor force, and finally those unmarried and not in the labor force (Verbrugge and Madans 1985). On the whole, then, wives who work outside the home are mentally and physically healthier than those who, for whatever reasons, do not but would like to work outside the home.

Social Policy and Coping Strategies

As we shall detail below, there are many strategies that couples can use to deal with the problems of dual-income families. But government also has an important role, because social policies can either help or thwart the effort to construct a meaningful family life when both husband and wife work. *Family-friendly social policies emerged as women's participation in the labor force surged during the 1960s and after* (Gilbert 2005). Family-friendly policies are designed to make it easier for people to deal with the competing demands of work and family life. For example, employers can offer their workers **flextime** arrangements (McGregor 2006). That is, the workers can have flexible rather than a rigid work hours. And some employers are finding that they even need flexibility in the flextime arrangements they offer in order to accommodate the differing needs of different workers. Flexible work hours are particularly important for working parents, who may then be able to adjust their work schedules so that at least one parent is always at home with the children.

Another family-friendly policy is the federal Family and Medical Leave Act of 1993. It requires employers to give an employee up to 12 weeks of unpaid leave during any 12-month period if the employee is giving birth, or is adopting a child, or needs to be a caretaker for an immediate family member with a serious health problem, or needs a medical leave for his or her own health problem. Of course, an unpaid leave means a financial burden, yet in 2004 California became the first state in the nation to mandate a paid maternity leave for women (Wisensale 2006).

Companies as well as government can institute family-friendly policies (Widener 2007). For example, some companies provide child care facilities for their employees. Some offer more benefits than those mandated by government policies. The point with all such policies, whether mandated by government or instituted by a company, is to allow parents to participate in the workforce in a way that not only fulfills the parents' career aspirations, but also facilitates the proper care and support of children and aging parents.

Even with family-friendly policies in effect, dual-income families still face a daunting set of tasks (Gilbert 2005). They can, therefore, benefit from using certain coping strategies to deal with various problems. Both dual-income and dual-career families can attain high levels of satisfaction when they employ strategies such as making family fun one of their priorities, keeping work problems from spilling over into family life, keeping life relatively simple, and being effective time managers (Haddock et al. 2001).

Studies of women in dual-income families note a number of ways that the women handle problems of time management and self-care (McLaughlin, Cormier, and Cormier 1988; Tiedje 2004). Time management strategies are those that enable a woman to control her personal and professional time. Self care strategies are those that enable a woman to care for her physical and emotional well-being. The more women used the strategies, the better their marital adjustment and the lower their levels of distress.

For *time-management,* the coping strategies include

- Do more than one task at a time.
- Have contingency plans.
- Say "no" to additional time demands.
- Break large jobs down into smaller subtasks.
- Budget your time so that you are not overwhelmed.
- Make a priority list of your tasks.
- Ask the family to help.
- Leave work in the workplace; don't bring it home.
- Make "to-do" lists.
- Utilize outside help.

For *self care,* the coping strategies include

- Give yourself permission to be a less-than-perfect housekeeper.
- Allow special time for each child.
- Eat nutritionally balanced meals.
- Engage in family activities.
- Give yourself permission to be a less-than-perfect mother.
- Give yourself permission to be a less-than-perfect wife.
- Stress quality rather than quantity time.
- Interact with spouse.
- Lower standards for housework.
- Take time for yourself to do something you enjoy.
- Engage in a hobby.
- Attend social or community group meetings.
- Exercise.

Twenty-eight percent of the women said that they never exercised. Every other strategy was used at least to some extent by the great majority of the women.

It is interesting to note that the self care strategies include giving oneself permission to be less than perfect as a housekeeper, wife, and mother. In other words, the women who are coping well have learned to avoid trying to be "superwomen." They know that they cannot be all things to all people. As a result, they are able to work outside the home, enjoy a family, and still maintain their personal well-being.

SUMMARY

Since industrialization, "his" work has mainly been to function as a provider and "her" work has been to care for the home. But in the industrial economy, only paid labor has been defined as work.

Since the 1960s, women have gone into the labor force in increasing numbers. Most married as well as single women now work outside the home; the most dramatic increase in labor force participation has occurred among married women with children under the age of 6. Women may take jobs or enter careers. Those who are employed become part of either a dual-earner or dual-career family. Dual-career families include three types of marital roles: traditional, participant, and role-sharing. The commuter marriage is a special form of the dual-career family and poses a serious challenge to the maintenance of intimacy.

Women who choose employment outside the home do so for a variety of reasons. They work for economic reasons (including consumerism and the desire for financial security), for the fulfillment that work brings, or for the power gained.

Home and work affect each other. Problems can arise from home-to-work spillover or work-to-home spillover. Both men and women experience conflicting demands from home and work.

Dual-income families face a number of challenges. One is the issue of equity, especially in relationship to household responsibilities. Progress has been made, but husbands and wives still do not assume equal shares of the responsibilities even when the wife as well as the husband is involved in a career. Other important challenges include the issue of children and child care, the costs of both parents working (including the effects on children), time management, and role negotiation.

Dual-income families can have as much satisfaction as single-income families. If the various challenges are addressed successfully, the couple can have high marital satisfaction as well as a number of other benefits from the arrangement.

Work is an integral part of our well-being. Wives and mothers who want to work and gain employment tend to find themselves assuming a heavier load of responsibilities. They still prefer to work and are more satisfied if they have employment. Men still tend to think of themselves as responsible to be providers and may have ambivalent feelings about cutting back on their hours or becoming house-husbands. But the life satisfaction of both men and women in dual-income families can be as high as it is for those in other arrangements.

Both social policy and individual coping strategies are important in helping the dual-income family to cope with their challenges. Family-friendly social policies, including those mandated by government and those instituted by companies, facilitate the ability of dual-income couples to construct a meaningful family life. Individual coping strategies, such as time-management skills and self care, are also important.

Principles for Enhancing Intimacy

1. Women today have numerous role options available to them. Women can choose among career, marriage, and motherhood—or any combination of these. They can decide to stay at home or continue to work outside the home after they have children. Increased confusion, however, often accompanies enlarged options as individuals struggle to decide what is the best pattern for their lives. When faced with such choices, it is vital for you to gain an understanding of your needs as well as those of your spouse and to consider carefully your personal and your shared goals.

2. It is very important to negotiate role expectations before marriage. Each person needs to define clearly what role he or she expects to play in the marriage and what the role of the other will be. Then, compromises need to be negotiated. Be aware that the roles you decide on are not etched in stone. The process of negotiation and compromise will be repeated throughout your marriage as circumstances change.

3. Women who decide to combine the responsibilities of job, children, and home must recognize and come to terms with the enormity of their tasks and their own limitations. They can't do everything equally well all of the time. If you choose to assume these roles, you need to make a list of priorities, reduce your expectations, eliminate the less valuable tasks, and seek help when necessary.

4. Research indicates that husbands in dual-income marriages do not share equally in family work. It is important that housework—including child care—be viewed as "our" work and not just "her" work. Otherwise, the wife may have a sense of inequity.

5. Often because she is not a wage earner, the work of the homemaker is not highly valued by society or, for that matter, by her husband. If a woman chooses to stop work and stay at home after having children, her husband needs to support her in this choice and acknowledge the valuable task she is performing. He also needs to encourage his wife to see friends, find ways of retaining career ties, and generally maintain interests outside the home. In this way, she will avoid the feelings of isolation that often plague homemakers.

KEY TERMS

ON THE WEB   Work and Home

Through a mixture of personal choice and economic necessity, the dual-income family has replaced the single-income family as the dominant type of family unit today. Married couples with and without children must adjust to increased stresses coming from competition between career and personal goals and responsibilities. Two Web sites that address the challenges and issues involved in the dual-income family are:

www.mhhe.com/lauer7e

National Partnership for Women and Families
http://www.nationalpartnership.org

This site provides information—including clips from television programs and other news sources, legislation, and proposed policies—about the varied problems of the dual-income family.

WFC Resources
http://www.workfamily.com

This site focuses on ways that employers can create a workplace that's both supportive and effective. The resources include the Work-Life *Newsbrief*, needs assessment tools, and a wealth of news and information about work and family.

Using these two sites, and others, enlarge your understanding with the following projects:

1. Compare the family-friendly policies of other nations with those of the United States. What kinds of benefits are offered working parents in other countries that would help U.S. families? Would you support policies that offer such benefits? Why or why not?

2. Imagine that you are called to testify before Congress. Using information from these two sites and others, write down the new policies you would urge Congress to adopt to help dual-income families. Give a clear rationale and provide any supporting evidence for each policy you propose.

part four

~ INTIMACY IN FAMILIES ~

At some point or other in our lives, we all face the task of establishing meaningful intimate relationships with someone other than a partner. As children, we strive to maintain intimacy with our parents. Once married, most of us will have children. Bringing children into the home poses new challenges and new tasks in our quest for intimacy.

As with the marital relationship, meaningful intimate relationships are not guaranteed simply because a group of people live together in the same house. In some ways, in fact, the challenge of intimacy is more difficult as the family grows. In this fourth part, then, we will examine family life over the life cycle, including the child-rearing years.

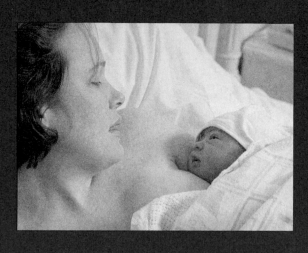

12

~ BECOMING A PARENT ~

After reading and studying chapter 12, you should be able to

1 Discuss the ways in which the birth rate, the ideal number of children, and sex preference have changed over the past few decades.

2 Explain why some people decide to have children and others choose to remain childless.

3 Outline the reasons for infertility.

4 Describe the process that infertile couples go through in coping with the knowledge of their infertility.

5 Discuss the various options that infertile couples have for obtaining a child.

6 Describe the stresses involved in raising children and the effect of this stress on marital satisfaction.

7 Compare and contrast men's and women's experience of parenting.

8 Summarize the three primary styles of parenting.

9 Explain the consequences of parental behavior on the well-being of children.

10 Describe the advantages and liabilities of parenting at a later age.

What is your initial reaction to the various options mentioned in this chapter—artificial insemination (do you feel differently about AIH and AID?), in vitro fertilization, surrogate mothers, and adoption? Which would be acceptable to you and which would be unacceptable? Why?

Select one of the options and make some notes about your feelings. Then research it in the popular literature. Use the *Readers' Guide to Periodical Literature* to find articles. Begin with the latest issue available and work back in time until you have found at least 10 articles that deal with your option.

How is the option treated in the popular literature? What kinds of legal and ethical problems are posed by that option?

What are the effects of the option on people's well-being? What arguments pro and con are offered? How do the attitudes reflected in the popular articles compare with your own feelings? Did anything you read change any of your feelings? If so, how?

If the class participates in this project, set up a debate using the information gathered in this text and the popular sources. Some students should take a strong pro position and others a strong con position. Discuss such things as the ethical, legal, interpersonal (quality of the couple's intimacy), and personal consequences of the option. As a class respond and vote on the preferred option. ✾

Someone once said that a new baby is total demand at one end and total irresponsibility at the other. If so, who would want one of those creatures around the house? Actually, most married people do, though most people want fewer children than did past generations of parents. In this chapter, we shall look at changing patterns of childbearing, why most people want children, and why some do not. We will examine the problem of infertility. We will see how people cope with involuntary childlessness or the loss of a child through death or spontaneous abortion. We will briefly discuss some of the relatively new technologies to help people who would have remained childless in the past.

Children have significant consequences for the quality of our lives. We will discuss those consequences, along with the somewhat different parenting experiences of men and women. Finally, we will explore the consequences of differing parenting styles for the well-being of children.

CHANGING PATTERNS OF CHILDBEARING

We saw in chapter 1 that the **birth rate** in the United States has declined considerably during this century. In fact, since the early 1970s, the birth rate has been below the **replacement level,** the rate necessary to keep the population stable. This assumes that there will be no increase because of immigration or a declining death rate. This is unlikely in the United States. In some European nations, however, the total population has declined because of birth rates lower than the replacement level.

Birth Rates

We pointed out in chapter 1 that the birth rate has fluctuated considerably (see figure 1.2). The rate declined dramatically from the mid-1950s to the mid-1970s, leveled off and increased somewhat in the late 1980s, then dropped again in the early 1990s. Since 1995, the rate has fluctuated very slightly between about 14 and 15 births per 1,000 population. A declining or lowered birth rate does not necessarily mean fewer total births. After 1975, the number of live births rose because of the rise in the number of women of childbearing age (the baby boomers). To some extent, the increased birth rate of the late 1980s resulted from increases among both white and black women ages 35 to 44 who had delayed childbearing (Haub 1992). But most of the increase occurred among women under the age of 30.

In general, birth rates are higher among the poor and minorities than among nonpoor whites. Comparing racial and ethnic groups, as figure 12.1 shows, Hispanics have

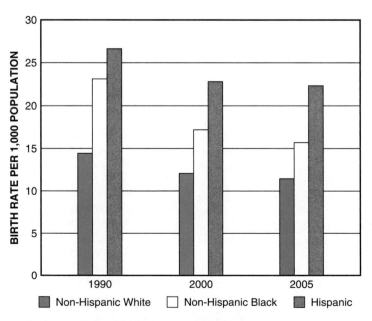

FIGURE 12.1 Birth Rates, 1990–2005
Source: U.S. Census Bureau 2008:78.

the highest rate, followed by African Americans and white Americans. The dramatic decline after the mid-1950s occurred in all the groups. Thus, while minority birth rates are higher than those of whites, all groups have lower rates than they did in the past. This is reflected in the declining proportion of families of all racial/ethnic groups with three or more children and the increasing proportion with no children (table 12.1). Uniformly, then, Americans are having fewer children.

Table 12.2 shows an overall profile of women who had children in 2006. Note that the birth rate is highest among Hispanics, those who are married, and those who are in the lower socioeconomic strata (as measured by level of income).

Preferences for Size and Sex

One thing that affects the birth rate is the preferred size of one's family, the ideal number of children. That ideal has changed over time. Since the 1930s, the Gallup Organization has periodically asked people about the ideal size of a family. In 1936, the first year of the survey, two-thirds of Americans said that three or more children is the ideal, and the mean number was 3.6. By 2007, 52 percent said

that two children is the ideal, and the mean preferred number was 2.5 (Carroll 2007). Those who said the ideal is three or more children varied by religious identification: 36 percent of Protestants, 34 percent of Catholics, and 21 percent of those with no religious affiliation preferred three or more children.

These changing preferences for family size are reflected in actual birth rates. According to the U.S. Census Bureau (2006), the proportion of women who ended their childbearing years with four or more children was 35.9 percent in 1976 but only 10.8 percent in 2004. At the other end of the scale, the proportion who had no children was 10.2 percent in 1976 and 19.3 percent in 2004.

Sex preference is also a factor in birth rates. In most nations, including the United States, if people could have only one child, more would prefer to have a boy than a girl. National data show that when there is a preference, it affects birth rates. People who prefer a boy, for instance, may have more children than they initially expected if their first one or two children are girls. Those who have more than one child are likely to want at least one of each sex. Thus, women with different-sex children are more likely to stop childbearing than women with same-sex

TABLE 12.1   Families, by Number of Own Children under 18 Years Old, 1970–2006

Year	Number (1,000)	Percent distribution			
		No children	One child	Two children	Three or more children
All Families					
1970	51,586	44	18	17	20
1980	59,550	48	21	19	12
1990	66,090	50	21	19	10
2006	77,402	53	20	18	9
White Families					
1970	42,261	45	18	18	19
1980	52,243	49	21	19	11
1990	56,590	53	20	18	9
2006	63,401	54	19	17	9
Black Families					
1970	4,887	39	18	15	29
1980	6,184	38	23	20	18
1990	7,470	41	25	19	14
2006	9,047	45	25	18	11
Asian Families					
2006	3,208	50	21	22	7
*Hispanic Families**					
1970	2,004	30	20	19	31
1980	3,029	31	22	23	23
1990	4,840	37	23	21	19
2006	9,862	38	23	22	17

*Hispanic persons may be of any race.
Source: U.S. Census Bureau 1994:64 and 2008:67.

TABLE 12.2 Social and Economic Characteristics of Women Who Gave Birth in 2006

Characteristic	Number of women (1,000)	Total births per 1,000 women
Total	61,683	67.0
Racial/Ethnic Group:		
White Non-Hispanic	38,532	61.8
Black	8,896	57.7
Asian	3,145	56.6
Hispanic*	9,141	82.2
Marital Status:		
Currently married		
(Husband present)	26,499	93.2
Widowed or divorced	4,920	26.2
Never married	27,730	44.3
Labor force status:		
Employed	39,961	51.4
Unemployed	2,728	61.2
Not in labor force	18,994	92.3
Family income:		
Under $10,000	3,878	86.9
$10,000 to $19,999	4,984	77.4
$20,000 to $24,999	2,903	76.8
$25,000 to $29,999	2,989	61.9
$30,000 to $34,999	3,236	62.4
$35,000 to $49,999	7,571	63.9
$50,000 to $74,999	10,724	65.7
$75,000 and over	15,421	61.5

*Hispanic persons may be of any race.
Source: U.S. Census Bureau 2008:89.

children, a tendency that is stronger for highly educated than for less-educated women (Yamaguchi and Ferguson 1995). In other words, if a couple has two children of the same sex, they may have a third child in the hope of having an opposite-sex offspring even though their ideal was two children.

TO BEAR OR NOT TO BEAR

Do you want to have children? Why or why not? Think about the matter a bit before you read the following materials. Reflect on how your own thoughts compare with those of others.

Why People Want to Have Children

As we pointed out in chapter 4, some people who have children do not want them, at least not at the time of conception. As many as 1 of every 10 children born each year is unwanted when he or she is conceived. On the other hand, the overwhelming number of people say they want to have children at some point in their lives. In the Gallup poll about ideal family size, only 1 percent said that the ideal is no children at all (Carroll 2007). The desire for children is so strong in many couples that both the husband and the wife may grieve for two years or more following a pregnancy loss (Stinson et al. 1992). The wife's grief is likely to be stronger and last longer than the husband's, however.

Children add to parents' sense of personal fulfillment.

Why do people want to have children? The reasons are many (Schoen et al. 1997). One or more of the following reasons may motivate a particular couple.

Experience of Happiness in a Family. If you grew up in a family that provided you with meaningful experiences, you are likely to want to have your own family. We all tend to try to recreate the situations that made us happy in the past. If you associate happiness with family life, therefore, you are likely to want your own family.

Personal Fulfillment. Having children may be perceived as adding not only to our happiness but also to our fulfillment as humans. Some people believe that the experience of having a child is unique, that it adds a dimension to life that is unparalleled by any other. Friends who have children may convey that impression to you. The mass media may reinforce it through stories of parents who find ultimate joy in the experience of childbirth.

The fulfillment, of course, comes not only at the time of birth but also through the child-rearing years. To love and be loved, to share in the growing child's delights of discovery and learning, and to shape the life of another are unique experiences that many people find personally fulfilling. A professional man, deeply involved in his career, said to us, "I can't conceive of my life without my children." Although he is very successful, he finds his children to be an indispensable part of his growth.

Personal and Family Legacy. Many if not most of us want to leave our imprint on the world in some way. In addition, there is a desire to carry on the family line. Frequently, these desires only awaken as you get older, but at some point you are likely to experience them. Children arc thc mcans of satisfying thosc desires. They are your personal legacy to humanity. And they are the extension of your family line.

The importance of family legacy is illustrated by the attorney who told us that she insisted on retaining her maiden name and wanted to have children with that name. "My parents had three girls," she said. "If I don't keep my maiden name and have children by that name, it will die out. And that would deeply hurt my father."

Personal Status. In some cultures, having children is a means of achieving high status in the community. Among the ancient Jews, for example, a woman was not considered fully human until she bore a son. In some contemporary societies, women still gain status by bearing children,

and men gain status (demonstrating their manhood) by fathering children.

For some Americans, having children is also an avenue to higher status. The enhanced status may come from family members, friends, or colleagues. After all, to both achieve in your work and fulfill the responsibilities of parenthood means that you are a very competent person.

Religious Beliefs. Those who identify with an organized religion are more likely to want children than those who do not. Most religions are strongly profamily. Some religions, such as Roman Catholicism and Mormonism, stress theological reasons for people having large families. A couple strongly committed to such a religious faith may feel that they are fulfilling the will of God by having not merely one but many children.

Social Expectations. When we ask why people "want" children, we need to recognize that there are some who have children without necessarily either wanting or not wanting them. That is, they do not think much about the matter in such terms. They believe that everyone who is married should have children as a matter of course because that is normal and typical. In our society, there are in fact many pressures, some subtle and some not-so-subtle, for married people to have children.

While the expectations are changing somewhat, it is still true that married people are expected to have children. No couple, after all, has to explain why they decided to have a baby. But explanations are usually in order if a couple decides not to have children. Moreover, a couple that announces a forthcoming child is likely to be greeted with smiles and congratulations. A couple that declares their intention to remain child-free is likely to be greeted with quizzical looks and perhaps frowns.

There is, then, a certain amount of stigma attached to married couples who opt to remain child-free (Park 2003). In fact, when 274 undergraduate students read descriptions of couples, they rated the childless in less-positive terms regardless of the reasons for the childlessness (Lamastro 2001)!

The Child-Free Option

In spite of all the reasons for having children, and in spite of the fact that the great bulk of Americans say the ideal is to have one or more children, increasing numbers of couples have opted to be child-free. There is an interesting sex difference in attitudes about childlessness, however: Women are more likely than men to have positive attitudes (Koropeckyj-Cox and Pendell 2007). And the gap between men's and women's attitudes is greater at higher educational levels. The increasingly positive stance of women at higher educational levels is reflected in birth rates. Among women aged 40 to 44 years in 2004, 17 percent of those with a high school education and 24 percent of those with a college degree were childless (Biddlecom and Martin 2006). In addition to education, women who remain childless tend to have higher incomes, work experience, and lower religiosity (Abma and Martinez 2006).

Still, the choice is not an easy one for most people. One well-educated woman told us, "I have agonized more and cried more about this decision than any I have ever made." But just as there are many reasons why people want to have children, there are also many reasons why they decide to remain child-free. For any particular couple, the reasons are likely to include one or more of the following.

Personal Fulfillment.   Not everyone believes that fulfillment comes best through children. Not everyone believes that being childless will leave you lonely and depressed in old age. Indeed, childlessness per se does not make elderly people more lonely or depressed than they would be if they had children (Zhang and Hayward 2001). Many people find fulfillment through their children. Others opt to remain child-free in order that they may find fulfillment through their work, their interests, and/or their adult relationships. Children require time and energy that they prefer to put into other pursuits, those they believe more likely to yield personal satisfaction and growth.

Focus on Career.   People strongly committed to a career, and particularly the dual-career couple, may prefer to remain child-free. As we noted in the last chapter, dual-career couples face some difficult questions when they decide to have children. For some, the questions themselves are reason enough not to have children. Neither the husband nor the wife may be willing to use time and energy for child-rearing tasks.

As this suggests, women who are not career oriented and those who tend to agree that women should take care of the home and that men should be breadwinners are more likely to become mothers and to have more than one child.

Economic Costs of Children.   In addition to time and energy, children cost a great deal of money. Some people feel that the costs are not worth the benefits, that the economic costs will outweigh whatever satisfactions they gain from becoming parents. The U.S. Department of

Agriculture estimates the cost of raising children. In 2007, the Department estimated that the cost for a couple in the middle range of income to raise a child from birth through age 17 would be $197,700 (the cost would vary by where the child lives, what kind of school the child would attend, etc.) (Lino 2007).

There are indirect as well as direct costs. Consider the fact that children may narrow the range of economic opportunities parents have. Women in particular may have to make career compromises if they have children. Men, too, may be constrained in their careers if, for example, a move that would mean career advancement must be deferred because of children's school needs. For example, a child may be one year away from graduating from a primary or secondary school. Or a child may be in a program that is unavailable in the new area. Such opportunity costs are economic as well as personal; the family may lose a considerable amount of potential income.

The costs continue, of course, at least until the children have finished their education. For those who expect their children to get a college education, the costs go up considerably. Taking all the costs—both direct and indirect—into consideration, how much does a child require? One estimate is that the total cost of a middle-class child born in the late 1990s will be $1,455,581 (Longman 1998)!

Focus on the Marriage.   Some people feel that children will detract from the marital relationship, and they prefer to focus their energies on that relationship (Ramu and Tavuchis 1986). Those in child-free marriages talk about the freedom they have and the continuing romance and sex in their relationships. They feel that they are able to spend more time together and develop a more intimate relationship than would be possible with children. Joan, an artist in her 40s, expresses her feelings this way:

> My husband and I have talked about having children many times. But we realized that we were talking about this because other people expected us to have children as much as from our own desires. I guess I would like to have children eventually, but we both have careers and we cherish our marriage. I don't want to sacrifice my marriage to the children. I've seen other people do that. We won't. Our relationship means too much to us.

Doubts About Parenting Skills.   Clearly, not everyone makes a good parent. Good parenting requires certain skills, and some people question whether they have those skills. They feel that they do not want to be parents unless they can do a good job, and they're not sure

Personal

To Be a Parent? The Agonies of the Decision

Lori and Ben are in their late 20s. She is a graduate student in biology, and he is a practicing engineer. Lori talks about their struggle with the question of whether to have children. As with many couples, it has not been a settled question for them. Through their years together, they have both changed in their attitudes. And although they seem to be in agreement now, the issue continues to trouble them:

I think that both of us would like to have children once I'm finished with school and have gotten my career started. We've made a decision to wait until then. And we think we might have two children. It is interesting that our attitudes have changed over the years. Ben absolutely did *not* want children when we were first married. But I assumed that we would have them anyway after three or four years. I

thought he would probably change his mind.

But as I progressed in college and became more career-oriented, my attitude changed and became like his. I decided that I preferred to pursue my career and not get involved with the hassles of a family. However, by then Ben had changed. He had gotten much more warm-hearted and affectionate with children. When we were first married, he had a kind of dread of them. He felt they were too much responsibility and too much of a burden. I always had a more tender feeling about children, but now I've gotten to feel somewhat more fearful of the vast responsibility that's involved. Maybe that's because we've both finally come to a point where we agree that we will have children. But I'm not sure how it's going to work out with both of us pursuing careers.

Anyway, something really interesting happened this past week. I've always religiously taken my birth-control pills. We've been very responsible. We didn't want any unplanned pregnancy. But a few days ago I accidentally dropped my pill between the kitchen counter and the stove. I got Ben to move the stove away from the wall so I could retrieve it. But we couldn't find it. I would have joyfully popped that peach-colored pill into my mouth even though it had fallen into a thick layer of dust. But it was lost.

I realized that my panic over losing the pill showed that I'm not ready yet for motherhood. I expect to feel differently in a few years. I really do want to have children. And Ben says he is now definitely ready. Life is sure complicated, isn't it?

they can cope with the demands of parenting. As a graduate student put it, "I would love to be a mother, but I don't think I have the patience to deal with children. I just don't think I would be a good enough mother." Her desire to mother was not stronger than her doubts about her skills, so she opted to remain child-free.

INVOLUNTARY CHILDLESSNESS

If this were a perfect world, those who wanted children would have them, and those who didn't would not. But just as there are a substantial number of unwanted pregnancies, there are a substantial number of people who want children but who cannot bear their own.

Infertility

Infertility is usually defined as the inability to conceive after a year of unprotected sexual intercourse. Infertility does not mean that a couple has no children. Sometimes

people have one or more children, desire still more, but are unable for various reasons to conceive again.

As many as one of every six couples may be affected by infertility (Peterson, Gold, and Feingold 2007). This means that millions of U.S. couples and U.S. women who want to have a first or an additional child cannot do so. Some are able to bear with medical assistance. Others remain infertile.

What causes infertility? Numerous factors are involved. Sustained exposure to environmental factors, such as toxic chemicals, can render an individual sterile. Sexually transmitted diseases can damage a woman's fallopian tubes. Infections from intrauterine contraceptive devices have made some women infertile. Both men and women can suffer from infertility. Let us look briefly at the more common types.

Female infertility can be due to **endometriosis,** a disease in which the tissue that lines the inside of the uterus begins to grow outside as well. The growth may prevent the sperm from meeting the egg in the fallopian tubes.

The causes of endometriosis are unknown. It tends to affect women in their 20s and 30s who have not had children. It can frequently be corrected by drugs or surgery.

Various other conditions also can cause blockage of the fallopian tubes, thus preventing conception. Scar tissue from inflammations is a common cause of blocked tubes. The blockage sometimes can be removed through surgery.

A third reason that a woman may be infertile is that she doesn't **ovulate** properly; that is, her body does not release the egg as it should. Drugs may correct this situation.

Finally, a woman's body, for various reasons, may hinder the sperm or even kill it. Again, drug therapy may be effective in resolving the problem. Or the couple may be able to make use of some of the new technologies available.

Male infertility is somewhat less common than female but also may arise from a number of different factors. Males are infertile generally because they have a low sperm count or because their sperm do not swim as fast as they should. Low sperm counts may result from injury, infection (particularly from having mumps after childhood), exposure to radiation, birth defects, or a variety of other disorders (Masters, Johnson, and Kolodny 1988). Sperm production also may be decreased by alcohol and drug use, including some prescription drugs. Finally, environmental pollutants may depress sperm count. Some or all of these factors are probably involved in a substantial drop in sperm counts in the United States and Europe since the 1930s (Schulte 1997). Male infertility sometimes can be treated through drugs or surgery.

Coping with Infertility

If you strongly desire to have a child but are unable to conceive after a year or more of unprotected sexual relations, you may find yourself struggling to cope with this unexpected situation. Most of us believe that if we want to have children, we can. When we want to and find that we cannot, we are likely to be quite distressed (McQuillan et al. 2003).

Infertility, in other words, is not merely a biological condition. It deeply affects people. Among other things, a couple unable to conceive may experience lowered self-esteem, anxiety, depression, sexual problems, and questions about their identity and the meaning of their lives (Gonzalez 2000; Daniluk 2001; Peterson, Gold, and Feingold 2007). In fact, those unable to conceive may experience a process of grief similar to that endured when a loved one dies (Deveraux and Hammerman 1998).

Technology has opened up many new options for those who are infertile.

The first stage of the process is *surprise.* People simply do not expect to be infertile, particularly those who are achievement oriented and think of themselves as capable of dealing adequately with the obstacles of life. Surprise is followed by *denial,* a sense that "this can't happen to me." Then there is *anger,* anger because of the pain and inconvenience of the tests, anger at the pressures from family and friends, anger at the inappropriate comments of people, and perhaps anger at those who seem to have children easily or those who have them but don't want them.

Guilt is the fourth stage. Some people may feel that God is punishing them for their sins. Some find other ways to blame themselves for the condition. *Depression* is a typical fifth part of the process. There is a sense of loss, a sadness, perhaps even a sense of despair. Associated with the sense of loss is *grief.* Those who are infertile grieve because they cannot produce another living being, in a way that people grieve when they lose a living being. Unfortunately, while those who lose someone through death are expected to grieve openly, that may be more difficult for the infertile. After all, their loss is not of an actual but only a potential person. As such, it may not be viewed as a real and significant loss by many people.

The final stage of the process is *resolution.* A couple may resolve its situation in a number of ways. Some may accept the fact that they will not have children and get on with their lives. Most will probably first attempt various other ways to have a child. As we shall see in the sections that follow, however, using new technologies or going the route of adoption can be very expensive and frustrating. Many couples do not fully resolve their infertility for years. Those with a strong relationship will ultimately be strengthened for having worked through the crisis; those with weak bonds may break up.

OPTIONS FOR THE INFERTILE

Those who are infertile and who want children or more children than they already have can choose from a variety of options. In the mid-1990s, about 15 percent of the women of reproductive age had used some kind of infertility service, including medical advice, tests, drugs, surgery, or other kinds of treatment (Abma et al. 1997). The services can be very expensive, running into tens of thousands of dollars for some couples.

Artificial Insemination

Artificial insemination is the injection of sperm into a woman's reproductive tract. To result in conception, of course, the procedure must be carried out at the time the woman is ovulating (releasing an egg). Artificial insemination uses either the husband's semen (abbreviated AIH) or that of an anonymous donor (abbreviated AID).

AIH is useful when the husband's sperm count is low. The physician can take a larger amount of sperm from several ejaculations. AIH also can be done using fresh semen and inserting it into the vagina at the mouth of the uterus. Only a small portion of the sperm get to that location during intercourse, so the chances of conception are enhanced by the AIH procedure.

If the husband is sterile or his sperm count is exceptionally low, AID may be used (this is also an option for single women and for lesbian couples who want a child). The couple will normally select a donor from an anonymous list that gives information about health, intelligence, and various physical characteristics. If fresh semen is used, the pregnancy rate with AID is about 75 percent; the rate is around 60 percent when frozen semen from a sperm bank is used (Masters, Johnson, and Kolodny 1988:146).

AID is less acceptable to people than AIH. Some religions view the procedure as morally wrong. Even the courts have occasionally defined it as adultery. Some men feel humiliated; some women are reluctant to have another man be the biological father of their children. One way that a couple may minimize potential problems is to have the physician mix the sperm of the husband with that of a donor so that the couple can't be sure who the natural father is. Generally, however, men whose wives conceive by AID assume the father's role with enthusiasm.

In Vitro Fertilization

If the infertility is due to damaged or blocked fallopian tubes and the condition cannot be corrected, the couple may opt for **in vitro fertilization.** In this procedure, the eggs are removed from the woman's body. Fertility drugs may be used to facilitate the development of healthy eggs and to control the timing of ovulation (Sher et al. 1995). The use of the drugs poses a number of risks, including the possibility of multiple fetuses, various side effects, and ovarian tumors and cancer (National Cancer Institute 1998). The issue of ovarian cancer is debatable, however, because the research is still inconclusive.

Once the eggs are removed from the woman's body, they are fertilized with sperm in a laboratory. The resulting embryo is then implanted in the woman's uterus.

The first case of in vitro fertilization leading to pregnancy and birth of a child occurred in England. In 1978, Louise Brown was born as a result of the work of Doctors Patrick Steptoe and Robert Edwards. The Brown baby was the first success after more than a decade of research and more than 30 failed attempts.

Since 1978, fertility clinics have opened up around the world. Of the tens of thousands of women who have tried to conceive through in vitro fertilization, how many have succeeded? The clinics have varying success rates, but probably average around 20 percent. The success rate depends in part upon a woman's age. For those under the age of 35 years, the success rate is 32 percent, while those aged 40 years and more have a success rate of only 8 percent (Vastag 2001). However, if a woman opts for a donor egg rather than her own, the success rate is around 40 percent regardless of her age.

The risks associated with in vitro fertilization go beyond the possibility of failure, however. Medical researchers who compared infants conceived naturally with those conceived through in vitro fertilization reported that major birth defects occurred twice as often among the latter group (9.0 percent vs. 4.2 percent of the babies; Hansen et al. 2002).

Some people are opposed to in vitro fertilization on the grounds that it violates God's way or the "natural" way. Some people also are disturbed by the fact that clinics normally fertilize a number of eggs. The first step in the procedure is to give the woman daily hormone injections to stimulate egg production. Thus, the woman produces a number of eggs, and each is fertilized. Extra fertilized eggs may be discarded (in some the cells are not dividing normally anyway). To some people, this is the same as abortion—in other words, they see it as a form of murder because they regard the fertilized egg as a human.

For other people, however, procedures such as in vitro fertilization mean that they have the opportunity to become parents. Without the procedure, they would not have children of their own. To deny them the use of the procedure is to deny them the opportunity to have biologically related children.

Surrogate Mothers

When the wife is infertile or incapable of carrying a child, a couple may opt for a surrogate mother (Ciccarelli and Beckman 2005). The surrogate mother is a woman who volunteers to carry the baby of the couple and give the infant to them at the time of birth. The arrangement is typically arranged through a legal contract. The total cost can range from $25,000 to $100,000. Nearly all the women identified by researchers as surrogate mothers have a child or children of their own, and most are married or with a partner. They tend to view the arrangement not as a way to earn money, but as a way to give the gift of parenthood to those who would otherwise be deprived of that experience.

The surrogate mother may be inseminated with the husband's sperm or, if the husband is also infertile, with the sperm of a donor. If the wife still has functioning ovaries, she can provide an egg, use in vitro fertilization, and have the resulting embryo implanted in the surrogate mother.

As with all the possibilities discussed in this section, the option of a surrogate mother is controversial. In part, each option may present problems because technology has become available before legal and ethical guidelines have been developed to deal with various complications. Two cases during the 1980s illustrate some of the complex and painful problems involved with surrogate motherhood.

The first case occurred in 1983. A Michigan woman gave birth to a deformed baby. A New York man had contracted with her to have a child by AID but rejected it when he discovered it was deformed. He believed that he had firm legal grounds for the rejection because he was not the child's biological father. The surrogate mother didn't want the child, either. Newspaper headlines pointed out that the nation now had an "unclaimed" infant. Eventually, the surrogate mother agreed to keep the child. Future cases may be more difficult if both parties are adamant in their refusal to accept such a child.

The second case occurred in 1986 after Mary Beth Whitehead of New Jersey gave birth to "Baby M." She had contracted with a couple to act as a surrogate mother and had been inseminated with the sperm of the husband. After the girl was born, Whitehead didn't want to give her up. She felt she had a right to keep the child because she was the biological mother. She and her husband fled with the girl to Florida. Ultimately, a New Jersey court awarded the girl to the couple who had contracted for her, honoring the biological father's rights and arguing that Whitehead must honor the contract she had signed.

Adoption

Adoption offers another option to the infertile. About 2.1 million children, or 2.5 percent of all children of householders, are adopted (Kreider 2003). Because of the cost of adoption, adopted children live in homes with a higher-than-average median income. Three percent of households with adopted children have three or more adopted children and another 15 percent have two adopted children. Figure 12.2 shows the race and Hispanic origin of adopted children.

There are not enough U.S. children to supply the demand. An increasing number of adopted children are foreign-born. According to a national survey conducted by the Census Bureau, 13 percent of adopted children are foreign-born, with nearly half born in Asia (Kreider 2003). The largest number come from Korea, which accounts for a little more than a fifth of all foreign-born adopted children.

Gay and lesbian as well as heterosexual couples are interested in adopting children (Padgett 2007). Americans are about evenly divided on the issue of whether such couples should be allowed to adopt. As of this writing, ten states allow such adoptions even though they do not allow same-sex marriages. One of the objections is that all children should have both a mother and a father in the home while growing up. However, a

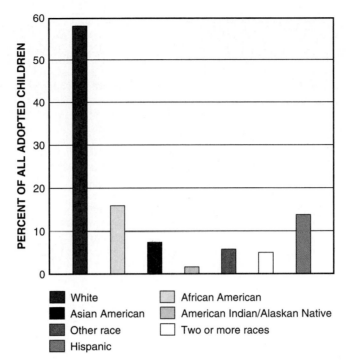

FIGURE 12.2   Race and Hispanic Origin of Adopted Children

Source: Kreider 2003.

study of lesbian mothers found that the women had decided even before their children were born that they wanted some kind of male involvement with the children (Goldberg and Allen 2007). Children adopted by a gay or lesbian couple, then, are not necessarily prevented from having both sexes involved in their lives, any more than the large number of children of single mothers necessarily lack adult males in their lives.

Children may be adopted either through an agency or through a private adoption. Governmental agencies are the least expensive way to adopt a child, because the adoptive parents only pay the legal fees involved. But their requirements are very strict, the time involved is long (usually a minimum of nine months, and it may stretch into years), and the number of children available is small. Private agencies can handle the matter in less time, but they are more expensive.

Instead of going through an agency, some people attempt a private adoption, through either a physician or a lawyer who specializes in private adoptions. Those who use the services of a lawyer may engage in what is called an *open adoption,* which became fairly common in the 1980s. Open adoptions are in sharp contrast to the secretive processes of the past. If you adopted a child through

an agency in past years, you would not know the biological parents, and they would not know you. The secrecy would, in theory, protect the child, the adoptive parents, and the biological parents. The mother, who was frequently unwed, would not have to bear the stigma of having a child without a husband, and she could get on with her life. The adoptive parents would not have to worry about the mother wanting to have a close relationship with her child at some point in the future. And the child would not be caught between the two sets of parents.

But the secretive procedures so common in the past overlooked one important fact: Adopted children generally get to a point at which they want to know about their biological parents. In fact, some adopted adolescents become preoccupied with the fact of their adoption, leading to a certain amount of alienation from the adoptive parents (Kohler, Grotevant, and McRoy 2002). Children also may grieve the loss of their natural parents and suffer from depression and low self-esteem (Smith and Brodzinsky 2002).

In the long run, adopted children function as well as those raised by their natural parents (Borders, Penny, and Portnoy 2000; van Ijzendoorn, Juffer, and Poelhuis

What Do You Think?

*There is disagreement about **whether spanking is a useful form of discipline for young children.** What follows are pro and con arguments. What do you think?*

Pro

Spanking is a useful form of discipline for young children because

- parents cannot reason with them at such an early age.
- it does no physical harm while teaching them that there are consequences for behavior.
- it increases their respect for parental authority.
- it is often the only way to teach them to avoid doing dangerous things.
- it is a way for parents to say, "I care about you and about the kind of person you become."

Con

Spanking is not a useful form of discipline for young children because

- it leads children to accept violence.
- those who are spanked are more likely than others to become physically abusive.
- it makes parents into people of power rather than of love.
- it punishes rather than teaches.
- it generates feelings of shame, guilt, and worthlessness.

2005). In fact, adopted children tend to have an advantage in that the couples who adopt generally are in the higher socioeconomic classes and invest more resources into the children's lives (perhaps to compensate the children for their lack of biological parents) (Hamilton, Cheng, and Powell 2007).

Adopted children are likely to go through a phase during which the fact of their adoption and the desire to know or know about their natural parents is an intense concern. They may even insist on their right to have information about their genetic heritage. In many cases, they have won the right to such information and have helped to change the laws. Adopted children who have a reunion with their biological parents and other birth relatives may or may not want to have a close relationship with them (Gladstone and Westhues 1998). But that does not affect either their desire or their right to know their biological family.

An open adoption avoids the problem of the adopted child's desire to know about his or her genetic heritage. The open adoption may involve anything from a minimal exchange of information to extensive contact with the birth mother both before and after the child is born (Grotevant et al. 1994). The following case illustrates extensive contact.

Sandra is a young woman who became pregnant while unmarried. She did not want to have an abortion, but she was financially and emotionally unable to care for a baby. She contacted a lawyer who specialized in open adoptions. The Smiths, a couple in their late 30s, were unable to have children but badly wanted them. They had contacted the same lawyer. The lawyer gave Sandra eight biographies of couples who wanted to adopt; the Smiths were one of the eight.

Sandra was three months pregnant at the time. She selected the Smiths. The lawyer then arranged for a meeting between Sandra and the Smiths. Sandra felt that she had made the right choice. Thereafter, the Smiths and Sandra met on a weekly basis. The Smiths went with Sandra to her Lamaze classes and were present at the birth. The boy is now about 6 months old. Sandra and the Smiths are friends. The Smiths will tell their son about his mother when he is older. He will have the opportunity to meet her and interact with her. At this point, they are negotiating about the amount of time that Sandra will spend with the boy.

The adoption cost about the same as one through a private agency. Both Sandra and the Smiths are quite happy with the arrangement. This is not to say that there will be no problems in the future, but open adoptions seem to work well for many people. Most couples studied in open adoption situations report being satisfied and confident that the birth mother will not try to reclaim her child (Grotevant et al. 1994).

CHILDREN AND THE QUALITY OF LIFE

The reasons given previously for why people want to have children imply that the children will enhance people's quality of life. What does the evidence say?

The Stresses of Raising Children

Clearly, raising children is a demanding and sometimes agonizing task (Bird 1997). Stress, in the form of emotional and physical strain and tension, will be experienced by all parents at some time and by a few a good deal of the time. A study of adolescent mothers of preschool children found that about 30 percent of the mothers reported high levels of stress at one or more of six measurement points over a 2½-year period (Larson 2004). The stress level may vary by gender. A study of 90 Israeli couples noted that the mothers had significantly higher levels of negative emotions related to parenting than did the fathers (Scher and Sharabany 2005). However, while mothers may have higher levels, fathers also experience the stress of child-rearing and the associated emotional consequences such as depression (Bronte-Tinkew, Moore, Matthews, and Carrano 2007).

Further evidence of the stress of parenting is seen in the numerous support groups that have been developed to help parents. Support groups are needed because there is very little formal training available for the task,

even though most people agree that raising a child is one of the most important and challenging jobs that one ever undertakes.

Support groups are available to help at virtually every stage of parenting. Both national and local groups exist. Depending on the area where you live, you can find groups that deal with parenting generally or specific aspects of parenting. For example, the La Leche League offers women an opportunity to meet to learn about breast feeding and to share practical mothering tips. Children are viewed as assets, and the purpose is to enhance the quality of mothering. There are other groups that focus on positive methods of discipline. Toughlove is a support group that provides support to those who have problems with adolescents. Parent education classes also are available in local school districts. They furnish aid in such matters as sex education, communication skills, and helping the child in school. Parents Without Partners is a support group for single parents. Parents Anonymous offers help to those who abuse or who fear they are about to abuse their children. Various other groups offer specialized help and support to those suffering from depression after delivery, to parents of multiples, to parents of hyperactive children, and to parents of children with learning disabilities.

The stresses of child rearing may begin as soon as the infant is brought home. Most people respond to a baby

Parenting is stressful as well as gratifying.

with tenderness, but babies can evoke frustration as well—frustration that affects both mothers and fathers (Barnett, Brennan, and Marshall 1994). For one thing, a good many infants have "cry-fuss" and sleep problems during the first two years (Wake et al. 2006). But such problems are only a part of the challenges new parents face. A study of over 100 mothers and fathers of infants three to five months old found a number of sources of stress (Ventura 1987). About a third of the mothers and two-thirds of the fathers described stresses that resulted from their multiple-role demands (the typical problems of the dual-income family). The effort to meet adequately the demands of work, marriage, and children can be exhausting.

The care of the infant is also stressful:

> The infant's fussy behavior in relation to feeding or soothing techniques was the major stress reported by 35 percent of mothers and 20 percent of fathers (Ventura 1987:27).

Mothers said they often felt guilty, helpless, or angry when trying to care for a fussy infant. Fathers felt stress because they didn't know what to do when the infant would not sleep or respond to their attempts to soothe it. Some of the subjects (14 percent of mothers and 11 percent of fathers) also reported being stressed with each other. They had increased marital conflict and less frequent sexual relations and felt a lack of support from each other since the arrival of the baby.

As the infant grows, there are always "daily hassles" that are stressful to parents (Crnic and Booth 1991). For example, a group of parents of 5-year-olds noted such things as continually cleaning up kids' messes; nagging, whining, or complaining by the children; kids not listening and not obeying without being nagged; kids interrupting adult conversation or interaction; and struggles over going to bed at night (Crnic and Greenberg 1990).

The bulk of parents agree that the teen years are the most difficult of all. But parenting stress can occur at any age. A five-year study of 2,500 Massachusetts women

Systems Theory Applied

reported that 39 percent identified children as their primary source of stress (Mehren 1988). The stress can get intense when the marriage itself is troubled and one parent enlists a child into a coalition against the other parent. This situation, called *triangulation* by *systems theorists,* only increases the problems of the family and may require therapy in order to help both the child and the marriage (Broderick 1993).

The stress of parenting does not necessarily cease when the children are grown. For instance, when adult children have serious problems in their lives, their parents are likely to experience lowered personal and relational well-being (Greenfield and Marks 2006). And having an adult child return to live in the home can be more stressful than having a child leave home (Lauer and Lauer 1999b).

The return home of an adult child raises such issues as control (do the parents have any control over the child's schedule, activities, etc.?), division of labor (is the child obligated to help around the house?), differing preferences (which TV program to watch?), and privacy (as one woman said, "We're back to having sex when our son is asleep or out, which isn't very often.").

Children and Marital Satisfaction

Are children, then, hazardous to marriage? Do they inevitably detract from the quality of the marital relationship? We know that first-born children tend to increase the stability of marriages through their preschool years (Waite and Lillard 1991). But does that mean that the marriage is still as satisfying as it was or just that the parents are "hanging in there" for the sake of the children?

Many studies have confirmed the conclusion of Lewis and Spanier (1979) that marital satisfaction declines during the child-rearing years (Twenge, Campbell, and Foster 2003). The decline in satisfaction is most pronounced among parents of infants. Also, the more children a couple has, the greater decline the parents are likely to experience.

On the other hand, a decline is not inevitable. Children provide the couple with satisfactions that can balance or override the problems associated with parenting (Tseng et al. 2003). Thus, Belsky and Kelly (1994) studied 250 new parents during their first postbaby year and found four different patterns: For slightly less than 13 percent, marital satisfaction declined severely; 38 percent experienced a moderate decline; 30 percent reported no change; and 19 percent experienced an improvement. Those with improved marital satisfaction are likely to be more educated, be married longer, and have higher levels of income (Belsky and Rovine 1990).

Conflict Theory Applied

When Belsky and Kelly (1994) sought to identify the cause of decline that occurred in roughly half of the couples, they found the problem was not rooted in stress related to the baby's behavior. Rather, two things are involved in the decline.

The first is the fact that the baby brings typical male–female differences into focus. We have seen that men and women generally have a certain number of *diverse and even contradictory ways of feeling and thinking*. These differences can come into sharp focus when parents are confronted with the important and demanding task of caring for a baby.

The second factor involved in the decline is that some of the mechanisms that the parents had previously used to deal with their differences are no longer available to them. For example, disagreement about whose career was more important was previously dealt with by simply not talking about it. When the baby comes, the disagreement can no longer be avoided because at least one of the parents may have to put his or her career on the "parent-track." Similarly, differences about the division of labor in the home may have been averted by hiring a housekeeper. When the baby comes, there may be insufficient income for a housekeeper and the couple must confront their differences and work them out so that there is a sense of equity. Thus, wives whose husbands are more involved in the child-rearing tasks are also more satisfied with their marriages (Kalmijn 1999; Grote, Clark, and Moore 2004).

But there are other factors involved in the decline in marital satisfaction. Being too tired for sexual relations is a common problem among parents during the first six months or more after birth (Ahlborg, Dahloof, and Hallberg 2005). And couples who kept diaries of their time use before and after the birth of a child reported changes in relational patterns that affected their satisfaction (Monk et al. 1996). The mothers were more likely than the fathers to feel less satisfied with the marriage, mainly because they had so little time to themselves. The fathers were more likely to feel depression than lower satisfaction, mainly because they had less time alone with their wives.

Some babies, of course, are easier to care for than others. Some children seem to be easier to rear than others. The greater the stress of parenting, whatever the age of the children, the more likely the parents feel diminished well-being both personally and in their marriage (Lavee, Sharlin, and Katz 1996).

In sum, there is a tendency for marital satisfaction to decline somewhat after children are born and throughout the child-rearing years, a tendency that holds true not only for whites but also for racial and ethnic minorities such as African Americans (Crohan 1996).

We will comment further about marital satisfaction and children in the next chapter, but four points should be made here about those couples who experience a decline in marital satisfaction after the birth of a child.

First, most research has shown that not only couples with children but also couples generally report a decline in marital satisfaction during the first two decades (McHale and Huston 1985). A study of changes in 98 couples over the first two and a half years of marriage reported that both the parents and the childless couples tended to report a decline in feelings of love, marital satisfaction, shared activities, and frequency of positive interaction with each other (MacDermid, Huston, and McHale 1990).

Second, to say that satisfaction is lower is not to say that people are dissatisfied. After all, satisfaction is at a peak in the first flush of marriage. If it changes at all, it is most likely to go down. But it does not go down to the point of dissatisfaction for the majority of couples.

Third, at least some of the couples who experience a decline were already having serious problems before the baby came. When an unhappy couple has a child, however, they are less likely to get divorced in the next few years (White, Booth, and Edwards 1986). For at least some couples, then, the transition to parenthood does not mean that a happy marriage becomes an unhappy one, but that an unhappy marriage becomes even more unhappy.

Finally, in some cases marital satisfaction actually goes up after the couple has children. And in the long run, children are likely to contribute to the stability and satisfaction a couple experience. In her study of marriages of 50-plus years, Alford-Cooper (1998:78) reported that 57 percent of the couples said that their children contributed to the success of their unions, and most of the couples "regarded child rearing as one of the happiest, most meaningful experiences of their lives."

The Satisfactions of Raising Children

In spite of the problems and the stresses, most people continue to want children. And the great majority of those who are parents indicate that the experience has given them great satisfaction. This happens even when the parents lack some of the resources we would all prefer to have. Thus, a study of 60 African American mothers with lower-than-average income and education found that they enjoyed being parents and that they were perceived by themselves and their children to be successfully fulfilling their roles (Strom et al. 1990). And a study that compared biological parents, adoptive parents, and stepparents found among all three groups of parents less depression after the child came into their lives (Ceballo et al. 2004).

In a review of the research literature, Ann Goetting (1986) drew a number of conclusions, including the following:

- Generally, satisfaction with the parental role is very high.
- Women report more fulfillment as parents than do men, but they also see parenthood as more burdensome and restrictive.
- Women are more satisfied with parenthood when they also are able to fulfill whatever aspirations for work or career they have.
- Maternal satisfaction is higher to the extent that the woman has the social support of friends.

Recent research shows that these findings are still valid. For example, a national study reported that almost 81 percent said they are very satisfied with their lives as mothers and another 16 percent said they are somewhat satisfied (Erickson and Aird 2005). The women also expressed satisfaction with the amount of responsibility they have for their children and with the amount of emotional support they get. The women did recognize that parenting involves stress and concern for the future, but more than 93 percent said that they experience a love for their children that is unlike any other love they have known in their lives.

The extent to which the bearing and caring of children is satisfying depends on a number of factors. A couple who wants and plans for the child is likely to be more satisfied afterward than one for whom the child is unplanned and/or unwanted. Couples who have a good relationship, including meaningful communication and satisfying experiences of love and affection, are more likely to maintain high marital quality and also to have higher levels of parenting satisfaction (Harriman 1986; Rogers and White 1998). Finally, both marital and parental satisfaction are likely to be higher when the father is more involved with the baby (Goldberg, Michaels, and Lamb 1985; Levy-Skiff 1994).

What about the satisfaction of raising adopted children? The evidence is somewhat mixed. In some cases, such as for those who adopted neglected infants from Eastern European countries, the stress of parenting has been severe. The children often exhibited behavioral problems that did not cease after being with their adopted parents in a loving home (Talbot 1998; Mainemer, Gilman, and Ames 1998). Still, the majority of children adopted from other nations turn out to be well-adjusted, although they are referred more often than others to mental health services (Juffer and van Ijzendoorn 2005).

For other situations, the research is sparse and the evidence is not consistent. Drawing on national data, but having only 72 adopted children and their adoptive parents in the sample, three researchers found no significant differences between the adopted children and parents and a matched set of biological children and parents on such things as the parents' well-being, parental attitudes toward family life, frequency of the need for discipline, and parental views of the children's adjustment (Borders, Black, and Pasley 1998).

In contrast, many earlier studies have found a higher rate of both emotional and behavioral problems among adopted children (see, e.g., Brodzinsky et al. 1984; Kotsopoulous et al. 1988). More recently, Feigelman (1997) used national data to compare 101 adoptees with those raised in disrupted homes and those raised by both biological parents. Both the adopted children and those from disrupted homes had more problem behaviors during adolescence than did those raised by both biological parents. However, by adulthood, the adoptees were similar to those raised by both biological parents in terms of such things as educational attainment, occupation, and marital stability.

While the issue is important to those millions of couples who are infertile, then, we cannot say with certainty whether adopting a child will be as satisfying an experience as having your own child. Clearly, there are both risks and potential rewards whatever you do.

In sum, while couples are likely to experience some decline in marital satisfaction during the childbearing years, that does not mean that they are dissatisfied with their marriages. Moreover, the amount of decline that occurs depends on a number of factors, including the quality of their relationships before the bearing of children. And the satisfactions of parenting seem, for most people, to outweigh the stresses and problems.

PARENTING: HER EXPERIENCE AND HIS EXPERIENCE

As we have noted, mothers perceive the experience of parenting as more demanding, more constricting, but also more rewarding than do fathers. That suggests that mothers and fathers have somewhat different experiences of being parents.

Her Experience

"M is for the million things she gave me" begins a parody of an old song about mother. For many mothers, it seems that there are indeed a million things to give. There are also a million things to do. Motherhood is above all a consuming experience. Mothers are expected to be the primary caregivers in our society, even if they are working full-time outside the home (Wilson et al. 1990). Fathers may come and go, but mothers are expected to nurture their children nearly every day, year in and year out.

There is, in fact, an assumption by many people that mothers are far better equipped than fathers to care for the physical and emotional needs of children. "There is something special about mothers," a man told us as he reflected on his own experiences. "They relate to you in a way that no one else in the world ever does." That may be true. Indeed, mothers make a unique contribution to our well-being. In general, mothers are more involved in both getting and giving support, particularly emotional support, than are fathers (Marks and McLanahan 1993). But fathers also make important contributions. It is not fair to women to make them feel that their children will suffer greatly if they are not incessantly there to care for their children's needs.

Nevertheless, it is mothers who give a disproportionate share of themselves to the rearing of the children. Compared to fathers, mothers spend more overall time, engage in more multitasking and physical labor, keep a more rigid timetable, spend more time alone with the children, and have more overall responsibility for child care (Craig 2006). And these differences tend to remain even when the mother works full time. One estimate of the relative amounts of time spent in a typical two-parent, two-child home is that from birth until the child is 18, the mother will spend between 13,729 and 15,439 hours in child care while the father will spend between 4,150 and 4,415 hours (Zick and Bryant 1996). Incidentally, the number of hours for both mothers and fathers increased from the 1960s to the late 1990s (Sayer, Bianchi, and Robinson 2004). Mothers increased their participation in their children's developmental activities, while fathers increased the amount of time they gave to routine child care and to playing with their children.

There are some negative consequences of the more intense involvement of mothers with their children. Compared to fathers, mothers have higher levels of distress and anger, a diminished social network, less discretionary time, and a greater range of tasks (Bird 1997; Munch, McPherson, and Smith-Lovin 1997; Nomaguchi and Milkie 2003). Mothers risk diminished mental health if they have too little emotional support, have difficulty paying for child care, or spend an excessive amount of time with their children (Mistry et al. 2007). On the other hand, there are also positive consequences. In the long run, women may receive more psychological benefits from child rearing than do men (Bird 1997). Children

tend to communicate more with and disclose more to their mothers than to their fathers. Mothers, thus, may have a more sustained kind of intimacy with their children. And the overall experience of mothering may enhance a woman's sense of her own worth and help her establish a meaningful identity (McMahon 1995; Erickson and Aird 2005).

Thus, it is not surprising that a survey of 22,000 mothers found that 72 percent said they would have children again (Rosen 1990). And 93 percent said they were as happy as or happier than they were before they became mothers.

His Experience

Fatherhood was a relatively neglected topic until recent years. Increasingly, researchers are examining the role of the father and the father's experience of parenting. Interestingly, a study of child-rearing books reported that minimal discussion is given to fathers, and the father's role is often portrayed as more voluntary and negotiable than the mother's (Fleming and Tobin 2005). Researchers, in

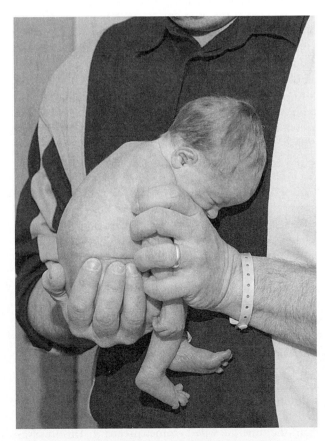

Fathers involved with their children from birth are more active in child care as the child grows.

contrast, not only find fathers capable of nurturing behavior, but also argue that the father's involvement in child rearing is as important as the mother's for the child's healthy development (Biller 1993; National Institute of Child Health and Human Development 2004). The more, for instance, a father is involved in the care of a preschooler, the fewer problems that child is likely to have in school (Aldous and Mulligan 2002). And the more a father is involved with his adolescent child (e.g., talking over important decisions, listening to the adolescent's point of view, knowing with whom the adolescent spends time, and attending events and activities that are important to the adolescent), the fewer behavioral problems the adolescent will have (Carlson 2006).

Fortunately, then, fathers now both desire and practice greater involvement in child rearing than fathers did in previous generations (Bolzan, Gale, and Dudley 2004; Sayer, Bianchi, and Robinson 2004). There are some racial/ethnic differences, however (Yeung et al. 2001). On weekends, Hispanic fathers spend more time with their children than do white fathers, who, in turn, spend more time than do black fathers.

The greater involvement occurs from the beginning of pregnancy. Shapiro (1987) interviewed 227 expectant and recent fathers and found seven major fears and concerns. The first was queasiness. The men were concerned about maintaining their composure and being helpful during the birth process. Some feared that they would faint or get sick. Second, the men worried about the increased responsibility, the loss of what seemed like a comparatively free and easy life. Another concern revolved about the medical procedures. The men disliked the dehumanizing atmosphere of examinations and felt that medical personnel regarded them as out of place. Fourth, more than half of the men were concerned about whether they were truly the child's father. This fear was rooted in a general insecurity surrounding the momentous event rather than in any real doubts about the wife's fidelity. Fifth, the men worried about the possibility of damage or death to the wife and/or the child. The sixth concern involved the marital relationship. The men feared that the child would replace them as the focus of their wife's attention or that the marital relationship would be permanently altered to a less intimate form. Finally, the men became aware of the fragile nature of life and the importance of not dying and leaving the child without their support.

Fathers, then, are emotionally involved with the child from the time the wife becomes pregnant. This involvement is beneficial for the fathers as well as their children. The more that fathers are involved with their children, the

more satisfied they are with their lives, the closer their ties with their communities, and the more connected they are with their families (Eggebeen and Knoester 2001).

The extent to which fathers are involved with their children depends on, in addition to the racial/ethnic differences, a number of factors. Fathers who are more concerned with adult issues, such as the amount of time they have for various activities, their health, sexual satisfaction, and their own mortality, tend to be less involved with their children, less confident of their parental role, and less likely to use positive child-rearing practices (De Luccie and Davis 1991). Fathers who are satisfied with their marriages are likely to be more involved with their children (Harris and Morgan 1991). When the children are in the preadolescent and adolescent stages, fathers tend to be much more involved with their sons than their daughters (Starrels 1994).

Egalitarian fathers tend to be more involved with their children than are traditional fathers (Bulanda 2004). And religious fathers are more involved and report higher-quality relationships than do nonreligious fathers (King 2003; Petts 2007). The higher involvement of religious fathers is true for both those who are married and those who are divorced, although divorced noncustodial fathers tend to lose some involvement with their children and feel both less competent and less satisfied with their roles as fathers (Minton and Pasley 1996).

PARENTING AND THE WELL-BEING OF CHILDREN

If you feel good about yourself and are doing well in life, you probably grew up in a home with one or two warm, loving parents. Parents are not the only influences in your life, but the way they relate to you is very important for your well-being. Among other things, you are likely to be more trusting and to have better relationships with romantic partners (Black and Schutte 2006). Even your physical health benefits. Adults who perceive their relationship with their parents as having been warm and loving are less likely to suffer from such ailments as heart disease, hypertension, ulcers, and alcoholism (Russek and Schwartz 1997). The way that our parents relate to us tends to set the tone of our future lives.

Styles of Parenting

Many good books are available on appropriate and healthy parenting techniques. Here we will briefly look at three basic approaches to parenting that can have quite different effects on the children (Baumrind 1967).

In **authoritarian parenting,** the approach is to exercise maximum control and to expect unquestioning obedience. Children may perceive such parents as rejecting and as refusing to give them any autonomy. Parent–child interaction is not the give-and-take of a developing relationship but the giving of orders by a superior to a subordinate. In case of infraction of the rules, discipline is likely to be both severe and physical.

In **authoritative parenting,** the approach is to put boundaries on acceptable behavior within a warm, accepting context. Children are likely to perceive such an atmosphere as one that encourages their autonomy, controls their behavior moderately, and allows them to express their opinions and develop their own decision-making ability. Parent–child interaction is generally characterized by affection, a certain amount of give-and-take, but relatively clear expectations for the children's behavior.

Finally, in **permissive parenting,** the approach is to minimize any control. Children are encouraged to make their own decisions and develop their independence with few or no parental constraints or guidance. Parent–child interaction may consist of parental acceptance and approval of whatever the children decide to do.

Types of Discipline

Discipline can be generally categorized as aversive or nonaversive (Regalado et al. 2004). Aversive discipline includes yelling and spanking. Nonaversive discipline involves such things as taking away toys, requiring the child to take a "time out," and offering explanations for why a behavior is unacceptable.

In a national survey of children between the ages of 4 and 35 months, parents were questioned about their use of the two kinds of discipline (those with infants between 4 and 18 months were only asked about the use of aversive discipline) (Regalado et al. 2004). Thirteen percent of the parents acknowledged using "yelling"either often or sometimes to discipline the four- to nine-month-old infants. The percentages rose to 47 for parents of 10- to 18-month-olds, and 67 percent for 19- to 35-month-olds. Two percent of the parents said they sometimes spanked their four- to nine-month-old children. Eleven percent spanked 10- to 18-month-old children, and 26 percent spanked 19- to-35-month-old children. Results for nonaversive methods among the parents of 19- to 35-month-old children were 56 percent often or sometimes took toys away; 70 percent often or sometimes used a time out; and 90 percent often or sometimes used explanations.

The results varied by a number of factors. African Americans were most likely to use spanking and yelling. Whites were most likely to use toy removal and time out.

Yelling was more common among mothers 20 years and older than among those younger than 20, but adolescent parents were twice as likely as older parents to use spanking. Spanking was also more common among those in the lower income brackets.

Overall, parents tend to use both aversive and nonaversive methods of discipline by a child's third year. While they tend to favor nonaversive methods over spanking, yelling is used as frequently as giving time outs and taking away toys in the third year. The use of spanking is of particular concern and has been the focus of a good deal of research. Is corporal punishment appropriate or is it counterproductive? Let's look at the debate.

The Corporal Punishment Debate

Corporal punishment is associated mainly with authoritarian parenting, but people who are authoritative or even permissive may occasionally resort to some form of corporal punishment. In addition to spanking, corporal punishment includes such things as striking, shaking, beating with an object, and severe abuse. No one approves of abuse, but child-rearing experts disagree on the milder forms of corporal punishment such as spanking.

The issue is important because national data show that most children will experience corporal punishment at some point in their lives. Two researchers found that during a one-year period, slightly over a third of parents admitted hitting their infants (under a year old), 94 percent said they had used corporal punishment on 4- and 5-year-olds, and more than 40 percent used corporal punishment on 13-year-olds (Straus and Stewart 1999). The extent to which corporal punishment was used varied by racial/ethnic group and by social class, with greater prevalence among African Americans than whites and among those in the lower social classes. Severe rather than mild punishment is also more likely among those in the lower social classes (Dietz 2000).

Those who use corporal punishment say they find support for the practice from workshops, pediatricians, books, magazines, newspapers, and, to a lesser extent, relatives and friends (Walsh 2002). In fact, if you log on to the Internet and type in either "corporal punishment" or "spanking," you will find numerous sites that justify and recommend spanking as a form of discipline. You also will find many sites that disapprove.

The question is, therefore, should or should not parents use corporal punishment? Does it have adverse effects? Or is it an effective way to discipline children? Unfortunately, there is no clear answer from the research. Some researchers find no adverse effects and even some beneficial ones (such as more compliance and less fighting) when nonabusive spanking is employed (Larzelere 2000). Other researchers find both short-term and long-term detrimental effects from corporal punishment and urge that it never be used (Straus 2001). An analysis of a number of studies concluded that corporal punishment did yield higher levels of immediate compliance, but also higher levels of aggression and lower levels of mental health in the children (Gershoff 2002). A study of children at three months and in first grade found behavior problems associated with corporal punishment (Mulvaney and Mebert 2007). Research on fifth and sixth grade students also reported that harsh discipline—both physical and verbal discipline—was associated with behavior problems (McKee et al. 2007). Research on 649 students from three New England colleges found more symptoms of depression among those who had experienced some kind of corporal punishment when they were 13 years old (Turner and Muller 2004). And a study of a sample of college students found that those who had experienced the highest level of physical punishment while growing up also

reported more family conflict, more negative relationships with parents, more family worries, more depressive symptoms, and more negative social relationships (Leary, Kelley, Morrow, and Mikulka 2007).

However, there are factors that can intervene in the relationship between the punishment and the outcomes (see Comparison). McLoyd and Smith (2002) reported that the detrimental effects of spanking occurred when children had low levels but not when they had high levels of warmth and emotional support from the mother. Other researchers found even more complicated relationships (Harper, Brown, Arias, and Brody 2006). High levels of corporal punishment by the father led to more child aggression and depression, regardless of the amount of mother support. But lower levels of the father's corporal punishment diminished the amount of depression when the mother gave the child support. In contrast, when the mother engaged in the corporal punishment and the father offered strong support, the child was less likely to engage in aggression. But corporal punishment

Comparison

Corporal Punishment and Child Aggression in Singapore

As noted in the text, U.S. studies find that a number of factors intervene in the relationship between corporal punishment of a child and the child's likelihood of experiencing emotional problems such as depression and behavioral problems such as aggression. Sim and Ong (2005) studied the relationship in Singapore among a group of 286 Chinese preschool children. Preschoolers in Singapore are typically four to six years old, At that age, parents tend to believe that corporal punishment is appropriate, and among the Chinese in Singapore such punishment may take the more severe form of caning and/or slapping.

Does such corporal punishment lead to child aggression? The researchers included a number of different kinds of aggression in their questions to the children's teachers: physical aggression such as starting a fight with another

child or hitting a child who was teasing him or her; verbal aggression such as teasing, name-calling, and blaming other children; and bullying by getting others to gang up on a classmate or threatening other children.

Children who were caned or slapped did exhibit higher levels of aggression. But the effects differed depending on the specific form of punishing (caning or slapping), on who did it (the father or mother), on the sex of the child, and on the child's perception of whether the parents were rejecting (disliking, disapproving, or resenting) him or her. Thus,

• Caning by the father was associated with higher levels of aggression.
• Caning by the mother was associated with aggression only when she was low in rejection.

• Slapping by the father was associated with aggression only with daughters and only when he was low in rejection.
• Slapping by the mother was associated with aggression but only with sons.

Low rejection, of course, means higher emotional support, which means that the Singapore results are contrary to the findings of U.S. studies. Why would Singapore children who experience more support also be more likely to become aggressive when they are severely punished? The researchers speculate that perhaps the children respect their parents because of the support, believe therefore that the parents' behavior must be right, and conclude that aggression is an appropriate way to relate to others.

by the mother was associated with child depression regardless of the amount of support the child received from the father.

What, then, can be said about the use of corporal punishment? Clearly, the effects depend upon a number of factors. Strong support and high levels of warmth by one parent mitigates the effects of the corporal punishment by the other parent. The less harsh the punishment, the less likely it is to have detrimental effects. Severe punishment or frequent punishment over many years is likely to be detrimental. But in our judgment, the occasional, mild spanking of a child in the preschool years will probably have no adverse consequences and may even help the discipline process. We also believe that corporal punishment should always be a last resort, that parents should make every effort to use other ways to discipline children.

Parental Behavior and Children's Adjustment

The three different styles of parenting have very different consequences. Interestingly, children who perceive their parents as permissive also rate them as less accepting and warm than those who perceive their parents as authoritative (Johnson, Shulman, and Collins 1991). Those with authoritarian parents tend to have lower self-esteem and school achievement and more behavioral problems in school than those with authoritative parents (Bronstein et al. 1996; Ackerman et al. 2003).

Controversy exists over whether children should ever be spanked.

In general, an authoritative parenting style seems to produce the most responsible and well-adjusted children. Children from authoritarian homes tend to be less well-adjusted and to have problems of trusting others, while those from permissive homes may lack self-control and the ability to adapt well to situations in which others have authority over them. In contrast, those from authoritative homes report a higher quality of family life, do better academically, are more self-reliant, have less anxiety and depression, are less likely to get involved in delinquent behavior and drug use, are less at risk for early sexual behavior, have better moral reasoning capability, and report more life satisfaction (Bronstein et al. 1996; Gray and Steinberg 1999; Bronte-Tinkew, Moore, and Carrano 2006; Kapungu, Holmbeck, and Paikoff 2006; Milevsky, Schlechter, Netter, and Keehn 2007).

One reason for the positive outcomes of authoritative parenting is that adolescents who report their parents as authoritative are likely to be involved with peers who refrain from drug use and other behavior that is contrary to adult norms (Durbin et al. 1993). In other words, adolescents from authoritative homes tend to choose friends who prefer generally to conform to their parents' expectations for behavior.

The importance of parental behavior in children's adjustment begins early in life and involves both mother and father. Infants as young as 5 months are more at ease in social situations when they have been cared for and played with by their fathers. When fathers are substantially engaged in the care of their children, those children exhibit more intellectual competence, more empathy, higher levels of self-control and self-esteem, a greater degree of social competence, and higher levels of psychological well-being than do those with less father involvement (Lamb 1997; Videon 2005). A study of adolescents found that the father's acceptance was the most important predictor of the child's effective functioning outside the home (Forehand and Nousianinen 1993). And a study involving a national sample of 471 young adults reported that closeness to fathers made an important contribution to the respondents' happiness, life satisfaction, and emotional health (Amato 1994).

Similarly, mothers' interaction with their infants is important to the children's adjustment (Solomon 2000; Sturgess, Dunn, and Davies 2001). In other words, both parents are important to the child's development and adjustment throughout life. Whether that adjustment is a healthy one depends to a considerable extent on the parenting style.

Parental Behavior and Self-Esteem

If you are well-adjusted, of course, you are most likely to have high self-esteem, the evaluation of yourself as someone of worth. But self-esteem is important for all aspects of your life, not just your adjustment to social situations. A number of researchers have specifically looked at the kind of parental behavior that is related to the development of self-esteem.

A pioneering study of the development of self-esteem was done by Morris Rosenberg (1965), who examined more than 5,000 high school students in New York. Among his findings were the following:

- Adolescents with close relationships with their fathers are more likely to have high self-esteem than those with more distant relationships.
- Only children have higher self-esteem than children with siblings (only children are likely to have a closer relationship with their parents).
- Parental interest in the adolescent, such as knowing the adolescent's friends, being concerned about grades, and conversing with the child during meals, is correlated with higher self-esteem.

Subsequent studies have affirmed the importance of parents, particularly of their warmth, communication, acceptance and involvement in their children's lives (see, e.g., Barber, Chadwick, and Oerter 1992; Roberts and Bengtson 1996; Deutsch, Servis, and Payne 2001; Laible and Carlo 2004). When mothers and fathers are clearly interested in and concerned about their children, they convey a message of the importance and value of their children. And children who know they are deeply valued tend to have higher self-esteem.

A Final Note: Is Older Better in Parenting?

It is difficult for a teenager to be a competent parent because the teenaged parent is, in many ways, a child raising a child. Fortunately, as we have seen, the tendency to delay child-bearing means that fewer children are likely to be raised by very young parents. But can the delaying of parenthood be carried too far? Are there also negative consequences from becoming a parent when you are older? Such questions took on new meaning in 1996 when a 63-year-old woman, who had lied about her age, used in vitro fertilization to become pregnant and give birth to her first child (Kalb 1997).

There is not much research to answer the question of whether there are negative consequences from being older when you become a parent. A study that compared 84 "late"(mean age of 35), 138 "on-time"(mean age of 29), and 82 "early"(mean age of 24) fathers found that the "late" fathers tended to be more highly involved with their children and to have more positive feelings about parenting (Cooney et al. 1993). An assessment of 69 families in which the first child came after the age of 35 concluded that most of the parents "were more satisfied, less stressed, and reported better functioning than their non-delaying counterparts" (Garrison et al. 1997:288). And a study of young adults born to older parents concluded that both older fathers and older mothers are closer with their children than are younger mothers and fathers (Drenovsky and Meshyock 2000). It may be that older parents are more nurturing and mature in dealing with their infants and young children and thereby more likely to develop a particularly close relationship with them.

The most intensive study was that of sociologist Monica Morris (1988), who addressed the questions by looking at a sample of adults who were "last-chance children"; that is, they were the children of women who waited until their late 30s or early 40s to have them. The results were mixed. Some of the subjects reported a variety of problems. Indeed, it is not difficult to imagine that life would be different if you were born to a 42-year-old woman and a 61-year-old man. A man who was such a child said that he didn't have a childhood. His parents never bought him toys. They dressed him up instead of letting him play in jeans in the park. He never played baseball with his father or had the rough-and-tumble activities that his friends had with their parents. He feels as if he didn't even have a real relationship with them. They both died when he was in his teens, long before he was old enough to have an adult conversation with them.

The fear of one or both parents dying was expressed by a number of the subjects in Morris's study. The subjects also talked, like the man mentioned, about what they missed. And they mentioned embarrassing incidents, like being taken for the grandchildren of their parents.

But some also believed that having older parents was a positive experience. In fact, the sample of 22 was almost evenly divided on whether the experience was positive or negative. Those who perceived it to be positive reflected on such things as the wisdom and stability of their parents, qualities that helped them to feel more comfortable and secure. Nevertheless, only two of them strongly endorsed the idea of having their own children at an advanced age.

Increasing numbers of children are born to women who are 35 or older. Older parents have to recognize some of the problems, anxieties, and embarrassments their children are likely to face and have to take steps to minimize them. Older parents have much to offer children in the way of security and stability. But they have to work a little harder to make sure that their children do not miss out on important things that their peers have and that their children do not endure added anxieties and embarrassments because of their parents' older age.

SUMMARY

Birth rates have declined. The decline has occurred among the poor as well as the rich and minorities (except among Hispanic women) and whites. The decline mirrors a lower ideal family size reported by Americans.

Among the reasons that people want to have children are the experience of happiness in a family, personal fulfillment, personal and family legacy, personal status, religious beliefs, and social expectations. Among the reasons for remaining child-free are personal fulfillment, a focus on career, the economic costs of children, a focus on the marriage, and doubts about parenting skills.

Many married couples are infertile. Infertility results from a variety of causes, including environmental toxins and sexually transmitted diseases. Among women, common causes of infertility are endometriosis, other conditions that cause blockage of the fallopian tubes, improper ovulation, and a bodily reaction against sperm. Among men, infertility is somewhat less common but is generally due to a low sperm count. Infections, injuries, exposure to radiation, excessive drug and alcohol use, and birth defects are among the causes of low sperm counts.

Those who discover that they are infertile may go through a process similar to what we experience after loss through death. The process is characterized by surprise, denial, anger, guilt, depression, and grief. The infertile couple also may experience marital strain.

There are technologies that can help many of the infertile. Artificial insemination, in vitro fertilization, and surrogate mothers are alternative ways to have a baby. These methods are expensive and may pose some legal and psychological problems. Adoption is also available, although the number of couples wanting to adopt is far greater than the number of children available. In recent years, open adoptions have become more common.

Raising children is stressful, as illustrated by the number of support groups available to help parents. The stress begins as soon as the child is brought home. Marital problems may increase, and marital satisfaction will probably go down during the child-rearing years; but the satisfactions are such that most parents indicate they would go through the process again.

The experience of parenting is somewhat different for men and women. Women tend to find joy in their children but not in the tasks of motherhood. Women tend to be more involved than men in the lives of their children. Men, however, are equally capable of nurturing behavior. Expectant fathers have many anxieties that they tend not to share with others. Men spend a higher proportion of time in play with children than do mothers. They are playmates as well as caretakers.

Three basic styles of parenting are the authoritarian, the authoritative, and the permissive. Authoritarian parents exercise maximum control and provide minimal warmth. Authoritative parents provide warmth in the context of clear expectations. Permissive parents provide little or no guidance or rules. Authoritative parenting tends to produce the most well-adjusted children.

Discipline may be aversive (such as yelling or spanking) or nonaversive (such as giving time outs, taking away toys, and giving explanations). Both types tend to be used by the time the child is 3 years old. Whether the use of corporal punishment is valuable or harmful is debated by researchers and child care experts.

Parental behavior is important for the child's adjustment. Both parents must relate warmly and intimately with the child for maximal adjustment and for the child's self-esteem.

Those who become parents somewhat later have much to offer children in the way of stability and security. But they also confront unique problems. They and their children will have to deal with a number of problems, anxieties, and embarrassments arising from their age.

Principles for Enhancing Intimacy

1. To have or not to have children is a serious decision. It is a decision with which each spouse needs to feel comfortable. Therefore, the best time to begin discussion about this decision is before you marry. People sometimes marry with the assumption that their spouse wants a family of two, three, or more children. When the matter then comes up for serious debate, they are often surprised that their assumptions were not correct. In fact, they may find that their partner wants no children at all. It is best not to make assumptions about this important matter. Talk it out and arrive at an understanding before the wedding.

2. Flexibility is a requirement in a successful marriage; certainly this is true where decisions about parenting are concerned, because people do change their minds. Even people who are most adamant about not having children sometimes, when they mature, reverse their decision. Similarly, even the individual most enthusiastic about eventually becoming a parent may change his or her mind in light of new personal or professional commitments. Couples, thus, need not only begin discussing this important matter before their wedding but also continue to do so afterward.

3. Becoming a parent is a demanding, lifelong commitment and must be entered into seriously. A baby radically changes your life. The responsibilities are tremendous—a new life is completely dependent on you. You will not be able to go and come as freely as when there were just you and your partner. But keep in mind that the responsibilities are balanced by the joys and satisfactions of parenthood.

4. Child-rearing patterns are changing with the erosion of traditional roles and the increase in the number of dual-career couples. Today fathers as well as mothers are involved in nurturing and caring for their children. This is a fortunate change and should be encouraged, for fathers make a unique contribution to the development of their children.

5. If you want to have a baby and seem unable to conceive, don't give up hope. Many options are available for infertile couples today. Patience and determination are required to find a workable solution. However, also be aware that the search for a solution will likely be expensive, and your spouse may be unwilling to consider some of the options available.

KEY TERMS

artificial insemination   *267*
authoritarian parenting   *277*
authoritative parenting   *277*
birth rate   *260*

endometriosis   *265*
infertility   *265*
in vitro fertilization   *267*
ovulate   *266*

permissive parenting   *277*
replacement level   *260*

ON THE WEB   Becoming a Parent

As noted in the text, certain kinds of parenting are much more beneficial than are others for the well-being of both parents and children. In general, the authoritative style of parenting works best. It would be considered a healthy or positive form of parenting. But how does that translate into everyday behavior with the children? For example, what about discipline? A good deal of controversy exists about corporal punishment. Can you ever use any form of corporal punishment and still engage in a healthy parenting style? You can explore the meaning of healthy or positive parenting and the debate about corporal punishment on the following two sites:

www.mhhe.com/lauer7e

Positive Parenting

http://www.positiveparenting.com

While publicizing the Positive Parenting program that may be purchased for teaching groups of parents, this site also offers a useful newsletter, success stories, numerous articles, and links to other sites that explain and encourage positive parenting.

Kids Health for Parents

http://www.kidshealth.org/parent/emotions/behavior/discipline.html

This site emphasizes the need for differing kinds of discipline at different ages. It also strongly discourages the use of physical punishment such as spanking.

Using these two sites and others, enlarge your understanding with the following projects:

1. Go to the Positive Parenting site and compile a list of ten tips for healthy parenting. Present your list to the class, and discuss how the tips fit into the idea of authoritative parenting. Include a tip about physical punishment, and defend your position to the class.
2. Use the two sites above and search the Internet for other sites that deal with the issue of corporal punishment of children. You can find a number of sites that urge parents to spank their children. Write a paper that gives the rationale used by both those who advocate and those who repudiate spanking. State and justify your own position on the matter.

13

~ THE FAMILY LIFE CYCLE ~

LEARNING OBJECTIVES

After reading and studying chapter 13, you should be able to

1 Outline the stages of the family life cycle.

2 Summarize the types of changes that take place in each stage of the cycle.

3 Describe the effect of social changes on the family life cycle.

4 Discuss the strengths and tasks of the newly married couple.

5 Describe the challenges facing the family with young children.

6 Analyze the strains and stresses as well as the satisfactions experienced by parents and children in the family with adolescents.

7 Explain how the empty-nest stage can be a time of renewal and enrichment for both the marriage and the family.

8 Describe the various types of grandparents and their functions.

9 Discuss the shift of roles in the aging family.

10 Summarize the challenges of retirement, sex, children, and death in the aging family.

In this chapter, we note the importance of rites of passage in family life. Family rituals are also an important tool in creating family solidarity and providing family members with meaningful experiences of interaction. Unlike rites of passage, rituals occur frequently and regularly. How many rituals do you observe in your family? How are they observed? What were some of the most meaningful rituals to you in your family of origin? How many of them do you, or do you plan to, use in your own nuclear family?

When thinking of rituals, consider what your family did on holidays, on certain special days, and regularly as a part of family life. Here are some examples:

Holidays:

New Year's Eve	Christmas
Labor Day	Mother's and Father's Days
Memorial Day	Hanukkah
Thanksgiving	Independence Day
Easter or Passover	

Special days:

birthdays	graduation
anniversaries	weddings
confirmation or Bar Mitzvah or Bat Mitzvah	baptism vacations

Other rituals:

mealtime activities	bedtime rituals
family recreation activities	family religious activities

Talk to someone of another race or another ethnic background about the rituals in his or her family. How do they compare with yours? Are there different rituals for boys and girls? If so, how would you evaluate that practice?

If the entire class participates in this project, a number of people should describe the rituals that were most meaningful to their family. Then discuss which of the rituals you would like to incorporate in your own families. ❧

"You aren't the person I married." Usually this statement indicates dissatisfaction, but it could be made by every husband and wife in the nation. We change continuously throughout our lives, and our relationships change as well. In some cases, people change without conscious effort. In other cases, people may deliberately initiate change in order to improve their marital relationship (Brillinger 1985). For instance, they may try to improve their communication skills or work on certain unrealistic attitudes or expectations. At any rate, once the change has occurred, spouses are no longer the same as at the time of their wedding.

In other words, if we ask how satisfied people are with their marriages, if we inquire into communication patterns or styles and kinds of conflict or any one of numerous aspects of family life, the answer will differ somewhat depending on how long the people have been married. In this chapter, we will look at family life as a process, as a set of relationships that inevitably changes over time. They change in terms of such things as interaction patterns, feelings about each other, division of labor in the home, and expectations about behavior. There are, of course, continuities as well as changes, but it is the changes that we shall focus on here. Change is crucial to intimacy; depending on how the individuals change, intimacy in the family can be weakened or strengthened. People can grow apart as they change, or they can grow closer together. We will examine changing relationships in terms of the family life cycle. And we will look at some of the particular challenges, problems, and satisfactions that people face at differing points in the family life cycle.

THE FAMILY LIFE CYCLE

The notion of a life cycle can be applied to all of life, including nonhuman life. From stars to forests, from humans to insects, from nations to organizations, we find identifiable life cycles. That is, we can trace the process from birth to death. And a family, like a star or forest, is different at varying points along the process.

The Meaning of the Family Life Cycle

What is the difference between a family composed of a couple with an infant and a couple with an adolescent? As it happens, the difference can be dramatic in terms of the experiences of the people involved. There are differing challenges and differing problems. These considerations are the focus of the study of the **family life cycle.**

Carter and McGoldrick (1989) identified six stages in the family life cycle, each of which focuses on at least two generations (table 13.1). The six stages they identify are points at which family members enter or leave the system. These stages include (1) the unattached young adult, (2) the newly married couple, (3) the family with young children, (4) the family with adolescents, (5) the launching and moving on, and (6) the family in later life. Carter and McGoldrick discussed the ways in which families must alter their attitudes and relationships in order to adapt to the varying stages.

For instance, in the family with an unattached young adult, there is the challenge of accepting the parent–child separation that must occur. Three changes are necessary for that challenge to be successfully met. First, each family member must view the young adult as an individual, someone with a life of his or her own that is separate from that of the family. Second, the young adult must develop close relationships with his or her peers. And third, the young adult must become established in some kind of work or a career.

What Changes Occur over the Family Life Cycle?

It is not merely the challenges and problems that change from one stage of the family life cycle to another. Our relationships with each other also change. We have noted in earlier chapters such changes as the lower marital satisfaction that occurs during the child-rearing years and the changing nature of relationships with children as they grow. Relationships also change when wives enter, leave, or re-enter the labor force. And relationships change as the individuals in the family each become more mature, acquire new interests, gain new perspectives, and so forth.

This is not to say that everything is totally different as people move through the various life stages. For example, a study of 160 couples who came to a family therapy clinic found that the presenting problems were generally the same regardless of the number of years the couples had been married (Miller et al. 2003). And at all stages, wives tended to report more problems in their relationships than did husbands. The proportion of husbands and wives who reported a particular problem as occurring "very often" or "often" is shown in figure 13.1

TABLE 13.1 Stages of the Family Life Cycle

Family life cycle stage	Emotional process of transition: Key principles	Second-order changes in family status required to proceed developmentally
(1) Between families: The unattached young adult	Accepting parent–offspring separation	(a) Differentiation of self in relation to family of origin (b) Development of intimate peer relationships (c) Establishment of self in work
(2) The joining of families through marriage: The newly married couple	Commitment to new system	(a) Formation of marital system (b) Realignment of relationships with extended families and friends to include spouse
(3) The family with young children	Accepting new members into the system	(a) Adjusting marital system to make space for child(ren) (b) Taking on parenting roles (c) Realignment of relationships with extended family to include parenting and grandparenting roles
(4) The family with adolescents	Increasing flexibility of family boundaries	(a) Shifting of parent–child relationships to permit adolescent to move in and out of system (b) Refocus on midlife marital and career issues (c) Beginning shift toward concerns for older generation
(5) Launching children and moving on	Accepting a multitude of exits from and entries into the family system	(a) Renegotiation of marital system as a dyad (b) Development of adult relationships between grown children and parents (c) Realignment of relationships to include in-laws and grandchildren (d) Dealing with disabilities and death of parents (grandparents)
(6) The family in later life	Accepting the shifting of generational roles	(a) Maintaining own and/or couple functioning and interests in face of physiological decline: exploration of new familial and social role options (b) Support for a more central role for middle generation (c) Making room in the system for the wisdom and experience of the elderly: supporting the older generation without overfunctioning for them (d) Dealing with loss of spouse, siblings, and other peers and preparation for own death (e) Life review and integration

Source: From Betty Carter and Monica McGoldrick, *The Changing Family Life Cycle: A Framework for Family Therapy.* 2nd ed. Copyright © 1989 by Allyn and Bacon. Reprinted with permission.

for five of the more frequently named problem areas. Note that except for the issue of money among those married 10 or more years, more wives than husbands identified each of the five topics as a problem. But note also that the extent to which each of the problems occurs varies by the number of years of marriage. In sum, whatever characteristic of family life you are interested in, you must understand it in the context of where it occurs in the family life cycle.

Social Change and the Family Life Cycle

Your experiences in passing through the family life cycle will depend on a number of things, including the kinds of change that occur in society. In chapter 1, we identified a number of changes that have occurred since about the middle of the last century (premarital sex, births to unmarried women, cohabitation, etc.). Such changing

patterns of relationships are associated with such social changes as altered social norms about sex and about whether and when people ought to get married, an economy that makes it difficult for many people to buy a home, increased longevity that (among other things) increases the amount of time people may live alone and the number of people who will have to care for aging parents, and so on.

Consider, for example, the experience of the death of a parent or of a child. While the death of a child is usually far more traumatic than the death of a parent, the latter is also a source of stress and emotional struggle (Marks, Jun, and Song 2007). A parent's death, however, is now likely to occur much later in a child's life than it used to, because improved nutrition and health care have made a dramatic difference in the **death rate.** At the turn of the twentieth century, more than half of children experienced

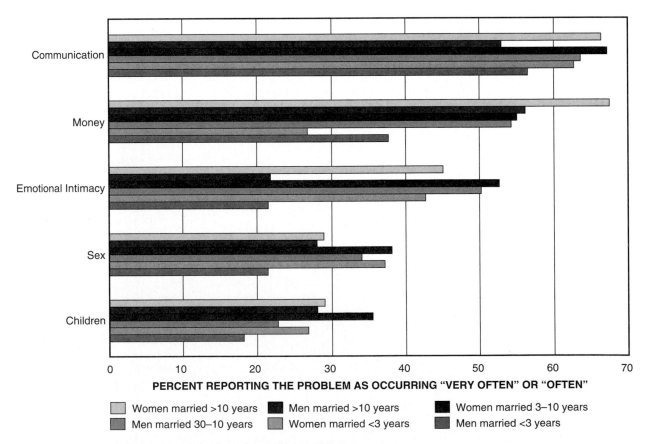

FIGURE 13.1 **Problem Areas of 160 Couples in Therapy**
Source: Adapted from Miller et al. 2003.

the death of a parent while the children were still in their teens. Now you may not have to cope with the death of a parent until you are in the fourth, fifth, or sixth stage of the family life cycle.

Similarly, parents are far less likely to face the death of a child. In 1900, parents had a better than even chance of experiencing the death of a child. Now relatively few parents have such an experience. The infant death rate is 6.8 per thousand live births, which is less than a third of the rate even as late as 1970 (National Center for Health Statistics 2007a).

A second example of change involves grandparenthood. With increased life expectancy, an increasing number of Americans are experiencing grandparenthood. More, an increasing number have grandchildren living with them. Nearly 6 million U.S. grandparents have grandchildren younger than 18 living with them (Tillery 2007). And 43 percent of those who have grandchildren living with them are responsible for most of the basic needs (food, shelter, and clothing) of their grandchildren.

However, fewer women today are both the mother of a small child and a grandmother. Women are completing their childbearing at an earlier age than they did in the past. There is now more likely to be a sequence than an overlapping of roles.

A third change relates to marital disruption and remarriage. A widespread belief exists that marital disruption is far more prevalent than it was in the past. Actually, the rate of disruption has not changed much. Rather, it is the reason for the disruption that has changed (Pinsof 2002). Before the twentieth century, death of a spouse was the common way for a marriage to end. In 1900, two-thirds of marriages ended because of the death of a partner within 40 years. Since 1974, more marriages end because of divorce than death.

There are differing consequences to disruption by divorce than by death. In discussing the consequences with people who have experienced one or both, the authors found that many insist that it is more difficult to adjust to divorce than it is to death. If, then, the rate of disruption is about the same, the experience is not.

The incidence of remarriage is also affected. The death of a spouse may put one person into the marriage market; divorce may put two. But after the age of 40, males are more likely than females to remarry (Coleman, Ganong, and Fine 2000). In part this is due to the sex ratio and in part to the tendency of men to marry women younger than themselves. The net effect is that a man is likely to spend the last part of his life with a wife, while a woman is more likely to spend the last part of her life alone or in an institution.

Loss and grief are part of the sixth stage of the family life cycle.

THE NEWLY MARRIED:
A FAMILY WITHOUT CHILDREN

You will recall that we considered the first stage of the family life cycle in chapter 5 in our discussion of the single adult. The second stage of the family life cycle occurs when a couple marries. What are the characteristics of this stage in the family cycle, and what are the important challenges a couple faces as they establish a marital system?

Newly married couples tend to have certain relational strengths that enable them to deal with the challenges and problems of forming a new family unit (Schramm, Marshall, Harris, and Lee 2005). Among other things, they are likely to have a high degree of mutual trust. They respect and appreciate each other. They are committed to the marriage. They enjoy high levels of affection for each other. To the extent that their sexual life meets the wife's initial expectations and remains at a frequency desired by the husband, they have a satisfying sexual relationship (McNulty and Fisher 2007). They engage in a good deal of self-disclosure, sharing their thoughts and feelings. And they are likely to have few serious conflicts. Such qualities mean that they have a strong foundation for beginning their life together as a married couple.

One of the important tasks facing the newly married couple is that of forming their own marital system (Wallerstein 1994). That is, when you marry you have to decide on a whole range of matters for your own newly formed family. In the past, the roles of husband and wife were not as ambiguous as they are now. In the 1950s, for example, the husband was expected to be the breadwinner, and the wife was expected to be the homemaker. Today, the roles must be negotiated, including everything from questions about balancing work and marriage to the matter of who will shop for food and prepare dinners (Schramm, Marshall, Harris, and Lee 2005; Bove and Sobal 2006). Interestingly, in a study of 20 newly married couples, Bove and Sobal (2006) found that in just under half of the unions both partners shared in foodwork tasks, while in the rest one partner—equally likely to be the husband or the wife—assumed primary responsibility.

Every newly married couple, then, must address a whole range of questions. Many of them deal with practical matters of work, dealing with debts brought into the marriage, housework, and so on. But there are also many important questions involving the ways you will relate to each other. Will you openly show both positive and negative feelings? Will you give both positive and negative feedback about each other (the importance of this question is seen in the fact that your partner is likely to adjust his or her self-view to be consistent with the feedback you give [Cast and Cantwell 2007])? Will you each take responsibility for your own actions? Will you

What Do You Think?

There is disagreement about **whether sex is fundamental to the marital happiness of long-term marriages.** *What follows are pro and con arguments. What do you think?*

Pro

Sex is fundamental to marital happiness in long-term marriages because

- you never outgrow your need for sex.
- it maintains intimacy.
- the lack of sexual desire usually means indifference to your partner.
- it affirms your spouse's attractiveness and desirability.
- it keeps both spouses attentive to each other's needs.

Con

Sex is not fundamental to marital happiness in long-term marriages because

- it becomes much less important as you age.
- companionship is more important than passion.
- with time you learn to value the whole person and not just his or her sexuality.
- marital happiness depends on such things as compatibility more than on sex.
- it is too often tied up with power struggles and conflict.

deal openly with problems? Will you resolve normal conflicts without causing each other undue stress? If and when you have children, will you freely admit to them when you are wrong? Will you allow them to express views different from yours? Will you consciously strive to maintain a warm and supportive atmosphere in the home? And so on.

One of the more important tasks is establishing a pattern of resolving conflicts. It is important for two reasons. First, as we pointed out in chapter 10, dealing with conflict in a way that is acceptable to each of you is crucial to your marital satisfaction and to the stability of your relationship. And, second, the pattern you establish in the first year of marriage is likely to be the pattern you maintain throughout your marriage (Schneewind and Gerhard 2002).

In building a marital system, a couple will tend to model their relationship after the one or the other of their families of origin. Look again at the series of questions we just raised. How would you answer them in terms of the way your parents behaved? How would you answer them in terms of your ideal for your own marriage?

If your ideals vary from what your parents did, you may choose to reject the model of your family of origin, though this is probably the exception rather than the rule. It may be difficult to know or to agree on what kind of model to use as a substitute. In such cases, it is easy to fall back on what is familiar. Nevertheless, there are couples who consciously opt for a different model when they are uncomfortable with that of their families of origin. As, for instance, a husband told us,

> My wife and I both came from families where our parents argued loudly and vociferously with each other. We both disliked that, and we decided that we would not do this. We have very few arguments but when we do disagree, we make a strong effort to talk about things calmly and get the matter settled as quickly as possible.

The spouses had similar experiences in their family of origin, but each had agreed to find an alternative way in their marriage.

In any case, a central task at this stage is to establish your own marital system, your own way of relating and dealing with the various problems and processes of family life. You will probably model some of your patterns on those of your family of origin. You should be aware, however, that some of those patterns may not work well for you and that unless you consciously decide to do otherwise, you will follow them even though they are not effective for your family.

In establishing your own marital system, you also will have to deal with the dilemma posed by your need for closeness and the danger of **fusion.** A fused relationship is one in which boundaries between people become blurred, in the sense that the individuals are overinvolved with each other such that they have difficulty making their own decisions or having their own opinions (Skowron and Schmitt 2003). Fused individuals function as one person rather than as two individuals in an intimate relationship. Fusion happens when, in the quest for intimacy, an individual tries to get close to another but goes to the extreme. In a fused marriage, for example, the spouses may always feel the same thing in every situation, may be unwilling to engage in activities without the other, may be unable to make separate and contrary judgments about things, and so forth. Fusion in a relationship will lead sooner or later to difficulties and even to a loss of intimacy in the relationship. Another central task of the newly married couple, then, is to form an intimate union without a loss of individual identity.

THE FAMILY WITH YOUNG CHILDREN

In the third stage of the family life cycle, the couple commits itself to an additional person and to changes in the family system. Spouses face the challenge of the new roles of mother and father as well as those of husband and wife. Initially, they may find great joy in the birth of their child. However, as we saw in the last chapter, the "blessed event" has its problems as well as its blessings. Parents have a host of challenges and tasks facing them as they rear their children (Halfon, McLearn, and Schuster 2002; Blumberg, Halfon, and Olson 2004). From weaning the child from the breast or the bottle to toilet training to preparing the child (and the parents) for going to school, young children present their parents with a continuing series of new responsibilities.

The family strengths we mentioned previously tend to remain high at this stage, but the couple is likely to rate its marital communication as lower. And marital satisfaction starts to decline. Again, this does not mean that the partners are unhappy, but only that they are less happy than at other stages. It is probable that the increased attention and energy that the wife gives to the children and the increasing demand by employed wives for husbands to share in the family work account for the lower satisfaction.

The same factors are involved in the declining marital satisfaction of wives at this stage. That is, they are consumed with the endless tasks of parenthood. They may be frustrated with their husbands' reluctance to share the family work. And they may have little time or energy for working at their intimate relationships with their husbands. In good part, this reflects the strains of mothering. As pointed out earlier, women tend to assume a disproportionate share of the added work when a child comes into the family. Gjerdingen and Center (2005) studied 128 couples during pregnancy and six months after the birth of a first child. They found that the time devoted to their varied responsibilities after the birth increased 64 percent for the mothers and 37 percent for the fathers. The mothers were more likely than the fathers to decrease their work hours outside the home, but had significantly larger increases in child care (48.9 hours per week, compared to 25.7 hours per week for the fathers). They also perceived less sharing of household chores after the birth.

Another factor that strains marital satisfaction at this stage is the extent of perceived agreement between the spouses. White (1987) looked at eight issues in family life: preferred family size, how children should be disciplined, whether to spend leisure time with friends or family, equality in financial contributions to the family, equal sharing of household chores, perceived equity in the relationship, whether a wife should have an abortion without the husband's consent, and whether a mother with small children should enter the labor force.

While the wives in White's sample tended to see more overall agreement in this stage than they did in the previous one (newly married), the husbands' perceptions of agreement dropped sharply. Actually, when comparing

 Symbolic Interactionist Theory Applied

the responses of husbands and wives, it was clear that the couples' agreement on the eight issues went up. But whether the husbands *defined the agreement as going up* is as important as whether it actually went up. In point of fact, the husbands perceived a much lower level of agreement and, consequently, they reported a lower level of marital satisfaction.

We noted in the last chapter that marital satisfaction increases for some couples in the child-rearing years. This is likely to be true for those with strong marriages before the children come and with those who engage in certain helpful kinds of behavior. "Helpful" behavior includes such things as establishing meaningful family rituals and maintaining a high level of involvement in child rearing on the part of the father (Levy-Skiff 1994; Landau 2007).

THE FAMILY AT MIDLIFE: ADOLESCENTS AND AGING PARENTS

Three areas of concern can make the fourth stage—the family at midlife—particularly problematic. These areas are aging parents, adolescent children, and midlife concerns.

By 2006, 37.3 million Americans, 12.4 percent of the population, were age 65 or older (U.S. Census Bureau 2008:8). The proportion varied considerably among racial/ethnic groups: 13.5 percent of non-Hispanic whites, 8.3 percent of African Americans, 8.9 percent of Asian Americans, and 5.4 percent of Hispanics were 65 or older in 2006. The population as a whole is much older than when the nation began. In the late eighteenth century, the median age of the population was about 16 years; by 2006, the median age was 36.4 years. The median age has fluctuated some, but has continued on a generally upward trend. This aging reflects such things as increasing longevity, later age for marriage and childbearing, and fewer children per family (Fussell 2002).

At the midlife stage, the effects of this aging population are increasingly evident. People must deal with their aging parents, which may include caring for parents who become ill, disabled, or frail (Levande, Herrick, and Sung 2000). In addition, rates of illness and death also increase for people in their midlife years, bringing loss and the strain of caregiving to many families. At the same time, the children are growing older and reaching adolescence; parents face the challenge of allowing their children to form independent identities and establish a wider range of intimate relationships. And while all this is going on, the spouses face their own midlife concerns about their marriage and their careers. Not surprising, then, that this fourth stage is often an agitated clash of varied turbulent processes.

The Needs of Adolescents

Adolescence is a time of important physical, intellectual, and role changes (Steinberg 2007). Physically, adolescents change in size and appearance and develop the capacity to engage in sexual relations and reproduce. Intellectually, the adolescent develops the capacity to think more logically and more abstractly. This means that the family now has another individual who can think and reason at a more adult level. The role change involves the transition out of childhood and the changed expectations about rights and responsibilities that people have for the adolescent as he or she emerges into adulthood. These new expectations give the adolescent a different position both in the family and in the larger society.

At adolescence, then, parents and children must work out a new system. Adolescents prefer more egalitarian relationships with their parents, and because of the changes they experience, they have a basis for advancing that preference. Whereas children may obey simply on the basis of a parental "because I say so," adolescents are likely to be dissatisfied with such statements. Adolescents want to deal with parental expectations on the basis of reason, fairness, and mutual respect.

Adolescents also need increasing autonomy and independence. They are striving to establish their own identity, to find out what kind of persons they are. They need to test their abilities and explore their future options. In the process, they may shift their focus from family to friends and peers. It isn't that they reject the family but that they find the perspectives of those outside the family to be an important part of their quest for their own identity.

Parent–Child Problems

Because *conflict arises out of opposing needs and interests,* the unique needs of adolescents make this stage one of increasing conflict and decreased closeness with parents (McGue, Elkins, Walden, and Iacono 2005). The changes tend to be more intense for girls than for boys. The way the conflict is handled is important for the adolescent's well-being, because excessive and poorly handled conflict can adversely affect the adolescent's future romantic relationships (Overbeek et al. 2007). Ultimately, how families manage the conflict depends upon the quality of family life before adolescence. Families that are warm and supportive will generally keep the conflict at minimal or moderate levels and parent–adolescent relationships will gradually improve, while families with hostile, coercive atmospheres will generally have intense conflict that tends to worsen (Rueter and Conger 1995).

Conflict Theory Applied

What do adolescents and their parents fight about? The most frequent sources of conflict, according to a national survey, are everyday matters such as helping around the house, family relations, school, and dress (Barber 1994). Contrary to some popular notions, drug use and sex are seldom the issues of the conflict. And these conclusions hold true for African Americans and Hispanics as well as for whites.

Maintaining good communication between parents and children is particularly important in adolescence (Shearer, Crouter, and McHale 2005). A study of 339 high-school students found that those students who perceived good communication with their parents reported lower rates of delinquency and less serious kinds of delinquency (Clark and Shields 1997). Unfortunately, communication problems tend to be more serious during adolescence than at other stages. Parents may complain that they don't understand their children, who, in turn, complain that they don't understand their parents. Mothers perceive more satisfying communication with adolescents than do fathers. Mothers particularly see the parent–child communication as more open. Adolescents themselves agree with that assessment, perceiving better and more open communication with their mothers than with their fathers.

Parents also report stress from increased financial problems. Children become increasingly expensive as they age. By the time of adolescence, the costs of food, clothing, medical care, automobiles, education, and so on are at a peak for many families.

Adolescents see most of their stress arising from daily hassles with parents. They report increasing arguments about household chores, increased pressure to achieve (either academically or in sports), hassles about using the family car and doing things with the family, and arguments over their selection of friends and social activities.

Emerging Adulthood

Family life experts now identify a new stage of development called early or emerging adulthood (Arnett 2000; Furstenberg et al. 2004). Emerging adulthood refers to the period from the late teens through the mid- to late-20s. It is not merely "extended adolescence." In contrast to adolescence, the child has less parental control and is free to engage in independent exploration of various facets of life (Arnett 2004). During emerging adulthood, the young person is not married, has not become a parent, and is not in a career line. In other words, emerging adults have not yet taken on the full set of responsibilities of adulthood.

What are they doing? Some are still pursuing their education. Some are working, but not in what they regard as a career or even a long-term area of employment. Some are developing romantic relationships. Some move out of the parental home but return for one or more periods of time (Cohen et al. 2003). Emerging adults, in short, are drifting and dabbling rather than pursuing the typical goals of adulthood.

The proportion of those who entered full adulthood by the age of 30 dropped dramatically over the last part of the twentieth century (Furstenberg et al. 2004). If we define adults as those who have left home, finished school, are married, have one or more children, and are financially independent, then 65 percent of 30-year-old men and 77 percent of 30-year-old women in 1960 were adults. By 2000, the figures were 31 percent of 30-year-old men and 46 percent of 30-year-old women.

Being an emerging adult is not a time of fun and games rather than of responsibility. Rather, there are high rates of depression and of feelings of being overwhelmed by life (Apter 2001; Berry 2004). And the depression and sense of being overwhelmed is probably related to the difficulties of finding employment that enables an individual to afford housing for family life and maintain an acceptable standard of living (Furstenberg et al. 2004). To do so requires a college degree, and completing a degree is taking longer than it did in the past. Moreover, even when you have a degree, you may not obtain employment that will enable you to support a family in the near future.

In other words, the new stage of emerging adulthood does not reflect a generation that is shrinking away from responsibility. Rather, it reflects social and economic conditions that make it increasingly difficult for individuals to fulfill all the conditions of adulthood.

Caring for Aging Parents

Parents who have responsibilities for adolescent children and aging parents at the same time are the **"sandwich generation."** They also may have other relatives or friends

Those in the "sandwich generation" have responsibilities for both their children and their aging parents.

in need of some kind of help. One estimate is that 44 percent of Americans in the 45- to 55-year age group have at least one living parent and one child under age 21 (Pierret 2006). Of course, not all who have both a living parent and a minor child are giving care to the parent. But a substantial number are. The care can take the form of co-residence (the parent or parents live with the child), financial help, and/or time given to various caretaking tasks (providing companionship, help with shopping, medical appointments, housecleaning, etc.). Table 13.2 shows the proportion who give these kinds of care to both children and parents. Depending on how we define the sandwich generation, from about 1 in 9 to 1 in 3 women in the 45- to 56-year-old age group are caught in it.

Many of those caring for an impaired parent also work outside the home; such a situation is stressful and the stress increases with the amount of time the caregiving requires (Starrels et al. 1997). Physical and emotional exhaustion, putting a career on hold, and cutting back on leisure activities are among the potential consequences of caregiving that produce the stress. In addition, women who give up or cut back on work to care for a parent put themselves at risk for poverty in later life because of the difficulty of getting back into the labor force and the toll taken on their health (Wakabayashi and Donato 2006).

It is not surprising that more than 70 percent of those in a national survey supported the idea of tax credits for caregivers, and nearly 60 percent supported a requirement that employers give time off without pay to caregivers (Silverstein and Parrott 2001). Support was stronger among those who were current caregivers; they knew from experience the need for measures to alleviate the stress.

There are parents who, anticipating future needs for care, voluntarily move to a continuing care retirement community (Krout et al. 2002). Their reasons include

TABLE 13.2 Proportion of 45- to 56-Year-Old Women Caring for Parents and Children

Type of care (Given both to parents and to children)	Percent of women
Co-residence	1.1
Aid of 100 hours or more per year	4.1
Aid of $200 or 100 hours/year or more	14.2
Aid of 500 hours or more per year	1.4
Aid of $1000 or 500 hours/year or more	6.2
Co-residence or in support facility (parents) or at college (children), or aid of $200 or 100 hours/year or more	33.1

Source: Pierret (2006:7)

freedom from maintaining a home, the guarantee of whatever long-term care they need in the future, and the satisfaction of knowing they will not be a burden to their children. Most parents, however, continue to rely on their children.

A growing number of Americans, therefore, are turning to some kind of formal care rather than assuming all the burdens of caregiving themselves (Spillman and Pezzin 2000). They may hire part-time or full-time help for their parents. They may call on community resources, such as Meals on Wheels.

The vast majority of the aged are cared for by family members alone, or combined with community services, for the remainder of their lives. But for those who require specialized or extensive care, or who have no family members to care for them, institutionalization may be the only alternative. By 2004, nearly 1.5 million Americans, most of them women, were in a nursing home (National Center for Health Statistics 2007b). Some spend a short time there before returning to their homes. Others, however, spend their final days in nursing facilities.

Placing your parents in an institution is likely to be a painful process. Few if any people go willingly or easily. In addition to the elderly parent's resistance, there is the problem of the quality of care in the nursing home. There are homes that provide outstanding care, but others give inadequate care or even abusive treatment to their residents. Although nursing homes are regulated, a government investigation of nursing homes in 10 states found that two-thirds of them were cited for practices harmful to residents and had committed at least one more serious offense within two years of the original charge (Bates 1999). The offenses included such things as

- failure to notify doctors of serious breathing problems.
- failure to treat anxiety and depression.
- negligence in treating bed sores.
- failure to report or record serious injuries from falls.

When institutionalization is required, then, a thorough investigation of the nursing facility should be made.

The Couple's Midlife Concerns

In addition to facing responsibilities for their children and their parents, the couple in stage four faces marital and personal challenges. The most common midlife marital problems involve financial concerns, dealing with the children, and the sexual relationship (Henry and Miller 2004). In other words, the same issues that are the most common sources of conflict in earlier years may continue to be a challenge at midlife.

Midlife is also a time when people become increasingly concerned about their own aging process. They face issues of their appearance, physical competency, and health. The importance of health to an individual's quality of life increases significantly around the age of 35. It isn't that health actually tends to deteriorate at that age but that people become aware of its importance and get more concerned about it.

At midlife, a change also occurs in the way that people view life. They begin to think in terms of how much time they have left rather than how much has already occurred. Possibilities for change seem limited. For example, they may feel that they no longer have options for a career change and that they are bound to continue in whatever career they have until retirement. There may be a yearning for some new excitement or new direction, but there appear to be few if any opportunities to fulfill these desires. In some cases, people's marriages may appear to be stale and a handicap to further growth and/or excitement in life. One or both partners of a couple may seriously think about the possibility of separation or divorce in order to pursue new relationships.

Perhaps all of this sounds familiar. It is a description of some of the things that happen to people who wrestle with the so-called midlife crisis. Not everyone has a midlife crisis, but everyone faces a set of challenges and concerns at midlife.

For men, Levinson and his associates (1978) have identified four fundamental concerns. First is the concern with mortality. Men think more about the fact that they are growing older and will die. Some men resist the process vigorously, using dress, cosmetics, exercise, diet, new relationships, new behavior patterns, or plastic surgery in an effort to stay youthful.

A second concern is the hunger to be creative, to leave the world some legacy that will last. Third, men may begin to explore the feminine side of their nature and experience increasing concern for family and relationships (as opposed to career and achievement). Fourth is the need to be attached to and separate from the social environment. That is, men have a need to both be involved with their world as well as have time to nurture their inner life. In their 20s and 30s, men tend to be primarily consumed with making their way in the world and in their work. At midlife, however, it becomes important to attain a more equal balance between attachment and separateness.

Although Levinson's work focused on men, women also deal with midlife issues. Women tend to reach the midlife crisis point sooner than men, usually around the age of 35 (Brehony 1996). At that point, a woman may feel that she faces her last opportunity to accomplish certain things in her life. She also may experience important changes, such as her last child going to school and the prospective end of her childbearing years. With the tasks of mothering requiring less of her time, a woman may begin to focus more attention on her own needs and development.

Women as well as men face the possibility of a "midlife crisis" or of the kinds of concerns that can lead to the crisis (Shellenbarger 2005). Like men, women who undergo a midlife crisis may break up their marriage or have an extramarital affair. Even apart from a midlife crisis, women tend to develop their masculine side and think more about creative achievements and their need to be assertive and to explore. They may return to school, start a career, or pursue interests for which they had no time during their child-rearing years.

In short, both men and women at midlife face a new set of challenges and concerns that may alter the course of their lives. How they deal with these various issues is crucial to their life satisfaction.

Satisfaction at Midlife

Obviously, the intersection of the turmoil of adolescence with the parental crisis of midlife creates a fertile climate for considerable family strain and for diminished satisfaction with life. But, for a number of reasons, many people find a high degree of satisfaction (Westerhof and Barrett 2005; Greenfield and Marks 2007; Peterson and Duncan 2007). Among other things, life satisfaction is likely to be higher for those who have a sense of achieving something creative and worthwhile in their lives, for those who closely identify with and are active in a religious group, and those who simply feel younger than their actual age (suggesting that they are in excellent health).

Furthermore, in spite of the strains, intense conflict between parents and their adolescent children is not inevitable. Most adolescents report positive relationships with parents (Moore et al. 2004). More than four out of five agree that they think highly of their fathers and mothers, and more than three-fourths say they enjoy spending time with their parents. In addition, the majority of girls say they want to be like their mothers, and the majority of boys agree that they want to be like their fathers.

When families do have conflict, it may partly be due to a lack of **rites of passage** (Quinn, Newfield, and Protinsky 1985; Broderick 1993). A rite of passage marks a significant time of change in an individual's life. In many preindustrial cultures, the transition to adulthood is marked by a rite of passage. For example, an adolescent male may undergo some kind of physical test, such as a period of isolation or beating by adult men, that marks the end of childhood and his entry into the world of adults. We may find these rites of passage unappealing because they involve varying degrees of anxiety and pain. Still, they clearly indicated when an individual passed from childhood to adulthood.

In our society, there are some markers of this transition. For example, attaining the age when you can get a driver's license may be a rite of passage, but it depends on how it is handled in a family. In some families, the new right may be granted with reluctance or not at all. Or it may be treated as little more than the result of living a certain number of years rather than as a significant accomplishment. To be effective, a rite of passage should treat the event as an achievement that brings with it higher status and greater responsibility and privileges.

Thus, one of the ways that families can deal with conflicts and problems is to institute rites of passage. Consider the following case of a single mother and her adolescent daughter (Quinn, Newfield, and Protinsky 1985). Mrs. Ward, the mother, was a widow raising her 15-year-old daughter, Diane, alone. Diane's father was killed when she was 4. Her uncle served as a kind of surrogate father to her, but he was killed in a military accident when she was 9. Mrs. Ward didn't realize how traumatic each of these losses was for Diane. She didn't take Diane's grieving seriously. She tried to take over both parental roles by being a strict disciplinarian and maintaining total control.

But maintaining control meant that Diane's attempts to grow up were thwarted. Her mother defined any efforts on Diane's part to act like an adult as premature. Their conflict culminated in Diane's attempted suicide. At the time of the attempt, Diane had just graduated from junior high after a three-year struggle with her math courses and a number of behavioral problems at school. The therapist suggested a rite of passage. He said it was time for the family to move to a new stage of their lives. He helped them plan a party to celebrate Diane's school achievements and her entrance into senior high. The party would also allow them each to meet new people. Following the party, Diane and her mother began to make significant progress.

A party as a formal recognition is, of course, only one way that a family can institute its own rites of passage. The point is that there is great value to all members of the family to have some kind of ceremony that carries with it recognition by both parents and children that a new phase has been reached and that this new phase means that the adolescent has achieved something significant and is now endowed with a higher status and new privileges and responsibilities. Such rites of passage may occur profitably a number of times during the adolescent years.

THE LAUNCHING AND EMPTY-NEST STAGE

In stage five, the couple must deal with the children moving out and being on their own. This can be a problem for both the children and the parents (Lauer and Lauer 1999b). Family therapists stress the *need for "differentiation,"* the need for each member of the family to be an autonomous individual as well as an integral part of an intimate group (Bowen 1978). As we noted previously in our discussion of the problem of fusion in

Systems Theory Applied

a newly married couple, a fulfilling intimate relationship is a relationship of interdependence, not of merging and loss of individuality. Fusion can occur between children and parents as well as between spouses. At some point, then, it is important that the children pursue their individual lives by leaving the home. The children seem to sense this to a somewhat greater extent than their parents; a study of high school seniors found that they were more likely than their parents to expect they would establish their own residences before getting married (Goldscheider and Goldscheider 1993). In fact, an independent residence before marriage has become a sign of adult status for young adults.

The age at which a young adult leaves the parental home depends on a number of factors, including the quality of the parent–child relationship, the child's employment status, the parents' marital status, and the status of the child's intimate relationships (engaged or planning to cohabit, e.g.; Goldscheider 1997). Because increasing numbers of adult children are leaving the parental home for nonmarital reasons, a substantial number return to the parental home for varying periods of time, creating a new set of challenges for both parents and children (Lauer and Lauer 1999b).

When the children leave, the parent–child relationship changes (Lauer and Lauer 1999b). Generally, the relationship is likely to become closer, more supportive, and less conflicted (Aquilino 1997). Moreover, in their interviews with more than a thousand people in upstate New York, Logan and Spitze (1996) found that adult children and their parents engage in a great deal of care for each other, with the parents tending to give more help in the form of household tasks to their adult children than they receive. The situation only reverses when the parents become ill or infirm, and the children become their parents' caregivers. Clearly, family ties are likely to remain strong throughout the family life cycle.

Delayed Launching and Boomerang Children

Some couples never experience, or have little time to experience, the empty nest. For various reasons, the launching may be delayed. As table 13.3 shows, after age 45 there is a dramatic decline in the proportion of family households with children. But three-fourths of families where the householder is 45 to 49 years, and one-fourth where the householder is 75 or older, still have children in the home. And whatever the age of the householder, some family households have children older than 25 years and some have children younger than 12 years. Of course, there are a number of different situations represented in the numbers. An older male householder may have a younger wife and a second family that involves young children. A couple may be caring for a disabled or mentally ill older child. The family may have fused relationships that include an adult child who never married. Or the child may be one of the "boomerang" children that we shall discuss below.

What are the consequences of an adult child remaining at home rather than establishing an independent residence? The answer may vary by racial/ethnic background. In some Asian and Hispanic cultures, for example, young adults are expected to live with their parents until they marry. Thus, a study of parents in Canada reported that 50 percent of parents born in South or Central America

TABLE 13.3 Percent of Family Households with Children

Percent of Families	Age of Householder				
	45–49	50–54	55–64	65–74	75+
With own children, any age	76.5	60.1	35.2	22.6	24.9
With own children under 25 years	73.8	53.2	21.3	4.1	1.4
With own children under 12 years	25.8	10.2	2.9	0.9	0.6

Source: U.S. Census Bureau 2007a.

and 60 percent of parents born in Asia had adult children living at home, compared to only 22 percent of parents born in Canada (Turcotte 2006). And while we know of no research on the matter, we have heard from Hispanic students that it is not uncommon for a young mother and her husband to live with parents and that an adult child who returns to the nest is more likely to be greeted with joy than with reluctance or concern.

Even for those parents from other cultural backgrounds, the experience may add some frustrations but still be basically satisfying (Turcotte 2006). A study of U.S. college students living at home found that the students complained of such things as a lack of privacy, financial dependence, and disagreements over such things as sharing the car, high telephone expenses, using the bathroom, and dealing with different schedules (Strom and Strom 2005). In addition, the parents expressed concern over their continuing financial support and the issue of whether the child had become a grownup. At the same time, both the students and their parents talked about the benefits of the arrangement, such as having more time together and giving the students a financial base while they completed their education.

A somewhat different situation involves the "boomerang" child, the adult who returns home after having left to live independently. It may be a college graduate who hasn't yet found work or whose income isn't sufficient for independent living. It may be a child who divorced or who suffered a job loss or who is trying to recover from an addiction. It may be a child who has experienced serious health problems and needs the parents' care. It could be a child who has returned to the home town to pursue a career there and needs to live for a time with the parents until he or she is able to find housing. And so on.

In the Canadian study, a fourth of the adult children who were living with their parents were boomerang children (Turcotte 2006). And there were somewhat different consequences for the parents than for those whose children had never yet left home. For one thing, parents with boomerang children were more likely than others to be frustrated with the amount of time taken up by the children. They were less likely to agree strongly that having children had made them happier people. However, the parents of boomerang children experienced no more frequent conflict than did other parents.

The experience with boomerang children, therefore, is not strikingly different from the experience of delayed launching. In either case, the parents tend to find the situation to be more positive than negative, even though there may be some added stress, frustration, and conflict.

The Couple Together Again

When the couple finally does have an empty nest, the initial reaction is likely to be one of mixed emotions, with grief yielding sooner or later to relief and happiness because of the new opportunities and options that open up (Rubenstein 2007). Before the joy of the adventure of a fresh phase of life can be experienced, however, the couple will usually experience a time of grieving over the loss. And some will grieve more than others.

Men as well as women may find it painful for the children to leave. A psychology professor put it this way:

> Two of the most painful times I remember are when our oldest child announced he was leaving home to go to college and when our youngest did the same. With the oldest, it meant that the family was beginning to break up. With the youngest, it meant a loss of a special kind of parenting that I valued, that day-to-day involvement with the kids.

This man had a good relationship with both his children and his wife. This may seem to make the launching more painful, but actually it can be more difficult for those who haven't had the best family life. For example, those who have poor marital relationships are likely to find the empty nest disagreeable (Lauer and Lauer 1999b). Also, men who have been very work minded may be well established in their careers and now would like to devote more time to their children. But the children are leaving, and the men are left with the disappointment of a relationship that can never be.

Women who have invested themselves totally, or nearly so, in child rearing also will find the empty nest painful (Lauer and Lauer 1999b). The woman who had little other than motherhood to occupy herself during the earlier stages may find this stage a deeply painful one. She may have fulfilled her intimacy needs in her relationships with her children. She even may feel somewhat estranged from her husband because she has neglected the marriage. And even if there is no estrangement, she may find that her husband is too involved with work or his career to take the place of the children in her life. She desperately needs new challenges, new tasks, new intimate relationships, but she may be at a loss as to where to find them.

But how many women, or men for that matter, come to the empty-nest stage and find it empty of meaning as well as of children? Certainly not the majority. To the contrary, most people, both men and women, report that it is a time of increased marital satisfaction and renewal for their marriage (Lauer and Lauer 1999b). A combination of reduced parental and work responsibilities as people age leads to enhanced marital satisfaction (Orbuch et al. 1996).

Personal

An Empty-Nest High

Mark is a building contractor who has been married 26 years. A year ago, the last of his four children left home for college. Mark and his wife, Jeri, are devoted parents and have had a close family life. How would they deal with the empty nest? Mark tells us:

We've always had a great time as a family. I must admit that I had mixed feelings when my first kid—my oldest daughter—got married. I had to battle the feeling that an intruder had come and disrupted our family. But at least we still had three other kids. Then marriage and college finally got to all of them. When my youngest girl left for college, my wife and I went with her to help her get settled in the dormitory. We both cried most of the way back home. Our nest was depressingly empty.

At first, I tried to deal with it by increasing my workload. Jeri works with me in the business and she also has been active in the League of Women Voters and our church. She got even more active in the first few months of our empty nest.

That caused some problems. Instead of growing closer together and supporting each other, we were becoming strangers. We irritated each other. We weren't happy with our nest being empty, but neither of us was helping the other to cope with it.

I don't know how long we might have gone on that way. But one day Jeri said to me, "Mark, we're heading for serious trouble." That shocked me. I knew it, but I didn't want to admit it. And I didn't know she felt the same way. We talked about it. We agreed that we needed to get back to work on our marriage. We knew some other couples who talked about how much they were enjoying themselves since their kids were gone. Why couldn't we?

We decided that we would stop burying our sadness in work and start exploring this new stage of life. So we started doing things together. We took a few weekend trips. We almost shocked ourselves when we took off from the office one afternoon and went home, made love, went out to dinner, and took in a show. That was it! I suddenly realized what a great life we have. It still feels a little strange to come home and not have anyone there, or for things to be so quiet at night. But I want to tell you that we're on a second honeymoon. We're learning things about each other and exploring things together and just thoroughly enjoying ourselves.

I guess the thing is that life just isn't as serious as it was when the kids were at home. I don't worry about things. Even when the kids were grown, Jeri and I both worried if they were out real late or if they were going to a party where everyone was drinking a lot or even if they didn't seem to be eating properly. We don't even think about those things now. We're just having fun.

For most people, then, stage five represents a time of increasing marital satisfaction and renewed family strength (Levenson, Carstensen, and Gottman 1993). Husbands perceive a sharp increase in agreement on various issues at this stage (White 1987). Wives begin to spend less time in housework (Rexroat and Shehan 1987). There may be a sexual renewal in the marriage as the couple realizes that they can express themselves sexually in a more relaxed and private way. There may be a sense of new freedom—fewer responsibilities, less financial strain, less family work. The marriage may become more egalitarian than it was during the child-rearing years. And whatever grief is involved in the children leaving may be more than compensated by pride in their achievements and the satisfactions of having parented them.

Overall, then, the empty nest is likely to be a stage that is gratifying and filled with a new zest for living. The psychologist quoted previously had more to say: "What I discovered, however, was that just being with my wife again was great. We're having a ball! I love my children dearly, and I can't imagine being without them, but life has never been any better than it is now."

Grandparenthood

Increasing numbers of people are experiencing the grandparent role. Some people become grandparents as early as their 40s. Among those 65 and older, about three-fourths are grandparents. Although the pride of grandparents is legendary in our society, manifesting itself in everything from pins to bumper stickers that say, "Ask me about my

When the last child leaves home, a couple must come to terms with their marital relationship for the future.

grandchildren" or "Happiness is being a grandparent," not everyone welcomes the role. Some grandparents resist the implication of their own aging. Some do not want to get involved in the child care aspects that are frequently expected of them. But for the most part, grandparenting is a positive experience in people's lives (Kaufman and Elder 2003). In fact, grandparents suffer emotionally, including becoming depressed, if they are deprived of contact with their grandchildren for any reason (Drew and Silverstein 2007).

Types of Grandparents.   Grandparents relate in differing ways to their grandchildren, depending in part on the kind of relationship the grandparents had with their own grandparents and in part on the age of the grandparents (King and Elder 1997; Silverstein and Marenco 2001). There are five different types of grandparent: the formal, the fun seeker, the surrogate parent, the reservoir of family wisdom, and the distant figure.

The *formal* grandparent has definite ideas of the role and clearly distinguishes it from the parental role. Formal grandparents may occasionally indulge the child and do some babysitting, but they basically let child care duties remain in the hands of the parents. They show constant interest in the grandchild but do not offer advice on parenting.

The *fun seeker* establishes an informal, playful relationship with the grandchild, joining the child in play almost like a playmate.

The *surrogate parent* assumes the responsibilities of child care. Increasing numbers of grandparents are functioning as surrogate parents to some degree, including growing numbers who have total responsibility for child care (Simmons 2001). A third or more of the grandparents care for their grandchildren five or more years, and more than half of the grandparents are in the labor force. The factors leading to care by grandparents include parental divorce, illness, drug addiction, child abuse, and neglect (Goodman and Silverstein 2001). When grandparents coparent with the parents—particularly among Hispanics—they can form an emotionally close and satisfying family group (Goodman and Silverstein 2006; Goodman 2007). Grandparents who must function as surrogate parents and assume total responsibility, on the other hand, must deal with significant changes in their lifestyles and their relationships. They may have to re-enter the job market or extend their working hours to compensate for the additional costs (Wang and Marcotte 2007). They may be more vulnerable to various physical and emotional problems from the stress of parenting their grandchildren (Williamson, Softas-Nall, and Miller 2003; Goodman and Silverstein 2006). However, a study of grandmothers who were parenting their grandchildren found that the grandmothers saw themselves as wiser, more relaxed, and more involved than they were as parents (Dolbin-MacNab 2006). And a large-scale study reported no dramatic or widespread negative consequences for grandparents' health or health behavior (Hughes, Waite, LaPierre, and Luo 2007). In short, while the grandparent who becomes a surrogate parent will undoubtedly have some additional stress and challenges, the overall experience is more likely to be gratifying than detrimental to his or her well-being.

The *reservoir of family wisdom* is a grandparent who acts as a source of special skills and resources for the grandchild. Both the parents and the grandchildren are subordinate to this grandparent. Everyone defers to his or her judgment. This role, incidentally, seems to be rare.

Finally, the *distant figure* is the grandparent who has kindly but rare contact with the child. The distant figure may be separated by distance or by choice. In any case, contact is infrequent and brief.

What Grandparents Do for Us.   As the preceding suggests, the idea of grandparenthood as being simply pleasure without responsibility grossly underestimates the role that grandparents play in our lives. Parents may find grandparents helpful in providing various kinds of support, including practical help in child rearing, giving grandchildren a sense of their heritage, providing emotional and financial support, and passing along to grandchildren knowledge and wisdom about everyday living (Dunning 2006; Ruby et al. 2007). We should note that this can be a delicate role to play for grandparents, since the line between support and interference is not always clear. If the behavior is defined as interference, conflict may arise between parents and grandparents.

Conflict can also occur in the grandparent–grandchild relationship, but grandparents are more likely to provide important benefits to their grandchildren. Data from a national sample, for example, show that the closer the grandchildren feel to their grandparents, the less likely they are to have depressive symptoms (Ruiz and Silverstein 2007). And grandchildren themselves report a number of ways that their grandparents have influenced their development. Grandparents help them to get a sense of their own identity by linking them up with their heritage. Grandparents help adolescents understand their own parents better and may function as confidants for the adolescents when the latter are unwilling for some reason to talk with their parents about a matter. Adolescents tend to view grandparents in warm, comfortable, and supportive terms. When they have such a relationship with grandparents, they are likely to develop more positive attitudes toward older people and also about their own aging.

When asked about the relationship with their grandparents, young adults agree that it is very important to them. They get a certain amount of emotional gratification from it. A survey of 391 young adult grandchildren (mean age of 19.1 years) reported the following reasons as important factors in feeling close to grandparents: enjoying their personalities; enjoying shared activities with them; experiencing their appreciation, attention, and support; and relating to them as models, teachers, advisers, and sources of inspiration (Kennedy 1991). Another study, of 171 Canadian undergraduates, looked at the relationship the young people had with grandparents with whom they were close and not as close (Boon and Brussoni 1996). The students indicated that the grandparents with whom they were close were influential in their lives, that they had frequent contact with those grandparents and

Many older couples find retirement an opportunity to pursue their interests.

shared a number of activities with them, and that all of these experiences were important to them.

In sum, while the grandparent–grandchild relationship is not as intense as the parent–child one, it is a unique and potentially highly gratifying relationship that is important in the lives of both grandparents and grandchildren. It is a form of intimacy that enhances the quality of life.

THE AGING FAMILY

In the aging family, there is a shift of roles. The middle generation, the children of the aging couple, take on a more central role in the family. The aging couple must cope with various challenges and problems, including retirement, the death of friends and siblings, and their own physical decline. Eventually, one of the spouses is likely to face the challenge of living alone. But this stage, like every other, has its satisfactions as well as its problems.

Retirement

Retirement can be a critical time for a couple. When a married individual first retires, marital quality tends to go down because of the adjustments required (Moen, Kim, and Hofmeister 2001). The retired individual has to adjust to a new role, which may include the loss of the highly valued role of worker. The couple has to adjust to an altered schedule. If both spouses have been working and only one retires, they are likely to experience more conflict in their relationship as they try to adapt to the situation.

In part, adjusting well to retirement depends on whether the retirement is a voluntary one. Those forced to retire because of age or other factors will have a more difficult time adjusting. This can place a strain on a marriage. A depressed man, for example, who sits around the house all day and grieves over a forced retirement can create considerable frustration and tension in the home.

Once the initial adjustment has been made, however, marital quality tends to go up (Moen, Kim, and Hofmeister 2001). Among a sample of 421 retired subjects and their spouses, researchers found that 77 percent of the retirees reported retirement satisfaction and 59 percent of couples reported joint satisfaction (Smith and Moen 2004). High levels of joint satisfaction are less likely if one spouse remains employed when the other has retired (Szinovacz and Davey 2005). Satisfaction also depends on such things as whether retirement was voluntary, the couples' financial status, and the extent to which the couple engage in joint, meaningful activities.

Marital Relations

A couple in the sixth stage is more likely to be oriented maritally than parentally. That is, spouses are likely to focus more of their time and energy on their relationship with each other than on that with their children and grandchildren. Their marriage is likely to be more egalitarian as the husband increases his share of the housework, particularly once he is retired (Solomon, Acock, and Walker 2004).

The couple may continue to have an active and meaningful sex life during this stage, especially if the marriage relationships generally is a good one (Hawton, Gath, and Day 1994). Comedians and popular beliefs reinforce the notion that sexuality vanishes from our lives at some point in the aging process. However, as we pointed out in chapter 4, people can have sexual relations throughout life. It is not true that older people lack sexual desire, or that they are physically incapable of having sexual relations. The idea that meaningful, and even exciting, sexual experiences necessarily cease at some point in an individual's life is a myth. In fact, contrary to the notion that the sexual drive is one of the first to diminish with age, sexuality is actually one of the last functions to decline (Trudel, Turgeon, and Piche 2000).

In contrast to the jokes and myths, therefore, sex may be an important part of the aging couple's marital relationship. For couples with long-standing problems, of course, age can be an excuse for ceasing sexual activity. But there are no inherent physiological reasons for sex to stop. Actually, the majority of married people over the age of 70 report having sex, sometimes as often as twice a week or more.

In general, then, how much satisfaction is there with marriage at this stage? For most couples, it tends to be high, higher in fact than at any stage since the couple was first married (Trudel, Turgeon, and Piche 2000). And this is particularly true for those couples who have egalitarian attitudes (Kaufman and Taniguchi 2006). There are, however, fluctuations by age. In an older study, Gilford (1984) found that satisfaction was highest among those in the 63- to 69-year age group (she measured satisfaction in terms of the amount of positive interaction and negative sentiment expressed by couples). Those between 55 and 62 and those between 70 and 90 had somewhat lower levels of satisfaction. She speculated that the reason for the higher levels among those 63 to 69 was that it is the "honeymoon" stage after retirement that allows the spouses to enjoy such resources as "leisure time, inclination to spend it together and with adult children, good health, and adequate income with which to enhance marital lifestyle and negotiate marital happiness" (Gilford 1984:331).

Other Relationships

Although the aging couple is more maritally than parentally oriented, family relationships are still very important. The great majority of adults over 65 live with someone else, primarily with spouses or other relatives. The great majority also live within a short distance of at least one child. The elderly prefer to maintain their own homes rather than live with their children. This is a shift from the past. In the mid-nineteenth century, nearly 70 percent of the elderly lived with adult children (Ruggles 2007). Now, only a small minority of people are involved in intergenerational coresidence.

But while not likely to live with their adult children, the elderly still tend to have frequent contact with them. Of course, the contact can be of differing kinds (van Gaalen and Dykstra 2006). Those with a history of strained,

Comparison

Caring for Elderly Family Members on Malo

One of the problems facing all societies is the care of the aged. Responsibility for this care generally falls to the family although, in the United States, this responsibility is frequently assigned to nursing homes. Malo is an island in the South Pacific whose inhabitants are relatively poor by U.S. standards. As in the United States, people on Malo are considered in need of caregiving when they clearly cannot be self-sufficient. But who assumes the caregiving responsibility? The Maloese have a saying that "Men stay on the land and women leave it." That is, when a woman marries, she is expected to move to her husband's village and become a part of his land. Her sons will belong to that land, but her daughters will marry onto other lands.

The spouse is responsible for caring for his or her aged partner. If the spouse dies, caregiving is assumed by daughters-in-law and, only if necessary, by daughters. Men do not get involved in this caregiving. In fact, a man is not supposed to touch his mother and thus cannot take care of her. Nor is a man supposed to care for his sister, brother, father's father, or various other family members. The man's responsibility is generally only for his wife. The reason for this arrangement, which the Maloese take very seriously, is the belief that certain embodiments of males and females are very different and are not supposed to come into contact with each other.

Even though they have clearly defined rules, the Maloese can experience conflict when dealing with the elderly. A daughter's first obligation, for instance, is to her husband's family. But she is likely still to have emotional ties to her own parents and other relatives. No society yet, including Malo, has provided a system for care of elderly family members that relieves people of having to make difficult choices (Rubinstein 1994).

---

troubled relationships with their children may continue in the same pattern when the children are adults. They will relate to each other in ways that are more hurtful than helpful (Coleman 2007). For some of these, any contact will likely be a negative one (e.g., argumentative or distasteful). For others, the contact may reflect little more than the children's sense of obligation (e.g., call dad to wish him a happy birthday even though both the child and the father know it's a ritual done without affection). And for still others, there may be some kind of support (e.g., financial or helping with errands) but, again, without any affection.

The relationship with adult children that enhances the quality of life is one marked by genuine affection and respect. It will be the kind of harmonious relationship that exists between friends (van Gaalen and Dykstra 2006). And the most satisfying relationship will be one in which there is reciprocity between parent and child (Lowenstein, Katz, and Gur-Yaish 2007). That is, in accord with equity theory, both the parents and the children will contribute in some way to the relationship. When the role of the child is primarily to give help to the parent, with the parent giving little in return, the relationship is not as satisfying.

Although children play a major role in the experiences of intimacy of older adults, other relationships are also important. Whatever people's age, the maintenance of intimate ties is essential to a high quality of life (Bowling and Gabriel 2007). The aged do not need as many close relationships as they had when they were younger. Nor do they need the frequency of interaction they once had. Rather, they need, and tend to choose, contact with a smaller number of others whom they find satisfying, whether family members or friends (Berg, Hassing, McClearn, and Johansson 2006).

Thus, the elderly may include in their network of intimate friends siblings (in some cases, even when they have not been that close to their siblings earlier in their lives), other relatives, and old or new friends. Friends can be found in organizations such as church and local senior centers (Aday, Kehoe, and Farney 2006). In effect, those who make close friends may create a surrogate family, something quite important to the elderly who never married or had children or whose relatives are few and distant (McDill, Hall, and Turell 2006). Whether the network of intimate relationships includes a spouse and/or other family members, or just friends, the effect is to enhance the quality of life and promote better physical and emotional health (Sheare and Fleury 2006).

Death of a Spouse

At every age level, women are more likely than men to face the death of a spouse, and the likelihood becomes increasingly greater in the older age groups (figure 13.2).

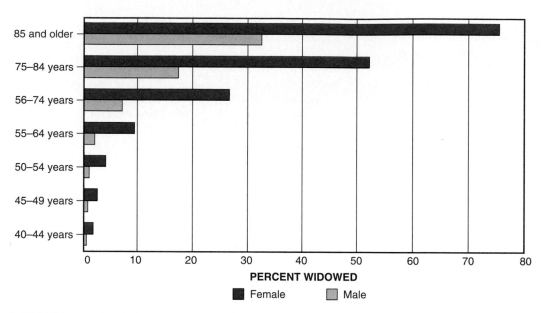

FIGURE 13.2   Proportion Widowed, by Age, 2006
Source: U.S. Census Bureau 2007a.

Although men tend to have a harder time adjusting to the death of a spouse than do women (because older men tend to lean more heavily than do women on their spouses for support and intimacy), the death of a spouse is always traumatic and typically entails a time of emotional and physical distress. Distress is diminished though not eliminated by a helpful social support network (Miller et al. 1998).

There are various reasons for the distress. For one thing, there is the loss of intimacy. A relationship that, for most married people, is the most intimate relationship of all has been severed. There is also a loss of identity. One is no longer a husband or a wife, a role that has occupied a major portion of one's life. What will take the place of that role? The problem is intensified because there tends to be a somewhat negative connotation to the term *widow* or *widower*.

The surviving spouse also must go through a grieving process. A study of grief among 141 older people who lost a spouse identified three different patterns (Ott, Lueger, Kelber, and Prigerson 2007). The "common" pattern (49 percent of the sample) involved elevated levels of grief and depression that diminished over time. The "resilient" pattern (34 percent of the sample) was characterized by relatively low levels of grief and depression. And the "chronic" pattern (17 percent of the sample) had the highest levels of grief and depression and both short-term and long-term negative health consequences.

The negative health consequences of grief include both emotional and physical health problems, including higher rates of depression, anxiety disorders, cardiovascular disease, and cancer (Onrust and Cuijpers 2006; Hart et al. 2007). In fact, the death rate from major diseases is higher among the bereaved.

For the majority of people who sooner or later work through their grief, the process begins with a period of confusion, which includes some lapse of memory, difficulty in concentrating, and wandering thoughts. There is likely to be an intense feeling of loneliness, even in those who have children. We heard a woman try to console her newly widowed friend by reminding the friend, "At least you have your children." The widow replied, "It's not the same as your mate. It's just not the same." Eventually, the children may help assuage the grief and provide a source of support and renewed interest in life. But the remaining spouse typically has to wrestle with difficult periods of loneliness. And depression tends to accompany the loneliness. On top of all this may be practical worries as well—financial concerns or who will do some of the chores that the spouse formerly handled.

Eventually, the surviving spouse is likely to work through his or her grief and begin to pursue a new life (Bonanno et al. 2002). There are ways to facilitate the process, all of which involve relationships. One way, for example, is to do volunteer work—not immediately, but at least within a few years. Volunteer work protects people against depression and increases their sense of well-being (Yunqing 2007).

A study of 75 widows ages 60 to 90, reported that those who were more successful in resolving their grief had discussed a number of important matters with their spouses, family, or friends prior to the spouse's death (Hansson and Remondet 1987). Specifically, they had talked about finances, family reactions, their own feelings, how their lives might change, and how their friendships might be affected. Discussion with the spouse was possible because most widows (and widowers) have some period of warning. Of course, such discussion requires the spouses to continue to engage in self-disclosure to the very end and not engage in a game of pretending that the dying spouse will recover. Those widows who had discussed the issues not only resolved their grief more quickly but were better adjusted some years later and reported better physical and emotional health than the others.

Many individuals get on with their lives by dating and eventually marrying again (Carr 2004). A study of 249 widows and 101 widowers concluded that those who were either in a new romance or remarried 25 months after the spouse's death were emotionally healthier than those who were still uninvolved with someone new (Schneider et al. 1996). The chances for widows to remarry, especially those who are older, is less than that for widowers. Those who do remarry tend to have higher morale than those who do not. The main reasons men give for remarrying are for companionship and to be cared for; the main reasons women give for remarrying are for companionship and love. The quest for intimacy never ends.

SUMMARY

The idea of the family life cycle is based on the notion that families, like everything else, go through a process from birth through growth to decline and death. A useful way of conceptualizing the family life cycle is to look at ways that families must alter their attitudes and relationships in order to adapt to each of six stages:

1. the young unattached adult
2. the newly married couple
3. the family with young children
4. the family at midlife: adolescents and aging parents
5. the stage of launching children and moving on
6. the family in later life

Both cyclical and linear changes of many kinds occur over these stages, including marital satisfaction, empathy, discussion, and regard.

Our experiences in passing through the family life cycle are affected by social changes. Some important changes in recent times are the lowered likelihood of experiencing the death of one's parents or of a child, the increased likelihood of being a grandparent, and the increased likelihood of facing marital disruption because of divorce rather than death, which also means a greater likelihood of experiencing remarriage.

The newly married couple tends to have a high level of certain family strengths, including self-disclosure, loyalty, trust, and respect. One of the couple's important tasks is forming its own marital system.

The couple with young children faces the challenge of taking on the roles of mother and father as well as husband and wife and of enlarging the family system to include other people. Marital satisfaction is likely to be lower at this stage.

The couple at midlife faces multiple challenges: dealing with adolescent children, including those who are in the emerging adulthood stage; caring for aging parents; and dealing with their own concerns about their own aging, their marriage, and their employment. Although this tends to be the most stressful stage of the family life cycle, there are ways to enhance satisfaction, including the use of rites of passage.

In the launching and empty-nest stage, the couple must deal with the children moving out. They must come to terms again with their marital relationship and its future. Women are more likely than men to find the empty nest stressful because they tend to invest themselves more in the child-rearing process. But the majority of people report the empty nest as a time of increased marital satisfaction and renewed family strength.

Grandparenthood is likely to occur in the fifth stage. There are different kinds of grandparents, including the formal, the fun seeker, the surrogate parent, the reservoir of family wisdom, and the distant figure. The grandparent–grandchild relationship can be highly gratifying for both generations.

The aging family involves a shift of roles, with the middle generation taking on a more central place in the family. Retirement occurs at this stage. People may adjust well to, or even welcome, retirement when it is voluntary. Marital problems can arise if the new roles are not worked out satisfactorily.

Couples in the sixth stage tend to be maritally rather than parentally oriented. The marriage is likely to become more egalitarian. The couple may continue to have an active and meaningful sex life. And marital satisfaction is likely to be at its highest point since the couple's early years together. Family relationships are still important. Contact with children tends to be frequent.

Women are far more likely than men to experience the death of a spouse. People go through the grieving process in various ways. Most deal with their grief and get on with their lives, but some endure chronic grief and suffer various kinds of emotional and physical health problems. Getting involved in volunteer work is a healthy way to deal with the loss. Also, those who talk over various matters with the dying spouse make a better adjustment to the death than do others. Many eventually remarry, although widows are less likely to do so than are widowers. Companionship is one of the most common reasons that both men and women remarry after the death of a spouse.

Principles for Enhancing Intimacy

1. Change is inevitable in our family relationships. Yet we are often surprised and generally resist change when it occurs. And unfortunately, many intimate relationships are strained beyond repair by the onslaught of change. It is vital, therefore, that you understand and prepare for the alterations that typically occur during the family life cycle. Anticipating some of the challenges at each stage of the process will help you cope when they actually take place.

2. At every stage of life, there are opportunities for personal as well as family growth. Growth comes from taking responsibility for yourself, opening yourself to others and to new experiences, taking advantage of available resources, and persevering in the face of difficulties. If we affirm personal growth, our capacity for genuine intimacy with others will increase.

3. One of the major tasks facing newly married couples is to develop their own family system. This is not an easy job. For example, couples are often uncertain and anxious about how and when to establish holiday traditions that are theirs and separate from those of their families of origin. In order to accomplish this most effectively, the couple needs to discuss the matter thoroughly, come to an understanding of what they want, and then gradually introduce these plans to their families.

4. Children can affect the marriage relationship of their parents at various stages in the family life cycle. They bring joy and pain, fun and responsibility. They also can consume much of the attention of one or both of their parents. Unless the parents are vigilant, their relationship to each other can suffer from neglect. Thus, spouses need always to reserve time for themselves as a couple, work at their marriage, and prepare for the time when the two of them will be alone together once again.

5. If these are difficult times, remember there's hope. If you are experiencing problems and frustrations in a particular stage of your family life cycle, it is useful to remember that this time will pass. And if you confront the difficulties and work through them, your family system eventually will be stronger.

KEY TERMS

adolescence   *292*
death rate   *288*

family life cycle   *286*
fusion   *291*

rites of passage   *296*
sandwich generation   *294*

ON THE WEB The Family Life Cycle

This chapter outlines and describes the transition phases and challenges associated with married and unmarried families. The six stages that are discussed are not the only way to conceptualize the family life cycle. You could have fewer or more stages. Moreover, the discussion of many of the issues and challenges is necessarily abbreviated—whole books have been written, for example, on the caregiving task of those in the sandwich generation. You can explore these issues and challenges further in the following two sites:

www.mhhe.com/lauer7e

U.S. Department of Health and Human Services
http://www.hhs.gov/aging

This is the Department of Health and Human Services' site on aging issues, including both data and discussions of such topics as health, nursing homes, safety, Medicare and Medicaid, and caregiving.

Ask Dr. Gayle
http://www.askdrgayle.com/flc1.html

At this site, you will find a discussion of the family life cycle that employs seven rather than six stages. Each stage is described and illustrated with case studies. At the end of part two of the discussion is an exercise that you can take or give to others to discuss the stress involved in the various stages.

Using these two sites, enlarge your understanding with the following projects:

1. Go to the government site and call up the resources on caregiving. Assign different aspects to a number of students in your class, form a panel, and make a brief presentation to the class. Give the students an opportunity to ask questions. Alternatively, you could use the materials to set up a debate: Caregiving: Responsibility of the Family or the Government?

2. Study the seven stages described on the Ask Dr. Gayle site. Is this a more or less useful categorization than the six stages discussed in the text? Justify your conclusion.

3. Use the exercise at the end of the Ask Dr. Gayle site to explore the stress at the various stages. Give the exercise to a number of older adults. Ask them to describe the nature of the added stress at the stages they identify. Are there particular stages that are typically named as more stressful? What are the reasons for the stress? What did you learn from them that can be of help to you in the future?

part five

~ CHALLENGES TO INTIMACY ~

philosopher speculated that the family might one day become an obsolete institution. By contrast, an anthropologist speculated that, if civilization were ever wiped out in a nuclear holocaust, the last man on earth would spend his dying days searching through the rubble for his family. We believe the anthropologist was closer to reality than was the philosopher. Most people try to maintain intimate relationships, especially family relationships, and they endure a great deal of suffering before they break such relationships.

In this final section, we will look at some of the crises that strain intimacy in the family. The crises can lead either to disruption or to an enhanced intimacy. Then we will discuss what happens when, in spite of the tendency to hang on, a decision is made to terminate the marital relationship. Finally, we will talk about the nature of and problems in the reconstituted family. The need for family intimacy is so strong that most divorced people try again to establish a meaningful family life. As the anthropologist suggested, in spite of the high rate of disruption in our society, people fundamentally value and strive to create and maintain families.

14

~ FAMILY CRISES ~

LEARNING OBJECTIVES

After reading and studying chapter 14, you should be able to

1 Explain how stressful events can result in a family crisis.

2 Discuss the various types of stressor events.

3 Define *alcohol abuse* and show how it affects the quality of family life.

4 Describe the extent and types of violence in families.

5 Define *child abuse* and *incest* and tell why these occur.

6 Explain the causes of spouse and parent abuse.

7 Discuss the consequences of abuse for families.

8 Relate the reasons that the same type of crisis can have different consequences in different families.

9 Describe how denial, avoidance, and scapegoating are ineffective ways of coping with a crisis.

10 Discuss the five tools for effective coping with a crisis.

What can you do if you have a drinking problem or if you are in a family with someone who abuses alcohol? Alcoholics Anonymous (AA) is the best known and one of the most effective self-help organizations for alcoholics. Al-Anon and Alateen are organizations for the spouses and children of alcoholics. They help the individual cope with the difficulties of living with an alcoholic.

There are self-help groups today to deal with all kinds of problems that can create a crisis in a family, ranging from groups that help people with different kinds of addictions (such as gambling) to those that help people who have various kinds of emotional problems. There are groups for the overweight, the unemployed, and the abused.

Locate some kind of self-help group in your community (the telephone directory is a good place to begin) and get permission to visit a group meeting. Note the way that the group works to help each member cope with problems. Ask one of the people attending if you can interview him or her for your class project.

Tell the person that you are particularly interested in how his or her experience relates to family life—both the family of origin and the current family of which the individual is a part. Explore the following questions:

1. What kinds of experiences in the family of origin seemed to contribute to the problem, if any?
2. What kinds of experiences in the current family contributed to the problem, if any?
3. Did anyone else in the family or the family of origin have a similar problem?
4. How did the problem affect family life, including the marital relationship and relations with children?

If the entire class participates in this project, see if you can come up with any common factors in the family background of the people and any common consequences for family life. Do different kinds of problems seem to have different sources and consequences? Why or why not? ✽

For days, wildfires raged through our area. We had to evacuate our home for nearly a week. When we returned, we discovered that hundreds of homes had burned down in our neighborhood. Driving around, words like "disaster" and "crisis" kept coming to mind. Yet a smile brought a moment of relief as we drove by one burned-down home. The owner had put up a homemade sign with the words, "Termite free at last."

That owner had employed one of the ways that people cope with a crisis—the use of humor. Did the humor mean the owner felt no pain? Or shrugged the incident off and got on with life? Or was not in a crisis? Not at all. The sign was a way of saying, "This isn't going to defeat us. We'll deal with it." Having their home burn down is one way a family can find itself in a crisis. Fortunately, it is not a common way. But crisis does come to every family at some point. In this chapter, we will discuss some of the crises that come to families and threaten intimacy. We will look at greater length at two kinds of crises that are widespread: alcohol and other drug abuse and violence. These two problems involve severe trauma in the family. Finally, we will see how people deal with crises, including both successful and unsuccessful methods of coping.

SOURCES OF FAMILY CRISES

Have you ever experienced what you would call a family crisis? If so, what was the nature of that crisis? What caused it? If you posed these questions to other people, you might hear of some differing kinds of crises than you have experienced. In any case, crises are closely linked with stressful events and/or behavior.

Stress and Crisis

In their efforts to understand diverse family responses to stressful events, family scholars have used the ABCX model developed by Reuben Hill (1958). Hill (1949) began his work by studying the **stress** endured by families during war. He developed the ABCX family crisis model to try to account for differential success in coping. In essence, A is the **stressor event** and the hardships it produces. B is the management of the stress through coping resources that the family has. Since an important aspect of the impact of stress is *the way in which the stressful situation is defined,* C

Symbolic Interactionist Theory Applied

refers to the family's definition of the event. A, B, and C interact to produce X, the crisis.

For example, let us say that two families, the Smiths and the Joneses, face the stressor of unemployment (A). The Smiths define it as undesirable but also as a challenge (C), and they decide that each family member will try to find work and will do something to save money (B). The interaction of these three produces no serious crisis for them (X). The Joneses, on the other hand, define the event as a disaster (C). They expect the father to find a new job immediately and to do something to avoid any serious change in their lifestyle (B). The interaction of these three is a crisis (X).

The two examples are simplified, of course. In fact, the model itself is somewhat simplified, because there are other elements that may be important in the outcome of a stressor. Recognizing this, McCubbin and Patterson (1983) proposed a Double ABCX model. They relabeled the A factor as *family demands.* There are three components to family demands. One is the *stressor.* The second is the *hardships* that accompany the stressor (such as increasing financial problems when a parent is unemployed). Third, there are *pileups,*

> the residuals of family tension that linger from unresolved prior stressors or that are inherent in ongoing family roles such as being a parent or spouse (McCubbin and Patterson 1983:279).

This model has been shown to explain the differential adaptation of women with severe physical disabilities (Florian and Danagoor 1994), the ways families function when a member is recovering from a stroke (Clark 1999), the adjustment of Korean mothers to their children's cancer (Han 2003), and the stress of parents of children with intellectual or physical disabilities (Saloviita, Italinna, and Leinonen 2003; Xu 2007).

It is important to recognize the place of pileups or prior strains. A stressor does not occur in a vacuum but in the context of ongoing life. Suppose, for instance, that you learned more about the Smiths and the Joneses, the two families introduced in the preceding example. What if the unemployment of Mr. Smith occurred while there were few other strains, while that of Mr. Jones occurred in the midst of family illness and at a point when the oldest daughter was preparing to go to college? Clearly, we need to know something about what is going on in a family at the time of the stressor event to fully understand its response to that stressor.

Pauline Boss (2001), who has made extensive studies of family stress, concluded that many families in crisis are not sick families but are simply facing a greater volume of stress than they, or most other families, can handle. Boss also argued that families today are under more pressure than those of the past. Indeed, you only need to reflect on the changes discussed in chapter 1 and the challenges and demands discussed in subsequent chapters to recognize the complexity and difficulty of family life today. In addition, there are the daily hassles that are qualitatively different from those of previous generations: the traffic, the hectic schedules of children, the inordinately high cost of housing, the threats of violence and terrorist activities, and so on.

In other words, there are numerous commonplace tensions and strains in most of our lives. If some additional stressors in the form of unemployment, serious illness, or severe personal or interpersonal problems occur, their cumulative effect can lead to illness in the family (Bigbee 1992) or to some kind of crisis of well-being. Nearly all of us will experience such a crisis, if not a series of crises, because it is unlikely that anyone can live in a family for an extended period of time without encountering periods of severe stress.

Stressor Events

As we discuss the stressor events that can bring about a family crisis, it is important to keep in mind that the events per se are not sufficient to cause serious problems. As the model indicates, the context in which the event occurs, the way that the family defines the event, and the resources the family has for dealing with it are all crucial to the outcome. Still, it is important to be aware of the kinds of events that are likely to cause a family crisis.

Types of Stressor Events. What kinds of stressor events are most likely to result in a family crisis? Some of the common ones that you may face include the death of a family member, a serious illness or accident to a family member, unemployment of a family member, an unwanted pregnancy, a miscarriage, a move to a new location, serious personal problems such as emotional illness or alcohol abuse by a family member, and serious interpersonal problems such as abuse, infidelity, or a broken engagement within the family.

Stressor events can be classified in terms of various dimensions as shown in table 14.1. Thus, a stressor event can arise from within or outside of the family. It can be an expected or an unpredictable event, controllable or uncontrollable. For example, international and national shifts in the markets for agricultural products create economic hardship for U.S. farmers that leads to stress in many farm families and increases aggression and depression among farm children (Elder et al. 1992). These shifts are external, nonnormative, nonvolitional,

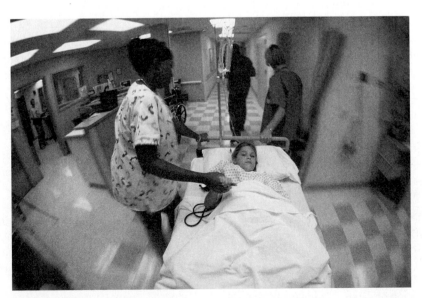

Every family must deal with times of stress and crisis.

TABLE 14.1 Types of Stressor Events

Internal	External
Events that begin from someone inside the family, such as getting drunk, suicide, or running for election	Events that begin from someone or something outside the family, such as earthquakes, terrorism, the inflation rate, or cultural attitudes toward women and minorities
Normative	**Nonnormative**
Events that are expected over the family life cycle, such as birth, launching an adolescent, marriage, aging, or death	Events that are unexpected, such as winning a lottery, getting a divorce, dying young, war, or being taken hostage; often but not always disastrous
Ambiguous	**Nonambiguous**
Events for which you can't get the facts and that are so unclear that you're not even sure that it's happening to you and your family	Events for which clear facts are available (what is happening, when, how long, and to whom)
Volitional	**Nonvolitional**
Events that are wanted and sought out, such as a freely chosen job change, a college entrance, or a wanted pregnancy	Events that are not sought out but just happen, such as being laid off or the sudden loss of someone loved
Chronic	**Acute**
A situation that has long duration, such as diabetes, chemical addiction, or racial discrimination	An event that lasts a short time but is severe, such as breaking a limb, losing a job, or flunking a test
Cumulative	**Isolated**
Events that pile up, one right after the other, so that there is no resolution before the next one occurs; a dangerous situation in most cases	An event that occurs alone, at least with no other events apparent at that time, that can be pinpointed easily

Source: From Pauline Boss, *Family Stress Management.* Copyright © 1988 Sage Publications, Inc., Newbury Park, CA. Reprinted by permission of Sage Publications, Inc.

and acute. They may be ambiguous or nonambiguous to the farmers, depending on their understanding of market trends.

As table 14.1 indicates, stressor events can be freely chosen (the volitional category) as well as imposed. A businessman shared an example with us:

> I was excited about getting a new job in a new city. But for the first few months on that job, I was really distressed. I thought I had made the biggest mistake of my life.

Stressor Events and the Family Life Cycle. As you would expect, the kinds of things most likely to be important stressors vary somewhat over the family life cycle. Among young, recently wed couples, work and financial strains are most common. Changing jobs or careers, becoming dissatisfied with one's job or career, having problems with people on the job, and taking on additional responsibilities at work are all potential sources of stress for the young couple. As we noted in chapter 11, there is a kind of contagion across work and family roles, such that stress in one area tends to spill over into the other. In some cases, a self-perpetuating cycle can be set up: Work stress is brought home, creating marital problems that make effective work problematic and cause further difficulty at work, aggravating the individual's stress, and so forth.

During the early childbearing years, financial strains are the most common. There are increased demands on the family's income for such things as food, clothing, and medical and dental care. Major purchases, such as homes and cars, are made, putting the family deeply into debt. The couple may have to take out additional loans or refinance their debt to cover the increased expenses of the growing family.

While financial pressures tend to lessen somewhat as the children grow, time demands generally increase. Additional stress can arise from the growing number of outside activities in which the children are involved. There is a sense that an increasing number of tasks around the home are simply not being done. These problems continue as the children grow into adolescence, at which point financial strains again may become severe.

By the time the couple has reached the empty-nest stage, time demands again are generally the prime source of stress with emphasis on chores that do not get done. In addition, difficulties with the sexual relationship, financial problems, decreasing satisfaction with work, and illness and death become more likely. Finally, in the retirement stage, financial problems once again become the most likely source of stress.

It is important to realize three things. First, some problems, such as financial strains, tend to be common at all stages. Second, the previous discussion does not include all the stressors that may occur but simply indicates the stressors most frequently named by people at various stages. Finally, as indicated by the nonnormative sources in table 14.1, such stressors as serious illness are unpredictable. Although serious illness is more likely to occur in the later years, it may happen at any time.

Not All Stressors Are Equal. What is the worst thing that could happen to you? You can probably think of some undesirable events that you could deal with relatively easily, others that would be much more difficult to cope with, and perhaps one or more that would make you feel like life was no longer worth living. In other words, the various stressors do not affect us equally. In fact, the same stressor may affect different people in different ways. Unemployment, for example, may be devastating to one person and a welcome break to another depending on circumstances. Caring for a chronically disabled family member, such as an Alzheimer's patient, is more or less difficult depending on such things as how close the caregiver feels to the patient and the extent to which the caregiver perceives that others understand what it is like to care for such a patient (Barber, Fisher, and Pasley 1990).

In spite of varying reactions, when we look at how large numbers of people respond to stressors, we can rank order the varied stressors in terms of severity. The Family Inventory of Life Events and Changes (FILE) is one effort to identify the severity (McCubbin and Patterson 1983). The researchers who developed FILE worked in the context of the Double ABCX model of stress. Thus, the instrument is an effort to measure the pileups in a family during the course of a year. It measures not only the number but also the severity of stressors that accumulate and that can bring a family to the point of crisis.

The death of a child is one of the most severe crises a family can face.

FILE taps into nine important types of stressors in family life. Intrafamily strains include tensions between family members and the strains of parent–child relationships. The other types of stressors are marital strains, pregnancy and childbearing strains, finance and business strains, work-family transitions and strains, illness and family care strains, family losses (loss of member or friend or a breakdown in the relationships), family transitions in and out (members of the family moving out or back into the home or engaging in a serious involvement of some kind outside the family), and family legal strains. The total of all these nine strains, weighted according to their severity, result in a "family pileup" score. Given a sufficiently high score, most families are likely to experience difficulty in coping.

What are the most severe stressors? Ranked in terms of difficulty of adjusting, table 14.2 shows the 15 most severe. At the upper end of the scale are loss through

TABLE 14.2 The 15 Most Severe Family Stressors
(numbers are a measure of relative severity)

Death of a child	99
Death of a spouse/parent	98
Separation or divorce of spouse/parent	79
Physical or sexual abuse or violence between family members	75
Family member becomes physically disabled or chronically ill	73
Spouse/parent has an affair	68
Family member jailed or sent to juvenile detention	68
Family member dependent on alcohol or drugs	66
Pregnancy of an unmarried family member	65
Family member runs away from home	61
Family member seems to have an emotional problem	58
Increased sexual problems in the marriage	58
Increased difficulty handling a disabled or chronically ill family member	58
Married child separates or gets a divorce	58
Family member picked up by police or arrested	57

Source: From Hamilton I. McCubbin and Joan M. Patterson, "Stress: The Family Inventory of Life Events and Changes" in *Marriage and Family Assessment: A Sourcebook for Family Therapy,* pp. 285–86. Copyright © 1983 Erik Filsinger. Reprinted by permission of Erik Filsinger.

death or divorce or separation. The most stressful of all, the death of a child, not only tends to strain the marriage but also increases the risk of a first psychiatric hospitalization (Li et al. 2005). The risk is higher for mothers than for fathers. In fact, the mother's risk can stay elevated for five years or more after the child's death.

At the lower end of the scale are such things as purchase of an automobile or other major item (19); increased strain on income for food, clothing, energy, and home care (21); increased strain on income for children's education (22); and increased strain on income for medical and dental expenses (23). It is important to realize that the numbers, which are measures of relative severity, are averages for large numbers of people. The same event can have a quite different impact on different individuals, depending on a number of other factors. One factor is the time of life when the event occurs. For example, if a parent dies when you are a teenager, the impact is likely to be far more severe than when you are in your 50s or 60s.

Another factor is the nature of your relationships at the time of the event. For example, among those who have begun the task of giving care to a parent, there is a greater decline in happiness and more depressive symptoms among those who have also have a higher level of marital disagreement (Choi and Marks 2006).

The impact of the various stressors, then, will differ somewhat from one individual to another depending on the circumstances. But their *relative* severity will generally

reflect these numbers. The impact will also differ depending on the chain of other consequences that follow from them. For instance, consider the stress of having a child with autism. Dealing with such a problem in of itself is quite stressful. But some families spend so much money on therapy and medical intervention that they jeopardize their future financial security and some even go into bankruptcy as they strive to care for their autistic child (Sharpe and Baker 2007).

In other words, a family in crisis may have to cope with not a single but multiple problems. An interesting finding from the research using FILE relates to the amount of pileup at various stages of the family life cycle. Again, keep in mind that the figures are averages for large numbers of families. You may or may not have the same experience in your own family. But looking at families generally, the researchers found that the highest amount of stress (pileup) tends to occur during the time when the family is in the transition from having children in the home to the empty nest. During this "launching" stage, there tend to be more stressors than at any other time in the family life cycle. At this point, there is the stress of disrupting the home through children leaving for marriage or school and the likelihood of increased financial strain to cover the expenses of these events. It is also a time of life when one of the parents may be considering a change in jobs or career and when serious illness becomes more likely.

The lowest overall stress scores tend to occur in the retirement stage, and the second lowest are in the empty-nest stage of the family life cycle. It is not without some cause that the later years of life are sometimes termed the *golden* years. If grandmothers and grandfathers seem more relaxed and better able to flow with the events of life, it is in part because they are enjoying a time of life in which there are fewer stressor events with which they must cope.

ABUSE OF ALCOHOL AND OTHER DRUGS IN THE FAMILY

Drug abuse, particularly the abuse of alcohol (which is a drug, incidentally), ranks high on the list of family stressors. Although many of the studies we cite focused on either alcohol or on other drugs, the stressful consequences for family life are similar regardless of which drug is involved in the abuse.

Extent of Drug Abuse

We will define **drug abuse** as the improper use of alcohol or other drugs to the degree that the consequences are defined as detrimental to the user and the family. In the case of alcohol, it is excessive drinking and not merely the use that creates problems. In the case of other drugs, it is any use because the drugs are illegal.

A national survey reported that over the year prior to the research 33.9 percent of college students and 32.1 percent of young adults had used some kind of illicit drug at least once (Johnston, O'Malley, Bachman, and Schulenberg 2006). Other than alcohol, marijuana was by far the most likely drug to be used. But alcohol, even more used, was consumed at least once by 82.1 percent of college students and 84.4 percent of young adults. In addition, 66.2 percent of college students and 65.7 percent of young adults admitted they had been drunk at least once during the year. The extensive abuse of alcohol has led some experts to call alcohol abuse the nation's foremost health problem. Alcohol abuse is responsible for 4 percent of all deaths among men and 1.5 percent of all deaths among women (Rivara et al. 2004).

Drug use begins at an early age. In the survey, more than a third of twelfth grade students and 28.7 percent of tenth grade students acknowledged the use of an illicit drug. And nearly half of the twelfth graders and over a third of the tenth graders admitted being drunk at least once during the year. Drug abuse generally is more common among white than black adolescents and decreases among adolescents as their level of religiosity goes up (Wallace et al. 2007).

It is not surprising, then, that 37 percent of Americans say that drinking has been a source of trouble in their families (Maguire and Pastore 2004). And the problem is not just that the parents are abusers, but that *many adolescent children have a drinking problem*. In fact, alcohol abuse and dependence is one of the most common psychiatric disorders among adolescents (Thatcher and Clark 2006).

Drug Abuse and the Quality of Family Life

Drug abuse seriously detracts from the quality of family life. When a child is the abuser, the family experiences considerable stress and conflict. As a mother of an adolescent boy who was heavily into smoking marijuana told us:

> This is just tearing us up. My husband and I are trying desperately to find some way to help Brad break the habit. His grades at school have gone way down, and he doesn't seem to be interested in anything except hanging out with his pot-smoking friends. We're terrified that it's going to ruin his entire life. But we don't know what to do. We can't be with him 24 hours a day. Worse, my husband and I don't always agree on how to help him, so we wind up arguing with each other instead of doing something useful for Brad.

It is more likely, however, that the family must deal with parental rather than with child drug abuse. When one or both parents are drug abusers, the consequences can include frequent arguments, inadequate parenting, physical and emotional abuse, health problems, problem behavior by the children, and marital and family disruption (Deming, Chase, and Karesh 1996; Elkins et al. 2004; Haugland 2005; Collins, Ellickson, and Klein 2007).

Alcohol abuse affects millions of Americans and their families.

The consequences depend in part on whether the husband or wife or both are drug abusers. One study found an association with alcohol dependence, conduct disorder, and major depression among adolescents who avoided a mother who was abusing drugs or whose mother got angry while abusing drugs (Ohannessini et al. 2004). No such consequences were found among those who avoided a drug-abusing father or whose father got angry while using drugs. However, the researchers did find a tendency toward alcohol dependence among those adolescents who were concerned about either a father's or mother's drug abuse. An Australian study that looked at parental alcohol abuse reported an association between father's but not mother's abuse and children's delinquency (Grekin, Brennan, and Hammen 2005). The consequences may vary, therefore, but drug abuse by either parent has negative effects on the children.

Some families with an abuser seem to function fairly normally when not drinking. The family can communicate with each other, enjoy family functions, carry on family work, and so forth. But when the abuser is using, the whole character of family life is likely to change.

In the case of alcohol abuse, for example, at the very least the drinker is likely to become more negative and critical with his or her spouse while drinking. At worst, the abuser may become physically or emotionally abusive of his or her spouse. There is a strong relationship between alcohol abuse and both the physical and verbal abuse of an intimate partner (Caetano, Nelson, and Cunradi 2001; Eckhardt 2007).

In many families, particularly when the abuse is long-term, there are negative consequences whether or not the abuser is drinking. Such families resemble those that have a high degree of dissatisfaction and a large number of disagreements. In other words, the atmosphere in a family in which there is an abuser of alcohol is likely to feature a great deal of tension, considerable dissatisfaction, and frequent conflict (Testa and Leonard 2001).

In addition, the spouses and children of the abusers may develop various physical and emotional problems. Wives of alcoholic men may become heavy drinkers themselves (Gilbert 2003). In any case, they are likely to experience long-term personal and marital problems, such as unsatisfactory sexual relations, abusive behavior, conflict, physical and emotional health problems, and victimization and injury (Halford et al. 2001; Maharajh and Ali 2005; Dawson, Grant, Chou, and Stinson 2007).

With regard to children, while the majority who come from a home with one or more drug abusers are not doomed to some kind of pathology, they are more vulnerable to a variety of behavioral and emotional problems (Jones and Houts 1992; Sher and Gershuny 1997; Loukas et al. 2001; Bancroft et al. 2004; Altshuler 2005). Among other things, children in such families are more likely than others to

- say their parents cannot provide consistent practical and emotional care for them.
- experience a shortened childhood because of assuming early responsibility for their own and other family members' well-being.
- be the victims of emotional and physical abuse.
- blame themselves for their parents' problems.
- perceive less parental warmth and concern.
- have a conduct disorder or become delinquent.
- become abusers of drugs themselves.
- display higher rates of hyperactivity.
- have problems with schoolwork.
- report higher rates of health problems.
- have higher rates of anxiety and depression.

The negative consequences of drug abuse do not quickly disappear simply because the parent stops abusing. A study that compared sons of recovering alcoholic and nonalcoholic fathers reported that the sons of the recovering alcoholics were more compulsive, insecure, fearful, subdued, and detached (Whipple and Noble 1991).

When the children become adults, their past experience in a drug-abusing home can continue to trouble them. A good deal of research has looked at the problems of adult children of alcoholics (though not at adult children of those who abuse other drugs). A group of Hispanic adult children of alcoholics reported more physical health problems than Hispanic adults from nonalcoholic homes (Harman and Arbona 1991). Other research shows that adult children of alcoholics have higher rates of anxiety and depression, lower levels of self-esteem, and higher rates of alcoholism themselves (Tweed and Ryff 1991; Domenico and Windle 1993; Schuckit and Smith 1996; Olmsted, Crowell, and Waters 2003). Finally, the adult children of alcoholics have more relational problems. Their dating experiences are less satisfying (Larson and Reedy 2004). They have a higher need for control and lower relationship satisfaction (Beesley and Stoltenberg 2002). They are less likely than others to marry, and when they do marry they tend to have lower levels of marital and family satisfaction, higher levels of marital conflict, and a greater chance of marital disruption (Domenico and Windle 1993; Watt 2002). Clearly, the abuser is engaged not merely in a self-destructive process but also in a process that may detract from both the immediate and the long-term quality of life of other family members.

Family Problems and Drug Abuse

If drug abuse can lead to family problems, family problems also can lead to drug abuse. A cohesive, healthy family life inhibits drug abuse (Wilens et al. 2002). But when there are disturbed relationships within the home, one of the family members may resort to heavy drinking or to other drugs in an effort to cope with the stress. Young women who are physically abused by an intimate partner are at increased risk for heavy drinking (Martino, Collins, and Ellickson 2005). A husband or wife with serious marital problems may resort to abuse of alcohol or other drugs. Children may abuse alcohol or other drugs—either as children or when they become adults—where there is a high level of conflict between parents; physical, emotional, or sexual abuse; or the disruption of divorce (Kang, Magura, and Shapiro 1994; Wolfinger 1998; Downs, Capshew, and Rindels 2004; Rutger et al. 2005). The drug abuse in such situations is an effort to cope with a frustrating, stressful situation. Like other inappropriate coping methods, it is counterproductive. It is a way of escape, rather than a way of confronting the problem and pursuing some constructive resolution.

If family problems result in a member becoming a drug abuser, the family may get caught in a vicious circle in which the problems and the abuse feed on and sustain each other. That is, the difficulties lead the member to drug abuse, and the drug abuse intensifies the problems and creates additional ones. The added stress perpetuates the drug abuse, and the drug abuse continues to aggravate the problems. Once the pattern is established, it tends to be self-perpetuating.

Moreover, drug abuse can take its toll across a number of generations. Kayla, a graduate student in her 30s, has alcoholic grandparents on both sides of her family. Although neither of her parents abused alcohol, the effects of the grandparents' abuse have continued in the family:

> To this day, I see my mother struggling to establish her own identity and my father striving to free himself from the emotional tyranny of an alcoholic father. Growing up in alcoholic families, my parents didn't know how to deal with things like sickness, job loss, moving, or family conflict. Whenever they faced a crisis, they would lean on me as the oldest child to help resolve it. I grew up feeling overly responsible and quite inadequate.

Kayla married a man who was from an alcoholic family. She knows now that she looked to him to give her the nurturing she never got from her family, and he looked to her to be the capable and competent individual that he never had in his family. They were both wrong. Their marriage alternated between coldness and stormy passions and between self-blame and blaming the other. It eventually ended in divorce.

Kayla's experience illustrates one of the more insidious consequences of drug abuse in a family. The inadequate parenting that results when there is an abuser can have negative effects through subsequent generations.

VIOLENCE IN FAMILIES

Next to death, separation, and divorce, family violence is the most difficult experience people have to cope with (table 14.2). It is easy to understand the severity of the trauma. After all, we expect our families to be a source of comfort and support, a refuge from an often difficult world. For the refuge to become a violent battleground is, as one person told us, "like discovering that God is a malevolent tormentor rather than a loving Father."

We shall be looking primarily at **physical abuse,** but we should keep in mind that **emotional abuse** also occurs and always accompanies physical abuse. Emotional abuse includes such things as the threat of physical abuse and ridicule. Some victims report that the emotional abuse was more damaging to them than the physical abuse (Follingstad et al. 1990).

The Extent of Violence

If the bright side of intimate relationships is their potential for enhancing our well-being, the dark side is their potential for destruction because of physical and emotional abuse. The rates of physical abuse against intimates decreased after the 1980s. Still, a national survey reported that nearly 750,000 women and 125,000 men said they were abused by a current or former spouse or a boyfriend or girlfriend in 2004 (Catalano 2006). American Indian women have the highest rate of abuse. Whites have the lowest, with African Americans and Hispanics in between (Caetano, Field, Ramisetty-Mikler, and McGrath 2005). Rates also vary across socioeconomic lines. A study of very poor mothers, most of whom were of Puerto Rican descent, found that nearly two-thirds had experienced intimate partner violence at some time during their adult lives (Bassuk, Dawson, and Huntington 2006).

Even pregnant women are not safe from abuse. According to a national study of pregnant women, 33 percent of mothers and 40 percent of fathers are subjected to some kind of intimate partner abuse during or after the pregnancy (Charles and Perreira 2007). Hispanic women and those no longer romantically involved with the fathers of their children are the most likely to be abused. Some women first experience violence from an intimate partner when they become pregnant (Sagrestano et al. 2004). And among those who are abused, both the frequency and severity of abuse are likely to increase after the woman becomes pregnant (Burch and Gallup 2004).

Women are the victims of intimate violence in other nations as well. A survey of violence from male partners in Quebec, Canada, found that 6.1 percent of women were physically abused and 6.8 percent were sexually abused (Rinfret-Raynor et al. 2004). And a United Nations report concluded that at least one out of every three women in the world will experience physical or sexual abuse during their lifetimes (Sev'er, Dawson, and Johnson 2004)! Rates of intimate violence against pregnant women tend to be higher in the developing countries than in the industrialized nations (Campbell, Garcia-Moreno, and Sharps 2004).

Child Abuse

Some researchers define violence to include mild forms such as spanking, and as a result they find that the majority of parents use some form of violence against their children. We are concerned here, however, with more severe forms of violence that fall into the category of **child maltreatment,** which includes a range of behavior from depriving children of some of the necessities of life to severe physical injury (figure 14.1). Physical abuse includes physical acts that lead to or could lead to physical injury.

Sexual abuse includes using a child for sexual gratification or for making money (through such things as child pornography or prostitution). Psychological abuse involves verbal attacks or emotional deprivation that causes or could cause behavioral or emotional problems in the child. Neglect is the failure, whether deliberate or unintended, to provide a child with basic needs such as food, water, shelter, and medical attention (medical neglect).

Since 2002, the number of substantiated cases of child maltreatment has remained about the same—around 900,000 (Federal Interagency Forum on Child and Family Statistics 2007). Many more are reported each year but not substantiated or not yet substantiated. As shown in figure 14.1, about two-thirds of the cases involve some kind of neglect. The rates are higher for girls and for infants 3 years and under. African Americans have the highest rates, followed by American Indians, whites, Hispanics, and Asian Americans (whose rate is quite low).

It is difficult, of course, to identify emotional maltreatment in the absence of other forms of abuse. Using a national sample to study "psychological aggression," two researchers found that 90 percent of the parents admitted using one or more forms of such aggression by the time the child was 2 years old (Straus and Field 2003). The researchers' definition of psychological aggression included shouting, yelling, threatening to hit or spank, swearing at the child, threatening to send the child away or out of the house, and calling the child a derogatory name. The last three items were labeled "severe" psychological aggression. Ten to 20 percent of parents acknowledged using severe aggression on toddlers, and 50 percent used it on teenagers.

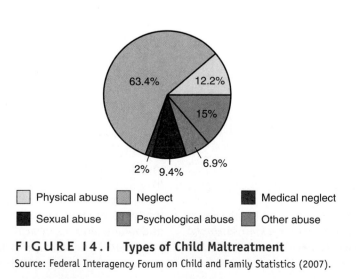

FIGURE 14.1 Types of Child Maltreatment
Source: Federal Interagency Forum on Child and Family Statistics (2007).

In a broader sense, children may be said to be abused when they live in an abusive atmosphere. Thus, a survey of 8,629 adults in a health plan asked whether they had ever had one or more of 10 adverse experiences. The experiences included childhood physical, emotional, and sexual abuse, emotional and physical neglect, witnessing domestic violence, witnessing parental marital discord, and living with someone in the home who was a drug abuser, a criminal, or mentally ill (Dong et al. 2004). Two-thirds of the respondents had experienced at least one of the 10, and the great majority of those had experienced two or more of the 10.

What kind of parent abuses his or her own children? A prototype would be one who is single, is young (around 30 or less), has been married for fewer than 10 years, had his or her first child before the age of 18, and is unemployed or employed part-time. Among the married, spouse abusers also are far more likely to be child abusers than are those who do not abuse their spouses (Ross 1996). And the more times someone has abused a spouse, the more likely that person is a child abuser as well. Women are slightly more likely to abuse children than are men, probably because women are more intensely involved with children (and the rates of child abuse are higher in single-parent, which for the most part means single-mother, families). Child abusers tend to have lower self-esteem than others, to define their children as more troublesome, to have serious financial problems, to have poorer mental health, to have low levels of social support, and to have a large number of stressor events in their lives (Whipple and Webster-Stratton 1991; Kolko et al. 1993; Coohey 2000; Berger 2005). Abusers are also more likely than nonabusers to have been abused themselves as children.

Incest

Incest, a special form of child abuse, is any type of exploitive sexual contact between relatives in which the victim is under 18 years of age. It is difficult to know exactly how many people are the victims of incest.

Father–daughter incest, when it occurs, usually begins early—when the daughter is between the ages of 6 and 11. Typically, the father will justify the incest in terms of love and care and define himself as a considerate and fair person (Gilgun 1995) even though he initiates sexual relations with his daughter by force or by intimidation. Incest is a horrifying experience to the victim, who, among other things, is likely to suffer from low self-esteem, conduct problems in school, and, when she grows up, problems of relating to men in a meaningful way and ongoing struggles with low self-esteem and depression (Jackson et al. 1990; Dadds et al. 1991).

Why doesn't the daughter rebel and refuse? We need to realize both how powerless and how responsible for family well-being girls tend to feel. For instance, Becky, an editor, is still "overwhelmed" as she discusses her experience. She remembers the intense conflict between her parents, and her mother finally being hospitalized for a period of time. She was about 11 years old, and "sex was not even the subject for jokes with my circle of friends. I hardly thought about it." When her father approached her for sex, she was passive. She "didn't react to the incest as a sexual act but as a way to keep the family together." When Becky yielded to her father, things seemed better in the home. "I desperately wanted harmony in my family and every other need became subordinate to that." When Becky's father asked her if she wanted him to return to her bedroom after each sexual encounter, she told him no. But she continued to allow him to use her. And she has spent the years since then trying to work through the agony of being betrayed by a man to whom she looked for support and unconditional love.

Mother–son incest seems to be quite rare. Other forms of incest, such as that between brother and sister and uncles and nieces and other relatives, occur, but we do not know how widespread they are. We do know, however, that most incestuous relationships are a betrayal of trust and lead to long-term problems for the victim. For example, a report on a small number of women who had experienced brother–sister incest noted that the women felt "isolation, secrecy, shame, anger, and poor communication" in their families (Canavan, Meyer, and Higgs 1992).

Finally, there is brother–sister incest. We don't know how much brother–sister incest exists, but we do know that, like all incest, it is traumatic for the victim (Sheinberg and Fraenkel 2001). Having been betrayed by a sibling, the victims have difficulty developing a sense of loyalty and trust in others, including even other members of their own family. An anthology of experiences of women who were victims of sibling incest when they were young repeatedly tells of coercive tactics and underscores the fact that the incest was typically not about sex or pleasure but about power and control (Shaw 2000).

Spouse Abuse

The term *spouse abuse* is likely to conjure up the image of a man beating a woman. There are two things we need to keep in mind. First, the abuse may be emotional or both physical and emotional. National samples show that for both kinds of abuse, the rates of husband-to-wife and wife-to-husband abuse are roughly the same (Johnson 2005).

Second, however, the equal rates of abusing one's partner must be interpreted in the light of two additional

Abused wives suffer both physical and emotional trauma.

facts. One is that women are more likely to suffer injury from physical abuse, and they suffer more emotionally than men do from being the victims of abuse (Umberson et al. 1998; Felson and Cares 2005). The other is that women who assault their husbands are likely to have been previously beaten by their husbands. A wife's violence is often a form of self-defense (Melton and Belknap 2003).

In looking at rates of husbands' abuse, it is also important to keep in mind the distinction between **intimate terrorism** and situational violence (Johnson and Leone 2005). Situational violence may occur infrequently. The victims of intimate terrorism, on the other hand, suffer frequent, long-term episodes of violence. They will probably be injured, have emotional problems, use painkillers, and miss work or other important events to stay home and recover. *Whether the abuse is intimate terrorism or situational violence, however, many experts agree that the victim should leave the abuser.* For one thing, infrequent does not mean mild; the violence may erupt without warning and be intense (Roberts 2006). For another thing, the violence may escalate over time. Unfortunately, leaving either kind of violent relationship may be difficult especially for a woman who has children, or who does not have a job that will support her, or who lacks resources in the form of sympathetic family members or friends who will help her.

The severity of intimate terrorism raises the question, What kind of man would inflict such harm on his wife? Researchers have found that a male abuser tends to be young (between 18 and 24 years); be unemployed or employed part-time; have a lower level of education; live at the poverty level; worry about finances; be dissatisfied with life; have been married fewer than 10 years; have been physically punished as a child; be insecure and jealous and have frequent conflict with his wife; and abuse alcohol or other drugs (Straus and Yodanis 1996; Brookoff et al. 1997; DeMaris et al. 2003; Benson and Fox 2004). He abuses his wife emotionally as well as physically. He views battered women in negative terms, as somehow deserving of their plight (Eisikovits et al. 1991). He believes that the man should be the head of the family, but he lacks the resources to be dominant in his own family. Thus, he assaults his wife in order to establish his control over her (Felson and Messner 2000; Atkinson, Greenstein, and Lang 2005). As this suggests, the lack of an egalitarian relationship increases the chances of physical abuse. It also increases the chances of emotional abuse. There are higher rates of emotional abuse in marriages where the wife is employed and the husband is unemployed, or where the wife has more education or earns 65 percent or more of the family income (Kaukinen 2004).

A counterpart to the question of what kind of man would abuse his wife is the question, Why would a woman allow herself to be repeatedly assaulted? Why does she stay in the relationship? In some cases, women lack (or believe that they lack) the economic means to leave. In an effort to retain some economic security or to make the relationship ultimately work out, they may be willing to tolerate abuse as long as it does not become too severe or involve their children.

In other cases, women have fallen into what Donald Dutton (1987) called a *social trap*. Thus, the abused woman begins her marriage with the same expectations as others—long-term happiness and fulfillment and her own heavy responsibility for such an outcome and for the emotional state of her husband. The violent episodes, which typically begin in the first year of marriage, are less severe at first and are likely to be followed by strong expressions of regret from the husband. She may therefore view the violence as an anomaly. At first, she does not expect the violence to continue. Eventually, she realizes that it will, but by that time she has developed a strong commitment to the man. She is determined to make the relationship succeed. A "traumatic bonding" occurs, a bonding that is facilitated by the fact that the abuse occurs intermittently and may be followed by effusive apologies and promises to change.

Finally, some women develop the **battered woman syndrome.** The battered woman syndrome is somewhat controversial, but has been used in the defense of women who eventually kill their abuser. The syndrome has two components (Terrance and Matheson 2003). First, after being repeatedly abused, a woman may believe she is unable to control the abuse. She has learned from experience that she is helpless. Even if she were to leave, she thinks, she has no way to support herself (and her children if she has any) and in any case her abuser would find her and perhaps kill her. The second component is that the violence continues, and the woman becomes aware of any cues that it might occur. She lives in terror of those times. In between, when the abuser may seem like a normal, caring person, she submits to him and strives to please him in the hope of deferring future violence.

Women with the battered woman syndrome may re-experience a battering as if it were occurring again even when it isn't (Walker 2006). They may try to deal with the emotional terror by avoiding activities, people, and their own feelings. And they are likely to have disrupted relationships and problems with sexuality and intimacy. Because of such consequences, some experts treat the battered woman syndrome as a form of posttraumatic stress disorder.

Parent Abuse

The abuse of parents by their children (of any age from adolescence through adulthood) is under-researched even though the rates are fairly high, particularly by white adolescents against their mothers (Walsh and Krienert 2007). Both adolescent and adult male children inflict physical as well as emotional abuse on their parents (Eckstein 2004; Stewart, Burns, and Leonard 2007). A study of 445 white and Hispanic youth in California found that the whites were more likely than the Hispanics to hit a parent and that those who did assault parents were likely to be bored with school, have low self-esteem, and be less happy than others (Paulson, Coombs, and Landsverk 1990).

When older parents are abused, the most likely victim is, again, a white female, and the most likely abuser is also a female (because women rather than men are generally the caregivers). Adult women who abuse their elderly mothers often are going through some kind of personal crisis such as an addiction, illness, or financial problems. Perhaps as many as a half a million to a million elderly parents a year are victims of abuse.

Consequences of Abuse

In the short-term, of course, abuse involves serious physical and emotional damage. But abuse also tends to have serious long-term consequences. Let us look first at the consequences for children. Abuse has both short-term and long-term detrimental effects on children (DuCharme, Koverola, and Battle 1997; Garnefski and Arends 1998; Shonk and Cicchetti 2001; Ethier, Lemelin, and Lacharite 2004; Thrane, Hoyt, Whitbeck, and Yoder 2006; Schilling, Aseltine, and Gore 2007). Detrimental effects during the growing-up years include:

- greater likelihood of running away from home and living on the streets.
- behavior problems at home and at school.
- higher levels of anger and aggression.
- lower intellectual and academic development.
- emotional problems, including anxiety, depression, and thoughts of, and attempts at, suicide.
- abuse of alcohol and other drugs.
- problems of low self-esteem.
- health problems, including higher rates of chronic diseases.
- feelings of isolation, difficulty in trusting others, difficulty in forming meaningful intimate relationships, and lower levels of intimacy in the relationships.
- generalized unhappiness.

What Do You Think?

*There is disagreement about **whether you should stay with an abusive spouse.** What follows are pro and con arguments. What do you think?*

Pro

You should stay with an abusive spouse because

- marriage is for better or worse.
- your continued faithfulness will eventually help your spouse change.
- if you leave, your spouse will find you and abuse you even more severely.
- if you change whatever you have done to provoke the problem, your spouse will stop the abuse.
- the abuser is always sorry and asks for forgiveness, and forgiveness is something spouses must give to each other.

Con

You should not stay with an abusive spouse because

- he or she will not change without professional help.
- you will put your health and even your life at risk.
- it will only encourage further abuse.
- you put your children in harm's way.
- staying is an admission of your own guilt rather than your love for your mate.

Interestingly, a study of sexually abused boys and girls found that the adverse consequences were greater for the boys than for the girls in terms of much higher rates of aggression, drug abuse, and suicidal thoughts and behavior (Garnefski and Arends 1998). The reasons for the sex differences are unknown.

Many of these problems continue to plague the abused when they become adults. They are more likely to become abusers themselves than are those who were not abused as children (Swinford et al. 2000; Kwong et al. 2003). They have higher rates of anxiety disorders, depression, alcohol and other drug abuse, antisocial behavior, and other emotional problems (MacMillan et al. 2001; Whiffen and MacIntosh 2005; Lo and Cheng 2007). They have higher rates of physical as well as mental illness, including (for women) chronic pain (Najman, Nguyen, and Boyle 2007; Walsh, Jamieson, MacMillan, and Boyle 2007; Young, Harford, Kinder, and Savell 2007). Women who were abused also have more negative attitudes and feelings about marriage and are less likely to marry or to be in a stable, cohabiting relationship (Cherlin et al. 2004; Larson and LaMont 2005). And those who do marry are more likely to divorce (Colman and Widom 2004).

Spouse abuse also has detrimental consequences. Abused wives have higher rates of death, injury, disability, chronic pain, drug abuse, and reproductive problems (Plichta 2004). Both emotional and physical abuse depress marital satisfaction and inhibit intimacy (Arias, Lyons, and Street 1997; Lawrence and Bradbury 2001). Abused wives, compared to those not abused, have lower self-esteem and higher rates of anxiety and depression (Haj-Yahia 2000; Christian-Herman, O'Leary, and Avery-Leaf 2001). The emotional damage is underscored by the fact that only about 2 women in 1,000 think seriously about suicide in any one year, but about 46 *abused* women in 1,000 think about suicide frequently. One of the bitter ironies of the abusive relationship is that the woman's reaction to the abuse—for example, her depression—may be used to justify further beatings. In other words, the victim is blamed for the violence used against her.

We should note that *witnessing* violence as well as being victimized by it have harmful consequences. Children who witness violence between their parents or between parents and siblings will suffer even if they are not themselves abused. Such children may suffer from both psychological and social maladjustment, and their problems may continue into adulthood (Henning et al. 1996). Thus, those who witness violence in their homes are more likely than others to

- suffer from depression and other emotional problems and to have recurring problems of depression when they become adults (Kessler and Magee 1994; Graham-Bermann and Levendosky 1998; Davies, DiLillo, and Martinez 2004).

Comparison

Intimate Partner Abuse in Canada

Abuse of an intimate partner—a spouse or cohabiting partner—is a concern in other nations as well as the United States. In Canada, a government survey found that more than a million citizens have been shoved, beaten, strangled, or subjected to some other kind of physical abuse by a spouse or cohabiting partner (Cryderman 2000). Roughly 8 percent of women and 7 percent of men said that they had experienced violence at least once during the previous five-year period. The rate for women was slightly higher than the U.S. figure of 6 percent and considerably higher than

the U.S. figure of less than 2 percent for men (Rennison 2001).

As in the United States, in Canada the rates of intimate partner violence declined through the 1990s, and the abuse was more common among the young (under 25 years of age) and those cohabiting. Also, women were far more likely to suffer serious damage from the violence. Three times as many women as men die from domestic violence in Canada. And five times as many women as men fear for their lives and require medical attention after an attack.

The greater harm suffered by women is reflected in the greater

extent to which men use more severe forms of abuse. According to the survey, men were more likely than women to be slapped, kicked, bit, and hit with something. But women were more likely than men to be pushed, shoved, beaten, choked, threatened with a gun or knife, and sexually assaulted.

Some of the acts of violence were attempts to control the partner. Others were defensive or retaliatory. Thus, intimate partner abuse in Canada is very similar to that in the United States but apparently is more widespread.

- have lower social and cognitive competence and more health problems (Onyskiw 2003).
- have higher rates of delinquent activities and other behavior problems (Kruttschnitt and Dornfeld 1993; O'Keefe 1994).
- have more violence in their own relationships as adults (McNeal and Amato 1998).

It seems that children learn from watching their parents that those who love you also hit you and that this is an appropriate way to get your way and to deal with stress.

REACTING TO CRISES

As we have discussed, about one-third of abused children will grow up to become abusers; about two-thirds will not. Clearly, people react in different ways to family crises. The point we wish to stress in this section is that whatever the particular crisis you face, there are always alternative ways of dealing with it. You can't control all of the things that happen in your life, but you can control the way you respond to them. This doesn't mean that you can avoid the trauma of crises. It does mean, as we will show in the final section of this chapter, that you can avoid long-term, adverse consequences. In fact, it is possible to turn the crisis into something that yields long-term, positive consequences (figure 14.2).

Whatever the type of crisis faced, different families will have somewhat different reactions. In some cases, an event may be a crisis for some families or some family members but not for others. Consider, for example, a perinatal loss (miscarriage, stillbirth, or infant death). To what extent is that a crisis? It varies, depending on the extent to which family members feel attachment:

> Some family members will feel very strongly attached to an embryo, fetus, or newborn, even to the mere idea of a child. These people may grieve a perinatal loss quite intensely. Other people, even those who consider an embryo, a fetus, or a newborn fully human, may feel relatively little attachment to it and grieve its loss little if at all (Rosenblatt and Burns 1986:237).

Among those who grieve after a perinatal loss, the reactions vary. Women are likely to experience depression for a year or more after a miscarriage (Robinson et al. 1994). In some cases of perinatal loss, the grief may continue for decades. A woman who lost a 2-month-old son 42 years previously told an interviewer that she still thought about him every day (Rosenblatt and Burns 1986:243). She still had some feelings of sorrow, though she also had some pleasant memories. Overall, perhaps as many as one-fifth of those with a perinatal loss have long-term grief to some extent. The husband and wife may not feel the grief equally, and that can cause marital problems (Schwab 1992; Najman et al. 1993).

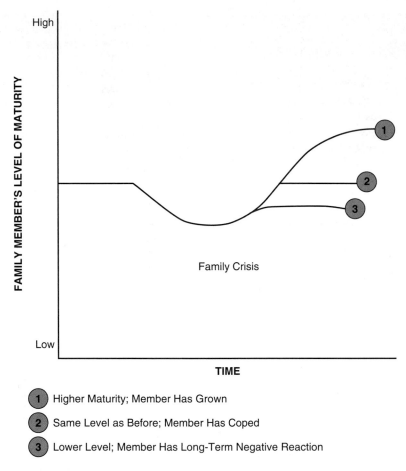

	1	Higher Maturity; Member Has Grown
	2	Same Level as Before; Member Has Coped
	3	Lower Level; Member Has Long-Term Negative Reaction

FIGURE 14.2 **Differing Outcomes of a Family Crisis**

In contrast to perinatal loss, having a child die or succumb to a life-threatening illness like cancer is likely to be a crisis for every family. A study of 31 couples who had lost an infant reported that, even after two years, the couples reported less marital intimacy and significantly less sexual intimacy than they had before the loss (Gottlieb, Lang, and Amsel 1996). Still, the majority of marriages survive the stress of a child's death and may even be strengthened in the long run (Schwab 1998).

Whatever the crisis, the initial reaction will be one of added stress and lowered life satisfaction. And for some people, these are long term. Couples with children who have chronic health problems, for example, have higher rates than other parents of marital dissatisfaction and depressive symptoms (Berge, Patterson, and Rueter 2006). People who are responsible for caring for an elderly parent with dementia are at increased risk for developing such health problems as cardiovascular disease (Mausbach et al. 2007). And while a study of women who were sexually abused as children found that the majority perceived some benefits from their efforts to cope with the experience, 29 percent said it was not possible for them to draw any positive meaning from it (Wright, Crawford, and Sebastian 2007).

In other words, people respond in all three ways shown in figure 14.2. All try to cope in some way with crisis, but clearly there are both helpful and unhelpful ways of coping. Specifically, then, what mechanisms and resources do families use to cope with a crisis? And which coping patterns are constructive? Which lead to the higher level of maturity of family members as indicated by path one in figure 14.2? That is our final topic.

COPING PATTERNS

Whatever you do in the face of a crisis is a coping pattern. Even if you do nothing, that is one way of trying to cope. Perhaps doing nothing is a way of saying there really is no crisis. Or perhaps it is based on the belief that time will heal all things, so that you need only hold on and wait it out. Unfortunately, doing nothing is not usually an effective coping pattern. Other patterns are also ineffective, and we need to be aware of them as well as of those that are more useful.

Ineffective Coping Patterns

"Ineffective" does not mean that a coping pattern does not work for an individual or family. Rather, it means that it is not a pattern that typically will yield long-term, constructive outcomes. Those who use an ineffective coping pattern may follow path three in figure 14.2. The members of those families are functionally less capable after a crisis. They have not coped effectively, and, as a result, their growth as individuals and as a family is set back. What kinds of coping patterns are likely to result in path three?

Denial. Denial is perhaps the most common of the ineffective coping patterns. Denial is a defense mechanism in which people will not believe what they observe. For example, a woman may be married to an alcoholic but refuse to accept the fact that he has a drinking problem. She may believe that he will stop drinking as soon as his work stress eases, that he doesn't drink any more than most other men, or that the problem is exaggerated by others and not really as serious as they say. Whatever her rationale, she denies that he is an alcoholic and thereby delays a constructive confrontation with the problem.

We should note that denial is both normal and perhaps helpful in the initial stage of some crises (Boss 2001). For example, denial is typically the initial response to the death of a loved one or to the news of a terminal illness. The denial may serve the useful purpose of giving the individual a chance to collect his or her thoughts and resources in order to deal with the problem constructively.

When denial is a temporary measure that enables family members to mobilize their resources, it is useful. When denial becomes a long-term pattern of ignoring the problem, it is destructive. The family that continues to ignore the symptoms of illness in father or mother, the financial disaster that looms because of parental unemployment, or the abuse that father inflicts on his wife or the children is a family that will inevitably reap a bitter harvest of emotional and physical damage.

One of the ways to break out of denial is for some member of the family to openly admit that there is a problem. Parents may have to tell their children frankly about the difficulties they face because of unemployment.

Children may have to talk frankly with their parents about problems of alcohol or physical abuse. Boss (2001) provides some examples:

- Dad, I love you, but I don't like the way you act when you're drunk. I would like you to stop because I care about you. If you don't stop, I won't hang around since it hurts me too much to see you that way.
- Mom, as your kid, I have to tell you that I can't stand watching you and Dad fight any more. If you don't call the cops the next time Dad hits you, I will.
- Grandpa, I know how sick you are. I just want you to know that I love you and that I will miss you when you die. Is there anything I can do for you now?

Once everyone admits that there is a problem, the family can begin to work together to find the best way to deal with it.

Avoidance. Admitting the existence of a problem is not sufficient, however. Sometimes people acknowledge that the problem exists, but they avoid confronting and dealing with it. Avoidance occurred, for instance, among those parents we noted in the previous section, who reacted to their child's cancer by drinking excessively or having an affair. They didn't deny the cancer, but they didn't act in a way to deal constructively with their own and their family's distress.

Avoidance can be used in any kind of crisis. It has been found among those trying to cope with their own cancer and those at risk for cancer (Derks et al. 2005; Fry and Prentice-Dunn 2005). It is used by those who have to live with a drug abuser. It is common among the victims of physical and emotional abuse. Usually, avoidance is counterproductive. Those who drink, for example, may increase their drinking as a way of coping with crises (Moos et al. 2004). Those who are abused simply prolong their victimization by avoiding a confrontation with the situation. And those at risk for a particular disease increase their risk by forgoing regular medical care.

At the same time, like denial, avoidance is not always a dysfunctional way of coping. There may be times when avoidance is necessary in order to give the family time to mobilize their resources. If, in other words, avoidance means a temporary delay in confronting the problem, it may be useful. If avoidance means long-term refusal to deal with the problem, it can have the same disastrous results as denial.

Scapegoating. Sometimes people admit a problem but feel that they have to find someone or something to blame. They select a family scapegoat to bear the brunt of the responsibility for the problem. A young woman who experienced a miscarriage told us that her suffering was intensified by the queries of some family members and acquaintances who asked such things as whether she had overexerted herself or taken proper care of herself. In other words, they suggested that her own behavior was to blame for the loss.

Scapegoating is an insidious way to respond to crisis. It boils down to selecting one of the victims of the crisis and further victimizing that person. We offered an example of this earlier when we pointed out that a man often uses the reaction of his beaten wife as an excuse for further beating.

Scapegoating, unlike denial and avoidance, is not even useful in the short run. Rather, it is a way of shifting responsibility so that one does not have to feel guilt or personal responsibility for resolving the crisis. Thus, if the family blames the father's unemployment on his own inept work habits, then other members of the family do not have to sacrifice or worry about the family's financial problems. On the other hand, if a father blames the kids for draining his energies so that he cannot do his work properly, then he has shifted the responsibility to the rest of the family.

The Foundation of Effective Coping

If a crisis occurs in a family that is not functioning well to begin with, the family may not be able to marshall the resources necessary to deal effectively with the crisis. To put the matter another way, a family is most likely to cope effectively with problems or crises when the members have worked together to develop certain family strengths. The strengths become a foundation on which the family can stand together and deal with crises.

The family that has developed strengths is likely to be a **resilient family,** one that can resist disruption in the face of change and cope effectively with crises. The strengths that help make a family resilient include the following (McCubbin and McCubbin 1988; Conger and Conger 2002):

- accord, or relationships that foster problem-solving and manage conflict well.
- celebrations, including birthdays, religious days, and other special events.
- communication, including both beliefs and emotions.
- good financial management.
- hardiness, which includes commitment to the family, the belief that family members have control over their lives, and a sense that the family can deal with all changes.

Family celebrations build emotional strength that is useful for dealing with crises.

- health, both physical and emotional.
- shared leisure activities.
- acceptance of each member's personality and behavior.
- a social support network of relatives and friends.
- sharing routines such as family meals and chores.
- traditions that carry over from one generation to another.

Families that have worked at developing these strengths will be in a position to deal effectively with stressors and with crises.

Tools for Effective Coping

In our research on how people master life's unpredictable crises (Lauer and Lauer 1988), we found a number of tools that people use to deal with everything from divorce to abuse to serious illness. We were particularly interested in how people deal with a crisis in a way to follow path one in figure 14.2 rather than path two or three.

The following are path one tools, those that enable people to confront a crisis and eventually emerge at a higher level of functioning. For any particular crisis, one or a number of these tools may be useful.

Take Responsibility. In contrast to denial, avoidance, and scapegoating, effective coping begins when you take responsibility for yourself and your family. Taking responsibility means not only that you will not deny or avoid the problem or blame others, but also that you will not play the victim game. That is, even though you may have been victimized by something or someone, you will not continue to act as a victim—hurt, oppressed, exploited, in pain, and helpless.

If the crisis is some kind of family disruption, such as death or divorce, taking responsibility means charting a new course as an alternative to playing the victim game. For example, Amy, a Mormon woman, felt victimized by her husband of 24 years when he abruptly told her he wanted a divorce. After her initial shock and grief, she decided to accept the responsibility for her own life:

> My first step was to resolve not to become a woman wrapped up in her past, clinging to it like a life raft. I wanted to be able to move beyond the hurt and pain and make something special out of my life. I began by taking a real-estate course and getting my license.

In some cases, taking responsibility may involve confrontation. Drug abusers, for example, are notoriously resistant to admitting they need help. One way to motivate them to get the professional help they need is for family members to confront the abuser in an intervention session (Landau et al. 2004). By family consensus, the abuser is told that he or she has a severe problem, needs professional help, and faces certain consequences (including losing the support and any co-dependent behavior of the rest of the family) if he or she does not address the problem.

Affirm Your Own and Your Family's Worth. A crisis assaults people's self-esteem. This makes it more difficult to deal with the crisis. It is important to believe in yourself and in your ability to deal with difficult situations in order to be effective in a crisis. In a crisis, you may have to remind yourself that you and your family are people with strengths and the capacity to cope effectively.

A woman who stayed in an abusive relationship for years told us that one of her problems was her sense of being a worthless individual. The husband who abused her suggested that there was something about her that made him violent, something defective or deficient in

her that made her deserve to be beaten. Her ability to deal with the critical situation began one day when she decided to stop viewing herself as somehow deserving the abuse. She had seen some information about abusive relationships and realized that she was a victim rather than a worthless person. She affirmed her own worth, which meant that being beaten was no longer tolerable. She left her husband and began a new life in another state.

Balance Self-Concern with Other-Concern. We have said that you must take responsibility for your own well-being. That doesn't mean you should ignore the well-being of others. The totally self-focused life is as self-destructive as the totally other-focused life. Someone who stays in an abusive relationship because "my spouse needs me" may be too other-focused. Someone who leaves a spouse simply because "I want my space so I can grow" may be too self-focused.

Exchange Theory Applied

A crisis tends not only to attack our self-esteem but also to throw us into self-absorption. Some people get so enmeshed in the crisis that they seem neither to listen to nor to care about others in the family. If all family members become self-absorbed, the situation can become hazardous to both marital and familial well-being. Each member may *perceive inequity,* for each may be expecting the others to give support and, finding none, may feel abandoned by the family—a sense of "I've put a lot into this family and now, when I need help, I'm getting nothing in return." Dealing effectively with a crisis requires a healthy amount of both self-concern and other-concern on the part of at least some, and ideally all, family members.

In a study of families in which a child had died of cancer two to nine years earlier, the researchers found that families that handled the crisis best were those in which the individual family members were aware of the grieving of other members and made efforts to empathize and support them (Davies et al. 1986). Families with a poorer adjustment, on the other hand, tended to have members who focused on their own personal grief without relating that grief to other family members:

> It seemed as if each person was carrying the burden of grief all alone and there seemed to be a lack of empathy for how the other members were doing (Davies et al. 1986:302).

Learn the Art of Reframing. Reframing, or redefining the meaning of something, is a way of changing your perspective on a situation. It isn't the situation that is changed but the way that you look at it. In essence, you learn to redefine something that you had defined as troublesome as adaptive and useful. The technique can help you overcome a variety of problems (Easley and Epstein 1991).

Reframing is not denial. It is based on the fact that people can look at any situation in various ways. You can see a crisis as an intruder that has robbed you of a measure of peace and happiness, or you can define the crisis as an obstacle that will ultimately lead to your growth as you overcome it (Urcuyo et al. 2005).

Celia, an undergraduate student, had a crisis situation in her family when she was still in high school. Her father had begun to drink heavily. He was having problems at his work. The drinking, of course, only exacerbated the problems and put his job in jeopardy. Celia was preparing to go to college and feared that she could not go if her father lost his job. Then one day her mother sat down with her and helped her reframe the situation:

> "This may mean that you won't go to college when you thought," her mother said. "But it doesn't mean you won't go. At the most, it means you will have to wait for a year or so. But you *will* go. Furthermore, I want you to see this for what it is. It isn't a disaster. In fact, it may be the best lesson you ever learn, in school or out of school. Your father picked the wrong way to deal with the problem. But if we just condemn him, we will also pick the wrong way to deal with it. He needs us to help him now. We're going to do that."

Celia, as the oldest child, worked with her mother to firmly help her father cut back on his drinking. They gave him extra attention and support. Eventually, his work stress eased, and the family made it through the crisis. Celia went to college as she had planned. In good part, it was her mother's reframing of the situation that made the difference.

Find and Use Available Resources. Every family has numerous internal and external resources to which it can turn in a time of crisis. Family members themselves are internal resources. That is, family members can be a source of emotional support for each other. Internal resources also include all of the family strengths we identified earlier, such as open communication of both beliefs and feelings. As long as family members can talk to each other freely and openly about a situation, they are not likely to fall into the unhealthy traps of avoidance or denial.

For many families, religious beliefs are an important resource (Belavich and Pargament 2002; Ai et al. 2004). Religious beliefs can be a basis for reframing crises. Religious beliefs also provide family members with hope for an acceptable outcome and with strength for enduring the trauma until the crisis is resolved.

External resources include such things as the extended family, friends, books, self-help groups, and therapists. There are also numerous community resources that are designed to help people through crises of every kind.

For example, a study of coping strategies used by parents of autistic children found that those who coped well found encouragement and support from such sources as friends, other families with similar problems, and various community agencies and programs (Twoy, Connolly, and Novak 2007). Similarly, research on fathers of chronically ill children reported that the fathers found a number of strategies very helpful, including reading about the problem, getting information, examining various options, and evaluating differing choices (Hovey 2005).

Still, the question comes up of how someone gets in touch with these varied external resources. A place to begin is quite simple—the yellow pages of the telephone directory. Help may be found listed under the specific problem or a more general category. For example, our local directory has listings for "alcoholism information and treatment centers," "drug abuse and addiction information," "women's organizations and services" (which includes a domestic violence hotline and a number for a rape and family violence resource center), and "social and human services for individuals and families."

The clergy and school counselors are also helpful in identifying community resources. As a student told us:

> I struggled for years trying to deal with an alcoholic father. My mother died when I was 7, and my sister and I soon started taking care of him. He never got abusive with us, but he was unreliable, often depressed and withdrawn, and of no help to us whatever. When my sister got fed up and moved away, I was stuck with taking care of him and it was really getting me down. I'm not religious, but I was walking by this Methodist church one day and on an impulse I went in and met the minister. It turned out that his church sponsored a group for people like me who are trying to cope with alcoholic parents! I joined it right away. It's been a tremendous help to me.

Not everyone can find help that quickly and easily. But the point is that most communities have an abundance of resources to help individuals and families through all kinds of crises.

Using the available resources along with other coping strategies we have discussed can enable a family to emerge from a crisis at a higher level of functioning than it had before the crisis. Indeed, the very meaning of effective coping is that the individual will achieve a new level of maturity and that the family will attain a new level of intimacy.

Personal

Things Were Terribly Still

Kim is in her early 20s. She has been married for five years. Phil, her husband, works as an electronics engineer. Their daughter was 4 years old when Kim got pregnant again. Kim and Phil were very happy. Both wanted a large family. However, the "blessed event" turned into a crisis for them, a crisis for which they needed some outside help:

I was so happy when I got pregnant that I prepared a nursery in rainbow colors for the baby. Phil and I were really excited as the due date approached. He loved to put his hand on my stomach and feel the baby moving. He wanted a boy so he could go fishing with him. And our daughter looked forward to a baby brother or sister.

A few weeks before the baby was due, I felt sick to my stomach. The doctor thought I had a virus and needed to get more rest. But a few days later, I suddenly realized that things were terribly still inside me. I went to the doctor immediately. She decided to induce labor. Phil was with me when I delivered a stillborn baby boy. An autopsy showed that our son had a chromosomal disorder.

We were devastated. We spent 45 minutes with our son, holding and touching him. We said goodbye to him, and the nurse asked if we wanted her to take a picture. We said no, but I regret it now. It would mean a lot to me to have a picture of that child.

I left the hospital the next morning. Phil got a week off from work. Our son's name was to be Bradley. We had him cremated and held a memorial service at the beach. We scattered his ashes in the Pacific Ocean.

The first week, we spent most of our time talking and crying about it. When Phil went back to work, he tried to act macho about it all. He told everyone that we were fine and that everything was going to be all right. But I was upset all the time. I began to feel depressed and guilty. We went for genetic tests. But we are not at high risk for genetic defects. Phil didn't want to talk about it any more. He reminded me that we could have more children.

Phil and I were really close before Bradley's death. Even right afterward. But as time went on, we grew apart. We couldn't seem to communicate. And we didn't have much sex. I spent most of my time with our daughter, and Phil spent more time at work and watching television.

We talked about another child, but I don't think either of us wanted to take the risk. I talked about it with my doctor one day, and she suggested that before we try to have another child we should attend Healing Hearts, a self-help group for people who have had a child die. Phil refused to go at first. He told me to go, that he was fine and didn't need it. So I went alone. It helped me a lot. I kept asking Phil and he finally agreed to go. Toward the end of his first meeting, he broke down and cried for several minutes. He finally began to open up and talk about how he really felt.

It's been five months now since Bradley died. We still go to Healing Hearts. We're also working on our relationship with each other. We're beginning to feel intimate with each other again. Some day we will try to have another child. We're still scared, but we're working at it. We're a lot more mature, and I think we have a new kind of respect for each other.

SUMMARY

Family crises are associated with various kinds of stressful events and/or behavior. A family in crisis is not necessarily a sick family but may be a family overwhelmed by a stressor or piled-up stressors in accord with the ABCX and Double ABCX models. Some of the common stressor events are death, serious illness, accidents, loss of work, an unwanted pregnancy, moving, alcohol abuse, and interpersonal problems, such as abuse and infidelity.

The kinds of stressors people face vary over the family life cycle. Not all stressors are equally severe; rather, they range in severity from such highly stressful events as a death in the family to the mildly stressful event of a major purchase.

Drug abuse, and particularly alcohol abuse, ranks high on the list of family stressors. A substantial number of Americans say that the abuse of alcohol or other drugs has been a problem in their family. A variety of short-term and long-term negative consequences result when a family member abuses drugs. Family problems contribute to, as well as result from, drug abuse.

Next to death, separation, and divorce, family violence is the most difficult experience people confront. Millions of U.S. adults and children endure violence in their homes. A substantial proportion of abused children are 5 years old or younger, with females slightly more likely than males to be abused. The typical abusive parent is single, is young (around 30 or under), has been married for less than 10 years, had his or her first child before the age of 18, and is unemployed or employed part-time.

Incest is a form of abuse more likely to happen to girls than boys. Incest usually begins when the child is between 6 and 11. Father–daughter incest is the most common form, tending to occur in families in which the marital relationship has broken down and the father has many stressors and a problem relating meaningfully and sexually with an adult.

Spouse abuse may involve either husband or wife being the victim, but the damage is likely to be more severe for abused wives. Women stay in an abusive relationship because they believe they lack the resources to leave, or they have fallen into a social trap and developed a "traumatic bonding" to their husbands, or they have developed the battered woman syndrome.

Parent abuse occurs from both adolescent and adult children. The abuse may be physical, emotional, or both. White females are most likely to be victimized by a child, and a daughter is more likely than a son to be the abuser.

Abuse results in short-term physical and emotional damage. It also tends to have serious long-term consequences. Victims may have to undergo therapy to work through their trauma. Witnessing abuse as well as enduring it can perpetuate violence in family life.

People react to crises in different ways. We cannot control the events that occur in our lives, but we can control the way we respond to them. Ineffective coping patterns are ways of response that leave people at a lower level of functioning after a crisis. Denial, avoidance, and scapegoating are ineffective coping patterns. Effective coping is facilitated by developing family strengths. It involves such things as taking responsibility, affirming individual and family worth, balancing self-concern with other-concern, learning the art of reframing, and finding and using available resources.

Principles for Enhancing Intimacy

1. When you or your family is undergoing major stress, avoid deliberately adding on other sources of pressure. Multiple stresses can be a lethal combination that can threaten any individual or intimate relationship. If you should lose your job, for example, it is probably a bad time to buy a new car or go on a diet. Or if your marriage is undergoing difficulties of one sort or another, it is not a good time to make a major career change or decide to have a baby.

2. Keep your economic house in order. Financial difficulties are a continuing source of stress throughout the family life cycle. By maintaining realistic expectations, careful budgeting, and avoiding the excessive use of credit, families can reduce financial strains and enhance their well-being and stability.

3. Alcohol abuse is difficult to cope with alone. If you are an abuser, organizations like AA can provide needed assistance. If someone in your family abuses alcohol, you also can benefit from a support group like Al-Anon.

4. Family violence—whatever its form and whoever its victim—results in serious physical and emotional damage. If the damage is to be minimized, family violence must be acknowledged and then dealt with as quickly and effectively as possible. It is not possible to have true intimacy in the context of violence.

5. Remember that you can cope with a crisis in your family. Even the most difficult situation offers the possibility of long-term, positive consequences. Indeed, by using effective coping strategies, you can transform the crisis into an opportunity for personal growth and enhanced intimacy.

KEY TERMS

battered woman syndrome   *323*
child maltreatment   *320*
drug abuse   *316*
emotional abuse   *319*

incest   *321*
intimate terrorism   *322*
physical abuse   *319*
reframing   *329*

resilient family   *328*
stress   *312*
stressor event   *312*

ON THE WEB   Family Crises

As society becomes increasingly complex and as economic as well as personal challenges grow, so does the potential for stress and crisis. Increases in poverty lead to increased levels of drug abuse, violence, and sexual abuse, which all dramatically impact the way people cope in families. It is quite likely that you have had contact with, or know of, a family that has had to deal with the problem of drug or alcohol abuse or of violence in the home. It is helpful, therefore, to be as knowledgeable as possible about these two crises, for your knowledge may enable you to help yourself or someone you care about. Two useful sites are:

www.mhhe.com/lauer7e

eMedicineHealth

http://www.emedicinehealth.com/alcoholism/article_em.htm

This site contains information on the causes, symptoms, and treatment of alcoholism, and offers links to other sites with additional information.

MedLine Plus

http://www.nlm.nih.gov/medlineplus/domesticviolence.html

A service of the U.S. Library of Medicine and the National Institutes of Health, this site has a wealth of information, including links to other sites, about all forms of domestic violence.

Using these two sites, enlarge your understanding with the following projects:

1. Use the eMedicineHealth site (including the links) to address the following questions about alcoholism and family life. How is everyday family life affected by an alcoholic member? How do some families help maintain a member's addiction? What are the consequences for children of growing up with an alcoholic parent? What can a family do to help an alcoholic member stop drinking?

2. The text has less information on the abuse of parents (or elder abuse) than it has on other kinds of abuse. At the MedLine Plus site, gather information on parent (or elder) abuse. You may need to go to other sites as well. Using the materials in the text, compare what you find about abuse of parents with spousal and child abuse in terms of rates or frequency, severity, causes, and consequences.

~ SEPARATION AND DIVORCE ~

LEARNING OBJECTIVES

After reading and studying chapter 15, you should be able to

1 Relate the trends in the rate of and grounds for divorce in U.S. society.

2 Explain the four periods in marital dissolution.

3 Identify the six "stations" that people often experience when they divorce.

4 Discuss the sociodemographic factors that contribute to the failure of a marriage.

5 Summarize the interpersonal factors that lead to divorce.

6 Describe the positive and negative effects of divorce for adults.

7 Discuss the impact of divorce on children.

8 Contrast and compare the differing reaction of boys and girls to the divorce of their parents.

9 Review the prevailing pattern of custody arrangements and show how it has changed over time.

10 Identify the ways in which parents and children can best cope with divorce.

Attend a local divorce court for a day. Write down your observations of what is happening. Note the expressions on the faces of the couples, lawyers, and judge. To what extent can you sense the trauma of divorce from the proceedings of the court? Note the outcomes of the various cases. What are the similarities and differences? If possible, see if you can obtain court records from a time when divorce was an adversarial process. Compare some of the proceedings with those you have observed. What differences are there? Which system do you think works best?

Finally, find someone who has recently been through a divorce. Discuss that person's recollections of the court proceedings. How did the person feel during the court session? How does the person feel about the legal aspects of divorce generally? How would that person change the legal system to make divorce more equitable or less painful for people? Do you agree or disagree with the divorced person's position? Why?

If divorce court proceedings in your locale are not available, an alternative option would be to write the history of a divorce you are familiar with. It might be the divorce of your parents, another relative, or a friend or even your own. The four periods—recognition, discussion, action, and postdissolution—of divorce may provide a useful device for organizing your account. 🌼

Is divorce ever good for you? Is it ever good for children? In the short run, the answer to both questions is "no" for most people. We say "most" because there are cases in which divorce can be a health-saving or even a life-saving event for an abused wife. It can be a form of social and emotional deliverance for a child victimized by a highly conflicted family life. Some marriages should *not* last.

At the same time, many marriages end that could have turned out to be satisfying. According to Waite and Gallagher (2000), the majority of couples who are unhappy can work through their problems and have a happy union within five years. Of course, this means that a minority won't be happy even if they try to work through their problems. In the long run, then, the answer to the question of whether divorce is ever good for you varies. The question of whether a divorce would be good for you or whether it would be good for your children is not easy to answer.

For example, consider one student's account of her parents' divorce:

> My most painful experience when I was growing up was when my parents got a divorce. My greatest pain wasn't the actual breakup. That was the best thing to happen. They had always fought. And so getting a divorce made all of our lives easier. The pain I experienced was deciding whom to live with.

Another undergraduate told us that the stress in her life was dramatically reduced when her parents divorced and, as a result, the quality of her life greatly improved. But others talk about the pain, the loss, the emptiness. Disrupting an intimate relationship is never easy, even when the relationship is defined as a destructive one (recall that people tend to stay in abusive relationships for long periods of time).

In this chapter, we will look closely at what has become a common experience for Americans: the disruption of an intimate relationship through separation and/or divorce. We will examine first the trends in divorce. Then we will discuss the process of "uncoupling." We will talk about some of the causes and correlates of divorce; the effects on spouses, parents, and children; and, finally, how people work through the issues raised by the disruption.

DIVORCE TRENDS

Americans are troubled about the number of divorces in the nation. About a fourth of Americans believe that divorce is morally wrong (Polling Report 2008). A good

many others believe that a high rate of divorce is a serious threat because stable families are the foundation of a healthy society. Just how high is the rate in the United States? Articles and commentators in the media continue to decry the "fact" that half of all marriages end in divorce, which, as we pointed out in chapter 1, is not true. It is true, however, that your chances of divorce are higher in the United States than in any other Western country (Schoen and Canudas-Romo 2006).

Divorce Rates

The government has measured the **divorce rate** in two ways: as the number of divorces per 1,000 population and as the number of divorces per 1,000 married women 15 years and older. While the latter gives us a somewhat better estimate of the proportion of marriages that fail, the data are not collected and published regularly. However, the pattern of the two figures is quite similar to that shown for rate per 1,000 population in figure 15.1. We know, therefore, the general trend of divorce rates. We also know that more than a million couples divorce each year, although we do not know the precise number because the figures are based on state reports and a few states no longer tabulate the data.

With regard to the trends, figure 15.1 shows the dramatic increase in rates in the 1960s and 1970s, with the peak coming from 1979 to 1981. In 1974, for the first time in our history, more marriages ended in divorce than through the death of a spouse. Although many people believe that the high rates of the 1970s and early 1980s were a striking break with tradition, there has actually been a fairly regular trend over the past century or so, a trend represented by a rising curve. There are variations, of course: Those who married during the 1950s have lower-than-expected rates of divorce, while those who married during the 1960s and 1970s have higher-than-expected rates (where *expected* means the rate we would have according to the long-term trend line). However, the high rates of the 1970s are modest rather than dramatic deviations from the long-term trend.

After 1980, rates tended to decline as marriages became more stable (Heaton 2002). By 2006, the rate per 1,000 population was 3.6, a number lower than any since 1970. As table 15.1 shows, the rate per 1,000 married women shows the same pattern.

The table also shows the proportion of Americans who are divorced during particular years. Of course, these figures do not tell us how many people have *ever* been separated or divorced. Some of those who are reported as divorced in a particular year will be married

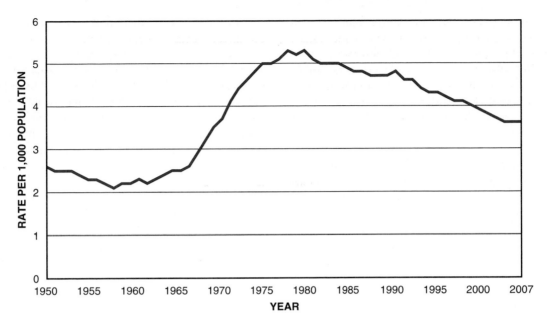

FIGURE 15.1   U.S. Divorce Rates, 1950–2007

Sources: Statistical Abstract of the United States, various editions; Eldridge and Sutton 2007.

TABLE 15.1   Divorces, 1960–2006

	1960	1965	1970	1975	1980	1985	1990	1995	2000	2006
Total (1,000)	393	479	708	1026	1189	1190	1182	1169	n.a.	n.a.
Rate per 1,000 Married Women, 15 Years and Older	9.2	10.6	14.9	20.3	22.6	21.7	20.9	19.8	18.8	17.9*
Percent divorced, 18 yrs and over:										
Male	2.0	2.5	2.5	3.7	5.2	6.5	7.2	8.3	8.8	9.1
Female	2.9	3.3	3.9	5.3	7.1	8.7	9.3	10.3	10.8	11.6

n.a. = not available.

*Rate for 2004.

Sources: Statistical Abstract of the United States, various editions; National Marriage Project 2007.

in another year and vice versa. By 2004, 20.7 percent of men and 22.9 percent of women had experienced divorce at some point in their lives (U.S. Census Bureau, Survey of Income and Program Participation 2007). Of first marriages that do end in divorce, about half break up within the first eight years.

Divorce rates also vary by race/ethnicity, with 47 percent of black non-Hispanic women, 34 percent of Hispanic women, 32 percent of white non-Hispanic women, and 20 percent of Asian women divorcing within 10 years of a first marriage. These figures reflect the fact that the decline in divorce rates since 1980 has not occurred equally for all racial groups; in fact, the rate for African

Americans has increased somewhat since the late 1980s (Sweeney and Phillips 2004).

Changing Grounds for Divorce

For what legal reasons can you attain a divorce? State rather than federal laws answer that question. In the past, the states provided many different answers. For example, in the nineteenth century, South Carolina did not allow divorce at all, while New York allowed it only on the grounds of adultery (Degler 1980). Some states permitted more lenient grounds than others. As a result, people often established temporary residence in order to make use of a state's more liberal divorce laws. At one time or another, Pennsylvania, Ohio, South Dakota, North Dakota, and Nevada, among others, made it relatively easy for people to establish residence and obtain a divorce (Day and Hook 1987). However, only middle- and upper-class people could typically afford to pursue a divorce under such conditions.

In response to the increase in divorces, states have changed divorce laws. The changes reflect a different perspective on divorce—that it is essentially an individual rather than a government-controlled decision. Because it is viewed as an individual decision, states have abandoned the adversarial approach to divorce, an approach that assumes one of the spouses is at fault. In the past, "fault" could have referred to such things as adultery, insanity, imprisonment, or cruelty. In any case, the plaintiff had to provide evidence to show that the partner was at fault. When both spouses wanted the divorce, they might agree to lie or present false evidence in order to comply with the law.

In the 1970s, California and New York began the trend toward no-fault divorce, which is now practiced in all states. In **no-fault divorce,** no proof for divorce is needed. Neither spouse accuses the other of impropriety or immorality. Rather, the marriage is deemed unworkable and therefore is dissolved. Some states allow either spouse to initiate the divorce unilaterally, while others require mutual consent.

The purpose of no-fault divorce laws was to remove some of the acrimony and pain from the process. In many cases, they have achieved that aim. However, the laws have generated controversy and opposition (Gallagher and Whitehead 1997). Opponents point out that they make divorce easier to obtain at a time when there is a need to save marriages rather than to foster divorce. Moreover, no-fault laws empower the spouse who wishes to leave but make the other spouse relatively helpless; some people, therefore, advocate a five-year waiting period when the no-fault divorce may be contested by one of the spouses.

On the other hand, proponents argue that the laws not only remove acrimony but also *make divorce a more equitable process*, and Americans strongly believe in *equity*. The process is more equitable because settlements are not made on the basis of someone having been wronged but on the basis of need. The settlement does not presume that the man should continue to support the woman nor that the woman should assume total care of any children.

Exchange Theory Applied

To many Americans, no-fault divorce appears to make divorce too easy. A majority of Americans are convinced that making divorce more difficult will be better for our society. In the late 1990s, a number of groups, mostly associated with conservative Christian causes, began to promote the idea of **"covenant marriage."** Those who enter a covenant marriage make a legal contract that they will not seek divorce except for abuse or adultery. If they want to divorce for any other reasons, they agree to first have counseling and wait two years before finalizing the decision.

Three states—Arizona, Arkansas, and Louisiana—have passed covenant marriage bills. Similar legislation was introduced in a number of other states but did not pass. Although the founders of the movement claim that 50,000 couples were in covenant marriages by 2006, the idea has not appealed to people other than some conservative Christians (Monkerud 2006). There is no reason to believe that large numbers of Americans will opt for covenant marriages.

In fact, there is little evidence that covenant marriages achieve the aim of greater stability and satisfaction. A researcher who tracked 600 newlywed couples, half of whom were in covenant marriages, reported after the first two years of the study that about 50 divorces occurred and a fourth of those were covenant marriages (Perina 2002). Another research effort looked at the question of whether a covenant marriage would offset the negative effects of cohabitation on marriage (discussed in chapter 7). Examining a sample of Louisiana marriages that included both covenant and standard arrangements, the researchers found that covenant marriage did not moderate the amount of marital instability, unhappiness, or divorce among those who had cohabited prior to marriage (Brown, Sanchez, Nock, and Wright 2006).

In short, although the evidence is sparse, covenant marriages do not appear to fare better than standard marriages. Of course, we do not know what will happen over a longer time span. Perhaps covenant marriages are as fragile as others over the first years of marriage (which is all we can study at this point), but are more likely to endure among those married eight or more years. But for now there is little enthusiasm for, and little reason to be enthusiastic about, covenant marriage as a way to add stability and satisfaction to marital relationships.

THE PROCESS OF UNCOUPLING

What happens in a family that is in the process of breaking up? What stages bring an intimate relationship to the point of disruption? What is the meaning of

What Do You Think?

*There is disagreement about **whether divorce should be more difficult to obtain.** What follows are pro and con arguments. What do you think?*

Pro	Con
Divorce should be more difficult to obtain because	Divorce should not be more difficult to obtain because
• stable families are the foundation of a stable society.	• that would force some people to stay in meaningless or even abusive marriages.
• couples need to learn to work through difficulties.	• divorce is only harmful to the society if people believe it is, and accepting divorce eliminates the damage it can cause.
• most marriages that break up could have lasted and become fulfilling if the partners had tried harder.	• this would mean an increase in extramarital affairs.
• it is extremely traumatic for children.	• there is no point in adding to the pain of a bad marriage by making it more difficult to end it.
• it leaves couples with a sense of failure, a fear of future commitments, and possible long-term trauma.	• the quicker you can leave a bad marriage, the sooner you can get into a fulfilling and lasting one.

the disruption? Researchers have identified a number of features in the process that are common to most divorcing couples. They also tend to apply to cohabiting and same-sex couples who break up after living together for a number of years.

Toward Marital Dissolution

While few if any of those who "fall in love" expect to fall out of it, many do. They may experience disaffection, which is

> the gradual loss of emotional attachment, including a decline in caring about the partner, an emotional estrangement, and an increasing sense of apathy and indifference toward one's spouse (Kayser 1993:6).

Dissolution may follow such disaffection. Not all disaffected people divorce, and not all divorces involve disaffection. When people do divorce, for whatever reason, four phases tend to mark the process: recognition, discussion, action, and postdissolution (Ponzetti and Cate 1986).

Recognition. Recognition begins when one or both spouses become aware of serious problems. A spouse may feel discontent or dissatisfaction and realize that the feeling is sufficiently strong to call the relationship into question. Frequently, recognition occurs when marital stress and open conflict are followed by a period of cold war between the spouses.

However, the period of recognition may occur very early. In her interviews with disaffected people who divorced, Kayser (1993:29) concluded that "the ink is barely dry on the marriage license when doubts and disillusionment about marriage and the partner can begin to set in." Forty percent of her respondents said that doubts occurred within the first six months, and 60 percent had doubts within the first year.

What caused such doubts? The most frequent causes given by Kayser's respondents were the spouse's controlling behavior, lack of responsibility, and lack of emotional support. Controlling behavior involves such things as making decisions without consulting the spouse or taking into account the spouse's opinion. Lack of responsibility refers to such things as driving while drunk, getting fired from a job for just cause, spending excessive amounts of time with friends, and leaving children unattended. Lack of emotional support involves behavior that suggests a lack of concern and care for the spouse, particularly during such stressful times as pregnancy, childbirth, or the death of a family member.

These early doubts intensified when the troubling behavior continued, leading to anger, hurt, and disillusionment. The offended spouse became deeply aware of

 Symbolic Interactionist Theory Applied

his or her partner's flaws and recognized that the marriage had taken an unexpected and undesirable turn. In some cases,

Typically, divorce is an emotionally devastating experience.

the offended spouse believed that the partner had changed after the marriage. What had mainly changed, Kayser (1993:33) notes, was not the partner "but the *respondent's perception" of his or her partner.* The changed perception led to a definition of the marriage as moving in a very different direction than expected and than could be tolerated.

Discussion. Discussion is the period during which one or both spouses begin to share the marital problems with others—friends, relatives, a counselor, and often each other. The discussion is not merely a sharing of information but an opportunity to redefine the relationship. The partner may be defined in negative terms, and the history of the relationship may be reconstructed as a series of negative experiences. Gratifying experiences also may be redefined: "Yes, we had a good time on that trip but that was only because we were with friends."

Discussion with the partner involves the breaking down of the pretense that all is well with the marriage. The initiator, the partner who first feels but doesn't openly acknowledge discontent, finally discloses that discontent and does so with sufficient force and clarity that the partner cannot deny the fact that the marriage is in serious trouble. With such a confrontation, conflict increases significantly in the discussion period (Ponzetti and Cate 1986). One of the functions of such conflict is to maintain the relationship for a time. Conflict at least means that there is interaction. But the conflict also serves to underscore that there are problems in the relationship.

During the discussion period, the discontented spouse will find a "transitional person," someone who can help him or her move from the old life to a new one. The transitional person may be a temporary lover but also may be a friend who can provide emotional support. The problem with the relationship has now become a public matter.

Some effort may be made to save the marriage during this period. Once the confrontation has taken place and the problem is openly acknowledged, the noninitiating partner may ask for an opportunity to try to save the relationship. The initiator feels that he or she has already tried but may be willing to give the partner a chance to try also. Yet in many cases, the odds are against any change for the better. The initiator has been making the transition to a new life for a period of time. The initiator is already a somewhat different person, with a new ideology, perhaps new friends, and new commitments. Many initiators tell their partners during this period, "You don't know me any more." If the initiator has gone far enough in the process of transition to a new life, he or she may allow the partner to try to save the relationship but will not allow the partner to succeed. Letting the noninitiating partner try but fail can be a way of getting him or her to agree that the intimate bond has been severed irreparably.

Action. In the period of action, one of the spouses secures a lawyer in order to legally dissolve the marriage. Many are already preparing for independence by such things as paying their own bills and not relying on their partner for emotional support or companionship (Kayser 1993). Separation is also likely in this period. There are a number of reasons why a married couple might separate for a period of time, including military deployment and incarceration. Here, we are only dealing with the separation that occurs in a troubled marriage where one or both partners are considering divorce. Such separation does not necessarily lead to divorce. Some couples are able to use it as a cooling-off period that allows them to deal more rationally with their differences and effect a reconciliation. A couple may also get involved in a long-term, unresolved separation. They neither reconcile nor divorce.

Often, however, separation does culminate in a divorce. The partners may or may not have anticipated and/or desired divorce as the outcome. The separation may occur either before or after a lawyer is consulted. In any case, separation is likely to be a difficult experience, a form of a grieving process with all the pain (including even suicidal thoughts) involved in loss (Knox and Corte 2007).

Once separated, most women make the transition to divorce quickly: 84 percent do it within three years and 91 percent do it within five years (Bramlett and Mosher 2002). Actually, although some people advocate, and some states mandate, a mandatory time of separation before divorce in order to maximize the possibility of reconciliation, longer times of separation are associated with increased rates of violence between the partners (Stolzenberg and D'Alessio 2007). The risk of such violence indicates that it is best to have a short time between the separation and the divorce.

The likelihood of divorce following separation varies by race and ethnicity (Bramlett and Mosher 2002). White women are more likely to divorce once they are separated than are African Americans or Hispanics. As many as 15 percent of Hispanic and black couples who separate remain in separation for the long term (10 or more years).

Difficulties mount once a lawyer is secured and the divorce petition is filed. At this point in the process, couples frequently struggle over such things as division of property and child custody. Moreover, they often are anxious about the separation and have lingering uncertainties about whether dissolution is really in their best interests.

This period also can last much longer than people anticipate if there are disagreements about the settlement. For example, community property laws do not make financial settlements an automatic matter. Thus, there can be considerable wrangling over the division of property and intense bitterness about the outcome.

Postdissolution. The postdissolution period begins when both spouses accept the fact that the marriage has ended. During this period, the spouses probably will think about reasons for the divorce and construct some acceptable rationale for what has happened. Many people do not accept completely the fact that the marriage has ended until the former spouse is coupled with a new partner.

The Six Stations of Divorce

Paul Bohannan (1970) discussed divorce in terms of six "stations," or six different experiences that people are likely to have. Marriage, he pointed out, makes us feel good in part because we have been selected, out of all those available, by someone to be an intimate partner. Divorce, by contrast, makes you feel "so awful," in part, because "you have been deselected" (Bohannan 1970:33). To some extent, deselection occurs in each of the six different stations of divorce.

The *emotional* divorce involves a loss of trust, respect, and affection for each other. Rather than supporting each other, the spouses act in ways to hurt, to frustrate, to lower self-esteem. The spouses grate on each other. Each is visible evidence to the other of failure and rejection.

The *legal* divorce, in which a court officially brings the marriage to an end, is the only one of the six stations that provides a tangible benefit to the partners: relief from the legal responsibilities of the marriage and the right to remarry. The legal divorce also can help partners feel free of other kinds of obligations, such as that of caring for a sick partner. Legal divorce may follow a period of separation, but increasingly couples opt directly for divorce rather than trial separation.

The *economic* divorce involves settlement of the property. The division of property is rarely an easy matter. Actually, economic settlements were easier under the adversary system, in which one of the parties was at fault and therefore "owed" the other compensation. The economic divorce is likely to be painful for at least three reasons. First, there are never enough assets for each partner to feel that he or she is getting all that is needed to continue living at a comfortable level. Second, there can be considerable acrimony over who gets what—the condo, the silver, a favorite painting, and so forth. And third, there is likely to be a sense of loss as each partner realizes that he or she must live in the future without some familiar and cherished possessions.

The *co-parental* divorce is experienced by those with children—about two-thirds of all couples. Decisions must be made about who will have custody, visitation rights, and continuing parental responsibilities. This is perhaps the most tragic part of the divorce (see the discussion on the consequences of divorce for children later in the chapter), particularly when the parents use their children as weapons against each other or even fail to protect them from the conflict and bitterness of the struggle.

The *community* divorce means that each of the partners leaves one community of friends and relations and enters another. A newly divorced person may feel uncomfortable with some of the friends he or she shared with the former spouse, especially if there is a feeling that the friends were more sympathetic with the former spouse. Relationships with former in-laws may cease or become minimal and strained. The process of changing from one community of relationships to another is likely to be difficult and frequently leaves the individual feeling lonely and isolated for a period of time.

Finally, the *psychic* divorce is the central separation that occurs—the individual must accept the disruption of the relationship and regain a sense of being an individual rather than a part of an intimate couple. Eventually, as the healing process takes place, the individual will begin to feel whole again. But he or she can only feel whole to the extent that the psychic divorce is final; that is, to the extent that there is a distancing from both the positive and negative aspects of the broken relationship.

CAUSES AND CORRELATES OF DIVORCE

As we noted in chapter 1, the great majority of Americans place a high value on marriage and family life. And a large majority indicate satisfaction with their own marriages. Why, then, is the divorce rate as high as it is? What factors make it more or less likely that someday you may be involved in a divorce?

Sociodemographic Factors

If a couple files for divorce, you might wonder what the spouses did to bring about the breakup. Social scientists have found that it is not just what people do that helps account for the failure of a marriage, but also such things as their socioeconomic status, race, religion, and other sociodemographic factors.

Socioeconomic Status. An inverse relationship exists between socioeconomic status and divorce rates. That is, the higher your status, the less likely you are to divorce. Higher status generally means more education and higher income and vice versa. Thus, when the wife works but has a low income, or when the wife is not working and the husband has a low income, the chances of marital disruption are higher (Ono 1998). Similarly, a study of women over a 20-year period found that the divorce

rates were highest among those with less than a high school education and lowest among those with four or more years of college (Martin 2006). In fact, although the divorce rate has declined overall, it actually rose for those without a high school diploma. Finally, data from the National Center for Health Statistics showed that the proportion of women divorced within 15 years of marriage was 65 percent for those in families with less than $25,000 annual income, 40 percent for those with family income between $25,000 and $49,999, and 31 percent for those with a family income of $50,000 or more (Bramlett and Mosher 2002).

Undoubtedly, the financial pressures on those in lower income brackets add to the instability of their marriages. Research in the Netherlands also found financial problems to be associated with higher divorce rates (Poortman 2005).

Age at Marriage. In earlier chapters, we pointed out that one's age at marriage is related to marital stability. The younger you are when you marry, the greater your chances of divorce (Amato and Rogers 1997). The National Center for Health Statistics data showed that 59 percent of women who married when they were younger than 18 years, compared to 25 percent who were 25 years or older, experienced marital disruption within 15 years (Bramlett and Mosher 2002). In part, younger age at marriage is associated with higher rates of breakup because early marriage is detrimental to high educational attainment (South 1995). This, in turn, generally means lower income levels.

There is one factor, however, that appears to alter the relationship between young age and the probability of divorce. When researchers looked at the gender ideologies of a sample of ever-married women, they found that the relationship between young age and higher rates of divorce varied by ideology (Davis and Greenstein 2004). They divided the women into three types of gender ideology. Traditional women were those who agreed that a woman's place is in the home, that she finds fulfillment in raising her children and taking care of her home, and that outside employment carries the risk of negative consequences (such as juvenile delinquency). Nontraditional women disagreed with such ideas. And a group the researchers called "transitional" agreed in part and disagreed in part.

The researchers found that age at first marriage did not affect the likelihood of divorce for nontraditional women. Very young transitional women, however, were 57 percent more likely to experience marital disruption than transitional women who married in their early 20s.

Religious people are less likely to have their marriages end in divorce.

And traditional women who married younger than 18 were twice as likely to divorce as those who married at the ages of 22 to 24. Whether a woman's age at marriage affects her chances of divorce, then, depends upon her beliefs about gender roles. Women who expect home and family to fulfill all their needs, and who grow up in a culture where divorce is common, may be willing to break up the marriage when the expected fulfillment doesn't happen.

Race.   African Americans are more likely both to separate and to divorce than are whites. In fact, African Americans have higher rates than any other racial group in the United States (Bramlett and Mosher 2002). Asian Americans have the lowest rate (a little over half the rate of whites and Hispanics). The greatest differences between African Americans and others occur in the lower socioeconomic levels, but they exist at all levels. Some scholars

have suggested that because of their experience of low income, job instability, and high unemployment rates, African Americans have learned to depend less on marriage and more on the extended kin network for support. This may have established a cultural tradition in which marriage is less central and in which there is thus less commitment to the marital relationship. An alternative explanation is that African Americans still have to deal with overt and covert discrimination and rejection, leading them to be more likely to have a pileup of stressor events in their lives. The pileup, in turn, places greater strains on their marriages than on those of other races.

Social Integration.   **Social integration** is a state of relative harmony and cohesion in a group. People who are members of an integrated group have an important source of support, a buffer against stress. We would expect, then, that social integration would help to minimize the divorce rates. Evidence exists to support that conclusion.

Religious groups provide one source of social integration. In addition, religion places great value on the family. It is reasonable to expect, therefore, that the more religious people are, the less likely they are to divorce. Indeed, people who are members of churches and who attend services are less likely to divorce than are nonmembers (Amato and Rogers 1997; Bramlett and Mosher 2002; Mullins, Brackett, Bogie, and Pruett 2006). As figure 15.2 shows, not only are there differences in divorce to the extent that people say religion is important to them but also according to their religious affiliation. Catholics have the lowest divorce rates among Christians, followed by fundamentalists (very conservative Protestants) and other Protestants. All groups have considerably lower rates than those who say they have "no religion."

Social integration occurs in more than religious groups, of course. Using data from a national survey, three researchers found that "normative integration" (measured by the number of nondivorced people who are significant to the individual) is associated with lower divorce rates and that "communicative integration" (measured by the number of friends and organizational memberships the individual has) is associated with a slightly lower divorce rate among those married seven years or less (Booth, Edwards, and Johnson 1991).

Children also can be an integrating factor. Marital stability tends to grow with increasing family size up to the third child but declines when family size is five or more children (Heaton 1990). Perhaps the strains of a

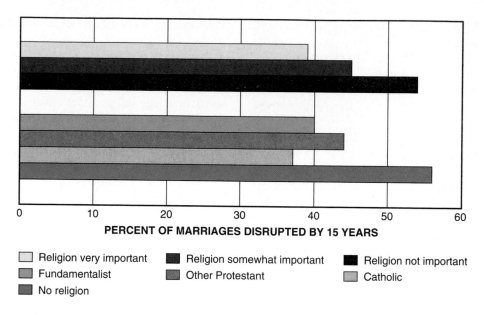

FIGURE 15.2   Divorce and Religion
Source: Bramlett and Mosher 2002.

large number of children outweigh the tendency for children to integrate a family. The integrating power of children also may vary by their gender. Using national data, Katzev, Warner, and Acock (1994) found that mothers with at least one son reported a significantly lower propensity to divorce than mothers who only had girls.

If social integration tends to minimize divorce, the lack of integration should be associated with higher rates of divorce. This may help explain why those whose parents divorced have a much higher rate of divorce themselves (Amato and DeBoer 2001). Coming from a background of disruption, they have not learned to place a high value on lifelong commitment to a partner.

Lacking the integrating power of offspring, childless couples are more prone to divorce (Weinberg 1990). People also get into a situation with less integration when they move to a new community. There they are likely to be cut off from friends and family and may not become an integral part of religious or other community organizations for some time. Thus, those who move a good deal are at greater risk for marital disruption.

Changing Norms and Roles. Divorce has become more acceptable over time, both in the United States and many other nations. In the United States, we have a "divorce culture" that is rooted in our individualism and insistence on personal happiness (Whitehead 1997; Coontz 2007). Individual happiness takes priority over

couple well-being. In a national survey, nearly half the respondents agreed that divorce is usually the best solution when couples can't seem to work out their problems. In addition, over two-thirds disagreed with the idea that people who don't get along should stay in a marriage for the sake of the children (Jacques 1998). Because Americans marry in order to be happy, they opt for divorce and look for happiness in a new relationship if their present marriage does not fulfill their expectations. Earlier in our history, a successful marriage was one that lasted and produced offspring. Now, a successful marriage is one that facilitates the happiness and well-being of both partners. No-fault divorce laws reflected this ideal of personal happiness for both partners. And while, as discussed earlier, the laws may have achieved some desired ends, they also are associated with an increased divorce rate of roughly 10 percent (Allen and Gallagher 2007).

In addition, the changing roles of women are associated with higher divorce rates. Over the past few decades, as noted earlier, the divorce rates have gone down among highly educated women and up among those with the least education. Associated with this trend are more negative attitudes toward divorce among the highly educated (who used to be the most permissive group of women) and more permissive attitudes among those with the least education (Martin and Parashar 2006). Nevertheless, it is still true that women as a whole are more likely than men to initiate divorce, and they do so in England, Wales, and Canada as well as in the United States (Buckle, Gallup, and Rodd 1996; Amato and Previti 2003). Both the higher rates and the tendency of women to initiate divorce are associated with the increasing economic independence of women (South 2001). In particular, wives who earn as much as or more than their husbands have higher rates of separation and divorce (Heckert, Nowak, and Snyder 1998). Of course, those with a strong commitment and a satisfying marriage will not seek a divorce. Rather, it is those in unhappy marriages who use their financial independence to escape from the union (Sayer and Bianchi 2000). In addition, women have varied ideologies about their roles, and only those with nontraditional gender ideologies show a positive relationship between number of work hours and divorce rate (Green-stein 1995).

One other way in which roles relate to marital breakup involves premarital sexual relations: Women who are sexually active before marriage have a considerably higher rate of divorce than those who are virgins (Kahn and London 1991). This may reflect differing norms about roles, the fact that

> women who continue to hold traditional attitudes about marriage are less likely than other women to consider both premarital sex and divorce as acceptable options for themselves (Kahn and London 1991:853).

Interpersonal Factors

These various sociodemographic factors are important, of course, because they have a bearing on the way that people interact. Ultimately, however, it is the interaction that leads to disruption. If we focus on the interaction itself, rather than on the sociodemographic variables that underlie the interaction, what do we find?

Complaints. When people in a national sample were asked why their marriages ended in a divorce, the most common reason given was infidelity (Amato and Previti 2003). **Infidelity,** which is sexual and/or emotional unfaithfulness to one's partner, is one of the most severe marital stressors, greatly increasing the chances of divorce (Cano, O'Leary, and Heinz 2004). A relatively recent form is Internet infidelity (Whitty 2005). Some have found their spouse's obsession with a virtual partner so consuming that it was as damaging to the marriage as a traditional affair. Internet infidelity underscores the fact that emotional infidelity is as harmful as sexual infidelity to a marriage. We should note here that infidelity of any kind is both a cause and a consequence of low marital quality (Previti and Amato 2004). In some cases, it may be

impossible to know whether the infidelity or the low marital quality came first, but, in any event, they feed on each other and significantly raise the probability of divorce.

In addition to infidelity, a number of other complaints are given by those who divorce, complaints that are offered not only by Americans but those in other nations as well (Patterson and Kim 1991; Amato and Rogers 1997; Amato and Previti 2003; Lowenstein 2005; Bodenmann et al. 2007):

- communication problems.
- lack of emotional support.
- emotional and physical abuse.
- falling out of love or growing apart.
- unsatisfactory sex.
- constant conflict.
- financial problems.
- falling in love with someone else.
- boredom with the marriage.
- alcohol or other drugs.
- incompatibility.

Conflict. Some marriages are characterized by intense conflict. The conflict is pervasive; the couple argues over nearly everything. The conflict may involve both severe (infidelity) and trivial (who takes the garbage out) issues.

Few, if any, people are comfortable and happy living in a situation of continual conflict. The situation may be compounded by a lack of conflict management skills. That is, the partners may get into a vicious circle in which the inability to resolve early conflicts acceptably only exacerbates subsequent conflicts. Thus, a conflict that may begin over a trivial issue may be an opportunity to bring back a severe issue that is still unresolved.

In addition to the sheer amount of conflict, the way the couple handles the conflict is crucial. John Gottman and Robert Levenson (2000) observed 79 couples talking together about three topics: events of the day, a matter on which the couple had ongoing disagreement, and a mutually agreed on, pleasant topic. The couples had been married an average of five years. The researchers contacted the couples four years later to see how they were doing.

Nine of the couples divorced early, an average of 7.4 years after marriage. Thirteen couples divorced a little later, an average of 13.9 years after marriage. The researchers found that the way the couples discussed the three topics predicted the outcomes. Those who divorced early had negative affect while discussing the topic on which they disagreed. They engaged in the kind of destructive messages we discussed in chapter 9. Those who divorced later lacked positive affect (e.g., taking a problem-solving approach and using humor or laughing) while discussing both the topic on which they disagreed and events of the day. The negative affect of the first group and the lack of positive affect in the second group were ways of dealing with conflict that disrupted the marriages.

Changed Feelings and Perspectives. Although many who divorce have a great deal of conflict, many do not. The marital bond erodes from decay, not from war. The marriage ends because feelings change—the couple no longer love each other, no longer have respect for each other, or no longer enjoy being together.

One of the possible reasons for the slow, nonconflicted erosion of a marriage is changed perspectives. We all change throughout our lives. Two people who begin a marriage with similar perspectives may find themselves changing in ways that make them less compatible. They no longer enjoy doing the same things. They are no longer the same two people who were married, and unfortunately, neither likes very much the way that the other has changed.

For example, Marie and Don were married as teenagers. He was in engineering school, and she was preparing to be a teacher. A few years later, Don realized that he didn't like engineering. He was restless and decided that having a child might make his life more meaningful. Although they had always talked about having a family, Marie was happy with her teaching and decided she didn't want children yet. She worked with

---

Comparison

Divorce, Japanese Style

Divorce rates have tended to go up throughout the world and have risen faster in some countries than they have in the United States. In Japan, as in the United States, divorce rates began to rise rapidly during the 1960s. By the end of the 20th century, the number of divorces each year had doubled. About one in three marriages now ends in divorce in Japan. A writer who interviewed divorced Japanese couples identified three causes: a greater acceptance of divorce in Japanese society, greater opportunities for women outside the home, and women's changing attitudes. In the following selection, the writer talks about the changing attitudes of women:

Women are no longer satisfied with being glorified housemaids and cooks. They want to live more rewarding lives now that they can expect to live longer ones. . . . Even more important, however, may be the changing character of these divorces. There has been a rapid increase in divorces among middle-aged couples and among couples with children. No longer are children the bond that keeps a marriage going. . . .

Another change in the character of divorce is relatively new: They are initiated by the wife. For a long time it was assumed that only the husband had the prerogative to make such a selfish demand. In the Edo period (1603–1868), a husband could easily get rid of his wife by handing her a letter of divorce called a *mikudarihan* (three and a half lines). Today, however, 60 percent of the divorce cases that are brought to the family courts come from wives. Japanese men, accustomed to being lord of the manor, are having difficulty adjusting to this new fact of life.

Socioeconomic change has not only changed the nature of divorce in Japan; it has created certain types of divorce that may be unique to this country. One of these is the nondivorce divorce, which happens to couples who have grown miles apart in heart and mind and yet continue to live under the same roof, appearing to be a normal married couple to the outside world but barely on speaking terms within their own home. . . .

If the husband's fear of social stigma has created the nondivorce, the wife's capacity for submission has created the retirement divorce. Mr. and Ms. B divorced when he was 57, she, 49. They had been married 28 years and had a son, 26, and a daughter, 24. Ms. B decided to get a divorce some 10 years before she finally carried it out. She waited so long because she wanted to see her children through college and felt that she should continue fulfilling her role as wife as long as her husband was working. . . . Once she had set a target date, Ms. B began to save money in small amounts. Since she would be the one asking for a divorce, she had no intention of demanding a settlement from her husband. Not that she wasn't entitled. Having sacrificed most of her life to this man, it would not be strange to demand at least half of his hefty retirement pay. But that wouldn't be honorable, she thought.

Source: Yamashita Katsutoshi. Reprinted by permission.

children all day and felt that they fulfilled whatever maternal instincts she had. She began to wonder if she would ever want children of her own. Don resented Marie's changed perspective. In his restlessness, he quit his job and went back to school to study social work. Marie felt uncomfortable with his new aspirations. She resented the fact that he would probably work for less money than he got as an engineer. They agreed to a trial separation. Within six months, Marie filed for divorce. They never argued much. They simply watched each other change, and neither liked the changes of the other.

Emotional Problems. One of the consequences of divorce is likely to be an increase in emotional problems. But not all problems are the result of the divorce. Some exist before and contribute to the deterioration of the relationship. Recall the *principle of circularity* in sys-

Systems Theory Applied

tems theory—for many things it is not a case of *a* causing *b*, but of *a* causing *b*, which causes more *a*, which causes more *b*, and so on. Thus, a partner's emotional problems can lead to a deterioration of the marriage, and as the marriage grows more troubled, the emotional problems intensify, causing the marriage to deteriorate even more.

Although it is not always possible in a particular case to know whether the deterioration or the emotional problem came first, research has shown that a pre-existing emotional problem can lead to marital disintegration. The National Center for Health Statistics data on women reported significant differences in divorce rates depending on whether a woman had ever had a generalized anxiety disorder (Bramlett and Mosher 2002). Fifty-five percent of women who had ever had such a disorder divorced within 15 years, compared to 39 percent of those who had not experienced a disorder.

EFFECTS OF DIVORCE ON SPOUSES/PARENTS

We began the chapter with the question, "Is divorce ever good for you?" The answer, we suggested, is "yes" and "no." There will probably be short-term negative effects. There may be long-term positive effects. The intensity of the effects depends on such things as gender and whether the individual is the initiator or the one left. Generally, initiators are likely to be more positive about the divorce than are the ones left, and females adjust better to a divorce than do males (Black et al. 1991; Diedrick

1991; Sakraida 2005). Most studies focus on the negative consequences of divorce, but there are positive ones as well. We will look at the latter first.

Positive Outcomes

Although it is unlikely that anyone, even the initiator, finds divorce a painless process, there are long-term and sometimes short-term positive outcomes. Personal growth, optimism, spiritual comfort, and improved communication and conflict skills are among the benefits perceived by divorced people (Schneller and Arditti 2004; Sakraida 2005). And those in high-distress marriages may report increased happiness following the divorce (Amato and Hohmann-Marriott 2007).

Even if the divorce is a very traumatic experience, most people will eventually (within two to three years) adapt in a constructive way to their situation (Hetherington 2003). And some will view the divorce as a positive turning point, perhaps even a necessary step in their own well-being. For instance, Heather, who runs an art gallery, believes that her divorce set her on the road to autonomy for the first time in her life (Lauer and Lauer 1988:129). She had not established her independence before getting married:

> I switched from parental control to marital control. At the age of thirty, I began to gain autonomy. At thirty-two, I rebelled. At forty, I finally became a person. I mean I finally became me, Heather, an independent human being.

She became that "independent human being" by leaving a marriage with a domineering man. She says that she feared being on her own and hesitated leaving him, but she "had to yank that safety net of marriage in order to realize that I can survive without it."

Not everyone is equally likely to have such a positive outcome. Veevers (1991) searched the literature to identify factors associated with divorce being a personality-enhancing or growth experience. In summary, divorce is more likely to be positive for females, particularly those with a high level of education; those who are relatively young; those in relatively short-lived marriages; those who define the divorce as normal rather than as an abnormal failure; those with adequate income; and those holding to more nontraditional gender and marital roles. In addition, a positive outcome is more likely for those with good social support (Garvin, Kalter, and Hansell 1993; Greeff and van der Merwe 2004).

Health Problems

Not all outcomes are positive, even in the long run. Problems with physical and emotional health are common

Therapy may be needed to cope with a divorce.

among people who are in the process of divorcing. Moreover, sometimes these problems last for years or even decades after the divorce is final. Physical health problems occur because the stress of the divorce tends to suppress the functioning of the body's immune system (Gottman 1994).

Although some emotional difficulties may be present before and contribute to a divorce, the process is sufficiently stressful to create such problems. Divorced people have higher rates of suicide, accidents, physical and mental health problems (including anxiety and depression), and alcoholism (Wasserman 1990; Hetherington 1993; Richards, Hardy, and Wadsworth 1997; Hilton and Kopera-Frye 2004; Chatav and Whisman 2007). Divorced people also report themselves as less happy and as having more insecurity in their relationships (Kurdek 1991; Schneller and Arditti 2004).

The negative effects of divorce are greatest for those who have young children in the home at the time of the divorce, especially for the women (Williams and Dunne-Bryant 2006). There are also some other gender differences in reactions to the divorce.

Men grieve the loss involved in divorce differently than do women (Baum 2003). They tend to start the grieving process later, mourn the loss of home and children more than the loss of their wives, and express their grief in behavior rather than in words or other obvious ways to express grief. Men are also more likely to drink excessively, while women are more likely to exhibit depression and hostility (Hilton and Kopera-Frye 2004).

The stress of a divorce is great because it involves the disruption of an intimate relationship. There is a sense of loss. There are uncertainties about the future, about the individual's network of relationships, and perhaps about the decision to divorce. The prospect of such a radical change in one's life tends to create a certain amount of anger, depression, and guilt.

How long do such negative emotions last? Typically, it takes anywhere from two to four years to work through a divorce. However, if the individual does not cope well, the problems may go on for decades or even a lifetime (Lauer and Lauer 1988:122). In a long-term study of 60 families disrupted by divorce, the researchers found that a fourth of the mothers and a fifth of the fathers were still struggling 10 years after their divorces (Wallerstein and Blakeslee 1989). The researchers discovered something else of importance: The parents tended to be chronically disorganized and had difficulty meeting the demands of parenting. Other research supports that conclusion. A study of 45 toddlers concluded that the divorced mothers provided their children with less stimulation than did married mothers (Poehlmann and Fiese 1994). Older children may even find their divorced parents leaning on them for support; the children, in effect, become parents to their own parents (Wallerstein and Blakeslee 1989).

Financial Problems

The purpose of no-fault divorce laws was to make marital disruption a more equitable process. Initially, the economic effect of no-fault divorce tended to increase the standard of living of the men and decrease that of the women. For women who had sole custody of their children, financial problems were frequently exacerbated by the ex-husband's unwillingness to give child support. Many divorced mothers had to resort to public assistance.

More recent research, however, indicates that divorce is not likely to be financially beneficial for men nor to be as financially detrimental to women as it once was (McKeever and Wolfinger 2001). It is still true that divorced mothers who have custody of their children do not generally have as high a standard of living as their ex-husbands (Bianchi, Subaiya, and Kahn 1999). The gap between the women and the men is smaller, however, among those women who work full-time and among those whose ex-husbands provide regular child support. And the economic status of men who divorce also tends to go down (McManus and Diprete 2001). For one thing, the men lose the income generated by their ex-wives. For another, they are more likely than in the past to have compulsory or voluntary child support payments. Those men who relied on their ex-wives for only a very small portion of their incomes may experience a stronger economic status and a higher standard of living after divorce. Others, however, experience a decline. Their decline may not be as sharp as that of their ex-wives, but both men and women who divorce are likely to have financial problems.

It is not difficult to see why financial problems are common. Assuming that both partners were working prior to the divorce and that both maintain their employment, they face a situation of substantially higher debts with no increase in income. The debts arise because of such things as legal bills, moving expenses, and a second household. Thus, Terri, a middle-aged, divorced mother with custody of her two children, put it this way:

> Even with the little child support I get from my ex, our lifestyle is totally different. We don't eat out any more. We don't take vacations. I had to take my children out of their private school and put them in a public school. We've cut way back on our clothes budget. Our health insurance is not nearly as good as what we had through my ex-husband's job. I could go on, but the bottom line is that we're living a different life and every day we have to deal with financial concerns and pressures.

Interaction between Former Spouses

A divorce doesn't necessarily end interaction between former spouses. If children are involved in the divorce, of course, at least some contact between the ex-spouses is likely, although having children also means the contact probably will be less friendly and involve more quarreling than contact between the childless (Masheter 1991). A Dutch study of 1,791 divorced people found that nearly half still had contact with the ex 10 years after the divorce (Fischer, De Graaf, and Kalmijn 2005). Those with children were more likely than those without to maintain the contact.

In a U.S. study of 80 couples, about one of five had relatively high degree of coparental interaction a year after the divorce, and another 59 percent reported a moderate amount of interaction (Ahrons and Wallisch 1987). By three years after the divorce, however, only one in 10 of the respondents reported a continuing high degree of interaction. Among other things, the couples said that they interacted to share major decisions about the children; discuss children's personal, school, and medical problems; discuss children's progress and accomplishments; and talk about childrearing problems generally. Nearly half of the ex-spouses spent time together with their children for the first year after divorce, but the number dropped to 30 percent two years later.

On matters other than parenting, the ex-spouses had less interaction. Still, after one year, about a fourth continued to interact with each other every few months. They talked about such things as new experiences, their families (other than the children), old friends, personal problems, and finances. For many people, then, the relationship continues, at least to some extent, even after divorce.

Of course, the quality of the interaction between ex-spouses varies considerably. Psychologist Constance Ahrons found four types of relationships between 98 pairs of ex-spouses: fiery foes, angry associates, cooperative colleagues, and perfect pals (Stark 1986). About a fourth were fiery foes, those who had minimal contact with each other and who became bitter and angry when they did interact. Fiery foes try to avoid each other. Another fourth were angry associates, those who could tolerate being in the same place with the ex-spouse but who still felt so angry and bitter that they could not interact pleasantly. The largest group, 38 percent, were cooperative colleagues. They had a moderate amount of interaction and could mutually support each other. They strove to get along for the children's sake. Finally, the perfect pals comprised 12 percent of the sample. Like cooperative colleagues, they were child-centered and tried to put the interests of their children above any anger or frustration they still had. But perfect pals were much more involved with each other than were cooperative colleagues. Neither partner had remarried. They enjoyed each other's company. They might telephone to share

Personal

"My Whole World Was Lost"

Divorce is generally painful but particularly so when one of the partners doesn't expect it. In some cases, the "secret" is so well kept that a spouse is stunned by the announcement that the marriage is over. Craig, a 40-year-old salesman, had that experience. He describes his feelings:

> Even though we had been having a few problems and seeing a marriage counselor, I was really caught by surprise. I came home from work one day to discover that my wife and children were gone. I felt like hell and nearly powerless to change the situation. They were gone, and what was I to do? I made several attempts to get my wife to return, but she wouldn't consider it. Two days later, I was served with divorce papers.
>
> I had to deal with the reality. It was over. I blamed myself. I blamed her mother. I even blamed the marriage counselor that we had visited. I reached for anything that would take the pain away. I was hurt and I wanted my family back.
>
> I kept hoping things would get better. But they didn't. I wanted to see my children as often as I could, but that became an impossibility. Then one day I thought of a way that I might at least see them. My wife had moved in with her mother, and across from their house was a school with a track. I started jogging at the school so that I could be near my children and maybe even get a glimpse of them at times. But I was jogging too early in the morning. I decided to join the YMCA, which was just a block from their house. I could jog there any time of the day.
>
> The jogging track at the Y had piped in music, and everyday I would hear the same song about how somebody had done somebody else wrong. I was not only running to the music but living its harsh message. I hurt in places deep in my soul. Sometimes I cried. My whole world was lost, and I couldn't get it back. I returned to the only place that I could remember that left me feeling good about myself—my church.
>
> The court date finally arrived, and the judge gave custody to my ex-wife. However, I was awarded liberal visitation rights. My ex-wife sometimes tried to make excuses and keep me from picking up the children on weekends. That went on for 14 years. It was only recently that I finally forgave her for the pain and suffering I have endured. I have remarried, and my new wife is helping me with her love and patience. I am finally beginning to trust people again.

exciting news with each other. They maintained a fairly active involvement in each other's life even though they were not trying to reestablish the marriage.

EFFECTS OF DIVORCE ON CHILDREN

One of the reasons given by some people for remaining in an unhappy marriage is to protect their children. Most people are aware that divorce can be a very painful experience for children. Still, is it always better for children if their parents' marriage is intact? Just how painful is divorce for the children? These questions take on increasing importance in an age when the number of children affected by divorce is enormous. By 2006, nearly 3 of 10 of the 73.7 million U.S. children under the age of 18 lived with only one parent or with neither parent (U.S. Census Bureau 2008:65). While many of the 10.5 million single parents in the nation had never been married, a substantial number were the result of divorce. How are the children affected by divorce?

Short-Term Effects

In the short term, children are likely to suffer a variety of physical and emotional problems when their parents divorce. In cases of abuse or intense and constant conflict, as we indicated earlier, parental separation and divorce are beneficial to the children (Booth and Amato 2001; Strohschein 2005). Most of the time, however, the short-term consequences are negative.

Among the negative consequences identified by researchers are the following:

- Initial reactions to parental separation may include intense anger, self-blame, fears about the future, and loyalty conflicts as the child is pressured to take sides in the parental battle (Healy, Stewart, and Copeland 1993; Hetherington 1993).
- Children from divorced families have more physical and emotional health problems than those from intact families (Guidubaldi and Cleminshaw 1985; Strohschein 2005).

Supportive, warm parenting minimizes the negative effects of divorce on children.

- Children from divorced families rate themselves lower in social competence, and, in fact, are likely to be less sociable, have fewer friends, and be less responsive at home, school, and play (Baker, Barthelemy, and Kurdek 1993; Amato 2001; Lindsey, Colwell, Frabutt, and MacKinnon-Lewis 2006).
- Children from divorced families have lower self-esteem and are more likely to be anxious, depressed, and withdrawn than those in intact families (Dawson 1991; Amato 2001).
- Children from divorced families are more likely to have eating problems and disorders (Wynn and Bowering 1990).
- Children from divorced families tend to receive less maternal warmth and empathy (the conflict and pain of most divorces leave little energy for nurturing children), which contributes to various emotional and behavior problems (Kline, Johnston, and Tschann 1991).
- Intact-family children have fewer absences at school; higher popularity ratings; higher IQ, reading, spelling, and math scores, and fewer behavioral problems at school than do children from divorced families (Dawson 1991; Downey 1994; Ham 2004; Cavanagh and Huston 2006).
- Adolescents from divorced families tend to have higher rates of substance abuse; poorer academic performance; higher rates of dropout from school; higher rates of antisocial behavior; and more negative attitudes about marriage (Needle, Su, and Doherty 1990; Sandefur, McLanahan, and Wojtkiewicz 1992; Hoffmann and Johnson 1998; Jeynes 2001; Breivik and Olweus 2005; Dennison and Koerner 2006).

These various consequences are understandable. Disruptions in intimate relationships are very stressful for all of us. In fact, the turmoil that typically precedes separation and divorce is itself a disruption. Thus, some of the consequences begin while the home is still intact (Sun and Li 2001).

The disruption may be even more stressful for children than it is for parents because children have no control over what is happening to them and see no long-term benefits to the disruption. Thus, they react with anger, depression, and anxiety, and this emotional turbulence interferes with other aspects of their lives.

Long-Term Effects

By long-term, we mean effects that last into late adolescence and beyond. In fact, a study over a 20-year period that used a national sample reported adverse effects from the divorce of an individual's grandparents (Amato and Cheadle 2005). In particular, the divorce of grandparents was associated with lower education, more marital problems, and weaker ties between parents and grand-parents, a pattern that was repeated between the grand-children and their parents when their parents divorced. Thus, negative effects stretched across at least three generations!

But we need to exercise caution, for the evidence is mixed and somewhat controversial, fueled by two books that seem to come to contradictory conclusions. Based on a 25-year longitudinal study of 60 cases of divorce, Wallerstein, Lewis, and Blakeslee (2001) concluded that the most serious detrimental effects of divorce occur when the children become adults and try to form their own intimate relationships. Based on their longitudinal research with nearly 1,400 families, Hetherington and Kelly (2002) concluded that the great majority (75 to 80 percent) of children of divorce exhibit little if any long-term damage from the experience. They function quite well as adults.

The dispute is not whether long-term effects exist. They do. The question is how detrimental they are and what proportion of children suffer the long-term detrimental consequences. We can't answer the question with certainty, but we will give an overview of the evidence.

First, we need to reiterate the point that the long-term effects can be beneficial as well as detrimental. Some children, both in the short and the long run, are better off if their parents divorce. Rates of depression, withdrawal, and other problems are higher for those who live in a home of persistent conflict and unhappiness than those in single-parent homes (Amato and Booth 1991; Jekielek 1998; Strohschein 2005). Based on their 12-year longitudinal study, three researchers sum up the relationship between parental conflict, divorce, and the long-term well-being of the children as follows (Amato, Loomis, and Booth 1995). Where the level of parental conflict is high, children have higher levels of well-being as young adults if the parents divorce. Where the level of parental conflict is low, the children are better off if the parents stay together. If the parents do not divorce, the more their conflict, the lower the level of well-being of the children as young adults.

While some children may actually be better off, parental divorce is more likely to be associated with long-term negative consequences (Cartwright 2005). The severity of the consequences depends on a number of factors. In both the short and the long run, children will adjust better if the custodial parent functions well, the children have regular contact with the noncustodial

parent, and the children's exposure to conflict between the parents has been minimal (Furstenberg and Cherlin 1991). Some of the possible consequences of poor adjustment include the following:

- Compared to those from intact homes, adults whose parents divorced tend to have lower levels of psychological well-being (higher levels of depression and lower life satisfaction), family well-being (lower marital quality and higher chances of divorce), socioeconomic well-being (lower educational attainment, income, and occupational prestige), and physical health (Amato and Keith 1991a; Kessler and Magee 1993; Powell and Parcel 1997; Ross and Mirowsky 1999; Wolfinger 2000; Teachman 2004). The lower socioeconomic well-being applies to white males, white females, black females, and, to a somewhat lesser extent, Hispanic females but not to black or Hispanic males (Amato and Keith 1991b). Higher levels of depression are more likely among African Americans than whites whose parents divorced but not among Hispanics, perhaps because of the close-knit extended Hispanic family (Amato 1991). Researchers also have found long-term negative effects on emotional health in a longitudinal study of people in Britain (Cherlin, Chase-Lansdale, and McRae 1998), a survey of 1,656 Finnish subjects (Palosaari, Aro, and Laippala 1996), and interviews with 12,537 Australians (Rodgers, Power, and Hope 1997). The negative impact of divorce on children's well-being may be independent of culture.
- College students from divorced families have significantly more sexual partners and more negative attitudes toward marriage than do students from intact families (Gabardi and Rosen 1991).
- Compared to those from intact families, adults from divorced families have less sense of personal power, view their families of origin in more negative terms, and are likely to have poorer relationships with parents (particularly their fathers) and siblings (Aquilino 1994a; Booth and Amato 1994; Cooney 1994; White 1994; Milevsky 2004). The negative impact on parent–child relations also occurs if the divorce takes place after the children are already adults (Aquilino 1994b).
- Divorce tends to reduce attachment to the noncustodial parent (Cooney and Uhlenberg 1990). If the parents had a highly conflicted relationship, the adult child may be close to neither of them (Sobolewski and Amato 2007).

- A smaller proportion of those from disrupted than from intact homes report themselves as "very happy" and as generally satisfied with their lives (Marquardt and Glenn 2001).
- Those from disrupted homes have lower levels of trust and altruistic love, various difficulties in intimate relationships such as more conflict and anxiety about love and commitment, and a lower likelihood of marrying (Jacquet and Surra 2001; Tallman, Rotolo, and Gray 2001; Wallerstein 2005; Chen et al. 2006).
- Those from disrupted homes have a higher risk of premature mortality across the life span (Tucker et al. 1997). A long-term study found that adult children of divorced parents have a one-third greater chance of dying earlier than those whose parents remained married until they were at least 21 years old (Friedman et al. 1995). The predicted median age at death for men was 76 years for those from divorced homes and 80 years for those from intact homes; the predicted median age for women was 82 years for those from divorced homes and 86 years for those from intact homes.

Gender Differences

Will you handle the divorce of your parents better if you are a girl or a boy? As with the consequences generally, the evidence is mixed. It would appear that in some ways it is more difficult for boys and in other ways it is more difficult for girls.

A good deal of research has suggested that a divorce is harder on boys, perhaps because of the lack of a same-sex parent (most children of divorce live with the mother). The boy's need for a father, a male role model, intensifies during adolescence. It would be reasonable to conclude that the boy's unmet needs are a factor in his behavior. A study that used national data, however, found no benefits for either boys or girls who lived in same-sex as opposed to opposite-sex homes (Downey and Powell 1993).

At any rate, some researchers have argued that girls appear to adjust more easily to divorce than do boys. Boys from divorced homes exhibit significantly more problematic behavior than do boys from intact homes; no such differences are found among girls (Hetherington 1993). Boys also take a longer time to adjust than do girls. Boys' problems are less, however, if the conflict between their divorced parents is relatively low (Amato and Rezac 1994).

Another reason suggested for the greater difficulty of boys adjusting to a divorce is that boys tend to be more aggressive than girls at all ages. Divorce tends to raise the level of aggression in both boys and girls, but

the increase may "push the boy's behavior past acceptable limits while an increase in a girl's aggressive behavior might still not be labeled problematic behavior" (Lowery and Settle 1985:458).

It may be that the problems girls have in adjusting to divorce are just different rather than less than those of boys. A study of high school seniors found that those from divorced homes had lower levels of academic achievement than those from intact homes, and the result was more pronounced for girls than for boys (Ham 2004). Another study looked at the reactions of adolescents to their mother's anger (the anger of those divorced, particularly of the partner who did not initiate the divorce, can be intense and lasting) (Dreman 2003). Adolescent girls whose mothers had high levels of anger had more behavioral problems; high maternal anger did not affect adolescent boys' behavior. Finally, a Canadian study reported increased levels of aggression in both boys and girls as a result of divorce, but the boys engaged in more physical aggression, including misconduct and destruction of property, while the girls resorted to indirect aggression that was not as noticeable (Ram and Hou 2005).

Still other research has found few differences between boys and girls—both are affected adversely, though not always in precisely the same way or to the same degree (Sun and Li 2002). And that, until and unless additional research clarifies the issue, is our conclusion.

CHILD CUSTODY

At the beginning of this chapter, we quoted the undergraduate student who said that the most painful part of her parents' divorce was deciding with whom to live. She was forced to make a decision that could only hurt regardless of who she chose:

> I was daddy's girl but mother's baby. My sister wanted to live with Mom and so did I. But my Dad wanted me to live with him. I didn't want to be apart from my sister and my mom. So one day all four of us sat down to legalize where we'd live. My Dad asked me who I wanted to live with. I didn't want to answer. It just killed me. I was only 10 years old. When I finally answered, it was awful. My Dad broke down and began to cry. That was the first time I'd ever seen him cry. It was devastating to me to have my Dad feel so disappointed with me.

Custody arrangements can be very painful for both the parents and the children. For the children, any kind of arrangement involves some type of loss. For parents, losing all physical custody can be particularly painful. Thus, a study of divorced fathers found that those who had full or joint physical custody had much better emotional well-being than those who were noncustodial or who had legal status but no physical presence of the children (Bokker, Farley, and Bailey 2005). Interestingly, the arrangements have changed over time. Until relatively recently, the only arrangement was **sole custody,** in which one of the parents is given the responsibility for the care and raising of the child. Before the early part of the twentieth century, the parent who got such custody was the father. Fathers were the economic heads of the family and were presumed to be in a better position to care for the needs of the children.

Increasingly in the twentieth century, however, mothers were granted custody under the "tender years" doctrine, the notion that the child's well-being is maximized by the mother's care. By 1925, the phrase "best interests of the child" was incorporated into state laws. Until the mid-1960s, then, mothers were generally given custody, and they won custody in more than 90 percent of contested cases (Ihinger-Tallman and Pasley 1987). Unless a father could show that his former wife was unstable or unable to provide proper care, the courts routinely gave custody to the mother. The role of the father was reduced to providing financial support and to some visitation rights. Then fathers began to ask for more.

After the mid-1960s, an increasing number of fathers won the right to sole custody. A study of 509 cases in Michigan found that fathers were more likely to get custody when the children were older (especially if the oldest child was male) and the father was the plaintiff (Fox and Kelly 1995). Fathers as well as mothers may find the separation from their children to be extremely painful. Indeed, divorced fathers who have custody of their children are less depressed, are less anxious, and have fewer problems of adjustment than those without custody (Stewart, Schwebel, and Fine 1986).

Why not, then, find another alternative, one that allows both parents to continue to be involved in some way in their children's lives? **Joint custody,** an arrangement in which both parents continue to share the responsibility for the care and raising of the children, is an attempt to provide a better solution. In 1980, California adopted a joint custody arrangement. Other states soon followed suit.

A number of states now award joint custody unless there is some compelling reason to do otherwise. The way in which joint custody actually works out in daily life varies somewhat (Ihinger-Tallman and Pasley 1987). The children may spend some time each day at two different homes, various amounts of time during the week at two different homes, differing periods of the time in each of two homes, or alternate years in each of the two homes. In other cases, joint custody does not even require shared living arrangements but is rather joint legal custody in which both parents are involved in important decisions in their child's life.

Does joint custody resolve the problems? Does it at least provide a better way to deal with the issues? The answer seems to be "yes." In an analysis of studies that compared children in sole-custody versus joint-custody situations, Bauserman (2002) found that those in joint custody were better adjusted than those in sole custody. Joint-custody children were more satisfied. They were able to avoid the struggle with the sense of loss that afflicts children in sole-custody arrangements. And adolescents whose nonresident fathers remain highly involved with them are less likely to experience school failure (Menning 2006).

Joint custody is also more satisfying to the parents, who report less current and past conflict than do sole-custody parents (Bauserman 2002). Fathers who have joint custody are more satisfied than noncustodial fathers because they have more contact with their children (Arditti 1992). And joint custody means a greater likelihood of complying with child-support obligations and of elimination of the problem of visitation denial (Seltzer 1991; Bender 1994).

Parental satisfaction is crucial, for the adjustment of children depends in large part on the way in which the parents relate to them and to each other (Maccoby and Mnookin 1992). Joint custody, of course, means that the ex-spouses will continue to interact more than they would have under sole custody. If their interaction is one of ongoing conflict, the joint-custody arrangement may be worse for the child than sole custody. If the parents can relate to each other without anger and conflict, the children will usually prefer joint custody. They find the benefits of maintaining intimate contact with both parents worth the hassles of living alternately in two homes.

COPING WITH THE DISRUPTION

How can both parents and children cope effectively with the disruption of their intimate relationships? How can they maximize their chances of eventually turning the divorce into something positive for themselves?

For children, adjustment depends in part on the adjustment and the behavior of their parents (Spruijt, Goede, and Vandervalk 2004; Wood, Repetti, and Roesch 2004). Adolescents do best when they are able to maintain strong ties with both the mother and the father; they have fewer emotional and relational problems than those with weak ties, particularly those with weak ties to both parents (King and Sobolewski 2006).

Children's well-being is enhanced when fathers pay child support and exercise warm, authoritative parenting (Amato and Gilbreth 1999). Children also adjust better when the custodial parent is well-adjusted (Silitsky 1996). The mother is particularly important in the child's adjustment, even when she does not have sole custody (Buchanan, Maccoby, and Dornbusch 1996). Whatever else happens, one of the prime needs of the children is a stable home and a loving, supportive mother. The children also need to understand what the disruption is about (so that they don't, among other things, blame themselves), and the parents need to beware of becoming so preoccupied with their own concerns that they are unaware of their children's concerns—which are likely to be different from their own (Stewart et al. 1997).

As you would expect from our discussion about parental conflict, children adjust better to the extent that the divorce reduces the conflict between the parents. Under a sole-custody arrangement, children's adjustment is better if there is frequent contact with the noncustodial parent and if the custodial parent is satisfied with the noncustodial parent's relationship with the children. Obviously, children benefit when their parents grow beyond the anger and bitterness of the divorce and establish cordial relations. Finally, adolescent children adjust better to the extent that they are able to talk with their parents about their feelings and the stress they are experiencing (Afifi, Huber, and Ohs 2006). Parents can help their adolescent children by encouraging them to speak freely and openly and by responding in an understanding, supportive way.

How can parents cope with divorce and develop a relationship that is helpful to their children? To begin with, ex-spouses need to be open about their feelings and work through the anger, guilt, and anxiety that attend the disruption of an intimate relationship. Such feelings should not be repressed or denied; that only delays adjustment. Blaming someone for the disruption is generally unprofitable. Neither self-blame nor other-blame pays off in terms of adjusting well. Initially, of course, condemning the ex-spouse may be a

Children adjust to a divorce better if their parents can be cordial to each other.

part of venting one's anger. But eventually each of the partners must get beyond blaming and get on with the business of constructing a new life with new intimate relationships.

Divorced parents also will help their children adjust to the extent that they have a sense of control over their child-rearing responsibilities. A study of 58 divorced mothers found that those who perceived themselves as being in control had children with higher self-esteem and fewer physical and psychological problems than mothers who perceived less control (Machida and Holloway 1991). Parents who have problems with such control can find help in various books and classes on parenting.

Finally, the parents will adjust well to a divorce, and thereby help their children to adjust, to the extent that they are able to define it as an opportunity for growth. We have seen examples of how divorce can block growth, leading to long-term stagnation as the individual persists in anger, bitterness, and depression. But divorce also can be an opportunity. In our study of watersheds in people's lives, we found that those who successfully coped with a divorce came to a point at which they defined the disruption as an important step in their growth (Lauer and Lauer 1988:125). For instance, a number of women told about how divorce allowed them for the first time in their lives to test their capacity for self-sustained living. The discovery of their capacity for independence was an exhilarating experience. The pain of disruption eventually led to the excitement of self-discovery. For many people, then, a divorce becomes the beginning of a new journey into fulfillment, a journey that includes both personal growth and meaningful intimate relationships.

SUMMARY

The divorce rate increased dramatically in the 1960s and 1970s, with the peak coming from 1979 to 1981. Since 1981 the rate of divorce has tended to decline. The grounds for divorce are set by the states, all of which now have no-fault laws.

The process of uncoupling is marked by four time periods: recognition, discussion, action, and postdissolution. In the recognition period, one partner senses that the relationship is deteriorating but may not openly confront the other. In the discussion period, the marital problems may be shared with outsiders as well as the spouse. The history of the relationship may be redefined in terms of a series of negative experiences. The initiator is making the transition to a new life. The action period involves legal steps to formally dissolve the marriage. This is a difficult period, involving the struggle over such things as division of property, child custody, and ambivalent feelings. The postdissolution period begins when both spouses accept the fact that the marriage is over.

Bohannan has identified six experiences that people are likely to have in divorce. Divorce involves an emotional, legal, community, and psychic separation and an economic and co-parental (for those with children) settlement.

Divorce is more likely for those of lower socioeconomic status, those married at a younger or later age, African Americans, and those who lack membership in an integrated group, such as a religious group. Changed laws and attitudes and the changing roles of women are associated with higher divorce rates. At an interpersonal level, divorce is associated with various complaints, such as infidelity and conflict over personalities and finances. Some divorces are the result of changed feelings about the partner, and some result from a spouse's emotional problems.

Divorce can have positive as well as negative outcomes. For some, a divorce is a positive turning point in personal well-being. But numerous negative outcomes are likely, including short-term and in some cases long-term health problems and, particularly for women, financial problems. Divorce doesn't necessarily end interaction between the spouses, though the quality of the interaction varies considerably.

Divorce has both short-term and long-term effects on children. In the short run, children are likely to suffer various physical, behavioral, and emotional problems. Over the long run, there may be positive outcomes for children, especially if the home was marked by intense and continual conflict. In some ways, children from disrupted homes are no different from those from intact homes in the long run. But there also can be some long-term negative consequences, including lower levels of educational and occupational achievement, problematic relationships with the noncustodial parent, problems with trust, and depression.

Some researchers believe that girls adjust more easily than boys to the divorce of parents. But both girls and boys suffer adverse effects, though not always in precisely the same way or to the same degree.

Child custody arrangements can be painful for both parents and children. Sole custody is giving way to joint custody in many states. The type of custody can affect the child's adjustment to the divorce. Some evidence exists that joint custody, while not solving all the problems, does have benefits for both the children and the parents. Children's adjustment to the divorce depends in part on the behavior of the parents. If the divorce reduces conflict significantly, children adjust better. The parents will adjust better to the extent that they work through their feelings and are able to define the divorce as an opportunity to grow.

Principles for Enhancing Intimacy

Although divorce can have a potentially damaging impact on children, the following principles suggest some ways in which parents can help their offspring and maximize the probability of maintaining meaningful, intimate relations.

1. Be open and straightforward when discussing the divorce with children. Children sometimes blame themselves for a parental divorce. Don't deny the marital difficulties that led to the divorce; rather, help your children see the situation as clearly as possible.

2. Avoid blaming anyone for the divorce. Make sure the children know they are not to blame. But don't heap blame on the other spouse. The children probably want to continue to love and interact with both parents. Don't make that difficult for them.

3. Help the children understand that neither parent is divorcing them. Don't ask them to choose the parent with whom they want to live. Let them know that both parents continue to love them even though the family will no longer be living together.

4. Let the children vent their emotions, including any anger, fear, and guilt they feel. Being open about their feelings will help them work through the disruption.

5. Avoid unnecessary changes. Children will usually benefit by staying in the same neighborhood and school in the period immediately following a divorce.

KEY TERMS

covenant marriage   *338*
divorce rate   *336*
infidelity   *345*

joint custody   *354*
no-fault divorce   *338*
social integration   *343*

sole custody   *354*

ON THE WEB   Separation and Divorce

Divorce has become a commonplace experience in U.S. society. This is, in part, an outcome of the supremacy of individual values and choices over governmental regulation, social roles, and social norms. Economic factors, however, as well as issues related to social status are as important to the issue of divorce as is personal choice. Whatever the factors involved, though, divorce is a painful process, as illustrated by the massive number of Internet sites set up to help those thinking about, going through, or trying to recover from a divorce.

www.mhhe.com/lauer7e

Two useful sites are:

Divorce Magazine
http://www.divorcemag.com

This site offers subscription to the magazine, but also has news, advice, statistics, and articles from past issues of the magazine that you can freely access.

Divorce Net
http://www.divorcenet.com

This is also a comprehensive Web site, including legal aspects of divorce in each of the states and links to resources concerning all aspects of divorce.

Using these two sites, enlarge your understanding with the following projects:

1. At the Divorce Magazine site, find articles on divorce recovery. Using material from the articles and the text, make a presentation to the class entitled "Ten tips on how to recover from a divorce."
2. Go to the Divorce Net site and peruse the legal aspects of divorce (such as custody, child support, debt, property division, etc.) in the state where you live. Do the same for two other states—one with roughly the same population as yours and another that is much smaller or larger. What are the similarities and differences? Does size or region of the states seem to make any difference? Evaluate the laws in the three states in terms—as you see it—of fairness and helpfulness to those divorcing.

∼ REMARRIAGE AND STEPFAMILIES ∼

LEARNING OBJECTIVES

After reading and studying chapter 16, you should be able to

1 Classify the various types of remarriage.
2 Give the demographic characteristics of remarriages and stepfamilies.
3 Evaluate the prospects for those who remarry.
4 Discuss the processes of courting and choosing a partner for those who remarry.
5 Summarize the reasons that people choose to remarry.

6 Explain the myths and the challenges of remarriage.
7 Contrast and compare the general quality of remarriages to first marriages.
8 Describe the complexities and difficulties that confront stepfamilies.
9 Discuss the stepparent–stepchild relationship.
10 Summarize the ways in which a stepfamily can cope with its difficulties and foster satisfying relationships.

Little research has been done on how people move toward a second marriage. What is it like to date? How has the experience of divorce affected dating and courtship patterns and preparatory steps toward marriage? What kind of expectations do people have for their second marriage?

Interview someone in your family or someone you know who has been divorced and remarried. Write an account of the person's remarriage experience, beginning with the time immediately after the divorce. Ask the following questions:

1. After the divorce, how did you feel about the prospect of dating or getting involved in a new relationship?
2. When, why, and how did you start dating again?
3. What problems did you encounter with dating again? How did your feelings and behavior on dates compare with those before your first marriage?

4. What made you decide to get remarried?
5. What did you do to try to make sure that the second marriage would work out better than the first?
6. What did you learn from the first marriage that you think will help you in the second one?
7. Looking back on it now, what would you do differently if you could do it all over?
8. What are you doing now, in this marriage, that is different from your first marriage?
9. What advice would you give to young men and women who are looking toward their first marriage?

If the entire class participates in this project, see if there are any common elements in the answers. In what ways, if any, do your findings differ from those presented in the text?

There is a song that says that love is better the "second time around." If this is true, millions of Americans are living out the ecstasy of a loving relationship in second marriages. A more cynical view was expressed by the eighteenth-century writer Samuel Johnson, who called remarriage the "triumph of hope over experience." If this is true, millions of Americans are living in the disillusionment of a second marriage.

The actual experiences of those who remarry, as we shall see, are somewhere between these two extremes. Remarriage has its own unique potential and its own unique problems. In this chapter, we will look at the extent of remarriage, the experiences and hopes that lead up to it, and the prospects and pitfalls involved in it. We will look in some detail at the various issues raised by a **stepfamily**—a remarriage involving children. Finally, we will examine some ways in which people can maximize the probability of a positive outcome when they remarry and live in a stepfamily.

TYPES AND NUMBER OF REMARRIAGES AND STEPFAMILIES

How many people do you know who have remarried or who are living in a stepfamily? The chances are good that either you or someone you know has had such an experience. When we discuss remarriages and stepfamilies, we are talking about a significant proportion of the U.S. population. But considerable diversity exists among the remarried. We will look first at the various types and then at some related statistics.

Types of Remarried Couples

There are many ways to classify remarried couples. For instance, men and women come to remarriage from a variety of situations. At the time of remarriage, the man and woman were in one of five different conditions: single, divorced or widowed with no children, divorced or widowed with custody of children, divorced or widowed without custody of children, or divorced or widowed with custody of some children but not others. Such a classification yields 24 different types of remarriages (the number is 24 rather than 25 because two single people do not constitute a remarriage).

The possible combinations could be further multiplied if we added those who have adult children no longer living at home and those who have had more than one divorce. The important point here is that each combination is likely to produce different outcomes. As we shall see, the prospects for a stable and satisfying union are quite different for a single woman who marries a divorced man who has custody of his children versus those for a marriage between two divorced people

Stepfamilies are increasingly common.

without children versus those for a marriage between two divorced parents, each of whom has custody.

As may already be clear, remarried life and especially stepfamily life can become incredibly complicated. The network of relationships expands enormously. Consider the problems of a divorced woman who has custody of her children marrying a divorced man who has custody of his children. There may be ex-spouses to deal with, grandparents who are still very attached to the children, other relatives of the ex-spouses with whom there were close relationships, new stepparent relationships, and new stepsibling relations to work through. It is likely to be a difficult process at best.

Demographics of Remarriage and Stepfamilies

Of the more than two million Americans who divorce each year, the majority will eventually remarry. Half of those who remarry after a divorce do so within a little over three years—the median is 3.6 years for men and 3.5 years for women (U.S. Census Bureau, Survey of Income and Program Participation 2007). Widowed people also remarry. Among those ever married, 12.5 percent of men and 13.6 percent of women have been married twice, and 3.2 percent of men and 3.1 percent of women have been married three or more times (Kreider 2005).

Somewhat similar results have been found in Canada (Wu and Schimmele 2005). About 42 percent of women and 54 percent of men enter a second union within five years of a divorce. Initially, more opt for cohabitation than for marriage, however, and widows are less likely than others to remarry.

The probability of remarriage varies by a number of factors (Bramlett and Mosher 2002). For women, the rates of remarriage are highest for white divorced women and lowest for black divorced women. Remarriage is more likely for women who were younger than 25 years at the time of the divorce, who live in nonmetropolitan areas, and who live in communities with low rates of male unemployment and poverty.

Government data on the living arrangements of children show that 62.2 percent live with both biological parents, 7.0 percent have a stepparent, 0.8 percent have adoptive parents (Kreider and Fields 2005). The remaining 30 percent live with a single parent, or some combination of biological, step-, and adoptive parents, or other relatives or foster parents. Nearly 5.1 million children, then, live in stepfamilies. The proportion varies by racial/ethnic group (figure 16.1), with white, non-Hispanic children having the highest rate of living in a stepfamily and Asian

American children having the lowest. Among all groups, the biological mother-stepfather arrangement is far more common than the biological father-stepmother.

What are the prospects for those who remarry? In general, the rate of divorce for remarrieds is slightly higher than that for first marriages. However, the higher rate may hold true only in the early years of the remarriage; a second marriage that lasts 15 years or more has the same probability of breakup as a first marriage of the same duration (Clarke and Wilson 1994). In other words, remarriages are only more fragile than first marriages in the first 15 years.

A number of factors bear on the probability of a remarriage breaking up (Bramlett and Mosher 2002). African Americans have higher rates than whites. In addition, divorce is more likely among women who were younger than 25 years at the time of the remarriage, who lacked a two-parent home throughout childhood, who live in poor communities, and who had children at the time of remarriage.

The presence of children at remarriage is particularly important. Using national data, White and Booth (1985) concluded that when one spouse was remarried and the other had been single, the chances for divorce were not significantly greater than they were for unions in which both partners were in a first marriage. But the chances increased 50 percent if both partners were previously married but without children and another 50 percent if both partners were previously married and one or both brought stepchildren into the marriage. The presence of stepchildren is particularly destabilizing for remarriages. If the remarried couple has children of their own, however, the second marriage is less likely to break up (Wineberg 1992).

One other type of remarriage that is unstable is that involving an individual who is in a serial-marriage pattern. **Serial marriage** refers to three or more marriages that occur as a result of repeated divorces or widowhood. As noted earlier, a little over 3 percent of Americans who have ever been married have been in three or more marriages.

DÉJÀ VU: DATING AND MATE SELECTION REVISITED

Those who remarry must go through the processes of dating and mate selection again. Although we think of dating and mate selection as something that occurs mainly in adolescence and the 20s, millions of Americans repeat the process at other times in their lives.

How is dating at 40 or 50 or 60 different from what it was in youth? As we pointed out in chapter 5, the reasons that older people date as well as some of their experiences

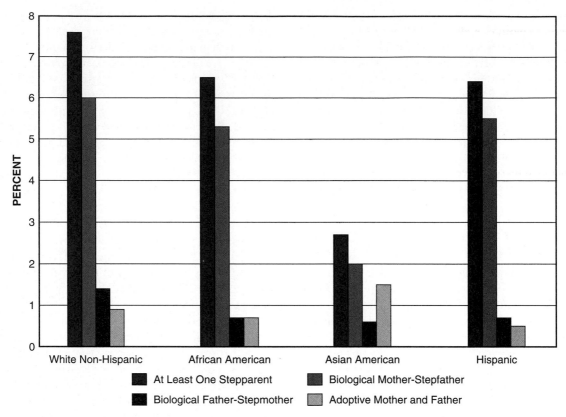

FIGURE 16.1 Proportion of Children Living with Step- and Adoptive Parents
Source: Kreider and Fields 2005.

are the same as those of younger people. Whatever your age, you are likely to date because you want to establish an intimate relationship, generally one that will culminate in marriage.

Is it any easier to date when you are older? Perhaps not. As a divorced man of 50 put it, "I felt like a kid again. The same anxiety. The same awkwardness whenever the conversation stopped. The same questions about what I should or shouldn't do." The man was experiencing only one of the problems that the divorced face in dating. There may be problems of children and limited money because of alimony and/or child support as well as a sense of impatience to establish a new relationship and a reluctance to waste time on one that is going nowhere.

Most people whose marriages have been disrupted by divorce or death would like to marry again. We already have noted that the majority of those divorced intend to remarry. A study of those widowed found smaller proportions who thought about remarrying and some gender differences (Carr 2004). Six months after a spouse's death, significantly more men (30 percent) than

women (16 percent) wanted to remarry some day and even fewer (17 percent of men and 6 percent of women) were interested in dating. By 18 months after the death, however, the proportion interested in dating rose to 37 percent of the men and 15 percent of the women.

Those who want to remarry must go through the process of dating, even though many prefer to shorten the process as much as possible. The problem is, as therapists point out (Sager et al. 1983), a certain amount of time is needed between the disruption of one marriage and the initiation of another. Widows and widowers who remarry too quickly may not have had time to work through their grief and loss, and may be emotionally unprepared to forge the bonds of intimacy with someone new. The divorced who remarry too quickly may not have time to work through their pain and disappointment, completely sever ties with the ex-spouse, or learn from the failed relationship. The popular notion of avoiding a "rebound" marriage is sound because an old relationship can adversely affect a new one. Yet if the time between marriages is too long, problems also can develop.

For example, in a remarriage of a person who has had long-time custody of a child, it may be difficult for the new spouse to break into the existing parent–child relationship. Unfortunately, many parents do not discuss dating issues with their children (Sumner 1997). They may proceed with a relationship that will eventually be stressed or disrupted because they will be forced to choose who will get priority in their lives—a child or a new mate.

While there is no set amount of time that is ideal in every situation, in general a period of from three to five years before remarriage seems optimal. This should allow the divorced or widowed individual sufficient time to work through the emotional pain and to experience a number of relationships.

A study of divorcing custodial parents found that half had dated before the divorce filing, and within a year after the filing had, on the average, two new partners (Anderson et al. 2004). Nationally, 15 percent of women remarry within a year after a divorce, and by three years 39 percent have remarried (Bramlett and Mosher 2002). This relatively rapid reentry into marriage is one of the factors in the greater instability of remarriages.

What do the divorced do to prepare for remarriage? Knowing the vulnerability of marriages, what steps do they take to minimize the possibility of a second breakup? Not a great deal, according to the little evidence we have. Ganong and Coleman (1989) asked 100 men and 105 women about their preparation for a second marriage. The majority (59 percent) simply lived together. They tested their capacity to be a family through a period of cohabitation. About a fourth of the men and 38 percent of the women received counseling. A little over half of the men and 72 percent of the women sought advice from written materials (such as self-help books) and from friends.

An important way of preparing for any marriage, including a second one, is for the couple to discuss significant issues and potential problems. The researchers found that the couples in their study did not discuss many of the issues regarded as important by stepfamily experts (Ganong and Coleman 1989:30). Children from a previous marriage, the most frequently mentioned issue, were discussed by 56 percent of the couples. Less than a fourth said they talked about the next most frequently named topic—finances. Thirteen percent said they didn't seriously discuss any issues:

> Responses to other questions seemed to reinforce the sense that these couples were either overly optimistic or naive (Ganong and Coleman 1989:30).

Some people cooperate more in their second marriages than they did in their first.

If these results are generally true, then people are not taking the necessary steps to ensure stability and satisfaction in their second marriages.

WHY REMARRY?

People remarry for many of the same reasons that they married the first time. In particular, people wish to establish an intimate relationship:

> We find the promise of a caring and loving relationship to be the prime motivation for remarriage (Sager et al. 1983:61).

The most frequently given reason of 205 men and women, that "it was time," probably reflects the felt need for intimacy (figure 16.2). As figure 16.2 shows, those who remarry also have some reasons that are different from those in first marriages. Thus, parents with custody of their children may be motivated by the desire to find suitable co-parents.

In chapter 8 we discussed private contracts, assumptions, and expectations that each partner has for the

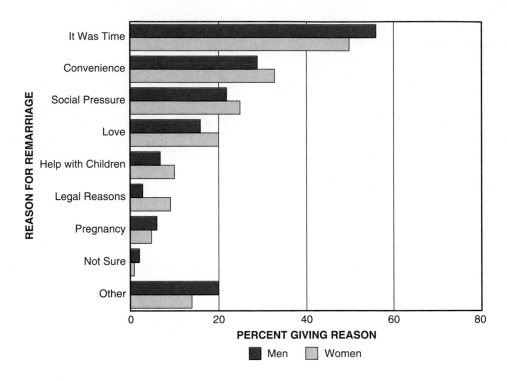

FIGURE 16.2   **Reasons for Remarriage Offered by 205 Men and Women**
Source: Data from L. H. Ganong and M. Coleman, *Family Relations* 38:30, 1989.

other in the marital relationship. People also bring their private contracts to remarriage. Based on clinical experience, Clifford Sager and his associates (1983:67–68) have identified some of the common expectations in remarriage. Those who remarry tend to assume and expect that the new spouse will

1. be loyal, devoted, and faithful, providing a kind of romantic love and intimacy that occurred when the first marriage was at its best (or that was lacking altogether in the first marriage).
2. help nurture and discipline the children.
3. provide companionship and relief from the loneliness of being single.
4. help deal with problems and stresses and gain, or regain, the order and stability of a two-parent family.
5. be committed to making this marriage last.

Depending on age and circumstances, those who remarry also may expect to have shared children (even if one or both bring children to the marriage).

In some cases, the private contract may be unrealistic. It may, in essence, say to the other, "I expect you to do everything for me that my former spouse didn't. I expect

this to be the marriage 'made in heaven' that I didn't have before." Ideally, however, those who remarry will be more realistic, avoiding fanciful illusions and maintaining flexibility about roles in order to maximize the chances of success.

ISSUES IN RECOUPLING

What is it like to remarry? What are the problems and prospects the second time around? Is it just as demanding? Does it ever get any easier? Remarriage, like marriage for the first time, requires insight and effort if it is to succeed. Unfortunately, many people enter a second marriage holding on to certain mythical beliefs that can be detrimental.

The Myths of Remarriage

We act on what we believe, not necessarily on what

Symbolic Interactionist Theory Applied

is true or appropriate or helpful. As in the case of first marriages, those who remarry may act on the basis of myths. Coleman and Ganong (1985) have identified a number of remarriage myths that can detract from the quality of the new union. These myths may be held by those in the legal system, churches, and helping professions as well as by friends and family members. They also appear in the popular media.

Things Must Work Out. People in first marriages tend to believe this also, but there may be a quality of desperation in those who are remarrying. They insist on "getting it right" the second time. Or they believe that everything will work out because this time it is *really* love. But if insistence or confidence were sufficient, second marriages would not break up at a slightly higher rate than first marriages.

Consider Other People First. In remarriage, an individual may believe that success this time demands that he or she put personal needs secondary to those of spouse or children. But trying to fulfill everyone's needs is frustrating, stressful, and probably impossible. The problems of remarriage are not resolved by either partner denying his or her own needs.

Be an Individual First and a Couple Second. This is the opposite of the myth of always considering others first. It is held by those who felt that they suffered in a first marriage because they didn't care for their own needs. They believe that they must "look out for number one" regardless of what that means for the marital relationship.

Focus on the Positive and Forget Criticism. Some people who remarry believe that if they had followed this rule in their first marriage, it might have succeeded. They may be determined to follow it in the second marriage. As a result, they may

> "walk on eggs" rather than confront, challenge, or argue with other family members. Pseudomutuality may lead to unhappiness and feelings of powerlessness and alienation rather than unity (Coleman and Ganong 1985:117).

Avoid Mistakes of the Past. When things are not going well in the second marriage, some believe that they need to remember mistakes made in the first marriage and avoid repeating them. But, again, this may be a way of avoiding the realities of the present. It is an effort to keep working at the past relationship rather than an attempt to build a new and unique relationship in the present.

Marriage Makes People Happier. Of course, it is true that the married tend to be happier than the unmarried.

But remarriage, like marriage, is not a magic elixir that guarantees happiness or your money back. For some who remarry, happiness becomes even more of an imperative in the second than the first marriage, an aspect of the notion that this time it *has* to work out. A related myth is the idea that if the couple is happy, everyone else will be happy. But friends, grandparents, ex-spouses, and children may react very differently to the remarriage, and the happiness of the spouses cannot be separated from those reactions.

The Challenges of Remarriage

Those who remarry are likely to differ from those in a first marriage in a number of ways. They may be older and, therefore, in a different phase of their life cycles than those marrying for the first time. They may have different ideas about the meaning of love. They have experience in marriage. They know the pain of divorce. Having been hurt by a previous marital relationship, they tend to want more autonomy for themselves in such matters as child-rearing and financial decisions (Allen et al. 2001). In addition, they must deal with a number of issues that are unique to a remarriage.

Complex Kin Relationship and Ambiguous Roles. The acquisition of a whole new set of kin relationships, including steprelations, combined with ambiguity about many of the roles, can create considerable uncertainty and confusion for those involved in a remarriage (Hobart 1991; Lauer and Lauer 1999a; Michaels 2007). Many a stepparent has had to deal with the retort, "You aren't my *real* parent." And many a spouse in a remarriage has had to contend with a partner's continuing relationship with an ex-spouse. No social norms exist for such relationships. What is appropriate? What is expected?

Consider the following case reported by Sager and his associates (1983). Mrs. Prince was single when she met Mr. Prince, who was divorced and the father of two school-age children who lived with their mother. Problems began early in Mr. Prince's second marriage. He felt that his wife resented his children and the time and money he spent on them. She complained that he talked constantly on the telephone with his ex-wife, as often as several times during a day. She also resented the fact that they couldn't be with her parents on holidays because his parents wanted to see his children. The problems seemed monumental, and the couple eventually went to a therapist to try to work out the difficulties resulting from their complex family situation.

Unresolved Emotional Issues Related to the First Marriage. In addition to problematic relationships, there may be unresolved emotional issues from the first marriage and the divorce that continue to nag people and to affect their relationships. Whether positive (lingering desire for the ex-spouse) or negative (anger) feelings are involved, emotional attachment to the divorced spouse diminishes the intimacy in the remarriage (Gold, Bubenzer, and West 1993; Falke and Larson 2007). The emotional attachment comes out in various ways. For example, a husband may react to something his wife says or does because it reminds him of a problem or situation in his first marriage. He may shout at wife number two, but he is really still battling with wife number one. A woman had the habit of shrugging at either of two acceptable options for recreation. Her shrug meant, "I don't care. I'll be happy doing either as long as I'm with you." To her husband, however, it had been a sign of scorn from his first wife, and he still found himself reacting angrily, as he had to his first wife.

Another example of how unresolved emotional issues continue to affect people is the difficulty that some have in developing trust in the remarriage. Trust is crucial to the well-being of an intimate relationship, but the failure of a first marriage is frequently a crisis of trust for people. Having found their trust in the first spouse betrayed, they must work hard to learn to trust a second spouse.

Adjustment of Children. As we noted earlier, children pose perhaps the biggest problem to a remarriage. In the past, remarriage generally meant a spouse had died. Now, the children are more likely to have continuing relationships with both biological parents as well as a stepparent. The problems can be severe; we shall discuss them in detail shortly.

Financial Issues. Financial issues are likely to loom almost as large as children as a source of stress in remarriages (Hobart 1991). Financial problems can be complex and painful because of obligations to ex-spouses and children. Plus, questions arise about the inheritance rights of children and stepchildren. Such problems raise the issue of *equity, and if partners do not feel that the financial arrangements are equitable, the marriage will be severely strained.*

How, then, can family finances be managed in a way that is equitable? Should the couple have only separate accounts, only joint accounts, or a combination of separate and joint accounts? If everything is in a joint account, for example, the spouses put their total income (including any alimony and child support) into the account and allocate it among family members according to need instead of according to who earned what. The use of separate accounts suggests a safeguarding of resources for personal use and one's own children.

For example, one couple, Sheila and Harry, have separate accounts. Sheila has three sons and Harry has a daughter. The daughter does not live with them. Harry gives Sheila money each week for his share of food and household expenses. Sheila adds a much larger amount that she gets in child support and uses the total to run the home and pay for her sons' expenses. Harry pays fixed expenses, such as the mortgage and utilities. He also supports his own child.

Which arrangement, then, works best? Exchange theory suggests that, because of diverse circumstances, different couples will need different arrangements in order to feel equity. In other words, none of the arrangements is intrinsically superior to the others. A study of 91 remarried couples supports that conclusion (Pasley, Sandras, and Edmondson 1994). The researchers reported no differences in satisfaction or happiness among couples using one or the other of the three types of arrangements.

Legal Issues. Although the biological children and the ex-spouse may all have legal rights, what of stepchildren? There are no laws specific to stepparent–stepchild relationships. Some couples, therefore, may opt for a premarital agreement that takes into account what each has brought to the marriage and that protects each spouse as well as the children of each and any children they may have in common. This may require negotiation and a rather complex agreement. But the complexity of the arrangement is a reflection of the intricacies of the multiple relationships of remarriage.

The Quality of Remarried Life

What can you anticipate in a second marriage in terms of the quality of marital life? First, the same factors that lead to satisfaction in a first marriage are also important in any subsequent marriage. Thus, cohabitation tends to diminish the satisfaction and stability of a first marriage, and it tends to do the same with remarriage (Xu, Hudspeth, and Bartkowski 2006). Similarly, the quality of a remarriage depends upon such things as the couple's consensus on important topics, a social support network of friends and family, financial stability, the

Personal

"My Husband's First Wife Is Straining My Marriage"

Judy, an ebullient young woman in her early 30s, fell in love with and married Kurt, a divorced man with a teenaged daughter by his first wife, Eve. Judy and Kurt have a child of their own and are expecting a second. They are caught up in conflict between their relationships and the legal system, and as a result, their marriage is strained:

Kurt has been divorced for over 10 years. During most of that time he paid Eve $300 dollars a month for Sharon's child support and half of the costs for her dance lessons and other activities. He also has had to pay all of her medical and dental expenses. A year ago, Sharon decided to move in with us. That meant that Kurt would no longer have to pay child support

to Eve. Because of Kurt's and my salaries, however, Eve wouldn't have to contribute to Sharon's support while she lived with us.

Six months after she moved in, Sharon decided to go back and live with her mother. Eve told Kurt that she had a letter from a therapist recommending that she not work due to stress-related illnesses. She would continue to work until Sharon moved back, but at that time, she would have to quit. She implied that she would need more child support because of not being able to work.

I went to a lawyer to see if I had any rights about my salary not being used to help support Sharon. And what I found out was not encouraging. The law says that

Kurt's first responsibility is to Eve and Sharon. Because of my salary, more of Kurt's can be used to support Sharon. But this is going to cause a good deal of financial strain for us.

I feel like I'm being punished for being successful. The law is letting Eve steal from us. I don't blame Sharon. In fact, we're pretty good friends. But Kurt and I suspect that Eve's so-called problems are just a way of making things difficult for us and easy for herself. We're both angry, and we find ourselves getting irritable with each other at times. Eve is straining our marriage. The law supports her. And we don't quite know how to handle it at this point.

way stepchildren and other new relationships are handled, the nature of the relationship with the ex-spouse or ex-spouses, and the extent to which there are enjoyable, shared family activities (Hutchinson, Afifi, and Krause 2006; Falke and Larson 2007).

Second, failure in a first marriage has no necessary bearing on the quality of a second marriage (Johnson and Booth 1998). In a sense, a second marriage is a fresh start. It, too, can fail. But it also can be a much better marriage, one that lasts and is fulfilling to both spouses.

Third, people who remarry have high levels of intimacy and high-quality relationships in terms of such things as amount of interaction, amount of tension in the relationship, number of disagreements, and level of happiness (White and Booth 1985). Satisfaction is higher when the remarriage is perceived as more equitable (Buunk and Mutsaers 1999).

In at least one way, however, the quality of remarried life differs: The remarried are more divorce-prone in the sense that they think more about divorce, talk more about their marital problems with others, and are more likely to report a decline in marital quality in the first

eight years (Booth and Edwards 1992). The decline in marital quality is not dramatic, but it may take less to bring about a divorce among those who have experienced a previous decline and divorce. Those in remarriages also tend to have less interaction with parents and in-laws (Booth and Edwards 1992). Thus, they are less likely to have an important support group when problems arise.

Finally, remarried couples may not deal with conflict as effectively as the first-married. Remarriage and stepchildren do not produce more marital conflict than occurs in a first marriage (MacDonald and DeMaris 1995). But the remarried may not handle the conflict as well (Halford, Nicholson, and Sanders 2007). (Of course, the poor handling of conflict could have been a factor in the breakup of the first marriage also.) In a comparative study of 33 first-married and 33 remarried couples, Larson and Allgood (1987) reported that the remarried were more likely to use unproductive problem-solving strategies, such as shouting and anger, during conflict. The researchers suggested that the less effective conflict management may be due to the greater number of challenges and problems faced by remarried couples, incompatibility resulting from patterns

Comparison

Repartnering in Australia

Data provided on the Australian Bureau of Statistics Web site show that, as in the United States, marriage and divorce rates have both declined somewhat in recent years. However, the Australian marriage and divorce rates (5.9 and 2.6 per 1,000 population in 2000) are both lower than in the United States (8.3 and 4.1). Most Americans who have ever divorced are currently married (Kreider and Fields 2002). And women are slightly more likely than men to remarry.

In Australia, a random survey of 650 people who had divorced obtained information on "repartnering"; that is, on divorced people remarrying, cohabiting, or having a committed intimate relationship with someone but not living in the same home as that person (Hughes 2000). In particular, the researcher investigated whether gender, economic status, and children make a difference in repartnering.

They do. In contrast to the U.S. situation, Australian men were more likely to repartner than were women. According to the researchers, this may

reflect the fact that women with primary responsibility for children were less likely than other women to repartner, while having primary responsibility for children had no effect on men's likelihood of repartnering. The older a woman's children, however, the more likely she was to repartner.

Economic status also affected the chances of repartnering, which was more common among those in the middle statuses than those at either the high or the low end of the economic spectrum. Both men and women with high levels of income and property were less likely than those with middle levels to repartner. When they did, the men were likely to remarry, while the women tended to cohabit or to maintain a noncohabiting relationship. Among the women, this lower rate of remarriage may reflect a desire for more autonomy in an intimate relationship (a desire noted in the text as also common among Americans who remarry).

Men and women at the lower economic levels were also less likely than

those at middle levels to repartner. Their low rates may stem from the fact that they are socially marginalized by their economic position. They have fewer opportunities to meet people and establish relationships. And those they meet also may have limited resources, which results in a fragile economic base for building an intimate relationship.

Overall, Australian men and women spend less of their lives in marriage than they did formerly. As the Australian Bureau of Statistics sums it up, if present trends continue, an average man will spend 42 years single, 28 years married, 5 years divorced, and 2 years widowed; an average woman will spend 40 years single, 29 years married, 7 years divorced, and 6 years widowed.

Nevertheless, adult Australians, like their U.S. counterparts, still spend most of their lives in cohabitation, marriage, or, if they divorce, some form of repartnering.

---

established and remaining from the first marriage, or the lack of social norms for problem solving in remarriage.

If there are special challenges, there also may be unique strengths in second marriages. Some evidence exists that those who remarry have a better balance between self-interest and other-interest than they had in their first marriages (Smith et al. 1991). The husbands have learned to focus more on the interests of their wives, while the wives have learned something about the importance of caring for their own interests as well as those of their husbands. Thus, remarrieds may be somewhat more nontraditional in their gender-role orientation. This would explain, at least in part, why husbands in remarried families contribute significantly more than husbands in first marriages to the household tasks of cooking, meal cleanup, shopping,

laundry, and housecleaning (Ishii-Kuntz and Coltrane 1992; Sullivan 1997).

What about relationships with ex-spouses? How do they affect remarriage? Contrary to what some think, complete isolation from ex-spouses is not necessarily the best arrangement. Of course, such contact can cause disruption in remarriage if not handled properly. Nevertheless, women who have friendly contact with their ex-husbands, particularly when children are involved, express more satisfaction with remarriage than do others (Hobart 1990; Weston and Macklin 1990).

In sum, the marital relationship of the remarried can be as satisfying as that of the first-married. By the same token, second marriages break down for the same reasons as first marriages. However, the remarried are more likely than the first-married to divorce. The reason, as we

What Do You Think?

*There is disagreement about **whether second marriages are more likely than first marriages to be fulfilling.** What follows are pro and con arguments. What do you think?*

Pro	Con
Second marriages are more likely than first marriages to be fulfilling because	Second marriages are not more likely than first marriages to be fulfilling because

Pro

Second marriages are more likely than first marriages to be fulfilling because

- you learn from the mistakes of the first marriage.
- you are older, more experienced, and better prepared.
- you don't want to fail again so you try harder.
- you are not as idealistic and unrealistic about what to expect.

Con

Second marriages are not more likely than first marriages to be fulfilling because

- you are as likely to repeat the mistakes of the first marriage as you are to learn from them.
- giving up on the first marriage makes it easier to give up on the second as well.
- all marriages—whether the first or the fifth—have the same kinds of problems and challenges.
- second marriages frequently involve stepchildren, and stepfamilies are the most troublesome of all unions.

have noted, is likely to be found in the total family system, particularly in the relationships with children and stepchildren. We need, then, to look closely at the problems encountered in stepfamilies.

LIVING IN A STEPFAMILY

What exactly is it about stepfamilies that makes them more vulnerable to breaking up than others? In the first place, a stepfamily is built upon loss—the loss of the earlier family with its unique identity, history, and shared expectations (Lauer and Lauer 1999a). Stepfamilies also present people with numerous, often unanticipated, adjustments with loyalty conflicts (e.g., between one's spouse and one's children or between one's stepparent and one's biological parent) and with problems of resources (e.g., a stepfather may pay child support for his biological children, putting a financial strain on the stepfamily [Arnaut 2000]). In this section, we will look at the challenges posed by the stepfamily life cycle, by the structure of the stepfamily, and by the troublesome stepparent–stepchild relationship.

The Stepfamily Life Cycle

In a nine-year study of over 200 stepfather families, Bray and Kelly (1998) found three phases in the first 10 years of stepfamily life. The first phase involves the "turbulent first two years." Even stepfamilies that turn out to be satisfying in the future tend to experience a good deal of turmoil and conflict in the first two years. In fact, a significant number of adults who recall both the divorce of their parents and the remarriage of one or both of their parents say that the remarriage was more stressful for them than was the divorce (Ahrons 2007).

An important source of trouble in the first phase is the unrealistic expectations that people bring to the stepfamily. We call them "fantasy expectations," expectations that reflect our love of fairy-story endings—"they all lived happily ever after" (Lauer and Lauer 1999a). They include such things as, "We will be a normal family again"; "We will all love each other from the start"; and "We won't have the problems that other stepfamilies have because we all get along well." But even when people seem to get along well before the parent and stepparent marry, unanticipated struggles and problems can emerge once the stepfamily is formed.

For a stepfamily is not like a biological family. As we noted earlier, the stepfamily is built upon loss. It involves complicated and troublesome relationships that grow out of the loss. Research with a group of adolescents found that their experience of moving into stepfamilies was generally a negative one (Stoll, Arnaut, Fromme, and Felker-Thayer 2005). The youth felt powerless. They believed they had little or no say in the matter. They disliked having their home, their relationships, and the routines and rules of their lives altered. And they resented the reduced time of intimacy with their biological custodial parent. It is not surprising, then, that among adolescents the transition into a stepfamily is associated with an increased risk of initiating alcohol use (Kirby 2006).

In the second phase, from the third to the fifth year, stepfamilies are in the "golden period" (Bray and Kelly 1998). The challenges and problems of the first two years have been addressed or at least are no longer as troublesome as they were (if the family is still together). In this phase, stepfamily life seems finally to become the circle of intimacy that family members had hoped for. One thing that facilitates the relative harmony in this phase is the fact that stepchildren are frequently in the period of latency (between the ages of 8 and 11), which is one of the calmest periods of childhood. Also, the family members have now had a chance to work through some of the many issues (mealtimes, bedtimes, who has the right to discipline, how much time shall be given to the marriage as opposed to parenting, etc.) that have to be negotiated in stepfamily life.

Unfortunately, the tranquil phase doesn't last. From about the sixth year on, the stepfamily enters the phase of "singing in the rain" (Bray and Kelly 1998). It's a time when some things (like the marital relationship) continue to get better, while other matters (like stepparenting) become troublesome again, particularly if the stepchildren are now entering their teen years. A danger at this point is that the couple may attribute their difficulties to the fact of being a stepfamily rather than to the typical problems of all families with teenagers (Lauer and Lauer 1999a). In spite of some renewed difficulties, however, most stepfamilies at this stage have the stability and strengths to keep the family intact.

The Structure of the Stepfamily

Stepfamilies function somewhat differently than other families because of certain structural differences. These structural differences make the stepfamily a greater challenge to the quest for intimacy.

Complexity.   Stepfamilies are more complex because of the increased number of relationships. Thus, greater interpersonal skills are necessary in the stepfamily as people must deal with ex-spouses, the parents of ex-spouses (who are also grandparents), and various new steprelations. An additional point to keep in mind is that the complexity is there from the start. The spouses in a stepfamily have no child-free period of time in which to adjust to each other and build their marital relationship. Rather, they are immediately beset with an intricate and potentially troublesome set of relationships that can put considerable strain on their marriage.

Children also face a complex situation. Family therapist Virginia Satir (1972) wrote of an adolescent girl who was "alternately crazy and depressed." She lived with her mother and stepfather but alternated weekends with her father and his fiancée, her maternal grandparents, and her paternal grandparents. At each place, she was asked to tell about what went on at the other places and told to keep quiet about what was discussed "here." The girl was the unwitting victim of a network of jealous and angry people.

The girl was also caught up in **loyalty conflicts.** A loyalty conflict is the internal stress that results when contradictory commitments are expected from different family members. Loyalty conflicts are particularly likely in stepfamilies, and especially for children who feel caught between the contrary expectations of a custodial and noncustodial parent, or between parents and stepparents (Afifi 2003). Who gets the child's primary commitment? To whom should the child be most loyal? The child who loves and/or wants and needs to be accepted by all the family members who create the loyalty conflict is caught in the midst of a very painful dilemma.

Ambiguous Family Boundaries.   **Family boundary** is a concept from family *systems theory* that *refers to rules about who is a member of the family and how much each* *member participates in family life.* When family boundaries are ambiguous, there is likely to be stress and various problems in family functioning. Unfortunately, boundary ambiguity is much more likely in stepfamilies (Stewart 2005; Doodson and Morley 2006).

For instance, in her study of 60 adolescents whose parents had divorced, Gross (1986) found four ways of defining family. A third of the adolescents defined family in terms of *retention.* They named both biological parents as part of the family but did not include a stepparent. They considered stepparents mainly as outsiders who "just weren't related." Thirteen percent defined their families in terms of *substitution.* They excluded the missing biological parent and included the stepparent as a family member. However, they did not completely regard the stepparent as a parent. The stepparent was a family member but not a total replacement for a parent.

A fourth of the adolescents chose a third category, *reduction,* in which they defined the family in terms of the biological parents with whom they were living. Some were living with a stepparent but didn't include that person, while others were living with a single parent and excluded the nonresidential parent.

Finally, 28 percent of the adolescents defined family in terms of *augmentation,* identifying both biological parents and any stepparent as family members. They saw the stepparent as an addition to the family. Those who fell into this category tended to move freely between the homes of their biological parents and reported little hostility between the parents.

There are, then, differences in the way that the children of divorce define the boundaries of their family. Parents also may have vague ideas of exactly who is and who isn't a part of "our family." The problem may be compounded by pressures to make the boundaries more open than family members prefer. For example, there may be pressure to allow a nonresidential child to visit whenever he or she wants. Life in such a stepfamily really gets complicated if the child's biological parent views the child as a family member who should be able to enter freely into the home and other family members view the nonresidential child as an outsider who needs permission to enter the home.

Normative Ambiguity.   Fewer cultural norms exist to deal with life in the stepfamily than in the intact family. This means that there must be a good deal more negotiation. What, precisely, is the role of a stepparent? What if the stepparent and the nonresidential biological parent differ on appropriate behavior for the child? What do stepparents and stepchildren call each other? How much interaction with an ex-spouse is appropriate? What obligations remain to relatives of an ex-spouse with whom one has had close ties in the past?

All such questions must be worked out by each stepfamily. No cultural norms prescribe the behavior. It is not surprising, then, that in a study of 65 adolescents and young adults from stepfather families, the subjects were about evenly divided over whether the mother should give priority to the children or to both the children and the stepfather (Moore and Cartwright 2005). Thus, different children had different ideas about what should be normative. In the most difficult situations, there may even be as many different ideas about norms and roles in the stepfamily as there are people in it. Nor is there any help from the legal system. Residential stepparents actually have fewer legal rights than legal guardians or foster parents, and there is no consistent definition of the functions, rights, or obligations of stepparents toward their stepchildren (Malia 2005).

Stepparents and Stepchildren

What do the terms *stepparent* and *stepchild* mean to you? Is your initial reaction positive, neutral, or negative? As increasing numbers of people experience stepparenting, attitudes may be improving (Keshet 1990).

But students generally tend to react negatively to the very terms *stepparent* and *stepchild*. They believe that stepparents are both less obligated and less likely than either biological or adoptive parents to be supportive in various situations requiring parent–child interaction (Schwebel, Fine, and Renner 1991). And 45.5 percent of a sample of university students believed that children who live with a stepfather are at greater risk for sexual and physical abuse than are children who live with biological fathers (Claxton-Oldfield and Whitt 2003).

These negative perceptions may be rooted, at least in part, in experience. Analysis of data from a national survey showed the stepparents report significantly fewer activities with and positive responses to children than do biological parents (Thomson, McLanahan, and Curtin 1992). Stepfathers are likely to engage in less play, private talks, and projects with children than are biological fathers (Marsiglio 1991). Nevertheless, stereotyping the stepfamily in negative terms does not help members adjust easily to each other. Children are being pulled into something that they have learned to think of as negative. It would not be surprising, then, if many children entered the stepfamily with pessimism and the expectation of problems.

Older children may pose more problems for a stepparent than do younger children. Some evidence exists that stepparents have less positive relationships with older than with younger stepchildren (Hobart 1987). Even the adult children of those who remarry may create problems for a couple. A 45-year-old woman whose 69-year-old mother remarried some years after being widowed admitted that she had problems accepting her stepfather:

> One reason I got so upset was that I felt like Mom's new husband was just after her money—Dad's money. Her new husband gave his house to his son and then moved in with Mom. I remember Dad saying that he didn't mind dying because he knew that his grandchildren and his great-grandchildren would be running around that house just like I did when I was little. But he left the house to Mom. If she dies first, I'm afraid her new husband will get everything and my children and grandchildren will lose what my dad expected them to have.

Whatever their age, stepchildren can resent and resist a stepparent coming into the family.

Stepfathering.   Because of custody arrangements over the past few decades, stepfathering with custody of the child has been more common than stepmothering with custody. How do stepfathers regard their performance? Apparently not very well. They tend to see themselves as less competent than either their wives or their stepchildren see them. They feel more inadequate in maintaining close physical and emotional contact with stepchildren than do biological fathers with their own children. Still, Marsiglio (1992) found in a national survey that over half of stepfathers disagree that it is harder to love stepchildren than one's own children. The survey also showed that stepfathers who have both stepchildren and their own children in the same household and who have a happy relationship with their partner are more likely to say that they feel "fatherlike" toward the stepchildren and report better relationships with their stepchildren.

Having good relationships with both a stepfather and the nonresident father are important for the child's well-being (White and Gilbreth 2001; King 2006, 2007). Stepfathers who engage in shared activities with their adolescent stepchildren, for example, tend to enhance the children's emotional well-being (Yuan and Hamilton 2006).

It is, therefore, encouraging to note that many stepfathers are satisfied with their roles and experience a positive parenting experience. In fact, many stepfathers are as involved with their stepchildren as their biological children and relate to the stepchildren as though they were their own (Hofferth and Anderson 2003; Marsiglio 2004). Such a positive parenting experience is more likely to happen when (Ihinger-Tallman and Pasley 1987; Fine, Ganong, and Coleman 1997; Everett 1998) the following are true:

- They have prior, involved parenting experience with their natural children.
- They frequently engage in parenting behavior and view their parenting as their right and their responsibility.
- They communicate often and well with their stepchildren.
- Their wives support them in their involvement with and discipline of stepchildren.

Discipline of stepchildren is a particularly problematic area (Newman 1994; Lauer and Lauer 1999a). The child may resent discipline from a stepfather. In fact, stepchildren tend to believe that it is the mother's rather than the stepfather's responsibility to discipline them (Moore and Cartwright 2005). If the stepfather takes primary responsibility for discipline in the face of the stepchild's resentment, or if he participates in the discipline and he and the mother disagree about how the child should be disciplined, the outcome is likely to be disruptive to the marriage and the family. A study of 50 stepfather families reported that stepfather–adolescent relationships were best when both the stepfather and the adolescents perceived stepfather–mother agreement about parenting of the adolescents (Skopin, Newman, and McKenry 1993).

In spite of the stepfathers' perceptions and the problems that can arise, a number of studies have reported no significant differences between stepfather and intact families in such things as perceptions of family conflict and the quality of family relationships (Ganong and Coleman 1988). The majority of stepchildren say that they like their stepparents and get along well with them. Adults who were raised in stepfamilies seem to get along as well in family relationships as those raised in intact families.

Disciplining is one of the more problematic tasks for a stepfather.

Stepmothering. In a study of stepfamilies, mothers reported themselves responding as positively to their stepchildren as to their biological children (Fine, Voydanoff, and Donnelly 1993). Nevertheless, the family with a stepmother is the most likely to be conflicted and poorly adjusted (Ganong and Coleman 1994).

A survey of 104 undergraduates reported that those in stepmother families perceived less relationship quality, less support, and more conflict with their stepmother than those who lived with their biological mothers (Pruett, Calsyn, and Jensen 1993). The challenge of stepmothering is not helped by the fact that there is a long cultural tradition of the "wicked stepmother." In addition, there are abundant illustrations of disastrous efforts at stepmothering. A woman whose marriage broke up because of stepchildren tells about the agony:

> I was in my early 20s when I married a man with two kids, one 8 and one 12. He had joint custody with his wife. I tried from the first to be their friend. Eventually the boy and I developed a good relationship. But the girl would have none of it. She never would look at me or talk to me directly if she could avoid it. I remember one time I suggested we all go camping on the next weekend. I thought it would be a good family activity. She turned to her father and said, "Does *she* have to go along?" He told her yes, because "she's my wife." They were talking about me as if I wasn't even in the room. My husband never tried to get her to change her behavior towards me. He was afraid she might stop spending time with us. I didn't want to make him choose between me and his daughter. So I left him.

Stepmothering does seem to be more troublesome than stepfathering. Perhaps one factor in this is that stepmothering is more likely than stepfathering to involve a noncustodial relationship. When the stepchild is in the home, the stepmother rather than the child's father is likely to have the extra work of cleaning and cooking. The stepmother is called on to assume a burden that will have little or no emotional benefit to her. Not only is the stepchild not hers, but she may feel left out because the father is involving his ex-wife more than her in the parenting process.

In spite of such difficulties, stepmothering isn't necessarily a painful experience. Many stepmothers have very positive experiences with their stepchildren, and the majority of stepchildren have satisfying relationships with stepmothers. Crohn (2006) interviewed 19 young women, 19 to 25 years of age, who had positive relationships with their stepmothers. She found five styles of stepmothering, each of which worked well in terms of a positive relationship. Whatever the style, all of the women agreed that a primary factor in the positive relationship was that

the stepmother did not try to usurp the role of the biological mother. Apart from that, the styles were quite different.

The most common style was that of "an older close friend." These stepmothers had a close relationship with their stepdaughters, and were affectionate and loving. They did not attempt to control their stepchildren; rather, they used suggestions rather than directives when trying to enforce family rules. Another style was that of "a type of kin." Stepdaughters described these stepmothers as being like a cousin or sister or aunt. Some of these stepmothers were like valued guides or mentors to their stepchildren.

A third style was of that of "a peer-like girlfriend." These stepmothers were significantly younger than the biological parents, and were likely to share similar interests in music and food. Two of the young women identified a style of "my father's wife." These stepmothers were disengaged. The relationship was civil but minimal. Finally, one young woman described her stepmother as "like another mother." She said her stepmother was very nurturing (unlike her career-oriented biological mother) and that she felt good when people thought her stepmother was her biological mother.

Stepchildren and the Marital Relationship. Stepparents are more likely than biological parents to perceive strains on their marriage from the parenting experience (Falke and Larson 2007). White and Booth (1985) reported that those with stepchildren in their homes are more likely than others to prefer living apart from the children and to perceive the children as giving them problems. They are also less likely to be satisfied with their spouse's relationship with their children. Finally, they are more prone to see the marriage as having a negative effect on the children and more likely to say that if they could do it all over, they would not have married. In fact, 15 percent of those with stepchildren said they wouldn't have married, compared with only 6 percent of those without stepchildren. Not surprisingly, those with stepchildren reported somewhat less marital happiness than others.

Wives are more likely to see their marital relationship affected by their husbands' relationships with the children (his children, her children, or their children) than vice versa (Hobart and Brown 1988). Marital satisfaction also is affected by the type of family. Satisfaction is significantly lower when both spouses bring children to the marriage than when only one has children by a previous marriage (Clingempeel 1981). Satisfaction also is significantly affected by the living arrangements of the stepchildren. Stepmothers who have the least amount of difficulty and

Everyone adjusts better when the biological parent and stepparent get along.

report the highest amount of marital satisfaction are those who have live-in stepchildren rather than stepchildren who visit the home. While a live-in stepchild does not necessarily make for an easy situation, stepmothers apparently find it easier to develop a close relationship with the live-in child. Thus, the greater frequency of problems with stepmothers than stepfathers may be rooted in the fact that most stepmothers do not have live-in stepchildren.

There are a variety of reasons stepchildren can adversely affect the marital relationship (Sager et al. 1980; Lauer and Lauer 1999a). The stepfamily is an instant creation rather than a gradual process of pregnancy, birth, and the development of intimate relationships from the beginning of the child's life. Coming into an instant family and dealing with the challenges and issues of that stage of the family life cycle may not be fully compatible with the stepparent's individual stage of life. As one stepmother put it,

> I do my best. I really like my stepdaughter. But I find myself still thinking about the fact that I'm raising another woman's child. And meanwhile, I'm trying to establish my career. It's not quite fair. But I remind myself that I do like her and that she is my husband's child.

Another factor that complicates the stepfamily is that the ex-spouse and his or her parents may continue to have input into the children's lives. This can contribute to divided loyalties. The stepchild may like the stepparent but get conflicting guidance from the stepparent and the absent biological parent or may simply feel that liking the stepparent too much is disloyalty to the absent biological parent.

In addition, the stepchild may still be suffering from the emotional trauma of loss of the absent parent. In such cases, the stepchild may act out his or her anger against the stepparent. Even when the child is consulted about the remarriage, the child may feel resentment. The biological parent, then, is torn between loyalty to the child and loyalty to the new spouse.

Adjustment of Stepchildren. The evidence on the adjustment children make to stepfamily life is mixed. A number of earlier studies reported various positive findings. For example, researchers found that stepchildren have no more negative attitudes toward themselves or others than do children in intact families and that stepchildren are no lower in self-esteem, psychological functioning, or academic achievement than those in intact families (Ihinger-Tallman and Pasley 1987; Ganong and Coleman 1993; Thomson, Hanson, and McLanahan 1994). More recent research has found that stepchildren are more likely than others to spend time in jail, have higher levels of depressive symptoms, and have lower levels of academic achievement (Harper and McLanahan 2004; Barrett and Turner 2005; Jeynes 2006). The lower academic achievement could be explained by the lack of resources (parental education and income) rather than by living in a stepfamily per se (Downey 1995). And lumping stepmother families with stepfather families could confound findings, because Fine and Kurdek (1992) found fewer problems among those living with stepfathers than those living with stepmothers.

Most of the research, however, has examined the short-term effects of stepfamily life on stepchildren. What about the longer-term consequences? Surveys carried out by the National Opinion Research Center asked respondents about their living arrangements at the age of 16. Beer (1988) pooled results from a 12-year period and found some interesting differences depending on whether the respondents lived with both biological parents, a father and a stepmother, or a mother and stepfather (table 16.1). Males from intact families scored better than those from stepfamilies on 7 of 10 of the measures, while females from intact families scored better than others on 5 of the measures. A close examination of table 16.1 shows that no simple conclusions can be drawn. In some things, people from stepfamilies scored better than those from intact families. Overall, both males and females from intact families had somewhat better emotional adjustment (as defined by the five items

in the survey) than did those from stepfamilies. And males from intact families had better social adjustment. But an intact family yielded little or no advantage to female social adjustment or to the familial adjustment of males or females.

Another interesting finding in table 16.1 is the differences between the backgrounds of stepfathers and stepmothers. In spite of the research that shows that stepmothers have more problems with children, only the females from stepmother families reported less adjustment than those from stepfather families. For males, those from stepmother families scored higher than those from stepfather families on 6 of the 10 measures. Finally, note that males from stepfather families and females from stepmother families were much less likely than others to say that they are very happy and had the lowest scores on a majority of the 10 measures. It may be, then, that the most difficult time for children occurs when the stepparent is the same sex as the stepchild.

Family Functioning

Apart from the stepparent–stepchild relationship, how do people see the stepfamily as a whole? How well does the stepfamily function? A study of 631 college students reported that those from stepfamilies perceived less cohesion and more stress in family life than did those from intact families (Kennedy 1985). Using a smaller

TABLE 16.1 Long-Term Adjustment by Type of Family Background

	Males at age 16, lived with			Females at age 16, lived with		
	Mother and father	Father and stepmother	Mother and stepfather	Mother and father	Father and stepmother	Mother and stepfather
Emotional adjustment	Percent					
Say they are very happy	34	38	23	39	24	34
Believe most people try to be helpful	51	41	43	60	56	57
Believe most people try to be fair	63	66	54	69	66	60
Believe most people can be trusted	51	41	41	46	44	42
Find life exciting	50	34	44	44	32	49
Social adjustment						
Are very satisfied with job	50	43	41	51	48	50
Get a very great deal of satisfaction from friendships	29	27	24	35	25	37
Respond "no" when asked if they drink more than they should	52	49	48	69	73	55
Familial adjustment						
Are very happily married	70	65	66	67	57	67
Get a very great deal of satisfaction from family life	42	43	36	47	30	49

sample of 28 intact and 28 stepfamilies, Pink and Wampler (1985) obtained ratings from both parents and adolescent children and also found lower levels of cohesion in the step-families. In addition, the stepfamily respondents reported lower levels of adaptability, the family's ability to deal successfully with differing problems and situations. Finally, stepfamilies tend to have more conflict between members than do biological families (Jenkins et al. 2005).

Thus, stepfamilies tend to have less closeness between members and less ability to change when confronted with stress than do intact families. The same results, plus some additional findings, were reported by four researchers who compared 106 intact with 108 stepfamilies (Peek et al. 1988). The stepfamilies scored lower not only on cohesion and adaptability but also on expressiveness (the extent to which people feel free to express their feelings to other family members), ability to manage conflict effectively, problem-solving skills, openness of communication, and the quality of relationships.

Again, it is important to emphasize that these results do not mean that stepfamilies are all in trouble. Lower scores do not mean pathological scores. The point is not that life in a stepfamily is miserable. The point is that stepfamilies tend to function at a somewhat lower level than intact families. You will probably not be damaged by living in a stepfamily; you may not, however, have the same experience of family closeness and flexibility as someone who grows up in an intact family.

On the other hand, stepfamilies have a number of potential strengths (Coleman, Ganong, and Gingrich 1985). The divorced parent may feel less harassed by financial problems and child-rearing responsibilities when he or she remarries. The children of divorce may benefit more from the stepfamily than the single-parent experience. In fact, children from stepfamilies are more like those from intact families than are children from single-parent families.

In stepfamilies, new people with new ideas and skills are encountered—sources of new opportunities for children. Children also once again have a model of marriage and of adult intimacy. Having seen one marriage break up, they may benefit by a second marriage that shows them that adults can have a stable and happy relationship.

The merging of two families in the stepfamily means that children come into a situation that requires a good deal of negotiation and flexibility. They may learn much about how and how not to cope with other people in situations that require the working out of differences. As a result, stepchildren can be more accommodating and adaptable in their adult relationships.

In sum, stepfamily life has both advantages and disadvantages. Overall, your chances of growing up in a stable and healthy environment are somewhat less in a stepfamily than in an intact family. But in those stepfamilies that function well, the outcome will be similar to that of the well-functioning intact family. In fact, Bray and Kelly (1998) found that the great majority of the children they studied were functioning well academically, personally, and socially after 10 years in a stepfamily.

MAKING IT WORK

Tanya is a 34-year-old secretary who is expecting her first child. She is in her second marriage. At the age of 20, she married her high school sweetheart. The union lasted six years. "It was a clear example of the conflict-habituated marriage," she recalls. "We were both pulling our own way and expecting the other to 'prove how much you love me.'" At one point, they moved to a different state, hoping the move would give their marriage a fresh start. When it didn't, her husband moved back, but Tanya remained where she was. They divorced. She met another man and remarried a year later. She is delighted: "It was, and continues to be, six and one-half years later, wonderful to have someone with whom I can truly share my life. With him, I have found the intimacy that is so important for well-being and growth."

Clearly, not everyone who remarries will have Tanya's experience. But second marriages, including those involving stepfamilies, can work out well and be stable and satisfying. In our study of long-term marriages, about 10 percent of the couples involved a remarriage (Lauer and Lauer 1986). What factors are at work in those second marriages and stepfamilies that succeed?

First, as far as the marriage itself is concerned, the same factors that make a first marriage work well also apply to a second marriage. For example, communication skills are as important to marital satisfaction in stepfamilies as in marriages generally (Beaudry et al. 2004). It is also important to continually nurture the marriage (Lebey 2004). As a therapist told us, some remarried couples make the mistake of giving priority to the needs of their children over their needs as a couple. He suggests that parents in a remarriage set aside a minimum amount of time each day and some special times on weekends when they can be alone. One of the best things a couple can do for their children, he notes, is to show them that their parent and stepparent care about each other and need to spend time together to enrich their marriage. It is also one of the best things they can do for their relationship as husband and wife.

Second marriages, like first marriages, need careful nurturing.

Furthermore, stepfamilies work well to the extent that they confront and adequately respond to a number of challenges and tasks (Lauer and Lauer 1999a), including the following:

- Help each other deal with feelings of loss that arise out of the disruption of the previous families.
- Replace fantasy expectations with realistic ones.
- Develop a sense of family identity, including the sense that "We are a family" rather than "We are a stepfamily."
- Assist each other in working through such loyalty conflicts as when children are torn between a desire to maintain a close relationship with the natural parent and to develop one with the stepparent.

- Resolve any lingering issues with ex-spouses.
- Develop stepparenting rules and behaviors that are acceptable to everyone.
- Be aware of, and responsive to, the feelings and needs of each member of the stepfamily.
- Nurture a strong marital relationship.

In sum, remarriage and the stepfamily represent another effort to create meaningful intimate relationships after the first effort has failed. The task is no easier the second time. On the contrary, it is more difficult. But millions of Americans have already shown that it can be done. A failed quest for intimacy does not mean that the quest is fruitless. With patience, understanding, and hard work, fulfilling intimate relationships are within the grasp of each of us.

SUMMARY

People may enter a remarriage from one of five different situations. One partner may have been single. And one or both partners may have been divorced or widowed with no children, divorced or widowed with custody of children, divorced or widowed without custody of children, or divorced or widowed with custody of some children but not others. Most Americans who divorce each year will remarry, and many of the remarriages will involve children. The divorce rate is slightly higher among second than first marriages when both partners were married previously, and it is even higher when one or both partners bring children to the marriage.

Second marriages fare better if there is a period of three to five years of dating after the divorce. Those who remarry tend to spend less time in dating and engagement to second spouses. They also do little to prepare for a second marriage other than living together, though some get counseling or seek advice from friends or books. People remarry for the same reasons they marry the first time; in addition, some may be looking for suitable stepparents for their children.

Some myths about remarriage can be detrimental to the relationship. There are also challenges and issues that are peculiar to remarriage. The kin relations are complex and the roles may be ambiguous. There may be unresolved emotional issues from the first marriage. Issues of children and finances and legal matters also arise.

The quality of remarried life depends on such things as companionship, feelings, and satisfaction with parenting. Remarried people tend to report as satisfying relationships as those in first marriages.

Life in a stepfamily typically involves a phase of turmoil, followed by a phase of relative harmony and then another phase of difficulties. Stepfamilies are unique because of their complexity (the large number of relationships involved), ambiguous family boundaries, and normative ambiguity. The very term *stepfamily* has negative connotations for many people.

Stepfathers tend to feel inadequate. Their stepchildren report less support, control, and discipline from them than do children of biological fathers. Yet the relationship tends to improve over time and become more like that with a biological father. Discipline is a particularly problematic area. The majority of stepchildren say they like stepparents and get along well with them, though boys have an easier time than girls in adjusting to stepfamily life.

Stepmothers have less positive relationships with stepchildren than do stepfathers. Still a majority of their stepchildren report satisfying relationships. One of the reasons stepmothering poses more problems than stepfathering is it is more likely to involve a noncustodial relationship.

Stepparents are more likely than biological parents to perceive strains on the marriage from the parenting experience, and satisfaction is significantly lower when both spouses bring children to the marriage. Noncustodial stepchildren tend to create more problems than those who live in the stepfamily.

In spite of the problems, the majority of children in stepfamilies are satisfied with their stepparents. In the long run, however, both males and females from intact families have somewhat better emotional adjustment and males have somewhat better social adjustment than those who grow up in stepfamilies. There tends to be less cohesion, less adaptability, and more stress in stepfamilies. Stepfamilies also have strengths, particularly compared with single-parent families.

The same factors that make a first marriage work well also apply to a second marriage. For the stepfamily to work well, the various members must work together through a set of challenges and tasks that range from clearing away unrealistic expectations to forming a family identity.

Principles for Enhancing Intimacy

The following suggestions, published by the U.S. Department of Health, Education, and Welfare (1978), are very useful principles for dealing with the special problems of being a stepparent:

1. Let the relationship with stepchildren develop gradually. Don't force it. Remember that both stepparents and stepchildren need time to adjust.

2. Don't try to replace the lost parent. Try to be an additional parent to the child.

3. Expect a confusion of various feelings in each member of the stepfamily. Anxiety, ambivalence, feelings of divided loyalties, love, caring, and other feelings will all be mixed together over the course of creating the new family unit.

4. Be prepared for comparisons with the absent parent. Work out with your spouse what is best for you and the stepchildren and stand by it.

5. You will need support from your spouse in rearing the children. It is important that the two of you agree. Raising children is a difficult task; raising someone else's children can be even harder.

6. Make every effort to be open, fair, and honest with both stepchildren and children. Openly acknowledge good relations between stepsiblings.

7. Try to recognize and admit your need for help if the situation becomes too difficult for you. We all need help at times. Numerous counselors and organizations are available to help people with the difficult task of stepparenting.

KEY TERMS

family boundary *370*
loyalty conflict *370*

serial marriage *361*

stepfamily *360*

ON THE WEB   Remarriage and Stepfamilies

If you have experienced remarriage in your personal life as a marriage partner, stepchild, or grandparent, you know that the challenges associated with remarriage are many. And the challenges of creating a satisfying stepfamily life are not only numerous but very difficult. A number of organizations and Web sites exist to help people with the challenges. Two useful Web sites are:

www.mhhe.com/lauer7e

Remarriage
http://www.remarriage.com

Designed to help those who are thinking about, are in the process of, or have already engaged in remarriage, this site offers helpful articles and information about both remarriage and stepfamily life.

Stepfamily Foundation
http://www.stepfamily.org

This site offers information and statistics on various aspects of stepfamily life.

Using these two sites and others, enlarge your understanding with the following projects:

1. Use the Remarriage site and others that you identify through a search engine, to gather materials about remarriage. Imagine that a good friend, who lives in another city and who has been divorced for two years, writes you about falling in love again. Your friend is thinking about remarriage, but is concerned because the first marriage failed. Write a letter that gives some helpful guidance, including both the perils and the promises of a second marriage that you have gleaned from your Internet search.

2. From materials at the Stepfamily Foundation site, along with the discussion in your text, summarize the major challenges facing stepfamily life and the resources available to deal with those challenges. Identify two or three stepfamilies, and interview a member of each of them about their experience of these challenges and resources. Note similarities and differences between the Internet and text materials and information from your interviews.

3. Use a search engine to find information about stepfamilies in other nations and about the support groups available to them. Summarize what you find. Make a report to the class, comparing your findings with the text materials on stepfamilies in the United States.

EPILOGUE

THE QUEST REVISITED: WHY BOTHER?

The last three chapters—family crises, separation and divorce, remarriage and the stepfamily—illustrate the dark side of the quest for intimacy. One student reacted to them with a hint of frustration in his voice:

> Why bother? Maybe we'd all be better off if we just did our own thing and not worry about trying to make a go of it in a family. I'm looking forward to my career and think I'll make a go of it. But I'm not so sure about marriage—whether I can build a good marriage and have a family that doesn't drive me nuts with all kinds of problems.

To be sure, he can't know that. For that matter, he can't know that he'll have a career that will be as fulfilling and lasting as he anticipates. Everything in life carries risk. Is the quest for intimacy worth the risks involved?

Let's go back to chapter 1. There we noted the research that shows not only our need for intimacy, but the ways in which intimate relationships—even though they are never flawless or trouble free—can enhance our physical and emotional well-being. So our response to the student is: "Yes, intimacy is risky. But if you shy away from the quest, you will miss out on the most important source, the very foundation, of a richly fulfilling life."

Here are three more reasons for our response. The Pew Research Center (2007a) did a national survey to determine where people find fulfillment. They asked people to rate various matters on a scale of 0 to 10, where 10 meant the most important to their personal happiness and fulfillment. The proportion giving a "10" varied as follows: 85 percent named their relationship with minor children; 81 percent named their relationship with their spouse or partner; 74 percent said their relationship with adult children; 56 percent gave a 10 to relationship with mother and 43 percent said relationship with father; and 37 percent named relationship with friends. Only 31 percent named the things they did in their free time, and job or career was given a 10 by just 23 percent.

Second, in a study of the quality of life of older adults, two researchers found that the most important factor in a high quality of life was satisfaction with personal relationships, followed by health and sexual activity (Robinson and Molzahn 2007). And third, some years ago we asked hundreds of people to tell us of one or two experiences of joy they had in their lives. We collected and analyzed over a thousand experiences. The most frequent response was to relate a joyous experience that involved an intimate relationship. The response of a married woman sums it all up well. She and her husband have had their share of arguments, differences, and struggles (including job loss and disagreement over when to start having children). But:

> I just enjoy being with Larry. I feel little twinges of joy when we come home at night and see each other. I feel more joy when he does things or says things to let me know that he loves me. . . . Looking back over our time together, I feel I really came alive with Larry.

To be sure, this epilogue isn't a standard textbook approach. But we are so convinced of the importance of intimate relationships for your well-being that we wanted to share these final words with you. By all means, pursue your quest for intimacy! Hopefully, it will be the most rewarding quest you ever undertake.

GLOSSARY

abortion expulsion of the fetus from the uterus

accommodation in conflict theory, the neglect of your own interests in order to pursue the interests of the other

adolescence the years, basically the teens, of the transition from puberty to adulthood

agape love that is action on the behalf of someone's well-being, independently of one's feelings for the other person

androgyny possession of both traditional masculine (instrumental) and traditional feminine (expressive) traits

anxious/ambivalent attachment style the effort to maintain high levels of closeness and love in the context of anxiety over rejection or abandonment

arranged marriage a marriage in which the parents have chosen the spouse for their child

artificial insemination injection of sperm into a woman's reproductive tract

assortative mating marriage between people who are similar on one or more characteristics

authoritarian parenting style of parenting with strong control, minimal affection, and the expectation of unquestioning obedience

authoritative parenting style of parenting with warmth and acceptance in the context of clear rules and boundaries about what is acceptable behavior

avoidance in conflict theory, minimum concern for either your own interests or those of the other person

avoidant attachment style attempt to retain control of one's life by maintaining a certain amount of distance from one's partner

battered woman syndrome a psychological state in which an abused woman submits to continuing abuse because she believes herself helpless to escape the abuser

birth rate number of births per 1,000 women in the child-bearing years (15–44 years of age)

bisexual having sexual relations with either sex or both together

child maltreatment physical, sexual, or emotional abuse or neglect of a child

coercive power ability to influence someone with the threat of punishment

cohabitation living with someone in an intimate, sexual relationship without being legally married

collaboration in conflict theory, a high degree of concern for both your own interests and the interests of the other person

commitment a promise of dedication to a relationship in which there is an emotional attachment to another person who has made the same promise

communication the use of language and nonverbal signs to create shared meaning between two or more people

commuter marriage dual-career marriage in which the spouses live in different areas

companionate love affection for and commitment to someone with whom one is deeply involved

competition in conflict theory, a high degree of concern for your own interests and low concern for the interests of the other person

compromise in conflict theory, a satisfactory level of concern about both your own interests and those of the other person

conflict theory focuses on contradictory interests, inequalities, and the resulting conflict and change

contraception use of devices or techniques to prevent fertilization

covenant marriage a marriage based on a legal contract in which the partners agree not to divorce except for abuse or adultery; for any other grounds, they agree to certain provisions such as mandatory counseling and a waiting period before finalizing the divorce

cunnilingus oral stimulation of the female genitals

death rate the number of deaths per 1,000 population

decode to interpret the words of someone so that you understand the other's ideas and feelings

definition of the situation if a situation is defined as real, it will have real consequences

divorce rate the number of divorces per 1,000 population or the number of divorces per 1,000 married women 15 years and older

drug abuse improper use of alcohol or other drugs such that the consequences are detrimental to the user and the family

dual-career family   family in which both spouses are in careers and have a commitment to work that has a long-term pattern of mobility

dual-earner family   family in which both spouses are involved in paid work outside the home and one or both view the work only as a job rather than a career

dual-income family   a family in which both spouses are involved in paid work outside the home

egalitarian marriage   a marriage in which husband and wife can both be employed and have an equal voice in making decisions

ejaculation   discharge of semen from the penis during orgasm

emotional abuse   acts or words that are used to control or demean another person and that create emotional deprivation or trauma

emotional loneliness   having fewer intimate relationships than you desire

encode   to put ideas and feelings into words that will convey their meaning to someone else

endometriosis   disease in which the tissue that lines the inside of the uterus grows outside as well

equity   fairness, in the sense that people are rewarded in proportion to their contributions

eros   sexual love

exchange theory   views social interaction as a cost-benefit analysis in which people try to keep their costs lower than their rewards

expert power   ability to influence someone with special knowledge or expertise

expressive traits   those traits, associated with the traditional female gender role, that facilitate good relationships

extended family   group of three or more generations formed as an outgrowth of the parent–child relationship

familism   value of family living

family   group united by marriage, cohabitation, blood, and/or adoption in order to satisfy intimacy needs and/or bear and socialize children

family boundary   systems theory concept, referring to rules about who is a member of the family and how each member participates in family life

family life cycle   a description of typical changes and functioning in family life from the stage of the unattached young adult to the stage of the family in later life

family of origin   family into which one is born

family-to-work spillover   adverse effects on work performance because of family demands or problems

fellatio   oral stimulation of the male genitalia

flextime   an arrangement in which an employer offers workers flexible working hours

fusion   in interpersonal relationships, a blurring of the boundaries between people

gays   male homosexuals

gender   social male or female, as distinguished from the biological male or female

gender role   behavior associated with the status of being male or female

gender-role orientation   conception of the self as having some combination of masculine and feminine traits

hanging out   casual and sometimes spontaneous getting together of groups for having fun

heterogamy   marriage between people who are dissimilar in social and demographic characteristics

heterosexual   having sexual preference for persons of the opposite sex

homogamy   marriage between people who are similar in social and demographic characteristics

homophobia   irrational fear of homosexuality

homosexual   having sexual preference for persons of the same sex; someone who privately or overtly considers himself or herself a homosexual

hooking up   various kinds of sexual behavior from kissing to sexual intercourse between two people who are not committed to each other

hypergamy   marriage with someone who is from a higher socioeconomic background

impotence   inability of a male to get or sustain an erection

incest   any type of exploitive sexual contact between relatives in which the victim is under 18 years of age

infatuation   strong, romantic feelings for someone you don't know well and to whom you have no commitment

infertility   failure to conceive after one year of unprotected intercourse

infidelity   sexual and/or emotional unfaithfulness to one's partner

informational power   ability to influence someone by arguing in terms of his or her best interests

institution   collective, regularized solution to a problem of social life, such as economic or family arrangements

instrumental traits   those traits, associated with the traditional male gender role, that facilitate goal achievement

integration   state of being a significant and meaningful part of some group

intimacy   relationship characterized by mutual commitment, affection, and sharing

intimate terrorism   frequent, long-term abuse that tends to lead to physical injuries and emotional problems

in vitro fertilization   removal of eggs from a woman's body, fertilizing them with sperm in a laboratory, and implanting the resulting embryo in the woman's uterus

jealousy   negative emotional reaction to a real or imagined threat to a love relationship

joint custody arrangement in which both divorced parents continue to share responsibility for the care and raising of their children

labor force all civilians who are employed or who are unemployed but able and desirous of work

legitimate power ability to influence someone because of one's authoritative position

lesbians female homosexuals

life partner an individual with whom one lives in a committed sexual relationship through marriage or another consensual arrangement

loneliness feeling of isolation from desired relationships

loyalty conflict the internal stress that results when contradictory commitments are expected from different family members

ludus playful love

mania possessive, dependent love

marriage rate proportion of unmarried women, ages 15 and above, who get married during a year

marriage squeeze a shortage of acceptable mates for one sex or the other

matrilineal characteristic of descent traced through the female line

media in communication, the verbal and nonverbal means of conveying meaning to someone

misattribution of arousal attributing the wrong emotion to physical arousal

monogamy marriage to one person at a time

myth a belief that is accepted uncritically

network family support group of nonkin others

no-fault divorce a divorce granted without requiring either spouse to prove marital misconduct on the part of the other

nonverbal cues facial expressions, body position, gestures, and paralanguage (inflection, rate, and loudness of speaking, etc.) that communicate meaning

norms expected patterns of behavior

nuclear family group composed of husband, wife, and children, if any

occupational sex segregation the clustering of men and women in different occupations

orgasm third phase of the sexual response cycle in which there is a sudden discharge of sexual tension

ovulate to release an egg from the ovary

passionate love preoccupation with and intense longing for union with a particular other

patrilineal characteristic of descent traced through the male line

penis male sex organ

permissive parenting style of parenting with little or no guidance or control

philia the kind of love that exists between friends

physical abuse any act that causes physical harm or injury to someone

polyandry marriage of a woman to two or more husbands

polygamy marriage of one person to two or more people of the opposite sex

polygyny marriage of a man to two or more wives

postnuptial agreement a legal document that specifies how the couple's assets will be divided if they divorce, but is entered into after the couple is married

power ability to get someone to think, feel, or act in a way that he or she would not have done spontaneously

pragma a logical kind of love

prenuptial agreement a legal document that specifies, for people who are getting married, such matters as how assets will be distributed in the event of divorce or death, how premarital debts will be paid, what insurance coverage to have, and other matters agreed upon by both parties

promiscuity characteristic of frequent and indiscriminate sexual relations with many partners

propinquity nearness in place

rape carnal knowledge of a female forcibly and against her will

rapport harmonious and comfortable relationship with someone

reactance theory theory that a person will resist coercion to behave in a certain way even when the behavior is consistent with the person's attitudes

referent power ability to influence someone because he or she identifies with and desires to please you

refractory period period of time after ejaculation by the male during which he cannot have another orgasm

reframing redefining the meaning of something in order to make it more acceptable

replacement level the birth rate necessary to keep the population level stable

resilient family family that can resist disruption in the face of change and cope effectively with crises

resource theory theory that the balance of power in a marriage reflects the relative resources of each spouse

reward power ability to influence someone by offering rewards

rites of passage ceremonies that recognize significant times of change in an individual's life

role-making the process of working out the nature of particular roles

sandwich generation those who have responsibilities for both adolescent children and aging parents

secure attachment style the willingness to get close to others and feel secure in the relationship.

self-concept totality of an individual's beliefs and attitudes about himself or herself

self-disclosure honest revealing of oneself to another

semen fluid that carries the sperm and is ejaculated during orgasm

serial marriage three or more marriages as a result of repeated divorces

sex an individual's biological identification as male or female

sex ratio number of males per 100 females

sexism prejudice or discrimination against someone because of his or her sex

sexual aggression any kind of unwanted sexual activity

sexual dysfunction impairment of the physical responses in sexual activity

sexual harassment unwelcome sexual advances, requests for sexual favors, and other sexual behavior that either results in punishment when the victim resists or creates a hostile environment

social class social group consisting of people with similar income, education, and occupational prestige

social integration state of relative harmony and cohesion in a group

social loneliness having less interaction with others than you desire

socialization process of learning to function effectively in a group

sole custody arrangement in which the responsibility for the care and raising of children after a divorce is given to one

static interference of some kind with accurate communication

status prestige attached to a particular position in society

stepfamily remarriage in which one or both of the spouses has children from a previous marriage

sterilization Surgical procedure that prevents fertilization

storge the kind of love that exists between parents and their children

stress biological reaction to adverse conditions or experiences that disturbs well-being

stressor event any situation or condition or set of circumstances that causes stress

symbolic interaction theory views humans as cognitive creatures who are influenced and shaped by their interaction experiences

systems theory focuses on social systems and how their interdependent parts maintain order

testes male reproductive glands that hang in the scrotum

theory a set of related propositions that comprise an explanation of social phenomena

time pressure feelings of frustration and anxiety because of insufficient time to fulfill one's responsibilities and desires

undifferentiated characteristic of perception of one's self as low on both masculine and feminine traits

vagina canal leading from the uterus to the vulva (exterior part of the female genitals); passage for menstrual flow, for giving birth, and for receiving the penis during heterosexual intercourse

values things preferred because they are defined as being worthy and desirable

wedding a public ceremony that validates and celebrates a couple's marriage

work-to-family spillover adverse effects on family life because of work demands or problems

REFERENCES

Abel, E. L., M. Kruger, and L. Burd. 2002. "Effects of Maternal and Paternal Age on Caucasian and Native American Preterm Births and Birth Weights." *American Journal of Perinatology* 19:49–54.

Abma, J., A. Driscoll, and K. Moore. 1998. "Young Women's Degree of Control over First Intercourse." *Family Planning Perspectives* 30:12–18.

Abma, J. C., and G. M. Martinez. 2006. "Childlessness among Older Women in the United States." *Journal of Marriage and Family* 68:1045–56.

Abma, J. C., G. M. Martinez, W. D. Mosher, and B. S. Dawson. 2004. "Teenagers in the United States: Sexual Activity, Contraceptive Use, and Childbearing." *Vital Health Statistics* 23.

Abma, J. C., and F. L. Sonenstein. 2001. "Sexual Activity and Contraceptive Practices among Teenagers in the United States, 1968 and 1995." *Vital Health Statistics* 23(21).

Abma, J. C., et al. 1997. "Fertility, Family Planning, and Women's Health." *Vital and Health Statistics* 23(19).

Ackerman, B. P., E. Brown, and C. E. Izard. 2003. "Continuity and Change in Levels of Externalizing Behavior in School of Children from Economically Disadvantaged Families." *Child Development* 74:694–709.

Adamczyk, A., and J. Felson. 2006. "Friends' Religiosity and First Sex." *Social Science Research* 35:924–47.

Adams, J. M., and W. H. Jones. 1997. "The Conceptualization of Marital Commitment: An Integrative Analysis." *Journal of Personality and Social Psychology* 72:1177–96.

Adams, K. B., S. Sanders, and E. A. Auth. 2004. "Loneliness and Depression in Independent Living Retirement Communities." *Aging and Mental Health* 8:475–85.

Adams, S., J. Kuebli, P. A. Boyle, and R. Fivush. 1995. "Gender Differences in Parent-Child Conversations about Past Emotions." *Sex Roles* 33:309–23.

Adams-Curtis, L. E., and G. B. Forbes. 2004. "College Women's Experiences of Sexual Coercion." *Trauma, Violence & Abuse* 5:91–122.

Aday, R. H., G. C. Kehoe, and L. A. Farney. 2006. "Impact of Senior Center Friendships on Aging Women Who Live Alone." *Journal of Women and Aging* 18:57–73.

Afifi, T. D. 2003. "'Feeling Caught' in Stepfamilies." *Journal of Social and Personal Relationships* 20:729–65.

Afifi, T. D., F. N. Huber, and J. Ohs. 2006. "Parents' and Adolescents' Communication with Each Other about Divorce-Related Stressors and Its Impact on Their Ability to Cope Positively with the Divorce." *Journal of Divorce & Remarriage* 45:1–30.

Agliata, D., and S. Tantleff-Dunn. 2004. "The Impact of Media Exposure on Males' Body Image." *Journal of Social and Clinical Psychology* 23:7–22.

Ahlborg, T., L. Dahloof, and R. M. Hallberg. 2005. "Quality of the Intimate and Sexual Relationship in First-Time Parents Six Months after Delivery." *Journal of Sex Research* 42:167–74.

Ahlborg, T., L. Persson, and L. Hallberg. 2005. "Assessing the Quality of the Dyadic Relationship in First-Time Parents." *Journal of Family Nursing* 11:19–37.

Ahrons, C. R. 2007. "Family Ties after Divorce: Long-Term Implications for Children." *Family Process* 46:53–65.

Ahrons, C. R., and L. S. Wallisch. 1987. "The Relationship between Former Spouses." In D. Perlman and S. Duck, eds. *Intimate Relationships: Development, Dynamics, and Deterioration*, pp. 269–96. Beverly Hills, CA: Sage.

Ai, A. L., C. Peterson, T. N. Tice, S. F. Bolling, and H. G. Koenig. 2004. "Faith-Based and Secular Pathways to Hope and Optimism Subconstructs in Middle-Aged and Older Cardiac Patients." *Journal of Health Psychology* 9:435–52.

Alba, R. D., and R. M. Golden. 1986. "Patterns of Ethnic Marriage in the United States." *Social Forces* 65:202–23.

Aldous, J., and G. M. Mulligan. 2002. "Fathers' Child Care and Children's Behavior Problems." *Journal of Family Issues* 23:624–47.

Alessandri, S. M. 1992. "Effects of Maternal Work Status in Single-Parent Families on Children's Perception of Self and Family and School Achievement." *Journal of Experimental Child Psychology* 54:417–33.

Alford-Cooper, F. 1998. *For Keeps: Marriages That Last a Lifetime*, Armonk, NY: M. E. Sharpe.

Al-Johar, D. 2005. "Muslim Marriages in America." *Muslim World* 95:557–74.

Allen, A., and T. Thompson. 1984. "Agreement, Understanding, Realization, and Feeling Understood as Predictors of Communicative Satisfaction in Marital Dyads." *Journal of Marriage and the Family* 46:915–21.

Allen, D. W., and M. Gallagher. 2007. "Does Divorce Law Affect the Divorce Rate?" *iMAPP Research Brief* 1:1–29.

Allen, E. S., et al. 2001. "Decision-Making Power, Autonomy, and Communication in Remarried Spouses Compared with First-Married Spouses." *Family Relations* 50:326–34.

Aloni, M., and F. J. Bernleri. 2004. "Is Love Blind? The Effects of Experience and Infatuation on the Perception of Love." *Journal of Nonverbal Behavior* 28:287–95.

Alternatives to Marriage Project. 2002. "About the Alternatives to Marriage Project." Alternatives to Marriage Project Web site.

Altman, I., and J. Ginat. 1996. *Polygamous Families in Contemporary Societies.* Cambridge, UK: Cambridge University Press.

Altschuler, S. J. 2005. "Drug-Endangered Children Need a Collaborative Community Response." *Child Welfare* 84:171–90.

Amato, P. R. 1987. "Family Processes in One-Parent, Stepparent, and Intact Families: The Child's Point of View." *Journal of Marriage and the Family* 49:327–37.

Amato, P. R. 1991. "Parental Absence During Childhood and Depression in Later Life." *The Sociological Quarterly* 32:543–56.

Amato, P. R. 1994. "Father-Child Relations, Mother-Child Relations, and Offspring Psychological Well-Being in Early Adulthood." *Journal of Marriage and the Family* 56:1031–42.

Amato, P. R. 2001. "Children of Divorce in the 1990s." *Journal of Family Psychology* 15:355–70.

Amato, P. R. 2004. "Tension between Institutional and Individual Views of Marriage." *Journal of Marriage and Family* 66:959–65.

Amato, P. R., and T. D. Afifi. 2006. "Feeling Caught between Parents: Adult Children's Relations with Parents and Subjective Well-Being." *Journal of Marriage and Family* 68:222–35.

Amato, P. R., and A. Booth. 1991."Consequences of Parental Divorce and Marital Unhappiness for Adult Well-Being." *Social Forces* 69:895–914.

Amato, P. R., and A. Booth. 1995. "Changes in Gender Role Attitudes and Perceived Marital Quality." *American Sociological Review* 60:58–66.

Amato, P. R., and A. Booth. 2001. "The Legacy of Parents' Marital Discord." *Journal of Personality and Social Psychology* 81:627–38.

Amato, P. R., and J. Cheadle. 2005. "The Long Reach of Divorce: Divorce and Child Well-Being across Three Generations." *Journal of Marriage and the Family* 67:191–206.

Amato, P. R., and D. D. DeBoer. 2001. "The Transmission of Marital Instability across Generations." *Journal of Marriage and the Family* 63:1038–51.

Amato, P. R., and J. G. Gilbreth. 1999. "Nonresident Fathers and Children's Well-Being." *Journal of Marriage and the Family* 61:557–73.

Amato, P. R., and B. Hohmann-Marriott. 2007. "A Comparison of High- and Low-Distress Marriages That End in Divorce." *Journal of Marriage and Family* 69:621–38.

Amato, P. R., D. R. Johnson, A. Booth, and S. J. Rogers. 2003. "Continuity and Change in Marital Quality between 1980 and 2000." *Journal of Marriage and the Family* 65:1–22.

Amato, P. R., and B. Keith. 1991a. "Parental Divorce and Adult Well-Being: A Meta-Analysis." *Journal of Marriage and the Family* 53:43–58.

Amato, P. R., and B. Keith. 1991b. "Separation from a Parent during Childhood and Adult Socioeconomic Attainment." *Social Forces* 70:187–206.

Amato, P. R., L. S. Loomis, and A. Booth. 1995. "Parental Divorce, Marital Conflict, and Offspring Well-Being during Early Adulthood." *Social Forces* 73:895–915.

Amato, P. R., and D. Previti. 2003."People's Reasons for Divorcing: Gender, Social Class, the Life Course, and Adjustment." *Journal of Family Issues* 24:602–26.

Amato, P. R., and S. J. Rezac. 1994. "Contact with Nonresident Parents, Interparental Conflict, and Children's Behavior." *Journal of Family Issues* 15:191–207.

Amato, P. R., and S. J. Rogers. 1997. "A Longitudinal Study of Marital Problems and Subsequent Divorce." *Journal of Marriage and the Family* 59:612–24.

Ambert, A. M. 1982."Differences in Children's Behavior toward Custodial Mothers and Custodial Fathers." *Journal of Marriage and the Family* 44:73–86.

Anderberg, P., M. Lepp, A. Berglund, and K. Segesten. 2007. "Preserving Dignity in Caring for Older Adults." *Journal of Advanced Nursing* 59:635–43.

Anderson, D. A., and M. Hamilton. 2005. "Gender Role Stereotyping of Parents in Childrens' Picture Books." *Sex Roles* 52:145–51.

Anderson, E. R., S. M. Greene, L. Walker, C. A. Malerba, M. S. Forgatch, and D. S. DeGarmo. 2004. "Ready to Take a Chance Again: Transitions into Dating among Divorced Parents." *Journal of Divorce and Remarriage* 40:61–75.

Anderson, P. B., and J. S. Savage. 2005. "Social, Legal, and Institutional Context of Heterosexual Aggression by College Women." *Trauma, Violence & Abuse* 6:130–40.

Applewhite, M. 2005. "Understanding Infatuation and Devotion." *Human Development* 26:16–20.

Apter, T. 2001. *The Myth of Maturity.* New York: W. W. Norton.

Aquilino, W. S. 1994a. "Impact of Childhood Family Disruption on Young Adults' Relationships with Parents." *Journal of Marriage and the Family* 56:295–313.

Aquilino, W. S. 1994b. "Later Life Parental Divorce and Widowhood: Impact on Young Adults' Assessment of Parent-Child Relations." *Journal of Marriage and the Family* 56:908–22.

Aquilino, W. S. 1997. "From Adolescent to Young Adult: A Prospective Study of Parent-Child Relations during the Transition to Adulthood." *Journal of Marriage and the Family* 59:670–86.

Araujo, A. B., B. A. Mohr, and J. B. McKinlay. 2004. "Changes in Sexual Function in Middle-Aged and Older Men." *Journal of the American Geriatrics Society* 52:1502–09.

Arditti, J. A. 1992. "Differences between Fathers with Joint Custody and Noncustodial Fathers." *American Journal of Ortho-Psychiatry* 62:186–95.

Arias, I., C. M. Lyons, and A. E. Street. 1997. "Individual and Marital Consequences of Victimization." *Journal of Family Violence* 12:193–210.

Armistead, L., M. Wierson, and R. Forehand. 1990. "Parent Work and Early Adolescent Development." *Journal of Early Adolescence* 10:260–78.

Arnaut, G. L. 2000. "A Qualitative Analysis of Stepfamilies." *Journal of Divorce and Remarriage* 33:11–28.

Arnett, J. J. 2000. "Emerging Adulthood." *American Psychologist* 55:469–80.

Arnett, J. J. 2004. "Emerging Adulthood." *Chronicle of Higher Education,* November 12.

Aronson, S. R., and A. C. Huston. 2004. "The Mother-Infant Relationship in Single, Cohabiting, and Married Families." *Journal of Family Psychology* 18:5–18.

Arriaga, X. B., and V. A. Foshee. 2004. "Adolescent Dating Violence." *Journal of Interpersonal Violence* 19:162–80.

Arriaga, X. B., J. T. Reed, W. Goodfriend, and C. R. Agnew. 2006. "Relationship Perceptions and Persistence." *Journal of Personality and Social Psychology* 91:1045–65.

Artis, J. E. 2007. "Maternal Cohabitation and Child Well-Being among Kindergarten Children." *Journal of Marriage and Family* 69:222–36.

Asakawa, K. 2001. "Family Socialization Practices and Their Effects on the Internalization of Educational Values for Asian and White American Adolescents."*Applied Developmental Science* 5:184–94.

Atkinson, M. P., T. N. Greenstein, and M. M. Lang. 2005. "For Women, Breadwinning Can Be Dangerous." *Journal of Marriage and Family* 67:1137–48.

Avellar, S., and P. J. Smock. 2005. "The Economic Consequences of the Dissolution of Cohabiting Unions." *Journal of Marriage and Family* 67:315–27.

Aylor, B., and M. Dainton. 2004. "Biological Sex and Psychological Gender as Predictors of Routine and Strategic Relational Maintenance." *Sex Roles* 50:689–97.

Bachu, A., and M. O'Connell. 2001. "Fertility of American Women: June 2000." *Current Population Reports.* Washington, DC: Government Printing Office.

Bagarozzi, D. A. 1990. "Marital Power Discrepancies and Symptom Development in Spouses: An Empirical Investigation." *American Journal of Family Therapy* 18:51–64.

Bailey, J. M., D. Bobrow, M. Wolfe, and S. Mikach. 1995. "Sexual Orientation of Adult Sons of Gay Fathers." *Developmental Psychology* 31:124–29.

Bailey, W. C., C. Hendrick, and S. S. Hendrick. 1987. "Relation of Sex and Gender Role to Love, Sexual Attitudes, and Self-Esteem." *Sex Roles* 16:637–48.

Baillargeon, R. H., et al. 2007. "Gender Differences in Physical Aggression." *Developmental Psychology* 43:13–26.

Baker, A. K., K. J. Barthelemy, and L. A. Kurdek. 1993. "The Relation between Fifth and Sixth Graders' Peer-Rated Classroom Social Status and Their Perceptions of Family and Neighborhood Factors." *Journal of Applied Developmental Psychology* 14:547–56.

Bales, A. 1929. "A Course in Home Economics for College Men." *Journal of Home Economics* 21:427–28.

Ball, F. L., P. Cowan, and C. P. Cowan. 1995. "Who's Got the Power? Gender Differences in Partners' Perceptions of Influence during Marital Problem-Solving Discussions." *Family Process* 34:303–21.

Bancroft, A., S. Wilson, S. Cunningham-Burley, K. Backett-Milburn, and H. Masters. 2004. *Parental Drug and Alcohol Misuse.* Edinburgh, Scotland: Joseph Rowntree Foundation.

Bancroft, J., L. Carnes, E. Janssen, D. Goodrich, and J. S. Long. 2005. "Erectile and Ejaculatory Problems in Gay and Heterosexual Men." *Archives of Sexual Behavior* 34:285–97.

Banse, R. 2004. "Adult Attachment and Marital Satisfaction." *Journal of Social and Personal Relationships* 21:273–82.

Barber, B. K. 1994. "Cultural, Family, and Personal Contexts of Parent-Adolescent Conflict." *Journal of Marriage and the Family* 56:375–86.

Barber, B. K., B. A. Chadwick, and R. Oerter. 1992."Parental Behaviors and Adolescent Self-Esteem in the United States and Germany." *Journal of Marriage and the Family* 54:128–41.

Barber, C. E., B. L. Fisher, and K. Pasley. 1990. "Family Care of Alzheimer's Disease Patients: Predictors of Subjective and Objective Burden." *Family Perspective* 24:289–309.

Barber, J. S., and W. G. Axinn. 1998. "Gender Role Attitudes and Marriage among Young Women." *Sociological Quarterly* 39:11–31.

Barna Group. 2004. "The Barna Group Survey." The Barna Group Web site.

Barnett, R. C., R. T. Brennan, and N. L. Marshall. 1994. "Gender and the Relationship between Parent Role Quality and Psychological Distress." *Journal of Family Issues* 15:229–52.

Barnett, R. C., N. L. Marshall, S. W. Raudenbush, and R. T. Brennan. 1993. "Gender and the Relationship between Job Experiences and Psychological Distress: A Study of Dual-Earner Couples." *Journal of Personality and Social Psychology* 64:794–806.

Barnett, R. C., and C. Rivers. 1996. *She Works/He Works: How Two-Income Families Are Happier, Healthier, and Better-Off.* San Francisco, CA: Harper San Francisco.

Barret, R. L., and B. E. Robinson. 1990. *Gay Fathers.* Lexington, MA: D. C. Heath.

Barrett, A. E., and W. H. Raskin. 2002. "Trajectories of Gender Role Orientations in Adolescence and Early Childhood." *Journal of Health and Social Behavior* 43:451–68.

Barrett, A. E. 1999. "Social Support and Life Satisfaction among the Never Married." *Research on Aging* 21:46–72.

Barrett, A. E., and R. J. Turner. 2005. "Family Structure and Mental Health." *Journal of Health and Social Behavior* 46:156–69.

Barton, P. E. 2006. "The Dropout Problem." *Educational Leadership* 63:14–18.

Bartsch, R. A., T. Burnett, T. R. Diller, and E. Rankin-Williams. 2000. "Gender Representation in Television Commercials." *Sex Roles* 43:735–43.

Basile, K. C. 2002. "Prevalence of Wife Rape and Other Intimate Partner Sexual Coercion in a Nationally Representative Sample of Women." *Violence and Victims* 5:511–24.

Bassuk, E., R. Dawson, and N. Huntington. 2006. "Intimate Partner Violence in Extremely Poor Women." *Journal of Family Violence* 21:387–99.

Bates, S. 1999. "Nursing Home Horrors." *AARP Bulletin* (September):9–11.

Batson, C. D., Z. Qian, and D. T. Lichter. 2006. "Interracial and Intraracial Patterns of Mate Selection among America's Diverse Black Populations." *Journal of Marriage and Family* 68:658–72.

Baum, C. L. 2004. "The Long-Term Effects of Early and Recent Maternal Employment on a Child's Academic Achievement." *Journal of Family Issues* 25:29–60.

Baum, N. 2003. "The Male Way of Mourning Divorce." *Clinical Social Work Journal* 31:37–50.

Baumbusch, J. L. 2004. "Unclaimed Treasures: Older Women's Reflections on Lifelong Singlehood." *Journal of Women and Aging* 16:105–21.

Baumeister, R. F., K. R. Catanese, and K. D. Vohs. 2001. "Is There a Gender Difference in Strength of Sex Drive?" *Personality and Social Psychology Review* 5:242–73.

Baumrind, D. 1967. "Child Care Practices Anteceding Three Patterns of Preschool Behavior." *Genetic Psychology Monographs* 75:43–88.

Bauserman, R. 2002. "Child Adjustment in Joint-Custody versus Sole-Custody Arrangements." *Journal of Family Psychology* 16:91–102.

Baxter, J. 2005. "To Marry or Not to Marry." *Journal of Family Issues* 26:300–21.

Beach, S. R. H., and A. Tesser. 1993. "Decision Making Power and Marital Satisfaction: A Self-Evaluation Maintenance Perspective." *Journal of Social and Clinical Psychology* 12:471–94.

Beaudry, M., J. Boisvert, M. Simard, C. Parent, and M. Blais. 2004. "Communication a Key to Meeting the Challenges of Stepfamilies." *Journal of Divorce and Remarriage* 42:85–104.

Beck, Aaron T. 1988. *Love Is Never Enough.* New York: Harper & Row.

Beer, W. 1988. "New Family Ties: How Well Are We Coping?" *Public Opinion,* March/April, pp. 14–15, 57.

Beesley, D., and C. Stoltenberg. 2002. "Control, Attachment Style, and Relationship Satisfaction among Adult Children of Alcoholics." *Journal of Mental Health Counseling* 24:281–98.

Belavich, T. G., and K. I. Pargament. 2002. "The Role of Attachment in Predicting Spiritual Coping with a Loved One in Surgery." *Journal of Adult Development* 9:13–29.

Bellah, R. N., R. Madsen, W. M. Sullivan, A. Swidler, and S. M. Tipton. 1985. *Habits of the Heart: Individualism and Commitment in American Life.* New York: Harper & Row.

Belsky, J. 2002. "Developmental Risks (Still) Associated with Early Child Care." *Journal of Child Psychology and Psychiatry* 42:845–59.

Belsky, J., et al. 2007. "Are There Long-Term Effects of Early Child Care?" *Child Development* 78:681–701.

Belsky, J., and J. Kelly. 1994. *The Transition to Parenthood.* New York: Delacorte Press.

Belsky, J., and M. Rovine. 1990. "Patterns of Marital Change across the Transition to Parenthood: Pregnancy to Three Years Postpartum." *Journal of Marriage and the Family* 52:5–19.

Bem, S. L. 1974. "The Measurement of Psychological Androgyny." *Journal of Consulting and Clinical Psychology* 42:155–62.

Bender, W. N. 1994. "Joint Custody: The Option of Choice." *Journal of Divorce and Remarriage* 21:115–31.

Benson, M. L., and G. L. Fox. 2004. "When Violence Hits Home." National Institute of Justice Research Brief, NIJ Web site.

Bereczkei, T. 1996. "Mate Choice, Marital Success, and Reproduction in a Modern Society." *Ethology and Sociobiology* 17:17–35.

Berg, A. I., L. B. Hassing, G. E. McClearn, and B. Johansson. 2006. "What Matters for Life Satisfaction in the Oldest-Old?" *Aging and Mental Health* 10:257–64.

Berge, J. M., J. M. Patterson, and M. Rueter. 2006. "Marital Satisfaction and Mental Health of Couples with Children with Chronic Health Conditions." *Families, Systems & Health* 24:267–85.

Berger, L. M. 2005. "Income, Family Characteristics, and Physical Violence toward Children." *Child Abuse and Neglect* 29:107–33.

Bernard, J. 1972. *The Future of Marriage.* New York: World.

Berry, D. S., and K. M. Miller. 2001. "When Boy Meets Girl: Attractiveness and the Five-Factor Model in Opposite-Sex Interactions." *Journal of Research in Personality* 35:62–77.

Berry, D. 2004. "The Relationship between Depression and Emerging Adulthood." *Advances in Nursing Science* 27:53–69.

Berscheid, E., and E. Walster. 1974. "A Little Bit about Love." In T. L. Huston, ed., *Foundations of Interpersonal Attraction,* pp. 355–81. New York: Academic Press.

Berthiaume, M., H. David, J. F. Saucier, and F. Borgeat. 1996. "Correlates of Gender Role Orientation during Pregnancy and the Postpartum. *Sex Roles* 35:781–800.

Bessenoff, G. R., and R. E. Del Priore. 2007. "Women, Weight, and Age: Social Comparison to Magazine Images across the Lifespan." *Sex Roles* 56:215–22.

Betchen, S. J. 2006. "Husbands Who Use Sexual Dissatisfaction to Balance the Scales of Power in Their Dual-Career Marriages." *Journal of Family Psychotherapy* 17:19–35.

Bianchi, S. M., M. A. Milkie, L. C. Sayer, and J. P. Robinson. 2000. "Is Anyone Doing the Housework? Trends in the Gender Division of Household Labor." *Social Forces* 79:191–228.

Bianchi, S. M., J. P. Robinson, and M. A. Milkie. 2006. *Changing Rhythms of American Family Life.* New York: Russell Sage Foundation.

Bianchi, S. M., L. Subaiya, and J. R. Kahn. 1999. "The Gender Gap in the Economic Well-Being of Nonresident Fathers and Custodial Mothers." *Demography* 36:195–203.

Biddlecom, A., and S. Martin. 2006. "Childless in America." *Contexts* 5:54–5.

Bienvenu, M. J., Sr. 1978. *A Counselor's Guide to Accompany a Marital Communications Inventory.* Saluda, NC: Family Life.

Bigbee, J. L. 1992. "Family Stress, Hardiness, and Illness: A Pilot Study." *Family Relations* 41:212–17.

Bigner, J. J., and R. B. Jacobsen. 1989. "Parenting Behaviors of Homosexual and Heterosexual Fathers." *Journal of Homosexuality* 18:173–86.

Biller, H. B. 1993. *Fathers and Families: Paternal Factors in Child Development.* Westport, CT: Auburn House.

Billingham, R. E., P. B. Perera, and N. A. Ehlers. 2005. "College Women's Rankings of the Most Undesirable Marriage and Family Forms." *College Student Journal* 39:749–53.

Binstock, G., and A. Thornton. 2003. "Separations, Reconciliations, and Living Apart in Cohabiting and Marital Unions." *Journal of Marriage and the Family* 65:432–43.

Bird, C. E. 1997. "Gender Differences in the Social and Economic Burdens of Parenting and Psychological Distress." *Journal of Marriage and the Family* 59:809–23.

Bird, C. E. 1999. "Gender, Household Labor, and Psychological Distress." *Journal of Health and Social Behavior* 40:32–45.

Birditt, K. A., and K. L. Fingerman. 2003. "Age and Gender Differences in Adults' Descriptions of Emotional Reactions to Interpersonal Problems." *Journal of Gerontology Series B* 58:237–45.

Birnbaum, G. E., O. Cohen, and V. Wertheimer. 2007. "Is It All About Intimacy? Age, Menopausal Status, and Women's Sexuality." *Personal Relationships* 24:167–85.

Bischoping, K. 1993. "Gender Differences in Conversation Topics, 1922–1990." *Sex Roles* 28:1–18.

Bitter, R. G. 1986. "Late Marriage and Marital Instability: The Effects of Heterogeneity and Inflexibility." *Journal of Marriage and the Family* 48:631–40.

Bittman, M., P. England, L. Sayer, N. Folbre, and G. Matheson. 2003. "When Does Gender Trump Money? Bargaining and Time in Household Work." *American Journal of Sociology* 109:186–214.

Black, K. A., and E. D. Schutte. 2006. "Recollections of Being Loved." *Journal of Family Issues* 27:1459–80.

Black, L. E., M. M. Eastwood, D. H. Sprenkle, and E. Smith. 1991. "An Exploratory Analysis of the Construct of Leavers versus Left as It Relates to Levinger's Social Exchange Theory of Attractions, Barriers, and Alternative Attractions." *Journal of Divorce and Remarriage* 15:127–39.

Black, M. M., H. Dubowitz, and R. H. Starr Jr. 1999. "African American Fathers in Low Income, Urban Families." *Child Development* 70:967–79.

Blair, S. L. 1993. "Employment, Family, and Perceptions of Marital Quality among Husbands and Wives." *Journal of Family Issues* 14:189–212.

Blair, S. L., and Z. Qian. 1998. "Family and Asian Students' Educational Performance." *Journal of Family Issues* 19:355–74.

Blake, B. J., and L. Bentov. 2001. "Geographical Mapping of Unmarried Teen Births and Selected Sociodemographic Variables." *Public Health Nursing* 18:33–39.

Blakemore, J. E. O., and R. E. Centers. 2005. "Characteristics of Boys' and Girls' Toys." *Sex Roles* 53:619–33.

Blakemore, J. E. O., C. A. Lawton, and L. R. Vartanian. 2005. "I Can't Wait to Get Married: Gender Differences in the Drive to Marry." *Sex Roles* 53:327–35.

Blalik, C. 2007. "Weddings Are Not the Budget Drains Some Surveys Suggest." *Wall Street Journal,* August 24.

Blanchflower, D. G., and A. J. Oswald. 2004. "Money, Sex, and Happiness: An Empirical Study." *NBER Working Paper No. w10499.* National Bureau of Economic Research Web site.

Blood, R. O., Jr., and D. M. Wolfe. 1960. *Husbands and Wives.* New York: Free Press.

Blumberg, S. J., N. Halfon, and L. M. Olson. 2004. "The National Survey of Early Childhood Health." *Pediatrics* 113:1899–906.

Bodenmann, G., et al. 2007. "The Role of Stress in Divorce." *Journal of Social and Personal Relationships* 24:707–28.

Bohannan, P. 1970. *Divorce and After.* New York: Doubleday.

Bohannan, P. 1985. *All the Happy Families: Exploring the Varieties of Family Life.* New York: McGraw-Hill.

Bokker, P., R. Farley, and W. Bailey. 2005. "The Relationship between Custodial Status and Emotional Well-Being among Recently Divorced Fathers." *Journal of Divorce and Remarriage* 44:83–98.

Bolzan, N., F. Gale, and M. Dudley. 2004. "Time to Father." *Social Work and Health Care* 39:67–88.

Bonanno, G. A., et al. 2002. "Resilience to Loss and Chronic Grief." *Journal of Personality and Social Psychology* 83:1150–64.

Bond, J. T. 2002. *The National Study of the Changing Workforce.* Families and Work Institute Web site.

Boon, S. D., and M. J. Brussoni. 1996. "Young Adults' Relationships with Their 'Closest' Grandparents: Examining Emotional Closeness." *Journal of Social Behavior and Personality* 11:439–58.

Booth, A., and P. R. Amato. 1994. "Parental Marital Quality, Parental Divorce, and Relations with Parents." *Journal of Marriage and the Family* 56:21–34.

Booth, A., and P. R. Amato. 2001. "Parental Predivorce Relations and Offspring Postdivorce Well-Being." *Journal of Marriage and the Family* 63:197–212.

Booth, A., and J. N. Edwards. 1992. "Starting Over: Why Remarriages Are More Unstable." *Journal of Family Issues* 13:179–94.

Booth, A., J. N. Edwards, and D. R. Johnson. 1991. "Social Integration and Divorce." *Social Forces* 70:207–24.

Booth, C. L., et al. 2002. "Child-Care Usage and Mother-Infant 'Quality Time.'" *Journal of Marriage and the Family* 64:16–26.

Booth, R., and M. Jung. 1998. *Romancing the Net: A "Tell-All" Guide to Love Online.* Rocklin, CA: Prima.

Borders, L. D., L. K. Black, and B. K. Pasley. 1998. "Are Adopted Children and Their Parents at Greater Risk for Negative Outcomes?" *Family Relations* 47:237–41.

Borders, L. D., J. M. Penny, and F. Portnoy. 2000. "Adult Adoptees and Their Friends: Current Functioning and Psychosocial Well-Being." *Family Relations* 49:407–18.

Boss, P. 2001. *Family Stress Management.* 2nd ed. Beverly Hills, CA: Sage.

Bosworth, H. B., et al. 2000. "The Relationship of Social Support, Social Networks and Negative Events with Depression in Patients with Coronary Artery Disease." *Aging and Mental Health* 4:253–58.

Botkin, D. R., and M. O. Weeks. 2000. "Changing Marriage Role Expectations: 1961–1996." *Sex Roles* 42:933–42.

Bouchard, G. 2006. "Cohabitation versus Marriage." *Journal of Divorce & Remarriage* 46:107–17.

Bove, C. F., and J. Sobal. 2006. "Foodwork in Newly Married Couples." *Food, Culture and Society* 9:69–89.

Bowen, M. 1978. *Family Therapy in Clinical Practice.* New York: Jason Aronson.

Bowling, A., and Z. Gabriel. 2007. "Lay Theories of Quality of Life in Older Age." *Ageing & Society* 27:827–48.

Bowman, K. 2001. "Poll-Pourri: Opinions on Romance." *Women's Quarterly,* Winter, pp. 15–16.

Boyer, D., and D. Fine. 1992. "Sexual Abuse as a Factor in Adolescent Pregnancy and Child Maltreatment." *Family Planning Perspectives* 24:4–11.

Boyle, J. 1995. "Survey Indicates Most Women Want to Work but to Work Less." *San Diego Union-Tribune,* May 13.

Bozett, F. W. 1989. "Gay Fathers: A Review of the Literature." *Journal of Homosexuality* 18:137–62.

Brady, S. S., and B. L. Halpern-Feisher. 2007. "Adolescents' Reported Consequences of Having Oral Sex versus Vaginal Sex." *Pediatrics* 119:229–36.

Bramlett, M. D., and S. J. Blumberg. 2007. "Family Structure and Children's Physical and Mental Health." *Health Affairs* 26:549–58.

Bramlett, M. D., and W. D. Mosher. 2002. *Cohabitation, Marriage, Divorce, and Remarriage in the United States.* National Center for Health Statistics Web site.

Brannon, R. 1976. "The Male Sex Role: Our Culture's Blueprint for Manhood, What It's Done for Us Lately." In D. David and R. Brannon, eds., *The Forty-Nine Percent Majority: The Male Sex Role,* pp. 1–45. Reading, MA: Addison-Wesley.

Brand, R., C. Markey, A. Mills, and S. Hodges. 2007. "Sex Differences in Self-Reported Infidelity and Its Correlates." *Sex Roles* 57:101–09.

Brand, S., M. Luethi, A. von Planta, M. Hatzinger, and E. Holsboer-Trachsler. 2007. "Romantic Love, Hypomania, and Sleep Pattern in Adolescents." *Journal of Adolescent Health* 41:69–76.

Brandt, S. 2004. "Religious Homogamy and Marital Satisfaction." *Sociological Viewpoints* 20:11–20.

Brantley, A., D. Knox, and M. E. Zusman. 2002. "When and Why Gender Differences in Saying 'I Love You' among College Students." *College Student Journal* 36:614–16.

Bray, J., and J. Kelly. 1998. *Stepfamilies.* New York: Broadway Books.

Brayfield, A. 1995. "Juggling Jobs and Kids: The Impact of Employment Schedules on Fathers' Caring for Children." *Journal of Marriage and the Family* 57:321–32.

Brehm, J. W. 1966. *A Theory of Psychological Reactance.* New York: Academic Press.

Brehony, K. A. 1996. *Awakening at Midlife.* New York: Riverhead Books.

Breivik, K., and D. Olweus. 2005. "Adolescent's Adjustment in Four Post-Divorce Family Structures." *Journal of Divorce & Remarriage* 44:99–124.

Brennan, E. M., et al. 2007. "Employed Parents of Children with Mental Health Disorders." *Families in Society* 88:115–23.

Brescoll, V. L., and E. L. Uhlmann. 2005. "Attitudes toward Traditional and Nontraditional Parents." *Psychology of Women Quarterly* 29:436–45.

Brewer, R. 1997. "Living on Both Sides of the Fence: Gay Male Couples with Children." *Progress: Family Systems Research and Therapy* 6:137–50.

Brillinger, M. E. 1985. "Marital Satisfaction and Planned Change." *Family Perspective* 19:35–43.

Brimhall, A. S., and M. H. Butler. 2007. "Intrinsic vs. Extrinsic Religious Motivation and the Marital Relationship." *American Journal of Family Therapy* 35:235–49.

Broderick, C. B. 1993. *Understanding Family Process: Basics of Family Systems Theory.* Newbury Park, CA: Sage.

Brodzinsky, D. M., D. E. Schechter, A. M. Braff, and L. M. Singer. 1984. "Psychological and Academic Adjustment in Adopted Children." *Journal of Consulting and Clinical Psychology* 52:582–90.

Bromberger, J. T., and K. A. Matthews. 1994. "Employment Status and Depressive Symptoms in Middle-Aged Women." *American Journal of Public Health* 84:202–6.

Bronner, G., C. Peretz, and M. Ehrenfeld. 2003. "Sexual Harassment of Nurses and Nursing Students." *Journal of Advanced Nursing* 42:637–44.

Bronstein, P., et al. 1996. "Family and Parenting Behaviors Predicting Middle School Adjustment." *Family Relations* 45:415–26.

Bronte-Tinkew, J., K. A. Moore, and J. Carrano. 2006. "The Father-Child Relationship, Parenting Styles, and Adolescent Risk Behaviors in Intact Families." *Journal of Family Issues* 27:850–81.

Bronte-Tinkew, J., K. A. Moore, G. Matthews, and J. Carrano. 2007. "Symptoms of Major Depression in a Sample of Fathers of Infants." *Journal of Family Issues* 28:61–99.

Brookoff, D., K. O'Brien, C. S. Cook, and T. D. Thompson. 1997. "Characteristics of Participants in Domestic Violence." *Journal of the American Medical Association* 277:1369–73.

Brown, P. M. 1995. *The Death of Intimacy: Barriers to Meaningful Interpersonal Relationships.* New York: Haworth.

Brown, S. L. 2000a. "Fertility Following Marital Dissolution." *Journal of Family Issues* 21:501–24.

Brown, S. L. 2000b. "The Effect of Union Type on Psychological Well-Being." *Journal of Health and Social Behavior* 41:241–55.

Brown, S. L. 2004. "Family Structure and Child Well-Being: The Significance of Parental Cohabitation." *Journal of Marriage and the Family* 66:351–67.

Brown, S. L. 2005. "How Cohabitation Is Reshaping American Families." *Contexts* 4:33–37.

Brown, S. L. 2006. "Family Structure Transitions and Adolescent Well-Being." *Demography* 43:447–61.

Brown, S. L., and A. Booth. 1996. "Cohabitation versus Marriage: A Comparison of Relationship Quality." *Journal of Marriage and the Family* 58:668–78.

Brown, S. L., G. R. Lee, and J. R. Bulanda. 2006. "Cohabitation among Older Adults." *Journals of Gerontology Series B* 61B:71–79.

Brown, S. L., L. A. Sanchez, S. L. Nock, and J. D. Wright. 2006. "Links between Premarital Cohabitation and Subsequent Marital Quality, Stability, and Divorce." *Social Science Research* 35:454–70.

Browning, J. R., E. Hatfield, D. Kessler, and T. Levine. 2000. "Sexual Motives, Gender, and Sexual Behavior." *Archives of Sexual Behavior* 29:135–54.

Bryant, A. N. 2003. "Changes in Attitudes toward Women's Roles." *Sex Roles* 48:131–42.

Bryant, C. M., R. D. Conger, and J. M. Meehan. 2001. "The Influence of in-Laws on Change in Marital Success." *Journal of Marriage and the Family* 63:614–26.

Buchanan, C. M., E. Maccoby, and S. M. Dornbusch. 1996. *Adolescents after Divorce*. Cambridge, MA: Harvard University Press.

Buckle, L., G. G. Gallup Jr., and Z. A. Rodd. 1996. "Marriage as a Reproductive Contract." *Ethology and Sociobiology* 17:363–77.

Buddie, A. M., and M. Testa. 2005. "Rates and Predictors of Sexual Aggression among Students and Nonstudents." *Journal of Interpersonal Violence* 20:713–24.

Buehler, C., and J. M. Gerard. 2002. "Marital Conflict, Ineffective Parenting, and Children's and Adolescents' Maladjustment." *Journal of Marriage and the Family* 64:78–92.

Bulanda, J. R., and S. L. Brown. 2007. "Race-Ethnic Differences in Marital Quality and Divorce." *Social Science Research* 36:945–67.

Bulanda, R. E. 2004. "Paternal Involvement with Children." *Journal of Marriage and the Family* 66:40–45.

Bulcroft, R. A., and K. A. Bulcroft. 1993. "Race Differences in Attitudinal and Motivational Factors in the Decision to Marry." *Journal of Marriage and the Family* 55:338–55.

Bullers, S. 1999. "Selection Effects in the Relationship between Women's Work/Family Status and Perceived Control." *Family Relations* 48:181–88.

Bunker, B. B., J. M. Zubek, V. J. Vanderslice, and R. W. Rice. 1992. "Quality of Life in Dual-Career Families: Commuting versus Single-Residence Couples." *Journal of Marriage and the Family* 54:399–407.

Burch, R. L., and G. G. Gallup Jr. 2004. "Pregnancy as a Stimulus for Domestic Violence." *Journal of Family Violence* 19:243–47.

Burchinal, M. R., et al. 2000. "Cognition and Language: The Relation of Child Care to Cognitive and Language Development." *Monographs of the Society for Research in Child Development* 71:960–80.

Burden, D. S. 1986. "Single Parents and the Work Setting: The Impact of Multiple Job and Homelife Responsibilities." *Family Relations* 35:37–43.

Burdette, A. M., C. G. Ellison, D. E. Sherkat, and K. A. Gore. 2007. "Are There Religious Variations in Marital Infidelity?" *Journal of Family Issues* 28:1553–81.

Bureau of Justice Statistics. 2007. "Intimate Partner Violence in the U. S." Bureau of Justice Statistics Web site.

Bureau of Labor Statistics. 2007a. *American Time Use Survey*. Bureau of Labor Statistics Web site.

Bureau of Labor Statistics. 2007b. "Employment Characteristics of Families in 2006." *News Release*, Bureau of Labor Statistics Web site.

Burford, H. C., L. A. Foley, P. G. Rollins, and K. S. Rosario. 1996. "Gender Differences in Preschoolers' Sharing Behavior." *Journal of Social Behavior and Personality* 11:17–25.

Burleson, M. H., W. R. Trevathan, and M. Todd. 2007. "In the Mood for Love or Vice Versa?" *Archives of Sexual Behavior* 36:357–68.

Burley-Allen, M. 1995. *Listening: The Forgotten Skill*. 2nd ed. New York: John Wiley & Sons.

Burnett, P. C., and W. J. Demnar. 1996. "The Relationship between Closeness to Significant Others and Self-Esteem." *Journal of Family Studies* 2:121–29.

Buss, D. M. 2000. *The Dangerous Passion: Why Jealousy Is as Necessary as Love and Sex*. New York: Free Press.

Buss, D. M., T. K. Shackelford, L. A. Kirkpatrick, and R. J. Larsen. 2001. "A Half Century of Mate Preferences." *Journal of Marriage and the Family* 63:491–503.

Buunk, B., and R. G. Bringle. 1987. "Jealousy in Love Relationships." In D. Perlman and S. Duck, eds., *Intimate Relationships: Development, Dynamics, and Deterioration*, pp. 123–47. Beverly Hills, CA: Sage.

Buunk, B., and W. Mutsaers. 1999. "Equity Perceptions and Marital Satisfaction in Former and Current Marriages." *Journal of Social and Personal Relationships* 16:123–32.

Caetano, R., C. A. Field, S. Ramisetty-Mikler, and C. McGrath. 2005. "The 5-Year Course of Intimate Partner Violence Among White, Black, and Hispanic Couples in the United States." *Journal of Interpersonal Violence* 20:1039–57.

Caetano, R., S. Nelson, and C. Cunradi. 2001. "Intimate Partner Violence, Dependence Symptoms and Social Consequences from Drinking among White, Black, and Hispanic Couples in the United States." *American Journal on Addictions* 10:60–69.

Cairney, J., M. H. Boyle, E. L. Lipman, and Y. Racine. 2004. "Single Mothers and the Use of Professionals for Mental Health Care Reasons." *Social Science & Medicine* 59:2535–47.

Callan, V. J. 1986. "Single Women, Voluntary Childlessness and Perceptions about Life and Marriage." *Journal of Biosocial Science* 18:479–87.

Calvert, S. L., et al. 2005. "Gender Differences in Preadolescent Children's Online Interactions." *Journal of Applied Developmental Psychology* 24:627–44.

Campbell, J., C. Garcia-Moreno, and P. Sharps. 2004. "Abuse during Pregnancy in Industrialized and Developing Countries." *Violence against Women* 10:770–89.

Canavan, M. M., W. J. Meyer III, and D. C. Higgs. 1992. "The Female Experience of Sibling Incest." *Journal of Marital and Family Therapy* 18:129–42.

Cano, A., K. D. O'Leary, and W. Heinz. 2004. "Short-Term Consequences of Severe Marital Stressors." *Journal of Social and Personal Relationships* 21:419–30.

Caplow, T., H. M. Bahr, B. A. Chadwick, R. Hill, and M. H. Williamson. 1982. *Middletown Families: Fifty Years of Change and Continuity.* Minneapolis: University of Minnesota Press.

Cardoza, D. 1991. "College Attendance and Persistence among Hispanic Women: An Examination of Some Contributing Factors." *Sex Roles* 24:133–47.

Carli, L. L. 1999. "Gender, Interpersonal Power, and Social Influence." *Journal of Social Issues* 55:81–99.

Carlson, M. J. 2006. "Family Structure, Father Involvement, and Adolescent Behavioral Outcomes." *Journal of Marriage and Family* 68:137–54.

Carr, D. 2004. "The Desire to Date and Remarry among Older Widows and Widowers." *Journal of Marriage and Family* 66:1051–68.

Carr, D. 2007. "Body Work." *Contexts* 6:58.

Carr, P. L., K. C. Gareis, and R. C. Barnett. 2003. "Characteristics and Outcomes for Women Physicians Who Work Reduced Hours." *Journal of Women's Health* 12:399–410.

Carroll, J. 2007. "Americans: 2.5 Children Is 'Ideal' Family Size." Gallup Poll Web site.

Carroll, L., and R. Anderson. 2002. "Body Piercing, Tattooing, Self-Esteem, and Body Investment in Adolescent Girls." *Adolescence* 37:627–37.

Carter, E. A., and M. McGoldrick. 1989. *The Changing Family Life Cycle: A Framework for Family Therapy.* 2nd ed. Boston: Allyn and Bacon.

Cartwright, C. 2005. "Young Adults' Perceptions of Impact of Parental Divorce." *Journal of Divorce and Remarriage* 44:125–43.

Casper, L. 1997. "My Daddy Takes Care of Me! Fathers as Care Providers." *Current Population Reports*, P70–90, September.

Caspi, A., B. R. E. Wright, T. E. Moffitt, and P. A. Silva. 1998. "Early Failure in the Labor Market: Childhood and Adolescent Predictors of Unemployment in the Transition to Adulthood." *American Sociological Review* 63:424–51.

Cassidy, M. L., and B. O. Warren. 1996. "Family Employment Status and Gender Role Attitudes." *Gender & Society* 10:312–29.

Cast, A. D., and A. M. Cantwell. 2007. "Identity Change in Newly Married Couples." *Social Psychology Quarterly* 70:172–85.

Castaneda, D. M. 1993. "The Meaning of Romantic Love among Mexican-Americans." *Journal of Social Behavior and Personality* 8:257–72.

Catalano, S. 2006. *Intimate Partner Violence in the United States.* Bureau of Justice Statistics Web site.

Catanzarite, L., and V. Ortiz. 2002. "Too Few Good Men? Available Partners and Single Motherhood among Latinas, African Americans, and Whites." *Hispanic Journal of Behavioral Sciences* 24:278–95.

Cate, R., and A. I. Sugawara. 1986. "Sex Role Orientation and Dimensions of Self-Esteem among Middle Adolescents." *Sex Roles* 15:145–58.

Caughlin, J. P., and R. S. Malis. 2004. "Demand/Withdraw Communication between Parents and Adolescents." *Journal of Social and Personal Relationships* 21:125–48.

Cavalcanti, H. B., and D. Schleef. 2001. "The Melting Pot Revisited: Hispanic Density and Economic Achievement in American Metropolitan Regions." *Hispanic Journal of Behavioral Sciences* 23:115–22.

Cavanagh, S. E., and A. C. Huston. 2006. "Family Instability and Children's Early Problem Behavior." *Social Forces* 85:551–81.

Ceballo, R. 2004. "From Barrios to Yale: The Role of Parenting Strategies in Latino Families." *Hispanic Journal of Behavioral Sciences* 26:171–86.

Ceballo, R., J. E. Lansford, A. Abbey, and A. J. Stewart. 2004. "Gaining a Child: Comparing the Experiences of Biological Parents, Adoptive Parents, and Stepparents." *Family Relations* 53:38–48.

Centers for Disease Control. 2001. "Congenital Syphilis—United States, 2000." *Morbidity and Mortality Weekly Report* 573–77.

Centers for Disease Control. 2007. "Cases of HIV Infection and AIDS in the United States and Dependent Areas, 2005." Centers for Disease Control Web site.

Chafetz, J. S. 1974. *Masculine/Feminine or Human?* Itasca, IL: F. E. Peacock.

Chang, E., et al. 2006. "What Do They Want in Life? The Life Goals of a Multi-Ethnic, Multi-Generational Sample of High School Seniors." *Journal of Youth and Adolescence* 35:302–13.

Charles, P., and K. M. Perreira. 2007. "Intimate Partner Violence during Pregnancy and 1-Year Post-Partum." *Journal of Family Violence* 22:609–19.

Charles, R. 2001. "Is There Any Empirical Support for Bowen's Concepts of Differentiation of Self?" *American Journal of Family Therapy* 29:279–92.

Charny, I. W., and S. Parnass. 1995. "The Impact of Extramarital Relationships on the Continuation of Marriages." *Journal of Sex and Marital Therapy* 21:100–15.

Chassin, L., A. Zeiss, K. Cooper, and J. Reaven. 1985. "Role Perceptions, Self-Role Congruence and Marital Satisfaction in Dual-Worker Couples with Preschool Children." *Social Psychology Quarterly* 48:301–11.

Chatav, Y., and M. A. Whisman. 2007. "Marital Dissolution and Psychiatric Disorders." *Journal of Divorce & Remarriage* 47:1–13.

Chelune, G. J., L. B. Rosenfeld, and E. M. Waring. 1985. "Spouse Disclosure Patterns in Distressed and Nondistressed Couples." *American Journal of Family Therapy* 13:24–32.

Chen, H., et al. 2006. "Predicting Conflict within Romantic Relationships during the Transition to Adulthood." *Personal Relationships* 13:411–27.

Cherlin, A. J. 2004. "The Deinstitutionalization of American Marriage." *Journal of Marriage and Family* 66:848–61.

Cherlin, A. J., et al. 2004. "The Influence of Physical and Sexual Abuse on Marriage and Cohabitation." *American Sociological Review* 69:768–89.

Cherlin, A. J., P. L. Chase-Lansdale, and C. McRae. 1998. "Effects of Parental Divorce on Mental Health throughout the Life Course." *American Sociological Review* 63:239–49.

Choi, H., and N. F. Marks. 2006. "Transition to Caregiving, Marital Disagreement, and Psychological Well-Being." *Journal of Family Issues* 27:1701–22.

Choi, N. 2004. "Sex Role Group Differences in Specific Academic and General Self-Efficacy." *Journal of Psychology* 138:149–59.

Choo, P., T. Levine, and E. Hatfield. 1996. "Gender, Love Schemas, and Reactions to Romantic Break-Ups." *Journal of Social Behavior and Personality* 5:143–60.

Chowdhury, F. I., and F. Trovato. 1994. "The Role and Status of Women and the Timing of Marriage in Five Asian Countries." *Journal of Comparative Family Studies* 25:143–57.

Christensen, A., K. Eldridge, A. Catta-Preta, V. R. Lim, and R. Santagata. 2006. "Cross-Cultural Consistency of the Demand/Withdraw Interaction Pattern in Couples." *Journal of Marriage and Family* 68:1029–44.

Christsensen, S. A., and R. B. Miller. 2006. "Areas of Desired Change among Married Midlife Individuals." *Journal of Couple and Relationship Therapy* 5:35–57.

Christian-Herman, J. L., K. D. O'Leary, and S. Avery-Leaf. 2001. "The Impact of Severe Negative Events in Marriage on Depression." *Journal of Social and Clinical Psychology* 20:24–40.

Ciccarelli, J. C., and L. J. Beckman. 2005. "Navigating Rough Waters: An Overview of Psychological Aspects of Surrogacy." *Journal of Social Issues* 61:21–43.

Ciccarone, D. H., et al. 2003. "Sex without Disclosure of Positive HIV Serostatus in a US Probability Sample of Persons Receiving Medical Care for HIV Infection." *American Journal of Public Health* 93:949–54.

Cicerello, A., and E. P. Sheehan. 1995. "Personal Advertisements: A Content Analysis." *Journal of Social Behavior and Personality* 10:751–56.

Clark, C. 2005. "Preventive Measures." *San Diego Union-Tribune,* March 8.

Clark, M. S. 1999. "The Double ABCX Model of Family Crisis as a Representation of Family Functioning after Rehabilitation from Stroke." *Psychology, Health and Medicine* 4:203–20.

Clark, R. A., et al. 2004. "Initial Encounters of Young Men and Women." *Sex Roles* 50:699–709.

Clark, R. D., and G. Shields. 1997. "Family Communication and Delinquency." *Adolescence* 32:81–92.

Clarke, S. C., and B. F. Wilson. 1994. "The Relative Stability of Remarriages." *Family Relations* 43:305–10.

Claxton-Oldfield, S., and L. Whitt. 2003. "Child Abuse in Stepfather Families." *Journal of Divorce and Remarriage* 40:17–33.

Clay, C. M., et al. 2007. "Black Women and White Women: Do Perceptions of Childhood Family Environment Differ?" *Family Process* 46:243–56.

Clearfield, M. W., and N. M. Nelson. 2006. "Sex Differences in Mothers' Speech and Play Behavior With 6-0, 9-0, and 14-Month-Old Infants." *Sex Roles* 54:127–37.

Clements, M. L., S. M. Stanley, and H. J. Markman. 2004. "Before They Said 'I Do': Discriminating among Marital Outcomes over 13 Years." *Journal of Marriage and the Family* 66:613–26.

Clements, R., and C. H. Swensen. 2000. "Commitment to One's Spouse as a Predictor of Marital Quality among Older Couples." *Current Psychology* 19:110–19.

Clingempeel, W. G. 1981. "Quasi-Kin Relationships and Marital Quality in Stepfather Families." *Journal of Personality and Social Psychology* 41:890–901.

Cockrum, J., and P. White. 1985. "Influences on the Life Satisfaction of Never-Married Men and Women." *Family Relations* 34:551–56.

Cohan, C. L., and S. Kleinbaum. 2002. "Toward a Greater Understanding of the Cohabitation Effect." *Journal of Marriage and the Family* 64:184–92.

Cohany, S. R., and E. Sok. 2007. "Trends in Labor Force Participation of Married Mothers of Infants." *Monthly Labor Review,* February, 9–16.

Cohen, L. L., and R. L. Shotland. 1996. "Timing of First Sexual Intercourse in a Relationship." *Journal of Sex Research* 33:291–99.

Cohen, P., S. Kasen, H. Chen, C. Hartmark, and K. Gordon. 2003. "Variations in Patterns of Developmental Transitions in the Emerging Adulthood Period." *Developmental Psychology* 39:657–69.

Coleman, J. 2007. *When Parents Hurt: Compassionate Strategies When You and Your Grown Child Don't Get Along.* New York: Harper Collins.

Coleman, M., and L. H. Ganong. 1985. "Remarriage Myths: Implications for the Helping Professions." *Journal of Counseling and Development* 64:116–20.

Coleman, M., L. Ganong, and M. Fine. 2000. "Reinvestigating Remarriage: Another Decade of Progress." *Journal of Marriage and the Family* 62:1288–307.

Coleman, M., L. H. Ganong, and R. Gingrich. 1985. "Stepfamily Strengths: A Review of Popular Literature." *Family Relations* 34:583–89.

Coley, A., and Z. Todd. 2002. "Gender-Linked Differences in the Style and Content of E-Mails to Friends." *Journal of Language & Social Psychology* 21:380–92.

Collins, K. A., K. M. Cramer, and J. A. Singleton-Jackson. 2005. "Love Styles and Self-Silencing in Romantic Relationships." *Guidance and Counseling* 20:139–46.

Collins, N. L., M. L. Cooper, A. Albino, and L. Allard. 2002. "Psychosocial Vulnerability from Adolescence to Adulthood." *Journal of Personality* 70:965–1008.

Collins, R. L., P. L. Ellickson, and D. J. Klein. 2007. "The Role of Substance Use in Young Adult Divorce." *Addiction* 102:786–94.

Colman, R. A., and C. S. Widom. 2004. "Childhood Abuse and Neglect and Adult Intimate Relationships." *Child Abuse and Neglect* 28:1133–51.

Coltrane, S. 2000. "The Perpetuation of Subtle Prejudice: Race and Gender Imagery in 1990s Television Advertising." *Sex Roles* 42:363–89.

Condon, R. G., and P. R. Stern. 1993. "Gender-Role Preference, Gender Identity, and Gender Socialization among Contemporary Inuit Youth." *Ethos* 21:384–416.

Conger, R. D., and K. J. Conger. 2002. "Resilience in Midwestern Families." *Journal of Marriage and the Family* 64:361–73.

Constantine, M. G. 2006. "Perceived Family Conflict, Parental Attachment, and Depression in African American Female Adolescents." *Cultural Diversity and Ethnic Minority Psychology* 12:697–709.

Constantine, M. G., and S. M. Blackmon. 2002. "Black Adolescents' Racial Socialization Experiences." *Journal of Black Studies* 32:322–35.

Coohey, C. 2000. "The Role of Friends, In-laws, and Other Kin in Father-Perpetrated Child Physical Abuse." *Child Welfare* 79:373–402.

Cooney, T. M. 1994. "Young Adults' Relations with Parents: The Influence of Recent Parental Divorce." *Journal of Marriage and the Family* 56:45–56.

Cooney, T. M., F. A. Pedersen, S. Indelicato, and R. Palkovitz. 1993. "Timing of Fatherhood: Is 'On-Time' Optimal?" *Journal of Marriage and the Family* 55:205–15.

Cooney, T. M., and P. Uhlenberg. 1990. "The Role of Divorce in Men's Relations with Their Adult Children after Mid-life." *Journal of Marriage and the Family* 52:677–88.

Coontz, S. 1997. *The Way We Really Are: Coming to Terms with America's Changing Families.* New York: Basic Books.

Coontz, S. 2005. *Marriage, a History: From Obedience to Intimacy.* New York: Viking.

Coontz, S. 2007. "The Origins of Modern Divorce." *Family Process* 46:7–16.

Cooperman, N. A., J. H. Arnsten, and R. S. Klein. 2007. "Current Sexual Activity and Risky Sexual Behavior in Older Men with or at Risk for HIV Infection." *AIDS Education & Prevention* 19:321–33.

Cornell Law School. 2007. "Marriage Laws of the Fifty States, District of Columbia and Puerto Rico." Cornell Law School Web site.

Corrigan, P. W., and S. M. Phelan. 2004. "Social Support and Recovery in People with Serious Mental Illnesses." *Community Mental Health Journal* 40:513–23.

Cortez, K. 1996. "My Two Moms: Issues and Concerns of Lesbian Couples Raising Sons." *Progress: Family Systems Research and Therapy* 5:37–50.

Craig, L. 2006. "Does Father Care Mean Fathers Share?" *Gender & Society* 20:259–81.

Crawford, M., and D. Popp. 2003. "Sexual Double Standards." *Journal of Sex Research* 40:13–26.

Crnic, K. A., and C. L. Booth. 1991. "Mothers' and Fathers' Perceptions of Daily Hassles of Parenting across Early Childhood." *Journal of Marriage and the Family* 53:1042–50.

Crnic, K. A., and M. T. Greenberg. 1990. "Minor Parenting Stresses with Young Children." *Child Development* 61:1628–37.

Crockett, L. J., and B. A. Randall. 2006. "Linking Adolescent Family and Peer Relationships to the Quality of Young Adult Romantic Relationships." *Journal of Social and Personal Relationships* 23:761–80.

Crohan, S. E. 1992. "Marital Happiness and Spousal Consensus on Beliefs about Marital Conflict: A Longitudinal Investigation." *Journal of Social and Personal Relationships* 9:89–102.

Crohan, S. E. 1996. "Marital Quality and Conflict across the Transition to Parenthood in African American and White Couples." *Journal of Marriage and the Family* 58:933–44.

Crohn, H. M. 2006. "Five Styles of Positive Stepmothering from the Perspective of Young Adult Stepdaughters." *Journal of Divorce & Remarriage* 46:119–34.

Crosby, J. F. 1991. *Illusion and Disillusion: The Self in Love and Marriage.* 4th ed. Belmont, CA: Wadsworth.

Crowder, K. D., and S. E. Tolnay. 2000. "A New Marriage Squeeze for Black Women: The Role of Racial Intermarriage by Black Men." *Journal of Marriage and the Family* 62:792–807.

Cryderman, K. 2000. "StatsCan Survey Chronicles Abuse among Both Sexes." *Calgary Herald,* July 26.

Cullen, L. T. 2007. "Till Work Do Us Part." *Time,* October 8, 63–64.

Cummings, E. M. 1994. "Marital Conflict and Children's Functioning." *Social Development* 3:16–36.

Cunningham, M. 2001. "The Influence of Parental Attitudes and Behaviors on Children's Attitudes toward Gender and Household Labor in Early Adulthood." *Journal of Marriage and the the Family* 63:111–22.

Cunningham, M. 2007. "Influences of Women's Employment on the Gendered Division of Household Labor Over the Life Course." *Journal of Family Issues* 28:422–44.

Cutrona, C. E. 2004. "A Psychological Perspective: Marriage and the Social Provisions of Relationships." *Journal of Marriage and Family* 66:992–99.

Cutrona, C. E., et al. 2003. "Neighborhood Context and Financial Strain as Predictors of Marital Interaction and Marital Quality in African American Couples." *Personal Relationships* 10:389–409.

Dadds, M., M. Smith, Y. Webber, and A. Robinson. 1991. "An Exploration of Family and Individual Profiles Following Father-Daughter Incest." *Child Abuse and Neglect* 15:575–86.

Dainton, M. 1999. "African-American, European-American, and Biracial Couples' Meanings for and Experiences in Marriage." In T. J. Socha and R. C. Diggs, eds., *Communication, Race, and Family.* Mahwah, NJ: Lawrence Erlbaum Associates.

Dang, A., and M. S. Frazer. 2005. "Black Same-Sex Couple Households in the 2000 U.S. Census." *Western Journal of Black Studies* 29:521–30.

Daniluk, J. C. 2001. "Reconstructing Their Lives: A Longitudinal, Qualitative Analysis of the Transition to Biological

Childlessness for Infertile Couples." *Journal of Counseling & Development* 79:439–50.

Davies, B., J. Spinetta, I. Martinson, S. Mc-Clowry, and E. Kulenkamp. 1986. "Manifestations of Levels of Functioning in Grieving Families." *Journal of Family Issues* 7:297–313.

Davies, C. A., D. DiLillo, and I. G. Martinez. 2004. "Isolating Adult Psychological Correlates of Witnessing Parental Violence." *Journal of Family Violence* 19:369–77.

Davis, K. C., W. H. George, and J. Norris. 2004. "Women's Responses to Unwanted Sexual Advances." *Psychology of Women Quarterly* 28:333–42.

Davis, K. E. 1985. "Near and Dear: Friendship and Love Compared." *Psychology Today* 19:22–28.

Davis, S., and L. D. Pearce. 2007. "Adolescents' Work-Family Gender Ideologies and Educational Expectations." *Sociological Perspectives* 50:249–71.

Davis, S. N., and T. N. Greenstein. 2004. "Interactive Effects of Gender Ideology and Age at First Marriage on Women's Marital Disruption." *Journal of Family Issues* 25:658–82.

Davis, S. N., T. N. Greenstein, and J. P. G. Marks. 2007. "Effects of Union Type on Division of Household Labor." *Journal of Family Issues* 28:1246–72.

Davis-Brown, K., Salamon, S., and Surra, C. 1987. "Economic and Social Factors in Mate Selection: An Ethonographic Analysis of an Agriculture Community." *Journal of Marriage and the Family* 49:41–55.

Dawson, D. A. 1991. "Family Structure and Children's Health and Well-Being: Data from the 1988 National Health Interview Survey on Child Health." *Journal of Marriage and the Family* 53:573–84.

Dawson, D. A., B. F. Grant, S. P. Chou, and F. S. Stinson. 2007. "The Impact of Partner Alcohol Problems on Women's Physical and Mental Health." *Journal of Studies on Alcohol* 68:66–75.

Day, R. D., and D. Hook. 1987. "A Short History of Divorce: Jumping the Broom—and Back Again." *Journal of Divorce* 10:57–73.

de Anda, D., R. M. Becerra, and E. Fielder. 1990. "In Their Own Words: The Life Experiences of Mexican-American and White Pregnant Adolescents and Adolescent Mothers." *Child and Adolescent Social Work Journal* 7:301–18.

De Luccie, M. F., and Albert J. Davis. 1991. "Do Men's Adult Life Concerns Affect Their Fathering Orientations?" *Journal of Psychology* 125:175–88.

Dean-Church, L., and F. D. Gilroy. 1993. "Relation of Sex-Role Orientation to Life Satisfaction in a Healthy Elderly Sample." *Journal of Social Behavior and Personality* 8:133–40.

Deffenbacher, J. L., D. M. Deffenbacher, R. S. Lynch, and T. L. Richards. 2003. "Anger, Aggression, and Risky Behavior." *Behaviour Research and Therapy* 41:701–17.

Degler, C. N. 1980. *At Odds: Women and the Family in America from the Revolution to the Present.* New York: Oxford University Press.

Dehle, C., D. Larsen, and J. E. Landers. 2001. "Social Support in Marriage." *American Journal of Family Therapy* 29:307–24.

DeLeire, T., and A. Kalil. 2005. "How Do Cohabiting Couples with Children Spend Money?" *Journal of Marriage and Family* 67:286–95.

DeMaris, A., M. L. Benson, G. L. Fox, T. Hill, and J. Van Wyk. 2003. "Distal and Proximal Factors in Domestic Violence." *Journal of Marriage and the Family* 65:652–67.

DeMaris, A., and G. L. Greif. 1992. "The Relationship between Family Structure and Parent-Child Relationship Problems in Single Family Households." *Journal of Divorce and Remarriage* 18:55–77.

DeMaris, A., and K. V. Rao. 1992. "Premarital Cohabitation and Subsequent Marital Stability in the United States: A Reassessment." *Journal of Marriage and the Family* 54:178–90.

DeMeis, D. K., and H. W. Perkins. 1996. " 'Supermoms' of the Nineties: Homemaker and Employed Mothers' Performance and Perceptions of the Motherhood Role." *Journal of Family Issues* 17:777–92.

Deming, M. P., N. D. Chase, and D. Karesh. 1996. "Parental Alcoholism and Perceived Levels of Family Health among College Freshmen." *Alcoholism Treatment Quarterly* 14:47–57.

Demos, J. 1968. "Families in Colonial Bristol, Rhode Island: An Exercise in Historical Demography." *William and Mary Quarterly* 25:34–61.

DeNavas-Walt, C., B. D. Proctor, and J. Smith. 2007. *Income, Poverty, and Health Insurance Coverage in the United States: 2006.* Washington, DC: Government Printing Office.

Dennison, R. P., and S. S. Koerner. 2006. "About Marriage: The Influence of Maternal Disclosures and Adolescent Gender." *Journal of Divorce & Remarriage* 45:31–49.

Derks, W., et al. 2005. "Differences in Coping Style and Locus of Control between Older and Younger Patients with Head and Neck Cancer." *Clinical Otolaryngology and Allied Sciences* 30:186–92.

Derlega, V. J., S. Metts, S. Petronio, and S. T. Margulis. 1993. *Self-Disclosure.* Newbury Park, CA: Sage.

Dervic, K., et al. 2004. "Religious Affiliation and Suicide Attempt." *American Journal of Psychiatry* 161:2303–8.

Deutsch, F. M., L. J. Servis, and J. D. Payne. 2001. "Paternal Participation in Child Care and Its Effects on Children's Self-Esteem and Attitudes toward Gendered Roles." *Journal of Family Issues* 22:1000–24.

Deveraux, L., and A. J. Hammerman. 1998. *Infertility and Identity.* San Francisco, CA: Jossey-Bass.

Dew, J. 2007. "Two Sides of the Same Coin? The Differing Roles of Assets and Consumer Debt in Marriage." *Journal of Family and Economic Issues* 28:89–104.

Dickson, F. C., P. C. Hughes, and K. L. Walker. 2005. "An Exploratory Investigation into Dating among Later-Life Women." *Western Journal of Communication* 69:67–82.

DiClemente, R., et al. 2004. "Efficacy of an HIV Prevention Intervention for African American Adolescent Girls." *Journal of the American Medical Association* 292:171–79.

Diedrick, P. 1991. "Gender Differences in Divorce Adjustment." *Journal of Divorce and Remarriage* 14:33–45.

Diekman, A. B., and S. K. Murnen. 2004. "Learning to Be Little Women and Little Men." *Sex Roles* 50:373–85.

Dietz, T. L. 2000. "Disciplining Children." *Child Abuse & Neglect* 24:1529–42.

Dillaway, H., and C. Broman. 2001. "Race, Class, and Gender Differences in Marital Satisfaction and Divisions of Household Labor among Dual-Earner Couples." *Journal of Family Issues* 22:309–27.

Ding, C. S., K. Song, and L. I. Richardson. 2007. "Do Mathematical Gender Differences Continue?" *Educational Studies* 40:279–95.

Dion, K. K., and K. L. Dion. 1991. "Psychological Individualism and Romantic Love." *Journal of Social Behavior and Personality* 6:17–33.

Dion, K. L., and K. K. Dion. 1993. "Gender and Ethnocultural Comparisons in Styles of Love." *Psychology of Women Quarterly* 17:463–73.

Divakaruni, C. 2000. "Uncertain Objects of Desire." *Atlantic Monthly*, March, pp. 22–27.

Doherty, K. T. 1998. "A Mind of Her Own: Effects of Need for Closure and Gender on Reactions to Nonconformity." *Sex Roles* 38:801–20.

Dolan, K. A., and H. Niven. 2005. "A Review of HIV Prevention among Young Injecting Drug Users." *Harm Reduction Journal* 2:5.

Dolbin-MacNab, M. L. 2006. "Just Like Raising Your Own? Grandmothers' Perceptions of Parenting a Second Time Around." *Family Relations* 55:564–75.

Dolcini, M. M., et al. 1996. "Cognitive and Emotional Assessments of Perceived Risk for HIV among Unmarried Heterosexuals." *AIDS Education & Prevention* 8:294–307.

Domenico, D., and M. Windle. 1993. "Intrapersonal and Interpersonal Functioning among Middle-Aged Female Adult Children of Alcoholics." *Journal of Consulting and Clinical Psychology* 61:659–66.

Donald, K. L., et al. 2003. "Comparison between American Indian and Non-Indian out-of-Home Placements." *Families in Society* 84:267–74.

Dong, M., et al. 2004. "The Interrelatedness of Multiple Forms of Childhood Abuse, Neglect, and Household Dysfunction." *Child Abuse and Neglect* 28:771–84.

Doodson, L., and D. Morley. 2006. "Understanding the Roles of Non-Residential Stepmothers." *Journal of Divorce & Remarriage* 45:109–30.

Doohan, E. M., and V. Manusov. 2004. "The Communication of Compliments in Romantic Relationships." *Western Journal of Communication* 68:170–94.

Doucet, J., and R. H. Aseltine Jr. 2003. "Childhood Family Adversity and the Quality of Marital Relationships in Young Adulthood." *Journal of Social and Personal Relationships* 20:818–42.

Downey, D. B. 1994. "The School Performance of Children from Single-Mother and Single-Father Families: Economic or Interpersonal Deprivation?" *Journal of Family Issues* 15:129–47.

Downey, D. B. 1995. "Understanding Academic Achievement among Children in Stephouseholds." *Social Forces* 73:875–94.

Downey, D. B., P. B. Jackson, and B. Powell. 1994. "Sons versus Daughters: Sex Composition of Children and Maternal Views on Socialization." *Sociological Quarterly* 35:33–50.

Downey, D. B., and B. Powell. 1993. "Do Children in Single-Parent Households Fare Better Living with Same-Sex Parents?" *Journal of Marriage and the Family* 55:55–71.

Downs, B. 2003. *Fertility of American Women: June 2002.* Washington, DC: Government Printing Office.

Downs, W. R., T. Capshew, and B. Rindels. 2004. "Relationships between Adult Women's Alcohol Problems and Their Childhood Experiences of Parental Violence and Psychological Aggression." *Journal of Studies on Alcohol* 65:336–44.

Doyle, A. B., and D. Markiewicz. 2005. "Parenting, Marital Conflict and Adjustment from Early- to Mid-Adolescence." *Journal of Youth and Adolescence* 34:97–110.

Drass, K. A. 1986. "The Effect of Gender Identity on Conversation." *Social Psychology Quarterly* 49:294–301.

Dreman, S. 2003. "Family Cohesiveness, Flexibility and Maternal Anger." *Journal of Divorce and Remarriage* 39:65–89.

Dreman, S., and H. Ronen-Eliav. 1997. "The Relation of Divorced Mothers' Perceptions of Family Cohesion and Adaptability to Behavior Problems in Children." *Journal of Marriage and the Family* 59:324–31.

Drenovsky, C. K., and M. Meshyock. 2000. "Young Adults' Perception of Their Relationship with Parents." *International Social Science Review* 75:15–22.

Drew, L. M., and M. Silverstein. 2007. "Grandparents' Psychological Well-Being after Loss of Contact with Their Grandchildren." *Journal of Family Psychology* 21:372–79.

Driver, J. L., and J. M. Gottman. 2004. "Daily Marital Interactions and Positive Affect during Marital Conflict among Newlywed Couples." *Family Process* 43:301–14.

DuCharme, J., C. Koverola, and P. Battle. 1997. "Intimacy Development: The Influence of Abuse and Gender." *Journal of Interpersonal Violence* 12:590–99.

Duck, S. 1994. *Meaningful Relationships: Talking Sense and Relating.* Newbury Park, CA: Sage.

Dugosh, J. W. 2000. "On Predicting Relationship Satisfaction from Jealousy." *Current Research in Social Psychology* 5:254–63.

Duncan, G. J., B. Wilkerson, and P. England. 2006. "Cleaning Up Their Act: The Effects of Marriage and Cohabitation on Licit and Illicit Drug Use." *Demography* 43:691–710.

Dunn, M. S., R. T. Bartee, and M. A. Perko. 2003. "Self-Reported Alcohol Use and Sexual Behaviors of Adolescents." *Psychological Reports* 92:339–48.

Dunning, A. 2006. "Grandparents—an Intergenerational Resource for Families." *Journal of Intergenerational Relationships* 4:127–35.

Durant, W. 1954. *Our Oriental Heritage.* New York: Simon and Schuster.

Durbin, D. L., N. Darling, L. Steinberg, and B. B. Brown. 1993. "Parenting Style and Peer Group Membership among

European-American Adolescents." *Journal of Research on Adolescence* 3:87–100.

Durkheim, E. 1933. *The Division of Labor in Society,* trans. George Simpson. New York: Free Press.

Dush, C. M. K., and P. R. Amato. 2005. "Consequences of Relationship Status and Quality for Subjective Well-Being." *Journal of Social and Personal Relationships* 22:607–27.

Dush, C. M. K., C. L. Cohan, and P. R. Amato. 2003. "The Relationship between Cohabitation and Marital Quality and Stability." *Journal of Marriage and the Family* 65:539–49.

Dutton, D. G. 1987. "Wife Assault: Social Psychological Contributions to Criminal Justice Policy." In S. Oskamp, ed., *Family Processes and Problems: Social Psychological Aspects,* pp. 238–61. Beverly Hills, CA: Sage.

Dwyer, K. M. 1990. "Characteristics of Eighth-Grade Students Who Initiate Self-Care in Elementary and Junior High School." *Pediatrics* 86:448–54.

Dyk, P. A. H. 1987. "Graduate Student Management of Family and Academic Roles." *Family Relations* 36:329–32.

Eagly, A. H. 1978. "Sex Differences in Influenceability." *Psychological Bulletin* 85:86–116.

Earle, K. A. 2000. *Child Abuse and Neglect: An Examination of American Indian Data.* Portland, OR: National Indian Child Welfare Association.

Easley, M. J., and N. Epstein. 1991. "Coping with Stress in a Family with an Alcoholic Parent." *Family Relations* 40:218–24.

East, P. L., M. E. Felice, and M. C. Morgan. 1993. "Sisters' and Girlfriends' Sexual and Childbearing Behavior: Effects on Early Adolescent Girls' Sexual Outcomes." *Journal of Marriage and the Family* 55:953–63.

Eaton, D. K., et al. 2006. "Youth Risk Behavior Surveillance–United States, 2005." *Morbidity and Mortality Weekly Report* 55:1–78.

Eaton, D. K., K. S. Davis, L. Barrios, N. C. Brener, and R. K. Noonan. 2007. "Associations of Dating Violence Victimization with Lifetime Participation, Co-Occurrence, and Early Initiation of Risk Behaviors among U.S. High School Students." *Journal of Interpersonal Violence* 22:585–602.

Eckhardt, C. I. 2007. "Effects of Alcohol Intoxication on Anger Experience and Expression among Partner Assaultive Men." *Journal of Consulting and Clinical Psychology* 75:61–71.

Eckstein, D. 2004. "The 'A's and 'H's of Healthy and Unhealthy Relationships." *Family Journal* 12:414–18.

Eckstein, D., and L. L. Grassa. 2005. "For Couples and Families: The Non-Violent Relationship Questionnaire." *Family Journal* 13:205–211.

Eckstein, N. 2004. "Emergent Issues in Families Experiencing Adolescent-to-Parent Abuse." *Western Journal of Communication* 68:365–88.

Edin, K., and M. Kefalas. 2005. "Unmarried with Children" *Contexts* 4:16–22.

Edwards, R., and M. A. Hamilton. 2004. "You Need to Understand My Gender Role." *Sex Roles* 50:491–504.

Eggebeen, D., and C. Knoester. 2001. "Does Fatherhood Matter for Men?" *Journal of Marriage and the Family* 63:381–93.

Eggebeen, D., A. R. Snyder, and W. D. Manning. 1996. "Children in Single-Father Families in Demographic Perspective." *Journal of Family Issues* 17:441–64.

Eisikovits, Z. C., J. L. Edleson, E. Guttmann, and M. Sela-Amit. 1991. "Cognitive Styles and Socialized Attitudes of Men Who Batter: Where Should We Intervene?" *Family Relations* 40:72–77.

Elder, G. H., Jr., R. D. Conger, E. M. Foster, and M. Ardelt. 1992. "Families under Economic Pressure." *Journal of Family Issues* 13:5–37.

Eldridge, R. I., and P. D. Sutton. 2007. "Births, Marriages, Divorces, and Deaths." *National Vital Statistics Reports* 56, no. 1.

Elkins, I. J., M. McGue, S. Malone, and W. G. Iacono. 2004. "The Effect of Parental Alcohol and Drug Disorders on Adolescent Personality." *American Journal of Psychiatry* 161:670–76.

Elliott, M. 1996. "Impact of Work, Family, and Welfare Receipt on Women's Self-Esteem in Young Adulthood." *Social Psychology Quarterly* 59:80–95.

Ellis, B. J., et al. 2003. "Does Father Absence Place Daughters at Special Risk for Early Sexual Activity and Teenage Pregnancy?" *Child Development* 74:801–21.

Emmers-Sommer, T. M. 2004. "The Effect of Communication Quality and Quantity Indicators on Intimacy and Relational Satisfaction." *Journal of Social and Personal Relationships* 21:399–411.

Emmers-Sommer, T. M., P. Pauley, A. Hanzal, and L. Triplett. 2006. "Love, Suspense, Sex, and Violence." *Sex Roles* 55:311–20.

Erickson, M. F., and E. G. Aird. 2005. *The Motherhood Study.* New York: Institute for American Values.

Erickson, R. J. 1993. "Reconceptualizing Family Work: The Effect of Emotion Work on Perceptions of Marital Quality." *Journal of Marriage and the Family* 55:888–900.

Erwin, P. G. 1999. "Love Attitudes and Romantic Involvement." *Perceptual and Motor Skills* 88:317–18.

Espenshade, T. J., and W. Ye. 1994. "Differential Fertility within an Ethnic Minority: The Effect of 'Trying Harder' among Chinese-American Women." *Social Problems* 41:97–106.

Essien, E. J., A. F. Meshack, R. J. Peters, G. Ogungbade, and N. I. Osemene. 2005. "Strategies to Prevent HIV Transmission among Heterosexual African-American Women." *International Journal of Equity and Health* 17:4–8.

Ethier, L. S., J. Lemelin, and C. Lacharite. 2004. "A Longitudinal Study of the Effects of Chronic Maltreatment on Children's Behavioral and Emotional Problems." *Child Abuse and Neglect* 28:1265–78.

Evans, L., and K. Davies. 2000. "No Sissy Boys Here: A Content Analysis of Masculinity in Elementary School Reading Textbooks." *Sex Roles* 42:255–70.

Everett, L. W. 1998. "Factors That Contribute to Satisfaction or Dissatisfaction in Stepfather-Stepchild Relationships." *Perspectives in Psychiatric Care* 34:25–36.

Ezra, M. 2003. "Factors Associated with Marriage and Family Formation Processes in Southern Ethiopia." *Journal of Comparative Family Studies* 34:509–30.

Falke, S., and J. Larson. 2007. "Premarital Predictors of Remarital Quality." *Contemporary Family Therapy* 29:9–23.

Fang, W., and Sen Q. 2006. "Longitudinal Effects of Parenting on Children's Academic Achievement in African American Families." *Journal of Negro Education* 75:415–29.

Federal Bureau of Investigation. 2002. *Crime in the United States: 2002.* FBI Web site.

Federal Interagency Forum on Child and Family Statistics. 2007. *America's Children: Key National Indicators of Well-Being.* Washington, DC: Government Printing Office.

Feigelman, W. 1997. "Adopted Adults: Comparisons with Persons Raised in Conventional Families." *Marriage and Family Review* 25:199–23.

Feinberg, M. E., M. L. Kan, and E. M. Hetherington. 2007. "The Longitudinal Influence of Coparenting Conflict on Parental Negativity and Adolescent Maladjustment." *Journal of Marriage and Family* 69:687–702.

Felmlee, D., S. Sprecher, and E. Bassin. 1990. "The Dissolution of Intimate Relationships: A Hazard Model." *Social Psychology Quarterly* 53:13–30.

Felson, R. B., and A. C. Cares. 2005. "Gender and the Seriousness of Assaults on Intimate Partners and Other Victims." *Journal of Marriage and Family* 67:1182–95.

Felson, R. B., and S. F. Messner. 2000. "The Control Motive in Intimate Partner Violence." *Social Psychology Quarterly* 63:86–94.

Ferguson, S. J. 2000. "Challenging Traditional Marriage: Never Married Chinese American and Japanese American Women." *Gender & Society* 14:136–59.

Figueroa-Moseley, C. D. V., C. T. Ramey, B. Keltner, and R. G. Lanzi. 2006. "Variations in Latino Parenting Practices and Their Effects on Child Cognitive Developmental Outcomes." *Hispanic Journal of Behavioral Sciences* 28:102–14.

Fine, M. A., L. H. Ganong, and M. Coleman. 1997. "The Relation between Role Constructions and Adjustment among Stepfathers." *Journal of Family Issues* 18:503–25.

Fine, M. A., and L. A. Kurdek. 1992. "The Adjustment of Adolescents in Stepfather and Stepmother Families." *Journal of Marriage and the Family* 54:725–36.

Fine, M. A., P. Voydanoff, and B. W. Donnelly. 1993. "Relations between Parental Control and Warmth and Child Well-Being in Stepfamilies." *Journal of Family Psychology* 7:222–32.

Finer, L. B. 2007. "Trends in Premarital Sex in the United States, 1954–2003." *Public Health Reports* 122:73–8.

Finer, L. B., L. F. Frohwirth, L. A. Dauphinee, S. Singh, and A. M. Moore. 2005. "Reasons U.S. Women Have Abortions." *Perspectives on Sexual & Reproductive Health* 37:110–18.

Fingerson, L. 2005. "Do Mothers' Opinions Matter in Teens' Sexual Activity?" *Journal of Family Issues* 26:947–74.

Fisher, H. 2004. *Why We Love: The Nature and Chemistry of Romantic Love.* New York: Henry Holt & Co.

Fischer, H. E., et al. 2006. "Romantic Love: A Mammalian Brain System for Mate Choice." *Philosophical Transactions of the Royal Society B* 361:2173–86.

Fischer, T. F., P. M. De Graaf, and M. Kalmijn. 2005. "Friendly and Antagonistic Contact between Former Spouses after Divorce." *Journal of Family Issues* 26:1131–63.

Fischtein, D. S., E. S. Herold, and S. Desmarais. 2007. "How Much Does Gender Explain in Sexual Attitudes and Behaviors?" *Archives of Sexual Behavior* 36:451–61.

Fitchen, J. M., and O. Cohen. 1995. "Divorced Fathers Raise Their Children by Themselves." *Journal of Divorce & Remarriage* 23:55–73.

Fitzgerald, L. F. 1993. "Sexual Harassment: Violence against Women in the Workplace." *American Psychologist* 48:1070–76.

Fivush, R. 2000. "Gender Differences in Parent-Child Emotion Narratives." *Sex Roles* 42:233–53.

Flack, W. F. Jr. 2007. "Risk Factors and Consequences of Unwanted Sex among University Students." *Journal of Interpersonal Violence* 22:139–57.

Flaste, R. 1991. "Sidelined by Loneliness." *New York Times Magazine,* April 28.

Fleming, L. M., and D. J. Tobin. 2005. "Popular Child-Rearing Books: Where Is Daddy?" *Psychology of Men and Masculinity* 61:18–24.

Fletcher, G. J. O., J. M. Tither, C. O'Louglin, M. Friesen, and N. Overall. 2004. "Warm and Homely or Cold and Beautiful? Sex Differences in Trading Off Traits in Mate Selection." *Personality and Social Psychology Bulletin* 30:659–72.

Florian, V., and N. Danagoor. 1994. "Personal and Familial Adaptation of Women with Severe Physical Disabilities." *Journal of Marriage and the Family* 56:735–46.

Fluehr-Lobban, C., and L. Bardsley-Sirois. 1990. "Obedience (TA'A) in Muslim Marriage: Religious Interpretation and Applied Law in Egypt." *Journal of Comparative Family Studies* 21:39–53.

Follingstad, D. R., L. L. Rutledge, B. J. Berg, and E. S. Hause. 1990. "The Role of Emotional Abuse in Physically Abusive Relationships." *Journal of Family Violence* 5:107–20.

Forbes, G. B., L. E. Adams-Curtis, B. Rade, and P. Jaberg. 2001. "Body Dissatisfaction in Women and Men." *Sex Roles* 44:461–84.

Forbes, G. B., L. E. Adams-Curtis, A. H. Pakalka, and K. B. White. 2006. "Dating Aggression, Sexual Coercion, and Aggression-Supporting Attitudes among College Men as a Function of Participation in Aggressive High School Sports." *Violence Against Women* 12:441–55.

Ford, C. S., and F. A. Beach. 1951. *Patterns of Sexual Behavior.* New York: Harper Torchbooks.

Forehand, R., and S. Nousianinen. 1993. "Maternal and Paternal Parenting: Critical Dimensions in Adolescent Functioning." *Journal of Family Psychology* 7:213–21.

Forste, R., and K. Tanfer. 1996. "Sexual Exclusivity among Dating, Cohabiting, and Married Women." *Journal of Marriage and the Family* 58:33–47.

Fossett, M. A., and K. J. Kiecolt. 1993. "Mate Availability and Family Structure among African Americans in U.S. Metropolitan Areas." *Journal of Marriage and the Family* 55:288–302.

Foubert, J. D., and B. K. Sholley. 1996. "Effects of Gender, Gender Role, and Individualized Trust on Self-Disclosure." *Journal of Social Behavior and Personality* 11:277–88.

Fouts, G., and K. Burggraf. 2000. "Television Situation Comedies: Female Weight, Male Negative Comments, and Audience Reactions." *Sex Roles* 42:925–32.

Fowers, B. J. 1991. "His and Her Marriage: A Multivariate Study of Gender and Marital Satisfaction." *Sex Roles* 24:209–21.

Fowers, B. J. 1996. "Predicting Marital Success for Premarital Couple Types Based on PREPARE." *Journal of Marital and Family Therapy* 22:103–19.

Fowers, B. J., and D. H. Olson. 1986. "Predicting Marital Success with PREPARE: A Predictive Validity Study." *Journal of Marital and Family Therapy* 12:403–13.

Fox, G. L., and R. F. Kelly. 1995. "Determinants of Child Custody Arrangements at Divorce." *Journal of Marriage and the Family* 57:693–708.

Franco, J. L., L. Sabattini, and F. J. Crosby. 2004. "Anticipating Work and Family." *Journal of Social Issues* 60:755–66.

Frank, R. 2007. "Rise of Postnups." *Wall Street Journal,* June 9.

Franklin, D. L., S. E. Smith, and W. E. P. McMiller. 1995. "Correlates of Marital Status among African American Mothers in Chicago Neighborhoods of Concentrated Poverty." *Journal of Marriage and the Family* 57:141–52.

Franzoi, S. L., and J. R. Klaiber. 2007. "Body Use and Reference Group Impact." *Sex Roles* 56:205–14.

Frazier, P., N. Arikian, S. Benson, and A. Losoff. 1996. "Desire for Marriage and Life Satisfaction among Unmarried Heterosexual Adults." *Journal of Social and Personal Relationships* 13:225–39.

Freud, S. 1949. *Three Essays on the Theory of Sexuality.* Trans. J. Strachey. London: Imago Publishing Co.

Frederick, D. A., et al. 2007. "Desiring the Muscular Ideal: Men's Body Satisfaction in the United States, Ukraine, and Ghana." *Psychology of Men & Masculinity* 8:103–17.

Frederick, D. A., G. B. Forbes, K. E. Grigorian, and J. M. Jarcho. 2007. "Gender and Ethnic Differences in Self-Objectification and Body Satisfaction among 2,206 Undergraduates." *Sex Roles* 57:317–27.

Frias, S. M., and R. J. Angel. 2005. "The Risk of Partner Violence among Low-Income Hispanic Subgroups." *Journal of Marriage and Family* 67:552–64.

Friedman, H. S., et al. 1995. "Psychosocial and Behavioral Predictors of Longevity." *American Psychologist* 50:69–78.

Friedman, S., and C. Weissbrod. 2005. "Work and Family Commitment and Decision-Making Status among Emerging Adults." *Sex Roles* 53:317–25.

Frieze, I. H., et al. 2003. "Gender-Role Attitudes in University Students in the United States, Slovenia, and Croatia." *Psychology of Women Quarterly* 27:256–61.

Frisco, M. L. 2005. "Parental Involvement and Young Women's Contraceptive Use." *Journal of Marriage and the Family* 67:110–21.

Frisco, M. L., and K. Williams. 2003. "Perceived Housework Equity, Marital Happiness, and Divorce in Dual-Earner Households." *Journal of Family Issues* 24:51–73.

Fromm, E. 1956. *The Art of Loving.* New York: Bantam.

Fry, R. B., and S. Prentice-Dunn. 2005. "Effects of Coping Information and Value Affirmation on Responses to a Perceived Health Threat." *Health Communication* 17:133–47.

Fu, V. K. 2007. "How Many Melting Pots? Intermarriage, Panethnicity, and the Black/non-Black Divide in the United States." *Journal of Comparative Family Studies* 38: 215–37.

Fu, X., J. Tora, and H. Kendall. 2001. "Marital Happiness and Inter-racial Marriage." *Journal of Comparative Family Studies* 32:47–60.

Fuligni, A. J., T. Yip, and V. Tseng. 2002. "The Impact of Family Obligation on the Daily Activities and Psychological Well-Being of Chinese American Adolescents." *Child Development* 73:302–14.

Fuller-Thomson, E., and M. Minkler. 2005. "American Indian/Alaskan Native Grandparents Raising Grandchildren." *Social Work* 50:131–39.

Furstenberg, F., Jr., and A. J. Cherlin. 1991. *Divided Families: What Happens to Children When Parents Part.* Cambridge, MA: Harvard University Press.

Furstenberg, F. F., Jr., S. Kennedy, V. C. McLoyd, R. G. Rumbaut, and R. A. Settersten Jr. 2004. "Growing Up Is Harder to Do." *Contexts* 3:33–41.

Fussell, E. 2002. "The Transition to Adulthood in Aging Societies." *Annals of the American Academy of Political and Social Science* 580:16–39.

Gabardi, L., and L. A. Rosen. 1991. "Differences between College Students from Divorced and Intact Families." *Journal of Divorce and Remarriage* 15:175–91.

Gable, S. L., H. T. Reis, E. A. Impett, and E. R. Asher. 2004. "What Do You Do When Things Go Right? The Intrapersonal and Interpersonal Benefits of Sharing Positive Events." *Journal of Personality and Social Psychology* 87:228–45.

Gaelick, L., G. V. Bodenhausen, and R. S. Wyer Jr. 1985. "Emotional Communication in Close Relationships." *Journal of Personality and Social Psychology* 49:1246–65.

Gallagher, M., and B. D. Whitehead. 1997. "End No-Fault Divorce?" *First Things,* August/September.

Ganong, L. H., and M. Coleman. 1988. "Do Mutual Children Cement Bonds in Stepfamilies?" *Journal of Marriage and the Family* 50:687–98.

Ganong, L. H., and M. Coleman. 1989. "Preparing for Remarriage: Anticipating the Issues, Seeking Solutions." *Family Relations* 38:28–33.

Ganong, L. H., and M. Coleman. 1993. "A Meta-Analytic Comparison of the Self-Esteem and Behavior Problems of Stepchildren to Children in Other Family Structures." *Journal of Divorce and Remarriage* 19:143–63.

Ganong, L. H., and M. Coleman. 1994. *Remarried Family Relationships.* Thousand Oaks, CA: Sage.

Garcia, C. 2005. "Buscando Trabajo: Social Networking among Immigrants from Mexico to the United States." *Hispanic Journal of Behavioral Sciences* 27:3–22.

Garcia, L. T., and C. Markey. 2007. "Matching in Sexual Experience for Married, Cohabiting, and Dating Couples." *Journal of Sex Research* 44:250–55.

Gardner, R. M., R. G. Sorter, and B. N. Friedman. 1997. "Developmental Changes in Children's Body Images." *Journal of Social Behavior and Personality* 12:1019–36.

Garnefski, N., and E. Arends. 1998. "Sexual Abuse and Adolescent Maladjustment." *Journal of Adolescence* 21:99–107.

Garner, P. W., S. Robertson, and G. Smith. 1997. "Preschool Children's Emotional Expressions with Peers: The Roles of Gender and Emotion Socialization." *Sex Roles* 36:675–91.

Garrett, W. R. 1982. *Seasons of Marriage and Family Life.* New York: Holt, Rinehart & Winston.

Garrison, M. C. B., L. B. Blalock, J. J. Zarski, and P. B. Merritt. 1997. "Delayed Parenthood: An Exploratory Study of Family Functioning." *Family Relations* 46:281–90.

Garvin, V., N. Kalter, and J. Hansell. 1993. "Divorced Women: Factors Contributing to Resiliency and Vulnerability." *Journal of Divorce and Remarriage* 21:21–39.

Gatrell, C. 2007. "Whose Child Is It Anyway? The Negotiation of Paternal Entitlements within Marriage." *Sociological Review* 55:352–72.

Gaunt, R. 2006. "Couple Similarity and Marital Satisfaction." *Journal of Personality* 74:1401–20.

Gazmararian, J. A., S. A. James, and J. M. Lepkowski. 1995. "Depression in Black and White Women: The Role of Marriage and Socioeconomic Status." *Annals of Epidemiology* 5:455–63.

Ge, X., G. H. Elder Jr., M. Regnerus, and C. Cox. 2001. "Pubertal Transitions, Perceptions of Being Overweight, and Adolescents' Psychological Maladjustment." *Social Psychology Quarterly* 64:363–75.

Gee, G. C., et al. 2007. "The Association between Self-Reported Racial Discrimination and 12-Month DSM-IV Mental Disorders among Asian Americans Nationwide." *Social Science & Medicine* 64:1984–96.

Gelissen, J. 2004. "Assortative Mating after Divorce." *Social Science Research* 33:361–84.

Gershoff, E. T. 2002. "Corporal Punishment by Parents and Associated Child Behaviors and Experiences." *Psychological Bulletin* 128:539–79.

Gershuny, J., M. Bittman, and J. Brice. 2005. "Exit, Voice, and Suffering: Do Couples Adapt to Changing Employment Patterns?" *Journal of Marriage and Family* 67:656–65.

Gerson, K., and J. A. Jacobs. 2004. "The Work-Home Crunch." *Contexts* 3:29–37.

Gibbons, J. L., M. Lynn, and D. A. Stiles. 1997. "Cross-National Gender Differences in Adolescents' Preferences for Free-Time Activities." *Cross-Cultural Research* 31:55–69.

Gibson, C. 2001. "Nation's Median Age Highest Ever." Press Release, U.S. Census Bureau, Census Bureau Web site.

Gilbert, L. A. 1993. *Two Careers/One Family.* Newbury Park, CA: Sage.

Gilbert, N. 2003. "My Husband Made Me Do It." *Times Higher Education Supplement,* Issue 1605, p. 10.

Gilbert, N. 2005. "Family Life: Sold on Work." *Society* 42:12–17.

Gilford, R. 1984. "Contrasts in Marital Satisfaction Throughout Old Age: An Exchange Theory Analysis." *Journal of Gerontology* 39:325–33.

Gilgun, J. F. 1995. "We Shared Something Special: The Moral Discourse of Incest Perpetrators." *Journal of Marriage and the Family* 57:265–81.

Gilliam, M. L. 2007. "The Role of Parents and Partners in the Pregnancy Behaviors of Young Latinas." *Hispanic Journal of Behavioral Sciences* 29:50–67.

Giordano, P. C., W. D. Manning, and M. A. Longmore. 2005. "The Romantic Relationships of African-American and White Adolescents." *The Sociological Quarterly* 46:545–68.

Gjerdingen, D. K., and B. A. Center. 2005. "First-Time Parents' Postpartum Changes in Employment, Childcare, and Housework Responsibilities." *Social Science Research* 34:103–16.

Gladstone, J., and A. Westhues. 1998. "Adoption Reunions: A New Side of Intergenerational Family Relationships." *Family Relations* 47:177–84.

Glascock, J., and C. Preston-Schreck. 2004. "Gender and Racial Stereotypes in Daily Newspaper Comics." *Sex Roles* 51:423–31.

Glass, J., and L. E. Nath. 2006. "Religious Conservatism and Women's Market Behavior Following Marriage and Childbirth." *Journal of Marriage and Family* 68:611–29.

Glenn, N. D. 1987. "Social Trends in the United States: Evidence from Sample Surveys." *Public Opinion Quarterly* 51:S109–S126.

Glenn, N. D. 1992. "What Does Family Mean?" *American Demographics,* June, pp. 30–37.

Goetting, A. 1986. "Parental Satisfaction: A Review of Research." *Journal of Family Issues* 7:83–109.

Goetting, A. 1990. "Patterns of Support among In-Laws in the United States." *Journal of Family Issues* 11:67–90.

Gold, J. M., D. L. Bubenzer, and J. D. West. 1993. "Differentiation from Ex-Spouses and Stepfamily Marital Intimacy." *Journal of Divorce and Remarriage* 19:83–95.

Gold, S. J. 1993. "Migration and Family Adjustment: Continuity and Change among Vietnamese in the United States." In H. P. McAdoo, ed., *Family Ethnicity: Strength in Diversity.* Newbury Park, CA: Sage.

Goldberg, A. E., and K. R. Allen. 2007. "Imagining Men: Lesbian Mothers' Perceptions of Male Involvement during the Transition to Parenthood." *Journal of Marriage and Family* 69: 352–65.

Goldberg, A. E., and M. Perry-Jenkins. 2007. "The Division of Labor and Perception of Parental Roles." *Journal of Social and Personal Relationships* 24:297–318.

Goldberg, M. 1987. "Patterns of Disagreement in Marriage." *Medical Aspects of Human Sexuality* 21:42–52.

Goldberg, W. A., G. Y. Michaels, and M. E. Lamb. 1985. "Husbands' and Wives' Adjustment to Pregnancy and First Parenthood." *Journal of Family Issues* 6:483–503.

Goldman, N., et al. 2004. "Sex Differentials in Biological Risk Factors for Chronic Disease." *Journal of Women's Health* 13:393–403.

Goldscheider, C., and W. D. Mosher. 1991. "Patterns of Contraceptive Use in the United States: The Importance of Religious Factors." *Studies in Family Planning* 22:102–15.

Goldscheider, F. 1997. "Recent Changes in U.S. Young Adult Living Arrangements in Comparative Perspective." *Journal of Family Issues* 18:708–24.

Goldscheider, F. K., and C. Goldscheider. 1993. *Leaving Home before Marriage: Ethnicity, Familism, and Generational Relationships.* Madison: University of Wisconsin Press.

Goldstein, J. R., and C. T. Kenney. 2001. "Marriage Delayed or Marriage Forgone? Cohort Forecasts of First Marriage for U.S. Women." *American Sociological Review* 66:506–19.

Goleman, D. 1986. "Two Views of Marriage Explored: His and Hers." *New York Times,* April 1.

Golombok, S., and F. Tasker. 1996. "Do Parents Influence the Sexual Orientation of Their Children?" *Developmental Psychology* 32:3–11.

Golombok, S., et al. 2003. "Children with Lesbian Parents: A Community Study." *Developmental Psychology* 39:20–33.

Gonzalez, L. O. 2000. "Infertility as a Transformational Process." *Issues in Mental Health Nursing* 21:619–33.

Goodman, C. C. 2007. "Family Dynamics in Three-Generation Grandfamilies." *Journal of Family Issues* 28:355–79.

Goodman, C. C., and M. Silverstein. 2001. "Grandmothers Who Parent Their Grandchildren." *Journal of Family Issues* 22:557–78.

Goodman, C. C., and M. Silverstein. 2006. "Grandmothers Raising Grandchildren." *Journal of Family Issues* 27:1605–26.

Gordon, R. A., R. Kaestner, and S. Korenman. 2007. "The Effects of Maternal Employment on Child Injuries and Infectious Disease." *Demography* 44:307–33.

Gottlieb, L. 2006. "How Do I Love Thee?" *The Atlantic Monthly,* March, pp. 58–70.

Gottlieb, L. N., A. Lang, and R. Amsel. 1996. "The Long Term Effects of Grief on Marital Intimacy Following an Infant's Death." *Omega* 33:1–19.

Gottman, J. M. 1994. *What Predicts Divorce?* Hillsdale, NJ: Lawrence Erlbaum Associates.

Gottman, J. M., J. Coan, S. Carrere, and C. Swanson. 1998. "Predicting Marital Happiness and Stability from Newlywed Interactions." *Journal of Marriage and the Family* 60:5–22.

Gottman, J. M., and L. J. Krokoff. 1989. "Marital Interaction and Satisfaction: A Longitudinal View." *Journal of Consulting and Clinical Psychology* 57:47–52.

Gottman, J. M., and R. W. Levenson. 2000. "The Timing of Divorce." *Journal of Marriage and the Family* 62:737–45.

Gottman, J. M., et al. 2003. "Correlates of Gay and Lesbian Couples' Relationship Satisfaction and Relationship Dissolution." *Journal of Homosexuality* 45:23–43.

Graham-Bermann, S. A., and A. A. Levendosky. 1998. "Traumatic Stress Symptoms in Children of Battered Women." *Journal of Interpersonal Violence* 13:111–28.

Grant, J. D., et al. 2007. "Spousal Concordance for Alcohol Dependence." *Alcoholism Clinical and Experimental Research* 31:717–28.

Gray, M. R., and L. Steinberg. 1999. "Unpacking Authoritative Parenting." *Journal of Marriage and the Family* 61:574–87.

Greeff, A. P., and T. De Bruyne. 2000. "Conflict Management Style and Marital Satisfaction." *Journal of Sex and Marital Therapy* 26:321–34.

Greeff, A. P., and S. van der Merwe. 2004. "Variables Associated with Resilience in Divorced Families." *Social Indicators Research* 68:59–75.

Greenfield, E. A., and N. F. Marks. 2006. "Linked Lives: Adult Children's Problems and Their Parents' Psychological and Relationship Well-Being." *Journal of Marriage and Family* 68:442–54.

Greenfield, E. A., and N. F. Marks. 2007. "Religious Social Identity as an Explanatory Factor for Associations between More Frequent Formal Religious Participation and Psychological Well-Being." *International Journal for the Psychology of Religion* 17: 245–59.

Greenstein, T. N. 1995. "Gender Ideology, Marital Disruption and the Employment of Married Women." *Journal of Marriage and the Family* 57:31–42.

Gregoire, A. 2000. "Assessing and Managing Male Sexual Problems." *Western Journal of Medicine* 172:49–50.

Grekin, E. R., P. A. Brennan, and C. Hammen. 2005. "Parental Alcohol Use Disorders and Child Delinquency." *Journal of Studies on Alcohol* 66:14–22.

Gross, P. 1986. "Defining Post-Divorce Remarriage Families: A Typology Based on the Subjective Perceptions of Children." *Journal of Divorce* 10:205–17.

Grossman, M., and W. Wood. 1993. "Sex Differences in Intensity of Emotional Experience." *Journal of Personality and Social Psychology* 65:1010–22.

Grote, N. K., M. S. Clark, and A. Moore. 2004. "Perceptions of Injustice in Family Work." *Journal of Family Psychology* 18:480–92.

Grote, N. K., K. E. Naylor, and M. S. Clark. 2002. "Perceiving the Division of Family Work to Be Unfair." *Journal of Family Psychology* 16:510–22.

Grotevant, H. I., et al. 1994. "Adoptive Family System Dynamics: Variations by Level of Openness in the Adoption." *Family Process* 33:125–46.

Grover, K. J., C. S. Russell, W. R. Schumm, and L. A. Paff-Bergen. 1985. "Mate Selection Processes and Marital Satisfaction." *Family Relations* 34:383–86.

Guarnero, P. A. 2007. "Family and Community Influences on the Social and Sexual Lives of Latino Gay Men." *Journal of Transcultural Nursing* 18:12–18.

Guastello, D. D., and S. J. Guastello. 2003. "Androgyny, Gender Role Behavior, and Emotional Intelligence among College Students and Their Parents." *Sex Roles* 49:663–73.

Gueorguieva, R. V., et al. 2001. "Effect of Teenage Pregnancy on Educational Disabilities in Kindergarten." *American Journal of Epidemiology* 154:212–20.

Guidubaldi, J., and H. Cleminshaw. 1985. "Divorce, Family Health, and Child Adjustment." *Family Relations* 34:35–41.

Guilamo-Ramos, V., et al. 2006. "The Content and Process of Mother-Adolescent Communication about Sex in Latino Families." *Social Work Research* 30:169–81.

Guilamo-Ramos, V., et al. 2007. "Parenting Practices among Dominican and Puerto Rican Mothers." *Social Work* 52:17–30.

Guldner, G. 2003. *Long Distance Relationships*. Corona, CA: J.F. Milne Publications.

Gupta, S. 2006. "The Consequences of Maternal Employment during Men's Childhood for Their Adult Housework Performance." *Gender & Society* 20:60–86.

Gwanfogbe, P. N., W. R. Schumm, M. Smith, and J. L. Furrow. 1997. "Polygyny and Marital Life Satisfaction." *Journal of Comparative Family Studies* 28:55–71.

Gwinnell, E. 1998. *Online Seductions: Falling in Love with Strangers on the Internet*. New York: Kodansha.

Haddock, S. A., T. S. Zimmerman, S. J. Ziemba, and I. R. Current. 2001. "Ten Adaptive Strategies for Family and Work Balance." *Journal of Marital and Family Therapy* 27:445–58.

Hahn, J., and T. Blass. 1997. "Dating Partner Preferences." *Journal of Social Behavior and Personality* 12:595–610.

Haj-Yahia, M. M. 2000. "Implications of Wife Abuse and Battering for Self-Esteem, Depression, and Anxiety as Revealed by the Second Palestinian National Survey on Violence against Women." *Journal of Family Issues* 21:435–63.

Halfon, N., T. McLearn, and M. Schuster, eds. 2002. *Child Rearing in America: Challenges Facing Parents with Young Children*. New York: Cambridge University Press.

Hahm, C. H., M. Lahiff, and R. M. Barreto. 2006. "Asian American Adolescents' First Sexual Intercourse." *Perspectives on Sexual and Reproductive Health* 38:28–36.

Halford, W. K., K. Hahlweg, and M. Dunne. 1990. "The Cross-Cultural Consistency of Marital Communication Associated with Marital Distress." *Journal of Marriage and the Family* 52:487–500.

Halford, W. K., J. Nicholson, and M. Sanders. 2007. "Couple Communication in Stepfamilies." *Family Process* 46:471–83.

Halford, W. K., J. Price, A. B. Kelly, R. Bouma, and R. M. Young. 2001. "Helping the Female Partners of Men Abusing Alcohol." *Addiction* 96:1497–1508.

Hall, J., N. Murphy, and M. Mast. 2006. "Recall of Nonverbal Cues." *Journal of Nonverbal Behavior* 30:141–55.

Halpern, C. T., et al. 2001. "Partner Violence among Adolescents in Opposite-Sex Romantic Relationships." *American Journal of Public Health* 91:1679–85.

⌐n, B. D. 2004. "The Effects of Divorce and Remarriage on Academic Achievement of High School Seniors." *Journal ⌐rce and Remarriage* 42:159–78.

Hamer, J., and K. Marchioro. 2002. "Becoming Custodial Dads: Exploring Parenting Among Low-Income and Working-Class African American Fathers." *Journal of Marriage and the Family* 64:116–29.

Hamilton, B. 1996. "Ethnicity and the Family Life Cycle: The Chinese-American Family." *Family Therapy* 23:199–212.

Hamilton, B. E., J. A. Martin, and S. J. Ventura. 2006. "Births: Preliminary Data for 2005." National Center for Health Statistics Web site.

Hamilton, L., S. Cheng, and B. Powell. 2007. "Adoptive Parents, Adaptive Parents: Evaluating the Importance of Biological Ties for Parental Investment." *American Sociological Review* 72:95–116.

Hamilton, M.C., D. Anderson, M. Broaddus, and K. Young. 2006. "Gender Stereotyping and Under-representation of Female Characters in 200 Popular Children's Picture Books." *Sex Roles* 55:757–65.

Han, H. 2003. "Korean Mothers' Psychosocial Adjustment to Their Children's Cancer." *Journal of Advanced Nursing* 44:499–506.

Han, W. 2005. "Maternal Nonstandard Work Schedules and Child Cognitive Outcomes." *Child Development* 76:137–54.

Han, W.-J., J. Waldfogel, and J. Brooks-Gunn. 2001. "The Effects of Early Maternal Employment on Later Cognitive and Behavioral Outcomes." *Journal of Marriage and the Family* 63:336–54.

Hanna, B. 2001. "Negotiating Motherhood: The Struggles of Teenage Mothers." *Journal of Advanced Nursing* 34:456–64.

Hansen, G. L. 1985a. "Dating Jealousy among College Students." *Sex Roles* 12:713–19.

Hansen, G. L. 1985b. "Perceived Threats and Marital Jealousy." *Social Psychology Quarterly* 48:262–68.

Hansen, M., J. J. Kurinczuk, C. Bower, and S. Webb. 2002. "The Risk of Major Birth Defects after Intracytoplasmic Sperm Injection and In Vitro Fertilization." *New England Journal of Medicine* 346:725–30.

Hanson, S. M. 1986. "Healthy Single Parent Families." *Family Relations* 35:125–32.

Hansson, R. O., and J. H. Remondet. 1987. "Relationships and the Aging Family: A Social Psychological Analysis." In S. Oskamp, ed., *Family Processes and Problems: Social Psychological Aspects*, pp. 262–83. Beverly Hills, CA: Sage.

Harding, D. J., and C. Jencks. 2003. "Changing Attitudes toward Premarital Sex." *Public Opinion Quarterly* 67:211–26.

Harknett, K., and S. S. McLanahan. 2004. "Racial and Ethnic Differences in Marriage after the Birth of a Child." *American Sociological Review* 69:790–811.

Harman, M. J., and C. Arbona. 1991. "Psychological Adjustment among Hispanic Adult Children of Alcoholics: An Exploratory Study." *Hispanic Journal of Behavioral Sciences* 13:105–12.

Harper, C. C., and S. S. McLanahan. 2004. "Father Absence and Youth Incarceration." *Journal of Research on Adolescence* 14:369–97.

Harper, F. W. K., A. M. Brown, I. Arias, and G. Brody. 2005. "Corporal Punishment and Kids." *Journal of Family Violence* 21:197–207.

Harpster, P., and E. Monk-Turner. 1998. "Why Men Do Housework: A Test of Gender Production and the Relative Resources Model." *Sociological Focus* 31:45–59.

Harriman, L. C. 1986. "Marital Adjustment as Related to Personal and Marital Changes Accompanying Parenthood." *Family Relations* 35:233–39.

Harris, C. R. 2002. "Sexual and Romantic Jealousy in Heterosexual and Homosexual Adults." *Psychological Science* 13:7–12.

Harris, I. M. 1995. *Messages Men Hear: Constructing Masculinities.* Bristol, PA: Taylor & Francis.

Harris, K. M., and S. P. Morgan. 1991. "Fathers, Sons, and Daughters: Differential Paternal Involvement in Parenting." *Journal of Marriage and the Family* 53:531–44.

Harris, O., and R. R. Miller, eds. 2003. *Impacts of Incarceration on the African American Family.* New Brunswick, NJ: Transaction Publishers.

Harris, T. L., and R. Schwab. 1990. "Sex-Role Orientation and Personal Adjustment." *Journal of Social Behavior and Personality* 5:473–79.

Harrison, D. J. 2004. "Dangerous Medicine." *New York Times,* November 19.

Hart, C. L., D. J. Hole, D. A. Lawlor, G. D. Smith, and T. F. Lever. 2007. "Effect of Conjugal Bereavement on Mortality of the Bereaved Spouse in Participants of the Renfew/ Paisley Study." *Journal of Epidemiology and Community Health* 61:455–60.

Hart, K. 2007. "Love by Arrangement." *Journal of the Royal Anthropological Institute* 13:345–62.

Harvey, J. H., and A. L. Weber. 2002. *Odyssey of the Heart: Close Relationships in the 21st Century.* Mahwah, NJ: Lawrence Erlbaum Associates.

Hatch, L. R., and K. Bulcroft. 2004. "Does Long-Term Marriage Bring Less Frequent Disagreements?" *Journal of Family Issues* 25:465–95.

Hatfield, E., and R. L. Rapson. 1993. "Historical and Cross-Cultural Perspectives on Passionate Love and Sexual Desire." *Annual Review of Sex Research* 4:67–97.

Hatfield, E., and S. Sprecher. 1986. "Measuring Passionate Love in Intimate Relationships." *Journal of Adolescence* 9:383–410.

Hatoum, I. J., and D. Belle. 2004. "Mags and Abs: Media Consumption and Bodily Concerns in Men. *Sex Roles* 51:397–407.

Haub, C. 1992. "The Late 1980's Baby Boomlet: Delayed Childbearing or Not?" *Population Today* 20:3.

Haugland, B. S. M. 2005. "Recurrent Disruptions of Rituals and Routines in Families with Paternal Alcohol Abuse." *Family Relations* 54:225–41.

Haveman, R., and B. L. Wolfe. 1994. *Succeeding Generations.* New York: Russell Sage Foundation.

Hawkley, L. C., M. H. Burleson, G. G. Berntson, and J. T. Cacioppo. 2003. "Loneliness in Everyday Life." *Journal of Personality and Social Psychology* 85:105–20.

Hawkins, D. N., and A. Booth. 2005. "Unhappily Ever After: Effects of Low-Quality Marriages on Well-Being." *Social Forces* 84:445–65.

Hawton, K., D. Gath, and A. Day. 1994. "Sexual Function in a Community Sample of Middle-Aged Women with Partners: Effects of Age, Marital, Socioeconomic, Psychiatric, Gynecological, and Menopausal Factors." *Archives of Sexual Behavior* 23:375–95.

Haynes, F. E. 2000. "Gender and Family Ideals." *Journal of Family Issues* 21:811–37.

Healy, J. M., A. J. Stewart, and A. P. Copeland. 1993. "The Role of Self-Blame in Children's Adjustment to Parental Separation." *Personality and Social Psychology Bulletin* 19:279–89.

Heaton, T. B. 1990. "Marital Stability throughout the Child-rearing Years." *Demography* 27:55–63.

Heaton, T. B. 2002. "Factors Contributing to Increasing Marital Stability in the United States." *Journal of Family Issues* 23:392–409.

Heaton, T. B., and S. L. Albrecht. 1991. "Stable Unhappy Marriages." *Journal of Marriage and the Family* 53:747–58.

Hecht, M. L., P. J. Marston, and L. K. Larkey. 1994. "Love Ways and Relationship Quality in Heterosexual Relationships." *Journal of Social and Personal Relationships* 11:25–43.

Heckert, D. A., T. C. Nowak, and K. A. Snyder. 1998. "The Impact of Husbands' and Wives' Relative Earnings on Marital Disruption." *Journal of Marriage and the Family* 60:690–703.

Heiman, J. R. 2002. "Sexual Dysfunction." *Journal of Sex Research* 39:73–78.

Henderson-King, D. H., and J. Veroff. 1994. "Sexual Satisfaction and Marital Well-Being in the First Years of Marriage." *Journal of Social and Personal Relationships* 11:509–34.

Hendrick, S. S., and C. Hendrick. 1987. "Love and Sex Attitudes and Religious Beliefs." *Journal of Social and Clinical Psychology* 5:391–98.

Hendrick, S. S., and C. Hendrick. 1992. *Romantic Love.* Newbury Park, CA: Sage.

Hendrick, S. S., C. Hendrick, and N. L. Adler. 1988. "Romantic Relationships: Love, Satisfaction, and Staying Together." *Journal of Personality and Social Psychology* 54:980–88.

Hendrix, L. 1997. "Quality and Equality in Marriage: A Cross-Cultural View." *Cross-Cultural Research* 31:201–25.

Henning, K., H. Leitenberg, P. Coffey, and T. Turner. 1996. "Long-Term Psychological and Social Impact of Witnessing Physical Conflict between Parents." *Journal of Interpersonal Violence* 11:35–51.

Henretta, J. C. 2007. "Early Childbearing, Marital Status, and Women's Health and Mortality after Age 50." *Journal of Health and Social Behavior* 48:254–66.

Henry, R., and R. Miller. 2004. "Marital Problems Occurring in Midlife." *American Journal of Family Therapy* 32:405–17.

Hensley, W. E. 1996. "The Effect of a Ludus Love Style on Sexual Experience." *Social Behavior and Personality* 24:205–12.

Herring, C., and K. R. Wilson-Sadberry. 1993. "Preference or Necessity? Changing Work Roles of Black and White Women, 1973–1990." *Journal of Marriage and the Family* 55:314–25.

Hertz, R. 2006. *Single by Chance, Mothers by Choice.* New York: Oxford University Press.

Hesse-Biber, S. 1996. *Am I Thin Enough Yet? The Cult of Thinness and the Commercialization of Identity.* New York: Oxford University Press.

Hester, C. 1996. "The Relationship of Personality, Gender, and Age to Adjective Check List Profiles of the Ideal Romantic Partner." *Journal of Psychological Type* 36:28–35.

Hetherington, E. M. 1993. "An Overview of the Virginia Longitudinal Study of Divorce and Remarriage with a Focus on the Early Adolescent." *Journal of Family Psychology* 7:39–56.

Hetherington, E. M. 2003. "Intimate Pathways: Changing Patterns in Close Personal Relationships across Time." *Family Relations* 32:318–31.

Hetherington, E. M., and J. Kelly. 2002. *For Better or for Worse: Divorce Reconsidered.* New York: W. W. Norton.

Hetsroni, A. 2000. "Choosing a Mate in Television Dating Games." *Sex Roles* 42:83–106.

Hettrich, E. L., and K. D. O'Leary. 2007. "Females' Reasons for Their Physical Aggression in Dating Relationships." *Journal of Interpersonal Violence* 22:1131–43.

Hildebrandt, E., and S. T. Kelber. 2005. "Perceptions of Health and Well-Being among Women in a Work-Based Welfare Program." *Public Health Nursing* 22:506–14.

Hill, E. J., et al. 2006. "Researching the 60-Hour Dual-Earner Workweek." *American Behavioral Scientist* 49:1184–1203.

Hill, R. 1949. *Families under Stress.* New York: Harper & Row.

Hill, R. 1958. "Generic Features of Families under Stress." *Social Casework* 49:139–50.

Hill, S. 2001. "Class, Race, and Gender Dimensions of Child Rearing in African American Families." *Journal of Black Studies* 31:494–508.

Hilton, J. M., and K. Kopera-Frye. 2004. "Patterns of Psychological Adjustment among Divorced Custodial Parents." *Journal of Divorce and Remarriage* 41:1–30.

Himsel, A. J., and W. A. Goldberg. 2003. "Social Comparisons and Satisfaction with the Division of Housework." *Journal of Family Issues* 24:843–66.

Hinchliff, S., and M. Gott. 2004. "Intimacy, Commitment, and Adaptation: Sexual Relationships within Long-Term Marriages." *Journal of Social and Personal Relationships* 21:595–609.

Hinze, S. W. 2004. "'Am I Being Over-Sensitive?' Women's Experience of Sexual Harassment during Medical Training." *Health* 8:101–27.

Hirokawa, K., A. Yagi, and Y. Miyata. 2004. "An Examination of Masculinity-Femininity Traits and Their Relationships to Communication Skills and Stress-Coping Skills." *Social Behavior and Personality* 32:731–40.

Hobart, C. 1987. "Parent-Child Relations in Remarried Families." *Journal of Family Issues* 8:259–77.

Hobart, C. 1990. "Relationships between the Formerly Married." *Journal of Comparative Family Studies* 21:81–97.

Hobart, C. 1991. "Conflict in Remarriages." *Journal of Divorce and Remarriage* 15:69–86.

Hobart, C., and D. Brown. 1988. "Effects of Prior Marriage Children on Adjustment in Remarriage: A Canadian Study." *Journal of Comparative Family Studies* 19:381–96.

Hochschild, A. R. 1997. *The Time Bind: When Work Becomes Home and Home Becomes Work.* New York: Metropolitan Books.

Hoelter, L. F., W. G. Axinn, and D. J. Ghimire. 2004. "Social Change, Premarital Nonfamily Experiences, and Marital Dynamics." *Journal of Marriage and the Family* 66:1131–51.

Hofferth, S. L. 2003. "Race/Ethnic Differences in Father Involvement in Two-Parent Families: Culture, Context, or Economy." *Journal of Family Issues* 24:185–216.

Hofferth, S. L., and K. G. Anderson. 2003. "Are All Dads Equal? Biology versus Marriage as a Basis for Paternal Investment." *Journal of Marriage and the Family* 65:213–32.

Hoffmann, J. P. 2006. "Family Structure, Community Content, and Adolescent Problem Behaviors." *Journal of Youth and Adolescence* 35:867–80.

Hoffmann, J. P., and R. A. Johnson. 1998. "A National Portrait of Family Structure and Adolescent Drug Use." *Journal of Marriage and the Family* 60:633–45.

Hohmann-Marriott, B. E. 2006. "Shared Beliefs and the Union Stability of Married and Cohabiting Couples." *Journal of Marriage and Family* 68:1015–28.

Hollist, D. R., and W. H. McBroom. 2006. "Family Structure, Family Tension, and Self-Reported Marijuana Use." *Journal of Drug Issues* 36:975–98.

Holman, T. B., and B. D. Li. 1997. "Premarital Factors Influencing Perceived Readiness for Marriage." *Journal of Family Issues* 18:124–44.

Hong, L. K., and R. W. Duff. 1997. "Relative Importance of Spouses, Children, and Friends in the Life Satisfaction of Retirement Community Residents." *Journal of Clinical Geropsychology* 3:275–82.

Hosain, G. M., and N. Chatterjee. 2005. "Beliefs, Sexual Behaviours and Preventive Practices with Respect to HIV/AIDS among Commercial Sex Workers in Daulatdia, Bangladesh." *Public Health* 119:371–81.

Hossain, Z., and J. L. Roopnarine. 1993. "Division of Household Labor and Child Care in Dual-Earner African-American Families with Infants." *Sex Roles* 29:571–83.

Houts, L. A. 2005. "Young Women's First Voluntary Sexual Intercourse." *Journal of Family Issues* 26:1082–1102.

Houts, R. M., E. Robins, and T. L. Huston. 1996. "Compatibility and the Development of Premarital Relationships." *Journal of Marriage and the Family* 58:7–20.

Hovell, M., et al. 1994. "Family Influences on Latino and Anglo Adolescent Sexual Behavior." *Journal of Marriage and the Family* 56:973–86.

Hovey, J. K. 2005. "Fathers Parenting Chronically Ill Children." *Issues in Comprehensive Pediatric Nursing* 28:83–95.

Howard, D. E., and M. O. Wang. 2003. "Risk Profiles of Adolescent Girls Who Were Victims of Dating Violence." *Adolescence* 38:1–14.

Howard, J. A., P. Blumstein, and P. Schwartz. 1986. "Sex, Power, and Influence Tactics in Intimate Relationships." *Journal of Personality and Social Psychology* 51:102–9.

Hughes, J. 2000. "Repartnering after Divorce." *Family Matters* no. 55. Australian Institute of Family Studies Web site.

Hughes, M. E., L. J. Waite, T. A. LaPierre, and Y. Luo. 2007. "All in the Family: The Impact of Caring for Grandchildren on

Grandparents' Health." *Journals of Gerontology Series B* 62B:S108–119.

Hull, K. E. 2006. *Same-Sex Marriage: The Cultural Politics of Love and Law.* Cambridge, UK: Cambridge University Press.

Hunt, M. 1974. *Sexual Behavior in the 1970s.* Chicago: Playboy Press.

Huppe, M., and M. Cyr. 1997. "Division of Household Labor and Marital Satisfaction of Dual Income Couples According to Family Life Cycle." *Canadian Journal of Counselling* 31:145–62.

Hurtz, W., and K. Durkin. 1997. "Gender Role Stereotyping in Australian Radio Commercials." *Sex Roles* 36:103–13.

Huston, T. L., S. M. McHale, and A. C. Crouter. 1986. "When the Honeymoon's Over: Changes in the Marriage Relationship over the First Year." In R. Gilmour and S. Duck, eds., *The Emerging Field of Personal Relationships*, pp. 109–32. Hillsdale, NJ: Lawrence Erlbaum Associates.

Hutchinson, E. O. 2000. "Nine Habits Every Black Dad Should Have." *Family Digest.* Family Digest Web site.

Hutchison, R., and M. McNall. 1994. "Early Marriage in a Hmong Cohort." *Journal of Marriage and the Family* 56:579–90.

Hutchinson, S. I., T. Afifi, and S. Krause. 2006. "The Family That Plays Together Fares Better." *Journal of Divorce & Remarriage* 46:21–48.

Hyde, J. S. 2005. "The Gender Similarities Hypothesis." *American Psychologist* 60:581–92.

Hyde, J. S., and J. D. DeLamater. 2007. 10th edition. New York: McGraw-Hill.

Hyde, J. S., and M. C. Linn. 2006. "Gender Similarities in Mathematics and Science." *Science* 314:599–600.

Ihinger-Tallman, M., and K. Pasley. 1987. *Remarriage.* Beverly Hills, CA: Sage.

Impett, E. A., and L. A. Peplau. 2002. "Why Some Women Consent to Unwanted Sex with a Dating Partner." *Psychology of Women Quarterly* 26:360–70.

Inman-Amos, J., S. S. Hendrick, and C. Hendrick. 1994. "Love Attitudes: Similarities between Parents and between Parents and Children." *Family Relations* 43:456–61.

Institute for American Values. 2002. *Why Marriage Matters.* New York: Institute for American Values.

Isaac, R., and A. Shah. 2004. "Sex Roles and Marital Adjustment in Indian Couples." *International Journal of Social Psychiatry* 50:129–41.

Isay, R. A. 2006. *Commitment and Healing: Gay Men and the Need for Romantic Love.* New York: John Wiley & Sons.

Ishii-Kuntz, M., and S. Coltrane. 1992. "Remarriage, Stepparenting, and Household Labor." *Journal of Family Issues* 13:215–33.

Iuliano, A. D., I. S. Speizer, J. Santelli, and C. Kendall. 2006. "Reasons for Contraceptive Nonuse at First Sex and Unintended Pregnancy." *American Journal of Health Behavior* 30:92–102.

Jackson, A. P., and R. Scheines. 2005. "Single Mothers' Self-Efficacy, Parenting in the Home Environment, and Children's Development in a Two-Wave Study." *Social Work Research* 29:7–21.

Jackson, J. L., K. S. Calhoun, A. E. Amick, H. M. Maddever, and V. L. Habif. 1990. "Young Adult Women Who Report

Childhood Intrafamilial Sexual Abuse: Subsequent Adjustment." *Archives of Sexual Behavior* 19:211–21.

Jacobsen, R. B., and J. J. Bigner. 1991. "Black versus White Single Parents and the Value of Children." *Journal of Black Studies* 21:302–12.

Jacques, J. M. 1998. "Changing Marital and Family Patterns." *Sociological Perspectives* 41:381–411.

Jacquet, S. E., and C. A. Surra. 2001. "Parental Divorce and Premarital Couples." *Journal of Marriage and Family* 63:627–38.

Jaffe, D. H., O. Manor, Z. Eisenbach, and Y. D. Neumark. 2007. "The Protective Effect of Marriage on Mortality in a Dynamic Society." *Annals of Epidemiology* 17:540–47.

Jaffee, S., et al. 2000. "Why Are Children Born to Teen Mothers at Risk for Adverse Outcomes in Young Adulthood?" *Developmental Psychopathology* 13:377–97.

Jaffee, S. R., T. E. Moffitt, A. Caspi, and A. Taylor. 2003. "Life with (or without) Father." *Child Development* 74:109–26.

Jambunathan, S., D. C. Burts, and S. Pierce. 2000. "Comparisons of Parenting Attitudes among Five Ethnic Groups in the United States." *Journal of Comparative Family Studies* 31:395–406.

Jang, S. J. 2002. "Race, Ethnicity, and Deviance." *Sociological Forum* 17:647–80.

Janssen, E., D. Carpenter, and C. A. Graham. 2003. "Selecting Films for Sex Research: Gender Differences in Erotic Film Preference." *Archives of Sexual Behavior* 32:243–51.

Javaid, G. A. 1993. "The Children of Homosexual and Heterosexual Single Mothers." *Child Psychiatry and Human Development* 23:235–48.

Jekielek, S. M. 1998. "Parental Conflict, Marital Disruption, and Children's Emotional Well-Being." *Social Forces* 76:905–35.

Jenkins, J., A. Simpson, J. Dunn, J. Rasbash, and T. G. O'Connor. 2005. "Mutual Influence of Marital Conflict and Children's Behavior Problems." *Child Development* 76:24–39.

Jennison, K. M., and K. A. Johnson. 2001. "Parenting Alcoholism as a Risk Factor for DSM-IV–Defined Alcohol Abuse and Dependence in American Women." *American Journal of Drug and Alcohol Abuse* 27:349–74.

Jervolino, A. C., M. Hines, S. E. Golombok, J. Rust, and R. Plomin. 2005. "Genetic and Environmental Influences on Sex-Typed Behavior during the Preschool Years." *Child Development* 76:826–40.

Jeynes, W. H. 2001. "The Effects of Recent Parental Divorce on Their Children's Consumption of Alcohol." *Journal of Youth and Adolescence* 30:305–19.

Jeynes, W. H. 2006. "The Impact of Parental Remarriage on Children." *Marriage & Family Review* 40:75–102.

Joebgen, A. M, and M. H. Richards. 1990. "Maternal Education and Employment: Mediating Maternal and Adolescent Emotional Adjustment." *Journal of Early Adolescence.* 10:329–43.

John, D. 1996. "Women's Reports of Men's Childcare Participation." *Journal of Men's Studies* 5:13–30.

John, R. 1997. "Native American Families." In C. H. Mindel, R. W. Habenstein, and R. Wright, Jr., eds. *Ethnic Families in America.* 4th edition. Upper Saddle River, NJ: Prentice-Hall.

Johnson, B. M., S. Shulman, and W. A. Collins. 1991. "Systemic Patterns of Parenting as Reported by Adolescents." *Journal of Adolescent Research* 6:235–52.

Johnson, D. R., and A. Booth. 1998. "Marital Quality: A Product of the Dyadic Environment or Individual Factors?" *Social Force* 76:883–905.

Johnson, H. D., J. C. LaVoie, and M. Mahoney. 2001. "Interparental Conflict and Family Cohesion." *Journal of Adolescent Research* 16:304–18.

Johnson, H. D., et al. 2007. "Identity as a Moderator of Gender Differences in the Emotional Closeness of Emerging Adults' Same- and Cross-Sex Friendships." *Adolescence* 42:1–23.

Johnson, M. P. 2005. "Domestic Violence: It's Not about Gender–Or Is It?" *Journal of Marriage and Family* 67:1126–30.

Johnson, M. P., and J. M. Leone. 2005. "The Differential Effects of Intimate Terrorism and Situational Couple Violence." *Journal of Family Issues* 26:322–49.

Johnson, S. 1994. "Love: The Immutable Longing for Contact." *Psychology Today*, March/April, pp. 32–37.

Johnson, S. M., and E. O'Connor. 2002. *The Gay Baby Boom: The Psychology of Gay Parenthood*. New York: New York University Press.

Johnston, L. D., P. M. O'Malley, J. G. Bachman, and J. E. Schulenberg. 2006. *Monitoring the Future: National Survey Results on Drug Use*. National Institute on Drug Abuse Web site.

Jones, D. 2007. "A Culture of Romance." *New Scientist* 193:15.

Jones, D. C. 2004. "Body Image among Adolescent Girls and Boys." *Developmental Psychology* 40:823–35.

Jones, D. C., N. Bloys, and M. Wood. 1990. "Sex Roles and Friendship Patterns." *Sex Roles* 23:133–45.

Jones, D. C., and R. Houts. 1992. "Parental Drinking, Parent-Child Communication, and Social Skills in Young Adults." *Journal of Studies on Alcohol* 53:48–56.

Jones, D. C., T. H. Vigfusdottir, and Y. Lee. 2004. "Body Image and the Appearance Culture among Adolescent Girls and Boys." *Journal of Adolescent Research* 19:323–39.

Jones, E. F., and J. D. Forrest. 1992. "Contraceptive Failure Rates Based on the 1988 NSFG." *Family Planning Perspectives* 24:12–19.

Jones, G. W. 2005. "The 'Flight from Marriage' in South-East and East Asia." *Journal of Comparative Family Studies* 36:93–119.

Jose, P. E., and W. J. McCarthy. 1988. "Perceived Agentic and Communal Behavior in Mixed-Sex Group Interactions." *Personality and Social Psychology Bulletin* 14:57–67.

Juffer, F., and M. H. van Ijzendoorn. 2005. "Behavior Problems and Mental Health Referrals of International Adoptees." *Journal of the American Medical Association* 293:2501–15.

Juliusdottir, S. 1997. "An Icelandic Study of Five Parental Life Styles." *Journal of Divorced Remarriage* 26:87–103.

Kaestle, C. E., and C. T. Halpern. 2007. "What's Love Got to Do with It? Sexual Behaviors of Opposite-Sex Couples Through Emerging Adulthood." *Perspectives on Sexual and Reproductive Health* 39:134–40.

Kageyama, Y. 2004. "More Japanese Women Defying Culture, Delaying Marriage." *San Diego Union-Tribune*, November 23.

Kahn, A. S. 1984. *Social Psychology*. Dubuque, IA: Wm. C. Brown.

Kahn, J. R., and K. A. London. 1991. "Premarital Sex and the Risk of Divorce." *Journal of Marriage and the Family* 53:845–55.

Kalb, C. 1997. "How Old Is Too Old?" *Newsweek*, May 5.

Kalichman, S.C., et al. 2007. "Changes in HIV Treatment Beliefs and Sexual Risk Behaviors among Gay and Bisexual Men." *Health Psychology* 26:650–56.

Kalmijn, M. 1991. "Shifting Boundaries: Trends in Religious and Educational Homogamy." *American Sociological Review* 56:786–800.

Kalmijn, M. 1994. "Mother's Occupational Status and Children's Schooling." *American Sociological Review* 59:257–75.

Kalmijn, M. 1999. "Father Involvement in Childrearing and the Perceived Stability of Marriage." *Journal of Marriage and the Family* 61:409–21.

Kalmijn, M., and H. Flap. 2001. "Assortative Meeting and Mating: Unintended Consequences of Organized Settings for Partner Choices." *Social Forces* 80:661–70.

Kamo, Y., and E. L. Cohen. 1998. "Division of Household Work between Partners." *Journal of Comparative Family Studies* 39:147–58.

Kanaan, M., and K. Avraham. 2005. "Breaking the Barriers." *New Scientist* 185:48–51.

Kanemasa, Y., J. Taniguchi, I. Daibo, and M. Ishimori. 2004. "Love Styles and Romantic Love Experiences in Japan." *Social Behavior and Personality* 32:265–82.

Kang, S. Y., S. Magura, and J. L. Shapiro. 1994. "Correlates of Cocaine/Crack Use among Inner-City Incarcerated Adolescents." *American Journal of Drug and Alcohol Abuse* 209:413–29.

Kao, T. A., B. Guthrie, and C. Loveland-Cherry. 2007. "An Intergenerational Approach to Understanding Taiwanese American Adolescent Girls' and Their Mothers' Perceptions about Sexual Health." *Journal of Family Nursing* 13:312–32.

Kaplan, R. M., and R. G. Kronick. 2006. "Marital Status and Longevity in the United States Population." *Journal of Epidemiology and Community Health* 60:760–65.

Kapungu, C., G. N. Holmbeck, and R. L. Paikoff. 2006. "Longitudinal Association between Parenting Practices and Early Sexual Risk Behaviors among Urban African American Adolescents." *Journal of Youth and Adolescence* 35:783–94.

Kasian, M., and S. L. Painter. 1992. "Frequency and Severity of Psychological Abuse in a Dating Population." *Journal of Interpersonal Violence* 7:350–64.

Katzev, A. R., R. L. Warner, and A. C. Acock. 1994. "Girls or Boys? Relationship of Child Gender to Marital Instability." *Journal of Marriage and the Family* 56:89–100.

Kaufman, C., J. Beals, C. Mitchell, P. Lemaster, and A. Fickensher. 2004. "Stress, Trauma, and Risky Sexual Behaviour among American Indians in Young Adulthood." *Culture, Health & Sexuality* 6:301–18.

Kaufman, G. 2005. "Gender Role Attitudes and College Students' Work and Family Expectations." *Gender Issues* 22:58–71.

Kaufman, G., and G. H. Elder, Jr. 2003. "Grandparenting and Age Identity." *Journal of Aging Studies* 17:269–82.

Kaufman, G., and H. Taniguchi. 2006. "Gender and Marital Happiness in Later Life." *Journal of Family Issues* 27:735–57.

Kaufman, G., and F. Goldscheider. 2007. "Do Men 'Need' a Spouse More Than Women?" *The Sociological Quarterly* 48:29–46.

Kaukinen, C. 2004. "Status Compatibility, Physical Violence, and Emotional Abuse in Intimate Relationships." *Journal of Marriage and the Family* 66:452–71.

Kaura, S. A., and C. M. Allen. 2004. "Dissatisfaction with Relationship Power and Dating Violence Perpetration by Men and Women." *Journal of Interpersonal Violence* 19:576–88.

Kaura, S. A., and B. J. Lohman. 2007. "Dating Violence Victimization, Relationship Satisfaction, Mental Health Problems, and Acceptability of Violence." *Journal of Family Violence* 22:367–81.

Kawakami, N., R. E. Roberts, E. S. Lee, and S. Araki. 1995. "Changes in Rates of Depressive Symptoms in a Japanese Working Population." *Psychological Medicine* 25:1181–90.

Kayser, K. 1993. *When Love Dies: The Process of Marital Disaffection.* New York: Guilford.

Keene, J. R., and J. R. Reynolds. 2005. "The Job Costs of Family Demands." *Journal of Family Issues* 26:275–99.

Kelley, J. E., M. A. Lumley, and J. C. Leisen. 1997. "Health Effects of Emotional Disclosure in Rheumatoid Arthritis Patients." *Health Psychology* 16:331–40.

Kennedy, G. E. 1985. "Family Relationships as Perceived by College Students from Single-Parent, Blended, and Intact Families." *Family Perspective* 19:117–26.

Kennedy, G. E. 1991. "Grandchildren's Reasons for Closeness with Grandparents." *Journal of Social Behavior and Personality* 6:697–712.

Kernes, J. L., and R. T. Kinnier. 2005. "Psychologists' Search for the Good Life." *Journal of Humanistic Psychology* 45:82–105.

Keshet, J. K. 1990. "Cognitive Remodeling of the Family: How Remarried People View Stepfamilies." *American Journal of Orthopsychiatry* 60:196–203.

Kesner, J. E., and P. C. McKenry. 2001. "Single Parenthood and Social Competence in Children of Color." *Families in Society* 82:136–45.

Kessler, R. C., and W. J. Magee. 1993. "Childhood Adversities and Adult Depression: Basic Patterns of Association in a U.S. National Survey." *Psychological Medicine* 23:679–90.

Kessler, R. C., and W. J. Magee. 1994. "Childhood Family Violence and Adult Recurrent Depression." *Journal of Health and Social Behavior* 35:13–27.

Khawaja, M., and R. R. Habib. 2007. "Husbands' Involvement in Housework and Women's Psychosocial Health." *American Journal of Public Health* 97:860–66.

Kibria, N. 1993. *Family Tightrope: The Changing Lives of Vietnamese Americans.* Princeton, NJ: Princeton University Press.

Kibria, N. 1994. "Household Structure and Family Ideologies: The Dynamics of Immigrant Economic Adaptation among Vietnamese Refugees." *Social Problems* 41:81–95.

Kiecolt, K. J. 2003. "Satisfaction with Work and Family Life." *Journal of Marriage and the Family* 65:23–35.

Kiger, P. 2003. "What Men Want from Marriage." *Ladies' Home Journal,* June, pp. 112–18.

Kilborn, P. T. 2004. "Alive, Well, and on the Prowl." *New York Times,* March 7.

Kim, H. K., and P. C. McKenry. 2002. "The Relationship between Marriage and Psychological Well-Being." *Journal of Family Issues* 23:885–911.

Kim, J., and E. Hatfield. 2004. "Love Types and Subjective Well-Being." *Social Behavior and Personality* 32:173–82.

Kim, J. L., and L. M. Ward. 2007. "Silence Speaks Volumes: Parental Sexual Communication among Asian American Emerging Adults." *Journal of Adolescent Research* 22:3–31.

King, J., J. Beals, S. M. Manson, and J. E. Trimble. 1992. "A Structural Equation Model of Factors Related to Substance Abuse among American Indian Adolescents." *Drugs and Society* 6:253–68.

King, L. A. 1993. "Emotional Expression, Ambivalence over Expression, and Marital Satisfaction." *Journal of Social and Personal Relationships.* 10:601–7.

King, V. 2003. "The Influence of Religion on Fathers' Relationships with Their Children." *Journal of Marriage and the Family* 65:382–95.

King, V. 2006. "The Antecedents and Consequences of Adolescents' Relationships with Stepfathers and Nonresident Fathers." *Journal of Marriage and Family* 68:910–28.

King, V. 2007. "When Children Have Two Mothers: Relationships with Nonresident Mothers, Stepmothers, and Fathers." *Journal of Marriage and Family* 69:1178–93.

King, V., and G. H. Elder Jr. 1997. "The Legacy of Grandparenting: Childhood Experiences with Grandparents and Current Involvement with Grandchildren." *Journal of Marriage and the Family* 59:848–59.

King, V., and M. E. Scott. 2005. "A Comparison of Cohabiting Relationships among Older and Younger Adults." *Journal of Marriage and Family* 67:271–85.

King, V., and J. M. Sobolewski. 2006. "Nonresident Fathers' Contributions to Adolescent Well-Being." *Journal of Marriage and Family* 68:537–57.

Kinsey, A. C., W. B. Pomeroy, and C. E. Martin. 1948. *Sexual Behavior in the Human Male.* Philadelphia: Saunders.

Kinsey, A. C., W. B. Pomeroy, C. E. Martin, and P. H. Gebhard. 1953. *Sexual Behavior in the Human Female.* Philadelphia: Saunders.

Kinsfogel, K. M., and J. H. Grych. 2004. "Interparental Conflict and Adolescent Dating Relationships." *Journal of Family Psychology* 18:505–15.

Kirby, J. B. 2006. "From Single-Parent Families to Stepfamilies." *Journal of Family Issues* 27:685–711.

Kiser, S., and S. Whitehornc. 2005. "Beauty Browsing." *Prevention,* March.

Kleinplatz, P., M. McCarrey, and C. Kateb. 1992. "The Impact of Gender-Role Identity on Women's Self-Esteem, Lifestyle Satisfaction and Conflict." *Canadian Journal of Behavioural Science* 24:333–47.

Kline, M., J. R. Johnston, and J. M. Tschann. 1991. "The Long Shadow of Marital Conflict: A Model of Children's

Post-Divorce Adjustment." *Journal of Marriage and the Family* 53:297–309.

Knapp, M. L., and J. A. Hall. 2001. *Nonverbal Communication in Human Interaction.* Belmont, CA: Wadsworth.

Knox, D., R. Breed, and M. Zusman. 2007. "College Men and Jealousy." *College Student Journal* 41:494–98.

Knox, D., and U. Corte. 2007. "'Work It Out/See a Counselor'; Advice from Spouses in the Separation Process." *Journal of Divorce & Remarriage* 48:79–90.

Knox, D., M. E. Zusman, K. McGinty, and D. A. Abowitz. 2003. "Weddings: Some Data on College Student Perceptions." *College Student Journal* 37:197–200.

Koball, H. L. 2004. "Crossing the Threshold: Men's Incomes, Attitudes toward the Provider Role, and Marriage Timing." *Sex Roles* 51:387–95.

Kohler, J. K., H. D. Grotevant, and R. G. McRoy. 2002. "Adopted Adolescents' Preoccupation with Adoption." *Journal of Marriage and the Family* 64:93–104.

Kohn, A. 1988. "Girl Talk, Guy Talk." *Psychology Today,* February, pp. 65–66.

Kolko, D. J., A. E. Kazdin, A. M. Thomas, and B. Day. 1993. "Heightened Child Physical Abuse Potential: Child, Parent, and Family Dysfunction." *Journal of Interpersonal Violence* 8:169–92.

Konner, M. 1982. "She & He." *Science 82,* September, pp. 54–61.

Koropeckyj-Cox, T., and O. Pendell. 2007. "The Gender Gap in Attitudes about Childlessness in the United States." *Journal of Marriage and Family* 69:899–915.

Kostanski, M., and E. Guilone. 2006. "The Impact of Teasing on Children's Body Image." *Journal of Child and Family Studies* 16:307–19.

Kotsopoulous, S., et al. 1988. "Psychiatric Disorders in Adopted Children." *American Journal of Orthopsychiatry* 58:608–12.

Kouri, K. M., and M. Lasswell. 1993. "Black-White Marriages: Social Change and Intergenerational Mobility." *Marriage and Family Review* 19:241–55.

Krafchick, J. L., T. S. Zimmerman, S. A. Haddock, and J. H. Banning. 2005. "Best-Selling Books Advising Parents about Gender." *Family Relations* 54:84–100.

Kramer, E. 2004. "Cohabitation: Just a Phase?" *Psychology Today,* September/October, pp. 28–32.

Kreeger, K. Y. 2002. "Deciphering How the Sexes Think." *Scientist,* January 21, pp. 28–33.

Kreider, R. M. 2003. *Adopted Children and Stepchildren: 2000.* Washington, DC: Government Printing Office.

Kreider, R. M. 2005. *Number, Timing, and Duration of Marriages and Divorces: 2001.* Washington, DC: Government Printing Office.

Kreider, R. M., and J. Fields. 2005. *Living Arrangements of Children: 2001.* U.S. Census Bureau Web site.

Kreider, R. M., and J. M. Fields. 2002. *Number, Timing, and Duration of Marriages and Divorces: 1996.* Washington, DC: Government Printing Office.

Krishnakumar, A., and C. Buehler. 2000. "Interparental Conflict and Parenting Behaviors." *Family Relations* 49:25–44.

Krout, J. A., P. Moen, H. H. Holmes, J. Oggins, and N. Bowen. 2002. "Reasons for Relocation to a Continuing Care Retirement Community." *Journal of Applied Gerontology* 21:236–56.

Kruttschnitt, C., and M. Dornfeld. 1993. "Exposure to Family Violence: A Partial Explanation for Initial and Subsequent Levels of Delinquency?" *Criminal Behavior and Mental Health* 3:61–75.

Kuhn, D. 2006. "Does the Asian Success Formula Have a Downside?" *Education Week* 25:29.

Kulczycki, A., and A. P. Lobo. 2002. "Patterns, Determinants, and Implications of Intermarriage among Arab Americans." *Journal of Marriage and the Family* 64:202–10.

Kurdek, L. A. 1991. "The Relations between Reported Well-Being and Divorce History, Availability of a Proximate Adult, and Gender." *Journal of Marriage and the Family* 53:71–78.

Kurdek, L. A. 1994. "Areas of Conflict for Gay, Lesbian, and Heterosexual Couples: What Couples Argue About Influences Relationship Satisfaction." *Journal of Marriage and the Family* 56:923–34.

Kurdek, L. A. 1995. "Predicting Change in Marital Satisfaction from Husbands' and Wives' Conflict Resolution Styles." *Journal of Marriage and the Family* 57:153–64.

Kurdek, L. A. 2001. "Differences between Heterosexual-Non-parent Couples and Gay, Lesbian, and Heterosexual-Parent Couples." *Journal of Family Issues* 22:727–55.

Kurdek, L. A. 2004. "Are Gay and Lesbian Cohabiting Couples *Really* Different from Heterosexual Married Couples?" *Journal of Marriage and Family* 66:880–900.

Kurdek, L. A. 2005. "Gender and Marital Satisfaction Early in Marriage." *Journal of Marriage and Family* 67:68–84.

Kurylo, M., and S. Gallant. 2000. "Hostility and Cardiovascular Reactivity in Women during Self-Disclosure." *International Journal of Behavioral Medicine* 7:271–85.

Kuttler, A. F., and A. M. La Greca. 2004. "Linkages among Adolescent Girls' Romantic Relationships, Best Friendships, and Peer Networks." *Journal of Adolescence* 27:395–414.

Kwiatoski, D. 2007. "Throwing a Wedding, 2007." *Hudson Valley Business Journal,* July 30.

Kwong, M. J., K. Bartholomew, A. J. Z. Henderson, and S. J. Trinke. 2003. "The Intergenerational Transmission of Relationship Violence." *Journal of Family Psychology* 17:288–301.

Kyvig, D. E. 2004. *Daily Life in the United States, 1920–1940.* Chicago: Ivan R. Dee.

Lacey, R. S., A. Reifman, J. P. Scott, S. M. Harris, and J. Fitzpatrick. 2004. "Sexual-Moral Attitudes, Love Styles, and Mate Selection." *Journal of Sex Research* 41:121–27.

Laeng, B., R. Mathisen, and J. Johnsen. 2007. "Why Do Blue-Eyed Men Prefer Women with the Same Eye Color?" *Behavioral Ecology and Sociobiology* 61:371–84.

Laible, D. J., and G. Carlo. 2004. "The Differential Relations of Maternal and Paternal Support and Control to Adolescent Social Competence, Self-Worth, and Sympathy." *Journal of Adolescent Research* 19:759–82.

Lall, R. R. 2006. "Waiting for a Sexual Revolution." *New Statesman* 135:28–29.

Lamb, M. E., ed. 1997. *The Role of the Father in Child Development*. 3rd ed. New York: John Wiley & Sons.

Lambert, S. 2005. "Gay and Lesbian Families: What We Know and Where to Go from Here." *The Family Journal* 13:43–51.

Lambert, T. A., A. S. Kahn, and K. J. Apple. 2003. "Pluralistic Ignorance and Hooking Up." *Journal of Sex Research* 40:129–33.

Lamm, H., and U. Wiesmann. 1997. "Subjective Attributes of Attraction." *Personal Relationships* 4:271–84.

Lance, L. M. 2004. "Attitudes of College Students toward Contraceptives." *College Student Journal* 38:579–86.

Landau, J., et al. 2004. "Outcomes with the ARISE Approach to Engaging Reluctant Drug- and Alcohol-Dependent Individuals in Treatment." *American Journal of Drug and Alcohol Abuse* 30:711–48.

Landau, J. 2007. "Enhancing Resilience: Families and Communities as Agents for Change." *Family Process* 46:351–65.

Landry, B. 2002. *Black Working Wives*. Berkeley, CA: University of California Press.

Laner, M. R., and N. A. Ventrone. 2000. "Dating Scripts Revisited." *Journal of Family Issues* 21:488–500.

Lang, H. 2005. "The Trouble with Day Care." *Psychology Today*, June, pp. 17–18.

Langer, L. M., G. J. Warheit, and L. P. McDonald. 2001. "Correlates and Predictors of Risky Sexual Practices among a Multi-Racial/Ethnic Sample of University Students." *Social Behavior and Personality* 29:133–44.

Lanier, C., and L. Huff-Corzine. 2006. "American Indian Homicide." *Homicide Studies* 10: 181–94.

Lanz, J. B. 1995. "Psychological, Behavioral, and Social Characteristics Associated with Early Forced Sexual Intercourse among Pregnant Adolescents." *Journal of Interpersonal Violence* 10:188–200.

LaPlante, D., and N. Ambady. 2003. "On How Things Are Said." *Journal of Language and Social Psychology* 22:434–41.

Larson, J. H. 2000. *Should We Stay Together?* San Francisco: Jossey-Bass.

Larson, J. H., and S. M. Allgood. 1987. "A Comparison of Intimacy in First-Married and Remarried Couples." *Journal of Family Issues* 8:319–31.

Larson, J. H., and T. B. Holman. 1994. "Premarital Predictors of Marital Quality and Stability." *Family Relations* 43:228–37.

Larson, J. H., and C. LaMont. 2005. "The Relationship of Childhood Sexual Abuse to the Marital Attitudes and Readiness for Marriage of Single Young Adult Women." *Journal of Family Issues* 26:415–30.

Larson, J. H., and B. M. Reedy. 2004. "Family Process as a Mediator of the Negative Effects of Parental Alcoholism on Young Adult Dating Relationships." *American Journal of Family Therapy* 32:289–304.

Larson, N. C. 2004. "Parenting Stress among Adolescent Mothers in the Transition to Adulthood." *Child and Adolescent Social Work Journal* 21:457–76.

Larzelere, R. E. 2000. "Child Outcomes of Nonabusive and Customary Physical Punishment by Parents." *Clinical Child and Family Psychology Review* 3:199–222.

Laslett, P. 1977. *Family Life and Illicit Love in Earlier Generations*. Cambridge, UK: Cambridge University Press.

Lasswell, M. 1985. "Illusions Regarding Marital Happiness." *Medical Aspects of Human Sexuality* 19:144–58.

Lauer, J. C., and R. H. Lauer. 1986. *'Til Death Do Us Part: How Couples Stay Together*. New York: Haworth.

Lauer, J. C., and R. H. Lauer. 1993. *No Secrets? How Much Honesty Is Good for Your Marriage?* Grand Rapids, MI: Zondervan.

Lauer, J. C., and R. H. Lauer. 1999a. *Becoming Family: How to Build a Stepfamily That Really Works*. Minneapolis, MN: Augsburg.

Lauer, J. C., and R. H. Lauer. 1999b. *How to Survive and Thrive in an Empty Nest*. Oakland, CA: New Harbinger.

Lauer, R. H., and W. H. Handel. 1983. *Social Psychology: The Theory and Application of Symbolic Interactionism*. 2nd ed. Englewood Cliffs, NJ: Prentice Hall.

Lauer, R. H., and J. C. Lauer. 1983. *The Spirit and the Flesh: Sex in Utopian Communities*. Metuchen, NJ: Scarecrow Press.

Lauer, R. H., and J. C. Lauer. 1988. *Watersheds: Mastering Life's Unpredictable Crises*. New York: Little, Brown.

Lauer, R. H., and J. C. Lauer. 2008. *Social Problems and the Quality of Life*. 11th ed. New York: McGraw-Hill.

Lauer, R. H., J. C. Lauer, and S. T. Kerr. 1990. "The Long-Term Marriage: Perceptions of Stability and Satisfaction." *International Journal of Aging and Human Development* 31:189–95.

Laumann, E. O., R. T. Michael, J. H. Gagnon, and S. Michaels. 1994. *The Social Organization of Sexuality*. Chicago: University of Chicago Press.

Laurenceau, J., L. F. Barrett, and M. J. Rovine. 2005. "The Interpersonal Process Model of Intimacy in Marriage." *Journal of Family Psychology* 19:314–23.

Lavee, Y., and D. H. Olson. 1993. "Seven Types of Marriage." *Journal of Marital and Family Therapy* 19:325–40.

Lavee, Y., S. Sharlin, and R. Katz. 1996. "The Effect of Parenting Stress on Marital Quality." *Journal of Family Issues* 17:114–35.

Lawrence, E., and T. N. Bradbury. 2001. "Physical Aggression and Marital Dysfunction." *Journal of Family Psychology* 15:135–54.

Lawson, H. M., and K. Leck. 2006. "Dynamics of Internet Dating." *Social Science Computer Review* 24:189–208.

Layng, A. 2000. "American Indians: Trading Old Stereotypes for New." *USA Today*, July.

Le, C. N. 2005. "Interracial Dating and Marriage: U.S.-Raised Asian Americans." *Asian-Nation*, March 17.

Le, T. N., and G. D. Stockdale. 2005. "Individualism, Collectivism, and Delinquency in Asian American Adolescents." *Journal of Clinical Child and Adolescent Psychology* 34:681–91.

Leahey, E., and G. Guo. 2001. "Gender Differences in Mathematical Trajectories." *Social Forces* 80:713–32.

Leary, C. E., M. L. Kelley, J. Morrow, and P. J. Mikulka. 2007. "Parental Use of Physical Punishment as Related to Family Environment, Psychological Well-Being, and Personality in Undergraduates." *Journal of Family Violence* 23:1–7.

Leary, M. R., and W. E. Snell Jr. 1988. "The Relationship of Instrumentality and Expressiveness to Sexual Behavior in Males and Females." *Sex Roles* 18:509–22.

Lebey, B. 2004. *Remarried with Children: Ten Secrets for Successfully Blending and Extending Your Family.* New York: Bantam.

Lederer, W. J., and D. D. Jackson. 1968. *The Mirages of Marriage.* New York: W. W. Norton.

Lee, G.R., and J. R. Bulanda. 2005. "Change and Consistency in the Relation of Marital Status to Personal Happiness." *Marriage and Family Review* 38:69–84.

Lee, G. R., and L. R. Petersen. 1983. "Conjugal Power and Spousal Resources in Patriarchal Cultures." *Journal of Comparative Family Studies* 14:23–38.

Lee, J. A. 1973. *The Colors of Love: An Exploration of the Ways of Loving.* Don Mills, Ontario: New Press.

Lee, S. M., and K. Yamanaka. 1990. "Patterns of Asian-American Intermarriages and Marital Assimilation." *Journal of Comparative Family Studies* 21:287–305.

Leeb, R. T., and F. G. Rejskind. 2004. "Here's Looking at You, Kid! Study of Perceived Gender Differences in Mutual Gaze Behavior in Young Infants." *Sex Roles* 50:1–14.

Leigh, B. C., M. T. Temple, and K. F. Trocki. 1993. "The Sexual Behavior of U.S. Adults: Results from a National Survey." *American Journal of Public Health* 83:1400–08.

Leman, P. J., S. Ahmed, and L. Ozarow. 2005. "Gender, Gender Relations, and the Social Dynamics of Children's Conversations." *Developmental Psychology* 41:64–74.

Lemieux, R., and J. L. Hale. 2000. "Intimacy, Passion, and Commitment among Married Individuals." *Psychological Reports* 87:941–48.

Lemieux, R., and J. L. Hale. 2002. "Cross-Sectional Analysis of Intimacy, Passion, and Commitment." *Psychological Reports* 90:1009–14.

Leslie, L. A. 2000. "Selecting a Child Care Center: What Really Matters to Parents?" *Child and Youth Care Forum* 29:299–322.

Leslie, L. A., and B. L. Letiecq. 2004. "Marital Quality of African American and White Partners in Interracial Couples." *Personal Relationships* 11:559.

Levande, D. I., J. M. Herrick, and K-T. Sung. 2000. "Eldercare in the United States and South Korea." *Journal of Family Issues* 21:632–51.

Levant, R., and G. Kopecky. 1994. *Masculinity Reconstructed: Changing the Rules of Manhood at Work, in Relationships, and in Family Life.* New York: Dutton.

Leve, L. D., and B. I. Fagot. 1997. "Gender-Role Socialization and Discipline Processes in One- and Two-Parent Families." *Sex Roles* 36:1–21.

Levenson, R. W., L. L. Carstensen, and J. M. Gottman. 1993. "Long-Term Marriage: Age, Gender, and Satisfaction." *Psychology and Aging* 8:301–13.

Levine, J. A., H. Pollack, and M. E. Comfort. 2001. "Academic and Behavioral Outcomes among the Children of Young Mothers." *Journal of Marriage and the Family* 63:355–69.

Levinger, G. 1965. "Marital Cohesiveness and Dissolution: An Integrative Review." *Journal of Marriage and the Family* 27:19–28.

Levinson, D. J., C. N. Darrow, E. B. Klein, M. H. Levinson, and B. McKee. 1978. *The Seasons of a Man's Life.* New York: Alfred A. Knopf.

Levy-Skiff, R. 1994. "Individual and Contextual Correlates of Marital Change across the Transition to Parenthood." *Developmental Psychology* 30:591–601.

Lewandowski, G. W., Jr., and A. P. Aron. 2004. "Distinguishing Arousal from Novelty and Challenge in Initial Romantic Attraction between Strangers. *Social Behavior and Personality* 32:361–72.

Lewis, C. S. 1960. *The Four Loves.* New York: Harcourt Brace Jovanovich.

Lewis, K. G., and S. Moon. 1997. "Always Single and Single Again Women." *Journal of Marital and Family Therapy* 23:115–34.

Lewis, R. A., and G. B. Spanier. 1979. "Theorizing about the Quality and Stability of Marriage." In W. R. Burr, R. Hill, F. I. Nye, and I. L. Reiss, eds., *Contemporary Theories about the Family. Vol. 1.* New York: Free Press.

Lewis, R. W., et al. 2004. "Epidemiology/Risk Factors of Sexual Dysfunction." *Journal of Sexual Medicine* 1:35–39.

Lewis, T., R. Lannon, and E. Amini. 2001. *A General Theory of Love.* New York: Vintage Books.

Li, J. H., and R. A. Wojtkiewicz. 1994. "Childhood Family Structure and Entry into First Marriage." *The Sociological Quarterly* 35:247–68.

Li, J. H., et al. 2005. "Hospitalization for Mental Illness among Parents after the Death of a Child." *New England Journal of Medicine* 352:1190–96.

Lichter, D. T., D. K. McLaughlin, G. Kephart, and D. J. Landry. 1992. "Race and the Retreat from Marriage: A Shortage of Marriageable Men?" *American Sociological Review* 57:781–99.

Lichter, E. L., and L. A. McCloskey. 2004. "The Effects of Childhood Exposure to Marital Violence on Adolescent Gender-Role Beliefs and Dating Violence." *Psychology of Women Quarterly* 28:344–56.

Lightbody, P., G. Siann, R. Stocks, and D. Walsh. 1996. "Motivation and Attribution at Secondary School: The Role of Gender." *Educational Studies* 22:13–25.

Liker, J. K., and G. H. Elder Jr. 1983. "Economic Hardship and Marital Relations in the 1930s." *American Sociological Review* 48:343–59.

Lin, C., and W. T. Liu. 1993. "Intergenerational Relationships among Chinese Immigrant Families from Taiwan." In H. P. McAdoo, ed., *Family Ethnicity: Strength in Diversity.* Newbury Park, CA: Sage.

Lindau, S.T., et al. 2007. "A Study of Sexuality and Health among Older Adults in the United States." *The New England Journal of Medicine* 357:762–74.

Lindner, K. 2004. "Images of Women in General Interest and Fashion Magazine Advertisements from 1955 to 2002." *Sex Roles* 51:409–21.

Lindsey, E. W., M. J. Colwell, J. M. Frabutt, and C. MacKinnon-Lewis. 2006. "Family Conflict in Divorced and Non-Divorced Families." *Journal of Social and Personal Relationships* 23:45–63.

Lindsey, E. W., and J. Mize. 2001. "Contextual Differences in Parent-Child Play." *Sex Roles* 44:155–76.

Lino, M. 2007. *Expenditures on Children by Families, 2006.* Alexandria, VA: U. S. Department of Agriculture.

Lippa, R. A. 2007. "The Preferred Traits of Mates in a Cross-National Study of Heterosexual and Homosexual Men and Women." *Archives of Sexual Behavior* 36:193–208.

Lo, C. C., and T. C. Cheng. 2007. "The Impact of Childhood Maltreatment on Young Adults' Substance Abuse." *American Journal of Drug & Alcohol Abuse* 33:139–46.

Logan, J. R., and G. D. Spitze. 1996. *Family Ties: Enduring Relations between Parents and Their Grown Children.* Philadelphia, PA: Temple University Press.

Lonczak, H. S., D. M. Donovan, A. Fernandez, G. A. Marlatt, and L. Austin. 2007. "Family Structure and Substance Use among American Indian Youth." *Families, Systems and Health* 25:10–22.

Long, V. O. 1986. "Relationship of Masculinity to Self-Esteem and Self-Acceptance in Female Professionals, College Students, Clients, and Victims of Domestic Violence." *Journal of Consulting and Clinical Psychology* 54:323–27.

Longman, P. J. 1998. "The Cost of Children." *U. S. News and World Report,* March 27.

Longmore, M. A., W. D. Manning, and P. C. Giordano. 2001. "Preadolescent Parenting Strategies and Teens' Dating and Sexual Initiation." *Journal of Marriage and the Family* 63:322–35.

Loscocco, K., and G. Spitze. 2007. "Gender Patterns in Provider Role Attitudes and Behavior." *Journal of Family Issues* 28:934–54.

Lott, D. A. 1999. "The New Flirting Game." *Psychology Today,* January, pp. 42–45.

Loukas, A., et al. 2001. "Parental Distress as a Mediator of Problem Behaviors in Sons of Alcohol-Involved Families." *Family Relations* 50:293–301.

Low, J., and P. Sherrard. 1999. "Portrayal of Women in Sexuality and Marriage and Family Textbooks." *Sex Roles* 40:309–18.

Lowenstein, A., R. Katz, and N. Gur-Yaish. 2007. "Reciprocity in Parent-Child Exchange and Life Satisfaction among the Elderly." *Journal of Social Issues* 63:865–83.

Lowenstein, L. F. 2005. "Causes and Associated Features of Divorce as Seen by Recent Research." *Journal of Divorce and Remarriage* 42:153–71.

Lowery, C. R., and S. A. Settle. 1985. "Effects of Divorce on Children: Differential Impact of Custody and Visitation Patterns." *Family Relations* 34:455–63.

Lowndes, L. 1997. *How to Make Anyone Fall in Love with You.* New York: McGraw-Hill.

Luo, S., and E. C. Klohnen. 2005. "Assortative Mating and Marital Quality in Newlyweds." *Journal of Personality and Social Psychology* 88:304–26.

Luster, T., and S. A. Small. 1994. "Factors Associated with Sexual Risk-Taking Behaviors among Adolescents." *Journal of Marriage and the Family* 56:622–32.

Lye, D. N., and T. J. Biblarz. 1993. "The Effects of Attitudes toward Family Life and Gender Roles on Marital Satisfaction." *Journal of Family Issues* 14:157–88.

Lykken, D. T., and A. Tellegen. 1993. "Is Human Mating Adventitious or the Result of Lawful Choice? A Twin Study of Mate Selection." *Journal of Personality and Social Psychology* 65:56–68.

Lysova, A. V. 2007. "Dating Violence in Russia." *Russian Education and Society* 49:43–59.

MacCallum, F., and S. Golombok. 2004. "Children Raised in Fatherless Families from Infancy." *Journal of Child Psychology & Psychiatry & Allied Disciplines* 45:1407–20.

Maccoby, E. E., and R. Mnookin. 1992. *Dividing the Child: Social and Legal Dimensions of Custody.* Cambridge, MA: Harvard University Press.

MacDermid, S. M., T. L. Huston, and S. M. McHale. 1990. "Changes in Marriage Associated with the Transition to Parenthood: Individual Differences as a Function of Sex-Role Attitudes and Changes in the Division of Household Labor." *Journal of Marriage and the Family* 52:475–86.

MacDonald, W. L., and A. DeMaris. 1995. "Remarriage, Step-Children, and Marital Conflict: Challenges to the Incomplete Institutionalization Hypothesis." *Journal of Marriage and the Family* 57:387–98.

MacGeorge, E. L., A. R. Graves, B. Feng, S. J. Gillihan, and B. R. Burleson. 2004. "The Myth of Gender Cultures." *Sex Roles* 50:143–75.

Machida, S., and S. D. Holloway. 1991. "The Relationship between Divorced Mothers' Perceived Control over Child Rearing and Children's Post-Divorce Development." *Family Relations* 40:272–78.

Mackay, J. 2001. "How Does the United States Compare with the Rest of the World in Human Sexual Behavior?" *Western Journal of Medicine* 174:429–33.

Mackey, R. A., M. A. Diemer, and B. A. O'Brien. 2000. "Psychological Intimacy in the Lasting Relationships of Heterosexual and Same-Gender Couples." *Sex Roles* 43:201–27.

Mackey, R. A., M. A. Diemer, and B. A. O'Brien. 2004. "Relational Factors in Understanding Satisfaction in the Lasting Relationships of Same Sex and Heterosexual Couples." *Journal of Homosexuality* 47:111–36.

Mackey, R. A., and B. A. O'Brien. 1995. *Lasting Marriages: Men and Women Growing Together.* Westport, CT: Praeger.

MacMillan, H. L., et al. 2001. "Childhood Abuse and Lifetime Psychopathology in a Community Sample." *American Journal of Psychiatry* 158:1878–83.

Maggini, C., E. Lundgren, and E. Leuci. 2006. "Jealous Love and Morbid Jealousy." *Acta Biomedica* 77:137–46.

Maguire, K., and A. L. Pastore, eds. 2004. *Sourcebook of Criminal Justice Statistics.* Washington, DC: Government Printing Office.

Maharajh, H. D., and A. Ali. 2005. "Aggressive Sexual Behaviour of Alcohol-Dependent Men." *Alcoholism Treatment Quarterly* 23:101–6.

Mainemer, H., L. C. Gilman, and E. W. Ames. 1998. "Parenting Stress in Families Adopting Children from Romanian Orphanages." *Journal of Family Issues* 19:164–80.

Majumdar, R. 2004. "Looking for Brides and Grooms." *Journal of Asian Studies* 63:911–35.

Malandro, L. A., and L. Barker. 1983. *Nonverbal Communication.* Reading, MA: Addison-Wesley.

Malia, S. E. C. 2005. "Balancing Family Members' Interests Regarding Stepparent Rights and Obligations." *Family Relations* 54:298–319.

Malinowski, B. 1932. *The Sexual Life of Savages in Northwestern Melanesia.* London: George Routledge.

Malone-Colon, L. 2007. "Responding to the Black Marriage Crisis." *Research Brief No. 6.* Institute for American Values Web site.

Mandara, J., C. B. Murray, and T. N. Joyner. 2005. "The Impact of Father's Absence on African American Adolescents' Gender Role Development." *Sex Roles* 53:207–20.

Manning, W. D. 2001. "Childbearing in Cohabiting Unions." *Family Planning Perspectives* 33:217–23.

Manning, W. D., M. A. Longmore, and P. C. Giordano. 2007. "The Changing Institution of Marriage: Adolescents' Expectations to Cohabit and to Marry." *Journal of Marriage and Family* 69:559–75.

Manning, W. E. 2004. "Children and the Stability of Cohabiting Couples." *Journal of Marriage and the Family* 66:674–89.

Manusov, V., K. Floyd, and J. Kerssen-Griep. 1997. "Yours, Mine, and Ours: Mutual Attributions for Nonverbal Behaviors in Couples' Interactions." *Communication Research* 24:234–60.

Marano, H. E., and E. Strand. 2003. "Points of Departure." *Psychology Today,* July/August, pp. 48–49.

Markey, C. N., P. M. Markey, and L. L. Birch. 2004. "Understanding Women's Body Satisfaction." *Sex Roles* 51:209–16.

Markey, C. N., and P. M. Markey. 2005. "Relations between Body Image and Dieting Behaviors." *Sex Roles* 53:519–30.

Markman, H., S. Stanley, and S. L. Blumberg. 1994. *Fighting for Your Marriage.* San Francisco, CA: Jossey-Bass.

Marks, M., and R. C. Fraley. 2005. "The Sexual Double Standard." *Sex Roles* 52:175–86.

Marks, M. J., and R. C. Fraley. 2006. "Confirmation Bias and the Sexual Double Standarad." *Sex Roles* 54:19–26.

Marks, N. F., H. Jun, and J. Song. 2007. "Death of Parents and Adult Psychological and Physical Well-Being." *Journal of Family Issues* 28:1611–38.

Marks, N. F., and S. S. McLanahan. 1993. "Gender, Family Structure, and Social Support among Parents." *Journal of Marriage and the Family* 55:481–93.

Markstrom-Adams, C. 1989. "Androgyny and Its Relation to Adolescent Psychosocial Well-Being: A Review of the Literature." *Sex Roles* 5/6:325–40.

Marquardt, E., and N. Glenn. 2001. *Hooking Up, Hanging out and Hoping for Mr. Right.* New York: Institute for American Values.

Marsiglio, W. 1991. "Paternal Engagement Activities with Minor Children." *Journal of Marriage and the Family* 53:973–86.

Marsiglio, W. 1992. "Stepfathers with Minor Children Living at Home." *Journal of Family Issues* 13:195–214.

Marsiglio, W. 2004. "When Stepfathers Claim Stepchildren." *Journal of Marriage and the Family* 66:22–39.

Martin, K. A. 1998. "Becoming a Gendered Body: Practices of Preschools." *American Sociological Review* 63:494–511.

Martin, P. D., G. Specter, D. Martin, and M. Martin. 2003. "Expressed Attitudes of Adolescents toward Marriage and Family Life." *Adolescence* 38:359–67.

Martin, S. P. 2006. "Trends in Marital Dissolution by Women's Education in the United States." *Demographic Research* 15:537–60.

Martin, S. P., and S. Parashar. 2006. "Women's Changing Attitudes toward Divorce: 1974–2002." *Journal of Marriage and Family* 68:29–40.

Martino, S. C., R. L. Collins, and P. L. Ellickson. 2005. "Cross-Lagged Relationships between Substance Use and Intimate Partner Violence among a Sample of Young Adult Women." *Journal of Studies on Alcohol* 66:139–48.

Masheter, C. 1991. "Postdivorce Relationships between Ex-Spouses: The Roles of Attachment and Interpersonal Conflict." *Journal of Marriage and the Family* 53:103–10.

Massoni, K. 2004. "Modeling Work: Occupational Messages in *Seventeen* Magazine." *Gender & Society* 18:47–65.

Masters, W. H., V. E. Johnson, and R. C. Kolodny. 1988. *Human Sexuality.* 3rd ed. Glenview, IL: Scott, Foresman and Company.

Mathews, C. A., and V. I. Reus. 2001. "Assortative Mating in the Affective Disorders." *Comprehensive Psychiatry* 42:257–62.

Matthews, L. S., R. D. Conger, and K. A. S. Wickrama. 1996. "Work-Family Conflict and Marital Quality." *Social Psychology Quarterly* 59:62–79.

Mattingly, M. J., and S. M. Bianchi. 2003. "Gender Differences in the Quantity and Quality of Free Time." *Social Forces* 81:999–1030.

Maume, D. J. 2006. "Gender Differences in Restricting Work Efforts Because of Family Responsibilities." *Journal of Marriage and Family* 68:859–69.

Mausbach, B. T., et al. 2007. "Depression and Distress Predict Time to Cardiovascular Disease in Dementia Caregivers." *Health Psychology* 26:539–44.

May, K., and A. Riley. 2002. "Sexual Function after 60." *Journal of the British Menopause Society* 8:112–15.

Maylor, E. A., et al. 2007. "Gender and Sexual Orientation Differences in Cognition Across Adulthood." *Archives of Sexual Behavior* 36:235–49.

McAdoo, J. L. 1985/1986. "Black Perspective on the Father's Role in Child Development." *Marriage and Family Review* 9:117–33.

McAdoo, J. L. 1993. "Decision Making and Marital Satisfaction in African American Families." In H. P. McAdoo, ed., *Family Ethnicity: Strength in Diversity.* Newbury Park, CA: Sage.

McBride, C. K., R. L. Paikoff, and G. N. Holmbeck. 2003. "Individual and Familial Influences on the Onset of Sexual Intercourse among Urban African American Adolescents." *Journal of Consulting and Clinical Psychology* 71:159–67.

McCabe, K. M., R. Clark, and D. Barnett. 1999. "Family Protective Factors among Urban African American Youth." *Journal of Clinical Child Psychology* 28:137–50.

McCall, M. E., and N. J. Struthers. 1994. "Sex, Sex-Role Orientation and Self-Esteem as Predictors of Coping Style." *Journal of Social Behavior and Personality* 9:801–10.

McCarthy, G. 1999. "Attachment Style and Adult Love Relationships and Friendships." *British Journal of Medical Psychology* 72:305–21.

McConkey, D. 2001. "Whither Hunter's Culture War? Shifts in Evangelical Morality, 1988–1998." *Sociology of Religion* 61:149–74.

McCormack, K. 2007. "Careers: The Goods on Generation Y." *Business Week,* June 26.

McCubbin, H. I., and M. A. McCubbin. 1988. "Typologies of Resilient Families: Emerging Roles of Social Class and Ethnicity." *Family Relations* 37:247–54.

McCubbin, H. I., and J. M. Patterson. 1983. "Stress: The Family Inventory of Life Events and Changes." In E. E. Filsinger, ed., *Marriage and Family Assessment: A Sourcebook for Family Therapy,* pp. 275–98. Beverly Hills, CA: Sage.

McDaniel, P. 2001. "Shrinking Violets and Caspar Milquetoasts." *Journal of Social History* 34:547–71.

McDermott, J. F., Jr., and C. Fukunaga. 1977. "Intercultural Family Interaction Patterns." In W. Tseng, J. F. McDermott Jr., and T. W. Maretzki, eds., *Adjustment in Intercultural Marriage,* pp. 81–92. Honolulu: University Press of Hawaii.

McDill, T., S. K. Hall, and S. C. Turell. 2006. "Aging and Creating Families." *Journal of Women & Aging* 18:37–50.

McDonald, T. W., and L. M. Kline. 2004. "Perceptions of Appropriate Punishment for Committing Date Rape." *College Student Journal* 38:44–56.

McGregor, J. 2006. "Flextime: Honing the Balance." *Business Week,* December, 11.

McGue, M., I. Elkins, B. Walden, and W. G. Iacono. 2005. "Perceptions of the Parent-Adolescent Relationship." *Developmental Psychology* 41:971–84.

McHale, S. M., and T. L. Huston. 1985. "The Effect of the Transition to Parenthood on the Marriage Relationship." *Journal of Family Issues* 6:409–33.

McKee, L., et al. 2007. "Harsh Discipline and Child Problem Behaviors." *Journal of Family Violence* 22:187–96.

McKeever, M., and N. H. Wolfinger. 2001. "Reexamining the Economic Costs of Marital Disruption for Women." *Social Science Quarterly* 82:202–17.

McKenry, P. C., and M. A. Fine. 1993. "Parenting Following Divorce: A Comparison of Black and White Single Mothers." *Journal of Comparative Family Studies* 24:99–111.

McKinnon, J., and E. Grieco. 2001. "Nation's Asian and Pacific Islander Population Profiled by Census Bureau." Press release, Census Bureau Web site.

McLanahan, S., and G. Sandefur. 1994. *Growing Up with a Single Parent: What Hurts, What Helps.* Cambridge, MA: Harvard University Press.

McLaughlin, M., L. S. Cormier, and W. H. Cormier. 1988. "Relation between Coping Strategies and Distress, Stress, and Marital Adjustment of Multiple-Role Women." *Journal of Counseling Psychology* 35:187–93.

McLoyd, V. C., T. E. Jayaratne, R. Ceballo, and J. Borquez. 1994. "Unemployment and Work Interruption among African American Single Mothers: Effects on Parenting and Adolescent Socioemotional Functioning." *Child Development* 65:562–89.

McLoyd, V. E., and J. Smith. 2002. "Physical Discipline and Behavior Problems in African American, European American, and Hispanic Children." *Journal of Marriage and the Family* 64:40–53.

McMahon, M. 1995. *Engendering Motherhood: Identity and Self-Transformation in Women's Lives.* New York: Guildford Press.

McManus, P. A., and T. A. DiPrete. 2001. "Losers and Winners: The Financial Consequences of Separation and Divorce for Men." *American Sociological Review* 66:246–68.

McMullin-Coyne, S. 2005. "Hotels Say 'I Do' to Destination Weddings, Ring in Profits." *Hotel & Motel Management,* February 21.

McNeal, C., and P. R. Amato. 1998. "Parents' Marital Violence: Long-Term Consequences for Children." *Journal of Family Issues* 19:123–39.

McNulty, J. K., and T. D. Fisher. 2007. "Gender Differences in Response to Sexual Expectancies and Changes in Sexual Frequency." *Archives of Sexual Behavior* 36:768–77.

McPherson, M., L. Smith-Lovin, and J. M. Cook. 2001. "Birds of a Feather: Homophily in Social Networks." *Annual Review of Sociology* 27:415–44.

McQuillan, J., A. L. Greil, L. White, and M. C. Jacob. 2003. "Frustrated Fertility: Infertility and Psychological Distress among Women." *Journal of Marriage and the Family* 65:1007–18.

Mead, M. 1969. *Sex and Temperament in Three Primitive Societies.* New York: Dell.

Mead, R. 2007. *One Perfect Day: The Selling of the American Wedding.* New York: Penguin.

Mednick, M. T. 1987. "Single Mothers: A Review and Critique of Current Research." In S. Oskamp, ed., *Family Processes and Problems: Social Psychological Aspects,* pp. 184–201. Beverly Hills, CA: Sage.

Mehl, M. R., S. Vazire, N. Ramirez-Esparza, R. B. Slatcher, and J. W. Pennebaker. 2007. "Are Women Really More Talkative Than Men?" *Science* 317:82.

Mehren, E. 1988. "New Study Downplays the Effects of Menopause." *Los Angeles Times,* June 14, 1988.

Meier, A. M. 2003. "Adolescents' Transition to First Intercourse, Religiosity, and Attitudes about Sex." *Social Forces* 81:1031–52.

Melton, H. C., and J. Belknap. 2003. "He Hits, She Hits." *Criminal Justice and Behavior* 30:328–48.

Menning, C. L. 2006. "Nonresident Fathering and School Failure." *Journal of Family Issues* 27:1356–82.

Menninger, K. 1942. *Love Against Hate.* New York: Harcourt, Brace, and Co.

Mennino, S. F., B. A. Rubin, and A. Brayfield. 2005. "Home-to-Job and Job-to-Home Spillover." *Sociological Quarterly* 46:107–14.

Merchant, R. H., and M. M. Lala. 2005. "Prevention of Mother-to-Child Transmission of HIV." *Indian Journal of Medical Research* 121:589–601.

Meston, C. M., and D. M. Buss. 2007. "Why Humans Have Sex." *Archives of Sexual Behavior* 36:477–507.

Meston, C. M., and P. F. Frohlich. 2003. "Love at First Fright." *Archives of Sexual Behavior* 32:537–44.

Metz, M. E., and B. W. McCarthy. 2007. "The 'Good-Enough Sex' Model for Couple Satisfaction." *Sexual and Relationship Therapy* 22:351–62.

Meyer, C. J. 1987. "Stress: There's No Place Like a First Home." *Family Relations* 36:198–203.

Michaels, M. L. 2007. "Remarital Issues in Couple Therapy." *Journal of Couple & Relationship Therapy* 6:125–39.

Mickelson, K. D., R. C. Kessler, and P. R. Shaver. 1997. "Adult Attachment in a Nationally Representative Sample." *Journal of Personality and Social Psychology* 73:1092–106.

Mikulincer, M. 1998. "Attachment Working Models and Sense of Trust." *Journal of Personality and Social Psychology* 74:1209–24.

Milevsky, A. 2004. "Perceived Parental Marital Satisfaction and Divorce." *Journal of Divorce and Remarriage* 41:115–28.

Milevsky, A., M. Schlechter, S. Netter, and D. Keehn. 2006. "Maternal and Paternal Parenting Styles in Adolescents." *Journal of Child and Family Studies* 16:39–47.

Miller, B. C. 2002. "Family Influences on Adolescent and Contraceptive Behavior." *Journal of Sex Research* 39:22–26.

Miller, N. B., V. L. Smerglia, D. S. Gaudet, and G. C. Kitson. 1998. "Stressful Life Events, Social Support, and the Distress of Widowed and Divorced Women." *Journal of Family Issues* 19:181–203.

Miller, R. B., J. B. Yorgason, J. G. Sandberg, and M. B. White. 2003. "Problems that Couples Bring to Therapy." *American Journal of Family Therapy* 31:395–407.

Miller, W. M., et al. 2004. "Prevalence of Chlamydial and Gonococcal Infections among Young Adults in the United States." *Journal of the American Medical Association* 291:2229–36.

Mills, R., and R. Mills. 1996. "Adolescents' Attitudes toward Female Gender Roles." *Adolescence* 31:735–45.

Minton, C., and K. Pasley. 1996. "Fathers' Parenting Role Identity and Father Involvement." *Journal of Family Issues* 17:26–45.

Mirowsky, J. 2005. "Age at First Birth, Health, and Mortality." *Journal of Health and Social Behavior* 46:32–50.

Mistry, R., G. D. Stevens, H. Sareen, R. De Vogli, and N. Halfon. 2007. "Parenting-Related Stressors and Self-Reported Mental Health of Mothers with Young Children." *American Journal of Public Health* 97:1261–68.

Mitchell, C. M., et al. 2007. "Cumulative Risk for Early Sexual Initiation among American Indian Youth." *Journal of Research on Adolescence* 17:387–412.

Mitka, M. 1998. "Viagra Leads as Rivals Are Moving Up." *Journal of the American Medical Association* 280 (July 8):119.

Moen, P., J. E. Kim, and H. Hofmeister. 2001. "Couples' Work/Retirement Transitions, Gender, and Marital Quality." *Social Psychology Quarterly* 64:55–71.

Mollborn, S. 2007. "Making the Best of a Bad Situation: Material Resources and Teenage Parenthood." *Journal of Marriage and Family* 69:92–104.

Monk, T. H., M. J. Essex, N. A. Snider, and M. H. Klein. 1996. "The Impact of the Birth of a Baby on the Time Structure and Social Mixture of a Couple's Daily Life and Its Consequences for Well-Being." *Journal of Applied Social Psychology* 26:1237–58.

Monkerud, D. 2006. "Covenant Marriage on the Rocks." *Humanist,* May/June, pp. 39–40.

Montgomery, B. M. 1981. "The Form and Function of Quality Communication in Marriage." *Family Relations* 30:21–30.

Montgomery, M. J. 2005. "Psychosocial Intimacy and Identity: From Early Adolescence to Emerging Adulthood." *Journal of Adolescent Research* 20:346–74.

Montgomery, M. J., and G. T. Sorell. 1997. "Differences in Love Attitudes across Family Life Stages." *Family Relations* 46:55–61.

Moore, C. G., et al. 2007. "The Prevalence of Violent Disagreements in U.S. Families." *Pediatrics* 119:S68–76.

Moore, K. A., L. Guzman, E. Hair, L. Lippman, and S. Garrett. 2004. "Parent-Teen Relationships and Interactions." *ChildTrends Research Brief,* #2004–25.

Moore, M. R., and P. L. Chase-Lansdale. 2001. "Sexual Intercourse and Pregnancy among African American Girls in High-Poverty Neighborhoods." *Journal of Marriage and the Family* 63:1146–57.

Moore, S., and C. Cartwright. 2005. "Adolescents' and Young Adults' Expectations of Parental Responsibilities." *Journal of Divorce and Remarriage* 43:111–30.

Moos, R. H., K. Schulte, P. Brennan, and B. S. Moos. 2004. "Ten-Year Patterns of Alcohol Consumption and Drinking Problems among Older Women and Men." *Addiction* 99:829–38.

Morash, M., B. Hoan, Z. Yan, and K. Holtfreter. 2007. "Risk Factors for Abusive Relationships." *Violence Against Women* 13:653–75.

Morgan, E. S. 1966. *The Puritan Family.* New York: Harper Torchbooks.

Moriarty, P. H., and L. D. Wagner. 2004. "Family Rituals That Provide Meaning for Single-Parent Families." *Journal of Family Nursing* 10:190–210.

Morokoff, P. J., and R. Gilliland. 1993. "Stress, Sexual Functioning, and Marital Satisfaction." *Journal of Sex Research* 30:43–53.

Morris, M. 1988. *Last-Chance Children: Growing Up with Older Parents.* New York: Columbia University Press.

Morrison-Beedy, D. 1997. "Correlates of HIV Risk Appraisal in Women." *Annals of Behavioral Medicine* 19:36–41.

Mosher, W. D., A. Chandra, and J. Jones. 2005. "Sexual Behavior and Health Measures: Men and Women 15–44 Years of Age, United States, 2002." *Advance Data from Vital and Health Statistics,* Centers for Disease Control Web site.

Mosher, W. D., G. M. Martinez, A. Chandra, J. C. Abma, and S. J. Willson. 2004. "Use of Contraception and Use of Family Planning Services in the United States: 1982–2002." *Advance Data for Vital and Health Statistics,* No. 350, December 10.

Mueller, D. P., and P. W. Cooper. 1986. "Children of Single Parent Families: How They Fare as Young Adults." *Family Relations* 35:169–76.

Muller, C. 1995. "Maternal Employment, Parent Involvement, and Mathematics Achievement among Adolescents." *Journal of Marriage and the Family* 57:85–100.

Mullins, L. C., K. P. Brackett, D. W. Bogie, and D. Pruett. 2006. "The Impact of Concentrations of Religious Denominational Affiliations on the Rate of Currently Divorced in Counties in the United States." *Journal of Family Issues* 27:976–1000.

Mulvaney, M. K., and C. J. Mebert. 2007. "Parental Corporal Punishment Predicts Behavior Problems in Early Childhood." *Journal of Family Psychology* 21:389–97.

Munch, A., J. M. McPherson, and L. Smith-Lovin. 1997. "Gender, Children, and Social Contact: The Effects of Childrearing for Men and Women." *American Sociological Review* 62:509–20.

Murdaugh, C., S. Hunt, R. Sowell, and I. Santana. 2004. "Domestic Violence in Hispanics in the Southeastern United States." *Journal of Family Violence* 19:107–15.

Murphy, M., K. Glaser, and E. Grundy. 1997. "Marital Status and Long-Term Illness in Great Britain." *Journal of Marriage and the Family* 59:156–64.

Murstein, B., and R. G. Brust. 1985. "Humor and Interpersonal Attraction." *Journal of Personality Assessment* 49:637–40.

Myers, D. G. 2004. *Psychology.* 7th ed. New York: Worth Publishers.

Myers, J. B., J. Madathil, and L. R. Tingle. 2005. "Marriage Satisfaction and Wellness in India and the United States." *Journal of Counseling and Development* 83:183–90.

Myers, S. M. 2006. "Religious Homogamy and Marital Quality." *Journal of Marriage and Family* 68:292–304.

Najman, J., M. Nguyen, and F. Boyle. 2007. "Sexual Abuse in Childhood and Physical and Mental Health in Adulthood." *Archives of Sexual Behavior* 36:666–75.

Najman, J. M., J. C. Vance, F. Boyle, and G. Embleton. 1993. "The Impact of a Child Death on Marital Adjustment." *Social Science and Medicine* 37:1005–10.

National Cancer Institute. 1998. "Fertility Drugs as a Risk Factor for Ovarian Cancer." NCI Web site.

National Center for Education Statistics. 2004. *Trends in Educational Equity of Girls & Women: 2004.* National Center for Education Statistics Web site.

National Center for Health Statistics. 2007a. *Health, United States, 2007.* NCHS Web site.

National Center for Health Statistics. 2007b. *National Health Care Surveys.* NCHS Web site.

National Institute of Child Health and Human Development. 2001. "Child Care and Common Communicable Illnesses." *Archives of Pediatrics and Adolescent Medicine* 155:481–88.

National Institute of Child Health and Human Development. 2004. "Fathers' and Mothers' Parenting Behavior and Beliefs as Predictors of Children's Social Adjustment in the Transition to School." *Journal of Family Psychology* 18:628–38.

National Institute of Justice. 2004. *Violence against Women: Identifying Risk Factors.* Washington, DC: Government Printing Office.

National Marriage Project. 2003. *The State of Our Unions: 2003.* The National Marriage Project Web site.

National Marriage Project. 2007. *The State of Our Unions.* National Marriage Project Web site.

National Opinion Research Center. 1999. "Marital Bliss." *Public Perspective,* April/May, p. 38.

Needle, R. H., S. S. Su, and W. J. Doherty. 1990. "Divorce, Remarriage, and Adolescent Substance Use: A Prospective and Longitudinal Study." *Journal of Marriage and the Family* 52:157–69.

Neergaard, L. 2000. "FDA Approves Abortion Pill, RU-486." Associated Press release, September 28.

Negy, C., and D. K. Snyder. 2000. "Relationship Satisfaction of Mexican American and Non-Hispanic White American Interethnic Couples." *Journal of Marital & Family Therapy* 26:293–304.

Nelson, A. 2004. *You Don't Say: Navigating Nonverbal Communication between the Sexes.* Upper Saddle River, NJ: Prentice Hall.

Nelson, M. K. 2005. *The Social Economy of Single Motherhood: Raising Children in Rural America.* New York: Routledge.

Nelson, N. W., and A. M. Van Meter. 2007. "Measuring Written Language Ability in Narrative Samples." *Reading & Writing Quarterly* 3:287–309.

Neto, F. 2007. "Love Styles: A Cross-Cultural Study of British, Indian, and Portuguese College Students." *Journal of Comparative Family Studies* 38:239–54.

Neto, F., et al. 2000. "Cross-Cultural Variations in Attitudes toward Love." *Journal of Cross-Cultural Psychology* 31:626–35.

Netting, N. S. 2006. "Two-Lives, One Partner: Indo-Canadian Youth between Love and Arranged Marriages." *Journal of Comparative Family Studies* 37:129–46.

Newman, M. 1994. *Stepfamily Realities.* Oakland, CA: New Harbinger Publications.

Nicolosi, A., D. B. Glasser, S. C. Kim, K. Marumo, and E. O. Laumann. 2005. "Sexual Behavior and Dysfunction and Help-Seeking Patterns in Adults Aged 40–80 Years in the Urban Population of Asian Countries." *BJU International* 95:609–14.

Nieto, D. S. 1990. "The Custodial Single Father: Who Does He Think He Is?" *Journal of Divorce* 13:27–43.

Niraula, B. B. 1994. "Marriage Changes in the Central Nepali Hills." *Journal of Asian and African Studies* 29:91–109.

Nock, S. L. 1995. "A Comparison of Marriages and Cohabiting Relationships." *Journal of Family Issues* 16:53–76.

Noller, P., J. A. Feeney, D. Bonnell, and V. J. Callan. 1994. "A Longitudinal Study of Conflict in Early Marriage." *Journal of Social and Personal Relationships* 11:233–52.

Nomaguchi, K. M. 2006. "Maternal Employment, Nonparental Care, Mother-Child Interactions, and Child Outcomes during Preschool Years." *Journal of Marriage and Family* 68:1341–69.

Nomaguchi, K. M., and M. A. Milkie. 2003. "Costs and Rewards of Children: The Effects of Becoming a Parent on Adults' Lives." *Journal of Marriage and Family* 65:356–74.

Nomaguchi, K. M., and M. A. Milkie. 2006. "Maternal Employment in Childhood and Adults' Retrospective Reports of Parenting Practices." *Journal of Marriage and Family* 68:573–94.

Nomaguchi, K. M., M. A. Milkie, and S. M. Bianchi. 2005. "Time Strains and Psychological Well-Being." *Journal of Family Issues* 26:756–92.

Nye, F. I. 1988. "Fifty Years of Family Research, 1937–1987." *Journal of Marriage and the Family* 50:305–16.

Oakley, A. 1974. *Sociology of Housework.* New York: Pantheon.

Obeidallah, D. A., S. M. McHale, and R. K. Silbereisen. 1996. "Gender Role Socialization and Adolescents' Reports of Depression: Why Some Girls and Not Others?" *Journal of Youth & Adolescence* 25:775–85.

O'Connell, A. 1993. "Voices from the Heart: The Developmental Impact of a Mother's Lesbianism on Her Adolescent Children." *Smith College Studies in Social Work* 63:281–99.

O'Connor, M. L. 1998. "Religion Plays a Growing Role in White Teenagers' Sexual Decision-Making." *Family Planning Perspectives* 30:295–96.

Oggins, J. 2003. "Topics of Marital Disagreement among African-American and Euro-American Newlyweds." *Psychological Reports* 92:419–25.

Ohalete, N. 2007. "Adolescent Sexual Debut." *Journal of Black Studies* 37:737–52.

Ohannessian, C. M., et al. 2004. "Parental Substance Use Consequences and Adolescent Psychopathology." *Journal of Studies on Alcohol* 65:725–30.

Ojcius, D. M., T. Darville, and P. M. Bavoil. 2005. "Can Chlamydia Be Stopped?" *Scientific American,* May, pp. 72–79.

O'Keefe, M. 1994. "Linking Marital Violence, Mother-Child/Father-Child Aggression, and Child Behavior Problems." *Journal of Family Violence* 9:63–78.

O'Keefe, M. 1997. "Predictors of Dating Violence among High School Students." *Journal of Interpersonal Violence* 12:546–68.

Olmstead, R. E., S. M. Guy, P. M. O'Malley, and P. M. Bentler. 1991. "Longitudinal Assessment of the Relationship between Self-Esteem, Fatalism, Loneliness, and Substance Use." *Journal of Social Behavior and Personality* 6:749–70.

Olmsted, M. E., J. A. Crowell, and E. Waters. 2003. "Assortative Mating among Adult Children of Alcoholics and Alcoholics." *Family Relations* 52:64–71.

Olson, J. E., I. H. Frieze, and E. G. Detlefsen. 1990. "Having It All? Combining Work and Family in a Male and a Female Profession." *Sex Roles* 23:515–33.

Olson, M. R., and J. A. Haynes. 1993. "Successful Single Parents." *Families in Society* 74:259–67.

Olson, S. L., and V. Banyard. 1993. "Stop the World So I Can Get Off for a While: Sources of Daily Stress in the Lives of Low-Income Single Mothers of Young Children." *Family Relations* 42:50–56.

Ono, H. 1998. "Husbands' and Wives' Resources and Marital Dissolution." *Journal of Marriage and the Family* 60:674–89.

Ono, H. 2003. "Women's Economic Standing, Marriage Timing, and Cross-National Contexts of Gender." *Journal of Marriage and the Family* 65:275–86.

Onrust, S. A., and P. Cuijpers. 2006. "Mood and Anxiety Disorders in Widowhood." *Aging & Mental Health* 10:327–34.

Onyskiw, J. E. 2003. "Domestic Violence and Children's Adjustment." *Journal of Emotional Abuse* 3:11–45.

Orbuch, T. L., and L. Custer. 1995. "The Social Context of Married Women's Work and Its Impact on Black Husbands and White Husbands." *Journal of Marriage and the Family* 57:333–45.

Orbuch, T. L., J. S. House, R. P. Mero, and P. S. Webster. 1996. "Marital Quality over the Life Course." *Social Psychology Quarterly* 59:162–71.

Oropesa, R. S. 1997. "Development and Marital Power in Mexico." *Social Forces* 75:1291–317.

Orthner, D. K. 1990. "Parental Work and Early Adolescence: Issues for Research and Practice." *Journal of Early Adolescence* 10:246–59.

Osborne, C., W. D. Manning, and P. J. Smock. 2007. "Married and Cohabiting Parents' Relationship Stability: A Focus on Race and Ethnicity." *Journal of Marriage and Family* 69:1345–66.

Osborne, R. 2004. "Asian Pacific American Heritage Month." U. S. Census Bureau Press Release.

Otis, M. D., S. S. Rostosky, E. D. B. Riggle, and R. Hamrin. 2006. "Stress and Relationship Quality in Same-Sex Couples." *Journal of Social and Personal Relationships* 23:81–99.

Ott, C. H., R. J. Lueger, S. T. Kelber, and H. G. Prigerson. 2007. "Spousal Bereavement in Older Adults." *Journal of Nervous and Mental Disorders* 195:332–41.

Overbeek, G., H. Stattin, A. Vermulst, H. Thao, and R. Engels. 2007. "Parent-Child Relationships, Partner Relationships, and Emotional Adjustment." *Developmental Psychology* 43:429–37.

Padgett, T. 2007. "Gay Family Values." *Time,* July 5, pp. 51–52.

Pagano, M., and B. Hirsch. 2007. "Friendships and Romantic Relationships of Black and White Adolescents." *Journal of Child and Family Studies* 16:347–57.

Palosaari, U., H. Aro, and P. Laippala. 1996. "Parental Divorce and Depression in Young Adulthood." *Acta Psychiatrica Scandinavica* 93:20–26.

Parcel, T. L., and E. Menaghan. 1994. *Parents' Job and Children's Lives.* New York: Aldine de Gruyter.

Parish, W. L., Y. Luo, E. O. Laumann, M. Kew, and Z. Yu. 2007. "Unwanted Sexual Activity among Married Women in Urban China." *Journal of Sex Research* 44:158–71.

Park, H. H. 2006. "The Economic Well-Being of Households Headed by a Grandmother as Caregiver." *Social Service Review* 80:264–95.

Park, K. 2003. "Stigma Management among the Voluntarily Childless." *Sociological Perspectives* 45:21–45.

Parke, R. D. 2004. "Development in the Family." *Annual Review of Psychology* 55:365–99.

Parsons, J. T., P. N. Halkitis, D. Bimbi, and T. Borkowski. 2000. "Perceptions of the Benefits and Costs Associated with Condom Use and Unprotected Sex among Late Adolescent College Students." *Journal of Adolescence* 23:377–91.

Partners Task Force for Gay & Lesbian Couples. 2002. "Domestic Partnership Benefits." Partners Task Force for Gay & Lesbian Couples Web site.

Pasley, K., E. Sandras, and M. E. Edmondson. 1994. "The Effects of Financial Management Strategies on Quality of Family Life in Remarriage." *Journal of Family and Economic Issues* 15:53–70.

Patrick, S., J. N. Sells, F. G. Giordano, and T. R. Tollerud. 2007. "Intimacy, Differentiation, and Personality Variables as Predictors of Marital Satisfaction." *The Family Journal* 15:359–67.

Patterson, C. J. 1995. "Families of the Baby Boom: Parents' Division of Labor and Children's Adjustment." *Developmental Psychology* 31:115–23.

Patterson, C. J. 2000. "Family Relationships of Lesbians and Gay Men." *Journal of Marriage and the Family* 62:1052–69.

Patterson, J., and P. Kim. 1991. *The Day America Told the Truth.* Englewood Cliffs, NJ: Prentice Hall.

Paul, E. L., B. McManus, and A. Hayes. 2000. " 'Hookups': Characteristics and Correlates of College Students' Spontaneous and Anonymous Sexual Experiences." *Journal of Sex Research* 37:76–88.

Pauli-Pott, U., and D. Beckmann. 2007. "On the Association of Interparental Conflict with Developing Behavioral Inhibition and Behavior Problems in Early Childhood." *Journal of Family Psychology* 21:529–32.

Paulson, M. J., R. H. Coombs, and J. Landsverk. 1990. "Youth Who Physically Assault Their Parents." *Journal of Family Violence* 5:121–33.

Paulson, S. E., J. J. Koman, and J. P. Hill. 1990. "Maternal Employment and Parent-Child Relations in Families of Seventh Graders." *Journal of Early Adolescence* 10:279–95.

Payne, F. D. 1987. " 'Masculinity,' 'Femininity,' and the Complex Construct of Adjustment." *Sex Roles* 17:359–72.

Payne, J. W. 2007. "Going with Plan B." *The San Diego Union-Tribune,* January 9.

Peek, C. W., N. J. Bell, T. Waldren, and G. T. Sorrell. 1988. "Patterns of Functioning in Families of Remarried and First-Married Couples." *Journal of Marriage and the Family* 50:699–708.

Peele, S., and A. Brodsky. 1976. *Love and Addiction.* New York: New American Library.

Peragallo, N., et al. 2005. "A Randomized Clinical Trial of an HIV-Risk-Reduction Intervention among Low-Income Latina Women." *Nursing Research* 54:108–18.

Peretti, P. O., and R. R. Abplanalp Jr. 2004. "Chemistry in the College Dating Process." *Social Behavior and Personality* 32:47–54.

Peretti, P. O., and B. C. Pudowski. 1997. "Influence of Jealousy on Male and Female College Daters." *Social Behavior and Personality* 25:155–60.

Perina, K. 2002. "Covenant Marriage: A New Marital Contract." *Psychology Today,* March/April, p. 18.

Perrin, E. C. 2002. "Technical Report: Coparent or Second-Parent Adoption by Same-Sex Parents." *Pediatrics* 109:341–44.

Perry-Jenkins, M., and K. Folk. 1994. "Class, Couples, and Conflict: Effects of the Division of Labor on Assessments of Marriage in Dual-Earner Families." *Journal of Marriage and the Family* 56:165–80.

Perry-Jenkins, M., R. L. Repetti, and A. C. Crouter. 2000. "Work and Family in the 1990s." *Journal of Marriage and the Family* 62:981–98.

Person, E. S. 2006. *Dreams of Love and Fateful Encounters.* New York: American Psychiatric Publishing.

Petersen, L. R., and G. V. Donnenwerth. 1997. "Secularization and the Influence of Religion on Beliefs about Premarital Sex." *Social Forces* 75:1071–90.

Peterson, B. D., L. Gold, and T. Feingold. 2007. "The Experience and Influence of Infertility." *The Family Journal* 15:251–57.

Peterson, B. E., and L. E. Duncan. 2007. "Midlife Women's Generativity and Authoritarianism." *Psychology & Aging* 22:411–19.

Peterson, J. L., and N. Zill. 1986. "Marital Disruption, Parent-Child Relationships, and Behavior Problems in Children." *Journal of Marriage and the Family* 48:295–307.

Petts, R. J. 2007. "Religious Participation, Religious Affiliation, and Engagement with Children among Fathers Experiencing the Birth of a New Child." *Journal of Family Issues* 28:1139–61.

Pew Research Center. 2006a. *Are We Happy Yet?* Pew Research Center Web site.

Pew Research Center. 2006b. *Families Drawn Together by Communication Revolution.* Pew Research Center Web site.

Pew Research Center. 2006c. *Who's Feeling Rushed?* Pew Research Center Web site.

Pew Research Center. 2007a. *As Marriage and Parenthood Drift Apart, Public Is Concerned about Social Impact.* Pew Research Center Web site.

Pew Research Center. 2007b. *Fewer Mothers Prefer Full-Time Work.* Pew Research Center Web site.

Pew Research Center. 2007c. *Modern Marriage: "I Like Hugs. I Like Kisses. But What I Really Love Is Help With the Dishes."* Pew Research Center Web site.

Pfaff, D., ed. 2002. *Hormones, Brain and Behavior.* San Diego, CA: Academic Press.

Phillips, J. A., and M. M. Sweeney. 2005. "Premarital Cohabitation and Marital Disruption among White, Black, and Mexican American Women." *Journal of Marriage and Family* 67:296–314.

Phua, V. C., and G. Kaufman. 2003. "The Crossroads of Race and Sexuality: Date Selection among Men in Internet 'Personal' Ads." *Journal of Family Issues* 24:981–94.

Phua, V. C., G. Kaufman, and K. S. Park. 2001. "Strategic Adjustments of Elderly Asian Americans." *Journal of Comparative Family Studies* 32:263–82.

Pienta, A. M., M. D. Hayward, and K. R. Jenkins. 2000. "Health Consequences of Marriage for the Retirement Years." *Journal of Family Issues* 21:559–86.

Pierret, C. R. 2006. "The 'Sandwich Generation': Women Caring for Parents and Children." *Monthly Labor Review* 129:3–9.

Pilon, M. 1994. "Types of Marriage and Marital Stability: The Case of the Moba-Gurma of North Togo." In C. Bledsoe and G. Pison, eds., *Nuptiality in Sub-Saharan Africa.* Oxford, UK: Clarendon Press.

Pines, A., and E. Aronson. 1983. "Antecedents, Correlates, and Consequences of Sexual Jealousy." *Journal of Personality* 51:108–35.

Pink, J. E. T., and K. S. Wampler. 1985. "Problem Areas in Stepfamilies: Cohesion, Adaptability, and the Step-Father–Adolescent Relationship." *Family Relations* 34:327–35.

Pinsof, W. M. 2002. "The Death of 'Till Death Us Do Part'; The Transformation of Pair-Bonding in the 20th Century." *Family Process* 41:135–57.

Pittman, F. 1993. "Beyond Betrayal: Life after Infidelity." *Psychology Today,* May/June, pp. 33–38.

Plant, E. A., K. C. Kling, and G. L. Smith. 2004. "The Influence of Gender and Social Role on the Interpretation of Facial Expressions." *Sex Roles* 51:187–96.

Plichta, S. B. 2004. "Intimate Partner Violence and Physical Health Consequences." *Journal of Interpersonal Violence* 19:1296–323.

Pneuman, R. W., and M. E. Bruehl. 1982. *Managing Conflict.* Englewood Cliffs, NJ: Prentice Hall.

Poehlmann, J. A., and B. H. Fiese. 1994. "The Effects of Divorce, Maternal Employment, and Maternal Social Support on Toddlers' Home Environments." *Journal of Divorce and Remarriage* 22:121–31.

Pogarsky, G., T. P. Thornberry, and A. J. Lizotte. 2006. "Developmental Outcomes for Children of Young Mothers." *Journal of Marriage and Family* 68:332–44.

Polling Report. 2008. Poll results. The Polling Report Web site.

Pollock, A. D., A. H. Die, and R. G. Marriott. 1990. "Relationship of Communication Style to Egalitarian Marital Role Expectations." *Journal of Social Psychology* 130:619–24.

Ponzetti, J. J., Jr., and R. M. Cate. 1986. "The Developmental Course of Conflict in the Marital Dissolution Process." *Journal of Divorce* 10:1–15.

Poortman, A. 2005. "How Work Affects Divorce." *Journal of Family Issues* 26:168–95.

Pope, H. G., Jr., K. A. Phillips, and R. Olivardia. 2001. *Adonis Complex: The Secret Crisis of Male Body Obsession.* New York: Free Press.

Popenoe, D., and B. D. Whitehead. 1999. *Should We Live Together?* New Brunswick, NJ: The National Marriage Project.

Potts, M. K. 1997. "Social Support and Depression among Older Adults Living Alone." *Social Work* 42:348–62.

Powell, M. A., and T. L. Parcel. 1997. "Effects of Family Structure on the Earnings Attainment Process: Differences by Gender." *Journal of Marriage and the Family* 59:419–33.

Prather, J. E. 1990. "'It's Just as Easy to Marry a Rich Man as a Poor One.' Students' Accounts of Parental Messages about Marital Partners." *Mid-American Review of Sociology* 14:151–62.

Presser, H. B. 1994. "Employment Schedules among Dual-Earner Spouses and the Division of Household Labor by Gender." *American Sociological Review* 59:348–64.

Pressman, S. D., et al. 2005. "Loneliness, Social Network Size, and Immune Response to Influenza Vaccination in College Freshmen." *Health Psychology* 24:297–306.

Previti, D., and P. R. Amato. 2004. "Is Infidelity a Cause or a Consequence of Poor Marital Quality?" *Journal of Social and Personal Relationships* 21:217–30.

Proulx, C. M., H. M. Helms, and C. Buehler. 2007. "Marital Quality and Personal Well-Being." *Journal of Marriage and Family* 69:576–93.

Pruett, C. L., R. J. Calsyn, and F. M. Jensen. 1993. "Social Support Received by Children in Stepmother, Stepfather, and Intact Families." *Journal of Divorce and Remarriage* 19:165–79.

Putnam, R. D. 2001. *Bowling Alone: The Collapse and Revival of American Community.* New York: Simon & Schuster.

Qian, Z. 2005. "Breaking the Last Taboo: Interracial Marriage in America." *Contexts* 4:33–37.

Qian, Z., and D. T. Lichter. 2007. "Social Boundaries and Marital Assimilation: Interpreting Trends in Racial and Ethnic Intermarriage." *American Sociological Review* 72:68–94.

Qian, Z., and S. H. Preston. 1993. "Changes in American Marriage, 1972 to 1987: Availability and Forces of Attraction by Age and Education." *American Sociological Review* 58:482–95.

Quackenbush, R. L. 1990. "Sex Roles and Social-Sexual Effectiveness." *Social Behavior and Personality* 18:35–39.

Queen, S. A., R. W. Habenstein, and J. S. Quadagno. 1985. *The Family in Various Cultures.* 5th ed. New York: Harper & Row.

Quilliam, S. 2005. *Body Language: Learning to Read and Use the Body's Secret Signals.* Richmond Hill, Ontario, Canada: Firefly.

Quinn, N. 1982. "'Commitment' in American Marriage: A Cultural Analysis." *American Ethnologist* 9:775–98.

Quinn, W. H., N. A. Newfield, and H. O. Protinsky. 1985. "Rites of Passage in Families with Adolescents." *Family Process* 24:101–11.

Quinsey, Vernon L., et al. 1996. "Adult Attachment Style and Partner Choice." *Personal Relationships* 3:117–36.

Quintero, A., and R. Koestner. 2006. "What Valentine Announcements Reveal about the Romantic Emotions of Men and Women." *Sex Roles* 55:767–73.

Radmacher, K., and M. Azmitia. 2006. "Are There Gendered Pathways to Intimacy in Early Adolescents' and Emerging Adults' Friendships?" *Journal of Adolescent Research* 21: 415–48.

Raghavan, R., L. M. Bogart, M. N. Elliott, K. D. Vestal, and M. A. Schuster. 2004. "Sexual Victimization among a National Probability Sample of Adolescent Women." *Perspectives on Sexual and Reproductive Health* 36:225–32.

Rainie, L., and M. Madden. 2006. *Not Looking for Love: Romance in America.* Pew Research Center Web site.

Raj, A., and J. G. Silverman. 2003. "Immigrant South Asian Women at Greater Risk for Injury from Intimate Partner Violence." *American Journal of Public Health* 93:435–37.

Raley, R. K., and J. Bratter. 2004. "Not Even If You Were the Last Person on Earth." *Journal of Family Issues* 25:167–81.

Raley, S. B., M. J. Mattingly, and S. M. Bianchi. 2006. "How Dual Are Dual-Income Couples?" *Journal of Marriage and Family* 68:11–28.

Ram, B., and F. Hou. 2005. "Sex Differences in the Effects of Family Structure on Children's Aggressive Behavior." *Journal of Comparative Family Studies* 36:329–41.

Ramu, G. N., and N. Tavuchis. 1986. "The Valuation of Children and Parenthood among the Voluntarily Childless and Parental Couples in Canada." *Journal of Comparative Family Studies* 17:99–116.

Rashotte, L. S., and M. Webster. 2005. "Gender Status Beliefs." *Social Science Research* 34:618–33.

Raty, H., and L. Snellman. 1997. "Children's Images of an Intelligent Person." *Journal of Social Behavior and Personality* 12:773–84.

Raven, B. H., R. Centers, and A. Rodrigues. 1975. "The Bases of Conjugal Power." In R. Cromwell and D. Olson, eds., *Power in Families*, pp. 217–32. New York: Halstead Press.

Razdan, A. 2003. "What's Love Got to Do with It?" *Utne*, May–June, pp. 68–70.

Red Horse, J. G., et al. 2000. *Family Preservation: Concepts in American Indian Communities*. Portland, OR: National Indian Child Welfare Association.

Reed, J. M. 2006. "Not Crossing the 'Extra Line': How Cohabitors with Children View Their Unions." *Journal of Marriage and Family* 68:1117–31.

Regalado, M., H. Sareen, M. Inkelas, L. S. Wissow, and N. Halfon. 2004. "Parents' Discipline of Young Children." *Pediatrics* 113:1952–58.

Regan, P. C., R. Durvasula, L. Howell, O. Ureno, and M. Rea. 2004. "Gender, Ethnicity, and the Developmental Timing of First Sexual and Romantic Experiences." *Social Behavior and Personality* 32:667–76.

Regan, P. C., J. L. Lyle, A. L. Otto, and J. Anupama. 2003. "Pregnancy and Changes in Female Sexual Desire." *Social Behavior and Personality* 31:603–12.

Regnerus, M. D., and L. B. Luchies. 2006. "The Parent-Child Relationship and Opportunities for Adolescents' First Sex." *Journal of Family Issues* 27:159–83.

Reiss, I. L., and G. R. Lee. 1988. *Family Systems in America*. 4th ed. New York: Holt, Rinehart & Winston.

Rennison, C. M. 2001. *Intimate Partner Violence and Age of Victim, 1993–99*. Washington, DC: U.S. Department of Justice.

Repetti, R. L., S. E. Taylor, and T. E. Seeman. 2002. "Risky Families: Family Social Environments and the Mental and Physical Health of Offspring." *Psychological Bulletin* 128:330–66.

Retherford, R. D., N. Ogawa, and R. Matsukura. 2001. "Late Marriage and Less Marriage in Japan." *Population and Development Review* 27:65–67.

Rexroat, C., and C. Shehan. 1987. "The Family Life Cycle and Spouses' Time in Housework." *Journal of Marriage and the Family* 49:737–50.

Reynolds, J., M. Wetherell, and S. Taylor. 2007. "Choice and Chance: Negotiating Agency in Narratives of Singleness." *Sociological Review* 55:331–51.

Rhee, S., J. Chang, and J. Rhee. 2003. "Acculturation, Communication Patterns, and Self-Esteem among Asian and Caucasian American Adolescents." *Adolescence* 38:749–68.

Rhoades, G. K., S. M. Stanley, and H. J. Markman. 2006. "Pre-engagement Cohabitation and Gender Asymmetry in Marital Commitment." *Journal of Family Psychology* 20:553–60.

Ricciuti, H. N. 2004. "Single Parenthood, Achievement, and Problem Behavior in White, Black, and Hispanic Children." *Journal of Educational Research* 97:56–67.

Richards, L. N., and C. J. Schmiege. 1993. "Problems and Strengths of Single-Parent Families: Implications for Practice and Policy." *Family Relations* 42:277–85.

Richards, M., R. Hardy, and M. Wadsworth. 1997. "The Effects of Divorce and Separation on Mental Health in a National UK Birth Cohort." *Psychological Medicine* 27:1121–28.

Richmond, V. P. 1995. "Amount of Communication in Marital Dyads as a Function of Dyad and Individual Marital Satisfaction." *Communication Research Reports* 12:152–59.

Rickert, V. I., C. M. Wiemann, R. D. Vaughan, and J. W. White. 2004. "Rates and Risk Factors for Sexual Violence among an Ethnically Diverse Sample of Adolescents." *Archives of Pediatric and Adolescent Medicine* 158:1132–39.

Ridley, M. 2003. *Nature Via Nurture: Genes, Experience, and What Makes Us Human*. New York: Harper Collins.

Riedmann, A. 1995. "Lesbian and Gay Male Families." Primis 4:66–83.

Riggio, H. R. 2004. "Parental Marital Conflict and Divorce, Parent-Child Relationships, Social Support, and Relationship Anxiety in Young Adulthood." *Personal Relationships* 11:99–114.

Riggs, D. S. 1993. "Relationship Problems and Dating Aggression: A Potential Treatment Target." *Journal of Interpersonal Violence* 8:18–35.

Riggs, D. S., and M. B. Caulfield. 1997. "Expected Consequences of Male Violence against Their Female Dating Partners." *Journal of Interpersonal Violence* 12:229–40.

Riley, L. A., and Glass, J. L. 2002. "You Can't Always Get What You Want—Infant Care Preferences and Use among Employed Mothers." *Journal of Marriage and the Family* 64:2–15.

Rinfret-Raynor, M., et al. 2004. "A Survey on Violence against Female Partners in Quebec, Canada." *Violence against Women* 10:709–28.

Risman, B. J. 1986. "Can Men 'Mother'? Life as a Single Father." *Family Relations* 35:95–102.

Rivara, F. P., M. M. Garrison, B. Ebel, C. A. McCarty, and D. A. Christakis. 2004. "Mortality Attributable to Harmful Drinking in the United States, 2000." *Journal of Studies on Alcohol* 65:530–36.

Roberts, A. R. 2006. "Classification Typology and Assessment of Five Levels of Woman Battering." *Journal of Family Violence* 21:521–27.

Roberts, R. E. L., and V. L. Bengtson. 1996. "Affective Ties to Parents in Early Adulthood and Self-Esteem across 20 Years." *Social Psychology Quarterly* 59:96–106.

Robinson, G. E., R. Stirtzinger, D. E. Stewart, and E. Ralevski. 1994. "Psychological Reactions in Women Followed for 1 Year after Miscarriage." *Journal of Reproductive and Infant Psychology* 12:31–36.

Robinson, J., and G. Godbey. 1998. "No Sex, Please . . . We're College Graduates." *American Demographics*, February.

Robinson, J. G., and A. E. Molzahn. 2007. "Sexuality and Quality of Life." *Journal of Gerontological Nursing* 33:19–27.

Roche, K. M., et al. 2005. "Parenting Influences on Early Sex Initiation among Adolescents." *Journal of Family Issues* 26:32–54.

Rodgers, B., C. Power, and S. Hope. 1997. "Parental Divorce and Adult Psychological Distress." *Journal of Child Psychology and Psychiatry* 38:867–72.

Rogers, S. J., and L. K. White. 1998. "Satisfaction with Parenting: The Role of Marital Happiness, Family Structure, and Parents' Gender." *Journal of Marriage and the Family* 60:293–308.

Rokach, A. 2001. "Strategies of Coping with Loneliness throughout the Lifespan." *Current Psychology* 20:3–11.

Rokach, A., and M. Sharma. 1996. "The Loneliness Experience in Cultural Context." *Journal of Social Behavior and Personality* 11:827–39.

Rolison, G. L. 1992. "Black, Single Female-Headed Family Formation in Large U.S. Cities." *The Sociological Quarterly* 33:473–81.

Ronfeldt, H. M., R. Kimerling, and I. Arias. 1998. "Satisfaction with Relationship Power and the Perpetration of Dating Violence." *Journal of Marriage and the Family* 60:70–78.

Rose, P. 1983. *Parallel Lives: Five Victorian Marriages.* New York: Vintage.

Rosen, M. D. 1990. "The American Mother: A Landmark Survey for the 1990s." *Ladies' Home Journal,* May, pp. 132–36.

Rosen-Grandon, J. R., J. E. Myers, and J. A. Hattie. 2004. "The Relationship between Marital Characteristics, Marital Interaction Processes, and Marital Satisfaction." *Journal of Counseling & Development* 82:58–68.

Rosenberg, M. 1965. *Society and the Adolescent Self-Image.* Princeton, NJ: Princeton University Press.

Rosenberg, M. B., and L. Leu, eds. 2003. *Nonviolent Communication: A Language of Life.* 2nd ed. Encinitas, CA: PuddleDancer Press.

Rosenblatt, P. C., and L. H. Burns. 1986. "Long-Term Effects of Perinatal Loss." *Journal of Family Issues* 7:237–53.

Rosenblatt, P. C., T. A. Karis, and R. D. Powell. 1995. *Multiracial Couples: Black & White Voices.* Thousand Oaks, CA: Sage.

Rosenbluth, S. C., J. M. Steil, and J. H. Whitcomb. 1998. "Marital Equality: What Does It Mean?" *Journal of Family Issues* 19:227–44.

Rosenfeld, M. J., and B. Kim. 2005. "The Independence of Young Adults and the Rise of Interracial and Same-Sex Unions." *American Sociological Review* 70:541–62.

Rosin, H. M., and K. Korabik. 1990. "Marital and Family Correlates of Women Managers' Attrition from Organizations." *Journal of Vocational Behavior* 37:104–20.

Rosip, J., and J. A. Hall. 2004. "Knowledge of Nonverbal Cues, Gender, and Nonverbal Decoding Accuracy." *Journal of Nonverbal Behavior* 28:267–86.

Ross, C. E. 1991. "Marriage and the Sense of Control." *Journal of Marriage and the Family* 53:831–38.

Ross, C. E., and J. Mirowsky. 1999. "Parental Divorce, Life-Course Disruption, and Adult Depression." *Journal of Marriage and the Family* 61:1034–45.

Ross, L. E., and A. C. Davis. 1996. "Black-White College Student Attitudes and Expectations in Paying for Dates." *Sex Roles* 35:43–56.

Ross, S. M. 1996. "Risk of Physical Abuse to Children of Spouse Abusing Parents." *Child Abuse and Neglect* 10:589–98.

Rostosky, S. S., B. L. Wilcox, M. L. C. Wright, and B. A. Randall. 2004. "The Impact of Religiosity on Adolescent Sexual Behavior." *Journal of Adolescent Research* 19:677–97.

Rotenberg, K. J., and S. Korol. 1995. "The Role of Loneliness and Gender in Individuals' Love Styles." *Journal of Social Behavior and Personality* 10:537–46.

Rotenberg, K. J., V. A. Shewchuk, and T. Kimberley. 2001. "Loneliness, Sex, Romantic Jealousy, and Powerlessness." *Journal of Social and Personal Relationships* 18:55–79.

Rothbaum, F., G. Morelli, M. Pott, and Y. Liu-Constant. 2000. "Immigrant-Chinese and Euro-American Parents' Physical Closeness with Young Children." *Journal of Family Psychology* 14:334–48.

Roxburgh, S. 2004. " 'There Just Aren't Enough Hours in the Day': The Mental Health Consequences of Time Pressure." *Journal of Health and Social Behavior* 45:115–31.

Roxburgh, S. 2006. "I Wish We Had More Time to Spend Together. . . ." *Journal of Family Issues* 27:529–53.

Rubenstein, C. 2007. *Beyond the Mommy Years: Empty Nest, Full Life.* New York: Springboard Press.

Rubin, Z. 1970. "Measure of Romantic Love." *Journal of Personality and Social Psychology* 16:265–73.

Rubinstein, R. L. 1994. "Culture, Caregiving, and the Frail Elderly on Malo, Vanuatu." *Journal of Cross-Cultural Gerontology* 9:355–68.

Ruby, M., C. Kenner, J. Jessel, E. Gregory, and T. Arju. 2007. "Gardening with Grandparents." *Early Years: Journal of International Research and Development* 27:131–44.

Rueter, M. A., and R. D. Conger. 1995. "Antecedents of Parent-Adolescent Disagreements." *Journal of Marriage and the Family* 57:435–48.

Ruggles, S. 2007. "The Decline of Intergenerational Coresidence in the United States: 1850 to 2000." *American Sociological Review* 72:964–89.

Ruiz, S. A., and M. Silverstein. 2007. "Relationships with Grandparents and the Emotional Well-Being of Late Adolescent and Young Adult Grandchildren." *Journal of Social Issues* 63:793–808.

Rusbult, C. E. 1987. "Responses to Dissatisfaction in Close Relationships." In D. Perlman and S. Duck, eds., *Intimate Relationships: Development, Dynamics, and Deterioration,* pp. 209–37. Beverly Hills, CA: Sage.

Russek, L. G., and G. E. Schwartz. 1997. "Feelings of Parental Caring Predict Health Status in Midlife: A 35-Year Follow-up of the Harvard Mastery of Stress Study." *Journal of Behavioral Medicine* 20:1–13.

Russell, B. L., and D. L. Oswald. 2001. "Strategies and Dispositional Correlates of Sexual Coercion Perpetrated by Women." *Sex Roles* 45:103–15.

Rutger, C. M. E., A. A. Vermulst, J. S. Dubas, S. M. Bot, and J. Gerris. 2005. "Long-Term Effects of Family Functioning and Child Characteristics on Problem Drinking in Young Adulthood." *European Addiction Research* 11:32–37.

Sabatelli, R. M., and S. Bartle-Haring. 2003. "Family-of-Origin Experiences and Adjustment in Married Couples." *Journal of Marriage and the Family* 65:159–69.

Sabatelli, R. M., and E. F. Cecil-Pigo. 1985. "Relational Interdependence and Commitment in Marriage." *Journal of Marriage and the Family* 47:931–37.

Sack, W. H., M. Beiser, G. Baker-Brown, and R. Redshirt. 1994. "Depressive and Suicidal Symptoms in Indian School Children: Findings from the Flower of Two Soils." *American Indian and Alaska Native Mental Health Research* 4:81–96.

Sagarin, B. J., and R. E. Guadagno. 2004. "Sex Differences in the Contexts of Extreme Jealousy." *Personal Relationships* 11:319–28.

Sager, C. J., H. S. Brown, H. Crohn, T. Engel, E. Rodstein, and L. Walker. 1983. *Treating the Remarried Family.* New York: Brunner/Mazel.

Sager, C. J., H. Steer, H. Crohn, E. Rodstein, and E. Walker. 1980. "Remarriage Revisited." *Family and Child Mental Health Journal* 6:19–33.

Saginak, K. A., and M. A. Saginak. 2005. "Balancing Work and Family: Equity, Gender, and Marital Satisfaction." *Family Journal* 13:162–66.

Sagrestano, L. M., D. Carroll, A. C. Rodriguez, and B. Nuwayhid. 2004. "Demographic, Psychological, and Relationship Factors in Domestic Violence during Pregnancy in a Sample of Low-Income Women of Color." *Psychology of Women Quarterly* 28:309–16.

Sagrestano, L. M., C. L. Heavey, and A. Christensen. 1999. "Perceived Power and Physical Violence in Marital Conflict." *Journal of Social Issues* 55:65–79.

Sakraida, T. 2005. "Divorce Transition Differences of Midlife Women." *Issues in Mental Health Nursing* 26:225–49.

Saloviita, T., M. Italinna, and E. Leinonen. 2003. "Explaining the Parental Stress of Fathers and Mothers Caring for a Child with Intellectual Disability." *Journal of Intellectual Disability Research* 47:300–12.

Sampson, R. J., J. D. Morenoff, and S. Rauderbush. 2005. "Social Anatomy of Racial and Ethnic Disparities in Violence." *American Journal of Public Health* 95:224–32.

Sandefur, G. D., S. McLanahan, and R. A. Wojtkiewicz. 1992. "The Effects of Parental Marital Status during Adolescence on High School Graduation." *Social Forces* 71:103–21.

Sandfort, T. G. M., M. Morr, J. S. Hirsch, and J. Santelli. 2008. "Long-Term Health Correlates of Timing of Sexual Debut." *American Journal of Public Health* 98:155–61.

Santelli, J. S., B. Morrow, J. E. Anderson, and L. D. Lindberg. 2006. "Contraceptive Use and Pregnancy Risk among U.S. High School Students, 1991-2003." *Perspectives on Sexual and Reproductive Health* 38:106–11.

Santi, L. L. 1987. "Change in the Structure and Size of American Households: 1970 to 1985." *Journal of Marriage and the Family* 49:833–37.

Sapolsky, R. M. 2004. "Of Mice, Men, and Genes." *Natural History,* May, pp. 21–31.

Sapp, S. G., W. J. Harrod, and L. Zhao. 1996. "Leadership Emergence in Task Groups with Egalitarian Gender-Role Expectations." *Sex Roles* 34:65–80.

Sarkisian, N., and N. Gerstel. 2004. "Kin Support among Blacks and Whites: Race and Family Organization." *American Sociological Review* 69:812–37.

Sarkisian, N., M. Gerena, and N. Gerstel. 2007. "Extended Family Integration among Euro and Mexican Americans." *Journal of Marriage and Family* 69:40–54.

Satir, V. 1972. *Peoplemaking.* Palo Alto, CA: Science and Behavior Books.

Sawhill, I. V. 2006. "Teenage Sex, Pregnancy, and Nonmarital Births." *Gender Issues* 23:48–59.

Sayer, L. C. 2005. "Gender, Time and Inequality: Trends in Women's and Men's Paid Work, Unpaid Work and Free Time." *Social Forces* 84:285–303.

Sayer, L. C., and S. M. Bianchi. 2000. "Women's Economic Independence and the Probability of Divorce." *Journal of Family Issues* 21:906–43.

Sayer, L. C., S. M. Bianchi, and J. P. Robinson. 2004. "Are Parents Investing Less in Children? Trends in Mothers' and Fathers' Time with Children." *American Journal of Sociology* 110:1–43.

Sbarra, D. A., and R. E. Emery. 2005. "The Emotional Sequelae of Nonmarital Relationship Dissolution." *Personal Relationships* 12:213–32.

Scarf, M. 1987. *Intimate Partners: Patterns in Love and Marriage.* New York: Ballantine.

Schachner, D. A., and P. R. Shaver. 2004. "Attachment Dimensions and Sexual Motives." *Personal Relationships* 11:179–95.

Schachter, S., and J. E. Singer. 1962. "Cognitive, Social, and Physiological Determinants of Emotional State." *Psychological Review* 69:379–99.

Scher, A., and R. Sharabany. 2005. "Parenting Anxiety and Stress." *Journal of Genetic Psychology* 166:203–13.

Schilling, E., R. Aseltine, and S. Gore. 2007. "Young Women's Social and Occupational Development and Mental Health in the Aftermath of Child Sexual Abuse." *American Journal of Community Psychology* 40:109–24.

Schneewind, K. A., and A.-K. Gerhard. 2002. "Relationship Personality, Conflict Resolution, and Marital Satisfaction in the First 5 Years of Marriage." *Family Relations* 51:63–71.

Schneider, D. S., P. A. Sledge, S. R. Shuchter, and S. Zisook. 1996. "Dating and Remarriage over the First Two Years of Widowhood." *Annals of Clinical Psychiatry* 8:51–57.

Schneller, D. P., and J. A. Arditti. 2004. "After the Breakup." *Journal of Divorce and Remarriage* 42:1–37.

Schoen, R., et al. 1997. "Why Do Americans Want Children?" *Population and Development Review* 23:333–58.

Schoen, R., and V. Canudas-Romo. 2006. "Timing Effects on Divorce." *Journal of Marriage and Family* 68:749–58.

Schoen, R., and Y. A. Cheng. 2006. "Partner Choice and the Differential Retreat from Marriage." *Journal of Marriage and Family* 68:1–10.

Schoen, R., S. J. Rogers, and P. R. Amato. 2006. "Wives' Employment and Spouses' Marital Happiness." *Journal of Family Issues* 27:506–28.

Schooler, D., L. M. Ward, A. Merriwether, and A. Caruthers. 2004. "Who's That Girl: Television in the Body Image Development of Young White and Black Women." *Psychology of Women Quarterly* 28:38.

Schrader, D. 1990. "A Refined Measure of Interpersonal Communication Competence: The Inventory of Communicator Characteristics." *Journal of Social Behavior and Personality* 5:343–55.

Schramm, D. G., J. P. Marshall, V. W. Harris, and T. R. Lee. 2005. "After 'I Do': The Newlywed Transition." *Marriage & Family Review* 38:45–67.

Schredl, M., et al. 2004. "Content Analysis of German Students' Dreams: Comparison to American Findings." *Dreaming* 13:237–43.

Schubot, D. B. 2001. "Date Rape Prevalence among Female High School Students in a Rural Midwestern State during 1993, 1995, and 1997." *Journal of Interpersonal Violence* 16:291–96.

Schuck, A. M. 2005. "Explaining Black-White Disparity in Maltreatment." *Journal of Marriage and Family* 67:543–51.

Schuckit, M. A., and T. L. Smith. 1996. "An 8-Year Followup of 450 Sons of Alcoholic and Control Subjects." *Archives of General Psychiatry* 53:202–10.

Schulte, B. 1997. "Huge Drop in Sperm Count Reported." *Los Angeles Daily News*, November 24.

Schulz, M. S., P. A. Cowen, C. P. Cowen, and R.T. Brennan. 2004. "Coming Home Upset: Gender, Marital Satisfaction, and the Daily Spillover of Workday Experience Into Couple Interactions." *Journal of Family Psychology* 18:250–63.

Schwab, R. 1992. "Effects of a Child's Death on the Marital Relationship." *Death Studies* 16:141–54.

Schwab, R. 1998. "A Child's Death and Divorce." *Death Studies* 22:445–68.

Schwartz, C. R., and R. D. Mare. 2005. "Trends in Educational Assortative Marriage from 1940 to 2003." *Demography* 42:621–46.

Schwartz, P. 2002. "Love Is Not All You Need." *Psychology Today*, May/June, pp. 56–62.

Schwebel, A. I., M. A. Fine, and M. A. Renner. 1991. "A Study of Perceptions of the Stepparent Role." *Journal of Family Issues* 12:43–57.

Schwetz, B. A. 2002. "New Contraceptive Patch." *Journal of the American Medical Association* 287:2347.

Secret, M., and C. Peck-Heath. 2004. "Maternal Labor Force Participation and Child Well-Being in Public Assistance Families." *Journal of Family Issues* 25:520–41.

Seligman, M. E. P. 1998. *Learned Optimism.* New York: Free Press.

Seltzer, J. A. 1991. "Legal Custody Arrangements and Children's Economic Welfare." *American Journal of Sociology* 96:895–929.

September, A. N., et al. 2001. "The Relation between Well-Being, Imposter Feelings, and Gender Role Orientation among Canadian University Students." *Journal of Social Psychology* 141:218–32.

Serquina-Ramiro, L. 2005. "Physical Intimacy and Sexual Coercion among Adolescent Intimate Partners in the Philippines." *Journal of Adolescent Research* 20:476–96.

Sev'er, A., M. Dawson, and H. Johnson. 2004. "Lethal and Nonlethal Violence against Women by Intimate Partners." *Violence against Women* 10:563–76.

Shackelford, T. K., et al. 2004. "Romantic Jealousy in Early Adulthood and Later Life." *Human Nature* 15:283–300.

Shackelford, T. K., and J. Mouzos. 2005. "Partner Killing by Men in Cohabiting and Marital Relationships." *Journal of Interpersonal Violence* 20:1310–24.

Shafii, T., K. Stovel, and K. Holmes. 2007. "Association between Condom Use at Sexual Debut and Subsequent Sexual Trajectories." *American Journal of Public Health* 97:1090–95.

Shagle, S. C., and B. K. Barber. 1993. "Effects of Family, Marital, and Parent-Child Conflict on Adolescent Self-Derogation and Suicidal Ideation." *Journal of Marriage and the Family* 55:964–74.

Shapiro, A. F., J. M. Gottman, and S. Carrere. 2000. "The Baby and the Marriage: Identifying Factors That Buffer Against Decline in Marital Satisfaction after the First Baby Arrives." *Journal of Family Psychology* 14:59–70.

Shapiro, B. L., and J. C. Schwarz. 1995. "Date Rape: Its Relationship to Trauma Symptoms and Sexual Self-Esteem." *Journal of Interpersonal Violence* 12:407–19.

Shapiro, J. L. 1987. "The Expectant Father." *Psychology Today*, January, pp. 36–42.

Sharlin, S. A. 1996. "Long-Term Successful Marriages in Israel." *Contemporary Family Therapy* 18:225–42.

Sharpe, D. L., and D. L. Baker. 2007. "Financial Issues Associated with Having a Child with Autism." *Journal of Family and Economic Issues* 28:247–64.

Sharpsteen, D. J., and L. A. Kirkpatrick. 1997. "Romantic Jealousy and Adult Romantic Attachment." *Journal of Personality and Social Psychology* 72:627–40.

Shaw, R., ed. 2000. *Not Child's Play: An Anthology on Brother-Sister Incest.* Takoma Park, MD: Lunchbox Press.

Sheare, N., and J. Fleury. 2006. "Social Support Promoting Health in Older Women." *Journal of Women & Aging* 18:3–17.

Shearer, C. L., A. C. Crouter, and S. M. McHale. 2005. "Parents' Perceptions of Changes in Mother-Child and Father-Child Relationships during Adolescence." *Journal of Adolescent Research* 20:662–84.

Shehan, C. L., E. W. Bock, and G. R. Lee. 1990. "Religious Heterogamy, Religiosity, and Marital Happiness: The Case of Catholics." *Journal of Marriage and the Family* 52:73–79.

Shehan, C. L., M. A. Burg, and C. A. Rexroat. 1986. "Depression and the Social Dimensions of the Full-Time Housewife Role." *Sociological Quarterly* 27:403–21.

Sheinberg, M., and P. Fraenkel. 2001. *The Relational Trauma of Incest.* New York: Guilford Press.

Sheldon, K. M. 2007. "Gender Differences in Preferences for Singles Ads That Proclaim Extrinsic versus Intrinsic Values." *Sex Roles* 57:119–29.

Shellenbarger, S. 2003. "The New Prenup: Planning Whose Job Comes First, Who Stays Home with Kids." *The Wall Street Journal*, June 26.

Shellenbarger, S. 2005. *The Breaking Point: How Female Midlife Crisis Is Transforming Today's Women.* New York: Henry Holt and Co.

Sher, G., V. M. Davis, J. Stoess, and V. A. Marriage. 1995. *In Vitro Fertilization: The A.R.T. of Making Babies.* New York: Facts on File, Inc.

Sher, K. J., and B. S. Gershuny. 1997. "The Role of Childhood Stressors in the Intergenerational Transmission of Alcohol Use Disorders." *Journal of Studies on Alcohol* 58:414–27.

Sherkat, D. E. 2004. "Religious Intermarriage in the United States: Trends, Patterns, and Predictors." *Social Science Research* 33:606–25.

Shonk, S. M., and D. Cicchetti. 2001. "Maltreatment, Competency Deficits, and Risk for Academic and Behavioral Maladjustment." *Development Psychology* 37:3–17.

Shook, N. J., D. A. Gerrity, J. Jurich, and A. E. Segrist. 2000. "Courtship Violence among College Students." *Journal of Family Violence* 15:1–22.

Shumway, D. R. 2003. *Modern Love: Romance, Intimacy, and the Marriage Crisis.* New York: New York University Press.

Sieving, R.E., M.E. Eisenberg, S. Pettingell, and C. Skay. 2006. "Friends' Influence on Adolescents' First Sexual Intercourse." *Perspectives on Sexual and Reproductive Health* 38:13–19.

Silitsky, D. 1996. "Correlates of Psychosocial Adjustment in Adolescents from Divorced Families." *Journal of Divorce and Remarriage* 26:151–69.

Sillars, A. L., L. Roberts, K. E. Leonard, and T. Dun. 2000. "Cognition during Marital Conflict." *Journal of Social and Personal Relationships* 17:479–502.

Silliman, B., and W. R. Schumm. 2004. "Adolescents' Perceptions of Marriage and Premarital Couples Education." *Family Relations* 53:513–20.

Sills, J. 1984. *How to Stop Looking for Someone Perfect and Find Someone to Love.* New York: St. Martin's.

Silverman, J. G., A. Raj, and K. Clements. 2004. "Dating Violence and Associated Sexual Risk and Pregnancy among Adolescent Girls in the United States." *Pediatrics* 114:220–25.

Silverman, J. G., A. Raj, L. A. Mucci, and J. E. Hathaway. 2001. "Dating Violence against Adolescent Girls and Associated Substance Use, Unhealthy Weight Control, Sexual Risk Behavior, Pregnancy, and Suicidality." *Journal of the American Medical Association* 286:572–79.

Silverstein, M., and A. Marenco. 2001. "How Americans Enact the Grandparent Role across the Family Life Course." *Journal of Family Issues* 22:493–522.

Silverstein, M., and T. M. Parrott. 2001. "Attitudes toward Government Policies That Assist Informal Caregivers." *Research on Aging* 23:349–74.

Sim, T. N., and L. P. Ong. 2005. "Parent Physical Punishment and Child Aggression in a Singapore Chinese Preschool Sample." *Journal of Marriage and Family* 67:85–99.

Simmons, T. 2001. "Multigeneral Households Number 4 Million According to Census 2000." Press Release, Census Bureau Web site.

Simon, B. L. 1987. *Never Married Women.* Philadelphia: Temple University Press.

Simon, R. W. 2002. "Revisiting the Relationship among Gender, Marital Status, and Mental Health." *American Journal of Sociology* 107:1065–95.

Simon, R. W., and L. E. Nath. 2004. "Gender and Emotion in the United States: Do Men and Women Differ in Self-Reports of Feelings and Expressive Behavior?" *American Journal of Sociology* 109:1137–76.

Simons, R. L., K.-H. Lin, and L. C. Gordon. 1998. "Socialization in the Family of Origin and Male Dating Violence." *Journal of Marriage and the Family* 60:467–78.

Simpson, J. A. 1990. "Influence of Attachment Styles on Romantic Relationships." *Journal of Personality and Social Psychology* 59:971–80.

Sinha, G. 2004. "The Identity Dance." *Psychology Today*, March/April, pp. 52–62.

Skaldeman, P. 2006. "Converging or Diverging Views of Self and Other: Judgment of Relationship Quality in Married and Divorced Couples." *Journal of Divorce and Remarriage* 44:145–60.

Skinner, K. B., S. J. Bahr, D. R. Crane, and V. R. A. Call. 2002. "Cohabitation, Marriage, and Remarriage: A Comparison of Relationship Quality over Time." *Journal of Family Issues* 23:74–90.

Skopin, A. R., B. M. Newman, and P. McKenry. 1993. "Influences on the Quality of Stepfather-Adolescent Relationships." *Journal of Divorce and Remarriage* 19:181–96.

Skowron, E. A., and T. A. Schmitt. 2003. "Assessing Interpersonal Fusion." *Journal of Marital and Family Therapy* 29:209–22.

Slonim-Nevo, V., and A. Al-Krenawi. 2006. "Success and Failure among Polygamous Families." *Family Process* 45:311–30.

Small, S. A., and T. Luster. 1994. "Adolescent Sexual Activity: An Ecological, Risk-Factor Approach." *Journal of Marriage and the Family* 56:181–92.

Smith, D. B., and P. Moen. 2004. "Retirement Satisfaction for Retirees and Their Spouses." *Journal of Family Issues* 25:262–85.

Smith, D. S. 1985. "Wife Employment and Marital Adjustment: A Cumulation of Results." *Family Relations* 34:483–90.

Smith, D. W., and D. M. Brodzinsky. 2002. "Coping with Birthparent Loss in Adopted Children." *Journal of Child Psychology and Psychiatry* 43:213–23.

Smith, M. L., G. W. Cottrell, F. Gosselin, and P. G. Schyns. 2005. "Transmitting and Decoding Facial Expressions." *Psychological Science* 16:284–89.

Smith, R. M., M. A. Goslen, A. J. Byrd, and L. Reece. 1991. "Self-Other Orientation and Sex-Role Orientation of Men and Women Who Remarry." *Journal of Divorce and Remarriage* 14:3–32.

Smock, P. J. 2000. "Cohabitation in the United States." *Annual Review of Sociology* 26:1–20.

Sniezek, T. 2005. "Is It Our Day or the Bride's Day? The Division of Wedding Labor and Its Meaning for Couples." *Qualitative Sociology* 28:215–34.

Sobolewski, J. M., and P. R. Amato. 2007. "Parents' Discord and Divorce, Parent-Child Relationships and Subjective Well-Being in Early Adulthood." *Social Forces* 85:1105–24.

Solie, L. J., and L. J. Fielder. 1987/1988. "The Relationship between Sex Role Identity and a Widow's Adjustment to the Loss of a Spouse." *Omega* 18:33–40.

Solomon, C. R., A. C. Acock, and A. J. Walker. 2004. "Gender Ideology and Investment in Housework." *Journal of Family Issues* 25:1050–71.

Solomon, D. H., L. K. Knobloch, and M. A. Fitzpatrick. 2004. "Relational Power, Marital Schema, and Decisions to Withhold Complaints." *Communication Studies* 55:146–67.

Solomon, M. 2000. "The Fruits of Their Labors: A Longitudinal Exploration of Parent Personality and Adjustment in Their Adult Children." *Journal of Personality* 68:281–308.

Solomon, S. D., and J. R. T. Davidson. 1997. "Repairing the Shattered Self." *Journal of Clinical Psychiatry* 58:5–11.

Solomon, S. E., E. D. Rothblum, and K. F. Balsam. 2005. "Money, Housework, Sex, and Conflict." *Sex Roles* 52:561–75.

Sorenson, K. A., S. M. Russell, D. J. Harkness, and J. H. Harvey. 1993. "Account-Making, Confiding, and Coping with the Ending of a Close Relationship." *Journal of Social Behavior and Personality* 8:73–86.

Sotile, W. M., and M. O. Sotile. 2004. "Physicians' Wives Evaluate Their Marriages, Their Husbands, and Life in Medicine." *Bulletin of the Menninger Clinic* 68:39–59.

South, S. J. 1995. "Do You Need to Shop Around? Age at Marriage, Spousal Alternatives, and Marital Dissolution." *Journal of Family Issues* 16:432–49.

South, S. J. 2001. "Time-Dependent Effects of Wives' Employment on Marital Dissolution." *American Sociological Review* 66:226–45.

South, S. J., and E. P. Baumer. 2000. "Deciphering Community and Race Effects on Adolescent Premarital Childbearing." *Social Forces* 78:1379–409.

Spain, D., and S. M. Bianchi. 1996. *Balancing Act: Motherhood, Marriage, and Employment among American Women.* New York: Russell Sage Foundation.

Speakman, J. R., K. Djafarian, J. Stewart, and D. M. Jackson. 2007. "Assortative Mating for Obesity." *American Journal of Clinical Nutrition* 86:316–23.

Speckhard, A. C., and V. M. Rue. 1992. "Postabortion Syndrome: An Emerging Public Health Concern." *Journal of Social Issues* 48:95–119.

Spelke, E. S. 2005. "Sex Differences in Intrinsic Aptitude for Mathematics and Science?" *American Psychologist* 60:950–58.

Spence, J. T., and R. L. Helmreich. 1978. *Masculinity and Femininity: Their Psychological Dimensions, Correlates, and Antecedents.* Austin: University of Texas Press.

Spillman, B. C., and L. E. Pezzin. 2000. "Potential and Active Family Caregivers." *Milbank Quarterly* 78:347–74.

Spitze, G., and K. Trent. 2006. "Gender Differences in Adult Sibling Relations in Two-Child Families." *Journal of Marriage and Family* 68:977–92.

Spraggins, R. E. 2003. *Women and Men in the United States: March 2002.* Washington, DC: Government Printing Office.

Sprecher, S. 2001. "Equity and Social Exchange in Dating Couples." *Journal of Marriage and the Family* 63:599–613.

Sprecher, S. M., and P. C. Regan. 1998. "Passionate and Companionate Love in Courting and Young Married Couples." *Sociological Inquiry* 68:163–85.

Sprecher, S., M. Schmeeckle, and D. Felmlee. 2006. "The Principle of Least Interest: Inequality in Emotional Involvement in Romantic Relationships." *Journal of Family Issues* 27:1255–80.

Sprecher, S., and M. Toro-Morn. 2002. "A Study of Men and Women from Different Sides of Earth to Determine If Men Are from Mars and Women Are from Venus in Their Beliefs about Love and Romantic Relationships." *Sex Roles* 46:131–47.

Spruijt, E., M. D. Goede, and I. Vandervalk. 2004. "Frequency of Contact with Nonresident Fathers and Adolescent Well-Being." *Journal of Divorce and Remarriage* 40:77–90.

Stack, S., and J. R. Eshleman. 1998. "Marital Status and Happiness: A 17–Nation Study." *Journal of Marriage and the Family* 60:527–36.

Stafford, L., and D. J. Canary. 2006. "Equity and Interdependence as Predictors of Relational Maintenance Strategies." *Journal of Family Communication* 6:227–54.

Stanley, S. C., H. J. Markman, and S. W. Whitton. 2002. "Communication, Conflict, and Commitment." *Family Process* 41:659–76.

Staples, R. 1988. "The Emerging Majority: Resources for Nonwhite Families in the United States." *Family Relations* 37:348–54.

Stark, E. 1986. "Friends Through It All." *Psychology Today,* May, pp. 54–60.

Starrels, M. E. 1994. "Gender Differences in Parent-Child Relations." *Journal of Family Issues* 15:148–65.

Starrels, M. E., B. Ingersoll-Dayton, D. W. Dowler, and M. B. Neal. 1997. "The Stress of Caring for a Parent: Effects of the Elder's Impairment on an Employed, Adult Child." *Journal of Marriage and the Family* 59:860–72.

Steil, J., and K. Weltman. 1991. "Marital Inequality: The Importance of Resources, Personal Attributes, and Social Norms on Career Valuing and the Allocation of Domestic Responsibilities." *Sex Roles* 24:161–79.

Steinberg, L. 2007. *Adolescence.* New York: McGraw-Hill.

Stennes, L. M., M. M. Burch, M. G. Sen, and P. J. Bauer. 2005. A Longitudinal Study of Gendered Vocabulary and Communicative Action in Young Children." *Developmental Psychology* 41:75–88.

Sternberg, R. J. 1987. "Liking versus Loving: A Comparative Evaluation of Theories." *Psychological Bulletin* 102:331–45.

Sternberg, R. J. 1999. *Love Is a Story: A New Theory of Relations.* New York: Oxford University Press.

Sternberg, R. J., and D. M. Dobson. 1987. "Resolving Interpersonal Conflicts: An Analysis of Stylistic Consistency." *Journal of Personality and Social Psychology* 52:794–812.

Sternglanz, R. W., and B. M. Depaulo. 2004. "Reading Nonverbal Cues to Emotions." *Journal of Nonverbal Behavior* 28:245–66.

Stets, J. E. 1993. "The Link between Past and Present Intimate Relationships." *Journal of Family Issues* 14:236–60.

Stevens, D., G. Kiger, and P. J. Riley. 2001. "Working Hard and Hardly Working: Domestic Labor and Marital Satisfaction among Dual-Earner Couples." *Journal of Marriage and the Family* 63:514–26.

Stevens, D. P., K. L. Minnotte, S. E. Mannon, and G. Kiger. 2007. "Examining the 'Neglected Side of the Work-Family Interface'." *Journal of Family Issues* 28:242–62.

Stewart, A. J., A. P. Copeland, N. L. Chester, J. E. Malley, and N. C. Barenbaum. 1997. *Separating Together: How Divorce Transforms Families.* New York: Guilford.

Stewart, J. R., A. I. Schwebel, and M. A. Fine. 1986. "The Impact of Custodial Arrangement on the Adjustment of Recently Divorced Fathers." *Journal of Divorce* 9:55–65.

Stewart, M., A. Burns, and R. Leonard. 2007. "Dark Side of the Mothering Role: Abuse of Mothers by Adolescent and Adult Children." *Sex Roles* 56:183–91.

Stewart, S. D. 2005. "Boundary Ambiguity in Stepfamilies." *Journal of Family Issues* 26:1002–29.

Stewart, S., H. Stinnett, and L. B. Rosenfeld. 2000. "Sex Differences in Desired Characteristics of Short-Term and Long-Term Relationship Partners." *Journal of Social and Personal Relationships* 17:843–53.

Stiffman, A., et al. 2007. "American Indian Youth: Personal, Familial, and Environmental Strengths." *Journal of Child and Family Studies* 16:331–46.

Stinson, K. M., J. N. Lasker, J. Lohmann, and L. J. Toedter. 1992. "Parents' Grief Following Pregnancy Loss: A Comparison of Mothers and Fathers." *Family Relations* 41:218–23.

Stohs, J. H. 1995. "Predictors of Conflict over the Household Division of Labor among Women Employed Full-Time." *Sex Roles* 33:257–76.

Stoll, B. M., G. L. Arnaut, D. K. Fromme, and J. A. Felker-Thayer. 2005. "Adolescents in Stepfamilies." *Journal of Divorce & Remarriage* 44:177–89.

Stolzenberg, L., and S. J. D'Alessio. 2007. "The Effect of Divorce on Domestic Crime." *Crime & Delinquency* 53:281–302.

Stoneley, P. 2003. *Consumerism and American Girls' Literature, 1860–1940.* New York: Cambridge University Press.

Story, L. B., and R. Repetti. 2006. "Daily Occupational Stressors and Marital Behavior." *Journal of Family Psychology* 20:690–700.

Strassberg, D. S., and S. Holty. 2003. "An Experimental Study of Women's Internet Personal Ads." *Archives of Sexual Behavior* 32:253–60.

Straus, J. 2006. "Lone Starts." *Psychology Today,* May/June, pp. 84–92.

Straus, M. A. 2001. "New Evidence for the Benefits of Never Spanking." *Society* 38:52–60.

Straus, M. A. 2004. "Prevalence of Violence against Dating Partners by Male and Female University Students Worldwide." *Violence against Women* 10:790–811.

Straus, M. A., and C. J. Field. 2003. "Psychological Aggression by American Parents." *Journal of Marriage and the Family* 65:795–808.

Straus, M. A., and J. H. Stewart. 1999. "Corporal Punishment by American Parents." *Clinical Child and Family Psychology Review* 2:55–70.

Straus, M. A., and C. L. Yodanis. 1996. "Corporal Punishment in Adolescence and Physical Assaults on Spouses in Later Life." *Journal of Marriage and the Family* 58:825–41.

Strazdins, L., M. S. Clements, R. J. Korda, D. H. Broom, and R. M. D'Souza. 2006. "Unsociable Work? Nonstandard Work Schedules, Family Relationships, and Children's Well-Being." *Journal of Marriage and Family* 68:394–410.

Strohschein, L. 2005. "Parental Divorce and Child Mental Health Trajectories." *Journal of Marriage and Family* 67:1286–1300.

Strom, P. S., and R. D. Strom. 2005. "Parent-Child Relationships in Early Adulthood." *Community College Journal of Research and Practice* 29:517–29.

Strom, R., D. Griswold, S. Strom, P. Collinsworth, and J. Schmid. 1990. "Perceptions of Parenting Success by Black Mothers and Their Preadolescent Children." *Journal of Negro Education* 59:611–22.

Strough, J., J. P. Leszczynski, T. L. Neely, J. A. Flinn, and J. Margrett. 2007. "From Adolescence to Later Adulthood: Femininity, Masculinity, and Androgyny in Six Age Groups." *Sex Roles* 57:385–96.

Stuart, F. M., D. C. Hammond, and M. A. Pett. 1987. "Inhibited Sexual Desire in Women." *Archives of Sexual Behavior* 16:91–106.

Sturgess, W., J. Dunn, and L. Davies. 2001. "Young Children's Perceptions of Their Relationships with Family Members." *International Journal of Behavioral Development* 25:521–29.

Substance Abuse and Mental Health Services Administration. 2007. "The NSDUH Report: Sexually Transmitted Diseases and Substance Use." Rockville, MD: Government Printing Office.

Sugar, M. H. 1994. *When Mothers Work, Who Pays?* New York: Greenwood.

Sullivan, D. A. 2001. *Cosmetic Surgery: The Cutting Edge of Commercial Medicine in America.* New Brunswick, NJ: Rutgers University Press.

Sullivan, M. 2005. *The Family of Woman: Lesbian Mothers, Their Children, and the Undoing of Gender.* Berkeley and Los Angeles: University of California Press.

Sullivan, O. 1997. "The Division of Housework about 'Remarried' Couples." *Journal of Family Issues* 18: 205–23.

Sumner, W. C. 1997. "The Effects of Parental Dating on Latency Children Living with One Custodial Parent." *Journal of Divorce and Remarriage* 27:137–57.

Sun, Y., and Y. Li. 2001. "Marital Disruption, Parental Investment, and Children's Academic Achievement." *Journal of Family Issues* 22:27–62.

Sun, Y., and Y. Li. 2002. "Children's Well-Being during Parents' Marital Disruption Process." *Journal of Marriage and Family* 64:472–88.

Sung, B. L. 1990. "Chinese American Intermarriage." *Journal of Comparative Family Studies* 21:337–52.

Surra, C. A., and D. K. Hughes. 1997. "Commitment Processes in Accounts of the Development of Premarital Relationships." *Journal of Marriage and the Family* 59:5–21.

Swaab, D. F., W. C. J. Chung, F. P. M. Kruijver, M. A. Hofman, and T. A. Ishunina. 2001. "Structural and Functional Sex Differences in the Human Hypothalamus." *Hormones and Behavior* 40:93–98.

Swanson, J. M., and C. W. Chentiz. 1993. "Regaining a Valued Self: The Process of Adaptation to Living with Genital Herpes." *Qualitative Health Research* 3:270–97.

Sweeney, M. M., and J. A. Phillips. 2004. "Understanding Racial Differences in Marital Disruption." *Journal of Marriage and the Family* 66:639–50.

Swensen, C. H., and G. Trahaug. 1985. "Commitment and the Long-Term Marriage." *Journal of Marriage and the Family* 47:939–45.

Swim, J. K., L. L. Hyers, L. L. Cohen, and M. J. Ferguson. 2001. "Everyday Sexism: Evidence for its Incidence, Nature, and Psychological Impact from Three Daily Diary Studies." *Journal of Social Issues* 57:31–53.

Swinford, S. P., A. DeMaris, S. A. Cernkovich, and P. C. Giordano. 2000. "Harsh Physical Discipline in Childhood and Violence in Later Romantic Involvements." *Journal of Marriage and the Family* 62:508–19.

Szinovacz, M., and A. Davey. 2005. "Retirement and Marital Decision Making." *Journal of Marriage and Family* 67:387–98.

Talbot, M. 1998. "Attachment Theory: The Ultimate Experiment." *The New York Times Magazine,* May 24.

Tallman, I., T. Rotolo, and L. N. Gray. 2001. "Continuity or Change? The Impact of Parents' Divorce on Newly Married Couples." *Social Psychology Quarterly* 64:333–46.

Tannen, D. 1990. *You Just Don't Understand: Women and Men in Conversation.* New York: William Morrow.

Tashiro, T., and P. Frazier. 2003. " 'I'll Never Be in a Relationship Like That Again': Personal Growth Following Romantic Relationship Breakups." *Personal Relationships* 10:113–28.

Tasker, F., and S. Golombok. 1997. "Young People's Attitudes toward Living in a Lesbian Family: A Longitudinal Study of Children Raised by Post-Divorce Lesbian Mothers." *Journal of Divorce & Remarriage* 28:183–202.

Taylor, R., L. Chatters, C. Hardison, and A. Riley. 2001. "Informal Social Support Networks and Subjective Well-Being." *Journal of Black Psychology* 27:1–12.

Teachman, J. D. 2004. "The Childhood Living Arrangements of Children and the Characteristics of Marriages." *Journal of Family Issues* 25:86–111.

Teleki, J. K., and S. Buck-Gomez. 2002. "Child Care and Early Education." *Early Childhood Education Journal* 29:161–66.

Tenenbaum, H. R., and C. Leaper. 2003. "Parent-Child Conversations about Science: The Socialization of Gender Inequities?" *Developmental Psychology* 39:34–47.

Terrance, C., and K. Matheson. 2003. "Undermining Reasonableness." *Psychology of Women Quarterly* 27:37–45.

Testa, M., and K. E. Leonard. 2001. "The Impact of Husband Physical Aggression and Alcohol Use on Marital Functioning." *Violence and Victims* 16:507–16.

Thatcher, D. L., and D. B. Clark. 2006. "Adolescent Alcohol Abuse and Dependence." *Current Psychiatry Reviews* 2:159–77.

Thompson, E. H., C. Grisanti, and J. H. Pleck. 1985. "Attitudes toward the Male Role and Their Correlates." *Sex Roles* 13:413–27.

Thompson, L. Y., et al. 2005. "Dispositional Forgiveness of Self, Others, and Situations." *Journal of Personality* 73:313–60.

Thompson, M. P., I. Arias, K. C. Basile, and S. Desai. 2002. "The Association between Childhood Physical and Sexual Victimization and Health Problems in Adulthood in a Nationally Representative Sample of Women." *Journal of Interpersonal Violence* 17:1115–29.

Thomson, E., and U. Colella. 1992. "Cohabitation and Marital Stability: Quality or Commitment." *Journal of Marriage and the Family* 54:259–68.

Thomson, E., T. L. Hanson, and S. S. McLanahan. 1994. "Family Structure and Child Well-Being: Economic Resources vs. Parental Behaviors." *Social Forces* 73:221–42.

Thomson, E., S. S. McLanahan, and R. B. Curtin. 1992. "Family Structure, Gender, and Parental Socialization." *Journal of Marriage and the Family* 54:368–78.

Thornton, A., and L. Young-DeMarco. 2001. "Four Decades of Trends in Attitudes toward Family Issues in the United States: The 1960s through the 1990s." *Journal of Marriage and the Family* 63:1009–37.

Thrane, L. E., D. R. Hoyt, L. B. Whitbeck, and K. A. Yoder. 2006. "Impact of Family Abuse on Running Away." *Child Abuse & Neglect* 30:1117–28.

Tichenor, V. J. 1999. "Status and Income as Gendered Resources: The Case of Marital Power." *Journal of Marriage and the Family* 61:638–50.

Tichenor, V. 2005. "Maintaining Men's Dominance: Negotiating Identity and Power When She Earns More." *Sex Roles* 53:191–205.

Tidwell, M.-C. O., H. T. Reis, and P. R. Shaver. 1996. "Attachment, Attractiveness, and Social Interaction." *Journal of Personality and Social Psychology* 71:729–45.

Tiedje, L. B. 2004. "Processes of Change in Work/Home Incompatibilities." *Journal of Social Issues* 60:787–800.

Tiggemann, M., and B. McGill. 2004. "The Role of Social Comparison in the Effect of Magazine Advertisements on Women's

Mood and Body Dissatisfaction." *Journal of Social and Clinical Psychology* 23:23–44.

Tiggemann, M., Y. Martins, and A. Kirkbride. 2007. "Oh to Be Lean and Muscular: Body Image Ideals in Gay and Heterosexual Men." *Psychology of Men & Masculinity* 8:15–24.

Tillery, D. E. 2007. "Grandparents Day 2007: Sept. 9." Press Release. Washington, DC: U.S. Census Bureau.

Tjaden, P., N. Thoennes, and C. J. Allison. 1999. "Comparing Violence over the Life Span in Samples of Same-Sex and Opposite-Sex Cohabitants." *Violence and Victims* 14:413–25.

Tolmacz, R. 2004. "Attachment Style and Willingness to Compromise When Choosing a Mate." *Journal of Social and Personal Relationships* 21:267–72.

Tomaskovic-Devey, D., et al. 2006. "Documenting Desegregation: Segregation in American Workplaces by Race, Ethnicity, and Sex, 1966-2003." *American Sociological Review* 71:565–88.

Treas, J., and D. Giesen. 2000. "Sexual Infidelity among Married and Cohabiting Americans." *Journal of Marriage and the Family* 62:48–60.

Trent, K., and K. Crowder. 1997. "Adolescent Birth Intentions, Social Disadvantage, and Behavioral Outcomes." *Journal of Marriage and the Family* 59:523–35.

Trimberger, E. K. 2005. *The New Single Woman*. Boston: Beacon Press.

Trudel, G., L. Turgeon, and L. Piche. 2000. "Marital and Sexual Aspects of Old Age." *Sexual and Relationship Therapy* 15:381–406.

Truman, D. M., D. M. Tokar, and A. R. Fischer. 1996. "Dimensions of Masculinity: Relations to Date Rape Supportive Attitudes and Sexual Aggression in Dating Situations." *Journal of Counseling & Development* 74:555–62.

Tseng, L. L., C. D. H. Harvey, K. A. Duncan, and R. Sommer. 2003. "The Effects of Children, Dual Earner Status, Sex Role Traditionalism, and Marital Structure on Marital Happiness over Time." *Journal of Family and Economic Issues* 24:5–26.

Tucker, J. S., H. S. Friedman, J. E. Schwartz, and M. H. Criqui. 1997. "Parental Divorce: Effects on Individual Behavior and Longevity." *Journal of Personality and Social Psychology* 73:381–91.

Tucker, P., and A. Aron. 1993. "Passionate Love and Marital Satisfaction at Key Transition Points in the Family Life Cycle." *Journal of Social and Clinical Psychology* 12:135–47.

Turcotte, M. 2006. "Parents with Adult Children Living at Home." *Canadian Social Trends* 80:2–10.

Turner, B. F., and C. G. Adams. 1988. "Reported Change in Preferred Sexual Activity over the Adult Years." *Journal of Sex Research* 25:289–303.

Turner, H. A. 2006. "Stress, Social Resources, and Depression among Never-Married and Divorced Rural Mothers." *Rural Sociology* 71:479–504.

Turner, H. A., D. Finkelhor, and R. Ormrod. 2007. "Family Structure Variations in Patterns and Predictors of Child Victimization." *American Journal of Orthopsychiatry* 77:282–95.

Turner, H. A., and K. Kopiec. 2006. "Exposure to Interparental Conflict and Psychological Disorder among Young Adults." *Journal of Family Issues* 27:131–58.

Turner, H. A., and P. A. Muller. 2004. "Long-Term Effects of Child Corporal Punishment on Depressive Symptoms in Young Adults." *Journal of Family Issues* 25:761–82.

Turner, M. J., C. R. Young, and K. I. Black. 2006. "Daughters-in-Law and Mothers-in-Law Seeking Their Place Within the Family." *Family Relations* 55:588–600.

Turner, P. H., L. Scadden, and M. B. Harris. 1990. "Parenting in Gay and Lesbian Families." *Journal of Gay and Lesbian Psychotherapy* 1:55–66.

Tweed, S. H., and C. D. Ryff. 1991. "Adult Children of Alcoholics: Profiles of Wellness amidst Distress." *Journal of Studies on Alcohol* 52:133–41.

Twenge, J. M., W. K. Campbell, and C. A. Foster. 2003. "Parenthood and Marital Satisfaction: A Meta-analytic Review." *Journal of Marriage and Family* 65:574–83.

Twoy, R., P. M. Connolly, and J. M. Novak. 2007. "Coping Strategies Used by Parents of Children with Autism." *Journal of the American Academy of Nurse Practitioners* 19: 251–60.

Uchitelle, L. 1998. "Still Married to the Job." *New York Times,* April 20.

Ullman, S. E., and L. R. Brecklin. 2003. "Sexual Assault History and Health-Related Outcomes in a National Sample of Women." *Psychology of Women Quarterly* 27:46–57.

Umberson, D., K. Anderson, J. Glick, and A. Shapiro. 1998. "Domestic Violence, Personal Control, and Gender." *Journal of Marriage and the Family* 60:442–52.

Umberson, D., K. Williams, D.A. Powers, H. Liu, and B. Needham. 2006. "You Make Me Sick: Marital Quality and Health over the Life Course." *Journal of Health and Social Behavior* 47:1–16.

Unger, J. B., G. B. Molina, and L. Teran. 2000. "Perceived Consequences of Teenage Childbearing among Adolescent Girls in an Urban Sample." *Journal of Adolescent Health* 26:205–12.

United Nations Statistics Division. 2005. "Marriages and Crude Marriage Rates, by Urban/Rural Residence: 1998-2002." United Nations Statistics Division Web site.

Upchurch, D. M., C. S. Aneshensel, C. A. Sucoff, and L. Levy-Storms. 1999. "Neighborhood and Family Contexts of Adolescent Sexual Activity." *Journal of Marriage and the Family* 61:920–33.

Urbaniak, G. C., and P. R. Kilmann. 2003. "Physical Attractiveness and the 'Nice Guy Paradox': Do Nice Guys Really Finish Last?" *Sex Roles* 49:413–26.

Urcuyo, K. R., A. E. Boyers, C. S. Carver, and M. H. Antoni. 2005. "Finding Benefit in Breast Cancer." *Psychology and Health* 20:175–92.

U.S. Census Bureau. 1975. *Historical Statistics of the United States, Colonial Times to 1970*. Washington, DC: Government Printing Office.

U.S. Census Bureau. 1989. *Statistical Abstract of the United States, 1989*. Washington, DC: Government Printing Office.

U.S. Census Bureau. 1994. *Statistical Abstract of the United States, 1994.* Washington, DC: Government Printing Office.

U.S. Census Bureau. 2004/2005. *Statistical Abstract of the United States, 2004/2005.* Washington, DC: Government Printing Office.

U.S. Census Bureau. 2006. *Population Profile of the United States.* U.S. Census Bureau Web site.

U.S. Census Bureau. 2007a. *Families and Living Arrangements in 2006.* U.S. Census Bureau Web site.

U.S. Census Bureau. 2007b. *The American Community–American Indians and Alaska Natives: 2004.* U.S. Census Bureau Web site.

U.S. Census Bureau. 2007c. *Unmarried and Single Americans Week.* U.S. Census Bureau Web site.

U.S. Census Bureau. 2008. *Statistical Abstract of the United States.* U.S. Census Bureau Web site.

U.S. Census Bureau, Survey of Income and Program Participation. 2007. "Median Duration of Marriages for People 15 Years and Over by Sex, Race, and Hispanic Origin: 2004." U.S. Census Bureau Web site.

U.S. Department of Health, Education, and Welfare. 1978. *Yours, Mine, and Ours: Tips for Stepparents.* Washington, DC: Government Printing Office.

U.S. Department of Labor. 2007. *Women in the Labor Force: A Databook.* U.S. Department of Labor Web site.

Valiente, C. E., C. J. Belanger, and A. U. Estrada. 2002. "Helpful and Harmful Expectations of Premarital Interventions." *Journal of Sex and Marital Therapy* 28:71–77.

Van Baarsen, B., T. A. B. Snijders, J. H. Smit, and M. A. J. Van Dujin. 2001. "Lonely but Not Alone." *Educational and Psychological Measurement* 61:119–35.

van Gaalen, R., and P. A. Dykstra. 2006. "Solidarity and Conflict between Adult Children and Parents." *Journal of Marriage and Family* 68:947–60.

Vangelisti, A., and M. A. Banski. 1993. "Couples' Debriefing Conversations: The Impact of Gender, Occupation, and Demographic Characteristics." *Family Relations* 42:149–57.

Van Horn, M. L., S. L. Ramey, B. A. Mulvihill, and W. Y. Newell. 2001. "Reasons for Child Care Choice and Appraisal among Low-Income Mothers." *Child and Youth Care Forum* 30:231–49.

van Ijzendoorn, M. H., F. Juffer, and C. W. K. Poelhuis. 2005. "Adoption and Cognitive Devleopment." *Psychological Bulletin* 131:301–16.

Vastag, B. 2001. "Fertility Treatment Statistics." *Journal of the American Medical Association* 285:987.

Veevers, J. E. 1991. "Traumas versus Stress: A Paradigm of Positive versus Negative Divorce Outcomes." *Journal of Divorce and Remarriage* 15:99–126.

Ventura, J. N. 1987. "The Stresses of Parenthood Reexamined." *Family Relations* 36:26–29.

Ventura, S. J., J. C. Abma, W. D. Mosher, and S. K. Henshaw. "Recent Trends in Teenage Pregnancy in the United States, 1990–2002." *Health E-Stats.* National Center for Health Statistics Web site.

Verbrugge, L. M., and J. H. Madans. 1985. "Women's Roles and Health." *American Demographics* 8:35–39.

Videon, T. M. 2005. "Parent-Child Relations and Children's Psychological Well-Being." *Journal of Family Issues* 26:55–78.

Viki, G. T., D. Abrams, and P. Hutchison. 2003. "The 'True' Romantic: Benevolent Sexism and Paternalistic Chivalry." *Sex Roles* 49:533–37.

Villalba, J. A., M. Brunelli, L. Lewis, and D. Orfanedes. 2007. "Experiences of Latino Children Attending Rural Elementary Schools in the Southeastern U.S." *Professional School Counseling* 10:506–509.

Viorst, J. 1998. *Necessary Losses.* New York: Free Press.

Viscoli, C. M., et al. 2001. "Social Support as a Buffer to the Psychological Impact of Stressful Life Events in Women with Breast Cancer." *Cancer* 91:443–54.

Vittengi, J. R., and C. S. Holt. 2000. "Getting Acquainted: The Relationship of Self-Disclosure and Social Attraction to Positive Affect." *Journal of Social and Personal Relationships* 17:53–66.

Voydanoff, P., and B. W. Donnelly. 1999. "The Intersection of Time in Activities and Perceived Unfairness in Relation to Psychological Distress and Marital Quality." *Journal of Marriage and the Family* 61:739–51.

Voyer, D., C. Nolan, and S. Voyer. 2000. "The Relation Between Experience and Spatial Performance in Men and Women." *Sex Roles* 43:891–915.

Vuchinich, S. 1985. "Arguments, Family Style." *Psychology Today,* October, pp. 40–46.

Wade, J. C., and C. Brittan-Powell. 2001. "Men's Attitudes toward Race and Gender Equity." *Psychology of Men and Masculinity* 2:42–50.

Wahab, S., and L. Olson. 2004. "Intimate Partner Violence and Sexual Assault in Native American Communities." *Trauma, Violence, & Abuse* 5:353–66.

Waite, L., and M. Gallagher. 2000. *The Case for Marriage: Why Married People Are Happier, Healthier and Better Off Financially.* New York: Doubleday.

Waite, L. J., F. K. Goldscheider, and C. Witsberger. 1986. "Nonfamily Living and the Erosion of Traditional Family Orientations among Young Adults." *American Sociological Review* 51:541–54.

Waite, L. J., and K. Joyner. 2001. "Emotional Satisfaction and Physical Pleasure in Sexual Unions." *Journal of Marriage and the Family* 63:247–64.

Waite, L. J., and L. A. Lillard. 1991. "Children and Marital Disruption." *American Journal of Sociology* 96:930–53.

Wakabayashi, C., and K. M. Donato. 2006. "Does Caregiving Increase Poverty among Women in Later Life?" *Journal of Health and Social Behavior* 47:258–74.

Wake, M., et al. 2006. "Prevalence, Stability, and Outcomes of Cry-Fuss and Sleep Problems in the First 2 Years of Life." *Pediatrics* 117:836–42.

Walcott, D. D., H. D. Pratt, and D. R. Patel. 2003. "Adolescents and Eating Disorders." *Journal of Adolescent Research* 18:223–43.

Walker, A. J. 1996. "Couples Watching Television: Gender, Power, and the Remote Control." *Journal of Marriage and the Family* 58:813–23.

Walker, L. E. 2006. "Battered Woman Syndrome." *Annals of the New York Academy of Science* 1087:142–57.

Wallace, J. M. Jr., et al. 2007. "Religiosity and Adolescent Substance Use: The Role of Individual and Contextual Influences." *Social Problems* 54:308–27.

Waller, W. 1951. *The Family.* Revised by R. Hill. New York: Dryden Press.

Wallerstein, J. S. 1994. "The Early Psychological Tasks of Marriage." *American Journal of Orthopsychiatry* 64:640–50.

Wallerstein, J. S. 2005. "Growing Up in the Divorced Family." *Clinical Social Work Journal* 33:401–18.

Wallerstein, J. S., and S. Blakeslee. 1989. *Second Chances: Men, Women and Children a Decade after Divorce.* New York: Ticknor & Fields.

Wallerstein, J. S., J. Lewis, and S. Blakeslee. 2001. *The Unexpected Legacy of Divorce.* New York: Hyperion.

Walsh, C. A., E. Jamieson, H. MacMillan, and M. Boyle. 2007. "Child Abuse and Chronic Pain in a Community Survey of Women." *Journal of Interpersonal Violence* 22:1536–54.

Walsh, J. A., and J. L. Krienert. 2007. "Child-Parent Violence." *Journal of Family Violence* 22: 563–74.

Walsh, W. 2002. "Spankers and Nonspankers: Where They Get Information on Spanking." *Family Relations* 51:81–88.

Wang, Y., and D. E. Marcotte. 2007. "Golden Years? The Labor Market Effects of Caring for Grandchildren." *Journal of Marriage and Family* 69:1283–96.

Ward, R. A. 1993. "Marital Happiness and Household Equity in Later Life." *Journal of Marriage and the Family* 55:427–38.

Waring, E. M., and G. J. Chelune. 1983. "Marital Intimacy and Self-Disclosure." *Journal of Clinical Psychology* 39:183–90.

Wasserman, I. M. 1990. "The Impact of Divorce on Suicide in the United States: 1970–1983." *Family Perspective* 24:61–68.

Watson, D., et al. 2004. "Match Makers and Deal Breakers." *Journal of Personality* 72:1029–68.

Watt, T. T. 2002. "Marital and Cohabiting Relationships of Adult Children of Alcoholics." *Journal of Family Issues* 23:246–65.

Waxman, S. 2007. "Matchmakers Know Superstars Need Love, Too." *The New York Times,* May 6.

Weaver, C. N. 2003. "Happiness of Mexican Americans." *Hispanic Journal of Behavioral Sciences* 25:275–94.

Weger, H. 2005. "Disconfirming Communication and Self-Verification in Marriage." *Journal of Social and Personal Relationships* 22:19–31.

Weigel, D. J., K. K. Bennett, and D. S. Ballard-Reisch. 2003. "Family Influences on Commitment." *Personal Relationships* 10:453–74.

Weinberg, H. 1990. "Delayed Childbearing, Childlessness and Marital Disruption." *Journal of Comparative Family Studies* 21:99–110.

Weir, E. 2001. "Drug-Facilitated Date Rape." *Canadian Medical Association Journal* 165:1.

Wellings, K., et al. 2006. "Sexual Behavior in Context: A Global Perspective." *The Lancet* 368:1706–28.

West, J. 1945. *Plainville, U.S.A.* New York: Columbia University Press.

Westerhof, G. J., and A. E. Barrett. 2005. "Age Identity and Subjective Well-Being." *Journals of Gerontology Series B* 60B:S129–36.

Weston, C. A., and E. D. Macklin. 1990. "The Relationship between Former-Spousal Contact and Remarital Satisfaction in Stepfather Families." *Journal of Divorce and Remarriage* 14:25–47.

Whelan, D. L. 2007. "More Parents Reading to Their Preschoolers." *School Library Journal* 53:17.

Whiffen, V. E., and H. B. MacIntosh. 2005. "Mediators of the Link between Childhood Sexual Abuse and Emotional Distress." *Trauma, Violence, and Abuse* 6:24–39.

Whipple, E. E., and C. Webster-Stratton. 1991. "The Role of Parental Stress in Physically Abusive Families." *Child Abuse and Neglect* 15:279–91.

Whipple, S. C., and E. P. Noble. 1991. "Personality Characteristics of Alcoholic Fathers and Their Sons." *Journal of Studies on Alcohol* 52:331–37.

Whisman, M. A., and N. S. Jacobson. 1990. "Power, Marital Satisfaction, and Response to Marital Therapy." *Journal of Family Psychology* 4:202–12.

Whisman, M. A., K. C. Gordon, and Y. Chatav. 2007. "Predicting Sexual Infidelity in a Population-Based Sample of Married Individuals." *Journal of Family Psychology* 21:320–24.

Whisman, M.A., and L.A. Uebelacker. 2006. "Impairment and Distress Associated with Relationship Discord in a National Sample of Married or Cohabiting Adults." *Journal of Family Psychology* 20:369–77.

Whitbeck, L. B., K. A. Yoder, D. R. Hoyt, and R. D. Conger. 1999. "Early Adolescent Sexual Activity." *Journal of Marriage and the Family* 61:934–46.

White, J. M. 1987. "Marital Perceived Agreement and Actual Agreement over the Family Life Cycle." *Journal of Comparative Family Studies* 18:47–59.

White, L. 1994. "Growing Up with Single Parents and Stepparents: Long-Term Effects on Family Solidarity." *Journal of Marriage and the Family* 56:935–48.

White, L. K., and A. Booth. 1985. "Stepchildren in Remarriages." *American Sociological Review* 50:689–98.

White, L. K., A. Booth, and J. N. Edwards. 1986. "Children and Marital Happiness: Why the Negative Correlation?" *Journal of Family Issues* 7:131–47.

White, L. K., and J. G. Gilbreth. 2001. "When Children Have Two Fathers: Effects of Relationships with Stepfathers and Noncustodial Fathers on Adolescent Outcomes." *Journal of Marriage and the Family* 63:155–67.

Whitehead, B. D. 1997. *The Divorce Culture.* New York: Alfred A. Knopf.

Whitehead, B. D., and D. Popenoe. 2001. *The State of Our Unions: The Social Health of Marriage in America.* The National Marriage Project Web site.

Whitley, B. E. 1990. "College Student Contraceptive Use: A Multivariate Analysis." *Journal of Sex Research* 27:305–13.

Whitty, M. T. 2005. "The Realness of Cybercheating." *Social Science Computer Review* 23:57–67.

Whyte, M. K. 1990. *Dating, Mating, and Marriage.* New York: Aldine de Gruyt.

Widener, A. J. 2007. "Family-Friendly Policy: Lessons from Europe." *Public Manager* 36:57–61.

Wiederman, M. W., and E. R. Allgeier. 1996. "Expectations and Attributions Regarding Extramarital Sex among Young Married Individuals." *Journal of Psychology & Human Sexuality* 8:21–35.

Wiemann, C., et al. 2006. "Absent Fathers as Providers." *Child and Adolescent Social Work Journal* 23:617–34.

Wilcox, W. B., and S. L. Nock. 2006. "What's Love Got to Do with It? Equality, Equity, Commitment and Women's Marital Quality." *Social Forces* 84:1321–45.

Wilens, T. E., et al. 2002. "A Family Study of High-Risk Children of Opioid- and Alcohol-Dependent Parents." *American Journal on Addictions* 11:41–51.

Wilkie, J. R., M. M. Ferree, and K. S. Ratcliff. 1998. "Gender and Fairness: Marital Satisfaction in Two-Earner Couples." *Journal of Marriage and the Family* 60:577–94.

Willeto, A. A. 2007. "Native American Kids: American Indian Children's Well-Being Indicators for the Nation and Two States." *Social Indicators Research* 83:149–76.

Willetts, M. C. 2006. "Union Quality Comparisons between Long-Term Heterosexual Cohabitation and Legal Marriage." *Journal of Family Issues* 27:110–27.

Willi, J. 1997. "The Significance of Romantic Love for Marriage." *Family Process* 36:171–82.

Williams, D. E., and J. D. D'Alessandro. 1994. "A Comparison of Three Measures of Androgyny and Their Relationship to Psychological Adjustment." *Journal of Social Behavior and Personality* 9:469–80.

Williams, G. B. 2001. "Short-Term Grief after an Elective Abortion." *Journal of Obstetric, Gynecologic, and Neonatal Nursing* 30:174–83.

Williams, K., and A. Dunne-Bryant. 2006. "Divorce and Adult Psychological Well-Being." *Journal of Marriage and Family* 68:1178–96.

Williams, L. 2007. "Premarital Counseling." *Journal of Couple and Relationship Therapy* 6:207–17.

Williamson, J., B. Softas-Nall, and J. Miller. 2003. "Grandmothers Raising Grandchildren." *Family Journal* 11:23–32.

Wilmot, W. W., and J. L. Hocker. 2000. *Interpersonal Conflict.* 6th ed. New York: McGraw-Hill.

Wilson, G., and J. Cousins. 2003. "Partner Similarity and Relationship Satisfaction." *Sexual & Relationship Therapy* 18:161–70.

Wilson, M. D., M. Kastrinakis, L. J. D'Angelo, and P. Getson. 1994. "Attitudes, Knowledge, and Behavior Regarding Condom Use in Urban Black Adolescent Males." *Adolescence* 29:13–26.

Wilson, M. N., T. F. Tolson, I. D. Hinton, and M. Kiernan. 1990. "Flexibility and Sharing of Childcare Duties in Black Families." *Sex Roles* 22:409–25.

Wilson, S. M., and N. P. Madora. 1990. "Gender Comparisons of College Students' Attitudes toward Sexual Behavior." *Adolescence* 25:615–27.

Wineberg, H. 1992. "Childbearing and Dissolution of the Second Marriage." *Journal of Marriage and the Family* 54:879–87.

Wisensale, S. K. 2006. "California's Paid Leave Law." *Marriage & Family Review* 39:177–96.

Wolfinger, N. H. 1998. "The Effects of Parental Divorce on Adult Tobacco and Alcohol Consumption." *Journal of Health and Social Behavior* 39:254–69.

Wolfinger, N. H. 2000. "Beyond the Intergenerational Transmission of Divorce." *Journal of Family Issues* 21:1061–86.

Wolfinger, N. H. 2003. "Family Structure Homogamy." *Social Science Research* 32:80–97.

Women in Development. 1999. *Statistics on Women in Asia and the Pacific.* WID Web site.

Wood, D. B. 2001. "Latinos Redefine What It Means to Be 'Manly.'" *Christian Science Monitor,* July 16.

Wood, J., R. Repetti, and S. Roesch. 2004. "Divorce and Children's Adjustment Problems at Home and School." *Child Psychiatry and Human Development* 35:121–42.

Woodward, L., D. M. Fergusson, and L. J. Horwood. 2001. "Risk Factors and Life Processes Associated with Teenage Pregnancy." *Journal of Marriage and the Family* 63:1170–84.

Worchel, S., J. Cooper, and G. R. Goethals. 1991. *Understanding Social Psychology.* 5th ed. Pacific Grove, CA: Books/Cole.

Worthington, E. L., Jr., and M. Scherer. 2004. "Forgiveness Is an Emotion-Focused Coping Strategy That Can Reduce Health Risks and Promote Health Resilience." *Psychology and Health* 19:385–405.

Wright, D. W., and R. Young. 1998. "The Effects of Family Structure and Maternal Employment on the Development of Gender-Related Attitudes among Men and Women." *Journal of Family Issues* 19:300–14.

Wright, M. O., E. Crawford, and K. Sebastian. 2007. "Positive Resolution of Childhood Sexual Abuse Experiences." *Journal of Family Violence* 22:597–608.

Wrigley, J., and J. Dreby. 2005. "Fatalities and the Organization of Child Care in the United States." *American Sociological Review* 70:729–57.

Wu, Z., and C. Schimmele. 2005. "Repartnering after First Union Disruption." *Journal of Marriage and the Family* 67:27–36.

Wyatt, G. E., and M. Riederle. 1995. "The Prevalence and Context of Sexual Harassment among African American and White American Women." *Journal of Interpersonal Violence* 10:309–21.

Wynn, R. L., and J. Bowering. 1990. "Homemaking Practices and Evening Meals in Married and Separated Families with Young Children." *Journal of Divorce and Remarriage* 14:107–23.

Xiong, Z., and D. F. Detzner. 2004–2005. "Southeast Asian Adolescents' Perception of Immigrant Parenting Practices." *Hmong Studies Journal* 5:1–20.

Xiong, Z., P. A. Eliason, D. F. Detzner, and M. J. Cleveland. 2005. "Southeast Asian Immigrants' Perceptions of Good Adolescents and Good Parents." *Journal of Psychology* 139:159–75.

Xu, X., C. D. Hudspeth, and J. P. Bartkowski. 2006. "The Role of Cohabitation in Remarriage." *Journal of Marriage and Family* 68:271–74.

Xu, X., and C. S. Lai. 2004. "Gender Ideologies, Marital Roles, and Marital Quality in Taiwan." *Journal of Family Issues* 25:318–55.

Xu, Y. 2007. "Empowering Culturally Diverse Families of Young Children with Disabilities: The Double ABCX Model." *Early Childhood Education Journal* 34:431–37.

Yamaguchi, K., and L. R. Ferguson. 1995. "The Stopping and Spacing of Childbirths and Their Birth-History Predictors." *American Sociological Review* 60:272–98.

Yeh, H., F. O. Lorenz, K. A. S. Wickrama, R.D. Conger, and G. H. Elder. 2006. "Relationships among Sexual Satisfaction, Marital Quality, and Marital Instability at Midlife." *Journal of Family Psychology* 20:339–43.

Yelsma, P., and C. T. Brown. 1985. "Gender Roles, Biological Sex, and Predisposition to Conflict Management." *Sex Roles* 12:731–47.

Yelsma, P., and S. Marrow. 2003. "An Examination of Couples' Difficulties with Emotional Expressiveness and Their Marital Satisfaction." *Journal of Family Communication* 3:41–62.

Yeung, W. J., J. F. Sandberg, P. E. David-Kean, and S. L. Hofferth. 2001. "Children's Time with Fathers in Intact Families." *Journal of Marriage and the Family* 63:136–54.

Young, M. 2000. "Sexual Satisfaction among Married Women." *American Journal of Health Studies* 16:24–34.

Young, M. S., K. Harford, B. Kinder, and J. K. Savell. 2007. "The Relationship between Childhood Sexual Abuse and Adult Mental Health among Undergraduates." *Journal of Interpersonal Violence* 22:1315–31.

Youngblade, L. M. 2003. "Peer and Teacher Ratings of Third- and Fourth-Grade Children's Social Behavior as a Function of Early Maternal Employment." *Journal of Child Psychology & Psychiatry & Allied Disciplines* 44:477–88.

Yount, K. M. 2005a. "Resources, Family Organization, and Domestic Violence against Married Women in Minya, Egypt." *Journal of Marriage and Family* 67:579–96.

Yount, K. M. 2005b. "Women's Family Power and Gender Preference in Minya, Egypt." *Journal of Marriage and Family* 67:410–28.

Yuan, A. S. V., and H. A. Hamilton. 2006. "Stepfather Involvement and Adolescent Well-Being." *Journal of Family Issues* 27:1191–1213.

Youthography. 2007. "In the Spring a Young Person's Fancy Turns to. . . ." Youthography Web site.

Yunqing, L. 2007. "Recovering from Spousal Bereavement in Later Life: Does Volunteer Participation Play a Role?" *Journals of Gerontology Series B* 62B:S257–66.

Zakowski, S. G., et al. 2003. "Social Barriers to Emotional Expression and Their Relations to Distress in Male and Female Cancer Patients." *British Journal of Health Psychology* 8:271–86.

Zaleski, E. H., and K. M. Schiaffino. 2000. "Religiosity and Sexual Risk-Taking Behavior during the Transition to College." *Journal of Adolescence* 23:223–27.

Zamboni, B. D., and I. Crawford. 2007. "Minority Stress and Sexual Problems among African-American Gay and Bisexual Men." *Archives of Sexual Behavior* 36:569–78.

Zhan, M., and S. Pandey. 2004. "Postsecondary Education and Economic Well-Being of Single Mothers and Single Fathers." *Journal of Marriage and Family* 66:661–73.

Zhang, Z., and M. D. Hayward. 2001. "Childlessness and the Psychological Well-Being of Older Persons." *Journal of Gerontology* 56:S311–20.

Zick, C. D., and W. K. Bryant. 1996. "A New Look at Parents' Time Spent in Child Care: Primary and Secondary Time Use." *Social Science Research* 25:260–80.

Zick, C. D., W. K. Bryant, and E. Osterbacka. 2001. "Mothers' Employment, Parental Involvement, and the Implications for Intermediate Child Outcomes." *Social Science Research* 30:25–49.

Zinn, M. B., and B. Wells. 2000. "Diversity within Latino Families." In D. H. Demo, K. R. Allen, and M. A. Fine, eds., *Handbook of Family Diversity.* New York: Oxford University Press.

Zucker, A. N., et al. 2001. "Smoking in College Women: The Role of Thinness Pressures, Media Exposure, and Critical Consciousness." *Psychology of Women* 25:233–41.

Zuo, J., and Y. Bian. 2001. "Gendered Resources, Division of Housework, and Perceived Fairness—A Case in Urban China." *Journal of Marriage and the Family* 63:1122–33.

PHOTO CREDITS

Part Openers

Part 1, p. 1: BananaStock/PictureQuest; Part 2, p. 105: Banana-Stock/age fotostock; Part 3, p. 169: Colin Paterson/Getty Images; Part 4, p. 257: Skip Nall/Getty Images; Part 5, p. 309: The McGraw-Hill Companies, Inc./Jill Braaten, photographer

Chapter 1

Opener, p. 3: BananaStock/PictureQuest; page 5: BananaStock/PunchStock; p. 7, Digital Vision/Getty Images; p. 13: Banana-Stock/PunchStock; p. 18: Rim Light/PhotoLink/Getty Images

Chapter 2

Opener, p. 25: Andersen Ross/Getty Images; p. 28: Hurd Evan/Corbis; p. 29: Brand X Pictures/PunchStock; p. 40: Digital Vision; p. 44: Scott T. Baxter/Getty Images; p. 48: Digital Vision/PunchStock

Chapter 3

Opener, p. 55: PunchStock; p. 60: Getty Images; p. 67: Stockbyte/PunchStock; p. 73: Hollingsworth/PunchStock

Chapter 4

Opener, p. 77: Stockbyte/PunchStock; p. 80: BananaStock/PunchStock; p. 81: Keith Brofsky/Getty Images; p. 85: Creatas/PunchStock; p. 95: PhotoDisc/Getty Images; p. 99: The McGraw-Hill Companies, Inc./Christopher Kerrigan, photographer

Chapter 5

Opener, p. 107: Stockbyte/PunchStock; p. 111: Royalty-Free/Corbis; p. 114: Ryan McVay/Getty Images; p. 117: Brand X Pictures; p. 121: Image Source

Chapter 6

Opener, p. 127: Stockbyte/PunchStock; p. 129: Thinkstock; p. 133: Royalty-Free/Corbis; p. 138: Royalty-Free/Corbis

Chapter 7

Opener, p. 147: Comstock Images/Jupiterimages; p. 151: C. Borland/PhotoLink/Getty Images; p. 157: Royalty-Free/Corbis; p. 161: Comstock Images; p. 164: Royalty-Free/Corbis

Chapter 8

Opener, p. 171: Nancy R. Cohen/Getty Images; p. 175: Stockbyte; p. 180: Janis Christie/Getty Images; p. 184: Digital Vision/Getty Images

Chapter 9

Opener, p. 191: Eric Audras/Photoalto/PictureQuest; p. 194: Monica Lau/Getty Images; p. 199: Brand X Pictures/PunchStock; p. 205: PhotoLink/Getty Images; p. 208: Royalty-Free/Corbis

Chapter 10

Opener, p. 213: BananaStock/PunchStock; p. 216: Eyewire/Getty Images; p. 218: Royalty-Free/Corbis; p. 225: Ryan McVay/Getty Images; p. 228: Royalty-Free/Corbis; p. 232: Ryan McVay/Getty Images

Chapter 11

Opener, p. 235: Ryan McVay/Getty Images; p. 240: Mark Thornton/Getty Images; p. 244: Image Source/PictureQuest; p. 247: BananaStock; p. 251: Photodisc/Getty Images

Chapter 12

Opener, p. 259: Brand X Pictures/Jupiterimages; p. 262: Ryan McVay/Getty Images; p. 266: Comstock/Getty Images; p. 271: BananaStock/PunchStock; p. 275: The McGraw-Hill Companies, Inc./Bob Coyle, photographer; p. 279: Comstock/Corbis

Chapter 13

Opener, p. 285: Royalty-Free/Corbis; p. 289: Marmaduke St. John/Alamy; p. 294: Hill Street Studios/Brand X Pictures/Jupiterimages; p. 300: Digital Vision/Getty Images; p. 301: Photodisc

Chapter 14

Opener, p. 311: Photodisc Collection/Getty Images; p. 313: Creatas/PunchStock; p. 315: Royalty-Free/Corbis; p. 317: Emma Lee/Life File/Getty Images; p. 322: BananaStock/PunchStock; p. 328: Image 100/Corbis

Chapter 15

Opener, p. 335: PhotoLink/Getty Images; p. 340: McGraw-Hill Companies, Inc./Gary He, photographer; p. 343: Photo-Disc/Getty Images; p. 348: Geoff Manasse/Getty Images; p. 351: PhotoDisc/PunchStock; p. 355: Stockbyte

Chapter 16

Opener, p. 359: Comstock Images; p. 360: Ryan McVay/Getty Images; p. 363: Ryan McVay/Getty Images; p. 372: ER Productions/Brand X Pictures/Jupiterimages; p. 374: Jack Hollingsworth/Getty Images

Name Index

SUBJECT INDEX

Lewis & Clark
Journey to Another America

edited by Alan Taylor

Missouri Historical Society Press

7710 Carondolet Avenue, Suite 125, St. Louis, Missouri 63105
published in the United States of America by
Missouri Historical Society Press
P.O. Box 11940, St. Louis, Missouri 63112-0040

Major funding support is provided by the National Endowment for the
Humanities.

07 06 05 04 03   5 4 3 2 1

Library of Congress Cataloging-in-Publication Data

Lewis and Clark : journey to another America / edited by Alan Taylor.
                              p. cm.
Includes bibliographical references (p.   ) and index.
              ISBN 1-883982-48-0 (alk. paper)
            1. Lewis and Clark Expedition (1804–1806) 2. West (U. S.) — Discovery and
exploration. 3. West (U. S.) — Description and travel.
I. Taylor, Alan, 1955–
              F592.7.L694 2003
              917.804'2—dc21   2003000344

Printed and bound in Canada by Friesens

Design by Robyn Morgan
Cover design by Caitlin McQuade

Title page photograph by Bob Little, Allied Photocolor, 1980.
Photographs on pages 9, 10, 21, 39, 53, 54, 94, 113, 136, 153, 162, 171, 188, 190, 202, 209
© Missouri Historical Society, all rights reserved.

Contents

Foreword

Since 1982, OASIS has focused on enriching the lives of mature adults by offering challenging programs in the humanities, the arts, technology, wellness, and volunteer service.

In 1993, with the support of the National Endowment for the Humanities, OASIS presented *Reemerging Russia: Search for Identity*, a discussion series that explored a Russia emerging in the wake of the fall of the Berlin Wall. In 1999, again with assistance from the National Endowment for the Humanities, OASIS developed *The Peoples of Russia and China*, which examined catalysts of change within Russian and Chinese society during the last several decades. These programs touched the lives of more than 100,000 adults through classes that explored quality scholarship on topics that were pertinent to their lives and futures.

Once again, with support from the National Endowment for the Humanities, OASIS is pleased to present a new approach to the scholarship about the expedition of Meriwether Lewis and William Clark two centuries ago. This book of essays is designed to stimulate rich discussion and to explore the expedition and the complexity and change that abounded in North America at the turn of the nineteenth century. *Lewis & Clark: Journey to Another America* is designed to encourage OASIS participants to connect personally with the exciting drama of the expedition in the way that best suits their own interests.

The journey of Lewis and Clark and its impact on American history are also a part of the intergenerational component of this program. It will give older adults a wonderful opportunity and creative materials and resources to learn more about the expedition with children in kindergarten through fifth grade. A Web page will enhance the educational value of the program to learners inside and outside the OASIS network.

We wish to thank the National Endowment for the Humanities for their major funding support and commitment to the OASIS mission. We also wish to thank the Missouri Historical Society, a major partner in this project, for publishing *Lewis & Clark: Journey to Another America* and for their continuing support with the implementation of the program.

OASIS also wishes to acknowledge Alan Taylor, Professor of American History at University of California–Davis, who provided editorial oversight; and David Konig, Professor of History (and Law, by courtesy) at Washington University; and Peter Kastor, Professor of American Culture Studies at Washington University, who served as historical consultants. We would like to recognize all the authors and other experts who contributed to this program; their involvement helped create a successful journey in exploring the America of Lewis and Clark and in learning the impact the expedition made on the America of the present and future. Finally, special recognition is given to the May Department Stores Company and its foundation for its magnificent contributions to OASIS and its programs for twenty years.

We invite you to participate and learn more about the incredible journey of 1804.

—MARYLEN MANN
President, The OASIS Institute

Introduction

Peter J. Kastor
Washington University in St. Louis

The Object of your mission is to explore the Missouri river, &
such principal stream of it, as, by it's course and communication with the waters of the Pacific ocean, whether the
Columbia, Oregan, Colorado or any other river may offer the
most direct & practicable water communication across this
continent for the purpose of commerce.
—Thomas Jefferson, instructions to Meriwether Lewis

With these words Thomas Jefferson dispatched a small collection of men on a journey of staggering proportions. Jefferson included the passage near the start of the orders he wrote to Meriwether Lewis on June 20, 1803. Jefferson explained that "what follows will respect your proceedings after your departure from the United States." What followed in Jefferson's letter was a detailed set of instructions. What followed for Lewis and the men who joined him was a venture lasting two years that covered more than six thousand miles, a venture that remains not only a compelling story but also a fascinating way to learn about a very different time.

Consider some of the questions that surround the Lewis and Clark Expedition, beginning with the most obvious one: Why would Thomas Jefferson send these men, including a personal friend, on such a hazardous venture? Consider as well the other questions that came during or after the expedition: How did Lewis and Clark select their supplies? How did Lewis and Clark interact with each other and with the other members of the expedition? What did the Indians they met along the way think of Lewis and Clark or the country they represented? Finally, how is it that we know so much about the Lewis and Clark Expedition, and why does it remain such a compelling story?

The answers to all these questions do not emerge strictly from the details of the expedition. Instead, making sense of the Lewis and Clark Expedition requires a more general under-standing of North America at the turn of the nineteenth century, a time of considerable uncertainty and change. Likewise, seemingly abstract concepts such as scientific theory, international relations, and cultural differences become clearer when examined in the particular context of the Lewis and Clark Expedition.

For all these reasons, the essays that constitute this anthology do more than retell the story of the Lewis and Clark Expedition. Instead, this anthology provides a means to *understand* the expedition. My own goal in this introduction is to provide a foundation for reading those essays. I want to introduce not only the key themes of the anthology but also the venture itself, with a condensed chronology of the expedition.

The essays in this anthology use the expedition as a springboard for engaging a broad series of subjects. Many of the essays function in pairs that consider the way that Indians and Euro-Americans examined the same thing. For example, James Lewis and Wendel Cox examine U.S. and Indian foreign policy, respectively. Likewise, James Ronda provides an overview of cultural dynamics among the Indians whom Lewis and Clark encountered by looking at three different Indian leaders in three different parts of North America. Peter Onuf provides a general overview of the political dynamics within the United States by exploring the way Americans talked about the West. Moving beyond the particulars of nineteenth-century America, Angela Cavender Wilson explores the ways that Indians have remembered European and later Euro-American expansion in North America, while Betty Houchin Winfield details the public perception of the Lewis and Clark Expedition among those Euro-Americans. Other essays examine more discrete subjects. David Konig describes Thomas Jefferson's scientific interest in the American West. Conevery Bolton Valenčius explores the way people in nineteenth-century America conceived of the environment. Fred Fausz examines the fur trade, a powerful force in the West that Lewis and Clark explored. Finally, William Skelton provides a portrait of the army officer corps that produced Meriwether Lewis and William Clark.

Most essays begin with a quotation from Jefferson's June 1803 instructions to Meriwether Lewis. In many cases, the authors have chosen to compare these passages to selections from the journals that Lewis and Clark kept along the way.

These pairings show how the Corps of Discovery (as Lewis coined the expedition) attempted to translate Jefferson's abstract ideas into practical realities. These quotations also show just how diffuse the goals of the expedition were, for while each paragraph of Jefferson's instructions seems to flow logically to the next, the skillful writing of those instructions belied a considerable breadth of tasks.

Since the instructions are so important to the way the authors have approached the subject of the Lewis and Clark Expedition, they appear in their entirety at the end of this anthology, along with related documents. Maps are also included to show just how little the residents of the United States knew about the American West as well as how much they learned through the expedition.

Those illustrations are also vital for the difficult task of recapturing two very different times, one before the expedition and another after. In 1800, few people living east of the Mississippi could imagine the land to the west. They literally could not "see" that landscape in their minds because they had so little information with which to create a picture. Meanwhile, the residents west of the Mississippi had only the vaguest understanding of the United States. The Lewis and Clark Expedition transformed this situation. The expedition was always a two-way process of exploration, as the members of the expedition learned about the people and the landscape of the North American West, while the Indians who acted as their hosts received their own introduction to the infant republic taking shape in the East.

Before and after is equally important for understanding the expedition itself, for the best way to think of Lewis and Clark's journey is to think of it as two expeditions. The first marked the culmination of Jefferson's scientific and commercial interests in the last quarter of the eighteenth century, an expedition that for all its elaborate planning looked like it would never occur. Then, in 1803, seemingly distant diplomatic events enabled the expedition to proceed and transformed its purposes.

The first incarnation of the expedition was indeed Jefferson's brainchild. The ink was hardly dry on the Declaration of Independence when Jefferson began dreaming of an expedition to the West. As David Konig shows in his essay, Jefferson's interest in the West included a lengthy and frustrated effort to launch an American scientific expedition.

A. Arrowsmith. *A Map Exhibiting All the New Discoveries in the Interior Parts of North America.* London, January 1, 1795. Geography and Maps Division, Library of Congress.

Jefferson had scientific reasons, but he had practical motivations as well. The absence of any detailed information seemed to create real problems for the infant republic. Jefferson became convinced that effective development of the West would provide prosperity for individual Americans and for the nation as a whole, while ineffective management would lead to chaos and disunion.

Despite his continental interests, the "West" that occupied most of Jefferson's time was the land between the Appalachian Mountains and the Mississippi River. Like most Americans, Jefferson doubted that the United States could or even should acquire land west of the Mississippi at any time in the immediate future. Nonetheless, Jefferson believed that Americans were likely to trade in that region. The Ohio and Mississippi River valleys were already the foundation of a vigorous trade that connected the West to the Atlantic seaboard, the Caribbean, and Europe. Jefferson hoped that western waterways would provide a similar avenue to the Pacific Ocean, the fabled Northwest Passage that had been the obsession of European explorers in North America.

This combination of scientific interest and commercial aspiration constituted the foundation of Jefferson's plan for a western expedition. In 1801, he finally had the means. Following a bitterly disputed election that eventually was decided in the House of Representatives, Jefferson became the third president of the United States. With full command of the federal government's resources, Jefferson could begin assembling an expedition that would answer scientific as well as commercial mysteries.

Jefferson began discussing this expedition with Meriwether Lewis, his private secretary and a captain in the U.S. Army. In January 1803, Jefferson began a low-key effort to build support for the expedition. In a lengthy, secret message to

Congress focusing on Indian affairs east of the Mississippi, Jefferson added that "The river Missouri, & the Indians inhabiting it, are not as well known as is rendered desireable by their connection with the Missisipi, & consequently with us." Jefferson saw specific benefits to acquiring information on the Missouri River and the Indians who lived along its banks, explaining that "it is however understood that the country on that river is inhabited by numerous tribes, who furnish great supplies of furs & peltry to the trade of another nation carried on in a high latitude, through an infinite number of portages and lakes, shut up by ice through a long season." In a subtle, almost offhand suggestion of an expedition that he was, in fact, already actively planning, Jefferson predicted that

> an intelligent officer with ten or twelve chosen men, fit for the enterprize and willing to undertake it, taken from our posts, where they may be spared without inconvenience, might explore the whole line, even to the Western ocean, have conferences with the natives on the subject of commercial intercourse, get admission among them for our traders as others are admitted, agree on convenient deposits for an interchange of articles, and return with the information acquired in the course of two summers.[1]

Jefferson further explained that all this would be possible for a mere $2,500. Congress appropriated the money, and Jefferson dispatched Lewis for a rushed education in Philadelphia, then the center of scientific learning in the United States. Lewis also began the process of deciding which people and what equipment he would take with him. Among his first decisions was to contact William Clark and ask him to join the planning of the expedition.

Lewis, Clark, and Jefferson had plenty in common. All three men came from Virginia, more specifically from

Portrait of Meriwether Lewis wearing what he called "the most eligant peice of Indian dress I ever saw." The cape, made of otter fur and white weasel skins, is probably the one that Cameahwait gave him during his visit with the Shoshones. Engraving by Strickland after St. Memin (painted 1807) published in *Analectic Magazine and Naval Chronicle*, 1816. Missouri Historical Society Photograph and Print Collection.

Albemarle County. This was no mere coincidence. As a man without sons at a time when many people doubted the long-term viability of the American republican experiment, Jefferson was eager to cultivate young leaders. Although Jefferson honestly had claimed to choose these men on the basis of intellectual ability rather than birth, he nonetheless started his search close to home, usually selecting young men he knew either personally or through family connections.

Portrait of William Clark. Oil on canvas attributed to John Wesley Jarvis, ca. 1810. Photograph by David Schultz, Missouri Historical Society.

These sorts of connections were particularly important in planning the expedition. When Jefferson explained his instructions by stating that "what follows will respect your proceedings after your departure from the United States," he acknowledged that he would have to trust Lewis's discretion.

It was not only their Virginia origins or personal connections that made Jefferson confident in trusting Lewis and Clark. All three men also were wedded to the federal government. A fierce defender of the union, Jefferson the president attempted to build a federal system that would promote security and prosperity while respecting the individual liberties of white settlers. Meanwhile, Lewis and Clark built careers as federal employees. Born in 1774 and 1770, respectively, Lewis and Clark both had joined the U.S. Army in the 1790s. Lewis stayed and retained his commission after becoming Jefferson's secretary. Clark tired of the Army in 1796 and resigned his commission. He regretted the decision, however, and when Lewis asked him to join the expedition, Clark eagerly accepted. What followed was a period of considerable frustration for Clark, who had been promised a captain's commission but was retained as a lieutenant. One of Lewis's most important decisions was to refer to Clark as his "co-captain," ignoring the War Department's decision in the interest of a united command. It was an odd situation, however, because when the two men first met almost a decade before, Clark had been Lewis's commander.

By the summer of 1803, Lewis and Clark were hard at work planning for the expedition. They purchased supplies and recruited men, all with Jefferson's keen support. Their enthusiasm was all the more striking because they had no reason to believe they actually would be able to proceed. After all, the United States did not own the land west of the Mississippi.

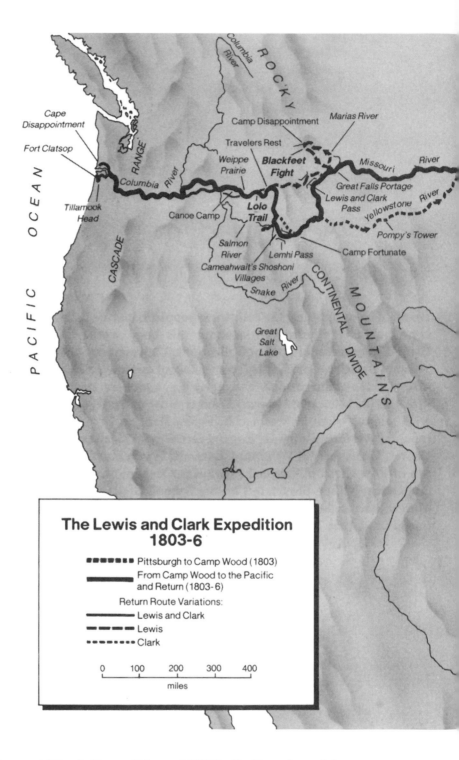

Map of the Lewis and Clark Expedition, 1803–6. Reprinted from David Lavender's *The Way to the Western Sea* with permission of the author.

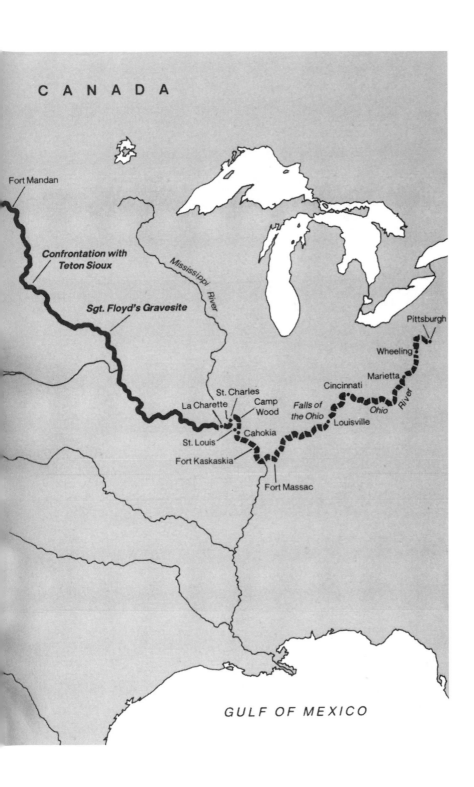

CANADA

Fort Mandan

Confrontation with Teton Sioux

Sgt. Floyd's Gravesite

Mississippi River

St. Charles
La Charette
Camp Wood
Falls of the Ohio
Louisville
Cahokia
St. Louis
Fort Kaskaskia
Fort Massac

Cincinnati
Marietta
Wheeling
Pittsburgh
Ohio River

GULF OF MEXICO

As James Lewis explains in his essay on American foreign policy, France owned the region between the Mississippi and the Rocky Mountains but gave direct administration to Spain, while Spain owned outright the land from the Continental Divide west to the Pacific. In addition, it was the Indians of North America who wielded direct authority over much of this area, and Wendel Cox details the elaborate diplomatic system that reigned in the North American interior. As a result, the United States sought Spanish permission to send an expedition through land owned by France, where Indians were, in fact, in charge. The Spanish rejected the American request and not without good reason. Consider the situation: Many Spanish officials were convinced that the United States was an aggressive country bent on territorial acquisition. While the Spanish fears were, in 1803, exaggerated, they were not illogical. Consider as well what Jefferson proposed—a military mission into the heart of North America to form new alliances between the United States and the Indians—and the Spanish decision seems all the more reasonable.

So at the very moment Jefferson wrote his instructions with so much confidence, the expedition seemed to be heading nowhere. The route Jefferson had chosen—the Missouri River—hardly gave much room to hide. Jefferson's original expedition, a commercial and scientific venture to foreign territory, was dead in its tracks.

The transformation of the situation had nothing to do with the United States or with Spain. Instead, it was slaves in search of their freedom and a European dictator who enabled Lewis and Clark to proceed. By the spring of 1803, Napoleon Bonaparte had concluded that he could no longer control the island colony of Saint Domingue, where an army of slaves and free people of color had overthrown French rule and would soon declare themselves the independent Republic of Haiti. Napoleon had reacquired Louisiana in 1800 as a source of raw materials and a defensive point for the more lucrative colony of Saint Domingue. Without Saint Domingue, there was no reason to keep Louisiana. Napoleon informed American negotiators that he would sell not only New Orleans but also his entire holdings on the North American mainland.

The Louisiana Purchase coincided with Jefferson and Lewis's planning for the expedition. Indeed, they overlapped almost perfectly. As James Lewis explains, Jefferson and Lewis proceeded on the assumption that somehow the expedition would be able to move forward despite Spanish objections. Unknown to them, the solution—in the form of the Louisiana Purchase agreement—was making its lengthy passage across the Atlantic Ocean. On July 4, 1803, Jefferson wrote more instructions to amend the directive he had written to Lewis a few weeks earlier. This additional set of instructions detailed how Lewis should negotiate with the Indians of the Pacific Coast. He explained to Lewis that after traversing the North American interior, "you may find it imprudent to hazard a return the same way, and be forced to seek a passage round by sea, in such vessels as you may find on the Western coast. But you will be without money, without clothes, & other necessaries.… Your resource in that case can only be the credit of the United States."[2] On that very day, Jefferson received news of the Louisiana Purchase. The following day, he wrote a letter to his son-in-law Thomas Mann Randolph explaining that American negotiators had "signed a treaty with France, ceding to us the island of N. Orleans and all of Louisiana.… This removes from us the greatest source of danger to our peace."[3] It also removed the greatest impediment for Lewis and Clark.

The Fourth of July was already a day of national celebration, and the news of the Louisiana Purchase could not have come at a more appropriate time. Still, the Louisiana Purchase was not what the Americans sought or even what they necessarily wanted. The purchase transformed the expedition, giving it new importance and expanded goals. It was no longer a small venture to satisfy American foreign trade and Jefferson's private interests. It was now a surveying expedition that would map the new land the United States had acquired. It was also a diplomatic expedition in two critical ways. First, it would provide accurate information on the North American landscape at a time when the United States and Spain were arguing about the boundaries of the Louisiana Purchase. Second, Lewis and Clark were supposed to make the Indians they encountered acknowledge the sovereignty of the U.S. government.

If nothing else, the Lewis and Clark Expedition was supposed to help Americans understand just what they had acquired from France. This was no small affair at a time when rumors abounded of a strange and fantastic land in the North American West. For example, a pamphleteer named David Ramsay claimed that "the greatest portion enjoys a salubrious air; and is so fertile, as to be equal to the support of a population, far exceeding the many millions which inhabit Great-Britain, Ireland, France, Spain, and Portugal—I had almost said all Europe."[4] Other reports were more extravagant. Several newspapers described a great mountain of salt.[5] In a sarcastic take on this and other stories, the *Connecticut Courant* reported "a considerable lake of pure *Whiskey*, which is said very nearly to resemble good old *Irish Usquebaugh*. Should this rumour prove to be well founded, it is believed that most of our newly imported citizens will speedily remote to that country for the sake of securing the free navigation of those *waters*."[6]

These sorts of reports made the Lewis and Clark Expedition seem all the more important. During the summer and fall of 1803, Lewis and Clark continued recruiting men and gathering equipment. In the winter of 1803, they moved the entire operation to western Illinois, where they awaited the transfer of Upper Louisiana in March 1804. (The United States took charge in Lower Louisiana, the region corresponding roughly to the current state of Louisiana, in December 1803.) On May 14, 1804, the Corps of Discovery began its ascent of the Missouri River, crowded into an odd collection of canoes and one large vessel called the keelboat. Patrick Gass, a member of the expedition who kept a detailed journal of his own, reported the event in these melodramatic terms: "the best authenticated accounts informed us, that we were to pass through a country possessed by numerous, powerful and warlike nations of savages, of gigantic stature, fierce, treacherous and cruel; and particularly hostile to white men. And fame had united with tradition in opposing mountains to our course, which human enterprize and exertion would attempt in vain to pass."[7]

Historians occasionally have disputed the exact number of men on the expedition, but the total was probably forty-seven. Several of these men were temporary, hired to help the corps reach the Upper Missouri. Members of the expedition came from numerous backgrounds. Some, like Lewis and Clark, were from Virginia or other Mid-Atlantic states, while others had been born in the francophone culture of Louisiana. Most were of European ancestry but not all. A number of the Louisiana Creoles were of mixed French-Indian ancestry. Clark also brought his slave, York, promising him freedom. While Clark informed York that freedom would have to await their return from the West, York soon found that the considerable demands facing the expedition afforded him a status unusual for slaves.

What followed for these men was a grueling ascent of the Missouri River. In August 1804 the expedition suffered its only death when Sergeant Charles Floyd died, most likely of a burst appendix. By October, the men had reached an area near Bismarck, North Dakota, where they constructed a fort near the villages of the Mandan Indians and waited through the winter. It was in North Dakota that another product of Franco-Indian parentage, Toussaint Charbonneau, joined the expedition after convincing Lewis and Clark of his considerable linguistic skills. Lewis and Clark eventually were disappointed with Charbonneau and found instead that his teenage wife, Sacagawea, possessed far more useful knowledge. Sacagawea's own background was confusing: born a Shoshone Indian, she had been captured and raised by the Hidatsas.

The Mandan winter proved vital. Lewis and Clark dispatched the temporary employees and pruned the corps of its most unreliable or difficult members. The remaining men congealed into an effective team. Equally important, extensive contact with the Mandans transformed Lewis and Clark's fundamental antagonism toward Indians into a more accommodating posture. Although their belief in racial superiority persisted, Lewis and Clark did become more perceptive in their understanding of Indians and more likely to conciliate at moments of conflict. This change made them more detailed observers of Indian life and may well have saved their lives by making them better diplomats.

The expedition that left the Mandan villages in April 1805 consisted of twenty-three people including a baby boy named Jean Baptiste, born to Sacagawea two months before. The Corps of Discovery followed the Missouri River to the Continental Divide where, only after the most difficult effort, it managed to reach the waters feeding the Columbia River. They made a quick descent of the Columbia, reaching the Pacific Coast in November 1805. Once again the corps built a winter settlement, and once again they were dependent on their hosts, in this case the Clatsop Indians of the Pacific Northwest. But the Mandan and Clatsop winters were only extended versions of the kind of contact that occurred throughout the expedition. This was a crowded frontier. Not only were Lewis and Clark in regular contact with Indians, but those Indians were well aware of their American neighbors. Indeed, as James Ronda shows, the Indians of North America engaged in their own exploration, using the Lewis and Clark Expedition to learn about the United States.

The information that Lewis and Clark acquired served them well on the return trip. In just six months, from March to September 1806, Lewis and Clark went from the Pacific Northwest back to St. Louis. Lewis and Clark dismissed their men and proceeded to Washington, where they reported to Jefferson in person. The expedition was over, but its aftermath actually helps explain what had transpired from 1804 to 1806.

The members of the expedition dispersed. Many of them remained in the West, pursuing lives as trappers, traders, and merchants. Several died in violent encounters with Indians, caught in the numerous disputes that emerged as the newcomers to the West attempted to impose their own terms onto the Indians who lived there. For most of these men, the expedition was an unusual excursion but not a fundamental change in their lives. Many had spent their adult lives on the frontiers of North America, and they felt no compunction to leave.

Meanwhile, Lewis and Clark found that the expedition created considerable political opportunities. In 1807, Jefferson dispatched both men back to the West, Lewis as governor of the Louisiana Territory (the American successor to the old European colony of Upper Louisiana) and Clark as the commander of the territorial militia and an Indian agent. As Betty Winfield explains in her essay, those appointments brought mixed results. Lewis was a failure as a territorial governor and in 1809 committed suicide. Clark's public career was far more successful, including a lengthy tenure as territorial governor from 1813 to 1820, during which he helped complete Missouri's transformation from territory to state. For much of this time, however, Clark had failed in his promise to free York. Once they returned from the expedition, Clark reverted to the traditional slaveholder he had been before 1804. York pleaded with Clark either to be freed or to be hired to a master in Kentucky, where York's wife was enslaved. It was not until 1809 that Clark sent York to Kentucky and not until the 1810s that he freed York (exactly when remains open for debate). York then disappeared from the documentary record, and subsequent stories describe occupations ranging from a businessman in Kentucky to a chief among the Crow Indians.

Rather than concern himself with York, Clark chose to focus on other affairs. Besides his growing responsibilities in the Louisiana Territory, Clark was working hard at editing the journals of the expedition. Several members of the Corps of Discovery kept journals, each of which usually consisted of a series of short, leather-bound books. (Patrick Gass rushed his own version of the expedition into print in 1807.) In addition, Lewis and Clark had personally collected a host of plant and animal samples while drawing numerous maps for distinct portions of the journey. They had no intention of publishing all this material. Instead, they hoped to produce a concise narrative synthesizing the work of numerous men. Along the way, Lewis and Clark worked with editor Nicholas Biddle, a Philadelphia banker of extraordinary wealth who would have been thoroughly out of place on the expedition itself. The task of synthesizing all this material was a daunting one, and Lewis's own failure to make progress on the project may help account for his suicide.

Clark stayed with the project, adding an exquisite map that combined his and Lewis's observations with geographic knowledge from earlier expeditions. In 1814, a Philadelphia printer published the first full-length account of the expedition based on the journals, entitled *History of the Expedition*

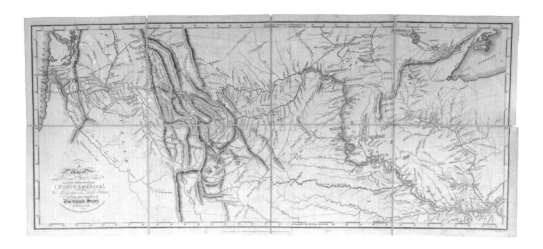

William Clark completed this four-foot-wide map after the completion of the expedition. Samuel Lewis copied it for publication in 1814. Some experts have called this the most important document produced by the expedition. It is one of the first maps showing a more accurate picture of the Rocky Mountains. *Map of Lewis and Clark's Track across the Western Portion of North America ... From Travels to the Source of the Missouri River and Across the American Continent.* London: Longman, Hurst, Rees, Orme, and Brown, 1814. Missouri Historical Society Library.

Under the Command of Captains Lewis and Clark, to the Sources of the Missouri, thence across the Rocky mountains and down the river Columbia to the Pacific Ocean performed during the years 1804–5–6 by order of the government of the United States. It was a long title and, by modern standards, an ungainly one. Yet it was typical for the kind of travel narratives that proliferated in the first half of the nineteenth century. The book was substantially different from the journals themselves. Gone were the occasional passages—most of them by Lewis—that reported emotional reactions to the landscape or the fears of expedition members at moments of particular challenge. Those passages, among the most compelling to modern readers, seemed entirely inappropriate, almost superfluous, two centuries ago.

Although many Americans knew about the Corps of Discovery, they eventually lost interest. The *History of the Expedition* went out of print, and the original journals remained scattered. Lewis and Clark deposited the largest single collection at the American Philosophical Society, where it still resides today. But other materials found their way to public repositories like the National Archives and the Library of Congress, as well as a variety of other private collections. Scraps of material related to the expedition still emerge from time to time.

Only at the end of the nineteenth century did people actually begin to read the firsthand records of the expedition. It was a time of particular interest in the founding generation of the United States. Publishers had released the first large-scale editions of the letters of men such as George Washington, Thomas Jefferson, and James Madison. Meanwhile, an editor named Reuben Gold Thwaites set out to republish the narratives of western travel. In addition to republishing the *History of the Expedition* and dozens of other published accounts from the eighteenth and nineteenth centuries, in 1904 Thwaites compiled a seven-volume collection of the original journals from the Lewis and Clark Expedition.

When people read journals of the expedition today, they are usually reading abridged versions of the material that Thwaites first edited more than a century ago. Quite a different project is nearing completion at the University of Nebraska Press, where a team of editors is systematically publishing all of the firsthand accounts of the expedition. The result, a thirteen-volume collection, combines the text of Lewis, Clark, and other members of the expedition, as well as the numerous illustrations that recorded visually what Lewis and Clark concluded they could not sufficiently capture in words.

The journals are a matter of no small importance because they are the means through which we now understand the Lewis and Clark Expedition. The lives of people such as York, Sacagawea, and the other members of the Corps of Discovery are so difficult to recapture because records like the journals are so rare. The journals are more than the window to the expedition. Through constant republication, they have created links connecting modern readers to seemingly distant events.

While Lewis and Clark recognized the importance of the expedition, they had no way of grasping the eventual popularity of the journals. They struggled against their own limitations as writers to express with sufficient clarity just what they had done. One of Lewis's first efforts came more than three years after Jefferson wrote his June 1803 instructions. Writing triumphantly from St. Louis soon after the corps returned in 1806, Lewis informed that president that "it is with pleasure that I announced to you the safe arrival of myself and party … at this place with our papers and baggage. In obedience to your orders, we have penitrated the Continent of North America to the Pacific Ocean, and sufficiently explored the interior of the country to affirm with confidence that we have discovered the most practicable rout which does exist across the continent."[8] The letter marked an appropriate response to Jefferson's instructions. Lewis began where Jefferson did, emphasizing the central goal of acquiring geographic knowledge that would serve American commerce. Despite his reference to a "most practicable rout," he was forced to admit that there was no Northwest Passage. Nonetheless, having "sufficiently explored the interior of the country," they could deliver a wealth of knowledge to their fellow countrymen. Likewise, the men and their papers were intact. Not only had they survived the expedition, but could deliver the materials that remain with us today.

Notes

1   Jefferson to Congress, January 18, 1803, *A Compilation of the Messages and Papers of the Presidents, 1789–1897*, ed. James D. Richardson (Washington, D.C.: Government Printing Office, 1900).

2   Jefferson to Lewis, July 4, 1804, *Letters of the Lewis and Clark Expedition, with Related Documents 1783–1854*, ed. Donald T. Jackson 2 vols. (Urbana: University of Illinois Press, 1962), 1:105–6.

3   Jefferson to Thomas Mann Randolph, July 5, 1803, Thomas Jefferson Papers, Library of Congress, reel 46.

4   David Ramsay, *An Oration on the Cession of Louisiana to the United States*, eds. Shaw and Shoemaker (Charleston, S.C.: W. P. Young, 1804), 6–8.

5   *Alexandria Advertiser*, December 30, 1803; *Connecticut Courant*, December 7, 1803; *National Aegis*, December 7, 1803; *Scioto Gazette*, December 3, 1803.

6   *Connecticut Courant*, December 7, 1803.

7   Patrick Gass, *Gass's Journal of the Lewis and Clark Expedition* (Chicago: A. C. McClurg and Co., 1904).

8   Lewis to Jefferson, September 23, 1806, *Letters of the Lewis and Clark Expedition* 1:319–20.

Suggested Readings

Clark, William. *Dear Brother: Letters of William Clark to Jonathan Clark.* Edited by James J. Holmberg. New Haven, Conn.: Yale University Press, 2002.

Foley, William E. *The Genesis of Missouri: From Wilderness Outpost to Statehood.* Columbia: University of Missouri Press, 1989.

Furtwangler, Albert. *Acts of Discovery: Visions of America in the Lewis and Clark Journals.* Urbana: University of Illinois Press, 1993.

Jackson, Donald T. *Thomas Jefferson and the Stony Mountains: Exploring the West from Monticello.* Urbana: University of Illinois Press, 1981.

Lewis, James E., Jr. *The American Union and the Problem of Neighborhood: The United States and the Collapse of the Spanish Empire, 1783–1829.* Chapel Hill: University of North Carolina Press, 1998.

Lewis, Meriwether, and William Clark. *The History of the Lewis and Clark Expedition.* Edited by Elliott Coues. Reprint. New York: Dover Publications, 1979.

Madison, James. *The Papers of James Madison.* Edited by Robert J. Brugger et al. Secretary of State Series. Charlottesville: University Press of Virginia, 1986–.

Nobles, Gregory H. *American Frontiers: Cultural Encounters and Continental Conquest.* New York: Hill and Wang, 1997.

Ronda, James P. *Lewis and Clark among the Indians.* Lincoln: University of Nebraska Press, 1984. Reprint. Lincoln: University of Nebraska Press, 2002.

Thorne, Tanis C. *The Many Hands of My Relations: French and Indians on the Lower Missouri.* Columbia: University of Missouri Press, 1996.

Thomas Jefferson's Scientific Project and the American West

David Thomas Konig
Washington University in St. Louis

July the 30th Monday [1804].... Jo. Fields Killed a Brarow or as the Ponie [Pawnee] call it Cho car tooch, this animale burrows in the ground & feeds on Bugs and flesh principally the little Dogs of the Prarie, also Something of the Vegetable Kind[.] [H]is Shape & Size is like that of a Beever, his head Mouth &c is like a Dog with its ears Cut off, his tale and hair like that of a Ground hog[.] Something longer and lighter, his interals like a Hogs, his Skin thick & loose, white & hair Short under its belly, of the Species of the Bear, and it has a white Streake from its nose to its Sholders, the Toe nails of its fore feet which is large is 1 inch and $3/4$ qtr. long and those of his hind feet which is much Smaller is $3/4$ long. We have this animale Skined and Stuffed. Short legs, raseing himself just above the ground when in motion[.]

—William Clark, journal entry, describing the badger
Meriwether Lewis stuffed and sent to Thomas Jefferson

As Thomas Jefferson prepared his departure from Washington at the end of his embattled presidency in March 1809, he looked back with regret on the missed opportunities of the past eight years. "Nature intended me for the tranquil pursuits of science," he wrote to his friend Pierre Samuel du Pont de Nemours, and now he could once again enjoy "my supreme delight."[1] Looking forward to his return to Virginia, Jefferson would be reunited with the artifacts of humans and nature that he had collected and studied over the years, items that he had kept on display in the East Wing of the White House. Back in Monticello, he would arrange them in his home's foyer, the first things that he or anyone else would see upon entering Monticello. They were a restorative sight for eyes worn sore by the tedium of official correspondence.

Ironically, it was only Jefferson's political career that enabled him to collect many of those items. In perhaps the boldest move of his presidency, Jefferson had set in motion the fulfillment of a lifelong scientific curiosity by arranging for the purchase of the vast Louisiana Territory in 1803. The trans-Mississippi West had been an enduring fascination, dating from his childhood at Shadwell plantation on the edge of English settlement. For many Virginians such as his father, Peter Jefferson, the West long had inspired scientific speculation no less than it had attracted avid land speculation. Indian emissaries had passed through his home on their way to meet with English governors in Williamsburg, bringing with them lore about life, both animal and human, beyond the Blue Ridge Mountains that loomed behind them.

From both sides of his ancestry, Jefferson inherited an interest in what the unexplored regions of North America might reveal. His father had mapped much of the land to the west of Shadwell, and as a member of the Loyal Land Company he had surveyed and purchased western lands and had

Thomas Jefferson kept many of his natural history collections in the entrance hall at Monticello. The Monticello curator has tried to re-create how it might have looked in Jefferson's time. The buffalo robe on the left is a reproduction of a Mandan buffalo robe sent to Jefferson by Meriwether Lewis. On the walls are maps of Africa (ca. 1801) and Asia (ca. 1802). On the small table is the fossilized jawbone of the American mastodon excavated by William Clark in 1806 in a dig at Big Bone Lick, Kentucky. Jefferson wrote about this rich, ancient salt lick on the Ohio River in his *Notes on the State of Virginia*. From the collection of Monticello/Thomas Jefferson Foundation, Inc.

planned expeditions deep into the interior of the continent. Peter Jefferson's collaborator in cartography, Joshua Fry, possessed an intriguing map of North America drafted by Daniel Coxe, which showed the trans-Mississippi West providing travelers with easy routes by water and plain to the Pacific Ocean. Thomas's mother's father, Isham Randolph, had corresponded with the eminent English patron of science Peter Collinson, as well as with Collinson's American contact, the botanist John Bartram, who had collected and shipped across the Atlantic Ocean numerous specimens of plant varieties unknown in Europe. After his father's death, Thomas Jefferson was sent to study with James Maury, another investor in the Loyal Land Company interested in the West. Maury was captivated by the lure of the West and wrote of plans to send explorers "in search of that river Missouri, if that be the right name of it, in order to discover whether it had any communication with the Pacific Ocean."[2]

Jefferson thus accepted a long tradition that assumed as an article of faith that the rivers of North America derived from a common source, and that finding such a source would enable its discoverer to make a short and easy portage from the headwaters of the eastward-flowing Missouri to those of another great river flowing westward and emptying into the Pacific. This idea was typical of the Enlightenment, a philosophy that asserted that nature exhibited a beneficent symmetry. The low and easily breached Appalachian Mountains, from which the Ohio River flowed westward and the Potomac River eastward, were thought to parallel a similar western chain—the Stony Mountains, as some called them—from which the Missouri flowed eastward, matched by what many confidently expected to be the "Oregon River" emptying into the Pacific. Like others of his time, he had little doubt of this. He believed the Blue Ridge Mountains to be the highest in North America; how could the Stony Mountains pose any more formidable barrier?

Jefferson's hunger for information about the West only increased in adulthood, as he became obsessed with the Enlightenment project of gathering information to better understand the workings of the material world. Deeply convinced that humankind, as part of the natural world, was governed by the same principles that "Nature and Nature's God" had ordained for all creation, he joined with other scientists of his era to amass the data whose analysis would yield knowledge useful for the betterment of humanity. After finding an Indian burial mound near Monticello, Jefferson wrote, he had "determined to open and examine it thoroughly." Years later, in his *Notes on Virginia*, his enthusiasm was still obvious as he recalled efforts "to satisfy myself" about "the aboriginal Indians" of the region. Seeking to understand their culture through their burial practices, he became one of the nation's first students of what today is called paleoanthropology when he carefully excavated the mound, layer by layer.

Jefferson's impulse and method typified the scientific spirit of the age. His descriptions were precise, and he held other observers to the same standards. Like other "natural philosophers" (the term "scientist" did not appear until the 1820s), he distrusted accounts based solely on legend or the imprecise reports of travelers who wrote unsystematically of curiosities and legends. As a member of the American Philosophical Society beginning in 1780 (and its president from 1797 to his death in 1826), he shared its view that the gathering of facts had "little use, when confined to mere speculation." For that reason, after his own excavations of Indian burial mounds he asked others to report similar sites and to provide only "very accurate descriptions of what they see of that kind," requesting that they do so "without forming any theories" that might affect the way they gathered and reported facts.[3]

Jefferson asked questions and recorded answers at an almost compulsive pace, believing that their accumulation would, at the very least, disabuse society of false beliefs and confining theories. Piling fact upon fact, he believed, would allow the "collisions of different hypotheses" so that "truth may be elicited and science advanced in the end." To describe Jefferson merely as a recorder of observations, therefore, vastly understates his efforts. It has been estimated that he may have written two thousand letters inquiring about or reporting on scientific matters. From 1764 almost to his death, he recorded in his *Garden Book* and (from 1774) his *Farm Book* when he planted and harvested his crops, the time of blooming of his flowers, and notations about soil, crop yield, and the condition of his slaves. Assembling some of his data for *Notes on Virginia*, he could boast of having made thousands of observations to support his generalizations about natural phenomena. Even during his trips to Williamsburg from 1772 to 1777 to practice law and add his voice to the movement for independence, he managed to record the speed and direction of the wind "two or three times in every day" as well as "the coolest and warmest point of the same day in each year" and the amount of rainfall. Climate, according to a widely studied science of the time known as phenology, was thought to influence biological phenomena and, indirectly, human life and society. Accurate observations, therefore, and what he called the "patient pursuit of facts," would inevitably contribute to the better understanding and improvement of humankind.

Accurate fact gathering was crucial if the West was to serve the useful goal of human betterment. If Jefferson's America was to be, as he described it, a "republic of science," it must not be forgotten that it was above all else a *republic*. That is, it was an unprecedented experiment in self-government, and anything that would protect or advance that goal stood as a priority for him. It was for much more than national pride, therefore, that he indignantly refuted French claims that the climate of North America had caused the degeneration of its native peoples, plants, and animals, and that it would, by extension, have the same baleful effect on its European settlers. Jefferson not only sought examples of American fauna larger in size than their European relatives but also sent specimens to France to prove it. Not content with those samples, he meticulously noted the size and weight of comparable species in his *Notes on Virginia*, listing among other examples the fact that the European beaver averaged 18.5 pounds in weight; its American cousin, 45. Jefferson rightly perceived that such Old World canards were the product of reactionary opposition to the progress of humankind in the New World, and he proudly identified his political radicalism with the scientific "insurrection" he saw all around him among progressive scientists. "Ignorance is preferable to error," he wrote in assailing the unthinking acceptance of dogma, "and he is less remote from the truth who believes nothing than he who believes what is wrong."[4]

But associating conventional wisdom with the decayed ancien régime became a secular faith almost as constraining as that of the reactionaries. Like many who rejected the corruptions of established religion, he made "Nature and Nature's God" his alternative faith. Just as the devout were to allow religious truth to imprint itself on the believer, Jefferson believed that one might allow Nature to do so with scientific truth. A beneficent Nature, for example, could never allow a species—part of God's natural creation—to become extinct, and thus the mammoth *must* still exist somewhere in North America. He was convinced that it only required patience and careful exploration to find it.

And it was in the West that such answers lay. Though he never ventured farther west than Harpers Ferry, Jefferson always remembered the plans that Maury and others had proposed for exploring and exploiting the trans-Mississippi West.

Indeed, American independence from Britain made the two nations rivals for the prize of knowing and using its vast resources. No sooner had the Treaty of Paris been ratified in 1783 than Jefferson wrote to George Rogers Clark that the British had raised "a large sum of money … for exploring the country from the Missisipi to California." Ever distrustful, he noted skeptically (and pessimistically),

> They pretend it is only to promote knoledge. I am afraid they have thoughts of colonising into that quarter. Some of us have been talking here in a feeble way of making the attempt to search that country. But I doubt whether we have enough of that spirit to raise the money. How would you like to lead such a party?[5]

Enfeebled by age and alcohol, Clark declined.

Jefferson's interest did not wane while he served in France as American minister but rather grew when he learned of Louis XVI's support of plans by Jean François de Lapérouse for an allegedly scientific search for the Northwest Passage. Fearing "some other design" such as colonization or trade, Jefferson asked John Paul Jones to investigate. In addition, Jefferson sought the aid of an ambitious Connecticut adventurer he met in Paris. Described by historians as a "soldier of fortune" or "part genius and part moongazer," John Ledyard became the first American to visit the Northwest when he sailed there with Captain James Cook's Pacific expedition in the late 1770s. Ledyard's account of the voyage included an extravagant description of the potential for American exploitation of a fur trade with the Far East. Jefferson had read Ledyard's book, and after abortive plans to send Ledyard back with John Paul Jones, he agreed to give his support— both diplomatic as well as financial—for him to trek overland alone from the east. When Spain refused to allow this expedition, Ledyard hatched and almost succeeded in a daring plan to travel overland eastward across Russia. Departing St. Petersburg without official approval, he was tracked down in Siberia by Russian agents and sent back home.

Returning to the United States in 1789, Jefferson resumed his political career as secretary of state and his membership in the American Philosophical Society (APS), the new nation's foremost promoter of scientific research. Within two years he was elected to the society's vice presidency, a post he retained even after withdrawing from political combat and leaving government in 1793. When he learned in 1792 that a French botanist, André Michaux, had proposed an overland expedition to the Northwest, he leapt at the opportunity. Raising money from fellow APS members and others—including George Washington—he drew up instructions for Michaux "to explore the country along the Missouri, & thence Westwardly to the Pacific ocean." Combining scientific with commercial inquiries, Jefferson more fully revealed his western project. Not only was Michaux "to find the shortest & most convenient route of communication between the U.S. and the Pacific Ocean," but he was also to make note of the "soil, rivers, [and] mountains" of the area as well as "its productions animal, vegetable, and mineral so far as they may be new to us & may also be useful or very curious." Trade would require good relations with the Indians, and as much for that reason as for scientific ones he also requested

> the names, numbers, & dwellings of the inhabitants, and such particularities as you can learn of their history, connection with each other, languages, manners, state of society & of the arts & commerce among them.

Yielding to his curiosity about reports of gigantic beasts roaming the West, he added that information on "the Mammoth is particularly recommended to your enquiries."[6]

Jefferson would have to look elsewhere for someone to fulfill his goal. Michaux, it turned out, was a spy as well as a botanist, and his mission to gather political information for France led him to turn back from Kentucky only shortly into his trip in 1793. Meanwhile, Jefferson's interest had been fueled by the voyage of an American sea captain on a private trading voyage. In 1792 Captain Robert Gray had sailed his *Columbia* into the mouth of a river, which he named after his vessel. But the American was not alone there, for he had met British captain George Vancouver also exploring the region, sailing more than a hundred miles upstream. Together, their findings seemed to confirm the existence of the great river of the West that everyone had expected to find. Moreover, Jefferson in 1802 read the travel account of—finally—a successful overland trek to the Pacific: Alexander Mackenzie of the British fur trading North West Company had crossed Canada and reached the ocean in 1793, and he concluded his account with a call for British colonization on the Pacific. Mackenzie believed that he, too, had reached the "great river of the West," though he had, in fact, discovered the Fraser River, which flows from the north and does not connect the Missouri River with the Pacific.

Jefferson had not been idle as these reports reached him. His presidential aide, Meriwether Lewis, was an army veteran with experience in the Old Northwest whom he trusted like a son. By 1802, possibly after reading Mackenzie's recently published account of his *Voyages from Montreal ... through the Continent of North America, to the Frozen* [Arctic] *and Pacific Oceans*, Jefferson had begun to plan a serious voyage of discovery across the Mississippi to the Pacific. But "Mr. Lewis's tour," as he cryptically referred to it, was to be like no other that he had contemplated and was to be mounted on a scale unheard of before. Dozens of men—soldiers in the service of the state—would accompany Captain Lewis, along with another Virginia veteran with western military experience:

the younger brother of George Rogers Clark, William Clark. To him fell the vitally important duty of mapping. Both Lewis and Clark had long wished to explore the West; they would be perfect complements to each other.

While Jefferson had instructed Michaux in general terms and had trusted the Frenchman's botanical training to provide adequate reporting on plants, he took steps to have Lewis in particular trained in a variety of skills to enable him to gather the most accurate and useful information. The president sent his new western explorer to Philadelphia early in 1803 for a crash program in science, where Lewis was instructed by the nation's leading scientists in botany, zoology, geology, Indian ethnography, celestial observation, and medicine. Jefferson prepared the way for Lewis by writing to such luminaries as botanists Caspar Wistar and Dr. Benjamin Smith Barton and physician Dr. Benjamin Rush, asking them to suggest "the most worthy" questions in their fields. They were happy to comply, and their suggestions unmistakably found their way into Jefferson's instructions.

By the time he drafted those instructions, however, the mission westward had taken on new meaning. In July 1803, Jefferson learned from his emissaries in France that their planned purchase of New Orleans now included the vast western lands that until now had been only a dream. What had been a literary or philosophical journey suddenly took on a much more pressing practical tone, and Jefferson now had more than science on his mind. Nevertheless, the expedition remained crucially important. In asking the questions he did, Jefferson showed himself typical of what has been called the "imperial science" of his age, in which the practical—that is, *commercial*—exploitation of new plants, minerals, and animals was seen as essential to a modern nation's expansion. The United States, after all, had separated from the world's greatest imperial power, which was itself exploring not only the Pacific Northwest in search of trade goods but also the entire Pacific and other oceans. As a new nation excluded from Britain's mercantile world, Jefferson's America desperately needed new sources of trade. He therefore left no doubt in the minds of the two captains as to their primary purpose:

> The object of your mission is to explore the Missouri River, & such principal stream of it, as by it's course & communication with the waters of the Pacific Ocean, may offer the most direct and practicable water communication across this continent, for the purposes of commerce.[7]

To assure unimpeded American movement across that continent, Jefferson commanded them to seek alliances with the Indians and "treat them in the most friendly & conciliatory manner" in order to foster "commercial intercourse" in "the articles of most desireable interchange for them & us," all of which he hoped would bring peace and stability for a *Pax Americana* in the region. They were, of course, to be especially alert to any marketable products "worthy of notice" such as "mineral productions" and "vegetable productions."

Practical diplomatic and commercial reasons certainly informed the Voyage of Discovery, but—perhaps for that very reason—its scientific purposes remained central. Science and diplomacy, science and trade, science and national survival: all of these were inseparable in Jefferson's mind, for they typified the spirit of an inquiring and acquisitive age. With much greater detail than he had asked of Michaux, Jefferson commanded the two officers,

> Your observations are to be taken with great pains & accuracy, to be entered distinctly, & intelligibly for others as well as for yourself, to comprehend all the elements necessary....

They responded with clarity, precision, and diligence. Lewis, while sailing down the Ohio to join Clark at Louisville, heard of an excavation of "mammoth" bones near Big Bone Lick, Kentucky, and asked permission to examine them. Allowed to take what he wished from the site, he packed specimens and sent them back to Jefferson along with his own comments and detailed descriptions so that "you may from thence draw your own inferences, and make your own deductions."

As they followed the Missouri upstream, the bounty of discoveries exceeded their anticipations. By the time they reached the High Plains of Nebraska and the Dakotas later in 1804, they had seen their first coyotes, mule deer, jackrabbits, and magpies, as well as the remarkable pronghorn. Centuries earlier, Spanish explorers had seen the pronghorn, too, but they had neglected to describe and measure it as Lewis did; their interest had been conquest and the spread of religion, and they paid little attention to scientific matters. After the long winter encampment with the Mandans in 1804–5, Lewis sent a huge cargo of boxed specimens of plant and animal life to the president, which were "accompanyed by their rispective labels expressing the days on which obtained, places where found, and also their virtues and properties when known." Lewis also sent four boxes and three trunks of Indian artifacts, but these were dwarfed in bulk by twenty-five crates of zoo-logical items, along with a caged prairie dog (identified as "a liveing burrowing Squirrel of the praries"), a sharp-tailed grouse, and four magpies. Forwarded from St. Louis to New Orleans and then by sea to Washington, the prairie dog and one magpie survived to delight Jefferson, and he prominently displayed them in the Executive Mansion.[8]

Adverse conditions made survival difficult, much less the careful recording of minutiae. Despite long gaps in his jour-nals, however, Lewis provided a wealth of accurate detail con-cerning his observations of flora and fauna. The captains

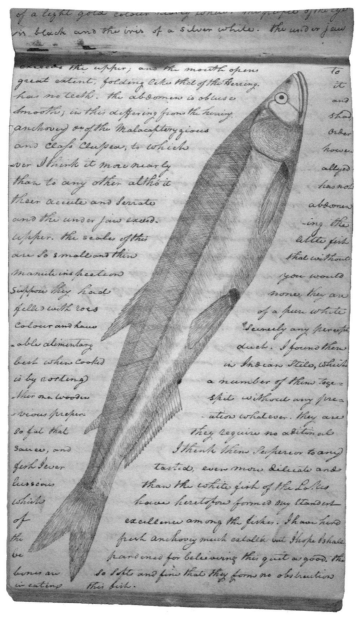

Lewis sketched this eulachon (a small fish related to smelt) during the winter of 1805–6. Lewis wrote on February 25, 1806, that these fish "were taken in great quantities in the Columbia R. about 40 miles above us by means of skiming or scooping nets. on this page I have drawn the likeness of them as large as life; it as perfect as I can make it with my pen and will serve to give a general idea of the fish." William Clark Papers, Missouri Historical Society Archives.

made every effort to provide the fullest information they could, ignoring physical discomfort when necessary. Recovering from the gunshot wound he had suffered from a nearsighted member of the party, Lewis admitted that "wrighting in my present situation is extreemly painful to me … however I must notice a singular Cherry which is found on the Missouri in the bottom lands about the beaver bends."[9] Clark maintained painstakingly precise geographical descriptions for mapping, and Lewis kept alert to anything of potential interest. Crossing the difficult and snow-covered Lolo Trail in September 1805 on an "excessively bad" path, and suffering from hunger such that they had to kill and eat one of their own colts, their efforts typified the loyalty they felt to their charge. Though wet, cold, and hungry, Clark managed to continue mapping their progress in great detail. Lewis took the trouble to record "a specimen of bird which I never had seen before." He wrote of this thrush,

> It was rather larger than a robbin, tho' much it's form and action. the colours were a blueish brown on the back the wings and tale black, as was a stripe above the croop ¾ of an inch wide in front of the neck, and two others of the same colour passed from it's eyes back along the sides of the head. the top of the head, neck brest and belly and butts of the wings were of a fine yellowish brick reed....[10]

Both captains demonstrated unexpected talents in their respective efforts, Clark at cartography and Lewis in his observations of nature. Four months after describing the thrush he had seen at Lolo Trail, Lewis examined a dead bird that one of his men brought to him. "I immediately recognized it," he wrote, "to be of the same kind of which I had seen in the Rocky mountains on the morning of the 20th of September last." He then proceeded to write a long (six times the length of his first entry) and minutely detailed description of the "beatifull little bird."[11] So precise were Lewis's efforts that later ornithologists were able to confirm his reports by comparison with their own.

Ingenuity and hard work marked their efforts, too. They instructed their men to report or to bring them examples of plant and animal life and went to great lengths to get the information they needed. They might lie down and kick their legs in the air to attract deer or order the flooding of prairie-dog tunnels to flush them out for capture. They also inquired about natural phenomena from the Indians they met, though the language barrier made this difficult and imprecise. Amazingly, neither captain spoke French; Clark later described the laborious method of communicating with the native peoples they encountered, as when they met the Flathead:

> I spoke in English to Labieche [Private Francis Labiche] … he translated it to Chaboneau [Toussaint Charbonneau, the husband of Sacagawea] in French— he to his wife in Minnetaree—she in Shoshone to the boy—the boy in Tushepaw to that nation.[12]

Because their instructions had emphasized that the "commerce which may be carried on with the people inhabiting the line you will pursue, renders a knoledge of these people important," the captains had been instructed "to make your-self acquainted, as far as a diligent pursuit of your journey shall admit," listing different areas of interest ranging from "the extent & limits of their possessions" to "the diseases prevalent among them, & the remedies they use." Lewis and Clark might ask, too, about "the state of morality, religion & information among them, as it may better enable those who endeavor to civilize & instruct them…." Lewis responded in true Jeffersonian fashion, devising a chart listing fifty tribes and nineteen questions to be answered about each. Indian ethnography, unfortunately, was probably the one area where the captains were not adequately equipped to make evaluations as objective as with flora, fauna, and geography. Although they made careful and accurate descriptions of Indian lodgings, for example, they often revealed an uncomprehending condescension in their accounts of Indian life and culture, especially matters religious or sexual. Even so, they also demonstrated a remarkable level of acceptance and objectivity for their age.

Lewis and Clark were on the cusp of a new era in science and exploration. Natural philosophers sought to replace anecdotal reports and preconceived notions with the more modern empirical notion based on the "patient pursuit of facts" and from which to "draw your own inferences, and make your own deductions." Clark made dozens of maps of their progress and meticulously recorded geographical detail as a guide to locating sites more precisely. In addition to his own observations and calculations, he added data from existing maps for regions he had not seen, including those of the recently explored Southwest by Zebulon Pike. The result revolutionized American notions of geography in general and of the West in particular. By giving accurate locations for the headwaters of the Missouri and Columbia Rivers—and by showing how each shrank to a trickle at its source—Clark made it clear that there existed no easy river-and-portage route to the Pacific. The map's display of the great mountain ranges of the West made this fact clearer still: the Stony Mountains were not a single narrow chain with convenient gaps but rather three chains. The mountains seen by sea captains from the Pacific were thus not the Rockies at all but rather the Cascades. Clark's efforts give meaning to the term "Corps of Discovery" because the corps had traversed and filled in vast areas of blank *terra incognita*. Unlike many Americans who to this day regard the voyage as having explored uninhabited regions, Clark recognized the presence of the American Indian and—significantly—recorded it on his maps. The West was not an empty wilderness, as he made clear with such notations as "Ricaras 3000 Souls" and the locations of abandoned sites of habitation.[13]

Like Jefferson, however, the explorers succumbed to many persistent ideas, and Clark's great map, though it transformed politics no less than it changed cartography, illustrates this two-sided mentality. Clark spent years in St. Louis perfecting his maps by seeking reports from other travelers. Not only did he incorporate information from veterans of the Corps of Discovery passing through the city, but he added information from fur traders and from other maps he acquired. Along with the invaluable data he accumulated, therefore, his master map perpetuated errors and misconceptions. Pike's reports, for example, noted a common source for the great rivers of the Southwest and reinforced Clark's belief in a major river south of the Columbia (just as the Yellowstone drained the region south of the Missouri). In 1806, when Indians showed Clark the river they called the Multnomah joining the Columbia at present-day Portland, Oregon (and now known as the Willamette River), he had incorrectly leapt to the conclusion that it originated far to the south, near the headwaters of the Colorado. When Clark read Pike's report, he remained as convinced as ever. It would take many more expeditions to disabuse Americans of such ideas, but they were on their way. Lewis and Clark had made that possible.

Notes

1   *The Correspondence of Jefferson and du Pont de Nemours* (Baltimore: John Hopkins University Press, 1931), 144.

2   Donald T. Jackson, "The West," in *Thomas Jefferson: A Reference Biography*, ed. Merrill D. Peterson (New York: Scribner, 1986), 369.

3   James P. Ronda, "Lewis & Clark and Enlightenment Ethnography," in *Westering Captains: Essays on the Lewis and Clark Expedition*, supplementary publication of *We Proceeded On* 9 (August 1990), 58.

4   Thomas Jefferson, *Notes on the State of Virginia*, ed. William Peden (1787; reprint, Chapel Hill: University of North Carolina Press, 1954), 53. For Jefferson's "comparative View of the Quadrupeds of Europe and of America," see ibid., 50–52.

5   Julian P. Boyd, ed., *The Papers of Thomas Jefferson* (Princeton, N.J.: Princeton University Press, 1952), 6:371.

6   Jefferson's instructions to Michaux are reprinted in Donald T. Jackson, *Thomas Jefferson and the Stony Mountains: Exploring the West from Monticello* (Urbana: University of Illinois Press, 1981), 75–78.

7   Jefferson's instructions are reprinted in *The Journals of Lewis and Clark*, ed. Bernard De Voto (Boston: Houghton Mifflin, 1953; reprint, New York: Mariner Books, 1997), 481–87.

8   Paul Russell Cutright, *Lewis and Clark: Pioneering Naturalists* (Urbana: University of Illinois Press, 1969; reprint, Greenwich, Conn.: Brompton Books, 1989), 121.

9   Ibid., 325.

10 Gary E. Moulton, ed., *The Journals of the Lewis and Clark Expedition*, 12 vols. (Lincoln: University of Nebraska Press, 1983–99), 5:217–18.

11 Ibid., 6:254.

12 Cutright, *Lewis and Clark*, 194.

13 Albert Furtwangler, *Acts of Discovery: Visions of America in the Lewis and Clark Journals* (Urbana: University of Illinois Press, 1993), 240.

Suggested Readings

Allen, John Logan. *Passage through the Garden: Lewis and Clark and the Image of the American Northwest.* Urbana: University of Illinois Press, 1975. Reprint. New York: Dover Publications, 1991.

Cutright, Paul Russell. *Lewis and Clark: Pioneering Naturalists.* Urbana: University of Illinois Press, 1969. Reprint. Greenwich, Conn.: Brompton Books, 1989.

Furtwangler, Albert. *Acts of Discovery: Visions of America in the Lewis and Clark Journals.* Urbana: University of Illinois Press, 1993. Reprint. Urbana: University of Illinois Press, 1999.

Jackson, Donald T. *Thomas Jefferson and the Stony Mountains: Exploring the West from Monticello.* Urbana: University of Illinois Press, 1981.

Miller, Charles L. *Jefferson and Nature: An Interpretation.* Baltimore: Johns Hopkins University Press, 1988. Reprint. Baltimore: Johns Hopkins University Press, 1993.

Ronda, James P. *Westering Captains: Essays on the Lewis and Clark Expedition.* Great Falls, Mont.: Lewis and Clark Trail Heritage Foundation, 1990.

"A Multitude of Indians"

Indian Country on the Eve of Lewis and Clark

James P. Ronda
University of Tulsa

In all your intercourse with the natives, treat them in the most friendly & conciliatory manner which their own conduct will admit; allay all jealousies as to the object of your journey, satisfy them of it's innocence, make them acquainted with the position, extent, character, peaceable & commercial dispositions of the U.S. of our wish to be neighborly, friendly & useful to them, & of our dispositions to a commercial intercourse with them.

> —Thomas Jefferson, instructions to Meriwether Lewis

[A] Cold morning Some wind the Black Cat, Chief of the Mandans Came to See us, he made Great inquiries respecting our fashions. he also Stated the Situation of their nation, he mentioned that a Council had been held the day before and it was thought advisable to put up with the recent insults of the Ossiniboins [Assiniboines] & Christonoes [Crees] until they were Convinced that what had been told thim by us Mr. Evins [the St. Louis trader John Thomas Evans] had deceived them & we might also, he promised to return & furnish them with guns & ammunition, we advised them to remain at peace & that they might depend upon Getting Supplies through the Channel of the Missouri, but it required time to put the trade in operation. The Assiniboins etc. have the trade of those nations in their power and treat them badly as the Soux does the Ricarees and they cannot resent for fear of loseing their trade.

—William Clark, journal entry, November 18, 1804

William Clark did not have to be told twice. No matter what some maps said about the West as an empty place—a place with neither homes nor homelands—he knew better. Years of experience on more eastern frontiers had prepared the future explorer to encounter a West that was more like a crowded neighborhood than an uninhabited wilderness. Heading up the Missouri River, Clark was ready to find Indian Country—a landscape filled with prosperous villages, extensive hunting territories, and well-traveled trading paths. Even before leaving Camp Wood outside St. Louis, Clark recognized that his community—the Corps of Discovery—would be moving through the lands and lives of other older and more established communities. He said as much the day before the expedition pointed itself up the Missouri. Clark predicted that the Corps of Discovery's "road across the continent" would take the explorers through "a multitude of Indians."[1] What those natives and newcomers thought about each other is at the very heart of the Lewis and Clark story.

When the Lewis and Clark Expedition pushed upriver in May 1804, the Corps of Discovery was not entering a country outside of time and beyond the reach of change. This was not a virgin land, an Eden untouched by human hands. Enchanted by the paintings of Karl Bodmer, George Catlin, and Paul Kane, it is easy for us to conjure up a Native American West in 1803 as paradise in a fallen world. But Mandans, Shoshones, and Clatsops were not remote and isolated from the rest of humankind. Trade, disease, and personal relationships made Indians neighbors to peoples in the farthest parts of that world. From the distance of two centuries we lose track of the profound changes that swept the American West in the last half of the eighteenth century. The Lewis and Clark Expedition both witnessed those changes and advanced them.

The Friends of Black Cat

Perhaps no one up the Missouri understood more about native worlds in transformation than Posecopsahe, known to Lewis and Clark as Black Cat. As headman, or *tia*, at the Mandan village of Ruptare—one of five Mandan and Hidatsa settlements on the Missouri in present-day North Dakota— Black Cat saw it all and struggled to make sense of what he had witnessed. Lewis and Clark recognized Black Cat as an astute observer of life on the northern Great Plains, describing him as a man of "integrity, firmness, intelligence, and perspicuity."[2] Whatever happened on the plains and along the river could be seen and felt from the place Black Cat called home. And Black Cat was more than a passive observer. As Clark recalled, whenever Black Cat visited Fort Mandan "he made Great inquiries respecting our fashions."[3]

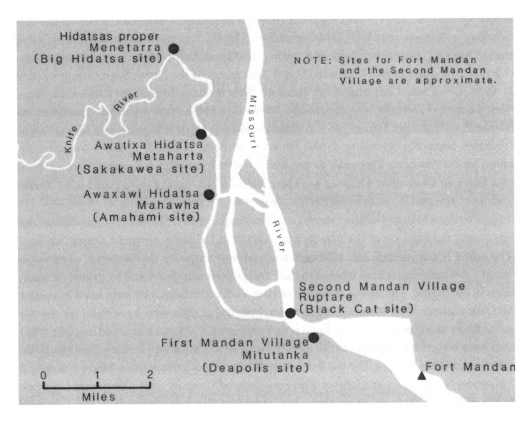

Knife River Indian Villages, August 25, 1804–April 6, 1805.
From *The Journals of the Lewis and Clark Expedition*, ed. Gary
Moulton. Vol. 3. Reprinted with permission of the University of
Nebraska Press.

Black Cat and his neighbors lived in a world where change
and the unpredictable seemed everywhere. How Black Cat
and other earth-lodge people responded to Lewis and Clark
was determined by those changes. And nothing spread
change more rapidly than epidemic disease. Everywhere he
looked, Black Cat saw what disease had wrought. Down the
Missouri in what is now South Dakota, Arikara villagers had
suffered the effects of one smallpox epidemic after another.
Black Cat would have agreed with Clark when he reported
that the Grand River Arikaras were a people "much reduced."[4]
Before the terrible pandemic of 1780–81 there were perhaps
twenty to thirty thousand Arikaras living in dozens of villages

along the Missouri. After the disease had burned itself out, 75 percent of the Arikaras were dead. And the depopulation had consequences for all to see and hear. When French trader Jean Baptiste Truteau visited the Arikaras in 1795 he saw firsthand the political results of the epidemics. Struck by the intense factionalism and bickering that marked Arikara life, Truteau discovered villages filled with disease survivors. Arikara leaders—another French trader called them "captains without companies"—were constantly engaged in verbal squabbling and open discord.[5] The tension was so great that some Arikaras moved south to live among the Pawnees, while others headed north to join the Mandans. Disease not only shaped the unruly world of Missouri River politics but also marked the very way the Arikaras and their neighbors spoke. Every visitor to the Grand River villages noted the many dialect and accent differences among the Arikaras, who had consolidated from many locations into just three villages. William Clark explained that there was "a difference in pronunciation and some difference of language" among the Arikaras and their neighbors.[6] St. Louis trader Pierre-Antoine Tabeau put it more forcefully: Arikaras lived and spoke in a "tower of Babel."[7] What happened to the Arikaras was part of Black Cat's past, and the future of his people as well.

At the end of the eighteenth century, wave after wave of smallpox and other contagious diseases swept up the Missouri River trench. The general western pandemic of 1780–81 was followed by disease assaults in the 1790s and 1801–2. As sedentary farmers living close to one another, the earth-lodge people were especially vulnerable to what epidemiologists call "virgin-soil epidemics." These were the disease outbreaks among populations without previous exposure to a particular illness and thus lacking sufficient immunities. Like the Arikaras, the Mandans had suffered considerable population loss. The 1780–81 pandemic was just the beginning of a ceaseless round of suffering and death that culminated in the disaster of 1837 when smallpox nearly destroyed the Mandans. A rapid population decline and increased fear from Sioux raids convinced Mandans living at the Heart River villages in present-day North Dakota to move north toward the Knife River and an uneasy alliance with the Hidatsas.

Diseases like smallpox were the invisible invaders. The more visible agents of change came later. While Sieur de la Vérendrye and his sons visited the Arikara and Mandan villages in 1738 and 1742, it was not until the late 1780s that Canadian and then French traders from St. Louis began to arrive. By 1794–95 traders representing the Hudson's Bay Company and the North West Company, as well as independent merchants, began to pay regular visits to the earth-lodge villages. In one way, traders such as Rene Jusseaume, David Thompson, and James Slater were nothing new in Black Cat's world. The Mandan and Hidatsa villages were already the center of a vast native exchange network anthropologists call the Middle Missouri River trade system. Traders from Canada and St. Louis simply fit their commercial schemes into the system that already existed. There was a pattern to the comings and goings of these bearded strangers. They were men—always men—and they came in small groups. In the half century before Lewis and Clark, the largest European trading expedition to the Mandan and Hidatsa villages numbered just ten. Little wonder that the sheer size of the Lewis and Clark party prompted both surprise and concern. The Canadians developed a seasonal trade cycle: arriving in the late fall or early winter, staying for a few weeks to do business, and then returning north. Only occasionally did a trader winter over, marry into a village family, and become known as a tenant or resident trader. Two of those men—Toussaint Charbonneau and Rene Jusseaume—came to play important roles in the Lewis and Clark story.

What those trading outsiders brought represented a force

for change every bit as powerful as the microbe invasion. European manufactured goods—especially guns, powder, knives, kettles, and awls—were part of earth-lodge life well before the 1730s. Sieur de la Verendrye reported that Assiniboine merchants were regularly bringing those goods to Mandan and Hidatsa consumers.[8] During the next half century what began as a trickle became a flood. By the time Lewis and Clark came to spend the winter of 1804–5 with them, Indians on the Missouri knew all about iron axes, glass beads, and shiny mirrors. By the late 1790s, thanks to suppliers from Canada and St. Louis, Black Cat's people were using European iron, brass, and textile goods as part of everyday life. Archaeological evidence reveals an astounding variety of objects—everything from iron arrow points and brass bracelets to heavy butcher knives and gun parts.[9] But what of the consequences of those goods on Mandan and Hidatsa life? Reflecting on that question, Lewis believed that Indians imputed spirit power to those items and considered white traders as "the most powerful persons in the nation."[10] But that medicine seemed to wear off quickly. Black Cat treated the trade goods brought by Lewis and Clark as objects in everyday life.

While a growing dependence on the products of the Industrial Revolution was a fact of life in Black Cat's world, it was also clear that native people were quick to adapt European objects to their own needs. Sewing thimbles, a common item in the trade, were sometimes pierced at the top and made into pendant earrings.[11] Perhaps the most intriguing example of trade-goods transformation came when Lewis and Clark offered the Mandans and Arikaras two corn grinders. The Mandans accepted the strange devices, but when Canadian trader Alexander Henry the Younger saw the grinder it was no longer recognizable. Instead, Mandans had salvaged the usable iron parts, employing the large piece as a pounder for making grease from buffalo bones.[12]

an earth lodge over
rough April 1834. The
or the Mandan family
Hutte des Mandan
n Chief). Steel engraving
n von Wied, *Travels in
s 1832–34*, London,

creasing power of the
traders and European
worked to give Black
unsettled future.
ggle for empire in the
conflict was still fresh
1796, John Thomas
nd commercial interests
ges and launched an
at limiting Canadian
ack Cat was probably

Karl Bodmer completed this portrait of Mandeh-Pahchu, a Mandan, in March 1834 at Fort Clark. Mandeh-Pahchu carries a wooden flute decorated with an otter fur. Steel engraving after Karl Bodmer, 1843. From Maximilian von Wied, *Travels in the Interior of North America in the Years 1832–34*. London, 1843. Missouri Historical Society Library.

among them—were given flags and medals as signs of Spanish rule. The headmen received these gifts, so Evans reported, with "the most sincere attachment to their great father the Spaniard and his chiefs."[13] Evans also made impressive promises about a profitable trade with St. Louis merchants. As fortune had it, Evans found it impossible to keep those promises. In fact, he barely escaped the village with his life when Canadian traders Rene Jusseaume and Baptiste La France convinced several Indians to assault him. Evans emerged unharmed, but at that moment it was plain that the Mandans had been divided by rival schemes of empire. Flags, medals, and the trade itself could draw Black Cat and his people into struggles beyond their control and with consequences unforeseen by anyone.

Seven years later, the memory of Evans and the conflict he sparked was still fresh in Black Cat's mind. Talking with Clark, Black Cat complained that Evans had deceived the Mandans. And it hardly had to be said that many in the lodges now suspected that the Americans were also deceivers.[14] Despite those bitter experiences, Black Cat and other village headmen found themselves once again drawn into the Great Plains contest for empire. This time the flags were American, the medals bore the likeness of an American president, and the gifts carried multiple meanings. Black Cat allowed Lewis and Clark to name him Grand Chief of the Mandans, a title that said more about American misconceptions than Mandan realities. What counted for Black Cat was the possibility that the Americans might make life less precarious. As he explained, the security of an American alliance would enable Mandans "to hunt without fear" and allow "our womin [to] work in the fields without looking every moment for the enimey."[15] Lewis and Clark had come to a part of Indian Country with a troubled past and an uncertain future. Black Cat greeted the American strangers warmly, accepted their tokens of friendship, but continued to worry about the future.

Cameahwait and the Guns of August

From a distance, life at the Lemhi Shoshone camps along the Continental Divide between present-day Montana and Idaho seemed the same year after year. Far from the main lines of trade, disease, and imperial conflict, the people of the Lemhi River appeared immune from the changes that were remaking Black Cat's world. Lemhi Shoshone life was shaped by a seasonal cycle of fishing in streams west of the Continental Divide and hunting buffalo out on the plains. That cycle reflected two distinct but not mutually exclusive cultural traditions. The older Southern Shoshone tradition was rooted in the lifeways of the Great Basin. Southern Shoshoneans clustered in small family groups, lived as hunter-gatherers, and built conical-shaped brush *wickiups*. Horses and guns played no part in the lives of these *agaideka'a*, the salmon and fish eaters. The Northern Shoshone tradition was much more recent, shaped in large part by the post-1700 northern Great Plains experience. This was the world of horses, guns, and buffalo. The Lemhi people lived in both worlds—fishing for part of the year and then joining their Flathead (Interior Salish) neighbors for the annual fall buffalo hunt. When Lewis and Clark met the Shoshones in August 1805 some were fishing as *agaideka'a* while others prepared to become *kut-sendeka'a*, the buffalo eaters.

To modern eyes, Lemhi Shoshone life might seem in perfect balance with an economy well suited to the resources at hand. But Cameahwait, chief of the Lemhi people, knew better. No fishing camp was secure from raiders; every buffalo hunt put Shoshones at risk of attack by well-armed enemies. This was a fragile world, one where survival was a daily gamble. Like Black Cat, Cameahwait saw change and the consequences of change everywhere. And how he understood change determined the way he and his people viewed the strangers from the east, those some Lemhis called "men with faces pale as ashes."[16]

Lewis and Clark never got to know Cameahwait as they did Black Cat but they did recognize him as "a man of Influence Sense [and] a great deel of Cincerity."[17] In council with Lewis the day after their first encounter, Cameahwait described a Lemhi people surrounded by enemies and struggling for survival. In his mind there was no greater force for change than firearms. Without guns, the Lemhi Shoshones were left "defenceless and an easy prey to ... bloodthirsty neighbors to the east of them, who being in possession of firearms hunt them without rispect to sex or age and plunder them of their horses on all occasions." Cameahwait reported that his people "were obliged to remain in the interior of those mountains at least two-thirds of the year ... sometimes living for weeks without meat and only a little fish, roots, and berries." Just looking at the Lemhi headman, "his ferce eyes and lank jaws grown meager for want of food," was enough to convince Lewis that Cameahwait was a man haunted by memories of violence and death at the hands of powerful enemies. In one of the most memorable lines in the Lewis and Clark journals, Cameahwait summed up all the hard-edged realities in his world. "If we had guns, we could then live in the country of the buffaloe and eat as our enemies do and not be compelled to hide in these mountains and live on roots and berries as the bear do."[18] As if to emphasize the promise of the gun, Cameahwait had taken as his war name Too-et-te-con'l, or Black Gun. Where once horses meant prosperity and security, now every warrior dreamed of guns, powder, and bullets.

For all his seeming isolation, Cameahwait was an astute observer of the shifting balance of power on the northern plains and Rocky Mountains. In an Indian Country increasingly dominated by horsemen with guns, the Lemhi people had horses but few guns. Lewis and Clark counted only three old North West Company trade guns among the Lemhis, probably obtained by way of Crow middlemen. Cameahwait's gun-toting enemies included Hidatsas, Atsinas, and the Piegan

Blackfeet. Of those, the Piegans were the best armed and the most aggressive. Blackfeet warriors possessed guns by the 1730s. In 1781 a Hudson's Bay Company trader reported that the Blackfeet had so much ammunition, "they don't know what to do with it," and that they went to war "every year."[19] Sudden attack from such well-armed raiders was a constant threat. In the spring of 1805, just months before Lewis and Clark arrived, the Lemhis suffered a devastating blow at the hands of the Atsinas. Twenty Shoshones were killed, and others were taken prisoner. The band lost valuable horses and all but one of their hide lodges.[20] Lewis and Clark soon heard about other raids, including ones in 1799 and 1804.[21]

The danger to Shoshones and Flatheads increased dramatically when they hunted buffalo during the late summer and fall. At a buffalo hunt around Three Forks, Sacagawea was kidnapped as a girl by Hidatsa warriors. One of Cameahwait's neighbors, the Salish chief Carrier, put their situation in simple terms for Canadian explorer David Thompson. "You are well aware when we go to hunt the Bison, we also prepare for war with the Pieagans and their allies; if we had ammunition we should already have been there, for the Cow Bison are now all fat, but we cannot go with empty Guns: we do not fear War, but we wish to meet our enemies well armed."[22] Cameahwait and Carrier knew that guns had transformed Indian Country. So long as they were gun hungry and powder poor, the Lemhis could see a future that promised only more raids, kidnappings, and life on the edge of starvation.

Cameahwait centered his attention on guns and the possibility that Americans might supply them. But he did not ignore the presence of other trade goods now flooding the plains and Rockies. After seeing the relative material wealth of the Mandans and Hidatsas, Lewis and Clark were struck by the seeming poverty of the Lemhis. Trade with the Crows and other native merchants brought only a handful of European items to the Lemhi camps. With an eye to future business, Lewis noted that the Shoshones had "a few indifferent knives, a few brass kettles, some arm bands of iron and brass, a few buttons, worn as ornaments in their hair, a spear or two of a foot in length, and some iron and brass arrow points." He also saw Spanish horse tack—bridle bits and stirrups—"tho these were but few."[23] These goods had come through native intermediaries; the Shoshones now wanted to do business directly with white traders. Lewis and Clark were eager to oblige, painting a glowing picture of trade connections and prosperity once the Lemhi people became part of the American system. Cameahwait's people looked at the objects carried by the American travelers and invested them with both material and spiritual meanings. Possessing such objects—whether beads or ironware or cloth—promised not only prestige and wealth but also a connection to powerful spirit forces. As Lewis explained later, "every article about us appeared to excite astonishment in their minds."[24] Astonishment was a prelude to desire—the desire for security and prosperity that Cameahwait believed only guns could provide.

Few scenes in the Lewis and Clark drama are more memorable than the first meeting between Lewis and Cameahwait on August 13, 1805. Lewis and his small scouting party had spent days searching for the Shoshones. For his part, Cameahwait knew at least a day before that strangers were in the neighborhood, and he now prepared to strike in defense of his people. Sometime during the morning, as the expedition worked its way through steep ravines in the Lemhi valley, Lewis and his party came upon three Shoshone women. One fled in terror but an elderly woman and a young girl sat quietly with their heads bowed, awaiting what seemed certain death. After reassuring them that he was not an enemy, Lewis offered mirrors, moccasin awls, face paint, and some beads. With the Shoshones as guides, Lewis and his men hiked toward what they believed was the main Indian camp.

Suddenly Cameahwait and some sixty mounted warriors gal-
loped into view. At that moment both Lewis and Cameahwait
made crucial decisions. First to act, Lewis left his gun behind
and walked toward the Indians waving an American flag. For all
of Lewis's bravado, it was Cameahwait who had to make the
life-or-death decision. There is no doubt that the Shoshones
could have killed Lewis's party with little loss to themselves.

With memories of the recent Atsina attack still fresh,
Cameahwait might have seen the Americans as the advance
party for more raiders from the east. But the objects Lewis gave
the Shoshone women gave him pause. Cameahwait looked at
them, talked with the women, and then decided that this was
the opportunity he had been searching for. In a journal entry
that would do any screenwriter proud, Lewis described what
happened next:

> These men then advanced and embraced me very
> affectionately in their way which is by putting their left
> arm over you wright sholder clasping your back, while
> they apply their left cheek to yours and frequently
> vociferate the word *ah-hi'-e, ah-hi'-e* that is, I am much
> pleased, I am much rejoiced. bothe parties now
> advanced and we wer all carresed and besmeared with
> their grease and paint till I was heartily tired of the
> national hug.[25]

But in all the talk and signs of friendship that followed, neither
Cameahwait nor his warriors could take their eyes off the guns.
As Cameahwait told Lewis some days later, "they had been long
anxious to see the whitemen that traded guns."[26] Now they had
come and Cameahwait believed guns would surely follow.

And so the promises were made and the deals were done.
Cameahwait agreed to provide the expedition with much-
needed horses and even made a nod toward Lewis's insistence

that American trade guns never be turned on other Indians. But it was the guns that made the difference. Cameahwait knew it, and sometime later Lewis and Clark came to know it as well. Almost a year later, as Lewis and a small scouting party camped with a group of Piegan Blackfeet along the Two Medicine River in present-day north-central Montana, the story of Cameahwait's guns took on greater importance. Around the campfire on the night of July 26, 1806, Lewis told the Piegans that their traditional enemies—the Shoshones, Nez Perce, and Kutenais—were now united by an American-inspired peace. Even more stunning was the announcement that these tribes would have American guns. The northern plains arms race now seemed certain to grow even more intense. But it was not geopolitics that sparked violence the next morning when the Piegans attempted to take expedition horses and guns. When the killing stopped and two Piegans lay dead, what happened next was all about Cameahwait's guns and American power. In an act of pure defiance, Lewis hung a peace-and-friendship medal around the neck of one dead Piegan "so that they might be informed who we were."[27] Cameahwait welcomed Lewis and Clark because he believed he knew who they were. They were the "whitemen gun traders" who could free the Lemhi people from fear and hunger. What Lewis announced at the Two Medicine River was yet another understanding of American identity. The "whitemen gun traders" were not in the West to free the Shoshones and their neighbors but to assert the claims of a new American empire.

Coboway and the Cloth Men

Thomas Jefferson thought about it as the place where the river of the West met the great western sea. For Lewis and Clark it was the end of the trail and the farthest place from home. Headman Coboway and those Clatsop Indian families who lived in eight large plank houses at what is now Point Adams near present-day Astoria, Oregon, knew the place simply as home. It was the village they called "where the pounded salmon is." This was a world shaped by the presence of the Pacific Ocean and the Columbia River. The ocean and the river were not barriers, keeping the outside world at bay. Rather, they connected the Clatsops and their neighbors to the wider world. And as fortune had it, the Clatsops lived in one of Indian Country's busiest and most cosmopolitan places. Cameahwait had never seen whites and possessed few European objects; Black Cat and Coboway knew white traders by name and had ready access to all sorts of manufactured goods. When Lewis and Clark built Fort Clatsop along the Netul River (now the Lewis and Clark River), the Americans became one more company in a long line of merchants and travelers to come knocking at Coboway's door.

An often-told Clatsop story explains their situation best. A trading ship, trying to cross the treacherous Columbia River bar, broke up and sank with all hands. But its cargo—including brass, copper, and iron—was salvaged from the wreck. Indians up the Columbia, eager for metal goods, came to the Clatsops for trade. As the story concludes, "the people [that is, the upriver Indians], bought this and the Clatsop became rich." The storyteller might have added that trade with the growing number of ships that successfully crossed the bar made the Clatsops a confident people as well.[28] Point Adams was neither a great maritime fur trade center like Nootka Sound nor a key Indian trading place like the Dalles on the Columbia. Instead, the Clatsops had the good fortune to live where the western branch of the Pacific plateau trade system met the burgeoning Pacific Ocean maritime fur trade. It was as if the Clatsops had built their village at the intersection of two important interstate highways. Centered at the Dalles, the Pacific plateau system brought together native people from throughout the greater Northwest to exchange everything from dried salmon and buffalo meat to textiles and ironware. Clark aptly described the Dalles as the "great mart of trade."[29] But as the Clatsop story suggested, it was the maritime fur trade that made the real difference. European ships first entered Coboway's world in 1792. In the years that followed, a steady procession of merchant vessels sailed the Columbia. Seeking furs for markets in China and Europe, the ships brought the Industrial Revolution to Coboway and his neighbors. Like Black Cat, Coboway was now a citizen of the world.

If Lewis and Clark thought they had stumbled into yet another part of the capitalist world, they soon learned otherwise. Trade—and the accumulation of material wealth—did shape Clatsop life and the way the Clatsops viewed outsiders. But the values and customs of that commerce often were unlike those in Boston, Williamsburg, or St. Louis. First, there was the matter of gender. While exceptions were everywhere, Lewis and Clark came from a commercial world dominated by men. In the Northwest Coast, trade was usually woman's work. This generalization was especially true in the maritime fur trade. Women owned the trade canoes that went out to meet ships from Boston or Bristol and then negotiated business arrangements with sea captains. Those deals were often sealed by intimate liaisons. A second difference involved the social boundaries between business and the rest of daily life. For many white Americans, business was often quite separate from family affairs, political affiliation, religious persuasion, or other social relationships. But for the Clatsops and their neighbors, trade was a way of life. Trading times, whether with sea captains or upriver at the Dalles, meant opportunities to socialize, to exchange songs and stories, and to court. Fur trader Alexander Ross described trading times at the Dalles as "the general theatre of gambling and roguery."[30] In this trading life, buying and selling were almost incidental. What counted for Clatsops was the social experience of bargaining. Theirs was a life that celebrated the dance of the deal; little wonder that Clark once described them as "close deelers."[31]

Meriwether Lewis experienced this dance when he tried to exchange a pocket watch, two knives, and "a considerable quantity of beads" for a small sea-otter skin. Lewis later admitted that he "did not much want" the pelt. What interested him were Clatsop economic values and customs. His native partner quickly sensed a deal in the making and asked for double the amount of beads Lewis initially offered. And not any beads would do. Clark's journal entry notes that the Clatsop man wanted blue beads, the sort most valued on the coast. After some time the bargaining grew cold and then faded away. But the next day the Clatsop was back, this time offering what Lewis reported as "a few stran[ds] of the same beads he had refused the day before." Misinterpreting the entire two-day enterprise, Lewis and Clark insisted that Clatsop business practices were rooted in "an avaricious all grasping disposition" that knew nothing of "usefulness or value."[32] They had seen the dance of the deal and either misunderstood the steps or thought it beneath them to play along. Whatever the reason, Lewis and Clark must have known that in this part of Indian Country, it was not business as usual.

Sometime in early December 1805 the Clatsops learned they had new neighbors. Oral tradition records that some Clatsops thought the strangers were raiders. Because the bearded strangers came well after the fur traders had come and gone, and because they came from the east and not from the ocean, there was real concern among the Clatsops. Others believed that they were *pah-shish-e-ooks*, or cloth men—the Chinook jargon word for the maritime fur traders. While Coboway did not make the first Clatsop visit to the fort, as headman it was plainly his responsibility to investigate what was going on along the banks of the Netul.

Coboway made his initial call to Fort Clatsop on December 12, 1805, and remained a constant visitor until the Corps of Discovery left in March 1806. Confident about his own place in the world, Coboway was prepared to deal with the newcomers just as he had other traders. Exploring Fort Clatsop, the headman found what he expected. There was much to convince him that the Corps of Discovery was nothing new and surely not a threat to his people. The things at Fort Clatsop—things that so fascinated interior tribes with less outside contact—seemed commonplace to Coboway. Fishhooks, iron pots, knives, guns, and textile clothing were all part of the material world Coboway knew well. Early in the history of the maritime fur trade some Indians speculated that the white traders were bears. But that notion quickly passed, and Coboway certainly recognized Lewis and Clark as human like himself. While it might have seemed odd to have a woman and a child with these traders, the presence of Sacagawea and Jean Baptiste evidently did nothing to change Coboway's mind about the identity of the Americans.

Throughout the winter of 1805–6, Coboway and his people treated Lewis and Clark as they had any other company of traders—or at least they tried to. Clatsops made regular trips to the fort, trading foodstuffs for ironware and cloth. A lively trade in sexual favors grew as well. One woman (known to Lewis and Clark as "the old Baud"), who was wife of Chinook Indian Delashelwilt, established what we might call a brothel on the north side of the Columbia River in mid-November 1805. When Lewis and Clark established Fort Clatsop on the south side of the river, she moved her operation closer to the men. Expedition member Patrick Gass admitted that the Clatsop women "frequently visited our quarters" and that sex was available "at an easy rate."[33] These exchanges fit the behavior that characterized economic relations between the Clatsops and the maritime fur traders, but there were differences that set Lewis and Clark apart from other visitors. Some were simple and obvious: Lewis and Clark came from the east, not the west; they came in December, well after fur traders had come and gone; they built a large, beached "ship house" on the banks of the Netul; and they did not seem to understand the complex trade rituals so important in Clatsop life. But those differences could be overlooked, and Coboway and his people did just that; they made allowances for the ill-mannered strangers and kept up regular visits to the fort.

Yet other distinctions could not so easily be ignored or explained. One of the most important was the way Lewis and Clark defined space and power. Both Black Cat and Coboway saw American explorers claim space, square it off, put wooden pickets around it, and then claim control over it. Lewis and Clark built Forts Mandan and Clatsop, named them after their neighbors, and then built walls and rules that partitioned the area. Lewis and Clark felt comfortable enough among the Mandans that the expedition's post had native visitors nearly every day. Many of those visitors, including Black Cat, stayed overnight. The story was quite different at Fort Clatsop. On the Northwest Coast the Americans were in a physical and cultural environment they neither liked nor understood. Endless days of rain, food that was either meager or spoiled, and an edginess born of boredom all conspired to make the expedition think of Fort Clatsop as their damp prison. Feeling surrounded by Indians they characterized as "troublesome," Lewis and Clark fashioned elaborate rules to govern the comings and goings of native people to the fort. Despite those restrictions, Coboway continued to visit his neighbors. Fur-trade captains often set strict rules when Indians came onboard ship; some allowed natives to trade only alongside merchant vessels. Coboway may have thought the fort rules were just another version of those shipboard regulations.

In March 1806, as time drew near for the expedition to leave, Lewis and Clark recognized that they would need extra canoes to take the party up the Columbia. Because they had failed to purchase them from their neighbors, the explorers decided on a different course. Evidently at the suggestion of either George Drouillard or Toussaint Charbonneau, Lewis and Clark detailed four men to secretly take canoes from Coboway's village. The Americans always boasted that they would severely punish any native thieves; now they had become thieves themselves. The expedition's justification for this bold act was that the Clatsops had not paid proper restitution for six elk shot by Drouillard and taken by Indians from his cache. In fact, restitution had been made a month earlier.[34] If Coboway knew what Lewis and Clark had done, he conveniently forgot it. On March 19, two days after the theft, Coboway paid one of his usual visits to the fort. In what must be the most brazen act in expedition history, Lewis and Clark gave Coboway a list of the members of the expedition and "a cirtificate of his good conduct and the friendly intercourse which he has maintained with us."[35] And in a moment of unintentional humor, Delashelwilt was given a certificate of "good deportment" and then "dispatched to his village with his female band."[36] Perhaps his wife and her employees deserved something as well.

For the next eight years, Coboway kept his scraps of paper, perhaps as souvenirs or links to powerful strangers. Those years brought more trading ships and, in 1811, the establishment of the first permanent American commercial outpost at Astoria. In mid-May 1814, with John Jacob Astor's Fort Astoria now in British hands, Coboway went to what was renamed Fort George to visit North West Company trader Alexander Henry the Younger. There had been a dispute over goods missing from the fort, and Coboway had agreed to recover them. As Coboway's reward, Henry offered some clothing and then—because he had seen them some days before—demanded the Lewis and Clark documents. Without hesitation, Coboway handed them over. Henry gave the Clatsop a North West Company certificate and then in a gesture filled with imperial symbolism and arrogance threw the American papers into the fire.[37] As the Lewis and Clark documents curled and crumbled in the fire, Coboway may have grasped something about the contest for empire that was already reshaping the West.

Apprehensive Mandans, hungry Shoshones, and confident Clatsops—all looked to their own parts of Indian Country and found reasons to welcome Lewis and Clark. Black Cat, Cameahwait, and Coboway knew that change was in the air. At the moment when Lewis and Clark arrived those changes seemed to promise a brighter future. Black Cat clutched his cherished American flag; Cameahwait dreamed of guns; and Coboway held on to that certificate from a distant Great Father. But the surest portent for the future was the peace-and-friendship medal Lewis hung around the neck of a dead Piegan. So the winds of change continued to blow through Indian Country. After Lewis and Clark they seemed to blow with more fury. As the ancient writer put it, "the wind blows where it chooses, and you hear the sound of it, but you do not know where it comes from or where it goes."

Notes

1 Gary E. Moulton, ed., *The Journals of the Lewis and Clark Expedition*, 12 vols. (Lincoln: University of Nebraska Press, 1983–99), 2:215. Hereafter cited as *JLCE*.

2 *JLCE*, 3:289.

3 *JLCE*, 3:237.

4 *JLCE*, 3:401.

5 Annie Heloise Abel, ed., *Tabeau's Narrative of Loisel's Expedition to the Upper Missouri* (Norman: University of Oklahoma Press, 1939), 44.

6 Donald T. Jackson, ed., *Letters of the Lewis and Clark Expedition, with Related Documents, 1783–1854*, 2d ed., 2 vols. (Urbana: University of Illinois Press, 1978), 2:537.

7 Abel, *Tabeau's Narrative*, 125.

8 Lawrence J. Burpee, ed., *Journals and Letters of Pierre Gaultier de Varennes de La Vérendrye and His Sons* (Toronto: Champlain Society, 1927), 323–24.

9 Richard A. Krause, *The Leavenworth Site: Archaeology of an Historic Arikara Community* (Lawrence: University of Kansas Publications in Anthropology, 1972), 67–84, 106–15; Donald J. Lehmer, *Introduction to Middle Missouri Archaeology* (Lincoln: National Park Service Anthropological Papers, 1971), 145–62.

10 Jackson, *Letters of the Lewis and Clark Expedition*, 2:698.

11 Lehmer, *Middle Missouri Archaeology*, 161.

12 Elliott Coues, ed., *New Light on the Early History of the Greater Northwest: The Manuscript Journals of Alexander Henry the Younger and of David Thompson*, 2 vols. (1897; reprint, Minneapolis: Ross and Haines, 1965), 1:329.

13 A. P. Nasatir, ed., *Before Lewis and Clark: Documents Illustrating the History of the Missouri*, 2 vols. (St. Louis: St. Louis Historical Documents Foundation, 1952), 2:496.

14 *JLCE*, 3:237.

15 *JLCE*, 3:219

16 James P. Ronda, *Lewis and Clark among the Indians* (Lincoln: University of Nebraska Press, 1984), 133.

17 *JLCE*, 5:114.

18 *JLCE*, 5:91.

19 E. E. Rich, ed., *Cumberland House Journals and Inland Journal, 1775–1782*, 2 vols. (London: Hudson's Bay Company Record Society, 1951–52), 1:262–63.

20 *JLCE*, 5:83.

21 *JLCE*, 5:83, 168; Atlas, map, 67 for location of the 1804 attack.

22 Richard Glover, ed., *David Thompson's Narrative, 1784–1812* (Toronto: Champlain Society, 1962), 380.

23 *JLCE*, 5:149.

24 *JLCE*, 5:112.

25 *JLCE*, 5:79.

26 *JLCE*, 5:92.

27 *JLCE*, 8:135.

28 Franz Boas, ed., *Chinook Texts*, Bureau of American Ethnology Bulletin 20 (Washington, D.C.: Government Printing Office, 1894), 277–78.

29 Jackson, *Letters of the Lewis and Clark Expedition*, 2:527.

30 Alexander Ross, *Adventures of the First Settlers on the Oregon or Columbia River* (1849; reprint, Lincoln: University of Nebraska Press, 1993), 127–28.

31 *JLCE*, 6:123.

32 *JLCE*, 6:164–65.

33 JLCE, 10:200; Ronda, *Lewis and Clark among the Indians*, 208–9.

34 Ronda, *Lewis and Clark among the Indians*, 210–11.

35 JLCE, 6:432.

36 JLCE, 6:429.

37 Coues, ed., *New Light*, 2:913, 915.

Suggested Readings

Ewers, John C. *The Blackfeet: Raiders of the Northwestern Plains*. Norman: University of Oklahoma Press, 1958.

Hunt, David C., et al. *Karl Bodmer's America*. Lincoln: University of Nebraska Press, 1984.

Madsen, Brigham D. *The Northern Shoshoni*. Caldwell, Idaho: Caxton Printers, 1980.

Meyer, Roy W. *The Village Indians of the Upper Missouri: The Mandans, Hidatsas, and Arikaras*. Lincoln: University of Nebraska Press, 1977.

Ronda, James P. *Lewis and Clark among the Indians*. Lincoln: University of Nebraska Press, 1984. Reprint. Lincoln: University of Nebraska Press, 2002.

Ruby, Robert H., and John A. Brown. *The Chinook Indians: Traders of the Lower Columbia River*. Norman: University of Oklahoma Press, 1976.

Truettner, William H. *The Natural Man Observed: A Study of Catlin's Indian Gallery*. Washington, D.C.: Smithsonian Institution Press, 1979.

The Professional Culture of the Lewis and Clark Army

William Skelton
University of Wisconsin–Stevens Point

In re-entering the U.S. and reaching a place of safety, discharge any of your attendants you may desire & deserve it, procuring for them immediate paiment of all arrears of pay & cloathing which may have incurred since their departure; & assure them that they shall be recommended to the liberality of the legislature for the grant of a soldier's portion of land each, as proposed in my message to Congress & repair yourself with your papers to the seat of government.
                    —Thomas Jefferson, instructions to Meriwether Lewis

"A fair day compelled to punish misconduct....

"A Sergeant and four men of the Party destined for the Missouri Expidition will convene at 11 oClock on the quarter Deck of the Boat, and form themselves into a Court Martial to hear and determine (in behalf of the Capt.) the evidences aduced against William Warner & Hugh Hall for being absent last night without leave; contrary to orders;—& John Collins 1st for being absent without leave—2nd for behaveing in an unbecoming manner at the Ball last night—3dly for Speaking in a language last night after his return tending to bring into disrespect the orders of the Commanding officer."

—William Clark, orderly book entry, May 17, 1804

In St. Louis on the early afternoon of March 9, 1804, a small crowd that included Meriwether Lewis and most of the French-speaking residents of the town gathered to witness a ceremony at the ramshackle wooden building serving as the government center for the Upper Louisiana Territory. Captain Amos Stoddard of the U.S. Army, acting as the diplomatic agent of both the United States and France, and Carlos Dehault Delassus, the Spanish official who had continued to administer the remote region during the brief period when it was under French sovereignty, formally signed the documents transferring Upper Louisiana to the United States. In an address the following day, Stoddard informed the residents that they were no longer subjects of a king but citizens of "a great community; the powers of whose Government are circumscribed and defined by charter, and the liberty of the citizen extended and secured," and he went on to instruct them on their new rights and duties.[1]

For the next seven months, while the Corps of Discovery toiled its way up the Missouri River, Stoddard served as the interim governor of Upper Louisiana, working to ease the anxieties of the inhabitants about American rule, maintain peace with the Indians, and sort out the maze of conflicting land claims inherited from the previous regime. Similarly, other Army officers, supported by detachments of troops, took possession of New Orleans and smaller settlements scattered throughout the eastern and southern portion of the vast Louisiana Purchase. In much of the region, they constituted the sole governmental authority until civilian territorial officials eventually superseded them.

The military role in the occupation of the Louisiana Purchase suggests a central fact about the U.S. regular army in the age of Jefferson: It was primarily a frontier police force rather than a disciplined professional army geared to foreign war. Its principal duties were preserving order on the Indian frontiers and international borders, extending governmental authority into newly acquired territories, and enforcing controversial federal laws. By the standard of today's armed forces, the Army was miniscule. During 1798–1800, when John Adams and the conservative Federalists waged an undeclared naval war against revolutionary France, the Army reached an authorized level of more than 12,000 officers and men. However, Thomas Jefferson and his Democratic Republican supporters considered a large standing army to be both an economic burden and a potential danger to liberty. In 1802 they reduced its strength to 3,287, including a commissioned officer corps of only 191.

A portion of the tiny peacetime force, comprising most of those units designated as artillery, occupied seacoast fortifications at port cities along the Atlantic seaboard, designed to repel a European invader. The greatest part of the army, however, was dispersed at isolated garrisons in the vast area west of the Appalachian Mountains—an archipelago of tiny islets strewn across thousands of miles of remote frontier. At the end of 1804, the largest concentrations of troops were at New Orleans (375) and Detroit (220). The remainder of the Army garrisoned forty-one posts spread from the Maine coast to the Louisiana-Texas border, only four of which contained more than 100 officers and men. The typical military post consisted of a handful of wooden buildings grouped around a small parade ground and surrounded by a log stockade, located in a clearing on the bank of a western river.

In the upper ranks of this far-flung army stood a small group of middle-aged veterans of the Revolutionary War who had learned their trade by practice, in the camps of George Washington's Continental Army. Representative of these men was Jacob Kingsbury, a Connecticut farmer's son who at age nineteen had enlisted as a private early in the Revolution. After five years of wartime service, he rose to ensign, the Army's lowest commissioned rank. Though he was discharged at the end of the war, he seized the first opportunity to resume his military career by accepting an appointment in the First American Regiment formed in 1784–85, the original unit from which the U.S. regular army would grow. He remained on duty for thirty more years, usually commanding frontier posts, and culminated his service as a colonel in the War of 1812, when he supervised the defense of the Connecticut coastline against British naval raids. Discharged for a second time in 1815, he appealed to the secretary of war for relief, plaintively explaining that he had been, "at the advanced age of sixty, turned out upon the world destitute of support" after a military career of more than forty years, "which is longer than any other officer or soldier of the United States."[2]

The middle- and lower-ranking officers of the Jeffersonian army were younger men in their twenties and thirties. Most had entered the Army during the 1790s, when it had expanded to deal with Indian troubles in the West and the prospect of war with Britain and France. Since political influence lubricated the Army appointment process, many were members of politically prominent families and close relatives of high-ranking Revolutionary figures. Meriwether Lewis, for example, was the son of a Continental Army officer, and William Clark's two older brothers had been Revolutionary heroes. Beginning in 1795, the Army provided some training to cadets and junior officers at a small artillery post on the bluffs overlooking the Hudson River at West Point, New York, and Congress officially established the U.S. Military Academy there in 1802. This school long remained on shaky ground, however, and it produced only forty-five graduates during Jefferson's presidency, many of whom did not continue in the Army. In the absence of systematic professional training, the great majority of junior officers acquired whatever military knowledge they possessed informally, by reading military manuals, drilling small detachments of troops, and observing the conduct of other officers in garrison and on the march.

In contrast to the long-term Revolutionary veterans in the senior grades, the careers of most middle-ranking and junior officers were brief. Disillusioned with garrison duty or unable to adjust to the minimal professional standards of the early Army, many resigned after a few years or even months, and others were forced out in the frequent reductions and reorganizations. Lewis and Clark, whose careers spanned twelve and seven years respectively, would qualify as seasoned veterans compared to many of their comrades-in-arms.

A yawning social chasm separated the army's enlisted men from the officer corps. Most of the privates and noncommissioned officers were farm workers, laborers, and artisans who had signed up for economic reasons in the eastern states. About one-fifth were immigrants, mainly from Ireland, and a few African Americans were scattered through the ranks.

Low pay ($5 a month for privates), chronic shortages of supplies and clothing, and unhealthy living conditions at frontier posts produced low morale and disciplinary problems. Desertion plagued the Army after the Revolution, though it seems to have abated somewhat in the early nineteenth century. The officers reacted to unrest in the ranks with a rigid code of corporal punishment, modeled after the draconian measures of the British and other European standing armies. Whipping up to one hundred lashes was the most common penalty prescribed by courts-martial. Other punishments included branding or tattooing with the letter designating the crime, repeatedly running the gauntlet between lines of soldiers wielding sticks or ramrods, and degrading ceremonies in which offenders were drummed out of the service at bayonet point with a noose around their necks after having their heads shaved. Even the most dedicated soldiers had little hope of higher rank, as promotions into the officer corps were rare in peacetime.

Fort Washington, Ohio, was a typical western fort, built in 1789, where Cincinnati now stands. Engraving from *Sketches and Statistics of Cincinnati* by Charles Cist, p. 44. From the collection of the Wisconsin Historical Society (WHi 4534).

During the early 1790s, the Army fought a brutal wilderness war against an alliance of Indian tribes centered in the present state of Ohio; in proportion to the numbers engaged it was perhaps the deadliest conflict in the Army's long history. This war ended in 1794, after General Anthony Wayne defeated the tribes in the Battle of Fallen Timbers, and for the next seventeen years the Army saw no combat whatsoever. Therefore, most regulars spent their careers in routine garrison duty. Fairly typical of the garrisons was Fort Defiance, established on the Maumee River in northwestern Ohio after Wayne's victory. A young Harvard-educated Army surgeon, Joseph G. Andrews, was stationed there in 1795, and his diary offers a window into peacetime Army life as Lewis and Clark probably experienced it. According to his monthly tabulations, the number of residents ranged between 68 and 166, including 5 to 8 commissioned officers and 55 to 149 enlisted men. The civilian residents included several women—mainly soldiers' wives and laundresses or the mistresses of officers, as no officers' wives are mentioned—one child, two supply contractors' agents, and an interpreter. In addition, the fort received many visitors: traders, delegations of Indians, and whites redeemed from Indian captivity in the aftermath of the recent war.

Fort Defiance was near forts that had been occupied since the Revolution by British troops, and Indian-white violence continued to flare in the surrounding forests. Thus military readiness was probably greater than at posts in more tranquil areas. Andrews's journal mentions evening parades and the punishment of enlisted men for derelictions of duty. One court-martial found two soldiers guilty of putting their muskets aside and sitting down while on guard and sentenced each to receive one hundred lashes. Desertion was a problem at Fort Defiance, but the isolation of the post in the midst of Indian Country seems to have kept it in check. When a private deserted in November 1795, the officers offered two Shawnee Indians a reward of $10 for capturing him alive and $20 for his scalp. One of the warriors returned the following day with the soldier's scalp and collected the reward as well as "many compliments from the officers."[3]

Andrews's journal describes considerable socializing among officers, civilians, and Indians. The officers spent their leisure time gardening, hunting, fishing, and visiting nearby Indian camps. On one occasion Andrews and another officer "raised & joined in a dance with the Tawney Ladies & Gentlemen."[4] The officers' social life revolved around the evening meal, and Andrews recorded the surprisingly diverse fare: corned beef, pork, chicken, fish, and wild game, as well as vegetables from the officers' gardens. Frequent allusions to heavy drinking and womanizing indicate that the officers cultivated a free-wheeling style of life. Andrews appears to have quarreled with a major over a woman, and he mentions the departure in October of the major and "Madam pro tem." Sexual relations between officers and Indian women seem to have been common. Late in December, a Delaware chief informed the post artillery officer, Lieutenant Piercy S. Pope, that his "Lady had that morning introduced to the world a young artillerist." When the officers applied for the "usual fee" on such occasions—a gallon of wine—Pope ungallantly denied paternity, "his first connection being in May last; & not withstanding all that could be said on the subject, would not be persuaded that it was possible for a child to be born in less than 9 [months] from the conception."[5]

For most officers, military service did not constitute an exclusive career, devoted to the undivided pursuit of professional duties. Pay was paltry—Army captains earned $633 a year, less than the salaries of junior clerks in the War Department—and officers lacking independent fortunes needed outside income to maintain a "respectable" lifestyle. Service in the West offered abundant opportunities for land speculation, trade, and other economic ventures. While at

Fort Michilimackinac on the Upper Great Lakes, for example, medical officer Francis LeBarron dabbled in the fur trade, serving as an agent of John Jacob Astor's American Fur Company, and operated a distillery and mill; he also held the office of civil judge. Jacob Kingsbury's holdings included farms in Connecticut, town lots in Marietta and Cincinnati, Ohio, and extensive western lands. Inevitably, the isolation of the garrisons and the haziness of ethical standards tempted some commanders to boost their income through fraud or the exploitation of enlisted men. In 1797, reports that officers were using unpaid soldier labor to raise crops for their personal profit led the Army's senior general to remind his subordinates that the "soldier by voluntary compact, becomes the servant of the state, but not the slave of an individual" and to require a wage of a third of a dollar a day for work performed outside of military duty.[6]

The officers of the early Army were a prickly and quarrelsome lot. The officer was rare whose career was not punctuated with bitter altercations with his comrades-in-arms, and a captain's description of Fort Norfolk would fit many garrisons: "Quarrelling slandering, Arresting & threatening of Arrests is common, & probably more on account of individual animosity than public good."[7] A number of factors contributed to this dissension: the diverse origins of the officers, who came from a wide range of regional and social backgrounds; the frequent expansions and contractions of the army and the brevity of most military careers, which retarded the growth of strong group loyalties; and the absence of a clearly established code of professional conduct. Perhaps the most important source of tension, however, was the prevailing ideal of military honor.

Drawn from the aristocratic values of contemporary European armies, honor had at its core an obsession with personal reputation—an officer's image in the eyes of his comrades-in-arms. Honor could require an officer to obey faithfully the orders of his superiors, eagerly seek distinction in combat, and take a paternalistic interest in the welfare of the enlisted men. It could also require him to resent suspected insults to himself, his regiment, or his profession, jealously guard the prerogatives of his rank, and maintain an ostentatious style of life appropriate to his station. In particular, honor demanded that an officer demonstrate unflinching physical courage on each and every occasion, and it led to touchy, individualistic behavior that often clashed with formal regulations.

The most dramatic feature of military honor was the habit of dueling. Although clearly banned by military law, dueling was widespread in the early Army and unofficially condoned by high commanders, who saw it as a way to settle quickly officers' disputes without the expense and inconvenience of courts-martial. In fact, reluctance to duel could bring an officer disgrace. In 1799 or 1800, a court-martial acquitted Major Adam Hoops of an assault on Captain Frederick Frye. The court did not deny that Hoops had struck Frye with a cane on a New York City street but considered the blow too light to be a violation of law. It then issued a lecture on honor—"the *Vital principle*, of every *military Establishment*" that should be "an article in the *Religion* of every *true Soldier*"— and chastised Frye for failing to demand satisfaction.[8] While only a minority of duels resulted in deaths, they almost certainly cost more officers' lives than did combat in the early decades of the regular Army.

A cherished principle of today's military profession holds that officers should avoid involvement in partisan politics and commit themselves to politically neutral national service. However, no such barrier separated the officer corps of the Jeffersonian army from the civilian political world. Officers of all ranks held strong partisan views and frequently engaged in civilian political matters. During the 1790s and early 1800s, the Army was a stronghold of the conservative Federalist Party. For one thing, nearly all the officers had been appointed by the Federalist administrations of George Washington and John Adams, which had considered political loyalty in making selections. Moreover, Federalist policy favored a strong central government and a relatively large standing army, views naturally popular in the officer corps. On taking office in 1801, Thomas Jefferson and his supporters expressed concern about the political reliability of the officer corps, but they attempted no major purge of their opponents. Late in his administration, however, when rising tensions with Great Britain led to an expansion of the Army, Jefferson appointed Democratic Republicans to the new officers' slots, and by the War of 1812 the Army had taken on a strongly Jeffersonian cast.

In particular, the Army's role as a frontier police force encouraged the blending of politics and military life. As noted earlier in this essay, the Army was involved deeply in the administration of the Louisiana Purchase and other newly acquired territories. Moreover, officers in the West routinely held such civil offices as local judge, postmaster, customs collector, land-office official, and Indian agent. Throughout the Jeffersonian era, the Army policed the thinly populated borderlands with Spanish Texas and Florida, politically unstable regions where American expansionists posing as patriotic revolutionaries continually sought to expel Spanish rule. Officers at the remote border posts, most of whom strongly favored expansionism, were enmeshed deeply in the plotting as well as in diplomatic negotiations with the harried Spanish authorities. At times their actions might well have plunged the nation into war.

The career of James Wilkinson, the early republic's most notorious intriguer, illustrates in an extreme way the political connections of the early officer corps. A veteran of the

General James Wilkinson, 1757–1825, in an engraving made from a 1797 portrait by Charles Willson Peale. From the collection of the Wisconsin Historical Society (WHi 4533).

Revolution, Wilkinson entered the regular Army in 1791, was promoted to brigadier general the following year, and continued in service until 1815, during most of which time he was the Army's highest ranking officer. At the same time, he was a double agent who received payments from Spain in exchange for his advice and influence in aiding Spain's efforts, first to pry Kentucky away from the Union and later to hold on to Texas and Florida. Charming, even charismatic, but intensely ambitious, Wilkinson engaged throughout his career in politically charged quarrels with other commanders. "There is a great division among the officers of the army concerning him," a major wrote in 1809. "Some are his warm advocates, whilst others are his deadly enemies."[9]

Although closely tied to the Federalist Party during the 1790s, Wilkinson quickly shifted his allegiance to the Democratic Republicans after Jefferson's election. In 1803–4, he served as co-commissioner for the transfer of New Orleans and the southern portion of the Louisiana Purchase to the United States. Appointed governor of the Upper Louisiana Territory in 1805, he soon became entangled in local political disputes, which centered mainly on disputed land claims, and territorial politics polarized into pro-Wilkinson and anti-Wilkinson factions. According to a territorial judge, Wilkinson and his officers threatened, challenged, arrested, and assaulted their opponents, and the judge personally feared for his life. Although he was repeatedly investigated for his Spanish connection and other shady dealings, Wilkinson managed to evade disclosure, and he responded to his critics by challenging them to duels.

Wilkinson's most notorious venture was the web of intrigue known as the Burr Conspiracy. Aaron Burr, Jefferson's former vice president, apparently hatched this murky and shifting plot in collusion with Wilkinson. Their goal seems to have been a private invasion of Spanish Mexico and West Florida and, less certainly, separation of a part of the trans-Appalachian West from the Union. A substantial portion of the officers stationed on the Lower Mississippi River were drawn into this plot and a related plot to launch an expedition against Spanish territory, perhaps financing it by seizing the banks and shipping in New Orleans. While commanding on the southwestern border late in 1806, Wilkinson apparently got cold feet about the scheme and decided to betray his fellow conspirator. He wrote Jefferson, warning that a powerful conspiracy was afoot to invade and subjugate Mexico, and he then rushed to New Orleans to quash the movement before Burr's expected arrival from the east. Professing shock that Army officers were involved, the wily general allowed some to clear themselves with a loyalty oath and held others in arrest. Wilkinson's action, together with a presidential proclamation denouncing the movement, destroyed whatever chance the plot had of success, and Burr was arrested and tried for treason. With characteristic guile, Wilkinson testified against Burr, while preventing his own role from coming to light.

Dispersed across half a continent and absorbed in frontier police duties, the little army of the early republic was a flawed institution—rigidly stratified by rank and privilege, plagued by low morale, and led by a collection of quarrelsome individualists who remained tied to the civilian political world. Nevertheless military force constituted the main instrument available to Thomas Jefferson in his efforts to forge a territorial empire in the interior of North America, and he turned to the Army in organizing the Corps of Discovery. From its inception, the expedition was a military enterprise, commanded by Army officers, recruited mainly from the Army's enlisted ranks, and subject to the rigorous discipline and harsh punishments of the regular service.

Despite the unpromising soil from which it grew, the Corps of Discovery functioned effectively as a military unit in the face of daunting adversity. One factor making for success was the administration's selection of personnel; Jefferson acted with great care in choosing the expedition's leaders, and he allowed the captains considerable latitude in recruiting their subordinates. Rather than a cross section of the rank and file, the expedition was composed of young, active, and highly motivated volunteers, some of whom had been inspired to enlist specifically by the prospect of western adventure. A second factor was the ability of the officers to lead by example rather than by threats and, after establishing their authority early in the expedition, to dispense altogether with the courts-martial and floggings so common in stationary garrisons. Probably the most important factor in the expedition's success, however, was circumstantial—the cohesion and comradeship that developed naturally from the grandness of the mission and the hardships endured. In a unit of about thirty men, charged with the awesome task of projecting the nation's power across a vast continent and faced with constant danger and privation, the rigid rank structure of the Army proved both unworkable and unnecessary, and Lewis and Clark transformed it gradually into a more flexible system based on trust, teamwork, and individual enterprise.

Notes

1   Amos Stoddard, Address to the People of Upper Louisiana, March 10, 1804, "Transfer of Upper Louisiana: Papers of Captain Amos Stoddard," *Glimpses of the Past* 2 (1934–35): 87–91.

2   Jacob Kingsbury to William H. Crawford, April 16, 1816, in James R. Jacobs, *Tarnished Warrior: Major-General James Wilkinson* (New York: Macmillan, 1938), 315.

3   Richard C. Knopf, ed., *A Surgeon's Mate at Fort Defiance: The Journal of Joseph Gardner Andrews* (Columbus: Ohio Historical Society, 1957), 77.

4   Ibid., 53.

5   Ibid., 69, 87.

6   General Orders, May 22, 1797, reissued July 15, 1808, file W-1808, Letters Received by the Secretary of War, Unregistered Series, 1789–1861, Records of the Office of the Secretary of War, RG 107, National Archives.

7   Capt. Benjamin Forsyth to Secretary of War, September 16, 1811, file F-112(5), Letters Received by the Secretary of War, Registered Series, 1801–1870, Records of the Office of the Secretary of War, RG 107, National Archives.

8   Decision of a court-martial of which Lt. Col. William S. Smith was president, n.d. [1799 or 1800], Alexander Hamilton Papers, Library of Congress.

9   Major John Fuller to his wife, July 28, 1809, John Fuller Papers, Ohio Historical Society, Columbus.

Suggested Readings

Caldwell, Norman W. "The Frontier Army Officer, 1794–1814." *Mid America* 37 (January 1955): 101–28.

Crackel, Theodore J. *Mr. Jefferson's Army: Political and Social Reform of the Military Establishment, 1801–1809.* New York: New York University Press, 1987.

Jacobs, James Ripley. *The Beginning of the U.S. Army, 1783–1812.* Princeton, N.J.: Princeton University Press, 1947.

———. *Tarnished Warrior: Major-General James Wilkinson.* New York: Macmillan, 1938.

Skelton, William B. *An American Profession of Arms: The Army Officer Corps, 1784–1861.* Lawrence: University Press of Kansas, 1992.

Stagg, J. C. A. "Soldiers in Peace and War: Comparative Perspectives on the Recruitment of the United States Army, 1802–1815." *William and Mary Quarterly* 3d ser., 57, no. 1 (January 2000): 79–120.

The Geopolitical Context of the Expedition

James E. Lewis, Jr.
Kalamazoo College

Your mission has been communicated to the Ministers here from France, Spain & Great Britain, and through them to their governments: and such assurances given them as to it's objects as we trust will satisfy them. the country of Louisiana having been ceded by Spain to France, the passport you have from the Minister of France, the representation of the present sovereign of the country, will be a protection with all it's subjects: And that from the Minister of England will entitle you to the friendly aid of any traders of that allegiance with whom you may happen to meet.

—Thomas Jefferson, instructions to Meriwether Lewis

I now have lost all hope of the waters of this river [the Marias] ever extending to N Latitude 50° though I still hope and think it more probable that both white earth river and milk river extend as far north as latd. 50°.

—Meriwether Lewis, journal entry, July 22, 1806

On successive Tuesdays in mid-January 1803, President Thomas Jefferson sent important messages to Congress. The first asked the Senate to advise and consent to dispatching James Monroe on a special diplomatic mission to Paris to address the crisis caused by France's reacquisition of the vast province of Louisiana from Spain. The second called upon both houses of Congress to fund the expedition across Louisiana up the Missouri River, "even to the Western ocean," that would shortly be known as the Lewis and Clark Expedition. These two requests were hardly unrelated. The uncertain, overlapping, and evolving diplomatic claims to western North America formed a key element in the geopolitical context of the expedition. At the same time, the relationship between Monroe's mission and the Lewis and Clark Expedition was not as simple as hindsight might suggest. To see the mission and the expedition as twin expressions of that confident expectation of the nation's continental future that would later be called "manifest destiny" is, quite simply, to misunderstand them.[1]

From its initial planning in January 1803 to its eventual return to St. Louis in September 1806, the expedition unfolded within a geopolitical context that was crowded and unstable. East of the Rocky Mountains, France, Spain, and Great Britain asserted claims or exercised influence. West of the Rockies, Lewis and Clark traveled through some of the most hotly contested lands in North America, as Spain, Great Britain, the United States, and Russia had each staked a claim in the region. Everywhere they went, moreover, the members of the expedition would pass through lands controlled or contested by one or more of the dozens of Indian nations between the Mississippi River and the Pacific Ocean. But the geopolitical context of the expedition extended far beyond western North America to include eastern Asia and western Europe. Across the Pacific was China, whose teas, silks, porcelains, and spices fueled hopes of finding a more direct and less costly trade route.

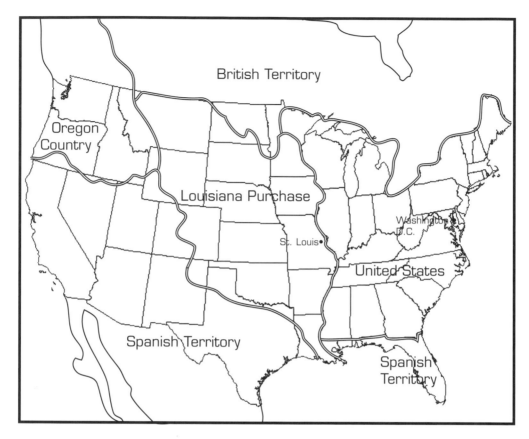

This map shows the approximate areas of the present-day United States that were claimed by different countries about the time of the Louisiana Purchase.

Across the Atlantic were France and Great Britain, whose descent into renewed warfare in the spring of 1803 meant new problems and opportunities for American policymakers.

Changing circumstances dramatically altered Jefferson's, and Lewis and Clark's, understanding of the context of the expedition over time. By examining their thinking at key points from early 1803 to late 1806, it becomes apparent that the expedition fit within a far more limited vision of national expansion than the concept of Manifest Destiny would suggest.

When Jefferson first proposed an exploring expedition to the Pacific in January 1803, the crisis over the French reacquisition of Louisiana framed his thinking. Colonized by France, Louisiana had been transferred to Spain in 1763. In 1800, the two powers had signed a new treaty restoring the province to France. In neither 1763 nor 1800 had they actually specified Louisiana's boundaries. But, in 1800, the province generally was believed to include the entire Mississippi watershed west of the river, the so-called island of New Orleans east of the river, and perhaps more of the Gulf Coast extending west toward Texas and east toward Florida. For Jefferson, his cabinet members, and many of their contemporaries, what was most alarming about the impending French return to Louisiana was the threat that it posed to the union of the American states east of the river, not to the prospect of future expansion west of the river. French control over the vast expanses of Louisiana west of the river mattered far less than French possession of New Orleans and the eastern bank of the Mississippi from the thirty-first parallel to the Gulf of Mexico (the Florida Parishes of modern Louisiana).

With New Orleans and the mouth of the Mississippi in French hands, Napoleon Bonaparte would have had the power to stop the trade down the river from Ohio, Kentucky, Tennessee, and the rest of the country west of the Appalachians.

"By holding the key to the commerce of the Mississippi," Secretary of State James Madison explained, France could "command the interests and attachments of the Western portion of the United States." With such a powerful source of influence over the economy of the West, France would have had the leverage to "controul the Atlantic portion also; or if that [could not] be done, to seduce the [West] into a separate Government, and a close alliance with herself." The American consul in New Orleans confirmed these fears. "No dependence ought to be placed on a majority of [western settlers]," Daniel Clark warned. They would leave the union "if even very slight advantages were held out" by the new owners of New Orleans.[2]

The administration's concerns shaped the instructions that Madison prepared for Monroe and Robert R. Livingston, Monroe's negotiating partner in France, in the spring of 1803. At no time before Monroe and Livingston agreed to the Louisiana Purchase in April did Jefferson and Madison express any interest in acquiring territory west of the river. The most that they ever hoped to purchase was all of the French and Spanish lands from New Orleans east (including both West and East Florida). They also would have accepted just New Orleans and West Florida (to either the Pearl or Perdido River), West Florida alone, or New Orleans alone. Madison even suggested at one point that Monroe and Livingston could simply purchase "space enough for a large commercial town and its appurtenances, on the banks of the river" near its mouth; there, the government could build, from scratch, its own emporium for western commerce.[3]

The initial plans for the Lewis and Clark Expedition, thus, were made at a time when Jefferson was more concerned about the present stability of the union east of the Mississippi than its future expansion west of the Mississippi. These plans also were made at a time when the formal transfer of Louisiana from Spain to France appeared imminent. Accordingly, Jefferson did not seem worried by the refusal of the Spanish minister in Washington to provide a passport for the expedition. A passport from the French minister—"the representation of the present sovereign of the country"—was expected to suffice to protect the expedition from governmental interference in the thousands of miles, going and coming, of its exploration of the Missouri River. A second passport from the British minister would provide additional protection and assistance if the expedition encountered British officials or traders. Beyond the Rockies, the expedition seemed unlikely to meet with the officials of any recognized nation.[4]

In the summer of 1803, Lewis stopped in Washington for his final consultation with Jefferson before heading west to lead the expedition. He reached the capital in mid-June, just as the first reports of Monroe's mission arrived from France. Contrary to all intentions or expectations, the fruits of this diplomacy seemed likely to be the purchase of all of Louisiana, as well as New Orleans. Warning him to keep the news "a perfect secret," Lewis apprised Clark on June 19 "that the whole of that immense country wartered by the Mississippi and it's tributary streams" soon would be sold to the United States. Official confirmation of the purchase reached Washington in early July, just a few days before Lewis set out for the West.[5]

Monroe and Livingston had agreed to the Louisiana Purchase even though they knew that they had exceeded their instructions. "Could we have procur'd a part of the territory," Monroe informed Madison, "we shod. never have thot. of getting the whole." But Napoleon would sell the province only in its entirety. Monroe and Livingston could only hope that Jefferson and Madison would see the same benefits from purchasing the whole territory that they did. To their great relief, the news of the purchase gave the president and the cabinet "much pleasure," according to the secretary of state.[6]

James Monroe was the fifth president of the United States, serving in that role from 1817 to 1825. In his earlier political career, he helped negotiate the Louisiana Purchase along with Robert R. Livingston. Steel engraving by C. Holl after Gilbert Stuart. Missouri Historical Society Photograph and Print Collection.

But the future of the vast new acquisition beyond the river remained undecided. Many Americans believed that this territory could not possibly be added to the union. Jefferson's Federalist opponents began arguing almost immediately that the entirety of Louisiana west of the river should be traded to Spain for all of its holdings east of the river, leaving the United States with New Orleans, the Floridas, and a permanent western border at the Mississippi. Jefferson quickly decided against this course. But, even before Lewis left Washington, the president had devised a plan that would have delayed white settlement of Louisiana for generations. Under his plan, all of Louisiana north of the thirty-first parallel would be reserved for the Indians. No more white settlement would be permitted in the region; any whites who already lived there— French, Spanish, or American—would be moved east of the river. The eastern Indians would be encouraged to exchange their lands for new lands beyond the river. This plan could solve the "Indian problem," open millions of acres east of the Mississippi to white settlement, and prevent Americans from streaming across the river, where they would prove difficult for either the federal or state governments to control. Jefferson's calculation that it would take "half a century" for Americans to "[fill] up all the vacant country on this side" of the river makes clear the limits to his continentalism on the verge of Lewis's departure.[7]

In time, Jefferson and the cabinet rejected this plan. When Lewis set out from Washington in early July 1803, however, he not only knew of Jefferson's plan but also had been charged by the president with determining its practicality. Lewis spent part of the ensuing winter investigating whether the current inhabitants of Louisiana could be persuaded to "withdraw" east of the river. He believed that most of the settlers could be "prevailed upon to come into this measure," though he worried that their inability to hold slaves on the east side of the river (where slavery was banned by the

Northwest Ordinance) would present an obstacle. As he prepared for the expedition in late 1803 and early 1804, Lewis easily could have expected that, for decades into the future, the acquisition of Louisiana by the United States would lead to less, not more, white settlement west of the Mississippi.[8]

In the short term, the Louisiana Purchase may have presented more obstacles than advantages for the expedition. Originally, Jefferson had acted as though he could safely ignore Spain's opposition to the expedition as long as he obtained a passport from France, which would soon assume control over the province. But French officials did not arrive in New Orleans or St. Louis as quickly as expected. Having sold Louisiana to the United States, moreover, Napoleon had no real interest in incurring the cost and difficulties of sending someone to take possession. At the same time, the Spanish government insisted that the Louisiana Purchase was invalid since its 1800 treaty with France explicitly stated that the province could not be sold or transferred to another party. Though justice was clearly on its side, Spain was simply too weak to oppose its French ally on this matter. But it was not too weak to obstruct American plans. Spanish officials refused to turn the province over to the United States directly, and they blocked Lewis's initial plan to set out in the fall of 1803 by refusing him permission to enter their territory.

It was not until December 1803 that the formal transfer of power from Spain to France to the United States took place in New Orleans and not until March 1804 that a similar event occurred in St. Louis. Two months later, the Lewis and Clark Expedition set sail up the Missouri from St. Charles. The geopolitical context of the expedition had changed dramatically in the fourteen months since Jefferson's initial message to Congress. France no longer figured into American thinking at all. Spain could once again be ignored, at least east of the Rockies, after having unexpectedly become a problem for a number of months. In contrast, the many native tribes west of the Mississippi assumed a new significance. "Being now become sovereigns of the country," Jefferson informed Lewis in January 1804, "we are authorised to propose to [the Indians] in direct terms the institution of commerce with them." In what was, perhaps surprisingly, the only meaningful revision of Lewis's original instructions, Jefferson directed him to inform the Indians "that their late fathers the Spaniards" had withdrawn their troops, abandoned their posts and lands, and "surrendered" their subjects and "that henceforward we become their fathers and friends."[9]

Great Britain also attained a new importance as a result of recent developments. Having purchased Louisiana, the United States would now need to fix a boundary with British Canada from the Lake of the Woods to the Rockies. Jefferson originally had shown far less interest in the northern than in the southern part of the Missouri watershed. British explorers already had proven that there was no easy transit across the Rockies north of the Missouri; there might be a simple portage somewhere between the Missouri's southern branches and the Rio Grande, however. The Louisiana Purchase gave the United States a solid claim to the entire Mississippi watershed, the northern limits of which could form at least the basis for a new boundary with British Canada. Jefferson recognized that as a result of the purchase, it had become "interesting to fix with precision by celestial observations the longitude & latitude of the sources" of the rivers that flowed into the Missouri and Mississippi. He did not expect Lewis and Clark to satisfy this desire in full, but they could provide valuable information for determining "the contour of our new limits."[10]

Even before the Louisiana Purchase raised these new issues, Jefferson had directed Lewis's attention to a problem in the old northern border. By the Treaty of Paris of 1783, the boundary with British Canada ran west from the Lake of the

Woods until it struck the Mississippi. But the treaty had been written with only a vague idea of the geography west of the Great Lakes. In the two decades since 1783, it had become fairly clear that a line running west from the Lake of the Woods (at almost fifty degrees north latitude) could not strike the Mississippi since its headwaters did not extend that far north. Jefferson never specifically redirected Lewis and Clark's interest from the "most Northern source of the Missisipi" to the most northern source of the Missouri. But, during the return journey, the explorers decided that Lewis should make a side trip up the Marias River to see if it reached as far north as fifty degrees. As Clark later explained: "The reason why it was wished that Maria's river should extend to 50° north was that … it was hoped that a river parallel to [the Mississippi] would go far enough north to satisfy the treaty boundary." If it could be shown that a branch of the Missouri extended as far north as the Lake of the Woods, Lewis and Clark reasoned, the United States could argue that the boundary with British Canada should run west from the lake at least as far as that river, rather than south from the lake to the Mississippi's source. While the Marias could not serve this purpose, Lewis believed, correctly, that the Milk River could.[11]

When the returning expedition, as Lewis tellingly put it, "reach[ed] the United States" in September 1806, the world looked quite different from when it had left twenty-eight months earlier. The war that had begun between Great Britain and France in the spring of 1803—a war that had helped to precipitate the sale of all of Louisiana—now threatened to engulf the United States. Having destroyed the French fleet in October 1805, the British navy ruled the ocean. Great Britain's efforts to use its naval power to inflict indirect damage on France meant that more and more American ships were falling prey to what seemed to Americans to be unreasonable limits on neutral trade. About the time that Lewis and Clark arrived in St. Louis, James Monroe and William Pinkney began negotiations in London in an unsuccessful attempt to stem the tide of abuses that seemed certain to lead to war.[12]

The danger of war appeared even more immediate on the United States' uncertain southwestern border. In September 1806, U.S. troops under General James Wilkinson and Spanish forces under Colonel Simón de Herrera eyed each other warily across a remote wilderness along the Sabine River. Wilkinson's orders were to prevent any Spanish encroachment east of the Sabine; Herrera's orders were to remain east of the river and check any American advance west of the Arroyo Hondo. It was not only these officers who knew that their conflicting orders meant war; their superiors in Washington, D.C., and Chihuahua, Mexico, knew as well. With American and Spanish negotiators trying to work out a treaty in Madrid, however, all parties were reluctant to initiate a war over a relatively small piece of territory miles from any real settlement. By late October, the two commanders in the field had arranged a compromise whereby the Americans would remain east of the Arroyo Hondo and the Spanish would remain west of the Sabine, with the intervening territory treated as "neutral ground" until the final boundary could be settled by treaty.

Wilkinson had decided to violate his orders and offer a compromise, in part, because he had received indications that former vice president Aaron Burr was preparing to head down the Mississippi with perhaps as many as seven thousand men. Both the precise goal of the so-called Burr Conspiracy and the exact role of General Wilkinson in it remain elusive to this day. There is no question, however, that during the fall of 1806, just as Lewis and Clark arrived in St. Louis, the vague rumors about Burr that had circulated for more than a year began to solidify around a single idea—that he intended to divide the union. Precisely how Burr might accomplish this end remained unclear. But many observers, including Jefferson, believed that Burr's calculations were the same as Napoleon's four years earlier. They expected Burr to try to capture New Orleans, control the mouth of the Mississippi, and exert economic pressure on the settlers west of the Appalachians in order to pry them from the union. In Jefferson's view, Burr hoped to "extend his empire to the Alleghany, [by] seizing on New Orleans as the instrument of compulsion for our western States." Burr's "empire" presumably also would have encompassed the entire Mississippi watershed west of the river—the recently acquired Louisiana Territory. Throughout the fall of 1806 and the ensuing winter, the Burr Conspiracy provoked concern in and out of government. In the end, little came of Burr's mysterious enterprise.[13]

When Lewis and Clark returned to St. Louis, they might also have detected a change in official thinking about the future of Louisiana. Through much of their absence, Jefferson had seemed committed to his earlier ideas about slowing white settlement west of the Mississippi. He had appointed General Wilkinson as governor of Louisiana Territory (which confusingly included all of the purchase except the modern state of Louisiana) because he considered a military government more appropriate than a civil one for this vast region. As late as December 1805, moreover, Wilkinson still believed that Jefferson wanted to encourage the removal of the territory's white settlers, other than those in the immediate vicinity of St. Louis, "to any other quarter within our Limits." By then, however, Jefferson's thinking may already have changed. He apparently had abandoned his plan of removing white settlers east of the river and had stopped writing of the Mississippi as a long-term boundary between Indians and whites. And he had indicated in his second inaugural address that he was willing to imagine both the settlement of Upper Louisiana "by our own brethren and children" and its eventual incorporation into the union.[14]

The Lewis and Clark Expedition did not find an easier

route to the riches of China. Nor did it produce a rush of settlement into Upper Louisiana. Nor did it fix an unchallenge-
able American claim to either the northern reaches of the
Missouri watershed or the entirety of the Columbia River
basin. Occurring within a geopolitical context that changed
repeatedly and rapidly between the winter of 1803 and the fall
of 1806, neither the Lewis and Clark Expedition nor the
Louisiana Purchase guaranteed that the vast region west of
the Mississippi would become a part of the United States.
Even twenty years after Lewis and Clark's return, many
Americans doubted whether the Upper Missouri would ever
be settled and whether the Pacific Northwest should ever be
added to the union. Ultimately, the establishment of
American claims and the enthusiasm for American settlement
in this region required the new domestic and international
contexts of the 1820s, 1830s, and 1840s. In these new contexts,
it was the mythic force of the expedition in American public
consciousness, rather than its actual impact on American
diplomatic claims, that proved most significant.

Notes

1   Jefferson, "Message to Congress," January 18, 1803, in Donald T. Jackson, ed., *Letters of the Lewis and Clark Expedition, with Related Documents, 1783–1854*, 2d ed., 2 vols. (Urbana: University of Illinois Press, 1978), 1:13.

2   Madison to Robert R. Livingston and James Monroe, March 2, 1803, *The Papers of James Madison*, eds. Robert J. Brugger, et al. Secretary of State Series, 6 vols. to date (Charlottesville: University Press of Virginia, 1986–), 4:366; Daniel Clark to Madison, April 27, 1803, in "Despatches from the United States Consulate in New Orleans, 1801–1803," *American Historical Review* 33 (January 1928): 340.

3   Madison to Livingston and Monroe, 4:377.

4   Jefferson, "Instructions to Lewis," June 20, 1803, in Donald T. Jackson, ed., *Letters of the Lewis and Clark Expedition, with Related Documents, 1783–1854*, 2d ed., 2 vols. (Urbana: University of Illinois Press, 1978), 1:61.

5   Ibid., Lewis to Clark, June 19, 1803, 1:59.

6   Monroe to Madison, May 14, 1803, *Papers of James Madison*, 4:610; Madison to Monroe, June 25, 1803, ibid., 5:117.

7   Jefferson to Du Pont de Nemours, November 1, 1803, *The Writings of Thomas Jefferson*, eds. Andrew A. Lipscomb and Albert Ellery Bergh, memorial edition, 20 vols. (Washington, D.C.: Thomas Jefferson Memorial Association, 1903–4), 10:423.

8   Lewis to Jefferson, December 28, 1803, *Letters of the Lewis and Clark Expedition*, 1:154.

9   Ibid., Jefferson to Lewis, January 22, 1804, 1:165.

10   Ibid., Jefferson to Lewis, November 16, 1803, 1:137.

11   Ibid., Jefferson, "Instructions to Lewis," June 20, 1803, 1:63; ibid., "The Nicholas Biddle Notes," c. April 1810, 2:544.

12   Lewis, journal entry, July 25, 1806, *The Journals of the Lewis and Clark Expedition*, ed. Gary E. Moulton, 12 vols. (Lincoln: University of Nebraska Press, 1983–99), 8:127.

13   Jefferson to Charles Clay, January 11, 1807, *Writings of Thomas Jefferson*, 11:133.

14   James Wilkinson to Jefferson, December 23, 1805, *Letters of the Lewis and Clark Expedition*, 1:274; Jefferson, "Second Inaugural Address," March 4, 1805, *Writings of Thomas Jefferson*, 3:378.

Suggested Readings

DeConde, Alexander. *This Affair of Louisiana*. New York: Charles Scribner's Sons, 1976.

Guiness, Ralph B. "The Purpose of the Lewis and Clark Expedition." *Mississippi Valley Historical Review* 20 (June 1933): 90–100.

Jackson, Donald T. *Thomas Jefferson and the Stony Mountains: Exploring the West from Monticello*. Urbana: University of Illinois Press, 1981.

Kaplan, Lawrence S. *Thomas Jefferson: Westward the Course of Empire*. Wilmington, Del.: SR Books, 1999.

Lyon, E. Wilson. *Louisiana in French Diplomacy, 1759–1804*. Norman: University of Oklahoma Press, 1934.

Onuf, Peter S. *Jefferson's Empire: The Language of American Nationhood*. Charlottesville: University Press of Virginia, 2000.

Tucker, Robert W., and David C. Hendrickson. *Empire of Liberty: The Statecraft of Thomas Jefferson*. New York: Oxford University Press, 1990.

Whitaker, Arthur Preston. *The Mississippi Question, 1795–1803: A Study in Trade, Politics, and Diplomacy*. New York: D. Appleton-Century Company, 1934.

A Journey's Beginning

The Corps of Discovery and the Diplomacy of Western Indian Affairs

J. Wendel Cox
University of Minnesota–Morris

In all your intercourse with the natives, treat them in the most friendly & conciliatory manner which their own conduct will admit; allay all jealousies as to the object of your journey, satisfy them of it's innocence, make them acquainted with the position, extent, character, peaceable & commercial dispositions of the U.S.[,] of our wish to be neighborly, friendly & useful to them, & of our disposition to a commercial intercourse with them; confer with them on the points most convenient as mutual emporiums, and the articles of most desireable interchange for them & us.

   —Thomas Jefferson, instructions to Meriwether Lewis

[Several Arikara leaders] promised to attend Strictly to what had been Said to them, and observed that they must trade with the Sieoux one more time to get guns and powder; that they had no guns or powder and had more horses than they had use for, after they got guns and powder that they would never again have anything to do with them &c. &c.

   —William Clark, journal entry, August 22, 1806

I.

The expedition of the Corps of Discovery was a physical journey, a mission for empire, commerce, and knowledge. It was also the beginning of another journey, one involving relationships between the United States and western Indian peoples begun with the meetings between Meriwether Lewis, William Clark, and the leaders and representatives of the peoples visited on the expedition's course. From its inception, the expedition had made diplomatic relationships with western Indians central to its objectives. As the United States acquired Louisiana from France, it also sought to bring the region's Indian peoples within its dominion and to describe the basis for their subsequent relationships. President Thomas Jefferson's instructions reflected the core elements of the relationship between the United States and Indian peoples from the expedition's travels to the present. He recognized the region's inhabitants, acknowledged their separate but circumscribed sovereignty, and admitted their prior claim to the land. And to this he added an obligation for the federal government to act as friend and protector to the peoples encompassed by the republic's newly enlarged boundaries.

During the latter half of the nineteenth century, when conquest, migration, and the relentless development of mining, ranching, and market-oriented agriculture transformed the West, these same principles were employed to secure tribal lands, erode tribal sovereignty, and subject Indian peoples to forced assimilation. Twentieth-century Indian peoples, building on the efforts of previous generations, responded by finding in the history of particular treaties, agreements, and executive orders, and in the persistence of their families and communities, the basis for contemporary tribal nations.

II.

For Jefferson, the West was essential to the American future. He envisioned it variously as a transcontinental link to the Pacific Ocean, home to an enlarged United States or other new republics, and, fleetingly, as a place for Indians removed from the eastern United States. But Jefferson also feared a European rival could jeopardize an American future in the West. Spain was an ideal neighbor, its still-extensive North American empire weak and its ability to resist the United States more and more dubious. France was a different matter, not solely for its own power: conflict between France and Britain might mean war in North America, and its resolution, most likely in Britain's favor, could see a British Louisiana. The United States would then face a British North America on its northern and western borders and perhaps the end to its desired western future. And so in these uncertain circumstances, Jefferson returned to his long-standing interest in an expedition to the West, now with an emphasis on a transcontinental route for American trade and the extension of an American presence.

While he contemplated these larger strategic interests, Jefferson remained mindful of the West's many Indian nations. The extension of American power would necessitate new relationships with distant tribes, and for the success of the transcontinental route, their alliance and trade. Such relationships were still more significant because Jefferson and others believed Britain also sought them, and British agents and their influence were widespread among the Indian nations of the Mississippi and Missouri Rivers. In the competition for western territories, Indians were crucial to American diplomacy.

Trade was considered an indispensable tool in diplomacy with Indian peoples, and Jefferson and his contemporaries believed it crucial to peace. Such conviction led to a succession

Jefferson peace-and-friendship medal like the ones that Lewis and Clark presented to Indian chiefs on their journey. They took three large medals, thirteen medium, and sixteen small ones. From the collection of the Jefferson National Expansion Memorial, National Park Service.

of laws, known as the Trade and Intercourse Acts, enacted between 1790 and 1834 to ensure a well-regulated Indian trade, to control movement into Indian lands, and to avoid unnecessary conflict. Such concerns also led to the creation of government-operated trading houses, established in 1796 and continuing until 1822, intended to supply Indian needs too important to leave to private interests. But trade was also a tool of power. As he planned the journey of the Corps of Discovery, Jefferson also instructed William Henry Harrison, governor of Indiana Territory, to extend trade on the most liberal terms possible, and in doing so, indebt Indian leaders, dispose them to sell tribal lands, and consequently extend an American presence to rival foreign pretensions in the West. In 1808, when reflecting on the conduct of Indian affairs in a letter to Meriwether Lewis, who had become governor of Missouri Territory, Jefferson reiterated the power of trade in Indian affairs, remarking that "commerce is the great engine by which we are to coerce them, & not war."[1]

Jefferson's initial instructions on the expedition's diplomatic mission to western Indians directed the captains to offer assurances of trade and amity and to provide information about the future trade with the United States. To the mission's foremost object, the discovery of a viable transcontinental route, Jefferson added the essential human context: "The commerce which may be carried on with the people inhabiting the line you will pursue, renders a knolege of those people important."[2] As the first quotation at the head of this essay makes plain, Jefferson counseled peace and constant reassurance of the expedition's peaceful intentions and commercial interests, including conference "on the points most convenient as mutual emporiums, and the articles of most desireable interchange for them & us."[3] To this Jefferson added that leaders of influence should be persuaded to travel to Washington. Parents might have their children sent to eastern schools, to the benefit of Indian peoples and the expedition's security. And Jefferson also recommended carrying matter for smallpox immunization. Tragically, the matter would be damaged and its potential benefit lost.

III.

The Corps of Discovery was encamped near St. Louis when word of the Louisiana Purchase arrived. In a letter dated January 22, 1804, Jefferson informed the captains of the successful transfer of New Orleans and the ongoing transfer of Louisiana. He also repeated the expedition's objectives, which remained the same, save for crucial changes to the diplomatic mission to the western Indian nations.

As Jefferson noted, the expedition would now cross a region claimed, at least in part, by the United States and meet with Indian nations encompassed by the republic's extended yet still uncertain boundaries. "When your instructions were penned," he wrote, "this new position was not so authentically known as to effect the complection of your instructions."[4] Jefferson now amended his instructions:

> Being now become sovereigns of the country, without however any diminution of the Indian rights of occupancy we are authorised to propose to them in direct terms the institution of commerce with them. It will now be proper you should inform those through whose country you will pass, or whom you may meet, that their late fathers the Spaniards have agreed to withdraw all their troops from all the waters & country of the Missisipi & Missouri, that they have surrendered to us all their subjects Spanish & French settled there, and all their posts & lands: that henceforward we become their fathers and friends, and that we shall endeavor that they shall have no cause to lament the change:

that we have sent you to enquire into the nature of the country & the nations inhabiting it, to know at what places and times we must establish stores of goods among them, to exchange for their peltries: that as soon as you return with the necessary information we shall prepare supplies of goods and persons to carry them and make the proper establishments: that in the mean time, the same traders who reside among or visit them, and who are now a part of us, will continue to supply them as usual: that we shall endeavor to become acquainted with them as soon as possible, and that they will find us faithful friends and protectors. Although you will pass through no settlements of Sioux (except seceders) yet you will probably meet with parties of them. On that nation we wish most particularly to make a friendly impression, because of their immense power, and because we learn they are very desirous of being on most friendly terms with us.[5]

Jefferson described the new character of relationships to be pursued with western Indians, altered the imperative of the expedition's diplomatic objects, and identified one Indian nation for special attention. And with these instructions, he also identified three fundamental principles for these relationships: first, a supreme American sovereignty and corresponding determination to claim an enlarged domestic sphere; second, a recognition of a circumscribed yet still significant Indian sovereignty and undiminished use of tribal lands; and third, a designation of Indian peoples as subject to the protection of the United States. Jefferson's instructions were a charter for relationships between the United States and western Indians.

The basis for the American assertion of a supreme sovereignty lay in the western legal tradition's doctrine of discovery, long employed in the Americas to subject indigenous peoples to their rule and to establish colonial claims as a right of Christian nations. (That religion serves as the legal foundation for relationships between the United States and Indian nations is rarely acknowledged. As the legal theorist Peter d'Errico observes, "It is concealed, as most foundations are."[6]) Jefferson's assertion of supreme American sovereignty created an exclusive relationship with the United States and rendered Indian peoples subject to the authority of the federal government, which had asserted its sole jurisdiction in Indian affairs from the time of the Revolution. Yet this relationship also understood Indian nations as distinct political communities and sovereigns in their own right. In short, the sovereignty of Indian communities at once was recognized and circumscribed—a condition extended to all peoples, regardless of their numbers, power, or remarkable diversity. Even the uniformity of the president's greeting and message, read by Lewis and Clark in their various counsels with western Indian peoples, reflected this prescription of a common political condition within the republic's bounds.

Critically, as Jefferson acknowledged, these claims made no intrusion on Indian use of tribal lands. Recognition of these rights was essential to later acquisition through legal means. To purchase lands from another via a treaty—a practice of Britain and other European powers continued by the United States—required a seller to have a prior claim to the land, if not an absolute and unconditional title. What the United States had already claimed in the East, and it would later claim in the West, was a right of preemption, or the federal government's exclusive right to purchase Indian lands. In practice, however, American interests in western lands were minimal as Lewis and Clark led their expedition westward. And so it remained until midcentury migration transformed those interests, first in the Pacific West and, shortly thereafter, in the vast interior.

Finally, Jefferson also extended a role for the United States to become the basis for the most significant challenge to Indian peoples in their dealings with the republic. Like others before and after, he employed a patriarchal metaphor to describe the federal government as "fathers and friends" to western Indian nations. This metaphor traded, in part, on the language of kinship Indian diplomats often employed to describe their own political relationships. (Some Indian diplomats, however, were careful or even pointed in their address of "brothers" when dealing with the United States.) Still more significant, the metaphor of fathers and children prescribed subordination, presumed wise and reasoned federal power, and envisioned a future transformation of children into adults. Throughout the republic's first one and a half centuries, this presumptuous benevolence, intent on transforming native peoples regardless of their own desires, dictated much of federal Indian policy.

IV.

If Jefferson's revised instructions embodied fundamental principles for relationships with western Indian nations, they also offered directions for the expedition's immediate diplo-matic objectives. Jefferson instructed Lewis and Clark to seek trade, amity, recognition of American ascendance, and the eventual exclusion of other powers. Consistent with his views, Jefferson also instructed the captains to make plain there would be no disruption of existing trade, and no occasion for dissatisfaction with this new relationship. And, finally, Jefferson identified the Sioux, whose power and presence made them a force of consequence on the northern plains, as an essential object of American diplomacy.

Jefferson intended the captains to pursue these objects in the present. Yet their diplomacy would almost always make its case in the future tense. Jefferson instructed Lewis and Clark to make a series of promises and guarantees—behind which lay assumptions about the power and position of the United States—at the time more ambition than fact and certainly unproved to western Indian nations. In contrast, Indian peoples negotiated in the present tense, acutely aware of their immediate interests, and also negotiated their relationships with one another. In responses ranging from polite indifference and genuine interest to plain and simple threat, those who met with Lewis and Clark always set their claims in this context, from the central and northern plains to the plateau and the Pacific Northwest.

Lewis and Clark Crossing South Dakota, 1804.
Chromolithograph from *St. Louis Globe-Democrat* Sunday Supplement, after painting by Frederick Mulhaupt, 1902.
Missouri Historical Society Photograph and Print Collection.

The best example of these circumstances can be found early in the expedition's journey, with Lewis and Clark's effort to do nothing less than fundamentally alter the existing balance of power on the northern plains. After the Teton Sioux rebuffed the expedition, the captains struck upon the idea of an Indian alliance, supported by American trade, as a counterpoint to Sioux power. To that end, they undertook an audacious effort involving the Mandans, the Hidatsas, and the Arikaras, three village societies long involved in trade and exchange with natives and newcomers throughout the region. Interest in Sioux trade, especially for arms, ammunition, and other goods gained through their connections to traders on the Minnesota and Mississippi Rivers, left the Arikaras little disposed to seek a relationship with the Mandans and the Hidatsas. To do so would incur Sioux wrath and end an important dimension of Arikara trade. But with the coming American trade, Lewis and Clark reasoned it would be possible to serve Arikara needs, as well as those of the Mandans and the Hidatsas, and to create the basis for such an alliance.

What Lewis and Clark were unable to overcome, and perhaps even to understand, was their own marginal position in such negotiation and the difficulty of mere promises to secure action and alliances in the present. In many respects, their assessment of Sioux power and diplomatic efforts with the Mandans, Hidatsas, and Arikaras reveal the captains to be apt students of regional affairs, capable of ready improvisation. Their plan was understandable and offered these parties a resolution to difficult circumstances. Indeed, in the mid-nineteenth century, the Mandans, Hidatsas, and Arikaras would create their own alliance in response to continued Sioux pressure—an alliance that became the basis for the Three Affiliated Tribes of today's Fort Berthold Reservation in western North Dakota. But during the winter of 1804–5, and again on their return from the Pacific in 1806, Lewis and Clark could not overcome present realities with future possibilities.

Although interested in the prospect of peace, Mandan, Hidatsa, and Arikara leaders distrusted one another, were cautious in their commitments, and did not yet see their interests served in a tenuous triple alliance. Moreover, the Arikaras were hardly in a position to abandon their crucial Sioux trade, however difficult it was, in favor of a promised but unproved American trade. Clark's journal entry for August 22, 1806, reproduced in part at this essay's beginning, captures the limits of American power on the northern plains, as Arikara leaders turned a future promise back on the explorers. As James Ronda has noted elsewhere of this event, "the captains had been put off in the best traditions of international diplomacy" and their plans thwarted.[7]

Lewis and Clark were quite successful in their other dealings with western Indian peoples, acquiring information, supplies, and assistance throughout the course of their journey. But the diplomatic objectives sought by the expedition remained largely unattained when the Corps of Discovery returned to St. Louis. During the years after the expedition, Lewis and, after him, Clark would express repeatedly their concern for the absence of American trade on the upper lengths of the Missouri River and their fear that the field had been left open to British traders. This anxiety would peak shortly after the War of 1812, with Secretary of War John C. Calhoun's effort to dispatch diplomatic missions to western Indians, employing a steamboat on the Missouri River as a means to demonstrate American power. The steamboat ran up on a sandbar, and so foundered the American drive to secure the northern plains from the specter of British influence. The federal government's concern with the region would wane after a diplomatic expedition in 1825 concluded no British presence or imminent threat existed, and even as the fur trade advanced during the late 1820s and early 1830s, the American military presence on the Upper Missouri River receded. Tensions remained in the Anglo-American relationship after the War of 1812, but in an age of nationalism and expansive visions of the republic's future, many American policymakers regarded British North America less as an enemy base than as an inevitable territorial acquisition. Energy and interest in Indian affairs turned to the continued removal of eastern Indians to places west of the Mississippi River. Western Indian affairs seemed remote, far beyond a permanent Indian frontier likely to persist for any foreseeable future.

But at midcentury that frontier disappeared with the acquisition of Oregon and, later, California and the Southwest. The distance between western Indians and American power closed, and a new round of negotiation began as a flood of migrants entered the West from several directions. Unlike the negotiation undertaken by Lewis and Clark, this effort was intent on securing Indian lands, obedience, and ultimately, assimilation. But it continued on the same premises extended by Jefferson and presented by the Corps of Discovery. Treaties were negotiated, first to describe tribal boundaries and then to concentrate populations and to secure land in California, Oregon, and Washington, and later in the plains and Southwest. In doing so, they haphazardly created the reservation system home to most Indian peoples by the late nineteenth century.

In that era, the past amity or enmity of western Indian nations was irrelevant. Convinced that Indians stood close to extinction, policymakers sought to destroy tribal identity to salvage a future for individuals. They suppressed traditional religious observance, including ceremonies essential to individual and collective life. They instituted compulsory education, requiring children to attend schools on reservations or distant boarding schools with long periods apart from friends, families, and community. And they allotted tribal lands to individuals and sold the remainder to non-Indians, creating conditions that led to a dramatic loss of lands on many allotted reservations. By the beginning of the twentieth century, diminished power, poverty, and wardship had eroded tribal sovereignty and led to the federal government's intrusion into almost every aspect of Indian life.

V.

Yet the effort to assimilate Indian peoples, so destructive to communities, families, and individual lives, also proved central to the creation of modern tribal life. Working within their communities, many Indian people bent, embraced, or ignored the intrusions of wardship. They fostered what remained of their independence and tribal sovereignty to secure communities from further encroachment and to retain a measure of control over their present and future. The steps in creating modern tribal nations were not always taken in perfect agreement, but even divided communities shared a common interest in persistence as distinct peoples. Parallel processes on many reservations make for ready comparison, but these experiences also occurred within the context of a tribe's own history, leaving a distinct cast to each contemporary western Indian nation.

At the same time, the recognition of common experiences, as well as education, religious movements, and extensive travel created a widespread identification among people from different Indian communities. Such identifications had occurred before, but in the twentieth century this new collective sensibility, or pan-Indianism, held fast. Pan-Indianism and a resurgent tribalism were not mutually exclusive, and they often reinforced each other in the recognition of common experience and significant differences. Twentieth-century Indians did not always agree on appropriate steps or ultimate ends; they did agree they had much to share with one another and might find strength in the collective address of their place in American society and their relationship with the United States. But successive generations would act in their own communities, in concert with one another and their eastern relatives, to continue a relationship begun with the passing of Lewis and Clark—and so it continues.

Notes

1   Jefferson to Lewis, August 21, 1808, *The Territory of Louisiana-Missouri, 1806–1814*, ed. Clarence Edwin Carter, vol. 14 of *The Territorial Papers of the United States* (Washington, D.C.: Government Printing Office, 1949), 220.

2   Jefferson to Lewis, June 20, 1803, *Letters of the Lewis and Clark Expedition, with Related Documents, 1783–1854*, ed. Donald T. Jackson, 2d ed., 2 vols. (Urbana: University of Illinois Press, 1978), 1:62.

3   Ibid., 1:61, 64.

4   Jefferson to Lewis, January 22, 1804, *Letters of the Lewis and Clark Expedition*, 1:165.

5   Ibid., 1:165–66.

6   Peter d'Errico, "Native Americans in America: A Theoretical and Historical Overview," in *American Nations: Encounters in Indian Country, 1850 to Present*, ed. Frederick E. Hoxie, Peter C. Mancall, and James H. Merrell (New York: Routledge, 2001), 489.

7   James P. Ronda, *Lewis and Clark among the Indians* (Lincoln: University of Nebraska Press, 1984), 50.

Suggested Readings

d'Errico, Peter. "Native Americans in America: A Theoretical and Historical Overview." In *American Nations: Encounters in Indian Country, 1850 to Present*, edited by Frederick E. Hoxie, Peter C. Mancall, and James H. Merrell. New York: Routledge, 2001.

Horsman, Reginald. *Expansion and American Indian Policy, 1783–1812*. East Lansing: Michigan State University Press, 1967. Reprint. Norman: University of Oklahoma Press, 1992.

Hoxie, Frederick E. "Exploring a Cultural Borderland: Native American Journeys of Discovery in the Early Twentieth Century." *Journal of American History* 79 (December 1992): 969–95.

Nichols, Roger L. *Indians in the United States and Canada: A Comparative History*. Lincoln: University of Nebraska Press, 1998.

Prucha, Francis Paul. *The Great Father: The United States Government and the American Indians*. Reprint, combined and unabridged Bison Books edition. Lincoln: University of Nebraska Press, 1995.

Wilkinson, Charles F. *American Indians, Time, and the Law: Native Societies in a Modern Constitutional Democracy*. New Haven, Conn.: Yale University Press, 1987.

Williams, Robert A., Jr. *The American Indian in Western Legal Thought: The Discourses of Conquest*. New York: Oxford University Press, 1990.

———. *Linking Arms Together: American Indian Treaty Visions of Law and Peace, 1600–1800*. New York: Oxford University Press, 1997.

"Pacific Intentions"

Lewis and Clark and the Western Fur Trade

J. Frederick Fausz
University of Missouri–St. Louis

Make ... [the Indians] acquainted with our wish to be neighborly, friendly & useful to them, & of our dispositions to a commercial intercourse with them; confer with them on the points most convenient as mutual emporiums, & the articles of most desireable interchange for them & us.
> —Thomas Jefferson, instructions to Meriwether Lewis

[W]e took care to make them [the Shoshones] a conspicuous object of our own good wishes and the care of our government. [W]e made them sensible of their dependance on the will of our government for every species of merchandize as well for their defence & comfort; and apprized them of the strength of our government....
> —Meriwether Lewis, journal entry, August 17, 1805

Among the many goals of the Lewis and Clark Expedition, the most practical one was to expand American commerce. The "pacific intentions" of the Corps of Discovery included the principal objective of finding an all-water route from St. Louis to the Pacific Ocean to export western furs to the rich markets of Asia. Even if the fabled Northwest Passage was not found, however, the United States could expect immense profits from a domestic fur trade with the Indian hunters who controlled the vast animal empire of the Louisiana Purchase territory. That secondary pacific intention was designed to pacify and satisfy distant native nations through commerce—America's first step in expanding its control over the West. The fur trade figured prominently in many aspects of the expedition—its planning and personnel, subsistence and survival—and the Indians who helped Lewis and Clark achieve their exploratory and scientific objectives often did so because of a promised commercial alliance with the United States.[1]

The information gathered by the Corps of Discovery had far-reaching consequences for the Indian trade, expanding its potential, profits, and popularity for two generations after 1806. The first Americans to follow Lewis and Clark went in search of fur fortunes, unleashing acquisitive and inquisitive processes that made the West an integral part of the United States well in advance of homesteading populations. Those developments had a devastating impact upon native populations that was unprecedented in the trans-Mississippi West, far more sinister and serious than the cultural changes previously experienced by trading tribes. As agents of the U.S. government and proponents of Jeffersonian ideology before, during, and after the expedition, Lewis and Clark advocated fur trading not as an end in itself but merely as a means for making Indians politically dependent and ultimately expendable. Because their distant discoveries included fertile lands and natural resources conducive to white settlement, Lewis and Clark viewed the Indian trade as a temporary expedient, being convinced by history that "savages in the hunter state" inevitably would be replaced by American farmers.

Two centuries before the Louisiana Purchase, the founding of Jamestown in 1607, Quebec in 1608, and Santa Fe in 1609 had initiated an intense competition among English, French, and Spanish colonists to claim and control territory throughout North America. The fur trade played a central role in those events by enticing Europeans to explore this continent in search of profitable fur-bearing animals, long extinct in their homelands and increasingly demanded by global markets. These agents of empire did not, of course, find a true wilderness teeming with animals free for the taking; Europeans always were intruding upon the homelands and natural resources of Indians, and only through negotiation and exchange with them could furs be obtained.

American Indians were the guardians of "soft gold" in every trade zone, jealously protecting the fur "capital" on their lands and harvesting a portion as "interest" each season to purchase European manufactures. In every successful fur trade, the cooperation and expertise of warrior-hunters was indispensable in procuring raw furs, while native women were equally essential in processing the stinking skins of fresh kills into the finished furs increasingly demanded by European, Asian, and American markets. Fur trading, at least initially, empowered Indian populations by bringing them novelties and necessities—European metal, cloth, and glass products; vermilion (mercury sulfide) from China; and often alcohol—to fulfill needs that their natural environments could not supply. Muskets and sharp metal blades were vitally important for defending territories and maintaining tribal sovereignty. At its best, the fur trade encouraged long-lasting, stable relationships of mutual respect and reciprocal benefit between European and Indian partners, avoiding divisive issues, such as religious beliefs and political sovereignty, to preserve harmonious commerce.

The revolutionizing impact of global capitalism, however, also could have destructive side effects for Indian populations—the rapid depletion of natural resources through overhunting; the expansion and escalation of more lethal warfare among competing "gun tribes"; the growing dependency on European products; and the spread of epidemic diseases and alcoholism through constant contact with foreign traders. At its worst, fur trading actually could accelerate the territorial dispossession, loss of independence, population decline, and cultural genocide that Indians had sought to avoid by doing business with Europeans in the first place.

When the United States purchased the Louisiana Territory from France, Thomas Jefferson knew well the best and worst aspects of the previous 250 years of North American fur trading. His own Chesapeake heritage featured classic cases of Indian decline through peaceful trade as well as aggressive warfare. Beginning in the 1580s, Thomas Harriot and John White, chroniclers of England's first colony at Roanoke Island, marveled at the "great store of Otters" and other furs that would "yeelde good profite." Harriot wrote that "Deare Skinnes dressed ... or undressed are to be had of the naturall inhabitants, thousands yeerely by way of trafficke for trifles." Harriot promoted the fur trade to attract English farmers to America, expecting that they quickly would make Indian hunters expendable and perhaps even extinct, because he knew firsthand how imported European diseases already had ravaged and reduced the native population. Twenty years later, the founders of Jamestown also believed that trade for the food and furs of the powerful Powhatan Indians was the best means to "induce ... Barbarous natures to a ... mutuall society with us," thus protecting the small, struggling Virginia colony in its infancy. The promise of commerce was a pacific intention that helped appease Indian populations until overwhelming numbers of white tobacco farmers conquered and dispossessed them once furs became less desirable than their lands.[2]

Jefferson's tabulations on near-extinct "aborigines" in his *Notes on the State of Virginia* (1785) confirmed how thoroughly Indians had been eradicated since 1607, as trading frontiers made way for settlement frontiers. By the 1750s, his Chesapeake countrymen already were planning expansion across the Alleghenies to the very banks of the Mississippi River. Between 1763 and 1795, Virginia's newest frontier encompassed the huge Ohio Country between Pittsburgh (Fort Duquesne, which George Washington helped wrest from the French) and the Illinois settlements that George Rogers Clark's Virginia "Long Knives" captured from the British in the 1770s. The Clark family epitomized Virginia's westward expansion when they moved to Kentucky as frontier farmers and Indian fighters seeking to become plantation gentry in the more affordable backcountry. At the 1795 Treaty of Greenville (Ohio), young Captain William Clark witnessed the surrender of Indians who had fought valiantly but futilely to resist white intrusion into the Old Northwest. Thousands of Shawnees, Delawares, Miamis, Mingoes, and other tribes would be forced across the Mississippi River, seeking a final refuge from American expansion—at least until the Louisiana Purchase. Virginia's colonial legacy of white farmers inheriting the lands of Indian hunters became national policy under President George Washington.

While Anglo-American settlers regarded fur trading as a temporary tactic leading ultimately to the conquest of territory, French Canadians followed a different course. With a small European population that did not seek to establish farming settlements beyond the St. Lawrence River, the French supported fur trading as its main industry and most dependable source of profitable exports. They pioneered a truly mutual society with essential Indian allies, who bolstered the economy

and defended the territory of New France. French frontiersmen (*coureurs de bois*) cultivated a far greater degree of cultural tolerance in their intercourse, both commercial and
sexual, with Indians than Anglo-American backwoodsmen
ever had. Testifying to the success of intercultural cooperation
across Canada, large numbers of French Indian mixed bloods
(*métis*) expanded the fur trade westward to the Pacific Ocean
and south to the Gulf of Mexico in the eighteenth century. The
Osages, Missourias, and Kansas along the Missouri River were
trading with French Canadians soon after 1700, and coureurs
de bois reached Santa Fe in 1739 and the Bighorn Mountains
of Wyoming by 1743. France's loss of Canada to Great Britain
in 1763 was a monumental setback and ultimately fatal for
many Indian tribes, but the French fur-trade model was far
from dead.

That fur-trading philosophy was critical in the development of early St. Louis, founded in 1764 by a merchant cartel
as the last French commercial settlement in North America.
It was the most strategically placed of all fur outposts south
of Canada, positioned midway along the Mississippi River
between the international market cities of Montreal and New
Orleans, with unrivaled access to the Missouri River—the
famous water highway to the riches of the "Fur West."
Established as a secular city focused solely on commerce,
without military motives or missionary objectives, St. Louis
represented the final stage in the evolution of successful and
mutually respectful French-Indian fur trading.

In the forty years prior to the Lewis and Clark Expedition,
the Osage Indians were the most essential factor in making
St. Louis the "Gateway to the West," controlling 100,000
square miles of hunting territory from their villages along
Missouri River tributaries. That powerful nation formed a
strong interethnic interest-group alliance of blood and business ties with the Laclède-Chouteau merchant family.

Solidified by extensive intermarriage and bicultural expertise, this long-term pelt partnership dominated all competitors in the lucrative, late-eighteenth-century fur trade of Upper Louisiana. With French muskets and metal tomahawks supplementing their famous orangewood bows, some fifteen hundred Osage warrior-hunters kept tribal enemies at bay while they harvested an unrivaled variety of furs—deer, buffalo, beaver, bear, and lush canine, feline, and weasel peltries—from three different ecosystems extending from southern Iowa to northern Texas, eastern Kansas to western Illinois. The Osages were supremely successful *commercial* fur harvesters and manufacturers—not subsistence hunters— who commuted from agricultural villages to procure and process animal skins for the coffeehouse auctions in Montreal, London, New Orleans, and Paris. The shaved and brain-tanned deerskins and buffalo hides manufactured by talented Osage women made the small, crude village of St. Louis an affluent, internationally respected boomtown long before the Louisiana Purchase. Noting the reliance on Osage buckskins as the main currency in St. Louis, a French visitor wrote in 1803 that "Indians are the true bankers of this region. Their peltries are the bills placed in circulation, and their hunting provides security for the fictitious specie upon which the merchants base their business.... [B]ows [and] guns ... secure this singular banking system."[3]

At the time of the Louisiana Purchase, the Osages and two dozen other Indian nations supplied furs to "Chouteau's Town" (St. Louis), from as far away as sixteen hundred miles. As the commercial capital of a vast inland empire and the central repository of critical knowledge about the West, St. Louis truly had achieved a society of multicultural interdependency. As such, it was the obvious choice to be the administrative center of America's new trans-Mississippi empire. In January 1804, William Clark reported to President Jefferson that the inhabitants of French Louisiana "appear anxious [about the U.S.

takeover] except the people of St. Louis, who are engaged in the Indian Trade." The Osages and their French Creole partners were reassured by Jefferson's pledge that their new American "fathers and friends" were committed "to the institution of commerce," and they willingly provided valuable information to Lewis and Clark that assisted the expedition.[4]

President Jefferson's plan to explore and exploit the Far West for commercial purposes was merely the latest in a long line of similar designs. Between 1794 and 1797, Spanish officials in St. Louis supported three failed attempts to reach the Pacific by fur trader Jacques Clamorgan's "Company of Discoverers and Explorers of the Missouri River." His main discovery was that most of the Upper Missouri Indians already were doing a booming business with resident French employees of British Canadian companies, with forts only 150 miles from the Dakotas. The Canadians were potent and rejuvenated traders after the French defeat in 1763, and the Scottish-dominated North West Company, formed in 1784, was giving London's 114-year-old Hudson's Bay Company a run for its money in several key regions. The British under Nor'wester Alexander Mackenzie in 1793 were the first to reach the Pacific Ocean by an overland route, adding the Oregon coast to their expanding trading territories to compete with both Russia and Spain. All land expeditions to the Pacific, however, lagged behind previous maritime explorations—e.g., Vitus Bering and the Russians (1742); Spanish ships from the Philippines (1765); English voyages by Captain James Cook (1778) and George Vancouver (1792–94); and American vessels (1792) captained by Robert Gray and others. The Pacific Northwest became a maritime magnet because it offered a double advantage: large quantities of the richest fur (sea otters) plus a direct ocean route to China, the world's largest and most lucrative market for North American furs. (Lewis and Clark missed a rare opportunity to observe and report on this coastal fur trade. They arrived at the mouth of the Columbia River in November 1805, after the October departure of the European ships, and they began their journey back to St. Louis in March 1806, just before the April return of the commercial fleets.)

As latecomers in the search for the Northwest Passage and with no prior experience in the complex, cutthroat business of fur trading, Lewis and Clark were woefully ill prepared to fulfill Jefferson's directives. Neither man had ventured beyond St. Louis, navigated the treacherous Missouri River, or haggled with savvy trading tribes long familiar with British products and multilingual Canadian métis. Recognizing their deficiencies, the young Virginians wisely supplemented their American army recruits in the Corps of Discovery with nearly a dozen French Creole boatmen (*voyageurs/engagés*) in addition to several other francophones with fur-trading experience: Pierre Cruzatte, a one-eyed French Omaha métis from St. Charles; Francois Labiche, either a métis or a mulatto skilled in tracking, hunting, and interpreting Indian languages; George "Drewyer" Drouillard, a French Shawnee métis born in Canada but recently living in Missouri who served as the primary hunter and translator of Indian sign language; Pierre Dorion, Sr., a Quebecois trader-interpreter in his fifties who had lived with the Yankton Sioux for two decades; Rene Jusseaume, or Jessaume, a French Canadian free trader fluent in the dialect of the Mandans, with whom he had lived for fifteen years; Jean Baptiste Le Page, a French Canadian familiar with the Black Hills and the Cheyenne tribe; and Toussaint Charbonneau, a veteran French Canadian employee of the North West Company, and long a resident with the Hidatsas-Minitarees. One of his young Indian wives was Sacagawea, a Shoshone captive of the Hidatsas whose linguistic skills and geographical knowledge also contributed to the success of Lewis and Clark's western "tour."

The items in this image are typical of the kind of goods taken by Lewis and Clark to trade with the Indians and to give as gifts. Left foreground: trade silver brooch. Right foreground: burning glass or magnifying glass (and leather case) used to start fires with the sun's rays. Left background: fire steel or striker (and leather case), used with a flint to start fires. Right background: metal trade ax, circa 1800 (found in Osage lands). Brooch and ax are from the author's collection. Other items are from the collection of William Guthman.

In addition to taking along vital cultural intermediaries with western experience, Lewis and Clark further improved their chances of success in commercial negotiations by stocking a sizable collection of "Indian presents" with proven appeal for trading tribes (see itemized list in appendix). In Philadelphia, Lewis spent $669.50 on standard trade items of glass, metal, and cloth, plus vermilion and tobacco, which represented the most costly category of preliminary supplies. However, the total expense of all Indian gifts, shipped west in fourteen bales and one box, was many times higher. Supplementing the familiar trade goods were specialty items designed as diplomatic gifts to tribal leaders—"Chief coats" (fancy U.S. Army officer uniforms), new peace-and-friendship medals with Jefferson's profile, other surplus medals from Washington's administration, and U.S. flags with fifteen stars and fifteen stripes. In addition, a portion of the supplies originally intended for the corpsmen's use—120 gallons of whiskey, muskets, swords, ammunition, uniforms, food, and other military stores—also were distributed to Indians as presents or as payments for services rendered. On other occasions, Lewis and Clark bartered medicine, medical treatment, made-to-order iron hatchets fabricated from an old stove, robes fashioned from a large U.S. flag, brass buttons from their own uniforms, Sacagawea's bead belt, and even animal skins dressed by corpsmen to sustain the expedition. In August 1805, Lewis and Clark distributed lyed cornmeal to the helpful Lemhi Shoshones, "which was the first they had ever eaten in their lives." Chief Cameahwait regretted the long delay until "they could be furnished with firearms ... as promised," but one impatient Shoshone seized the opportunity to sell a much-needed horse to Clark for his "Pistol," plus "100 balls Powder & a Knife."[5]

Lewis and Clark's "Corps of Volunteers for North Western Discovery" transported and distributed trade goods but were not actual fur traders, which confused and discouraged some

Indians. With four times the men of a typical trading expedition, the corps raised Indian hopes for a grand rendezvous only to disappoint them with small quantities of rather mundane merchandise and mere promises of a future commercial relationship with the United States. The tribes most desirous of an American trade alliance—the Otoes, Cheyennes, Shoshones, Flatheads, and Nez Perces—were the militarily weakest and least-experienced fur suppliers of their regions. They consistently requested firearms to defend against aggressive "British Indians," which presented diplomatic dilemmas for Lewis and Clark. Expanding an already lethal arms race in the West contradicted the pacific intention of promoting intertribal peace throughout the region, while favoritism shown to tribal underdogs alienated the strongest and richest trading tribes—the Teton Lakotas, Blackfeet, Gros Ventres, and Assiniboines—which were critically important to U.S. commercial objectives.

Throughout the expedition, the desire to promote trade was complicated by the goal to minimize conflict in a region where the same Indians monopolized the best furs and British guns. Based on preconceived prejudices, Lewis and Clark favored alliances with "culturally advanced" maize-growing, town-dwelling Mandans, Hidatsas, and Arikaras rather than the "wild," roving Lakota and Blackfeet hunters who were militarily and economically dominant. American objectives were thwarted regularly by long-flourishing British alliances within the complex, traditional Missouri River trade system. That intertribal trade network brought together thousands of Indians from a dozen different cultures for an annual summer rendezvous at the Mandan and Arikara villages in the Dakotas. Nomadic hunters bartered buffalo robes and meat for the vegetables of the village farmers, and a vast array of new or recycled European trade goods from Montreal, Michilimackinac, Hudson's Bay, St. Louis, and Santa Fe was exchanged among river, plains, and mountain tribes. Unfortunately, Lewis and

Clark missed this spectacular June gathering of native nations on both legs of their journey and never appreciated how endemic intertribal hostility was replaced by genuine hospitality at trading time. After futile efforts to impose a permanent peace or to win over the key British allies, Lewis and Clark gave the friendlier Mandan and Hidatsa farmers "plenty of Guns Powder and ball, and ... a cannon to defend themselves" against the "vilenous" Lakotas. Convinced that the Sioux were "bad people" and "pirates" who needed to be "well whip[p]ed" to secure Missouri River commerce for American merchants, the heavily armed Corps of Discovery merely confirmed the Lakotas' worst—and rational—fears about losing their trade monopoly to these young upstarts from a new nation. The failure of the expedition's Lakota diplomacy was a major blow to Jefferson's pacific intentions and presaged future decades of ruthless warfare in the West.[6]

The militant attitudes of Lewis and Clark as trained soldiers, coupled with their racial, cultural, and class prejudices as Virginia gentlemen, severely hindered many other prospects for fur-trade alliances. When their idealistic geopolitical goals confronted the realities of Indian Country, violent confrontations resulted—contradicting nineteenth-century portrayals of the expedition's "mild and pacific course of conduct." The corpse of a Gros Ventre warrior (sometimes believed to be a Piegan Blackfeet) was left with a Jefferson peace-and-friendship medal around his neck so that other Indians "might be informed who we were," Lewis wrote defiantly following the fatal skirmish along the Two Medicine River. That incident was merely the most extreme of several explosive encounters that could have resulted in other fatalities. Arrogantly ethnocentric toward Indians who were "Savage in every sens of the word," Lewis and Clark confused Indian fear with Indian respect, momentary compliance with lasting cooperation, and their own technological superiority with national supremacy. Clark taunted the

Lakotas with threats that "we Should kill them certainly" and reveled in the Clatsops' "very exalted opinion of us as marksmen and the Superior excellency of our rifles," which "will deter them from any acts of hostility." Threatening to kill Indians for even minor transgressions, such as stealing Lewis's dog, the military corps traversed the West with cocked rifles, drawn swords, loaded cannons, and an aggressive demeanor appropriate for soldiers but detrimental to the impression that Americans would be tolerant, permissive traders like the French.[7]

Lewis and Clark self-consciously symbolized "civilized man" in their encounters with "human nature [that was] ... allied with the brute creation." Lewis condemned the friendly Shoshones as "famished dogs" who ate raw deer entrails, and he described the acculturated and English-speaking Pacific Coast tribes as diseased and debased wretches who were "some of the most disgusting objects in nature." In those prejudicial contexts, Indians were not people who merited treatment as diplomatic equals, and the corps' ceremonial parleys consisted more of commandments than dialogues—always accentuated with a potent demonstration of American firepower. In village after village, Lewis and Clark spread the gospel of U.S. sovereignty by replacing familiar French, British, and Spanish flags with the Stars and Stripes; by officially recognizing or even creating chiefs (sometimes in error); and by proclaiming the new status of Indians as "children"—and subjects—of yet another "Great Father." Such presumptuous arrogance and military bravado discouraged many tribes from sending delegations to the distant capital of these dangerous strangers, a failure of the expedition deemed most regrettable by the intellectually curious president. Lacking firsthand Indian informants, Washington officials were forced to rely almost entirely on Lewis and Clark's biased assessments of "savages" and their sometimes-dubious contributions to a future American fur trade.[8]

Lewis and Clark seemed all too self-assured about how the Indian trade would turn out because they were guided by ancient preconceptions. During their "tour," they witnessed the full range of the fur trade's negative, corrupting impact on Indians—either treacherous and untrustworthy British allies who rejected American overtures, gun-hungry but backward tribes that would have to be taught how to prepare furs for market, or syphilitic prostitutes of the European "cloth men" in Oregon who exchanged traditional barbarity for acculturated depravity. These negative stereotypes reinforced Lewis and Clark's prejudgment that fur trading would represent merely a preliminary and temporary stage in the ultimate realization of an American settler empire in the West. Throughout their journals, Lewis and Clark sound more like real-estate agents than advocates of intercultural commerce, filling page after page with information on soil fertility, water quality, climate, timber, and mineral resources designed to facilitate the migration of American homesteaders. They reflected the progressive and ethnocentric ideology of the Jeffersonian Enlightenment, viewing magnificent virgin forests and immediately calculating how they could be leveled to create "an excellent waggon road." When they encountered a "fertill and hansome valley" along the Oregon coast—"*at this time* crowded with Indians"— they already envisioned "a settlement of 40 or 50 thousand souls if *properly cultivated* [emphasis added]." Such attitudes, of course, were not conducive to successful, long-lasting trade partnerships among equals from different cultural traditions. Lewis and Clark's prejudicial baggage left a more lasting impression on Indians than their meager stock of presents, making it difficult for Americans to compete in fur markets crowded with acculturated and tolerant coureurs de bois, half-Indian offspring, and immigrant Scots who preceded the Corps of Discovery and continued to flourish in its wake.[9]

During their twenty-eight-month, eight-thousand-mile expedition, the Corps of Discovery survived by adopting many traditional fur-trading practices—living off the land by hunting, storing goods in caches, negotiating in native dialects, spending winters in tribal towns, having sex with Indians, and dispensing standard trade goods to curry favor and sustain the expedition. Lewis and Clark noted the locations of the different ecosystems that supported deer, elk, beaver, bear, and buffalo, and they recorded fascinating data on Indian diversity and commercial potential (anchovy and salmon fishing, in addition to fur harvesting). Their single greatest failure, however, was the inability to respect or empathize with Indians as equals in the human family who had cultural traditions as valid as their own. The prejudices, armaments, and constant movement of the expedition precluded the development of intercultural trust and tolerance that was vital to sustainable commercial alliances. Other Americans, more appreciative of Indian cultures and contributions, would have to adapt to conditions in the Far West if it was ever going to become a profitable Fur West for the United States.

Nonetheless, Lewis and Clark made the critical first American survey of distant Indian Country, and their greatest legacy was in publicizing and promoting the prospects for western profits among their fellow citizens. Near the end of their journey, Lewis and Clark permitted John Colter to leave the corps so that he could join white trappers heading west, making him one of the earliest and most important mountain men. Less than a month after the expedition returned in September 1806, Lewis began advertising the great potential of the Fur West in newspapers across America. "I consider this Track across the continent as presenting immense advantages to the Fur Trade," he wrote. "[A]ll the furs collected in 9/10ths of the most valuable Fur Country of America may be conveyed to the Mouth of the Columbia & shipped from thence for the East Indies." Even though the expedition journals would not appear in any form until 1814 and were not published in their entirety until 1905, Lewis and Clark submitted official reports to the government, with detailed information on the furs that each tribe did or could contribute to U.S. commerce.[10]

At least some of that data was available to the general public as early as 1807—when veteran Spanish trader Manuel Lisa became the first St. Louis entrepreneur to act on this new knowledge. He pioneered a new American method of competing with the British by sending white trappers as well as white traders to tap the beaver bounty of the Rocky Mountains. Lisa established Fort Raymond at the mouth of the Bighorn River and sponsored explorations of other famous trapping regions—Yellowstone, Jackson's Hole, Pierre's Hole, and the Teton and Wind River ranges. Ex-corpsmen Colter, Drouillard, Charbonneau, Nathaniel Pryor, and John Potts played prominent roles as experienced frontiersmen working for Lisa and other fur enterprises. The Blackfeet's killing of Drouillard and

Fur Traders on the Missouri Attacked by Indians. Wood engraving from *Harper's Weekly*, 1868. Missouri Historical Society Photograph and Print Collection.

Potts and capture of Colter revealed that trading tribes resented Americans taking valuable animal skins from their territories, which was contrary to the traditional French model of Indian partnership.

Of even greater significance for western fur trading was the fact that Lewis and Clark became permanent residents and high government officials in St. Louis and directed the future course of American empire as they had always envisioned it. In 1808, Territorial Governor Lewis wrote a revealing treatise on "governing the Indian nations" of the West and conducting "trade and intercourse with the same." He proposed strict, even coercive, policies designed to regulate white traders through official licenses; to thwart foreign competition through government "factories" (trading forts strategically located at sites his expedition had discovered); and to encourage Indian dependence on American products—making them easier to control once they had material comforts to lose. An officially regulated Indian trade would become the first step in expanding U.S. control and full sovereignty over all aspects of life in the West. The government's involvement was already evident in the stockpiling of $60,000 worth of trade goods at Fort Bellefontaine, the army installation along the Lower Missouri just north of St. Louis. In 1809, Governor Lewis and Clark, by then superintendent of western Indian affairs and general of Missouri's territorial militia, became involved with fur trading more directly. Merging public office with personal opportunity, General Clark was a partner in the new St. Louis Missouri Fur Company, along with Lisa, the Chouteaus, Lewis's brother Reuben, and others. Governor Lewis granted that company a lucrative $7,000 government contract to escort the Mandan chief Sheheke/Shahake back home following his tour of the East. Those funds, however, also supported the transportation of company personnel and goods upriver in the pursuit of private profits and initiated criticisms about a blatant conflict of interest.[11]

Lewis and Clark's official and personal fascination with the Far West, both during and after the expedition, had ominous consequences for the Osages in the "Near West." In the November 1808 Treaty of Fort Osage, Governor Lewis and Superintendent Clark precipitously dispossessed those ever-loyal and still-profitable fur suppliers of fifty thousand square miles of prime hunting lands, conforming almost exactly to the present boundaries of the state of Missouri. The Osages thus became the first Indians west of the Mississippi to be removed from the path of American settlement precisely because their commercial dominance and military prowess made them targets of official machinations. In 1804, Jefferson considered the Osages to be "the great nation South of the Missouri ... [just] as the Sioux are the great [nation] North of that river. With these two powerful nations, we must stand well, because in their quarter we are miserably weak." When Americans became infected with Columbia River fur fever after 1806 and coveted Rocky Mountain beaver more than Missouri deerskins, the cooperative, productive Osages became expendable under Jefferson's expansionist policies. According to the president, "Commerce is the great engine by which we are to coerce them [the Indians] & not war," and given the military impotency of the United States west of the Mississippi, he found it expedient for "good and influential" Indians to "run into debt, because ... they become willing to lop [off debts to white traders] by a cession of lands." The exceedingly fertile Osage lands—a huge game park for fur harvesting that had never seen a plow—became a bigger prize than fur profits for the many thousands of Americans thronging into Missouri. Even though the Osages remained the largest and most-feared military force in Upper Louisiana, they could not hope to survive a joint assault by the old Indian rivals that Governor Lewis encouraged to attack them—especially since he had also embargoed their trade and suspended weapons shipments. They could not prevail against a cynical official strategy of "exchanging what they can spare & we want [land], for what we can spare and they want [manufactured products]." Like dozens of eastern tribes across several centuries, the Osages did not live far enough west to survive the expansion of land-hungry Americans. In Virginia's long history of "ethnic cleansing," Indian fur hunters and white farmers were incompatible and had never coexisted after whites achieved population dominance. Missouri had become yet another Virginia frontier and the Osages merely the latest victim of "progress."[12]

Late in his life, Clark admitted that his dispossession of the Osages in 1808 "was the hardest treaty on the Indians that he ever made, and that if he was damned hereafter it would be for making that treaty." The long-serving St. Louis superintendent of Indian affairs negotiated another thirty-seven treaties that forever altered the balance of power that had existed in 1804–6. His death in 1838 symbolized the end of the first phase of American expansion in the West. General Clark lived to see the rise and fall of dozens of fur outfits, endlessly destroying one another until only John Jacob Astor's American Fur Company survived as the sole monopolistic giant with global reach. Benefiting from the Lewis and Clark Expedition, that German immigrant was the only entrepreneur to fulfill Jefferson's vision of an ocean-to-ocean enterprise stretching to China. The mountain-man trappers who stole the Indians' valuable fur resources were nearly extinct by 1838—rendered expendable, like their beaver quarry, by shifting market demands. At the same time, thousands of Americans were heading to Oregon—not for furs but for the rich lands originally promoted by the Corps of Discovery. By 1838 as well, thousands of Indians recently had succumbed to devastating smallpox epidemics along the Missouri River trading routes; the faithful Mandans were reduced to fewer than two hundred people. When Clark died, the chiefs' portraits and tribal artifacts he had collected over a lifetime became haunting reminders of the catastrophes that had been visited upon the western Indians since the Corps of Discovery revolutionized their world only thirty-five years before.[13]

The Lewis and Clark Expedition changed the West forever. In an 1810 prospectus for the publication of the Corps of Discovery journals, editor Nicholas Biddle described the work as "an inquiry into the means of rendering the fur trade of North America more beneficial to the United States." If that had been all that Lewis and Clark did—and if they had done it sincerely—the consequences for the Indians may not have been so devastating. Because the expedition both fulfilled and furthered Jefferson's preconceived objectives, however, the "line of intercourse" from St. Louis to the Pacific was not restricted to fur trading alone. According to Biddle, the route pioneered by Lewis and Clark always was intended to be "the future path of civilization"—a highway designed to "receive ... the overflowing tide of our own population."[14]

Like Harriot and White 220 years earlier, Lewis and Clark journeyed across vast spaces and symbolically "back in time" to encounter and describe simpler societies and tempting territories that would provide a new future for their own countrymen. In both cases, first contacts with native populations imparted immediate knowledge that would lead to ultimate dominion over the lands and lives of the Indians. The Roanoke Indians in the 1580s were vulnerable to conquest because they were totally ignorant of the culture and country from which Harriot and White came. The Indians encountered by Lewis and Clark misjudged their motives, believing that the Americans would be as respectful of their talents and as tolerant of their cultures as the French had been. Accustomed to the society of faithful fur traders from Canada, they were ill prepared to deal with American assaults on their territory and sovereignty. Having demonstrated their indispensable value in fur trading, Indians were shocked to find that the Americans really had wanted their lands all along.

In their journey across space and time, two young Virginians, serving a Virginia president, explored the vast Louisiana Territory as if it were merely another in a long procession of Virginia frontiers previously cleared of Indians. Believing that the Indian trade in furs was trivial compared to providing lands for millions of their countrymen, Lewis and Clark took the first steps in integrating the West into the United States by advancing American democracy through Indian dispossession. New policies followed old patterns, as Lewis and Clark's colonial inheritance from the "Past of the East" became a national bequest to the "Future of the West."

Notes

1   Lewis, journal entry, September 22, 1805, *Original Journals of the Lewis and Clark Expedition 1804–1806*, ed. Reuben Gold Thwaites, 8 vols. (New York: Dodd, Mead & Co., 1904–5), 3:83.

2   Thomas Harriot, *A briefe and true report of the new found land of Virginia....* (Frankfort am Main, 1590), B2v–B3; Sir George Peckham, "A True Report...." *Voyages and Colonising Enterprises of Sir Humphrey Gilbert*, ed. David Beers Quinn, 2 vols. (London: Hakluyt Society, 1940), 2:452.

3   Carl J. Ekberg and William E. Foley, eds., *An Account of Upper Louisiana by Nicolas de Finiels* (Columbia: University of Missouri Press, 1989), 121.

4   Clark to William Croghan, January 15, 1804, *Letters of the Lewis and Clark Expedition, with Related Documents, 1783–1854*, ed. Donald T. Jackson, 2d ed., 2 vols. (Urbana: University of Illinois Press, 1978), 1:164; ibid., Jefferson to Lewis, January 22, 1804, 1:164–66.

5   Lewis, journal entry, August 17, 1805, *Original Journals*, 2:363; ibid., Clark, journal entry, August 28, 1805, 3:47.

6   Ibid., Clark, journal entry, August 30, 1806, 5:366–67.

7   "Mild and pacific" quotation is from Elliott Coues, ed., *The History of the Lewis and Clark Expedition*, 4 vols. (New York: Francis P. Harper, 1893), 3:943; Lewis, journal entry, July 27, 1806, *Original Journals*, 5:225; ibid., Clark, journal entry, February 1, 1806, 4:37; ibid., Clark, journal entry, August 30, 1806, 5:366; ibid., Clark, journal entry, January 24, 1806, 4:11. I believe that the two Indians killed by Lewis's party on July 27, 1806, were Gros Ventres and not Blackfeet. See the recent and definitive treatment by Robert A. Saindon, "The 'Unhappy Affair' on Two Medicine River," *We Proceeded On* 28, no. 3 (August 2002), 12–25.

8   Lewis, journal entry, August 16, 1805, *Original Journals*, 2:355.

9   Ibid., Clark, journal entry, July 8, 1806, 5:255; ibid., Clark, journal entry, November 5, 1805, 3:202; ibid., Lewis, journal entry, March 30, 1806, 4:220.

10   Jackson, *Letters of the Lewis and Clark Expedition*, 1:337.

11   Ibid., 2:695–719.

12   Ibid., Jefferson to Robert Smith, 1:200n; Jefferson to Lewis, August 21, 1808, in Anthony F. C. Wallace, *Jefferson and the Indians* (Cambridge, Mass.: Harvard University Press, 1999), 270; Jefferson, "Message to Congress," January 18, 1803, *Letters of the Lewis and Clark Expedition*, 11.

13   W. A. Croffut, ed., *Fifty Years in Camp and Field: Diary of Major-General Ethan Allen Hitchcock* (New York: G. P. Putnam's Sons, 1909), 140.

14   Biddle prospectus, *Letters of the Lewis and Clark Expedition*, 2:547.

Suggested Readings

Fausz, J. Frederick. "Becoming 'A Nation of Quakers': The Removal of the Osage Indians from Missouri." *Gateway Heritage* 20 (summer 2000), 28–39.

Foley, William E., and C. David Rice. *The First Chouteaus: River Barons of Early St. Louis.* Urbana: University of Illinois Press, 1983. Reprint. Urbana: University of Illinois Press, 2000.

Gibson, James R. *Otter Skins, Boston Ships, and China Goods: The Maritime Fur Trade of the Northwest Coast, 1785–1841.* Seattle: University of Washington Press, 1999.

Gilman, Carolyn. *Where Two Worlds Meet: The Great Lakes Fur Trade.* St. Paul: Minnesota Historical Society, 1982.

Jackson, Donald T. *Letters of the Lewis and Clark Expedition, with Related Documents, 1783–1854.* 2d ed., 2 vols. Urbana: University of Illinois Press, 1978.

Nasatir, A. P., ed. *Before Lewis and Clark: Documents Illustrating the History of the Missouri, 1785–1804.* 2 vols. Lincoln: University of Nebraska Press, 1990.

Robertson, R. G. *Competitive Struggle: America's Western Fur Trading Posts, 1764–1865.* Boise, Idaho: Tamarack Books, 1999.

Ronda, James P. *Lewis and Clark among the Indians.* Lincoln: University of Nebraska Press, 1984. Reprint. Lincoln: University of Nebraska Press, 2002.

Utley, Robert M. *A Life Wild and Perilous: Mountain Men and the Paths to the Pacific.* New York: Henry Holt Company, 1999.

Americans and Their Environments at the Time of Lewis and Clark

Conevery Bolton Valenčius
Washington University in St. Louis

One quarter of a mile in rear of our camp which was situated in a fine open grove of cotton wood [I] passed a grove of plumb trees loaded with fruit and now ripe, [and I] observed but little difference between this fruit and that of a similar kind common to the Atlantic States. [T]he trees are smaller and more thickly set. [T]his forrest of plumb trees garnish a plain about 20 feet more elivated than that on which we were encamped; this plane extends with the same bredth from the creek below to the distance of near three miles above parrallel with the river, and it is intirely occupied by the burows of the *barking squiril*...; this animal appears here in infinite numbers and the shortness and virdue of the grass gave the plain the appearance through-out it's whole extent of beatifull bowling green in fine order.
 —Meriwether Lewis, journal entry, September 17, 1804

Reading Meriwether Lewis's notes from the afternoon of September 17, 1804, when he split off from the main group and toured the countryside on his own, we modern people might easily relate to his experience. Lewis has what sounds like a lovely walk, through fruit trees just in season, on an "elivated," richly grassy plain above a creek, noticing animals that seem interesting and perhaps whimsical but not in any way threatening. What a nice way to spend part of a day!

Yet this modern perception betrays us. Lewis's walk *seems* familiar to us, but in fact he moved through this environment with an entirely different set of questions, preconceptions, and purposes than most of us would. Lewis's midday stroll, like the entire voyage on which he and his company were embarked, springs from a view of environments that was very much of his time and emphatically *not* of ours. Moreover, this brief excerpt points to many of the factors that defined Lewis's worldview—and that of his contemporaries. He and his company not only traveled over waterways but also defined places in relation to rivers, creeks, and other sources of water; he and his companions sought endlessly to interpret, to make known, and wherever possible to quantify the places they visited; and they brought with them values about the use of land—particularly about the positive qualities of settled, familiar, agricultural terrain—that colored everything they saw.

The Role of Waterways

We inhabitants of the early-twenty-first-century United States travel on roads and highways, occasionally by rail, and in the air. (Some of us may also travel in a more metaphorical sense on the Internet, but for most of us our travel is still quite literal!) Occasionally we might take cruises; however, these are by and large destinations in themselves. Few of us take a cruise ship to get somewhere fast or efficiently; we take a cruise to enjoy the journey, look at the sights, and savor the experience of being outside our normal, everyday lives.

By and large, we have lost our sense of rivers and waterways as the fundamental source of food, travel, and the exchange of goods and information. We have lost our sense that waterways were the main way in which we would communicate with or come to know other communities and other people.

For Americans of Lewis and Clark's time, however—as well as for many native peoples of the period—rivers were central to many people's livelihoods, and they were also fundamental to all exploration and cross-cultural contact. Rivers are accessible to individuals, traveling with the current or paddling themselves, even in small craft. They are amenable to small-scale explorations or to use by people without tremendous resources or financial backing. Numerous and diverse cultural groups capitalized on waterways in the era of the Corps of Discovery.

In the late eighteenth century, for instance, the Indian populations of what is now the southeastern United States included more than fifty thousand people in one hundred towns. These communities included the Cherokees, Creeks, Choctaws, Chickasaws, Seminoles, Caddos, and other groups, who spoke different languages and had different cultures and lifeways. Yet the diverse peoples of the North American Southeast were connected by a communications network of trails and waterways through which small villages could communicate with their allies, larger communities could engage in trade or political alliance, and individuals could explore and make personal contacts. This network of trails, rivers, creeks, and other waterways stretched for usual purposes for several hundred miles, and for important diplomatic or military purposes, they connected people one thousand to fifteen hundred miles distant.[1]

At the other edge of the continent, the peoples of what is now the Pacific Northwest were similarly dependent on their interconnected river systems. Historian Linda Nash noted in a discussion of the Skagit River that "Indians in this region traveled almost exclusively by canoe. So fully did they depend upon the river for movement that, prior to the arrival of whites, there had been no trails along the main channel."[2] People along the Columbia River and its tributaries traveled, bathed, fished, and communicated in and through their rivers; all cultural life was focused on waterways and the rich, nutritious salmon that coursed through them.[3]

For Americans of the period, waterways were just as crucial. Rivers, after all, carried freight downriver far more efficiently than people or work animals—especially given the poor state of most roads and trails in the early republic.[4] Farmers had to live near waterways to get their crops to market; everything from china cups to barrels of whiskey to the newly established U.S. mail had to travel primarily through and over watercourses.

Lewis and Clark traveled just before some of the explosion in use of waterways that came immediately later in the nineteenth century. In the first decades of the 1800s, investors began to realize that where nature had not had the "foresight" to create water connections, human beings could. In addition to roads, turnpikes (pay-as-you-go roads, often better maintained than free ones), and other overland connectors, in the first quarter of the nineteenth century, corporations, cities, and private investors began to build canals. The Erie Canal, built in 1817–25 to connect the 363 miles between the Upper Great Lakes and the Hudson River (and thus, the city of New York), was the most spectacular success of this period of canal building.[5]

The steam engine, too, soon helped transform the use of

the continent's major rivers, particularly the Mississippi, the Ohio, and the Lower Missouri. Although steam power was first developed in the late eighteenth century, it was not commercially applicable until the early 1800s. The first steamboat ascent from New Orleans, Louisiana, to Louisville, Kentucky, in 1816 was a major marker of transportation change. Suddenly people could, without having to use their own labor or draft animals to push, pull, or pole, take *up*stream heavy freight—especially the heavy and increasingly profitable freight of the South's white cotton. By 1840, more than five hundred boats served more than five thousand miles of the Ohio-Mississippi system.[6] Operating over the networks of waterways that laced across North America, such transit knit together the commercial power of the expanding United States.

In traveling up one of the continent's major rivers, searching for a water route to the Pacific Ocean, the Corps of Discovery carried out their era's imperative to make the best use of waterways to connect and to carry. Their whole mission reflected this focus on waterways. Even on a walk, Lewis situates himself in relation to "a fine open grove of cotton wood," a water-loving tree that in open western country is often the first (and sometimes the only) signal of a nearby creek or stream. He defines the stretch of ground over which he walks by how it connects with nearby waterways; he explains that he is on a plain that "extends with the same bredth from the creek below to … near three miles above parrallel with the river." Throughout the years of their journey, the corps would define themselves—and their whole expedition—in relation to rivers, creeks, and sources of flowing water. In so doing, they reflected their cultural context as well as the environments they sought to explore. Exploring the waterways of the great West, the expedition sprang from a different set of environmental priorities than we hold in the modern United States.[7]

Moreover, Lewis and Clark encountered other peoples and came to know them through water travel. Not only their entire route but also their whole cultural mapping of previously foreign cultures and nations was structured through the meandering routes of first the Missouri River, then the Clearwater, the Snake, and the great Columbia. They came to know groups of people along the river—the Mandans, the Hidatsas, and later the many tribes of the Pacific Northwest—precisely because those people, like Lewis and Clark, used and needed the rivers of their regions.[8]

As the French before them, and as many indigenous groups of their own time, Americans in this period came to know, understand, and assert power in North America largely through waterways. In addition, their mission of exploration

The Corps Leaving St. Charles. Since there are no visual records of the journey, artists have been free to represent their imagined view. In this mural, the artist represented the keelboat with a front cabin, which it did not have. The canoes are also pictured as birch bark, when dugouts would have been more accurately used. Photograph of a mural painted in 1963 by Charles Morganthaler. Courtesy of First Bank, St. Charles, Missouri.

and reporting was consistent with a broader American and European imperative of making known previously unknown territory.

The American Need to Interpret and Make Known

Unlike today's intrepid explorers, Lewis and Clark had no global positioning system to guide them. No satellite-created maps gave them reassuring images of their surroundings; no maps at all back in "Washington City" told them anything about the places they were attempting to reach.

In a context in which they knew little about where they would go, the Corps of Discovery took as a prime directive precisely that puzzle: to discover, to uncover, to make known to Americans much of the vast continent that remained unknown to them (although, as events would demonstrate, it was well known to many other societies). Lewis and Clark's cadre did not, however, embark upon this voyage uniquely or singularly; they were part of a broader Euro-American project of exploration and description. They also were committed to a way of making known the unknown that tells us much about their society's priorities and values. They went not simply as explorers but as quantifiers, committed to numerically tabulating and quantifying everything they could.

Tempting as it is to see Lewis and Clark as unique—and as uniquely *American*—in the larger sense the Corps of Discovery was one of a vast fleet of voyages that had set off since the early modern period to recover and bring home information about foreign places and foreign peoples. Many of these voyages are well known: Columbus's trip across the Atlantic to Hispaniola, Cook's exploration of the South Pacific, De Soto's exploration of what are now the Lower Mississippi states. Yet in addition to those trumpeted expeditions, many quieter and more mundane explorations were being launched from the world's metropolitan centers throughout the centuries preceding Jefferson's instructions to his two lieutenants. The eighteenth-century Swedish naturalist Carl Linnaeus sent off his students into the far reaches of South America and Asia to bring back samples of fruits and plants that could be cultivated to enrich Sweden's domestic exports. Intrepid artists such as seventeenth-century German craftswoman Maria Sibylla Merian braved tropical dangers to travel throughout South America painting beautiful illustrations of plants, birds, and insects to feed the growing scientific curiosity of Europe's literate elite.[9]

Indeed, in the United States, voyages of discovery and cultural contact were a sort of mini-industry by the early nineteenth century. Naturalists such as John J. Audubon, Henry Rowe Schoolcraft, and Thomas Nuttall spent months and even years in the early decades of the 1800s tramping through the American countryside to record their impressions of "new" regions' minerals, geology, birds, insects, creatures, medical plants, useful agricultural products, and native culture. And, in a voyage most closely linked with that of Lewis and Clark, President Thomas Jefferson charged George Hunter and William Dunbar with exploring the Lower Mississippi and Ouachita Rivers (now in Louisiana and southern Arkansas) in 1804–5.[10] To travel, to explore, and to make known was a fiery passion consuming many ambitious Americans and Europeans of the late eighteenth and early nineteenth centuries, one that combined political goals with personal drive and connected their own sense of manly bravery and virtue with the hard-headed calculations of expanded commerce and commercial profit.[11]

Lewis and Clark's journey demonstrates their goals. They were not simply to determine a river route to the western ocean but were to record and describe what they found. The description of the "barking squiril" from Lewis's journal excerpt was typical of the ways in which Lewis and Clark—like other explorers of their era—tried to convey to far-off, future readers all that they saw that was new and undescribed. (We would, by the way, be familiar with these small and prolific animals. Now identified as prairie dogs, they were before modern agricultural and pest-control methods a main feature of the ecosystems of the continent's great grasslands.)

Whenever possible, such explorers operated by analogy; something new was often described with reference to something known and familiar. The "grove of plumb trees loaded with fruit" through which Lewis walked, for instance, made sense to him in relation to familiar trees back home. He "observed but little difference between this fruit and that of a similar kind common to the Atlantic States." Such information helped the readers of expedition journals assess the likely agricultural potential, commercial markets, or other environmental resources of a place that they themselves had not seen.

Yet not all of Lewis and Clark's focus was on simple textual description. These explorers had in common with other Euro-American "discoverers" of their time not simply a shared impetus of exploration but a shared commitment to measurement and quantification. In their hand-hewn pirogues, along with roughly made clothing and sometimes-makeshift equipment, the expedition's leaders carried a variety of notebooks with which to write down and notate their trip, as well as a variety of tools and pieces of equipment with which to measure and quantify their environments. Lewis's requests for scientific and medical equipment went on for pages, and they included a quadrant; a "Mariner's Compas" as well as a smaller, portable, compass and two pole chains; thermometers; a "Cheap portable Microscope"; a foot-long brass scale; magnetic needles; measuring tape; hydrometers; a theodolite; and other instruments and writing equipment.[12] The journals of Lewis and Clark are full of notes about time of day, exact temperature (which they measured frequently with portable thermometers), and their latitude and longitude.

The excerpt from Lewis's journal that starts this essay is a good example of the ways in which the expedition's leaders tried constantly to quantify their surroundings, even in rough terms: Lewis was not simply walking across on a high plain, he was on "a plain about 20 feet more elivated than that on which we were encamped"; moreover, "this plane extends with the same bredth from the creek below to the distance of near three miles above parrallel with the river...." His distances were approximate guesses, but he did his best to

Scientific equipment used on journey. Lewis's watch and telescope and Clark's watch-chain compass and journals. Photograph by David Schultz, Missouri Historical Society.

describe a previously unknown world in terms that mapmakers, statisticians, economic thinkers, and other scientific and governmental readers could share and understand.

Human Beings in Their Environments

Meriwether Lewis, William Clark, and the people who traveled with them did not travel simply to new physical terrain. They also moved in imaginative terrain shaped by the expectations of their cultures. Lewis and Clark did not approach new environments as they would a blank slate; they brought with them powerful notions about the appropriate and moral uses of land.

First and foremost, the Corps of Discovery's leaders reflected a profound American commitment to *ordered* terrain. Land that was wild, raw, and savage (as they perceived it), such as swamps, dramatic gorges, old forests full of underbrush and rotting, fallen-down trees, was wasted land. Only land that was ordered—land put to good and productive use, with some sense of clear distinction between different types of plants and topography—was useful and therefore valuable and beautiful. We might contrast in our mind's eye two different environments. First, envision a marshy wetland created by a beaver dam: a stream broadens out to become a whole series of wide, shallow, interconnecting rivulets in which a profusion of young bushes, vines, and flowers grow, and old, dead trees and logs rot. Second, picture a neat, well-tended farm in which geometrically laid-out fields are bounded by well-painted fences that run in straight lines, and hedgerows are kept clipped back and do not run onto the fields or get confused with woodlands behind. These two different vistas—one complex, dense, hard to see through, and full of often-hidden and certainly not human-controlled life, and the other easy to see across, easy to bound and describe, and characterized by only one or two main plant species in each area—represent the "bad" and "good" ends of the environmental spectrum for most Americans of the turn of the nineteenth century.

Cultivated farmland—bounded in the distance, perhaps, by scenic woods or mountains but certainly not encroached upon by those uncontrollable environments—represented to most free Americans the ideal form of land. (People who lived and worked in slavery presumably held somewhat different assessments of the beauty of farmed terrain.) An orderly farm was a good use of land, a moral use of land. To farm a plot was to use it as God had intended.[13]

Even as American expeditionary parties fanned out across the continent seeking what was new and unknown, they therefore looked for what was familiar (like the plum trees) or what went along with their sense of propriety in land. Occasionally, they found it. Lewis notes in his day's journal, for instance, as he walked across a level grassy expanse in the fall of 1804, that "the shortness and virdue of the grass gave the plain the appearance throughout it's whole extent of beatifull bowling green in fine order." This approving description of land "in fine order," looking well cared for, with short-clipped, green grass, reflects the value Americans of his time placed on land that met their expectation for agricultural caretaking. His reference to a "bowling green" also called to mind the lawn-bowling games that were a popular form of entertainment for late-eighteenth-century gentlemen. Other, wilder spaces could be dramatic and even inspiring, but American settlement and community growth was understood to require quieter, orderly, more pastoral landscapes.

Even as they saw and recorded places new to them, Lewis and Clark moved in a world created at least partly by their own expectations. Yet in other ways, too, Lewis and Clark moved through environments of human beings. The journal entry quoted earlier is typical of many aspects of their environmental understanding, but it is misleading in some others: in particular, this is an excerpt in which there are no other people.

One thing that it is easy to forget as contemporary Americans—after all, our country now occupies the entire east-west expanse of a good stretch of the North American continent—is that the Corps of Discovery traveled almost the entire way through land claimed, used, named, and described by other people and other nations. Their own understanding of the places through which they moved thus was created in large part not only by their own observations, measurements, and experiences but also by their interactions and conversations with other people.

James Ronda, whose essay on American Indians appears earlier in this volume, has written an evocative and readable book about this aspect of the journey of the Corps of Discovery.[14] He argues that the expedition was defined throughout its travels—on the difficult upriver journey on the Missouri, in the wintering in the Mandan and Hidatsa villages near the great bend of the Missouri, in the rough passage over the mountainous spine of the continent, in the journey downriver through the densely populated regions of what is now the Pacific Northwest, and through all the long journey back home—by existing cultures along the way. Through interactions with other communities, he notes, the members of the Corps of Discovery found out about what to eat, how far they could travel, which peoples they would soon encounter, and what to expect upstream or downriver. Without these interactions, most of their observations would have been pointless. The whole purpose of the expedition was not simply to map out blank space but to create and foster commercial and diplomatic links with the nations to the west of the fledgling United States.

After all, Ronda notes, "the explorers proved the greatest tourist attraction in western America."[15] They were watched all along their way, and rumors of their trip spread upstream ahead of them far faster than they could travel. They moved in an environment defined by the trade, military, and cultural alliances of myriad peoples whom they did not well understand. Their growing knowledge of this political and social terrain was just as crucial as their record of the physical course of the Missouri, the location of Lemhi Pass, or the number of trade medallions they had given away. Moving into other peoples' frame of knowledge as they moved farther and farther from their own, Lewis and Clark traversed a terrain as defined by human relationships and human expectations as by winds, waters, and foreign species. In so doing, they helped create a new world for Americans, one filled suddenly with "barking" ground squirrels, wild falls, laborious new portages, and new and unfamiliar peoples.

Notes

1   Helen Hornbeck Tanner, "The Land and Water Communication Systems of the Southeastern Indians," in *Powhatan's Mantle: Indians in the Colonial Southeast*, eds. Peter H. Wood, Gregory A. Waselkov, and M. Thomas Hatley (Lincoln: University of Nebraska Press, 1989).

2   Linda Nash, "The Changing Experience of Nature: Historical Encounters with a Northwest River," *The Journal of American History* 86, no. 4 (2000): 1,600–29, n. 21.

3   Joseph E. Taylor III, *Making Salmon: An Environmental History of the Northwest Fisheries Crisis*, ed. William Cronon, Weyerhaeuser Environmental Books (Seattle: University of Washington Press, 1999); Richard White, *The Organic Machine* (New York: Hill and Wang, 1995).

4   John Opie, *Nature's Nation: An Environmental History of the United States* (Fort Worth, Tex.: Harcourt Brace College Publishers, 1998), 131.

5   D. W. Meinig, *Continental America 1800–1867*, vol. 2 of *The Shaping of America: A Geographical Perspective on 500 Years of History* (New Haven, Conn.: Yale University Press, 1993), 318–21; Opie, *Nature's Nation*, 131–32.

6   Meinig, *Continental America*, 323.

7   On water and the environment of the western United States, see Mark Reisner, *Cadillac Desert: The American West and Its Disappearing Water* (New York: Penguin Books, 1986); Donald Worster, *Rivers of Empire: Water, Aridity, and the Growth of the American West* (New York: Pantheon Books, 1985; reprint, New York: Oxford University Press, 1992).

8   James P. Ronda, *Lewis and Clark among the Indians* (Lincoln: University of Nebraska Press, 1984).

9   Lisbet Koerner, "'Should Coconuts Chance to Come into My Hands': Acclimatization Experiments," in *Linnaeus: Nature and Nation* (Cambridge, Mass.: Harvard University Press, 1999); Natalie Zemon Davis, "Metamorphoses: Maria Sibylla Merian," in *Women on the Margins: Three Seventeenth-Century Lives* (Cambridge, Mass.: Harvard University Press, 1995).

10   Robert J. Malone, "Everyday Science, Surveying, and Politics in the Old Southeast: William Dunbar and the Influence of Place on Natural Philosophy" (Ph.D. diss., University of Florida, 1996); John Francis McDermott, "The Western Journals of Dr. George Hunter, 1796–1805," *Transactions of the American Philosophical Association* 53, no. 4 (1963): 5–133.

11   Michael Dettelbach, "Humboldtian Science," and Janet Browne, "Biogeography and Empire," in *Cultures of Natural History*, eds. Nicolas Jardine, James A. Secord, and Emma Spary (Cambridge, England: Cambridge University Press, 1996).

12   "Lewis's List of Requirements," *Letters of the Lewis and Clark Expedition, with Related Documents, 1783–1854*, ed. Donald T. Jackson, 2d ed., 2 vols. (Urbana: University of Illinois Press, 1978), 1:69–75.

13   Conevery Bolton Valenčius, *The Health of the Country: How American Settlers Understood Themselves and Their Land* (New York: Basic Books, 2002).

14   Ronda, *Lewis and Clark among the Indians.*

15   Ibid., 221.

Suggested Readings

Berry, Wendell. *The Unsettling of America: Culture and Agriculture*. San Francisco: Sierra Club Books, 1977. Rev. ed. San Francisco: Sierra Club Books, 1996.

Cayton, Andrew R. L., and Fredrika J. Teute, eds. *Contact Points: American Frontiers from the Mohawk Valley to the Mississippi, 1750–1830*. Chapel Hill: University of North Carolina Press, 1998.

Cronon, William, ed. *Uncommon Ground: Rethinking the Human Place in Nature*. New York: W. W. Norton and Company, 1996.

Heat-Moon, William Least. *PrairyErth (A Deep Map)*. Boston: Houghton Mifflin, 1991.

Isenberg, Andrew C. *The Destruction of the Bison: An Environmental History, 1750–1920*. Edited by Donald Worster and Alfred W. Crosby. Studies in Environment and History. Cambridge, England: Cambridge University Press, 2000.

Price, Jennifer. *Flight Maps: Adventures with Nature in Modern America*. New York: Basic Books, 1999.

Vileisis, Ann. *Discovering the Unknown Landscape: A History of America's Wetlands*. Washington, D.C.: Island Press, 1997.

West, Elliott. *The Contested Plains: Indians, Goldseekers, and the Rush to Colorado*. Lawrence: University Press of Kansas, 1998.

White, Richard. *"It's Your Misfortune and None of My Own": A History of the American West*. Norman: University of Oklahoma Press, 1991.

Thomas Jefferson and the Expanding Union

Peter S. Onuf

University of Virginia

The interesting points of the portage between the heads of the Missouri & the water offering the best communication with the Pacific Ocean should also be fixed by observation, & the course of the water to the ocean, in the same manner as that of the Missouri.

—Thomas Jefferson, instructions to Meriwether Lewis

[A]t 11 A.M. we met a Captain McClellin late a Capt. of Artily. of the U States Army assending in a large boat. this gentleman an acquaintance of my friend Capt. Lewis was Somewhat astonished to see us return and appeared rejoiced to meet us. we found him a man of information and from whome we received a partial account of the political State of our country,... this Gentleman informed us that we had been long Since given out [up] by the people of the U S Generaly and almost forgotton, the President of the U. States had yet hopes of us;... he gave us Some Buisquit, Chocolate Sugar & whiskey, for which our party were in want and for which we made a return of a barrel of corn & much obliged to him. Capt. McClellin informed us that he was on reather a speculative expedition to the confines of New Spain, with the view to entroduce a trade with those people.

—William Clark, journal entry, September 17, 1806

Thomas Jefferson exulted in prospects for western exploration, settlement, and economic development. Though he never traveled west himself, he was a voracious reader of travel accounts and an armchair natural philosopher with an insatiable thirst for new knowledge. For Jefferson, the West was not a howling, dangerous wilderness but rather, as he called it in his first inaugural address, a "chosen country, with room enough for our descendants to the thousandth and thousandth generation."[1] Near the end of his life, Jefferson reaffirmed his faith in America's future. The progress of civilization was inscribed on the western landscape:

> I have observed this march of civilization advancing from the sea coast, passing over us like a cloud of light, increasing our knowledge and improving our condition, insomuch as that we are at this time more advanced in civilization here than the seaports were when I was a boy. And where this progress will stop no one can say. Barbarism has, in the meantime, been receding before the steady step of amelioration; and will in time, I trust, disappear from the earth.

This philosophy was what a later generation called Manifest Destiny: civilization and empire inexorably moved westward as expansion across space recapitulated progress through time. In Jefferson's panoramic vista, the ascending stages of historical development could be seen all at once, from "the earliest stage of association" among the "savages of the Rocky Mountains" to "the most improved state in our seaport towns."[2]

Yet the story did not have to turn out this way. Jefferson knew all too well that different outcomes were possible. The fragile union of independent American states could collapse, as it nearly did on the eve of his election in 1800. Without an effective union, the orderly expansion of westward settlement could be thwarted, as it had been during much of the colonial

Thomas Jefferson. Oil on canvas by Edward Percy Moran.
Missouri Historical Society Museum Collection. Photograph by
Allied Photocolor, 1990.

period, and perhaps even reversed. Or, more troubling still, the "semi-barbarous citizens" who swarmed across the frontiers could revert to savagery, subsisting all too easily on nature's bounty and turning their backs on civilization. Recognizing these realities, Jefferson did not hesitate to exercise the power of the federal state to shape and direct the progress of westward expansion.

Commerce

Fulfillment of Jefferson's prophetic vision depended on the expanding networks of trade that Captain McLellan and other enterprising Americans sought to foster. Without markets, why would settlers bother to produce surpluses? Without the reinforcement of common economic interests, how could political loyalties be sustained?

Jefferson's hostility to merchants is notorious—and hardly surprising for a tobacco planter who never could escape the thrall of debt to British creditors. For suspicious agrarians, merchants epitomized pure profit seeking; they lacked patriotic attachments to particular places, such as Jefferson's "country," Virginia, and therefore any sense of public responsibility. Farmers therefore were, as he famously wrote in *Notes on the State of Virginia*, "the chosen people of God, if ever he had a chosen people, whose breasts he has made his peculiar deposit for substantial and genuine virtue."[3] The independent husbandman relied on his "own soil and industry" for subsistence, while the dependence of all other classes begat "subservience and venality." Jefferson did not equate independence with isolation, for it was the farmer's virtue—his unfettered, uncorrupted natural sociability—that constituted the most durable bond of union. But here was the crux of Jefferson's paradox: farmers could never escape market relations, for society itself was dependent on—if not synonymous with—commerce, or "intercourse in the affairs of life." It was hardly surprising then that the agrarian Jefferson should look *eastward*, toward "our seaport towns," for progressively higher forms of civilization. It was through these towns that Americans were connected to the centers of European civilization and to the commercial opportunities of the Atlantic trade system.

Of course, Jefferson believed Americans certainly should keep their distance from European vice and corruption—this was the animating impulse of his expansionist faith. At the same time, however, he recognized the need to perfect and improve commercial ties between Old World and New World, to free trade from the distorting effects of mercantilist regulations and thus bring American producers and European consumers closer together. Jefferson's agrarianism juxtaposed virtuous farmers with avaricious merchants, but the territorial expansion that would create a great "empire of liberty" depended on a synthesis of his antithetical terms. In Jefferson's paradoxical vision, enterprising Americans would come together by moving apart. Americans, therefore, would have to develop a transportation and communication infrastructure across their vast continental domain. Providentially, nature showed the way; the great system of rivers would link farmers to distant markets, transforming inland trading centers into bustling "seaports." The cement of union was man's sociable nature, the tendency of independent individuals to associate for mutual protection and improvement and to exchange the fruits of their labors. But "nature" would have to be mapped and surveyed, mastered and improved, if man's natural potential was to be fulfilled. The first challenge was to clear the field of rival claimants.

External Enemies

The West was not simply a blank state during the early years of the republic. The Indian peoples who inhabited the region constituted formidable obstacles to the progress of American settlement. But they also possessed invaluable information about the continent and its resources that Jefferson and his countrymen sought to exploit. In return, Americans offered trade goods that were already familiar in Indian Country as well as the less-tangible promise of "civilization." In philanthropic moments, Jefferson looked forward to the assimilation of these native proprietors, imagining that one day they would "form one people with us, and we shall all be Americans."[4] But that prospect was distant at best, for the Indians were reluctant to give up their "barbarous" way of life—and the vast hunting grounds needed to support it. Too often, the new nation's enemies abetted them. As pawns of corrupt European empires, Indians tragically resisted the spread of republican civilization, their only hope for survival in the modern world.

In his inaugural address, Jefferson celebrated the happy fact that "a wide ocean" separated the New World from the "exterminating havoc" of the Old World. But Europe was very much present in the American hinterland, and its influence was felt—or imagined—in the belligerent posture of the "merciless Indian savages."[5] Jeffersonians conceived of conflicts along the frontier in ideological terms, imputing hostilities to the counter-Revolutionary, antirepublican principles of European imperial rivals and their Indian proxies. War against the Indians—even a war that would lead to their removal or extermination—thus was seen as yet another phase of the republican revolution against Old World tyranny and despotism. That Europeans would deploy "savage" auxiliaries against the Americans merely confirmed the Indians' reactionary antipathy to the progress of civilization; that they would align with corrupt Europeans rather than with their true countrymen, the Americans, showed that there was no place for them on the continent.

American Revolutionaries articulated the Enlightenment's faith in the progress of civilization in political terms. Adherence to republican principles, Jefferson's fundamental definition of Americanism, justified and disguised less-exalted means and motives. The geopolitical rivalries in the West that would determine the republic's future do not seem, in retrospect—or, to skeptical contemporaries—to have much to do with principles. The same enterprising impulses that attracted Americans—the fur trade, land speculation, the expansion of commercial agriculture—inspired European projects in the region. The great question was who would control the port of New Orleans and with it, the inland empire of the Mississippi River trade system. This issue was central in American politics from the time of the Revolution onward. The Revolutionary generation understood that the continuing union of east and west ultimately depended on extending American jurisdiction across the Appalachian Mountains, which depended on diplomacy and power politics.

Because enemies surrounded the new nation, its continuing expansion was by no means assured. Visionaries such as Jefferson might see the spread of republican institutions and the addition of new states to the federal union as inevitable, but no one expected the process to be smooth or peaceful. Patriotic Americans who celebrated the Louisiana Purchase were amazed and relieved that it came so cheaply, that war—the preemptive strike on New Orleans urged by Federalists, or the mass mobilization of American settlers threatened by political adventurers upriver—had not been necessary after all. Jefferson hoped to avoid armed conflict, less because of his pacifistic principles than because he feared, with good reason, that the Americans might lose and the union might collapse. One day, when American settlements spread thickly across the continent, the new nation would be impregnable. Once the landscape had been transformed and the patriotic attachments of an enterprising yeomanry were well secured, the United States would be, as Jefferson promised in his inaugural address, "the strongest Government on earth."[6] But that day had not yet arrived at the time of the Louisiana crisis, not even after the threat of a powerful French presence at the mouth of the Mississippi River was miraculously averted by the purchase. For the greatest threats to the survival of the union came from internal, not external sources.

Centrifugal Tendencies

For many contemporary commentators, including the anxious governors of neighboring empires, the spread of American settlements seemed to be an irresistible, almost natural force. When Americans insisted that the United States had a "natural right" to New Orleans and the mouth of the Mississippi, they warned that rapidly increasing frontier settlements eventually would enforce their demand for free trade on the river, whatever diplomats might decide. There was a strong undercurrent of anxiety in this expansionist rhetoric, for the American government was itself powerless to control the tide of settlement. And Jefferson knew that settlers' loyalties were tenuous, that economic interest could lead them to pledge allegiance to whatever power could secure them access to the Atlantic trade system. Commerce might draw Americans together in a harmonious union of interests, but it might just as easily divide them. Just as nature had to be improved to facilitate the spread of republican civilization, so trade had to be directed into the right channels. Jefferson and his fellow agrarians railed against merchants, the "foreign and false citizens" without patriotic attachments to their country who infested "our seaports" and were "planted in every little town and district of the interior country."[7] But it was equally and more ominously true that the loyalties of the "chosen people" themselves—the enterprising land speculators and commercial farmers who spearheaded expansion—were also for sale.

The problem of loyalties was central to the Revolution. Republicanism was a risky experiment; a people who abjured allegiance to the king also might turn against the governors they had chosen for themselves. One revolution could lead to another, fearful conservatives worried, and the result would be anarchy. Their concerns were justified. There were separatist movements in frontier regions of almost every state, from the Maine District of Massachusetts to the new state of Franklin in the western region of North Carolina, and though most separatists proclaimed their fealty to the Revolutionary cause (even while challenging the authority of the original states in the union), they sometimes looked to Britain or Spain for support in their political enterprises. The renegade state of Vermont (formerly the northeastern counties of New York) was most successful in pursuing an independent, potentially counter-Revolutionary "foreign" policy, entering into secret negotiations with the British while the Revolution was still in progress. Political adventurers in Kentucky conspired with Spanish officials in New Orleans even after their new state gained its independence from Virginia. Settlers found separatism attractive because they had serious grievances against the states that claimed jurisdiction over them, but they failed to establish effective legal and governmental institutions and offered little protection against Indian enemies. Conflict over land titles was the most compelling issue in almost every case, as the old states sought to protect the interests of land speculators who acted under their authority from the challenges of "foreign" squatters and speculators. Kentucky remained a hotbed of political discontent throughout the early national period precisely because there was so much confusion over conflicting land claims.

Conflicts of interest over land titles belied and inverted the Jeffersonian image of the virtuous and independent yeoman freeholder. The frontier farmer's patriotism could not be taken for granted as the solid foundation of a stable republican edifice; instead, it would be the result of the successful resolution of endemic jurisdictional conflicts. Sectional divisions among the old states also jeopardized the future of the union. If separatist movements generally reflected east-west tensions, focusing immediately on land and Indian policy, incipient sectionalism grew out of controversy over national commercial policy between northern mercantile interests and southern staple producers. The ultimate question in both cases was, how would different sectors of the economy and sections of the country best fit into the Atlantic trade system?

Controversy over the future of the West and over the continuing union of North and South came to a head in the late 1790s and in the first years of Jefferson's presidency. Chafing under the domination of northern High Federalists, Jeffersonian Republicans broached the possibility of secession in 1798; had the election impasse of 1800 not been resolved in their favor, they were prepared to jettison the federal Constitution and the union that it had created. Soon thereafter Spanish threats to close the Mississippi and rumors that Napoleon meant to erect a new French empire in the American hinterland revived anxieties about the political future of settlements in the Old Northwest Territory (Ohio), in the new states of Kentucky and Tennessee, and in the far-western reaches of Georgia.

Jefferson articulated his confident vision of America's future at a time when the new nation's prospects were more in doubt than they had been since the darkest days of the Revolution—or would again be until the eve of the Civil War. How could he say that this was "the strongest Government on earth," when its weaknesses were so manifest and divisions among Americans were so conspicuous?

Bonds of Union

It was the conventional wisdom of Jefferson's day, most influentially set forth by Montesquieu in his *Spirit of the Laws*, that republican government could survive and prosper only in small states. The principle of consent operated most effectively in compact societies where virtuous citizens could share common values and interests. The preservation of a large state, by this logic, required a powerful, even despotic government that could enforce its authority on distant provinces. How then could Americans hope to enjoy the benefits of republican self-government in a large, expanding federal union? Was "empire of liberty" a contradiction in terms?

For Jefferson the answer to the problem of size was not to be found in the kind of "energetic" central government Alexander Hamilton and his fellow High Federalists sought to create, but rather it was found in the patriotic attachments of citizens who fully embraced "federal and republican principles." Jefferson believed that order emerged spontaneously in a self-governing people when traditional distinctions between rulers and ruled were obliterated and citizens were conscious of their rights and duties. In his apotheosis of popular patriotism, Jefferson was a precocious nationalist, homogenizing differences in a transcendent conception of nationhood that counteracted the centrifugal tendencies of expansion. Precisely because a despotic central government did not seek to impose order, "every man, at the call of the law, would fly to the standard of the law, and would meet invasions of the public order as his own personal concern." The American Revolution demonstrated the power of patriotic appeals in time of crisis: when the distinction between "public" and "personal" dissolved, the power of the people was irresistible.

Jefferson was an astute political psychologist. He recognized that the United States did not have the coercive resources to govern recalcitrant and unruly frontier settlers; if they were to be governed at all, they would have to govern themselves. But this did not mean that there was no place for an active federal state in Jefferson's empire of liberty. To the contrary, it was incumbent on the U.S. government to clear the way for settlement through diplomatic negotiations with imperial neighbors—negotiations whose success depended on a credible threat of force. The goals of Jeffersonian diplomacy—to insulate the union from external danger and to provide space for expansion—justified the resort to any means necessary, as the Louisiana crisis and subsequent efforts to extend American jurisdiction in West Florida demonstrated. After all, the first law of nature was self-preservation; the need to secure vital national interests preempted

Emigration of Daniel Boone and His Family. Hand-colored lithograph by Regnier after George Caleb Bingham. Missouri Historical Society Photograph and Print Collection.

any moral or constitutional scruples. The future of the American nation depended on a statecraft that could create the kind of homogenous, empty space Jefferson imagined in his inaugural address, a "chosen country" for a "chosen people."

Jefferson's Indian policy also depended on the exercise of power, through diplomacy and war, to achieve the same goals. Ever responsive to the agitation of land-hungry settlers, Jefferson always gave highest priority to acquiring new lands. In peacetime, the threat of force could be concealed; market pressures led indebted Indians to relinquish their property voluntarily. Federal negotiators also offered aid and assistance to Indian efforts to become "civilized," often in collaboration with the philanthropic initiatives of Christian missionaries. The net result, whether in war or in peace, was to speed the retreat and removal of Indian nations as distinct political societies that could threaten the security of the federal republic or block its continuing expansion. If, in the process, a few civilized Indians blended into the tide of white settlement, all the better. In any case, however, the federal state played a central role, giving "nature" a powerful assist by clearing Indians off the land.

The paradox of expansion in Jeffersonian America was that a supposedly spontaneous, natural process depended so crucially on the exercise of state power. Government played a key role in collecting and circulating useful knowledge to facilitate settlement and economic development; in securing property rights and promoting commercial exchange by extending republican institutions and rule of law; and in promoting the internal improvements that enabled farmers and planters to get their surpluses to distant markets. Federal land policy was the centerpiece of this orderly, state-directed process of settlement and development. By surveying and selling the national domain according to the provisions of the

Congressional Land Ordinance of 1785 (based on a system
proposed by Jefferson and fellow committee members the
previous year), the land office provided critical information
that enabled settlers to make informed choices about recoup-
ing their investments in an expanding system of market relations. The purchaser of federal lands thus represented the
antithesis of the subsistence-oriented squatter, or "white
savage," who would have been perfectly content to live off the
land. Under the federal land system, enterprising and orderly
settlers were selected from the larger stream of potential
migrants; the government pledged to uphold their titles
against all other claimants, including squatters. Grateful for
this protection, citizens in the territories and new states
would rally to "the standard of the law" in time of crisis.

Jefferson's faith in popular patriotism thus was not based
on a naïvely optimistic conception of human nature.
Americans in newly settled frontier regions would *become*
good republicans as they sought to improve their condition
within established systems of economic and political opportunity. As Jefferson suggested, individual choices provided the
dynamic energy for expansion, but these choices were structured in ways that drew settlers together and, in doing so,
strengthened the union. By guaranteeing the rapid introduction of institutions of self-government, the territorial system
channeled political ambitions into statehood aspirations and
preempted the appeal of separatist movements—and foreign
alliances. The development of Republican Party organizations
in frontier areas rationalized the distribution of federal contracts and patronage to foster the emergence of local political
elites loyal to the union. If the achievement of statehood eliminated some of this federal largesse, it also opened a wide new
field for political ambition, both in state and federal politics.
That new states, despite their small populations, should enjoy
equal representation in the U.S. Senate constituted one of the
strongest bonds of union. Far from being kept in a permanent

state of colonial subjection, new western states were guaranteed equal standing in the union. Just as republicanism obliterated the traditional distinction between rulers and ruled, so an expanding federal union collapsed the traditional distance between center and periphery, metropolis and provinces.

Jefferson's vision of republican empire, of an expanding union of self-governing republics, represented a bold departure from historic precedents. But the vision—which invoked the beneficent operations of "nature" in a vast, fertile, virgin landscape and stipulated a virtuous, patriotic citizenry ready to exploit its gifts—was profoundly misleading. Both terms of Jefferson's equation were problematic: the "chosen country" had already been "chosen" by others, and the loyalties of American settlers were notoriously volatile. Any number of outcomes was possible—the "manifest destiny" of an expanding nation was only one of them, and it was not necessarily the most likely. To fulfill Jefferson's vision, the continent would have to be explored, surveyed, sold, settled, integrated into expanding market relations, and incorporated into the union on an equal basis. In all these areas, the federal government would play a decisive, continuing role.

Federal involvement in the development of the trans-Mississippi West grew out of diplomatic and scientific initiatives in Jefferson's first term. The Lewis and Clark Expedition helped open this vast domain to successive waves of adventurers, entrepreneurs, and settlers. To many contemporary commentators—and subsequent celebrants of America's Manifest Destiny—the rapid progress of republican "civilization" seemed spontaneous and inexorable, even "natural." Westward expansion, as Jefferson envisioned it in his first inaugural address, could be seen as the ultimate vindication of his conception of minimal, limited government, the form of government that best conformed to nature's laws. Yet now we can see clearly that Lewis and Clark were enacting much more human designs, projecting federal power into a contested region where European empires sought to establish their own influence and authority, and where native peoples sought to secure their ancestral lands. And the federal government would continue to play a critical, even essential role in fostering expansion as it protected vulnerable settlements, founded civil governments, distributed resources, and promoted economic development. Nowhere else in the far-flung republican empire did the federal government exercise such extensive powers. The mythology of popular sovereignty, limited government, and Manifest Destiny may indeed have been (and still be) so powerfully appealing to westerners, and to their countrymen generally, because it disguised and mystified the dependence of independent-minded, liberty-loving, self-governing Americans on the power of the federal state.

Notes

1   Jefferson, "First Inaugural Address," March 4, 1801, in Merrill D. Peterson, ed., *Thomas Jefferson: Writings* (New York: Library of America, 1984), 494.

2   Ibid., Jefferson to William Ludlow, September 6, 1824, 1,496–97.

3   Thomas Jefferson, *Notes on the State of Virginia*, ed. William Peden (Chapel Hill: University of North Carolina Press, 1954), Query XIX ("Manufactures"), 165.

4   Jefferson to Captain Hendrick, the Delawares, Mohicans, and Munries, December 21, 1808, *The Writings of Thomas Jefferson*, eds. Andrew A. Lipscomb and Albert Ellery Bergh, 20 vols. (Washington, D.C.: Thomas Jefferson Memorial Association, 1903–4), 16:452.

5   The phrase is taken from the Declaration of Independence, July 4, 1776, in *Thomas Jefferson: Writings*, 21.

6   Ibid., Jefferson, "First Inaugural Address," March 4, 1801, 493.

7   Jefferson to Elbridge Gerry, May 13, 1797, *Writings of Thomas Jefferson*, 9:383.

Suggested Readings

Jackson, Donald T. *Jefferson and the Stony Mountains: Exploring the West from Monticello.* Urbana: University of Illinois Press, 1981.

Limerick, Patricia Nelson. *The Legacy of Conquest: The Unbroken Past of the American West.* New York: W. W. Norton, 1987.

McCoy, Drew R. *The Elusive Republic: Political Economy in Jeffersonian America.* Chapel Hill: University of North Carolina Press, 1980.

Onuf, Peter S. *Statehood and Union: A History of the Northwest Ordinance.* Bloomington: Indiana University Press, 1987.

Sheehan, Bernard W. *Seeds of Extinction: Jeffersonian Philanthropy and the American Indian.* Chapel Hill: University of North Carolina Press, 1973.

Tucker, Robert W., and David C. Hendrickson. *Empire of Liberty: The Statecraft of Thomas Jefferson.* New York: Oxford University Press, 1990.

———. *Jefferson's Empire: The Language of American Nationhood.* Charlottesville: University Press of Virginia, 2000.

———. *The Origins of the Federal Republic: Jurisdictional Conflicts in the United States, 1775–1787.* Philadelphia: University of Pennsylvania Press, 1983.

Wallace, Anthony F. C. *Jefferson and the Indians: The Tragic Fate of the First Americans.* Cambridge, Mass.: Harvard University Press, 1999.

Weinberg, Albert K. *Manifest Destiny: A Study in Nationalist Expansionism in American History.* Baltimore: Johns Hopkins University Press, 1935.

Public Perception of the Expedition

Betty Houchin Winfield
University of Missouri–Columbia

"Huzzard! Huzzard! Huzzard! Here they come!" the boatmen shouted as they "plyed thear ores with great dexterity," wrote William Clark during those last expedition days of 1806.

The La Charette, St. Charles, and Cantonment Belle Fontaine settlers standing along the riverbanks cheered in the midst of the bursts of the blunderbuss and cannon booms. Forewarned, St. Louisians had waited and waited and waited. For some two and half years, they had waited. Not even President Thomas Jefferson knew the fate of the expedition. Like Ulysses, these travelers disappeared, only to return rugged in appearance and full of great adventures to tell.

And what a sight these men were that September 23 afternoon! They appeared to be Robinson Crusoes dressed entirely in buckskins. Strong in their movements and confident in their manner, the explorers swiftly rowed toward land. The original "voyage of discovery" of thirty-three men was missing only Sergeant Charles Floyd, who had died just months into the trip, and John Colter, who had turned back to the wilderness. The settlers could not wait to hear what had happened. Plied with questions, Captain Clark admitted, "I sleped but little last night."

Two days later at a St. Louis banquet and ball, these back-woodsmen awkwardly consumed wine and long-forgotten delicacies of French pastries. At that Christy's Inn celebration, the captains joined the toasts to Jefferson, his administration, the expedition, the men, the United States, and "Captains Lewis and Clark—Their perilous services endear them to every American heart."

Now, two centuries later, how did we know of these happenings? The exploration occurred before the telegraph, Associated Press, radio, television, satellite, and Internet. In 1806, St. Louis did not even have a newspaper. No reporter traveled with the expedition; only later nineteenth-century explorations included an official correspondent. America's early national era was a public oral culture and primarily a private recorded one. The men's accounts told in St. Louis taverns and the banquet toasts were faithfully recorded in letters sent east, then shared and subsequently printed in the nearest newspaper. Other newspapers reprinted those single-column stories over and over again, with small headlines and no visual images. Without the later cooperative news-gathering and wire services, newspapers freely exchanged news without fear of copyright infringement. The news stories would help the country understand and interpret the exploration. The initial newspaper accounts of the corps' return became the basis for a public perception about the far-off Lewis and Clark Expedition.

Before public opinion polls, such printed accounts, in one sense, publicly legitimized an event. The news stories competed with other possible news for scant newspaper space. The 1806 newspapers, numbering around three hundred, were limited by size, technology, and financial support. Except in the largest eastern cities, they were usually four-page weeklies, financially dependent upon the political parties and subscriptions. In fact, advertising was not then the major outside support; rather, printing contracts and legal notices controlled by the major political parties kept the papers afloat.

Unlike today, most of the American newspapers in 1806 overtly identified with a political party, as either Federalist or Republican. The partisan newspapers' content not only covered the major political events but also interpreted with a political slant the happenings in Congress, the presidency, and state and local politics.

During the Lewis and Clark Expedition, the most prominent newspaper was the tri-weekly *National Intelligencer* (*NI*). Led by an editor who could take shorthand, the *NI* was known for its accurate coverage of congressional proceedings, statements, and official documents. Before the advent of Washington correspondents, other newspapers regardless of party preference copied the *NI* stories verbatim, even though at times the *NI* served as Jefferson's mouthpiece. In general, the only people covered in the news, if mentioned at all, were the most newsworthy political figures: leaders and their associates in business, education, and religion. During this early national era, news accounts did not identify contemporary heroes.

In contrast, the nearly thirty American magazines that existed at the time carried more features about people. Without photographs or other visual depictions, readers depended on words for images. If the word *hero* was mentioned at all, it usually referred to an ancient Greek or Roman leader, biblical figure, or someone of Beowulf's era, as found in epic poetry. It would take another generation for American writers to refer to the Revolutionary War leaders and the country's founding fathers as heroes, and later, gentlemen of the Enlightenment. Most people, including city residents, shopkeepers, soldiers, women, Indians, and slaves, were virtually invisible. Among the rare exceptions were those news accounts identifying women and children captured by Indians, telling of Indian leaders during battles fought with American soldiers and settlers as the country expanded, and announcing particular slaves as "runaways."

When the Lewis and Clark Expedition returned in September 1806, the public may have recalled several previously published accounts about their exploration. In 1803, news stories had appeared about the Louisiana Purchase, the Federalists' opposition to expansion in general, and the controversy over the funding of the expedition. The president's instruction to Lewis was, in part, publicly political: to placate the Federalist opposition. "The object of your mission is to explore the Missouri river, & such principal stream of it ... or any other river may offer the most direct and practicable water communication across this continent for the purposes of commerce."[1] During the corps' preparations in 1803, the partisan news accounts emphasized Lewis as a leader and as Jefferson's secretary and agent. Except for references to soldier Clark, the news only implied that there would be other corps members as the expedition began.

As the men prepared to leave Wood's River in 1804, a *National Intelligencer* article told of their upcoming challenges and pointed out that Lewis had engaged three unnamed hunters whose "knowledge of the different tribes of Indians extended a considerable distance." This June 29 article also noted, "those hunters relate, that during their excursions they saw an Indian woman, who had been taken a prisoner from a nation who lived on the shores of the Pacific Ocean," and is the only contemporary possible news mention of Sacagawea before or after the exploration. This likely reference to Sacagawea would remain as illusive as she was to remain for almost a century.

Any public information about the corps traveled amazingly slowly, with a time lag of weeks, months, and even years between an event and the news account. The public first knew of the corps' 1804 progress, such as the treacherous ascent of the Missouri River, during 1805. The rest of the country did not learn through newspaper accounts of Floyd's death and the hostile Teton Sioux until long after the 1805 winter storms abated, the river ice melted, and the voyage had continued. From Fort Mandan in present-day North Dakota, the captains sent back the keelboat with reports, the men's letters, and scientific specimens in April 1805. In July, a Philadelphia magazine, the *Evening Fireside*, summarized letters from unidentified sources, referred to the captains, and included Lewis's report to Jefferson. This article gave value-ridden descriptions of "These enterprising young men," and pointed to their physical skills and health: "Our travelers experienced a severe winter" and "The party was in good health … only one man died on the journey," without giving his name.

The *Boston Centinel*, using information published in Frankfort, Kentucky, mentioned Floyd's River, named to perpetuate Charles Floyd, "Who died much regretted on the 20th of August." The *Centinel* also emphasized the captains' admirable leadership traits, "the men speak in the highest terms of the humanity, and the uncommon pains and attention to both Captains, Lewis and Clark, toward the whole of them...."[2] Yet, the newspapers did not display such stories prominently, and even the *National Intelligencer* placed Lewis's halfway report under a September headline, "Discoveries" and "Statistical View" among an account of the various western Indian nations and other explorations of the Red and Washita Rivers.[3]

When the corps finally did return a year later, newspapers throughout the country reported the explorers' feat and the joyous St. Louis reception. The *Frankfort (Kentucky) Palladium*, the nearest newspaper, used the letters sent east and broke the story. The *Palladium*'s account was repeated by other newspapers many times verbatim. For example, a letter from one unnamed St. Charles resident who wrote, "They were the first white people that ever visited that country" was copied in the weekly *Palladium* and reprinted in the *National Intelligencer*. Other letters published across the nation reported "Indians are as numerous on the Columbia as the whites are in any part of the U States" and "horses without number" among the Indians and the commercial possibilities, "the whole country furnishing valuable furs."

The *Frederickstown (Maryland) Herald* indicated the excitement over the men's return: "We stop the press to announce with the sincere pleasure, the following *Highly interesting intelligence*, Captains Lewis and Clark are just arrived, all in very good health." Even Federalist newspapers, despite previous opposition to the expedition, could not ignore the public response to the explorers' courage with the joyous return. The *Baltimore Federal Gazette* recounted, "When they arrived 3 cheers were fired" and described the corps' challenge: "They would have been here about the lst of August, but for the detention they met with from snow and frost in crossing mountains on which are eternal snows."[4]

Lewis's final report to Jefferson was first summarized in the *National Intelligencer* on October 27 and then reprinted. As to why Lewis had not sent men back from the Missouri River headwaters as Jefferson had requested, the article cited Lewis's explanation, "it was fortunate he sent no men back, since they owed their lives more than once to their numbers."

In one sense, the two captains framed their own news story by sending their own interpretation of their expedition to the nearest news outlet. Lewis, the better writer, wrote a letter draft for Clark to copy and send to Kentucky. Clark stated in his journal entry on September 24: "we rose early and commencd wrighting our letters. Capt Lewis wrote one to the president and I wrote Govr. Harrison & my friends in Kentucky and Sent of[f] George Drewyer with those letters...."

As the latest news account, Lewis and Clark's joint letter went to Clark's Kentucky brother, George, who shared it with the nearest newspapers. Initially printed in the *Frankfort Palladium* on October 6, Clark's letter was repeated in almost every newspaper's story of the explorers' return, with the same emphasis on the expedition's dangers and the corps' challenges, skills, and achievement.

America's newspaper-reading public, too, read the *Palladium*'s identical, initial laudatory congratulations "on the happy termination of an expedition, which will doubtless, be productive of incalculable commercial advantages in the western country" and "We are persuaded all think and feel alike on the courage, perseverance and prudent department displayed by this adventurous party." Much as a modern-day press release, Clark's letter highlighted the corps' accomplishments and attempted to establish the worth of their exploration for future accounts, years before their journals were to be published. Even magazines such as the November *Literary Magazine of American Register* (Philadelphia) repeated Clark's claims that "we were completely successful" and the erroneous statement, "we have discovered the best route which does exist across the continent of North America in that direction."

While Jefferson said in his annual December message to Congress that the expedition "had all the success which could have been expected," he hid his disappointment that the explorers had not found a northwestern river passage to the Pacific Ocean. The *National Intelligencer* news account grouped Lewis's report to the president together with other explorations of the Louisiana Territory to the Rocky Mountains and the Southwest. For the corps' feat, Jefferson wrote, "it is but justice to say, that Mssrs. Lewis and Clarke, and their brave companions, have, by this arduous service, deserved well of their country." The Federalist newspapers were not fooled. Despite the happiness over the explorers' safe return, the December 17 *Charleston Daily Courier* reported the "very unimportant discoveries of Lewis & Co on the Columbia, Missouri. And Red-river, concluding with recommending further appropriations for prosecuting these glorious discoveries."

For the next three months, the public followed via the press Lewis's travels from St. Louis to the U.S. capital, settlement by settlement, city by city. Residents along the way turned out to see Lewis and "his curious companions, a Mandan chief and several Osage Indians." News references repeated Lewis's and the Indians' arrivals and dribbled Lewis's whereabouts with this kind of announcement: "Captain Lewis, arrived at this place on Thursday last, and on Saturday morning proceeded on his journey to the city of Washington...." The captain's overnight stops became community dinners with congratulatory toasts and helped build anticipation for Lewis's triumphant return.

Clark, on the other hand, played down his own achievement. When communities gave tributes to him at various journey stops, he said, "Gentleman, we ought to assign the general safety of the party to a singular interposition of providence, and not to the wisdom of those who commanded the expedition." In fact, rather than go directly to the nation's capital for the celebration, Clark detoured to Virginia to court the woman who later would become his wife.

Three days after Lewis's homecoming arrival on December 28, the *National Intelligencer* reported that his return was met with "high satisfaction." The *NI* defended the exploration's worth: "Few expeditions have been conducted with more patience, perseverance, or success, and we have no doubt that the curiosity of the readers will be fully satisfied by the statements," which were to come from Lewis's published journals. The newspaper anticipated that the forthcoming work "would not merely gratify literary curiosity, but open views of great and immediate objects of national utility." The public, too, had been waiting for the corps' return and the account of all they had seen and done.

News organizations covered the lavish dinner given in Lewis's honor by the citizens of Washington, where attendants toasted the Constitution, the president, and Lewis and Clark and their brave companions. The country's best-known poet, Joel Barlow, celebrated the corps' feat, a "victory over wilderness, which is more interesting than that over man." Further, in an original ode to Lewis, Barlow urged that the great western river Columbia be renamed "Lewis," calling the expedition leader a hero, the only such reference printed at the time. "Let our Occident stream bear the young hero's name,"[5] Barlow proposed. Such puffery was too much for the Federalists, and one of them satirized the poem months later in the *Boston Monthly Anthology*. The writer, now believed to be Senator John Quincy Adams, poetically criticized Lewis and the exploration:

> What marvels on the way he found
> 　　*He'll* tell you, if inclin'd, sir—
> But I shall only now disclose
> 　　The things he *did not* find, sir.[6]

In that era of strong partisanship, such controversy was highly newsworthy and created discussions among the partisan readers.

During the winter and into the spring, the corps' return was *the* major news story. Jefferson wrote of the initial public response, "never did a similar event excite more joy thro' the United States." Newspapers such as the *National Intelligencer* also recounted that the House set up a committee "to inquire what compensation ought to be made to Messrs Lewis, and Clarke, and their brave companions"(January 5, 1807). The public later learned that Lewis's compensation bill of the land grants and pay amounted to $7,262 (March 11, 1807). The news stories told, too, of the Senate's approval of Lewis's appointment as governor of the Louisiana Territory and Clark's position as superintendent of Indian affairs of Louisiana Territory (March 4, 1807).

By the spring of 1807, several other corps members had become known because of the publication of expedition journals. The story began when Lewis published a series of announcements in the *NI* during March and April about an opportunity to join a list of subscribers for the printed journals. A call for subscriptions would tell the publisher how many copies to print. Lewis promised a map to be ready by the end of October 1807 and the first journal volume by January 1808, followed by two other volumes. He also included an open letter complaining about "several unauthorised and probably some spurious publications now preparing for the press, on the subject of my late tour to the Pacific Ocean by individual entirely unknown to me." Thus, he perpetuated the news story by increasing speculation about the unknown authors. He created public controversy by warning people to be "on guard with respect of such publications" and by adding that these works would "depreciate the worth of the work" he was preparing.

Lewis had given permission to only one other corps member to publish his journal. He wrote that Private Robert Frazier was "entirely unacquainted with the scientific

PROSPECTUS

OF

LEWIS AND CLARK's TOUR

TO THE

PACIFIC OCEAN,

THROUGH

THE INTERIOR OF THE CONTINENT OF NORTH AMERICA,

Performed by order of the Government of the United States,

during the Years 1804, 1805, & 1806.

THIS work will be prepared by Captain Meriwether Lewis, and will be divided into two parts, the whole comprised in three volumes octavo, containing from four to five hundred pages, each, printed on good paper, and a fair Pica type. The several volumes in succession will be put to press at as early periods as the avocations of the author will permit him to prepare them for publication.

PART THE FIRST—IN TWO VOLUMES.

VOLUME FIRST—

WILL contain a narrative of the voyage, with a description of some of the most remarkable places in those hitherto unknown wilds of America, accompanied by a Map of good size, and embellished with a view of the great cataract of the Missouri,—the plan, on a large scale, of the connected falls of that river, as also of those of the falls, narrows, and great rapids of the Columbia, with their several portages. For the information of future voyagers there will be added in the sequel of this volume, some observations and remarks on the navigation of the Missouri and Columbia rivers, pointing out the precautions which must necessarily be taken, in order to ensure success, together with an itinerary of the most direct and practicable rout across the continent of North America, from the confluence of the Missouri and Mississippi rivers to the discharge of the Columbia into the Pacific Ocean.

VOLUME SECOND—

WHATEVER properly appertains to geography, embracing a description of the rivers, mountains, climate, soil and face of the country; a view of the Indian nations distributed over that vast region, shewing their traditions, habits, manners, customs, national characters, stature, complexions, dress, dwellings, arms, and domestic utensils, with many other interesting particulars in relation to them: Also observations and reflections on the subjects of civilizing, governing and maintaining a friendly intercourse with those nations. A view of the fur trade of North America, setting forth a plan for its extension, and shewing the immense advantages which would accrue to the Mercantile interests of the United States, by combining the same with a direct trade to the East Indies through the continent of North America. This volume will be embellished with a number of plates illustrative of the dress and general appearance of such Indian nations as differ materially from each other; of their habitations; their weapons and habiliments used in war; their hunting and fishing apparatus; domestic utensils, &c. In an appendix there will also be given a diary of the weather, kept with great attention throughout the whole of the voyage, shewing also the daily rise and fall of the principal water-courses which were navigated in the course of the same.

PART THE SECOND—IN ONE VOLUME—

THIS part of the work will be confined exclusively to scientific research, and principally to the natural history of those hitherto unknown regions. It will contain a full dissertation on such subjects as have fallen within the notice of the author, and which may properly be distributed under the heads of Botany, Mineralogy, and Zoology, together with some strictures on the origin of Prairies, the cause of the muddiness of the Missouri, of volcanic appearances, and other natural phenomena which were met with in the course of this interesting tour. This volume will also contain a comparative view of twenty-three vocabularies of distinct Indian languages, procured by Captains Lewis and Clark on the voyage, and will be ornamented and embellished with a much greater number of plates than will be bestowed on the first part of the work, as it is intended that every subject of natural history which is entirely new, and of which there are a considerable number, shall be accompanied by an appropriate engraving illustrative of it.

THIS distribution of the work has been made with a view to the accommodation of every description of readers, and is here offered to the patronage of the public in such shape, that all persons wishing to become subscribers, may accommodate themselves with either of the parts, or the entire work, as it shall be most convenient to themselves.

Prospectus for the publication of the narrative of the Lewis and Clark Expedition, published by Lewis to seed subscriptions for the book he never wrote. Clark Family Collection. William Clark Papers. Missouri Historical Society Archives. Photograph by David Schultz, 1998.

matters" but would provide "merely a limited detail of our daily transactions." As a somewhat backhanded compliment, Lewis stated, "with respect to all unauthorized publications relative to his voyage, I presume that they cannot have stronger pretensions to accuracy of information than that of Robert Frazier."[7] Possibly intimidated, Frazier only published a prospectus. To this day, Frazier's journal remains lost, and only his map survives.

Six days later after Lewis's open letter, another corps member, Sergeant Patrick Gass, announced plans for the publication of his own account. In the March and April issues of the *Pittsburgh Gazette*, Gass's publisher issued a subscription call for a book by "one of the persons employed in the expedition." This prospectus quoted Lewis's certificate to the corps member: "as a tribute justly due to the merits of the said Patrick Gass, I declare ... my highest confidence and sincere thanks, while it eminently recommends him to the consideration and respect to his fellow citizens." Appearing to have the captain's approval, Gass's proposal also noted what appeared to be a joint effort by stating that around the campfire "several journals were brought together, compared, corrected and the blanks filled up." Now, the rush was on for the first insider's story. In contrast to Lewis's timetable, Gass promised delivery in two months. And, as compared to the captains' three volumes, Gass would publish only one journal. His book of around three hundred pages would cost $1. The cost of Lewis's journals was unknown at the time.

Given the slowness of the mail delivery, Gass's publisher, Pittsburgh bookseller David McKeehan, probably had not read Lewis's warning before advertising the call for subscriptions. In fact, with the captains' recent national acclaim, Lewis's outburst could be disastrous for the Gass journal. McKeehan quickly wrote a scathing response to Lewis in the *Pittsburgh Gazette*, attacking the corps' expedition and

Lewis's compensation: "These grants and rewards savor more of the splendid munificence of a Prince than the economy of a republican government." Few other newspapers printed McKeehan's letter even after the publisher offered as an inducement two copies of the Gass journals.[8]

The Gass publication, *A Journal of the Voyage & Travels of the Corps of Discovery*, de-emphasized Lewis and Clark and popularized the phrase "Corps of Discovery" in reference to the expedition. People were hungry for an immediate inside account, and being the first journal published, Gass's account immediately went through six editions, including ones in Paris and London (1807–12). Even though Gass received little money and almost a century later a *Dial* magazine reviewer pointed out "the name of Patrick Gass has never been written high in the list of American authors," Gass nonetheless

Captains Lewis and Clark Holding a Council with the Indians. From Patrick Gass, *A Journal of the Voyage & Travels of the Corps of Discovery.* Reprint of the 1811 edition. Chicago: A. C. McClurg and Company, 1904. Missouri Historical Society Library.

became known as a corps member. Despite Gass's unedu-
cated notes, edited by McKeehan, the *Dial* readers learned
that he was forever cheerful on the expedition, afterward saw
service in the War of 1812, married at sixty, fathered seven
children, and died in 1870 at ninety-nine years of age.[9]

Another "unauthorized" journal, a compilation of the
other men's letters and notes, followed, and it further satiated
the public's appetite for the official Lewis and Clark journals.
In fact, it was 1814, when the country was in the midst of a
war, when Clark and Philadelphia littérateur Nicolas Biddle
finally published the Lewis and Clark journals. Because of
wartime-prohibitive publication costs, Biddle abridged the
journals and omitted the scientific discoveries. By this time,
the war was *the* salient news; the Lewis and Clark exploration
was "old news." These journals did not sell well; only 1,417
copies were intact. Without the scientific discoveries in these
excerpted journals, Federalist criticisms gained credence: "the
expedition of Captains Lewis and Clark, tho fully successful,
has become a subject of federal ridicule," wrote the *Pittsburgh
Sun*. News of other western explorations and new inventions
of the Industrial Revolution soon surpassed the expedition
and even the members highlighted in the journals.

Rather than an emphasis on the expedition, news reports
instead featured the circumstances surrounding Lewis's initial
response to Gass's publication, his procrastination in publishing his journals, and the growing controversy that surrounded
him until his death. As governor of the Louisiana Territory,
Lewis struggled. Around St. Louis, it was apparent that Lewis
was unable to cope with territorial affairs, the St. Louis frontier life and politics, and the fiscal accountability of the new
Madison administration. At the same time, his relatives,
friends, and even Jefferson kept asking him about the journal
publication date. Lewis rarely communicated with Jefferson
and began drinking heavily. After receiving much criticism

for his territorial management, Lewis left St. Louis for Washington in September 1809 to raise money and to clear his name. During his fall overland trip along the Natchez Trace, Lewis's companions noted that he acted more and more strangely. On October 10, during an overnight stay in Tennessee at a wayside inn, Grinder's Stand, Lewis apparently shot himself in the head and below the breast. Lewis's reputation, forever frozen at age thirty-five, was based on his accomplishments as a young captain and the speculation about what he might have been. The *Richmond Enquirer* (November 17, 1809), in a heavy-line black column, recounted "the end of a brave and prudent officer, a learned scholar and a scientific gentleman...."

Lewis was buried at the site, and his violent death in that uninhabited area became an unsolved public mystery. Had he been murdered and robbed? Such rumors spread among residents along the trace and began to appear in print. The rumors gained such wide credence that they were discussed in the Tennessee legislature. Even editor Elliott Coues's 1893 expanded version of the Lewis and Clark journals referred to the mystery of Lewis's death.[10] The murder story persisted despite opposing evidence: Companions reported Lewis's mental instability all along this final journey. In fact, just prior to his St. Louis departure, Lewis had granted power of attorney to Clark and two other close friends to dispose of his property, and he had prepared his will shortly after leaving for Washington. Jefferson wrote his own verdict in a memoir to be included with the 1814 Lewis and Clark journal publication: "he did the deed which plunged his friends in affliction and deprived the country of one of her most valued citizens."

Until the end of the nineteenth century, the public perception was on Lewis's post-expedition leadership failure. Only later did the country begin to learn of the vast, virtually unknown scientific data of the original journals. Rather than just the expedition's captains, Lewis and Clark had been pioneer linguists and naturalists and indeed "explorers." It took the interpretations of historians in the 1940s and 1950s for the public to begin to understand the tremendous expedition findings and Lewis and Clark's considerable contributions.

As the two figures identified with western expansion throughout the nineteenth century, Lewis and Clark became the most recognizable corps members. By 1816, the public had been presented with the first printed image of Lewis. As a boost for sales of the official Lewis and Clark journals, the *Analectic Magazine and Naval Chronicle* used an engraving of a full-length portrait of Lewis in Indian dress, which accompanied a two-part series of journal excerpts and an abridged version of Jefferson's *Memoir*. Additional recognition soon followed. The Tennessee legislature renamed one of its state's counties after Lewis and built a public monument in his memory in 1848. Other states vying to honor Lewis named their counties and towns Lewis or Lewiston. Two colleges in Oregon and Idaho took Lewis and Clark's names. Jefferson's words defined Lewis's reputation, not just in 1814, but on that Tennessee monument and as a title of a best-selling book 187 years later: "His courage was undaunted: His firmness and perseverance yielded to nothing but impossibilities: a rigid disciplinarian, yet tender as a father of those committed to his charge: honest, disinterested, liberal, with a sound understanding and a scrupulous fidelity to truth."

Clark's recognition came not only as the expedition's co-leader but also for his public appointments and official honors during his next thirty years. Clark's name had always been paired with Lewis in all versions of expedition journals and in Jefferson's 1806 message to Congress. In 1807, Jefferson appointed Clark brigadier general of the Louisiana Territory militia as well as Indian agent. Clark later served as the territorial governor from 1813 to 1820, followed by an appointment as superintendent of Indian affairs from 1822 until his death in 1838 in St. Louis. Much admired as a territorial leader and a businessman, Clark surpassed the leadership reputation of his well-known soldier brother, George Rogers Clark. William Clark won the respect of Indians for his fairness; they called him chief "Red-head," and St. Louis "Red-head's town," even as he strove to assimilate the native peoples as the country expanded. When Clark died at age sixty-nine, his obituary appeared in the Missouri papers and elsewhere along with the poetry written for the occasion. Newspaper accounts cite Clark's funeral as one of the most impressive ever held in St. Louis.

Until the end of the nineteenth century, most of the other Corps of Discovery members remained invisible. In fact, history books and history texts, even children's books, ignored the expedition and the Corps of Discovery members until the twentieth century. In 1893, when editor Elliott Coues published a more complete edition of the official journals, he chose to highlight only the two captains and Gass in sketches. Coues called Gass, who lived until 1870, the last expedition survivor.

Yet York, Clark's slave, was still living at the time of Gass's death, however invisible to society. Never compensated with land grants or money, York, too, is mentioned in every edition of the journals, albeit not by name. "This nation never Saw a black man before," Clark wrote. The captains refer to his success as a hunter, a trader, a distraction, and an entertainer for the Indians. They mention his courage, strength, loyalty, and humor, along with his vote on an Oregon-coast winter site. The captains named two geographic features after him, including a small tributary stream into the Yellowstone River, York's Dry River. Clark finally granted York his freedom years after the expedition, and York became a freighting businessman in Kentucky and Tennessee for many years. When he died in 1879, a *New York Times* article told of the death of

"Ben," as York was also called. The headline, "The Lewis And Clark Expedition, Death Of 'Old Tom', Supposed To Be The Last Survivor," points mostly to York's association with the captains, primarily Lewis and the expedition. Only early in the twentieth century did artists such as Charles Russell include York in paintings. A 1985 biography, *In Search of York*, highlights York's important contribution to the corps' success.

Another corps member, John Colter, later became a fur trader and earned fame for his Yellowstone discoveries and his Rocky Mountain escapes from the Blackfeet Indians. Colter had been a valuable corps member, and the captains named two geographical sites after him: the Colter Falls below the Great Falls in present-day Montana and Colter's Creek, now the Potlatch River, in Idaho. Colter's refined orienting skills were valuable for the preparations of the 1814 publication of the journals and maps. Clark relied on Colter's description of Yellowstone, the Wind River, and other parts of the Rockies previously unrecorded. Credited as being the first white man to enter what is now Yellowstone National Park, Colter told unbelievable stories of the geothermal sights and the geysers, later called Colter's Hell. Colter was a mountain man, and his daring escapes from the Blackfeet began appearing publicly ten years after the expedition.[11] Later, Washington Irving's *The Rocky Mountains* (1836) recounted Colter's flight from the Blackfeet: Colter was stripped naked and barefoot but outran his captors through five miles of rocky, prickly pear cactus terrain and then wandered another two hundred miles before reaching Fort Raymond. Colter evaded death by the Blackfeet two other times, and by 1810 he had had enough. He married, settled on a farm near La Charette, close to Daniel Boone's Missouri place, and remained there until his 1813 death. A century later, numerous Colter biographies began appearing, emphasizing Colter's Yellowstone discoveries and mountain-man adventures but, alas, not his Corps of Discovery contributions.

By the twentieth century, the public had become more and more interested in the sole woman on the expedition, Sacagawea. Today, Sacagawea is one of the most-known expedition members, but during much of the nineteenth century she was invisible except for her presence in the journals. Newspaper references to Indians during much of that century were not informational but primarily confrontational, including negative accounts of uprisings and battles. Sacagawea's unusual name may have been one reason for her invisibility. It was difficult to pronounce, and each journal keeper had trouble saying it or spelling it. Some called her "the Squaw," "the Indian woman," or the "fur trader's woman." The captains spelled it out phonetically, "Sah-cah-gah-weah." They wrote of the painful birth of her son, Jean Baptiste, nicknamed "Pomp" after a dose of rattlesnake powder, and recorded her illnesses, her quiet endurance of the dangers and hardships, and her vote for a campsite along the Pacific Ocean. Clark called her "the pilot," attesting to her guidance skills and recognition of the Shoshone country. The journal keepers wrote that the presence of Sacagawea and her baby assured the Indians of the expedition's friendly intentions. They also wrote of her cool courage during a flash flood, when high winds nearly capsized the boat and she calmly recovered many valuable papers.

By 1904, Sacagawea had become *the* "new" news story connected with the Louisiana Purchase Exposition in St. Louis and the following year at the Lewis and Clark Exposition in Portland, Oregon. She became part of the centennial celebrations because of her role as a guide across the Continental Divide at Lemhi Pass. Plays, books, and magazine and journal articles highlighted her role to the point of mythmaking. All at once, statues and Charles Russell paintings depicted her. For the St. Louis exposition, New York sculptor Bruno Louis Zimm used a young Shoshone woman as a model for his Sacagawea monument. His statue set an agenda for other public monuments in other states, such as the ones along the Missouri River at Bismarck, North Dakota; at the convergence of the Snake and Clearwater Rivers at Lewiston, Idaho; and elsewhere. Annual celebrations are still held in her name at Lapwai, Idaho.

A 1904 *Century Magazine* included an illustration of Sacagawea along with Clark's 1806 letter to Charbonneau acknowledging her contribution: "Your woman who accompanied you on that long dangerous and fatiguing rout to the Pacific Ocean and back diserved a greater reward for her attention and services on the route than we had to power to give her at the Mandan." Sacagawea's role has captured the imagination of twentieth-century authors who add to the Sacagawea myth of just how important her linguistic and guidance skills were. Writers also place her as a kidnapped victim and slave of Charbonneau, as well as a strong woman, physically and mentally, who survived the rigors of crossing the mountains with a baby on her back.[12]

With few records about her except the journals, Sacagawea remains a mystery, even concerning her death. Is she the woman buried in the shadow of the Rockies at Wind River? A Wyoming state monument placed in the area in 1941 attested to her death there in 1884. Or, did she die in 1812, as one fur trader wrote from Fort Manuel to St. Louis? "This evening the Wife of Charbonneau a Snake Squaw, died of putrid fever she was a good and the best Woman in the fort, aged abt 25 years she left a fine infant girl." Historians generally follow the fur-trader's letter and Clark's note in his 1824–28 cash book listing the roster of the corps members. Clark marked, "Se Car Ja We Au Dead."[13] Clark must have known; as he had promised, he raised Sacagawea's children, the infant daughter, Lizette, Jean "Pomp" Baptiste, and her nephew, Toussaint.

In this new century, perhaps other expedition members will become known. With the Louisiana Purchase bicentennial, public perceptions are again raised about the Corps of Discovery's members and feats. New publications, celebrations, CD/ROMs, plays, operas, reenactments, artworks, Web sites, and even a fresh dollar coin give more interpretations about the Lewis and Clark Expedition. Such renewed notice of the expedition, public accounts, and speculations become part of the news coverage, far beyond those early, scant accounts in the magazines and partisan newspapers of 1806. With a renewed interest, the new media accounts will add to the public perceptions and perhaps fill the mysterious gaps of the Voyage of Discovery's story.

Notes

1 Jefferson to Lewis, June 20, 1803, Thomas Jefferson Papers, Library of Congress, 132:31–38.

2 "A Newspaper Account, Louisiana"; "Lexington, June 18, 1805," *Boston Centinel*, July 13, 1805.

3 *National Intelligencer*, September 26, 1805.

4 *Frankfurt Palladium*, October 9, 1806; *National Intelligencer*, November 2, 1806; "To the Editors of the *Baltimore Federal Gazette*, n.d., but copied in the *Philadelphia Gazette and Daily Advertiser*, October 27, 1806.

5 *National Intelligencer*, January 16, 1807.

6 *Monthly Anthology (Philadelphia)*, March 1807, 3.

7 *National Intelligencer*, March 18, 1807.

8 "Gass's Journal," *Pittsburgh Gazette*, November 16, 1807, p. l. See too Donald T. Jackson, "The Race to Publish Lewis and Clark," in *Voyages of Discovery: Essays on the Lewis and Clark Expedition*, ed. James P. Ronda (Helena: Montana Historical Society Press, 1998), 222.

9 Edwin Erle Sparks, "Patrick Gass, American Explorer," *The Dial* 37 (November 1, 1904): 270–71.

10   Elliott Coues, ed., *History of the Expedition under the Command of Lewis and Clark*, 4 vols. (New York: Frances P. Harper, 1893), 1:xiii–xlix, l–lv, lxii.

11   See also John Bradbury, *Travels in the Interior of America* (London: Sherwood, Neely, and Jones, 1817), 18–21, which recounted the story of Colter's escape.

12   Asebrit Sundquist, *Sacajawea and Co., The Twentieth-Century Fictional American Indian Women and Fellow Characters: A Study of Gender and Race* (Oslo, Norway: Solum Forlag A/S, 1991), 88–89.

13   "404a. Clark's List of Expedition Members," in Donald T. Jackson, ed., *Letters of the Lewis and Clark Expedition, with Related Documents, 1783–1854*, 2d ed., 2 vols. (Urbana: University of Illinois Press, 1978), 638–40.

Suggested Readings

Ambrose, Stephen E. *Undaunted Courage: Meriwether Lewis, Thomas Jefferson, and the Opening of the American West.* New York: Simon and Schuster, 1996.

Ames, William E. *History of the National Intelligencer.* Chapel Hill: University of North Carolina Press, 1972.

Appleman, Roy E. *Lewis and Clark's Transcontinental Exploration, 1804–1806.* Washington, D.C.: U.S. Department of the Interior, National Park Service, 1975.

Betts, Robert. *In Search of York: The Slave Who Went to the Pacific with Lewis and Clark.* Denver: Colorado Associated University Press, 1985.

Ronda, James P. *Lewis and Clark among the Indians.* Lincoln: University of Nebraska Press, 1984. Reprint. Lincoln: University of Nebraska Press, 2002.

———, ed. *Voyages of Discovery: Essays on the Lewis and Clark Expedition.* Helena: Montana Historical Press, 1998.

http://www.psb.org/lewisandclark/inside/corps.html

A New Encounter

The Native Oral Tradition and Lewis and Clark

Angela Cavender Wilson
Arizona State University

A blanket of darkness was settling on the winter village. The children eagerly anticipated the setting sun, knowing then that they could approach their favorite storyteller. As the mothers instructed, he would by now be fed and well rested after arriving the previous day from a nearby village. Knowing grandmothers lovingly wrapped select pieces of meat, delicacies, and prized possessions for their grandchildren to bring to the visitor. When it was finally time, the children paraded into the council lodge and quietly offered their small gifts to the old man. After settling themselves into stillness so as not to disturb the orator, they knew the stories would soon commence as the old man slowly pulled out his tobacco pouch and his pipe. While it seemed to take ages for him to fill his pipe, the children beamed as the elder closed his eyes and began to smoke. At last, the stories would begin....

William Clark and Meriwether Lewis, along with others from their imperial expedition, dutifully recorded details of their long journey by inscribing them on paper, using pen on field books and journals. Anticipating potential capitalist rewards resulting from this expedition, Thomas Jefferson directed the explorers, "The commerce which may be carried on with people inhabiting the line you will pursue, renders a knolege of those people important."[1] Lewis and Clark recorded, then, what they deemed valuable information regarding the Indians of the West and the landscape they inhabited. In producing these material artifacts, these explorers and diplomats created an ethnographic record that offered a rationale for the expedition. For the infant United States, this journey of scientific exploration and discovery justified any underlying expansionist agendas. The Corps of Discovery, therefore, created an important record that facilitated capitalist enterprises and, ultimately, burdened native peoples in the West with the yoke of colonialism. Lewis and Clark's momentous journey and the records originating from it forever changed the lives of the native peoples they encountered.

The native peoples met by Lewis and Clark, however, left different records to the future generations. Native historical records, since time immemorial, were kept orally by carefully trained individuals, often assisted by mnemonic devices such as winter counts, pictographs, notched and bundled sticks, song boards, and numerous accouterments depicting war records or individual accomplishments.

The education of storytellers started early. From the time they were young, they learned to listen attentively and hold those memories carefully in their minds. They learned to memorize quickly; the frequent repetition of the stories fostered quick mastering. To test their knowledge for veracity and completeness, they might be quizzed on the details of

Indian Painting on Skin. From Reuben Gold Thwaites, *Original Journals of the Lewis and Clark Expedition, 1804–1806.* Missouri Historical Society Library.

the story, or they might be asked to recite the stories to elders or younger siblings under an elder's supervision. In doing so, their elders could verify their success or recite the story yet again until they had it satisfactorily engraved into memory. In addition, they were taught to be astute observers of their surroundings. They would learn to remember tracks, signs of seasonal change, location of edible and medicinal plants, and the usual sounds of their surroundings. Indeed, they would be expected to use their knowledge to benefit the community, as its members might someday depend on them. These skills were not innate; they were carefully cultivated with a formality of training in accordance with native notions of appropriate education.

Aside from being the custodians of these physical survival skills, young native children trained within the oral tradition also were conduits of cultural tradition. Many indigenous people deemed their way of recording history more reliable and the superior way for them to remember their past; they believed the Creator had given them the method. Thus, in the transmission of stories through the generations, they fulfilled a divine obligation. The oral tradition served other important cultural functions as well. Oral narratives conveyed cultural morality and societal values. Through the actions of characters, the stories taught expected behavior. In addition, stories linked them to their nation, fostering both a sense of love for and loyalty to that nation as well as to the specific lineage and/or clan to which they belonged. Perhaps most important, the stories connected the living people to the land, teaching that people came *from* the land and therefore were to live *with* the land, which reaffirmed the concept of indigenousness. Thus, in perpetuating the oral tradition, a sense of identity was established, and individuals learned about their place in the world. Even today, despite all the assaults on cultural traditions, the oral tradition remains important among many native people.

When native peoples encountered the written word, many recognized its usefulness but did not view their lack of writing as proof of their inferiority or lack of civility. On the contrary, they often viewed the Euro-American dependency on writing and paper as a weakness—an attitude that persists among some believers in the oral tradition. The notion that people possess an inability to remember something unless it is written down is seen as a sign of a failing or an untutored mind.

Lewis and Clark had the opportunity to hear recited some of these native accounts, particularly by men of the Upper Missouri River such as Black Cat of the Mandan and Tatuckcopinreha of the Hidatsas. Perhaps Lewis and Clark were unaware of the important insights into native worldview these stories offered; they failed to record them in their journals and instead focused on capturing details of material culture. Undoubtedly they dismissed many of these stories as unimportant, relegated to the status of "myth" or "fiction" because of a lack of cross-cultural understanding. Lewis and Clark were not the last ones to dismiss native versions of their own history; indeed, the validity of native oral traditions still is debated hotly within academic circles.

This controversy transcends mere issues of training and reliability. In many ways, this debate pivots around fundamental notions of truth and perceptions of reality. Much of western culture, including the academic discipline of history, is based on the notion that there exists one truth about any given event in the past. Historians see their charge as coming as close as possible to that one truth, objectively interpreting those events by keeping close to what "actually happened." In fact, this philosophy is accepted so widely in western culture that it seems to be considered common sense. The idea that there might be other approaches to interpreting the past, or other truths, was perhaps as mind-boggling for Lewis and Clark as it is for many today.

Of course, there are other approaches to remembering and recounting the past, but even so, it is what is remembered and what is perceived to be true that creates the dissonance for many non-native people. Native oral traditions are easily accepted and even celebrated by non-native people when they align with western values, interpretations, and notions of reality. But when they deviate from the definitions of what is considered acceptable, they are rejected as fantasy from "primitive," "naïve," "simple-minded," or "uncivilized" natives. Native oral traditions often include aspects unexplainable by western scientific principles—things that might be referred to as "supernatural" in western culture. Native people seem to share a belief in the spiritual essence of every part of creation and a belief that human behavior is at least partially dictated by relationships with other spiritual beings. How these relationships are negotiated, how human beings have been influenced by other nonhuman beings, and how nonhumans act with thought and purpose, are all components of many oral narratives. These aspects are not included as a consequence of "myth" or "legend," but rather they are included because they reflect a native reality that all aspects of creation are important.

On the other hand, western culture has designed a hierarchy of the natural world—with humans reigning supreme over all other creatures—and thus operates largely on the basis of a belief in the fundamental inequality in parts of creation. To perpetuate that dominance, it has been necessary for other life-forms to be relegated to an inferior status by denying them their spirituality, consciousness, and even right to exist. Thus when native peoples relate accounts in which spirit beings play a prominent role, there is no framework familiar to many western peoples that can absorb this kind of information as another reality, and the stories are subsequently dismissed as fairy tales.

Interestingly, at the time of Lewis and Clark, native people also were bound by their conception of the world. For example, when a Shoshone man reported to people of his nation that while out riding he had seen people with faces as "pale as ashes," his observations were deemed absurd and were rejected. For some Shoshones, his report seemed beyond the realm of possibility for what was real in their world, or perhaps this particular Shoshone man was not considered a reliable source of information.

The Shoshone man was not the only one shocked by the strange appearance of those in the Lewis and Clark party.

A Nez Perce account, for example, relayed by Lizzie Lowery in 1952, recalled that the people of her village were afraid of the expedition's mules as well as the men's beards, never having seen facial hair before. Also surviving in that oral tradition was a story about a woman named Watkuese, who pleaded for the lives of the strangers when she heard the men among her people talking about killing the white men. Otis Halfmoon (Nez Perce), told a similar story but relayed that the expedition was saved from being killed because the native people were particularly afraid of the black man with them. Elizabeth Wilson (Nez Perce) corroborated both these stories, stating that the native men feared both the white men and the black man, and so they were going to kill them all. In Wilson's account, Watkuese relayed to the head chief her story of how white people had helped her return home after another tribe had captured her. When the chief brought Watkuese's story to the council, they agreed not to allow the killing of Lewis and Clark.

Oral traditions about Lewis and Clark did not begin with the expedition's arrival on native lands; instead they began with the dreams or visions of individuals among various native groups about the coming of white people. For example, in Halfmoon's account, several men had been given the same dream and caused them to make the prophecy that "some day strange people will come over the mountains from the rising sun. They will wear something on their heads with feathers on it. They will eat dogs. They will eat horses. They will mark out lands. They will plant things. They will come to Clearwater River. Some day they will make lots of trouble."[2] Thus, Lewis and Clark's arrival was viewed as the fulfillment of a prophecy. If Halfmoon's Nez Perce tribe had heeded the prophecy, they would have seen the expedition as the start of "lots of trouble."

The Nez Perce were not the only ones to find York, Clark's African American slave, alarming and fascinating. In 1953, Pierre Pichette (Flathead) relayed a story about how his people responded to the arrival of a group from the expedition camped along the Bitterroot River. His nation welcomed them, but York made a fearsome first impression—the Flatheads thought that he had painted himself in charcoal. Pichette said: "In those days it was the custom for warriors, when returning home from battle, to prepare themselves before reaching camp. Those who had been brave and fearless, the victorious ones in battle, painted themselves in charcoal. When the warriors returned to their camp, people knew at once which ones had been brave on the warpath. So the black man, they thought, had been the bravest of this party."[3] Furthermore, because the group's men had short hair—a sign of mourning among many native groups—the Flatheads believed the seven they encountered were in mourning for the remainder of their party, which the Flatheads believed must have been slaughtered. Just as the records left by the Lewis and Clark Expedition often reveal more about their own worldview as they describe American Indians, so too are native accounts more revealing about native worldview than about Lewis and Clark.

In this same account, Pichette recalled that the visitors did not take the robes bestowed to them, and the Flatheads believed that the Americans did not understand the robes were presents. Another Flathead, Sophie Moiese, recounted this same story and additionally noted that the party did not accept the dried meat and camas root given to them, clearly violating usual protocols of hospitality. While the Flatheads might have forgiven the strangers, even a century and a half later, they have not forgotten the details of their first impressions of the trespassers.

Other accounts, including one recorded by explorer Warren Ferris, illustrate that Lewis and Clark, on behalf of the United States, were involving themselves in an intricate system of trade, alliances, and territorial disputes already in existence. In a narrative provided to Ferris by a man named Faro (one attributed to the Shoshone today), Ferris described the consequences of the introduction of guns on intertribal warfare, especially when only in the possession of their enemies, saying, "For several moons we saw our best warriors almost daily falling around us, without our being able to avenge their deaths. Goaded by thirst for revenge, we often rushed forth upon our enemies, but they receded like the rainbow in proportion as we advanced, as ever remained at the same distance, whence they destroyed us by their deadly bolts, while we were utterly powerless to oppose them."[4] Their chief, Big Foot, compelled his people to leave their homeland and flee to the mountains, beyond the reach of their enemies, where they found safety and an abundance of food. Thus, when faced with white intruders from the Lewis and Clark Expedition who also possessed firearms, they initially felt fear but were also impressed with the strangers' kindness and their material goods. Even while being dazzled by the trinkets of the whites, such as the "solid water" that reflected their faces, the Shoshone were acutely aware that their own trade source was essential for obtaining firearms necessary to their survival. Just as Lewis and Clark depended on their hospitality and help, the Shoshone people knew that this relationship very well could determine their future.

The Lewis and Clark Expedition made its way into native oral traditions in other ways as well. For example, later in the nineteenth century, along the lower Columbia River, part of the hybrid Chinook jargon used for trading purposes reflected their encounter. One salutation became *clah hoh ah yah* or *clachouie*, apparently derived from the time when white men were greeted with the words "Clark, how are you?"[5]

Appropriately, the largest number of native oral accounts regarding the Lewis and Clark Expedition surrounds Sacagawea, one of the most famous native people in

American history. Interestingly, however, in the few documented accounts of stories she provided, she did not focus on
her "leading" or "guiding" the expedition (though many
accounts describe her role as such), but rather she emphasized aspects of her involvement that illustrated culturally
valued traits. For example, both Sacagawea's contemporary,
Susan Perry, and Sacagawea's grandson, Andrew Bazil, heard
her tell a story about providing dried meat to the whites,
saving them from starvation.

Debates still rage about whether Sacagawea died in 1812
at Fort Manuel, South Dakota, or whether she died at an old
age in 1884 after living by the name of Porivo at Wind River,
Wyoming. To confuse the matter, she is also known as Wadze-
wipe, or Lost Woman, by the Comanches with whom, accord-

Sacajawea Guiding the Lewis and Clark Expedition. Color lithograph after Alfred Russell, 1904. Missouri Historical Society
Photograph and Print Collection.

ing to many oral accounts, she lived for many years. Native accounts regarding her life and death seem to support her survival until the 1880s. As Grandma Herford (Shoshone) relayed in 1926:

> I truly believe that Porivo or Chief woman is the true and identical Sacajawea that guided and was inter-preter for the Lewis and Clark expedition; because she told of many experiences which she had encountered during her past life, otherwise no other person could have told of those experiences unless they had some similar experience.[6]

Generally among native people, empirical knowledge is valued highly; only individuals who have gained this kind of knowledge may authoritatively give accounts on that topic. Furthermore, once a respected individual gives those accounts, they are assumed to be trustworthy. Similarly, as Sacagawea's great-grandson James McAdams said, "Our tribe all know and have no doubt but that Sacagawea was the original Indian woman from where she said she was, that is, a member of the Lewis and Clark expedition. Personally, I would like to ask, what is all this fuss about?"[7] But there is a "fuss," or debate, because white written evidence—one entry in Clark's cash book and one in trader John C. Luttig's notes—makes reference to Sacagawea's death or to the death of the "Snake Squaw" of Toussaint Charbonneau (husband to Sacagawea and others). Scholars of Lewis and Clark generally favor the written evidence over the native oral versions despite an abundance of accounts from people who person-ally knew her and adamantly stated that Sacagawea, Porivo, and Wadze-wipe were the same person. McAdams continued, "There is no fraud in the statement which I am making to you, nor is there any fraud in this matter of identification of Sacajawea, the interpreter for Lewis and Clark. It is a true story. Fraud is not with the Indians in matters of this kind.

They do not put up a story just to have it startling and out-of-place."[8] McAdams's statement is testimony to the seriousness with which native people regard the spoken word and its veracity.

Considering the numerous native peoples that Lewis and Clark encountered, relatively few native oral accounts about the expedition have been documented. Travelers, explorers, and early ethnographers collected most of the indigenous oral accounts. While some undocumented oral accounts may still exist, a number of them from the time period no doubt have been lost because many native oral traditions have deteriorated in the past two centuries. At one time, the oral tradition worked successfully because its maintenance was a collective community process. People from any given town or community heard many of the same stories collectively, and in that way they could review the storytellers collectively. As a whole, they made sure that any given storyteller maintained the integrity of the account. In addition, gifted storytellers were recognized and celebrated; they achieved a special status within communities. Today, however, many oral traditions, though often still kept by gifted storytellers, are no longer shared collectively. Specific families or clans often transmit stories distinctive to their direct lineage. Among other native people, the oral tradition has deteriorated considerably and dangerously because of a number of factors, most significantly the dramatic population decline and assimilationist pressures.

Native peoples of North America have suffered some of the highest rates of extermination in the world, with death-rate estimates ranging from 90 to 99 percent from the time of initial contact. The majority of these deaths were caused by disease, often explained as an unfortunate consequence of contact with European or Euro-American explorers. The U.S. government and its citizens are not without blame, however.

It is now estimated that the United States destroyed 80 to 85 percent of native peoples within the first century of the nation's existence. By the end of the eighteenth century, many Americans, and certainly the American government, understood that native peoples suffered catastrophic deaths from diseases such as smallpox. (In fact, it was suggested by Attorney General Levi Lincoln to Thomas Jefferson that the expedition take a smallpox inoculation along for preventing disease among native populations.) They also understood that it was contact with Europeans that had caused these horrific population declines. Yet throughout the nineteenth century, Euro-Americans, including the government-sponsored Lewis and Clark Expedition, persisted in exploration and trade with native peoples and invasion of native lands without widely administering a preventive inoculation.

The native peoples of the Upper Missouri, so favored by Lewis and Clark, faced almost complete extinction because of European contact. Jean Baptiste Truteau, in his visit with the Arikara in 1795, documented that three epidemics already had devastated their population, reducing more than thirty villages to less than a handful. The Mandans, who had a population of about 15,000 in 1738, were reduced to 138 after the smallpox pandemic of 1836–40 (the result of the distribution of smallpox-infested blankets by the U.S. Army at Fort Clark, the first fort established by the Lewis and Clark Expedition). The Arikara lost half of their existing population in that same single epidemic. The United States could not claim that the death of the native peoples was an "unfortunate consequence" of contact. Clearly, by the beginning of the nineteenth century when Lewis and Clark set forth on their journey, the American government knew how diseases, including smallpox, were transmitted. Exploration, invasion, and settlement, along with the mass death of native peoples, must be viewed with this fact in mind.

Unfortunately, assault on native oral traditions did not end merely with physical destruction. The strong assimilationist governmental policies of the late nineteenth and early twentieth centuries, specifically the practice of boarding-school education, devastated native languages and the intergenerational transmission of stories in those languages. The government-sponsored schools forbade the children to speak their native languages, either by physical punishment or emotional abuse—associating the language closely with inferiority, shame, and humiliation. Hoping to spare their children from the hardships they had endured, many of those who remembered their language after years of institutionalization made the decision not to pass it on. No longer could children be raised freely according to native notions of education.

Amazingly, some oral traditions have survived and are valued highly, particularly among the elderly native population. However, even today elders lament the fact that the number of young people interested in the traditions is continually diminishing. When considering the expedition of Lewis and Clark, the dearth of native accounts provides a testament to the consequences of their exploration and the subsequent invasion and colonization of native peoples and their lands.

Notes

1   James P. Ronda, *Lewis and Clark among the Indians* (Lincoln: University of Nebraska Press, 1984), 3.

2   Ella Clark, *Indian Legends from the Northern Rockies* (Norman: University of Oklahoma Press, 1966), 70.

3   Ibid., 145.

4   Warren Angus Ferris, *Life in the Rocky Mountains: A Diary of Wanderings on the Sources of the Rivers Missouri, Columbia, and Colorado 1830–1835*, rev. ed. (Denver: Old West Publishing Company, 1983), 164.

5   Robert H. Ruby and John A. Brown, *The Chinook Indians: Traders of the Lower Columbia River* (Norman: University of Oklahoma Press, 1976), 150.

6   Grace Raymond Hebard, *Sacajawea: A Guide and Interpreter of the Lewis and Clark Expedition, with an Account of the Travels of Toussaint Charbonneau and of Jean Baptiste, the Expedition Papoose* (Glendale, Calif.: The Arthur H. Clark Company, 1957), 249.

7   Ibid., 280.

8   Ibid., 281.

Suggested Readings

Clark, Ella. *Indian Legends from the Northern Rockies.* Norman: University of Oklahoma Press, 1966.

Ferris, Warren Angus. *Life in the Rocky Mountains: A Diary of Wanderings on the Sources of the Rivers Missouri, Columbia, and Colorado 1830–1835.* Rev. ed. Denver: Old West Publishing Company, 1983.

Hebard, Grace Raymond. *Sacajawea: A Guide and Interpreter of the Lewis and Clark Expedition, with an Account of the Travels of Toussaint Charbonneau and of Jean Baptiste, the Expedition Papoose.* Glendale, Calif.: The Arthur H. Clark Company, 1957.

Ronda, James P. *Lewis and Clark among the Indians.* Lincoln: University of Nebraska Press, 1984.

Ruby, Robert, and John A. Brown. *The Chinook Indians: Traders of the Lower Columbia River.* Norman: University of Oklahoma Press, 1976.

Contributor Biographies

Alan Taylor (Ph. D., Brandeis University) is professor of American history at the University of California–Davis specializing in early American history and the history of the American West. He is the author of *William Cooper's Town: Power and Persuasion on the Frontier of the Early American Republic*, which won both the Pulitzer and Bancroft Prizes in 1996. He is also the author of *Liberty Men and the Great Proprietors: The Revolutionary Settlement on the Maine Frontier, 1760–1820* (1990) and *American Colonies: The Settling of North America* (2001).

Peter Kastor (Ph.D., University of Virginia) is a professor of American culture studies at Washington University, where he teaches both history and American culture. He is currently working on a book about the struggle to incorporate the people and land acquired through the Louisiana Purchase. He is also completing a brief book for the Lewis and Clark Heritage Trail Foundation that provides an introduction to the origin and significance of the Louisiana Purchase. In addition to teaching undergraduates, he has taught in Roots and the Chesapeake Seminar, both NEH-funded summer programs for teachers at the University of Virginia.

David Konig (Ph.D., Harvard University), is professor of history and law at Washington University, specializing in the development of law and legal institutions in early America and the evolution of American thought and society in that period. He has written on the colonial origins of American legal institutions and their role in the creation of a social order after independence. He is currently editing Thomas Jefferson's law notes for *The Papers of Thomas Jefferson* and is preparing a biography of Jefferson as a lawyer and an advocate of natural law.

James Ronda (Ph.D., University of Nebraska–Lincoln), holds the H. G. Barnard Chair in Western American History at the University of Tulsa and is a past president of the Western History Association. A specialist in the history of the exploration of the American West, he is the author of many books, essays, and articles. His most recent book is *Finding the West: Explorations with Lewis and Clark* (2001). He has been a consultant and on-screen commentator for several Lewis and Clark documentaries and is a member of the board of advisors of the International Center for Jefferson Studies at Monticello.

William Skelton (Ph.D., Northwestern University) recently retired from the University of Wisconsin–Stevens Point, where he was a member of the history faculty. Skelton is a specialist in the history of the U.S. Army and the author of numerous articles and book chapters on the origins of the military profession in the United States. During his career he received awards for teaching and scholarship from UW–Stevens Point and the Moncado Prize from the Society for Military History. In 1994, his book *An American Profession of Arms: The Army Officer Corps, 1784–1861* was awarded a Distinguished Book Award from that same society.

James E. Lewis, Jr. (Ph.D., University of Virginia) teaches at Kalamazoo College. He is currently writing a history of the Louisiana Purchase for Monticello and working on a book on the Burr Conspiracy. He is the author of *John Quincy Adams: Policymaker for the Union* and *The American Union and the Problem of Neighborhood: The United States and the Collapse of the Spanish Empire*, which won a 1999 *Choice* Outstanding Academic Book award.

J. Wendel Cox (Ph.D., University of Minnesota) is a visiting assistant professor of history in the social science division of the University of Minnesota–Morris. A student of Plains Indian history, he was the founding editor of the H-AMINDIAN H-Net discussion list and developer of H-AMINDIAN Web sites while a postdoctoral research associate at Arizona State University.

J. Frederick Fausz (Ph.D., The College of William and Mary) is an associate professor of history at the University of Missouri–St. Louis. His areas of special interest are Native Americans, colonial America, and early American fur trades. His publications include many articles on these topics, including "An 'Abundance of Blood Shed on Both Sides': England's First Indian War, 1609–1614" (1990) and "Becoming 'A Nation of Quakers': The Removal of the Osage Indians from Missouri" (2000), which won the Best Essay of the Year Awards from the Virginia Historical Society and the Missouri Conference on History, respectively.

Conevery Bolton Valenčius (Ph.D., Harvard University), is an assistant professor in history, American culture studies, and environmental studies at Washington University in St. Louis. Her research interests are in the connections between human health and environments; American environmental history; and the history of environmental sciences, broadly conceived. Her most recent book is *The Health of the Country: How American Settlers Understood Themselves and Their Land* (2002). Her current projects include an article on "Gender and the Economy of Health on the Santa Fe Trail" and a second book, *The River Ran Backward*, on the New Madrid earthquakes of 1811–12.

Peter S. Onuf (Ph.D., Johns Hopkins University) is the Thomas Jefferson Foundation professor of history at the University of Virginia and editor of *Jeffersonian Legacies.* He is the author and/or editor of many books, including *Jefferson's Empire: The Language of American Nationhood, Origins of the Federal Republic: Jurisdictional Controversies in the United States, 1775–1787,* and *Statehood and Union: A History of the Northwest Ordinance.*

Betty Houchin Winfield (Ph.D., University of Washington) is a professor of journalism at the University of Missouri–Columbia. She is an internationally recognized expert on the relationship between U.S. presidents and the press. Winfield is the author of *The Edward R. Murrow Heritage, FDR and the News Media,* and *BLEEP! Censoring Rock 'n' Rap Music,* as well as many other publications. In 1998, she won the University of Missouri System's Thomas Jefferson Award, and in 2002 she received an MU Faculty Alumni Award.

Angela Cavender Wilson (Ph.D., Cornell University) is a Wahpetunwan Dakota from the Upper Sioux Reservation in southwestern Minnesota. She is an assistant professor in the department of history at Arizona State University. Her research has focused on Dakota language and conceptions of history within the oral tradition; she has published numerous articles on her chosen topic. *Natives and Academics: Discussions on Researching and Writing About American Indians* included two of Wilson's essays and received the 1999 Critics' Choice Award from the American Educational Studies Association.

Appendix: The "Indian Presents" of the Lewis and Clark Expedition

Metal Wares

87	Peace medals of various sizes, featuring Jefferson or Washington
24	Pipe tomahawks (a specialty of the North American fur trades)
24	Squaw axes
36	Razors
264	Butcher knives
156	Other knives
150	Scissors
22	Files
144	Fire steels
1,152	Moccasin awls
5	Large canoe awls
55	Fish spears
2,800	Fish hooks
4,600	Needles
432	Curtain rings
288	Thimbles (including 111 tailors' steel needles)
1,500	Silver brooches
963	Hawk's bells, large and small
96	Earrings ("ear bobs")
26	Silver earrings
33	Lockets
72	Silver rings
40	Silver wrist/arm bands or bracelets
8	Silver "Moons" (officers' gorgets)
144	Iron combs
8	Brass kettles
2	Corn mills
14 lbs	Knitting pins
6.5 lbs	Sheet iron (for use in making ax blades)
12 lbs	Brass strips
12 lbs	Brass wire
10 lbs	Brads

Glass Goods

360	Pocket mirrors
96	Magnifying glasses ("Burning Glass" or "Fire-Starters")
33 lbs	Assorted trade beads, esp. sky blue
8	Mock garnets (colored glass "stones")

Cloth Products

15	"Chief coats" ("9 are Artillery Coats")
11	Hats, 6 with "Circle feathers & 5 Soldier's plumes"
15	Blankets (mostly blue)
44	Ruffled calico shirts

18	White shirts
48	Breechcloths
36	Tinsel hatbands
40 prs	Leggings, mostly scarlet
13 lbs	Handkerchiefs
17 lbs	Ribbons and bindings ("None-So-Pretty")
21 lbs	Thread
22 yds	Red flannel
47 yds	Scarlet cloth
40	Skeins of silk

Miscellaneous Items

500 lbs	Tobacco in 176 "Carrots"
63 lbs	Tobacco in 130 "Pigtail" rolls or "Twists"
19 lbs	Vermilion (mercury sulfide)—bright red pigment for face painting
10 lbs	Verdigris (copper sulfate)—green "copper rust" for face painting
8 lbs	Red Lead (for face painting)
8	Ivory Combs

These items were specifically designed for Indian gifts and do not include other things, such as liquor, firearms, a cannon, ammunition, "stove" axes, furs, and articles of corpsmen clothing that were also given or traded to the Indians during the expedition.

This itemization is based upon William Clark's longer and most complete list of presents, found in *Original Journals of the Lewis and Clark Expedition*, ed. Reuben Gold Thwaites (New York: Dodd, Mead, & Co., 1904–5) 6: 270–79.

Appendix: President Thomas Jefferson's Instructions to Captain Meriwether Lewis
(June 20, 1803)

To Meriwether Lewis esq. Capt. of the 1st regimt. of infantry of the U. S. of A.

Your situation as Secretary of the President of the U. S. has made you acquainted with the objects of my confidential message of Jan. 18, 1803 to the legislature; you have seen the act they passed, which, tho' expressed in general terms, was meant to sanction those objects, and you are appointed to carry them into execution.

Instruments for ascertaining, by celestial observations, the geography of the country through which you will pass, have been already provided. Light articles for barter and presents among the Indians, arms for your attendants, say for from 10. to 12. men, boats, tents, & other travelling apparatus, with ammunition, medecine, surgical instruments and provisions you will have prepared with such aids as the Secretary at War can yield in his department; & from him also you will recieve authority to engage among our troops, by voluntary agreement, the number of attendants above mentioned, over whom you, as their commanding officer, are invested with all the powers the laws give in such a case.

As your movements while within the limits of the U.S. will be better directed by occasional communications, adapted to circumstances as they arise, they will not be noticed here. What follows will respect your proceedings after your departure from the United states.

Your mission has been communicated to the ministers here from France, Spain & Great Britain, and through them to their governments; & such assurances given them as to its objects, as we trust will satisfy them. The country [of Louisiana] having been ceded by Spain to France, the passport you have from the minister of France, the representative of the present sovereign of the country, will be a protection with all its subjects; & that from the minister of England will entitle you to the friendly aid of any traders of that allegiance with whom you may happen to meet.

The object of your mission is to explore the Missouri river, & such principal stream of it, as, by it's course & communication with the waters of the Pacific Ocean, whether the Columbia, Oregan, Colorado or and other river may offer the most direct & practicable water communication across this continent, for the purposes of commerce.

Beginning at the mouth of the Missouri, you will take careful observations of latitude & longitude, at all remarke-able points on the river, & especially at the mouths of rivers, at rapids, at islands, & other places & objects distinguished by such natural marks & characters of a durable kind, as that they may with certainty be recognised hereafter. The courses of the river between these points of observation may be supplied by the compass the log-line & by time, corrected by the observations themselves. The variations of the compass too, in different places, should be noticed.

The interesting points of the portage between the heads of the Missouri, & of the water offering the best communication with the Pacific ocean, should also be fixed by observation, & the course of that water to the ocean, in the same manner as that of the Missouri.

Your observations are to be taken with great pains & accuracy, to be entered distinctly & intelligibly for others as well as yourself, to comprehend all the elements necessary, with the aid of the usual tables, to fix the latitude and longitude of the places at which they were taken, and are to be rendered to the war-office, for the purpose of having the calculations made concurrently by proper persons within the U.S. Several copies of these as well as of your other notes should be made at leisure times, & put into the care of the most trustworthy of your attendants, to guard, by multiplying them, against the accidental losses to which they will be exposed. A further guard would be that one of these copies be on the paper of the birch, as less liable to injury from damp than common paper.

The commerce which may be carried on with the people inhabiting the line you will pursue, renders a knolege of those people important. You will therefore endeavor to make yourself acquainted, as far as a diligent pursuit of your journey shall admit, with the names of the nations & their numbers;

the extent & limits of their possessions; their relations with other tribes of nations; their language, traditions, monuments;

their ordinary occupations in agriculture, fishing, hunting, war, arts, & the implements for these;

their food, clothing, & domestic accommodations;

the diseases prevalent among them, & the remedies they use;

moral & physical circumstances which distinguish them from the tribes we know;

peculiarities in their laws, customs & dispositions;

and articles of commerce they may need or furnish, & to what extent.

And, considering the interest which every nation has in extending & strengthening the authority of reason & justice among the people around them, it will be useful to acquire what knolege you can of the state of morality, religion, & information among them; as it may better enable those who endeavor to civilize & instruct them, to adapt their measure to the existing notions & practices of those on whom they are to operate.

Other objects worthy of notice will be

the soil & face of the country, it's growth & vegetable productions, especially those not of the U.S.

the animals of the country generally, & especially those not known in the U.S. the remains or accounts of any which may be deemed rare or extinct; the mineral productions of every kind; but more particularly metals, limestone, pit coal, & saltpetre; salines & mineral waters, noting the temperature of the last, & such circumstances as may indicate their character;

volcanic appearances;

climate, as characterized by the thermometer, by the proportion of rainy, cloudy, & clear days, by lightening, hail, snow, ice, by the access & recess of frost, by the winds prevailing at different seasons, the dates at which particular plants put forth or lose their flower, or leaf, times of appearance of particular birds, reptiles or insects.

Altho' your route will be along the channel of the Missouri, yet you will endeavor to inform yourself, by enquiry, of the character & extent of the country watered by it's branches, & especially on it's Southern side. The North river or Rio Bravo which runs into the gulph of Mexico, and the North river, or Rio colorado which runs into the gulph of California, are understood to be the principal streams heading opposite to the waters of the Missouri, and running Southwardly. Whether the dividing grounds between the Missouri & them are mountains or flatlands, what are their distance from the Missouri, the character of the intermediate country, & the people inhabiting it, are worthy of particular enquiry. The Northern waters of the Missouri are less to be enquired after, because they have been ascertained to a considerable degree, & are still in a course of ascertainment by English traders, and travellers. But if you can learn any thing certain of the most Northern source of the Missisipi, & of its position relatively to the lake of the woods, it will be interesting to us. Some account too of the path of the Canadian traders from the Missisipi, at the mouth of the Ouisconsin to where it strikes the Missouri, & of the soil and rivers in it's course, is desireable.

In all your intercourse with the natives, treat them in the most friendly & conciliatory manner which their own conduct will admit; allay all jealousies as to the object of your journey, satisfy them of its innocence, make them acquainted with the position, extent, character, peaceable & commercial dispositions of the U.S. of our wish to be neighborly, friendly & useful to them, & of our dispositions to a commercial intercourse with them; confer with them on the points most convenient as mutual emporiums, and the articles of most desireable interchange for them & us. If a few of their influential chiefs, within practicable distance, wish to visit us, arrange such a visit with them, and furnish them with authority to call on our officers, on their entering the U.S to have them conveyed to this place at the public expense. If any of them should wish to have some of their young people brought up with us, & taught such arts as may be useful to them, we will receive, instruct & take care of them. Such a mission, whether of influential chiefs or of young people, would give some security to your own party. Carry with you some matter of the kinepox; inform those of them with whom you may be, of it'[s] efficacy as a preservative from the small-pox; & instruct & incourage them in the use of it. This may be especially done wherever you winter.

As it is impossible for us to foresee in what manner you will be recieved by those people, whether with hospitality or hostility, so is it impossible to prescribe the exact degree of perseverance with which you are to pursue your journey. We value too much the lives of citizens to offer them to probable destruction. Your numbers will be sufficient to secure you against the unauthorised opposition of individuals or of small parties: but if a superior force, authorised, or not authorised, by a nation, should be arrayed against your further passage, and inflexibly determined to arrest it, you must decline its further pursuit, and return. In the loss of yourselves, we should lose also the information you will have acquired. By returning safely with that, you may enable us to renew the essay with better calculated means. To your own discretion therefore must be left the degree of danger you may risk, and the point at which you should decline, only saying we wish you to err on the side of your safety, and to bring back your party safe even it if be with less information.

As far up the Missouri as the white settlements extend, an intercourse will probably be found to exist between them & the Spanish post of St. Louis opposite Cahokia, or Ste. Genevieve opposite Kaskaskia. From still further up the river, the traders may furnish a conveyance for letters. Beyond that, you may perhaps be able to engage Indians to bring letters for the government to Cahokia or Kaskaskia, on promising that they shall there receive such special compensation as you shall have stipulated with them. Avail yourself of these means to communicate to us, at seasonable intervals, a copy of your journal, notes & observations, of every kind, putting into cypher whatever might do injury if betrayed.

Should you reach the Pacific ocean inform yourself of the

circumstances which may decide whether the furs of those parts may not be collected as advantageously at the head of the Missouri (convenient as it supposed to the waters of the Colorado & Oregan or Columbia) as at Nootka sound, or any other point of that coast; and that trade be consequently conducted through the Missouri & U.S. more beneficially than by the circumnavigation now practised.

On your arrival on that coast endeavor to learn if there be any port within your reach frequented by the sea-vessels of any nation, & to send two of your trusty people back by sea, in such way as shall appear practicable, with a copy of your notes: and should you be of opinion that the return of your party by the way they went will be eminently dangerous, then ship the whole, & return by sea, by way either of cape Horn, or the cape of good Hope, as you shall be able. As you will be without money, clothes or provisions, you must endeavor to use the credit of the U.S. to obtain them, for which purpose open letters of credit shall be furnished you, authorising you to draw upon the Executive of the U.S. or any of its officers, in any part of the world, on which draughts can be disposed of, & to apply with our recommendations to the Consuls, agents, merchants, or citizens of any nation with which we have intercourse, assuring them, in our name, that any aids they may furnish you, shall be honorably repaid, and on demand. Our consuls Thomas Hewes at Batavia in Java, Win. Buchanan in the Isles of France & Bourbon, & John Elmslie at the Cape of good Hope will be able to supply your necessities by draughts on us.

Should you find it safe to return by the way you go, after sending two of your party around by sea, or with your whole party, if no conveyance by sea can be found, do so; making such observations on your return, as may serve to supply, correct or confirm those made on your outward journey.

On re-entering the U.S. and reaching a place of safety, discharge any of your attendants who may desire & deserve it, procuring for them immediate paiment of all arrears of pay & cloathing which may have incurred since their departure, and assure them that they shall be recommended to the liberality of the legislature for the grant of a souldier's portion of land each, as proposed in my message to Congress: & repair yourself with papers to the seat of government.

To provide, on the accident of your death, against anarchy, dispersion, & the consequent danger to your party, and total failure of the enterprize, you are hereby authorised, by any instrument signed & written in your own hand, to name the person among them who shall succeed to the command on your decease, and by like instruments to change the nomination from time to time as further experience of the characters accompanying you shall point out superior fitness: and all the powers and authorities given to yourself are, in the event of your death, transferred to, & vested in the successor so named, with further power to him, and his successors in like manner to name each his successor, who, on the death of his predecessor, shall be invested with all the powers & authorities given to yourself.

Given under my hand at the city of Washington this 20th day of June 1803.

Th. Jefferson

Pr. U.S. of America

Donald T. Jackson, ed. *Letters of the Lewis and Clark Expedition, with Related Documents, 1783–1854,* 2d ed. 2 vols. (Urbana: University of Illinois Press, 1978).

Index

Adams, John Quincy, 74, 82, 186

American Fur Company, 139

American Philosophical Society, 22, 34

Andrews, Joseph G., 78-79

Arikaras, 49–50, 114–15, 131; epidemics, 49–50

Biddle, Nicholas, 20, 140, 191

Big Foot, 208

Black Cat (Posecopsahe), 47–55, 68, 203

Bodmer, Karl, 48, 53, 54

Bonaparte, Napoleon, 14–15, 91, 93, 96, 169

Burr Conspiracy, 84–85, 99–100

Burr, Aaron, 84–85, 99–100

Cameahwait, 9, 56–61, 68, 130

Canada, U.S. border with, 97–98

Catlin, George, 48

Charbonneau, Jean Baptiste "Pomp," 18, 65, 196, 197

Charbonneau, Lizette, 197

Charbonneau, Toussaint, 18, 41, 51, 67, 128, 210

Clark, George Rogers, 33, 36, 124, 194

Clark, William: attitude toward Indians, 18, 42–43, 47, 131–34, 139, 194; becomes involved in the expedition, 8, 36; commander of the territorial militia and Indian agent, 19, 137–39, 187, 193; death, 139, 194; expedition journals, 20–21, 191; expedition maps, 20, 21, 42–43; governor of the Louisiana Territory, 19–20, 193; journal entries, 26, 47, 73, 104, 160, 178; portrait, 10; relationship with Jefferson and Lewis, 8–11; superintendent of Indian affairs, 137, 193–94

Clatsops, 61–68

Coboway, 61–68

Colter, John, 135–37, 178, 195

Coues, Elliott, 192, 194

de Lapérouse, Jean François, 33

du Pont de Nemours, Pierre Samuel, 27

Dunbar, William, 151

Enlightenment, 29, 166

epidemics, effects of, 49–51, 139–40, 211–12

Evans, John Thomas, 53–55

Ferris, Warren, 207–8

Floyd, Charles, 17, 178, 182

Fort Clatsop, 62, 65, 66

Fort Defiance, 78

Fort Mandan, 48, 49, 66, 182

Frazier, Robert, 187–89

Fry, Joshua, 29

Gass, Patrick, 17, 65, 194; expedition journals, 20, 189–91; journal entries, 17

Gray, Robert, 35

Grinder's Stand, 192

Hidatsas, 49, 51–52, 114, 131, 149

Hudson's Bay Company, 51, 58, 127